American Government

AP* EDITION

American Government

Institutions & Policies

Thirteenth Edition

James Q. Wilson
University of California, Los Angeles, emeritus
Pepperdine University
Boston College

John J. DiIulio, Jr.
University of Pennsylvania

Meena Bose
Hofstra University

WADSWORTH
CENGAGE Learning

Australia • Brazil • Japan • Korea • Mexico • Singapore • Spain • United Kingdom • United States

American Government: Institutions and Policies, AP* Edition
James Wilson, John DiIulio, Meena Bose

Senior Publisher: Suzanne Jeans
Executive Editor: Carolyn Merrill
Development Editor: Rebecca Green
Associate Editor: Laura Ross
Media Editor: Laura Hildebrand
Editorial Assistant: Scott Greenan
Marketing Manager: Lydia LeStar
Marketing Program Manager: Caitlin Green
Marketing Coordinator: Lorreen Towle
Art Director: Linda May
Manufacturing Planner: Fola Orekoya
Senior Rights Acquisition Specialist: Jennifer Meyer Dare
VP, Director, Advanced and Elective Products Program: Alison Zetterquist
Editorial Coordinator, Advanced and Elective Products Program: Jean Woy
Production Service: Integra Software Services Pvt. Ltd.
Cover Image: ©Shutterstock
Compositor: Integra Software Services Pvt. Ltd.

Library of Congress Control Number: 2011940436

Student Edition:

ISBN-13: 978-1-111-83003-8

ISBN-10: 1-111-83003-7

Wadsworth
20 Channel Center Street
Boston, MA 02210
USA

Cengage Learning is a leading provider of customized learning solutions with office locations around the globe, including Singapore, the United Kingdom, Australia, Mexico, Brazil and Japan. Locate your local office at **international.cengage.com/region**

Cengage Learning products are represented in Canada by Nelson Education, Ltd. Cengage Learning products are represented in high schools by Holt McDougal, a division of Houghton Mifflin Harcourt.

To find online supplements and other instructional support, please visit **www.cengage.com.**

Instructors: Please visit **www.cengagebrain.com** and log in to access instructor-specific resources.

Printed in the United States of America
3 4 5 6 7 15 14 13

*AP and Advanced Placement Program are registered trademarks of the College Entrance Examination Board, which was not involved in the production of, and does not endorse, this product.

Part I
The American System 1

1 The Study of American Government 2
2 The Constitution 20
3 Federalism 50
4 American Political Culture 78
5 Civil Liberties 100
6 Civil Rights 130

Part II
Opinions, Interests, and Organizations 161

7 Public Opinion 162
8 Political Participation 182
9 Political Parties 202
10 Elections and Campaigns 234
11 Interest Groups 270
12 The Media 298

Part III
Institutions of Government 325

13 Congress 326
14 The Presidency 364
15 The Bureaucracy 408
16 The Judiciary 438

Part IV
The Politics of Public Policy 469

17 The Policymaking Process 470
18 Economic Policy 492
19 Social Welfare 514
20 Foreign and Military Policy 534
21 Environmental Policy 564

Part V
The Nature of American Democracy 581

22 Who Governs? To What Ends? 582

Preface xiii
About the Authors xix
A Letter from the Author xxi
Correlation for U.S. Government and Politics to *American Government, Thirteenth Edition* xxv
Preparing for the AP* Exam xxix
Taking the AP* U.S. Government and Politics Exam xxxi

PART I The American System 1

Chapter 1 The Study of American Government 2
What Is Political Power? 5
What Is Democracy? 7
Is Representative Democracy Best? 8
How Is Political Power Distributed? 10
Is Democracy Driven by Self-Interest? 12
What Explains Political Change? 12
The Nature of Politics 13

Chapter 2 The Constitution 20
The Problem of Liberty 21
The Colonial Mind 22
The Real Revolution 23
Weaknesses of the Confederation 24
The Constitutional Convention 25
The Lessons of Experience 25
The Framers 26
The Challenge 27
The Virginia Plan 28
The New Jersey Plan 28
The Compromise 29
The Constitution and Democracy 29
Key Principles 30
Government and Human Nature 31
The Constitution and Liberty 32
The Antifederalist View 33
Need for a Bill of Rights 36
The Constitution and Slavery 37
The Motives of the Framers 39
Economic Interests 39
The Constitution and Equality 40
Constitutional Reform: Modern Views 41
Reducing the Separation of Powers 41
Making the System Less Democratic 44
Who Is Right? 45

Chapter 3 Federalism 50
Why Federalism Matters 51
The Founding 52
A Bold, New Plan 53
Elastic Language 54
The Debate on the Meaning of Federalism 55
The Supreme Court Speaks 55
Nullification 55
Dual Federalism 56
State Sovereignty 57
Governmental Structure 59
Increased Political Activity 62
What the States Can Do 63
Federal-State Relations 63
Grants-in-Aid 63
Meeting National Needs 65
The Intergovernmental Lobby 66
Categorical Grants 66
Rivalry Among the States 67
Federal Aid and Federal Control 68
Mandates 68
Conditions of Aid 69
A Devolution Revolution? 70
Congress and Federalism 71

Chapter 4 American Political Culture 78
Political Culture 79
The Political System 81
The Persistence of Conflict 82
The Economic System 83
How We Compare: Comparing America with Other Nations 85
The Political System 85
The Economic System 86
The Civic Role of Religion 87
The Sources of Political Culture 88
The Culture War 89
Mistrust of Government 91
Civil Society 92
Political Tolerance 93

Chapter 5 Civil Liberties 100

Culture and Civil Liberties 102
Rights in Conflict 102
Cultural Conflicts 104
Applying the Bill of Rights to the States 105

Interpreting and Applying the First Amendment 106
Speech and National Security 107

What Is Speech? 109
Libel 109
Obscenity 109
Symbolic Speech 111

Commercial and Youthful Speech 112

Church and State 113
The Free-Exercise Clause 113
The Establishment Clause 114

Crime and Due Process 117
The Exclusionary Rule 118
Search and Seizure 118
Confessions and Self-Incrimination 121
Relaxing the Exclusionary Rule 121
Terrorism and Civil Liberties 122
Searches Without Warrants 124

Chapter 6 Civil Rights 130

The Black Predicament 132

The Campaign in the Courts 133
"Separate but Equal" 134
Can Separate Schools Be Equal? 134
Brown v. Board of Education 135

The Campaign in Congress 139
Racial Profiling 144

Women and Equal Rights 145
Sexual Harassment 147
Privacy and Sex 148

Affirmative Action 149
Equality of Results 149
Equality of Opportunity 149

Gays and the Constitution 154

PART II Opinions, Interests, and Organizations 161

Chapter 7 Public Opinion 162

Public Opinion and Democracy 163

What Is Public Opinion? 164
How Polling Works 165
How Opinions Differ 166

Political Socialization 167
Genes and the Family 167
Religion 169
The Gender Gap 170

Cleavages in Public Opinion 170
Social Class 171
Race And Ethnicity 172
Region 173

Political Ideology 173
Mass Ideologies: A Typology 174
Liberal and Conservative Elites 174

Political Elites, Public Opinion, and Public Policy 176

Chapter 8 Political Participation 182

A Close Look at Nonvoting 184

The Rise of the American Electorate 187
From State to Federal Control 187
Voter Turnout 190

Who Participates in Politics? 192
Forms of Participation 192
Participation: Causes and Meaning 193

Chapter 9 Political Parties 202

Parties—Here and Abroad 204

The Rise and Decline of the Political Party 206
The Founding 206
The Jacksonians 207
The Civil War and Sectionalism 208
The Era of Reform 208
Party Realignments 209
Party Decline 211

The National Party Structure Today 212
National Conventions 214

State and Local Parties 216
The Machine 217
Ideological Parties 218
Solidary Groups 218
Sponsored Parties 219
Personal Following 219

The Two-Party System 220

Minor Parties 222

Nominating a President 225
Are the Delegates Representative of the Voters? 225
Who Votes in Primaries? 226
Who Are the New Delegates? 226

Parties Versus Voters 229

Chapter 10 Elections and Campaigns 234

Campaigns Today 235
Better or Worse? 237
Here and Abroad 238

Presidential Versus Congressional Campaigns 238
Running for President 239
Getting Elected to Congress 241

Primary Versus General Campaigns 243
Two Kinds of Campaign Issues 244
Television, Debates, and Direct Mail 246

Money 249
The Sources of Campaign Money 249
Campaign Finance Rules 250
A Second Campaign Finance Law 252
New Sources of Money 255
Money and Winning 256

What Decides the Election? 257
Party 257
Issues, Especially the Economy 259
The Campaign 260
Finding a Winning Coalition 261

The Effects of Elections on Policy 264

Chapter 11 Interest Groups 270

The Birth of Interest Groups 273

Kinds of Organizations 274
Institutional Interests 274
Membership Interests 275
Incentives to Join 276
The Influence of the Staff 280

Interest Groups and Social Movements 280
The Environmental Movement 280
The Feminist Movement 280
The Union Movement 281
Upper-Class Bias? 282

The Activities of Interest Groups 283
Information 284
Earmarks 285
Public Support: The Rise of the New Politics 285
Money and PACs 286
The "Revolving Door" 289
Civil Disobedience 290

Regulating Interest Groups 291

Chapter 12 The Media 298

The Media and Politics 299

Journalism in American Political History 300
The Party Press 300
The Popular Press 300
Magazines of Opinion 302
Electronic Journalism 302
The Internet 304

The Structure of the Media 305
Degree of Competition 305
The National Media 306

Rules Governing the Media 307
Confidentiality of Sources 307
Regulating Broadcasting 308
Campaigning 309

Are the National Media Biased? 310
A Liberal Majority 310
Neutral and Objective? 311
Media's Influence 313

Government and the News 314
Prominence of the President 314
Coverage of Congress 314
Why Do We Have So Many News Leaks? 316
Sensationalism in the Media 317
Government Constraints on Journalists 318

PART III Institutions of Government 325

Chapter 13 Congress 326

Congress Versus Parliament 329

The Evolution of Congress 332

Who Is in Congress? 335
Gender and Race 335
Incumbency 337
Party 339

Representation and Polarization 340
Representational View 341
Organizational View 341
Attitudinal View 342

The Organization of Congress: Parties and Interests 343
Party Organizations 343
Party Voting 345
Caucuses 346

The Organization of Congress: Committees 346

The Organization of Congress: Staffs and Specialized Offices 348
Tasks of Staff Members 349
Staff Agencies 350

How a Bill Becomes Law 350
Introducing a Bill 350
Study by Committees 351
Floor Debate 352
Methods of Voting 354
Legislative Productivity 355
Reforming Congress 356

Chapter 14 The Presidency 364

Presidents and Prime Ministers 366

Divided Government 367
Does Gridlock Matter? 368
Is Policy Gridlock Bad? 369

The Powers of the President 370

The Evolution of the Presidency 372
Concerns of the Founders 372
The Electoral College 373
The President's Term of Office 373
The First Presidents 373
The Jacksonians 374
The Reemergence of Congress 375

The Power to Persuade 378
The Three Audiences 378
Popularity and Influence 380
The Decline in Popularity 382

The Power to Say No 383
Veto 383

Executive Privilege 384
Impoundment of Funds 385
Signing Statements 386

Presidential Character 386

The Office of the President 388
The White House Office 388
The Executive Office of the President 390
The Cabinet 390
Independent Agencies, Commissions, and Judgeships 391

Who Gets Appointed 392

The President's Program 394
Putting Together a Program 394
Attempts to Reorganize 397

Presidential Transition 398
The Vice President 398
Problems of Succession 399
Impeachment 400

How Powerful Is the President? 401

Chapter 15 The Bureaucracy 408

Distinctiveness of the American Bureaucracy 410

Proxy Government 411

The Growth of the Bureaucracy 412
The Appointment of Officials 412
A Service Role 413
A Change in Role 413

The Federal Bureaucracy Today 414
Recruitment and Retention 417
Personal Attributes 420
Do Bureaucrats Sabotage Their Political Bosses? 421
Culture and Careers 422
Constraints 422

Why So Many Constraints? 424
Agency Allies 425

Congressional Oversight 425
The Appropriations Committee and Legislative Committees 426
The Legislative Veto 427
Congressional Investigations 427

Bureaucratic "Pathologies" 428

Reforming the Bureaucracy 430

Chapter 16 The Judiciary 438

Judicial Review 440

The Development of the Federal Courts 441
National Supremacy and Slavery 441
Government and the Economy 442
Government and Political Liberty 444
The Revival of State Sovereignty 445

The Structure of the Federal Courts 446
Selecting Judges 447

The Jurisdiction of the Federal Courts 450

Getting to Court 452
Fee Shifting 453
Standing 453
Class-Action Suits 454

The Supreme Court in Action 455

The Power of the Federal Courts 457
The Power to Make Policy 457
Views of Judicial Activism 459
Legislation and the Courts 459

Checks on Judicial Power 460
Congress and the Courts 460
Public Opinion and the Courts 462

PART IV The Politics of Public Policy 469

Chapter 17 The Policymaking Process 470

Setting the Agenda 471
The Legitimate Scope of Government Action 472
Action by the States 474

Making a Decision 475

Majoritarian Politics: Distributed Benefits, Distributed Costs 476

Interest Group Politics: Concentrated Benefits, Concentrated Costs 477

Client Politics: Concentrated Benefits, Distributed Costs 478

Entrepreneurial Politics: Distributed Benefits, Concentrated Costs 479

The Case of Business Regulation 480
Majoritarian Politics 480
Interest Group Politics 482
Client Politics 482
Entrepreneurial Politics 484

Perceptions, Beliefs, Interests, and Values 486
Deregulation 487
The Limits of Ideas 488

Chapter 18 Economic Policy 492

The Politics of Economic Prosperity 495
What Politicians Try to Do 495

The Politics of Taxing and Spending 496

Economic Theories and Political Needs 498
Monetarism 498
Keynesianism 498
Planning 499
Supply-Side Tax Cuts 500
Did the Federal Government End the Recession? 500

The Machinery of Economic Policymaking 500
The Fed 501
Congress 502
Globalization 503

Spending Money 504
The Budget 504
Reducing Spending 505
Levying Taxes 506
The Rise of the Income Tax 507

Chapter 19 Social Welfare 514

Two Kinds of Social Welfare Programs 516
Social Welfare in the United States 518
Majoritarian Welfare Programs: Social Security and Medicare 521
Client Welfare Programs: Aid to Families with Dependent Children 526
Majoritarian Versus Client Politics 527

Chapter 20 Foreign and Military Policy 534

Kinds of Foreign Policy 536
The Constitutional and Legal Context 537
Presidential Box Score 537
Evaluating the Power of the President 539
Checks on Presidential Power 539
The Machinery of Foreign Policy 542
Foreign Policy and Public Opinion 543
Backing the President 544
Mass Versus Elite Opinion 545
Cleavages Among Foreign Policy Elites 546
How a Worldview Shapes Foreign Policy 546
Political Polarization 549
The Use of Military Force 550
War in Iraq 551
The Defense Budget 552
Total Spending 552
What Do We Get with Our Money? 554
The Structure of Defense Decision Making 557
Joint Chiefs of Staff 557
The Services 558
The Chain of Command 558
The New Problem of Terrorism 558
Iraq and Afghanistan 560

Chapter 21 Environmental Policy 564

Entrepreneurial Politics: Global Warming 566
Majoritarian Politics: Pollution from Automobiles 569
Interest Group Politics: Acid Rain 571
Client Politics: Agricultural Pesticides 572
The Environmental Uncertainties 574
The Results 577

PART V The Nature of American Democracy 581

Chapter 22 Who Governs? To What Ends? 582

Restraints on the Growth of Government 582
Relaxing the Restraints 583
The Old System 584
The New System 585
Consequences of Activist Government 587
The Influence of Structure 590
The Influence of Ideas 591

Appendixes
The Declaration of Independence A1
The Constitution of the United States A4
The Federalist No. 10 A21
The Federalist No. 51 A26
Presidents and Congresses, 1789–2009 A30
AP* Review Questions: Multiple Choice R1
AP* Practice Free-Response Questions E1
Glossary G1
Notes N1
Index I1

Preface

We wrote this textbook not only to explain to students how the federal government works but also to make clear how those institutions have developed over time and their effects on public policy. Unlike many authors, we explain the history of Congress, the presidency, the judiciary, and the bureaucracy because the politics we see today are different from those we would have seen a few decades ago. And, of course, change never stops: in another decade, federal politics may be very different from what they are today.

The book is current through mid-2011 and evaluates the immediate effect of the 2010 elections as well as the consequences for 2012.

SPECIAL FEATURES

As in the past, we illustrate our discussion with chapter-opening vignettes, landmark court decisions, and clear examples of politics in action. With the Thirteenth Edition, we now also begin each chapter with *Learning Objectives* that identify key questions for students to consider as they study the material, questions they should be able to answer after reading the chapter. The questions point out "What You Need to Know," followed by our thematic questions, "Who Governs?" and "To What Ends?" These questions and the answers to them are reexamined at the end of each chapter to help students assess their comprehension and review the material.

Like the previous AP* edition, this one includes an introduction to students about the AP* exam, with strategies for each type of question they will find, and a correlation chart that relates the topics of the AP* course to the pages of the text. New for this edition, we have added multiple-choice and free-response AP* Review Questions, created by Doug Henderson of Clear Lake High School, Houston, TX, so that students can practice for the exam. These can be found after the Appendix at the end of the book.

Compared to other modern democracies, America's basic constitutional framework has changed relatively little since the nation was founded. Yet America's political institutions have been quite dynamic, and certain shifts in public law and policy have been nothing short of dramatic. Each chapter's opening section now has a *Then and Now* feature intended to help sensitize students to this still-unfolding saga of continuity and change—the politics of financial crises in the 1780s and now (Chapter 1), the proliferation of interest groups (Chapter 11), the partisan polarization of Congress (Chapter 13), the rise of national social welfare policies (Chapter 19), and more.

We have expanded two features in this edition: *Research Frontiers* and *How We Compare*. *Research Frontiers* are short boxes in most chapters that highlight new findings about how politics works, ask readers to think critically about future implications, and challenge them to conduct their own research for deeper understanding. The *How We Compare* boxes evaluate how aspects of American democracy differ from governing philosophies and practices in other democracies.

Additional boxed features remain focused and clear. For example, the popular *What Would You Do?* boxes are designed to generate classroom discussion and debate. Each highlights an important policy question and briefly states the arguments for and against each option. *How Things Work* boxes give students an understanding of such procedures in American politics as amending the Constitution, becoming a U.S. citizen, and becoming a congressperson.

Thanks to the ever-evolving Internet, our students now have virtually limitless access to information on most subjects, including American government. Even when we are not searching for it or paying close attention, news, opinions, and entertainment concerning the latest in American politics stream into our lives. In some ways, this makes teaching and learning about our subject easier than it once was. But it also poses pedagogical challenges for teachers. Information is not knowledge. Instant analysis is no substitute for in-depth study. Strong opinions are hollow unless they are rooted in serious reflection and critical thinking. Thus, each chapter ends with *Questions to Consider* that address the *Learning Objectives* in the start of each chapter and offer further questions for students to consider as they prepare for class, writing assignments, and examinations. Within the end-of-chapter *To Learn*

*AP and the Advanced Placement Program are registered trademarks of the College Entrance Examination Board, which was not involved in the production of, and does not endorse, this product.

More sections, we have kept carefully selected Web resources and classic and contemporary suggested readings that identify key scholarship on each subject to further assist students in learning about American politics. Of course, the most important "examinations" of the material they study here will come later in their lives—lives that, we hope, will include ongoing and serious intellectual and civic engagement in American politics and government.

FOR USERS OF THE PREVIOUS EDITION

In addition to the new features, including updated tables, figures, citations, and photographs, as well as the most current information available throughout, significant chapter-by-chapter changes have been made as follows:

- Chapter 1: The *Research Frontiers* feature contains an introductory explanation of how political scientists explain political behavior. This is meant to show students that finding a good explanation is a complicated business.
- Chapter 2: An expanded discussion on the Framers' adoption of the Bill of Rights is included, in addition to a look at other countries' constitutions.
- Chapter 3: The *How We Compare* box evaluates how U.S. federalism differs from federalism in other democracies, and the *What Would You Do?* box examines how the national government and the states should share responsibility for public education.
- Chapter 4: Updated data are included on trust in the federal government and confidence in American institutions, and a new chart examines American civic health.
- Chapter 5: Includes new discussions on *Citizens United v. F.E.C., District of Columbia v. Heller,* and *McDonald v. Chicago,* and on "libel tourism."
- Chapter 6: An updated section on same-sex marriage, including a look at how the United States compares to other countries on this issue.
- Chapter 7: A look at how other countries view the United States and updated public opinion statistics throughout.
- Chapter 8: Includes a reworked section on the issue of nonvoting, a new *How We Compare* feature looking at laws on voting, and new data on the causes and meaning of participation.
- Chapter 9: Includes a new table on the rapidly rising costs to fund a successful congressional campaign in the 21st century, a discussion of the Tea Party movement in American politics, and an updated *Research Frontiers* box about the future of the Republican Party after the 2010 midterm elections.
- Chapter 10: A new box evaluating the 2010 midterm elections is included, as is a *How We Compare* box on public funding for national political campaigns.
- Chapter 11: New discussions on *Citizens United v. Federal Election Commission* and post-9/11 interest groups, updated financial data included throughout, an updated discussion on unions and the events of 2011, and a revised section on "Upper-Class Bias?"
- Chapter 12: A new *How We Compare* box examines freedom of the press in the United States and other advanced industrialized democracies, and the *Research Frontiers* box is updated to include recent examples of the uses and challenges of "digital democracy."
- Chapter 13: The chapter on Congress has been updated to account for the 2010 elections throughout and has also been thoroughly rewritten to streamline the chapter.
- Chapter 14: The Presidency chapter has been reorganized to bring together the sections on presidential power and persuasion, as well as the sections on White House organization and appointments. The *What Would You Do?* box has a new case study of presidential-congressional budget negotiations, and a new *Research Frontiers* box examines whether presidential public communications influence public opinion.
- Chapter 15: A new figure shows *The Growth of the Federal Government in Money, People, and Rules*, and the chapter includes an expanded discussion on congressional oversight.
- Chapter 16: Updated to include a look at the debate over the 2010 health care act's constitutionality, Elena Kagan's appointment to the Supreme Court, and how our courts compare to those in other countries.
- Chapter 17: Several examples updated for the Obama administration.
- Chapter 18: Thoroughly updated throughout to discuss the recent recession, deficit spending, and current tax policy, as well as a look at how taxation in the United States compares with taxation in other countries.
- Chapter 19: Updates on health care policy, Medicare, Social Security, and TANF.

- Chapter 20: Updates on the killing of Osama bin Laden, Afghanistan, and the role of the United States in the "Arab Spring" movements, as well as a new *How We Compare* feature on opinions on global issues and a new table on foreign policy position and party affiliation.
- Chapter 21: Includes updated data on public opinion about the environment, as well as a discussion of why the Obama administration has not followed through on campaign promises to enact major environmental policy reform.
- Chapter 22: The closing chapter leaves readers with a portrait of the current political landscape and tasks them with future examination of their government using the tools they've acquired.

LEARNING AND TEACHING ANCILLARIES

The program for *American Government*, Thirteenth Edition, includes a number of learning and teaching aids. These ancillaries provide instructors with useful course management and presentation tools and help students get the most from their American Government course.

PowerLecture DVD with JoinIn™ Student Response System and ExamView®

An all-in-one multimedia resource for class preparation, presentation, and testing, this DVD includes Microsoft® PowerPoint® slides, a Test Bank in both Microsoft® Word and ExamView® formats, an Instructor's Manual, and a Resource Integration Guide. The book-specific slides of lecture outlines, as well as photos, figures, and tables from the text, make it easy for you to assemble lectures for your course, while the media-enhanced slides for each chapter can be used on their own or easily integrated with the book-specific PowerPoint outlines. These media-enhanced slides include audio and video clips, as well as new animated learning modules illustrating key concepts, tables, statistical charts, and more. The Test Bank includes multiple-choice and essay questions, along with their answers and page references. An Instructor's Manual includes learning objectives, chapter outlines, discussion questions, class activities and projects suggestions, tips on integrating media into your class, suggested readings and Web resources, and a section especially designed to help teaching assistants and adjunct instructors. JoinIn™ offers book-specific "clicker" questions that test and track student comprehension of key concepts—political polling questions simulate voting and the results can be compared to national data, leading to lively discussions; Visual Literacy questions tied to images from the book add high-interest feedback during your lecture. Finally, the Resource Integration Guide outlines the resources available to instructors and students within the chapter-by-chapter framework of the book, suggesting how and when each supplement can be used to optimize learning. Contact your sales representative to receive a copy upon adoption.

AP* Teacher's Resource Guide

The AP* Teacher's Resource Guide, written by Karen Waples, Cherry Creek High School, Greenwood Village, CO, is based on the college Instructor's Resource Guide by Allen Trigger, Virginia Western Community College. It describes the AP* exam, offers recommendations to teachers, and suggests a pacing guide for the course. For each chapter of the text, it provides "AP* Focus" sections that offer suggestions for teaching particular topics and point out concepts that often appear on the exam.

Fast Track to a 5: Preparing for the AP* United States Government Examination

The Fast Track to a 5 is a test-preparation book by Karen Waples, Cherry Creek High School, Greenwood Village, Colorado. It includes information on the exam and strategies for answering each type of question, a diagnostic test, topic review chapters with practice questions, and two complete practice tests in AP* format. It can be purchased either with the text or separately.

AP Edition Political Science CourseMate with eBook

Cengage Learning's Political Science CourseMate brings course concepts to life with interactive learning, study tools, and exam preparation tools that support the printed textbook. Material from the Fast Track to a 5 guide has been integrated into the CourseMate product. An interactive eBook allows students to take notes, highlight, search, and interact with embedded media (such as quizzes, flashcards, and videos). Other resources include critical-thinking activities, simulations, animated learning modules, and interactive timelines. Ask your sales representative about available discounts.

Discovering State and Local Government: A Primer

Authors Wilson and DiIulio help students explore the politics of state and local government in this 48-page print supplement. Topics include: "who lives where" politics; American-style federalism; Jacksonians v. Progressives; constitutional and legal frameworks; state and local government structures; and the future of state and local government. Ask your sales representative about available discounts.

CourseReader: American Government

CourseReader for American Government is a fully customizable online reader that provides access to hundreds of readings, audio, and video selections from multiple disciplines. This easy-to-use solution allows you to select exactly the content you need for your courses, and is loaded with convenient pedagogical features like highlighting, printing, note taking, and audio downloads. *You* have the freedom to assign individualized content at an affordable price. CourseReader: American Government is the perfect complement to any class. Ask your sales representative about available discounts.

Instructor Companion Web Site

This password-protected Web site for teachers features all of the free student assets, plus an instructor's manual (learning objectives, chapter outlines, discussion questions, class activities and projects suggestions, tips on integrating media into your class, suggested readings and Web resources, and a section especially designed to help teaching assistants and adjunct instructors), and book-specific PowerPoint® presentations (lecture outlines, photos, and figures). Also included is the Instructor's Guide to YouTube. Organized by 15 topics, the guide follows the sequence of an American government course and includes a preface with tips on how to use Internet videos in class, links to video clips, clip descriptions, and discussion questions. Access from www.cengage.com/login.

Political Theatre DVD 2.0

Bring politics home to students with Political Theatre 2.0, up-to-date through the 2008 election season. This is the second edition of this three-DVD series and includes real video clips that show American political thought throughout the public sector. Clips include both classic and contemporary political advertisements, speeches, interviews, and more. Available to adopters of Cengage textbooks, version 2.0 provides added functionality with this updated edition. Ask your sales representative about available discounts.

JoinIn™ Student Response System—Political Theatre 2.0, 2nd Edition

For even more interaction, combine Political Theatre with the innovative teaching tool of a classroom response system through JoinIn™. Poll your students with questions created for you or create your own questions. Built within the Microsoft® PowerPoint® software, it's easy to integrate into your current lectures in conjunction with the "clicker" hardware of your choice.

The Wadsworth News DVD for American Government 2013, 1st Edition

This collection of two- to five-minute video clips on relevant political issues serves as a great lecture or discussion launcher. An introduction for context, as well as discussion questions, accompanies each clip.

Table of Contents:

1. AN INTRODUCTION TO AMERICAN DEMOCRACY

Video 1: Mongolia Embraces Democracy

Video 2: YouTube Provides Glimpse into Iranian Protests

2. THE BUREAUCRACY

Video 1: New Federal Safety Regulations for Deep Oil Drilling

Video 2: Federal Debt Ceiling Explained

3. CAMPAIGNS AND ELECTIONS

Video 1: Getting Out the Vote at the Iowa Caucuses

Video 2: President Obama Garners Support from Many Demographic Groups

Video 3: Obama Expands the Political Map

4. CIVIL LIBERTIES

Video 1: Protests at Military Funerals

Video 2: Protests in Wisconsin over Union Rights and Budget Cuts

5. CIVIL RIGHTS

Video 1: Arizona's New Immigration Law Causes Concern for Some

Video 2: The End of Don't Ask, Don't Tell

6. CONGRESS

Video 1: Lobbyists Garner Support for Special Interests

Video 2: Members of Congress Use Twitter to Reach Constituents

7. THE CONSTITUTION

Video 1: Republicans Use Courts to Try to Block Health Care Reform

8. DOMESTIC POLICY

Video 1: Immigrant Girl Thrives in School

Video 2: Illegal Immigrants Cost Taxpayers

Video 3: Reducing Dependence on Foreign Oil

9. FEDERALISM

Video 1: Federal Government Sues Arizona over Immigration Law

10. FOREIGN POLICY

Video 1: Afghanistan After bin Laden

Video 2: U.S.-Israeli Relations Hung Up on Settlements

11. INTEREST GROUPS

Video 1: Lobbyists Boost Power of Fannie Mae

Video 2: Pharmaceutical Industry Provides Lucrative Jobs for Former Members of Congress

12. THE JUDICIARY

Video 1: Mayor of Phoenix Uses Courts to Stop Immigration Law

13. MEDIA AND POLITICS

Video 1: President Obama Harnesses Social Networking for Campaigns and Governance

Video 2: Social Networking Advances Freedom in Middle East

14. POLITICAL PARTIES

Video 1: Congress and President Propose Alternative Deficit Reduction Plans

Video 2: Stalemate over Debt Ceiling

15. THE PRESIDENCY

Video 1: President Obama Uses Executive Orders to Reverse Bush Policies

Video 2: President Obama's Energy Policy Focuses on Long-Term Change

16. PUBLIC OPINION

Video 1: Exit Polls Project Winners and Demographic Trends

Video 2: The Difficulty of Predicting Iowa Caucus Outcomes

17. VOTING AND PARTICIPATION

Video 1: Inconsistencies in Voting Procedures from State to State

Video 2: Voting Machine Accountability in Question

ABC News DVD: Speeches by Barack Obama, 1st Edition

DVD of nine famous speeches by President Barack Obama, from 2004 through his inauguration, including his speech at the 2004 Democratic National Convention; his 2008 speech on race, "A More Perfect Union"; and his 2009 inaugural address. Speeches are divided into short video segments for easy, time-efficient viewing. This teacher supplement also features critical-thinking questions and answers for each speech, designed to spark classroom discussion. Ask your sales representative about available discounts.

Latino-American Politics Supplement, 2nd Edition

Schmidt/Shelley/Bardes/Ford/Maxwell/Crain/Santos

Ask your sales representative about available discounts. This updated 32-page supplement uses real examples to detail politics related to Latino Americans. Ask your sales representative about available discounts.

Instructor's Guide to YouTube for Political Science

Teachers have access to the Instructor's Guide to YouTube, which shows American government instructors where on the Internet to find videos that can be used as learning tools in class. Organized by 15 topics, the guide follows the sequence of an American Government course and includes a preface with tips on how to use Internet videos in class.

ACKNOWLEDGMENTS

A number of scholars reviewed the book and made useful suggestions for the Thirteenth Edition. They include:

Philip Aka, Chicago State University
Chuck Brownson, Stephen F. Austin High School
Zach Courser, Boston College
Matthew Eshbaugh-Soha, University of North Texas
Richard Grubbs, R.L. Paschal High School
Jeff Harmon, University of Texas at San Antonio
Junius Koonce, Edgecombe Community College
Randall McKeever, Forney ISD
Marvin Overby, University of Missouri
P. S. Ruckman, Rock Valley College
Randall Smith, Naperville Central High School
Greg Snoad, Mauldin High School

A number of scholars reviewed the previous two editions. They include:

Lucas Allen, Michigan State University
Roger Ashby, Peace College
Michael Baranowski, Northern Kentucky University
Jack Citrin, University of California, Berkeley
Stan Crippen, Riverside County Office of Education

Gregory Culver, University of Southern Indiana
Terri Fine, University of Central Florida
Glenn David Garrison, Collin County Community College—Spring Creek Campus
Kipling Hagopian
Kevin Hassett
Kathleen C. Hauger, Abington Senior High School
Stephen Kerbow, Southwest Texas Junior College
Halima Asghar Khan, Massasoit Community College
Young-Choul Kim, University of Evansville
Junius H. Koonce, Edgecombe Community College
William Lester, Jacksonville State University
Brad Lockerbie, University of Georgia
Anne F. Presley, McKinney High School
Gayle Randolph, Neosho County Community College
Donald Ranish, Antelope Valley College
Jonathan Roberts, Portland, OR, schools
P. S. Ruckman, Rock Valley College
Rebecca Small, Herndon High School
Jennifer Walsh, Azusa Pacific University
David Wigg, St. Louis Community College
Teresa Wright, California State University—Long Beach

Additional thanks go to Marc Siegal for his research assistance.

JAMES Q. WILSON

James Q. Wilson now teaches at Pepperdine University and Boston College. He is an emeritus professor of management and public policy at the University of California, Los Angeles, and from 1961 to 1987 was a professor of government at Harvard University. Raised in California, he received a B.A. degree from the University of Redlands and a Ph.D from the University of Chicago. Wilson is the author or coauthor of fourteen books, including *The Marriage Problem* (2002), *Moral Judgment* (1997), *The Moral Sense* (1993), *Bureaucracy* (1989), *Crime and Human Nature* (1985, with Richard J. Herrnstein), *Thinking about Crime* (1983), and *Political Organizations* (1974).

Wilson has served in a number of advisory posts in the federal government. He was chairman of the White House Task Force on Crime in 1967, chairman of the National Advisory Council on Drug Abuse Prevention in 1972–1973, a member of the Attorney General's Task Force on Violent Crime in 1981, and a member of the President's Foreign Intelligence Advisory Board in 1986–1990.

In 1977 the American Political Science Association conferred on him the Charles E. Merriam Award for advancing the art of government through the application of social science knowledge and in 1990 the James Madison Award for distinguished scholarship. In 1991–1992, he was President of the Association.

He is a Fellow of the American Academy of Arts and Sciences and a member of the American Philosophical Society. In 2003, Wilson received the Presidential Medal of Freedom, this nation's highest civilian award.

JOHN J. DIIULIO, JR.

John J. DiIulio, Jr., is a professor of political science at the University of Pennsylvania. From 1986 to 1999, he was a professor of politics and public affairs at Princeton University's Woodrow Wilson School of Public and International Affairs. He received B.A. and M.A. degrees from the University of Pennsylvania and M.A. and Ph.D degrees from Harvard University. He is the author, coauthor, or editor of a dozen books, including *Godly Republic* (2007), *Medicaid and Devolution* (1998, with Frank Thompson), *Deregulating the Public Service* (1994), and *Governing Prisons* (1987).

DiIulio advised both Vice President Al Gore and Governor George W. Bush during the 2000 presidential campaign. While on leave in academic year 2000–2001, he served as Assistant to the President of the United States. He has advised officials at the National Performance Review, the Office of Management and Budget, the General Accounting Office, the U.S. Department of Justice, and other federal agencies. He has served on the boards of Big Brothers Big Sisters of America and other nonprofit organizations.

In 1995, the Association of Public Policy Analysis and Management conferred on him the David N. Kershaw Award for outstanding research achievements and in 1987 he received the American Political Science Association's Leonard D. White Award in public administration. In 1991–1994, he chaired the latter association's standing committee on professional ethics. Since 2005, he has had a leading role in nonprofit initiatives to assist post-Katrina New Orleans.

MEENA BOSE

Meena Bose is Director of the Peter S. Kalikow Center for the Study of the American Presidency at Hofstra University, as well as the Peter S. Kalikow Chair in Presidential Studies and Professor of Political Science. She is the author of *Shaping and Signaling Presidential Policy: The National Security Decision Making of Eisenhower and Kennedy* (1998) and editor of the reference volume *The New York Times on the Presidency* (2009), *Votes to Victory: Winning and Governing the White House in the Twenty-First Century* (2011), and *President or King? Evaluating the Expansion of Presidential Power from Abraham Lincoln to George W. Bush* (forthcoming). She also is co-editor (with Rosanna Perotti) of *From Cold War to*

New World Order: The Foreign Policy of George H. W. Bush (2002), co-editor (with Mark Landis) of *The Uses and Abuses of Presidential Ratings* (2003), and co-editor (with John J. DiIulio, Jr.) of *Classic Ideas and Current Issues in American Government* (2007).

Bose was scholar-in-residence for a nonpartisan course sponsored by The Washington Center in connection with the 2008 Republican National Convention in Minneapolis, and she will be active in both of the Center's convention courses in 2012. She also has designed and taught several courses for Elderhostel, including "The Wisdom of Our Fathers: The Mount Rushmore Presidents."*Long Island Business News* selected her as one of the "Top 40 Under 40" leaders on Long Island in 2009.

Bose taught for six years at the United States Military Academy at West Point, where she also served as Director of American Politics in 2006. She previously taught at Hofstra University from 1996 to 2000 and represented the American Political Science Association on the Department of State's Historical Advisory Committee from 2001 to 2004. She earned her undergraduate degree in international politics from Penn State University (1990), and she received her master's (1992) and doctoral (1996) degrees in politics from Princeton University.

A Letter from the Author

WHY THIS TEXTBOOK?

This book first appeared in 1981 and has, I think, become better and better with every edition. A main reason for the improvement has been the suggestions from readers, teachers, and scholars asked to help improve it. I, and now with my coauthors, John DiIulio and Meena Bose, have corrected factual errors, put matters into clearer language, and added features that have made its main topics more accessible. I thank all of you who have helped out.

But there is another reason it has endured: it is written around certain key ideas that sustain the readers' interest and help them understand, not simply American government, but the reasons why government in this country is different from those in other, especially European, democracies. These ideas are our Constitution, our adversarial political culture, and a commitment to freedom and limited government.

The Constitution

The American Revolution and the Constitution, which was approved some years later, were not the results of a struggle between rival kings, an assertion of our ethnic or racial status, a rebuke to an established church, or the outcome of a battle between ambitious generals. In 1776 we were by and large (slaves being the big exception) one people with the same background and the same religion. There were no generals running around shooting cannons at each other. Rather, the Revolution reflected a commitment to certain principles, well stated by Thomas Jefferson in the Declaration of Independence, that were based on an idea of natural rights. We are, he wrote, created equal and endowed with certain unalienable rights, among which are life, liberty, and the pursuit of happiness. To ensure that the government respects those rights, it must first obtain the consent of the governed.

The Constitution was written by men preoccupied with liberty. To ensure it, they decided to separate the branches of government so that each one—the Congress, the president, and the Supreme Court—would share in almost every decision that would be made. To share, of course, means to argue. And argue they have. To add more opportunities for disagreement, the original view of federalism left the states with broad, but undefined, powers. Indeed, with few exceptions, the Constitution does not spell out which policies shall be under federal control and which under state control.

In most of Europe, there is no separation of powers; there is only one authority, parliament. It decides what polices shall be adopted and local governments are expected to do what parliament has decreed. In some countries, there are important state or provincial governments, but they are much less important in affecting public policy than are the American states. In this book we have tried to highlight these differences by putting in boxes that show how we compare to other democratic nations.

An Adversarial Nation

These constitutional arrangements and the mind-set that they encouraged gave rise to a political system in which we spend a lot of time criticizing one another. The late political scientist, Samuel P. Huntington, in his book *American Politics: The Promise of Disharmony*, points out that from the American Revolution down to the present we have gone through many periods of intense conflict followed, in many cases, with periods of relative calm. In 1775–1776 we argued about whether to dissolve our connection with England, in 1787 we argued about whether the new Constitution would protect personal liberty, in the middle of the 19th century we argued about whether slaves should be set free, in the late-19th century we argued about whether money should be made cheap by coining silver, in the 1920s we argued about Prohibition, in the 1960s we argued about almost everything (civil rights, the emancipation of youth, the war in Vietnam), and today we argue about whether the federal government is too large and too expensive.

Politics is often polarized in this country, but today's polarization is more visible than it was before because of the Internet, blogs, talk radio, and cable news programs that are on 24/7. We hear more about how we disagree than when the supporters of John Adams and Thomas Jefferson denounced one another in 1800 or the opponents and supporters of slavery not only denounced but started shooting at one another.

Contributing to polarization is the belief each of us has that our freedoms may be limited, and so we bring lawsuits against each other at an extraordinary rate, we mobilize supporters from sympathetic local and state governments, and we explain at length our grievances on talk shows and in op-eds. But restraining this adversarial impulse is the rarity with which we challenge the government by trying to shut it down. Compare antigovernment rhetoric in this country with mass strikes that shut down the government in France. It is, I think, ironic that people who believe in limited government are more reluctant to shut it down than people, such as those in France, who seem to believe in an all-powerful state.

We have had our share of public violence such as lynchings, shooting striking workers, attacks on abortion centers, and urban riots. But these events have not been attacks on the government but rather attacks on what the government either has done or has failed to do. What protects the government has been, to cite Huntington again, "the restraint of government power through fundamental law." One indicator of our skepticism of expanding the government to solve any problem has been the failure of many European ideologies, such as Marxism or fascism, to have much of an impact here. We certainly disagree with one another but not, for the most part, over "the substance of those beliefs than over how seriously to take those beliefs."

Commitment to Freedom

It may seem odd that in a nation with more than 300 million people made up of every imaginable ethnic, racial, and religious group we should get along with each other. But, with notable exceptions, we do. We have no good way of measuring our commitment to freedom; after all, we may value freedom on some issues and not value it so much on others. Our actions do not always match our beliefs. The Swedish sociologist, Gunnar Myrdal, called this the "American dilemma."

Over many decades our conception of who is entitled to freedom has changed. We are now more tolerant of racial, religious, and behavioral difference than once was the case. Perhaps the most interesting clue about the importance of freedom comes from the remarks of people in the armed services (the only part of the federal government that has grown sharply in its popularity) when they are asked why they are fighting in Afghanistan or Iraq. Their typical answer is that they are "defending freedom." In some ways this is an unusual response: how does one defend American freedom in two Middle Eastern countries? But in another way it is quite reasonable: they are saying that the military's central task is not to conquer land, acquire colonies, or seize resources, rather it is to protect what its members think is America's most important asset, the freedom its people enjoy.

When Americans were asked by the Pew Research Center whether they were "very proud" to be an American, 71 percent of the sample said yes. When British, French, German, Italian, and Japanese people were asked how they felt about their own countries, only 21 to 45 percent said they were proud. The same survey, in trying to find out why this difference in patriotism existed, asked questions about religion, the role of government, the causes of individual success, and how children should be taught; the differences in the answers were striking. In America, 94 percent said they believed in God, while in Britain, France, and Germany only about 50 to 60 percent gave the same answer. When asked whether it is more important for the government to provide a safety net or to let each person be left free to pursue his or her own goals, 58 percent of Americans preferred the latter while 57 to 71 percent of Europeans preferred the former. When asked what determines success in life, only one-third of Americans said that it was "forces beyond our control," while half to two-thirds of French, Italian, and German respondents said that it was outside forces. When asked whether children should be taught the value of hard work, 60 percent of Americans supported that but only one-third of British and Italian respondents agreed.

Clearly Americans differ on these measures from most Europeans. These differences may reflect differences in how people value freedom, but we cannot be confident of this because it is very hard to ask a meaningful question about "freedom" that is not connected to some specific issue, and of course there are countless such questions that might implicate how we value freedom. But we do know that most Western Europeans dislike American-style democracy and especially American business practices. Interestingly, most Eastern Europeans (for example, Czechs, Slovaks, and Poles) do like American-style democracy and business practices. Living for decades under Soviet rule may have given these Easterners a different view than that held by Westerners.

Naturally, this quick summary of what is distinctive about America neglects many issues. Part of the debate over President Obama's health care reform bill is an argument about whether or not this country should become more like Europe in how it delivers that service. This country has different policies toward abortion in part because here the Supreme Court decided the matter while abroad legislatures did. All of these differences are important; nevertheless, what is essential here is not who is right and who is wrong, but that the United States is a very different democracy than those we find abroad.

Conclusion

This book is an attempt to explain and give the historical and practical reasons for these differences. We are saying that America is a unique democracy, not necessarily the best one. That is for you to decide. Good luck.

Sincerely,

James Q. Wilson

Correlation for U.S. Government and Politics to *American Government: Institutions and Policies, 13th Edition*

TOPIC	CORRELATION TO *American Government: Institutions and Policies, 13th Edition*
I. Constitutional Underpinnings of United States Government	
A. Considerations that influenced the formulation and adoption of the Constitution	Pages 9, 20–41, 101–102, 332–334, 582–583
B. Separation of powers	Pages 25, 30–32, 41, 43–44, 47, 52, 164, 326, 329, 385, 582–583
C. Checks and balances	Pages 31, 326, 329, 369, 440, 460–462, 585
D. Federalism	Pages 30–32, 50–76, 164, 205, 326
E. Theories of democratic government	Pages 6–14, 16–17, 25–26, 29, 34, 40–45, 81–82, 85–86, 93

TOPIC	CORRELATION TO *American Government: Institutions and Policies, 13th Edition*
II. Political Beliefs and Behaviors	
A. Beliefs that citizens hold about their government and its leaders	Pages 4–9, 16, 32, 81–98, 162–164, 167–180, 471–476, 486–488
B. Processes by which citizens learn about politics	Pages 167–180, 235–238, 246–249, 298–324
C. The nature, sources, and consequences of public opinion	Pages 61, 162–180, 199, 235–236, 266, 285–286, 352, 460, 462–463
D. The ways in which citizens vote and otherwise participate in political life	Pages 182–199, 257–260, 263, 270–297
E. Factors that influence citizens to differ from one another in terms of political beliefs and behaviors	Pages 4, 79–97, 102–105, 130–159, 166–176, 244–249, 270–297, 471–476, 486–488

TOPIC	CORRELATION TO *American Government: Institutions and Policies, 13th Edition*
III. Political Parties, Interest Groups, and Mass Media	
A. Political parties and elections	
1. Functions	Pages 204–206, 257–264
2. Organization	Pages 216–225, 238–257
3. Development	Pages 187–192, 206–216
4. Effects on the political process	Pages 202–225, 264–266
5. Electoral Laws and systems	Pages 225–227, 234–268
B. Interest groups, including political action committees (PACs)	
1. The range of interests represented	Pages 270–283
2. The activities of interest groups	Pages 283–291
3. The effects of interest groups on the political process	Pages 10, 102–103, 280–293, 332, 425–426, 453, 477–478, 482, 571–572
4. The unique characteristics and roles of PACs in the political process	Pages 240, 249, 283–291
C. The mass media	
1. The functions and structure of the news media	Pages 300–310, 318–319
2. The impact of the news media on politics	Pages 176, 299–305, 310–319
3. The news media industry and its consequences	Pages 302–310, 313–319

TOPIC	CORRELATION TO *American Government: Institutions and Policies, 13th Edition*
IV. Institutions of National Government: The Congress, the Presidency, the Bureaucracy, and the Federal Courts	
A. The major formal and informal institutional arrangements of power	Pages 11–17, 30–31, 52–67, 326–363, 364–407, 408–437, 438–467
B. Relationships among these four institutions and varying balances of power	Pages 30–31, 41–44, 53–57, 326–329, 371–372, 383–386, 401, 438–440, 447–450, 457–462, 539-542, 582-585
C. Linkages between institutions and the following:	
1. Public opinion and voters	Pages 162–181, 192–196, 265–266, 285–286, 378–379, 462–463
2. Interest groups	Pages 249–257, 270–296
3. Political parties	Pages 202–206, 257–259, 330–331, 340–346
4. The media	Pages 234–239, 246–249, 298–323
5. State and local governments	Pages 51–68, 187–190, 216–220

TOPIC	CORRELATION TO *American Government: Institutions and Policies, 13th Edition*
V. Public Policy	
A. Policymaking in a federal system	Pages 8–10, 350–356, 470–488, 492–510, 515–520, 536–537, 557–558
B. The formation of policy agendas	Pages 78–85, 176–178, 224–225, 471–476, 504–510, 516–521, 583–587
C. The role of institutions in the enactment of policy	Pages 346–348, 350–356, 367–369, 394–398, 414–432, 440–446, 457–459
D. The role of the bureaucracy and the courts in policy implementation and interpretation	Pages 408–437, 438–467
E. Linkages between policy processes and the following:	
1. Political institutions and federalism	Pages 52, 59–63, 473–475
2. Political parties	Pages 205–206, 257–259, 496, 549
3. Interest groups	Pages 270–295, 472–473, 477–478, 482, 503–504, 536, 571–572
4. Public opinion	Pages 91–94, 173–178, 378–383, 462–463, 472–474
5. Elections	Pages 257–260, 264–266, 372–373, 378–383, 473, 495–496, 588
6. Policy networks	Pages 425, 484–486

TOPIC	CORRELATION TO *American Government: Institutions and Policies, 13th Edition*
VI. Civil Rights and Civil Liberties	
A. The development of civil liberties and civil rights by judicial interpretation	Pages 9, 36–37, 68–69, 105–127, 133-139, 143, 146, 438–445, 454–457
B. Knowledge of substantive rights and liberties	Pages 36–37, 83–84, 100–127, 130–156
C. The impact of the Fourteenth Amendment on the constitutional development of rights and liberties	Pages 37, 100, 105, 108, 126, 133–137, 145–153, 440–444

Preparing for the AP* Exam

Advanced Placement can be exhilarating. Whether you are taking an AP course at your school or you are working on AP independently, the stage is set for a great intellectual experience. As the school year progresses and you burrow deeper and deeper into the course work, you will begin to make connections between the ideas and concepts that form the basis of government and politics in the United States. Fleshing out those concepts is exciting. More exciting still is recognizing examples of these concepts in the media. More importantly, this course will prepare you to become a participatory citizen and informed voter.

But sometime after New Year's Day, when the examination begins to loom on a very real horizon, Advanced Placement can seem downright intimidating—in fact, offered the opportunity to take the examination for a lark, even adults long out of high school refuse. If you dread taking the test, you are in good company.

The best way to deal with an AP examination is to master it, not let it master you. If you can think of these examinations as a way to show off how your mind works, you have a leg up: attitude *does* help. If you are not one of those students, there is still a lot you can do to sideline your anxiety. Focused review and practice time will help you master the examination so that you can walk in with confidence and get a 5.

BEFORE THE EXAMINATION

By February, long before the exam, you need to make sure that you are registered to take the test. Many schools take care of the paperwork and handle the fees for their AP students, but check with your teacher or the AP coordinator to make sure that you are on the list. This is especially important if you have a documented disability and need test accommodations. If your family cannot afford to pay the full testing fee, do not be shy. Inform your AP coordinator. Reduced fees are available for those students who qualify. If you are studying AP independently, call AP Services at the College Board for the name of the local AP coordinator, who will help you through the registration process.

The evening before the exam is not a great time for partying. Nor is it a great time for cramming. If you like, look over class notes or drift through your textbook, concentrating on the broad outlines, not the small details, of the course.

The evening before the exam *is* a great time to get your things together for the next day. Sharpen a fistful of no. 2 pencils with good erasers for the multiple-choice section; set out several black or dark-blue ballpoint pens for the free-response questions; get a watch, as cell phones are not allowed in the testing room; get a piece of fruit or a power bar and a bottle of water for the break; make sure you have your Social Security number and whatever photo identification and admission ticket are required. Then relax. And get a good night's sleep.

On the day of the examination it is wise not to skip breakfast—studies show that students who eat a hot breakfast before testing get higher grades. Be careful not to drink a lot of liquids, necessitating a trip to the bathroom during the test. Breakfast will give you the energy you need to power you through the test—and more. You will spend some time waiting while everyone is seated in the right room for the right test, so prepare to be patient. Bring a high-energy snack to eat during the short break between Section I and Section II. The U.S. Government and Politics exam lasts for over two and a half hours. So be prepared for a long morning. You do not want to be distracted by a growling stomach or hunger pangs.

Leave your cell phone at home or in your locker. Be sure to wear comfortable clothes, taking along a sweater in case the heating or air-conditioning is erratic. Be sure, too, to wear clothes you like—everyone performs better when they think they look better—and by all means wear your lucky socks.

Now go get a 5.

---

*AP and the Advanced Placement Program are registered trademarks of the College Entrance Examination Board, which was not involved in the production of, and does not endorse, this product.

Taking the AP* U.S. Government and Politics Exam

The AP U.S. Government and Politics examination consists of two sections: Section I has 60 multiple-choice questions; Section II has four free-response questions. You will have 45 minutes for the multiple-choice portion. The questions are collected, and you will be given a short break. You then have 100 minutes for the free-response portion. You must write an essay for each of the four questions—some AP examinations allow you to choose among the free-response questions, but this is not one of them. Keep an eye on your watch and devote 25 minutes to each free-response question. Watch alarms are not allowed.

STRATEGIES FOR THE MULTIPLE-CHOICE SECTION

Here are some rules of thumb to help you work your way through the multiple-choice questions:

- **Answer every question** There are five possible answers for each question. Each correct answer is worth 1 point. There is no penalty for incorrect answers, so you should answer every question, even if you have to guess. Some students like to go through the exam quickly and answer the questions they know, and then go back to the more difficult questions. If you do this, be sure you mark the correct line on the answer sheet.
- **Read the question carefully** Pressured for time, many students make the mistake of reading the questions too quickly or merely skimming them. By reading a question carefully, you may already have some idea about the correct answer. You can then look for it in the responses. Careful reading is especially important in EXCEPT questions.
- **Eliminate any answer you know is wrong** You can write on the multiple-choice questions in the test book. As you read through the responses, draw a line through any answer you know is wrong.
- **Read all of the possible answers, then chose the most accurate response** AP examinations are written to test your precise knowledge of a subject. Sometimes there are a few probable answers but one of them is more specific. For example, the Fifteenth Amendment gave the vote to African Americans, but only men could vote at that time. An answer that referred to black men would be more correct than an answer that referred to all African Americans.
- **Avoid absolute responses** These answers often include the words "always" or "never." For example, the statement "Voter turnout in presidential elections is always slightly above 50 percent" is incorrect because in the 1996 presidential election, turnout was a little below 50 percent.
- **Mark and skip tough questions** If you are hung up on a question, mark it in the margin of the question book. You can come back to it later if you have time. Make sure you skip that question on your answer sheet too.

*AP and the Advanced Placement Program are registered trademarks of the College Entrance Examination Board, which was not involved in the production of, and does not endorse, this product.

TYPES OF MULTIPLE-CHOICE QUESTIONS

There are various kinds of multiple-choice questions. Here are some suggestions for how to approach each kind:

Classic/Best Answer Questions

This is the most common type of multiple-choice question. It simply requires you to read the question and select the most correct answer. For example:

1. How is the president of the United States usually selected?

    (A) by direct vote of the populace
    (B) by the House of Representatives
    (C) by the Senate
    (D) in a runoff election between the top two vote getters
    (E) by the Electoral College

ANSWER: E. The Electoral College usually selects the president, although the House of Representatives decides on the rare occasion when no candidate receives a majority of Electoral College votes. The word "usually" is very important in this question. This is a standard question that has one correct answer.

EXCEPT Questions

In the EXCEPT question, all of the answers are correct but one. The best way to approach these questions is as true/false. Mark a T or F in the margin next to each possible answer. There should be only one false answer, and that is the one you should select. For example:

1. Congress has the express power to do all of the following EXCEPT

    (A) lay and collect taxes
    (B) regulate interstate commerce
    (C) establish uniform standards for weights and measures
    (D) declare war
    (E) regulate intrastate commerce

ANSWER: E. Congress does not have the power to regulate intrastate commerce, so that is a false statement. You should have put an "F" next to it. All of the other statements are true.

List and Group Questions

In this type of question, there is a list of possible answers, and you must select the answer that contains the correct group of responses. These questions look hard, but you can simplify them by crossing out items from the list and then eliminating them in the answers below. For example:

1. According to the Constitution, as amended, which of the following is elected directly?

To approach the question, draw a line through choice I, because the president and vice president are not elected directly but are chosen by the Electoral College. Then cross out any response that contains choice I.

I. the president and vice-president

II. members of the House of Representatives

III. justices of the Supreme Court

IV. senators

    (A) I and II
    (B) II and III
    (C) I, II, and III
    (D) I and IV
    (E) II and IV

Continue to cross out items that are wrong and the responses that contain them. Justices of the Supreme Court are appointed, not elected. Draw a line through III and answer (B), which contains choice III, as well as through (C), which also contains choice III. Now you have narrowed down the possible responses.

ANSWER: E. Under the Constitution, including the Seventeenth Amendment, which provides for the direct election of senators, members of the House of Representatives and Senate are elected directly.

Chart/Graph Questions

These questions require you to examine the data on a chart or graph. While these questions are not difficult, spending too much time interpreting a chart or graph may slow you down. If a chart or graph is particularly difficult or detailed, consider skipping it and coming back to it later. Make sure you skip the question on your answer sheet as well. However, many graphs and charts are easy to decipher. First

Characteristics of Federal Civilian Employees, 1960 and 2005

Total number of employees 1960 2.2 million
2005 2.7 million

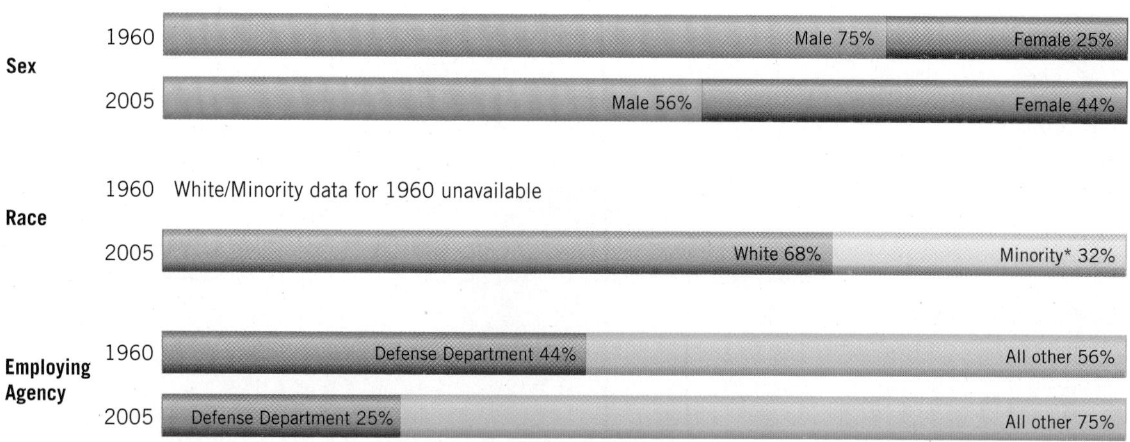

*Blacks, Native Americans, Hispanics, Asians, and Pacific Islanders

Sources: *Statistical Abstract of the United States, 1961*, 392–394; *Statistical Abstract of the United States, 2009*, Table 482.

read the question and all of the possible answers so that you know what you are looking for. Before you look at the chart, you may be able to eliminate some obviously incorrect responses. For example:

1. Which of the following statements does the figure above best support?
   (A) Due to affirmative action, ethnic minorities in the civil service are represented according to their percentage in the general population.
   (B) The percentage of civil servants working in the Defense Department increased from 1960 to 2005.
   (C) Because of gender discrimination, women are underrepresented in the bureaucracy.
   (D) The percentage of females in the bureaucracy has increased from 1960 to 2005.
   (E) There are more minorities in the bureaucracy than in any other branch of the federal government.

After reading the question and the responses, you could eliminate answer (A) without even reading the table; there is no affirmative action program that requires the federal civil service to reflect the population as a whole. After reading the table, eliminate choice (C) immediately—while discrimination may play a role, it is not addressed in the table, and the question requires you to find your answer from the table. You can eliminate answer (E) for the same reason—while there are more minorities in the bureaucracy than in any other branch of the federal government, the table does not contain information about the other branches, and you must answer the question using information from this table. Answer (B) is wrong because the percentage of civil servants working the Defense Department decreased.

ANSWER: D. As the table shows, the number of female civil servants increased from 25% in 1060 to 44% in 2005.

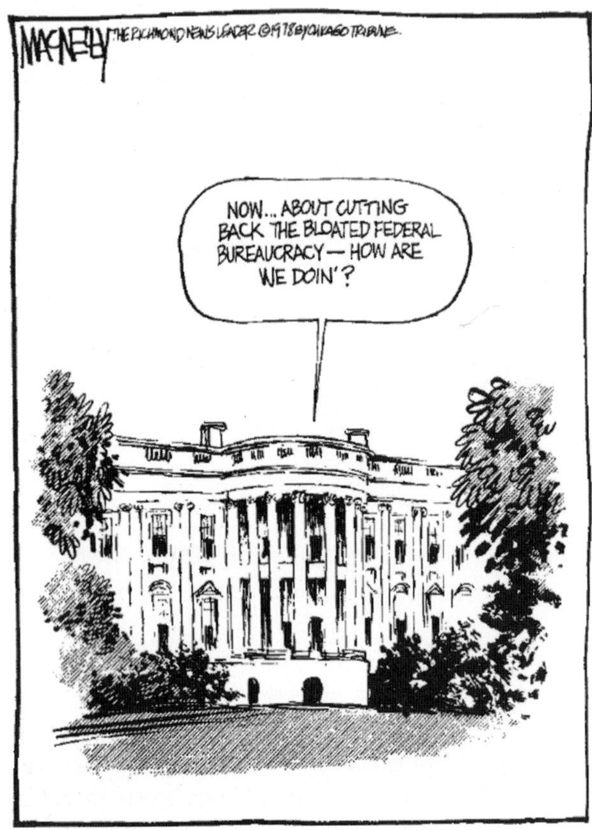

Political Cartoon Questions

These questions require you to interpret a political cartoon. Every political cartoon contains symbolism and a point of view. Examine the cartoon before you read the question and possible responses to determine what each part of the drawing represents and to identify the artist's viewpoint. For example:

1. What is the viewpoint expressed in the cartoon on this page
   - (A) One barrier to improving congressional control of the bureaucracy is the large number of federal agencies.
   - (B) One barrier to improving presidential control of the federal bureaucracy is that even the White House has become a large bureaucracy.
   - (C) The budget grows incrementally each year, and the result is a larger and larger bureaucracy.
   - (D) Although the bureaucracy has become very large, there are many people on the White House staff who would approve of cutting the bureaucracy.
   - (E) Neither the president nor his staff has any meaningful incentive to control the size of the federal bureaucracy.

ANSWER: B. The box on the left symbolizes the presidency (the president is speaking from the White House). The box on the right symbolizes the federal employees who work at the White House (all of the reactions to his comments are also coming from the White House). The viewpoint of the cartoonist is that although White House employees may claim to agree that the bureaucracy is hard to control, they are part of the problem.

Free-Response Questions

There are four mandatory free-response questions on the U.S. Government and Politics examination. At least one of the questions may require interpretation of a chart or graph. Essays for free-response questions can be written in any order. Whether you write the essays in or out of order, make sure you put the number of the question in the corner of each page of your essay booklet. Each free response question begins with a short introductory sentence. In the interest of time, do not re-write this on your paper. Following the introduction, free-response questions are broken into parts, such as (a), (b), (c), and (d). Label each part of your response.

Usually these are not traditional essay questions. Most free-response questions do not require an introduction or conclusion. Most do not even require a thesis. Many of these questions may be written in a bulleted or short-answer format. Although this may sound easier than writing a traditional essay, it is important that you know the material very well because these are targeted questions. Examination readers want specifics. They are looking for accurate information presented in clear, concise prose. You cannot mask vague information with elegant prose.

You will have a 100-minute block of time for this section, so watch your time. Allow 25 minutes for each question. Spend 5 minutes reading the question and jotting down a few words on each point you want to cover in your answer. Then spend 15 minutes writing your response. Save the last 5 minutes to read over your response to make sure you have covered each point with enough detail. If 25 minutes have passed and you are not finished with a question, leave some space, and start a new question on the next page. You can come back later if you have time.

Vocabulary

In answering the free-response questions, carefully read the question, and do exactly what it asks. It is important to note the word choices used in the questions:

- **Define:** to state the meaning of a word or phrase or to give a specific example. For instance, if a question asks you to define "iron triangle," the response is "An iron triangle is a close, advantageous relationship between an interest group, a congressional committee, and an administrative agency." Definitions are usually just one sentence.
- **Identify:** to select a factor, person, or idea and give it a name. For instance, if a question asks you to identify one advantage of incumbency, one possible response is "One advantage of incumbency is the opportunity to do *casework* for constituents."
- **Explain why/explain how:** to give a cause or reason. Explanations usually include the word *because.* For instance, if a question asks you why the ability to do casework gives incumbents an advantage, one possible response is "By doing casework, such as helping a constituent get her Social Security check, members of Congress are able to leave a favorable impression on members of their district. This increases their chances of reelection *because* they are able to get positive results for their constituents, who will vote for them in the next election."

SCORING FOR FREE-RESPONSE QUESTIONS

These questions are scored using a rubric that assigns points for each part of the answer. For example, if Part (a) requires you to identify and explain two factors, that part of the response will be worth 4 points (1 point for each identification and 1 point for each explanation). If Part (b) requires you to identify and explain one factor, that part of the response will be worth 2 points (1 point for the identification and 1 point for the explanation), for a total of 6 points possible on the question.

For the following free-response question you will find three sample responses—one excellent, one mediocre, and one poor—and an explanation of how the responses were scored.

QUESTION Congress has several ways of checking the power of the executive branch.

a. Identify and explain TWO formal powers that Congress may use to limit executive authority.

b. Identify and explain ONE informal power that Congress may use to limit executive authority.

Sample Essay 1

Part (a): The Constitution provides several formal, expressed powers that Congress can use to limit executive authority. One is by overriding a veto. When the president vetoes a bill passed by Congress, that bill does not usually become law. However, Congress may override a presidential veto by a two-thirds vote in each house. This limits presidential power, because the president does not have the final say over legislation. If enough members of Congress feel strongly enough about the legislation, it can still become law. Sometimes presidents are aware that their vetoes will be overridden and will sign bills they do not support in order to avoid the negative press that may come later with a defeat in Congress.

Another formal power that Congress has to limit executive authority is that Congress has the power to declare war. The president is commander in chief and has substantial authority in foreign affairs. He may commit troops for sixty days without congressional approval under the War Powers Act. However, for prolonged conflict, the president must turn to Congress to get an official declaration of war.

Part (b): An informal power that Congress has to limit executive authority is legislative oversight. Congress can conduct investigations and hold hearings to supervise the activities of the executive branch. This may pressure the executive to make changes in those agencies. For example, after Hurricane Katrina, Congress held hearings to investigate the effectiveness of the nation's disaster relief agencies.

SCORING 6/6. *In Part (a) the response identifies overriding a veto as a formal power of Congress*

(1 point for identification). The essay explains that by overriding a veto, presidential power is limited because the president does not have the final say over legislation (1 point for explanation).

The student also identifies the power to declare war as a check on the presidency (1 point for identification). The essay explains that presidential power is limited because the president must turn to Congress in prolonged conflicts (1 point for explanation). Part (a) earns all 4 points.

In Part (b) the essay identifies legislative oversight as an informal limit on the power of the executive (1 point for identification). The essay explains that this limits the power of executive agencies because their activities are investigated and their effectiveness may be challenged (1 point for explanation). Part (b) earns 2 points.

Sample Essay 2

Part (a): Under the Constitution, all appropriations bills must originate in the House. This means that the House has the power of the purse over executive proposals. This limits executive authority because Congress may reduce or eliminate funding altogether for presidential initiatives. Likewise, Congress must approve the budget. This limits executive authority because the president may not get everything he wants in his budget. This happened in 2004, when Congress cut President Bush's budget before it passed.

In addition, Congress may limit executive authority, because the Senate must ratify treaties. Although the executive branch negotiates treaties, often through the State Department, the Senate must ratify them in order to become law.

Part (b): One informal power that Congress has over the executive branch is the ability to go to the press. If Congress does not like a presidential proposal, a press conference can be held to get the public to oppose the president's policies.

SCORING 3/6. *In Part (a) the student is awarded 3 points. The essay identifies the power of the purse as a limitation on the executive (1 point for identification). The response explains that Congress can limit executive power by refusing to fund presidential initiatives by cutting the budget proposed by the president (1 point for explanation).*

The student also identifies Senate ratification of treaties as a limit on executive power (1 point for identification), but there is no meaningful explanation of how this limits presidential power.

In Part (b) the student does not receive any points. While congressional leaders may call press conferences as a way to put public pressure on the president, Congress is made up of 535 members. Congress as a whole cannot appeal to the press.

Sample Essay 3

Part (a): One formal power of Congress that limits the executive branch is the power to declare war. However, the president is the commander in chief. As a result, he is able to commit troops to foreign conflicts without a formal declaration of war. This is what Lyndon Johnson did during the Vietnam conflict.

Another formal power of Congress is the power to regulate interstate commerce. This gives Congress the power to enact laws affecting the economy. Such laws have been used to provide civil rights to African Americans, as well as to provide consumer protection nationwide.

Part (b): One informal power of Congress is the ability to support a president's reelection campaign. If the president does not do what Congress wants, it can oppose his reelection.

SCORING 1/6. *The student identifies the power to declare war as a limit on the executive (I point for identification). However, the essay does not explain how this power limits the president. Instead, it discusses how the president has not been limited by this power.*

While the power to regulate interstate commerce is a power of Congress, it does not generally limit the power of the presidency. The student does not earn any points for the rest of Part (a).

In Part (b) the response indicates that Congress may not support a president's reelection. While this may be true of individual members of Congress, it is not true of Congress as a whole. The student earns no points for Part (b).

American Government

evantravels/Shutterstock.com

Part 1

The American System

1 The Study of American Government 2

2 The Constitution 20

3 Federalism 50

4 American Political Culture 78

5 Civil Liberties 100

6 Civil Rights 130

In framing a government which is to be administered by men over men, the great difficulty lies in this: You must first enable the government to control the governed; and in the next place oblige it to control itself.

**** Federalist No. 51***

1 The Study of American Government

LEARNING OBJECTIVES

WHAT YOU NEED TO KNOW

- ☑ What is meant by "politics"?
- ☑ How is politics in the government different from politics in your family, school, or business?
- ☑ Can you give two definitions of *democracy*?
- ☑ How did Thomas Hobbes and John Locke differ about democracy?

WHO GOVERNS?

1. How is political power actually distributed in America?
2. What explains major political change?

TO WHAT ENDS?

1. What value or values matter most in American democracy?
2. Are trade-offs among political purposes inevitable?

As the 2012 U.S. national elections approached, Americans and their elected leaders hotly debated the federal government's spending, taxing, and future finances.

Some things never change.

THEN In 1786, a committee of Congress reported that since the Articles of Confederation were adopted in 1781, the state governments had paid only about one-seventh of the monies requisitioned by the federal government. The federal government was broke and sinking deeper into debt, including debt owed to foreign governments. Several states had financial crises, too.

In 1788, the proposed Constitution's chief architect, James Madison, argued that while the federal government needed its own "power of taxation" and "collectors of revenue," its overall powers would remain "few and defined" and its taxing power would be used sparingly.[1] In reply, critics of the proposed Constitution, including the famous patriot Patrick Henry, mocked Madison's view and predicted that if the Constitution were ratified, there would over time be "an immense increase of taxes" spent by an ever-growing federal government.[2]

NOW In 2010, a bipartisan presidential commission warned that by 2015, the federal government would be paying well over $300 billion a year in interest on a roughly $20 trillion national debt, much of it borrowed from foreign nations. The federal budget initially proposed for 2012 called for spending about $3.7 trillion, over a third of it in deficit spending. Projected total state government spending for 2012 was about $3 trillion as well, and many states' finances were a shambles.[3]

So, in the 1780s, as in the 2010s, nearly everyone agreed that government's finances were a huge mess and that bold action was required, and soon; but in each case,

then and now, there was no consensus about what action to take, or when.

This might seem odd. After all, at one level, the government's financial problems, including big budget deficits and revenue shortfalls, could be solved by simple arithmetic: either spend and borrow less, or tax more, or both.

But now ask: spend or borrow less for what, and raise taxes on whom, when, how, and by how much? For example, should we cut the defense budget but keep on funding health care programs, or the reverse? Or should we keep defense and health care funding where they are but reduce spending on environmental protection or homeland security? Should we perhaps increase taxes on the wealthy (define *wealthy*) and cut taxes for the middle class (define *middle class*), or . . . what?

Then, as now, the fundamental government finance problems were *political*, not mathematical. People disagreed not only over how much the federal government should tax and spend but also over whether in given areas it should be doing anything at all. For example, in 2011, the federal government nearly shut down, not mainly over disagreements between the two parties about how much needed to be cut from the federal budget (in the end, the agreed-to cuts totaled $38.5 billion), but primarily over whether any federal funding at all should go to certain relatively small-budget federal health, environmental, and other programs.

Thus, from the days of Madison and Henry right down to the present, debates over government finances often, at bottom, have been debates about the size, scope, competency, and legitimacy of the federal government, and about how to divide powers and responsibilities between the federal government and the state governments. Since the 1960s, political debates have grown ever more partisan and rancorous in part because there has been ever more government to fight about: America's total federal and state government spending has followed trends in other democratic nations in becoming a bigger and bigger share of the country's economy. For example, between 1960 and 2009, government spending in the U.S. rose from 27 percent to 42.2 percent of the nation's Gross Domestic Product (GDP, a measure of all the goods and services produced in a nation over a given period).[4] Over the same period, government spending as a percentage of GDP rose from 28.6 percent to 43.8 percent in Canada, from 17.5 percent to 39.7 percent in Japan, and from 31 percent to 52.7 percent in Sweden.[5] Between 2000 and 2009, government spending in the U.S. rose faster than it did in most European democracies, and by 2009 government spending per person was higher in the U.S. than it was in France, Germany, and the United Kingdom.[6]

Still, why way back then couldn't the differences over the Constitution be resolved in a snap, and why can't we now quickly come together over how to fix government finances and address other widely acknowledged problems?

The answer, in a word, is *politics.*

Politics exists in part because people normally differ about two things: who should govern, and the ends toward which they should work.

We want to know the answer to the first question because we believe that those who rule—their personalities and beliefs, their virtues and vices—will affect what they do to and for us. Many people think they already know the answer to the question, and they are prepared to talk and vote on that basis. That is their right, and the opinions they express may be correct. But they also may be wrong. Indeed, many of these opinions must be wrong because they are in conflict. When asked, "Who governs?" some people will say "the unions" and some will say "big business"; others will say "the politicians," "the people," or "the special interests." Still others will say "Wall Street," "the military," "crackpot liberals," "the media," "the bureaucrats," or "white males." Not all these answers can be correct—at least not all of the time.

How We Compare

Academic Freedom

You are reading a textbook on American government, but how is the freedom to study, teach, or do research protected from undue government interference? And how do European democracies protect academic freedom?

The U.S. Constitution does not mention academic freedom. Rather, in America, the federal and state courts have typically treated academic freedom, at least in tax-supported universities, as "free speech" strongly protected under the First Amendment.

In each of nine European nations, the constitution is silent on academic freedom, but various national laws protect it. In 13 other European nations, academic freedom is protected both by explicit constitutional language and by national legislation. But is academic freedom better protected in these nations than in either the United States or elsewhere in Europe?

Not necessarily. Germany's constitution states that "research and teaching are free" but subject to "loyalty to the constitution." Italy's constitution offers lavish protections for academic freedom, but its national laws severely restrict those same freedoms.

The United Kingdom has no written constitution, but its national laws regarding academic freedom (and university self-governance) are quite restrictive by American standards.

Source: Terence Karran, "Freedom in Europe: A Preliminary Analysis," *Higher Education Policy* 20 (2007): 289–313.

The answer to the second question is important because it tells us how government affects our lives. We want to know not only who governs, but what difference it makes who governs. In our day-to-day lives, we may not think government makes much difference at all. In one sense that is right, because our most pressing personal concerns—work, play, love, family, health—essentially are private matters on which government touches but slightly. But in a larger and longer perspective government makes a substantial difference. Consider: in 1935, 96 percent of all American families paid no federal income tax, and for the 4 percent or so who did pay, the average rate was only about 4 percent of their incomes. Today almost all families pay federal payroll taxes, and the average rate is about 21 percent of their incomes. Or consider: in 1960, in many parts of the country, African Americans could ride only in the backs of buses, had to use washrooms and drinking fountains that were labeled "colored," and could not be served in most public restaurants. Such restrictions have been almost eliminated, in large part because of decisions by the federal government.

It is important to bear in mind that we wish to answer two different questions, and not two versions of the same question. You cannot always predict what goals government will establish by knowing only who governs, nor can you always tell who governs by knowing what activities government undertakes. Most people holding national political office are middle-class, middle-aged, white Protestant males, but we cannot then conclude that the government will adopt only policies that are to the narrow advantage of the middle class, the middle-aged, whites, Protestants, or men. If we thought that, we would be at a loss to explain why the rich are taxed more heavily than the poor, why the War on Poverty was declared, why constitutional amendments giving rights to African Americans and women passed Congress by large majorities, or why Catholics and Jews have been appointed to so many important governmental posts.

This book is chiefly devoted to answering the question, Who governs? It is written in the belief that this question cannot be answered without looking at how government makes—or fails to make—decisions about a large variety of concrete issues. Thus in this book we shall inspect government policies to see what individuals, groups, and institutions seem to exert the greatest power in the continuous struggle to define the purposes of government. We shall see that power and purpose are inextricably intertwined.

What Is Political Power?

By **power** we mean the ability of one person to get another person to act in accordance with the first person's intentions. Sometimes an exercise of power is obvious, as when the president tells the air force that it cannot build a new bomber or orders soldiers into combat in a foreign land. Some claim it is exercised in subtle ways that may not be evident even to the participants, as when the president's junior speechwriters, reflecting their own evolving views, adopt a new tone when writing for their boss about controversial social issues like abortion. The speechwriters may not think they are using power—after all, they are the president's subordinates and may rarely see him face-to-face. But if the president lets their words exit his mouth in public, they have used power.

Power is found in all human relationships, but we shall be concerned here only with power as it is used to affect who will hold government office and how government will behave. This fails to take into account many important things. If a corporation closes a factory in a small town where it was the major employer, it is using power in ways that affect deeply the lives of people. When a university refuses to admit a student or a medical society refuses to license a would-be physician, it is also using power. But to explain how all these things happen would be tantamount to explaining how society as a whole, and in all its particulars, operates. We limit our view here to government, and chiefly to the American federal government. However, we shall repeatedly pay special attention to how things once thought to be "private" matters become "public"—that is, how they manage to become objects of governmental action. Indeed, one of the most striking transformations of American politics has been the extent to which, in recent decades, almost every aspect of human life has found its way onto the governmental agenda. In the 1950s, the federal government would have displayed no interest in a factory closing its doors, a university refusing an applicant, or a profession not accrediting a member. Now government actions can and do affect all these things.

People who exercise political power may or may not have the authority to do so. By **authority** we mean the right to use power. The exercise of rightful power—that is, of authority—is ordinarily easier than the exercise of power not supported by any persuasive claim of right. We accept decisions, often without question, if they are made by people who we believe have the right to make them; we may bow to naked power because we cannot resist it, but by our recalcitrance or our resentment we put the users of naked power to greater trouble than the wielders of authority. In this book, we will on occasion speak of "formal authority." By this we mean that the

power The ability of one person to get another person to act in accordance with the first person's intentions.

authority The right to use power.

right to exercise power is vested in a governmental office. A president, a senator, and a federal judge have formal authority to take certain actions.

What makes power rightful varies from time to time and from country to country. In the United States, we usually say a person has political authority if his or her right to act in a certain way is conferred by a law or by a state or national constitution. But what makes a law or constitution a source of right? That is the question of **legitimacy.** In the United States the Constitution today is widely, if not unanimously, accepted as a source of legitimate authority, but that was not always the case.

Much of American political history has been a struggle over what constitutes legitimate authority. The Constitutional Convention in 1787 was an effort to see whether a new, more powerful federal government could be made legitimate; the succeeding administrations of George Washington, John Adams, and Thomas Jefferson were in large measure preoccupied with disputes over the kinds of decisions that were legitimate for the federal government to make. The Civil War was a bloody struggle over the legitimacy of the federal union; the New Deal of Franklin Roosevelt was hotly debated by those who disagreed over whether it was legitimate for the federal government to intervene deeply in the economy. In our own day, even many citizens who take the same view on a hot-button topic like gay marriage disagree over whether it is legitimate to address the issue through an amendment to the Constitution that bans it nationally or whether the matter ought to be left for each state to decide.

legitimacy Political authority conferred by law or by a state or national constitution.

On one thing, however, virtually all Americans seem to agree: no exercise of political power by government at any level is legitimate if it is not in some sense democratic. That was hardly always the prevailing view. In 1787, as the Constitution was being debated, Alexander Hamilton worried that the new government he helped create might be too democratic, while George Mason, who refused to sign the Constitution, worried that it was not democratic enough. Today, however, almost everyone believes that democratic government is the only proper kind. Most people believe that American government is democratic; some believe that other institutions of public life—schools, universities, corporations, trade unions, churches—also should be run on democratic principles if they are to be

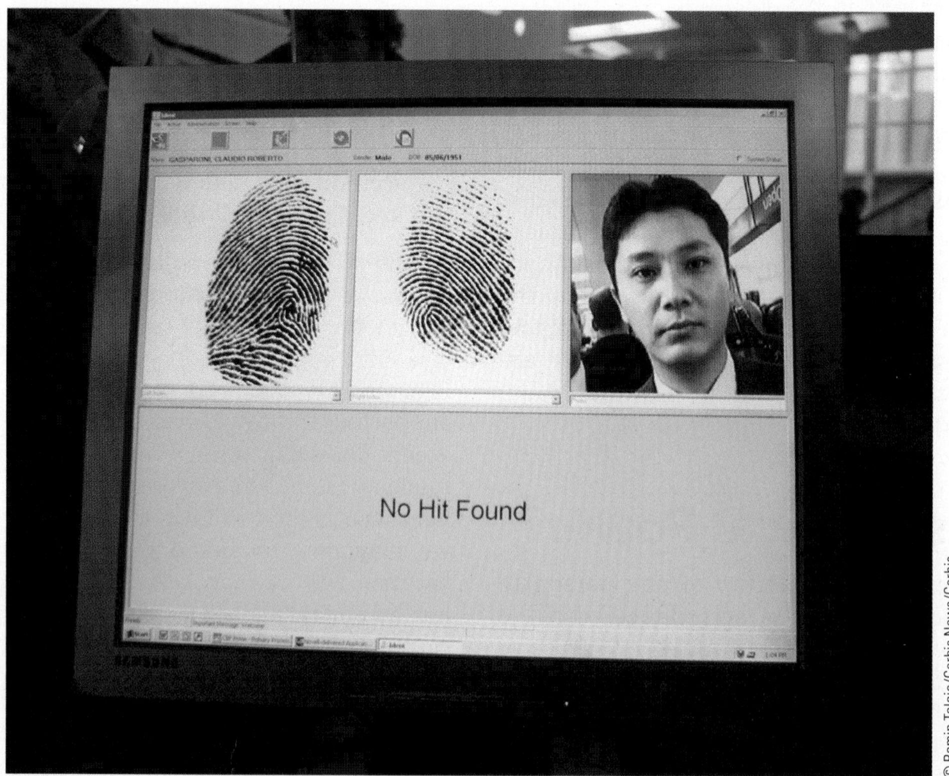

© Ramin Talaie/Corbis News/Corbis

To enter the United States, foreigners must now produce a photograph and fingerprints.

© GOLNAR MOTEVALLI/POOL/epa/Corbis

Afghan President Hamid Karzai has been backed by the United States but has also challenged American policy in Afghanistan.

legitimate; and some insist that promoting democracy abroad ought to be a primary purpose of U.S. foreign policy.

Whether democracy is the best way of governing all institutions and whether promoting democracy either has been or ought to be a major objective of U.S. foreign policy are both worthwhile questions. The former question goes beyond the scope of this book, but we will touch upon the latter question later in the text.

What Is Democracy?

Democracy is a word with at least two different meanings. First, the term *democracy* is used to describe those regimes that come as close as possible to Aristotle's definition—the "rule of the many."[7] A government is democratic if all, or most, of its citizens participate directly in either holding office or making policy. This often is called **direct or participatory democracy.** In Aristotle's time—Greece in the fourth century B.C.—such a government was possible. The Greek city-state, or *polis,* was quite small, and within it citizenship was extended to all free adult male property holders. (Slaves, women, minors, and those without property were excluded from participation in government.) In more recent times, the New England town meeting approximates the Aristotelian ideal. In such a meeting, the adult citizens of a community gather once or twice a year to vote directly on all major issues and expenditures of the town. As towns have become larger and issues more complicated, many town governments have abandoned the pure town meeting in favor of either the representative town meeting (in which a large number of elected representatives, perhaps 200–300, meet to vote on town affairs) or representative government (in which a small number of elected city councilors make decisions).

The second definition of *democracy* is the principle of governance of most nations that are called democratic. It was most concisely stated by the economist Joseph Schumpeter: "The democratic method is that institutional arrangement for arriving at political decisions in which individuals [that is, leaders] acquire the power to decide by means of a competitive struggle for the people's vote."[8] Sometimes this method is called, approvingly, **representative democracy;** at other times it is referred to, disapprovingly, as the elitist theory of democracy. It is justified by one or both of two

democracy The rule of the many.

direct or participatory democracy A government in which all or most citizens participate directly.

representative democracy A government in which leaders make decisions by winning a competitive struggle for the popular vote.

Can a Democracy Fight a War Against Terrorists?

On September 11, 2001, a date that will forevermore be referred to as 9/11, war came to the United States when terrorists crashed four hijacked airliners, filled with passengers, into the two towers of the World Trade Center in New York City, into the Pentagon in Washington, D.C., and into some empty land in Pennsylvania. About 3,000 people were killed.

How can a democratic nation respond to a war waged, not by an enemy nation, but by a loose collection of terrorists with cells in many parts of the world? America's new war against terrorism is much more difficult to fight than the one against Nazi Germany and the Japanese warlords in 1941.

- How can we reorganize the military so that it can respond swiftly and effectively against small targets?
- Is it constitutional to try captured terrorists in military tribunals?
- How much new law enforcement authority should be given to police and investigative agencies?
- Should America invade nations that support terrorists?

Over the last decade, these questions have raised profound challenges for American democracy. How would you begin to answer them?

Matt McDermott

Americans felt powerfully connected to their fellow citizens in the immediate aftermath of 9/11.

arguments: first, it is impractical, owing to limits of time, information, energy, interest, and expertise, for the people to decide on public policy, but it is not impractical to expect them to make reasonable choices among competing leadership groups. Second, some people (including, as we shall see in the next chapter, many of the Framers of the Constitution) believe direct democracy is likely to lead to bad decisions, because people often decide large issues on the basis of fleeting passions and in response to popular demagogues. This concern about direct democracy persists today, as seen from the statements of leaders who do not like what voters have decided. For example, voters in many states have rejected referenda that would have increased public funding for private schools. Politicians who opposed the defeated referenda spoke approvingly of the "will of the people," but politicians who favored them spoke disdainfully of "mass misunderstanding."

Is Representative Democracy Best?

Whenever the word *democracy* is used alone in this book, it will have the meaning Schumpeter gave it. As we discuss in the next chapter, the men who wrote the Constitution did not use the word *democracy* in that document. They wrote instead of a "republican form of government," but by that they meant what we call "representative democracy." Whenever we refer to that form of democracy involving the direct participation of all or most citizens, we shall use the term *direct* or *participatory* democracy.

For representative government to work, there must, of course, be an opportunity for genuine leadership competition. This requires in turn that individuals and parties be able to run for office, that communication (through speeches or the press, and in meetings) be free, and that the voters perceive that a meaningful choice exists. Many questions still remain to be answered. For instance: How many offices should be elective and how many appointive? How many candidates or parties can exist before the choices become hopelessly confused? Where will the money come from to finance electoral campaigns? There is more than one answer to such questions. In some European democracies, for example, very few offices—often just those in the national or local legislature—are elective, and much of the money for campaigning for these offices comes from the government. In the United States, many offices—executive and judicial as well as legislative—are elective, and most of the money the candidates use for campaigning comes from industry, labor unions, and private individuals.

Some people have argued that the virtues of direct or participatory democracy can and should be reclaimed even in a modern, complex society. This can be done either by allowing individual neighborhoods in big cities to govern themselves (community control) or by requiring those affected by some government program to participate in its formulation (citizen participation). In many states, a measure of direct democracy exists when voters can decide on referendum issues—that is, policy choices that appear on the ballot. The proponents of direct democracy defend it as the only way to ensure that the "will of the people" prevails.

The Framers of the Constitution did not think that the "will of the people" was synonymous with the "common interest" or the "public good." They strongly favored representative democracy over direct democracy. They believed that government should mediate, not mirror, popular views and that elected officials should represent, not register, majority sentiments. They supposed that most citizens did not have the time, information, interest, and expertise to make reasonable choices among competing policy positions. They suspected that even highly educated people could be manipulated by demagogic leaders who played on their fears and prejudices. They granted that representative democracy often proceeds slowly and prevents sweeping changes in policy, but they cautioned that a government capable of doing great good quickly also can do great harm quickly. They agreed that majority opinion should figure in the enactment of many or most government policies, but they insisted that the protection of civil rights and civil liberties—the right to a fair trial; the freedom of speech, press, and religion; or the right to vote itself—ought never to hinge on a popular vote. Above all, they embraced representative democracy because they saw it as a way of minimizing the chances that power would be abused either by a tyrannical popular majority or by self-serving officeholders.

The Framers were powerfully influenced by philosophers who had discussed democracy. Aristotle, who lived four centuries before Christ, defined democracy as the rule of the many; that is, rule by ordinary people, most of whom would be poor. But democracy can, he suggested, easily decay into an oligarchy (the rule of the rich) or a tyranny (the rule of a despot). To prevent this, a good political system will be a mixed regime, combining elements of democracy and oligarchy: most people will vote, but talented people will play a large role in managing affairs.

But the decisive influence on the Framers was wielded by John Locke, the 17th-century English writer who argued against powerful kings and in favor of popular consent.[9] People can exist in a state of nature—that is, without any ruler—so long as they can find enough food to eat and a way to protect themselves. But food may not be plentiful and, as a result, life may be poor and difficult.

The human desire for self-preservation will lead people to want a government that will enable them to own property and thereby to increase their supply of food. But unlike his English rival, Thomas Hobbes, Locke did not think it necessary to have an all-powerful government. Hobbes had argued that people live in a "war of all against all" and so an absolute, supreme ruler was essential to prevent civil war.[10] Locke disagreed: people can get along with one another if they can securely own their farms and live off what they produce.

A decent government must exist with the consent of the governed and be managed by majority rule. To prevent a majority from hurting a minority of the people, Locke wrote, the government should separate its powers, with different and competing legislative and executive branches.

As we shall see in the next chapter, what the Framers tried to do in 1787 was to create a government that would protect freedom and private property. And as with Aristotle, they hoped they had created a moderate regime that would simultaneously safeguard people and leave them alone.

How is Political Power Distributed?

The second question asks how political power has actually been distributed in America's representative democracy. Scholars differ in their interpretations of the American political experience. Where some see a steady march of democracy, others see no such thing; where some emphasize how voting and other rights have been steadily expanded, others stress how they were denied to so many for so long, and so forth. Short of attempting to reconcile these competing historical interpretations, let us step back now for a moment to our definition of representative democracy and four competing views about how political power has been distributed in America.

Representative democracy is defined as any system of government in which leaders are authorized to make decisions—and thereby to wield political power—by winning a competitive struggle for the popular vote. It is obvious then that very different sets of hands can control political power, depending on what kinds of people can become leaders, how the struggle for votes is carried on, how much freedom to act is given to those who win the struggle, and what other sorts of influence (besides the desire for popular approval) affect the leaders' actions.

elite Persons who possess a disproportionate share of some valued resource, like money or power.

class view View that the government is dominated by capitalists.

power elite view View that the government is dominated by a few top leaders, most of whom are outside of government.

bureaucratic view View that the government is dominated by appointed officials.

In some cases, the leaders will be so sharply constrained by what most people want that the actions of officeholders will follow the preferences of citizens very closely. We shall call such cases examples of *majoritarian politics* wherein elected officials are the delegates of the people, acting as the people (or a majority of them) would act were the matter put to a popular vote. The issues handled in a majoritarian fashion can be only those sufficiently important to command the attention of most citizens, sufficiently clear to elicit an informed opinion from citizens, and sufficiently feasible to address so that what citizens want done can in fact be done.

When circumstances do not permit majoritarian decision making, then some group of officials will have to act without knowing (and perhaps without caring) exactly what people want. Indeed, even on issues that do evoke a clear opinion from a majority of citizens, the shaping of the details of a policy will reflect the views of those who are sufficiently motivated to go to the trouble of becoming active participants in policymaking. These active participants usually will be a small, and probably an unrepresentative, minority. Thus the actual distribution of political power, even in a democracy, will depend importantly on the composition of the political elites who are actually involved in the struggles over policy. By **elite** we mean an identifiable group of persons who possess a disproportionate share of some valued resource—in this case, political power.

There are at least four ways of describing political elites: (1) elites reflect a dominant social class; (2) a group of business, military, labor union, and elected officials controls all decisions; (3) appointed bureaucrats run everything; and (4) representatives of a large number of interest groups are in charge.

The first view began with the theories of Karl Marx who, in the 19th century, argued that governments were dominated by business owners (the "bourgeoisie") until a revolution replaced them with rule by laborers (the "proletariat").[11] But strict Marxism has collapsed in most countries. Today a **class view,** though it may take some inspiration from Marx, is less dogmatic and emphasizes the power of "the rich" or the leaders of multinational corporations.

The second theory ties business leaders together with whatever other elites concern some people: top military officials, labor union leaders, mass media executives, and the heads of a few special-interest groups. This **power elite view** argues that American democracy is dominated by a few top leaders, many of them wealthy or privately powerful, who do not hold elective office.[12]

The third concept is that appointed officials run everything despite the efforts of elected officials and the public to control them. The **bureaucratic view** was first set forth by the German scholar Max Weber (1864–1920). He argued that the modern state, in order to become successful, puts its affairs in the hands of appointed bureaucrats whose competence is essential to the management of complex affairs.[13] These officials, invisible to most people, have mastered the written records and legislative details of the government and do more than just implement democratic policies: they actually make those policies.

RESEARCH FRONTIERS

How to Explain Political Behavior

In this book, most chapters will have a box called "Research Frontiers" that calls attention to new puzzles or findings about American government and politics. You can use these ideas for discussing issues or doing your own research.

But here, in the first such box, let us start by thinking about what a serious student of politics does. Contrary to what you may see on television or read in a Web blog, political scientists do not spend much time trying to tell you who the next Democratic or Republican presidential candidates will be. (In fact, before the 2008 election almost everybody who wrote about this got it wrong: they thought Hillary Clinton would run against Rudolph Giuliani.)

What political scientists do is to try to explain what has happened. Something has occurred (for example, most Hispanics voted for Barack Obama in 2008) and we try to figure out what caused this. Among the possible causes of this voting behavior are low incomes, a desire for changes in immigration laws, high unemployment rates, living in a big city, and so on.

What most people call an effect (for example, how Hispanics voted) and what they call a cause (for example, income or unemployment) are called something else by political scientists (and by most scholars). The effect is called a *dependent variable* and the causes are called *independent variables*. A variable is dependent if it changes because of changes in independent variables. In school or college, some people are more popular than others. You can easily think of reasons why a person is popular: he or she is physically attractive, has a warm personality, or is good at sports. Being popular does not make you attractive, engaging, or skilled; it is having these traits that makes you popular. In short, changes in an independent variable cause changes in the dependent variable.

The problem for scholars is that there is rarely one independent variable that produces the dependent variable. Let's go back to Hispanic voting behavior. We know from opinion polls that Hispanics from Cuba are much more likely to vote Republican than are those from Mexico. There is also evidence that Hispanics who have lived in this country for several generations are less likely to have liberal political views than those who arrived very recently. Moreover, Hispanics who have embraced a fundamentalist Protestant faith are less likely to be Democrats than those who have remained Roman Catholics.

If we want to explain Hispanic voting behavior, we have to use several independent variables: country of origin, time in America, and religious beliefs. There are probably even more independent variables that may be relevant. So now we face a problem: how much does each independent variable affect Hispanic voting behavior? Answering that question requires some complicated statistical techniques. Since this isn't a course on statistics, we won't bother you with this.

But whenever in the chapters you are about to read you come across some behavior you want to explain, bear in mind that a complete explanation will require you to look at several causes, and discuss with the instructor how best to sort them out.

The fourth view argues that political resources—such as money, prestige, expertise, and access to the mass media—have become so widely distributed that no single elite, no social class, no bureaucratic arrangement, can control them.[14] Political power is instead based on a **pluralist view.** In the United States, political resources are broadly shared in part because there are so many governmental institutions (cities, states, school boards) and so many rival institutions (legislatures, executives, judges, bureaucrats) that no single group can dominate most, or even much, of the political process.

pluralist view The belief that competition among all affected interests shapes public policy.

As you go through this book, we will evaluate these rival theories and indicate under what circumstances one or the other is true. A more precise statement of how policies are made can be found in Chapter 17.

Is Democracy Driven by Self-Interest?

Of the four views of how political power has been distributed in the United States, the pluralist view does the most to reassure one that America has been, and continues to be, a democracy in more than name only. But the pluralist view, not less than the other three, may lead some to the cynical conclusion that, whichever view is correct, politics is a self-seeking enterprise in which everybody is out for personal gain. Though there is surely plenty of self-interest among political elites (at least as much as there is among college or high school students!), it does not necessarily follow that the resulting policies will be wholly self-serving. Nor does it follow that democracy itself is driven mainly or solely by people's baser motives or selfish desires.

For one thing, a policy may be good or bad independent of the motives of the person who decided it, just as a product sold on the market may be useful or useless regardless of the profit-seeking or wage-seeking motives of those who produced it. For another thing, the self-interest of individuals often is an incomplete guide to their actions. People must frequently choose between two courses of action, neither of which has an obvious "payoff" to them. We caution against the cynical explanation of politics that Americans seem especially prone to adopt. Alexis de Tocqueville, the French author of a perceptive account of American life and politics in the early 19th century, noticed this trait among us.

> *Americans . . . are fond of explaining almost all the actions of their lives by the principle of self-interest rightly understood. . . . In this respect I think they frequently fail to do themselves justice; for in the United States as well as elsewhere people are sometimes seen to give way to those disinterested and spontaneous impulses that are natural to man; but the Americans seldom admit that they yield to emotions of this kind; they are more anxious to do honor to their philosophy than to themselves.*[15]

The belief that people will usually act on the basis of their self-interest, narrowly defined, is a theory to be tested, not an assumption to be made. Sometimes, as happened in New York City on September 11, 2001, elected officials, government workers, and average citizens behave in ways that plainly transcend personal or professional self-interest. There are countless other far less dramatic but still telling examples of people acting publicly in ways that seem anything but self-interested. To understand why people behave as they do, it is not enough to know their incomes or their jobs; one must also know something about their attitudes, their allies, and the temper of the times. In short, political preferences cannot invariably be predicted simply by knowing economic or organizational position.

Yet another reason to resist interpreting American democracy as if it were always and everywhere driven by narrowly self-interested individuals and groups is that many of the most important political happenings in U.S. history—the revolutionary movement of the 1770s and 1780s, the battle for civil rights in the 1950s and 1960s, to name just two—were led against long odds by people who risked much knowing that they might not succeed and suspecting that, even if they did succeed, generations might pass before their efforts truly benefited anyone. As we shall see, self-interest figures mightily in politics, but so do ideas about the common good and public-spirited behavior.

What Explains Political Change?

When we see American democracy from the perspective of the past, we will find it hard to accept as generally true any simple interpretation of politics. Economic interests, powerful elites, entrenched bureaucrats, competing pressure groups, and morally impassioned individuals have all played a part in shaping our government and its policies. But the great shifts in the character of our government—its size, scope, institutional arrangements, and the direction of its policies—have reflected complex and sometimes sudden changes in elite or mass *beliefs* about what government is supposed to do.

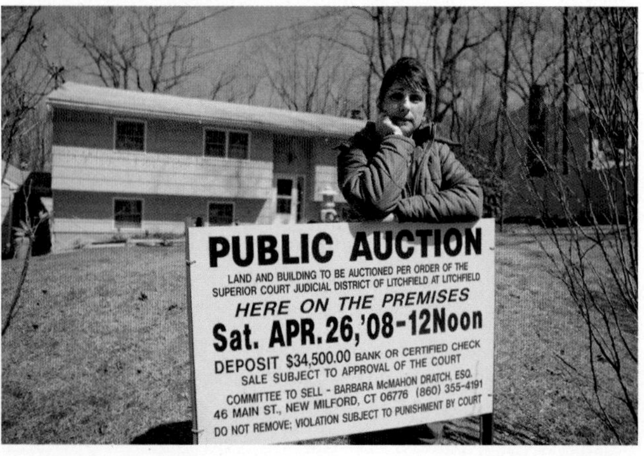

Enigma/Alamy

When thousands of people could no longer pay their mortgages, a major recession occurred.

In the 1920s, it was widely assumed that the federal government would play a small role in our lives. From the 1930s through the 1970s, it was generally believed that the federal government would try to solve whatever social or economic problem existed. From 1981 through 1988, the administration of Ronald Reagan sought to reverse that assumption and to cut back on the taxes Washington levied, the money it spent, and the regulations it imposed. It is clear that no simple theory of politics is likely to explain both the growth of federal power after 1932 and the effort to cut back on that power starting in 1981. Every student of politics sooner or later learns that the hardest things to explain usually are the most important ones.

Take the case of foreign affairs. During certain periods in our history we have taken an active interest in the outside world—at the time the nation was founded, when France and England seemed to have it in their power to determine whether or not America would survive as a nation; in the 1840s, when we sought to expand the nation into areas where Mexico and Canada had claims; in the late 1890s, when many leaders believed we had an obligation to acquire an overseas empire in the Caribbean and the Pacific; and in the period from the 1940s to the 1960s, when we openly accepted the role of the world's police officer. At other times America has looked inward, spurning opportunities for expansion and virtually ignoring events that in other periods would have been a cause for war, or at least mobilization. Today, America seems to be looking outward once again, spurred, on the one side, by unprecedented terrorist attacks against the country and, on the other side, by historic opportunities to make new friends with old foreign foes.

Deep-seated beliefs, major economic developments, and widely shared (or competing) opinions about what constitutes the dominant political problem of the time shape the nature of day-to-day political conflict. What this means is that, in any broad historical or comparative perspective, politics is not just about "who gets what," though that is part of the story. It is about how people, or elites claiming to speak for people, define the public interest. Lest one think that such definitions are mere window dressing, bear in mind that on occasion men and women have been prepared to fight and die for one definition or another. Suppose you had been alive in 1861. Do you think you would have viewed slavery as a matter of gains and losses, costs and benefits, winners and losers? Some people did. Or do you think you would have been willing to fight to abolish or preserve it? Many others did just that. The differences in these ways of thinking about such an issue are at least as important as how institutions are organized or elections conducted.

The Nature of Politics

Ideally, political scientists ought to be able to give clear answers, amply supported by evidence, to the questions we have posed about American democracy, starting with "who governs?" In reality they can (at best) give partial, contingent, and controversial answers. The reason is to be found in the nature of our subject. Unlike economists, who assume that people have more or less stable preferences and can compare ways of satisfying those preferences by looking at the relative prices of various goods and services, political scientists are interested in how preferences are formed, especially for those kinds of services, such as national defense or pollution control, that cannot be evaluated chiefly in terms of monetary costs.

Understanding preferences is vital to understanding power. Who did what in government is not hard to find out, but who wielded power—that is, who made a difference in the outcome and for what reason—is much harder to discover. *Power* is a word that conjures up images of deals, bribes, power plays, and arm-twisting. In fact, most power exists because of shared understanding, common friendships, communal or organizational loyalties, and different degrees of prestige. These are hard to identify and almost impossible to quantify.

Nor can the distribution of political power be inferred simply by knowing what laws are on the books or what administrative actions have been taken. The enactment of a consumer protection law does not mean that consumers are powerful, any more than the absence of such a law means that corporations are powerful. The passage of such a law could reflect an aroused public opinion, the lobbying of a small group claiming to speak for consumers, the ambitions of a senator, or the intrigues of one business firm seeking to gain a competitive advantage over another. A close analysis of what the law entails and how it was passed and administered is necessary before much of anything can be said.

This book will avoid sweeping claims that we have an "imperial" presidency (or an impotent one), an "obstructionist" Congress (or an innovative one), or "captured" regulatory agencies. Such labels do an injustice to the different roles that presidents, members of Congress, and administrators play in different kinds of issues and in different historical periods.

The view taken in this book is that judgments about institutions and interests can be made only after one has seen how they behave on a variety of important issues or potential issues, such as economic policy, the regulation of business, social welfare, civil rights and liberties, and foreign and military affairs. The policies adopted or blocked, the groups heeded or ignored, the values embraced or rejected—these constitute the raw material out of which one can fashion an answer to the central questions we have asked: Who governs? and To what ends?

The way in which our institutions of government handle social welfare, for example, differs from the way other democratic nations handle it, and it differs as well from the way our own institutions once treated it. The description of our institutions in Part III will therefore include not only an account of how they work today but also a brief historical background on their workings and a comparison with similar institutions in other countries. There is a tendency to assume that how we do things today is the only way they could possibly be done. In fact, there are other ways to operate a government based on some measure of popular rule. History, tradition, and belief weigh heavily on all that we do.

Although political change is not always accompanied by changes in public laws, the policy process is arguably one of the best barometers of changes in who governs. In Chapter 17, we offer a way of classifying and explaining the politics of different policy issues. The model we present there has been developed, refined, and tested over more than two decades (longer than most of our readers have been alive!). Our own students and others have valued it mainly because, they have found, it helps to answer such questions about who governs: How do political issues get on the public agenda in the first place? How, for example, did sexual harassment, which was hardly ever discussed or debated by Congress, burst onto the public agenda? Once on the agenda, how does the politics of issues like income security for older Americans—for example, the politics of Social Security, a program that has been on the federal books since 1935 (see Chapter 19)—change over time? And if, today, one cares about expanding civil liberties (see Chapter 5) or protecting civil rights (see Chapter 6), what political obstacles and opportunities will one likely face, and what role will public opinion, organized interest groups, the media, the courts, political parties, and other institutions likely play in frustrating or fostering one's particular policy preferences, whatever they might be?

Peek ahead, if you wish, to the book's policy chapters, but understand that the place to begin a search for how power is distributed in national politics and what purposes that power serves is with the founding of the federal government in 1787: the Constitutional Convention and the events leading up to it. Though the decisions of that time were not made by philosophers or professors, the practical men who made them had a philosophic and professorial cast of mind, and thus they left behind a fairly explicit account of what values they sought to protect and what arrangements they thought ought to be made for the allocation of political power.

WHAT WOULD YOU DO?

MEMORANDUM

To: *Governor Steve Finore*

From: *Edward Heron, chief policy adviser*

Subject: *Initiative repeal*

You have supported several successful initiatives (life imprisonment for thrice-convicted violent felons, property tax limits), but you have never publicly stated a view on the initiative itself, and the repeal proposal will probably surface during tomorrow's press briefing.

News »

Legal and Policy Experts Call for a Ban on Ballot Initiatives

A report released yesterday and signed by more than 100 law and public policy professors statewide urges that the state's constitution be amended to ban legislation by initiative. The initiative allows state voters to place legislative measures directly on the ballot by getting enough signatures. The initiative "has led to disastrous policy decisions on taxes, crime, and other issues," the report declared.

Arguments for a ban:

1. Ours is a representative, not a direct, democracy in which voters elect leaders and elected leaders make policy decisions subject to review by the courts.
2. Voters often are neither rational nor respectful of constitutional rights. For example, many people demand both lower taxes and more government services, and polls find that most voters would prohibit people with certain views from speaking and deprive all persons accused of a violent crime from getting out on bail while awaiting trial.
3. Over the past 100 years, hundreds of statewide ballot initiatives have been passed in twenty-four states. Rather than giving power to the people, special-interest groups have spent billions of dollars manipulating voters to pass initiatives that enrich or benefit them, not the public at large.

Arguments against a ban:

1. When elected officials fail to respond to persistent public majorities favoring tougher crime measures, lower property taxes, and other popular concerns, direct democracy via the initiative is legitimate, and the courts can still review the law.
2. More Americans than ever have college degrees and easy access to information about public affairs. Studies find that most average citizens are able to figure out which candidates, parties, or advocacy groups come closest to supporting their own economic interests and personal values.
3. All told, the 24 states that passed laws by initiative also passed thousands more laws by the regular legislative process (out of tens of thousands of bills they considered). Studies find that special-interest groups are severely limited in their ability to pass new laws by initiative, while citizens' groups with broad-based public support are behind most initiatives that pass.

Your decision:

Favor ban ____________ Oppose ban ____________

LEARNING OBJECTIVES

WHAT YOU NEED TO KNOW

☑ What is meant by "politics"?

Politics occurs because people disagree and the disagreement must be managed. Disagreements over many political issues, including disputes over government budgets and finances, are often at bottom disagreements over what government should or should not do at all.

☑ How is politics in the government different from politics in your family, school, or business?

Governmental politics is different from private politics because the government, unlike the family, school, or business, can make decisions that bind us all.

☑ Can you give two definitions of *democracy*?

Democracy can mean either that everyone votes on all government issues (direct democracy) or that the people elect representatives to make most of these decisions (representative democracy).

☑ How did Thomas Hobbes and John Locke differ about democracy?

Thomas Hobbes thought democracy was impossible because the self-interest of people required an all-powerful government to prevent a "war of all against all"; John Locke, by contrast, believed that people, though self-interested, can get along with one another if they consent to the government and it is ruled by the majority.

RECONSIDERING WHO GOVERNS?

1. How is political power actually distributed in America?

Some believe that political power in America is monopolized by wealthy business leaders, by other powerful elites, or by entrenched government bureaucrats. Others believe that political resources such as money, prestige, expertise, organizational position, and access to the mass media are so widely dispersed in American society, and the governmental institutions and offices in which power may be exercised so numerous and varied, that no single group truly has all or most political power. In this view, political power in America is distributed more or less widely. No one, however, argues that political resources are distributed equally in America.

2. What explains major political change?

The great shifts in the character of American government—its size, scope, institutional arrangements, and the direction of its policies—have reflected complex and sometimes sudden changes in elite or mass beliefs about what government is supposed to do. For instance, before Franklin Roosevelt's New Deal, most leaders and citizens did not automatically look to the federal government to improve the economy, and many doubted that Washington had any legitimate role to play in managing economic affairs. Today, however, leaders in both political parties assume that Washington must help reduce unemployment, create jobs, and otherwise actively manage the country's economy. The federal government now has policies on street crime, the environment, homeland security, and many other issues that were not on the federal agenda a half-century (or, in the case of homeland security, a mere decade) ago.

RECONSIDERING TO WHAT ENDS?

1. What value or values matter most in American democracy?

The Framers of the Constitution had their vision of American democracy and favored certain values, but neither they nor the Constitution specify what values matter most or how best to make trade-offs among or between competing political ends.

2. Are trade-offs among political purposes inevitable?

Yes. For instance, the government cannot spend more on health care without spending less on something else we may also desire—college loans, police patrols, or toxic waste cleanups. Nor can it maximize one value or purpose (say respecting the rights of persons suspected or accused of terrorist acts) without minimizing others (like liberty and associated legal rights). And, even if everyone agreed that the same one value—say liberty—was supreme, we could not all exercise it at the same time or to the fullest or just as we pleased without all losing it in the bargain: if everybody is at liberty to shout simultaneously, nobody is at liberty to be heard individually. We often cannot have more of some things we desire without having less of other things we desire, too. That is as true in politics and government, and as true for American democracy, as it is in other parts of life.

QUESTIONS TO CONSIDER

1. **How, if at all, does the rise of the Internet and average citizens' now virtually limitless access to information undercut many or most of the reasons for which the Framers of the Constitution favored representative democracy over direct democracy, and would you favor a majority-ruled, "direct digital democracy"?**
2. **Is democracy in any form sufficient to protect the rights and liberties of an unpopular minority of citizens, and in what ways do you think that the Constitution keeps American democracy from becoming "two wolves and a sheep deciding what's for supper"?**
3. **How is power distributed in the nongovernmental bodies that you know best (schools, religious groups, sports teams, businesses, social clubs, and others), and are many or most organized "democratically" or not?**
4. **Who are the federal, state, and local legislators who represent the community where you now reside (members of Congress, state senators and representatives, and members of the county, city, or town council or government), what is the party affiliation of each member, how long has each been in office, and what issue is he or she best known for?**
5. **Does your home state, the state in which you now reside, or a nearby state allow ballot initiatives or referenda, and, if so, what are the most recent examples (win or lose, by a lot or by a little, and highly controversial or not)?**
6. **How does the "nature of politics" differ between the United States and the United Kingdom with respect to how each nation's central government decides on how much to spend each year, and which has cut spending more deeply over the last three years?**

TO LEARN MORE

Banfield, Edward C. *Political Influence*. New York: Free Press, 1961. A method of analyzing politics—in this case, in the city of Chicago—comparable to the approach adopted in this book.

Crick, Bernard, *The American Science of Politics*. London: Routledge & Kegan Paul, 1959. A critical review of the methods of studying government and politics.

Marx, Karl, and Friedrich Engels. "The Manifesto of the Communist Party." In *The Marx-Engels Reader*, 2d ed., edited by Robert C. Tucker. New York: Norton, 1978, 469–500.

Schumpeter, Joseph A. *Capitalism, Socialism, and Democracy*. 3d ed. New York: Harper Torchbooks, 1950, chs. 20–23. A lucid statement of the theory of representative democracy and how it differs from participatory democracy.

Truman, David B. *The Governmental Process*. 2d ed. New York: Knopf, 1971. A pluralist interpretation of American politics.

Weber, Max. *From Max Weber: Essays in Sociology*. Translated and edited by H. H. Gerth and C. Wright Mills. London: Routledge & Kegan Paul, 1948, ch. 8. A theory of bureaucracy and its power.

2 The Constitution

LEARNING OBJECTIVES

WHAT YOU NEED TO KNOW

- ☑ Why was a Bill of Rights adopted so soon after the ratification of the Constitution?
- ☑ Why did so many authors of the Constitution fear factions?
- ☑ Why did the Framers agree on the idea of a separation of powers?

WHO GOVERNS?

1. What is the difference between a democracy and a republic?
2. What branch of government has the greatest power?

TO WHAT ENDS?

1. Does the Constitution tell us what goals the government should serve?
2. Whose freedom does the Constitution protect?

THEN When the Philadelphia convention was held in Philadelphia in 1787, its members were all white men. They were not chosen by popular election, and a few famous men, such as Patrick Henry of Virginia, refused to attend. One state, Rhode Island, sent no delegates at all. They met in secret and there was no press coverage. The delegates met to remedy the defects of the Articles of Confederation, under which the rebellious colonies had been governed, but instead of fixing the Articles they wrote an entirely new constitution. They then publicized it and said that it would go into effect once it had been ratified, not by state legislatures, but by popular conventions in at least nine states.

NOW Suppose you think we should have a new constitutional convention to remedy what you and others think are defects in the present document. As you will see later in this chapter, some critics want the Constitution to create here something like the parliamentary system of government one finds in Great Britain, while others want one that weakens the federal government by (for example) having a requirement that the budget be balanced or setting a limit on how much money it can raise in taxes each year. Now try to imagine your answers to these questions: How would delegates be picked? How many would there be? Is there any way to limit what the new convention does? Should the meeting be covered by live television, and should the delegates be free to send emails and Twitter messages to outsiders?

The goal of the American Revolution was liberty. It was not the first revolution with that object; it may not have been the last; but it was perhaps the clearest case of a people altering the political order violently, simply in order to protect their liberties. Subsequent revolutions had more complicated, or utterly different, objectives. The French Revolution in 1789 sought not only liberty, but "equality and fraternity." The Russian Revolution (1917) and the Chinese Revolution (culminating in 1949) chiefly sought equality and were little concerned with liberty as we understand it.

Steve McAlister/Getty Images

The Problem of Liberty

What the American colonists sought to protect when they signed the Declaration of Independence in 1776 were the traditional liberties to which they thought they were entitled as British subjects. These liberties included the right to bring their legal cases before truly independent judges rather than ones subordinate to the king; to be free of the burden of having British troops quartered in their homes; to engage in trade without burdensome restrictions; and, of course, to pay no taxes voted by a British Parliament in which they had no direct representation. During the ten years or more of agitation and argument leading up to the War of Independence, most colonists believed their liberties could be protected while they remained a part of the British Empire.

Slowly but surely opinion shifted. By the time war broke out in 1775, a large number of colonists (though perhaps not a majority) had reached the conclusion that the colonies would have to become independent of Great Britain if their liberties were to be assured. The colonists had many reasons for regarding independence as the only solution, but one is especially important: they no longer had confidence in the English constitution. This constitution was not a single document but rather a collection of laws, charters, and traditional understandings that proclaimed the liberties of British subjects. Yet these liberties, in the eyes of the colonists, were regularly violated despite their constitutional protection. Clearly, then, the English constitution was an inadequate check on the abuses of political power. The revolutionary leaders sought an explanation of the insufficiency of the constitution and found it in human nature.

THE COLONIAL MIND

"A lust for domination is more or less natural to all parties," one colonist wrote.[1] Men will seek power, many colonists believed, because they are ambitious, greedy, and easily corrupted. John Adams denounced the "luxury, effeminacy, and venality" of English politics; Patrick Henry spoke scathingly of the "corrupt House of Commons"; and Alexander Hamilton described England as "an old, wrinkled, withered, worn-out hag."[2] This was in part flamboyant rhetoric designed to whip up enthusiasm for the conflict, but it was also deeply revealing of the colonial mind. Their belief that English politicians—and by implication, most politicians—tended to be corrupt was the colonists' explanation of why the English constitution was not an adequate guarantee of the liberty of the citizens. This opinion was to persist and, as we shall see, profoundly affect the way the Americans went about designing their own governments.

The liberties the colonists fought to protect were, they thought, widely understood. They were based not on the generosity of the king or the language of statutes but on a "higher law" embodying "natural rights" that were ordained by God, discoverable in nature and history, and essential to human progress. These rights, John Dickinson wrote, "are born with us; exist with us; and cannot be taken away from us by any human power."[3] There was general agreement that the essential rights included life, liberty, and property long before Thomas Jefferson wrote them into the Declaration of Independence. (Jefferson changed "property" to "the pursuit of happiness," but almost everybody else went on talking about property.)

This emphasis on property did not mean the American Revolution was thought up by the rich and wellborn to protect their interests or that there was a struggle between property owners and the propertyless. In late-18th-century America, most people (except the black slaves) had property of some kind. The overwhelming majority of citizens were self-employed—as farmers or artisans—and rather few people benefited financially by gaining independence from England. Taxes were higher during and after the war than before, trade was disrupted by the conflict, and debts mounted perilously as various expedients were invented to pay for the

Signing the Declaration of Independence, painted by John Trumbull.

struggle. There were, of course, war profiteers and those who tried to manipulate the currency to their own advantage, but most Americans at the time of the war saw the conflict clearly in terms of political rather than economic issues. It was a war of ideology.

Everyone recognizes the glowing language with which Jefferson set out the case for independence in the second paragraph of the Declaration:

> *We hold these truths to be self-evident, that all men are created equal, that they are endowed by their Creator with certain unalienable Rights, that among these are Life, Liberty, and the pursuit of Happiness.—That to secure these rights, Governments are instituted among Men, deriving their just powers from the consent of the governed—that whenever any Form of Government becomes destructive of these ends, it is the Right of the People to alter or to abolish it, and to institute new Government, having its foundation on such principles, and organizing its powers in such form, as to them shall seem most likely to effect their Safety and Happiness.*

What almost no one recalls, but what are an essential part of the Declaration, are the next 27 paragraphs, in which Jefferson listed, item by item, the specific complaints the colonists had against George III and his ministers. None of these items spoke of social or economic conditions in the colonies; all spoke instead of specific violations of political liberties. The Declaration was in essence a lawyer's brief prefaced by a stirring philosophical claim that the rights being violated were **unalienable**—that is, based on nature and Providence, and not on the whims or preferences of people. Jefferson, in his original draft, added another complaint—that the king had allowed the slave trade to continue *and* was inciting slaves to revolt against their masters. Congress, faced with so contradictory a charge, decided to include a muted reference to slave insurrections and omit all reference to the slave trade.

unalienable A human right based on nature or God.

THE REAL REVOLUTION

The Revolution was more than the War of Independence. It began before the war, continued after it, and involved more than driving out the British army by force of arms. The *real* Revolution, as John Adams afterward explained in a letter to a friend, was the "radical change in the principles, opinions, sentiments, and affections of the people."[4] This radical change had to do with a new vision of what could make political authority legitimate and personal liberties secure. Government by royal prerogative was rejected; instead, legitimate government would require the consent of the governed. Political power could not be exercised on the basis of tradition but only as a result of a direct grant of power contained in a written constitution. Human liberty existed before government was organized, and government must respect that liberty. The legislative branch of government, in which the people were directly represented, should be superior to the executive branch.

These were indeed revolutionary ideas. No government at the time had been organized on the basis of these principles. And to the colonists such notions were not empty words but rules to be put into immediate practice. In 1776, eight states adopted written constitutions. Within a few years, every former colony had adopted one except Connecticut and Rhode Island, two states that continued to rely on their colonial charters. Most state constitutions had detailed bills of rights defining personal liberties, and most placed the highest political power in the hands of elected representatives.

Written constitutions, representatives, and bills of rights are so familiar to us now that we forget how bold and unprecedented those innovations were in 1776. Indeed, many Americans did not think they would succeed: such arrangements would be either so strong that they would threaten liberty or so weak that they would permit chaos.

The 11 years that elapsed between the Declaration of Independence and the signing of the Constitution in 1787 were years of turmoil, uncertainty, and fear. George Washington had to wage a bitter, protracted war without anything resembling a strong national government to support him. The supply and financing of his army were based on a series of hasty improvisations, most badly administered and few adequately supported by the fiercely independent states. When peace came, many parts of the nation were a shambles. At least a quarter of New York City was in ruins, and many other communities were nearly devastated. Though the British lost the war, they still were powerful on the North American continent, with an army available in Canada (where many Americans loyal to Britain had fled) and a large navy at sea. Spain claimed the Mississippi River valley and occupied what are now Florida and California. Men who had left their farms to fight came back to discover themselves in debt with no money and heavy taxes. The paper money printed to finance the war was now virtually worthless.

Figure 2.1
North America in 1787

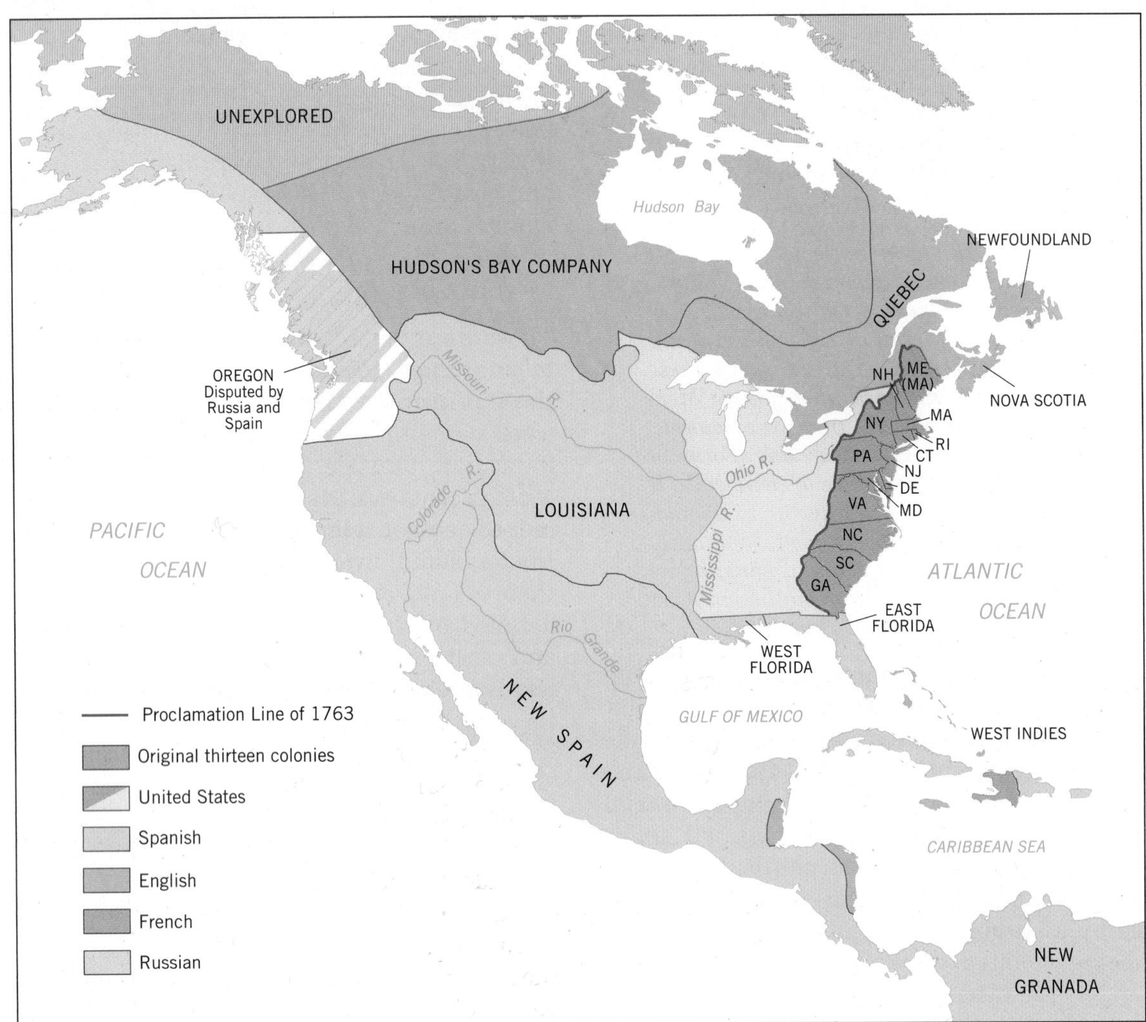

WEAKNESSES OF THE CONFEDERATION

The 13 states had formed only a faint semblance of a national government with which to bring order to the nation. The **Articles of Confederation,** which went into effect in 1781, created little more than a "league of friendship" that could not levy taxes or regulate commerce. Each state retained its sovereignty and independence, each state (regardless of size) had one vote in Congress, nine (of 13) votes were required to pass any measure, and the delegates who cast these votes were picked and paid for by the state legislatures. Congress did have the power to make peace, and thus it was able to ratify the treaty with England in 1783. It could coin money, but there was precious little to coin; it could appoint the key army officers, but the army was small and dependent for support on independent state militias; it was allowed to run the post office, then, as now, a thankless task that nobody else wanted. John Hancock, who in 1785 was elected to the meaningless office of "president" under the Articles, never showed up to take the job. Several states claimed the unsettled lands in the West, and they occasionally pressed those claims with guns. Pennsylvania and Virginia went to war near Pittsburgh, and Vermont threatened to become part of Canada. There was no national judicial system to settle these or other claims among the states. To amend the Articles of Confederation, all 13 states had to agree.

Articles of Confederation A weak constitution that governed America during the Revolutionary War.

Many of the leaders of the Revolution, such as George Washington and Alexander Hamilton, believed a stronger national government was

Bettmann/CORBIS

In 1775, British and American troops exchange fire in Lexington, Massachusetts, the first battle of the War of Independence.

essential. They lamented the disruption of commerce and travel caused by the quarrelsome states and deeply feared the possibility of foreign military intervention, with England or France playing one state off against another. A small group of men, conferring at Washington's home at Mount Vernon in 1785, decided to call a meeting to discuss trade regulation. That meeting, held at Annapolis, Maryland, in September 1786, was not well attended (no delegates arrived from New England), and so another meeting, this one in Philadelphia, was called for the following spring—in May 1787—to consider ways of remedying the defects of the Confederation.

The Constitutional Convention

The delegates assembled at Philadelphia at the **Constitutional Convention,** for what was advertised (and authorized by Congress) as a meeting to revise the Articles; they adjourned four months later having written a wholly new constitution. When they met, they were keenly aware of the problems of the confederacy but far from agreeing as to what should be done about those problems. The protection of life, liberty, and property was their objective in 1787 as it had been in 1776, but they had no accepted political theory that would tell them what kind of national government, if any, would serve that goal.

Constitutional Convention A meeting in Philadelphia in 1787 that produced a new constitution.

THE LESSONS OF EXPERIENCE

They had read ancient and modern political history, only to learn that nothing seemed to work. James Madison spent a good part of 1786 studying books sent to him by Thomas Jefferson, then in Paris, in hopes of finding some model for a workable American republic. He took careful notes on various confederacies in ancient Greece and on the more modern confederacy of the United Netherlands. He reviewed the history of Switzerland and Poland and the ups and downs of the Roman republic. He concluded that there was no model; as he later put it in one of the *Federalist* papers, history consists only of beacon lights "which give warning of the course to be shunned, without pointing out that which ought to be pursued."[5] The problem seemed to be that confederacies were too weak to govern and tended to collapse from internal dissension, while all stronger forms of government were so powerful as to trample the liberties of the citizens.

STATE CONSTITUTIONS

Madison and the others did not need to consult history, or even the defects of the Articles of Confederation, for illustrations of the problem. These could be found in the government of the American states at the time. Pennsylvania and Massachusetts exemplified two aspects of the problem. The Pennsylvania constitution, adopted in 1776, created the most radically democratic of the new state regimes. All power was given to a one-house (unicameral) legislature, the Assembly, the members of which were elected annually for one-year terms. No legislator could serve more than four years. There was no governor or president, only an Executive Council that had few powers. Thomas Paine, whose pamphlets had helped precipitate the break with England, thought the Pennsylvania constitution was the best in America, and in France philosophers hailed it as the very embodiment of the principle of rule by the people. Though popular in France, it was a good deal less popular in Philadelphia. The Assembly disfranchised the Quakers, persecuted conscientious objectors to the war, ignored the requirement of trial by juries, and manipulated the judiciary.[6] To Madison and his friends, the Pennsylvania constitution demonstrated how a government, though democratic, could be tyrannical as a result of concentrating all powers into one set of hands.

The Massachusetts constitution, adopted in 1780, was a good deal less democratic. There was a clear separation of powers among the various branches of government, the directly elected governor could veto acts of the legislature, and judges served for life. Both voters and elected officials had to be property owners; the governor, in fact, had to own at least £1,000 worth of property. The principal office-holders had to swear they were Christians.

SHAYS'S REBELLION

But if the government of Pennsylvania was thought too strong, that of Massachusetts seemed too weak, despite its "conservative" features. In January 1787, a group of ex–Revolutionary War soldiers and officers, plagued by debts and high taxes and fearful of losing their property to creditors and tax collectors, forcibly prevented the courts in western Massachusetts from sitting. This became known as **Shays's Rebellion,** after one of the officers, Daniel Shays. The governor of Massachusetts asked the Continental Congress to send troops to suppress the rebellion, but it could not raise the money or the manpower. Then he turned to his own state militia, but discovered he did not have one. In desperation, private funds were collected to hire a volunteer army, which marched on Springfield and, with the firing of a few shots, dispersed the rebels, who fled into neighboring states.

Shays's Rebellion A 1787 rebellion in which ex–Revolutionary War soldiers attempted to prevent foreclosures of farms as a result of high interest rates and taxes.

Shays's Rebellion, occurring between the aborted Annapolis and the coming Philadelphia conventions, had a powerful effect on opinion. Delegates who might have been reluctant to attend the Philadelphia meeting, especially those from New England, were galvanized by the fear that state governments were about to collapse from internal dissension. George Washington wrote a friend despairingly: "For God's sake, if they [the rebels] have real grievances, redress them; if they have not, employ the force of government against them at once."[7] Thomas Jefferson, living in Paris, took a more detached view: "A little rebellion now and then is a good thing," he wrote. "The tree of liberty must be refreshed from time to time with the blood of patriots and tyrants."[8] Though Jefferson's detachment might be explained by the fact that he was in Paris and not in Springfield, there were others, like Governor George Clinton of New York, who shared the view that no strong central government was required. (Whether Clinton would have agreed about the virtues of spilled blood, especially his, is another matter.)

THE FRAMERS

The Philadelphia convention attracted 55 delegates, only about 30 of whom participated regularly in the proceedings. One state, Rhode Island, refused to send anyone. The convention met during a miserably hot Philadelphia summer, with the delegates pledged to keep their deliberations secret. The talkative and party-loving Benjamin Franklin was often accompanied by other delegates to make sure that neither wine nor his delight in telling stories would lead him to divulge delicate secrets.

Those who attended were for the most part young (Hamilton was 30; Madison 36) but experienced. Eight delegates had signed the Declaration of Independence, seven had been governors, 34 were lawyers and reasonably well-to-do, a few were wealthy. They were not "intellectuals," but men of practical affairs. Thirty-nine had served in the ineffectual Congress of the Confederation; a third were veterans of the Continental Army.

Some names made famous by the Revolution were conspicuously absent. Thomas Jefferson and John Adams were serving as ministers abroad; Samuel Adams was ill; Patrick Henry was chosen to attend but refused, commenting that he "smelled a rat in Philadelphia, tending toward monarchy."

The key men at the convention were an odd lot. George Washington was a very tall, athletic man who was the best horseman in Virginia and who impressed everyone with his dignity despite decaying teeth and big eyes. James Madison was the very opposite: quite short with a frail body and not much of an orator, but possessed of one of the best minds in the country. Benjamin Franklin, though old and ill, was the most famous American in the world as a scientist and writer and always displayed shrewd judgment, at least when sober. Alexander Hamilton, the illegitimate son of a French woman and a Scottish merchant, had so strong a mind and so powerful a desire that he succeeded in everything he did, from being Washington's aide during the Revolution to a splendid secretary of the treasury during Washington's presidency.

The convention produced not a revision of the Articles of Confederation, as it had been authorized to do, but instead a wholly new written constitution creating a true national government unlike any that had existed before. That document is today the world's oldest written national constitution. Those who wrote it were neither saints nor schemers, and the deliberations were not always lofty or philosophical—much hard bargaining, not a little confusion, and the accidents of personality and time helped shape the final product. The delegates were split on many issues—what powers should be given to a central government, how the states should be represented, what was to be done about slavery, the role of the people—each of which

© Bettmann/Corbis

Shays's Rebellion in western Massachusetts in 1786–1787 stirred deep fears of anarchy in America. The ruckus was put down by a hastily assembled militia, and the rebels were eventually pardoned.

was resolved by a compromise. The speeches of the delegates (known to us from the detailed notes kept by Madison) did not explicitly draw on political philosophy or quote from the writings of philosophers. Everybody present was quite familiar with the traditional arguments and, on the whole, well read in history. But though the leading political philosophers were only rarely mentioned, the debate was profoundly influenced by philosophical beliefs, some formed by the revolutionary experience and others by the 11-year attempt at self-government.

From the debates leading up to the Revolution, the delegates had drawn a commitment to liberty, which, despite the abuses sometimes committed in its name, they continued to share. Their defense of liberty as a natural right was derived from the writings of the English philosopher John Locke and based on his view that such rights are discoverable by reason. In a "state of nature," Locke argued, all men cherish and seek to protect their life, liberty, and property. But in a state of nature—that is, a society without a government—the strong can use their liberty to deprive the weak of theirs. The instinct for self-preservation leads people to want a government that will prevent this exploitation. But if the government is not itself to deprive its subjects of their liberty, it must be limited. The chief limitation on it, he said, should derive from the fact that it is created, and governs, by the consent of the governed. People will not agree to be ruled by a government that threatens their liberty; therefore, the government to which they freely choose to submit themselves will be a limited government designed to protect liberty.

The Pennsylvania experience as well as the history of British government led the Framers to doubt whether popular consent alone would be a sufficient guarantor of liberty. A popular government may prove too weak (as in Massachusetts) to prevent one faction from abusing another, or a popular majority can be tyrannical (as in Pennsylvania). In fact, the tyranny of the majority can be an even graver threat than rule by the few. In the former case, there may be no defenses for the individual—one lone person cannot count on the succor of public opinion or the possibility of popular revolt.

The problem, then, was a delicate one: how to devise a government strong enough to preserve order but not so strong that it would threaten liberty. The answer, the delegates believed, was not "democracy" as it was then understood. To many conservatives in the late 18th century, democracy meant mob rule—it meant, in short, Shays's Rebellion (or, if they had been candid about it, the Boston Tea Party). On the other hand, *aristocracy*—the rule of the few—was no solution, since the few were likely to be self-seeking. Madison, writing later in the *Federalist* papers, put the problem this way:

> *If men were angels, no government would be necessary. If angels were to govern men, neither external nor internal controls on government would be necessary. In framing a government which is to be administered by men over men, the great difficulty lies in this: you must first enable the government to control the governed; and in the next place oblige it to control itself.*[9]

Striking this balance could not be done, Madison believed, simply by writing a constitution that set limits on what government could do. The example of British rule over the colonies proved that laws and customs were inadequate checks on political power. As he expressed it, "A mere demarcation on parchment of the constitutional limits [of government] is not a sufficient guard against those encroachments which lead to a tyrannical concentration of all the powers of government in the same hands."[10]

The Challenge

The resolution of political issues, great and small, often depends crucially on how the central question is phrased. The delegates came to Philadelphia in general agreement that there were defects in the

Articles of Confederation that ought to be remedied. Had they, after convening, decided to make their business that of listing these defects and debating alternative remedies for them, the document that emerged would in all likelihood have been very different from what in fact was adopted. But immediately after the convention had organized itself and chosen Washington to be its presiding officer, the Virginia delegation, led by Governor Edmund Randolph but relying heavily on the draftsmanship of James Madison, presented to the convention a comprehensive plan for a wholly new national government. The plan quickly became the major item of business at the meeting; it, and little else, was debated for the next two weeks.

THE VIRGINIA PLAN

When the convention decided to make the **Virginia Plan** its agenda, it had fundamentally altered the nature of its task. The business at hand was not to be the Articles and their defects, but rather how one should go about designing a true national government. The Virginia Plan called for a strong national union organized into three governmental branches—the legislative, executive, and judicial. The legislature was to be composed of two houses, the first elected directly by the people and the second chosen by the first house from among the people nominated by state legislatures. The executive was to be chosen by the national legislature, as were members of a national judiciary. The executive and some members of the judiciary were to constitute a "council of revision" that could veto acts of the legislature; that veto, in turn, could be overridden by the legislature. There were other interesting details, but the key features of the Virginia Plan were two: (1) a national legislature would have supreme powers on all matters on which the separate states were not competent to act, as well as the power to veto any and all state laws; and (2) at least one house of the legislature would be elected directly by the people.

Virginia Plan Proposal to create a strong national government.

New Jersey Plan Proposal to create a weak national government.

THE NEW JERSEY PLAN

As the debate went on, the representatives of New Jersey and other small states became increasingly worried that the convention was going to write a constitution in which the states would be represented in both houses of Congress on the basis of population. If this happened, the smaller states feared they would always be outvoted by the larger ones, and so, with William Paterson of New Jersey as their spokesman, they introduced a new plan. The **New Jersey Plan** proposed to amend, not replace, the old Articles of Confederation. It enhanced the power of the national government (though not as much as the Virginia Plan), but it did so in a way that left the states' representation in Congress unchanged from the Articles—each state would have one vote. Thus not only would the interests of the small states be protected, but Congress itself would remain to a substantial degree the creature of state governments.

If the New Jersey resolutions had been presented first and taken up as the major item of business, it is quite possible they would have become the framework for the document that finally emerged. But they were not. Offered after the convention had been discussing the Virginia Plan for two weeks, the resolutions encountered a reception very different from what they would have received if introduced earlier. The debate had the delegates already thinking in terms of a national government that was more independent of the states, and thus it had accustomed them to proposals that, under other circumstances, might have seemed quite radical. On June 19, the first decisive vote of the convention was taken: seven states preferred the Virginia Plan, three states the New Jersey Plan, and one state was split.

With the tide running in favor of a strong national government, the supporters of the small states had to shift their strategy. They now began to focus their efforts on ensuring that the small states could not be outvoted by the larger ones in Congress. One way was to have the members of the lower house elected by the state legislatures rather than the people, with each state getting the same number of seats rather than seats proportional to its population.

The debate was long and feelings ran high, so much so that Benjamin Franklin, at 81 the oldest delegate

Andre Jenny/Alamy

Independence Hall in Philadelphia.

present, suggested that each day's meeting begin with a prayer. It turned out that the convention could not even agree on this: Hamilton is supposed to have objected that the convention did not need "foreign aid," and others pointed out that the group had no funds with which to hire a minister. And so the argument continued.

THE COMPROMISE

Finally, a committee was appointed to meet during the Fourth of July holidays to work out a compromise, and the convention adjourned to await its report. Little is known of what went on in that committee's session, though some were later to say that Franklin played a key role in hammering out the plan that finally emerged. That compromise, the most important reached at the convention, and later called the **Great Compromise** (or sometimes the Connecticut Compromise), was submitted to the full convention on July 5 and debated for another week and a half. The debate might have gone on even longer, but suddenly the hot weather moderated, and Monday, July 16, dawned cool and fresh after a month of misery. On that day, the plan was adopted: five states were in favor, four were opposed, and two did not vote.* Thus, by the narrowest of margins, the structure of the national legislature was set as follows:

Great Compromise Plan to have a popularly elected House based on state population and a state-selected Senate, with two members for each state.

- A House of Representatives consisting initially of 65 members apportioned among the states roughly on the basis of population and elected by the people.
- A Senate consisting of two senators from each state to be chosen by the state legislatures.

The Great Compromise reconciled the interests of small and large states by allowing the former to predominate in the Senate and the latter in the House. This reconciliation was necessary to ensure there would be support for a strong national government from small as well as large states. It represented major concessions on the part of several groups. Madison, for one, was deeply opposed to the idea of having the states equally represented in the Senate. He saw in that a way for the states to hamstring the national government and much preferred some measure of proportional representation in both houses. Delegates from other states worried that representation on the basis of population in the House of Representatives would enable the large states to dominate legislative affairs. Although the margin by which the compromise was accepted was razor-thin, it held firm. In time, most of the delegates from the dissenting states accepted it.

After the Great Compromise, many more issues had to be resolved, but by now a spirit of accommodation had developed. When one delegate proposed having Congress choose the president, another, James Wilson, proposed that he be elected directly by the people. When neither side of that argument prevailed, a committee invented a plan for an "electoral college" that would choose the president. When some delegates wanted the president chosen for a life term, others proposed a seven-year term, and still others wanted the term limited to three years without eligibility for reelection. The convention settled on a four-year term with no bar to reelection. Some states wanted the Supreme Court picked by the Senate; others wanted it chosen by the president. They finally agreed to let the justices be nominated by the president and then confirmed by the Senate.

Finally, on July 26, the proposals that were already accepted, together with a bundle of unresolved issues, were handed over to the Committee of Detail, consisting of five delegates. This committee included Madison and Gouverneur Morris, who was to be the chief draftsman of the document that finally emerged. The committee hardly contented itself with mere "details," however. It inserted some new proposals and made changes in old ones, drawing for inspiration on existing state constitutions and the members' beliefs as to what the other delegates might accept. On August 6, the report—the first complete draft of the Constitution—was submitted to the convention. There it was debated, item by item, revised, amended, and finally, on September 17, approved by all 12 states in attendance. (Not all *delegates* approved, however; three, including Edmund Randolph, who first submitted the Virginia Plan, refused to sign.)

The Constitution and Democracy

A debate continues to rage over whether the Constitution created, or was even intended to create, a democratic government. The answer is complex. The Framers did not intend to create a "pure democracy"—one in which the people rule directly.

* The states in favor were Connecticut, Delaware, Maryland, New Jersey, and North Carolina. Those opposed were Georgia, Pennsylvania, South Carolina, and Virginia. Massachusetts was split down the middle; the New York delegates had left the convention. New Hampshire and Rhode Island were absent.

For one thing, the size of the country and the distances between settlements would have made that physically impossible. But more importantly, the Framers worried that a government in which all citizens directly participate, as in the New England town meeting, would be a government excessively subject to temporary popular passions and one in which minority rights would be insecure. They intended instead to create a **republic,** by which they meant a government in which a system of representation operates. In designing that system, the Framers chose, not without argument, to have the members of the House of Representatives elected directly by the people. Some delegates did not want to go even that far. Elbridge Gerry of Massachusetts, who refused to sign the Constitution, argued that though "the people do not want [that is, lack] virtue," they often are the "dupes of pretended patriots." Roger Sherman of Connecticut agreed. But George Mason of Virginia and James Wilson of Pennsylvania carried the day when they argued that "no government could long subsist without the confidence of the people," and this required "drawing the most numerous branch of the legislature directly from the people." Popular elections for the House were approved: six states were in favor, two opposed.

republic A government in which elected representatives make the decisions.

judicial review The power of the courts to declare laws unconstitutional.

federalism Government authority shared by national and local governments.

But though popular rule was to be one element of the new government, it was not to be the only one. State legislatures, not the people, would choose the senators; electors, not the people directly, would choose the president. As we have seen, without these arrangements, there would have been no Constitution at all, for the small states adamantly opposed any proposal that would have given undue power to the large ones. And direct popular election of the president would clearly have made the populous states the dominant ones. In short, the Framers wished to observe the principle of majority rule, but they felt that, on the most important questions, two kinds of majorities were essential—a majority of the voters and a majority of the states.

The power of the Supreme Court to declare an act of Congress unconstitutional—**judicial review**—is also a way of limiting the power of popular majorities. It is not clear whether the Framers intended that there be judicial review, but there is little doubt that in the Framers' minds the fundamental law, the Constitution, had to be safeguarded against popular passions. They made the process for amending the Constitution easier than it had been under the Articles but still relatively difficult.

An amendment can be proposed either by a two-thirds vote of both houses of Congress *or* by a national convention called by Congress at the request of two-thirds of the states.* Once proposed, an amendment must be ratified by three-fourths of the states, either through their legislatures or through special ratifying conventions in each state. Twenty-seven amendments have survived this process, all of them proposed by Congress and all but one (the Twenty-first Amendment) ratified by state legislatures rather than state conventions.

In short, the answer to the question of whether the Constitution brought into being a democratic government is yes, if by *democracy* one means a system of representative government based on popular consent. The degree of that consent has changed since 1787, and the institutions embodying that consent can take different forms. One form, rejected in 1787, gives all political authority to one set of representatives, directly elected by the people. (That is the case, for example, in most parliamentary regimes, such as Great Britain, and in some city governments in the United States.) The other form of democracy is one in which different sets of officials, chosen directly or indirectly by different groups of people, share political power. (That is the case with the United States and a few other nations where the separation of powers is intended to operate.)

KEY PRINCIPLES

The American version of representative democracy was based on two major principles, the separation of powers and federalism. In America, political power was to be shared by three separate branches of government; in parliamentary democracies, that power was concentrated in a single, supreme legislature. In America, political authority was divided between a national government and several state governments—**federalism**—whereas in most European systems authority was centralized in the national government. Neither of these principles was especially controversial at Philadelphia. The delegates began their work in broad agreement that separated powers and some measure of federalism were necessary, and both the Virginia and New Jersey plans

* There have been many attempts to get a new constitutional convention. In the 1960s, 33 states, one short of the required number, requested a convention to consider the reapportionment of state legislatures. In the 1980s, efforts were made to call a convention to consider amendments to ban abortions and to require a balanced federal budget.

enumerated powers Powers given to the national government alone.

reserved powers Powers given to the state government alone.

concurrent powers Powers shared by the national and state governments.

checks and balances Authority shared by three branches of government.

contained a version of each. How much federalism should be written into the Constitution was quite controversial, however.

Under these two principles, governmental powers in this country can be divided into three categories. The powers given to the national government exclusively are the delegated or **enumerated powers.** They include the authority to print money, declare war, make treaties, conduct foreign affairs, and regulate commerce among the states and with foreign nations. Those given exclusively to the states are the **reserved powers** and include the power to issue licenses and to regulate commerce wholly within a state. Those shared by both the national and the state governments are called **concurrent powers** and include collecting taxes, building roads, borrowing money, and having courts.

GOVERNMENT AND HUMAN NATURE

The desirability of separating powers and leaving the states equipped with a broad array of rights and responsibilities was not controversial at the Philadelphia convention because the Framers' experiences with British rule and state government under the Articles had shaped their view of human nature. These experiences had taught most of the Framers that people would seek their own advantage in and out of politics; this pursuit of self-interest, unchecked, would lead some people to exploit others. Human nature was good enough to make it possible to have a decent government based

How Things Work

Checks and Balances

The Constitution creates a system of *separate* institutions that *share* powers. Because the three branches of government share powers, each can (partially) check the powers of the others. This is the system of **checks and balances.** The major checks possessed by each branch are listed below.

Congress

1. Can check the president in these ways:
   a. By refusing to pass a bill the president wants
   b. By passing a law over the president's veto
   c. By using the impeachment powers to remove the president from office
   d. By refusing to approve a presidential appointment (Senate only)
   e. By refusing to ratify a treaty the president has signed (Senate only)
2. Can check the federal courts in these ways:
   a. By changing the number and jurisdiction of the lower courts
   b. By using the impeachment powers to remove a judge from office
   c. By refusing to approve a person nominated to be a judge (Senate only)

The President

1. Can check Congress by vetoing a bill it has passed
2. Can check the federal courts by nominating judges

The Courts

1. Can check Congress by declaring a law unconstitutional
2. Can check the president by declaring actions by him or his subordinates unconstitutional or not authorized by law

In addition to these checks specifically provided for in the Constitution, each branch has informal ways of checking the others. For example, the president can try to withhold information from Congress (on the grounds of "executive privilege"), and Congress can try to get information by mounting an investigation.

The exact meaning of the various checks is explained in Chapter 13 on Congress, Chapter 14 on the presidency, and Chapter 16 on the courts.

on popular consent, but it was not good enough to make it inevitable.

One solution to this problem would be to improve human nature. Ancient political philosophers such as Aristotle believed that the first task of any government was to cultivate virtue among the governed. Many Americans were of the same mind. To them, Americans would first have to become good people before they could have a good government. Samuel Adams, a leader of the Boston Tea Party, said that the new nation must become a "Christian Sparta." Others spoke of the need to cultivate frugality, industry, temperance, and simplicity.

But to James Madison and the other architects of the Constitution, the deliberate cultivation of virtue would require a government too strong and thus too dangerous to liberty, at least at the national level. Self-interest, freely pursued within reasonable limits, was a more practical and durable solution to the problem of government than any effort to improve the virtue of the citizenry. He wanted, he said, to make republican government possible "even in the absence of political virtue."

separation of powers Constitutional authority is shared by three different branches of government.

faction A group with a distinct political interest.

Federalists Those who favor a stronger national government.

Antifederalists Those who favor a weaker national government.

Madison argued that the very self-interest that leads people toward factionalism and tyranny might, if properly harnessed by appropriate constitutional arrangements, provide a source of unity and a guarantee of liberty. This harnessing was to be accomplished by dividing the offices of the new government among many people and giving to the holder of each office the "necessary means and personal motives to resist encroachments of the others." In this way, "ambition must be made to counteract ambition" so that "the private interest of every individual may be a sentinel over the public rights."[11]

If men were angels, all this would be unnecessary. But Madison and the other delegates pragmatically insisted on taking human nature pretty much as it was, and therefore they adopted "this policy of supplying, by opposite and rival interests, the defect of better motives."[12] The **separation of powers** would work, not in spite of the imperfections of human nature, but because of them.

So also with federalism. By dividing power between the states and the national government, one level of government can serve as a check on the other. This should provide a "double security" to the rights of the people: "The different governments will control each other, at the same time that each will be controlled by itself."[13] This was especially likely to happen in America, Madison thought, because it was a large country filled with diverse interests—rich and poor, Protestant and Catholic, northerner and southerner, farmer and merchant, creditor and debtor. Each of these interests would constitute a **faction** that would seek its own advantage. One faction might come to dominate government, or a part of government, in one place, and a different and rival faction might dominate it in another. The pulling and hauling among these factions would prevent any single government—say, that of New York—from dominating all of government. The division of powers among several governments would give to virtually every faction an opportunity to gain some—but not full—power.

The Constitution and Liberty

A more difficult question is whether the Constitution created a system of government that would respect personal liberties. And that in fact is the question that was debated in the states when the document was presented for ratification. The proponents of the Constitution called themselves the **Federalists** (though they might more accurately have been called "nationalists"). The opponents came to be known as the **Antifederalists** (though they might more accurately have been called "states' righters").* To be put into effect, the Constitution had to be approved at ratifying conventions in at least nine states. This was perhaps the most democratic feature of the Constitution: it had to be accepted, not by the existing Congress (still limping along under the Articles of Confederation), nor by the state legislatures, but by special conventions elected by the people.

Though democratic, the process established by the Framers for ratifying the Constitution was technically illegal. The Articles of Confederation, which still governed, could be amended only with the approval of all 13 state legislatures. The Framers

* To the delegates a truly "federal" system was one, like the New Jersey Plan, that allowed for very strong states and a weak national government. When the New Jersey Plan lost, the delegates who defeated it began using the word *federal* to describe their plan even though it called for a stronger national government. Thus men who began as "Federalists" at the convention ultimately became known as "Antifederalists" during the struggle over ratification.

wanted to bypass these legislatures because they feared that, for reasons of ideology or out of a desire to retain their powers, the legislators would oppose the Constitution. The Framers wanted ratification with less than the consent of all 13 states because they knew that such unanimity could not be attained. And indeed the conventions in North Carolina and Rhode Island did initially reject the Constitution.

THE ANTIFEDERALIST VIEW

The great issue before the state conventions was liberty, not democracy. The opponents of the new Constitution, the Antifederalists, had a variety of objections but were in general united by the belief that liberty could be secure only in a small republic in which the rulers were physically close to—and closely checked by—the ruled. Their central objection was stated by a group of Antifederalists at the ratifying convention in an essay published just after they had lost: "a very extensive territory cannot be governed on the principles of freedom, otherwise than by a confederation of republics."[14]

Figure 2.2

Ratification of the Federal Constitution by State Conventions, 1787–1790

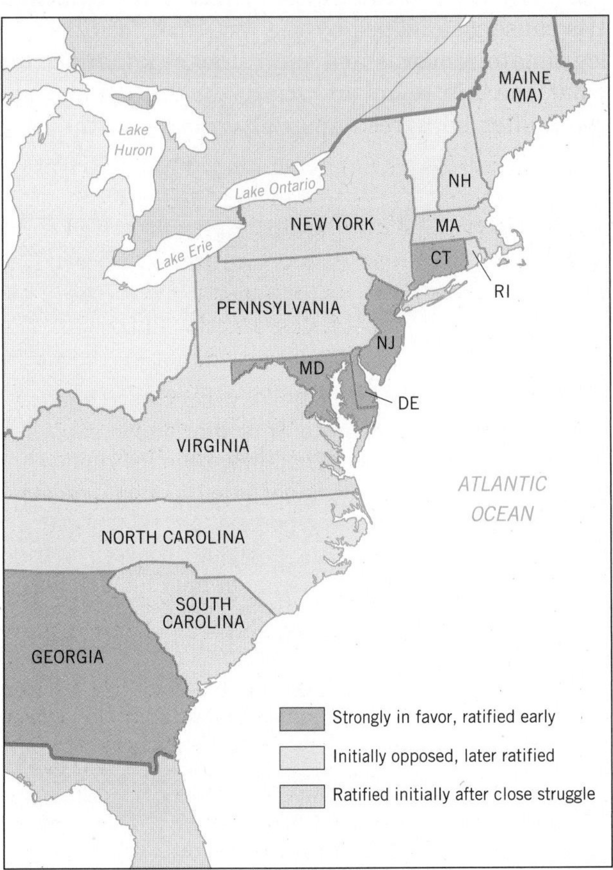

These dissenters argued that a strong national government would be distant from the people and would use its powers to annihilate or absorb the functions that properly belonged to the states. Congress would tax heavily, the Supreme Court would overrule state courts, and the president would come to head a large standing army. (Since all these things have occurred, we cannot dismiss the Antifederalists as cranky obstructionists who opposed without justification the plans of the Framers.) These critics argued that the nation needed, at best, a loose confederation of states, with most of the powers of government kept firmly in the hands of state legislatures and state courts.

But if a stronger national government was to be created, the Antifederalists argued, it should be hedged about with many more restrictions than those in the constitution then under consideration. They proposed several such limitations, including narrowing the jurisdiction of the Supreme Court, checking the president's power by creating a council that would review his actions, leaving military affairs in the hands of the state militias, increasing the size of the House of Representatives so that it would reflect a greater variety of popular interests, and reducing or eliminating the power of Congress to levy taxes. And some of them insisted that a *bill of rights* be added to the Constitution.

James Madison gave his answer to these criticisms in *Federalist* No. 10 and No. 51 (reprinted in the Appendix). It was a bold answer, for it flew squarely in the face of widespread popular sentiment and much philosophical writing. Following the great French political philosopher Montesquieu, many Americans believed liberty was safe only in small societies governed either by direct democracy or by large legislatures with small districts and frequent turnover among members.

Madison argued quite the opposite—that liberty is safest in *large* (or as he put it, "extended") republics. In a small community, he said, there will be relatively few differences in opinion or interest; people will tend to see the world in much the same way. If anyone dissents or pursues an individual interest, he or she will be confronted by a massive majority and will have few, if any, allies. But in a large republic there will be many opinions and interests; as a result, it will be hard for a tyrannical majority to form or organize, and anyone with an unpopular view will find it easier to acquire allies. If Madison's argument seems strange or abstract, ask yourself the following question: if I have an unpopular opinion, an exotic lifestyle, or an unconventional interest, will I find greater security living in a small town or a big city?

By favoring a large republic, Madison was not trying to stifle democracy. Rather, he was attempting to show how democratic government really works, and what can make it work better. To rule, different interests must come together and form a **coalition**—that is, an alliance. In *Federalist* No. 51, he argued that the coalitions that formed in a large republic would be more moderate than those that formed in a small one because the bigger the republic, the greater the variety of interests, and thus the more a coalition of the majority would have to accommodate a diversity of interests and opinions if it hoped to succeed. He concluded that in a nation the size of the United States, with its enormous variety of interests, "a coalition of a majority of the whole society could seldom take place on any other principles than those of justice and the general good." Whether he was right in that prediction is a matter to which we shall return repeatedly.

coalition An alliance of factions.

The implication of Madison's arguments was daring, for he was suggesting that the national government should be at some distance from the people and insulated from their momentary passions, because the people did not always want to do the right thing. Liberty was threatened as much (or even more) by public passions and popularly based factions as by strong governments. Now the Antifederalists themselves had no very lofty view of human nature, as is evidenced by the deep suspicion with which they viewed "power-seeking" officeholders. What Madison did was take this view to its logical conclusion, arguing that if people could be corrupted by office, they could also be corrupted by factional self-interest. Thus the government had to be designed to prevent both the politicians and the people from using it for ill-considered or unjust purposes.

To argue in 1787 against the virtues of small democracies was like arguing against motherhood. Moreover, the Federalists' counterargument involved many steps: representative democracy over direct democracy; a large republic over a small republic; diversity of economic, religious, and other interests over homogeneity of such interests; and barriers, not boosts, to majority group formation and influence. Still, the Federalists prevailed, probably because many citizens were convinced that a reasonably strong national government was essential if the nation were to stand united against foreign enemies, facilitate commerce among the states, guard against domestic insurrections, and keep one faction from oppressing another. The political realities of the moment and the recent bitter experiences with the Articles probably counted for more in ratifying the Constitution than Madison's arguments. His cause was helped by the fact that, for all their legitimate concerns and their uncanny instinct for what the future might bring, the Antifederalists could offer no agreed-upon alternative to the new

The *Federalist* Papers

In 1787, to help win ratification of the new Constitution in the New York state convention, Alexander Hamilton decided to publish a series of articles defending and explaining the document in the New York City newspapers. He recruited John Jay and James Madison to help him, and the three of them, under the pen name "Publius," wrote 85 articles that appeared from late 1787 through 1788. The identity of the authors was kept secret at the time, but we now know that Hamilton wrote 51 of them, Madison 26, and Jay five, and that Hamilton and Madison jointly authored three.

The *Federalist* papers probably played only a small role in securing ratification. Like most legislative battles, this one was not decisively influenced by philosophical writings. But these essays have had a lasting value as an authoritative and profound explanation of the Constitution. Though written for political purposes, the *Federalist* has become the single most important piece of American political philosophy ever produced. Ironically, Hamilton and Madison were later to become political enemies; even at the Philadelphia convention they had different views of the kind of government that should be created. But in 1787–1788, they were united in the belief that the new constitution was the best that could have been obtained under the circumstances.

Although Hamilton wrote most of the *Federalist* papers, Madison wrote the two most famous articles—Nos. 10

(continued)

and 51, reprinted in the Appendix. After you have finished this chapter, turn to the Appendix and try to read them. On your first reading of the papers, you may find Madison's language difficult to understand and his ideas overly complex. The following pointers will help you decipher his meaning.

In *Federalist* No. 10, Madison begins by stating that "a well constructed Union" can "break and control the violence of faction." He goes on to define a *faction* as any group of citizens who attempt to advance their ideas or economic interests at the expense of other citizens, or in ways that conflict with "the permanent and aggregate interests of the community" or "public good." Thus what Madison terms "factions" are what we today call "special interests."

One way to defeat factions, according to Madison, is to remove whatever causes them to arise in the first place. This can be attempted in two ways. First, government can deprive people of the liberty they need to organize: "Liberty is to faction what air is to fire." But that is surely a cure "worse than the disease." Second, measures can be taken to make all citizens share the same ideas, feelings, and economic interests. However, as Madison observes, some people are smarter or more hard-working than others, and this "diversity in the faculties" of citizens is bound to result in different economic interests as some people acquire more property than others. Consequently, protecting property rights, not equalizing property ownership, "is the first object of government." Even if everyone shared the same basic economic interests, they would still find reasons "to vex and oppress each other" rather than cooperate "for their common good." Religious differences, loyalties to different leaders, even "frivolous and fanciful distinctions" (not liking how other people dress or their taste in music) can be fertile soil for factions. In Madison's view, people are factious by nature; the "causes of faction" are "sown" into their very being.

Madison thus proposes a second and, he thinks, more practical and desirable way of defeating faction. The way to cure "the mischiefs of faction" is not by removing its causes but by "controlling its effects." Factions will always exist, so the trick is to establish a form of government that is likely to serve the public good through the even-handed "regulation of these various and interfering interests." Wise and public-spirited leaders can "adjust these clashing interests and render them all subservient to the public good," but, he cautions, "enlightened statesmen will not always be at the helm." (Madison implies that "enlightened statesmen"—such as himself, Washington, and Jefferson—were at the "helm" of government in 1787.)

Madison's proposed cure for the evils of factions is in fact nothing other than a republican form of government. Use the following questions to guide your own analysis of Madison's ideas. Why does Madison think the problem of a "minority" faction is easy to handle? Conversely, why is he so troubled by the potential of a majority faction? How does he distinguish direct democracy from republican government? What is he getting at when he terms elected representatives "proper guardians of the public weal," and why does he think that "extensive republics" are more likely to produce such representatives than small ones?

When you are finished with *Federalist* No. 10, try your hand at *Federalist* No. 51. You will find that the ideas in the former paper anticipate many of those in the latter. And you will find many points on which you may or may not agree with Madison. For example, do you agree with his assumption that people—even your best friends or college roommates—are factious by nature? Likewise, do you agree with his view that government is "the greatest of all reflections on human nature"?

By attempting to meet the mind of James Madison, you can sharpen your own mind and deepen your understanding of American government.

Constitution. In politics, then as now, you cannot beat something with nothing.

But this does not explain why the Framers failed to add a bill of rights to the Constitution. If they were so preoccupied with liberty, why didn't they take this most obvious step toward protecting liberty, especially since the Antifederalists were demanding it? Some historians have suggested that this omission was evidence that liberty was not as important to the Framers as they claimed. In fact, when one delegate suggested that a bill of rights be drawn up, the state delegations at the convention unanimously voted the idea down. There were several reasons for this.

First, the Constitution, as written, *did* contain a number of specific guarantees of individual liberty, including the right of trial by jury in criminal cases and the privilege of the writ of habeas corpus. The liberties guaranteed in the Constitution (before the **Bill of Rights** was added) are listed on the following (turn) page.

Bill of Rights First ten amendments to the Constitution.

- Writ of **habeas corpus** may not be suspended (except during invasion or rebellion).
- No **bill of attainder** may be passed by Congress or the states.
- No **ex post facto law** may be passed by Congress or the states.
- Right of trial by jury in criminal cases is guaranteed.
- The citizens of each state are entitled to the privileges and immunities of the citizens of every other state.
- No religious test or qualification for holding federal office is imposed.
- No law impairing the obligation of contracts may be passed by the states.

habeas corpus An order to produce an arrested person before a judge.

bill of attainder A law that declares a person, without a trial, to be guilty of a crime.

ex post facto law A law that makes an act criminal although the act was legal when it was committed.

Second, most states in 1787 had bills of rights. When Elbridge Gerry proposed to the convention that a federal bill of rights be drafted, Roger Sherman rose to observe that it was unnecessary because the state bills of rights were sufficient.[15]

But third, and perhaps most important, the Framers thought they were creating a government with specific, limited powers. It could do, they thought, only what the Constitution gave it the power to do, and nowhere in that document was there permission to infringe on freedom of speech or of the press or to impose cruel and unusual punishments. Some delegates probably feared that if any serious effort were made to list the rights that were guaranteed, later officials might assume that they had the power to do anything not explicitly forbidden.

NEED FOR A BILL OF RIGHTS

Whatever their reasons, the Framers made at least a tactical and perhaps a fundamental mistake. It quickly became clear that without at least the promise of a bill of rights, the Constitution would not be ratified. Though the small states, pleased by their equal representation in the Senate, quickly ratified (in Delaware, New Jersey, and Georgia, the vote in the conventions was unanimous), the battle in the large states was intense and the outcome uncertain. In Pennsylvania, Federalist supporters dragged boycotting Antifederalists to the legislature in order to ensure a quorum was present so a convention could be called. There were rumors of other rough tactics.

In Massachusetts, the Constitution was approved by a narrow majority, but only after key leaders promised to obtain a bill of rights. In Virginia, James Madison fought against the fiery Patrick Henry, whose climactic speech against ratification was dramatically punctuated by a noisy thunderstorm outside. The Federalists won by 10 votes. In New York, Alexander Hamilton argued the case for six weeks against the determined opposition of most of the state's key political leaders; he carried the day, but only by three votes, and then only after New York City threatened to secede from the state if it did not ratify. By June 21, 1788, the ninth state—New Hampshire—had ratified, and the Constitution was law.

Many people think that the first Congress moved quickly to adopt a Bill of Rights—that is, the first ten amendments to the Constitution—in order to satisfy demands made in state ratifying conventions that this be done. Unfortunately, that is not quite right. Of the many criticisms made of the proposed Constitution, hardly any referred to civil liberties. Take, for example, the Massachusetts convention. Several critics, including John Hancock, said they would vote to ratify the document if the new members of Congress did all they could to get nine amendments adopted. But these amendments had nothing to do with free speech or a free press. Instead, they involved the size of the House of Representatives, congressional influence on local elections, the power of Congress to impose taxes, and the need for grand juries in criminal cases.[16] Other speakers wanted an amendment that would have House members stand for election every year. Critics in other states made the same arguments.

Despite the bitterness of the ratification struggle, the new government that took office in 1789–1790, headed by President Washington, was greeted enthusiastically. By the spring of 1790, all 13 states had ratified. There remained, however, the task of fulfilling the promise of amending the document. To that end, James Madison introduced into the first session of the First Congress a set of proposals, 12 of which were approved by Congress; 10 of these were ratified by the states and went into effect in 1791. But with only a few exceptions, these bore no relationship to the criticisms made in the state conventions. On what, then did Madison base them? Probably on the Virginia Declaration of Rights, written by George Mason and Madison, and unanimously approved by the Virginia legislature in 1776. These amendments, which no one called a

How Things Work

The Bill of Rights

The First Ten Amendments to the Constitution Grouped by Topic and Purpose

Protections Afforded Citizens to Participate in the Political Process

Amendment 1: Freedom of religion, speech, press, and assembly; the right to petition the government.

Protections Against Arbitrary Police and Court Action

Amendment 4: No unreasonable searches or seizures.

Amendment 5: Grand jury indictment required to prosecute a person for a serious crime.

No "double jeopardy" (being tried twice for the same offense).

Forcing a person to testify against himself or herself prohibited.

No loss of life, liberty, or property without due process.

Amendment 6: Right to speedy, public, impartial trial with defense counsel and right to cross-examine witnesses.

Amendment 7: Jury trials in civil suits where value exceeds $20.

Amendment 8: No excessive bail or fines, no cruel and unusual punishments.

Protections of States' Rights and Unnamed Rights of People

Amendment 9: Unlisted rights are not necessarily denied.

Amendment 10: Powers not delegated to the United States or denied to states are reserved to the states.

Other Amendments

Amendment 2: Right to bear arms.

Amendment 3: Troops may not be quartered in homes in peacetime.

Bill of Rights as late as 1792, did not limit the power of state governments over citizens, only the power of the federal government. Later, the Fourteenth Amendment, as interpreted by the Supreme Court, extended many of the guarantees of the Bill of Rights to cover state governmental action.

THE CONSTITUTION AND SLAVERY

Though black slaves amounted to one-third of the population of the five southern states, nowhere in the Constitution can one find the word *slave* or *slavery*.

To some, the failure of the Constitution to address the question of slavery was a great betrayal of the promise of the Declaration of Independence that "all men are created equal." For the Constitution to be silent on the subject of slavery, and thereby to allow that odious practice to continue, was to convert, by implication, the wording of the Declaration to "all white men are created equal."

It is easy to accuse the signers of the Declaration and the Constitution of hypocrisy. They knew of slavery, many of them owned slaves, and yet they were silent. Indeed, British opponents of the independence movement took special delight in taunting the colonists about their complaints of being "enslaved" to the British Empire while ignoring the slavery in their very midst.

Increasingly, revolutionary leaders during this period spoke to this issue. Thomas Jefferson had tried to get a clause opposing the slave trade put into the Declaration of Independence. James Otis of Boston had attacked slavery and argued that black as well as white men should be free. As revolutionary fervor mounted, so did northern criticism of slavery. The Massachusetts legislature and then the Continental Congress voted to end the slave trade; Delaware prohibited the importation of slaves; Pennsylvania voted to tax it out of existence; and Connecticut and Rhode Island decided that all slaves brought into those states would automatically become free.

Slavery continued unabated in the South, defended by some whites because they thought it right, by others because they found it useful. But even in the South there were opponents, though rarely conspicuous ones. George Mason, a large Virginia slaveholder and a delegate to the convention, warned prophetically that "by an inevitable chain of causes and effects, providence punishes national sins [slavery] by national calamities."[17]

The blunt fact, however, was that any effort to use the Constitution to end slavery would have meant the end of the Constitution. The southern states would never have signed a document that seriously interfered with slavery. Without the southern states, there would have been a continuation of the Articles of Confederation, which would have left each state entirely sovereign and thus entirely free of any prospective challenge to slavery.

Thus the Framers compromised with slavery; political scientist Theodore Lowi calls this their Greatest Compromise.[18] Slavery is dealt with in three places in the Constitution, though never by name. In determining the representation each state was to have in the House, "three-fifths of all other persons" (that is, of slaves) are to be added to "the whole number of free persons."[19] The South originally wanted slaves to count fully even though, of course, none would be elected to the House; they settled for counting 60 percent of them. The Great (or Connecticut) Compromise favored smaller states, which were mostly northern, by giving each state two senators; but the three-fifths compromise even more strongly favored the South's slaveholding states. For example, apportioned according to its free population, the southern states would have had a combined total of 33 House seats rather than the 47 they claimed. The three-fifths compromise is behind the fact that southern-born presidents, House leaders, and Supreme Court justices generally dominated antebellum American national government.[20]

The convention also agreed not to allow the new government by law or even constitutional amendment to prohibit the importation of slaves until 1808.[21] The South thus had 20 years in which it could acquire more slaves from abroad; after that, Congress was free (but not required) to end the importation. Finally, the Constitution guaranteed that if a slave were to escape his or her master and flee to a nonslave state, the slave would be returned by that state to "the party to whom . . . service or labour may be due."[22]

The unresolved issue of slavery was to prove the most explosive question of all. Allowing slavery to continue was a fateful decision, one that led to the

North Wind Picture Archives/Alamy

Deck of a slave ship captured in 1860. Thousands of slaves died on such ships.

How We Compare

Does a Constitution Guarantee Freedom?

You may think that the best protection for individual freedom is for a nation to have a written constitution. After all, a constitution is supposed to limit governmental action. But if you look around the world you will see that a constitution is not enough.

Here are three nations that do not have a written constitution and yet personal freedom is well established:

Israel New Zealand United Kingdom

And here are three nations with a written constitution where personal freedom is rare:

Iran North Korea Russia

What else must nations have in order to ensure personal freedom?

worst social and political catastrophe in the nation's history—the Civil War. The Framers chose to sidestep the issue in order to create a union that, they hoped, would eventually be strong enough to deal with the problem when it could no longer be postponed. The legacy of that choice continues to this day.

The Motives of the Framers

The Framers were not saints or demigods. They were men with political opinions who also had economic interests and human failings. It would be a mistake to conclude that everything they did in 1787 was motivated by a disinterested commitment to the public good. But it would be an equally great mistake to think that what they did was nothing but an effort to line their pockets by producing a government that would serve their own narrow interests. As in almost all human endeavors, the Framers acted out of a mixture of motives. What is truly astonishing is that economic interests played only a modest role in their deliberations.

ECONOMIC INTERESTS

Some of the Framers were wealthy; some were not. Some owned slaves; some had none. Some were creditors (having loaned money to the Continental Congress or to private parties); some were deeply in debt. For nearly a century, scholars have argued over just how important these personal interests were in shaping the provisions of the Constitution.

In 1913 Charles Beard, a historian, published a book—*An Economic Interpretation of the Constitution*—arguing that the better-off urban and commercial classes, especially those members who held the IOUs issued by the government to pay for the Revolutionary War, favored the new Constitution because they stood to benefit from it.[23] But in the 1950s, that view was challenged by historians who, after looking carefully at what the Framers owned or owed, concluded that one could not explain the Constitution exclusively or even largely in terms of the economic interests of those who wrote it.[24] Some of the richest delegates, such as Elbridge Gerry of Massachusetts and George Mason of Virginia, refused to sign the document, while many of its key backers—James Madison and James Wilson, for example—were men of modest means or heavy debts.

In the 1980s, a new group of scholars, primarily economists applying more advanced statistical techniques, found evidence that some economic considerations influenced how the Framers voted on some issues during the Philadelphia convention. Interestingly, however, the economic position of the *states* from which they came had a greater effect on their votes than did their *own* monetary condition.[25]

We have already seen how delegates from small states fought to reduce the power of large states and how those from slaveowning states made certain that the Constitution would contain no provision that would threaten slavery.

But contrary to what Beard asserted, the economic interests of the Framers themselves did not dominate the convention. Some delegates owned a lot of public debt they had purchased for low prices. A strong national government of the sort envisaged by the Constitution was more likely than the weak Continental Congress to pay off this debt at face value, thus making the delegates who owned it much richer. Despite this, the ownership of public debt had no significant effect on how the Framers voted in Philadelphia. Nor did the big land speculators vote their interests. Some, such as George Washington and Robert Morris, favored the Constitution, while others, such as George Mason and William Blount, opposed it.[26]

In sum, the Framers tended to represent their states' interests on important matters. Since they were picked by the states to do so, this is exactly what one would expect. If they had not met in secret, perhaps they would have voted even more often as their constituents wanted.

With the grave and enormous exception of slavery, the Framers usually did not vote their own respective economic interests.

At the popularly elected state ratifying conventions, economic factors played a larger role. Delegates who were merchants, who lived in cities, who owned large amounts of western land, who held government IOUs, and who did not own slaves were more likely to vote to ratify the new Constitution than delegates who were farmers, who did not own public debt, and who did own slaves.[27] There were plenty of exceptions, however. Small farmers dominated the conventions in some states where the vote to ratify was unanimous.

Though interests made a difference, they were not simply elite interests. In most states, the great majority of adult white males could vote for delegates to the ratifying conventions. This means that women and blacks were excluded from the debates, but by the standards of the time—standards that did not change for over a century—the ratification process was remarkably democratic.

THE CONSTITUTION AND EQUALITY

Ideas counted for as much as interests. At stake were two views of the public good. One, espoused by the Federalists, was that a reasonable balance of liberty, order, and progress required a strong national government. The other, defended by the Antifederalists, was that liberty would not be secure in the hands of a powerful, distant government; freedom required decentralization.

Today that debate has a new focus. The defect of the Constitution, to some contemporary critics, is not that the government it created is too strong but that it is too weak. In particular, the national government is too weak to resist the pressures of special interests that reflect and perpetuate social inequality.

This criticism reveals how our understanding of the relationship between liberty and equality has changed since the Founding. To Jefferson and Madison, citizens naturally differed in their talents and qualities. What had to be guarded against was the use of governmental power to create unnatural and undesirable inequalities. This might happen, for example, if political power was concentrated in the hands of a few people (who could use that power

RESEARCH FRONTIERS

The Founding Debate over Church and State

Over the last decade, diverse scholars have begun to rediscover how competing views about religion and government shaped the debate between the Federalists and the Antifederalists.

In present-day political vernacular, the Antifederalists were the day's religious conservatives. Many Antifederalist leaders condemned the Constitution's no-religious-test provision (Article VI) and denounced the First Amendment because it forbade the Congress from establishing Christianity or any other religion as the national religion.

In stark contrast, most Federalists, even the orthodox Reverend John Witherspoon, agreed with James Madison that the Constitution should permit, and the national government should promote, religious pluralism. In *Federalist* No. 51, Madison argued that "the security for civil rights" consisted in "the multiplicity of interests" just as "that for religious rights" consisted in "the multiplicity of sects."

Scholars have argued about the religious views of the Founders for many years. Some have said they were religious while others have said they were atheists, agnostics, or Deists who believe there is a God but one who does not intervene in human affairs.

We now know that George Washington was not a Deist but rather a fairly typical late 18th-century Anglican. On the other hand, Thomas Jefferson was a Deist. During his two terms as our first president, Washington set many important precedents regarding the relationship between government and religion.

Unlike the Antifederalists, Washington, Witherspoon, Madison, and most other Federalists believed that any religious groups including their own might degenerate into what Madison, in *Federalist* No. 10, famously defined as "factions" that threaten "the rights of other citizens" and thwart the national interest or common good.

In defeating Antifederalist demands that the Constitution privilege Anglo-Protestants, neither Washington nor most other Federalists advocated a total separation between church and state, but neither did they deny the need for government diligence in checking what Madison, in *Federalist* No. 10, termed "a zeal for different opinions concerning religion."

- Do you think the fact that America today is home to over 300 million citizens representing scores of different Christian and other religious traditions, including tens of millions of citizens who are religiously unaffiliated, vindicates the Federalist vision?
- What might a "neo-Antifederalist" argue regarding church and state in America today?
- Finally, do a little research to find out what each of the three most recent presidents—Bill Clinton, George W. Bush, and Barack Obama—have argued about the relationship between religion and government.

Source: Peter R. Henriques, *Realistic Visionary: A Portrait of George Washington* (University of Virginia Press, 2008); Tara Ross and Joseph C. Smith, Jr., *Under God: George Washington and the Question of Church and State* (Spence, 2008); John J. DiIulio, Jr., *Godly Republic: A Centrist Blueprint for America's Faith-Based Future* (University of California Press, 2007); Peter A. Lillback, *George Washington's Sacred Fire* (Providence Forum Press, 2006); Michael Novak and Jana Novak, *Washington's God: Religion, Liberty, and the Father of Our Country* (Basic Books, 2006).

to give themselves special privileges) or if it was used in ways that allowed some private parties to acquire exclusive charters and monopolies. To prevent the inequality that might result from having too strong a government, its powers must be kept strictly limited.

Today, some people think of inequality quite differently. To them it is the natural social order—the marketplace and the acquisitive talents of people operating in that marketplace—that leads to undesirable inequalities, especially in economic power. The government should be powerful enough to restrain these natural tendencies and produce, by law, a greater degree of equality than society allows when left alone.

To the Framers, liberty and (political) equality were not in conflict; to some people today, these two principles are deeply in conflict. To the Framers, the task was to keep government so limited as to prevent it from creating the worst inequality—political privilege. To some modern observers, the task is to make government strong enough to reduce what they believe is the worst inequality—differences in wealth.

Constitutional Reform: Modern Views

Almost from the day it was ratified, the Constitution has been the object of debate over ways in which it might be improved. These debates have rarely involved the average citizen, who tends to revere the document even if he or she cannot recall all its details. Because of this deep and broad popular support, scholars and politicians have been wary of attacking the Constitution or suggesting many wholesale changes. But such attacks have occurred. During the 1980s—the decade in which we celebrated the bicentennial of its adoption—we heard a variety of suggestions for improving the Constitution, ranging from particular amendments to wholesale revisions. In general there are today, as in the 18th century, two kinds of critics: those who think the federal government is too weak and those who think it is too strong.

REDUCING THE SEPARATION OF POWERS

To the first kind of critic, the chief difficulty with the Constitution is the separation of powers. By making every decision the uncertain outcome of the pulling and hauling between the president and Congress, the Constitution precludes the emergence—except perhaps in times of crisis—of the kind of effective national leadership the country needs. In this view, our nation today faces a number of challenges that require prompt, decisive, and comprehensive action. Our problem is gridlock. Our position of international leadership, the dangerous and unprecedented proliferation of nuclear weapons among the nations of the globe, and the need to find ways of stimulating economic growth while reducing our deficit and conserving our environment—all these situations require the president be able to formulate and carry out policies free of some of the pressures and delays from interest groups and members of Congress tied to local interests.

Not only would this increase in presidential authority make for better policies, these critics argue, it would also help the voters hold the president and his party accountable for their actions. As matters now stand, nobody in government can be held responsible for policies: everybody takes the credit for successes and nobody takes the blame for failures. Typically the president, who tends to be the major source of new programs, cannot get his policies adopted by Congress without long delays and much bargaining, the result of which often is some watered-down compromise that neither the president nor Congress really likes but that each must settle for if anything is to be done at all.

Finally, critics of the separation of powers complain that the government agencies responsible for implementing a program are exposed to undue interference from legislators and special interests. In this view, the president is supposed to be in charge of the bureaucracy but in fact must share this authority with countless members of Congress and congressional committees.

Not all critics of the separation of powers agree with all these points, nor do they all agree on what should be done about the problems. But they all have in common a fear that the separation of powers makes the president too weak and insufficiently accountable. Their proposals for reducing the separation of powers include the following:

- Allow the president to appoint members of Congress to serve in the cabinet (the Constitution forbids members of Congress from holding any federal appointive office while in Congress).
- Allow the president to dissolve Congress and call for a special election (elections now can be held only on the schedule determined by the calendar).
- Allow Congress to require a president who has lost its confidence to face the country in a special election before his term would normally end.

Were Women Left Out of the Constitution?

In one sense, yes: Women were mentioned nowhere in the Constitution when it was written in 1787. Moreover, Article I, which set forth the provisions for electing members of the House of Representatives, granted the vote to those people who were allowed to vote for members of the lower house of the legislature in the states in which they resided. In no state at the time could women participate in those elections. In no state could they vote in any elections or hold any offices. Furthermore, wherever the Constitution uses a pronoun, it uses the masculine form—*he* or *him*.

In another sense, no: Wherever the Constitution or the Bill of Rights defines a right that people are to have, it either grants that right to "persons" or "citizens," not to "men," or it makes no mention at all of people or gender. For example:

- "The *citizens* of each State shall be entitled to all privileges and immunities of citizens of the several States."

  [Art. I, sec. 9]

- "No *person* shall be convicted of treason unless on the testimony of two witnesses to the same overt act, or on confession in open court."

  [Art. III, sec. 3]

- "No bill of attainder or ex post facto law shall be passed."

  [Art. I, sec. 9]

- "The right of the *people* to be secure in their persons, houses, papers, and effects, against unreasonable searches and seizures, shall not be violated."

  [Amend. IV]

- "No *person* shall be held to answer for a capital, or otherwise infamous crime, unless on presentment or indictment of a grand jury . . . nor shall any *person* be subject for the same offense to be twice put in jeopardy of life or limb; . . . nor be deprived of life, liberty, or property, without due process of law."

  [Amend. V]

- "In all criminal prosecutions the *accused* shall enjoy the right to a speedy and public trial, by an impartial jury."

  [Amend. VI]

Moreover, when the qualifications for elective office are stated, the word *person,* not *man,* is used.

- "No *person* shall be a Representative who shall not have attained to the age of twenty-five years."

  [Art. I, sec. 2]

- "No *person* shall be a Senator who shall not have attained to the age of thirty years."

  [Art. I, sec. 3]

- "No *person* except a natural born citizen . . . shall be eligible to the office of President; neither shall any *person* be eligible to that office who shall not have attained to the age of thirty-five years."

  [Art. II, sec. 1]

In places, the Constitution and the Bill of Rights used the pronoun *he*, but always in the context of referring back to a *person* or *citizen*. At the time, and until quite recently, the male pronoun was often used in legal documents to refer generically to both men and women.

Thus, though the Constitution did not give women the right to vote until the Nineteenth Amendment was ratified in 1920, it did use language that extended fundamental rights, and access to office, to women and men equally.

Of course, what the Constitution permitted did not necessarily occur. State and local laws denied to women rights that in principle they ought to have enjoyed. Except for a brief period in New Jersey, no women voted in statewide elections until, in 1869, they were given the right to cast ballots in territorial elections in Wyoming.

When women were first elected to Congress, there was no need to change the Constitution; nothing in it restricted officeholding to men.

When women were given the right to vote by constitutional amendment, it was not necessary to amend any existing language in the Constitution, because nothing in the Constitution itself denied women the right to vote; the amendment simply added a new right:

- "The right of citizens of the United States to vote shall not be denied or abridged by the United States or any state on account of sex."

  [Amend. XIX]

Source: Adapted from Robert Goldwin, "Why Blacks, Women and Jews Are Not Mentioned in the Constitution," *Commentary* (May 1987): 28–33.

- Require the presidential and congressional candidates to run as a team in each congressional district; thus a presidential candidate who carries a given district could be sure the congressional candidate of his party would also win in that district.
- Have the president serve a single six-year term instead of being eligible for up to two four-year terms; this would presumably free the president to lead without having to worry about reelection.
- Lengthen the terms of members of the House of Representatives from two to four years so that the entire House would stand for reelection at the same time as the president.[28]

Some of these proposals are offered by critics out of a desire to make the American system of government work more like the British parliamentary system, in which, as we shall see in Chapters 13 and 14, the prime minister is the undisputed leader of the majority in the British Parliament. The parliamentary system is the major alternative in the world today to the American separation-of-powers system.

amendment A new provision in the Constitution that has been ratified by the states.

Both the diagnosis and the remedies proposed by these critics of the separation of powers have been challenged. Many defenders of our present constitutional system believe that nations, such as Great Britain, with a different, more unified political system have done no better than the United States in dealing with the problems of economic growth, national security, and environmental protection. Moreover, they argue, close congressional scrutiny of presidential proposals has improved these policies more often than it has weakened them. Finally, congressional "interference" in the work of government agencies is a good way of ensuring that the average citizen can fight back against the bureaucracy; without that so-called interference, citizens and interest groups might be helpless before big and powerful agencies.

Each of the specific proposals, defenders of the present constitutional system argue, would either make matters worse or have, at best, uncertain effects. Adding a few members of Congress to the president's cabinet would not provide much help in getting his program through Congress; there are 535 senators and representatives, and probably only about half a dozen would be in the cabinet. Giving either the president or Congress the power to call

How Things Work

Ways of Amending the Constitution

Under Article V, there are two ways to *propose* **amendments** to the Constitution and two ways to *ratify* them.

To Propose an Amendment

1. Two-thirds of both houses of Congress vote to propose an amendment, *or*
2. Two-thirds of the state legislatures ask Congress to call a national convention to propose amendments.

To Ratify an Amendment

1. Three-fourths of the state legislatures approve it,

or

2. Ratifying conventions in three-fourths of the states approve it.

Some Key Facts

- Only the first method of proposing an amendment has been used.
- The second method of ratification has been used only once, to ratify the Twenty-first Amendment (repealing Prohibition).
- Congress may limit the time within which a proposed amendment must be ratified. The usual limitation has been seven years.
- Thousands of proposals have been made, but only 33 have obtained the necessary two-thirds vote in Congress.
- Twenty-seven amendments have been ratified.
- The first 10 amendments, ratified on December 15, 1791, are known as the Bill of Rights.

a special election in between the regular elections (every two or four years) would cause needless confusion and great expense; the country would live under the threat of being in a perpetual political campaign with even weaker political parties. Linking the fate of the president and congressional candidates by having them run as a team in each district would reduce the stabilizing and moderating effect of having them elected separately. A Republican presidential candidate who wins in the new system would have a Republican majority in the House; a Democratic candidate winner would have a Democratic majority. We might as a result expect dramatic changes in policy as the political pendulum swung back and forth. Giving presidents a single six-year term would indeed free them from the need to worry about reelection, but it is precisely that worry that keeps presidents reasonably concerned about what the American people want.

MAKING THE SYSTEM LESS DEMOCRATIC

The second kind of critic of the Constitution thinks the government does too much, not too little. Though the separation of powers at one time may have slowed the growth of government and moderated the policies it adopted, in the last few decades government has grown helter-skelter. The problem, these critics argue, is not that democracy is a bad idea but that democracy can produce bad, or at least unintended, results if the government caters to the special-interest claims of the citizens rather than to their long-term values.

To see how these unintended results might occur, imagine a situation in which every citizen thinks the government grows too big, taxes too heavily, and spends too much. Each citizen wants the government made smaller by reducing the benefits other people get—but not by reducing the benefits he or she gets. In fact, such citizens may even be willing to see their own benefits cut, provided everybody else's are cut as well, and by a like amount.

line-item veto An executive's ability to block a particular provision in a bill passed by the legislature.

But the political system attends to individual wants, not general preferences. It gives aid to farmers, contracts to industry, grants to professors, pensions to the elderly, and loans to students. As someone once said, the government is like an adding machine: during elections candidates campaign by promising to do more for whatever group is dissatisfied with what the incumbents are doing for it. As a result, most elections bring to office men and women committed to doing more for somebody. The grand total of all these additions is more for everybody. Few politicians have an incentive to do less for anybody.

To remedy this state of affairs, these critics suggest various mechanisms, but principally a constitutional amendment that would either set a limit on the amount of money the government could collect in taxes each year or require that each year the government have a balanced budget (that is, not spend more than it takes in in taxes), or both. In some versions of these plans, an extraordinary majority (say, 60 percent) of Congress could override these limits, and the limits would not apply in wartime.

The effect of such amendments, the proponents claim, would be to force Congress and the president to look at the big picture—the grand total of what they are spending—rather than just to operate the adding machine by pushing the "add" button over and over again. If they could spend only so much during a given year, they would have to allocate what they spend among all rival claimants. For example, if more money were to be spent on the poor, less could then be spent on the military, or vice versa.

Some critics of an overly powerful federal government think these amendments will not be passed or may prove unworkable; instead, they favor enhancing the president's power to block spending by giving him a **line-item veto.** Most state governors can veto a particular part of a bill and approve the rest using a line-item veto. The theory is that such a veto would better equip the president to stop unwarranted spending without vetoing the other provisions of a bill. In 1996, President Clinton signed the Line Item Veto Act, passed by the 104th Congress. But despite its name, the new law did not give the president full line-item veto power (only a change in the Constitution could confer that power). Instead the law gave the president authority to selectively eliminate individual items in large appropriations bills, expansions in certain income-transfer programs, and tax breaks (giving the president what budget experts call *enhanced rescission authority*). But it also left Congress free to craft bills in ways that would give the president few opportunities to veto (or *rescind*) favored items. For example, Congress could still force the president to accept or reject an entire appropriations bill simply by tagging on this sentence: "Appropriations provided under this act (or title or section) shall not be subject to the provisions of the Line Item Veto Act." In *Clinton et al. v. New York et al.* (1998), the Supreme Court struck down the 1996 law, holding 6 to 3 that the Constitution does not allow the president to cancel specific items in tax and spending legislation. Clinton's successor, President George W. Bush, championed the line-item veto, but to no avail; and, when asked about the line-item veto in February 2009, President Barack Obama's press secretary, Robert Gibbs, quipped that the new president would "love to take that for a test drive."

Finally, some critics of a powerful government feel that the real problem arises not from an excess of "adding-machine" democracy but from the growth in the power of the federal courts, as described in Chapter 16. These critics would like to devise a set of laws or constitutional amendments that would narrow the authority of federal courts.

The opponents of these suggestions argue that constitutional amendments to restrict the level of taxes or to require a balanced budget are unworkable, even assuming—which they do not—that a smaller government is desirable. There is no precise, agreed-upon way to measure how much the government spends or to predict in advance how much it will receive in taxes during the year; thus defining and enforcing a "balanced budget" is no easy matter. Since the government can always borrow money, it might easily evade any spending limits. It has also shown great ingenuity in spending money in ways that never appear as part of the regular budget.

The line-item veto may or may not be a good idea. Unless the Constitution is amended to permit it, future presidents will have to do without it. The states, where some governors have long had the veto, are quite different from the federal government in power and responsibilities. Whether a line-item veto would work as well in Washington, D.C., as it does in many state capitals is something that we may simply never know.

Finally, proposals to curtail judicial power are thinly veiled attacks, the opponents argue, on the ability of the courts to protect essential citizen rights. If Congress and the people do not like the way the Supreme Court has interpreted the Constitution, they can always amend the Constitution to change a specific ruling; there is no need to adopt some across-the-board limitation on court powers.

WHO IS RIGHT?

Some of the arguments of these two sets of critics of the Constitution may strike you as plausible or even entirely convincing. Whatever you may ultimately decide, decide nothing for now. One cannot make or remake a constitution based entirely on abstract reasoning or unproven factual arguments. Even when the Constitution was first written in 1787, it was not an exercise in abstract philosophy but rather an effort to solve pressing, practical problems in the light of a theory of human nature, the lessons of past experience, and a close consideration of how governments in other countries and at other times had worked.

Just because the Constitution is over 200 years old does not mean it is out-of-date. The crucial questions are these: How well has it worked over the long sweep of American history? How well has it worked compared to the constitutions of other democratic nations?

The only way to answer those questions is to study American government closely—with special attention to its historical evolution and to the practices of other nations. That is what this book is about. Of course, even after close study, people will still disagree about whether our system should be changed. People want different things and evaluate human experience according to different beliefs. But if we first understand how, in fact, the government works and why it has produced the policies it has, we can then argue more intelligently about how best to achieve our wants and give expression to our beliefs.

Kent Eanes/HBO/Everett Collection

In an excellent TV series, John Adams and George Washington discuss politics in the 18th century.

WHAT WOULD YOU DO?

MEMORANDUM

To: *Elizabeth Anthony, Arkansas state senate majority leader*

From: *George Morris, chief of staff*

Subject: *Proposal for a new constitutional convention*

In the 1990s, Arkansas and several other states approved term limits for their members of Congress, but the Supreme Court ruled in 1995 that states do not have this authority. Now term-limit advocates are pursuing a broader strategy, calling for states to approve legislation that would require Congress to consider several amendment proposals, including term limits and abolishing the Electoral College to permit the direct popular election of the president. The Arkansas General Assembly passed such a bill last week, and several senators in your party have declared their support.

News »

Twenty-Eight States Back Proposal for Constitutional Convention

Yesterday Pennsylvania's legislature approved a proposal for a constitutional convention, becoming the twenty-eighth state to do so. The Constitution states that Congress shall hold a convention for proposing amendments at the request of two-thirds of the state legislatures, but it has never happened in U.S. history. Six more states must approve for Congress to take action, and two announced yesterday that they plan to review similar proposals this week.

Arguments for:

1. Since the Twenty-second Amendment restricts presidents to two terms, members of Congress should face similar limits.
2. Term limits will ensure that national leaders do not become career politicians.
3. The public favors the direct popular election of the president; this constitutional convention would make possible abolishing the Electoral College.

Arguments against:

1. Limiting members of Congress to two terms would increase the power of lobbyists, congressional staffers, and administrative officials.
2. The Electoral College encourages a two-party system; a direct popular vote for the president would require runoff elections if no candidate won a majority.
3. The Constitutional Convention of 1787 was held in secret and involved only a few dozen people; today it would be heavily covered by the press and involve hundreds, perhaps thousands of people. No one knows what changes it might make.

Your decision:

Favor legislation _______________ Oppose legislation _______________

LEARNING OBJECTIVES

WHAT YOU NEED TO KNOW

☑ Why was a Bill of Rights adopted so soon after the ratification of the Constitution?

A Bill of Rights was adopted by the First Congress because so many states had asked for amendments in exchange for their votes to ratify the Constitution. But what they got was quite different from what they requested. James Madison, in writing the amendment, used much of the language of the Virginia Declaration of Rights.

☑ Why did so many authors of the Constitution fear factions?

Many Framers, but especially Madison, feared factions because human nature divides people, and when they are divided they are likely to oppose one another and so threaten the chances of arriving at the common good.

☑ Why did the Framers agree on the idea of a separation of powers?

Almost all of the Framers agreed that our government should be based on the separation of powers among its three branches because such a system would provide better checks on power than what they had experienced with England.

RECONSIDERING WHO GOVERNS?

1. What is the difference between a democracy and a republic?

A democracy means rule by the people; direct democracy means letting every important issue be decided by popular vote. A republic is a government in which authority has been given to elected representatives. The United States is a republic in which members of the House of Representatives are selected in democratic elections, members of the Senate (at least initially) were selected by state legislatures, and the courts are staffed by appointed judges.

2. What branch of government has the greatest power?

Initially, Congress had the most authority. As we shall see in later chapters, the president and the federal courts grew in power, but even so Congress remains the most important institution.

RECONSIDERING TO WHAT ENDS?

1. Does the Constitution tell us what goals the government should serve?

Not really. The preface tells us what the Founders hoped the federal government would do, but that preface has no legal authority. By and large, the government has to set its own goals.

2. Whose freedom does the Constitution protect?

It was intended to protect everybody's freedom, except that of slaves. To create a national government, it was necessary that the Constitution do nothing about slavery, but without the Constitution, there would have been no national government to challenge slavery during the Civil War. Though women are not mentioned, in fact there is nothing in the Constitution to prevent them from holding national office or from voting in federal elections. Voting was to be decided by each state until the passage of a constitutional amendment (the Nineteenth, ratified in 1920) that prohibited the states from denying the vote to women.

QUESTIONS TO CONSIDER

1. **Read your state's constitution and summarize how it is like and how it differs from the federal Constitution.**
2. **Only once were state ratifying conventions used to ratify a constitutional amendment (the Twenty-First). Learn why that happened.**

TO LEARN MORE

To find historical and legal documents:

TeachingAmericanHistory.org

National Constitution Center:

www.constitutioncenter.org

Congress:

thomas.loc.gov/ (choose Historical Documents)

To look at court cases about the Constitution:

Cornell University: **www.law.cornell.edu/supct**

Bailyn, Bernard. *The Ideological Origins of the American Revolution*. Cambridge: Harvard University Press, 1967. A brilliant account of how the American colonists formed and justified the idea of independence.

Becker, Carl L. *The Declaration of Independence*. New York: Vintage, 1942. The classic account of the meaning of the Declaration.

Beeman, Richard. *Plain, Honest Men: The Making of the American Constitution*. New York: Random House, 2009. The best account ever written about what happened in Philadelphia.

Federalist papers. By Alexander Hamilton, James Madison, and John Jay. The definitive edition, edited by Jacob E. Cooke, was published in Middletown, Conn., in 1961, by the Wesleyan University Press.

Goldwin, Robert A., and William A. Schambra, eds. *How Capitalistic Is the Constitution?* Washington, D.C.: American Enterprise Institute, 1982. Essays from different viewpoints discussing the relationship between the Constitution and the economic order.

___. *How Democratic Is the Constitution*? Washington, D.C.: American Enterprise Institute, 1980. Collection of essays offering different interpretations of the political meaning of the Constitution.

Maier, Pauline. *Ratification: The People Debate the Constitution, 1787–1788.* New York: Simon and Schuster, 2010. Not only is this a marvelous study of ratification, but it also is virtually the only one in existence. A splendid, comprehensive account.

McDonald, Forrest. *Novus Ordo Seclorum.* Lawrence: University of Kansas Press, 1985. A careful study of the intellectual origins of the Constitution. The Latin title means "New World Order," which is what the Framers hoped they were creating.

Sheldon, Garrett W. *The Political Philosophy of James Madison.* Baltimore: Johns Hopkins University Press, 2001. Masterful account of Madison's political thought and its roots in classical republicanism and Christianity.

Storing, Herbert J. *What the Anti-Federalists Were For.* Chicago: University of Chicago Press, 1981. Close analysis of the political views of those opposed to the ratification of the Constitution.

Wood, Gordon S. *The Creation of the American Republic.* Chapel Hill: University of North Carolina Press, 1969. A detailed study of American political thought before the Philadelphia convention.

___. *The Radicalism of the American Revolution*. New York: Knopf, 1992. Magisterial study of the nature and effects of the American Revolution and the relationship between the socially radical Revolution and the Constitution.

3 Federalism

LEARNING OBJECTIVES

WHAT YOU NEED TO KNOW

☑ Why does the United States have federalism?

☑ How has American federalism evolved from the founding to the present?

☑ Which level of government does federalism favor, the national government or the states?

WHO GOVERNS?

1. Where is sovereignty located in the American political system?
2. How is power divided between the national government and the states under the Constitution?

TO WHAT ENDS?

1. What competing values are at stake in federalism?
2. Who should decide which matters ought to be governed mainly or solely by national laws?

THEN When the Framers drafted the Constitution, the Antifederalists opposed it primarily on the grounds that it gave too much power to the national government. As Cato No. 3 (likely written by New York Governor George Clinton) states, people are likely to have weaker attachments to a distant central government than to the states that govern their everyday lives. The Antifederalists recognized the limitations of the Articles of Confederation, but they feared that the Constitution sacrificed liberty and civic responsibility with its vast expansion of the power of the national government.

NOW While the Federalists prevailed over the Antifederalists with the ratification of the Constitution, history suggests that the Antifederalist concerns may have been justified. The federal government has increasingly taken on responsibilities in areas that traditionally were the province of state governments, such as social-welfare policy, education, health care, and a minimum wage. States may have some flexibility in implementing policies, but the national government sets the direction in many more policy areas today than it did originally, and as the Antifederalists feared, we have a large standing army and activist courts. These changes may have contributed to the current polarization in American politics. But new developments do not mean the Constitution was wrong, only that politics and circumstances have changed. And the changes may have been greatest in the relations between the federal and state governments—that is, in federalism.

Like most average citizens, Susette Kelo, a nurse from New London, Connecticut, was not deeply interested in politics and government. But that changed when city officials condemned her little wood-frame home with a view of the Long Island Sound estuary. City officials took it and her neighbors' houses because they wanted

to redevelop the area with pricey townhouses, upscale shopping malls, and a huge hotel. Kelo sued the city all the way to the U.S. Supreme Court.

But in *Kelo v. City of New London* (2005), the justices decided, by a 5 to 4 majority, that the Constitution allows the government to seize property, not only for "public use" such as building highways, but also to "promote economic development" in a "distressed" community. Kelo and her neighbors were outraged, not least of all by the claim that their predominantly middle-class, waterside community was "distressed." But they had lost in the nation's highest court. What more could they or their by-then growing throng of sympathizers all across the country do?

Why Federalism Matters

Plenty, as it turned out. Before the ink had dried on the *Kelo* opinion, public protests, Internet letter-writing campaigns, and grassroots lobbying efforts were begun. Eighteen months later, 34 states had tightened laws to make it much harder for local governments to seize property for economic development purposes.

Similarly, you might suppose that federal law decides the minimum wage that employers must pay to workers. But before Congress moved to raise it (from 1996 into 2007 the standard was $5.15 an hour), more than a half-dozen states had a minimum wage above the federal standard (for instance, $7.15 an hour in Pennsylvania).

Okay, you might think, but what about state and local government powers in relation to big federal bureaucracies or huge federal programs? Surely the national government leads in making, administering, and funding important public policies that cost lots of money, right? The short answer is, "It all depends." The main reason is federalism.

> ***federalism***
> Government authority shared by national and local governments.

Federalism can be defined as a political system in which the national government shares power with local governments (state governments in the case of the United States, but other subnational governments in the case of federal systems including Australia, India, and Switzerland).Constitutionally, in America's federal system, state governments have a specially protected existence and the authority to make final decisions over many governmental activities. Even today, after more than a century during which the government headquartered in Washington, D.C., has grown, state and local governments are not mere junior partners in deciding important public policy matters. The national government can pass, and the federal courts can uphold, laws to protect the environment, store nuclear waste, expand low-income housing, guarantee the right to an abortion, provide special services for the handicapped, or toughen public-school graduation standards. But whether and how such federal laws are followed or funded often involves decisions by diverse state and local government officials, both elected and appointed.

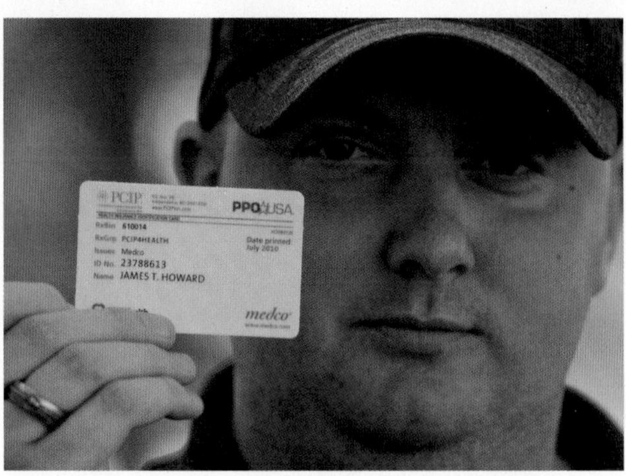

HEALTH/RISKPOOL REUTERS/Richard Carson

A man holds his card showing he is covered for a pre-existing medical condition. This program was part of the Affordable Care Act of 2010 ("Obamacare").

Federalism or federal-state relations may seem like an arcane or boring subject until you realize that it is behind many things that matter to many people: how much you pay in certain taxes, whether you can drive above 55 miles per hour on certain roadways, whether or where you can buy liquor, how much money gets spent on schools, whether all or most children have health insurance coverage, and much more. Federalism affects almost every aspect of crime and punishment in America (penalties for illegal drug sales vary widely from state to state, and persons convicted of murder are subject to the death penalty in some states but not in others). And, as we will see, federalism even figures in how certain civil liberties (Chapter 5) and civil rights (Chapter 6) are defined and protected (for instance, some state constitutions mention God, and some state laws specifically prohibit funding for religious schools).

Federalism matters, but how it matters has changed over time. In 1908, Woodrow Wilson observed that the relationship between the national government and the states "is the cardinal question of our constitutional system," a question that cannot be settled by "one generation, because it is a question of growth, and every successive stage of our political and economic development gives it a new aspect, makes it a new question."[1]

Since the adoption of the Constitution in 1787, the single most persistent source of political conflict has been the relations between the national and state governments. The political conflict over slavery, for example, was intensified because some state governments condoned or supported slavery, while others took action to discourage it. The proponents and opponents of slavery were thus given territorial power centers from which to carry on the dispute. Other issues, such as the regulation of business and the provision of social welfare programs, were in large part fought out, for well over a century, in terms of "national interests" versus "states' rights." While other nations, such as Great Britain, were debating the question of whether the national government *ought* to provide old-age pensions or regulate the railroads, the United States debated a different question—whether the national government *had the right* to do these things.

The Founding

The goal of the Founders seems clear: federalism was one device whereby personal liberty was to be protected. (The separation of powers was another.) The Founders feared that placing final political authority in any one set of hands, even in the hands of persons popularly elected, would so concentrate power as to risk tyranny. But they had seen what happened when independent states tried to form a compact, as under the Articles of Confederation; what the states put together, they could also take apart. The alliance among the states that existed from 1776 to 1787 was a confederation, that is, a system of government in which the people create state governments which in turn create and operate a national government (see Figure 3.1). Since the national government in a confederation derives its powers from the states, it is dependent on their continued cooperation for its survival. By 1786, that cooperation was barely forthcoming.

A BOLD, NEW PLAN

A federation—or a "federal republic," as the Founders called it—derives its powers directly from the people, as do the state governments. As the Founders envisioned it, both levels of government, the national and the state, would have certain powers, but neither would have supreme authority over the other. Madison, writing in *Federalist* No. 46, said that both the state and federal governments "are in fact but different agents and trustees of the people, constituted with different powers." In *Federalist* No. 28, Hamilton explained how he thought the system would work: the people could shift their support between state and federal levels of government as needed to keep the two in balance. "If their rights are invaded by either, they can make use of the other as the instrument of redress."

It was an entirely new plan, for which no historical precedent existed. Nobody came to the Philadelphia convention with a clear idea of what a federal (as opposed to a unitary or a confederal) system would look like, and there was not much discussion at Philadelphia of how the system would work in practice. Few delegates then used the word *federalism* in the sense in which we now employ it (it was originally used as a synonym for *confederation* and only later came to stand for something different).[2] The Constitution does not spell out the powers that the states are to have, and until the Tenth Amendment was added at the insistence of various states, there was not even a clause in it saying (as did the amendment) that "the powers not delegated to the United States by the Constitution, nor prohibited by it to the states, are reserved to the states respectively, or to the people." The Founders assumed from the outset that the federal government would have only those powers given to it by the Constitution; the Tenth Amendment was an afterthought, added to make that assumption explicit and allay fears that something else was intended.[3]

The Tenth Amendment has rarely had much practical significance, however. From time to time, the Supreme Court has tried to interpret that

Figure 3.1
Lines of Power in Three Systems of Government

UNITARY SYSTEM

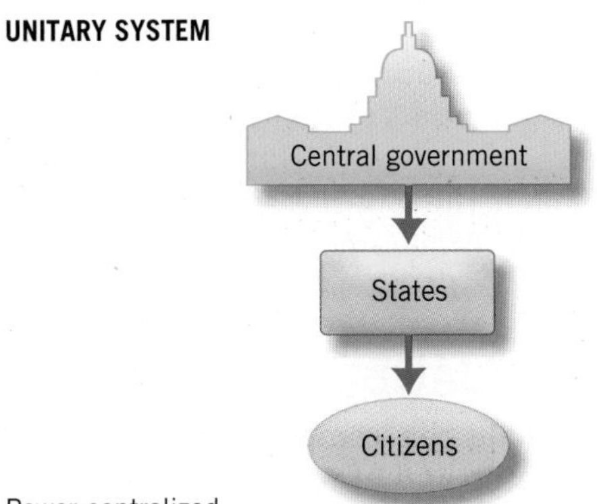

Power centralized.
State or regional governments derive authority from central government. Examples: United Kingdom, France.

FEDERAL SYSTEM

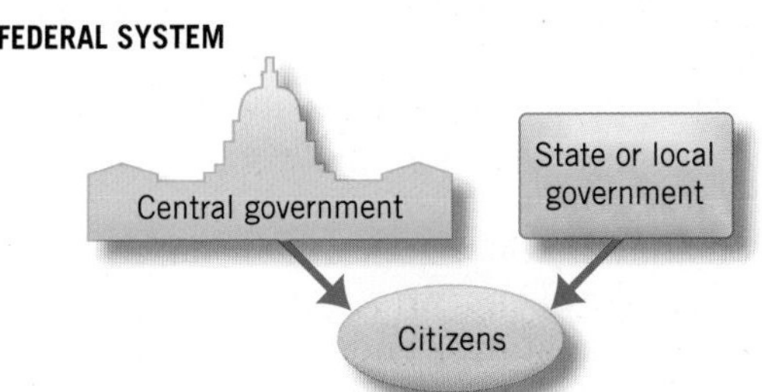

Power divided between central and state or local governments.
Both the government and constituent governments act directly upon the citizens.
Both must agree to constitutional change.
Examples: Canada, United States since adoption of Constitution.

CONFEDERAL SYSTEM (or CONFEDERATION)

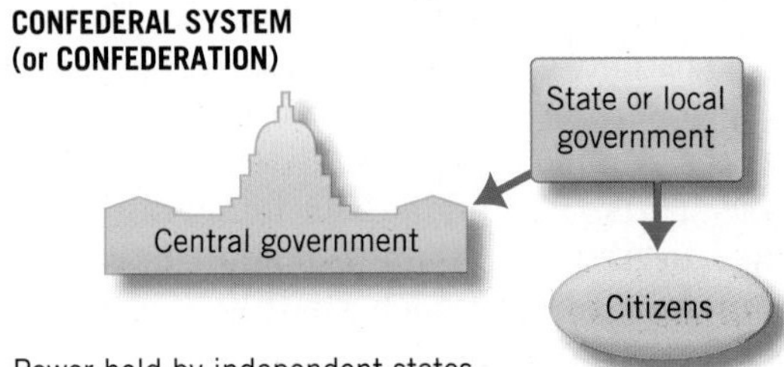

Power held by independent states.
Central government is a creature of the constituent governments.
Example: United States under the Articles of Confederation.

amendment as putting certain state activities beyond the reach of the federal government, but usually the Court has later changed its mind and allowed Washington to regulate such matters as the hours that employees of a city-owned mass-transit system may work. The Court did not find that running such a transportation system was one of the powers "reserved to the states."[4] But, as we explain later in this chapter, the Court has begun to give new life to the Tenth Amendment and the doctrine of state sovereignty.

ELASTIC LANGUAGE

The need to reconcile the competing interests of large and small states and of northern and southern states, especially as they affected the organization of Congress, was sufficiently difficult without trying to spell out exactly what relationship ought to exist between the national and state systems. For example, Congress was given the power to regulate commerce "among the several states." The Philadelphia convention would have gone on for four years rather than four months if the Founders had decided that it was necessary to describe, in clear language, how one was to tell where commerce *among* the states ended and commerce wholly *within* a single state began. The Supreme Court, as we shall see, devoted more than a century to that task before giving up.

Though some clauses bearing on federal-state relations were reasonably clear (see the box on page 58), other clauses were quite vague. The Founders knew, correctly, that they could not make an exact and exhaustive list of everything the federal government was empowered to do—circumstances would change, and new exigencies would arise. Thus they added the following elastic language to Article I: Congress shall have the power to "make all laws which shall be necessary and proper for carrying into execution the foregoing powers."

The Founders themselves carried away from Philadelphia different views of what federalism meant. One view was championed by Hamilton. Since the people had created the national government, since the laws and treaties made pursuant to the Constitution were "the supreme law of the land" (Article VI), and since the most pressing needs were the development of a national economy and the conduct of foreign affairs, Hamilton thought that the national government was the superior and leading force in political affairs and that its powers ought to be broadly defined and liberally construed.

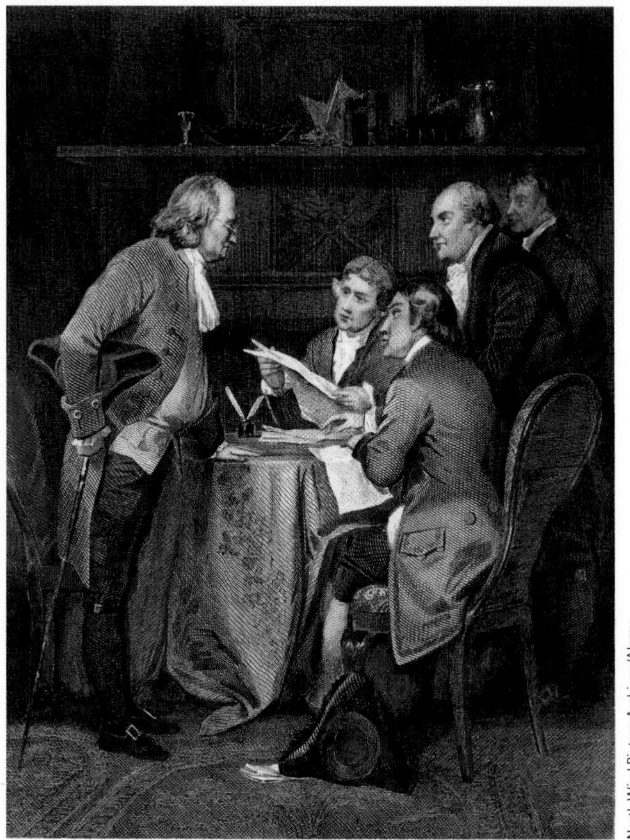
North Wind Picture Archives/Alamy

Benjamin Franklin, Thomas Jefferson, Livingston Adams, and Roger Sherman writing the Declaration of Independence.

The other view, championed by Jefferson, was that the federal government, though important, was the product of an agreement among the states; and though "the people" were the ultimate sovereigns, the principal threat to their liberties was likely to come from the national government. (Madison, a strong supporter of national supremacy at the convention, later became a champion of states' rights.) Thus the powers of the federal government should be narrowly construed and strictly limited. As Madison put it in *Federalist* No. 45, in language that probably made Hamilton wince, "The powers delegated by the proposed Constitution to the federal government are few and defined. Those which are to remain in the State governments are numerous and indefinite."

Hamilton argued for national supremacy, Jefferson for states' rights. Though their differences were greater in theory than in practice (as we shall see in Chapter 14, Jefferson while president sometimes acted in a positively Hamiltonian manner), the differing interpretations they offered of the Constitution were to shape political debate in this country until well into the 1960s.

The Debate on the Meaning of Federalism

The Civil War was fought, in part, over the issue of national supremacy versus states' rights, but it settled only one part of that argument—namely, that the national government was supreme, its sovereignty derived directly from the people, and thus the states could not lawfully secede from the Union. Virtually every other aspect of the national-supremacy issue continued to animate political and legal debate for another century.

THE SUPREME COURT SPEAKS

As arbiter of what the Constitution means, the Supreme Court became the focal point of that debate. In Chapter 16, we shall see in some detail how the Court made its decisions. For now it is enough to know that during the formative years of the new Republic, the Supreme Court was led by a staunch and brilliant advocate of Hamilton's position, Chief Justice John Marshall. In a series of decisions, he and the Court powerfully defended the national-supremacy view of the newly formed federal government.

The box on page 58 lists some landmark cases in the history of federal-state relations. Perhaps the most important decision was in a case, seemingly trivial in its origins, that arose when James McCulloch, the cashier of the Baltimore branch of the Bank of the United States, which had been created by Congress, refused to pay a tax levied on that bank by the state of Maryland. He was hauled into state court and convicted of failing to pay a tax. In 1819, McCulloch appealed all the way to the Supreme Court in a case known as *McCulloch v. Maryland.* The Court, in a unanimous opinion, answered two questions in ways that expanded the powers of Congress and confirmed the supremacy of the federal government in the exercise of those powers.

The first question was whether Congress had the right to set up a bank, or any other corporation, since such a right is nowhere explicitly mentioned in the Constitution. Marshall said that, though the federal government possessed only those powers enumerated in the Constitution, the "extent"—that is, the meaning—of those powers required interpretation. Though the word *bank* is not in that document, one finds there the power to manage money: to lay and collect taxes, issue a currency, and borrow funds. To carry out these powers, Congress may reasonably decide that chartering a national bank is "necessary and proper." Marshall's words were carefully chosen to endow the **"necessary and proper" clause** with the widest possible sweep:

> *Let the end be legitimate, let it be within the scope of the Constitution, and all means which are appropriate, which are plainly adapted to that end, which are not prohibited, but consistent with the letter and spirit of the Constitution, are constitutional.*[5]

The second question was whether a federal bank could lawfully be taxed by a state. To answer it, Marshall went back to first principles. The government of the United States was not established by the states, but by the people, and thus the federal government was supreme in the exercise of those powers conferred upon it. Having already concluded that chartering a bank was within the powers of Congress, Marshall then argued that the only way for such powers to be supreme was for their use to be immune from state challenge and for the products of their use to be protected against state destruction. Since "the power to tax involves the power to destroy," and since the power to destroy a federal agency would confer upon the states supremacy over the federal government, the states may not tax any federal instrument. Hence the Maryland law was unconstitutional.

"necessary and proper" clause Section of the Constitution allowing Congress to pass all laws "necessary and proper" to its duties, and which has permitted Congress to exercise powers not specifically given to it (enumerated) by the Constitution.

McCulloch won, and so did the federal government. Half a century later, the Court decided that what was sauce for the goose was sauce for the gander. It held that just as state governments could not tax federal bonds, the federal government could not tax the interest people earn on state and municipal bonds. In 1988, the Supreme Court changed its mind and decided that Congress was now free, if it wished, to tax the interest on such state and local bonds.[6] Municipal bonds, which for nearly a century were a tax-exempt investment protected (so their holders thought) by the Constitution, were now protected only by politics. So far Congress hasn't wanted to tax them.

NULLIFICATION

The Supreme Court can decide a case without settling the issue. The struggle over states' rights versus national supremacy continued to rage in Congress, during presidential elections, and ultimately on the battlefield. The issue came to center

How Things Work

The States and the Constitution

The Framers made some attempt to define the relations between the states and the federal government and how the states were to relate to one another. The following points were made in the original Constitution—before the Bill of Rights was added.

Restrictions on Powers of the States

States may not make treaties with foreign nations, coin money, issue paper currency, grant titles of nobility, pass a bill of attainder or an ex post facto law, or, without the consent of Congress, levy any taxes on imports or exports, keep troops and ships in time of peace, or enter into an agreement with another state or with a foreign power.

[Art. I, sec. 10]

Guarantees by the Federal Government to the States

The national government guarantees to every state a "republican form of government" and protection against foreign invasion and (provided the states request it) protection against domestic insurrection.

[Art. IV, sec. 4]

An existing state will not be broken up into two or more states or merged with all or part of another state without that state's consent.

[Art. IV, sec. 3]

Congress may admit new states into the Union.

[Art. IV, sec. 3]

Taxes levied by Congress must be uniform throughout the United States: they may not be levied on some states but not others.

[Art. I, sec. 8]

The Constitution may not be amended to give states unequal representation in the Senate.

[Art. V]

Rules Governing How States Deal with Each Other

"Full faith and credit" shall be given by each state to the laws, records, and court decisions of other states. (For example, a civil case settled in the courts of one state cannot be retried in the courts of another.)

[Art. IV, sec. 1]

The citizens of each state shall have the "privileges and immunities" of the citizens of every other state. (No one is quite sure what this is supposed to mean.)

[Art. IV, sec. 2]

If a person charged with a crime by one state flees to another, he or she is subjected to extradition—that is, the governor of the state that finds the fugitive is supposed to return the person to the governor of the state that wants him or her.

[Art. IV, sec. 2]

nullification The doctrine that a state can declare null and void a federal law that, in the state's opinion, violates the Constitution.

on the doctrine of **nullification.** When Congress passed laws (in 1798) to punish newspaper editors who published stories critical of the federal government, James Madison and Thomas Jefferson opposed the laws, suggesting (in statements known as the Virginia and Kentucky Resolutions) that the states had the right to "nullify" (that is, declare null and void) a federal law that, in the states' opinion, violated the Constitution. The laws expired before the claim of nullification could be settled in the courts.

Later the doctrine of nullification was revived by John C. Calhoun of South Carolina, first in opposition to a tariff enacted by the federal government and later in opposition to federal efforts to restrict slavery. Calhoun argued that if Washington attempted to ban slavery, the states had the right to declare such acts unconstitutional and thus null and void. This time the issue was settled—by war. The northern victory in the Civil War determined once and for all that the federal union is indissoluble and that states cannot declare acts of Congress unconstitutional, a view later confirmed by the Supreme Court.[7]

DUAL FEDERALISM

After the Civil War, the debate about the meaning of federalism focused on the interpretation of the commerce clause of the Constitution. Out of this debate

dual federalism Doctrine holding that the national government is supreme in its sphere, the states are supreme in theirs, and the two spheres should be kept separate.

emerged the doctrine of **dual federalism,** which held that though the national government was supreme in its sphere, the states were equally supreme in theirs, and that these two spheres of action should and could be kept separate. Applied to commerce, the concept of dual federalism implied that there were such things as *inter*state commerce, which Congress could regulate, and *intra*state commerce, which only the states could regulate, and that the Court could tell which was which.

For a long period the Court tried to decide what was interstate commerce based on the kind of business that was conducted. Transporting things between states was obviously interstate commerce, and so subject to federal regulation. Thus federal laws affecting the interstate shipment of lottery tickets,[8] prostitutes,[9] liquor,[10] and harmful foods and drugs[11] were upheld. On the other hand, manufacturing,[12] insurance,[13] and farming[14] were in the past considered *intra*state commerce, and so only the state governments were allowed to regulate them.

Such product-based distinctions turned out to be hard to sustain. For example, if you ship a case of whiskey from Kentucky to Kansas, how long is it in interstate commerce (and thus subject to federal law), and when does it enter intrastate commerce and become subject only to state law? For a while, the Court's answer was that the whiskey was in interstate commerce so long as it was in its "original package,"[15] but that only precipitated long quarrels as to what was the original package and how one is to treat things, like gas and grain, that may not be shipped in packages at all. And how could one distinguish between manufacturing and transportation when one company did both or when a single manufacturing corporation owned factories in different states? And if an insurance company sold policies to customers both inside and outside a given state, were there to be different laws regulating identical policies that happened to be purchased from the same company by persons in different states?

In time, the effort to find some clear principles that distinguished interstate from intrastate commerce was pretty much abandoned. Commerce was like a stream flowing through the country, drawing to itself contributions from thousands of scattered enterprises and depositing its products in millions of individual homes. The Court began to permit the federal government to regulate almost anything that affected this stream, so that by the 1940s not only had farming and manufacturing been redefined as part of interstate commerce,[16] but even the janitors and window washers in buildings that housed companies engaged in interstate commerce were now said to be part of that stream.[17]

Today lawyers are engaged in interstate commerce but professional baseball players are not. If your state has approved marijuana use for medical purposes, you can still be penalized under federal law even when the marijuana you consume was grown in a small pot in your backyard.[18]

STATE SOVEREIGNTY

It would be a mistake to think that the doctrine of dual federalism is entirely dead. Until recently, Congress, provided that it had a good reason, could pass a law regulating almost any kind of economic activity anywhere in the country, and the Supreme Court would call it constitutional. But in *United States v. Lopez* (1995), the Court held that Congress had exceeded its commerce clause power by prohibiting guns in a school zone.

The Court reaffirmed the view that the commerce clause does not justify any federal action when, in May 2000, it overturned the Violence Against Women Act of 1994. This law allowed women who were the victims of a crime of violence motivated by gender to sue the guilty party in federal court. In *United States v. Morrison,* the Court, in a five-to-four decision, said that attacks against women are not, and do not substantially affect, interstate commerce, and hence Congress cannot constitutionally pass such a law. Chief Justice William Rehnquist said that "the Constitution requires a distinction between what is truly national and what is truly local." The states, of course, can pass such laws, and many have.

The Court has moved to strengthen states' rights on other grounds as well. In *Printz v. United States* (1997), the Court invalidated a federal law that required local police to conduct background checks on all gun purchasers. The Court ruled that the law violated the Tenth Amendment by commanding state governments to carry out a federal regulatory program. Writing for the five-to-four majority, Justice Antonin Scalia declared, "The Federal government may neither issue directives requiring the states to address particular problems, nor command the states' officers, or those of their political subdivisions, to administer or enforce a Federal regulatory program. . . . Such commands are fundamentally incompatible with our constitutional system of dual sovereignty."

The Terms of Local Governance

Legally a **city** is a **municipal corporation** or **municipality** that has been chartered by a state to exercise certain defined powers and provide certain specific services. There are two kinds of charters: special-act charters and general-act charters.

A **special-act charter** applies to a certain city (for example, New York City) and lists what that city can and cannot do. A **general-act charter** applies to a number of cities that fall within a certain classification, usually based on city population. Thus in some states, all cities over 100,000 population will be governed on the basis of one charter, while all cities between 50,000 and 99,999 population will be governed on the basis of a different one.

Under **Dillon's rule,** the terms of these charters are to be interpreted very narrowly. This rule (named after a lawyer who wrote a book on the subject in 1911) authorizes a municipality to exercise only those powers expressly given, implied by, or essential to the accomplishment of its enumerated powers. This means, for example, that a city cannot so much as operate a peanut stand at the city zoo unless the state has specifically given the city that power by law or charter.

A **home-rule charter,** now in effect in many cities, reverses Dillon's rule and allows a city government to do anything not prohibited by the charter or state law. Even under a home-rule charter, however, city laws (called **ordinances**) cannot be in conflict with state laws, and the states can pass laws that preempt or interfere with what home-rule cities want to do.

There are in this country more than 87,500 local governments, only about a fifth (19,500) of which are cities or municipalities. **Counties** (3,000) are the largest territorial units between a state and a city or town. Every state but Connecticut and Rhode Island has county governments. (In Louisiana, counties are called *parishes,* in Alaska *boroughs.*)

The Court has also given new life to the Eleventh Amendment, which protects states from lawsuits by citizens of other states or foreign nations. In 1999, the Court shielded states from suits by copyright owners who claimed infringement from state agencies and immunized states from lawsuits by people who argued that state regulations create unfair economic competition. In *Alden v. Maine* (1999), the Court held that state employees could not sue to force state compliance with federal fair-labor laws. In the Court's five-to-four majority opinion, Justice Anthony M. Kennedy stated, "Although the Constitution grants broad powers to Congress, our federalism requires that Congress treat the states in a manner consistent with their status as residuary sovereigns and joint participants in the governance of the nation." A few years later, in *Federal Maritime Commission v. South Carolina Ports Authority* (2002), the Court further expanded states' sovereign immunity from private lawsuits. Writing for the five-to-four majority, Justice Clarence Thomas declared that dual sovereignty "is a defining feature of our nation's constitutional blueprint," adding that the states "did not consent to become mere appendages of the federal government" when they ratified the Constitution.

Landmark Cases

Federal-State Relations

- ***McCulloch v. Maryland* (1819):** The Constitution's "necessary and proper" clause permits Congress to take actions (in this case, to create a national bank) when it is essential to a power that Congress has (in this case, managing the currency).
- ***Gibbons v. Ogden* (1824):** The Constitution's commerce clause gives the national government exclusive power to regulate interstate commerce.
- ***Wabash, St. Louis and Pacific Railroad v. Illinois* (1886):** The states may not regulate interstate commerce.
- ***United States v. Lopez* (1995):** The national government's power under the commerce clause does not permit it to regulate matters not directly related to interstate commerce (in this case, banning firearms in a school zone).

Not all Court decisions, however, support greater state sovereignty. In 1999, for example, the Court ruled seven to two that state welfare programs may not restrict new residents to the welfare benefits they would have received in the states from which they moved. In addition, each of the Court's major prostate sovereignty decisions has been decided by a tenuous five-to-four margin. More generally, to empower states is not to disempower Congress, which, as it has done since the late 1930s, can still make federal laws on almost anything as long as it does not go too far in "commandeering" state resources or gutting states' rights.

New debates over state sovereignty call forth old truths about the constitutional basis of state and local government. In general, a state can do anything that is not prohibited by the Constitution or preempted by federal policy and that is consistent with its own constitution. One generally recognized state power is the **police power,** which refers to those laws and regulations, not otherwise unconstitutional, that promote health, safety, and morals. Thus the states can enact and enforce criminal codes, require children to attend school and citizens to be vaccinated, and restrict (subject to many limitations) the availability of pornographic materials or the activities of prostitutes and drug dealers.

police power State power to enact laws promoting health, safety, and morals.

Governmental Structure

Federalism refers to a political system in which there are local (territorial, regional, provincial, state, or municipal) units of government, as well as a national government, that can make final decisions with respect to at least some governmental activities and whose existence is specially protected. Almost every nation in the world has local units of government of some kind, if for no other reason than to decentralize the administrative burdens of governing. But these governments are not federal unless the local units exist independent of the preferences of the national government and can make decisions on at least some matters without regard to those preferences.

The United States, Canada, Australia, India, Germany, and Switzerland are federal systems, as are a few other nations. France, Great Britain, Italy, and Sweden are not: they are unitary systems, because such local governments as they possess can be altered or even abolished by the national government and cannot plausibly claim to have final authority over any significant governmental activities.

Sovereignty, Federalism, and the Constitution

Sovereignty means supreme or ultimate political authority: A sovereign government is one that is legally and politically independent of any other government.

A **unitary system** is one in which sovereignty is wholly in the hands of the national government, so that the states and localities are dependent on its will.

A **confederation or confederal system** is one in which the states are sovereign and the national government is allowed to do only that which the states permit.

A **federal system** is one in which sovereignty is shared, so that in some matters the national government is supreme and in other matters the states are supreme.

The Founding Fathers often took *confederal* and *federal* to mean much the same thing. Rather than establishing a government in which there was a clear division of sovereign authority between the national and state governments, they saw themselves as creating a government that combined some characteristics of a unitary regime with some of a confederal one. Or, as James Madison expressed the idea in *Federalist* No. 39, the Constitution "is, in strictness, neither a national nor a federal Constitution, but a composition of both." Where sovereignty is located in this system is a matter that the Founders did not clearly answer.

In this text, a **federal regime** is defined in the simplest possible terms—as one in which local units of government have a specially protected existence and can make some final decisions over some governmental activities.

The special protection that subnational governments enjoy in a federal system derives in part from the constitution of the country but also from the habits, preferences, and dispositions of the citizens and the actual distribution of political power in society. The constitution of the former Soviet Union in theory created a federal system, as claimed by that country's full name—the Union of Soviet Socialist Republics—but for most of their history, none of these "socialist republics" were in the slightest degree independent of the central government. Were the American Constitution the only guarantee of the independence of the American states, they would long since have become mere administrative subunits of the government in Washington. Their independence results in large measure from the commitment of Americans to the idea of local self-government and from the fact that Congress consists of people who are selected by and responsive to local constituencies.

"The basic political fact of federalism," writes David B. Truman, "is that it creates separate, self sustaining centers of power, prestige, and profit."[19] Political power is locally acquired by people whose careers depend for the most part on satisfying local interests. As a result, though the national government has come to have vast powers, it exercises many of those powers through state governments. What many of us forget when we think about "the government in Washington" is that it spends much of its money and enforces most of its rules not on citizens directly but on other, local units of government. A large part of the welfare system, all of the interstate highway system, virtually every aspect of programs to improve cities, the largest part of the effort to supply jobs to the unemployed, the entire program to clean up our water, and even much of our military manpower (in the form of the National Guard) are enterprises in which the national government does not govern so much as it seeks, by regulation, grant, plan, argument, and cajolery, to get the states to govern in accordance with nationally (though often vaguely) defined goals.

In France, welfare, highways, education, the police, and the use of land are all matters that are directed nationally. In the United States, highways and some welfare programs are largely state functions (though they make use of federal money), while education, policing, and land-use controls are primarily local (city, county, or special-district) functions.

Sometimes, however, confusion or controversy about which government is responsible for which functions surfaces at the worst possible moment and lingers long after attempts have been made to sort it all out. Sadly, in our day, that is largely what "federalism" has meant in practice to citizens from New Orleans and the Gulf Coast region.

Before, during, and after Hurricanes Katrina and Rita struck in 2005, federal, state, and local officials could be found fighting among themselves over everything from who was supposed to maintain and repair the levees to who should lead disaster relief initiatives. In the weeks after the

How We Compare

American-Style Federalism

The United States has always had a federal form of government. By contrast, most of the nearly 200 nations in existence today have never had a federal form of government.

Depending on how stringent are the criteria used to delineate federal from unitary systems, the United States is one of a dozen to two dozen nations that now have federal forms of government: America, Australia, Belgium, Brazil, Canada, Ethiopia, Germany, India, Malaysia, Mexico, Nigeria, Pakistan, Russia, South Africa, Spain, and Switzerland are on nearly every expert's list of federal nations.

But some of these nations (for instance, Belgium, Spain, and South Africa) once had unitary systems, and many nations that have federal forms of government are multiparty parliamentary democracies. By contrast, American-style federalism has shaped and been shaped by the country's separation-of-powers system (see Chapter 2) and its two-party electoral system.

In some federal nations, public opinion favors the national government over subnational governments: People in these countries tend to trust their national governments as much or more than they trust other levels of government; however, Americans tend to trust their state and local governments more than they trust Washington.

Sources: "Trust in Government Remains Low," Gallup Organization, September 2008; Richard Cole and John Kincaid, "Public Opinion on U.S. Federal and Intergovernmental Issues," *Publius* 36 (Summer 2006): 443–459; John Kincaid and G. Alan Tarr, eds., *Constitutional Origins, Structure, and Change in Federal Countries* (Montreal: McGill-Queens Press, 2005); Pradeep Chhibber and Ken Kollman, *The Formation of National Party Systems: Federalism and Party Competition in Canada, Great Britain, India, and the United States* (Princeton: Princeton University Press, 2004).

hurricanes hit, it was widely reported that the main first-responders and disaster relief workers came not from government, but from myriad religious and other charitable organizations. Not only that, but government agencies, such as the Federal Emergency Management Agency (FEMA), often acted in ways that made it harder, not easier, for these volunteers and groups to deliver help when and where it was most badly needed.

Federalism needs to be viewed dispassionately through a historical lens wide enough to encompass both its worst legacies (for instance, state and local laws that once legalized racial discrimination against blacks) and its best (for instance, blacks winning mayors' offices and seats in state legislatures when no blacks were in the U.S. Senate and not many blacks had been elected to the U.S. House).

Federalism, it is fair to say, has the virtues of its vices and the vices of its virtues. To some, federalism means allowing states to block action, prevent progress, upset national plans, protect powerful local interests, and cater to the self-interest of hack politicians. Harold Laski, a British observer, described American states as "parasitic and poisonous,"[20] and William H. Riker,

RESEARCH FRONTIERS

Which Governments Do We Trust?

In the United States, public trust in the federal government has dropped significantly since the 1960s. A 2010 Pew Research Center survey found that less than one quarter of the American population trusted the government to make the correct decisions all or most of the time. When this survey question was first asked in 1958, nearly three-fourths of the public responded positively to the same question. Such polling results are nothing new. But scholars who study public opinion on federalism have painted a more complicated picture. Since 1972, the long-term decline in public trust and confidence in Washington has not been matched by similar declines in public support for state and local governments.

For example, Richard L. Cole and John Kincaid have analyzed public opinion data on a wide range of issues:

- After 1972, the fraction of citizens who thought they got the most for their tax money from the federal government fell by 25 percent, while the fraction of citizens who thought they got the most for their tax money from state and local governments rose by 11 percent and 19 percent, respectively.
- After 1987, the fraction of citizens who expressed a "great deal" or a "fair amount" of trust and confidence in the federal government fell by 20 percent, while the fraction who expressed such support for state and local governments fell by 11 percent and 5 percent, respectively.
- Today, citizens are 50 percent more likely to express "not very much" trust and confidence in the federal government or "none at all" than they are to express the same negative view about local government.

The intergovernmental trust and confidence gap is especially wide between the federal government and local governments. Citizens of almost every demographic description are significantly more likely to express a "great deal" or a "fair amount" of trust and confidence in local government than to express such support for the federal government.

James Madison would not be surprised. In *Federalist* No. 46, he doubted that the American people would, in the "future, become more partial to the federal government" than to their respective state and local governments. The people might, he predicted, at times express "transient enthusiasm" for the federal government during wars or national crises, but their "attention and attachment" would ever be more inclined toward "their own particular governments."

- Madison would not be surprised, but are you?
- Do you have greater trust and confidence in the federal government or in state and local governments?
- Do you suppose most people you know feel much the way you do?

Sources: Pew Research Center for the People and the Press, "Distrust, Discontent, Anger and Partisan Rancor," April 18, 2010. Richard L. Cole and John Kincaid, "Public Opinion on U.S. Federal and Intergovernmental Issues," *Publius* 36 (Summer 2006): 443–459.

an American political scientist, argued that "the main effect of federalism since the Civil War has been to perpetuate racism."[21] By contrast, another political scientist, Daniel J. Elazar, argued that the "virtue of the federal system lies in its ability to develop and maintain mechanisms vital to the perpetuation of the unique combination of governmental strength, political flexibility, and individual liberty, which has been the central concern of American politics."[22]

So diametrically opposed are the Riker and Elazar views that one wonders whether they are talking about the same subject. They are, of course, but they are stressing different aspects of the same phenomenon. Whenever the opportunity to exercise political power is widely available (as among the 50 states, 3,000 counties, and many thousands of municipalities in the United States), it is obvious that in different places different people will make use of that power for different purposes. There is no question that allowing states and cities to make autonomous, binding political decisions will allow some people in some places to make those decisions in ways that maintain racial segregation, protect vested interests, and facilitate corruption. It is equally true, however, that this arrangement also enables other people in other places to pass laws that attack segregation, regulate harmful economic practices, and purify politics, often long before these ideas gain national support or become national policy.

The existence of independent state and local governments means that different political groups pursuing different political purposes will come to power in different places. The smaller the political unit, the more likely it is to be dominated by a single political faction. James Madison understood this fact perfectly and used it to argue (in *Federalist* No. 10) that it would be in a large (or "extended") republic, such as the United States as a whole, that one would find the greatest opportunity for all relevant interests to be heard. When William Riker condemns federalism, he is thinking of the fact that in some places the ruling factions in cities and states have opposed granting equal rights to African Americans. When Daniel Elazar praises federalism, he is recalling that, in other states and cities, the ruling factions have taken the lead (long in advance of the federal government) in developing measures to protect the environment, extend civil rights, and improve social conditions. If you live in California, whether you like federalism depends in part on whether you like the fact that California has, independent of the federal government, cut property taxes, strictly controlled coastal land use, heavily regulated electric utilities, and increased (at one time) and decreased (at another time) its welfare rolls.

INCREASED POLITICAL ACTIVITY

Federalism has many effects, but its most obvious effect has been to facilitate the mobilization of political activity. Unlike Don Quixote, the average citizen does not tilt at windmills. He or she is more likely to become involved in organized political activity if he or she feels a reasonable chance exists of having a practical effect. The chances of having such an effect are greater where there are many elected officials and independent governmental bodies, each with a relatively small constituency, than where there are few elected officials, most of whom have the nation as a whole for a constituency. In short, a federal system, by virtue of the decentralization of authority, lowers the cost of organized political activity; a unitary system, because of the centralization of authority, raises the cost. We may disagree about the purposes of organized political activity, but the fact of widespread organized activity can scarcely be doubted—or if it can be doubted, it is only because you have not yet read Chapters 8 and 11.

It is impossible to say whether the Founders, when they wrote the Constitution, planned to produce such widespread opportunities for political participation. Unfortunately they were not very clear (at least in writing) about how the federal system was supposed

Federalism has permitted experimentation. Women were able to vote in the Wyoming Territory in 1888, long before they could do so in most states.

to work, and thus most of the interesting questions about the jurisdiction and powers of our national and state governments had to be settled by a century and a half of protracted, often bitter, conflict.

WHAT THE STATES CAN DO

The states play a key role in social welfare, public education, law enforcement, criminal justice, health and hospitals, roads and highways, and managing water supplies. On these and many other matters, state constitutions are far more detailed and sometimes confer more rights than the federal one. For example, the California constitution includes an explicit right to privacy, says that noncitizens have the same property rights as citizens, and requires the state to use "all suitable means" to support public education.

Many state constitutions are now believed by some to be on the whole more progressive in their holdings on abortion rights (authorizing fewer restrictions on minors), welfare payments (permitting fewer limits on eligibility), employment discrimination (prohibiting discrimination based on sexual preference), and many other matters than federal courts generally are. As we saw in Chapter 2, the federal Constitution is based on a republican, not a democratic, principle: laws are to be made by the representatives of citizens, not by the citizens directly. But many state constitutions open one or more of three doors to direct democracy. About half of the states provide for some form of legislation by initiative. The **initiative** allows voters to place legislative measures (and sometimes constitutional amendments) directly on the ballot by getting enough signatures (usually between 5 and 15 percent of those who voted in the last election) on a petition. About half of the states permit the **referendum,** a procedure that enables voters to reject a measure adopted by the legislature. Sometimes the state constitution specifies that certain kinds of legislation (for example, tax increases) must be subject to a referendum whether the legislature wishes it or not. The **recall** is a procedure, in effect in more than 20 states, whereby voters can remove an elected official from office. If enough signatures are gathered on a petition, the official must go before voters, who can vote to leave the person in office, remove the person from office, or remove the person and replace him or her with someone else.

initiative Process that permits voters to put legislative measures directly on the ballot.

referendum Procedure enabling voters to reject a measure passed by the legislature.

recall Procedure whereby voters can remove an elected official from office.

grants-in-aid Money given by the national government to the states.

The existence of the states is guaranteed by the federal Constitution: no state can be divided without its consent, each state must have two representatives in the Senate (the only provision of the Constitution that may not be amended), every state is assured of a republican form of government, and the powers not granted to Congress are reserved for the states. By contrast, cities, towns, and counties enjoy no such protection; they exist at the pleasure of the states. Indeed, states have frequently abolished certain kinds of local governments, such as independent school districts.

This explains why there is no debate about city sovereignty comparable to the debate about state sovereignty. The constitutional division of power between them is settled: the state is supreme. But federal-state relations can be complicated, because the Constitution invites elected leaders to struggle over sovereignty. Which level of government has the ultimate power to decide where nuclear waste gets stored, how much welfare beneficiaries are paid, what rights prisoners enjoy, or whether supersonic jets can land at local airports? American federalism answers such questions, but on a case-by-case basis through intergovernmental politics and court decisions.

Federal-State Relations

Though constitutionally the federal government may be supreme, politically it must take into account the fact that the laws it passes have to be approved by members of Congress selected from, and responsive to, state and local constituencies. Thus what Washington lawfully may do is not the same thing as what it politically may wish to do.

GRANTS-IN-AID

The best illustration of how political realities modify legal authority can be found in federal **grants-in-aid.** The first of these programs began even before the Constitution was adopted, in the form of land grants made by the national government to the states in order to finance education. (State universities all over the country were built with the proceeds from the sale of these land grants; hence the name *land-grant colleges.*) Land grants were also made to support the building of wagon roads, canals, railroads, and flood-control projects. These measures

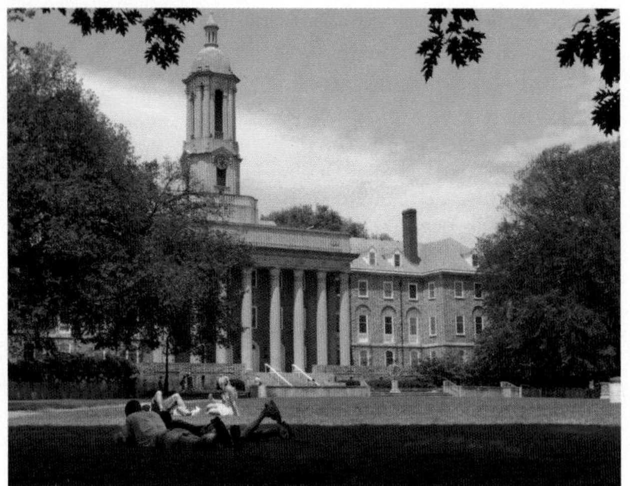
Johnny Stockshooter/Alamy

Some of the nation's greatest universities, such as Penn State, began as land-grant colleges.

Table 3.1 Federal Grants to State and Local Governments (2009)

The federal government spent $461 billion on grants to states in 2009.	
Among the biggest items:	
Medicaid	$268.3 billion
Income security	103.2 billion
Education and training	74 billion
Transportation	55.4 billion
Community development	17.4 billion

Source: Budget of the U.S. Government, Fiscal Year 2011, Historical Tables, Table 12.2.

were hotly debated in Congress (President Madison thought some were unconstitutional), even though the use to which the grants were put was left almost entirely to the states.

Cash grants-in-aid began almost as early. In 1808, Congress gave $200,000 to the states to pay for their militias, with the states in charge of the size, deployment, and command of these troops. However, grant-in-aid programs remained few in number and small in price until the 20th century, when scores of new ones came into being. Today, federal grants go to hundreds of programs, including such giant federal-state programs as Medicaid (see Table 3.1).

The grants-in-aid system, once under way, grew rapidly because it helped state and local officials resolve a dilemma. On the one hand, they wanted access to the superior taxing power of the federal government. On the other hand, prevailing constitutional interpretation, at least until the late 1930s, held that the federal government could not spend money for purposes not authorized by the Constitution. The solution was obviously to have federal money put into state hands: Washington would pay the bills; the states would run the programs.

Federal money seemed, to state officials, so attractive for four reasons. First, the money was there. Thanks to the high-tariff policies of the Republicans, Washington in the 1880s had huge budget surpluses. Second, in the 1920s, as those surpluses dwindled, Washington inaugurated the federal income tax. It automatically brought in more money as economic activity (and thus personal income) grew. Third, the federal government, unlike the states, managed the currency and could print more at will. (Technically, it borrowed this money, but it was under no obligation to pay it all back, because, as a practical matter, it had borrowed from itself.) States could not do this: if they borrowed money (and many could not), they had to pay it back, in full.

These three economic reasons for the attractiveness of federal grants were probably not as important as a fourth reason: politics. Federal money seemed to a state official to be "free" money. Governors did not have to propose, collect, or take responsibility for federal taxes. Instead, a governor could denounce the federal government for being profligate in its use of the people's money. Meanwhile, he or she could claim credit for a new public works or other project funded by Washington and, until recent decades, expect little or no federal supervision in the bargain.[23]

That every state had an incentive to ask for federal money to pay for local programs meant, of course, that it would be very difficult for one state to get money for a given program without every state's getting it. The senator from Alabama who votes for the project to improve navigation on the Tombigbee will have to vote in favor of projects improving navigation on every other river in the country if the senator expects his or her Senate colleagues to support such a request. Federalism as practiced in the United States means that when Washington wants to send money to one state or congressional district, it must send money to many states and districts.

Shortly after September 11, 2001, for example, President George W. Bush and congressional leaders in both parties pledged new federal funds to increase public safety payrolls, purchase the latest equipment to detect bioterror attacks, and so on. Since then, New York City and other big cities have received tens of millions of federal dollars for such purposes, but so have scores of smaller cities

Ethan Miller/Getty Images News/Getty Images

An airline passenger stands inside a device that searches electronically for any contraband.

and towns. The grants allocated by the Department of Homeland Security were based on so-called fair-share formulas mandated by Congress, which are basically the same formulas the federal government uses to allocate certain highway and other funds among the states. These funding formulas not only spread money around but also generally skew funding toward states and cities with low populations. Thus, Wyoming received seven times as much federal homeland security funding per capita as New York State did, and Grand Forks County, North Dakota (population 70,000), received $1.5 million to purchase biochemical suits, a semi-armored van, decontamination tents, and other equipment to deal with weapons of mass destruction.[24]

MEETING NATIONAL NEEDS

Until the 1960s, most federal grants-in-aid were conceived by or in cooperation with the states and were designed to serve essentially state purposes. Large blocs of voters and a variety of organized interests would press for grants to help farmers, build highways, or support vocational education. During the 1960s, however, an important change occurred: the federal government began devising grant programs based less on what states were demanding and more on what federal officials perceived to be important *national* needs (see Figure 3.2). Federal officials, not state and local ones, were the principal proponents of grant programs to aid the urban poor, combat crime, reduce pollution, and deal with drug abuse.

The rise in federal activism in setting goals and the occasional efforts, during some periods, to bypass state officials by providing money directly to cities or even local citizen groups, had at least two separate but related effects: one effect was to increase federal grants to state and local governments, and the other was to change the purposes to which those monies were put. Whereas federal aid amounted to less than 2 percent of state general revenue in 1927, by 2006 federal aid accounted for about 30 percent of state general revenue. About 17 percent of the entire federal budget was for grants to state and local governments (about 90 percent went directly to the states). The federal government spent $1,471 per capita on grants to state and local governments.

Figure 3.2

The Changing Purpose of Federal Grants to State and Local Governments

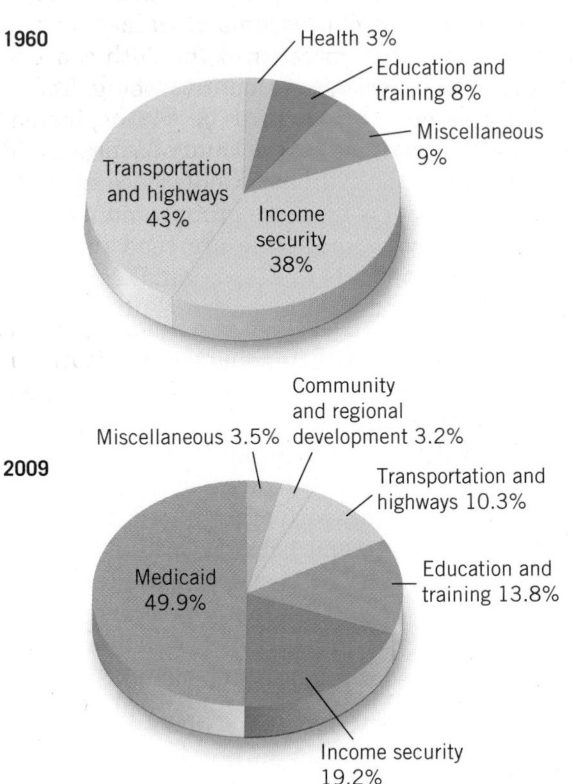

Note: Totals may not add up to 100 percent because of rounding.

Source: Budget of the U.S. Government, Fiscal Year 2011, Historical Tables, Table 12.2.

In 1960, about 3 percent of federal grants to state and local governments were for health care. Today, however, one federal-state health care program alone, Medicaid, accounts for nearly 50 percent of all federal grants. And whereas in 1960 more than 40 percent of all federal grants to state and local governments went to transportation (including highways), today only about 10 percent is used for that purpose (see Figure 3.2). Even in the short term, the purposes to which federal grants are put can shift; for example, after Hurricanes Katrina and Rita, federal grants for "community and regional development" spiked but were slated to return to pre-2005 levels by about 2011.

THE INTERGOVERNMENTAL LOBBY

State and local officials, both elected and appointed, began to form an important new lobby—the "intergovernmental lobby," made up of mayors, governors, superintendents of schools, state directors of public health, county highway commissioners, local police chiefs, and others who had come to count on federal funds.[25] Today, federal agencies responsible for health care, criminal justice, environmental protection, and other programs have people on staff who specialize in providing information, technical assistance, and financial support to state and local organizations, including the "Big 7": the U.S. Conference of Mayors; the National Governors Association; the National Association of Counties; the National League of Cities; the Council of State Governments; the International City/County Management Association; and the National Conference of State Legislatures. Reports by these groups and publications like *Governing* magazine are read routinely by many federal officials to keep a handle on issues and trends in state and local government.

National organizations of governors or mayors press for more federal money, but not for increased funding for any particular city or state. Thus most states, dozens of counties, and more than a hundred cities have their own offices in Washington, D.C. Some are small, some share staff with other jurisdictions, but a few are quite large and boast several dozen full-time employees. Back home, state and local governments have created new positions, or redefined old ones, in response to new or changed federal funding opportunities.

categorical grants Federal grants for specific purposes, such as building an airport.

The purpose of the intergovernmental lobby has been the same as that of any private lobby—to obtain more federal money with fewer strings attached. For a while, the cities and states did in fact get more money, but since the early 1980s their success in getting federal grants has been more checkered.

CATEGORICAL GRANTS

The effort to loosen the strings took the form of shifting, as much as possible, the federal aid from **categorical grants** to block grants. A categorical grant is one for a specific purpose defined by federal law: to build an airport or a college dormitory, for example, or to make welfare payments to low-income mothers. Such grants usually require that the state or locality put up money to "match" some part of the federal grant, though the amount of matching funds can be quite small (sometimes only 10 percent or less). Governors and mayors complained about these categorical grants because their purposes were often so narrow that it was impossible for a state to adapt federal grants to local needs. A mayor seeking federal money to build parks might have discovered that the city could get money only if it launched an urban-renewal program that entailed bulldozing several blocks of housing or small businesses.

One response to this problem was to consolidate several categorical or project grant programs into a single block grant devoted to some general purpose and with fewer restrictions on its use. Block grants began in the mid-1960s, when such a grant was created in the health field. Though many block grants were proposed between 1966 and 1980, only five were enacted. Of the three largest, one consolidated various categorical grant programs aimed at cities (Community Development Block Grants), another created a program to aid local law enforcement (Law Enforcement Assistance Act), and a third authorized new kinds of locally managed programs for the unemployed (CETA, or the Comprehensive Employment and Training Act).

In theory, block grants and revenue sharing were supposed to give the states and cities considerable freedom in deciding how to spend the money while helping to relieve their tax burdens. To some extent they did. However, for four reasons, neither the goal of "no strings" nor the one of fiscal relief was really attained. First, the amount of money available from block grants and revenue sharing did not grow as fast as the states had hoped nor as quickly as did the money available through categorical grants. Second, the federal government steadily increased the number of strings attached to the spending of this supposedly "unrestricted" money.

Third, block grants grew more slowly than categorical grants because of the different kinds of political coalitions supporting each. Congress and the federal bureaucracy liked categorical grants for the same reason the states disliked them—the specificity of these programs enhanced federal control over how the money was to be used. Federal officials, joined by liberal interest groups and organized labor, tended to distrust state governments. Whenever Congress wanted to address some national problem, its natural inclination was to create a categorical grant program so that it, and not the states, would decide how the money would be spent.

Fourth, even though governors and mayors like block grants, these programs cover such a broad range of activities that no single interest group has a vital stake in pressing for their enlargement. Categorical grants, on the other hand, often are a matter of life and death for many agencies—state departments of welfare, of highways, and of health, for example, are utterly dependent on federal aid. Accordingly, the administrators in charge of these programs will press strenuously for their expansion. Moreover, categorical programs are supervised by special committees of Congress, and as we shall see in Chapter 13, many of these committees have an interest in seeing their programs grow.

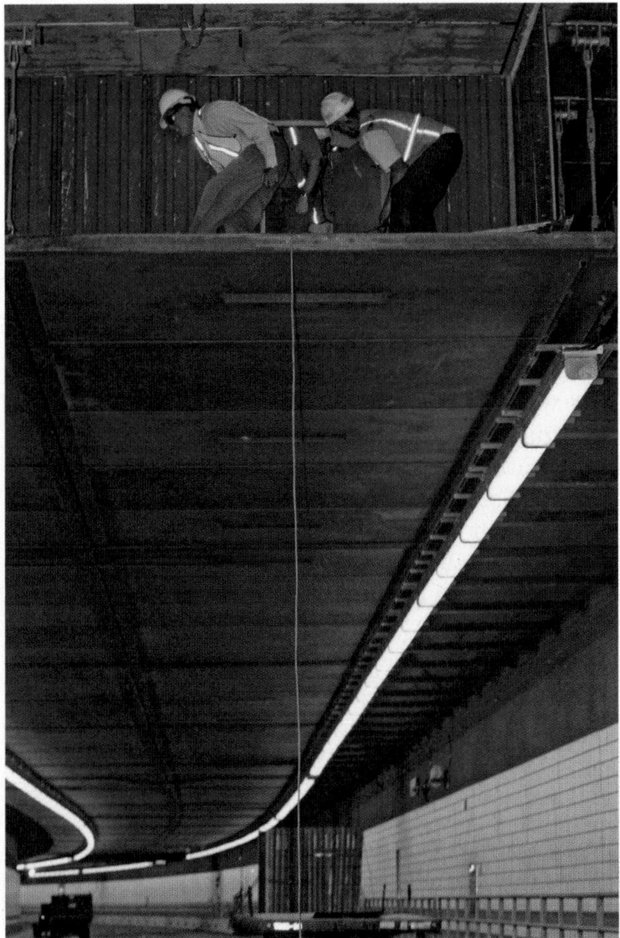

AP Images

Then-Governor Mitt Romney inspecting a roof that collapsed in "the Big Dig"—the tunnel under downtown Boston.

RIVALRY AMONG THE STATES

The more important federal money becomes to the states, the more likely the states are to compete among themselves for the largest share of it. For a century or better, the growth of the United States—in population, business, and income—was concentrated in the industrial Northeast. In recent decades, however, that growth—at least in population and employment, if not in income—has shifted to the South, Southwest, and Far West. This change has precipitated an intense debate over whether the federal government, by the way it distributes its funds and awards its contracts, is unfairly helping some regions and states at the expense of others. Journalists and politicians have dubbed the struggle as one between Snowbelt (or Frostbelt) and Sunbelt states.

Whether in fact there is anything worth arguing about is far from clear: the federal government has had great difficulty in figuring out where it ultimately spends what funds for what purposes. For example, a $1 billion defense contract may go to a company with headquarters in California, but much of the money may actually be spent in Connecticut or New York, as the prime contractor in California buys from subcontractors in the other states. It is even less clear whether federal funds actually affect the growth rate of the regions. The uncertainty about the facts has not prevented a debate about the issue, however. That debate focuses on the formulas written into federal laws by which block grants are allocated. These formulas take into account such factors as a county's or city's population, personal income in the area, and housing quality. A slight change in a formula can shift millions of dollars in grants in ways that favor either the older, declining cities of the Northeast or the newer, still-growing cities of the Southwest.

With the advent of grants based on distributional formulas (as opposed to grants for a particular project), the results of the census, taken every 10 years, assume monumental importance. A city or state shown to be losing population may, as a result, forfeit millions of dollars in federal aid. Senators and representatives now have access to computers that can tell them instantly the effect on their states and districts of even minor changes in a formula by which federal aid is distributed. These formulas rely on objective measures, but the exact measure is selected with an eye to its political consequences. There is nothing wrong with this in principle, since any political system must provide some benefits for everybody if it is to stay together. Given the competition among states in a federal system, however, the struggle over allocation formulas becomes especially acute.

Federal Aid and Federal Control

So important has federal aid become for state and local governments that mayors and governors, along with others, began to fear that Washington was well on its way to controlling other levels of government. "He who pays the piper calls the tune," they muttered. In this view, the constitutional protection of state government to be found in the Tenth Amendment was in jeopardy as a result of the strings attached to the grants-in-aid on which the states were increasingly dependent.

Block grants were an effort to reverse this trend by allowing the states and localities freedom to spend money as they wished. But as we have seen, the new device did not in fact reverse the trend. Categorical grants—those with strings attached—continued to grow even faster.

There are two kinds of federal controls on state governmental activities. The traditional control tells the state government what it must do if it wants to get some grant money. These strings often are called **conditions of aid.** The newer form of control tells the state government what it must do, period. These rules are called **mandates.** Most mandates have little or nothing to do with federal aid—they apply to all state governments whether or not they accept grants.

conditions of aid Terms set by the national government that states must meet if they are to receive certain federal funds.

mandates Terms set by the national government that states must meet whether or not they accept federal grants.

waiver A decision by an administrative agency granting some other part permission to violate a law or rule that would otherwise apply to it.

MANDATES

Most mandates concern civil rights and environmental protection. States may not discriminate in the operation of their programs, no matter who pays for them. Initially the antidiscrimination rules applied chiefly to distinctions based on race, sex, age, and ethnicity, but of late they have broadened to include physical and mental disabilities as well. Various pollution control laws require the states to comply with federal standards for clean air, pure drinking water, and sewage treatment.[26] Stated in general terms, these mandates seem reasonable enough. It is hard to imagine anyone arguing that state governments should be free to discriminate against people because of their race or national origin. In practice, however, some mandates create administrative and financial problems, especially when the mandates are written in vague language, thereby giving federal administrative agencies the power to decide for themselves what state and local governments are supposed to do.

But not all areas of public law and policy are equally affected by mandates. Federal-state disputes about who governs on such controversial matters as minors' access to abortion, same-sex marriage, and medical uses for banned narcotics make headlines. It is mandates that fuel everyday friction in federal-state relations, particularly those that Washington foists upon the states but funds inadequately or not at all. One 2006 study concluded that "the number of unfunded federal mandates is high in environmental policy, low in education policy, and moderate in health policy."[27] But why?

Some think that how much Washington spends in a given policy area is linked to how common federal mandates, funded or not, are in that same area. There is some evidence for that view. For instance, in recent years, annual federal grants to state and local governments for a policy area where unfunded mandates are pervasive—environmental protection—were about $4 billion, while federal grants for health care—an area where unfunded mandates have been less pervasive—amounted to about $200 billion. The implication is that when Washington itself spends less on something it wants done, it squeezes the states to spend more for that purpose. Washington is more likely to grant state and local governments waivers in some areas than in others. A **waiver** is a decision by an administrative agency granting some other party permission to violate a law or administrative rule that would otherwise apply to it. Generally, for instance, education waivers have been easy for state and local governments to get, but environmental protection waivers have proven almost impossible to acquire.[28]

However, caution is in order. Often, the more one knows about federal-state relations in any given area, the harder it becomes to generalize about present-day federalism's fiscal, administrative, and regulatory character, the conditions under which "permissive federalism" prevails, or whether new laws or court decisions will considerably tighten or further loosen Washington's control over the states.

Mandates are not the only way in which the federal government imposes costs on state and local governments. Certain federal tax and regulatory policies make it difficult or expensive for state and local governments to raise revenues, borrow funds, or privatize public functions. Other federal laws expose state and local governments to financial liability, and numerous federal court decisions and administrative regulations require state and local governments to do or not do various things, either by statute or through an implied constitutional obligation.[29]

It is clear that the federal courts have helped fuel the growth of mandates. As interpreted in this century by the U.S. Supreme Court, the Tenth Amendment provides state and local officials no protection against the march of mandates. Indeed, many of the more controversial mandates result not from congressional action but from court decisions. For example, many state prison systems have been, at one time or another, under the control of federal judges who required major changes in prison construction and management in order to meet standards the judges derived from their reading of the Constitution.

School-desegregation plans are the best-known example of federal mandates. Those involving busing—an unpopular policy—have typically been the result of court orders rather than of federal law or regulation.

Judges—usually, but not always, in federal courts—ordered Massachusetts to change the way it hires firefighters, required Philadelphia to institute new procedures to handle complaints of police brutality, and altered the location in which Chicago was planning to build housing projects. Note that in most of these cases nobody in Washington was placing a mandate on a local government; rather, a local citizen was using the federal courts to change a local practice.

The Supreme Court has made it much easier of late for citizens to control the behavior of local officials. A federal law, passed in the 1870s to protect newly freed slaves, makes it possible for a citizen to sue any state or local official who deprives that citizen of any "rights, privileges, or immunities secured by the Constitution and laws" of the United States. A century later, the Court decided that this law permitted a citizen to sue a local official if the official deprived the citizen of *anything* to which the citizen was entitled under federal law (and not just those federal laws protecting civil rights). For example, a citizen can now use the federal courts to obtain from a state welfare office a payment to which he or she may be entitled under federal law.

CONDITIONS OF AID

By far the most important federal restrictions on state action are the conditions attached to the grants the states receive. In theory, accepting these conditions is voluntary—if you don't want the strings, don't take the money. But when the typical state depends for a quarter or more of its budget on federal grants, many of which it has received for years and on which many of its citizens depend for their livelihoods, it is not clear exactly how "voluntary" such acceptance is. During the 1960s, some strings were added, the most important of which had to do with civil rights. But beginning in the 1970s, the number of conditions began to proliferate and has expanded in each subsequent decade to the present.

Some conditions are specific to particular programs, but most are not. For instance, if a state builds something with federal money, it must first conduct an environmental impact study, it must pay construction workers the "prevailing wage" in the area, it often must provide an opportunity for citizen participation in some aspects of the design or location of the project, and it must ensure that the contractors who build the project have nondiscriminatory hiring policies. The states and the federal government, not surprisingly, disagree about the costs and benefits of such rules. Members of Congress and federal officials feel they have an obligation to develop uniform national policies with respect to important matters and to prevent states and cities from misspending federal tax dollars. State officials, on the other hand, feel these national rules fail to take into account diverse local conditions, require the states to do things that the states must then pay for, and create serious inefficiencies.

What state and local officials discovered, in short, was that "free" federal money was not quite free after all. In the 1960s, federal aid seemed entirely beneficial; what mayor or governor would not want such money? But just as local officials found it attractive to do things that another level of government then paid for, in time federal officials learned the same thing. Passing laws to meet the concerns of national constituencies—leaving the cities and states to pay the bills and manage the problems—began to seem attractive to Congress.

Because they face different demands, federal and local officials find themselves in a bargaining situation in which each side is trying to get some benefit (solving a problem, satisfying a pressure group) while passing on to the other side most of the costs (taxes, administrative problems).

John Moore/Getty Images News/Getty Images

A National Guardsman watches over the U.S.-Mexico border in Arizona. The Guardsmen cannot make arrests but can call the Border Patrol.

The bargains struck in this process used to favor the local officials, because members of Congress were essentially servants of local interests: they were elected by local political parties, they were part of local political organizations, and they supported local autonomy. Beginning in the 1960s, however, changes in American politics that will be described in later chapters—especially the weakening of political parties, the growth of public-interest lobbies in Washington, and the increased activism of the courts—shifted the orientation of many in Congress toward favoring Washington's needs over local needs.

A Devolution Revolution?

In 1981, President Ronald Reagan tried to reverse this trend. He asked Congress to consolidate scores of categorical grants into just six large block grants. Congress obliged. Soon state and local governments started getting less federal money but with fewer strings attached to such grants. During the 1980s and into the early 1990s, however, many states also started spending more of their own money and replacing federal rules on programs with state ones.

With the election of Republican majorities in the House and Senate in 1994, a renewed effort was led by Congress to cut total government spending, roll back federal regulations, and shift important functions back to the states. The first key issue was welfare—that is, Aid to Families with Dependent Children (AFDC). Since 1935, there had been a federal guarantee of cash assistance to states that offered support to low-income, unmarried mothers and their children. In 1996, President Bill Clinton signed a new federal welfare law that ended any federal guarantee of support and, subject to certain rules, turned the management of the program entirely over to the states, aided by federal block grants.

These and other Republican initiatives were part of a new effort called devolution, which aimed to pass on to the states many federal functions. It is an old idea but one that actually acquired new vitality because Congress, rather than the president, was leading the effort. Members of Congress traditionally liked voting for federal programs and categorical grants; that way they could take credit for what they were doing for particular constituencies. Under its new conservative leadership, Congress, especially the House, was looking for ways to scale back the size of the national government. President Clinton seemed to agree when, in his 1996 State of the Union address, he proclaimed that the era of big national government was over.

But was it over? No. By 2010, the federal government was spending about $30,000 per year per household, which, adjusted for inflation, was its highest annual per-household spending level since World War II.[30] Federal revenues represented almost 30 percent of gross domestic product, close to the late 1970s annual average, and inflation-adjusted federal debt totals hit new highs. Adjusted for inflation, total spending by state and local governments also increased every year after 1996, as did state and local government debt.[31]

Devolution did not become a revolution. AFDC was ended and replaced by a block grant program called Temporary Assistance for Needy Families (TANF). But far larger federal-state programs, most notably Medicaid, were not turned into block grant programs. Moreover, both federal and state spending on most programs, including the block-granted programs, increased after 1996. Although by no means the only new or significant block grant, TANF now looked like the big exception that proved the rule. The devolution revolution was curtailed by public opinion. Today, as in 1996 and 2006, most Americans favor "shifting responsibility to the states," but not if that also means cuts in government programs that benefit most citizens (not just low-income families), uncertainty about who is eligible to receive benefits, or new hassles associated with receiving them.

Devolution seems to have resulted in more, not fewer, government rules and regulations. Research reveals that, in response to the federal effort to devolve responsibility to state and local governments, states have not only enacted new rules and regulations of their own, but also prompted Washington to issue new rules and regulations on environmental protection (especially greenhouse gas emissions) and other matters.[32]

Still, where devolution did occur, it has had some significant consequences. The devolution of welfare policy has been associated with dramatic decreases in welfare rolls. Scholars disagree about how much the drops were due to the changes in law and how much to economic conditions and other factors. Nor is it clear whether welfare-to-work programs have gotten most participants into decent jobs with adequate health benefits. But few now doubt that welfare devolution has made a measurable difference in how many people receive benefits and for how long.

Subject to state discretion, scores of local governments are now designing and administering welfare programs (job placement, child care, and others) through for-profit firms and a wide variety of nonprofit organizations, including local religious congregations. In some big cities, more than a quarter of welfare-to-work programs have been administered through public-private partnerships that have included various local community-based organizations as grantees.[33] By 2007, there was preliminary evidence that, at least in some states, such public-private partnerships were closer to the norm than they were only a half-decade or so earlier.[34]

A major challenge that states face in assuming more responsibilities for public programs is funding. By 2011, many states had lost the significant budget surpluses they had enjoyed just a few years ago and now faced enormous debt for the foreseeable future. While this was due in part to the national financial crisis, a longer-term factor was pension benefits for public employees, which are set by contract and can be changed only by mutual agreement between state governments and the unions that typically represent state and local officials. Consequently, several governors proposed restricting unions' collective-bargaining authority to balance budgets by reducing benefits. In Wisconsin, a gubernatorial proposal in 2011 to end some aspects of collective bargaining for public employees prompted huge protest rallies and led several state legislators who opposed the idea to flee the state for three weeks to avoid a vote (the bill passed anyway on a party-line vote). State legislators in Indiana did the same in response to a similar bill.

As states look to reduce costs, they need to consider which responsibilities are theirs to shoulder and which ones the federal government must bear. A 2011 study by the Government Accountability Office found extensive duplication of services both across federal government agencies and between the federal government and the states.[35] Areas of overlap include economic development, food regulation, and counterterrorism. But identifying bureaucratic overlap is easier than eliminating it (as we will see in Chapter 15), and federal public officials typically have very different views than their state counterparts about what qualifies as "wasteful" spending. Consequently, how states will address their long-term debt, and the implications for further devolution in policymaking, remains to be seen.

Congress and Federalism

Just as it remains to be seen whether the Supreme Court will continue to revive the doctrine of state sovereignty, so it is not yet clear whether the devolution movement will regain momentum, stall, or be reversed. But whatever the movement's fate, the United States will not become a wholly centralized nation. There remains more political and policy diversity in America than one is likely to find in any other large industrialized nation. The reason is not only that state and local governments have retained certain constitutional protections but also that members of Congress continue to think of themselves as the representatives of localities *to* Washington and not as the representatives *of* Washington to the localities. As we shall see in Chapter 13, American politics, even at the national level, remains local in its orientation.

But if this is true, why do these same members of Congress pass laws that create so many problems for, and stimulate so many complaints from, mayors and governors? One reason is that members of Congress represent different constituencies from the same localities. For example, one member of Congress from Los Angeles may think of the city as a collection of businesspeople, homeowners, and taxpayers, while another may think of it as a group of African Americans, Hispanics, and nature lovers. If Washington wants to simply send money to Los Angeles, these two representatives could be expected to vote together. But if Washington wants to impose mandates or restrictions on the city, these representatives might very well vote on opposite sides, each voting as his or her constituents would most likely prefer.

Another reason is that the organizations that once linked members of Congress to local groups have eroded. As we shall see in Chapter 9, the political parties, which once allowed many localities to speak with a single voice in Washington, have decayed to the point where most members of Congress now operate as free agents, judging local needs and national moods independently. In the 1960s, these needs and moods seemed to require creating new grant programs; in the 1970s, they seemed to require voting for new mandates; in the 1980s and 1990s, they seemed to require letting the cities and states alone experiment with new ways of meeting their needs; and today, some say they require rethinking devolution before it goes "too far."

There are exceptions. In some states, the parties continue to be strong, to dominate decision making in the state legislatures, and to significantly affect the way their congressional delegations behave. Democratic members of Congress from Chicago, for example, typically have a common background in party politics and share at least some allegiance to important party leaders.

But these exceptions are becoming fewer and fewer. As a result, when somebody tries to speak "for" a city or state in Washington, that person has little claim to any real authority. The mayor of Philadelphia may favor one program, the governor of Pennsylvania may favor another, and individual local and state officials—school superintendents, the insurance commissioner, public health administrators—may favor still others. In bidding for federal aid, those parts of the state or city that are best organized often do the best, and increasingly these groups are not the political parties but rather specialized occupational groups such as doctors or schoolteachers. If one is to ask, therefore, why a member of Congress does not listen to his or her state anymore, the answer is, "What do you mean by *the state?* Which official, which occupational group, which party leader speaks for the state?"

Finally, Americans differ in the extent to which we like federal as opposed to local decisions. When people are asked which level of government gives them the most for their money, relatively poor citizens are likely to mention the federal government first, whereas relatively well-to-do citizens are more likely to mention local government. If we add to income other measures of social diversity—race, religion, and region—there emerge even sharper differences of opinion about which level of government works best. It is this social diversity—and the fact that it is represented not only by state and local leaders but also by members of Congress—that keeps federalism alive and makes it so important. Americans simply do not agree on enough things, or even on which level of government ought to decide on those things, to make possible a unitary system.

WHAT WOULD YOU DO?

MEMORANDUM

To: *Secretary of Education Julie Dew*

From: *White House Special Assistant Jack Patrick*

Subject: *National curriculum for elementary and secondary schools*

As promised in her campaign platform, the president would like to expand upon the No Child Left Behind Act to develop a national curriculum for all elementary and secondary schoolchildren, beginning with high school, to better prepare students for the 21st-century workforce. The major arguments for and against this proposal follow. Will you present the initiative and address states' concerns at the National Governors Association next week?

News »

Expanding No Child Left Behind?

The president seeks a national curriculum for all K-12 schoolchildren. Many state school boards argue that federally mandated standards will do more harm than good.

Arguments for:

1. American jobs in the 21st century will require advanced skills in literacy, mathematics, and information technology that all schools must teach.
2. Variations in state curriculum standards leave students ill-prepared for college, which increasingly is a necessary credential for long-term employment.
3. If the national government does not invest in creating a uniform school curriculum now, then increased funding will be needed for remedial instruction later.

Arguments against:

1. States are better able to determine educational standards that will prepare their diverse populations for the workforce than the federal government.
2. Imposing a national curriculum will stifle state and local creativity in education, and will be so basic that it will make little difference in college preparation.
3. The national government has a history of imposing educational mandates on states with insufficient funding, and governors are skeptical of receiving sufficient funding to implement a national curriculum for students with varying needs successfully.
4. Expressly preempting more state laws could come back to bite us when it comes to state laws that we favor over contrary federal ones.

Your decision:

Support bill ________________ Oppose bill ________________

LEARNING OBJECTIVES

WHAT YOU NEED TO KNOW

☑ Why does the United States have federalism?

The Framers of the Constitution created a federal system of government for the United States because they wanted to balance the power of the central government with states that would exercise independent influence over most areas of people's lives, outside of national concerns such as defense, coining money, and so forth. Liberty would be protected by requiring the federal government to share power and authority with the states.

☑ How has American federalism evolved from the founding to the present?

Since the founding, the balance of power between the national government and the states has shifted over time. Overall, the federal government's power and responsibilities have increased, particularly with the expansion of programs in the 20th century. Still, states exercise broad latitude in implementing policies, and they frequently provide models for the federal government to consider in creating national policies.

☑ Which level of government does federalism favor, the national government or the states?

The short answer is, "it depends." In some areas, such as national defense and homeland security, the federal government dominates. In other areas, such as crime control and driving regulations, states primarily decide policy. And in some areas, such as education and health care, states traditionally have made policy decisions, but the federal government has become increasingly involved as such issues are deemed national priorities.

RECONSIDERING WHO GOVERNS?

1. Where is sovereignty located in the American political system?

Strictly speaking, the answer is "nowhere." Sovereignty means supreme or ultimate political authority. A sovereign government is one that is legally and politically independent of any other government. No government in America, including the national government headquartered in Washington, D.C., meets that definition. In the American political system, federal and state governments share sovereignty in complicated and ever-changing ways. Both constitutional tradition (the doctrine of dual sovereignty) and everyday politicking (fights over federal grants, mandates, and conditions of aid) render the national government supreme in some matters (national defense, for example) and the states supreme in others (education, for instance).

2. How is power divided between the national government and the states under the Constitution?

Early in American history, local governments and the states had most of it. In the 20th century, the national government gained power. In the last two decades, the states have won back some of their power because of Supreme Court decisions and legislative efforts to devolve certain federal programs to the states. But the distribution of power between the national government and the states is never as simple or as settled as it may appear.

RECONSIDERING TO WHAT ENDS?

1. What competing values are at stake in federalism?

Basically two: equality versus participation. Federalism means that citizens living in different parts of the country will be treated differently, not only in spending programs, such as welfare, but also in legal systems that assign in different places different penalties to similar offenses or that differentially enforce civil rights laws. But federalism also means that more opportunities exist for participation in making decisions—in influencing what is taught in the schools and in deciding where highways and government projects are to be built. Indeed, differences in public policy—that is, unequal treatment—are in large part the result of participation in decision making. It is difficult, perhaps impossible, to have more of one of these values without having less of the other.

2. Who should decide which matters ought to be governed mainly or solely by national laws?

In practice, the federal courts often have been the main or final arbiters of federalism. As we shall see in Chapter 6, it was the U.S. Supreme Court that decided to outlaw state and local laws that kept children in racially segregated public schools. Constitutional amendments initiated by members of Congress also have been used to apply legally enforceable national standards to matters once left to state or local governments. Examples would include the Twenty-sixth Amendment, which gave 18-year-old citizens the right to vote. Not surprisingly, when state and local officials have been permitted to decide, they usually have favored national laws or standards when that has served their political interests or desire for "free" money, but have decried them as "intrusive" or worse when that has not.

QUESTIONS TO CONSIDER

1. **Who decides whether a policy area is a national or state responsibility?**
2. **What are the strengths and weaknesses of American federalism for promoting democracy?**
3. **Why is federalism one of the central principles of American constitutionalism?**
4. **Which states have requested temporary exemptions from the 2010 health care law, and why?**
5. **Which states have the highest results on standardized tests in elementary and secondary education, and which have the lowest?**
6. **Which states face the greatest financial burdens in the coming year, and for which programs?**

TO LEARN MORE

State news: **www.stateline.org**

Council of State Governments: **www.csg.org**

National Governors Association: **www.nga.org**

Supreme Court decisions: **www.findlaw.com/casecode/supreme.html**

Beer, Samuel H. *To Make a Nation: The Rediscovery of American Federalism.* Cambridge: Harvard University Press, 1993. The definitive study of the philosophical bases of American federalism.

Conlan, Timothy. *From New Federalism to Devolution.* Washington, D.C.: Brookings Institution, 1998. A masterful overview of the politics of federalism from Richard Nixon to Bill Clinton.

Daniel, Ronald, Donald F. Kettl, and Howard Kureuther, eds. *On Risk and Disaster: Lessons from Hurricane Katrina.* Philadelphia: University of Pennsylvania Press, 2006. Several experts evaluate the government response.

Derthick, Martha N. *Keeping the Compound Republic.* Washington, D.C.: Brookings Institution, 2001. A masterful analysis of trends in American federalism from the Founding to the present.

Diamond, Martin. "The Federalist's View of Federalism." In *Essays in Federalism,* edited by George C.S. Benson. Claremont, Calif.: Institute for Studies in Federalism of Claremont Men's College, 1961, 21–64. A profound analysis of what the Founders meant by federalism.

Grodzins, Morton. *The American System.* Chicago: Rand McNally, 1966. Argues that American federalism has always involved extensive sharing of functions between national and state governments.

Melnick, R. Shep. *Between the Lines: Interpreting Welfare Rights.* Washington, D.C.: Brookings Institution, 1994. An examination of how trends in statutory interpretation have affected broader policy developments, including the expansion of the agenda of national government, the persistence of divided government, and the resurgence and decentralization of Congress.

Riker, William H. *Federalism: Origin, Operation, Significance.* Boston: Little, Brown, 1964. A classic explanation and critical analysis of federalism here and abroad.

Teske, Paul. *Regulation in the States.* Washington, D.C.: Brookings Institution, 2004. States have responded to devolution by adding new regulations of their own.

4 American Political Culture

LEARNING OBJECTIVES

WHAT YOU NEED TO KNOW

- ☑ What is American political culture?
- ☑ How does political culture differ from political ideology?
- ☑ Does the United States have a unique political culture compared to other advanced industrialized democracies?

WHO GOVERNS?

1. Do Americans trust their government?
2. Why do we accept great differences in wealth and income?

TO WHAT ENDS?

1. Why does our government behave differently than governments in countries with similar constitutions?

THEN In 1835, a French political official, Alexis de Tocqueville, visited the United States to conduct research on its prison systems. Based on two years of travel across the country, de Tocqueville wrote a two-volume study titled *Democracy in America* that continues to be one of the defining texts of American political culture. De Tocqueville argued that democracy endured in the United States because of geography, laws, and "the manners and customs of the people."[1] He concluded that the attitude of Americans about the merits of democracy was fundamental to its success here.

NOW In the 21st century, several issues divide Americans: how to address the rapidly growing national debt, how to battle terrorists, how to determine the appropriate scope of responsibility and power for the federal government, and so forth. But the political parties and interest groups (both of which we will discuss later in this textbook) that disagree about these issues share a common belief in preserving the principles of American constitutionalism—liberty, equality of opportunity, and so on—even if they differ over how to put those principles in practice. The Tea Party movement that has developed in recent years, for example, derives its name from a historic event in American politics, and its adherents claim that they seek to return American democracy to its founding principles. People in the United States may have very different views today of what democracy means for policymaking, but they continue to display the same veneration for democracy that de Tocqueville identified more than 175 years ago.

The United States, Great Britain, and France are all western nations with well-established representative democracies. Millions of people in each country (maybe including you) have been tourists in one or both of the other two countries. Ask any American who has spent time in either country "what's it like?" and you probably will hear generalizations about the "culture"—"friendly" or "cold," "very different" or "surprisingly like home," and so on.

But "culture" also counts when it comes to politics and government. Politically speaking, there are at least three major differences among and between countries: constitutional, demographic, and cultural. Each difference is important, and the differences tend to feed each other. Arguably, however, the cultural differences are not only the most consequential, but also often the trickiest to analyze. As we will see, that holds not only for cross-national differences between America and other countries, but also when it comes to deciphering political divides within America itself. And the differences usually endure over time.

Political Culture

Constitutional differences tend to be fairly obvious and easy to summarize. America and France each have a written constitution, while Great Britain does not. The United States separates powers between three equal branches of its national government. By contrast, the United Kingdom has a parliamentary system in which the legislature chooses a prime minister from within its own ranks. And France has a semi-presidential or quasi-parliamentary system divided into three branches: the president selects a prime minister from the majority party in the lower house of the parliament, and the prime minister exercises most executive powers.

Demographic differences are also straightforward. America is a large land with more than 300 million citizens. The dominant language is English, but millions of people also speak Spanish. About one-sixth of its population is Hispanic. More than 80 percent of its adults identify themselves as Christians, but they are divided between Catholics (about a quarter) and more than a dozen different Protestant denominations. By comparison, France and the United Kingdom are each home to about 60 million people and have small but growing immigrant and foreign-born subpopulations. Most French (more than 80 percent) are Catholic; most British belong to the Church of England (Anglican, the official state religion) or the Church of Scotland. But in neither country do many people go to church.

political culture A patterned and sustained way of thinking about how political and economic life ought to be carried out.

The differences among these three democracies go much deeper. Each country has a different **political culture**—a patterned and sustained way of thinking about how political and economic life ought to be carried out. Most Americans, British, and French think that democracy is good, favor majority rule, and believe in respecting minority rights. And few in each nation would say that a leader who loses office in an election has any right to retake office by force. Even so, their political cultures differ. Cross-national surveys consistently find that Americans are far more likely than the French or British to believe that everybody should be equal politically, but far less likely to think it important that everybody should be equal economically. For example, in one large survey, the French and British were more than twice as likely as Americans to agree that "it is government's responsibility to take care of the very poor," and less than a third as likely as Americans to agree that "government should *not* guarantee every citizen food and basic shelter."[2]

When it comes to ensuring political equality or equality before the law, Americans are more committed from an early age. For instance, a classic study compared how children aged 10 to 14 in the United States, Great Britain, and France responded to a series of questions about democracy and the law. They were asked to imagine the following:

> *One day the President (substitute the Queen in England, President of the Republic in France) was driving his car to a meeting. Because he was late, he was driving very fast. The police stopped the car. Finish the story.*[3]

The Granger Collection

Alexis de Tocqueville (1805–1859) was a young French aristocrat who came to the United States to study the American prison system. He wrote the brilliant *Democracy in America* (2 vols., 1835–1840), a profound analysis of our political culture.

The children from each country ended the story quite differently. French children declared that the president would not be reprimanded. British children said the queen would not be punished. But American children were most likely to say that the president would be fined or ticketed, just like any other person should be.

Cross-national differences wrought by political culture seem to be even sharper between America and such countries as Argentina, Brazil, Mexico, and the Philippines. Why do these countries, whose constitutions are very much like the American one, have so much trouble with corruption, military takeovers, and the rise of demagogues? Each of these nations has had periods of democratic rule, but only for a short period of time, despite having an elected president, a separately elected congress, and an independent judiciary.

Some have argued that democracy took root in the United States but not in other countries that copied its constitution because America offered more abundant land and greater opportunities for people.

Underwood & Underwood/CORBIS

At the height of immigration to this country, there was a striking emphasis on creating a shared political culture. Schoolchildren, whatever their national origin, were taught to salute this country's flag.

No feudal aristocracy occupied the land, taxes remained low, and when one place after another filled up, people kept pushing west to find new opportunities. America became a nation of small, independent farmers with relatively few landless peasants or indentured servants.

However, as Alexis de Tocqueville, the perceptive French observer of American politics, noted in the 1830s, much of South America contains fertile land and rich resources, but democracy has not flourished there. The constitution and the physical advantages of the land cannot by themselves explain the persistence of any nation's democratic institutions. Nor can they account for the fact that American democracy survived a Civil War and thrived as wave after wave of immigrants became citizens and made the democracy more demographically diverse. What can begin to account for such differences are the customs of the people—what de Tocqueville called their "moral and intellectual characteristics,"[4] and what social scientists today call political culture.

Japan, like the United States, is a democracy. But while America is an immigrant nation that often has favored open immigration policies, Japan remains a Japanese nation in which immigration policies are highly restrictive and foreign-born citizens are few. America, like Saudi Arabia, is a country in which most people profess religious beliefs, and many people identify themselves as orthodox believers. But America's Christian majority favors religious pluralism and church-state separation, while Saudi Arabia's Muslim majority supports laws that maintain Islam as the state religion. In Germany, courts have held that non-Christian religious symbols and dress, but not Christian ones, may be banned from schools and other public places. In France, the government forbids wearing any religious garb in schools. In the United States, such rulings or restrictions would be unthinkable.

THE POLITICAL SYSTEM

There are at least five important elements in the American view of the political system:

- *Liberty:* Americans are preoccupied with their rights. They believe they should be free to do pretty much as they please, with some exceptions, as long as they don't hurt other people.
- *Equality:* Americans believe everybody should have an equal vote and an equal chance to participate and succeed.
- *Democracy:* Americans think government officials should be accountable to the people.
- *Civic duty:* Americans generally feel people ought to take community affairs seriously and help out when they can.[5]
- *Individual responsibility:* A characteristically American view is that, barring some disability, individuals are responsible for their own actions and well-being.

By vast majorities, Americans believe that every citizen should have an equal chance to influence government policy and to hold public office, and they oppose the idea of letting people have titles such as "Lord" or "Duke," as in England. By somewhat smaller majorities, they believe people should be allowed to vote even if they can't read or write or vote intelligently.[6] Though Americans recognize that people differ in their abilities, they overwhelmingly agree with the statement that "teaching children that all people are really equal recognizes that all people are equally worthy and deserve equal treatment."[7]

At least three questions can be raised about this political culture. First, how do we know that the American people share these beliefs? For most of our history there were no public opinion polls, and even after they became commonplace, they were rather crude tools for measuring the existence and meaning of complex, abstract ideas. There is in fact no way to prove that values such as those listed above are important to Americans. But neither is there good reason for dismissing the list out of hand. One can infer, as have many scholars, the existence of certain values by a close study of the kinds of books Americans read, the speeches they hear, the slogans to which they respond, and the political choices they make, as well as by noting the observations of insightful foreign visitors. Personality tests as well as opinion polls, particularly those asking similar questions in different countries, also supply useful evidence, some of which will be reviewed in the following paragraphs.

Second, if these values are important to Americans, how can we explain the existence in our society of behavior that is obviously inconsistent with them? For example, if white Americans believe in equality of opportunity, why did so many of them for so long deny that equality to African Americans? That people act contrary to their professed beliefs is an everyday fact of life: people believe in honesty, yet they steal from their employers and sometimes underreport their taxable income. Besides values, self-interest and social circumstances also shape behavior. Gunnar Myrdal, a Swedish observer of American society, described race relations in this country as "an American dilemma" resulting from the conflict between the "American creed" (a belief in equality of opportunity) and American behavior (denying African Americans full citizenship).[8] But the creed remains important because it is a source of change: as more and more people become aware of the inconsistency between their values and their behavior, that behavior slowly changes.[9] Race relations in this country would take a very different course if instead of an abstract but widespread belief in equality there were an equally widespread belief that one race is inherently inferior to another.

The late political scientist, Samuel P. Huntington, put it this way: "Critics say that America is a lie because its reality falls so far short of its ideals. America is not a lie, it is a disappointment. And it can be a disappointment only because it is also a hope."[10]

Third, if there is agreement among Americans on certain political values, why has there been so much political conflict in our history? How could a people who agree on such fundamentals fight a bloody civil war, engage in violent labor-management disputes, take to the streets in riots and demonstrations, and sue each other in countless court battles? Conflict, even violent struggles, can occur over specific policies even among those who share, at some level of abstraction, common beliefs. Many political values may be irrelevant to specific controversies: there is no abstract value, for example, that would settle the question of whether steelworkers ought to organize unions. More important, much of our conflict has occurred precisely because we have strong beliefs that happen, as each of us interprets them, to be in conflict. Equality of opportunity seems an attractive idea, but sometimes it can be pursued only by curtailing personal liberty, another attractive idea. The states went to war in 1861 over one aspect of that conflict—the rights of slaves versus the rights of slaveowners.

Indeed, the Civil War illustrates the way certain fundamental beliefs about how a democratic regime ought to be organized have persisted despite bitter conflict over the policies adopted by particular governments. When the southern states seceded from the Union, they formed not a wholly different government but one modeled, despite some important differences, on the U.S. Constitution. Even some of the language of the Constitution was duplicated, suggesting that the southern states believed not that a new form of government or a different political culture ought to be created but that the South was the true repository of the existing constitutional and cultural order.[11]

Perhaps the most frequently encountered evidence that Americans believe themselves bound by common values and common hopes has been the persistence of the word *Americanism* in our political vocabulary. Throughout the 19th and 20th centuries, *Americanism* and *the American dream* were familiar terms not only in Fourth of July speeches but also in everyday discourse. For many years, the House of Representatives had a committee called the House Un-American Activities Committee. There is hardly any example to be found abroad of such a way of thinking: There is no "Britishism" or "Frenchism," and when Britons and French people become worried about subversion, they call it a problem of internal security, not a manifestation of "un-British" or "un-French" activities.

THE PERSISTENCE OF CONFLICT

We have ended slavery, endorsed civil rights, and expanded the scope of free discussion, but these gains have not ended political conflict. We argue about abortion, morality, religion, immigration, and affirmative action. Some people believe that core moral principles are absolute while others feel they are relative to the situation. Some people believe all immigrants should become like every other American while others argue that we should, in the name of diversity and multiculturalism, celebrate group differences.

Much depends on how we define a good citizen. Some people define them as persons who vote, pay their taxes, obey the law, and support the military; others describe them as skeptical of government and ready to join protest movements and boycott products they do not like. A recent study has suggested that these competing opinions reflect differences in age and

Table 4.1 Patriotism by Race and Ethnicity

Group	How strongly do you love America?
White	91%
Black	80
Hispanic	91

Source: Jack Citrin, et al., "Testing Huntington," *Perspectives on Politics* 5 (2007): 43. Data are from 2004 National Election Survey.

education. Older people, especially those who experienced the Great Depression and World War II, are more likely to take the first view, while those born between 1964 and 1984 and who have been to college are more likely to take the second.[12]

These two generations don't quite trust one another. The older generation thinks the younger one is alienated, distrustful, self-centered, and lacking in clear moral guidance. The younger group, often described as Generation X because they were born after the Baby Boomers, responds by saying that older people are rigid, conformist, overly supportive of the status quo, and too impressed by the military.

But these conflicts, though they affect every American, should not obscure the underlying level of agreement. Consider how different ethnic groups think about this country. When asked whether they "love" this country, the overwhelming majority of whites, blacks, and Hispanics say they do (see Table 4.1).

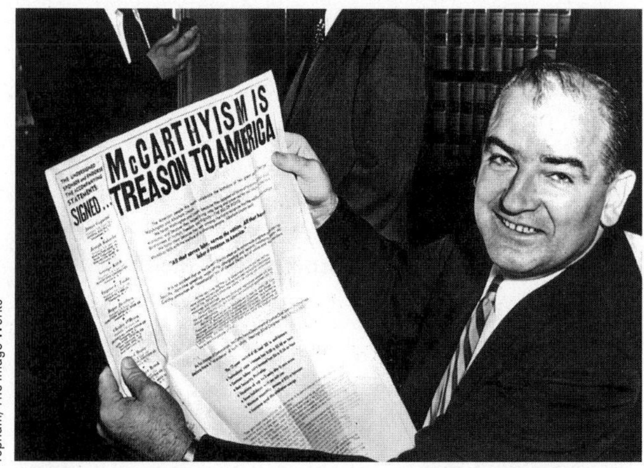

Topham/The Image Works

In the 1950s Senator Joseph McCarthy of Wisconsin was the inspiration for the word "McCarthyism" after his highly publicized attacks on alleged communists working in the federal government.

THE ECONOMIC SYSTEM

Americans judge the economic system using many of the same standards by which they judge the political system, albeit with some very important differences. As it is in American politics, liberty is important in the U.S. economy. Thus Americans support the idea of a free-enterprise economic system, calling the nation's economy "generally fair and efficient" and denying that it "survives by keeping the poor down."[13] However, there are limits to how much freedom they think should exist in the marketplace. People support government regulation of business in order to keep some firms from becoming too powerful and to correct specific abuses.[14]

Americans are more willing to tolerate economic inequality than political inequality. They believe in maintaining "equality of opportunity" in the economy but not "equality of results." If everyone has an equal opportunity to get ahead, then it is all right for people with more ability to earn higher salaries and for wages to be set based on how hard people work rather than on their economic needs. Hardly anyone is upset by the fact that Bill Gates, Warren Buffett, and Donald Trump are rich men. Although Americans are quite willing to support education and training programs to help disadvantaged people get ahead, they are strongly opposed to anything that looks like preferential treatment (for example, hiring quotas) in the workplace.[15]

The leaders of very liberal political groups, such as civil rights and feminist organizations, are more willing than the average American to support preferential treatment in the hiring and promoting of minorities and women. They do so because, unlike most citizens, they believe that whatever disadvantages minorities and women face are the result of failures of the economic system rather than the fault of individuals. Even so, these leaders strongly support the idea that earnings should be based on ability and oppose the idea of having any top limit on what people can earn.[16]

This popular commitment to economic individualism and personal responsibility may help explain how Americans think about particular public policies, such as welfare and civil rights. Polls show that Americans are willing to help people "truly in need" (this includes the elderly and the disabled) but not those deemed "able to take care of themselves" (this includes, in the public's mind, people "on welfare"). Also, Americans dislike preferential hiring programs and the use of quotas to deal with racial inequality.

RESEARCH FRONTIERS

Do Hispanics Embrace American Political Culture?

Hispanics are the largest and fastest-growing minority group in America. The nation's Hispanic population surpassed 48 million in 2009, representing about 16 percent of the total U.S. population. They comprise more than a third of the population in several states including California, New Mexico, and Texas.

In recent years, some analysts have asserted that Hispanic immigrants to the United States, the vast majority of whom come from Mexico, will remain strangers to American political culture. Among the most provocative of these analysts is Harvard political scientist Samuel P. Huntington, who has argued that the sheer number, concentration, and ostensible linguistic homogeneity of Hispanics in America will promote ethnic allegiances at odds with bedrock American beliefs about politics and government.

University of California at Berkeley political scientist Jack Citrin and other researchers tested Huntington's controversial contentions about Hispanic immigrants. Contrary to Huntington's dire predictions, all the evidence suggests that, if anything, Hispanic immigrants over time are far more likely to embrace and emulate, rather than to reject or refashion, American political culture.

- *Linguistic adaptation:* Regardless of age, educational level, or residential concentration, Hispanic immigrants from one generation to the next speak English as their first language (by the third generation, 71 percent are English-dominant).
- *Hyphenated-American identity:* Most Hispanics think of themselves as both American and Hispanic; and once Hispanic immigrants become citizens, they become far more likely to identify either as "just an American" or as "Hispanic-American."
- *Religiosity:* Measured by professed importance of religion and rates of church attendance, Hispanics are no more or less religious than non-Hispanic whites.
- *Patriotism:* 91 percent of Hispanic-Americans say they "love America," and 86 percent express "pride in the American flag."
- *Work ethic:* The higher the proportion of Hispanics living and working in a given state, the more likely it is that non-Hispanics will agree that Hispanics are especially hardworking.

Also contrary to Huntington's Mexican-specific thesis, the data analyses by Citrin and his colleagues, like most other recent empirical studies of the subject, suggest that generation-by-generation, Mexican-born Hispanic immigrants' social, economic, and personal ties to Mexico diminish.

In sum, the latest and best research offers this prediction: most Hispanic immigrant families, like most Italian and other European immigrant families into the early and mid-20th century, will continue to adapt, will adopt American political culture, and will make a hyphenated American identity all their own.

- Do a little research to discover the size and ethnic composition of the Hispanic population in your state. How, if at all, have debates about immigration figured in recent presidential elections or in local politics where you live?

Sources: Jack Citrin, et al., "Testing Huntington: Is Hispanic Immigration a Threat to American Identity?," *Perspectives on Politics* 5 (March 2007): 31–48; Samuel P. Huntington, *Who are We? The Challenges to America's National Identity* (Simon and Shuster, 2004); and U.S. Census Bureau, "Facts for Features," July 15, 2010.

At the core of these policy attitudes is a widely (but not universally) shared commitment to economic individualism and personal responsibility. Some scholars, among them Donald Kinder and David Sears, interpret these individualistic values as "symbolic racism"—a kind of plausible camouflage for antiblack attitudes.[17] But other scholars, such as Paul M. Sniderman and Michael Gray Hagen, argue that these views are not a smoke screen for bigotry or insensitivity but a genuine commitment to the ethic of self-reliance.[18] Since there are many Americans on both sides of this issue, debates about welfare and civil rights tend to be especially intense. What is striking about the American political culture is that in this country the individualist view of social policy is by far the most popular.[19]

Views about specific economic policies change. Americans now are much more inclined than they once were to believe that the government should help the needy and regulate business. But the commitment to certain underlying principles has been remarkably enduring. In 1924, almost half of the high school students in Muncie, Indiana, said that "it is entirely the fault of the man himself if he cannot succeed" and disagreed with the view that differences in wealth showed that the system was unjust. More than half a century later, the students in this same high school were asked the same questions again, with the same results.[20]

How We Compare: Comparing America with Other Nations

Americans like their own country more than people in European democracies like theirs. In Table 4.2, we see that 71 percent of Americans are proud to be an American compared to only 21 percent of Germans who are proud to be Germans. There are other differences as well: a majority of the French, Germans, and Italians think success in life is determined by forces outside an individual's own control; Americans deeply disagree. Most Americans think children should be taught the value of hard work and that a belief in God is necessary for morality; most western European countries have the opposite view.

America is not very popular abroad, but these data suggest that the reasons go well beyond the war in Iraq or the criticism of former president George W. Bush. Americans have very different views about important things than Europeans. Following are some examples drawn from politics, the economy, and religion.

THE POLITICAL SYSTEM

Sweden has a well-developed democratic government, with a constitution, free speech, an elected legislature, competing political parties, and a reasonably honest and nonpartisan bureaucracy. But the Swedish political culture is significantly different from ours; it is more deferential than participatory. Though almost all adult Swedes vote in national elections, few participate in politics in any other way. They defer to the decisions of experts and specialists who work for the government, rarely challenge governmental decisions in court, believe leaders and legislators ought to decide issues on the basis of "what is best" more than on "what the people want," and value equality as much as (or more than) liberty.[21] Whereas Americans are contentious, Swedes value harmony; while Americans tend to assert their rights, Swedes tend to observe their obligations.

The contrast in political cultures is even greater when one looks at a nation, such as Japan, with a wholly different history and set of traditions. One study compared the values expressed by a small number of upper-status Japanese with those of some similarly situated Americans. Whereas the Americans emphasized the virtues of individualism, competition, and equality in their political, economic, and social relations, the Japanese attached greater value to maintaining good relations with colleagues,

Table 4.2 Attitudes in the USA and Other Democracies

	Pride	Outside Control	Teach Value of Work	God and Morality
USA	71%	32%	60%	58%
Canada	66	35	51	30
Britain	45	48	38	25
France	38	54	50	13
Germany	21	68	22	33
Italy	38	66	Na	27

Key to columns:

Pride: "I am very proud to be a member of [country]"

Outside Control: "Success in life is determined by forces outside our control"

Teach Value of Work: "Children should be taught the value of hard work"

God and Morality: "It is necessary to believe in God to be moral"

Source: © 2006 by Andrew Kohut and Bruce Stokes. Reprinted by permission of Henry Holt and Company, LLC and the Pew Research Center.

having decisions made by groups, preserving social harmony, and displaying respect for hierarchy. The Americans were more concerned than the Japanese with rules and with treating others fairly but impersonally, with due regard for their rights. The Japanese, on the other hand, stressed the importance of being sensitive to the personal needs of others, avoiding conflict, and reaching decisions through discussion rather than the application of rules.[22]

civic duty A belief that one has an obligation to participate in civic and political affairs.

civic competence A belief that one can affect government policies.

A classic study of political culture in five nations found that Americans, and to a lesser degree citizens of Great Britain, had a stronger sense of **civic duty** (a belief that one has an obligation to participate in civic and political affairs) and a stronger sense of **civic competence** (a belief that one can affect government policies) than the citizens of Germany, Italy, or Mexico. More than half of all Americans and a third of all Britons believed the average citizen ought to "be active in one's community," compared to only a tenth in Italy and a fifth in Germany. Moreover, many more Americans and Britons than Germans, Italians, or Mexicans believed they could "do something" about an unjust national law or local regulation.[23] A more recent study of citizen participation in politics found that while America lagged behind Austria, the Netherlands, Germany, and the United Kingdom in voter participation, when it came to campaigning, attending political meetings, becoming active in the local community, and contacting government officials, Americans were as active—or substantially more active—than citizens elsewhere.[24]

Today the American people have less trust in government than they once did. But even so, popular confidence in political institutions remains higher here than in many places abroad. In cross-national surveys conducted in the United States and 16 other democracies, Americans expressed more confidence in public institutions (the police, the armed forces, the legal system, and the civil service) than the citizens of all but four other countries (Denmark, Ireland, Northern Ireland, and Norway), and greater confidence in private institutions (the church, major companies, the press, trade unions) than the citizens of any other nation.[25] In other cross-national surveys, Americans were more likely than the French or Germans to say they were "very patriotic" (see Figure 4.1). Of course, Americans know that their country has a lot of faults. But even the most disaffected voters believe the United States needs to change only certain policies, not its system of government.[26]

Figure 4.1
Political Culture in America and Other Democracies

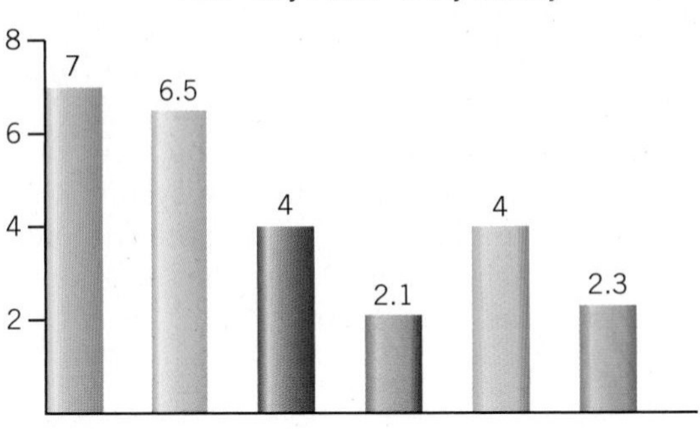

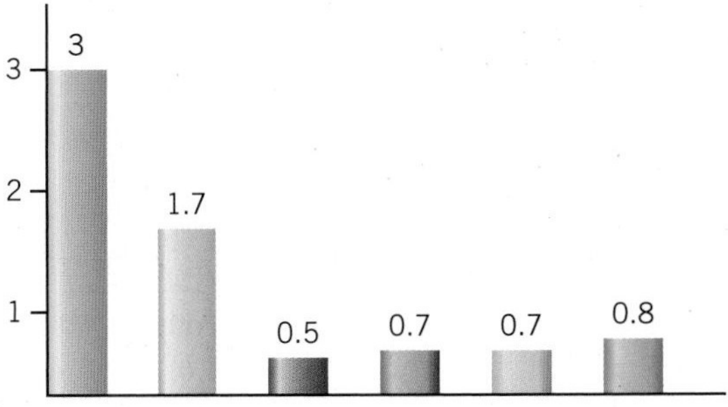

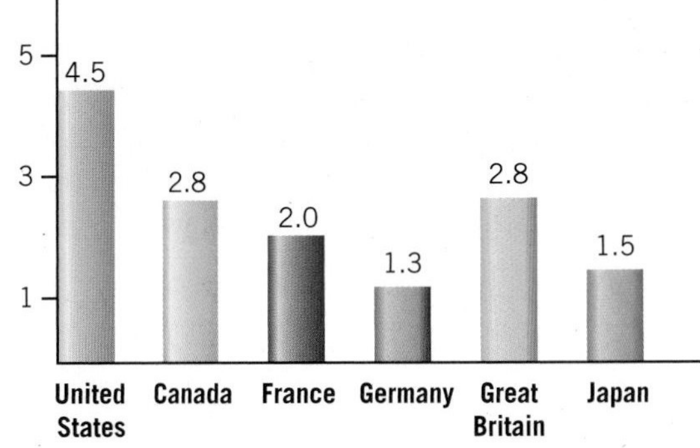

Sources: World Values Survey Wave 4; International Social Survey Program National Identity Module II (2003–2004)

THE ECONOMIC SYSTEM

The political culture of Sweden is not only more deferential than ours but also more inclined to favor equality of results over equality of opportunity. Sidney Verba and Gary Orren compared the views of Swedish and American trade union and political party leaders on a variety of economic issues. In both countries, the leaders were chosen from either blue-collar unions or the major liberal political party (the Democrats in the United States, the Social Democrats in Sweden).

The results are quite striking. By margins of four or five to one, the Swedish leaders were more likely to believe in giving workers equal pay than their

American counterparts. Moreover, by margins of at least three to one, the Swedes were more likely than the Americans to favor putting a top limit on incomes.[27]

Just what these differences in beliefs mean in dollars-and-cents terms was revealed by the answers to another question. Each group was asked what should be the ratio between the income of an executive and that of a menial worker (a dishwasher in Sweden, an elevator operator in the United States). The Swedish leaders said the ratio should be a little over two to one. That is, if the dishwasher earned $200 a week, the executive should earn no more than $440 to $480 a week. But the American leaders were ready to let the executive earn between $2,260 and $3,040 per week when the elevator operator was earning $200.

Americans, compared to people in many other countries, are more likely to think that freedom is more important than equality and less likely to think that hard work goes unrewarded or that the government should guarantee citizens a basic standard of living. These cultural differences make a difference in politics. In fact, there is less income inequality in Sweden than in the United States—the government sees to that.

THE CIVIC ROLE OF RELIGION

In the 1830s, de Tocqueville was amazed at how religious Americans were in comparison to his fellow Europeans. From the first days of the new Republic to the present, America has been among the most religious countries in the world. The average American is more likely than the average European to believe in God, to pray on a daily basis, and to acknowledge clear standards of right and wrong. [28]

Religious people donate more than three times as much money to charity as secular people, even when the incomes of the two groups are the same, and they volunteer their time twice as often. And this is true whether or not religious people go to church or synagogue regularly. Moreover, religious people are more likely to give money and donate time to nonreligious organizations, such as the Red Cross, than secular people.[29] It is clear that religion in America has a large effect on our culture.

It also affects our politics. The religious revivalist movement of the late 1730s and early 1740s (known as the First Great Awakening) transformed the political life of the American colonies. Religious ideas fueled the break with England, which, in the words of the Declaration of Independence, had violated "the laws of nature and nature's God." Religious leaders were central to the struggle over slavery in the 19th century and the temperance movement of the early 20th century.

Both liberals and conservatives have used the pulpit to promote political change. The civil rights movement of the 1950s and 1960s was led mainly by black religious leaders, most prominently Martin Luther King, Jr. In the 1980s, a conservative

Scott J. Ferrell/Congressional Quarterly/Alamy

A chaplain offers a prayer at a meeting of the U.S. Congress. Though having such a chaplain may appear to violate the separation of church and state, the Supreme Court has upheld it on grounds of "tradition."

religious group known as the Moral Majority advocated constitutional amendments that would allow prayer in public schools and ban abortion. In the 1990s, another conservative religious group, the Christian Coalition, attracted an enormous amount of media attention and became a prominent force in many national, state, and local elections.

Candidates for national office in most contemporary democracies mention religion rarely if they mention it at all. Not so in America. During the 2000 presidential campaign, for example, both Democratic candidate Al Gore and Republican candidate George W. Bush gave major speeches extolling the virtues of religion and advocating the right of religious organizations that deliver social services to receive government funding on the same basis as all other nonprofit organizations.

The general feeling about religion became apparent when a federal appeals court in 2002 tried to ban the Pledge of Allegiance because it contained the phrase "under God." There was an overwhelming and bipartisan condemnation of the ruling. To a degree that would be almost unthinkable in many other democracies, religious beliefs will probably continue to shape political culture in America for many generations to come. The Supreme Court, by deciding that the man who brought the case was not entitled to do so, left the Pledge intact without deciding whether it was constitutional.

The Sources of Political Culture

That Americans bring a distinctive way of thinking to their political life is easier to demonstrate than to explain. But even a brief, and necessarily superficial, effort to understand the sources of our political culture can help make its significance clearer.

The American Revolution, as we discussed in Chapter 2, was essentially a war fought over liberty: an assertion by the colonists of what they took to be their rights. Though the Constitution, produced 11 years after the Revolution, had to deal with other issues as well, its animating spirit reflected the effort to reconcile personal liberty with the needs of social control. These founding experiences, and the political disputes that followed, have given to American political thought and culture a preoccupation with the assertion and maintenance of rights. This tradition has imbued the daily conduct of U.S. politics with a kind of adversarial spirit quite foreign to the political life of countries that did not undergo a libertarian revolution or that were formed out of an interest in other goals, such as social equality, national independence, or ethnic supremacy.

The adversarial spirit of the American political culture reflects not only our preoccupation with rights but also our long-standing distrust of authority and of people wielding power. The colonies' experiences with British rule were one source of that distrust. But another, older source was the religious belief of many Americans, which saw human nature as fundamentally depraved. To the colonists, all of mankind suffered from original sin, symbolized by Adam and Eve eating the forbidden fruit in the Garden of Eden. Since no one was born innocent, no one could be trusted with power. Thus, the Constitution had to be designed in such a way as to curb the darker side of human nature. Otherwise, everyone's rights would be in jeopardy.

The contentiousness of a people animated by a suspicion of government and devoted to individualism could easily have made democratic politics so tumultuous as to be impossible. After all one must be willing to trust others with power if there is to be any kind of democratic government, and sometimes those others will be people not of one's own choosing. The first great test case took place around 1800 in a battle between the Federalists, led by John Adams and Alexander Hamilton, and the Democratic-Republicans, led by Thomas Jefferson and James Madison. The two factions deeply distrusted each other: the Federalists had passed laws designed to suppress Jeffersonian journalists; Jefferson suspected the Federalists were out to subvert the Constitution; and the Federalists believed Jefferson intended to sell out the country to France. But as we shall see in Chapter 9, the threat of civil war never materialized, and the Jeffersonians came to power peacefully. Within a few years, the role of an opposition party became legitimate, and people abandoned the idea of making serious efforts to suppress their opponents. By happy circumstance, people came to accept that liberty and orderly political change could coexist.

The Constitution, by creating a federal system and dividing political authority among competing institutions, provided ample opportunity for widespread—though hardly universal—participation in politics. The election of Jefferson in 1800 produced no political catastrophe, and those who had predicted one were, to a degree, discredited. But other, more fundamental features of American life contributed to the same end. One of the most important of these was religious diversity.

The absence of an established or official religion for the nation as a whole, reinforced by a constitutional prohibition of such an establishment and by the migration to this country of people with different religious backgrounds, meant that religious diversity was inevitable. Since there could be no orthodox or official religion, it became difficult for a corresponding political orthodoxy to emerge. Moreover, the conflict between the Puritan tradition, with its emphasis on faith and hard work, and the Catholic Church, with its devotion to the sacraments and priestly authority, provided a recurrent source of cleavage in American public life. The differences in values between these two groups showed up not only in their religious practices but also in areas involving the regulation of manners and morals, and even in people's choice of political party. For more than a century, candidates for state and national office were deeply divided over whether the sale of liquor should be prohibited, a question that arose ultimately out of competing religious doctrines.

Even though there was no established church, there was certainly a dominant religious tradition—Protestantism, and especially Puritanism. The Protestant churches provided people with both a set of beliefs and an organizational experience that had profound effects on American political culture. Those beliefs encouraged, or even required, a life of personal achievement as well as religious conviction: a believer had an obligation to work, save money, obey the secular law, and do good works. Max Weber explained the rise of capitalism in part by what he called the Protestant ethic—what we now sometimes call the work ethic.[30] Such values had political consequences, as people holding them were motivated to engage in civic and communal action.

Churches offered ready opportunities for developing and practicing civic and political skills. Since most Protestant churches were organized along congregational lines—that is, the church was controlled by its members, who put up the building, hired the preacher, and supervised the finances—they were, in effect, miniature political systems with leaders and committees, conflict and consensus. Developing a participatory political culture was undoubtedly made easier by the existence of a participatory religious culture. Even some Catholic churches in early America were under a degree of lay control. Parishioners owned the church property, negotiated with priests, and conducted church business.

All aspects of culture, including the political, are preserved and transmitted to new generations primarily by the family. Though some believe that the weakening of the family unit has eroded the extent to which it transmits anything, particularly culture, and has enlarged the power of other sources of values—the mass media and the world of friends and fashion, leisure, and entertainment—there is still little doubt that the ways in which we think about the world are largely acquired within the family. In Chapter 7, we shall see that the family is the primary source of one kind of political attitude—identification with one or another political party. Even more important, the family shapes in subtle ways how we think and act on political matters. Erik Erikson, the psychologist, noted certain traits that are more characteristic of American than of European families—the greater freedom enjoyed by children, for example, and the larger measure of equality among family members. These familial characteristics promote a belief, carried through life, that every person has rights deserving protection and that a variety of interests have a legitimate claim to consideration when decisions are made.[31]

The combined effect of religious and ethnic diversity, an individualistic philosophy, fragmented political authority, and the relatively egalitarian American family can be seen in the absence of a high degree of **class consciousness** among Americans. Class consciousness means thinking of oneself as a worker whose interests are in opposition to those of management, or vice versa. In this country, most people, whatever their jobs, think of themselves as "middle class."

class consciousness
A belief that you are a member of an economic group whose interests are opposed to people in other such groups.

Though the writings of Horatio Alger are no longer popular, Americans still seem to believe in the message of those stories—that the opportunity for success is available to people who work hard. This may help explain why the United States is the only large industrial democracy without a significant socialist party and why the nation has been slow to adopt certain welfare programs.

THE CULTURE WAR

Almost all Americans share some elements of a common political culture. Why, then, is there so much cultural conflict in American politics? For many years, the most explosive political issues have included abortion, gay rights, drug use, school prayer, and pornography. Viewed from a Marxist perspective, politics in the United States is utterly baffling: instead of two economic classes engaged in a bitter struggle over wealth, we have two cultural classes locked in a war over values.

As first formulated by sociologist James Davison Hunter, the idea is that there are, broadly defined,

orthodox A belief that morality and religion ought to be of decisive importance.

progressive A belief that personal freedom and solving social problems are more important than religion.

two cultural classes in the United States: the **orthodox** and the **progressive.** On the orthodox side are people who believe that morality is as important as, or more important than, self-expression and that moral rules derive from the commands of God or the laws of nature—commands and laws that are relatively clear, unchanging, and independent of individual preferences. On the progressive side are people who think that personal freedom is as important as, or more important than, certain traditional moral rules and that those rules must be evaluated in light of the circumstances of modern life—circumstances that are quite complex, changeable, and dependent on individual preferences.[32]

Most conspicuous among the orthodox are fundamentalist Protestants and evangelical Christians, and so critics who dislike orthodox views often dismiss them as the fanatical expressions of "the Religious Right." But many people who hold orthodox views are not fanatical or deeply religious or right-wing on most issues: they simply have strong views about drugs, pornography, and sexual morality. Similarly, the progressive side often includes members of liberal Protestant denominations (for example, Episcopalians and Unitarians) and people with no strong religious beliefs, and so their critics often denounce them as immoral, anti-Christian radicals who have embraced the ideology of secular humanism, the belief that moral standards do not require religious justification. But in all likelihood, few progressives are immoral or anti-Christian, and most do not regard secular humanism as their defining ideology.

Groups supporting and opposing the right to abortion have had many angry confrontations in recent years. The latter have been arrested while attempting to block access to abortion clinics; some clinics have been fire-bombed; and at least seven physicians have been killed. A controversy over what schoolchildren should be taught about homosexuals was responsible, in part, for the firing of the head of the New York City school system; in other states, there have been fierce arguments in state legislatures and before the courts over whether gay and lesbian couples should be allowed to marry or adopt children. Although most Americans want to keep heroin, cocaine, and other drugs illegal, a significant number of people want to legalize (or at least decriminalize) their use. The Supreme Court has ruled that there cannot be state-sponsored prayer in public schools, but this has not stopped many parents and school authorities from trying to reinstate school prayer, or at least prayer-like moments of silence. The discovery that a federal agency, the National Endowment for the Arts, had given money to support exhibitions and performances that many people thought were obscene led to a furious congressional struggle over the future of the agency.

Justin Sullivan/Getty Images News/Getty Images

Union members protest Wisconsin Governor Scott Walker's plan to restrict their collective bargaining rights.

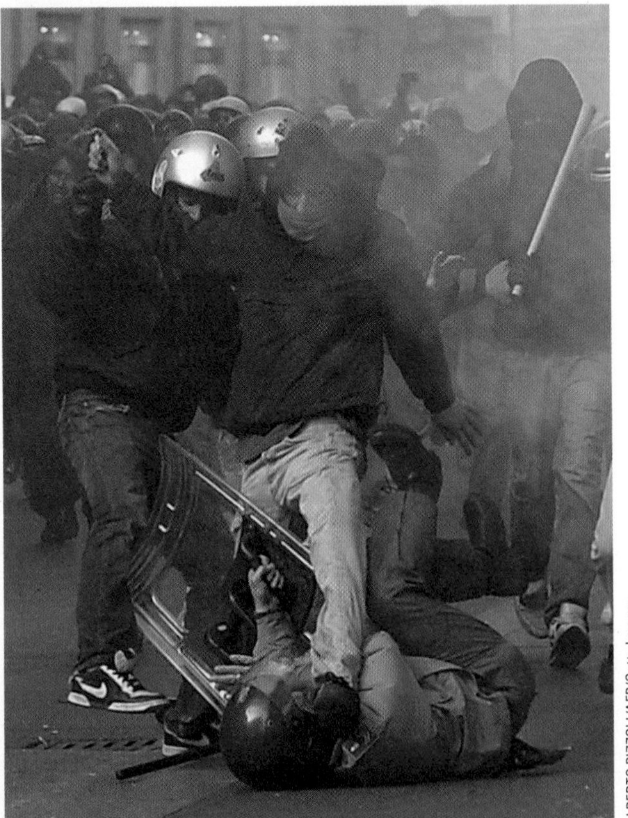

ALBERTO PIZZOLI/AFP/Getty Images

People stomp on a police officer in Rome as part of their demand for a change in the Italian government.

The culture war differs from other political disputes (over such matters as taxes, business regulations, and foreign policy) in several ways: money is not always at stake, compromises are almost impossible to arrange, and the conflict is more profound. It is animated by deep differences in people's beliefs about private and public morality—that is, about the standards that ought to govern individual behavior and social arrangements. It is about what kind of country we ought to live in, not just about what kinds of policies our government ought to adopt.

Two opposing views exist about the importance of the culture war. One view, developed by Morris Fiorina and others, holds that politically the culture war is a myth. While political leaders are polarized, most Americans occupy a middle position. Journalists write about the split between "blue states" (those that vote Democratic) and "red states" (those that vote Republican), but in fact popular views across both kinds of states on many policy issues are similar.[33]

The rival view, developed by Alan Abramowitz and others, holds that more and more people are choosing their party affiliations on the basis of the party's position on important issues. Moreover, a growing percentage of the public is politically engaged; that is, they do more to express their political views than simply vote.[34]

Choosing between these two theories will take time, as we watch what happens in future elections. But even now, popular attitudes about issues such as the use of military force abroad are already deeply polarized.

Mistrust of Government

One aspect of public opinion worries many people. Since the late 1950s, there has been a more or less steady decline in the proportion of Americans who say they trust the government in Washington to do the right thing. In the past, polls showed that about three-quarters of Americans said they trusted Washington most of the time or just about always. The percentage of people who say they trust the government has on occasion gone up (for example, when Ronald Reagan became president and again just after the 9/11 terrorist attacks), but by and large trust has been absent since at least the mid-1960s (see Figure 4.2).

Before we get too upset about this, we should remember that people are talking about government officials, not the system of government. Americans are much more supportive of the country and its institutions than Europeans are of theirs. Even so, the decline in confidence in officials is striking. There are all sorts of explanations for why it has happened. In the 1960s, there was our unhappy war in Vietnam; in the 1970s, President Nixon had to resign because of his involvement in the Watergate scandal; in the 1990s, President Clinton went through scandals that led to his impeachment by the House of Representatives (but was not convicted of that charge by the Senate); and in 2004 to 2007, President George W. Bush presided over a divisive war in Iraq.

But there is another way of looking at the matter. Maybe in the 1950s we had an abnormally *high* level of confidence in government, one that could

Figure 4.2
Trust in the Federal Government, 1958–2008

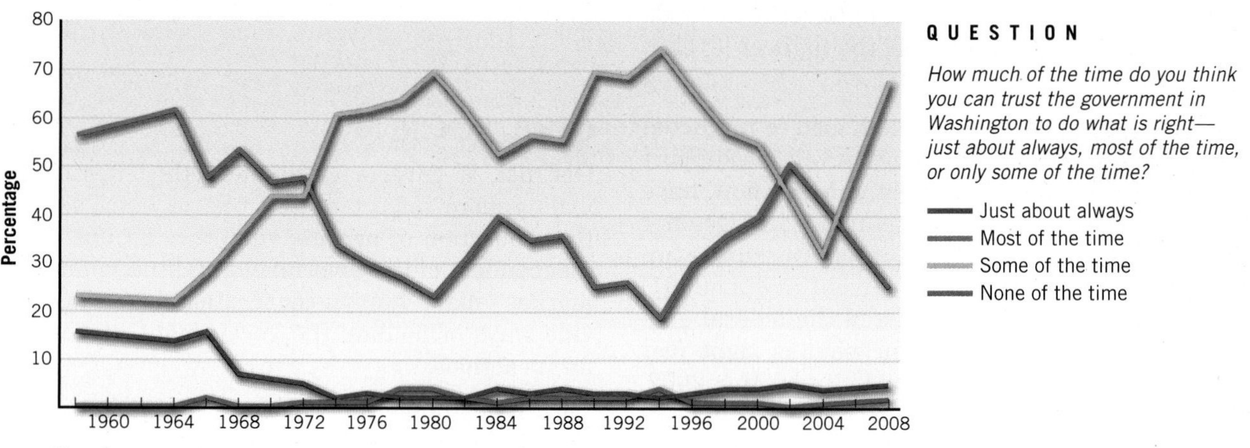

Source: University of Michigan, *The American National Election Studies*.

never be expected to last no matter what any president did. After all, when President Eisenhower took office in 1952, we had won a war against fascism, overcome the Depression of the 1930s, possessed a near monopoly of the atom bomb, had a currency that was the envy of the world, and dominated international trade. Moreover, in those days not much was expected out of Washington. Hardly anybody thought there should be important federal laws about civil rights, crime, illegal drugs, the environment, the role of women, highway safety, or almost anything else now on the national agenda. Since nobody expected much out of Washington, nobody was upset that they didn't get much out of it.

The 1960s and 1970s changed all of that. Domestic turmoil, urban riots, a civil rights revolution, the war in Vietnam, economic inflation, and a new concern for the environment dramatically increased what we expected Washington to do. And since these problems are very difficult ones to solve, a lot of people became convinced that our politicians couldn't do much.[35]

Those events also pushed the feelings Americans had about their country—that is, their patriotism—into the background. We liked the country, but there weren't many occasions when expressing that approval seemed to make much sense. But on September 11, 2001, when hijacked airliners were crashed by terrorists into the World Trade Center in New York City and the Pentagon in Washington, all of that changed. There was an extraordinary outburst of patriotic fervor, with flags displayed everywhere, fire and police heroes widely celebrated, and strong national support for our going to war in Afghanistan to find the key terrorist, Osama bin Laden, and destroy the tyrannical Taliban regime that he supported. By November of that year, about half of all Americans of both political parties said they trusted Washington officials to do what is right most of the time, the highest level in many years.

civil society Voluntary action that makes cooperation easier.

Those who had hoped or predicted that this new level of support would last, not ebb and flow, have been disappointed. In October 2001, 57 percent of Americans (up from just 29 percent in July 2001) said they trusted the federal government to do what is right just about always or most of the time. But by May 2002, only 40 percent expressed such trust in the federal government, and 57 percent said they trusted Washington only some of the time or never.

Table 4.3 Confidence in American Institutions

Institution	1973	2010
Churches	66%	48%
Public schools	58	34
Newspapers	39	25
Labor unions	30	20
Big business	26	19
Congress	42	11
The military	58	76

Source: Gallup Poll.

Only 12 percent of all Americans have a lot of confidence in Congress, but it—and the rest of the government—should not feel lonely. With few exceptions, Americans have lost confidence in many institutions. As Table 4.3 shows, newspapers, public schools, television news, and labor unions have all suffered a big drop during the last three decades. Only the military has gained support (71 percent of us say we have "a great deal" or "a lot" of confidence in it).

Because Americans are less likely than they once were to hold their leaders in high esteem, to have confidence in government policies, and to believe the system will be responsive to popular wishes, some observers like to say that Americans today are more "alienated" from politics. Perhaps this is true, but careful studies of the subject have not yet been able, for example, to demonstrate any relationship between overall levels of public trust in government or confidence in leaders, on the one hand, and the rates at which people come out to vote, on the other. There is, however, some evidence that the less voters trust political institutions and leaders, the more likely they are to support candidates from the nonincumbent major party (in two-candidate races) and third-party candidates.[36]

CIVIL SOCIETY

Distrust of governmental and other institutions makes more important the role of **civil society,** that collection of private, voluntary groups that—independent of the government and the commercial market—make human cooperation easier and provide ways of holding the government accountable for its actions.

The individualism of the American political culture makes civil society especially important. As we shall see in Chapter 11, Americans are more likely than people in other democracies to join voluntary groups. These organizations teach people how to cooperate, develop community-serving skills, and increase social capital. This last phrase refers to the connections people have with each other through friendship, personal contact, and group efforts.

Several scholars, such as Robert Putnam, argue that the more a community has social capital, the greater the level of trust among its members. And the more trust that exists, the easier it is to achieve common goals such as improving a neighborhood, combating intolerance, and producing useful projects outside of government. Putnam worries that our social capital may be decreasing because people are less and less likely to join voluntary associations. In Putnam's famous phrase, we once bowled in leagues; now we bowl alone. We once joined the PTA, the NAACP, and the Veterans of Foreign Wars; now we stay home and watch television or spend time on our computer.[37]

There are three qualifications to this argument. First, Americans still join more groups than people in most other democracies. Second, a general measure of civic health (that examines group membership and informal human contact) shows high engagement by group leaders (see Figure 4.3). Third, in ethnically and racially diverse communities, we "hunker down"—that is, we don't trust our neighbors, contribute to charities, cooperate with others, or join voluntary groups.[38] Just where we most need social capital, we do not have as much as we would like.

Figure 4.3

The American Civic Health Index, 2009

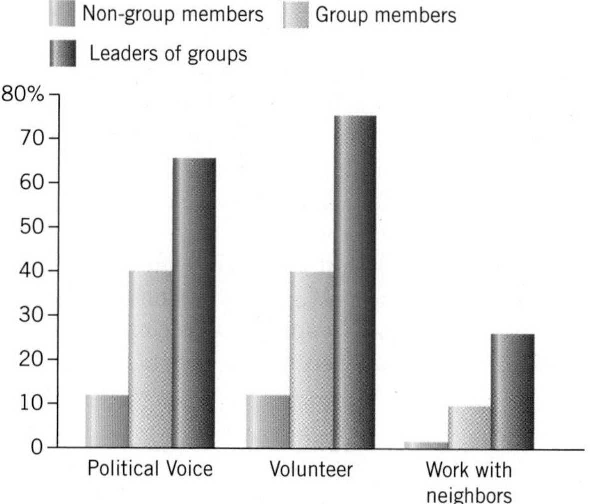

Source: 2010 Civic Health Assessment: Executive Summary, "Involvement by Group Membership," (Washington, D.C.: National Conference on Citizenship. (September 2010), p. 3. Used by permission.

Political Tolerance

Democratic politics depends crucially on citizens' reasonable tolerance of the opinions and actions of others. If unpopular speakers were always shouted down, if government efforts to censor newspapers were usually met with popular support or even public indifference, if peaceful demonstrations were regularly broken up by hostile mobs, if the losing candidates in an election refused to allow their victorious opponents to take office, then the essential elements of a democratic political culture would be missing, and democracy would fail. Democracy does not require perfect tolerance; if it did, the passions of human nature would make democracy forever impossible. But at a minimum, citizens must have a political culture that allows the discussion of ideas and the selection of rulers in an atmosphere reasonably free of oppression.

Public opinion surveys show that the overwhelming majority of Americans agree with concepts such as freedom of speech, majority rule, and the right to circulate petitions—at least in the abstract.[39] But when we get down to concrete cases, a good many Americans are not very tolerant of groups they dislike. Suppose you must decide which groups will be permitted to espouse their causes at meetings held in your community's civic auditorium. Which of these groups would *you* allow to run such a meeting?

1. Protestants holding a revival meeting
2. Right-to-life groups opposing abortion
3. People protesting a nuclear power plant
4. Feminists organizing a march for the Equal Rights Amendment
5. Gays organizing for homosexual rights
6. Atheists preaching against God
7. Students organizing a sit-in to shut down city hall

In general, Americans have become a bit more tolerant and more willing to tolerate public speech by communists, atheists, and homosexuals.[40] People are today more likely than in the past to say they are willing to vote for a qualified person who runs for president even if the candidate is a Catholic, a Jew, a woman, a black, or a homosexual.[41]

One person's civic intolerance can be another person's heartfelt display of civic concern. Most Americans believe that serious civic problems are rooted in a breakdown of moral values.[42] Correctly or not, most citizens worry that the nation is becoming too tolerant of behaviors that harm society, and they favor defending common moral standards over protecting individual rights.

Nonetheless, this majority tolerance for many causes should not blind us to the fact that for most of us, there is some group or cause from which we are willing to withhold political liberties—even though we endorse those liberties in the abstract.

If most people dislike one or another group strongly enough to deny it certain political rights that we usually take for granted, how is it that such groups (and such rights) survive? The answer, in part, is that most of us don't act on our beliefs. We rarely take the trouble—or have the chance—to block another person from making a speech or teaching school. Some scholars have argued that among people who are in a position to deny other people rights—officeholders and political activists, for example—the level of political tolerance is somewhat greater than among the public at large, but that claim has been strongly disputed.[43]

But another reason may be just as important. Most of us are ready to deny *some* group its rights, but we usually can't agree on which group that should be. Sometimes we can agree, and then the disliked group may be in for real trouble. There have been times (1919 to 1920, and again in the early 1950s) when socialists and communists were disliked by most people in the United States. The government on each occasion took strong actions against them. Today, fewer people agree that these left-wing groups are a major domestic threat, and so their rights are now more secure.

Finally, the courts are sufficiently insulated from public opinion that they can act against majority sentiments and enforce constitutional protections (see Chapter 16). Most of us are not willing to give all rights to all groups, but most of us are not judges.

These facts should be a sober reminder that political liberty cannot be taken for granted. Men and women are not, it would seem, born with an inclination to live and let live, at least politically, and many—possibly most—never acquire that inclination. Liberty must be learned and protected. Happily, the United States during much of its recent history has not been consumed by a revulsion for any one group that has been strong enough to place the group's rights in jeopardy.

Nor should any part of society pretend that it is always more tolerant than another. In the 1950s, for example, ultraconservatives outside the universities were attacking the rights of professors to say and teach certain things. In the 1960s and 1970s, ultraliberal students and professors inside the universities were attacking the rights of other students and professors to say certain things.

The American system of government is supported by a political culture that fosters a sense of civic duty, takes pride in the nation's constitutional arrangements, and provides support for the exercise of essential civil liberties (albeit out of indifference or diversity more than principle at times). In recent decades, mistrust of government officials (though not of the system itself) has increased, and confidence in their responsiveness to popular feelings has declined.

Although Americans value liberty in both the political system and the economy, they believe equality is important in the political realm. In economic affairs, they wish to see equality of opportunity but accept inequality of results.

Not only is our culture generally supportive of democratic rule, it also has certain distinctive features that make our way of governing different from what one finds in other democracies. Americans are preoccupied with their rights, and this fact, combined with a political system that (as we shall see) encourages the vigorous exercise of rights and claims, gives to our political life an *adversarial* style. Unlike Swedes or Japanese, we do not generally reach political decisions by consensus, and we often do not defer to the authority of administrative agencies. American politics, more than that of many other nations, is shot through at every stage with protracted conflict.

But as we shall learn in the next chapter, that conflict is not easily described as, for example, always pitting liberals against conservatives. Not only do we have a lot of conflict, it is often messy conflict, a kind of political Tower of Babel. Foreign observers sometimes ask how we stand the confusion. The answer, of course, is that we have been doing it for more than 200 years. Maybe our Constitution is two centuries old, not in spite of this confusion, but because of it. We shall see.

WHAT WOULD YOU DO?

MEMORANDUM

To: *White House Chief of Staff Omar McField*

From: *Secretary of Education Alexandra Clark*

Subject: *Civics education in schools*

The decline in political knowledge that Americans have about our governmental system is alarming. We need to work in partnership with Congress and the states to promote civic education in secondary schools. In her upcoming State of the Union message, the President needs to make a case for high school civics education and endorse the creation of a bipartisan task force to develop guidelines for such classes.

News »

U.S. Students Score Low Marks in Civics Study

A recent survey shows that only 24 percent of twelfth-graders scored proficient or higher in civics, a statistic that does not bode well for an informed and engaged U.S. citizenry.

Arguments for:

1. A recent survey finds that only about six of ten Americans can name the vice president, and more than half believe incorrectly that the Supreme Court prohibits public-school classes that compare world religions.
2. Schools have a responsibility to teach students the principles of American constitutionalism, such as federalism and separation of church and state.
3. If the federal government does not take the initiative in promoting civics education, then states will develop their own standards, which will weaken understanding of our shared political principles.

Arguments against:

1. Civics education needs to be incorporated into existing courses, not taught separately.
2. Individuals need to take responsibility for understanding the political system in which they live.
3. Based on their individual historical experiences, states are better prepared than the federal government to determine how the underlying principles of American politics should be taught in their classrooms.

Your decision:

Support ________________ Oppose ________________

LEARNING OBJECTIVES

WHAT YOU NEED TO KNOW

☑ What is American political culture?

American political culture refers to long-standing patterns in how people view government, politics, and the economy.

☑ How does political culture differ from political ideology?

American political culture refers to views about how government should function and its guiding principles, whereas political ideology refers to specific views about which programs and policies government should pursue.

☑ Does the United States have a unique political culture compared to other advanced industrialized democracies?

The question of whether the United States is "exceptional" among democracies sparks much debate among social scientists and historians, and while characteristics of American exceptionalism are difficult to identify and measure, surveys discussed in this chapter do show that Americans view government, politics, religion, and economics differently than citizens of other advanced industrialized democracies.

RECONSIDERING WHO GOVERNS?

1. Do Americans trust their government?

More than it sometimes appears. Compared to the 1950s, we are much less likely to think the government does the right thing or cares about what we think. But when we look at our system of government—the Constitution and our political culture—we are very pleased with it. Americans are much more patriotic than people in many other democracies. And we display a great deal of support for churches in large measure because we are more religious than most Europeans.

2. Why do we accept great differences in wealth and income?

We believe in equality of opportunity and not equality of results. Wealthy people may have more political influence than ordinary folks, but if we think they earned their money through their own efforts and if they follow legal rules, we have no complaint about their wealth.

RECONSIDERING TO WHAT ENDS?

1. Why does our government behave differently than governments in countries with similar constitutions?

Our political culture has imbued it with more tolerance and a greater respect for orderly procedures and personal rights than can be found in nations with constitutions like ours. We are willing to let whoever wins an election govern without putting up a fuss, and our military does not intervene.

QUESTIONS TO CONSIDER

1. **How do people in other nations view American democracy?**
2. **How have the American public's views about the meaning of such constitutional principles as liberty and equality for government policies evolved over time?**
3. **With the massive growth in the U.S. population in the last century, what are Americans' expectations for representative democracy, federalism, and public officials in the 21st century?**
4. **What are the central principles of American political culture, and how are they reflected in the founding documents of the United States, such as the Declaration of Independence, the Constitution, and the *Federalist/Antifederalist* papers?**
5. **How do Americans differ from citizens of other democracies in their views about government and politics, and what factors may help to explain this difference?**
6. **How can Americans differ so strongly in political ideology and still share the same political culture? How might growing political polarization in the United States pose risks for American political culture?**

TO LEARN MORE

Polling organizations that frequently measure aspects of political culture:

www.roper.com

www.gallup.com

U.S. Census Bureau: **www.census.gov**

Almond, Gabriel, and Sidney Verba. *The Civic Culture.* Princeton, N.J.: Princeton University Press, 1963. A survey of the political cultures of five nations—the United States, Germany, Great Britain, Italy, and Mexico—as they were in 1959.

Brooks, Arthur C. *Who Really Cares?* New York: Basic Books, 2006. Fascinating study of who gives to charities in America and Europe.

Hartz, Louis. *The Liberal Tradition in America.* New York: Harcourt Brace Jovanovich, 1955. A stimulating interpretation of American political thought since the Founding, emphasizing the notion of a liberal consensus.

Lipset, Seymour Martin. *The First New Nation.* Rev. ed. New York: Norton, 1979. How the origins of American society gave rise to the partially competing values of equality and achievement and the ways in which these values shape political institutions.

McClosky, Herbert, and John Zaller. *The American Ethos: Public Attitudes Toward Capitalism and Democracy.* Cambridge: Harvard University Press, 1984. Study of the ways in which Americans evaluate political and economic arrangements.

Nivola, Pietro S., and David W. Brady, eds. *Red and Blue Nation?* Washington, D.C.: Brookings Institution, 2006. Compares

5 Civil Liberties

LEARNING OBJECTIVES

WHAT YOU NEED TO KNOW

- ☑ What is meant by "selective incorporation"?
- ☑ Do high school students have the same rights in school as do adults out of school?
- ☑ Does "symbolic speech" have the same protection as does making a speech?

WHO GOVERNS?

1. Why do the courts play so large a role in deciding what our civil liberties should be?

TO WHAT ENDS?

1. Why not display religious symbols on government property?
2. If a person confesses to committing a crime, why is that confession sometimes not used in court?
3. Does the Patriot Act reduce our liberties?

THEN In 1803, President Thomas Jefferson wrote to the governor of Pennsylvania complaining about the "licentiousness" of newspapers and urging him and other state leaders to bring about "a few prosecutions of the most prominent offenders." This would, Jefferson said, have a "wholesome effect in restoring the integrity of the presses."[1] Today, a president writing such a letter to anyone, especially a governor, would be subject to intense criticism. Prosecuting publishers who had attacked the government would strike most people as outrageous.

NOW There are two differences between then and now. First, the Supreme Court decided in 1833, as you will see later in this chapter, that the Bill of Rights only restricted the federal government. All that limited what state governments could do about free speech, a free press, and religious freedom had to be found in state constitutions. This law changed after the ratification of the Fourteenth Amendment in 1868 and was (slowly) interpreted by the Supreme Court to mean that the states must also honor freedom for speeches, publications, and churches.

The second change occurred in the minds of the American people. Gradually, but especially in the 20th century, they acquired a libertarian view of personal freedom. The government at every level ought to leave people alone with respect to what they said, wrote, read, or worshipped.

If you think that civil liberties are only an issue for people who make inflammatory speeches, think again. Dogs trained to sniff out drugs go down your high school corridors and detect marijuana in some lockers. The school authorities open and search your locker without permission or a court order. You are expelled from school without any hearing. Have your liberties been violated?

Angry at what you consider unfair treatment, you decide to wear a cloth American flag sewn to the seat of your pants, and your fellow students decide to wear black armbands to class to protest how you were treated. The

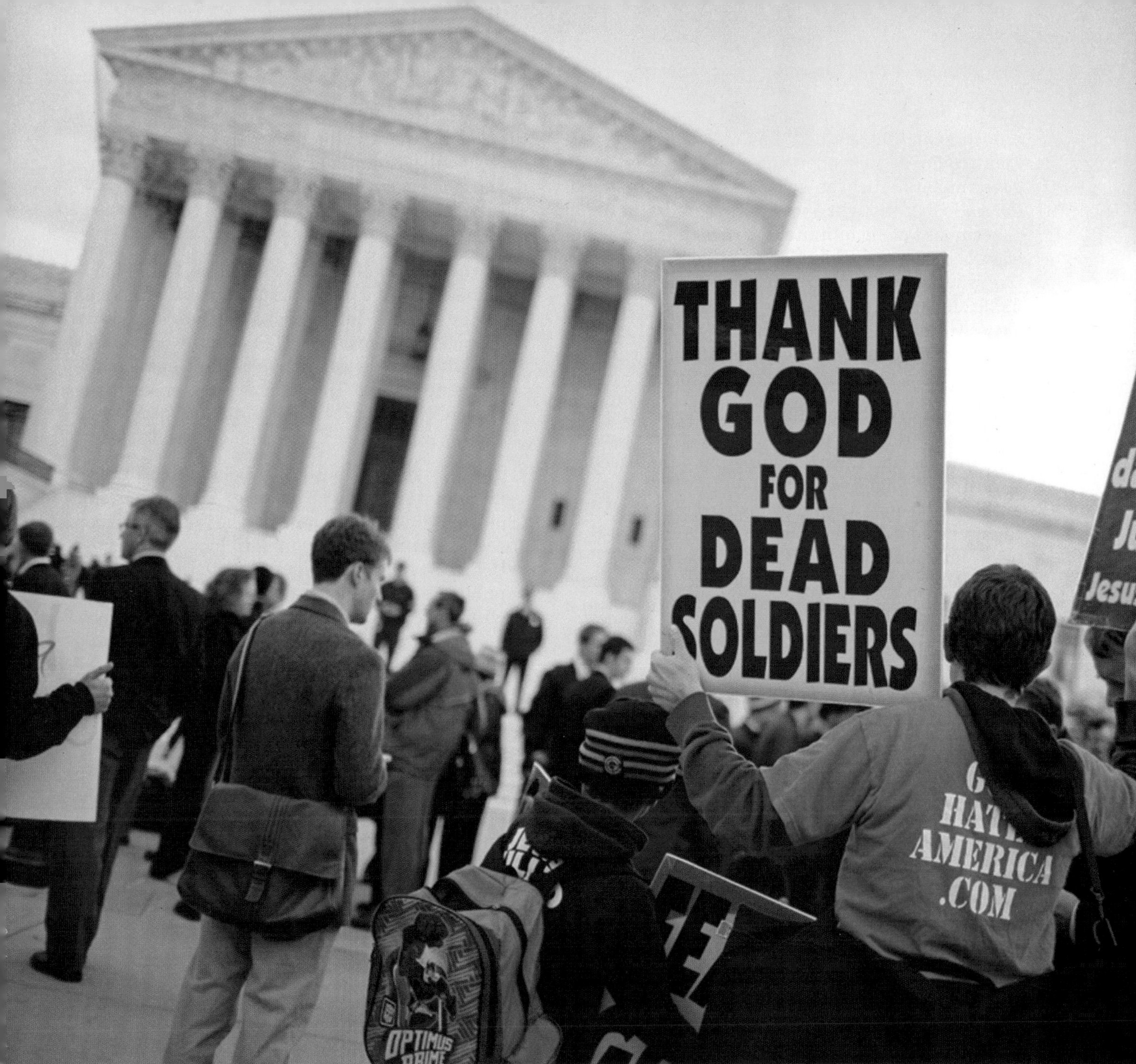

police arrest you for wearing a flag on your seat, and the school punishes your classmates for wearing armbands contrary to school regulations. Have your liberties, or theirs, been violated?

You go into federal court to find out. We cannot be certain how the court would decide the issues in this particular case, but in similar cases in the past the courts have held that school authorities can use dogs to detect drugs in schools and that these officials can conduct a "reasonable" search of you and your effects if they have a "reasonable suspicion" that you are violating a school rule. But they cannot punish your classmates for wearing black armbands, they cannot expel you without a hearing, and the state cannot make it illegal to treat the flag "contemptuously" (by sewing it to the seat of your pants, for example). In 2007, however, the Court allowed a school principal to punish a student for displaying a flag saying "Bong Hits 4 Jesus" that the official felt endorsed drug use during a school-supervised event. So a student's free-speech rights (and a school's authority to enforce discipline) now lie somewhere between disgracing a flag (okay) and encouraging drug use (not okay).[2]

Your claim that these actions violated your constitutional rights would have astonished the Framers of the Constitution. They thought they had written a document that stated what the federal government *could* do, not one that specified what state governments (such as school systems) *could not* do. And they thought they had created a national government of such limited powers that it was not even necessary to add a list—a bill of rights—stating what that government was forbidden from doing. It would be enough, for example, that the Constitution did not authorize the federal government to censor newspapers; an amendment prohibiting censorship would be superfluous.

The people who gathered in the state ratifying conventions weren't so optimistic. They suspected—rightly, as it turned out—that the federal government might well try to do things it was not authorized to do, and so they insisted that the Bill of Rights be added to the Constitution. But even they never imagined that the Bill of Rights would affect what *state* governments could do. Each state would decide that for itself, in its own constitution. And if by chance the Bill of Rights did apply to the states, surely its guarantees of free speech and freedom from unreasonable searches and seizures would apply to big issues—the freedom to attack the government in a newspaper editorial, for example, or to keep the police from breaking down the door of your home without a warrant. The courts would not be deciding who could wear what kinds of armbands or under what circumstances a school could expel a student.

Civil liberties are the protections the Constitution provides against the abuse of government power by, for example, censoring your speech. Civil rights, to be discussed in the next chapter, usually refers to protecting certain groups, such as women, gays, and African Americans, against discrimination. In practice, however, there is no clear line between civil liberties and civil rights. For example, is the right to an abortion a civil liberty or a civil right? In this chapter, we take a look at free speech, free press, religious freedom, and the rights of the accused. In the next one, we look at discrimination and abortion.

Culture and Civil Liberties

RIGHTS IN CONFLICT

We often think of "civil liberties" as a set of principles that protect the freedoms of all of us all of the time. That is true—up to a point. But in fact, the Constitution and the Bill of Rights contain a list of *competing* rights and duties. That competition becomes obvious when one person asserts one constitutional right or duty and another person asserts a different one. For example:

- At the funeral of a Marine killed in Iraq, Phelps and others from a church picketed it with signs saying "Thank God for Dead Soldiers" and other outrageous remarks. (The opening photo for this chapter shows such picketers outside the Supreme Court.) The Marine's father sued the church, claiming the picketers made him suffer. Free speech versus extreme emotional distress.
- The U.S. government has an obligation to "provide for the common defense" and, in pursuit of that duty, has claimed the right to keep secret certain military and diplomatic information. The *New York Times* claimed the right to publish such secrets as the "Pentagon Papers" without censorship, citing the Constitution's guarantee of freedom of the press. A duty and a right in conflict.
- Carl Jacob Kunz delivered inflammatory anti-Jewish speeches on the street corners of a Jewish neighborhood in New York City, suggesting, among other things, that Jews be "burnt in incinerators." The Jewish people living in that area were outraged. The New York police commissioner revoked Kunz's license to hold public meetings on the streets. When he continued to air his views on the public streets, Kunz was arrested for speaking without a permit. Freedom of speech versus the preservation of public order.

Even a disruptive high school student's right not to be a victim of arbitrary or unjustifiable expulsion is in partial conflict with the school's obligation to maintain an orderly environment in which learning can take place.

Political struggles over civil liberties follow much the same pattern as interest group politics involving economic issues, even though the claims in question are made by individuals. Indeed, there are formal, organized interest groups concerned with civil liberties. The Fraternal Order of the Police complains about restrictions on police powers, whereas the American Civil Liberties Union defends and seeks to enlarge those restrictions. Catholics have pressed for public support of parochial schools; Protestants and Jews have argued against it. Sometimes the opposed groups are entirely private; sometimes one or both are government agencies. Often their clashes end up in the courts. (When the Supreme Court decided the cases given earlier, Phelps, the *New York Times,* and Kunz all won.[3])

War has usually been the crisis that has restricted the liberty of some minority. For example:

- The Sedition Act was passed in 1798, making it a crime to write, utter, or publish "any false, scandalous, and malicious writing" with the intention of defaming the president, Congress, or the government or of exciting against the government "the hatred of the people." The occasion was a kind of half-war between the United States and France, stimulated by fear in this country of the violence following the French Revolution of 1789. The policy entrepreneurs were Federalist politicians who believed that Thomas Jefferson and his followers were supporters of the French Revolution and would, if they came to power, encourage here the kind of anarchy that seemed to be occurring in France.
- The Espionage and Sedition Acts were passed in 1917–1918, making it a crime to utter false statements that would interfere with the American military, to send through the mails material "advocating or urging treason, insurrection, or forcible resistance to any law of the United States," or to utter or write any disloyal, profane, scurrilous, or abusive language intended to incite resistance to the United States or to curtail war production. The occasion was World War I; the impetus was the fear that Germans in this country were spies and that radicals were seeking to overthrow the government. Under these laws, more than 2,000 persons were prosecuted (about half were convicted), and thousands of aliens were rounded up and deported. The policy entrepreneur leading this massive crackdown (the so-called Red Scare) was Attorney General A. Mitchell Palmer.
- The Smith Act was passed in 1940, the Internal Security Act in 1950, and the Communist Control Act in 1954. These laws made it illegal to advocate the overthrow of the U.S. government by force or violence (Smith Act), required members of the Communist Party to register with the government (Internal Security Act), and declared the Communist Party to be part of a conspiracy to overthrow the government (Communist Control Act). The occasion was World War II and the Korean War, which, like earlier wars, inspired fears that foreign agents (Nazi and Soviet) were trying to subvert the government. For the latter two laws, the policy entrepreneur was Senator Joseph McCarthy, who attracted a great deal of attention with his repeated (and sometimes inaccurate) claims that Soviet agents were working inside the U.S. government.

An Hispanic girl studies both English and Spanish in a bilingual classroom.

These laws had in common an effort to protect the nation from threats, real and imagined, posed by people who claimed to be exercising their freedom to speak, publish, organize, and assemble. In each case, a real threat (a war) led the government to narrow the limits of permissible speech and activity. Almost every time such restrictions were imposed, the Supreme Court was called upon to decide whether Congress (or sometimes state legislatures) had drawn those limits properly. In most instances, the Court tended to uphold the legislatures. But as time passed and the war or crisis ended, popular passions abated and many of the laws proved unimportant.

Though it is uncommon, some use is still made of the sedition laws. In the 1980s, various white supremacists and Puerto Rican nationalists were charged with sedition. In each case, the government alleged that the accused had not only spoken in favor of overthrowing the government but had actually engaged in violent actions such as bombings. Later in this chapter, we shall see how the Court has increasingly restricted the power of Congress and state legislatures to outlaw political speech; to be found guilty of sedition now, it usually is necessary to do something more serious than just talk about it.

CULTURAL CONFLICTS

In the main, the United States was originally the creation of white European Protestants. Blacks were, in most cases, slaves, and American Indians were not citizens. Catholics and Jews in the colonies composed a small minority, and often a persecuted one. The early schools tended to be religious—that is, Protestant—ones, many of them receiving state aid. It is not surprising that under these circumstances a view of America arose that equated "Americanism" with the values and habits of white Anglo-Saxon Protestants.

But immigration to this country brought a flood of new settlers, many of them coming from very different backgrounds (see Figure 5.1). In the mid-19th century, the potato famine led millions of Irish Catholics to migrate here. At the turn of the century, religious persecution and economic disadvantage brought more millions of people, many Catholic or Jewish, from southern and eastern Europe.

In recent decades, political conflict and economic want have led Hispanics (mostly from Mexico but increasingly from all parts of Latin America), Caribbeans, Africans, Middle Easterners, Southeast Asians, and Asians to cross our borders—some legally, some illegally. Among them have been Buddhists, Catholics, Muslims, and members of many other religious and cultural groups.

Ethnic, religious, and cultural differences have given rise to different views as to the meaning and scope of certain constitutionally protected freedoms. For example:

- Many Jewish groups find it offensive for a crèche (that is, a scene depicting the birth of Christ in a manger) to be displayed in front of a government building such as city hall at Christmastime, while many Catholics and Protestants regard such displays as an important part of our cultural heritage. Does a religious display on public property violate the First Amendment requirement that the government pass no law "respecting an establishment of religion"?

Figure 5.1
Annual Legal Immigration, 1850–2010

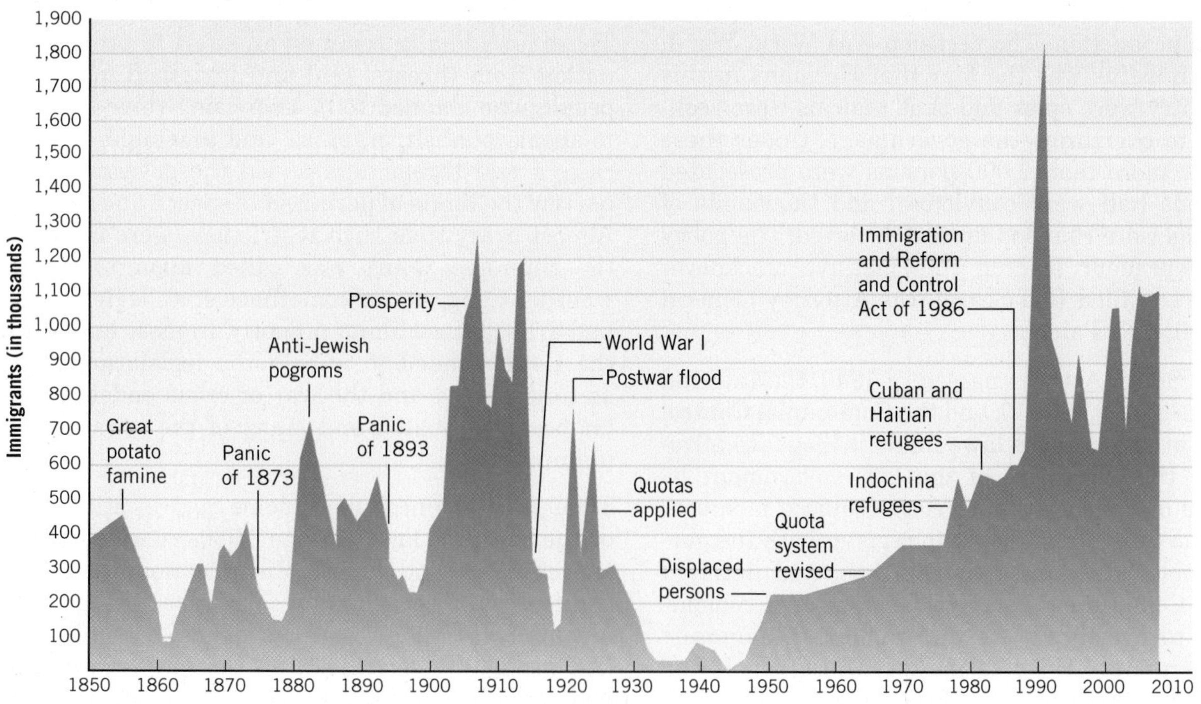

Note: Figures for 1989 and 1990 include persons granted permanent residence under the legalization program of the Immigration and Reform and Control Act of 1986.

Source: Data from Office of Immigration Statistics, *2010 Yearbook of Immigration Statistics* (Washington, D.C.: Department of Homeland Security, 2011), 1.

- Many English-speaking people believe that the public schools ought to teach all students to speak and write English, because the language is part of our nation's cultural heritage. Some Hispanic groups argue that the schools should teach pupils in both English and Spanish, since Spanish is part of the Hispanic cultural heritage. Is bilingual education constitutionally required?
- The Boy Scouts of America refuses to allow homosexual men to become scout leaders even though federal law says that homosexuals may not be the victims of discrimination. Many civil libertarians and homosexuals challenged this policy because it discriminated against gays, while the Boy Scouts defended it because their organization was a private association free to make its own rules. (The Supreme Court in 2000 upheld the Boy Scouts on the grounds of their right to associate freely.)

Even within a given cultural tradition there are important differences of opinion as to the balance between community sensitivities and personal self-expression. To some people the sight of a store carrying pornographic books or a theater showing a pornographic movie is deeply offensive; to others, pornography is offensive but such establishments ought to be tolerated to ensure that laws restricting them do not also restrict politically or artistically important forms of speech; to still others, pornography itself is not especially offensive. What forms of expression are entitled to constitutional protection?

APPLYING THE BILL OF RIGHTS TO THE STATES

For many years after the Constitution was signed and the Bill of Rights was added to it as amendments, the liberties these documents stated applied only to the federal government. The Supreme Court made this clear in a case decided in 1833.[4] Except for Article I which, among other things, banned ex post facto laws and guaranteed the right of habeas corpus, the Constitution was silent on what the states could not do to their residents.

This began to change a fter the Civil War when new amendments were ratified in order to ban slavery and protect newly freed slaves. The Fourteenth Amendment, ratified in 1868, was the most important addition. It said that no state shall "deprive any person of life, liberty, or property without **due process of law**" (a phrase now known as the "due process clause") and that no state shall "deny to any person within its jurisdiction the **equal protection of the laws**" (a phrase now known as the "equal protection clause").

Beginning in 1897, the Supreme Court started to use these two phrases as a way of applying certain rights to state governments. It first said that no state could take private property without paying just compensation, and then in 1925 held, in the *Gitlow* case, that the federal guarantees of free speech and free press also applied to the states. In 1937, it went much further and said in *Palko v. Connecticut* that certain rights should be applied to the states because, in the Court's words, they "represented the very essence of a scheme of ordered liberty" and were "principles of justice so rooted in the traditions and conscience of our people as to be ranked fundamental."[5]

The Supreme Court began the process of **selective incorporation** by which some, but not all, federal rights also applied to the states. But which rights are so "fundamental" that they ought to govern the states? There is no entirely clear answer to this question, but in general the entire Bill of Rights is now applied to the states except for the following:

- The right not to have soldiers forcibly quartered in private homes (Third Amendment)
- The right to be indicted by a grand jury before being tried for a serious crime (Fifth Amendment)
- The right to a jury trial in civil cases (Seventh Amendment)
- The ban on excessive bail and fines (Eighth Amendment)

The Second Amendment that protects "the right of the people to keep and bear arms" may or may not apply to the states. In 2008, the Supreme Court in *District of Columbia v. Heller* held for the first time that this amendment did not allow the federal government to ban the private possession of firearms. But the case arose in the District of Columbia, which is governed by federal law. The decision raised two questions: First, will this ban be incorporated so that it also applies to state governments? In 2010, the Supreme Court said in *McDonald v. Chicago* that the decision in the *Heller* case also applied to the states.[6] Second, will it still be possible to regulate gun purchases and gun use even if the government cannot ban guns? Based on other court cases, the answer appears to be yes.

due process of law Denies the government the right, without due process, to deprive people of life, liberty, and property.

equal protection of the law A standard of equal treatment that must be observed by the government.

selective incorporation The process whereby the Court has applied many parts of the Bill of Rights to the states.

RESEARCH FRONTIERS

Does "In-Your-Face" Television Affect Political Tolerance?

In a representative democracy, constitutional and related legal protections for free speech and other civil liberties ultimately depend on the degree to which average citizens are ready to respect each other's rights and willing to tolerate ideas that the majority dislikes or even despises.

Three separate but related lines of research examine how popular norms relating to political tolerance respecting free speech and other civil liberties arise, persist, and change.

The first and oldest line of research concerns a decades-old disjuncture in public attitudes toward civil liberties: wide majorities favor civil liberties including free speech and assembly, yet only about a third to half favor extending these liberties to groups they strongly dislike.

The second line of research tracks and analyzes changes in public attitudes. For example, in recent decades, there have been successive shifts in public attitudes regarding advocacy for homosexual rights and policies favoring gay rights: tolerance for the expression of homosexual rights has increased steadily, and in 2009, 59 percent of Americans favored allowing gays to serve openly in the military.

The third line of research attempts to understand more precisely how schooling, the media, and other influences determine mass levels of political toleration and openness to dissent.

One well-established finding here is that, other things equal, more formal schooling is associated with greater political tolerance even toward minority groups that one views as deplorable or even dangerous.

But a newer line of research probes how Americans perceive others whose political views they are strongly inclined to dispute or denounce. For example, through a series of experimental studies, University of Pennsylvania political scientist Diana C. Mutz has examined present-day "television discourse" in relation to whether average citizens respect and treat their "political foes" as a "legitimate opposition."

As Mutz observes, today much of the political debate carried on television tends to be "highly uncivil in tone," complete with accompanying camera work featuring facial close-ups that "intensify emotional reactions" in the viewing audience. This televised "in-your-face" politics succeeds in airing oppositional views, but, as Mutz concludes, it also "convinces people that the opposition is even less legitimate than they would have thought without any viewing."

- When, for whatever reasons, average citizens become less willing to perceive even moderate political opponents as legitimate, do they also thereby become less willing to respect or protect civil liberties exercised by citizens they view as "unworthy" or "extreme"? Researchers in various fields are just now asking that question. What is your best guess about what they will find?
- Do you think that newspapers and magazines are less prone to promote "in-your-face" politics than television?
- Do you suppose that "television discourse" was less polarizing in the past than it is today?

Source: Diana C. Mutz, "Effects of 'In-Your-Face' Television Discourse on Perceptions of a Legitimate Opposition," *American Political Science Review* 101, November 2007, pp. 623–635; "Opinion About Gays in the Military," Pew Research, March 25, 2009.

Interpreting and Applying the First Amendment

The First Amendment contains the language that has been at issue in most of the cases to which we have thus far referred. It has roughly two parts: one protecting **freedom of expression** ("Congress shall make no law . . . abridging the freedom of speech, or of the press, or the right of people peaceably to assemble, and to petition the government for a redress of grievances") and the other protecting **freedom of religion** ("Congress shall make no law respecting an establishment of religion; or abridging the free exercise thereof").

freedom of expression Right of people to speak, publish, and assemble.

freedom of religion People shall be free to exercise their religion, and government may not establish a religion.

prior restraint Censorship of a publication.

SPEECH AND NATIONAL SECURITY

The traditional view of free speech and a free press was expressed by William Blackstone, the great English jurist, in his *Commentaries,* published in 1765. A free press is essential to a free state, he wrote, but the freedom that the press should enjoy is the freedom from **prior restraint**—that is, freedom from censorship, or rules telling a newspaper in advance what it can publish. Once a newspaper has published an article or a person has delivered a speech, that paper or speaker has to take the consequences if what was written or said proves to be "improper, mischievous, or illegal."[7]

The U.S. Sedition Act of 1798 was in keeping with traditional English law. Like it, the act imposed no prior restraint on publishers; it did, however, make them liable to punishment after the fact. The act was an improvement over the English law, however, because unlike the British model, it entrusted the decision to a jury, not a judge, and allowed the defendant to be acquitted if he or she could prove the truth of what had been published. Although several newspaper publishers were convicted under the act, none of these cases reached the Supreme Court. When Jefferson became president in 1801, he pardoned the people who had been imprisoned under the Sedition Act. Though Jeffersonians objected vehemently to the law, their principal objection was not to the idea of holding newspapers accountable for what they published but to letting the *federal* government do this. Jefferson was perfectly prepared to have the *states* punish what he called the "overwhelming torrent of slander" by means of "a few prosecutions of the most prominent offenders."[8]

It would be another century before the federal government would attempt to define the limits of free speech and writing. Perhaps recalling the widespread opposition to the sweep of the 1798 act, Congress in 1917–1918 placed restrictions not on publications that were critical of the government but only on those that advocated "treason, insurrection, or forcible resistance" to federal laws or attempted to foment disloyalty or mutiny in the armed services.

In 1919, this new law was examined by the Supreme Court when it heard the case of Charles T. Schenck, who had been convicted of violating the Espionage Act because he had mailed circulars to men eligible for the draft, urging them to resist. At issue was the constitutionality of the Espionage Act and, more broadly, the scope of Congress's power to control speech. One view held that the First Amendment prevented Congress from passing *any* law restricting speech; the other held that Congress could punish dangerous speech. For a unanimous Supreme Court, Justice Oliver Wendell Holmes announced a rule by which to settle the matter. It soon became known as the **clear-and-present-danger test:**

> *The question in every case is whether the words used are used in such circumstances and are of such a nature as to create a clear and present danger that they will bring about the substantive evils that Congress has a right to prevent.*[9]

The Court held that Schenck's leaflets did create such a danger, and so his conviction was upheld. In explaining why, Holmes said that not even the Constitution protects a person who has been "falsely shouting fire in a theatre and causing a panic." In this case, things that might safely be said in peacetime may be punished in wartime.

The clear-and-present-danger test may have clarified the law, but it kept no one out of jail. Schenck went, and so did the defendants in five other cases in the period 1919–1927, even though during this time Holmes, the author of the test, shifted his position and began writing dissenting opinions in which he urged that the test had not been met and so the defendant should go free.

clear-and-present-danger test Law should not punish speech unless there was a clear and present danger of producing harmful actions.

Landmark Cases

Incorporation

- ***Gitlow v. New York* (1925):** Supreme Court says the First Amendment applies to states.
- ***Palko v. Connecticut* (1937):** Supreme Court says that states must observe all "fundamental" liberties.
- ***McDonald v. Chicago* (2010):** The Second Amendment that allows the people to keep and bear arms applies to state governments as well as the federal one.

Women picketed in front of the White House, urging President Warren Harding to release political radicals arrested during his administration.

In 1925, Benjamin Gitlow was convicted of violating New York's sedition law—a law similar to the federal Sedition Act of 1918—by passing out some leaflets, one of which advocated the violent overthrow of our government. The Supreme Court upheld his conviction but added, as we have seen, a statement that changed constitutional history: freedom of speech and of the press were now among the "fundamental personal rights" protected by the due process clause of the Fourteenth Amendment from infringements by *state* action.[10] Thereafter, state laws involving speech, the press, and peaceful assembly were struck down by the Supreme Court for being in violation of the freedom-of-expression guarantees of the First Amendment, made applicable to the states by the Fourteenth Amendment.[11]

The clear-and-present-danger test was a way of balancing the competing demands of free expression and national security. As the memory of World War I and the ensuing Red Scare evaporated, the Court began to develop other tests, ones that shifted the balance more toward free expression. Some of these tests are listed in the box on page 111.

But when a crisis reappears, as it did in World War II and the Korean War, the Court has tended to defer, up to a point, to legislative judgments about the need to protect national security. For example, it upheld the conviction of 11 leaders of the Communist Party for having advocated the violent overthrow of the U.S. government, a violation of the Smith Act of 1940.

This conviction once again raised the hard question of the circumstances under which words can be punished. Hardly anybody would deny that actually *trying* to overthrow the government is a crime; the question is whether *advocating* its overthrow is a crime. In the case of the 11 communist leaders, the Court said that the government did not have to wait to protect itself until "the *putsch* [rebellion] is about to be executed, the plans have been laid and the signal is awaited." Even if the communists were not likely to be successful in their effort, the Court held that specifically advocating violent overthrow could be punished. "In each case," the opinion read, the courts "must ask whether the gravity of the 'evil,' discounted by its improbability, justifies such invasion of free speech as is necessary to avoid the danger."[12]

But as the popular worries about communists began to subside and the membership of the Supreme Court changed, the Court began to tip the balance even farther toward free expression. By 1957, the Court made it clear that for advocacy to be punished, the government would have to show not just that a person believed in the overthrow of the government but also that he or she was using words "calculated to incite" that overthrow.[13]

By 1969, the pendulum had swung to the point where the speech would have to be judged likely to incite "imminent" unlawful action. When Clarence Brandenburg, a Ku Klux Klan leader in Ohio, made a speech before Klan members in which he called for "revengeance" [sic] against blacks and Jews (described with racial slurs) and called for a march on Washington, he was arrested and convicted for "advocating" violence. The U.S. Supreme Court reversed the conviction, holding that the First Amendment protects speech that abstractly advocates violence unless that speech will incite or produce "imminent lawless action."[14]

This means that no matter how offensive or provocative some forms of expression may be, this expression has powerful constitutional protections. In 1977, a group of American Nazis wanted to parade through the streets of Skokie, Illinois, a community with a large Jewish population. The residents, outraged, sought to ban the march. Many feared violence if it occurred. But the lower courts, under prodding from the Supreme Court, held that, noxious and provocative as the anti-Semitic slogans of the Nazis may be, the Nazi party had a constitutional right to speak and parade peacefully.[15]

Similar reasoning led the Supreme Court in 1992 to overturn a Minnesota statute that made it a crime to display symbols or objects, such as a Nazi swastika or a burning cross, that are likely to cause alarm or resentment among an ethnic or racial group, such as Jews or African Americans.[16] On the other hand, if you are convicted of actually hurting someone, you may be given a tougher sentence if it can be shown that you were motivated to assault them by racial or ethnic hatred.[17] To be punished for such a hate crime, your bigotry must result in some direct and physical harm and not just the display of an odious symbol.

Tim Boyle/Newsmakers/Getty Images News/Getty Images

A Ku Klux Klan member uses his constitutional right to free speech to utter "white power" chants in Skokie, Illinois.

What Is Speech?

If most political speaking or writing is permissible, save that which actually incites someone to take illegal actions, what *kinds* of speaking and writing qualify for this broad protection? Though the Constitution says that the legislature may make "no law" abridging freedom of speech or the press, and although some justices have argued that this means literally *no* law, the Court has held that there are at least four forms of speaking and writing that are not automatically granted full constitutional protection: libel, obscenity, symbolic speech, and false advertising.

LIBEL

A **libel** is a written statement that defames the character of another person. (If the statement is oral, it is called a *slander.*) The libel or slander must harm the person being attacked. In some countries, such as England, it is easy to sue another person for libel and to collect. In this country, it is much harder. For one thing, you must show that the libelous statement was false. If it was true, you cannot collect no matter how badly it harmed you.

A beauty contest winner was awarded $14 million (later reduced on appeal) when she proved that *Penthouse* magazine had libeled her. Actress Carol Burnett collected a large sum from a libel suit brought against a gossip newspaper. But when Theodore Roosevelt sued a newspaper for falsely claiming that he was a drunk, the jury awarded him damages of only six cents.[18]

libel Writing that falsely injures another person.

If you are a public figure, it is much harder to win a libel suit. A public figure such as an elected official, a candidate for office, an army general, or a well-known celebrity must prove not only that the publication was false and damaging but also that the words were published with "actual malice"—that is, with reckless disregard for their truth or falsity or with knowledge that they were false.[19] Israeli General Ariel Sharon was able to prove that the statements made about him by *Time* magazine were false and damaging but not that they were the result of "actual malice."

For a while, people who felt they had been libeled would bring suit in England against an American author. One Saudi leader sued an American author who had accused him of financing terrorism even though she had not sold her book in England (but word about it had been on the Internet). This strategy, called "libel tourism," was ended in 2010 when Congress unanimously passed and the president signed a bill that bars enforcement in U.S. courts of libel actions against Americans if what they published would not be libelous under American law.

OBSCENITY

Obscenity is not protected by the First Amendment. The Court has always held that obscene materials, because they have no redeeming social value and are calculated chiefly to appeal to one's sexual rather than political or literary interests, can be regulated by the state. The problem, of course, arises with the meaning of *obscene*. In the period from 1957 to 1968, the Court decided 13 major cases involving the definition of obscenity, which resulted in 55 separate opinions.[20] Some justices, such as Hugo Black, believed that the First Amendment protected all publications, even wholly obscene ones. Others believed that obscenity deserved no protection and struggled heroically to define the term. Still others shared the view of former Justice Potter Stewart, who objected to "hard-core pornography" but admitted that the best definition he could offer was "I know it when I see it."[21]

It is unnecessary to review in detail the many attempts by the Court at defining obscenity. The justices have made it clear that nudity and sex are not, by definition, obscene and that they will provide First Amendment protection to anything that has political, literary, or artistic merit, allowing the government to punish only the distribution of "hard-core pornography." Their most recent definition of this is as follows: to be obscene, the work, taken as a whole, must be judged by "the average person applying contemporary community standards" to appeal to the "prurient interest" or to depict "in a patently offensive way, sexual conduct specifically defined by applicable state law" and to lack "serious literary, artistic, political, or scientific value."[22]

After Albany, Georgia, decided that the movie *Carnal Knowledge* was obscene by contemporary local standards, the Supreme Court overturned the distributor's conviction on the grounds that the authorities in Albany failed to show that the film depicted "patently offensive hard-core sexual conduct."[23]

It is easy to make sport of the problems the Court has faced in trying to decide obscenity cases (one conjures up images of black-robed justices leafing through the pages of *Hustler* magazine, taking notes), but these problems reveal, as do other civil liberties cases, the continuing problem of balancing competing claims. One part of the community wants to read or see whatever it wishes; another part wants to protect private acts from public degradation. The first part cherishes liberty above all; the second values decency above liberty. The former fears that *any* restriction on literature will lead to *pervasive* restrictions; the latter believes that reasonable people can distinguish (or reasonable laws can require them to distinguish) between patently offensive and artistically serious work.

Anyone strolling today through an "adult" bookstore must suppose that no restrictions at all exist on the distribution of pornographic works. This condition does not arise simply from the doctrines of the Court. Other factors operate as well, including the priorities of local law enforcement officials, the political climate of the community, the procedures that must be followed to bring a viable court case, the clarity and workability of state and local laws on the subject, and the difficulty of changing the behavior of many people by prosecuting one person. The current view of the Court is that localities can decide for themselves whether to tolerate hard-core pornography; but if they choose not to, they must meet some fairly strict constitutional tests.

The protections given by the Court to expressions of sexual or erotic interest have not been limited to books, magazines, and films. Almost any form of visual or auditory communication can be considered "speech" and thus protected by the First Amendment. In one case, even nude dancing was given protection as a form of "speech,"[24] although in 1991 the Court held that nude dancing was only "marginally" within the purview of First Amendment protections, and so it upheld an Indiana statute that banned *totally* nude dancing.[25]

Of late some feminist organizations have attacked pornography on the grounds that it exploits and degrades women. They persuaded Indianapolis to pass an ordinance that defined pornography as portrayals of the "graphic, sexually explicit subordination of women" and allowed people to sue the producers of such material. Sexually explicit portrayals of women in positions of equality were not defined as pornography. The Court disagreed. In 1986, it affirmed a lower-court ruling that such an ordinance was a violation of the First Amendment because it represented a legislative preference for one form of expression (women in positions of equality) over another (women in positions of subordination).[26]

One constitutionally permissible way to limit the spread of pornographic materials has been to establish rules governing where in a city they can be sold. When one city adopted a zoning ordinance prohibiting an "adult" movie theater from locating within 1,000 feet of any church, school, park, or residential area, the Court upheld the ordinance, noting that the purpose of the law was not to regulate speech but to regulate the use of land. And in any case, the adult theaters still had much of the city's land area in which to find a location.[27]

With the advent of the Internet, it has become more difficult for the government to regulate obscenity. The Internet spans the globe. It offers an amazing variety of materials—some educational, some entertaining, some sexually explicit. But it is difficult to apply the Supreme Court's standard for judging whether sexual material is obscene—the "average person" applying "contemporary community standards"—to the Internet, because there is no easy way to tell what "the community" is. Is it the place where the recipient lives or the place where the material originates? And since no one is in charge of the Internet, who can

How Things Work

Testing Restrictions on Expression

The Supreme Court has employed various standards and tests to decide whether a restriction on freedom of expression is constitutionally permissible.

1. **Preferred position** The right of free expression, though not absolute, occupies a higher, or more preferred, position than many other constitutional rights, such as property rights. This is still a controversial rule; nonetheless, the Court always approaches a restriction on expression skeptically.
2. **Prior restraint** With scarcely any exceptions, the Court will not tolerate a prior restraint on expression, such as censorship, even when it will allow subsequent punishment of improper expressions (such as libel).
3. **Imminent danger** Punishment for uttering inflammatory sentiments will be allowed only if there is an imminent danger that the utterances will incite an unlawful act.
4. **Neutrality** Any restriction on speech, such as a requirement that parades or demonstrations not disrupt other people in the exercise of their rights, must be neutral—that is, it must not favor one group more than another.
5. **Clarity** If you must obtain a permit to hold a parade, the law must set forth clear (as well as neutral) standards to guide administrators in issuing that permit. Similarly, a law punishing obscenity must contain a clear definition of obscenity.
6. **Least-restrictive means** If it is necessary to restrict the exercise of one right to protect the exercise of another, the restriction should employ the least-restrictive means to achieve its end. For example, if press coverage threatens a person's right to a fair trial, the judge may only do what is minimally necessary to that end, such as transferring the case to another town rather than issuing a "gag order."

Cases cited, by item: (1) *United States v. Carolene Products,* 304 U.S. 144 (1938). (2) *Near v. Minnesota,* 283 U.S. 697 (1931). (3) *Brandenburg v. Ohio,* 395 U.S. 444 (1969). (4) *Kunz v. New York,* 340 U.S. 290 (1951). (5) *Hynes v. Mayor and Council of Oradell,* 425 U.S. 610 (1976). (6) *Nebraska Press Association v. Stuart,* 427 U.S. 539 (1976).

be held responsible for controlling offensive material? Since anybody can send anything to anybody else without knowing the age or location of the recipient, how can the Internet protect children? When Congress tried to ban obscene, indecent, or "patently offensive" materials from the Internet, the Supreme Court struck down the law as unconstitutional. The Court went even further with child pornography. Though it has long held that child pornography is illegal even if it is not obscene because of the government's interest in protecting children, it would not let Congress ban pornography involving computer-designed children. Under the 1996 law, it would be illegal to display computer simulations of children engaged in sex even if no real children were involved. The Court said "no." It held that Congress could not ban "virtual" child pornography without violating the First Amendment because, in its view, the law might bar even harmless depictions of children and sex (for example, in a book on child psychology).[28]

SYMBOLIC SPEECH

You cannot ordinarily claim that an illegal act should be protected because that action is meant to convey a political message. For example, if you burn your draft card in protest against the foreign policy of the United States, you can be punished for the illegal act (burning the card), even if your intent was to communicate your beliefs. The Court reasoned that giving such **symbolic speech** the same protection as real speech would open the door to permitting all manner of illegal actions—murder, arson, rape—if the perpetrator meant thereby to send a message.[29]

On the other hand, a statute that makes it illegal to burn the American flag is an unconstitutional infringement of free speech.[30] Why is there a difference between a draft card and the flag? The Court argues that the government has a right to run a military draft and so can

symbolic speech An act that conveys a political message.

"Symbolic speech:" When young men burned their draft cards during the 1960s to protest the Vietnam War, the Supreme Court ruled that it was an illegal act for which they could be punished.

protect draft cards, even if this incidentally restricts speech. But the only motive that the government has in banning flag-burning is to restrict this form of speech, and that would make such a restriction improper.

The American people were outraged by the flag-burning decision, and in response the House and Senate passed by huge majorities (380 to 38 and 91 to 9) a law making it a federal crime to burn the flag. But the Court struck this law down as unconstitutional.[31] Now that it was clear that only a constitutional amendment could make flag-burning illegal, Congress was asked to propose one. But it would not. Earlier members of the House and Senate had supported a law banning flag-burning with over 90 percent of their votes, but when asked to make that law a constitutional amendment they could not muster the necessary two-thirds majorities. The reason is that Congress is much more reluctant to amend the Constitution than to pass new laws. Several members decided that flag-burning was wrong, but not so wrong or so common as to justify an amendment.

Commercial and Youthful Speech

If people have a right to speak and publish, do corporations, interest groups, and children have the same right? By and large the answer is yes, though there are some exceptions.

When the attorney general of Massachusetts tried to prevent the First National Bank of Boston from spending money to influence votes in a local election, the Court stepped in and blocked him. The Court held that a corporation, like a person, has certain First Amendment rights. Similarly, when the federal government tried to limit the spending of a group called Massachusetts Citizens for Life (an antiabortion organization), the Court held that such organizations have First Amendment rights.[32] The Court has also told states that they cannot forbid liquor stores to advertise their prices and informed federal authorities that they cannot prohibit casinos from plugging gambling.[33]

When the California Public Utility Commission tried to compel one of the utilities it regulates, the Pacific Gas and Electric Company, to enclose in its monthly bills to customers statements written by groups attacking the utility, the Supreme Court blocked the agency, saying that forcing it to disseminate political statements violated the firm's free-speech rights. "The identity of the speaker is not decisive in determining whether speech is protected," the Court said. "Corporations and other associations, like individuals, contribute to the 'discussion, debate, and the dissemination of information and ideas' that the First Amendment seeks to foster." In this case, the right to speak includes the choice of what *not* to say.[34]

Even though corporations have some First Amendment rights, the government can place more limits on commercial than on noncommercial speech. The legislature can place restrictions on advertisements for cigarettes, liquor, and gambling; it can even regulate advertising for some less harmful products provided that the regulations are narrowly tailored and serve a substantial public interest.[35] If the regulations are too broad or do not serve a clear interest, then ads are entitled to some constitutional protection. For example, the states cannot bar lawyers from advertising or accountants from personally soliciting clients.[36]

A big exception to the free-speech rights of corporations and labor unions groups was imposed by the McCain-Feingold campaign finance reform law passed in 2002. Many groups, ranging from the American Civil Liberties Union and the AFL-CIO to the National Rifle Association and the Chamber of Commerce, felt that the law banned legitimate speech. Under its terms, organizations could not pay for "electioneering communications" on radio or television that "refer" to candidates for federal office within 60 days before the election. But the Supreme Court temporarily struck down these arguments, upholding the law in *McConnell v. Federal Election Commission*. The Court said ads that only

Landmark Cases

Free Speech and Free Press

- ***Schenck v. United States* (1919):** Speech may be punished if it creates a clear-and-present-danger test of illegal acts.
- ***Chaplinksy v. New Hampshire* (1942):** "Fighting words" are not protected by the First Amendment.
- ***New York Times v. Sullivan* (1964):** To libel a public figure, there must be "actual malice."
- ***Tinker v. Des Moines* (1969):** Public-school students may wear armbands to class protesting against America's war in Vietnam when such display does not disrupt classes.
- ***Miller v. California* (1973):** Obscenity defined as appealing to prurient interests of an average person with materials that lack literary, artistic, political, or scientific value.
- ***Texas v. Johnson* (1989):** There may not be a law to ban flag-burning.
- ***Reno v. ACLU* (1997):** A law that bans sending "indecent" material to minors over the Internet is unconstitutional because "indecent" is too vague and broad a term.
- ***FEC v. Wisconsin Right to Life* (2007):** Prohibits campaign finance reform law from banning political advocacy.
- ***Citizens United v. FEC* (2010):** The part of the McCain-Feingold campaign finance reform law that prevents corporations and labor unions from spending money on advertisements, independent of political candidates or parties, in political campaigns is unconstitutional.

mentioned but did not "expressly advocate" a candidate were ways of influencing the election. Some dissenting opinion complained that a Court that had once given free-speech protection to nude dancing ought to give it to political speech.[37] But seven years later, the Court, in *Citizens United v. Federal Election Commission,* decided that the part of the McCain-Feingold law that denied corporations and labor unions the right to run ads, independently of a political party's or candidate's campaign, about the election violated their rights to free speech under the Constitution.

Under certain circumstances, young people may have less freedom of expression than adults. In 1988, the Supreme Court held that the principal of Hazelwood High School could censor articles appearing in the student-edited newspaper. The newspaper was published using school funds and was part of a journalism class. The principal ordered the deletion of stories dealing with student pregnancies and the impact of parental divorce on students. The student editors sued, claiming their First Amendment rights had been violated. The Court agreed that students do not "shed their constitutional rights to freedom of speech or expression at the schoolhouse gate" and that they cannot be punished for expressing on campus their personal views. But students do not have exactly the same rights as adults if the exercise of those rights impedes the educational mission of the school. Students may lawfully say things on campus, as individuals, that they cannot say if they are part of school-sponsored activities, such as plays or school-run newspapers, that are part of the curriculum. School-sponsored activities can be controlled so long as the controls are "reasonably related to legitimate pedagogical concerns."[38]

Church and State

Everybody knows, correctly, the language of the First Amendment that protects freedom of speech and the press, though most people are not aware of how complex the legal interpretations of these provisions have become. But many people also believe, wrongly, that the language of the First Amendment clearly requires the "separation of church and state." It does not.

What that amendment actually says is quite different and maddeningly unclear. It has two parts. The first, often referred to as the **free-exercise clause,** states that Congress shall make no law prohibiting the "free exercise" of religion. The second, which is called the **establishment clause,** states that Congress shall make no law "respecting an establishment of religion."

free-exercise clause First Amendment requirement that law cannot prevent free exercise of religion.

establishment clause First Amendment ban on laws "respecting an establishment of religion."

THE FREE-EXERCISE CLAUSE

The free-exercise clause is the clearer of the two, though by no means is it lacking in ambiguity. It obviously means that Congress cannot pass a law prohibiting Catholics from celebrating Mass, requiring Baptists to become Episcopalians, or preventing Jews from holding a bar mitzvah. Since the First Amendment has been applied to the states via the due process clause of the Fourteenth Amendment, it means that state governments cannot pass such laws either. In general, the courts have treated religion like speech: you can pretty much do or say what you want so long as it does not cause some serious harm to others.

Even some laws that do not appear on their face to apply to churches may be unconstitutional if their enforcement imposes particular burdens on churches or greater burdens on some churches than others. For example, a state cannot apply a license fee on door-to-door solicitors when the solicitor is a Jehovah's Witness selling religious tracts.[39] By the same token, the courts ruled that the city of Hialeah, Florida, cannot ban animal sacrifices by members of an Afro-Caribbean religion called Santeria. Since killing animals generally is not illegal (if it were, there could be no hamburgers or chicken sandwiches served in Hialeah's restaurants, and rat traps would be unlawful), the ban in this case was clearly directed against a specific religion and hence was unconstitutional.[40]

Having the right to exercise your religion freely does not mean, however, that you are exempt from laws binding other citizens, even when the law goes against your religious beliefs. A man cannot have more than one wife, even if (as once was the case with Mormons) polygamy is thought desirable on religious grounds.[41] For religious reasons, you may oppose being vaccinated or having blood transfusions, but if the state passes a compulsory vaccination law or orders that a blood transfusion be given to a sick child, the courts will not block it on grounds of religious liberty.[42] Similarly, if you belong to an Indian tribe that uses a drug, peyote, in religious ceremonies, you cannot claim that your freedom was abridged if the state decides to ban the use of peyote, provided the law applies equally to all.[43] Since airports have a legitimate need for tight security measures, begging can be outlawed in them even if some of the people doing the begging are part of a religious group (in this case, the Hare Krishnas).[44]

Unfortunately, some conflicts between religious belief and public policy are even more difficult to settle. What if you believe on religious grounds that war is immoral? The draft laws have always exempted a conscientious objector from military duty, and the Court has upheld such exemptions. But the Court has gone further: it has said that people cannot be drafted even if they do not believe in a Supreme Being or belong to any religious tradition, so long as their "consciences, spurred by deeply held moral, ethical, or religious beliefs, would give them no rest or peace if they allowed themselves to become part of an instrument of war."[45] Do exemptions on such grounds create an opportunity for some people to evade the draft because of their political preferences? In trying to answer such questions, the courts often have had to try to define a religion—no easy task.

Judy Griesedieck/Time & Life Pictures/Getty Images

Public schools cannot organize prayers, but private ones can.

And even when there is no question about your membership in a bona fide religion, the circumstances under which you may claim exemption from laws that apply to everybody else are not really clear. What if you, a member of the Seventh-Day Adventists, are fired by your employer for refusing on religious grounds to work on Saturday, and then it turns out that you cannot collect unemployment insurance because you refuse to take an available job—one that also requires you to work on Saturday? Or what if you are a member of the Amish sect, which refuses, contrary to state law, to send its children to public schools past the eighth grade? The Court has ruled that the state must pay you unemployment compensation and cannot require you to send your children to public schools beyond the eighth grade.[46]

These last two decisions, and others like them, show that even the "simple" principle of freedom of religion gets complicated in practice and can lead to the courts' giving, in effect, preference to members of one church over members of another.

THE ESTABLISHMENT CLAUSE

What in the world did the members of the First Congress mean when they wrote into the First Amendment language prohibiting Congress from making a law "respecting" an "establishment" of religion? The Supreme Court has more or less consistently interpreted this vague phrase to mean that the Constitution erects a "wall of separation" between church and state.

That phrase, so often quoted, is not in the Bill of Rights nor in the debates in the First Congress that drafted the Bill of Rights; it comes from the pen of Thomas Jefferson, who was opposed to having the Church of England as the established church of his native Virginia. (At the time of the Revolutionary War, there were established churches—that is, official, state-supported churches—in at least eight of the 13 former colonies.) But it is not clear that Jefferson's view was the majority view.

During much of the debate in Congress, the wording of this part of the First Amendment was quite different and much plainer than what finally emerged. Up to the last minute, the clause was intended to read "no religion shall be established by law" or "no national religion shall be established." The meaning of those words seems quite clear: whatever the states may do, the federal government cannot create an official, national religion or give support to one religion in preference to another.[47]

But Congress instead adopted an ambiguous phrase, and so the Supreme Court had to decide what it meant. It has declared that these words do not simply mean "no national religion" but mean as well no government involvement with religion at all, even on a nonpreferential basis. They mean, in short, erecting a "wall of separation" between church and state.[48] Though the interpretation of the establishment clause remains a topic of great controversy among judges and scholars, the Supreme Court has more or less consistently adopted this **wall-of-separation** principle.

wall of separation Court ruling that government cannot be involved with religion.

Its first statement of this interpretation was in 1947. The case involved a New Jersey town that reimbursed parents for the costs of transporting their children to school, including parochial (in this case Catholic) schools. The Court decided that this reimbursement was constitutional, but it made it clear that the establishment clause of the First Amendment applied (via the Fourteenth Amendment) to the states and that it meant, among other things, that the government cannot require a person to profess a belief or disbelief in any religion; it cannot aid one religion, some religions, or all religions; and it cannot spend any tax money, however small the amount might be, in support of any religious activities or institutions.[49] The reader may wonder, in view of the Court's reasoning, why it allowed the town to pay for busing children to Catholic schools. The answer it gave is that busing is a religiously neutral activity, akin to providing fire and police protection to Catholic schools. Busing, available to public- and private-school children alike, does not breach the wall of separation.

Since 1947, the Court has applied the wall-of-separation theory to strike down as unconstitutional most efforts to have any officially conducted or sponsored prayer in public schools, even if it is nonsectarian,[50] voluntary,[51] or limited to reading a passage of the Bible.[52] Since 1992, it has even been unconstitutional for a public school to ask a rabbi or minister to offer a prayer—an invocation or a benediction—at the school's graduation ceremony. Since 2000, it has been unconstitutional for a student to lead a prayer at a public high school football game because it was done "over the school's public address system, by a speaker representing the student body, under the supervision of the school faculty, and pursuant to school policy."[53] The Court made it clear, however, that public-school students could pray voluntarily during school provided that the school or the government did not sponsor that prayer. Moreover, the

How We Compare

Church and State

The American government cannot pay for or endorse any church. By contrast, the national governments in England, Greece, Germany, Norway, and Sweden can. Moreover, until recently there were state-supported churches in France, Italy, and Spain. Despite the absence of any governmental support for churches in this country, attendance in churches and synagogues is very high—by some estimates, as much as 40 percent of our population goes to these institutions every week. By contrast, in countries that have or have had state-supported churches, church attendance is rare. Only 4 percent of the English and 5 percent of the French go to church at least once a week.

How would you explain high church attendance in a country where churches lack government backing and low attendance where they have that backing?

Court has held that laws prohibiting teaching the theory of evolution or requiring giving equal time to "creationism" (the biblical doctrine that God created mankind) are religiously inspired and thus unconstitutional.[54] A public school may not allow its pupils to take time out from their regular classes for religious instruction if this occurs within the schools, though "released-time" instruction is all right if it is done outside the public-school building.[55] The school prayer decisions in particular have provoked a storm of controversy, but efforts to get Congress to propose to the states a constitutional amendment authorizing such prayers have failed.

Almost as controversial have been Court-imposed restrictions on public aid to parochial schools, though here the wall-of-separation principle has not been used to forbid any and all forms of aid. For example, it is permissible for the federal government to provide aid for constructing buildings on denominational (as well as nondenominational) college campuses[56] and for state governments to loan free textbooks to parochial-school pupils,[57] grant tax-exempt status to parochial schools,[58] allow parents of parochial-school children to deduct their tuition payments on a state's income tax returns,[59] and pay for computers and a deaf child's sign language interpreter at private and religious schools.[60] But the government cannot pay a salary supplement to teachers who teach secular subjects in parochial schools,[61] reimburse parents for the cost of parochial-school tuition,[62] supply parochial schools with services such as counseling,[63] give money with which to purchase instructional materials, require that "creationism" be taught in public schools, or create a special school district for Hasidic Jews.[64]

The Court sometimes changes its mind on these matters. In 1985, it said the states could not send teachers into parochial schools to teach remedial courses for needy children, but 12 years later it decided they could. "We no longer presume," the Court wrote, "that public employees will inculcate religion simply because they happen to be in a sectarian environment."[65]

Perhaps the most important establishment-clause decision in recent times was the Court ruling that vouchers can be used to pay for children being educated at religious and other private schools. The case began in Cleveland, Ohio, where the state offered money to any family (especially poor ones) whose children attended a school that had done so badly that it was under a federal court order requiring it to be managed directly by the state superintendent of schools. The money, a voucher, could be used to send a child to any other public or private school, including one run by a religious group. The Court held that this plan did not violate the establishment clause because the aid went, not to the school, but to the families who were to choose a school.[66]

If you find it confusing to follow the twists and turns of Court policy in this area, you are not alone. The wall-of-separation principle has not been easy to apply, and the Court has begun to alter its position on church-state matters. The Court has tried to sort out the confusion by developing a three-prong test to decide under what circumstances government involvement in religious activities is improper.[67] That involvement is constitutional if it meets these tests:

1. It has a strictly secular purpose.
2. Its primary effect neither advances nor inhibits religion.
3. It does not foster an excessive government entanglement with religion.

No sooner had the test been developed than the Court decided that it was all right for the government of Pawtucket, Rhode Island, to erect a Nativity scene as part of a Christmas display in a local park. But five years later, it said Pittsburgh could not put a Nativity scene in front of the courthouse but could display a menorah (a Jewish symbol of Chanukah) next to a Christmas tree and a sign extolling liberty. The Court claimed that the crèche had to go (because, being too close to the courthouse, a government endorsement was implied) but the menorah could stay (because, being next to a Christmas tree, it would not lead people to think that Pittsburgh was endorsing Judaism).

When the Ten Commandments are displayed in or near a public building, a deeply divided Court has made some complicated distinctions. It held that it was unconstitutional for two Kentucky counties to put up the Ten Commandments in their courthouses because, the Court decided, the purpose was religious. It did no good for one Kentucky courthouse to surround the Ten Commandments with displays of the Declaration of Independence and the Star Spangled Banner so as to make the Commandments part of America's political heritage. The Court said it was still a religious effort, even though it noted that there was a frieze containing Moses in the Supreme Court's own building. (This, the opinion held, was not religious.) But when the Ten Commandments were put up outside the Texas state capitol, this was upheld. The justice, Stephen Breyer, who changed from opposing the Kentucky display to favoring the Texas one, said that in Texas the Commandments now revealed a secular message and, besides, nobody had sued to end this display for 40 years after the Commandments were erected.[68]

How Would You Decide?

Suppose you are on the Supreme Court. In each of the actual cases summarized below, you are asked to decide whether the First Amendment to the Constitution permits or prohibits a particular action. What would be your decision? (How the Supreme Court actually decided is given on page 120.)

Case 1: Jacksonville, Florida, passed a city ordinance prohibiting drive-in movies from showing films containing nudity if the screen was visible to passersby on the street. A movie theater manager protested, claiming he had a First Amendment right to show such films, even if they could be seen from the street. Who is correct?

Case 2: Dr. Benjamin Spock wanted to enter Fort Dix Military Reservation in New Jersey to pass out campaign literature and discuss issues with service personnel. The military denied him access on grounds that regulations prohibit partisan campaigning on military bases. Who is correct?

Case 3: A town passed an ordinance forbidding the placing of "For Sale" or "Sold" signs in front of homes in racially changing neighborhoods. The purpose was to reduce "white flight" and panic selling. A realty firm protested, claiming its freedom of speech was being abridged. Who is correct?

Case 4: A girl in Georgia was raped and died. A local television station broadcast the name of the girl, having obtained it from court records. Her father sued, claiming his family's right to privacy had been violated, and pointed to a Georgia law that made it a crime to broadcast the name of a rape victim. The television station claimed that it had a right under the First Amendment to broadcast the name. Who is correct?

Case 5: Florida passed a law giving a political candidate the right to equal space in a newspaper that had published attacks on him. A newspaper claimed that this violated the freedom of the press to publish what it wants. Who is correct?

Case 6: Zacchini is a "human cannonball" whose entire 15-second act was filmed and broadcast by an Ohio television station. Zacchini sued the station, claiming his earning power had been reduced by the film because the station showed for free what he charges people to see at county fairs. The station replied that it had a First Amendment right to broadcast such events. Who is correct?

Though the Court has struck down prayer in public schools, it has upheld prayer in Congress (since 1789, the House and Senate open each session with a prayer).[69] A public school cannot have a chaplain, but the armed services can. The Court has said that the government cannot "advance" religion, but it has not objected to the printing of the phrase "In God We Trust" on the back of every dollar bill.

These distinctions reflect the fact that the Court tends to use the wall-of-separation test when it deals with public schools but that it tries to strike a reasonable balance when it deals with Congress or state office buildings, perhaps because schools have a young and captive population whereas public forums have an adult and voluntary membership.

It is obvious that despite its efforts to set forth clear rules governing church-state relations, the Court's actual decisions are hard to summarize. It is deeply divided—some would say deeply confused—on these matters, and so the efforts to define the "wall of separation" will continue to prove to be as difficult as the Court's earlier efforts to decide what is interstate and what is local commerce (see Chapter 3).

Crime and Due Process

Whereas the central problem in interpreting the religion clauses of the First Amendment has been to decide what they mean, the central problem in interpreting those parts of the Bill of Rights that affect people accused of a crime has been to decide not only what they mean but also how to put them into effect. It is not obvious what constitutes an "unreasonable search," but even if we settle that question, we still must decide how best to protect people against such searches in ways that do not unduly hinder criminal investigations.

That protection can be provided in at least two ways. One is to let the police introduce in court evidence relevant to the guilt or innocence of a person, no matter how it was obtained, and then, after the case is settled, punish the police officer (or his or her superiors) if the evidence was gathered improperly (for example, by an unreasonable search). The other way is to exclude improperly gathered evidence from the trial in the first place, even if it is relevant to determining the guilt or innocence of the accused.

Most democratic nations, including England, use the first method; the United States uses the second. Because of this, many of the landmark cases decided by the Supreme Court have been bitterly controversial. Opponents of these decisions have argued that a guilty person should not go free just because the police officer blundered, especially if the mistake was minor. Supporters rejoin that there is no way to punish errant police officers effectively other than by excluding tainted evidence; moreover, nobody should be convicted of a crime except by evidence that is above reproach.[70]

exclusionary rule Improperly gathered evidence may not be introduced in a criminal trial.

Landmark Cases

Religious Freedom

- ***Pierce v. Society of Sisters* (1925):** Though states may require public education, they may not require that students attend only public schools.
- ***Everson v. Board of Education* (1947):** The wall-of-separation principle is announced.
- ***Zorauch v. Clauson* (1952):** States may allow students to be released from public schools to attend religious instruction.
- ***Engel v. Vitale* (1962):** There may not be a prayer, even a nondenominational one, in public schools.
- ***Lemon v. Kurtzman* (1971):** Three tests are described for deciding whether the government is improperly involved with religion.
- ***Lee v. Weisman* (1992):** Public schools may not have clergy lead prayers at graduation ceremonies.
- ***Santa Fe Independent School District v. Doe* (2000):** Students may not lead prayers before the start of a football game at a public school.
- ***Zelman v. Simmons-Harris* (2002):** Voucher plan to pay school bills is upheld.

THE EXCLUSIONARY RULE

The American method relies on what is called the **exclusionary rule.** That rule holds that evidence gathered in violation of the Constitution cannot be used in a trial. The rule has been used to implement two provisions of the Bill of Rights—the right to be free from unreasonable searches and seizures (Fourth Amendment) and the right not to be compelled to give evidence against oneself (Fifth Amendment).*

Not until 1949 did the Supreme Court consider whether to apply the exclusionary rule to the states. In a case decided that year, the Court made it clear that the Fourth Amendment prohibited the police from carrying out unreasonable searches and obtaining improper confessions but held that it was not necessary to use the exclusionary rule to enforce those prohibitions. It noted that other nations did not require that evidence improperly gathered had to be excluded from a criminal trial. The Court said that the local police should not improperly gather and use evidence, but if they did, the remedy was to sue the police department or punish the officer.[71]

But in 1961, the Supreme Court changed its mind about the use of the exclusionary rule. It all began when the Cleveland police broke into the home of Dollree Mapp in search of a suspect in a bombing case. Not finding him, they arrested her for possessing some obscene pictures found there. The Court held that this was an unreasonable search and seizure because the police had not obtained a search warrant, though they had had ample time to do so. Furthermore, such illegally gathered evidence could not be used in the trial of Mapp.[72] Beginning with this case—*Mapp v. Ohio*—the Supreme Court required the use of the exclusionary rule as a way of enforcing a variety of constitutional guarantees.

SEARCH AND SEIZURE

After the Court decided to exclude improperly gathered evidence, the next problem was to decide what evidence was improperly gathered. What happened to Dollree Mapp was an easy case: hardly anybody argued that it was reasonable for the police to break into someone's home without a warrant, ransack their belongings, and take whatever they could find

*We shall consider here only two constitutional limits—those bearing on searches and confessions. Thus we will omit many other important constitutional provisions affecting criminal cases, such as rules governing wiretapping, prisoner rights, the right to bail and to a jury trial, the bar on ex post facto laws, the right to be represented by a lawyer in court, the ban on "cruel and unusual" punishment, and the rule against double jeopardy.

WHAT WOULD YOU DO?

MEMORANDUM

To: *Rebecca Saikia, Supreme Court justice*

From: *David Wilson, law clerk*

Subject: *Patriot Act and libraries*

The Patriot Act allows the FBI to seek the records of possible terrorists from banks, businesses, and libraries. Many libraries claim this will harm the constitutional rights of Americans. You support these rights, but are also aware of the need to protect national security.

News »

High Court Hears from Libraries About War on Terror

Two public libraries have asked the Supreme Court to strike down provisions of the Patriot Act that allow the Federal Bureau of Investigation to see the borrowing records of persons who are under investigation.

Arguments for:

1. The Patriot Act does not target individuals who have not violated a criminal law and who do not threaten human life.
2. For the FBI to collect information about borrowers, it must first obtain permission from a federal judge.
3. Terrorists may use libraries to study and plan activities that threaten national security.

Arguments against:

1. Freedom of speech and expression are fundamental constitutional guarantees that should not be infringed.
2. The law might harm groups engaged in peaceful protests.
3. The law allows the government to delay notifying people that their borrowing habits are being investigated.

Your decision:

Uphold this provision ________________

Overturn this provision ________________

that might be incriminating. But that left a lot of hard choices still to be made.

When can the police search you without it being unreasonable? Under two circumstances—when they have a search warrant and when they have lawfully arrested you. A **search warrant** is an order from a judge authorizing the search of a place; the order must describe what is to be searched and seized, and the judge can issue it only if he or she is persuaded by the police that good reason **(probable cause)** exists to believe that a crime has been committed and that the evidence bearing on that crime will be found at a certain location. (The police can also search a building if the occupant gives them permission.)

In addition, you can be searched if the search occurs when you are lawfully arrested. When can you be arrested? You can be arrested if a judge has issued an arrest

search warrant A judge's order authorizing a search.

probable cause Reasonable cause for issuing a search warrant or making an arrest; more than mere suspicion.

How the Court Decided

The United States Supreme Court answered the questions on page 117 in the following ways:

Case 1: The drive-in movie won. The Supreme Court, 6–3, decided that the First Amendment protects the right to show nudity; it is up to the unwilling viewer on the public streets to avert his or her eyes.

Erznoznik v. Jacksonville, 422 U.S. 205 (1975)

Case 2: The military won. The Supreme Court, 6–2, decided that military reservations are not like public streets or parks, and thus civilians can be excluded from them, especially if such exclusion prevents the military from appearing to be the handmaiden of various political causes.

Greer v. Spock, 424 U.S. 828 (1976)

Case 3: The realty firm won. The Supreme Court, 8–0, decided that the First Amendment prohibits the banning of signs, even of a commercial nature, without a strong, legitimate state interest. Banning the signs would not obviously reduce "white flight," and the government has no right to withhold information from citizens for fear that they will act unwisely.

Linmark Associates, Inc. v. Willingboro, 431 U.S. 85 (1977)

Case 4: The television station won. The Court, 8–1, decided that the First Amendment protects the right to broadcast the names of rape victims obtained from public (that is, court) records.

Cox Broadcasting Corp. v. Cohn, 420 U.S. 469 (1975)

Case 5: The newspaper won. The Supreme Court decided unanimously that the First Amendment prohibits the state from intruding into the function of editors.

Miami Herald Publishing Co. v. Tornillo, 418 U.S. 241 (1974)

Case 6: Zacchini, the human cannonball, won. The Supreme Court, 5–4, decided that broadcasting the entire act without the performer's consent jeopardized his means of livelihood, even though the First Amendment would guarantee the right of the station to broadcast newsworthy facts about the act.

Zacchini v. Scripps-Howard Broadcasting Co., 433 U.S. 562 (1977)

warrant for you, if you commit a crime in the presence of a police officer, or if the officer has probable cause to believe you have committed a serious crime (usually a felony). If you are arrested and no search warrant has been issued, the police, and not a judge, decide what they can search. What rules should they follow?

In trying to answer that question, the courts have elaborated a set of rules that are complex, subject to frequent change, and quite controversial. In general the police, after arresting you, can search:

- You
- Things in plain view
- Things or places under your immediate control

As a practical matter, things "in plain view" or "under your immediate control" mean the room in which you are arrested but not other rooms of the house.[73] If the police want to search the rest of your house or a car parked in your driveway, they will first have to go to a judge to obtain a search warrant. But if the police arrest a college student on campus for drinking under age and then accompany that student back to his or her dormitory room so that the student can get proof that he or she was old enough to drink, the police can seize drugs in plain view in that room.[74] And if marijuana is growing in plain view in an open field, the police can enter and search that field even though it is fenced off with a locked gate and a "No Trespassing" sign.[75]

But what if you are arrested while driving your car—how much of it can the police search? The answer to that question has changed almost yearly. In 1979, the Court ruled that the police could not search a suitcase taken from a car of an arrested person, and in 1981 it extended this protection to any "closed, opaque container" found in the car.[76] But the following year, the Court decided that all parts of a car, closed or open, could be searched if the officers had probable cause to believe they contained contraband (that is, goods illegally possessed). And recently, the rules governing car searches have been relaxed even further. Officers who have probable cause to search a car can also search the things passengers are carrying in the car. And if the car is stopped to give the driver a traffic ticket, the car can be searched if the officer develops a "reasonable, articulable suspicion" that the car is involved in other illegal activity.[77]

In this confusing area of the law, the Court is attempting to protect those places in which a person has a "reasonable expectation of privacy." Your body is one such place, and so the Court has held that the police cannot compel you to undergo surgery to remove a bullet that might be evidence of your guilt or innocence in a crime.[78] But the police can require you to take a Breathalyzer test to see whether you have been drinking while driving.[79] Your home is another place where you have an expectation of privacy, but a barn next to your home is not, nor is your backyard viewed from an airplane, nor is your home if it is a motor home that can be driven away, and so the police need not have a warrant to look into these places.[80]

If you work for the government, you have an expectation that your desk and files will be private; nonetheless, your supervisor may search the desk and files without a warrant, provided that he or she is looking for something related to your work.[81] But bear in mind that the Constitution protects you only against *the government;* a private employer has a great deal of freedom to search your desk and files.

CONFESSIONS AND SELF-INCRIMINATION

The constitutional ban on being forced to give evidence against oneself was originally intended to prevent the use of torture or "third-degree" police tactics to extract confessions. But it has since been extended to cover many kinds of statements uttered not out of fear of torture but from lack of awareness of one's rights, especially the right to remain silent, whether in the courtroom or in the police station.

For many decades, the Supreme Court had held that involuntary confessions could not be used in federal criminal trials but had not ruled that they were barred from state trials. But in the early 1960s, it changed its mind in two landmark cases—*Escobedo* and *Miranda*.[82] The story of the latter and of the controversy that it provoked is worth telling.

Ernesto A. Miranda was convicted in Arizona of the rape and kidnapping of a young woman. The conviction was based on a written confession that Miranda signed after two hours of police questioning. (The victim also identified him.) Two years earlier, the Court had decided that the rule against self-incrimination applied to state courts.[83] Now the question arose of what constitutes an "involuntary" confession. The Court decided that a confession should be presumed involuntary unless the person in custody had been fully and clearly informed of his or her right to be silent, to have an attorney present during any questioning, and to have an attorney provided free of charge if he or she could not afford one. The accused could waive these rights and offer to talk, but the waiver must have been truly voluntary. Since Miranda did not have a lawyer present when he was questioned and had not knowingly waived his right to a lawyer, the confession was excluded from evidence in the trial and his conviction was overturned.[84]

Miranda was tried and convicted again, this time on the basis of evidence supplied by his girlfriend, who testified that he had admitted to her that he was guilty. Nine years later, he was released from prison; four years after that, he was killed in a barroom fight. When the Phoenix police arrested the prime suspect in Ernesto Miranda's murder, they read him his rights from a "Miranda card."

Everyone who watches cops-and-robbers shows on television probably knows the "Miranda warning" by heart (see the box on page 123). The police now read it routinely to people whom they arrest. It is not clear whether it has much impact on who does or does not confess or what effect, if any, it may have on the crime rate.

In time, the Miranda rule was extended to mean that you have a right to a lawyer when you appear in a police lineup[85] and when you are questioned by a psychiatrist to determine whether you are competent to stand trial.[86] The Court threw out the conviction of a man who had killed a child, because the accused, without being given the right to have a lawyer present and having undergone harsh questioning, had led the police to the victim's body.[87] You do not have a right to a Miranda warning, however, if while in jail you confess a crime to another inmate who turns out to be an undercover police officer.[88]

Some police departments have tried to get around the need for a Miranda warning by training their officers to question suspects before giving them a Miranda warning and then, if the suspect confesses, giving the warning and asking the same questions over again. But the Supreme Court has not allowed this and has struck the practice down.[89]

RELAXING THE EXCLUSIONARY RULE

Cases such as *Miranda* were highly controversial and led to efforts in Congress to modify or overrule the decisions by statute—without much coming of the attempts. But as the rules governing police conduct became increasingly more complex, pressure mounted to find an alternative. Some thought that any evidence should be admissible, with the question of police conduct left to lawsuits or other ways of punishing official misbehavior. Others felt that the exclusionary rule served a useful purpose but had simply become too technical to be an effective deterrent to police misconduct (the police cannot obey rules that they cannot understand). And still others felt that the exclusionary rule was a vital safeguard to essential liberties and should be kept intact. The Court has refused to let Congress abolish Miranda because it is a constitutional rule.[90]

good-faith exception An error in gathering evidence sufficiently minor that it may be used in a trial.

Public safety exception The police can question an un-Mirandized suspect if there is an urgent concern for public safety.

Inevitable discovery The police can use evidence if it would inevitably have been discovered.

The courts began to decide some cases in ways that modified while retaining the exclusionary rule. The police were given greater freedom to question juveniles.[91] If the police got a warrant they thought was valid but the judge had used the wrong form, they could use it under the **good faith exception**.[92] The Supreme Court has allowed the police to question a suspect without first issuing a Miranda warning if the questions were motivated by **overriding considerations of public safety**.[93] And the Court changed its mind about the killer who led the police to the victim's body. Under the **inevitable discovery** rule, the Court decided that if a victim will be discovered anyway, the evidence will not be excluded.[94]

TERRORISM AND CIVIL LIBERTIES

The attacks of September 11, 2001, raised important questions about how far the government can go in investigating and prosecuting individuals.

A little over one month after the attacks, Congress passed a new law, the USA Patriot Act, designed to increase federal powers to investigate terrorists.* Its main provisions are these:

- Telephone taps. The government may tap, if it has a court order, any telephone a suspect uses instead of having to get a separate order for each telephone.
- Internet taps. The government may tap, if it has a court order, Internet communications.
- Voice mail. The government, with a court order, may seize voice mail.
- Grand jury information. Investigators can now share with other government officials things learned in secret grand jury hearings.
- Immigration. The attorney general may hold any noncitizen who is thought to be a national security risk for up to seven days. If the alien cannot be charged with a crime or deported within that time, he or she may still be detained if he or she is certified to be a security risk.
- Money laundering. The government gets new powers to track the movement of money across U.S. borders and among banks.
- Crime. This provision eliminates the statute of limitation on terrorist crimes and increases the penalties.

About a month later, President Bush, by executive order, proclaimed a national emergency under which any noncitizen who is believed to be a terrorist or to have harbored a terrorist will be tried by a military, rather than a civilian, court. A military trial is carried on before a commission of military officers and not a civilian jury. The tribunal can operate in secret if classified information is used in evidence. Two-thirds of the commission must agree before the suspect can be convicted and sentenced. If convicted, the suspect can appeal to the secretary of defense and the president, but not to a civilian court. These commissions may eventually be used to try some of the men captured by the U.S. military during its campaign in Afghanistan against the Taliban regime and the al Qaeda terrorist network that was created by Osama bin Laden. The detainees held in a prison at our Guantanamo naval base in Cuba are not regarded by the Defense Department as ordinary prisoners of war.

The biggest legal issue created by this country's war on terrorism is whether the people we capture can be held by our government without giving them access to the courts. The traditional view, first announced during World War II, was that spies sent to this country by the Nazis could be tried by a military tribunal instead of by a civilian court. They were neither citizens nor soldiers, but "unlawful combatants."[95] The Bush administration relied on this view when it detained, in our military base in Guantanamo Bay, Cuba, men seized by American forces in Afghanistan. These men were mostly members of the al Qaeda terrorist movement or of the Taliban movement that governed Afghanistan

*The name of the law is an acronym derived from the official title of the bill, drawn from the first letters of the following capitalized words: Uniting and Strengthening America by Providing Appropriate Tools Required to Intercept and Obstruct Terrorism (USA Patriot).

How Things Work

The Miranda Rule

The Supreme Court has interpreted the due process clause to require that local police departments issue warnings of the sort shown below to people whom they are arresting.

PHILADELPHIA POLICE DEPARTMENT

STANDARD POLICE INTERROGATION CARD

WARNINGS TO BE GIVEN ACCUSED

We are questioning you concerning the crime of (state specific crime).

We have a duty to explain to you and to warn you that you have the following legal rights:

A. You have a right to remain silent and do not have to say anything at all.

B. Anything you say can and will be used against you in Court.

C. You have a right to talk to a lawyer of your own choice before we ask you any questions, and also to have a lawyer here with you while we ask questions.

D. If you cannot afford to hire a lawyer, and you want one, we will see that you have one provided to you free of charge before we ask you any questions.

E. If you are willing to give us a statement, you have a right to stop any time you wish.

75-Misc.-3 (Over)

(6-24-70)

Philadelphia Police Department

Ernesto A. Miranda was convicted in Arizona of rape and kidnapping. When the Supreme Court overturned the conviction, it issued a set of rules—the "Miranda rule"—governing how police must conduct an arrest and interrogation.

before American armed forces, together with Afghan rebels, defeated them. These men, none of them American citizens, argued that they were neither terrorists nor combatants. They demanded access to American courts. By a vote of six to three, the Supreme Court held that American courts can consider challenges to the legality of the detention of these men. The Court's opinion did not spell out what the courts should do when it hears such petitions.[96]

In another decision given the same day, the Supreme Court ruled on the case of an American citizen who apparently was working with the Taliban regime but was captured by our forces and imprisoned in South Carolina. The Court said that American citizens are entitled to a hearing before a neutral decision maker in order to challenge the basis for detention.[97]

That "neutral decision maker" was created in 2006 by a law authorizing military commissions to try alien enemy combatants. These are foreign fighters not in uniform, such as members of al Qaeda, who are captured by American forces. Each commission is to be composed of at least five military officers and is to allow the defendant certain fundamental rights (such as to see evidence and testify). Appeals from its decisions can be taken to the Court

Inside a cell at the terrorist prison in Guantanamo, where Muslim inmates receive a copy of the Koran, a chess set, and an arrow pointing toward Mecca.

of Military Review, whose members are selected by the secretary of defense. The federal appeals court for the District of Columbia and, if it wishes, the Supreme Court may hear appeals from the Court of Military Review.[98]

Military commissions have conducted hearings about the inmates in the Guantanamo prison. Some were released, some were held, and for some no decision has been made. Right after he became president, Barack Obama issued an order to close the Guantanamo prison. But there is a problem: What do you do with the inmates? While George W. Bush was president, 420 of the more than 700 inmates were released, but another 50 or so, though declared eligible for release, could not find a country willing to accept them. Where will they go?

When it was first passed in 2001, the Patriot Act made certain provisions temporary, perhaps to allay the fears of civil libertarians. When the act was renewed in March 2006, only a few changes were made and almost all of its provisions were made permanent.

In addition to the Patriot Act, Congress passed and the president signed in 2005 a law that requires all states by 2008 to comply with federal standards when they issue driver licenses. States, not Washington, pass out these licenses, but by mid-2008 the Real ID Act says that no federal agency, including those that manage security at airports, may accept a license or state identification card that does not have the person's photograph, address, signature, and full legal name based on documents that prove he or she is legally in this country. Some people think this amounts to a required national ID card.[99]

Landmark Cases

Criminal Charges

- ***Mapp v. Ohio* (1961):** Evidence illegally gathered by the police may not be used in a criminal trial.
- ***Gideon v. Wainwright* (1964):** Persons charged with a crime have a right to an attorney even if they cannot afford one.
- ***Miranda v. Arizona* (1966):** Court describes warning that police must give to arrested persons.
- ***United States v. Leon* (1984):** Illegally obtained evidence may be used in a trial if it was gathered in good faith without violating the principles of the *Mapp* decision.
- ***Dickerson v. United States* (2000):** The *Mapp* decision is based on the Constitution and cannot be altered by Congress passing a law.
- ***Rasul v. Bush* and *Hamdi v. Rumsfeld* (2004):** Terrorist detainees must have access to a neutral court to decide if they are legally held.

SEARCHES WITHOUT WARRANTS

For many decades, presidents of both parties authorized telephone taps without warrants when they believed the person being tapped was a foreign spy. Some did this to capture information about their political enemies. In 1978, Congress decided to bring this practice under legislative control. It passed the Foreign Intelligence Surveillance Act (FISA) that required the president to go before a special court, composed of seven judges selected by the Chief Justice, to obtain approval for electronic eavesdropping on persons who were thought to be foreign spies. The FISA court would impose a standard lower than that which governs the issuance of warrants against criminals. For criminals, a warrant must be based on showing "probable cause" that the person is engaged in a crime; for FISA warrants, the government need only show that the person is likely to be working for a foreign government.

In late 2005, the *New York Times* and other newspapers revealed that the National Security Agency (NSA), this country's code-breaking and electronic surveillance organization, had a secret program to intercept telephone calls and e-mail messages between certain people abroad and Americans. The Bush administration defended the program, arguing that the intercepts were designed, not to identify criminals or foreign spies, but to alert the country to potential terrorist threats. It could not rely on FISA because its procedures took too long and its standards of proof were too high. Critics of the program said that it imperiled the civil liberties of Americans.

The Supreme Court has never spoken on this matter, but every lower federal court, including the court that hears appeals from the FISA court, has agreed that the president, as commander in chief, has the "inherent authority" to conduct warrantless searches to obtain foreign intelligence information.[100] The administration also argued that after 9/11, when Congress passed a law authorizing the president to exercise "all necessary and appropriate" uses of military force, it included warrantless intercepts of terrorist communications.

In 2008, Congress passed a bill that allowed the government to intercept foreign communications with people in the United States provided the FISA court had approved the surveillance methods. But the administration could begin the surveillance before the FISA ruling was made if it declared the need to be urgent. However, if Americans living overseas are made the target of this surveillance, then there must first be a FISA warrant. In addition, private telephone and Internet companies that aided in the surveillance were exempt from lawsuits so long as they had received "substantial evidence" that the program was authorized by the president.

Civil liberties questions are in some ways like and in some ways unlike ordinary policy debates. Like most issues, civil liberties problems often involve competing interests—in this case, conflicting rights or conflicting rights and duties—and so we have groups mobilized on both sides of issues involving free speech and crime control. Like some other issues, civil liberties problems also can arise from the successful appeals of a policy entrepreneur, and so we have periodic reductions in liberty resulting from popular fears, usually aroused during or just after a war.

But civil liberties are unlike many other issues in at least one regard: more than struggles over welfare spending or defense or economic policy, debates about civil liberties reach down into our fundamental political beliefs and political culture, challenging us to define what we mean by religion, Americanism, and decency. The most important of these challenges focuses on the meaning of the First Amendment: What is "speech"? How much of it should be free? How far can the state go in aiding religion? How do we strike a balance between national security and personal expression? The zigzag course followed by the courts in judging these matters has, on balance, tended to enlarge freedom of expression.

Almost as important has been the struggle to strike a balance between the right of society to protect itself from criminals and the right of people (including criminals) to be free from unreasonable searches and coerced confessions. As with free-speech cases, the courts generally have broadened the rights at some expense to the power of the police. But in recent years, the Supreme Court has pulled back from some of its more sweeping applications of the exclusionary rule.

The resolution of these issues by the courts is political in the sense that differing opinions about what is right or desirable compete, with one side or another prevailing (often by a small majority). In this competition of ideas, federal judges, though not elected, often are sensitive to strong currents of popular opinion. When politics has produced new action against apparently threatening minorities, judges are inclined, at least for a while, to give serious consideration to popular fears and legislative majorities. And when no strong national mood is discernible, the opinions of elites influence judicial thinking (as described in Chapter 16).

At the same time, courts resolve political conflicts in a manner that differs in important respects from the resolution of conflicts by legislatures or executives. First, the very existence of the courts, and the relative ease with which one may enter them to advance a claim, facilitates challenges to accepted values. An unpopular political or religious group may have little or no access to a legislature, but it will have substantial access to the courts. Second, judges often settle controversies about rights not simply by deciding the case at hand, but rather by formulating a general rule to cover like cases elsewhere. This has an advantage (the law tends to become more consistent and better known) but a disadvantage as well: a rule suitable for one case may be unworkable in another. Judges reason by analogy and sometimes assume two cases are similar when in fact important differences exist. For example, a definition of "obscenity" or "fighting words" may suit one situation but be inadequate in another. Third, judges interpret the Constitution, whereas legislatures often consult popular preferences or personal convictions. However much their own beliefs influence what judges read into the Constitution, almost all of them are constrained by its language.

Taken together, the desire to find and announce rules, the language of the Constitution, and the personal beliefs of judges have led to a general expansion of civil liberties. As a result, even allowing for temporary reversals and frequent redefinitions, any value thought to hinder freedom of expression and the rights of the accused has generally lost ground to the claims of the First, Fourth, Fifth, and Sixth Amendments.

LEARNING OBJECTIVES

WHAT YOU NEED TO KNOW

☑ What is meant by "selective incorporation"?

"Selective incorporation" refers to the process the Supreme Court has followed in deciding which parts of the Bill of Rights, designed to limit only federal action, now also limit state action because they reflect a "fundamental value" that applies to the states by means of the Fourteenth Amendment's requirement that the rights of U.S. citizens shall not be abridged without due process of law, in a way that denies them the equal protection of the laws, or infringes their privileges and immunities.

☑ Do high school students have the same rights in school as do adults out of school?

High school students have many rights, but they can be limited when they use school property or are part of a school program.

☑ Does "symbolic speech" have the same protection as does making a speech?

"Symbolic speech," such as burning an American flag, is a statement that has constitutional protection, but other actions, such as burning a draft card, do not have such protection. The flag is not owned by the government and can be burned to make a statement, but a draft card is owned by the government and cannot be burned.

RECONSIDERING WHO GOVERNS?

1. Why do the courts play so large a role in deciding what our civil liberties should be?

The courts are independent of the executive and legislative branches, both of which will respond to public pressures. In wartime or in other crisis periods, people want "something done." The president and members of Congress know this. The courts usually are a brake on their demands. But the courts can make mistakes or get things confused, as many people believe they have with the establishment clause and the rights of criminal defendants.

RECONSIDERING TO WHAT ENDS?

1. Why not display religious symbols on government property?

The courts believe that putting on government property a single religious symbol, such as a Nativity scene, will make Americans believe the government endorses that religion.

if symbols from several different religions are displayed, no one will think government has endorsed any one of them. Putting "In God We Trust" on a ernment dollar bill is acceptable. Do not look for consistency here.

erson confesses to committing a crime, why is that confession sometimes ised in court?

nfession may not be used in court if it was improperly gathered by the e. Suspects may not be tortured, and they must be given the Miranda ning. There are other ways of protecting the right of people to be free of roper police procedures, such as admitting the confession in court and then ishing the officers who gathered it improperly. The American courts do not k that system would work in this country.

s the Patriot Act reduce our liberties?

re have not yet been any court tests of the law. Passed after 9/11, it roves the ability of the police to obtain search warrants and eliminates the ension between intelligence and law enforcement.

QUESTIONS TO CONSIDER

1. **Consider the issue of privacy and governmental searches of individuals' computer files. Describe in this case how you would balance civil liberties with the need for government authority. When or under what circumstances do you think government should be able to access and search an individual's computer files without his or her knowledge or consent? What limits, if any, would you place on government's ability to do this?**
2. **Think about your experiences with the issue of religion, prayer in school, and education. Were the religions of all students in your school represented? How would you have felt about the issue if the religions recognized were not yours?**
3. **List three situations where you think an individual's freedom of expression should be limited. Now, using the same cases, under what conditions do you think the same speech or expression should not be limited?**
4. **Do you think government should have the right to detain an individual indefinitely? Under what conditions would this be appropriate?**
5. **Give three examples of issues that have been affected by selective incorporation.**
6. **Given the pattern of civil liberty protections in the past, should we expect to see greater limitations placed on government or fewer protections for civil liberties in the future? Why or why not?**

TO LEARN MORE

Court cases: **www.law.cornell.edu**

Civil Rights Division of the Department of Justice: **www.usdoj.gov**

American Civil Liberties Union: **www.aclu.org**

Abraham, Henry J., and Barbara A. Perry, *Freedom and the Court,* 7th ed. New York: Oxford University Press, 1998. Analysis of leading Supreme Court cases on civil liberties and civil rights.

Amar, Akhil Reed. *The Constitution and Criminal Procedure: First Principles*. New Haven, Conn.: Yale University Press, 1997. A brilliant critique of how the Supreme Court has interpreted those parts of the Constitution bearing on search warrants, the exclusionary rule, and self-incrimination.

Berns, Walter. *The First Amendment and the Future of American Democracy*. New York: Basic Books, 1976. A look at what the Founders intended by the First Amendment that takes issue with contemporary Supreme Court interpretations of it.

Clor, Harry M. *Obscenity and Public Morality*. Chicago: University of Chicago Press, 1969. Argues for the legitimacy of legal restrictions on obscenity.

Levy, Leonard W. *Legacy of Suppression: Freedom of Speech and Press in Early American History*. Rev. ed. New York: Oxford University Press, 1985. Careful study of what the Founders and the early leaders meant by freedom of speech and press.

6 Civil Rights

LEARNING OBJECTIVES

WHAT YOU NEED TO KNOW

- ☑ If both African Americans and women benefit from civil rights, why do federal courts allow them to be treated somewhat differently?
- ☑ What is the difference between "strict scrutiny" and "intermediate scrutiny"?
- ☑ Legally, what is meant by sexual harassment?
- ☑ If sexual relations among gays cannot be banned, why is it that some organizations can ban gay people from membership?

WHO GOVERNS?

1. Since Congress enacts our laws, why has it not made certain that all groups have the same rights?
2. After the Supreme Court ended racial segregation in the schools, what did the president and Congress do?

TO WHAT ENDS?

1. If the law supports equality of opportunity, why has affirmative action become so important?
2. Under what circumstances can men and women be treated differently?

THEN In 1830, Congress passed a law requiring all Indians east of the Mississippi River to move to the Indian Territory west of the river, and the army set about implementing it. In the 1850s, a major political fight broke out in Boston over whether the police department should be obliged to hire an Irish officer. Until 1920, women could not vote in most elections. In the 1930s, the Cornell University Medical School had a strict quota limiting the number of Jewish students who could enroll. In the 1940s, the army, at the direction of President Franklin D. Roosevelt, removed all Japanese Americans from their homes in California and placed them in relocation centers far from the coast.

NOW Things have changed since those days. Now it would be inconceivable that the army would relocate Native Americans. Today no one can be denied entry into a police department by reason of race, ethnicity, or religion. And presently law enforcement is so preoccupied with treating even suspected terrorists (never mind all Muslims) fairly that even a man who was caught trying to blow up an passenger plane approaching Detroit was not sent immediately to a prison, but rather given the Miranda warning to

make it clear (as we saw in the last chapter) that he did not have to speak at all without a lawyer present.

Civil rights is about cases in which some group, usually defined along racial or ethnic lines, is denied access to facilities, opportunities, or services that are available to other groups. The pertinent question regarding civil rights is not whether the government has the authority to treat different people differently; it is whether such differences in treatment are reasonable. All laws and policies make distinctions among people—for example, the tax laws require higher-income people to pay taxes at a higher rate than lower-income ones—but not all such distinctions are defensible. The courts have long held that classifying people on the basis of their income and taxing them at different rates is quite permissible because such classifications are not arbitrary or unreasonable and are related to a legitimate public need (that is, raising revenue). Increasingly, however, the courts have said that classifying people on the basis of their race or ethnicity is unreasonable.[1] The tests the courts use are summarized in the box on page 143.

To explain the victimization of certain groups and the methods by which they have begun to overcome it, we shall consider chiefly the case of African Americans.

civil rights The rights of people to be treated without unreasonable or unconstitutional differences.

Black-white relations have in large measure defined the problem of civil rights in this country. Most of the landmark laws and court decisions have involved black claims. The strategies employed by or on behalf of African Americans have typically set the pattern for the strategies employed by other groups. At the end of this chapter, we shall look at the related but somewhat different issues of women's rights and gay rights.

The Black Predicament

Though constituting more than 12 percent of the population, African Americans until fairly recently could not in many parts of the country vote, attend integrated schools, ride in the front seats of buses, or buy homes in white neighborhoods.

Although today white citizens generally do not feel threatened when a black family moves into Cicero, Illinois, a black child goes to school at Little Rock Central High School, or a black group organizes voters in Neshoba County, Mississippi, at one time most whites in Cicero, Little Rock, and Neshoba County felt deeply threatened by these things (and some whites still do). This was especially the case in those parts of the country, notably the Deep South, where blacks often were in the majority. There the politically dominant white minority felt keenly the potential competition for jobs, land, public services, and living space posed by large numbers of people of another race. But even in the North, black gains often appeared to be at the expense of lower-income whites who lived or worked near them, not at the expense of upper-status whites who lived in suburbs.

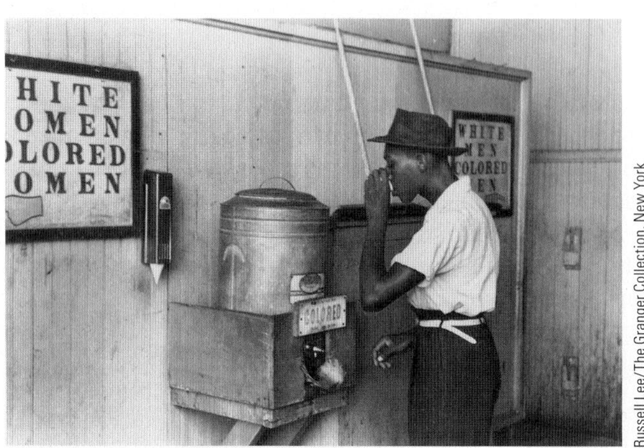

Segregated water fountain in Oklahoma City (1939).

Russell Lee/The Granger Collection, New York

African Americans were not allowed to vote at all in many areas; they could vote only with great difficulty in others; and even in those places where voting was easy, they often lacked the material and institutional support for effective political organization. If your opponent feels deeply threatened by your demands and can deny you access to the political system that will decide the fate of those demands, you are, to put it mildly, at a disadvantage. Yet from the end of Reconstruction to the 1960s—for nearly a century—many blacks in the South found themselves in just such a position.

To the dismay of those who prefer to explain political action in terms of economic motives, people often attach greater importance to the intangible costs and benefits of policies than to the tangible ones. Thus, even though the average black represented no threat to the average white, antiblack attitudes—racism—produced some appalling actions. Between 1882 and 1946, 4,715 people, about three-fourths of them African Americans, were lynched in the United States.[2] Some lynchings were carried out by small groups of vigilantes acting with much ceremony, but others were the actions of frenzied mobs. In the summer of 1911, a black man charged with murdering a white man in Livermore, Kentucky, was dragged by a mob to the local theater, where he was hanged. The audience, which had been charged admission, was invited to shoot the swaying body (those in the orchestra seats could empty their revolvers; those in the balcony were limited to a single shot).[3]

Though the public in other parts of the country was shocked by such events, little was done: lynching was a local, not a federal, crime. It obviously would not require many lynchings to convince African Americans in these localities that it would be foolhardy to try to vote or enroll in a white school. And even in those states where blacks did vote, popular attitudes were not conducive to blacks' buying homes or taking jobs on an equal basis with whites. Even among those professing to support equal rights, a substantial portion opposed African Americans' efforts to obtain them and federal action to secure them. In 1942, a national poll showed that only 30 percent of whites thought black and white children should attend the same schools; in 1956, the proportion had risen, but only to 49 percent, still less than a majority. (In the South, white support for school integration was even lower—14 percent favored it in 1956, about 31 percent in 1963.) As late as 1956, a majority of southern whites were opposed to integrated public transportation facilities. Even among whites who generally favored integration, there was in 1963 (*before* the ghetto riots) considerable opposition to the black civil rights movement: nearly half of the whites classified in a survey as moderate integrationists thought demonstrations hurt the black cause; nearly two-thirds disapproved of actions taken by the civil rights movement; and more than a third felt civil rights should be left to the states.[4]

In short, the political position in which African Americans found themselves until the 1960s made it difficult for them to advance their interests through a feasible legislative strategy; their opponents were aroused, organized, and powerful. Thus if black interests were to be championed in Congress or state legislatures, blacks would have to have white allies. Though some such allies could be found, they were too few to make a difference in a political system that gives a substantial advantage to strongly motivated opponents of any new policy. For that to change, one or both of two things would have to happen: additional allies would have to be recruited (a delicate problem, given that many white integrationists disapproved of aspects of the civil rights movement), or the struggle would have to be shifted to a policy-making arena in which the opposition enjoyed less of an advantage.

Partly by plan, and partly by accident, black leaders followed both of these strategies simultaneously. By publicizing their grievances and organizing a civil rights movement that (at least in its early stages) concentrated on dramatizing the denial to blacks of essential and widely accepted liberties, African Americans were able to broaden their base of support both among political elites and among the general public and thereby raise civil rights matters from a low to a high position on the political agenda. By waging a patient, prolonged, but carefully planned legal struggle, black leaders shifted decision-making power on key civil rights issues from Congress, where they had been stymied for generations, to the federal courts.

After this strategy had achieved some substantial successes—after blacks had become enfranchised and legal barriers to equal participation in political and economic affairs had been lowered—the politics of civil rights became more conventional. African Americans were able to assert their demands directly in the legislative and executive branches of government with reasonable (though scarcely certain) prospects of success. Civil rights became less a matter of gaining entry into the political system and more one of waging interest group politics within that system. At the same time, the goals of civil rights politics were broadened. The struggle to gain entry into the system had focused on the denial of fundamental rights (to vote, to organize, to obtain equal access to schools and public facilities); later the dominant issues were manpower development, economic progress, and the improvement of housing and neighborhoods.

The Campaign in the Courts

The Fourteenth Amendment was both an opportunity and a problem for black activists. Adopted in 1868, it seemed to guarantee equal rights for all: "No state shall make or enforce any law which shall abridge the privileges or immunities of citizens of the United States; nor shall any state deprive any person of life, liberty, or property, without due process of law; nor deny to any person within its jurisdiction the equal protection of the laws."

The key phrase was "equal protection of the laws." Read broadly, it might mean that the Constitution should be regarded as color-blind: no state law could have the effect of treating whites and blacks differently. Thus, a law segregating blacks and whites into separate schools or neighborhoods would be unconstitutional. Read narrowly, "equal protection" might mean only that blacks and whites had certain fundamental legal rights in common, among them the right to sign contracts, to serve on juries, or to buy and sell property, but otherwise they could be treated differently.

Historians have long debated which view Congress held when it proposed the Fourteenth Amendment. What forms of racial segregation, if any, were still permissible? Segregated trains? Hotels? Schools? Neighborhoods?

The Supreme Court took the narrow view. Though in 1880 it declared unconstitutional a West Virginia law requiring juries to be composed only of white males,[5] it decided in 1883 that it was unconstitutional for Congress to prohibit racial discrimination in public accommodations such as hotels.[6] The difference between the two cases seemed, in the eyes of the Court, to be this: serving on a jury was an essential right of citizenship that the state could not deny to any person on racial grounds without violating the Fourteenth Amendment, but registering at a hotel was a convenience controlled by a private person (the hotel owner), who could treat blacks and whites differently if he or she wished.

The major decision that determined the legal status of the Fourteenth Amendment for more than half a century was *Plessy v. Ferguson*. Louisiana had passed a law requiring blacks and whites to occupy separate cars on railroad trains operating in that state. When Adolph Plessy, who was seven-eighths white and one-eighth black, refused to obey the law, he was arrested. He appealed his conviction to the Supreme Court, claiming that the law violated the Fourteenth Amendment. In 1896, the Court rejected his claim, holding that the law treated both races equally even though it required them to be separate. The equal protection clause guaranteed political and legal but not social equality. "Separate-but-equal" facilities were constitutional because if "one race be inferior to the other socially, the Constitution of the United States cannot put them on the same plane."[7]

"SEPARATE BUT EQUAL"

Thus began the **separate-but-equal doctrine.** Three years later, the Court applied it to schools as well, declaring in *Cumming v. Richmond County Board of Education* that a decision in a Georgia community to close the black high school while keeping open the white high school was not a violation of the Fourteenth Amendment because blacks could always go to private schools. Here the Court seemed to be saying that not only could schools be separate, they could even be unequal.[8]

separate-but-equal doctrine The doctrine established in *Plessy v. Ferguson* (1896) that African Americans could constitutionally be kept in separate but equal facilities.

What the Court has made, the Court can unmake. But to get it to change its mind requires a long, costly, and uncertain legal battle. The National Association for the Advancement of Colored People (NAACP) was the main organization that waged that battle. Formed in 1909 by a group of whites and blacks in the aftermath of a race riot, the NAACP did many things, including lobbying in Washington and publicizing black grievances, especially in the pages of *The Crisis,* a magazine edited by W.E.B. Du Bois. But its most influential role was played in the courtroom.

It was a rational strategy. Fighting legal battles does not require forming broad political alliances or changing public opinion, tasks that would have been very difficult for a small and unpopular organization. A court-based approach also enabled the organization to remain nonpartisan. But it was a slow and difficult strategy. The Court had adopted a narrow interpretation of the Fourteenth Amendment. To get the Court to change its mind would require the NAACP to bring before it cases involving the strongest possible claims that a black had been unfairly treated—and under circumstances sufficiently different from those of earlier cases that the Court could find some grounds for changing its mind.

The steps in that strategy were these: First, persuade the Court to declare unconstitutional laws creating schools that were separate but obviously unequal. Second, persuade it to declare unconstitutional laws supporting schools that were separate but unequal in not-so-obvious ways. Third, persuade it to rule that racially separate schools were inherently unequal and hence unconstitutional.

CAN SEPARATE SCHOOLS BE EQUAL?

The first step was accomplished in a series of court cases stretching from 1938 to 1948. In 1938, the Court held that Lloyd Gaines had to be admitted to an all-white law school in Missouri because no black law school of equal quality existed in that state.[9] In 1948, the Court ordered the all-white University of Oklahoma Law School to admit Ada Lois Sipuel, a black, even though the state planned to build a black law school later. For education to be equal, it had to be equally available.[10] It still could be separate, however: the university admitted Ms. Sipuel but required her to attend classes in a section of the state capitol, roped off from other students, where she could meet with her law professors.

The second step was taken in two cases decided in 1950. Heman Sweatt, an African American, was treated by the University of Texas Law School much as Ada Sipuel had been treated in Oklahoma: "admitted" to the all-white school but relegated to a separate building. Another African American, George McLaurin, was allowed to study for his Ph.D in a "colored section" of the all-white University of Oklahoma. The Supreme Court unanimously decided that these arrangements were unconstitutional because, by imposing racially based barriers on the black students' access to professors, libraries, and other students, they created unequal educational opportunities.[11]

The third step, the climax of the entire drama, began in Topeka, Kansas, where Linda Brown wanted to enroll in her neighborhood school but could not because she was black and the school was by law reserved exclusively for whites. When the NAACP took her case to the federal district court in Kansas, the judge decided the black school Linda could attend was substantially equal in quality to the white school she could not attend and, therefore, denying her access to the white school was constitutional. To change that, the lawyers would have to persuade the Supreme Court to overrule the district judge on the grounds that racially separate schools were unconstitutional even if they were equal. In other words, the separate-but-equal doctrine would have to be overturned by the Court.

AP Images

Dorothy Counts, the first black student to attend Harding High School in Charlotte, N.C., tries to maintain her poise as she's taunted by shouting, gesticulating white students in September 1957.

It was a risky and controversial step to take. Many states, Kansas among them, were trying to make their all-black schools equal to those of whites by launching expensive building programs. If the NAACP succeeded in getting separate schools declared unconstitutional, the Court might well put a stop to the building of these new schools. Blacks could win a moral and legal victory but suffer a practical defeat—the loss of these new facilities. Despite these risks, the NAACP decided to go ahead with the appeal.

BROWN V. BOARD OF EDUCATION

On May 17, 1954, a unanimous Supreme Court, speaking through an opinion written and delivered by Chief Justice Earl Warren, found that "in the field of public education the doctrine of 'separate but equal' has no place" because "separate educational facilities are inherently unequal."[12] *Plessy v. Ferguson* was overruled, and "separate but equal" was dead.

The ruling was a landmark decision, but the reasons for it and the means chosen to implement it were as important and as controversial as the decision itself. There were at least three issues. First, how would the decision be implemented? Second, on what grounds were racially separate schools unconstitutional? Third, what test would a school system have to meet in order to be in conformity with the Constitution?

IMPLEMENTATION

The *Brown* case involved a class-action suit; that is, it applied not only to Linda Brown but to all others similarly situated. This meant that black children everywhere now had the right to attend formerly all-white schools. This change would be one of the most far-reaching and conflict-provoking events in modern American history. It could not be effected overnight or by the stroke of a pen. In 1955, the Supreme Court decided it would let local federal district courts oversee the end of segregation by giving them the power to approve or disapprove local desegregation plans. This was to be done "with all deliberate speed."[13]

In the South, "all deliberate speed" turned out to be a snail's pace. Massive resistance to desegregation broke out in many states. Some communities simply

WHAT WOULD YOU DO?

MEMORANDUM

To: *Justice Robert Gilbert*

From: *Ella Fitzgerald, law clerk*

Subject: *State support for predominantly black colleges*

Until school segregation ended, southern blacks could attend only all-black colleges. Now they are free to apply to previously all-white colleges, and these schools are integrated. But the traditional black colleges still exist, and very few whites apply to them. In 1992, the Supreme Court held that the state could not solve the problem by requiring a race-neutral admissions policy.* Now the Court must decide whether a predominantly black college can receive state support.

News »

Court to Rule on Black Colleges

The Supreme Court has announced that it will decide whether all-black colleges in the South can receive state support if there are too few whites attending them.

Arguments for:

1. These schools have a long tradition that ought to be preserved.
2. Many black students will learn better in an all-black environment.
3. African American organizations, in particular the United Negro College Fund, raise money for these schools.

Arguments against:

1. If the state once required single-race schools, it now has an obligation to dismantle them.
2. Race is a suspect classification, and no state program that chiefly serves one race can be allowed.

Your decision:

Allow all-black colleges ________________

Ban all-black colleges ________________

* *United States v. Fordice*, 505 U.S. 717 (1992).

defied the Court; some sought to evade its edict by closing their public schools. In 1956, more than 100 southern members of Congress signed a "Southern Manifesto" that condemned the *Brown* decision as an "abuse of judicial power" and pledged to "use all lawful means to bring about a reversal of the decision."

In the late 1950s and early 1960s, the National Guard and regular army paratroopers were used to escort black students into formerly all-white schools and universities. It was not until the 1970s that resistance collapsed and most southern schools were integrated. The use of armed force convinced people that resistance was futile; the disruption of the politics and economy of the South convinced leaders that it was imprudent; and the voting power of blacks convinced politicians that it was suicidal. In addition, federal laws began providing financial aid to integrated schools and withholding it from segregated ones. By 1970, only 14 percent of southern black schoolchildren still attended all-black schools.[14]

THE RATIONALE

As the struggle to implement the *Brown* decision continued, the importance of the rationale for that decision became apparent. The case was decided in a way that surprised many legal scholars.

Steve Shapiro/Black Star

In 1963, Governor George Wallace of Alabama stood in the doorway of the University of Alabama to block the entry of black students. Facing him is U.S. Deputy Attorney General Nicholas Katzenbach.

The Court could have said that the equal protection clause of the Fourteenth Amendment makes the Constitution, and thus state laws, color-blind. Or it could have said that the authors of the Fourteenth Amendment meant to ban segregated schools. It did neither. Instead, it said segregated education is bad because it "has a detrimental effect upon the colored children" by generating "a feeling of inferiority as to their status in the community" that may "affect their hearts and minds in a way unlikely ever to be undone."[15] This conclusion was supported by a footnote reference to social science studies of the apparent impact of segregation on black children.

Why did the Court rely on social science as much as or more than the Constitution in supporting its decision? Apparently for two reasons. One was the justices' realization that the authors of the Fourteenth Amendment may *not* have intended to outlaw segregated schools. The schools in Washington, D.C., were segregated when the amendment was proposed, and when this fact was mentioned during the debate, it seems to have been made clear that the amendment was not designed to abolish this segregation. When Congress debated a civil rights act a few years later, it voted down provisions that would have ended segregation in schools.[16] The Court could not easily base its decision on a constitutional provision that had, at best, an uncertain application to schools. The other reason grew out of the first. On so important a matter the chief justice wanted to speak for a unanimous court. Some justices did not agree that the Fourteenth Amendment made the Constitution color-blind. In the interests of harmony, the Court found an ambiguous rationale for its decision.

DESEGREGATION VERSUS INTEGRATION

That ambiguity led to the third issue. If separate schools were inherently unequal, what would "unseparate" schools look like? Since the Court had not said race was irrelevant, an "unseparate" school could be either one that blacks and whites were free to attend if they chose or one that blacks and whites in fact attended whether they wanted to or not. The first might be called a desegregated school, and the latter an integrated school. Think of the Topeka case. Was it enough that there was now no barrier to Linda Brown's attending the white school in her neighborhood? Or was it necessary that there be black children (if not Linda, then some others) actually going to that school together with white children?

As long as the main impact of the *Brown* decision lay in the South, where laws had prevented blacks from attending white schools, this question did not seem important. Segregation by law ***(de jure segregation)*** was now clearly unconstitutional. But in the North, laws had not kept blacks and whites apart; instead, all-black and all-white schools were the result of residential segregation, preferred living patterns, informal social forces, and administrative practices (such as drawing school district lines so as to produce single-race schools). This often was called segregation in fact ***(de facto segregation)***.

de jure *segregation* Racial segregation that is required by law.

de facto *segregation* Racial segregation that occurs in schools, not as a result of the law, but as a result of patterns of residential settlement.

In 1968, the Supreme Court settled the matter. In New Kent County, Virginia, the school board had created a "freedom-of-choice" plan under which every pupil would be allowed without legal restriction to attend the school of his or her choice. As it turned out, all the white children chose to remain in the all-white school, and 85 percent of the black children remained in the all-black school. The Court rejected this plan as unconstitutional because it did not produce the "ultimate end," which was a "unitary, nonracial system of education."[17] In the opinion written by Justice William Brennan, the Court seemed to be saying that the Constitution required actual racial mixing in the schools, not just the repeal of laws requiring racial separation.

This impression was confirmed three years later when the Court considered a plan in North Carolina under which pupils in Mecklenburg County (which includes Charlotte) were assigned to the nearest neighborhood school without regard to race. As a result, about half the black children now attended formerly all-white schools, with the other half attending all-black schools. The federal district court held that this was inadequate and ordered some children to be bused into more distant schools in order to achieve a greater degree of integration. The Supreme Court, now led by Chief Justice Warren Burger, upheld the district judge on the grounds that the court plan was necessary to achieve a "unitary school system."[18]

This case—*Swann v. Charlotte-Mecklenburg Board of Education*—pretty much set the guidelines for all subsequent cases involving school segregation. The essential features of those guidelines are as follows:

- To violate the Constitution, a school system, by law, practice, or regulation, must have engaged in discrimination. Put another way, a plaintiff must show an intent to discriminate on the part of the public schools.

Antibusing protesters buried a school bus (unoccupied) to dramatize their cause.

- The existence of all-white or all-black schools in a district with a history of segregation creates a presumption of intent to discriminate.
- The remedy for past discrimination will not be limited to freedom of choice, or what the Court called "the walk-in school." Remedies may include racial quotas in the assignment of teachers and pupils, redrawn district lines, and court-ordered busing.
- Not every school must reflect the social composition of the school system as a whole.

Relying on *Swann,* district courts have supervised redistricting and busing plans in localities all over the nation, often in the face of bitter opposition from the community. In Boston, the control of the city schools by a federal judge, W. Arthur Garrity, lasted for more than a decade and involved him in every aspect of school administration. One major issue not settled by *Swann* was whether busing and other remedies should cut across city and county lines. In some places, the central-city schools had become virtually all black. Racial integration could be achieved only by bringing black pupils to white suburban schools or moving white pupils into central-city schools. In a series of split-vote decisions, the Court ruled that court-ordered intercity busing could be authorized only if it could be demonstrated that the suburban areas as well as the central city had in fact practiced school segregation. Where that could not be shown, such intercity busing would not be required. The Court was not persuaded that intent had been proved in Atlanta, Detroit, Denver, Indianapolis, and Richmond, but it was persuaded that it had been proved in Louisville and Wilmington.[19]

The importance the Court attaches to intent means that if a school system that was once integrated becomes all black as a result of whites' moving to the suburbs, the Court will not require that district lines constantly be redrawn or new busing plans be adopted to adjust to the changing distribution of the population.[20] This in turn means that as long as blacks and whites live in different neighborhoods for whatever reason, there is a good chance that some schools in both areas will be heavily of one race. If mandatory busing or other integration measures cause whites to move out of a city at a faster rate than they otherwise would (a process often called "white flight"), then efforts to integrate the schools may in time create more single-race schools. Ultimately, integrated schools will exist only in integrated neighborhoods or where the quality of education is so high that both blacks and whites want to enroll in the school even at some cost in terms of travel and inconvenience.

Mandatory busing to achieve racial integration has been a deeply controversial program and has generated considerable public opposition. Surveys show that a majority of people oppose it.[21] As recently as 1992, a poll showed that 48 percent of whites in the Northeast and 53 percent of southern whites felt it was "not the business" of the federal government to ensure "that black and white children go to the same schools."[22] Presidents Nixon, Ford, and Reagan opposed busing; all three supported legislation to prevent or reduce it, and Reagan petitioned the courts to reconsider busing plans. The courts refused to reconsider, and Congress has passed only minor restrictions on busing.

The reason why Congress has not followed public opinion on this matter is complex. It has been torn between the desire to support civil rights and uphold the courts and the desire to represent the views of its constituents. Because it faces a dilemma, Congress has taken both sides of the issue simultaneously. By the late 1980s, busing was a dying issue in Congress, in part because no meaningful legislation seemed possible and in part because popular passion over busing had somewhat abated.

Then, in 1992, the Supreme Court made it easier for local school systems to reclaim control over their schools from the courts. In DeKalb County, Georgia (a suburb of Atlanta), the schools had been operating under court-ordered desegregation plans for many years. Despite this effort, full integration had not been achieved, largely because the county's neighborhoods had increasingly become either all black or all white. The Court held that local schools could not be held responsible for segregation caused solely by segregated living patterns and so the courts would have to relinquish their control over the schools. In 2007, the Court said race could not be the decisive factor in assigning students to schools that had either never been segregated (as in Seattle) or where legal segregation had long since ended (as in Jefferson County, Kentucky).[23]

Landmark Cases

Civil Rights

- **Dred Scott case, *Scott v. Sanford* (1857):** Congress had no authority to ban slavery in a territory. A slave was considered a piece of property.
- ***Plessy v. Ferguson* (1896):** Upheld separate-but-equal facilities for white and black people on railroad cars.
- ***Brown v. Board of Education* (1954):** Said separate public schools are inherently unequal, thus starting racial desegregation.
- ***Green v. County School Board of New Kent County* (1968):** Banned a freedom-of-choice plan for integrating schools, suggesting blacks and whites must actually attend racially mixed schools.
- ***Swann v. Charlotte-Mecklenburg Board of Education* (1971):** Approved busing and redrawing district lines as ways of integrating public schools.

The Campaign in Congress

The campaign in the courts for desegregated schools, though slow and costly, was a carefully managed effort to alter the interpretation of a constitutional provision. But to get new civil rights laws out of Congress required a far more difficult and decentralized strategy, one that was aimed at mobilizing public opinion and overcoming the many congressional barriers to action.

The first problem was to get civil rights on the political agenda by convincing people that something had to be done. This could be achieved by dramatizing the problem in ways that tugged at the conscience of whites who were not racist but were ordinarily indifferent to black problems. Brutal lynchings of blacks had shocked these whites, but lynchings were becoming less frequent in the 1950s.

Those leaders could, however, arrange for dramatic confrontations between blacks claiming some obvious right and the whites who denied it to them. Beginning in the late 1950s, these confrontations began to occur in the form of sit-ins at segregated lunch counters and "freedom rides" on segregated bus lines. At about the same time, efforts were made to get blacks registered to vote in counties where whites had used intimidation and harassment to prevent it.

The best-known campaign occurred in 1955–1956 in Montgomery, Alabama, where blacks, led by a young minister named Martin Luther King, Jr., boycotted the local bus system after it had a black woman, Rosa Parks, arrested because she refused to surrender her seat on a bus to a white man.

© Bettman/Corbis

AP Images

In 1960, black students from North Carolina Agricultural and Technical College staged the first "sit-in" when they were refused service at a lunch counter in Greensboro (left). Twenty years later, graduates of the college returned to the same lunch counter (right). Though prices had risen, the service had improved.

civil disobedience Opposing a law one considers unjust by peacefully disobeying it and accepting the resultant punishment.

These early demonstrations were based on the philosophy of **civil disobedience**—that is, peacefully violating a law, such as one requiring blacks to ride in a segregated section of a bus, and allowing oneself to be arrested as a result.

But the momentum of protest, once unleashed, could not be centrally directed or confined to nonviolent action. A rising tide of anger, especially among younger blacks, resulted in the formation of more militant organizations and the spontaneous eruption of violent demonstrations and riots in dozens of cities across the country. From 1964 to 1968, there were in the North as well as the South four "long, hot summers" of racial violence.

The demonstrations and rioting succeeded in getting civil rights on the national political agenda, but at a cost: many whites, opposed to the demonstrations or appalled by the riots, dug in their heels and fought against making any concessions to "lawbreakers," "troublemakers," and "rioters." In 1964 and again in 1968, more than two-thirds of the whites interviewed in opinion polls said the civil rights movement was pushing too fast, had hurt the black cause, and was too violent.[24]

In short, a conflict existed between the agenda-setting and coalition-building aspects of the civil rights movement. This was especially a problem since conservative southern legislators still controlled many key congressional committees that had for years been the graveyard of civil rights legislation. The Senate Judiciary Committee was dominated by a coalition of southern Democrats and conservative Republicans, and the House Rules Committee was under the control of a chairman hostile to civil rights bills, Howard Smith of Virginia. Any bill that passed the House faced an almost certain filibuster in the Senate. Finally, President John F. Kennedy was reluctant to submit strong civil rights bills to Congress.

Four developments made it possible to break the deadlock. First, public opinion was changing. As Figure 6.1 shows, the proportion of whites who were willing to have their children attend a school that was half black increased sharply (though the proportion of whites willing to have their children attend a school that was predominantly black increased by much less). About the same change could be found in attitudes toward allowing blacks equal access to hotels and buses.[25] Of course, support in principle for these civil rights measures was not necessarily the same as support in practice; nonetheless, clearly a major shift was occurring in popular approval of at least the principles of civil rights. At the leading edge of this change were young, college-educated people.[26]

Second, certain violent reactions by white segregationists to black demonstrators were vividly portrayed by the media, especially television, in ways that gave to the civil rights cause a powerful moral force. In May 1963, the head of the Birmingham police, Eugene "Bull" Connor, ordered his men to use attack dogs and high-pressure fire hoses to repulse a peaceful march by African Americans demanding desegregated public facilities and increased job opportunities. The pictures of that confrontation (such as the one on page 142) created a national sensation and contributed greatly to the massive participation, by whites and blacks alike, in the "March on Washington" that summer. About a quarter of

Figure 6.1

Attitudes toward white children's attending schools with different proportions of blacks.

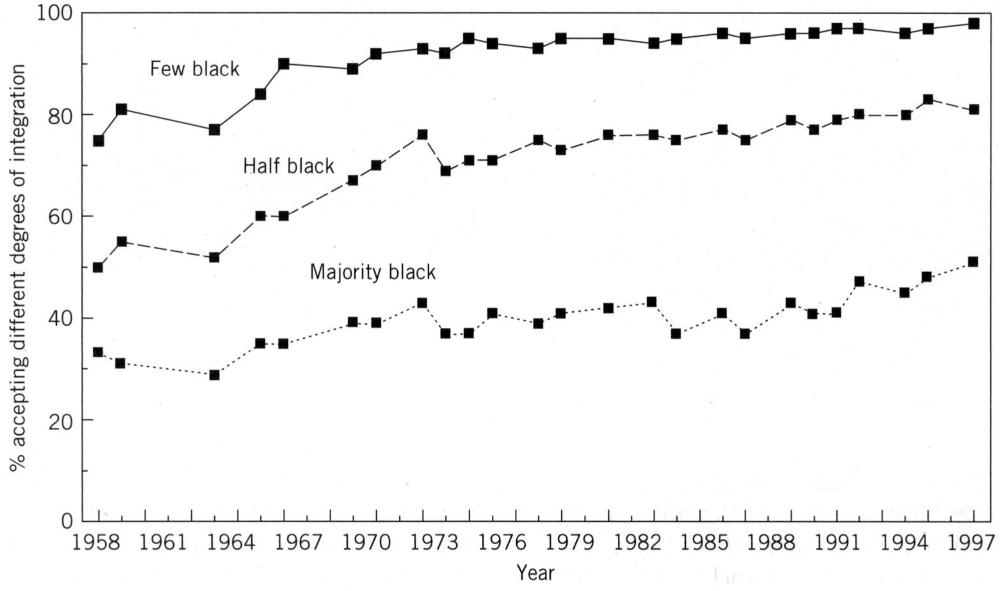

Source: Reprinted by permission of the publisher from Racial Attitudes in America by Howard Schuman, Charlotte Steeh, and Lawrence Bobo, p. 145, Figure 3.12. Cambridge, Mass.: Harvard University Press. Copyright © 1985, 1997 by the Presidents and Fellows of Harvard College.

a million people gathered in front of the Lincoln Memorial to hear Martin Luther King, Jr., deliver a stirring and widely hailed address, often called the "I Have a Dream" speech. The following summer in Neshoba County, Mississippi, three young civil rights workers (two white and one black) were brutally murdered by Klansmen aided by the local sheriff. When the FBI identified the murderers, the effect on national public opinion was galvanic; no white southern leader could any longer offer persuasive opposition to federal laws protecting voting rights when white law enforcement officers had killed students working to protect those rights. And the next year, a white woman, Viola Liuzzo, was shot and killed while driving a car used to transport civil rights workers. Her death was the subject of a presidential address.

Third, President John F. Kennedy was assassinated in Dallas, Texas, in November 1963. Many people originally (and wrongly) thought he had been killed by a right-wing conspiracy. Even after the assassin had been caught and shown to have left-wing associations, the shock of the president's murder—in a southern city—helped build support for efforts by the new president, Lyndon B. Johnson (a Texan), to obtain passage of a strong civil rights bill as a memorial to the slain president.

Fourth, the 1964 elections not only returned Johnson to office with a landslide victory but also sent a huge Democratic majority to the House and retained the large Democratic margin in the Senate. This made it possible for northern Democrats to outvote or outmaneuver southerners in the House.

The cumulative effect of these forces led to the enactment of five civil rights laws between 1957 and 1968. Three (1957, 1960, and 1965) were chiefly directed at protecting the right to vote; one (1968) was aimed at preventing discrimination in housing; and one (1964), the most far-reaching of all, dealt with voting, employment, schooling, and public accommodations.

The passage of the 1964 act was the high point of the legislative struggle. Liberals in the House had drafted a bipartisan bill, but it was now in the House Rules Committee, where such matters had often disappeared without a trace. In the wake of Kennedy's murder, a discharge petition was filed, with President Johnson's support, to take the bill out of committee and bring it to the floor of the House. But the Rules Committee, without waiting for a vote on the petition (which it probably realized it would lose), sent the bill to the floor, where it passed overwhelmingly. In the Senate, an agreement between Republican minority leader Everett Dirksen and President Johnson smoothed the way for passage in several important respects. The House bill was sent directly to the Senate floor, thereby bypassing the southern-dominated

AP Images

This picture of a police dog lunging at a black man during a racial demonstration in Birmingham, Alabama, in May 1963 was one of the most influential photographs ever published. It was widely reprinted throughout the world and was frequently referred to in congressional debates on the civil rights bill of 1964.

AFP/Getty Images

Martin Luther King, Jr., delivers his "I have a Dream" speech on the Washington, D.C., mall in 1963.

Judiciary Committee. Nineteen southern senators began an eight-week filibuster against the bill. On June 10, 1964, by a vote of 71 to 29, cloture was invoked and the filibuster ended—the first time in history that a filibuster aimed at blocking civil rights legislation had been broken.

Since the 1960s, congressional support for civil rights legislation has grown—so much so, indeed, that labeling a bill a civil rights measure, once the kiss of death, now almost guarantees its passage. For example, in 1984 the Supreme Court decided the federal ban on discrimination in education applied only to the "program or activity" receiving federal aid and not to the entire school or university.[27] In 1988, Congress passed a bill to overturn this decision by making it clear that antidiscrimination rules applied to the entire educational institution and not just to that part (say, the physics lab) receiving federal money. When President Reagan vetoed the bill (because, in his view, it would diminish the freedom of church-affiliated schools), Congress overrode the veto. In the override vote, every southern Democrat in the Senate and almost 90 percent of those in the House voted for the bill. This was a dramatic change from 1964, when more than 80 percent of the southern Democrats in Congress voted against the Civil Rights Act (see Figure 6.2).

This change partly reflected the growing political strength of southern blacks. In 1960, less than one-third of voting-age blacks in the South were registered to vote; by 1971 more than half were, and by 1984 two-thirds were. In 2001, more than 9,000 blacks held elective office (see Table 6.1). But this was only half of the story. Attitudes among white political elites and members of Congress had also changed. This was evident as early as 1968,

Figure 6.2

Growing Support Among Southern Democrats in Congress for Civil Rights Bills

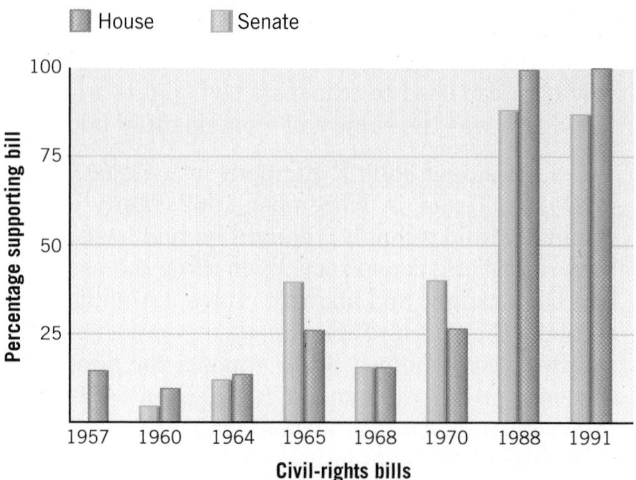

Source: Congressional Quarterly, *Congress and the Nation,* vols. 1, 2, 3, 7, 8.

Key Provisions of Major Civil Rights Laws

1957 **Voting** Made it a federal crime to try to prevent a person from voting in a federal election. Created the Civil Rights Commission.

1960 **Voting** Authorized the attorney general to appoint federal referees to gather evidence and make findings about allegations that African Americans were deprived of their right to vote. Made it a federal crime to use interstate commerce to threaten or carry out a bombing.

1964 **Voting** Made it more difficult to use devices such as literacy tests to bar African Americans from voting.

Public accommodations Barred discrimination on grounds of race, color, religion, or national origin in restaurants, hotels, lunch counters, gasoline stations, movie theaters, stadiums, arenas, and lodging houses with more than five rooms.

Schools Authorized the attorney general to bring suit to force the desegregation of public schools on behalf of citizens.

Employment Outlawed discrimination in hiring, firing, or paying employees on grounds of race, color, religion, national origin, or sex.

Federal funds Barred discrimination in any activity receiving federal assistance.

1965 **Voter registration** Authorized appointment by the Civil Service Commission of voting examiners who would require registration of all eligible voters in federal, state, and local elections, general or primary, in areas where discrimination was found to be practiced or where less than 50 percent of voting-age residents were registered to vote in the 1964 election.

Literacy tests Suspended use of literacy tests or other devices to prevent African Americans from voting.

1968 **Housing** Banned, by stages, discrimination in sale or rental of most housing (excluding private owners who sell or rent their homes without the services of a real-estate broker).

Riots Made it a federal crime to use interstate commerce to organize or incite a riot.

1972 **Education** Prohibited sex discrimination in education programs receiving federal aid.

1988 **Discrimination** If any part of an organization receives federal aid, no part of that organization may discriminate on the basis of race, sex, age, or physical handicap.

1991 **Discrimination** Made it easier to sue over job discrimination and collect damages; overturned certain Supreme Court decisions. Made it illegal for the government to adjust, or "norm," test scores by race.

Table 6.1 Increase in Number of Black Elected Officials

Office	1970	1991	2001
Congress and state legislatures	182	476	633
City and county offices	715	4,493	5,456
Judges and sheriffs	213	847	1,044
Boards of education	362	1,629	1,928
Total	1,472	7,445	9,061

Source: *Statistical Abstract of the United States, 2003, table 417.*

when Congress passed a law barring discrimination in housing even though polls showed that only 35 percent of the public supported the measure.

Civil rights is not an issue easily confined to schools, housing, and jobs. Sometimes it is extended to crime. When crack cocaine became a popular drug, it was cheap and easily sold on street corners. When the public demanded that the police get tough on crack dealers, arrests followed. Since the great majority of arrested dealers were black, there was a sharp increase in black drug dealers going to prison. Some blacks claimed they were being singled out by the

RESEARCH FRONTIERS

Civil Rights: Are Guns a Public Nuisance?

Some ideas about public policy grab media attention, garner political support, and go on to become public laws; other ideas never even make it on to the "public agenda." Political scientists have many different theories, taxonomies, and models about the policy process; and later in this book (Chapter 17) we offer our way of classifying and explaining the politics of issues ranging from economic policy to environmental policy.

When it comes to present-day civil rights policy dynamics, however, new research frontiers are being charted, not mainly by academic theorists, but by practitioner-scholars who have not merely studied change but helped to make it happen.

Take David Kairys, a Temple University law professor who was a full-time civil rights lawyer across four decades. In his 2008 memoir, Kairys illustrates how intricately intertwined with other issues civil rights policies tend to be; how post-1980 civil rights laws on racial discrimination and other matters have often shifted without any legislative changes; and how novel applications of old legal theories can spark new debates about how to define or enforce civil rights.

For example, in the Anglo-American legal tradition, a noisy blacksmith shop teeming with hot objects and other dangers could be declared a "public nuisance" and forced by local government authorities to shut down or pay damages even if it was there before anybody lived nearby, and even if it had always operated legally. But today, new questions arise: should otherwise law-abiding handgun manufacturers be sued by city officials for creating a "public nuisance," and do citizens have a civil right to live free from violence perpetrated with handguns?

In the late 1990s, the mayors of New Orleans, Chicago, Philadelphia, and several dozen other cities, joined in some cases by civil rights groups, brought "public nuisance" lawsuits against handgun manufacturers. In response, many state legislatures passed new laws exempting the handgun industry from these lawsuits; and, in 2005, the U.S. Congress enacted and President George W. Bush signed a new federal law granting the handgun industry broad legal immunity and rejecting related civil rights claims.

- Do you think that freedom from gun violence ought to be counted among "civil rights"?
- Do you think that permitting "public nuisance" or other lawsuits against otherwise law-abiding gun manufacturers might violate their "civil rights"?
- Do you think that a certain minimum standard of living, a certain minimum level of air quality, or a certain minimum degree of privacy ought to be considered a "civil right"?
- What, if any, contemporary issues do you think fall outside the domain of "civil rights," and why?

Source: David Kairys, *Philadelphia Freedom: Memoir of a Civil Rights Lawyer* (University of Michigan Press, 2008); John W. Kingdon, Agendas, *Alternatives, and Public Policies*, 2nd ed. (Pearson, 1997); James Q. Wilson, ed., *The Politics of Regulation* (Basic Books, 1980); Theodore J. Lowi, "American Business, Public Policy, Case Studies, and Political Theory," *World Politics* 16 (July 1964), pp. 677–715.

police because of their race. The Supreme Court disagreed, holding that no evidence had been presented to show that drug dealers of other races had not been prosecuted.[28]

RACIAL PROFILING

If law enforcement authorities are more likely to stop and question people because of their race or ethnicity, racial profiling occurs. At first glance, this would seem to be a bad idea. For example, African Americans often complain that they are stopped by the police for "driving while black." This complaint became a national issue in 1998 when the governor of New Jersey fired the head of the state police for saying blacks were stopped more frequently than whites because they broke the law more frequently. Soon President Clinton and later President Bush made statements condemning racial profiling.

But there is another side to this issue. Perhaps people of a certain race are more likely to break the speed limit or smuggle drugs in their cars; if that is the case, then stopping them more frequently, even if it means stopping more innocent people, may make sense. A study of police stops in Oakland, California, by the RAND Corporation showed that, at least in that city, officers stopped cars without knowing the race of the occupants because the share of blacks stopped at night, when the drivers could not been seen, was the same as the share stopped during the day when they could be seen.[29]

The terrorist attacks of 9/11 added a new dimension to the issue. If young Middle Eastern men are more likely to smuggle weapons onto airplanes, searching them more carefully than one searches an elderly white Caucasian woman may make sense. But federal officials are leery of doing anything that might get them labeled as "racial profilers."

Women and Equal Rights

The political and legal efforts to secure civil rights for African Americans were accompanied by efforts to expand the rights of women. There was an important difference between the two movements, however: whereas African Americans were arguing against a legal tradition that explicitly aimed to keep them in a subservient status, women had to argue against a tradition that claimed to be protecting them. For example, in 1908 the Supreme Court upheld an Oregon law that limited female laundry workers to a 10-hour workday against the claim that it violated the Fourteenth Amendment. The Court justified its decision with this language:

> *The two sexes differ in structure of body, in the functions to be performed by each, in the amount of physical strength, in the capacity for long-continued labor, particularly when done standing . . . the self-reliance which enables one to assert full rights, and in the capacity to maintain the struggle for subsistence. This difference justifies a difference in legislation and upholds that which is designed to compensate for some of the burdens which rest upon her.*[30]

The origin of the movement to give more rights to women was probably the Seneca Falls Convention held in 1848. Its leaders began to demand the right to vote for women. Though this was slowly granted by several states, especially in the West, it was not until 1920 that the Nineteenth Amendment made it clear that no state may deny the right to vote on the basis of sex. The great change in the status of women, however, took place during World War II when the demand for workers in our defense plants led to the employment of millions of women, such as "Rosie the Riveter," in jobs they had rarely held before. After the war, the feminist movement took flight with the publication in 1963 of *The Feminine Mystique* by Betty Friedan.

Congress responded by passing laws that required equal pay for equal work, prohibited discrimination on the basis of sex in employment and among students in any school or university receiving federal funds, and banned discrimination against pregnant women on the job.[31]

At the same time, the Supreme Court was altering the way it interpreted the Constitution. The key passage was the Fourteenth Amendment, which prohibits any state from denying to "any person" the "equal protection of the laws." For a long time the traditional standard, as we saw in the 1908 case, was a kind of protective paternalism. By the early 1970s, however, the Court had changed its mind. In deciding whether the Constitution bars all, some, or no sexual discrimination, the Court had a choice among three standards.

The first standard is the *reasonableness* standard. This says that when the government treats some classes of people differently from others—for example, applying statutory rape laws to men but not to women—the different treatment must be reasonable and not arbitrary.

The second standard is *intermediate scrutiny*. When women complained that some laws treated them unfairly, the Court adopted a standard somewhere between the reasonableness and strict scrutiny tests. Thus, a law that treats men and women differently must be more than merely reasonable, but the allowable differences need not meet the strict scrutiny test.

And so in 1971, the Court held that an Idaho statute was unconstitutional because it required that males be preferred over females when choosing people to administer the estates of deceased children. To satisfy the Constitution, a law treating men and women differently "must be reasonable, not arbitrary, and must rest on some ground of difference having a fair and substantial relation to the object of legislation so that all persons similarly circumstanced shall be treated alike."[32] In later decisions, some members of the Court wanted to make classifications based on sex inherently suspect and subject to the strict scrutiny test, but no majority has yet embraced this position.[33]

The third standard is *strict scrutiny*. This says that some instances of drawing distinctions between different groups of people—for example, by treating whites and blacks differently—are inherently suspect; thus, the Court will subject them to strict

How Things Work

How the Court Decides If You Discriminate

The Supreme Court has produced three different tests to decide if a government policy produces unconstitutional discrimination. Don't be surprised if you find it a bit hard to tell them apart.

1. **Rational basis** If the policy uses reasonable means to achieve a legitimate government goal, it is constitutional.

   Examples: If the government says you can't buy a drink until you are 21, this meets the rational basis test: the government wants to prevent children from drinking, and age 21 is a reasonable means to define when a person is an adult. And a state can ban advertising on trucks unless the ad is about the truck owner's own business.

2. **Intermediate scrutiny** If the policy "serves an important government interest" and is "substantially related" to serving that interest, it is constitutional.

   Examples: Men can be punished for statutory rape even if women are not punished because men and women are not "similarly situated." And men can be barred from entering hospital delivery rooms even though (obviously) women are admitted.

3. **Strict scrutiny** To be constitutional, the discrimination must serve a "compelling government interest," it must be "narrowly tailored" to attain that interest, and it must use the "least restrictive means" to attain it.

   Examples: Distinctions based on race, ethnicity, religion, or voting must pass the strict scrutiny test. You cannot bar black children from a public school or black adults from voting, and you cannot prevent one religion from knocking on your door to promote its views.

scrutiny to ensure they are clearly necessary to attain a legitimate state goal.

But sexual classifications can also be judged by a different standard. The Civil Rights Act of 1964 prohibits sex discrimination in the hiring, firing, and compensation of employees. The 1972 Civil Rights Act bans sex discrimination in local education programs receiving federal aid. These laws apply to *private,* and not just government, actions.

Over the years, the Court has decided many cases involving sexual classification. The following lists provide several examples of illegal sexual discrimination (violating either the Constitution or a civil rights act) and legal sexual distinctions (violating neither).

Landmark Cases

Women's Rights

- ***Reed v. Reed* (1971):** Gender discrimination violates the equal protection clause of the Constitution.
- ***Craig v. Boren* (1976):** Gender discrimination can be justified only if it serves "important governmental objectives" and is "substantially related to those objectives."
- ***Rostker v. Goldberg* (1981):** Congress can draft men without drafting women.
- ***United States v. Virginia* (1996):** State may not finance an all-male military school.

ILLEGAL DISCRIMINATION

- A state cannot set different ages at which men and women legally become adults.[34]
- A state cannot set different ages at which men and women are allowed to buy beer.[35]
- Women cannot be barred from jobs by arbitrary height and weight requirements.[36]
- Employers cannot require women to take mandatory pregnancy leaves.[37]
- Girls cannot be barred from Little League baseball teams.[38]

- Business and service clubs, such as the Junior Chamber of Commerce and Rotary Club, cannot exclude women from membership.[39]
- Though women as a group live longer than men, an employer must pay them monthly retirement benefits equal to those received by men.[40]
- High schools must pay the coaches of girls' sports the same as they pay the coaches of boys' sports.[41]

DECISIONS ALLOWING DIFFERENCES BASED ON SEX

- A law that punishes males but not females for statutory rape is permissible; men and women are not "similarly situated" with respect to sexual relations.[42]
- All-boy and all-girl public schools are permitted if enrollment is voluntary and quality is equal.[43]
- States can give widows a property-tax exemption not given to widowers.[44]
- The navy may allow women to remain officers longer than men without being promoted.[45]

The lower federal courts have been especially busy in the area of sexual distinctions. They have said that public taverns may not cater to men only and that girls may not be prevented from competing against boys in noncontact high school sports; on the other hand, hospitals may bar fathers from the delivery room. Women may continue to use their maiden names after marriage.[46]

In 1996, the Supreme Court ruled that women must be admitted to the Virginia Military Institute, until then an all-male state-supported college that had for many decades supplied what it called an "adversative method" of training to instill physical and mental discipline in cadets. In practical terms, this meant the school was very tough on students. The Court said that for a state to justify spending tax money on a single-sex school, it must supply an "exceedingly persuasive justification" for excluding the other gender. Virginia countered by offering to support an all-female training course at another college, but this was not enough.[47] This decision came close to imposing the strict scrutiny test, and so it has raised important questions about what could happen to all-female or traditionally black colleges that accept state money.

Perhaps the most far-reaching cases defining the rights of women have involved the draft and abortion. In 1981, the Court held in *Rostker v. Goldberg* that Congress may require men but not women to register for the draft without violating the due process clause of the Fifth Amendment.[48] In the area of national defense, the Court will give great deference to congressional policy (Congress had already decided to bar women from combat roles). For many years, women could be pilots and sailors but not on combat aircraft or combat ships. In 1993, the secretary of defense opened air and sea combat positions to all persons regardless of gender; only ground-troop combat positions are still reserved for men. The issue played a role in preventing the ratification of the Equal Rights Amendment to the Constitution, because of fears that it would reverse *Rostker v. Goldberg*.

SEXUAL HARASSMENT

When Paula Corbin Jones accused President Clinton of sexual harassment, the judge threw the case out of court because she had not submitted enough evidence such that, if the jury believed her story, she would have made a legally adequate argument that she had been sexually harassed.

What, then, is sexual harassment? Drawing on rulings by the Equal Employment Opportunities Commission, the Supreme Court has held that harassment can take one of two forms. First, it is illegal for someone to request sexual favors as a condition of employment or promotion. This is the "quid pro quo" rule. If a person does this, the employer is "strictly liable." Strict liability means the employer can be found at fault even if he or she did not know a subordinate was requesting sex in exchange for hiring or promotion.

Second, it is illegal for an employee to experience a work environment that has been made hostile or intimidating by a steady pattern of offensive sexual teasing, jokes, or obscenity. But employers are not strictly liable in this case; they can be found at fault only if they were "negligent"—that is, they knew about the hostile environment but did nothing about it.

In 1998, the Supreme Court decided three cases that made these rules either better or worse, depending on your point of view. In one, it determined that a school system was not liable for the conduct of a teacher who seduced a female student because the student never reported the actions. In a second, it held that a city was liable for a sexually hostile work environment confronting a female lifeguard even though she did not report this to her superiors. In the third, it decided that a female employee who was not promoted after having rejected the sexual advances of her boss could recover financial damages from the firm. But, it added, the firm could have avoided paying this bill if it had put in place an "affirmative defense" against sexual exploitation, although the Court never said what such a policy might be.[49]

Sexual harassment is a serious matter, but because there are almost no federal laws governing it, we are left with somewhat vague and often inconsistent court and bureaucratic rules to guide us.

PRIVACY AND SEX

Regulating sexual matters has traditionally been left up to the states, which do so by exercising their **police powers.** These powers include more than the authority to create police departments; they include all laws designed to promote public order and secure the safety and morals of the citizens. Some have argued that the Tenth Amendment to the Constitution, by reserving to the states all powers not delegated to the federal government, meant that states could do anything not explicitly prohibited by the Constitution. But that changed when the Supreme Court began expanding the power of Congress over business and when it started to view sexual matters under the newly discovered right to privacy.

police powers State power to effect laws promoting health, safety, and morals.

Until that point, it had been left up to the states to decide whether and under what circumstances a woman could obtain an abortion. For example, New York allowed abortions during the first 24 weeks of pregnancy, while Texas banned it except when the mother's life was threatened. That began to change in 1965 when the Supreme Court held that the states could not prevent the sale of contraceptives because by so doing it would invade a "zone of privacy." Privacy is nowhere mentioned in the Constitution, but the Court argued that it could be inferred from "penumbras" (literally, shadows) cast off by various provisions of the Bill of Rights.[50]

Eight years later the Court, in its famous *Roe v. Wade* decision, held that a "right to privacy" is "broad enough to encompass a woman's decision whether or not to terminate a pregnancy."[51] The case, which began in Texas, produced this view: during the first three months (or trimester) of pregnancy, a woman has an unfettered right to an abortion. During the second trimester, states may regulate abortions but only to protect the mother's health. In the third trimester, states might ban abortions.

In reaching this decision, the Court denied that it was trying to decide when human life began—at the moment of conception, at the moment of birth, or somewhere in between. But that is not how critics of the decision saw things. To them, life begins at conception, and so the human fetus is a "person" entitled to the equal protection of the laws guaranteed by the Fourteenth Amendment. People feeling this way began to use the slogans "right to life" and "pro-life." Supporters of the Court's action saw matters differently. In their view, no one can say for certain when human life begins; what one *can* say, however, is that a woman is entitled to choose whether or not to have a baby. These people took the slogans "right to choose" and "pro-choice."

Landmark Cases

Privacy and Abortion

- ***Griswold v. Connecticut* (1965):** Found a "right to privacy" in the Constitution that would ban any state law against selling contraceptives.
- ***Roe v. Wade* (1973):** State laws against abortion were unconstitutional.
- ***Webster v. Reproductive Health Services* (1989):** Allowed states to ban abortions from public hospitals and permitted doctors to test to see if fetuses were viable.
- ***Planned Parenthood v. Casey* (1992):** Reaffirmed *Roe v. Wade* but upheld certain limits on its use.
- ***Gonzales v. Carhart* (2007):** Federal law may ban certain forms of partial-birth abortion.

Almost immediately, the congressional allies of pro-life groups introduced constitutional amendments to overturn *Roe v. Wade,* but none passed Congress. Nevertheless, abortion foes did persuade Congress, beginning in 1976, to bar the use of federal funds to pay for abortions except when the life of the mother is at stake. This provision is known as the Hyde Amendment, after its sponsor, Representative Henry Hyde. The chief effect of the amendment has been to deny the use of Medicaid funds to pay for abortions for low-income women.

Despite pro-life opposition, the Supreme Court for 16 years steadfastly reaffirmed and even broadened its decision in *Roe v. Wade*. It struck down laws requiring, before an abortion could be performed, a woman to have the consent of her husband, an "emancipated" but underage girl to have the consent of her parents, or a woman to be advised by her doctor as to the facts about abortion.[52]

But in 1989, under the influence of justices appointed by President Reagan, the Court began in the *Webster* case to uphold some state restrictions on abortions. When that happened, many people predicted that in time *Roe v. Wade* would be overturned, especially if President George H.W. Bush was able to appoint more justices. He appointed two (Souter and Thomas), but *Roe* survived. The key votes were cast by Justices O'Connor, Souter, and Kennedy. In 1992, in its *Casey* decision, the Court by a vote of five to four explicitly refused to overturn *Roe,* declaring that there was a right to abortion. At the same time, however, it upheld a variety of restrictions imposed by the state of Pennsylvania on women seeking abortions. These included a mandatory 24-hour waiting period between the request for an abortion and the performance of it, the requirement that teenagers obtain the consent of one parent (or, in special circumstances, of a judge), and a requirement that women contemplating an abortion be given pamphlets about alternatives to it. Similar restrictions had been enacted in many other states, all of which looked to the Pennsylvania case for guidance as to whether they could be enforced. In allowing these restrictions, the Court overruled some of its own earlier decisions.[53] On the other hand, the Court did strike down a state law that would have required married women to obtain the consent of their husbands before having an abortion.

After a long political and legal struggle, the Court in 2007 upheld a federal law that bans certain kinds of partial-birth abortions. The law does not allow an abortion in which the fetus, still alive, is withdrawn until its head is outside the mother and then it is killed. But the law does not ban a late-term abortion if it is necessary to protect the physical health of the mother or if it is performed on an already dead fetus, even if the doctor has already killed it.[54]

There is one irony in all of this: "Roe," the pseudonym for the woman who started the suit that became *Roe v. Wade,* never had an abortion and many years later, using her real name, Norma McCorvey, became an evangelical Christian who published a book and started a ministry to denounce abortions.

Affirmative Action

A common thread running through the politics of civil rights is the argument between **equality of results** and equality of opportunity.

EQUALITY OF RESULTS

One view, expressed by most civil rights and feminist organizations, is that the burdens of racism and sexism can be overcome only by taking race or sex into account in designing remedies. It is not enough that people be given rights; they also must be given benefits. If life is a race, everybody must be brought up to the same starting line (or possibly even to the same finish line). This means that the Constitution is not and should not be color-blind or sex-neutral. In education, this implies that the races must actually be mixed in the schools, by busing if necessary. In hiring, it means that **affirmative action**—preferential hiring practices—must be used to find and hire women, African Americans, and other minorities. Women should not simply be free to enter the labor force; they should be given the material necessities (for example, free daycare) that will help them enter it. On payday, workers' checks should reflect not just the results of people's competing in the marketplace but the results of plans designed to ensure that people earn comparable amounts for comparable jobs. Of late, affirmative action has been defended in the name of diversity or multiculturalism—the view that every institution (firm, school, or agency) and every college curriculum should reflect the cultural (that is, ethnic) diversity of the nation.

EQUALITY OF OPPORTUNITY

The second view holds that if it is wrong to discriminate *against* African Americans and women, it is equally wrong to give them preferential treatment over other groups. To do so constitutes **reverse discrimination.** The Constitution and laws should be color-blind and sex-neutral.[55] In this view, allowing children to attend the school of their choice is sufficient; busing them to attain a certain racial mixture is wrong. Eliminating barriers to job opportunities is right; using numerical "targets" and "goals" to place minorities and women in specific jobs is wrong. If people wish to compete in the market, they should be satisfied with the market verdict concerning the worth of their work.

These two views are intertwined with other deep

affirmative action Programs designed to increase minority participation in some institutions (businesses, schools, labor unions, or government agencies) by taking positive steps to appoint more minority-group members.

reverse discrimination Using race or sex to give preferential treatment to some people.

equality of results Making certain that people achieve the same result.

How Things Work

Becoming a Citizen

For persons born in the United States, the rights of U.S. citizenship have been ensured, in constitutional theory if not in everyday practice, since the passage of the Fourteenth Amendment in 1868 and the civil rights laws of the 1960s. The Fourteenth Amendment conferred citizenship upon "all persons born in the United States . . . and subject to the jurisdiction thereof." Subsequent laws also gave citizenship to children born outside the United States to parents who are American citizens.

But immigrants, by definition, are not born with the rights of U.S. citizenship. Instead, those seeking to become U.S. citizens must, in effect, assume certain responsibilities in order to become citizens. The statutory requirements for naturalization, as they have been broadly construed by the courts, are as follows:

- Five years' residency, or three years if married to a citizen.
- Continuous residency since filing of the naturalization petition.
- Good moral character, which is loosely interpreted to mean no evidence of criminal activity.
- Attachment to constitutional principles. This means that potential citizens have to answer basic factual questions about American government (e.g., "Who was the first president of the United States?") and publicly denounce any and all allegiance to their native country and its leaders (e.g., Italy and the king of Italy), but devotion to constitutional principles is now regarded as implicit in the act of applying for naturalization.
- Being favorably disposed to "the good order and happiness of the United States."*

Today, about 97 percent of aliens who seek citizenship are successful in meeting these requirements and becoming naturalized citizens of the United States.

*8 U.S.C. 1423, 1427 (1970); *Girouard v. United States,* 328 U.S. 61 (1946).

equality of opportunity Giving people an equal chance to succeed.

philosophical differences. Supporters of **equality of opportunity** tend to have orthodox beliefs; they favor letting private groups behave the way that they want (and so may defend the right of a men's club to exclude women). Supporters of the opposite view are likely to be progressive in their beliefs and insist that private clubs meet the same standards as schools or business firms. Adherents to the equality-of-opportunity view often attach great importance to traditional models of the family and so are skeptical of daycare and federally funded abortions. Adherents to the equality-of-results view prefer greater freedom of choice in lifestyle questions and so take the opposite position on daycare and abortion.

Of course, the debate is more complex than this simple contrast suggests. Take, for example, the question of affirmative action. Both the advocates of equality of opportunity and those of equality of results might agree that there is something odd about a factory or university that hires no African Americans or women, and both might press it to prove that its hiring policy is fair. Affirmative action in this case can mean *either* looking hard for qualified women and minorities and giving them a fair shot at jobs *or* setting a numerical goal for the number of women and minorities that should be hired and insisting that that goal be met. Persons who defend the second course of action call these goals "targets"; persons who criticize that course call them "quotas."

The issue has largely been fought in the courts. Between 1978 and 1990, about a dozen major cases involving affirmative action were decided by the Supreme Court; in about half it was upheld, and in the other half it was overturned. The different outcomes reflect two things—the differences in the facts of the cases and the arrival on the Court of three justices (Kennedy, O'Connor, and Scalia) appointed by a president, Ronald Reagan, who was opposed to at least the broader interpretation of affirmative action. As a result of these decisions, the law governing affirmative action is now complex and confusing.

How Things Work

The Rights of Aliens

America is a nation of immigrants. Some have arrived legally, others illegally. An illegal, or undocumented, alien is subject to deportation. With the passage in 1986 of the Immigration Reform and Control Act, illegal aliens who have resided in this country continuously since before January 1, 1982, are entitled to amnesty—that is, they can become legal residents. However, the same legislation stipulated that employers (who once could hire undocumented aliens without fear of penalty) must now verify the legal status of all newly hired employees; if they knowingly hire an illegal alien, they face civil and criminal penalties.

Aliens—people residing in this country who are not citizens—cannot vote or run for office. Nevertheless, they must pay taxes just as if they were citizens. And they are entitled to many constitutional rights, even if they are in this country illegally. This is because most of the rights mentioned in the Constitution refer to "people" or "persons," not to "citizens." For example, the Fourteenth Amendment bars a state from depriving "*any person* of life, liberty, or property, without due process of law" and from denying "to *any person* within its jurisdiction the equal protection of the laws" [italics added]. As a result, the courts have held that:

- The children of illegal aliens cannot be excluded from the public school system.[1]
- Legally admitted aliens are entitled to welfare benefits.[2]
- Illegal aliens cannot be the object of reprisals if they attempt to form a labor union where they work.[3]
- The First Amendment rights of free speech, religion, press, and assembly and the Fourth Amendment protections against arbitrary arrest and prosecution extend to aliens as well as to citizens.[4]
- Aliens are entitled to own property.

The government can make rules that apply to aliens only, but they must justify the reasonableness of the rules. For example:

- The Immigration and Naturalization Service has broader powers to arrest and search illegal aliens than police departments have to arrest and search citizens.[5]
- States can limit certain jobs, such as police officer and schoolteacher, to citizens.[6]
- The president or Congress can bar the employment of aliens by the federal government.[7]
- States can bar aliens from serving on a jury.[8]
- Illegal aliens are not entitled to obtain a Social Security card.

[1] *Plyler v. Doe*, 457 U.S. 202 (1982).

[2] *Graham v. Richardson*, 403 U.S. 365 (1971).

[3] *Sure-Tan v. National Labor Relations Board*, 467 U.S. 883 (1984).

[4] *Chew v. Colding*, 344 U.S. 590 (1953).

[5] *United States v. Brignoni-Ponce*, 422 U.S. 873 (1975); *INS v. Delgado*, 466 U.S. 210 (1984); *INS v. Lopez-Mendoza*, 486 U.S. 1032 (1984).

[6] *Cabell v. Chavez-Salido*, 454 U.S. 432 (1982); *Foley v. Connelie*, 435 U.S. 291 (1978); *Amblach v. Norwick*, 441 U.S. 68 (1979).

[7] *Hampton v. Mow Sun Wong*, 436 U.S. 67 (1976).

[8] *Schneider v. New Jersey*, 308 U.S. 147 (1939).

Consider one issue: should the government be allowed to use a quota system to select workers, enroll students, award contracts, or grant licenses? In the *Bakke* decision in 1978, the Court said the medical school of the University of California at Davis could not use an explicit numerical quota in admitting minority students but could "take race into account."[56] So no numerical quotas, right? Wrong. Two years later, the Court upheld a federal rule that set aside 10 percent of all federal construction contracts for minority-owned firms.[57] All right, maybe quotas can't be used in medical schools, but they can be used in the construction industry. Not exactly. In 1989, the Court overturned a Richmond, Virginia, law that set aside 30 percent of its construction contracts for minority-owned firms.[58] Well, maybe the Court just changed its mind between 1980 and 1989. No. One year later it upheld a federal rule that gave preference to minority-owned firms in the awarding of broadcast licenses.[59] Then in 1993, it upheld the right of white contractors to challenge minority set-aside laws in Jacksonville, Florida.[60]

How Things Work

The Rights of the Disabled

In 1990, the federal government passed the Americans with Disabilities Act (ADA), a sweeping law that extended many of the protections enjoyed by women and racial minorities to disabled persons.

Who Is a Disabled Person?

Anyone who *has* a physical or mental impairment that substantially limits one or more major life activities (for example, holding a job), anyone who has a *record* of such impairment, or anyone who is *regarded* as having such an impairment is considered disabled.

What Rights Do Disabled Persons Have?

Employment Disabled persons may not be denied employment or promotion if, with "reasonable accommodation," they can perform the duties of that job. (Excluded from this protection are people who currently use illegal drugs, gamble compulsively, or are homosexual or bisexual.) Reasonable accommodation need not be made if this would cause "undue hardship" on the employer.

Government Programs and Transportation Disabled persons may not be denied access to government programs or benefits. New buses, taxis, and trains must be accessible to disabled persons, including those in wheelchairs.

Public Accommodations Disabled persons must enjoy "full and equal" access to hotels, restaurants, stores, schools, parks, museums, auditoriums, and the like. To achieve equal access, owners of existing facilities must alter them "to the maximum extent feasible"; builders of new facilities must ensure they are readily accessible to disabled persons, unless this is structurally impossible.

Telephones The ADA directs the Federal Communications Commission to issue regulations to ensure telecommunications devices for hearing- and speech-impaired people are available "to the extent possible and in the most efficient manner."

Congress The rights under this law apply to employees of Congress.

Rights Compared The ADA does not enforce the rights of disabled persons in the same way as the Civil Rights Act enforces the rights of African Americans and women. Racial or gender discrimination must end regardless of cost; denial of access to disabled persons must end unless "undue hardship" or excessive costs would result.

It is too early to try to make sense of these twists and turns, especially since a deeply divided Court is still wrestling with these issues and Congress (as with the Civil Rights Act of 1991) is modifying or superseding some earlier Court decisions. But a few general standards seem to be emerging. In simplified form, they are as follows:

- The courts will subject any quota system created by state or local governments to "strict scrutiny" and will look for a "compelling" justification for it.
- Quotas or preference systems cannot be used by state or local governments without first showing that such rules are needed to correct an actual past or present pattern of discrimination.[61]

A protest in Georgia over immigration laws.

- In proving there has been discrimination, it is not enough to show that African Americans (or other minorities) are statistically underrepresented among employees, contractors, or union members; you must identify the actual practices that have had this discriminatory impact.[62]
- Quotas or preference systems created by *federal* law will be given greater deference, in part because Section 5 of the Fourteenth Amendment gives to Congress powers not given to the states to correct the effects of racial discrimination.[63]
- It may be easier to justify in court a voluntary preference system (for example, one agreed to in a labor-management contract) than one that is required by law.[64]
- Even when you can justify special preferences in *hiring* workers, the Supreme Court is not likely to allow racial preferences to govern who gets *laid off*. A worker laid off to make room for a minority worker loses more than a worker not hired in preference to a minority applicant.[65]

Complex as they are, these rulings still generate a great deal of passion. Supporters of the decisions barring certain affirmative action plans hail these decisions as steps back from an emerging pattern of reverse discrimination. In contrast, civil rights organizations have denounced those decisions that have overturned affirmative action programs. In 1990, their congressional allies introduced legislation that would reverse several decisions. In particular, this legislation would put the burden of proof on the employer, not the employee, to show that the underrepresentation of minorities in the firm's workforce was the result of legitimate and necessary business decisions and not the result of discrimination. If the employer could not prove this, the aggrieved employee would be able to collect large damage awards. (In the past, he or she could collect only back pay.) In 1991, the bill was passed and was signed by President Bush.

In thinking about these matters, most Americans distinguish between compensatory action and preferential treatment. They define *compensatory action* as "helping disadvantaged people catch up, usually by giving them extra education, training, or services." A majority of the public supports this. They define preferential treatment as "giving minorities preference in hiring, promotions, college admissions, and contracts." Large majorities oppose this.[66] These views reflect an enduring element in American political culture—a strong commitment to individualism ("nobody should get something without deserving it") coupled with support for help for the disadvantaged ("somebody who is suffering through no fault of his or her own deserves a helping hand").

Where does affirmative action fit into this culture? Polls suggest that if affirmative action is defined as "helping," people will support it, but if it is defined as "using quotas," they will oppose it. On this matter, blacks and whites see things differently. Blacks think they should receive preferences in employment to create a more diverse workforce and to make up for past discrimination; whites oppose using goals to create diversity or to remedy past ills. In sum, the controversy over affirmative action depends on what you mean by it and on your racial identity.[67]

A small construction company named Adarand tried to get a contract to build guardrails along a highway in Colorado. Though it was the low bidder, it lost the contract because of a government policy that favors small businesses owned by "socially and economically disadvantaged individuals"—that is, by racial and ethnic minorities. In a five-to-four decision, the Court agreed with Adarand and sent the case back to Colorado for a new trial.

The essence of the Court's decision was that *any* discrimination based on race must be subject to strict scrutiny, even if its purpose is to help, not hurt, a racial minority. Strict scrutiny means two things:

- Any racial preference must serve a "compelling government interest."
- The preference must be "narrowly tailored" to serve that interest.[68]

To serve a compelling governmental interest, it is likely that any racial preference will have to remedy a clear pattern of past discrimination. No such pattern had been shown in Colorado.

This decision prompted a good deal of political debate about affirmative action. In California, an initiative was put on the 1996 ballot to prevent state authorities from using "race, sex, color, ethnicity, or national origin as a criterion for either discriminating against, or granting preferential treatment to, any individual or group" in public employment, public education, or public contracting. When the votes were counted, it passed. Michigan, Nebraska, and Washington have adopted similar measures, and other states may do so.

But the *Adarand* case and the passage of the California initiative did not mean affirmative action was dead. Though the federal Court of Appeals for the Fifth Circuit had rejected the affirmative action program of the University of Texas Law School,[69] the

Landmark Cases

Affirmative Action

- ***Regents of the University of California v. Bakke* (1978):** In a confused set of rival opinions, the decisive vote was cast by Justice Powell, who said that a quota-like ban on Bakke's admission was unconstitutional but that "diversity" was a legitimate goal that could be pursued by taking race into account.
- ***United Steelworkers v. Weber* (1979):** Despite the ban on racial classifications in the 1964 Civil Rights Act, this case upheld the use of race in an employment agreement between the steelworkers union and steel plant.
- ***Richmond v. Croson* (1989):** Affirmative action plans must be judged by the strict scrutiny standard that requires any race-conscious plan to be narrowly tailored to serve a compelling interest.
- ***Grutter v. Bollinger* and *Gratz v. Bollinger* (2003):** Numerical benefits cannot be used to admit minorities into college, but race can be a "plus factor" in making those decisions.
- ***Parents v. Seattle School District* (2007):** Race cannot be used to decide which students may attend especially popular high schools because this was not "narrowly tailored" to achieve a "compelling" goal.

Supreme Court did not take up that case. It waited for several more years to rule on a similar matter arising from the University of Michigan. In 2003, the Supreme Court overturned the admissions policy of the University of Michigan that had given to every African American, Hispanic, and Native American applicant a bonus of 20 points out of the 100 needed to guarantee admission to the University's undergraduate program.[70] This policy was not "narrowly tailored." In rejecting the bonus system, the Court reaffirmed its decision in the *Bakke* case made in 1978 in which it had rejected a university using a "fixed quota" or an exact numerical advantage to the exclusion of "individual" considerations.

But that same day, the Court upheld the policy of the University of Michigan Law School that used race as a "plus factor" but not as a numerical quota.[71] It did so even though using race as a plus factor increased by threefold the proportion of minority applicants who were admitted. In short, admitting more minorities serves a "compelling state interest," and doing so by using race as a plus factor is "narrowly tailored" to achieve that goal.

Gays and the Constitution

At first, the Supreme Court was willing to let states decide how many rights homosexuals should have. Georgia, for example, passed a law banning sodomy (that is, any sexual contact involving the sex organs of one person and the mouth or anus of another). Though the law applied to all persons, homosexuals sued to overturn it. In *Bowers v. Hardwick,* the Supreme Court decided, by a five-to-four majority, that there was no reason in the Constitution to prevent a state from having such a law. There was a right to privacy, but it was designed simply to protect "family, marriage, or procreation."[72]

But ten years later, the Court seemed to take a different position. The voters in Colorado had adopted a state constitutional amendment that made it illegal to pass any law to protect persons based on their "homosexual, lesbian, or bisexual orientation." The law did not penalize gays and lesbians; instead it said they could not become the object of specific legal protection of the sort that had traditionally been given to racial or ethnic minorities. (Ordinances to give specific protection to homosexuals had been adopted in some Colorado cities.) The Supreme Court struck down the Colorado constitutional amendment because it violated the equal protection clause of the federal Constitution.[73]

Now we faced a puzzle: a state can pass a law banning homosexual sex, as Georgia did, but a state cannot

Landmark Cases

Gay Rights

- ***Lawrence v. Texas* (2003):** State law may not ban sexual relations between same-sex partners.
- ***Boy Scouts of America v. Dale* (2000):** A private organization may ban gays from its membership.

adopt a rule preventing cities from protecting homosexuals, as Colorado did. The matter was finally put to rest in 2003. In *Lawrence v. Texas,* the Court, again by a five-to-four vote, overturned a Texas law that banned sexual contact between persons of the same sex. The Court repeated the language it had used earlier in cases involving contraception and abortion. If "the right to privacy means anything, it is the right of the individual, married or single, to be free from unwanted governmental intrusion" into sexual matters. The right of privacy means the "right to define one's own concept of existence, of meaning, of the universe, and of the mystery of human life." It specifically overruled *Bowers v. Hardwick.*[74]

The *Lawrence* decision had a benefit and a cost. The benefit was to strike down a law that was rarely enforced and if introduced today probably could not be passed. The cost was to create the possibility that the Court, and not Congress or state legislatures, might decide whether same-sex marriages were legal.

That same year, the Massachusetts Supreme Judicial Court decided, by a four-to-three vote, that gays and lesbians must be allowed to be married in the state.[75] The Massachusetts legislature responded by passing a bill that, if it becomes a state constitutional amendment, will reverse the state court's decision. For that to happen, the legislature would have to vote again on this matter, but that did not happen.

By mid-2011, six states and the District of Columbia had authorized same-sex marriages. In three it resulted from a court decision (Connecticut, Iowa, and Massachusetts), while in the others (the District, New Hampshire, New York, and Vermont) it was by vote of the legislature or city council. Several places have authorized "civil unions" for gays and lesbians.

In 2008 the California Supreme Court ruled, five to four, that the state's ban on same-sex marriage violated the state's constitution. In November of that year the voters were asked to decide whether the constitution should be amended to ban such marriages. The initiative (Proposition 8) passed. When the state supreme court was asked to decide whether this popular vote was binding, it upheld it but at the same time allowed existing same-sex marriages to remain in effect.

Many states have passed laws banning same-sex marriages, and in 1996 Congress enacted a bill, signed by President Clinton, called the Defense of Marriage Act. Under it, no state would have to give legal status to a same-sex marriage performed in another state, and it would define marriage as a lawful union of husband and wife. But state and federal laws on this matter could be overturned if the Supreme Court should decide in favor of same-sex marriage, using language that appears in the *Lawrence* case. That could be prevented by an amendment to the Constitution, but Congress is not willing to propose one and, if proposed, it is not clear the states would ratify it.

Private groups, however, can exclude homosexuals from their membership. In another five-to-four decision, the Supreme Court decided that the Boy Scouts of America could exclude gay men and boys because that group had a right to determine its own membership.[76]

How We Compare

Same-Sex Marriages at Home and Abroad

Same-sex marriages are legal in seven European countries: Belgium, Iceland, Netherlands, Norway, Portugal, Spain, and Sweden.

In the United States, they are legal in the District of Columbia and six states: Connecticut, Iowa, Massachusetts, New Hampshire, New York, and Vermont.

In Europe and America, northern nations and states are much more likely to legalize same-sex marriages than southern ones. What do you think may explain this?

People on both sides of the gay marriage issue gather in front of a California court while it considers arguments about a voter-backed ban on same-sex marriage.

The civil rights movement in the courts and in Congress profoundly changed the nature of African American participation in politics by bringing southern blacks into the political system so they could become an effective interest group. The decisive move was to enlist northern opinion in this cause, a job made easier by the northern perception that civil rights involved simply an unfair contest between two minorities—southern whites and southern blacks. That perception changed when it became evident the court rulings and legislative decisions would apply to the North as well as the South, leading to the emergence of northern opposition to court-ordered busing and affirmative action programs.

By the time this reaction developed, the legal and political system had been changed sufficiently to make it difficult if not impossible to limit the application of civil rights laws to the special circumstances of the South or to alter by legislative means the decisions of federal courts. Though the courts can accomplish little when they have no political allies (as revealed by the massive resistance to early school-desegregation decisions), they can accomplish a great deal, even in the face of adverse public opinion, when they have some organized allies (as revealed by their ability to withstand antibusing moves).

The feminist movement has paralleled in organization and tactics many aspects of the black civil rights movement, but with important differences. Women sought to repeal or reverse laws and court rulings that in many cases were ostensibly designed to protect rather than subjugate them. The conflict between protection and liberation was sufficiently intense to defeat the effort to ratify the Equal Rights Amendment.

The most divisive civil rights issues in American politics are abortion and affirmative action. From 1973 to 1989, the Supreme Court seemed committed to giving constitutional protection to all abortions within the first trimester; since 1989, it has approved various state restrictions on the circumstances under which abortions can be obtained.

There has been a similar shift in the Court's view of affirmative action. Though it will still approve some quota plans, it now insists they pass strict scrutiny to ensure they are used only to correct a proven history of discrimination, they place the burden of proof on the party alleging discrimination, and they be limited to hiring and not extended to layoffs. Congress has modified some of these rulings with new civil rights legislation.

LEARNING OBJECTIVES

WHAT YOU NEED TO KNOW

☑ **If both African Americans and women benefit from civil rights, why do federal courts allow them to be treated somewhat differently?**

The Supreme Court allows blacks and women to be treated somewhat differently because race is a skin color (and thus laws affecting it are subjected to strict scrutiny) while gender is a different body type (and so laws affecting it are subjected to intermediate scrutiny).

☑ **What is the difference between "strict scrutiny" and "intermediate scrutiny"?**

Strict scrutiny requires that a law be "narrowly tailored" and use "the least restrictive means" to serve a "compelling government interest." Intermediate scrutiny means that a law must be "substantially related" to serving "an important government interest."

☑ **Legally, what is meant by sexual harassment?**

Sexual harassment exists when an employer requests sexual favors in order to obtain employment or promotions or when an employee experiences a hostile or intimidating work environment that exists because of sexual teasing, jokes, or obscenity.

☑ **If sexual relations among gays cannot be banned, why is it that some organizations can ban gay people from membership?**

A private organization can ban gays from membership.

RECONSIDERING WHO GOVERNS?

1. **Since Congress enacts our laws, why has it not made certain that all groups have the same rights?**

   Congress responds to public demands. During much of our history, people have expected women, African Americans, Native Americans, and many other groups to be treated differently than others. The Bill of Rights is a check on congressional and state authority; to be effective, it must be enforced by independent courts.

2. After the Supreme Court ended racial segregation in the schools, what did the presi and Congress do?

For a while, not much. But in time, these institutions began spending federal mon and using federal troops and law enforcement officials in ways that greatly increa the rate of integration.

RECONSIDERING TO WHAT ENDS?

1. If the law supports equality of opportunity, why has affirmative action become so important?

There are several reasons. If there has been active discrimination in the past, affirmative action can be a way to help disadvantaged groups catch up. But the Supreme Court has also held, though by narrow majorities, that even when there not been a legacy of discrimination, pursuing "diversity" is a "compelling" interest real issue is what diversity means and how best to achieve it.

2. Under what circumstances can men and women be treated differently?

A difference in treatment can be justified constitutionally if the difference is fair, reasonable, and not arbitrary. Sex differences need not meet the "strict scrutiny" test. It is permissible to punish men for statutory rape and to bar them from hosp delivery rooms; men are different from women in these respects. Congress may dr men without drafting women.

QUESTIONS TO CONSIDER

1. How far should government be required to go or what obligation does government have to ensure the protection of the rights of the minority? Should government simply facilitate citizens holding each other accountable through the use of civil law or should government be actively monitoring and protecting the rights of the minority?
2. We know that discrimination has long-lasting negative effects for society. What can government do to remedy this? List three ideas of your own.
3. Explain why the Civil Rights Act of 1964 is considered the climax of the civil rights movement. Specifically, what did it entail and how were these requirements groundbreaking?
4. Why do you think the civil rights experience of Latinos and Native Americans has been so different from that of African Americans? What lessons can we learn from this for our expectation of how different groups may be treated in the future?
5. Given the numerical dominance of women in American society, why has it taken them so long to achieve their civil rights? What cultural beliefs or expectations may still be at work today that may affect the ability of women to attain equality?
6. What is the societal purpose of government recognition of the institution of marriage? Why does government sanction this form of contract? How does the issue of the gender of each participant in a given marriage fit into this discussion?
7. Think of the young people you know. At what age would you say they should be able to be tried as adults for serious crimes? On what basis are you making this determination?

TO LEARN MORE

Court cases: **www.law.cornell.edu**

Department of Justice: **www.usdoj.gov**

Civil rights organizations: National Association for the Advancement of Colored People: **www.naacp.org**

National Organization for Women: **www.now.org**

National Gay and Lesbian Task Force: **www.thetaskforce.org**

National Council of La Raza: **www.nclr.org**

American Arab Anti-Discrimination Committee: **www.adc.org**

Anti-Defamation League: **www.adl.org**

Branch, Taylor. *Parting the Waters: America in the King Years*. New York: Simon and Schuster, 1988. A vivid account of the civil rights struggle.

Flexner, Eleanor. *Century of Struggle: The Women's Rights Movement in the United States*. Rev. ed. Cambridge: Harvard University Press, 1975. A historical account of the feminist movement and its political strategies.

Foreman, Christopher A. *The African-American Predicament*. Washington, D.C.: Brookings Institution, 1999. Thoughtful essays on problems faced by African Americans today.

Franklin, John Hope. *From Slavery to Freedom,* 5th ed. New York: Knopf, 1980. A survey of black history in the United States.

Friedan, Betty. *The Feminine Mystique.* New York: Norton, 1963. Tenth anniversary edition, 1974. A well-known call for women to become socially and culturally independent.

Kluger, Richard. *Simple Justice*. New York: Random House/Vintage Books, 1977. Detailed and absorbing account of the school-desegregation issue, from the Fourteenth Amendment to the *Brown* case.

Kull, Andrew. *The Color-Blind Constitution.* Cambridge: Harvard University Press, 1992. A history of efforts, none yet successful, to make the Constitution color-blind.

Mansbridge, Jane J. *Why We Lost the ERA.* Chicago: University of Chicago Press, 1986. Explains why the Equal Rights Amendment did not become part of the Constitution.

Thernstrom, Stephan, and Abigail Thernstrom. *America in Black and White*. New York: Simon and Schuster, 1997. Detailed history and portrait of African Americans.

Wilhoit, Francis M. *The Politics of Massive Resistance*. New York: George Braziller, 1973. The methods—and ultimate collapse—of all-out southern resistance to school desegregation.

Woodward, C. Vann. *The Strange Career of Jim Crow*. New York: Oxford University Press, 1957. Brief, lucid account of the evolution of Jim Crow practices in the South.

evantravels/Shutterstock.com

Part 2

Opinions, Interests, and Organizations

7 Public Opinion 162

8 Political Participation 182

9 Political Parties 202

10 Elections and Campaigns 234

11 Interest Groups 270

12 The Media 298

The latent causes of faction are thus sown in the nature of man; and we see them everywhere brought into different degrees of activity, according to the different circumstances of civil society.

** Federalist No. 10*

7 Public Opinion

LEARNING OBJECTIVES

WHAT YOU NEED TO KNOW

☑ What is "public opinion" and how do we measure it?

☑ What is "political socialization" and how does it work?

☑ What is "political ideology" and how does it matter for what elites and the mass public believe?

WHO GOVERNS?

1. How does public opinion in America today vary by race, gender, and other differences?
2. What is political ideology, and how does it affect political behavior and influence public policy?

TO WHAT ENDS?

1. What role did the Framers of the Constitution think public opinion should play in American democracy?
2. When, if ever, should public policies mirror majority opinion?

Defined simply, **public opinion** refers to how people think or feel about particular things. In this chapter, we take a close look at what "public opinion" is, how it is formed, and how opinions differ. In later chapters, we examine the workings of political parties, interest groups, and government institutions and consider what impact they have on whether public opinion affects government policy. Let's begin this journey by recognizing how perspectives on the role public opinion is supposed to play in the country's representative democracy have changed since the nation was founded.

THEN The Founding Fathers believed that most average citizens lacked the time, information, energy, interest, and experience to decide on public policy. The Constitution's chief architect, James Madison, argued that direct popular participation in the decisions of government was a recipe for disaster, and that "it is the reason, alone, of the public that ought to control and regulate the government."[1] Madison and the other Framers looked to "the representatives of the people," most particularly the U.S. Senators who, in their original plan and until the Seventeenth Amendment was ratified in 1913, were not popularly elected, "as a defense to the people against their own temporary errors and delusions."[2]

NOW Try imagining any candidate for the U.S. Senate or, for that matter, for any federal, state, or local office, winning election or reelection, or maintaining high public approval ratings, after he or she had questioned "rule by the people" or doubted the majority's opinions the way that the Framers routinely, matter-of-factly, and publicly did.

Ironically, today about the only circumstances under which elected leaders can get away with sounding the least bit that way is when public opinion polls get the public talking about how little most people know about government or civics. That happened briefly in April 2011 when *Newsweek* magazine released the results of a twenty-five-item "U.S. Citizenship Test." Among other results, only 14 percent of the people knew that the U.S. House of Representatives has 435 voting members; only 39 percent knew that U.S. senators serve six-year terms; over a quarter did not know the name of the sitting vice president of the United States (at that time, Joe Biden); and only 12 percent could identify any one writer of *The Federalist Papers* (Madison, Alexander Hamilton, or John Jay).

Public Opinion and Democracy

In the Gettysburg Address, Abraham Lincoln said the United States has a government "of the people, by the people, and for the people." That suggests the

public opinion How people think or feel about particular things.

government should do what the people want. If that is the case, it is puzzling that:

- Today, the federal government is running budget deficits of over a trillion dollars a year, but most people want a balanced budget.
- In the 1970s, the Equal Rights Amendment to the Constitution was not ratified, but polls showed that most people supported it.
- Over the last several decades, most people have agreed that there should be a limit on the number of terms to which U.S. senators and members of the U.S. House of Representatives can be elected, but Congress has not approved term limits.

Some people, reflecting on the many gaps between what the government does and what the people want, may become cynical and think our system is democratic in name only. That would be a mistake. There are several very good reasons why government policy often appears to be at odds with public opinion.

First, it bears repeating that the Framers of the Constitution did not try to create a government that would do from day to day "what the people want." They created a government for the purpose of achieving certain substantive goals. The preamble to the Constitution lists six of these: "to form a more perfect Union, establish Justice, ensure domestic Tranquility, provide for the common defense, promote the general Welfare, and secure the Blessings of Liberty."

One means of achieving these goals was popular rule, as provided for by the right of the people to vote for members of the House of Representatives (and later for senators and presidential electors). But other means were provided as well: representative government, federalism, the separation of powers, a Bill of Rights, and an independent judiciary. These were all intended to be checks on public opinion. In addition, the Framers knew that in a nation as large and diverse as the United States there would rarely be any such thing as "public opinion"; rather there would be many "publics" (that is, factions) holding many opinions. The Framers hoped the struggle among these many publics would protect liberty (no one "public" would dominate) while at the same time permitting the adoption of reasonable policies that commanded the support of many factions.

Second, it is not as easy as one may suppose to know what the public thinks. We are so inundated these days with public opinion polls that we may imagine that they tell us what the public believes. That may be true on a few rather simple, clear-cut, and widely discussed issues, but it is not true with respect to most matters on which the government must act. The best pollsters know the limits of their methods, and citizens should know them as well.

AP Photo/Jim McKnight

Students at Marist College in New York call people in the state with poll questions.

What Is Public Opinion?

Some years ago, researchers at the University of Cincinnati asked 1,200 local residents whether they favored passage of the Monetary Control Bill. About 21 percent said they favored the bill, 25 percent said they opposed it, and the rest said they hadn't thought much about the matter or didn't know. But there was no such thing as the Monetary Control Bill. The researchers made it up. About 26 percent of the people questioned in a national survey also expressed opinions on the same nonexistent piece of legislation.[3] In many surveys, wide majorities favor expanding most government programs *and* paying less in taxes. On some issues, the majority in favor one month gives way to the majority opposed the next, often with no obvious basis for the shift.

How much confidence should we place in surveys that presumably tell us "what the American people think" about legislation and other issues, and how should we assess "public opinion"? For businesses, understanding how people think or feel about particular things—for example, knowing whether consumers are likely to want a new product or be willing to pay more for an old one—can spell the difference between profit and loss. In the early 20th century, corporations and marketing firms pioneered attempts to systematically measure public views, and political scientists were not far behind them.

The first major academic studies of public opinion and voting, published in the 1940s, painted a distressing picture of American democracy. The studies found that, while a small group of citizens knew lots about government and had definite ideas on many issues, the vast majority knew next to nothing about government and had only vague notions even on much-publicized public policy matters that affected them directly.[4] In the ensuing decades, however, other studies painted a somewhat more reassuring picture. These studies suggested that, while most citizens are poorly informed about government and care little about most public policy issues, they are nonetheless pretty good at using limited information (or cues) to figure out what policies, parties, or candidates most nearly reflect their values or favor their interests, and then acting (or voting) accordingly.[5]

The closer scholars have studied public opinion on particular issues, the less uniformed, indifferent, or fickle it has appeared to be. For example, a study by political scientist Terry M. Moe analyzed public opinion concerning whether the government should provide parents with publicly funded grants, or vouchers, that they can apply toward tuition at private schools. He found that although most people are unfamiliar with the voucher issue, "they do a much better job of formulating their opinions than skeptics would lead us to expect." When supplied with basic information, average citizens adopt "their positions for good substantive reasons, just as the informed do."[6]

HOW POLLING WORKS

If properly conducted, a survey of public opinion—popularly called a **poll**—can capture the opinions of 300 million citizens by interviewing as few as 1,500 of them. There are many keys to good polling: posing comprehensible questions (asking people about things they have some basis for forming an opinion about), wording questions fairly (not using "loaded" or "emotional" words or indicating what the "right" answer is), and others.

However, no poll, whatever it asks and however it is worded, can provide us with a reasonably accurate measure of how people think or feel unless the persons polled are a **random sample** of the entire population, meaning that any given voter or adult has an equal chance of being interviewed. Through a process called stratified or multistage area sampling, the pollster makes a list of all the geographical units in the country—say all the counties—and groups (or "stratifies") them by size of their population. The pollster then selects at random units from each group or stratum in proportion to its total population. Within each selected county, smaller and smaller geographical units (down to particular blocks or streets) are chosen, and then, within the smallest unit, individuals are selected at random (by, for example, choosing the occupant of every fifth house).

If this process is repeated using equally randomized methods, the pollster might get slightly different results. The difference between the results of two surveys or samples is called **sampling error.** For example, if one random sample shows that 70 percent of all Americans approve of the way the president is handling the job, and another random sample taken at the same time shows that 65 percent do, the sampling error is 5 percent.

Even if properly conducted, polls are hardly infallible. Since 1952, most major polls have in fact picked the winner of the presidential election. Likewise, **exit polls,** interviews with randomly selected voters conducted at polling places on election day in a representative sample of voting districts, have proven quite accurate. But as a

poll A survey of public opinion.

random sample Method of selecting from a population in which each person has an equal probability of being selected.

sampling error The difference between the results of random samples taken at the same time.

exit polls Polls based on interviews conducted on election day with randomly selected voters.

result of sampling error and for other reasons, it is very hard for pollsters to predict the winner in a close election.

For any population over 500,000, pollsters need to make about 15,000 telephone calls to reach a number of respondents (technically, the number computes to 1,065) sufficient to ensure that the opinions of the sample differ only slightly (by a 3 percent plus or minus margin) from what the results would have been had they interviewed the entire population from which the sample was drawn. That can be very expensive to do. Polling firms can economize by using smaller-than-ideal samples or by undersampling hard-to-contact people, but then they risk getting things wrong. As summarized in the "Research Frontiers" box, that is the story behind why so many 2008 presidential primary polls performed so poorly.

political socialization
Process by which background traits influence one's political views.

HOW OPINIONS DIFFER

Nobody fully understands how public opinion influences everything from who wins an election to what gets politicians' attention to whether given bills become law, but a few things are clear: some people care more about certain issues than other people do (*opinion saliency*); on some issues or choices, opinions are pretty steady, while on others they tend to be more volatile (*opinion stability*); and on some issues government seems to be largely in sync with popular views or majority sentiments, while on other issues it seems to be significantly out of sync (*opinion-policy congruence*). For example, most Americans had an opinion on U.S. involvement in Iraq, but some felt more strongly about it than others did, and opinions changed in response to news of positive or negative developments. In the mid-2000s, for example, many news reports on the situation in Iraq were negative, and mass public support for U.S. involvement fell.[7]

Studies also tell us that people with certain characteristics in common sometimes hold certain political beliefs in common. By no means do people with similar or even virtually identical family histories, religious affiliations, formal educations, or job experiences think or vote exactly the same way on all or most issues. But **political socialization**—the process by which personal and other background

RESEARCH FRONTIERS

How the 2008 Presidential Primary Polling Went Wrong

In 2008, opinion polls made a lot of mistakes during the primary contests. They picked the wrong Democratic and Republican winners in New Hampshire and made other bad judgments in California, South Carolina, and Wisconsin.

To figure out what went wrong, opinion experts studied the matter and reported in early 2009 on how several polling firms operated. Here is what they found:

Many polls thought Democrat Barack Obama would carry New Hampshire. Instead, Hillary Clinton did. They made this mistake because they did not spend the time and money to get and interview a representative sample of voters.

The pollsters did not reach out to find hard-to-locate voters; they interviewed too few union members and too many people without much schooling; and often they interviewed anyone who answered the telephone instead of the particular person named in the sample.

In part, these problems occurred because it is getting harder to conduct reliable polling. A lot of people use cell phones; some do not even own a regular home phone. How do you find them? And many people are getting tired of answering telephone polls, so they just hang up. How do you reach them?

Imagine you are trying to accurately poll students at your school.

- How big a sample should you have?
- How do you identify a representative sample?
- If you interview students by phone, what do you do if you can't find them or they hang up on you?

Source: American Association for Public Opinion Research, *Report of the Ad Hoc Committee on the 2008 Presidential Primary Polling* (March 2009).

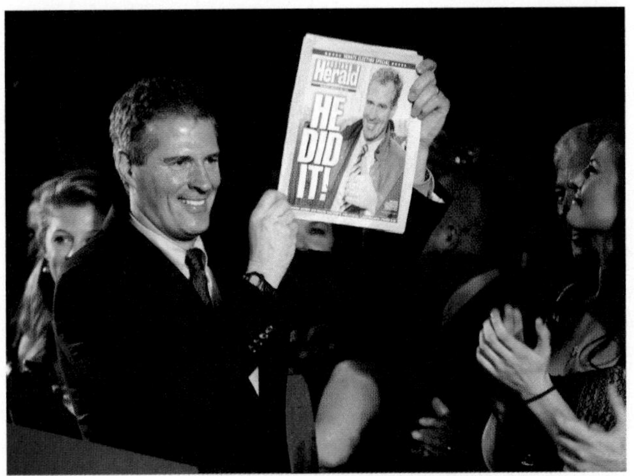

Robert Spencer/Getty Images News/Getty Images

Republican Scott Brown wins the election to fill the Senate seat once held by Ted Kennedy. He must stand for reelection in 2012.

traits influence one's views about politics and government—matters. It is behind the fact, to be discussed in the next section, that children tend to share their parents' party affiliations; and it helps to explain why, as we shall see, opinions seem to vary in interesting ways associated with class, race, religion, gender, and other characteristics.

elite People who have a disproportionate amount of some valued resource.

Research also has made clear that mass and elite opinions differ. By "elite" we do not mean people who are "better" than others. Rather, as discussed in Chapter 1, **elite** is a term used by social scientists to refer to people who have a disproportionate amount of some valued resource—money, schooling, prestige, political power, or whatever. Not only do political elites *know more* about politics than the rest of us, they *think differently* about it—they have different views and beliefs. As we explain later in this chapter, they are more likely than average citizens to hold a more or less consistent set of opinions about the policies government ought to pursue. The government attends more to the elite views than to popular views, at least on many matters.

How We Compare

Opinions on Americans

It is not surprising that most Americans have a favorable view of Americans; but what opinions on Americans are held by people in other countries?

By the same token, a majority of Americans typically expresses confidence in the U.S. president; but do majorities in other nations share that confidence?

For several years now, the Pew Global Attitudes Project has conducted sophisticated, in-depth opinion polls in dozens of nations. Below are two sets of selected results from its 2009 survey.

Percent with "a favorable view of the American people," 2009

Top Five	Bottom Five
1. United States 90%	1. Turkey 14%
2. Kenya 87%	2. Pakistan 20%
	2. Palestinian Territory 20%
3. South Korea 83%	3. Argentina 38%
4. Nigeria 76%	4. Jordan 39%
5. France 75%	5. Egypt 40%

Percent with "confidence in the U.S. president," 2009

Top Five & U.S.	Bottom Five
1. Kenya 94%	1. Pakistan 13%
2. Germany 93%	2. Palestinian Territory 23%
3. Canada 88%	3. Jordan 31%
4. Nigeria 88%	4. Turkey 33%
5. Britain 86%	5. Russia 37%
11. United States 74%	

Source: Data from Pew Charitable Trusts.

Political Socialization

GENES AND THE FAMILY

For a long time, scholars believed people acquired their political views from their families. There is a lot of truth in that argument. The great majority of high school students know the party affiliation of their parents, and only a tiny minority of children supports a party opposite that of their parents.[8]

But of late we have learned that genetic background also explains some of our political ideology, though rather little of our party affiliation. When we compare how identical twins (who are genetically the same) think about politics with how fraternal twins (who share only half of their genes) think about politics, we discover that identical twins are much

Bob Daemmrich/The Image Works

Children grow up learning, but not always following, their parents' political beliefs.

more likely to have similar political views than fraternal twins. Some research has found that about one-third of the differences among people about political beliefs comes from genetic makeup, but only one-tenth of these differences comes from family influences.[9]

These results should not surprise us. We know that children in the same family have different personalities even though they have the same parents. Genes play a big role in personality, as they also do in basic political beliefs. If you add together the big effect of genes and the smaller effect of parental influences, then half of our political views comes from our family backgrounds. The other half comes from our individual life experiences, such as the friends we acquire, the schools we attend, and what happens to us as adults.

But political beliefs are not necessarily the same as party affiliation. One can be a liberal or conservative Democrat, a liberal or conservative Republican. Studies that have shown that genes affect our political beliefs also suggest that they do not have much of an effect on our party affiliation. Whether we are Democrats, Republicans, or something else depends on what we learn from our parents.

The ability of the family to inculcate a strong sense of party identification has declined in recent years. The proportion of citizens who say they consider themselves Democrats or Republicans has become steadily smaller since the early 1950s. Accompanying this decline in partisanship has been a sharp rise in the proportion of citizens describing themselves as independents.[10]

Part of this change has resulted from the fact that young voters have always had a weaker sense of partisanship than older ones. But the youthfulness of the population cannot explain all the changes, for the decline in partisanship has occurred at all age levels. Those who reached voting age in the 1960s were less apt than those who matured in the 1950s to keep the party identification of their parents.[11] Moreover, as personal policy preferences develop into adulthood, the effects of parental socialization on the partisanship of children decrease gradually over time.[12]

There are also sizeable age-related differences in opinions on several issues. For example, in 2010 citizens under age 30 supported gay marriage by a margin of 24 percent more than those aged 65 and older.[13] In some ways, the opinions of younger citizens break old ideological molds. Compared to older Americans, for example, citizens aged 18 to 29 have been more likely to favor gay marriage and women's rights (generally labeled the liberal view), but also more likely to favor giving parents tax money in the form of vouchers for private or religious schools and letting people invest some of their Social Security contribution in the stock market (generally labeled the conservative view).[14] More generally, a majority of today's 18- to 24-year-olds thinks elected officials have priorities different from their own, but only one out of five thinks politics is not relevant to their lives at present (see Table 7.1).

Table 7.1 Young Adults on Politics and Politicians (2010)

Percent of 18- to 29-year-olds who agree that:	
politics has become too partisan	46%
elected officials don't have the same priorities I have	51%
getting involved in politics is an honorable thing to do	31%
people like me don't have any say about what government does	36%
it is difficult to find ways to be involved in politics	22%
politics is not relevant to my life right now	21%

Source: Institute of Politics, *The 17th Biannual Youth Survey on Politics and Public Service*, John F. Kennedy School of Government, Harvard University, Spring 2010.

Where do such views about politics come from? In most families, the dinner table is not a seminar in political philosophy but a place where people discuss school, jobs, dates, and chores. In some families, however, the dinner table is a political classroom. Studies of the participants in various student radical movements in the 1960s suggested that college radicals often were the sons and daughters of people who had themselves been young radicals; some commentators dubbed them the "red-diaper babies." Presumably, deeply conservative people come disproportionately from families that were also deeply conservative. This transfer of political beliefs from one generation to the next reflects both heredity and, to a lesser extent, family teaching.

RELIGION

One way in which the family forms and transmits political beliefs is by its religious tradition. Religious differences make for political differences, but the differences generally are more complicated than first meets the eye.

Although most Americans remain somewhat or deeply religious, most seriously question religion's role in politics and government.[15] Religious influences on public opinion are pronounced with respect to social issues like abortion or gay marriage, but they matter less on most other issues; and when a war is perceived to be going badly or the economy is in trouble, most Americans of all faiths or of no faith agree that these are the issues that matter most.[16]

Opinions about politics and government vary not only across but also within given religious traditions. For instance, Table 7.2 shows four Christian religious groups' respective opinions on four issues. As the table illustrates, white evangelicals and black Protestants hold similar views on environmental regulation, same-sex marriage, and faith-based initiatives, but differ over more aid to the poor. More generally, Table 7.3 shows that people of whatever religion who attend worship services regularly are considerably less likely to vote Democratic than otherwise comparable persons who attend worship services rarely or never.

Table 7.2 Opinions by Four Christian Groups on Four Issues (2009–2010)

	Tougher Environmental Regulations	Same-Sex Marriage	More Aid to the Poor	Letting Faith-Based Groups Apply for Government Funding
	Percent in favor			
All Americans	81	41	63	69
White Evangelicals	73	22	54	77
Black Protestants	79	26	81	84
White Catholics	86	49	58	81
Hispanic Catholics	89	40	77	N/A

Source: Adapted from Pew Forum on Religion and Public Life, *American Views on Religion, Politics, & Public Policy*, 2010, pp. 37, 41, and 46, and "Faith-Based Programs Still Popular, Less Visible," November 16, 2009, p. 2.

Table 7.3 Worship Service Attendance and the Probability of Voting Democratic (2000–2008)

	Probability of Voting for the Democratic Candidate		
Attendance at Worship Services	2000	2004	2008
More than once a week	34%	30%	33%
Once a week	44	39	43
A few times a month	54	49	54
A few times a year	64	59	65
Never	73	68	74

Source: Pew Forum on Religion and Public Life, *American Views on Religion, Politics & Public Policy*, 2010, p. 85.

gender gap Difference in political views between men and women.

THE GENDER GAP

Journalists often point out that women have "deserted" Republican candidates to favor Democratic ones. In some cases, this is true. But it would be more correct to say that men have "deserted" Democratic candidates for Republican ones. The **gender gap** is the difference in political views between men and women. That gap has existed for a long time, and it is a problem for both political parties.

Women obtained the right to vote in 1920 when the Nineteenth Amendment to the Constitution was ratified. Until 1980, women voted at significantly lower rates than men. Since 1980, however, women have voted at somewhat higher rates than men, a difference amplified by the fact that women are also a larger proportion of the voting-age population. In every presidential election from 1980 through 2008, women were more likely than men to favor the Democratic candidate.

As Table 7.4 shows, the Democratic advantage among women, especially women ages 18 to 29, has widened in recent years. Behind this gender gap in partisan self-identification are differences between men and women over prominent political issues and which issues matter most. For example, as results from the 2008 American National Election Survey suggested, women are 50 percent more likely than men to favor universal health care, nearly 50 percent more likely than men to favor same-sex marriage, somewhat more likely than men to say that abortion is an important issue, and somewhat less likely than men to approve of recent military interventions.

Cleavages in Public Opinion

The way in which political opinions are formed helps explain the cleavages that exist among these opinions and why these cleavages do not follow any single political principle but instead overlap and crosscut in bewildering complexity. If, for example, the United States lacked regional differences and was composed almost entirely of white Protestants who had never attended college, there would still be plenty of political conflict—the rich would have different views from the poor; workers would have different views from farmers—but that conflict would be much simpler to describe and explain. It might even lead to political parties that were more clearly aligned with competing political philosophies than those we now have. In fact, some democratic nations in the world today have a population very much like the one just described, and the United States itself, during the first half of the 19th century, was overwhelmingly white, Protestant, and without much formal schooling.

Table 7.4 Gender Gaps in Partisan Identification, 1992–2008

	Men			Women		
	Rep %	Dem %	D-R diff	Rep %	Dem %	D-R diff
All Voters						
2008	43	46	+3	33	56	+22
2004	48	43	-5	40	51	+11
2000	47	42	-5	38	51	+13
1996	49	43	-6	39	53	+14
1992	45	46	+1	40	52	+12
Voters Ages 18–29						
2008	38	52	+14	28	63	+35
2004	44	47	+3	36	54	+18
2000	46	44	-2	37	53	+16
1996	50	44	-6	38	55	+17
1992	52	42	-10	42	50	+8

Source: Pew Research Center for the People & the Press, *Gen Dems: The Party's Advantage Among Young Voters Widens,* April 28, 2008.

Today, however, there are crosscutting cleavages based on race, ethnicity, religion, region, and education, in addition to those created by income and occupation. To the extent that politics is sensitive to public opinion, it is sensitive to a variety of different and even competing publics. Not all these publics have influence proportionate to their numbers or even to their numbers adjusted for the intensity of their feelings. As will be described later, a filtering process occurs that makes the opinions of some publics more influential than those of others.

Whatever this state of affairs may mean for democracy, it creates a messy situation for political scientists. It would be so much easier if everyone's opinion on political affairs reflected some single feature of his or her life, such as income, occupation, age, race, or sex. Of course, some writers have argued that political opinion is a reflection of one such feature, social class, usually defined in terms of income or occupation, but that view, though containing some truth, is beset with inconsistencies: poor blacks and poor whites disagree sharply on many issues involving race; well-to-do Jews and well-to-do Protestants often have opposing opinions on social welfare policy; and low-income elderly people are much more worried about crime than low-income graduate students. Plumbers and professors may have similar incomes, but they rarely have similar views, and businesspeople in New York City often take a very different view of government than businesspeople in Houston or Birmingham.

In some other democracies, a single factor such as class may explain more of the differences in political attitudes than it does in the more socially heterogeneous United States. Most blue-collar workers in America think of themselves as "middle-class," whereas most such workers in Britain and France describe themselves as "working-class."

SOCIAL CLASS

Americans speak of "social class" with embarrassment. The norm of equality tugs at our consciences, urging us to judge people as individuals, not as parts of some social group (such as "the lower class"). Social scientists speak of "class" with confusion. They know it exists but quarrel constantly about how to define it: by income? occupation? wealth? schooling? prestige? personality?

Let's face up to the embarrassment and skip over the confusion. Truck drivers and investment bankers look different, talk differently, and vote differently. There is nothing wrong with saying that the first group consists of "working-class" (or "blue-collar") people and the latter of "upper-class" (or "management") people. Moreover, though different definitions of class produce slightly different groupings of people, most definitions overlap to such an extent that it does not matter too much which we use.

However defined, public opinion and voting have been less determined by class in the United States than in Europe, and the extent of class cleavage has declined in the last few decades in both the United States and Europe. In the 1950s, V. O. Key, Jr., found that differences in political opinion were closely associated with occupation. He noted that people holding managerial or professional jobs had distinctly more conservative views on social welfare policy and more internationalist views on foreign policy than manual workers.[17] During the next decade, this pattern changed greatly. Opinion surveys done in the late 1960s showed that business and professional people had views quite similar to those of manual workers on matters such as the poverty program, health insurance, American policy in Vietnam, and government efforts to create jobs.[18]

The voting patterns of different social classes also have become somewhat more similar. The differences in whether or not people vote, depending on their social class, have declined sharply since the late 1940s in the United States, France, Great Britain, and Germany and have declined moderately in Sweden.

Class differences remain, of course. Unskilled workers are more likely than affluent white-collar workers to be Democrats and to have liberal views on economic policy. And when economic issues pinch—for example, when farmers are hurting or steelworkers are being laid off—the importance of economic interests in differentiating the opinions of various groups rises sharply.

Still, many of the issues that now lead us to choose which party to support and that determine whether we think of ourselves as liberals or conservatives are noneconomic issues. In recent years, our political posture has been shaped by the positions we take on race relations, abortion, school prayer, environmentalism, and terrorism, issues that do not clearly affect the rich differently than the poor (or at least do not affect them as differently as do the union movement, the minimum wage, and unemployment). Moral, symbolic, and foreign policy matters do not divide rich and poor in the same way as economic ones. Thus, we have many well-off people who think of themselves as liberals because they take liberal positions on these noneconomic matters, and many not-so-well-off people who think of themselves as conservatives because that is the position they take on these issues.

RACE AND ETHNICITY

African Americans are overwhelmingly Democratic, though younger ones are a bit more likely than older ones to identify with the Republican party.[19] Younger blacks are also much more likely to support the idea of using school vouchers to pay for education than older ones.

There are sharp differences between white and black attitudes on many public policy questions. For example, blacks are much more likely than whites to support affirmative action, to think that the criminal justice system is biased against them, to oppose the use of military force, to doubt that we all should be willing to fight for our country, and to think that believing in God is essential for a person to be moral.[20]

But there are also many areas of agreement. Both blacks and whites want our courts to be tougher in handling criminals, oppose the idea of making abortion legal in all cases, agree that people have become too dependent on government aid, and think that everyone has it in their own power to succeed.[21]

Latinos are now the largest minority group in America, numbering over 50 million people. Unfortunately, studies of Latino public opinion have been called "small, disproportionately oriented toward immigration, and relatively silent on the influence of gender" and other possible intragroup opinion cleavages.[22] Likewise, despite the country's growing Asian population, there is as yet virtually no literature on Asian public opinion.

However, an early survey of ethnic groups in California, a state where fully one-third of all recent immigrants to this country live, gives us some hint of how Latinos and Asian Americans feel about political parties and issues. Latinos identify themselves as Democrats, but much less so than blacks, and Asian Americans are even more identified with the Republican party than Anglo whites. On issues such as spending on the military and welfare programs, prayer in public schools, and the imposition of the death penalty for murder, Asian American views are much more like those of Anglo whites than those of either blacks or Hispanics. Latinos are somewhat more liberal than Anglos or Asian Americans, but much less liberal than blacks, except with respect to bilingual education programs.[23]

Joe Raedle/Getty Images News/Getty Images

Marco Rubio, the Hispanic son of exiles from Cuba, is a conservative Republican elected from Florida to the United States Senate in 2010.

These figures, however, conceal important differences within these ethnic groups. For example, Japanese Americans are among the more conservative Asian Americans, whereas Korean Americans (perhaps because they are among the most recent immigrants) are more liberal. Similarly, Latinos, the fastest-growing ethnic group in the United States, are a diverse mix of Cuban Americans, Mexican Americans, Central Americans, and Puerto Ricans, each with distinct political views. Most studies of Latino voting show that people from Mexico vote heavily Democratic, those from Cuba mostly Republican, and those from Puerto Rico somewhere in between.[24] Local conditions also affect these views. Hispanics in Texas often vote for more conservative candidates than do those in California.

A majority of Latinos seem to favor bigger government, oppose making abortions generally available, and think that the Democratic party cares more about them and is better able to handle economic and other issues. But these views are complicated not only because Latinos come from many nations but also because some were born here and some abroad. For example, following the U.S. invasion of Iraq, most Latinos believed U.S. troops should be withdrawn, but there were important differences between the views of native-born and foreign-born Latinos.[25]

Latinos have less money and are younger than non-Hispanic white Americans. About four-fifths of all Latinos, but only half of all non-Hispanic whites, are younger than 45. It is possible that these differences affect their views.[26]

Despite the differences, there are broad areas of agreement between Latinos and non-Hispanic whites. Almost exactly the same percentage of both groups favor allowing people to invest some of their Social Security taxes into stock-market funds.[27] We would like to know more about these opinions, but pollsters have not yet fully explored Hispanic attitudes.

REGION

It is widely believed that geographic region affects political attitudes and in particular that southerners and northerners disagree significantly on many policy questions. At one time, white southerners were conspicuously less liberal than easterners, midwesterners, and westerners on questions such as aid to minorities, legalizing marijuana, school busing, and enlarging the rights of those accused of crimes. Although more conservative on these issues, they held views on economic issues similar to those of whites in other regions of the country. This helps to explain why the South was for so long a part of the Democratic party coalition: on national economic and social welfare policies, southerners expressed views not very different from those of northerners. That coalition was always threatened, however, by the divisiveness produced by issues of race and liberty.

The southern lifestyle is in fact different from that of other regions of the country. The South has, on the whole, been more accommodating to business enterprise and less so to organized labor than, for example, the Northeast; it gave greater support to the third-party candidacy of George Wallace in 1968, which was a protest against big government and the growth of national political power as well as against civil rights; and it was in the South that the greatest opposition arose to income-redistribution plans such as the Family Assistance Plan of 1969. Moreover, there is some evidence that white southerners became by the 1970s more conservative than they had been in the 1950s, at least when compared to white northerners.[28] Finally, white southerners have become less attached to the Democratic party: no Democratic candidate for president has won a majority of white southern votes since Lyndon Johnson did so in 1964; in 2008, Barack Obama won the presidency with about half the white vote nationally but only about 30 percent of the white vote in the South.

Since 1980, southern states have gained seats in the House of Representatives, with Florida and Texas alone each gaining a dozen. The opposite shift has occurred in much of the Northeast, with voters becoming somewhat more reliably Democratic in states like New York, Ohio, and Pennsylvania where populations and hence congressional delegations have been shrinking.

Political Ideology

Up to now the words *liberal* and *conservative* have been used as though everyone agrees on what they mean and as if they accurately describe general sets of political beliefs held by large segments of the population. Neither of these assumptions is correct. Like many useful words—*love, justice, happiness*—they are as vague as they are indispensable.

When we refer to people as liberals, conservatives, socialists, or radicals, we are implying that they have a patterned set of beliefs about how government and other important institutions in fact operate and how they ought to operate, and in particular about what kinds of policies government ought to pursue. These groups are said to display to some degree a **political ideology**—that is, a more or less consistent set of beliefs about what policies government ought to pursue.

political ideology A more or less consistent set of beliefs about what policies government ought to pursue.

Political scientists measure the extent to which people have a political ideology in two ways. The first is by seeing how frequently people use broad political categories (such as "liberal," "conservative," "radical") to describe their own views or to justify their preferences for various candidates and policies, and second, by seeing to what extent the policy preferences of a citizen are consistent over time or are based at any one time on consistent principles. This second method involves a simple mathematical procedure: measuring how accurately one can predict a person's view on a subject at one time based on his or her view on that subject at an earlier time, or measuring how accurately one can predict a person's view on one issue based on his or her view on a different issue. The higher the accuracy of such predictions (or correlations), the more we say a person's political opinions display "constraint" or ideology.

Despite annual fluctuations, ideological self-identification surveys show that over the last two decades, "conservative" and "moderate" have each been chosen by about 37 to 40 percent, while "liberal" has been chosen by about 20 percent.[29]

For three reasons, however, these self-identification survey averages do not really tell us much at all about how or whether most people think about politics in an ideological manner. First, except when asked by pollsters, most Americans do not actually employ the words *liberal, conservative,* or *moderate* in explaining or justifying their preferences for parties, candidates, or policies, and not many more than half can give plausible definitions of these terms. The vast majority of Americans simply do not think about politics in an ideological or very coherent manner.

Second, over the last decade, survey research scholars have rediscovered old truths about the limitations of polling as a window into "the public mind."[30] Public opinion polls must of necessity ask rather simple questions. The apparent "inconsistency" in the answers people give at different times may mean only that the nature of the problem and the wording of the question have changed. Or it could simply mean that many people consistently want from politics or government things that, as a practical matter, they cannot have, or at least cannot have all at once or at a price they are willing to pay—for instance, a bigger military, more expansive public health insurance coverage for all, and greater funding for public schools, but no military draft, no new or increased taxes, and no government budget deficits. Ideological liberals might consistently covet everything on that list except the bigger military, and be willing to pay higher taxes to get it. Ideological conservatives might want only the bigger military, but only if getting it requires no tax increases. But most citizens are more inclined to pick and choose their positions without regard to conventional liberal or conservative views, and without feeling any need to be "consistent."

Third, when surveyed in person (including by telephone), some people will hide what they think are socially or morally unacceptable self-identifications or positions behind a "don't know" or "middle-ground" response.[31] This can happen not only when the questions concern specific labels like "liberal" or "conservative," or particular issues like racial integration or immigration restrictions, but also when the questions seem to ask about fundamental values, patriotism, or "Americanism." As we saw in Chapter 4, most Americans share a distinctive political culture—a belief in freedom, in equality of political condition and economic opportunity, and in civic duty. Trying to determine precisely where political culture ends and ideology begins often is difficult or impossible.

MASS IDEOLOGIES: A TYPOLOGY

Partly in recognition of these and related limitations, pollsters have increasingly taken a fresh approach to documenting and analyzing average Americans' ideological cast and character. Essentially, rather than ask people to identify themselves as "liberal," "conservative," or "moderate," they ask people multiple questions about politics and government, and then use the answers to sort them into a half-dozen or more different groups.

The oldest ideological typology survey of this sort started in 1987 and has been updated three times since. (To see where you fit, you can take the survey for yourself at http://typology.people-press.org/typology.) Americans, it finds, are divided into nine different groups, each defined by certain key values (see Table 7.5). Measured by both their presence among registered voters and in the general population, "liberals" are the largest single ideological bloc. Together with "disadvantaged Democrats," they number nearly one in three registered voters and over a quarter of the general public.

But various types of conservatives ("social," "pro-government," and conservative Democrats), together with heavily Republican "enterprisers," comprise nearly one in two registered voters and over 40 percent of the general population. And nearly one in five Americans ("disaffected" plus "bystanders") hold views that lead them to be cynical about politics or pay it no mind. Dig deeper into the data on these nine groups (also available via the same Web site cited above), such as the related survey findings regarding each group's socioeconomic status and views on religion and other matters that affect politics, and you will see that the old three-way (liberal-conservative-moderate) self-identification surveys probably obscured more than they revealed about what most average Americans think about politics.

LIBERAL AND CONSERVATIVE ELITES

Although the terms *liberal* and *conservative* do not describe the political views held by most average Americans, they do capture the views held by many, perhaps most, people who are in the country's political elite. As we discussed in Chapter 1, every society has an elite, because in every society government officials have more power than ordinary folk, some persons make more money than others, and

Table 7.5 Ideology Typology: Nine Groups and Their Key Values

Key Values of Nine Groups	Registered Voters	Adult Population	Democrat/ Republican/ Independent
Liberals			
(Seculars; 60s Democrats)	19%	17%	59%/1%/40%
Pro-choice; diplomacy over military force; protect the environment			
Conservative Democrats			
(Socially Conservative Democrats; New Dealers)	15	14	89/0/11
Religion vital to morality; oppose same-sex marriage; support antipoverty programs			
Social Conservatives			
(Moralists)	13	11	0/82/18
Pro-life; assertive foreign policy; oppose welfare			
Upbeats			
(New Prosperity Independents)	13	11	39/5/56
Economic growth; pro-government and pro-business; pro-immigration			
Pro-Government Conservatives			
(Populist Republicans)	10	9	2/58/40
Government must promote morality; for antipoverty programs and business regulation			
Enterprisers			
(Staunch Conservatives)	10	9	1/81/18
Patriotic; antiregulation, including the environment			
Disaffecteds			
(Disaffected Voters)	10	9	30/2/68
Cynical about government; unhappy with own economic situation; anti-immigration			
Disadvantaged Democrats			
(Partisan Poor)	10	10	84/0/16
Extremely antibusiness; strong support for antipoverty programs; deep mistrust of elected leaders			
Bystanders			
(N/A)	0	10	22/22/56
Vote in single digits even in presidential elections; ignore most political news			

Source: Adapted from "Profiles of the Typology Groups: Beyond Red and Blue," Pew Research Center for the People and the Press, 2005.

some people are more popular than others. The former Soviet Union even had an official name for the political elite—the *nomenklatura.*

political elites Persons with a disproportionate share of political power.

In America, we often refer to **political elites** more casually as "activists"—people who hold office, run for office, work in campaigns or on newspapers, lead interest groups and social movements, and speak out on public issues. Being an activist is not an all-or-nothing proposition: people display differing degrees of activism, from full-time politicians to persons who occasionally get involved in a campaign (see Chapter 8). But the more a person is an activist, the more likely it is that he or she will display ideological consistency on the conventional liberal-conservative spectrum.

The reasons for this greater consistency seem to be information and peers. First, information: in general, the better informed people are about politics and the more interest they take in politics, the more likely they are to have consistently liberal or conservative views.[32] This higher level of information and interest may lead them to find relationships among issues that others don't see and to learn from the media and elsewhere what are the "right" things to believe. This does not mean there are no differences among liberal elites (or among conservative ones), only that the differences occur within a liberal (or conservative) consensus that is more well defined, more consistent, and more important to those who share it than would be the case among ordinary citizens.

Second, peers: politics does not make strange bedfellows. On the contrary, politics is a process of likes attracting likes. The more active you are in politics, the more you will associate with people who agree with you on some issues; and the more time you spend with those people, the more your other views will shift to match theirs.

The greater ideological consistency of political elites can be seen in Congress. As we shall note in Chapter 13, Democratic members of Congress tend to be consistently liberal, and Republican members of Congress tend to be consistently conservative—*far more* consistently than Democratic voters and Republican voters. By the same token, we shall see in Chapter 9 that the delegates to presidential nominating conventions are far more ideological (liberal in the Democratic convention, conservative in the Republican one) than is true of voters who identify with the Democratic or Republican party.

Still, on a large number of issues, the policy preferences of average Republican and Democratic voters do differ significantly from one another. Some political scientists argue that Republican and Democratic leaders in Congress are more polarized because voters are more polarized. Other political scientists, however, analyze the available polling and election data differently. They find that ideological changes among voters have been small while public opinion among Democrats voting in districts represented by Democrats and among Republicans voting in districts represented by Republicans has been remarkably stable. Which side is right? We have no data that allow us to compare in each district what voters think and how their representatives behave. To amass such data would require polls of perhaps 500 voters in each congressional district taken several years apart. Nobody thinks it is worth spending millions of dollars to interview more than 10,000 voters at different times just to answer this one academic puzzle.

norm A standard of right or proper conduct.

Political Elites, Public Opinion, and Public Policy

Though the elites and the public see politics in very different ways, and though there often are intense antagonisms between the two groups, the elites influence public opinion in at least two important ways.

First, elites, especially those in or having access to the media (see Chapter 12), raise and frame political issues. At one time, environmentalism was not on the political agenda; at a later time, not only was it on the agenda, but it also was near the top of governmental concerns. At some times the government has had little interest in what it should do in South Africa or Central America; at other times the government has been preoccupied with these matters. Just as world events help shape the political agenda, so also do political elites.

Two decades ago, a path-breaking study by John Zaller suggested that elite views shape mass views by influencing both what issues capture the public's attention and how those issues are debated and decided.[33] Subsequent studies in the 1990s hinted that, contrary to the myth of the pandering politician, what scholars of the subject call opinion-policy congruence (essentially the rate at which governments adopt crime, health, trade, and other policies supported by majorities in polls) had been declining, not rising, since 1980, a trend that could be interpreted to reflect greater elite influence over how policy options are presented to the public.[34] By the late 2000s, however, the rise of Internet campaigning and the political blogosphere, among other developments, had scholars debating anew the extent and means of elite influence over mass views and policy agendas.

Second, elites state the norms by which issues should be settled. (A **norm** is a standard of right or proper conduct.) By doing this, they help determine the range of acceptable and unacceptable policy options. For example, elites have for a long time emphasized that racism is wrong. Of late they have emphasized that sexism is wrong. Over a long period, the steady repetition of views condemning

WHAT WOULD YOU DO?

MEMORANDUM

To: *Bill Byron, U.S. senator*

From: *Dan Joyce, legislative assistant*

Subject: *Vote on "path-to-citizenship" immigration bill*

Your state has only a small illegal immigration problem, but voters have concerns about both maintaining law and order, and providing economic opportunities and a "path to citizenship" for people who have resided in this country for many years. As you contemplate both your vote on the bill and your possible presidential bid as a Republican, note that public opinion on the subject is divided by party, race, ethnicity, and religion. For example, an August 2010 Pew poll asked about priorities in dealing with illegal immigration: 47 percent of Republicans, 34 percent of Independents, and 21 percent of Democrats cited "better border security"; and 41 percent of Hispanics versus 19 percent of white evangelicals cited "creating a path to citizenship."

News »

U.S. House Considers Comprehensive Immigration Reform

The U.S. House of Representatives is weighing a bill that would result in the most comprehensive immigration reform in more than a decade. Proponents say it will both improve border security and provide opportunities for legal residency for more than 11 million illegal immigrants in the United States. The bill received a mixed reception, however, as critics denounced the provisions for illegal immigrants, saying they amount to "amnesty" for law breakers.

Arguments for:

1. Your state contains a small but slowly growing proportion of first-generation Americans, who favor a "path to citizenship" for immigrants who have lived in this country for years, regardless of their legal status.
2. Illegal immigrants often take menial jobs that nobody else wants, and contribute to the U.S. economy by paying taxes and buying goods and services.
3. A "path to citizenship," with fines and other penalties for being in the country illegally, is the most realistic option for individuals who have family and other long-term ties in the United States.

Arguments against:

1. Your party leaders oppose comprehensive immigration reform, saying that enhanced border security must be a higher priority.
2. Illegal immigrants take jobs away from native-born Americans and cost more in public services, such as education and emergency health care, than they contribute to the economy.
3. People who entered the country illegally must not be rewarded for breaking the law, and enforcement can be effective with sufficient resources.

Your decision:

Vote for bill ________________ Vote against bill ________________ racism and sexism will at least intimidate, and perhaps convince, those who are racist and sexist.

A recent example of this process has been the public discussion of AIDS and its relationship to homosexuality. The initial public reaction to AIDS was one of fear and loathing. But efforts to quarantine people infected with AIDS were met with firm resistance from the medical community and from other policy elites. The elites even managed to persuade some legislatures to bar insurance companies from testing insurance applicants for the disease.

There are limits to how much influence elites can have on the public. For instance, elites do not define economic problems—people can see for themselves the existence of unemployment, raging inflation, or high interest rates. Elite opinion may shape the policies, but it does not define the problem. Similarly, elite opinion has little influence on whether we think there is a crime or drug problem; it is, after all, *our* purses being snatched, cars being stolen, and children being drugged. On the other hand, elite opinion does define the problem as well as the policy options with respect to most aspects of foreign affairs; the public has little firsthand experience with which to judge what is going on in Iraq.

Because elites affect how we see some issues and determine how other issues get resolved, it is important to study the differences between elite and public opinion. But it is wrong to suppose that there is just one elite group, unified in interests and opinions. Just as there are many publics, and hence many public opinions, there are many elites, and hence many different elite opinions. Whether there is enough variety of opinion and influence among elites to justify calling our politics "pluralist" is one of the central issues confronting any student of government.

LEARNING OBJECTIVES

WHAT YOU NEED TO KNOW

☑ **What is "public opinion" and how do we measure it?**

Public opinion refers to how people think or feel about particular things, including but not limited to politics and government. Today, it is commonly measured by means of scientific survey research or polls based on random samples of given populations.

☑ **What is "political socialization" and how does it work?**

Political socialization refers to the process by which background traits influence one's political views. It works mainly through families, schools, and religious affiliations.

☑ **What is "political ideology" and how does it matter to what elites and the mass public believe?**

Political ideology is defined as a more or less consistent set of beliefs about what policies government ought to pursue. Elites are more prone to think ideologically than average citizens are, but there are mass ideologies, and the relationship between what diverse elites believe and what the public at large believes admits of no easy generalizations.

RECONSIDERING WHO GOVERNS?

1. How does public opinion in America today vary by race, gender, and other differences?

There are cleavages in American public opinion, but they change over time, and it is hard to generalize meaningfully about how they affect politics and government. For example, on some issues, the opinions of whites and blacks are similar or narrowing, but on other issues, wide opinion gaps remain between whites and blacks. Surprisingly, little major research exists on the opinions and partisan preferences of the country's over 50 million Latinos. People who attend worship services regularly are more conservative and far more likely to vote Republican in presidential elections than people who attend worship services rarely if ever. Women are far more sympathetic to liberal causes and Democratic candidates than men, but these so-called gender gaps in opinion and voting behavior are more pronounced in some elections than in others.

2. What is political ideology, and how does it affect political behavior and influence public policy?

Political ideology is a more or less consistent set of beliefs about the policies government ought to pursue. Political scientists measure the extent to which people have a political ideology by seeing how frequently people use broad political categories (such as "liberal" and "conservative") to describe their own views or to justify their preferences for candidates and policies. They also measure it by seeing to what extent the policy preferences of a citizen are consistent over time or are based at any one time on consi principles. Many scholars believe that Americans are becoming more ideological. On issues, for example, the policy preferences of average Republican and Democratic vot now differ significantly from one another. There is clear evidence that political elites more ideological today than they were just a generation or two ago. The government attends more to the elite views than to popular views, at least on many matters.

RECONSIDERING TO WHAT ENDS?

1. What role did the Framers of the Constitution think public opinion should play in American democracy?

Basically, a rather limited role. Turn to the Appendix and read *Federalist* No. 10 by Ja Madison. In it, Madison makes plain his view that the public interest is not always, o even often, the same as what most people demand from the government. Instead mer of Congress are to be "proper guardians of the public weal," representatives who serv permanent and aggregate interests" of the country. He holds that "the regulation of th various and interfering interests" is the "principal task" of representatives.

2. When, if ever, should public policies mirror majority opinion?

For most of us, the answer depends on the issue in question. (Which, if any, of the gaps between majority opinion and public policy on crime, education, or other pub issues would you wish to see closed?) When it comes to civil rights and civil liberti (see Chapters 5 and 6), few of us would be willing, strictly speaking, to trust our freedoms to a popular vote. On the other hand, few of us would consider our syste truly democratic if government only rarely did pretty much what most people war The Framers of the Constitution offer one principled answer. They believed tempo or transient popular majorities should carry little weight with representatives, bu persistent popular majorities—for example, ones that persist over the staggered t of House and Senate and over more than a single presidential term—should be he and in many, though not in all, cases heeded.

QUESTIONS TO CONSIDER

1. In general, how much do you suppose most people actually know about the issues on which they are polled?
2. Should elected officials constantly consult polls telling them what most of their constituents believe or favor, or should they campaign and govern with little or no regard for "what the polls say"?
3. Are some political elites liberal on some issues but conservative on others? Are you more liberal or conservative on social issues than you are on economic issues?
4. What do the latest public opinion polls indicate about how Americans feel about Congress and the president, and how high or low by historical standards is the level of public approval of each?
5. Jot down your own views on the issues of the day (abortion, school prayer, health care reform, environmental policy, and others) and then see what the latest surveys on these issues suggest about whether your views are held by a majority of people whose demographic description (age, gender, ethnicity, race, religion, and party affiliation) mirrors your own.
6. Is either liberal or conservative political ideology dominant in

your home state? If so, is there any evidence or even popular lore regarding how the state's policymaking has been affected by its dominant ideology?

7. Probe how given groups may contain within themselves complex and seemingly contradictory political views. For example, research how the views of American Catholics compare to the views of the Catholic Church's leaders (visit the Web site of the U.S. Conference of Catholic Bishops), and identify the issues on which the leaders favor the "liberal" position and those on which they favor the "conservative" position.

TO LEARN MORE

CBS News/*New York Times* poll:
Topics.nytimes.com/top/reference/timestopics/subjects/n/newyorktimes-poll-watch/

Gallup opinion poll: **www.gallup.com**

The Pew Research Center for the People & the Press: **www.people-press.org**

Rasmussen Reports: **www.rasmussenreports.com**

Roper Center for Public Opinion Research: **www.ropercenter.uconn.edu**

Wall Street Journal/NBC News poll: **topics.wsj.com/subject/W/wall-street-journal/nbc-news-polls/6052**

Berinsky, Adam J. *Silent Voices: Public Opinion and Political Participation in America.* Princeton, N.J.: Princeton University Press, 2004. Shows how opinion polls can bias the results and induce people with unpopular views to say "don't know."

Caplan, Bryan. *The Myth of the Rational Voter: Why Democracies Choose Bad Policies.* Princeton, N.J.: Princeton University Press, 2007. Democracy often lets people support economic policies that make them worse off.

Erikson, Robert S., and Kent L. Tedin. *American Public Opinion.* 5th ed. Boston: Allyn and Bacon, 1995. An excellent summary of how opinion is measured, what it shows, and how it affects politics.

Jennings, M. Kent, and Richard G. Niemi. *Generations and Politics.* Princeton, N.J.: Princeton University Press, 1981. A study of persistence and change in the political views of young adults and their parents.

___. *The Political Character of Adolescence: The Influence of Families and Schools.* Princeton, N.J.: Princeton University Press, 1974. A study of political attitudes among high school students.

Key, V. O., Jr. *The Responsible Electorate.* Cambridge: Harvard University Press, 1966. An argument, with evidence, that American voters are not fools.

Lewis-Beck, Michael S., et al. *The American Voter Revisited.* Ann Arbor, Mich.: University of Michigan Press, 2008. A careful comparison of how voters in the early 2000s compare to those in the mid-1950s.

Lipset, Seymour Martin. *Political Man: The Social Bases of Politics.* Garden City, N.Y.: Doubleday, 1959. An exploration of the relationship between society, opinion, and democracy in America and abroad.

Moe, Terry M. *Schools, Vouchers, and the American Public.* Washington, D.C.: Brookings Institution Press, 2001. A masterful study of how public opinion matters to education policy, suggesting that most people, with only slight information, form reasonable views.

Nie, Norman H., Sidney Verba, and John R. Petrocik. *The Changing American Voter.* Cambridge: Harvard University Press, 1976. Traces shifts in American voter attitudes since 1960.

Weissberg, Robert. *Polling, Policy, and Public Opinion.* New York: Palgrave Macmillan, 2002. A critique of what we think we know from opinion polling, showing the many ways in which polls can give us misleading answers.

Zaller, John. *The Nature and Origins of Mass Opinion.* Cambridge, England: Cambridge University Press, 1992. A path-breaking study of how the public forms an opinion, illustrating the ways in which elite views help shape mass views.

8 Political Participation

LEARNING OBJECTIVES

WHAT YOU NEED TO KNOW

- ☑ What is political participation?
- ☑ How are voter turnout rates measured?
- ☑ How, and how much, do most citizens participate?

WHO GOVERNS?

1. Who votes, who doesn't?
2. Why do some people participate in politics at higher rates than others?

TO WHAT ENDS?

1. How did the Framers of the Constitution think average citizens should participate in America's representative democracy?
2. Should today's college-age citizens participate more in politics?

Defined simply, **political participation** refers to the many different ways that people take part in politics and government: voting or trying to influence others to vote, joining a political party or giving money to a candidate for office, keeping informed about government or debating political issues with others, signing a petition, protesting a policy, advocating for a new law, or just writing a letter to an elected leader. Some scholars of the subject profess that, in addition to these activities, almost any form of civic engagement, like helping out at a local homeless shelter or attending a school board meeting, should count as political participation. And some believe that the rise of the Internet, political blogs, and social media make traditional ideas about what constitutes political participation obsolete.

But no matter how they define it, most academics who study political participation pay close attention to voting and begin with a puzzle: despite successive legal and other changes that might be expected to increase electoral participation, voter turnout rates in America today are lower than they were for previous generations, and scores of millions of Americans now sit out each presidential and midterm national election.

THEN In most states, well into the 19th century, only property-owning white males could vote. After the Civil War and into the mid-20th century, many states used all manner of stratagems to keep blacks from voting. Women did not receive the right to vote until 1920 when the Nineteenth Amendment to the Constitution was ratified. Before 1961, residents of the District of Columbia could not vote in presidential elections; the Twenty-Third Amendment to the Constitution gave them the right. Into the 1960s, most whites had only limited formal education; women and many minority groups faced legal, social, and other barriers or disincentives to voting; and there was nothing resembling today's steady stream of political news via multiple media outlets.

NOW National laws extend voter eligibility to all persons age 18 or older (courtesy of the Twenty-Sixth Amendment to the Constitution ratified in 1971). No state may restrict voting based on discriminatory tests, taxes, or residency requirements. In areas where many non-English speakers live, election authorities must supply ballots written in their own language. People in all fifty states can register to vote when applying for a driver's license, and most states now allow voters to vote by absentee ballot prior to election day even if they are not residing outside their home state. Many states also now permit people to register on the same day that they vote. Over the last half-century, formal education levels have risen among all groups, and news, information, and opinion about politics and government are just about everywhere one turns (or clicks).

And yet, between 1860 and 1900, the percentage of eligible voters participating in presidential elections ranged between 65 percent and 80 percent. By comparison, over the last several decades, the percentage of U.S. residents participating in presidential elections has dipped as low as half. Over the same period, voter turnout in midterm

political participation The many different ways that people take part in politics and government.

national elections has averaged below 50 percent. In 2006, the Democrats took majority-control of the U.S House of Representatives, and then in 2010, the Republicans won the House majority back from the Democrats; but in each of these two recent, power-shifting midterm national elections, about 80 million U.S. residents age 18 or older did not vote. Young voters, despite averaging more years of formal education, facing fewer legal barriers, and enjoying more access to information than any previous generation could have imagined, are nonetheless mostly nonvoters; for example, in the four midterm national elections since 1998, barely one in five 18- to 24 year-olds cast a ballot.

What explains nonvoting? Are voter turnout rates in America today really as bad as they seem, either in historical terms or relative to rates in other modern democracies; and what about other forms of political participation in America today?

A Close Look at Nonvoting

Start with the fact that there are at least two different ways to measure voter turnout, and they give different answers about the prevalence of nonvoting.[1] All U.S. residents age 18 or older constitute the **voting-age population (VAP).** But many residents of the United States who are of voting age (18 or older) are not, in fact, eligible to vote. Two such groups are noncitizens who reside in America and convicted felons who in most states are disenfranchised by state laws. Unlike the VAP, the **voting-eligible population (VEP)** measure excludes from the calculation U.S. residents age 18 or older who are not legally permitted to cast a ballot. For example, in 2008 the VAP numbered nearly 231 million, but that included about 18 million noncitizens and disenfranchised convicted felons. So, for example, measured by the VAP, the national voter turnout rate was 56.8 percent in 2008, but measured by the VEP it was 61.7 percent; and since 1948, as the percentage of the population age 18 and older that consists of noncitizens and disenfranchised convicted felons has grown, the gap between the VAP and the VEP measures of voter turnout has grown (see Table 8.1).

voting-age population (VAP) Citizens who are eligible to vote after reaching the minimum age requirement.

voting-eligible population (VEP) Citizens who have reached the minimum age to be eligible to vote, excluding those who are not legally permitted to cast a ballot.

registered voters People who are registered to vote.

Another important nuance about nonvoting concerns registered versus unregistered voters. Take a look at Table 8.2. Column A compares democratic nations in terms of the average percentage of their VAP that went to the polls in dozens of post-1945 national legislative (congressional or parliamentary) elections. The United States ranks dead last with 47.7 percent voter turnout.

Now, however, look at Column B. It compares the same nations in terms of percentage of **registered voters** (those eligible voters who have completed a registration form by a set date) who went to the polls in the same legislative elections. The United States still ranks low but looks somewhat better, with 66.5 percent registered voter turnout; and the registered voter turnout in post-1968 U.S. presidential elections is about 70 percent.

Table 8.1 Two Methods of Calculating Turnout in Presidential Elections, 1948–2008

Year	Voting-Age Population (VAP)	Voting-Eligible Population (VEP)
1948	51.1%	52.2%
1952	61.6	62.3
1956	59.3	60.2
1960	62.8	63.8
1964	61.9	62.8
1968	60.9	61.5
1972	55.2	56.2
1976	53.5	54.8
1980	52.8	54.7
1984	53.3	57.2
1988	50.3	54.2
1992	55.0	60.6
1996	48.9	52.6
2000	51.2	55.6
2004	55.0	60.0
2008	56.8	61.7

Source: Updated from Michael P. McDonald and Samuel L. Popkin, "The Myth of the Vanishing Voter," *American Political Science Review* 95 (December 2001): table 1, 966. Reprinted with permission of Cambridge University Press; Michael P. McDonald, "2008 General Election Turnout Rates," updated April 26, 2009, at http://elections.gmu.edu, accessed May 8, 2009.

Table 8.2 Two Ways of Calculating Voting Turnout, Here and Abroad

A		B	
	Turnout as Percentage of Voting-Age Population		Turnout as Percentage of Registered Voters
Italy	92.0%	Australia	94.5%
New Zealand	86.0	Belgium	92.5
Belgium	84.8	Austria	83.1
Austria	84.4	New Zealand	90.8
Australia	84.2	Italy	89.8
Sweden	84.1	Netherlands	87.5
Netherlands	83.8	Sweden	87.1
Denmark	83.6	Denmark	85.9
Canada	82.6	Germany	85.4
Germany	80.2	Norway	80.4
Norway	79.2	United Kingdom	75.2
United Kingdom	73.8	Canada	73.9
France	67.3	France	73.8
Switzerland	51.9	**United States**	**66.5**
United States	**47.7**	Switzerland	56.5

Source: Rafael Lopez Pintor, Maria Gratschew, and Kate Sullivan, "Voter Turnout Rates from a Comparative Perspective," in *Voter Turnout Since 1945: A Global Report* (Stockholm, Sweden: International Institute for Democracy and Electoral Assistance, 2002).

Nonvoting rates vary by age largely because voter registration rates vary by age. For example, in midterm and presidential elections alike, Americans ages 18 to 20 register at much lower rates and also fail to vote at much higher rates than do Americans age 65 and older (see Table 8.3). Yet the same data tell us that, without regard to age, citizens who register are highly likely to vote: for example, in the 2008 presidential election, only 20 percent of persons ages 18 to 20 who registered did not cast a ballot, and only 10 percent of persons age 65 and older who registered did not cast a ballot.

Still, simply getting more people registered to vote is not a cure-all for nonvoting, for in each national election since 2006, about half of all nonvoters were registered. When registered nonvoters were asked why they did not vote, three answers were most common: about a quarter of registered nonvoters said they were too busy or had scheduling conflicts (work or school mostly); about 12 percent cited family chores or obligations; and another 12 percent believed their vote would make no difference.[2]

In response to the number one reason why registered voters fail to vote (school, work, or other scheduling conflicts), some have proposed making election day a national holiday or holding national elections on weekends. Such proposals, though popular, remain only proposals; but all states now give voters the option to vote prior to election day via mail-in ballots, and by 2004 twenty-six states afforded voters the option of "no-fault" absentee voting, meaning that voters can vote absentee without having to demonstrate they are residing outside their home state or giving any other explanation. So far as most

Table 8.3 Voter Registration and Turnout by Age

Age	Percent Registered/Voted, Midterm Elections			
	1994	1998	2002	2006
18–20	37/17	32/14	33/15	37/17
21–24	46/22	35/19	43/19	45/22
25–34	52/32	52/28	50/27	50/28
65+	76/61	75/60	76/61	75/61
Age	**Percent Registered/Voted, Presidential Elections**			
	1996	**2000**	**2004**	**2008**
18–20	46/31	41/28	51/41	53/44
21–24	51/33	49/35	52/43	62/52
25–34	57/43	55/44	56/47	66/57
65+	77/67	76/68	77/69	77/70

Source: Adapted from U.S. Bureau of the Census, *Current Population Reports*, June 2008, Table 400.

researchers have been able to determine, and with a few dramatic exceptions (for example, Oregon's 1996 all-mail-in election for the U.S. Senate), the greater flexibility and convenience of these voting procedures has done little or nothing to increase voter turnout.[3]

If voter turnout rates are to rise substantially in the United States, then nonregistered voters must become registered to vote in ever greater numbers. In addition to the roughly 40 million registered nonvoters, another 40 million or so voting-age citizens were not registered to vote in each of several recent national elections.

In most European nations, registration is done for you—automatically—by the government. By contrast, in America, the entire burden of registering to vote falls on the individual voters: they must learn how and when and where to register; they must take the time and trouble to go somewhere and fill out a registration form; and they must register if they happen to move. It is costly to register to vote in this country and costless to register in other democracies; it should not be surprising that fewer people are registered here than abroad.

But would making it less burdensome to register necessarily result in higher percentages of Americans becoming registered voters *and* voting? In 1993, Congress passed a law designed to make it easier to register to vote. Known as the motor-voter law, the law allows people in all fifty states to register to vote when applying for driver's licenses and to provide registration through the mail and at some state offices that serve the disabled or provide public assistance (such as checks for eligible low-income families).

As with mail-in and absentee balloting, the evidence regarding the motor-voter law's impact on voter participation remains less than encouraging. In 2001, eight years after the law was enacted, millions of citizens had registered to vote via state motor vehicles bureaus or other state offices, but a study found "that those who register when the process is costless are less likely to vote."[4] By 2008, motor-voter law-related means of registration were widely used (see Figure 8.1). But between 1993 and 2008, while voter registration rates had increased somewhat over pre-1993 levels, there still was no solid evidence that the law had substantially increased voter turnout.

How We Compare

Laws on Voting

Ratified in 1971, the Twenty-Sixth Amendment to the U.S. Constitution forbids states to deny "on account of age" the right to vote to citizens who are age 18 or older. But most states deny voting rights to voting-age citizens who have been convicted of felony crimes. Relevant state laws vary; for instance, Kentucky and Virginia have largely maintained laws that disenfranchise felons for life, while Maine and Vermont have permitted certain presently incarcerated felons to vote.

The legal voting age in almost all other nations is also 18. In about a dozen other countries, however, the legal voting age has been 16 (as in Brazil) or 17 (as in Indonesia); and in about twenty other nations the legal voting age is 19 (as in South Korea), 20 (as in Japan), or 21 (as in Lebanon).

Some democracies (for example, the United Kingdom) deny prisoners the right to vote, but it is far more common for democracies to permit all prisoners (save, in some nations, persons convicted of electoral fraud or related crimes) to vote. America is almost alone among democracies in the extent to which laws deny ex-prisoners the right to vote.

America is also in the international minority with respect to laws on voter registration. In most other nations it is legally compulsory for voters to register; a central, regional, or local government, or, most commonly, a specialized "Electoral Management Body," is expressly responsible for registering voters in national elections.

In America, voter registration is not legally required, and under a diverse array of state laws, individual voting-age citizens remain responsible for registering to vote.

Source: ACE Electoral Knowledge Network and United Nations Development Program, data on Voter Registration and Voting Age, http://aceproject.org, accessed May 2010; "Felony Disenfranchisement in the United States," The Sentencing Project, September 2008.

Mounting a get-out-the-vote (GOTV) drive can make only a small difference depending on what tactic is used. In a 2008 study, political scientists Donald P. Green and Alan Gerber examined the findings from more than a hundred scientific studies of diverse GOTV tactics: door-to-door canvassing, leaflets, direct mail, e-mail, phone calls, radio ads, television ads, and election-day festivals.[5] Door-to-door canvassing and phone calls were the only two tactics

Figure 8.1
Method of Registration to Vote, 2008 Percent Distribution of Registered Voters

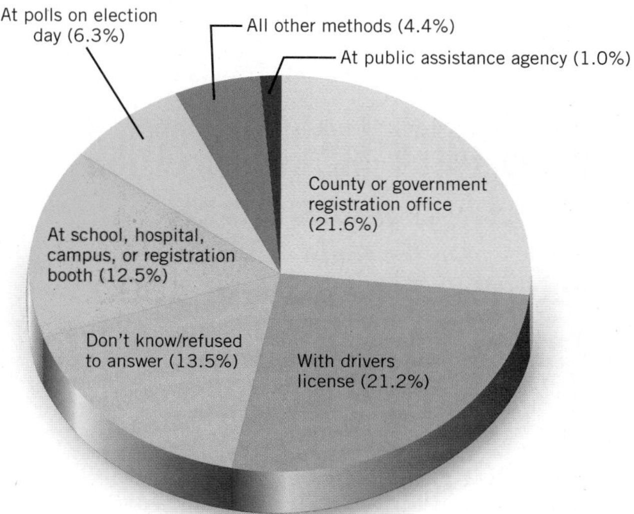

Source: U.S. Bureau of the Census, *Current Population Survey*, "Voting and Registration," November 2008.

that demonstrated statistically significant results; but even most prospective voters touched by these tactics did not turn out. In a separate 2008 study, they found that "social pressure" exerted through mailings increased turnout, yet 62 percent of those pressured still did not vote.[6]

Of course, voting is only one way of participating in politics. It is important (we could hardly be considered a democracy if nobody voted), but it is not all-important. Joining civic associations, supporting social movements, writing to legislators, fighting city hall—all these and other activities are ways of participating in politics. It is possible that, by these measures, Americans participate in politics *more* than most Europeans—or anybody else, for that matter. Moreover, it is possible that low rates of registration indicate that people are reasonably well satisfied with how the country is governed. If 100 percent of all adult Americans registered and voted (especially under a system that makes registering relatively difficult), it could mean that people were deeply upset about how things were run. In short, it is not at all clear whether low voter turnout is a symptom of political disease or a sign of political good health.

The important question about participation is not how much participation there is but how different kinds of participation affect the kind of government we get. This question cannot be answered just by looking at voter turnout, the subject of this chapter; it also requires us to look at the composition and activities of political parties, interest groups, and the media (the subjects of later chapters).

Nonetheless, voting is important. To understand why participation in American elections takes the form that it does, we must first understand how laws have determined who shall vote and under what circumstances.

The Rise of the American Electorate

It is ironic that relatively few citizens vote in American elections, since it was in this country that the mass of people first became eligible to vote. At the time the Constitution was ratified, the vote was limited to property owners or taxpayers, but by the administration of Andrew Jackson (1829–1837) it had been broadened to include virtually all white male adults. Only in a few states did property restrictions persist: they were not abolished in New Jersey until 1844 or in North Carolina until 1856. And, of course, African American males could not vote in many states, in the North as well as the South, even if they were not slaves. Women could not vote in most states until the 20th century; Chinese Americans were widely denied the vote; and being in prison is grounds for losing the franchise even today. Aliens, on the other hand, often were allowed to vote if they had at least begun the process of becoming citizens. By 1880, only an estimated 14 percent of all adult males in the United States could not vote; in England in the same period, about 40 percent of adult males were disfranchised.[7]

FROM STATE TO FEDERAL CONTROL

Initially, it was left entirely to the states to decide who could vote and for what offices. The Constitution gave Congress the right to pick the day on which presidential electors would gather and to alter state regulations regarding congressional elections. The only provision of the Constitution requiring a popular election was the clause in Article I stating that members of the House of Representatives be chosen by the "people of the several states."

Because of this permissiveness, early federal elections varied greatly. Several states picked their members of the House at large (that is, statewide) rather than by district; others used districts but elected more than one representative from each. Some had their elections in odd-numbered years, and some even required that a congressional candidate win a majority, rather than simply a plurality, of votes to be elected (when that requirement was in effect, runoff elections—in one case, as many as twelve—were necessary). Furthermore, presidential electors were at first picked by state legislatures rather than by the voters directly.

literacy test A requirement that citizens show that they can read before registering to vote.

poll tax A requirement that citizens pay a tax in order to register to vote.

grandfather clause A clause in registration laws allowing people who do not meet registration requirements to vote if they or their ancestors had voted before 1867.

white primary The practice of keeping blacks from voting in the southern states' primaries through arbitrary use of registration requirements and intimidation.

Congress, by law and constitutional amendment, has steadily reduced state prerogatives in these matters. In 1842, a federal law required that all members of the House be elected by districts; other laws over the years required that all federal elections be held in even-numbered years on the Tuesday following the first Monday in November.

The most important changes in elections have been those that extended the suffrage to women, African Americans, and 18-year-olds and made mandatory the direct popular election of U.S. senators. The Fifteenth Amendment, adopted in 1870, said that the "right of citizens of the United States to vote shall not be denied or abridged by the United States or by any state on account of race, color, or previous condition of servitude." Reading those words today, one would assume they gave African Americans the right to vote. That is not what the Supreme Court during the 1870s thought they meant. By a series of decisions, it held that the Fifteenth Amendment did not necessarily confer the right to vote on anybody; it merely asserted that if someone was denied that right, the denial could not be explicitly on the grounds of race. And the burden of proving that it was race that led to the denial fell on the black who was turned away at the polls.[8]

WHITE SUPREMACY!

Attention, White Men!

Grand Torch-Light Procession

At JACKSON,

On the Night of the

Fourth of January, 1890.

The Final Settlement of Democratic Rule and White Supremacy in Mississippi.

GRAND PYROTECHNIC DISPLAY!

Transparencies and Torches Free for all.

All in Sympathy with the Grand Cause are Cordially and Earnestly Invited to be on hand, to aid in the Final Overthrow of Radical Rule in our State.

Come on foot or on horse-back; come any way, but be sure to get there.

Brass Bands, Cannon, Flambeau Torches, Transparencies, Sky-rockets, Etc.

A GRAND DISPLAY FOR A GRAND CAUSE.

After Reconstruction ended in 1876, black voting shrank under the attacks of white supremacists.

This interpretation opened the door to three especially notorious but then-legal devices to keep blacks from voting. One was a **literacy test** (a large proportion of former slaves were illiterate); another was a requirement that a **poll tax** be paid (most former slaves were poor); and the third was the practice of keeping blacks from voting in primary elections (in the one-party South, the only meaningful election was the Democratic primary). To allow whites who were illiterate or poor to vote, a **grandfather clause** was added to the law, saying that a person could vote, even if he did not meet the legal requirements, if he or his ancestors voted before 1867 (blacks, of course, could not vote before 1867). When all else failed, blacks were intimidated, threatened, or harassed if they showed up at the polls.

Landmark Cases

Right to Vote

- ***Smith v. Allwright* (1944):** Since political parties select candidates for public office, they may not exclude blacks from voting in their primary elections.

Flip Schulke/CORBIS

After the Civil Rights Act of 1964 was passed, blacks and whites voted together in a small Alabama town.

There began a long, slow legal process of challenging in court each of these restrictions in turn. One by one, the Supreme Court set most of them aside. The grandfather clause was declared unconstitutional in 1915,[9] and the **white primary** finally fell in 1944.[10] Some of the more blatantly discriminatory literacy tests also were overturned.[11] The practical result of these rulings was slight: only a small proportion of voting-age blacks were able to register and vote in the South, and they were found mostly in the larger cities. A dramatic change did not begin until 1965, with the passage of the Voting Rights Act. This act suspended the use of literacy tests and authorized the appointment of federal examiners who could order the registration of blacks in states and counties (mostly in the South) where fewer than 50 percent of the voting-age population were registered or had voted in the last presidential election. It also provided criminal penalties for interfering with the right to vote.

Though implementation in some places was slow, the number of African Americans voting rose sharply throughout the South. For example, in Mississippi the proportion of voting-age blacks who registered rose from 5 percent to over 70 percent from 1960 to 1970. These changes had a profound effect on the behavior of many white southern politicians: Governor George Wallace stopped making pro-segregation speeches and began courting the black vote.

Women were kept from the polls by law more than by intimidation, and when the laws changed, women almost immediately began to vote in large numbers. By 1915, several states, mostly in the West, had begun to permit women to vote. But it was not until the Nineteenth Amendment to the Constitution was ratified in 1920, after a struggle lasting many decades, that women generally were allowed to vote. At one stroke, the size of the eligible voting population almost doubled. Contrary to the hopes of some and the fears of others, no dramatic changes occurred in the conduct of elections, the identity of the winners, or the substance of public policy. Initially, at least, women voted more or less in the same manner as men, though not quite as frequently.

The political impact of the youth vote was also less than expected. The Voting Rights Act of 1970 gave 18-year-olds the right to vote in federal elections beginning January 1, 1971. It also contained a provision lowering the voting age to 18 in state elections, but the Supreme Court declared this unconstitutional. As a result a constitutional amendment, the Twenty-sixth, was proposed by Congress and ratified by the states in 1971. The 1972 elections became the first in which all people between the ages of 18 and 21 could cast ballots (before then, four states

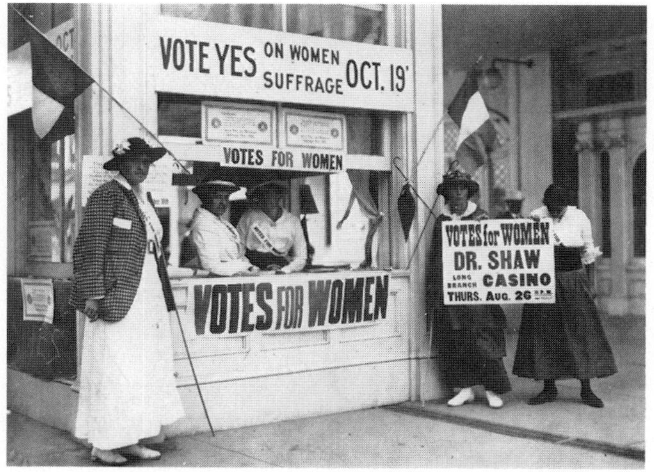

Library of Congress

The campaign to win the vote for women nationwide succeeded with the adoption of the Nineteenth Amendment in 1920.

had allowed those under 21 to vote). About 25 million people suddenly became eligible to participate in elections, but their turnout (42 percent) was lower than for the population as a whole, and they did not flock to any particular party or candidate.

Every presidential election year since 1972 has been accompanied by predictions that the "youth vote" is likely to surge. Such predictions were especially prevalent in 2008. In 2008, 23 million citizens under age 30, representing 52 percent of the 18- to 29-year-old voting population, voted. That was a higher fraction than in 1996 (37 percent), 2000 (41 percent), and 2004 (48 percent), but lower than 1972 (55 percent) and the same as 1992 (52 percent). Moreover, in every presidential election from 1996 through 2004, the under-30 youth vote accounted for 17 percent of the total election-day electorate; in 2008 the fraction rose, but only to 18 percent.

VOTER TURNOUT

The proportion of the voting-age population that has gone to the polls in presidential elections has remained about the same—between 50 and 63 percent of those eligible—at least since 1928, and appears today to be much smaller than it was in the latter part of the 19th century (see Figure 8.2). In every presidential election between 1860 and 1900, at least 70 percent of the eligible population apparently went to the polls, and in some years (1860 and 1876) almost 80 percent seem to have voted. Since 1900, in not a single presidential election has turnout reached 70 percent, and on two occasions (1920 and 1924), it did not even reach 50 percent.[12] Even outside the South, where efforts to disenfranchise African Americans make data on voter turnout especially hard to interpret, turnout seems to have declined: over 84 percent of the voting-age population participated in presidential elections in nonsouthern states between 1884 and 1900, but only 68 percent participated between 1936 and 1960, and even fewer have done so since 1960.[13]

Scholars have vigorously debated the meaning of these figures. One view is that this decline in turnout, even allowing for the shaky data on which the estimates are based, has been real and is the result of a decline of popular interest in elections and a weakening of the competitiveness of the two major parties. During the 19th century, according to this theory, the parties fought hard, worked strenuously to get as many voters as possible to the polls, afforded the mass of voters a chance to participate in party politics through caucuses and conventions, kept the legal barriers to participation (such as complex registration procedures) low, and looked forward to close, exciting elections. After 1896, by which time the South had become a one-party Democratic region and the North heavily Republican, both parties became more conservative, national elections usually resulted in lopsided victories for the Republicans, and citizens began to lose interest in politics because it no longer seemed relevant to their needs. The parties ceased functioning as organizations to mobilize the mass of voters and

Figure 8.2

Voter Participation in Presidential Elections, 1860–2008

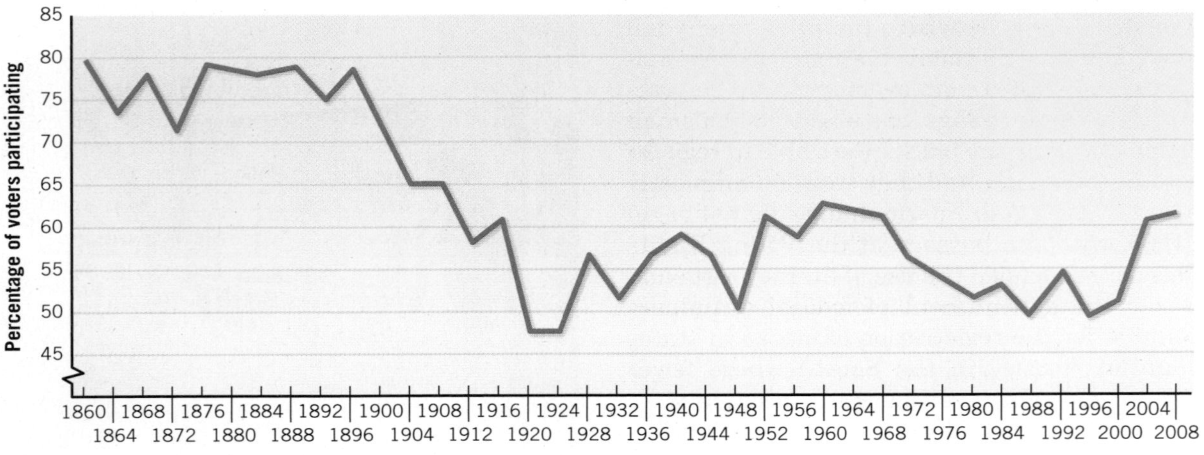

Note: Several southern states did not participate in the 1864 and 1868 elections.

Sources: For 1860–1928: Bureau of the Census, *Historical Statistics of the United States, Colonial Times to 1970,* part 2, 1071; 1932–1944: *Statistical Abstract of the United States, 1992,* 517; 1948–2000: Michael P. McDonald and Samuel L. Popkin, "The Myth of the Vanishing Voter," *American Political Science Review* 95 (December 2001): table 1, 966; 2004 and 2008 elections: American National Election Studies (ANES).

fell under the control of leaders, mostly conservative, who resisted mass participation.[14]

There is another view, however. It argues that the decline in voter turnout has been more apparent than real. Though elections were certainly more of a popular sport in the 19th century than they are today, the parties were no more democratic then than now, and voters then may have been more easily manipulated. Until around the beginning of the 20th century, voting fraud was commonplace, because it was easy to pull off. The political parties, not the government, printed the ballots; they often were cast in public, not private, voting booths; there were few serious efforts to decide who was eligible to vote, and the rules that did operate were easily evaded.

Under these circumstances, it was easy for a person to vote more than once, and the party machines made heavy use of these "floaters," or repeaters. "Vote early and often" was not a joke but a fact. The parties often controlled the counting of votes, padding the totals whenever they feared losing. As a result of these machinations, often the number of votes counted was larger than the number cast, and often the number cast was in turn larger than the number of individuals eligible to vote.

Around 1890, the states began adopting the **Australian ballot**. This was a government-printed ballot of uniform size and shape that was cast in secret, created to replace the old party-printed ballots cast in public. By 1910, only three states were without the Australian ballot. Its use cut back on (but certainly did not eliminate) vote buying and fraudulent vote counts.

In short, if votes had been legally cast and honestly counted in the 19th century, the statistics on election turnout might well be much lower than the inflated figures we now have.[15] To the extent that this is true, we may not have had a decline in voter participation as great as some have suggested. Nevertheless, most scholars believe that turnout probably did actually decline somewhat after the 1890s. One reason was that voter registration regulations became more burdensome: there were longer residency requirements; aliens who had begun but not completed the process of becoming citizens could no longer vote in most states; it became harder for African Americans to vote; educational qualifications for voting were adopted by several states; and voters had to register long in advance of the elections. These changes, designed to purify the electoral process, were aspects of the progressive reform impulse (described in Chapter 9) and served to cut back on the number of people who could participate in elections.

Australian ballot
A government-printed ballot of uniform dimensions to be cast in secret that many states adopted around 1890 to reduce voting fraud associated with party-printed ballots cast in public.

Strict voter registration procedures tended, like most reforms in American politics, to have unintended as well as intended consequences. These changes not only reduced fraudulent voting but also reduced voting generally, because they made it more difficult for certain groups of perfectly honest voters—those with little education, for example, or those who had recently moved—to register and vote. This was not the first time, and it will not be the last, that a reform designed to cure one problem created another.

Following the controversy over Florida's vote count in the 2000 presidential election, many proposals were made to overhaul the nation's voting system. In 2002, Congress passed a measure that for the first time requires each state to have in place a system for counting the disputed ballots of voters whose names were left off official registration lists. In addition, the law provides federal funds for upgrading voting equipment and procedures and for training election officials. But it stops short of creating a uniform national voting system. Paper ballots, lever machines, and punch-card voting systems will still be used in some places, while optical scan and direct recording electronic equipment will be used in others. Following the 2004 national elections, however, calls to overhaul the nation's voting system were more muted, partly because the popular vote for president was not terribly close (President Bush received 51 percent, John Kerry received 48 percent), and partly because in most states there were few reported problems.

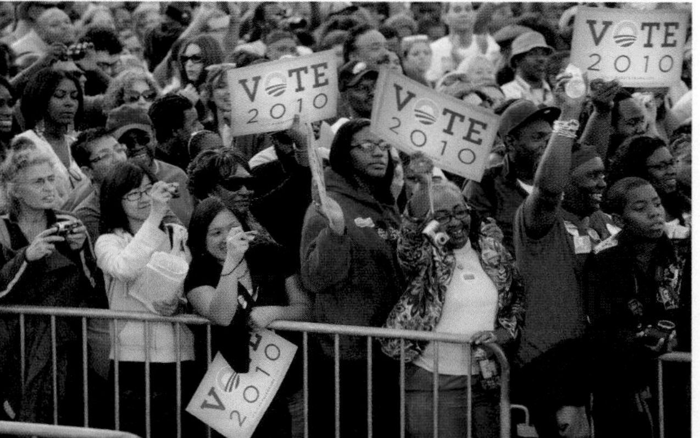

MIKE THEILER/EPA/Landov

In 2010 supporters of President Obama urged people to vote, but turnout fell and the Democrats suffered major losses.

Even after all the legal changes are taken into account, there seems to have been a decline in citizen participation in elections. Between 1960 and 1980, the proportion of voting-age people casting a ballot in presidential elections fell by about 10 percentage points, a drop that cannot be explained by how ballots were printed or how registration rules were rewritten. Nor can these factors explain why 1996 witnessed not only the lowest level of turnout (49 percent) in a presidential election since 1924 but also the single steepest four-year decline (from 55 percent in 1992) since 1920.

Actual trends in turnout aside, what if they gave an election and everyone came? Would universal turnout change national election outcomes and the content of public policy? It has long been argued that because the poor, less educated, and minorities are overrepresented among nonvoters, universal turnout would strongly benefit Democratic candidates and liberal causes. But a careful study of this question found that the "party of nonvoters" largely mirrors the demographically diverse and ideologically divided population that goes to the polls.[16]

activists People who tend to participate in all forms of politics.

Who Participates in Politics?

To understand better why voter turnout declined and what, if anything, that decline may mean, we must first look at who participates in politics.

FORMS OF PARTICIPATION

Voting is by far the most common form of political participation, while giving money to a candidate and being a member of a political organization are the least common. Many Americans exaggerate how frequently they vote or how active they are in politics. In a study by Sidney Verba and Norman Nie, 72 percent of those interviewed said they voted "regularly" in presidential elections.[17] Yet we know that since 1960, on average under 60 percent of the voting-age population has actually cast presidential ballots. Obviously, many people claim to have voted when in fact they have not. If people misreport their voting behavior, it is likely that they also misreport—that is, exaggerate—the extent to which they participate in other ways.

Indeed, most research shows that "politics is not at the heart of the day-to-day life of the American people."[18] Work, family, church, and other voluntary activities come first, both in terms of how Americans spend their time and in terms of the money they donate. For example, a study by Verba and others found that a higher proportion of citizens take part in nonpolitical than political activities: "More citizens reported giving time to church-related or charitable activities than indicated contacting a government official or working informally on a community problem, two of the most frequent forms of political participation beyond the vote."[19]

In an earlier study, Verba and Nie analyzed the ways in which people participate in politics and came up with six forms of participation that are characteristic of six different kinds of U.S. citizens. About one-fifth (22 percent) of the population is completely inactive: they rarely vote, they do not get involved in organizations, and they probably do not even talk about politics very much. These inactives typically have little education and low incomes and are relatively young. Many of them are African American. At the opposite extreme are the complete **activists,** constituting about one-ninth of the population (11 percent). These people are highly educated, have high incomes, and tend to be middle-aged rather than young or old. They tend to participate in all forms of politics.

Between these extremes are four categories of limited forms of participation. The *voting specialists* are people who vote but do little else; they tend not to have much schooling or income and to be substantially older than the average person. *Campaigners* not only vote but also like to get involved in campaign activities. They are better educated than the average voter, but what seems to distinguish them most is their interest in the conflicts, passions, and

Kayte Deioma/PhotoEdit

Young volunteers work rebuilding an area in Katrina-damaged New Orleans.

struggle of politics; their clear identification with a political party; and their willingness to take strong positions. *Communalists* are much like campaigners in social background but have a very different temperament: they do not like the conflict and tension of partisan campaigns. They tend to reserve their energy for community activities of a more nonpartisan nature—forming and joining organizations to deal with local problems and contacting local officials about these problems. Finally, there are some *parochial participants*, who do not vote and stay out of election campaigns and civic associations but are willing to contact local officials about specific, often personal, problems.[20]

PARTICIPATION: CAUSES AND MEANING

Whether participation takes the form of voting or being a complete activist, it is higher among people who have gone to college than it is among those who have not, higher among people who are employed than among the unemployed, and higher among whites and blacks than among Hispanics. The differences in voting rates for these groups are shown in Figure 8.3.

It is, however, far easier to describe differences in voting rates by schooling, employment status, race, and other characteristics than it is to explain them. Not long ago, political scientists thought they had a pretty firm handle on how education, occupation, race, gender, religion, political ideology, and other factors mattered to who votes.

For instance, a rich, older, professional woman with a graduate degree who strongly identifies as liberal or conservative and has strong partisan attachments is far more likely to vote than a poor, young, unemployed male who dropped out of high school and has no interest in politics. And, other things being equal, the more schooling one has—independent of age, occupation, race, or income—the more likely one is to vote.

All true, but the more sophisticated research into voting behavior has become—and the more that this research has attempted to explain not just intergroup differences but intragroup differences in

Figure 8.3

Voter Turnout in Presidential Elections, by Schooling, Employment, and Race, 1996–2008

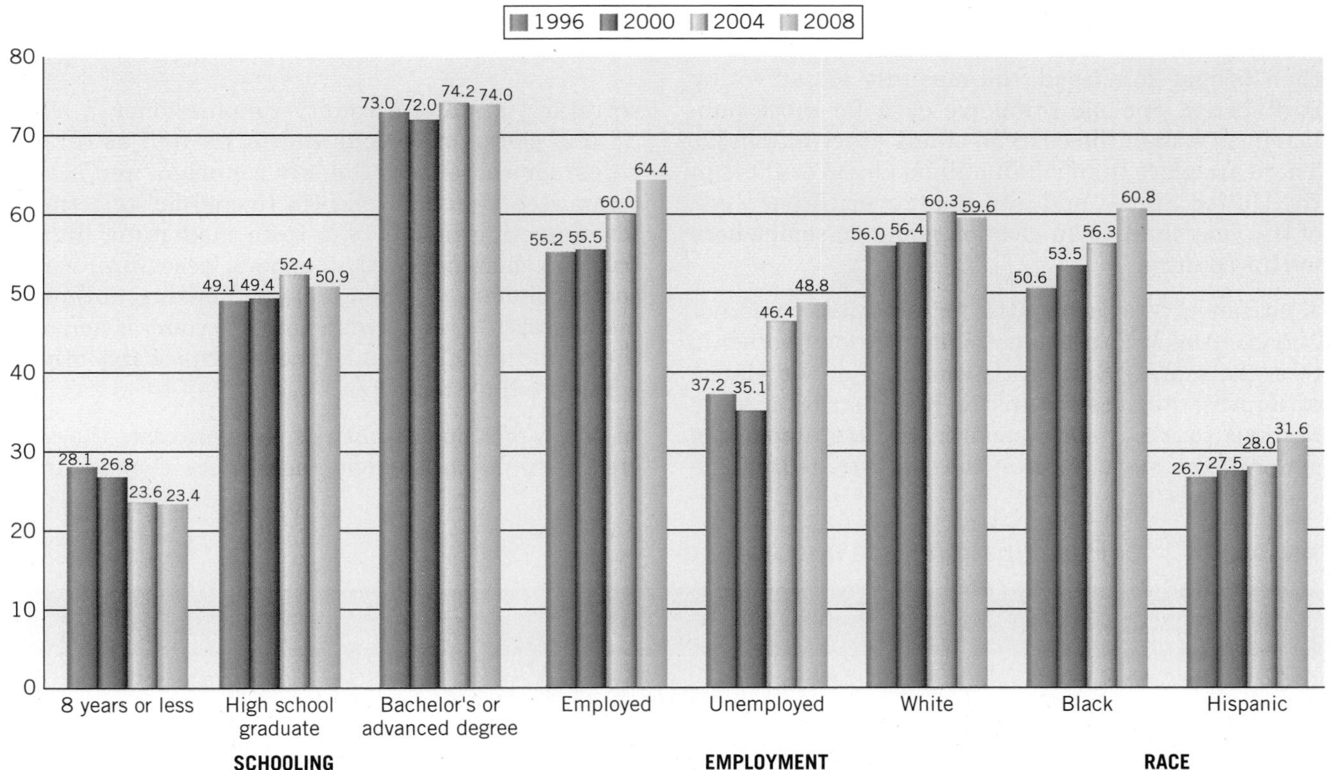

Source: Adapted from U.S. Bureau of the Census, *Current Population Reports*, June and November 2008.

voting behavior (some rich, old, politically engaged professional women don't vote; some poor, young, politically disaffected men do vote)—the less confidence we can retain in broad generalizations about the causes of participation.

One interesting explanation is religion. As the Research Frontiers box on page 195 explains, by at least some measures, religion does seem to boost participation in politics and in civic life more generally. Even with all the latest and best data at our disposal, however, it is wise to generalize with care: "religion increases participation" would be too sweeping, but "certain types of religious expression increase participation under some conditions" is about right.

The same caution applies when it comes to interpreting the meaning of participation. Although Americans are going to the polls less than earlier generations did, they are campaigning, contacting government officials, and (here the evidence is clearest, especially for younger Americans) volunteering and working on community issues no less and perhaps even more. And while the proportion of the population that votes is lower in the United States than in many other democracies, the percentage of Americans who engage in one or more political activities beyond voting is higher (see Table 8.4).

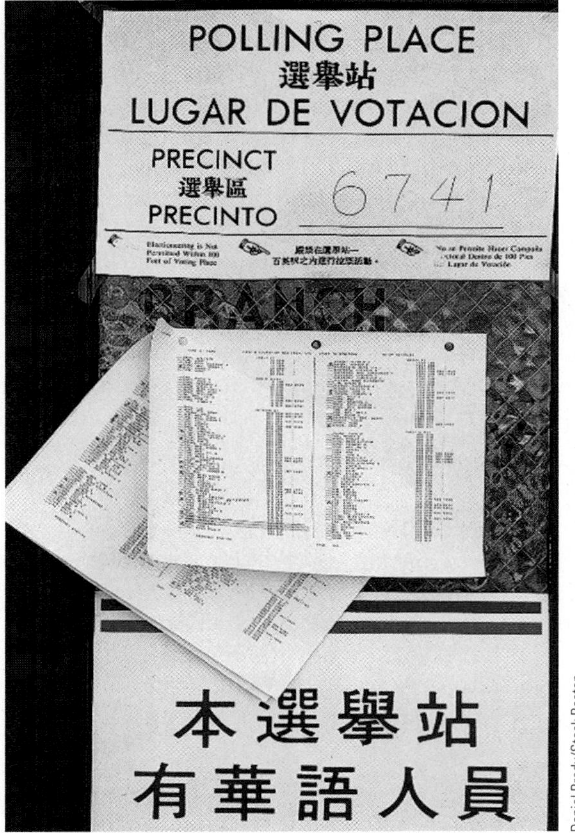

Daniel Brody/Stock Boston

In San Francisco, voting instructions are printed in English, Spanish, and Chinese.

Although we vote at lower rates in the United States than people do abroad, the meaning of our voting is different. For one thing, we elect far more public officials than the citizens of any other nation do. There are more than a half million elective offices in the United States, and just about every other week of the year there is an election going on somewhere in this country.

A citizen of Massachusetts, for example, votes not only for the U.S. president but also for two senators, the state governor, the member of the House of Representatives for his or her district, a state representative, a state senator, the state attorney general, the state auditor, the state treasurer, the secretary of state, a county commissioner, a sheriff, and clerks of various courts, as well as (in the cities) for the mayor, the city councilor, and school committee members and (in towns) for selectmen, town-meeting members, a town moderator, library trustees, health board members, assessors, water commissioners, the town clerk, housing authority members, the tree warden, and the commissioner of the public burial ground. (There are probably others whom we have forgotten.)

In many European nations, by contrast, the voters get to make just one choice once every four or

Table 8.4 Political Participation Here and Abroad

Percent of People Who . . .	USA	Rank Among Twenty Democracies	Outranked by . . .
Tried to persuade others to vote for a candidate	44%	2nd	Canada
Supported party by attending meeting, putting up poster	30%	2nd	Canada
Donated money to political group	21%	1st	None
Were contacted by party or candidate	47%	3rd	Canada, Ireland

Source: Professor Martin Wattenberg, University of California-Irvine, using data from the *Comparative Study of Electoral Systems.*

RESEARCH FRONTIERS

Does "Religion" Boost "Participation"?

For decades now, political scientists have studied participation in relation to income, race, gender, age, religion, marital status, and other variables. In recent years, however, scholars from many different disciplines have joined the fray, many with a special interest in understanding participation in relation to religion. What, if anything, have they discovered so far?

The cutting-edge studies of the subject are synthesized in a 2008 book co-authored by political scientist Corwin E. Smidt. The book's findings are fascinating but complicated. Start with religion in relation to civic participation:

- Americans vary not only by religious tradition, but also even within a given religious tradition according to their level of public religious practice (high or low) and their level of private religious practice (high or low).
- Other things (income, race, gender, age, marital status) being equal, mainline Protestants are more likely than citizens in most other religious traditions, and more likely than religiously unaffiliated citizens, to be members of voluntary associations.
- But regardless of religious tradition, persons whose form of religious expression involves high levels of both public and private religious practice are most likely to become voluntary association members.
- While religious citizens at all income levels give to charities at higher rates than otherwise comparable citizens who are religiously unaffiliated, the impact of religion on philanthropy is smaller than the impact of religion on volunteering.

What about religion in relation to political engagement?

- Religion is a significant factor in determining who votes and who doesn't, but no more significant than such variables as education and income.
- When it comes to attention to public matters, religion—other things being equal—generally is less important than education and age.
- Overall, "one's form of religious expression appears to be a stronger factor in shaping civic than in shaping political participation."

- Are you surprised by the finding that religion seems to matter more in relation to whether citizens volunteer or give to charity than it does to whether they vote or follow the political news?
- Smidt and his colleagues also reported that the same form of religious expression—namely, high levels of public and private religious practice—that is associated with higher rates of volunteering and donating is also associated with higher rates of political intolerance. Does that finding surprise you?
- What other questions about religion and participation do you think would be worth exploring?

Source: Corwin Smidt, et al., *Pews, Prayers, & Participation: Religion & Civic Responsibility in America* (Georgetown University Press, 2008).

five years: they can vote for or against a member of parliament. When there is only one election for one office every several years, that election is bound to assume more importance to voters than many elections for scores of offices. But one election for one office probably has less effect on how the nation is governed than many elections for thousands of offices. Americans may not vote at high rates, but voting affects a far greater part of the political system here than abroad.

The kinds of people who vote in the United States also are different from those who vote abroad. Since almost everybody votes in many other democracies, the votes cast there mirror almost exactly the social composition of those nations. Since only slightly over half of the voting-age population turns out even for presidential elections here, the votes cast in the United States may not truly reflect the country.

Latinos are the largest and fastest-growing minority group in America. Although they remain the most underrepresented group among all voters, the Latino share of the election-day electorate nearly doubled between 1996 (5 percent) and 2008 (9 percent). Until recently, little was known about the relationship between political participation and variables such as command of the language and involvement in non-political institutions such as workplaces, voluntary associations, and churches that provide information or impart skills relevant to politics.

But together with other recent research, a detailed 2008 study examined how ever more of the nation's Latino citizens are participating in politics in conjunction with their participation in diverse urban church communities.[21] Latino politics, it now seems clear, increasingly is taking shape as a form of hyphenated-American identity politics in which many Latino voters, including the young and the poor, not only gain information and hone politically relevant skills via church membership but also attach quasi-religious meaning to many forms of civic engagement.

The popular view that Americans don't vote as a result of apathy is not quite right. It is nearer to the truth to say that we don't all register to vote and don't always vote even when registered. There are many factors having nothing to do with apathy that shape our participation rates—age, race, party organization, the barriers to registration, and popular views about the significance of elections.

Compared to other nations, Americans vote at lower rates but more frequently and for many more offices, so elections make a bigger difference in the conduct of public affairs here than abroad. We also engage somewhat more frequently than people abroad in various nonelectoral forms of participation.

WHAT WOULD YOU DO?

MEMORANDUM

To: *Senator Henry Gilbert*

From: *Peter Clark, legislative analyst*

Subject: *Voting reform legislation*

In the 2000s, barely half of the electorate voted for president, and only a third or so cast ballots for congressional elections. In a few recent presidential primaries and statewide special elections, turnout has run 10 percent or below. Studies show that often citizens miss the opportunity to vote because of complications with work or child care. To address this problem, legislators from both parties support celebrating Veterans Day on election day, which would create a national holiday for voting. Eligible voters who do not go to the polls would be fined.

Arguments for:

1. This proposal honors veterans by recognizing their service with the fundamental requirement of representative democracy, rule by the people through voting.
2. A voting holiday ensures that people who cannot take off time from work or other responsibilities to vote have the opportunity to exercise their democratic right.
3. Imposing a fine for nonvoting sends a moral message that voting is a civic duty in a democracy. More citizens will feel morally obliged to vote if all citizens are legally obliged to do so.

Arguments against:

1. Just as veterans volunteer their service, so, too, should citizens volunteer to exercise their democratic responsibilities.
2. Voting is a right, but citizens have a civic duty to exercise that right, and the government should not, in effect, exercise that duty on their behalf. Moreover, people can vote by absentee ballot at their convenience.
3. Compulsory voting does not guarantee informed voting. It is both unwise and undemocratic to legally oblige people to vote.

News »

Congress Considers Voting Holiday to Honor Veterans and Nonvoting Fines to Increase Turnout

With bipartisan concern about maximizing voter turnout for the upcoming presidential election, both the House and the Senate are considering bills to combine Veterans Day with election day and/or impose fines on nonvoters. Members of Congress declare that increasing turnout is vital to the continued health of American democracy.

Your decision:

Vote for bill ____________ Vote against bill ____________

LEARNING OBJECTIVES

WHAT YOU NEED TO KNOW

☑ What is political participation?

Political participation refers to the many different ways that people take part in politics and government. Voting is one of the most common and widely studied forms of political participation.

☑ How are voter turnout rates measured?

There are at least two ways to measure voter turnout, by voting-age population (all residents age 18 and older) and voting-eligible population (all residents age 18 and older excluding noncitizens, disenfranchised convicted felons, and others who are not eligible to vote); voter turnout rates are higher when measured according to the voter-eligible population.

☑ How, and how much, do most citizens participate?

Most citizens vote at least on occasion in national elections and engage in one or more other forms of political participation, but maybe only one citizen in ten both votes regularly and participates regularly and in many different ways in politics and government.

RECONSIDERING WHO GOVERNS?

1. Who votes, who doesn't?

The most powerful determinants of voting are age (older people vote more than younger people) and education (college graduates vote more than high school graduates). Race makes a difference, but white rates, adjusted for income and other factors, are no longer consistently much higher than black rates; indeed, a higher percentage of blacks than whites voted in the 2008 presidential election.

2. Why do some people participate in politics at higher rates than others?

Older people and college graduates have learned to have a greater interest in politics, in part because they see ways in which government policies will affect them, and in part because they may have acquired a political ideology that makes politics intrinsically interesting. As we have seen, Americans vote less than people in most other democratic nations. That gap is in part the result of the failure of many Americans to register to vote; efforts to increase registration, such as the motor-voter law, have gotten more names onto the voting rolls, but often these new additions do not vote as frequently as other registered voters.

RECONSIDERING TO WHAT ENDS?

1. How did the Framers of the Constitution think average citizens should participate in America's representative democracy?

The Framers believed citizens should play an important but not the decisive role in the American Republic. They elect the House, but until the Constitution was amended in 1913, they did not elect the Senate; the president and senators, not ordinary people, select federal judges; and the president is chosen by electors. Over time, the system has become much more responsive to public opinion. Voters now help pick party candidates through party primaries, and their views are regularly solicited by opinion polls.

2. Should today's college-age citizens participate more in politics?

We would say yes, but the fact is that many young adults seem less disposed to traditional forms of political activity, including voting, than they are toward other types of civic engagement, such as community service or volunteer work. One forecast to ponder: unless youth voting rates increase relative to those of senior citizens, then, on election day 2020, persons 65 and older (about 22 percent of the general population) will cast a quarter of all ballots, while persons 18 to 29 (about 21 percent of the general population) will account for less than an eighth of the voting electorate.

QUESTIONS TO CONSIDER

1. **Do you think that most people your age are more likely to volunteer or do community service than they are to vote or get involved in political campaigns? How about you?**
2. **America has tens of thousands of federal, state, and local elected officials and millions of government workers (including the public employees known as public school teachers). But have you ever considered running for elected office one day or maybe working for a government agency? Why or why not?**
3. **What is your best guess as to why, despite having virtually unlimited access via the Internet and other media to news, information, and opinion, only a small fraction of young people are highly attentive to politics and government?**
4. **What was the voter turnout rate in your home state in the last three national elections, and how did it compare to the voter turnout rate nationally? Was there a significant difference between the national rate and the rate in your state, and what factors do you suppose might explain it?**
5. **Are convicted felons permitted to vote in your home state? If not, how many persons in your state today are not eligible to vote as a result, and is there any legislative effort underway to restore their voting rights?**
6. **Can you name your own members of the U.S. Congress (House and Senate), your state senator and representative, the mayor or other chief executive of your local government, and any two members of your city council or other local legislative body? If not, look them up and learn them.**

TO LEARN MORE

Information for voters:

DemocracyNet: **www.congress.org/congressorg/e4/**

League of Women Voters: **www.lwv.org/**

Voter Information Services: **www.vis.org/**

Women's Voting Guide: **www.womenvote.org/resources**

National Mail Voter Registration Form: **www.fec.gov/votregis/vr.shtml**

The Vanishing Voter: **www.vanishingvoter.org/**

Voter turnout statistics: **www.fec.gov/pages/electpg.htm**

Burnham, Walter Dean. *Critical Elections and the Mainsprings of American Politics.* New York: Norton, 1970. A classic argument about the decline of voter participation, linking it to changes in the economic system.

Eisner, Jane. *Taking Back the Vote: Getting American Youth Involved in Our Democracy.* Boston: Beacon Press, 2004. Highly readable account of why millennium-generation college-age Americans volunteer lots but vote little, with recommendations for getting young people more interested in politics.

Green, Donald P., and Alan S. Gerbec. *Get Out the Vote!: How to Increase Voter Turnout.* Washington, D.C.: Brookings Institution Press, 2nd edition, 2008. Excellent review of the evidence on what works—and what doesn't—to get more people to the polls.

Verba, Sidney, Norman H. Nie, and Jae-on Kim. *Participation and Political Equality.* Cambridge: Cambridge University Press, 1978. Classic comparative study of political participation in seven nations.

Wattenberg, Martin P. *Where Have All the Voters Gone?* Cambridge, MA: Harvard University Press, 2002. An insightful account of why voter turnout in America has lagged behind voter turnout in most other well-established democracies.

Wilson, Catherine E. *The Politics of Latino Faith: Religion, Identity, and Urban Community.* New York: New York University Press, 2008. Richly detailed study of how Latino religious life intersects with politics in three cities.

9 Political Parties

LEARNING OBJECTIVES

WHAT YOU NEED TO KNOW

- ☑ What is a political party, and why were the Framers of the Constitution concerned about their influence?
- ☑ Why does the United States have a two-party system?
- ☑ What are the prospects for a viable third party in the United States?

WHO GOVERNS?

1. How has America's two-party system changed, and how does it differ from the party systems of other representative democracies?
2. How much do parties affect how Americans vote?

TO WHAT ENDS?

1. Did the Founding Fathers think political parties were a good idea?
2. How, if at all, should America's two-party system be reformed?

From 2006 through 2008, Democratic Party leaders had reason to smile. They won control of the House and the Senate in 2006, and then they achieved unified government after Barack Obama won the 2008 presidential election. But in 2010, the Democrats lost a seat (and their filibuster-proof majority, which we will discuss in Chapter 13) in the Senate, after the Republican Party's upset victory in a special election in Massachusetts for the late Senator Ted Kennedy's seat. The Republican Party went on to regain control of the U.S. House of Representatives in the 2010 midterm elections, gaining more than 60 seats, and further reducing the Democratic majority in the Senate as well. What does the split in party control tell us about voter loyalties?

Very little, actually. Party loyalty of voters remains about what it has been for many decades. About one-third of voters say they are Democrats and another third say they are Republicans, with the rest describing themselves as independents. These numbers change a bit over time: beginning in 2006, the Republican share went down, and then when President Obama ran into trouble with his health care plan in 2010, the Republican affiliation increased a bit.

The central fact is that party attachment explains much but far from all of any election's results. Political parties must cope with economic conditions, personal popularity, crises in foreign policy, and various social issues. The attachment of voters to parties is weaker today than it was a century ago, but the very existence and endurance of political parties in the United States is significant, given how the Framers of the Constitution opposed them.

THEN The Founders disliked parties, thinking of them as "factions" motivated by ambition and self-interest. George Washington, dismayed by the quarreling between Alexander Hamilton and Thomas Jefferson in his cabinet, devoted much of his Farewell Address to condemning parties. This hostility toward parties was

understandable: the legitimacy and success of the newly created federal government were still very much in doubt. When Jefferson organized his followers to oppose Hamilton's policies, it seemed to Hamilton and *his* followers that Jefferson was opposing not just a policy or a leader but also the very concept of a national government. Jefferson, for his part, thought Hamilton was not simply pursuing bad policies but was subverting the Constitution itself. Before political parties could become legitimate, it was necessary for people to separate in their minds quarrels over policies and elections from disputes over the legitimacy of the new government itself. The ability to make that distinction was slow in coming; thus, parties were objects of profound suspicion, at first defended only as temporary expedients.

NOW American political parties are the oldest in the world, dating back to the first decade of the republic. They may be in decline, but they are not dead or dying. New parties (like the Green party launched in 2000 by consumer advocate Ralph Nader, or the Tea Party movement that developed after the 2008 presidential election) may come and go, but two parties, the Democratic and Republican, still dominate the country's campaigns and elections. Nor have party leaders been wholly replaced by media consultants, pollsters, or others whose profession is raising money or devising strategies for whichever candidates bid highest for their services. What distinguishes political parties from other groups, and why are they a fundamental feature of American politics?

Parties—Here and Abroad

A **political party** is a group that seeks to elect candidates to public office by supplying them with a label—a "party identification"—by which they are known to the electorate.[1] This definition is purposefully broad so that it will include both familiar parties (Democratic, Republican) and unfamiliar ones (Whig, Libertarian, Socialist Workers) and will cover periods in which a party is very strong (having an elaborate and well-disciplined organization that provides money and workers to its candidates) as well as periods in which it is quite weak (supplying nothing but the label to candidates). The label by which a candidate is known may or may not actually be printed on the ballot opposite the candidate's name: in the United States, it does appear on the ballot in all national elections but in only a minority of municipal ones; in Australia and Israel (and in Great Britain before 1969), it never appears on the ballot at all.

political party
A group that seeks to elect candidates to public office.

America's political parties do not matter as much, or in the same ways, as they once did. For instance, one reason voter turnout is higher abroad than in this country is that political parties in other democratic nations are more effective at mobilizing voters. The sense of belonging to a party and the inclination to vote the party ticket are greater in France, Italy, and Sweden than in the United States.

It was not always thus. At one time, being a Democrat or a Republican was a serious commitment that people did not make lightly or abandon easily. In those days, it would have been hard to find anything in Europe that could match the vote-getting power of such party organizations as those in Chicago, New York, and Philadelphia.

Parties in the United States are relatively weak today mainly because the laws and rules under which they operate have taken away much of their power at the same time that many voters have lost their sense of commitment to party identification. This weakening has proceeded unevenly, however, because our constitutional system has produced a decentralized party system just as it has produced a decentralized governmental system, with the result that parties are strong in some places and almost nonexistent in other places.

There are three political arenas in which parties may be found and in which changes in their strength may be assessed. A party exists as a *label* in the minds of the voters, as an *organization* that recruits and campaigns for candidates, and as a *set of leaders* who try to organize and control the legislative and executive branches of government. A powerful party is one whose label has a strong appeal for voters, whose organization can decide who will be candidates and how their campaigns will be managed, and whose leaders can dominate one or all branches of government.

American parties have become weaker in all three arenas. As a *label* with which voters identify, the parties probably are much weaker than they were in the 19th century but only somewhat weaker than they were 40 years ago (see Figure 9.1). In 1952, a total of 36 percent of the electorate identified strongly as Democrats (22 percent) or Republicans (14 percent), while a total of 23 percent of the electorate identified as independents. By 2004, total strong party identifiers had dropped to 33 percent of the electorate, while all independents had risen to 39 percent of the electorate. But the best evidence of weakening party identification is what voters *do*. As we shall see in the next chapter, in some elections many people vote split tickets—supporting a president from one party and members of Congress from the other.

As a *set of leaders* who organize government, especially Congress, political parties remain somewhat strong in ways that will be described in Chapter 13. As *organizations* that nominate and elect candidates, parties have become dramatically weaker since the 1960s. In most states, parties have very little control over who gets nominated to office. The causes and consequences of that change are the subject of this chapter.

In Europe, things are very different. Almost the only way a person can become a candidate for elective office is to be nominated by party leaders. Campaigns are run by the party, using party funds and workers, not by the candidate. Once in office, the elected officials are expected to vote and act together with other members of their party.

The principal criterion by which voters choose among candidates is their party identification or label. This has been changing somewhat of late: European

Figure 9.1
Decline in Party Identification, 1952–2008

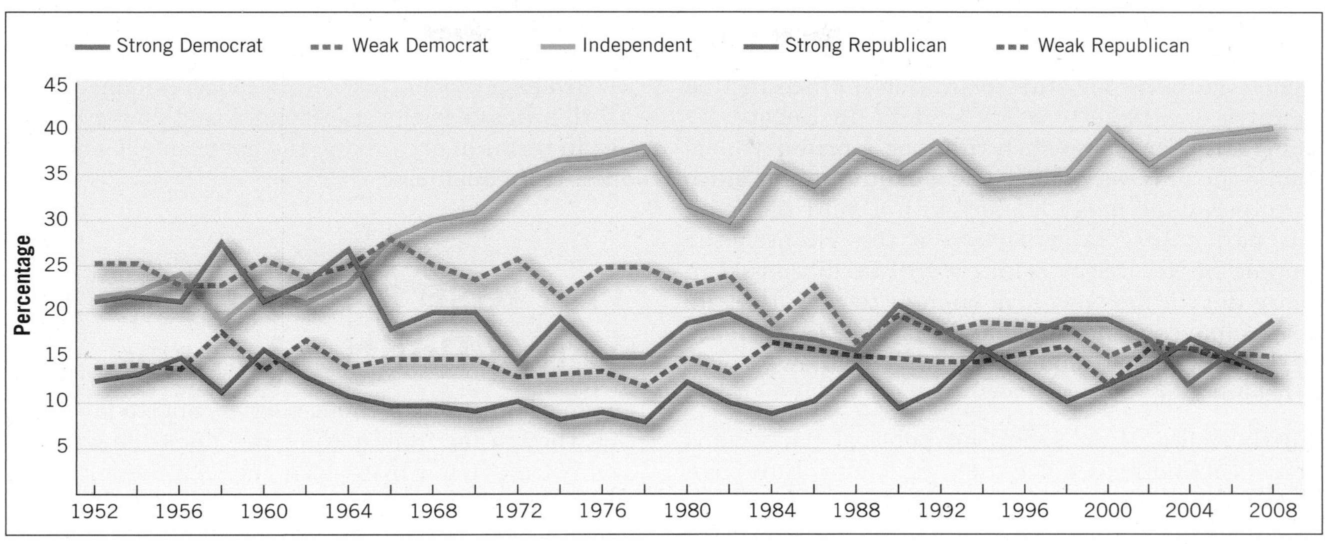

Source: American National Election Studies, Table 2A.1, "Party Identification, 1952–2008."

parties, like American ones, have not been able to count as heavily as in the past on party loyalty among the voters.

Several factors explain the striking differences between American and European political parties. First, the federal system of government in the United States decentralizes political authority and thus decentralizes political party organizations. For nearly two centuries, most of the important governmental decisions were made at the state and local levels—decisions regarding education, land use, business regulation, and public welfare—and thus it was at the state and local levels that the important struggles over power and policy occurred. Moreover, most people with political jobs—either elective or appointive—worked for state and local government, and thus a party's interest in obtaining these jobs for its followers meant it had to focus attention on who controlled city hall, the county courthouse, and the state capitol. Federalism, in short, meant political parties would acquire jobs and money from local sources and fight local contests. This, in turn, meant the national political parties would be coalitions of local parties, and though these coalitions would have a keen interest in capturing the presidency (with it, after all, went control of large numbers of federal jobs), the national party leaders rarely had as much power as the local ones. The Republican leader of Cuyahoga County, Ohio, for example, could often ignore the decisions of the Republican national chair and even the Ohio state chair.

Political authority in the United States has recently become far more centralized: the federal government now makes decisions affecting almost all aspects of our lives, including those—such as schooling and welfare—once left entirely in local hands. Yet the political parties have not become more centralized as a result. If anything, they have become even weaker and more decentralized. One reason for this apparent paradox is that in the United States, unlike in most other democratic nations, political parties are closely regulated by state and federal laws, and these regulations have weakened the power of parties substantially. Perhaps the most important of these regulations are those that prescribe how a party's candidates are selected.

There are so many political parties in France that in 2007 a woman could study pictures of twelve candidates to be president.

In the great majority of American states, the party leaders do not select people to run for office; by law, those people are chosen by the voters in primary elections. Though sometimes the party can influence who will win a primary contest, in general people running for state or national office in this country owe little to party leaders. In Europe, by contrast, there is no such thing as a primary election—the only way to become a candidate for office is to persuade party leaders to put your name on the ballot. In a later section of this chapter, the impact of the direct primary will be discussed in more detail; for now, it is enough to note that its use removes from the hands of the party leadership its most important source of power over officeholders.

Furthermore, if an American political party wins control of Congress, it does not—as in most European nations with a parliamentary system of government—also win the right to select the chief executive of the government. The American president, as we have seen, is independently elected, and this means that the president will choose his or her principal subordinates not from among members of Congress but from among persons out of Congress. Should the president pick a representative or senator for his or her cabinet, the Constitution requires that person to resign from Congress in order to accept the job. Thus, an opportunity to be a cabinet secretary is not an important reward for members of Congress, and so the president cannot use the prospect of that reward as a way of controlling congressional action. All this weakens the significance and power of parties in terms of organizing the government and conducting its business.

How We Compare

How Many Political Parties?

The United States has two political parties in Congress. Other countries have fewer or more parties in their national legislatures:

- China 1
- Canada 4
- United Kingdom 7
- Germany 6
- Mexico 8
- Russia 4
- Israel 16
- France 13
- Brazil 21 (more or less)
- India 43 (more or less)

Source: Arthur S. Banks, et al., *Political Handbook of the World: 2011* (Washington, D.C.: CQ Press, 2011).

The Rise and Decline of the Political Party

Our nation began without parties, and today's parties, though far from extinct, are about as weak as at any time in our history. In between the Founding and the present, however, parties arose and became powerful. We can see this process in four broad periods of party history: when political parties were created (roughly from the Founding to the 1820s); when the more or less stable two-party system emerged (roughly from the time of President Jackson to the Civil War); when parties developed a comprehensive organizational form and appeal (roughly from the Civil War to the 1930s); and finally when party "reform" began to alter the party system (beginning in the early 1900s but taking effect chiefly since the New Deal).

THE FOUNDING

The first organized political party in American history was made up of the followers of Jefferson, who, beginning in the 1790s, called themselves *Republicans* (hoping to suggest thereby that their opponents were secret monarchists).* The followers of Hamilton kept the label *Federalist*, which once referred to all supporters of the new Constitution (hoping to imply that their opponents were "Antifederalists," or enemies of the Constitution).

These early parties were loose caucuses of political notables in various localities, with New England strongly Federalist and much of the South passionately Republican. Jefferson and ally James Madison thought their Republican party was a temporary arrangement designed to defeat John Adams, a Federalist, in his bid to succeed

* The Jeffersonian Republicans were not the party that today we call Republican. In fact, present-day Democrats consider Jefferson to be the founder of their party.

Washington in 1796. (Adams narrowly defeated Jefferson, who, under the system then in effect, became vice president because he had the second most electoral votes.) In 1800, Adams's bid to succeed himself intensified party activity even more, but this time Jefferson won and the Republicans assumed office. The Federalists feared that Jefferson would dismantle the Constitution, but Jefferson adopted a conciliatory posture, saying in his inaugural address that "we are all Republicans, we are all Federalists."[2] It was not true, of course: the Federalists detested Jefferson, and some were planning to have New England secede from the Union. But it was good politics, expressive of the need that every president has to persuade the public that, despite partisan politics, the presidency exists to serve all the people.

So successful were the Republicans that the Federalists virtually ceased to exist as a party. Jefferson was reelected in 1804 with almost no opposition; Madison easily won two terms; James Monroe carried 16 out of 19 states in 1816 and was reelected without opposition in 1820. Political parties had seemingly disappeared, just as Jefferson had hoped. The parties that existed in these early years were essentially small groups of local notables. Political participation was limited, and nominations for most local offices were arranged rather casually.

Tennessee Historical Society

When Andrew Jackson ran for president in 1828, more than a million votes were cast for the first time in American history. This poster, from the 1832 election, was part of the emergence of truly mass political participation.

THE JACKSONIANS

What often is called the second party system emerged around 1824 with Andrew Jackson's first run for the presidency and lasted until the Civil War became inevitable. Its distinctive feature was that political participation became a mass phenomenon. For one thing, the number of voters to be reached had become quite large. Only about 365,000 popular votes were cast in 1824. But as a result of laws that enlarged the number of people eligible to vote and an increase in the population, by 1828 well over a million votes were tallied. By 1840, the figure was well over 2 million. (In England at this time, there were only 650,000 eligible voters.) In addition, by 1832 presidential electors were selected by popular vote in virtually every state. (As late as 1816, electors were chosen by the state legislatures, rather than by the people, in about half the states.) Presidential politics had become a truly national, genuinely popular activity; in many communities, election campaigns had become the principal public spectacle.

The party system of the Jacksonian era was built from the bottom up rather than—as during the period of the Founding—from the top down. No change better illustrates this transformation than the abandonment of the system of having caucuses composed of members of Congress nominate presidential candidates. The caucus system was an effort to unite the legislative and executive branches by giving the former some degree of control over who would have a chance to capture the latter. The caucus system became unpopular when the caucus candidate for president in 1824 ran third in a field of four in the general election. It was completely discredited that same year when Congress denied the presidency to Jackson, the candidate with the greatest share of the popular vote.

To replace the caucus, the party convention was invented. The first convention in American history was held by the Anti-Masonic party in 1831; the first convention of a major political party was held by the anti-Jackson Republicans later that year (it nominated Henry Clay for president). The Democrats held a convention in 1832 that ratified Jackson's nomination for reelection and picked Martin Van Buren as his running mate. The first convention to select a man who would be elected president and who was not already the incumbent president was held by the Democrats in 1836; they chose Van Buren.

THE CIVIL WAR AND SECTIONALISM

Though the party system created in the Jacksonian period was the first truly national system, with Democrats (followers of Jackson) and Whigs (opponents of Jackson) fairly evenly balanced in most regions, it could not withstand the deep split in opinion created by the agitation over slavery. Both parties tried, naturally, to straddle the issue, since neither wanted to divide its followers and thus lose the election to its rival. But slavery and sectionalism were issues that could not be straddled. The old parties divided and new ones emerged. The modern Republican Party (not the old Democratic-Republican party of Thomas Jefferson) began as a third party. As a result of the Civil War, it became a major party (the only third party ever to gain major-party status) and dominated national politics, with only occasional interruptions, for three-quarters of a century.

mugwumps* or *progressives Republican party faction of the 1890s to the 1910s, composed of reformers who opposed patronage.

Republican control of the White House, and to a lesser extent Congress, was in large measure the result of two events that gave to Republicans a marked advantage in the competition for the loyalties of voters. The first of these was the Civil War. This bitter, searing crisis deeply polarized popular attitudes. Those who supported the Union side became Republicans for generations; those who supported the Confederacy, or who had opposed the war, became Democrats.

As it turned out, this partisan division was nearly even for a while: though the Republicans usually won the presidency and the Senate, they often lost control of the House. There were many northern Democrats. In 1896, however, another event—the presidential candidacy of William Jennings Bryan—further strengthened the Republican party. Bryan, a Democrat, alienated many voters in the populous northeastern states while attracting voters in the South and Midwest. The result was to confirm and deepen the split in the country, especially North versus South, begun by the Civil War. From 1896 to the 1930s, with rare exceptions northern states were solidly Republican, southern ones solidly Democratic.

This split had a profound effect on the organization of political parties, for it meant that most states were now one-party states. As a result, competition for office at the state level had to go on *within* a single dominant party (the Republican party in Massachusetts, New York, Pennsylvania, Wisconsin, and elsewhere; the Democratic party in Georgia, Mississippi, South Carolina, and elsewhere). Consequently, there emerged two major factions within each party, but especially within the Republican party. One was composed of the party regulars—the professional politicians, the "stalwarts," the Old Guard. They were preoccupied with building up the party machinery, developing party loyalty, and acquiring and dispensing patronage—jobs and other favors—for themselves and their faithful followers. Their great skills were in organization, negotiation, bargaining, and compromise; their great interest was in winning.

The other faction, variously called **mugwumps** or **progressives** (or "reformers"), was opposed to the heavy emphasis on patronage; disliked the party machinery because it permitted only bland candidates to rise to the top; was fearful of the heavy influx of immigrants into American cities and of the ability of the party regulars to organize them into "machines;" and wanted to see the party take unpopular positions on certain issues (such as free trade). Their great skills lay in the areas of advocacy and articulation; their great interest was in principle.

At first the mugwumps tried to play a balance-of-power role, sometimes siding with the Republican party of which they were members, at other times defecting to the Democrats (as when they bolted the Republican party to support Grover Cleveland, the Democratic nominee, in 1884). But later, as the Republican strength in the nation grew, progressives within that party became increasingly less able to play a balance-of-power role, especially at the state level. If the progressives were to have any power, they came to believe, it would require an attack on the very concept of partisanship itself.

THE ERA OF REFORM

Progressives began to espouse measures to curtail or even abolish political parties. They favored primary elections to replace nominating conventions because the latter were viewed as manipulated by party bosses; they favored nonpartisan elections at the city level and in some cases at the state level as well; they argued against corrupt alliances between parties and businesses. They wanted strict voter registration requirements that would reduce voting fraud (but would also, as it turned out, keep ordinary citizens who found the requirements cumbersome from voting); they pressed for civil service reform to eliminate patronage; and they made heavy use of the mass media as a way of attacking the abuses of

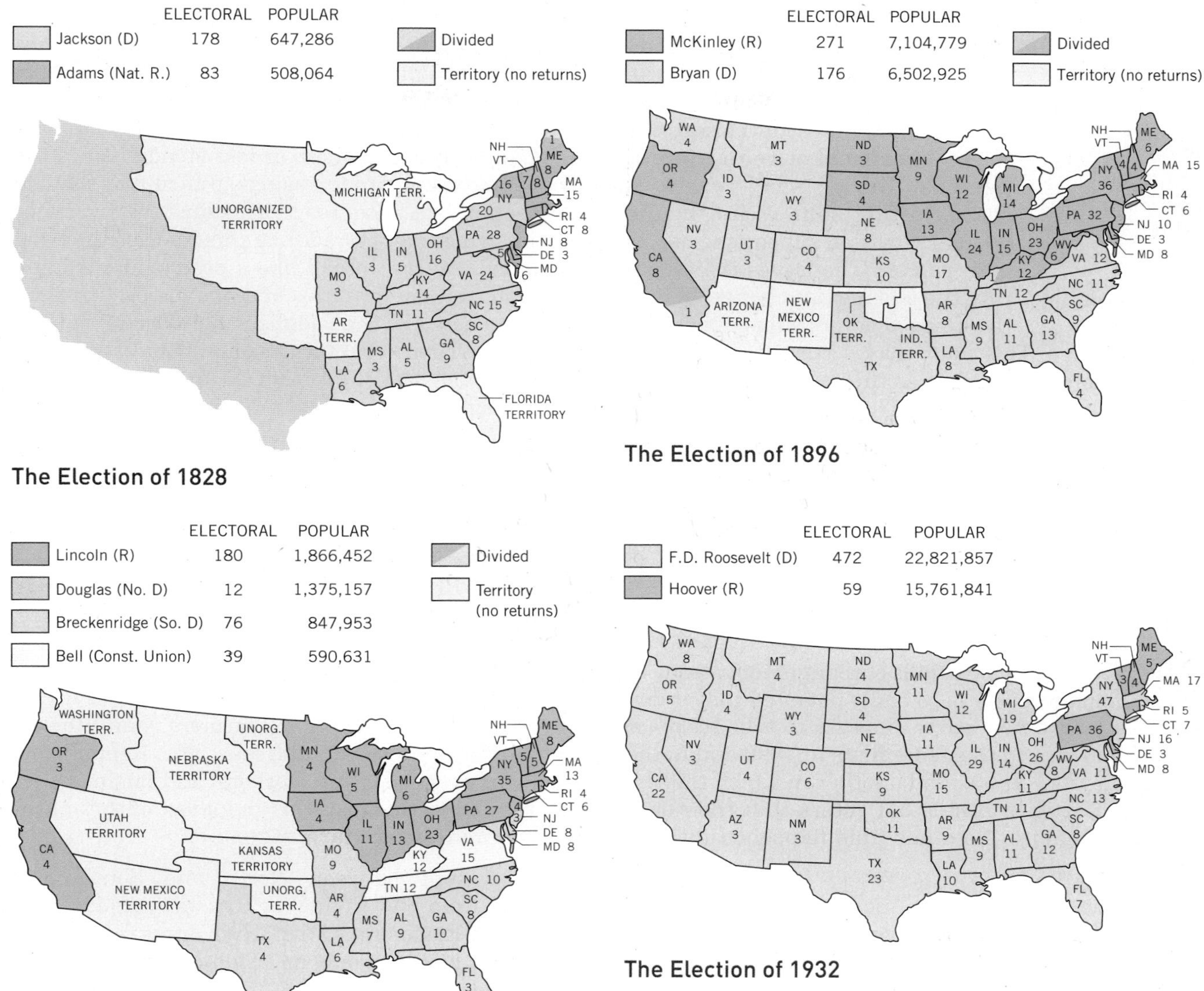

The Election of 1828

The Election of 1896

The Election of 1860

The Election of 1932

partisanship and of promoting their own ideas and candidacies.

The progressives were more successful in some places than in others. In California, for example, progressives led by Governor Hiram Johnson in 1910–1911 were able to institute the direct primary and to adopt procedures—called the *initiative* and the *referendum*—so citizens could vote directly on proposed legislation, thereby bypassing the state legislature. Governor Robert La Follette brought about similar changes in Wisconsin.

The effect of these changes was to reduce substantially the worst forms of political corruption and ultimately to make boss rule in politics difficult if not impossible. But they also had the effect of making political parties, whether led by bosses or by statesmen, weaker, less able to hold officeholders accountable, and less able to assemble the power necessary for governing the fragmented political institutions created by the Constitution. In Congress, party lines began to grow fainter, as did the power of congressional leadership. Above all, the progressives did not have an answer to the problem first faced by Jefferson: if there is not a strong political party, by what other means will candidates for office be found, recruited, and supported?

PARTY REALIGNMENTS

There have clearly been important turning points in the strength of the major parties, especially in the 20th century, when for long periods we have not so much had close competition between two parties

critical or ***realignment period*** A period when a major, lasting shift occurs in the popular coalition supporting one or both parties.

as we have had an alternation of dominance by one party and then the other. To help explain these major shifts in the tides of politics, scholars have developed the theory of **critical** or **realignment periods.** During such periods a sharp, lasting shift occurs in the popular coalition supporting one or both parties. The issues that separate the two parties change, and so the kinds of voters supporting each party change. This shift may occur at the time of the election or just after, as the new administration draws in new supporters.[3] There seem to have been five realignments so far, during or just after these elections: 1800, when the Jeffersonian Republicans defeated the Federalists; 1828, when the Jacksonian Democrats came to power; 1860, when the Whig party collapsed and the Republicans under Lincoln came to power; 1896, when the Republicans defeated William Jennings Bryan; and 1932, when the Democrats under Roosevelt came into office.

There are at least two kinds of realignments—one in which a major party is so badly defeated that it disappears and a new party emerges to take its place (this happened to the Federalists in 1800 and to the Whigs in 1856–1860), and another in which the two existing parties continue but voters shift their support from one to the other (this happened in 1896 and 1932).

The three clearest cases seem to be 1860, 1896, and 1932. By 1860, the existing parties could no longer straddle the fence on the slavery issue. The Republican party was formed in 1856 on the basis of clear-cut opposition to slavery; the Democratic party split in half in 1860, with one part (led by Stephen A. Douglas and based in the North) trying to waffle on the issue and the other (led by John C. Breckinridge and drawing its support from the South) categorically denying that any government had any right to outlaw slavery. The remnants of the Whig party, renamed the Constitutional Union party, tried to unite the nation by writing no platform at all, thus remaining silent on slavery. Lincoln and the antislavery Republicans won in 1860; Breckinridge and the pro-slavery Southern Democrats came in second. From that moment on, the two major political parties acquired different sources of support and stood (at least for a decade) for different principles. The parties that had tried to straddle the fence were eliminated. The Civil War fixed these new party loyalties deep in the popular mind, and the structure of party competition was set for nearly 40 years.

In 1896, a different kind of realignment occurred. Economics rather than slavery was at issue. A series of depressions during the 1880s and 1890s fell especially hard on farmers in the Midwest and parts of the South. The prices paid to farmers for their commodities had been falling more or less steadily since the Civil War, making it increasingly difficult for them to pay their bills. A bitter reaction against the two major parties, which were straddling this issue as they had straddled slavery, spread like a prairie fire, leading to the formation of parties of economic protest—the Greenbackers and the Populists. Reinforcing the economic cleavages were cultural ones: Populists tended to be fundamentalist Protestants; urban voters were increasingly Catholic.

Matters came to a head in 1896 when William Jennings Bryan captured the Democratic nomination for president and saw to it that the party adopted a Populist platform. The existing Populist party endorsed the Bryan candidacy. In the election, anti-Bryan Democrats deserted the party in droves to support the Republican candidate, William McKinley. Once again, a real issue divided the two parties: the Republicans stood for industry, business, hard money, protective tariffs, and urban interests; the Democrats for farmers, small towns, low tariffs, and rural interests. The Republicans won, carrying the cities, workers, and businesspeople; the Democrats lost, carrying most of the southern and midwestern farm states.

The old split between North and South that resulted from the Civil War was now replaced in part by an East versus West, city versus farm split.[4] It was not, however, only an economic cleavage—the Republicans had been able to appeal to Catholics and Lutherans who disliked fundamentalism and its hostility toward liquor and immigrants.

William Jennings Bryan giving a campaign speech during one of his three unsuccessful presidential campaigns.

This alignment persisted until 1932. Again change was triggered by an economic depression; again more than economic issues were involved. The New Deal coalition that emerged was based on bringing together into the Democratic party urban workers, northern blacks, southern whites, and Jewish voters. Unlike in 1860 and 1896, it was not preceded by any third-party movement; it occurred suddenly (though some groups had begun to shift their allegiance in 1928) and gathered momentum throughout the 1930s. The Democrats, isolated since 1896 as a southern and midwestern sectional party, had now become the majority party by finding a candidate and a cause that could lure urban workers, blacks, and Jews away from the Republican party, where they had been for decades. It was obviously a delicate coalition—blacks and southern whites disagreed on practically everything except their liking for Roosevelt; Jews and the Irish bosses of the big-city machines also had little in common. But the federal government under Roosevelt was able to supply enough benefits to each of these disparate groups to keep them loyal members of the coalition and to provide a new basis for party identification.

In short, an electoral realignment occurs when a new issue of utmost importance to the voters (slavery, the economy) cuts across existing party divisions and replaces old issues that formerly were the basis of party identification.

Some people wondered whether the election of 1980, since it brought into power the most conservative administration in half a century, signaled a new realignment. Many of President Reagan's supporters began talking of a "mandate" to adopt major new policies in keeping with the views of the "new majority." But Reagan won in 1980 less because of what he stood for than because he was not Jimmy Carter, and he was reelected in 1984 primarily because people were satisfied with how the country was doing, especially economically.[5]

Just because we have had periods of one-party dominance in the past does not mean we will have them in the future. Reagan's election could not have been a traditional realignment, because it left Congress in the hands of the Democratic Party. Moreover, some scholars are beginning to question the theory of critical elections, or at least the theory that they occur with some regularity.

Nevertheless, one major change has occurred of late—the shift in the presidential voting patterns of the South. From 1972 through 2008, the South was more Republican than the nation as a whole. The proportion of white southerners describing themselves to pollsters as "strongly Democratic" fell from more than one-third in 1952 to about one-seventh in 1984. There has been a corresponding increase in "independents." As it turns out, southern white independents have voted overwhelmingly Republican in recent presidential elections.[6] If you lump independents together with the parties for which they actually vote, the party alignment among white southerners has gone from 6 to 1 Democratic in 1952 to about 50/50 Democrats and Republicans. If this continues, it will constitute a major realignment in a region of the country that is growing rapidly in population and political clout.

In general, however, the kind of dramatic realignment that occurred in the 1860s or after 1932 may not occur again, because party labels have lost their meaning for a growing number of voters. For these people politics may *de*align rather than *re*align.

PARTY DECLINE

The evidence that the parties are decaying, not realigning, is of several sorts. We have already noted that the proportion of people identifying with one or the other party declined between 1960 and 1980. Simultaneously, the proportion of those voting a **split ticket** (as opposed to a **straight ticket**) increased.

split ticket Voting for candidates of different parties for various offices in the same election.

straight ticket Voting for candidates of the same party.

Split-ticket voting rose between 1952 and 1972 and hovered around 25 percent until it declined somewhat after 1992 (see Figure 9.2). For example, in 1988 more than *half* of all House Democrats were elected in districts that voted for Republican George Bush as president. This ticket splitting was greatest in the South, but it was common everywhere. If every district that voted for Bush had also elected a Republican to Congress, the Republican Party would have held a 2-to-1 majority in the House of Representatives. Ticket splitting creates divided government—the White House and Congress are controlled by different parties (see Chapter 14). Ticket splitting helped the Democrats keep control of the House of Representatives from 1954 to 1994.

Ticket splitting was almost unheard of in the 19th century, and for a very good reason. In those days, the voter was either given a ballot by the party of his choice and he dropped it, intact, into the ballot box (thereby voting for everybody listed on the ballot), or he was given a government-printed ballot that

Figure 9.2

Split-Ticket Voting for President/House, 1952–2008

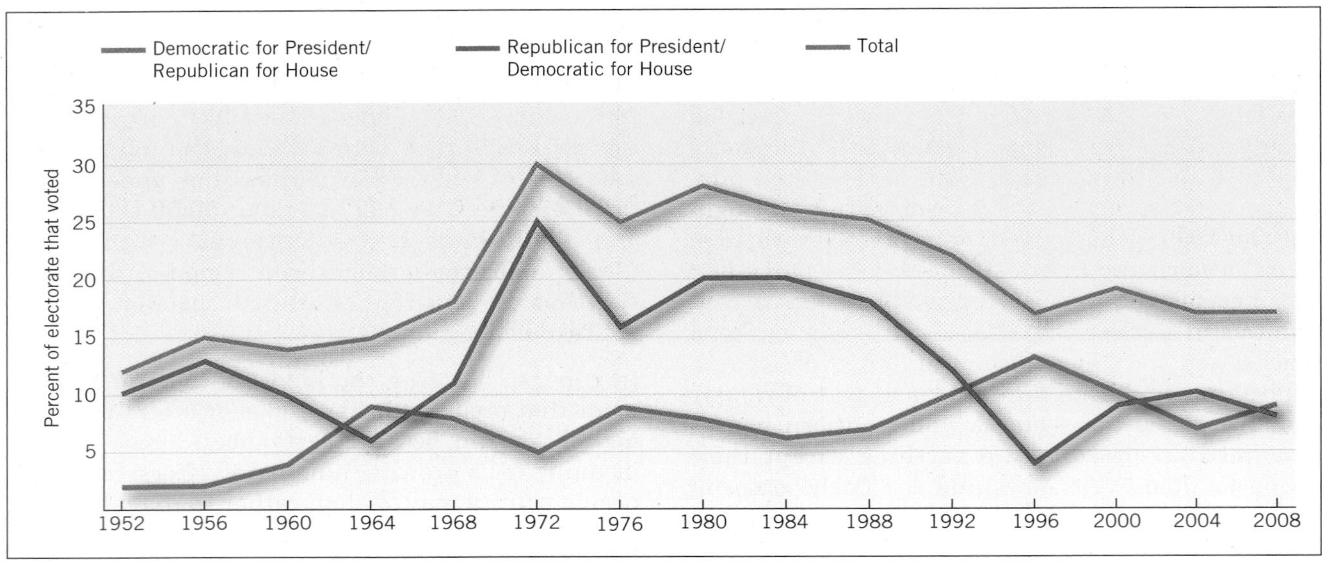

American National Election Studies, Table 9B.2, "Split-Ticket Voting for President/Congress, 1952–2008."

listed in columns all the candidates of each party. All the voter had to do was mark the top of one column in order to vote for every candidate in that column. (When voting machines came along, they provided a single lever that, when pulled, cast votes for all the candidates of a particular party.) Around the turn of the century progressives began to persuade states to adopt the **office-bloc** (or "Massachusetts") **ballot** in place of the **party-column** (or "Indiana") **ballot.** The office-bloc ballot lists all candidates by office; there is no way to vote a straight party ticket by making one mark. Not surprisingly, states using the office-bloc ballot show much more ticket splitting than those without it.[7]

office-bloc ballot A ballot listing all candidates of a given office under the name of that office; also called a "Massachusetts" ballot.

party-column ballot A ballot listing all candidates of a given party together under the name of that party; also called an "Indiana" ballot.

It would be a mistake, however, to conclude that parties have declined simply because many voters now split tickets in national elections. Despite many changes and challenges (see Figure 9.3), America's two-party system remains strong. In most elections—national, state, and local—voters registered as Democrats still vote for Democratic candidates, and voters registered as Republicans still vote for Republican candidates. In Congress, state legislatures, and city councils, members still normally vote along party lines. Local political machines have died, but, as we shall now explain, national party structures remain alive and well.

The National Party Structure Today

Since political parties exist at the national, state, and local levels, you might suppose they are arranged like a big corporation, with a national board of directors giving orders to state managers who in turn direct the activities of rank-and-file workers at the county and city level. Nothing could be further from the truth. At each level, a separate and almost entirely independent organization exists that does pretty much what it wants, and in many counties and cities there is virtually no organization at all.

State party organizations, all determined to pick their delegates to the presidential nominating convention first, have moved their primary elections to earlier and earlier dates. For example, the Iowa caucus and the New Hampshire primary in the 1980s were held in March; in 2008, they were held in January. California moved its primary from June to February. This front-loaded set of primaries has made the campaign much longer and more expensive, but the national party organizations have been almost powerless to prevent it.

Figure 9.3

Cleavages and Continuity in the Two-Party System

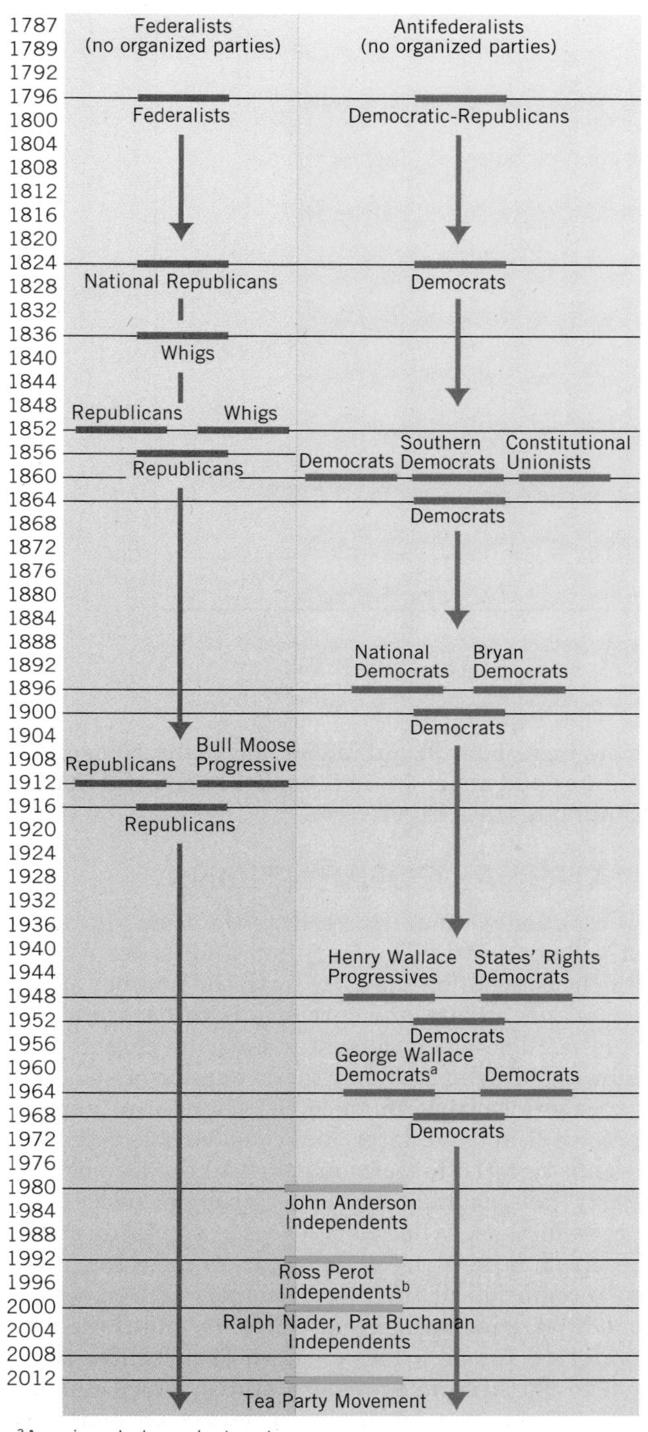

[a]American Independent party.

[b]United We Stand America or Reform Party.

On paper, the national Democratic and Republican parties look quite similar. In both parties, ultimate authority is in the hands of the **national convention** that meets every four years to nominate a presidential candidate. Between these conventions, party affairs are managed by a **national committee** made up of delegates from each state and territory. In Congress, each party has a **congressional campaign committee** that helps members of Congress running for reelection or would-be members running for an open seat or challenging a candidate from the opposition party. The day-to-day work of the party is managed by a full-time, paid **national chair** elected by the committee.

national convention A meeting of party delegates held every four years.

national committee Delegates who run party affairs between national conventions.

congressional campaign committee A party committee in Congress that provides funds to members and would-be members.

national chair Day-to-day party manager elected by the national committee.

For a long time, the two national parties were alike in behavior as well as description. The national chair, if his or her party held the White House, would help decide who among the party faithful would get federal jobs. Otherwise, the parties did very little.

But beginning in the late 1960s and early 1970s, the Republicans began to convert their national party into a well-financed, highly staffed organization devoted to finding and electing Republican candidates, especially to Congress. At about the same time, the Democrats began changing the rules governing how presidential candidates are nominated in ways that profoundly altered the distribution of power within the party. As a consequence, the Republicans became a bureaucratized party and the Democrats became a factionalized one. After the Republicans won four out of five presidential elections from 1968 to 1984 and briefly took control of the Senate, the Democrats began to suspect that maybe an efficient bureaucracy was better than a collection of warring factions, and so they made an effort to emulate the Republicans.

The Republicans had taken advantage of a new bit of technology—computerized mailings. They built up a huge file of names of people who had given or might give money to the party, usually in small amounts, and used that list to raise a big budget for the national party. The Republican National Committee (RNC) used this money to run, in effect, a national political consulting firm. Money went to

Figure 9.4
Cost of Winning a Congressional Election, 2002–2010

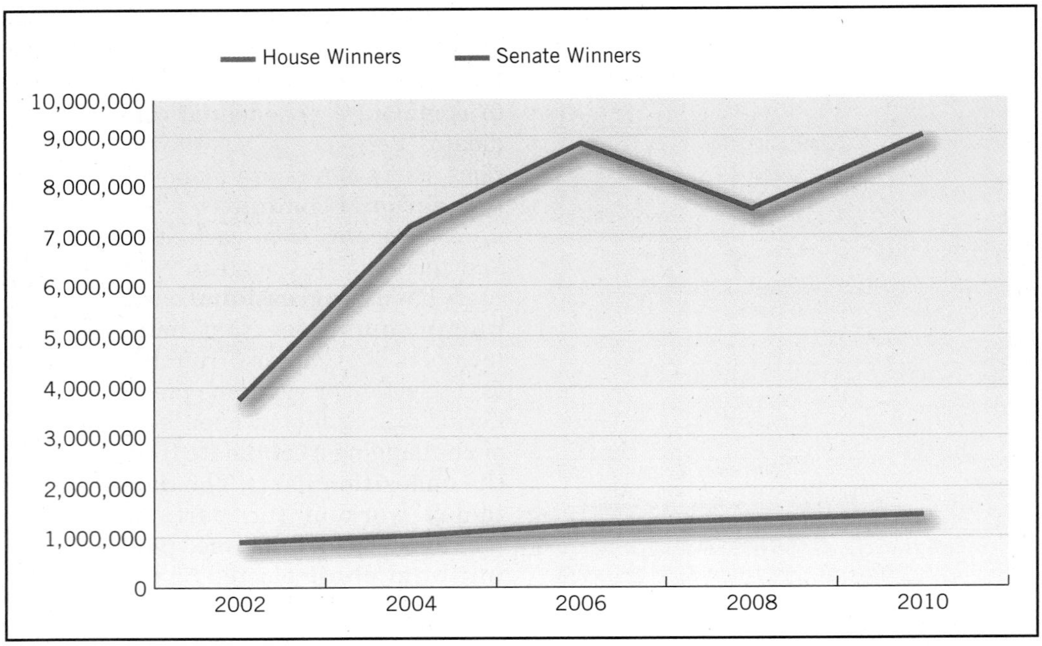

Source: Campaign Finance Institute, updated data from *Vital Statistics on Congress*, ed. Michael J. Malbin, Norman J. Ornstein, and Thomas E. Mann (Washington, D.C.: Brookings Institution Press, 2008).

recruit and train Republican candidates, give them legal and financial advice, study issues and analyze voting trends, and conduct national advertising campaigns on behalf of the party as a whole.

When the Democratic National Committee (DNC) decided to play catch-up, it followed the RNC strategy. Using the same computerized direct-mail techniques, the Democratic party committees—the National Committee, Senatorial Committee, and Congressional Committee—raised more money than ever before, though not as much as the Republicans. In 2004, the Democrats and their allies outspent the Republicans. The Democrats, like the Republicans, ship a lot of their national party money to state organizations to finance television ads supporting their parties.

Despite the recent enactment of campaign finance laws intended to check the influence of money on national elections, in 2004 both Democrats and Republicans redoubled efforts to raise *soft money*—that is, funds to aid parties (and their ads and polls). In the Democratic presidential primary, Howard Dean alone raised $30 million over the Internet with average contributions under $100. In 2010, new records were also set for spending on congressional races: the average cost for successful House candidates was more than $1.4 million, while the average cost for successful Senate candidates was close to $9 million. In contrast, the average numbers in 2002 were just under $1 million for successful House candidates and about $4.5 million for successful Senate candidates (see Figure 9.4).

NATIONAL CONVENTIONS

The national committee selects the time and place of the next national convention and issues a "call" for the convention that sets forth the number of delegates each state and territory is to have and the rules under which delegates must be chosen. The number of delegates and their manner of selection can significantly influence the chances of various presidential candidates, and considerable attention is thus devoted to these matters. In the Democratic Party, for example, a long struggle took place between those who wished to see southern states receive a large share of delegates to the convention, in recognition of their firm support of Democratic candidates in presidential elections, and those who preferred to see a larger share of delegates allotted to northern and western states, which, though less solidly Democratic, were larger or more liberal. A similar conflict within the Republican Party has pitted conservative Republican leaders in the Midwest against liberal ones in the East.

A compromise formula usually is chosen; nevertheless, over the years these formulas have gradually changed, shifting voting strength in the Democratic convention away from the South and toward the North and West and in the Republican convention away from the East and toward the South and Southwest. These delegate allocation formulas are but one sign (others will be mentioned later in this chapter) of the tendency of the two parties' conventions to move in opposite ideological directions—Democrats more to the left, Republicans more to the right.

The exact formula for apportioning delegates is extremely complex. For the Democrats, it takes into account the vote each state cast for Democratic candidates in past elections and the number of electoral votes of each state; for the Republicans, it takes into account the number of representatives in Congress and whether the state in past elections cast its electoral votes for the Republican presidential candidate and elected Republicans to the Senate, the House, and the governorship. Thus, the Democrats give extra delegates to large states, while the Republicans give extra ones to loyal states.

The way in which delegates are chosen can be even more important than their allocation. The Democrats, beginning in 1972, developed an elaborate set of rules designed to weaken the control over delegates by local party leaders and to increase the proportion of women, young people, African Americans, and Native Americans attending the convention. These rules were first drafted by a party commission chaired by Senator George McGovern (who later made skillful use of these new procedures in his successful bid for the Democratic presidential nomination). They were revised in 1974 by another commission, chaired by Barbara Mikulski, whose decisions were ratified by the 1974 midterm convention. After the 1976 election, a third commission, chaired by Morley Winograd, produced still another revision of the rules, which took effect in 1980. Then a fourth commission, chaired by North Carolina governor James B. Hunt, recommended in 1981 another set of rules, which became effective with the 1984 convention.

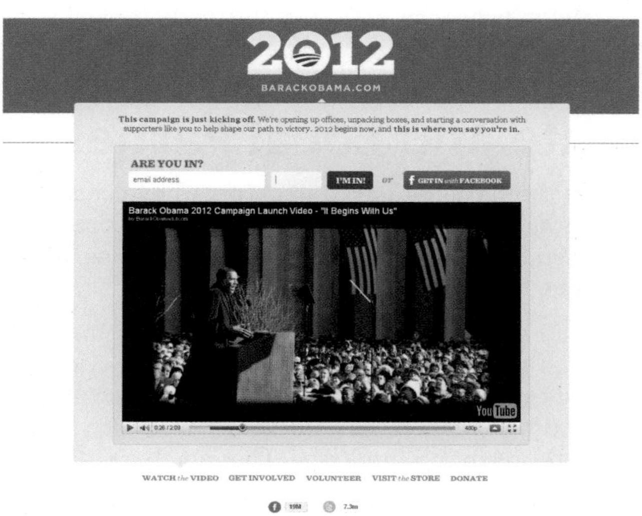

President Obama in 2011 used an e-mail and a video to tell his followers that he was going to run for reelection in 2012. Digital communication has become more important for both parties.

HO/Reuters/Landov

The general thrust of the work of the first three rules commissions was to broaden the antiparty changes started by the progressives at the beginning of the 20th century. Whereas the earlier reformers had tried to minimize the role of parties in the election process, those of the 1970s sought to weaken the influence of leaders within the party. In short, the newer reforms were aimed at creating *intra*party democracy as well as *inter*party democracy. Rules for the 1980 Democratic convention required:

- Equal division of delegates between men and women
- Establishment of "goals" for the representation of African Americans, Hispanics, and other groups in proportion to their presence in a state's Democratic electorate
- Open delegate selection procedures, with advance publicity and written rules
- Selection of 75 percent of the delegates at the level of the congressional district or lower
- No "unit rule" that would require all delegates to vote with the majority of their state delegation
- Restrictions on the number of party leaders and elected officials who could vote at the convention
- A requirement that all delegates pledged to a candidate vote for that candidate

In 1981, the Hunt Commission changed some of these rules—in particular, the last two—in order to increase the influence of elected officials and to make the convention a somewhat more deliberative body. The commission reserved about 14 percent of the delegate seats for party leaders and elected officials (the "**superdelegates**"), who would not have to commit themselves in advance to a presidential candidate, and it repealed the rule requiring that delegates pledged to a candidate vote for that candidate.

superdelegates Party leaders and elected officials who become delegates to the national convention without having to run in primaries or caucuses.

But the "reform" of the parties, especially the Democratic Party, has had far more profound consequences than merely helping one candidate or another. Before 1968, the Republican Party represented,

Table 9.1 Who Are the Party Delegates?

Characteristics of delegates to Democratic and Republican national conventions in 2008		
	Democrats	Republicans
Sex and Race		
Women	49%	32%
Blacks	23	2
Religion		
Protestant	<50	57
Catholic	25	30
Jewish	9	3
Education		
College degree and beyond	80	80
Postgraduate	41	35
Family Income		
Under $500,000	45	32
$500,000 and over	43	51
Belong to Union	25	5
Born-Again Christian	14	34
Gun Owner in Household	33	60

Source: 2008 CBS News/New York Times delegate polls.

essentially, white-collar voters and the Democratic Party represented blue-collar ones. After a decade of "reform," the Republican and the Democratic parties each represented two ideologically different sets of upper-middle-class voters (see Table 9.1). In the terminology of Chapter 7, the Republicans came to represent the more conservative wing of the traditional middle class and the Democrats the more leftist wing of the liberal middle class.

This was more troubling to the Democrats than the Republicans, because the traditional middle class is somewhat closer to the opinions of most citizens than the liberal middle class (and thus the Republican national convention more closely reflected public opinion than the Democratic national convention). And for whatever reason, the Republicans won five out of six presidential races between 1968 and 1988.

The DNC changed the rules for the 1992 campaign. Former DNC chair Ronald H. Brown (later President Clinton's secretary of commerce) won approval for three important requirements:

- The winner-reward systems of delegate distribution, which gave the winner of a primary or caucus extra delegates, were banned. (In 1988, fifteen states used winner-reward systems, including such vote-rich states as Florida, Illinois, New Jersey, and Pennsylvania.)
- The proportional representation system was put into use. This system divides a state's publicly elected delegates among candidates who receive at least 15 percent of the vote.
- States that violate the rules are now penalized with the loss of 25 percent of their national convention delegates.

Even though the Democrats have retreated a bit from the reforms of the 1960s and 1970s, the conventions of both parties have changed fundamentally, and probably permanently. Delegates once selected by party leaders are now chosen by primary elections and grassroots caucuses. As a result, the national party conventions are no longer places where party leaders meet to bargain over the selection of their presidential candidates; they are instead places where delegates come together to ratify choices already made by party activists and primary voters.

Most Americans dislike bosses, deals, and manipulation and prefer democracy, reform, and openness. These are commendable instincts. But such instincts, unless carefully tested against practice, may mislead us into supposing that anything carried out in the name of reform is a good idea. Rules must be judged by their practical results as well as by their conformity to some principle of fairness. Rules affect the distribution of power: they help some people win and others lose. Later in this chapter, we shall try to assess delegate selection rules by looking more closely at how they affect who attends conventions and which presidential candidates are selected there.

State and Local Parties

While the national party structures have changed, the grassroots organizations have withered. In between, state party systems have struggled to redefine their roles.

In every state, a Democratic and a Republican state party is organized under state law. Each typically consists of a state central committee, below which are county committees and sometimes city, town, or even precinct committees. The members of these committees are chosen in a variety of ways—sometimes in primary elections, sometimes by conventions, sometimes by a building-block process whereby people elected to serve on precinct or town committees choose the members of county committees, who in turn choose state committee members.

Knowing these formal arrangements is much less helpful than knowing the actual distribution of power in each state party. In a few places strong party bosses handpick the members of these committees; in other places, powerful elected officials—key state legislators, county sheriffs, or judges—control the committees. And in many places no one is in charge, so that either the party structure is largely meaningless or it is made up of the representatives of various local factions.

To understand how power is distributed in a party, we must first know what *incentives* motivate people in a particular state or locality to become active in a party organization. Different incentives lead to different ways of organizing parties.

THE MACHINE

A **political machine** is a party organization that recruits its members by the use of tangible incentives—money, political jobs, an opportunity to get favors from government—and is characterized by a high degree of leadership control over member activity. At one time, many local party organizations were machines, and the struggle over political jobs—patronage—was the chief concern of their members. Though Tammany Hall in New York City began as a caucus of well-to-do notables in the local Democratic party, by the late 19th century, it had become a machine organized on the basis of political clubs in each assembly district. These clubs were composed of party workers whose job it was to get out the straight party vote in their election districts and who hoped for a tangible reward if they were successful.

political machine A party organization that recruits members by dispensing patronage.

By permission of the Houghton Library/Harvard University

Ex-Senator George Washington Plunkitt of Tammany Hall explains machine politics from atop the bootblack stand in front of the New York County Courthouse around 1905.

And there were abundant rewards to hope for. During the 1870s, it was estimated that one out of every eight voters in New York City had a federal, state, or city job.[8] The federal bureaucracy was one important source of those jobs. The New York Customhouse alone employed thousands of people, virtually all of whom were replaced if their party lost the presidential election. The postal system was another source, and it was frankly recognized as such. When James N. Tyner became postmaster general in 1876, he was "appointed not to see that the mails were carried, but to see that Indiana was carried."[9] Elections and conventions were so frequent and the intensity of party competition so great that being a party worker was for many a full-time paid occupation.

Well before the arrival of vast numbers of poor immigrants from Ireland, Italy, and elsewhere, old-stock Americans had perfected the machine, run up the cost of government, and systematized voting fraud. Kickbacks on contracts, payments extracted from officeholders, and funds raised from businesspeople made some politicians rich but also paid the huge bills of the elaborate party organization. When the immigrants began flooding the eastern cities, the party machines were there to provide them with all manner of services in exchange for their support at the polls: the machines were a vast welfare organization operating before the creation of the welfare state.

The abuses of the machine were well known and gradually curtailed. Stricter voter registration laws reduced fraud, civil service reforms cut down the number of patronage jobs, and competitive bidding laws made it harder to award overpriced contracts to favored businesses. The Hatch Act (passed by Congress in 1939) made it illegal for federal civil service employees to take an active part in political management or political campaigns by serving as party officers, soliciting campaign funds, running for partisan office, working in a partisan campaign, endorsing partisan candidates, taking voters to the polls, counting ballots, circulating nominating petitions, or being delegates to a party convention. (They may still vote and make campaign contributions.)

These restrictions gradually took federal employees out of machine politics, but they did not end the machines. In many cities—Chicago, Philadelphia, and Albany—ways were found to maintain the machines even though city employees were technically under the civil service. Far more important than the various progressive reforms that weakened the machines were changes among voters. As voters grew in education, income, and sophistication, they depended less and less on the advice and leadership of local party officials. And as the federal government created a bureaucratic welfare system, the parties' welfare systems declined in value.

It is easy either to scorn the political party machine as a venal and self-serving organization or to romanticize it as an informal welfare system. In truth, it was a little of both. Above all, it was a frank recognition of the fact that politics requires organization; the machine was the supreme expression of the value of organization. Even allowing for voting fraud, in elections where party machines were active, voter turnout was huge: more people participated in politics when mobilized by a party machine than when appealed to via television or good-government associations.[10] Moreover, because the party machines were interested in winning, they would subordinate any other consideration to that end. This has meant that the machines usually were willing to support the presidential candidate with the best chance of winning, regardless of his policy views (provided, of course, that he was not determined to wreck the machines once in office). Republican machines helped elect Abraham Lincoln as well as Warren G. Harding; Democratic machines were of crucial importance in electing Franklin D. Roosevelt and John F. Kennedy.

The old-style machine is almost extinct, though important examples still can be found in the Democratic organization in Cook County (Chicago) and the Republican organization in Nassau County (New York). But a new-style machine has emerged in a few places. It is a machine in the sense that it uses money to knit together many politicians, but it is new in that the money comes not from patronage and contracts but from campaign contributions supplied by wealthy individuals and the proceeds of direct-mail campaigns.

IDEOLOGICAL PARTIES

At the opposite extreme from the machine is the **ideological party.** Where the machine values winning above all else, the ideological party values principle above all else. Where the former depends on money incentives, the latter spurns them. Where the former is hierarchical and disciplined, the latter usually is contentious and factionalized.

ideological party A party that values principled stands on issues above all else.

The most firmly ideological parties have been independent "third parties," such as the Socialist, Socialist Workers, Libertarian, and Right-to-Life parties. But there have been ideological factions within the Democratic and Republican parties as well, and in some places these ideological groups have taken over the regular parties.

In the 1950s and 1960s, these ideological groups were "reform clubs" within local Democratic and Republican parties. In Los Angeles, New York, and many parts of Wisconsin and Minnesota, issue-oriented activists fought to take over the party from election-oriented regulars. Democratic reform clubs managed to defeat the head of Tammany Hall in Manhattan; similar activist groups became the dominant force in California state politics.[11] Democratic club leaders were more liberal than rank-and-file Democrats, and Republican club leaders were often more conservative than rank-and-file Republicans.

The 1960s and 1970s saw these "reform" movements replaced by more focused social movements. The reform movement was based on a generalized sense of liberalism (among Democrats) or conservatism (among Republicans). With the advent of social movements concerned with civil rights, peace, feminism, environmentalism, libertarianism, and abortion, the generalized ideology of the clubs was replaced by the specific ideological demands of single-issue activists.

The result is that in many places, the party has become a collection of people drawn from various social movements. For a candidate to win the party's support, he or she often has to satisfy the "litmus test" demands of the ideological activists in the party. Democratic senator Barbara Mikulski put it this way: "The social movements are now our farm clubs."

With social movements as their farm clubs, the big-league teams—the Democrats and Republicans at the state level—behave very differently than they did when political machines were the farm clubs. Internal factionalism is more intense, and the freedom of action of the party leader (say, the chair of the state committee) has been greatly reduced. A leader who demands too little or gives up too much, or who says the wrong thing on a key issue, is quickly accused of having "sold out." Under these circumstances, many are "leaders" in name only.

SOLIDARY GROUPS

Many people who participate in state and local politics do so not in order to earn money or vindicate some cause, but simply because they find it fun. They enjoy the game, they meet interesting people, and they like the sense of being "in the know" and rubbing shoulders with the powerful. When people get together

solidary incentives The social rewards (sense of pleasure, status, or companionship) that lead people to join political organizations.

out of gregarious or game-loving instincts, they are responding to **solidary incentives;** if they form an organization, it is a solidary association.

Some of these associations were once machines. When a machine loses its patronage, some of its members—especially the older ones—may continue to serve in the organization out of a desire for camaraderie. In other cases precinct, ward, and district committees are built up on the basis of friendship networks. One study of political activists in Detroit found that most of them mentioned friendships and a liking for politics—rather than an interest in issues—as their reasons for joining the party organization.[12] Members of ward and town organizations in St. Louis County gave the same answers when asked why they joined.[13] Since patronage has declined in value and since the appeals of ideology are limited to a minority of citizens, the motivations for participating in politics have become very much like those for joining a bowling league or a bridge club.

The advantage of such groups is that they are neither corrupt nor inflexible; the disadvantage is that they often do not work very hard. Knocking on doors on a rainy November evening to try to talk people into voting for your candidate is a chore under the best of circumstances; it is especially unappealing if you joined the party primarily because you like to attend meetings or drink coffee with your friends.[14]

SPONSORED PARTIES

Sometimes a relatively strong party organization can be created among volunteers without heavy reliance on money or ideology and without depending entirely on people's finding the work fun. This type of **sponsored party** occurs when another organization exists in the community that can create, or at least sponsor, a local party structure. The clearest example of this is the Democratic Party in and around Detroit, which has been developed, led, and to a degree financed by the political-action arm of the United Auto Workers union. The UAW has had a long tradition of rank-and-file activism, stemming from its formative struggles in the 1930s, and since the city virtually is a one-industry town, it was not hard to transfer some of this activism from union organizing to voter organizing.

By the mid-1950s, union members and leaders made up over three-fourths of all the Democratic Party district leaders within the city.[15] On election day, union funds were available for paying workers to canvass voters; between elections, political work on an unpaid basis was expected of union leaders. Though the UAW–Democratic Party alliance in Detroit has not always been successful in city elections (the city is nonpartisan), it has been quite successful in carrying the city for the Democratic Party in state and national elections. Not many areas have organizations as effective or as dominant as the UAW that can bolster, sponsor, or even take over the weak formal party structure. Thus sponsored local parties are not common in the United States.

sponsored party A local or state political party largely supported by another organization in the community.

personal following The political support provided to a candidate on the basis of personal popularity and networks.

PERSONAL FOLLOWING

Because most candidates can no longer count on the backing of a machine, because sponsored parties are limited to a few unionized areas, and because solidary groups are not always productive, a person wanting to get elected often will try to form a **personal following** that will work for him or her during a campaign and then disband until the next election rolls around. Sometimes a candidate tries to meld a personal following with an ideological group, especially during the primary election campaign, when candidates need the kind of financial backing and hard work that only highly motivated activists are likely to supply.

To form a personal following, the candidate must have an appealing personality, a lot of friends, or a big bank account. The Kennedy family has all three, and the electoral success of the personal followings of John F. Kennedy, Edward M. Kennedy, Robert Kennedy, and Joseph P. Kennedy II are legendary. President George H. W. Bush also established such a following. After he left office, one son (Jeb) became governor of Florida and another one (George W.) became governor of Texas and the 43rd president of the United States.

Southern politicians who operate in one-party states with few, if any, machines have become grand masters at building personal followings, such as those of the Talmadge family in Georgia, the Long family in Louisiana, and the Byrd family in Virginia. But this strategy is increasingly followed wherever party organization is weak. The key asset is to have a known political name. This has helped the electoral victories of the son of Hubert Humphrey in Minnesota, the son and daughter of Pat Brown in California, the son of Birch Bayh in Indiana, the

The personal following of former President George H. W. Bush was passed on to his sons, George W. (left) and Jeb (right), both of whom became governors of large states, and the former of whom became president.

son of George Wallace in Alabama, and the son and grandson of Robert La Follette in Wisconsin.

By the mid-1980s, the traditional party organization—one that is hierarchical, lasting, based on material incentives, and capable of influencing who gets nominated for office—existed, according to political scientist David Mayhew, in only about eight states, mostly the older states of the Northeast. Another five states, he found, had faction-ridden versions of the traditional party organization.[16] The states in the rest of the country displayed the weak party system of solidary clubs, personal followings, ideological groups, and sponsored parties. What that meant could be seen in the composition of Democratic national conventions. In 1984, over half of the delegates were drawn from the ranks of the AFL-CIO, the National Education Association, and the National Organization for Women.[17] By 2004, both national party organizations and their respective conventions had been dominated for at least two decades by ideological groups and the like.

two-party system An electoral system with two dominant parties that compete in national elections.

plurality system An electoral system in which the winner is the person who gets the most votes, even if he or she does not receive a majority; used in almost all American elections.

The Two-Party System

With so many different varieties of local party organizations (or nonorganizations), and with such a great range of opinion found within each party, it is remarkable that we have had only two major political parties for most of our history. In the world at large a **two-party system** is a rarity; by one estimate only 15 nations have one.[18] Most European democracies are multiparty systems. We have only two parties with any chance of winning nationally, and these parties have been, over time, rather evenly balanced—between 1888 and 2004, the Republicans won 17 presidential elections and the Democrats 13. Furthermore, whenever one party has achieved a temporary ascendancy and its rival has been pronounced dead (as were the Democrats in the first third of the 20th century and the Republicans during the 1930s and the 1960s), the "dead" party has displayed remarkable powers of recuperation, coming back to win important victories.

At the state and congressional district levels, however, the parties are not evenly balanced. For a long time, the South was so heavily Democratic at all levels of government as to be a one-party area, while upper New England and the Dakotas were strongly Republican. All regions are more competitive today than once was the case. Parties are not as competitive in state elections as they are in presidential ones. States have rarely had, at least for any extended period, political parties other than the Democratic and Republican.

Scholars do not entirely agree on why the two-party system should be so permanent a feature of American political life, but two explanations are of major importance. The first has to do with the system of elections, the second with the distribution of public opinion.

Elections at every level of government are based on the plurality, winner-take-all method. The **plurality system** means that in all elections for representative, senator, governor, or president, and in almost all elections for state legislator, mayor, or city councilor, the winner gets the *most* votes, even if he or she does not get a *majority* of all votes cast. We are so familiar with this system that we sometimes forget there are other ways of running an election. For example, one could require that the winner get a majority of the votes, thus producing runoff elections if nobody got a majority on the first try. France does this in choosing its national legislature. In the first election, candidates for parliament who win an absolute majority of the votes cast are declared elected. A week later, remaining candidates who received at least one-eighth, but less than one-half of the vote, go into a runoff election; those who then win an absolute majority are also declared elected.

The French method encourages many political parties to form, each hoping to win at least one-eighth of the vote in the first election and then to enter into an alliance with its ideologically nearest rival in order to win the runoff. In the United States, the plurality system means that a party must make all the alliances it can before the first election—there is no second chance. Hence, every party must be as broadly based as possible; a narrow, minor party has no hope of winning.

The winner-take-all feature of American elections has the same effect. Only one member of Congress is elected from each district. In many European countries, the elections are based on proportional representation. Each party submits a list of candidates for parliament, ranked in order of preference by the party leaders. The nation votes. A party winning 37 percent of the vote gets 37 percent of the seats in parliament; a party winning 2 percent of the vote gets 2 percent of the seats. Since even the smallest parties have a chance of winning something, minor parties have an incentive to organize.

The most dramatic example of the winner-take-all principle is the electoral college (see Chapter 14). In every state but Maine and Nebraska, the candidate who wins the most popular votes in a state wins *all* of that state's electoral votes. In 1992, for example, Bill Clinton won only 45 percent of the popular vote in Missouri, but he got all of Missouri's 11 electoral votes because his two rivals (George H. W. Bush and Ross Perot) each got fewer popular votes. Minor parties cannot compete under this system. Voters often are reluctant to "waste" their votes on a minor-party candidate who cannot win.

The United States has experimented with other electoral systems. Proportional representation was used for municipal elections in New York City at one time and still is in use in Cambridge, Massachusetts. Many states have elected more than one state legislator from each district. In Illinois, for example, three legislators have been elected from each district, with each voter allowed to cast two votes, thus virtually guaranteeing that the minority party will be able to win one of the three seats. But none of these experiments has altered the national two-party system, probably because of the existence of a directly elected president chosen by a winner-take-all electoral college.

The presidency is the great prize of American politics; to win it, you must form a party with as broad appeal as possible. As a practical matter, this means there will be, in most cases, only two serious parties—one made up of those who support the party already in power, and the other made up of everybody else. Only one third party ever won the presidency—the Republicans in 1860—and it had by then pretty much supplanted the Whig party. No third party is likely to win, or even come close to winning, the presidency anytime soon. Despite the decline in mass party attachment, among Americans who actually vote in presidential elections, party voting is almost as strong today as it was in the early 1950s. As Table 9.2 shows, in the presidential elections of 1992 through 2008, the vast majority of Democrats voted for the Democrat, and the vast majority of Republicans voted for the Republican. Meanwhile, most independents voted for the winning Republican in 1988 and 2000, and pluralities of independents voted for the winning Democrat in 1992 and 1996 and again in 2008.

The second explanation for the persistence of the two-party system is found in the opinions of the voters. National surveys have found that most Americans see "a difference in what Democratic and Republican parties stand for."[19] For the most part, the majority has deemed Democrats better at handling such issues as poverty, the environment, and health care and the Republicans better at handling such issues as national defense, foreign trade, and crime; but voters generally have split on which party is best at handling the economy and taxes.[20] And when it comes to which party is best able to handle whatever individuals see as the "most important problem" facing the nation, normally about 15 percent to a quarter each choose either Democrats or Republicans, while about 45 to 55 percent answer "not much difference."[21]

Table 9.2 Party Voting in Presidential Elections

Party Affiliation of Voter	1992			1996			2000			2004			2008		
	Dem.	Rep.	Ind.	Dem.	Rep.	Ind.	Dem.	Rep.	Ind.	Dem.	Rep.	Ind.	Dem.	Rep.	Ind.
Democrat	82%	8%	10%	84%	10%	5%	85%	10%	3%	89%	11%	0%	89%	10%	0%
Republican	7	77	16	13	80	6	7	91	1	6	93	0	9	89	0
Independent	39	30	31	43	35	17	37	42	9	49	48	1	52	44	0

Source: Data from CNN exit polls for each year.

As we learned in Chapter 7, however, public opinion often is dynamic, not static. Mass perceptions concerning the parties are no exception. For instance, by 2004, a few years after President George W. Bush passed his No Child Left Behind education plan, Republicans cut into the Democrats' traditional slight edge in public school support concerning which party does better on public schools. After 2004, as the war in Iraq became unpopular, Republicans lost ground to Democrats on national defense. And on certain complicated or controversial issues, such as immigration policy, opinions can shift overnight in response to real or perceived changes in policy by those the public views as each party's respective leaders or spokespersons.

Though there have been periods of bitter dissent, most of the time most citizens have agreed enough to permit them to come together into two broad coalitions. There has not been a massive and persistent body of opinion that has rejected the prevailing economic system (and thus we have not had a Marxist party with mass appeal); there has not been in our history an aristocracy or monarchy (and thus there has been no party that has sought to restore aristocrats or monarchs to power). Churches and religion have almost always been regarded as matters of private choice that lie outside politics (and thus there has not been a party seeking to create or abolish special government privileges for one church or another). In some European nations, the organization of the economy, the prerogatives of the monarchy, and the role of the church have been major issues with long and bloody histories. So divisive have these issues been that they have helped prevent the formation of broad coalition parties.

But Americans have had other deep divisions—between white and black, for example, and between North and South—and yet the two-party system has endured. This suggests that our electoral procedures are of great importance—the winner-take-all, plurality election rules have made it useless for anyone to attempt to create an all-white or an all-black national party except as an act of momentary defiance or in the hope of taking enough votes away from the two major parties to force the presidential election into the House of Representatives. (That may have been George Wallace's strategy in 1968.)

For many years, there was an additional reason for the two-party system: the laws of many states made it difficult, if not impossible, for third parties to get on the ballot. In 1968, for example, the American Independent party of George Wallace found that it would have to collect 433,000 signatures (15 percent of the votes cast in the last statewide election) in order to get on the presidential ballot in Ohio. Wallace took the issue to the Supreme Court, which ruled, 6 to 3, that such a restriction was an unconstitutional violation of the equal protection clause of the Fourteenth Amendment.[22] Wallace got on the ballot. In 1980, John Anderson, running as an independent, was able to get on the ballot in all 50 states; in 1992, Ross Perot did the same. But for the reasons already indicated, the two-party system will probably persist even without the aid of legal restrictions.

Minor Parties

The electoral system may prevent minor parties from winning, but it does not prevent them from forming. Minor parties—usually called, erroneously, "third parties"—have been a permanent feature of American political life. Four major kinds of minor parties, with examples of each, are described in the box on page 223.

The minor parties that have endured are the ideological ones. Their members feel outside the mainstream of American political life and sometimes, as in the case of various Marxist parties, look forward to a time when a revolution or some other dramatic change in the political system will vindicate them. They usually are not interested in immediate electoral success and thus persist despite their poor showing at the polls. One such party, however, the Socialist party of Eugene Debs, won nearly 6 percent of the popular vote in the 1912 presidential election. During its heyday, 1,200 candidates were elected to local offices, including 79 mayors. Part of the Socialist appeal arose from its opposition to municipal corruption, its opposition to American entry into World War I, and its critique of American society. No ideological party has ever carried a state in a presidential election.

Apart from the Republicans, who quickly became a major party, the only minor parties to carry states and thus win electoral votes were one party of economic protest (the Populists, who carried five states in 1892) and several factional parties (most recently, the States' Rights Democrats in 1948 and the American Independent party of George Wallace in 1968). Though factional parties may hope to cause the defeat of the party from which they split, they have not always been able to achieve this. Harry Truman was elected in 1948 despite the defections of both the leftist progressives, led by Henry Wallace, and the right-wing Dixiecrats, led by J. Strom Thurmond. In 1968, it seems likely that Hubert Humphrey would have

How Things Work

Types of Minor Parties

1. **Ideological parties:** Parties professing a comprehensive view of American society and government radically different from the established parties. Most have been Marxist in outlook, but some are quite the opposite, such as the Libertarian party.

Examples:

Socialist party (1901 to 1960s)

Socialist Labor party (1888 to present)

Socialist Workers party (1938 to present)

Communist party (1920s to present)

Libertarian party (1972 to present)

Green party (1984 to present)

2. **One-issue parties:** Parties seeking a single policy, usually revealed by their names, and avoiding other issues.

Examples:

Free-Soil party—to prevent the spread of slavery (1848–1852)

American or "Know-Nothing" party—to oppose immigration and Catholics (1856)

Prohibition party—to ban the sale of liquor (1869 to present)

Woman's party—to obtain the right to vote for women (1913–1920)

3. **Economic-protest parties:** Parties, usually based in a particular region, especially involving farmers, that protest against depressed economic conditions. These tend to disappear as conditions improve.

Examples:

Greenback party (1876–1884)

Populist party (1892–1908)

4. **Factional parties:** Parties created by a split in a major party, usually over the identity and philosophy of the major party's presidential candidate.

Examples:

Split off from the Republican party:

"Bull Moose" Progressive party (1912)

La Follette Progressive party (1924)

Split off from the Democratic party:

States' Rights ("Dixiecrat") party (1948)

Henry Wallace Progressive party (1948)

American Independent (George Wallace) party (1968)

Split off from both Democrats and Republicans:

Reform party (Ross Perot)

Tea Party movement

lost even if George Wallace had not been in the race (Wallace voters would probably have switched to Nixon rather than to Humphrey, though of course one cannot be certain). It is quite possible, on the other hand, that a Republican might have beaten Woodrow Wilson in 1912 if the Republican party had not split in two (the regulars supporting William Howard Taft, the progressives supporting Theodore Roosevelt).

What is striking is not that we have had so many minor parties but that we have not had more. There have been several major political movements that did not produce a significant third party: the civil rights movement of the 1960s, the antiwar movement of the same decade, and, most important, the labor movement of the 20th century. African Americans were part of the Republican party after the Civil War and part of the Democratic party after the New Deal (even though the southern wing of that party for a long time kept them from voting). The antiwar movement found candidates with whom it could identify within the Democratic party (Eugene McCarthy, Robert F. Kennedy, George McGovern), even though it was a Democratic president, Lyndon B. Johnson, who was chiefly responsible for the U.S. commitment in Vietnam. After Johnson only narrowly won the

1968 New Hampshire primary, he withdrew from the race. Unions have not tried to create a labor party—indeed, they were for a long time opposed to almost any kind of national political activity. Since labor became a major political force in the 1930s, the largest industrial unions have been content to operate as a part (a very large part) of the Democratic Party.

One reason some potential sources of minor parties never formed such parties, in addition to the dim chance of success, is that the direct primary and the national convention made it possible for dissident elements of a major party—unless they become completely disaffected—to remain in the party and influence the choice of candidates and policies. The antiwar movement had a profound effect on the Democratic conventions of 1968 and 1972; African Americans have played a growing role in the Democratic Party, especially with the candidacy of Jesse Jackson in 1984 and 1988; only in 1972 did the unions feel that the Democrats nominated a presidential candidate (McGovern) unacceptable to them.

The impact of minor parties on American politics is hard to judge. One bit of conventional wisdom holds that minor parties develop ideas that the major parties later come to adopt. The Socialist party, for example, supposedly called for major social and economic policies that the Democrats under Roosevelt later embraced and termed the New Deal. It is possible the Democrats did steal the thunder of the Socialists, but it hardly seems likely that they did it because the Socialists had proposed these things or proved them popular. (In 1932, the Socialists received only 2 percent of the vote and in 1936 less than one-half of 1 percent.) Roosevelt probably adopted the policies in part because he thought them correct and in part because dissident elements within his *own* party—leaders such as Huey Long of Louisiana—were threatening to bolt the Democratic party if it did not move to the left. Even Prohibition was adopted more as a result of the efforts of interest groups such as the Anti-Saloon League than as the consequence of its endorsement by the Prohibition party.

The minor parties that have probably had the greatest influence on public policy have been the factional parties. Mugwumps and liberal Republicans, by bolting the regular party, may have made that party more sensitive to the issue of civil service reform; the Bull Moose and La Follette Progressive parties probably helped encourage the major parties to pay more attention to issues of business regulation and party reform; the Dixiecrat and Wallace movements probably strengthened the hands of those who wished to

Library of Congress/LC-DIG-pga-00130

© Bettman/Corbis

The Socialist party and the Progressive party were both minor parties, but their origins were different. The Socialist party was an ideological party; the "Bull Moose" Progressive party split off from the Republicans to support Theodore Roosevelt.

go slow on desegregation. The threat of a factional split is a risk that both major parties must face, and it is in the efforts that each makes to avoid such splits that one finds the greatest impact of minor parties, or at least that was the case in the 20th century.

In 1992 and again in 1996, Ross Perot led the most successful recent third-party movement. It began as United We Stand America and was later renamed the Reform party. Perot's appeal seemed to reflect a growing American dissatisfaction with the existing political parties and a heightened demand for bringing in a leader who would "run the government without politics." In 2000 and again in 2004, Ralph Nader led the Green party and rallied supporters by promising to remain above partisan politics and avoid making compromises if elected. Of course, it is no more possible to take politics out of governing than it is to take churches out of religion. Though unrealistic, some people seem to want policies without bargaining.

The Tea Party movement that has evolved in recent years is not a single national party, but it shares characteristics with minor parties: Tea Party supporters were active in the 2010 congressional midterm elections, and they seek to influence the national policy agenda. Although there are many groups within the movement with differing views, Tea Party activists seem to agree on the need to reduce taxes, government spending, budget deficits, and the national debt. They appear to have some influence within the Republican Party, where they have overturned a few establishment candidates for office whom they viewed as insufficiently dedicated to fiscal discipline. Whether the movement will turn into a cohesive minor party that shapes the major-party agenda remains to be seen.

Nominating a President

The major parties face, as we have seen, two contrary forces: one, generated by the desire to win the presidency, pushes them in the direction of nominating a candidate who can appeal to the majority of voters and who will thus have essentially middle-of-the-road views. The other, produced by the need to keep dissident elements in the party from bolting and forming a third party, leads them to compromise with dissidents or extremists in ways that may damage the party's standing with the voters.

The Democrats and Republicans have always faced these conflicting pressures, but of late they have become especially acute. When the presidential nomination was made by a party convention heavily influenced, if not controlled, by party leaders and elected officials, it was relatively easy to ignore dissident factions and pick candidates on the basis of who could win. The *electoral* objectives of the party were predominant. Often the result was that a faction left the party and ran a separate ticket—as in 1912, 1924, 1948, 1968, and 1980. Today the power of party leaders and elected officials within the parties is greatly diminished, with most delegates now selected by primary elections. A larger proportion of the delegates is likely to be more interested in issues and less amenable to compromise over those issues than formerly. In these circumstances, the *policy* interests of the party activists are likely important.

ARE THE DELEGATES REPRESENTATIVE OF THE VOTERS?

There would be no conflict between the electoral and policy interests of a political party if the delegates to its nominating convention had the same policy views as most voters, or at least as most party supporters. In fact, this is not the case: in parties, as in many organizations, the activists and leaders tend to have views different from those of the rank and file.[23] In American political parties in recent years, this difference has become very great.

In 1964, the Republican Party nominated the highly conservative Barry Goldwater for president. We have no opinion data for delegates to that convention as detailed and comprehensive as those available for subsequent conventions, but it seems clear that the Republican delegates selected as their nominee a person who was not the most popular candidate among voters at large and thus not the candidate most likely to win.

At every Democratic national convention since 1972, the delegates have had views on a variety of important issues vastly different from those of rank-and-file Democrats. On welfare, military policy, school desegregation, crime, and abortion, Democratic delegates expressed opinions almost diametrically opposed to those of most Democrats. The delegates to the 1980, 1984, and (to a lesser extent) 1988, 1992, 1996, 2000, and 2004 conventions were ideologically very different from the voters at large. The Democratic delegates were more liberal than the Democratic voters, and the Republican delegates were more conservative than the Republican voters.[24]

What accounts for the sharp disparity between delegate opinion (and often delegate candidate preference) and voter attitudes? Some blame the discrepancy on the rules, described earlier in this chapter, under which Democratic delegates are chosen, especially those that require increased representation for women, minorities, and the young. Close examination suggests this is not a complete explanation. For one thing, it does not explain

caucus A meeting of party members to select delegates backing one or another primary candidate.

why the Republicans nominated Goldwater in 1964 (and almost nominated Ronald Reagan instead of Gerald Ford in 1976). In addition, women, minorities, and youth have among them all shades of opinions: there are many middle-of-the-road women and young people, as well as very liberal or very conservative ones. (There are not many very conservative African Americans, at least on race issues, but there are certainly plenty who are moderate on race and conservative on other issues.) The question is why only *certain* elements of these groups are heavily represented at the conventions.

WHO VOTES IN PRIMARIES?

Maybe delegates are unrepresentative of the party rank and file because they are chosen in caucuses and primary elections whose participants are unrepresentative. Before 1972, most delegates were picked by party leaders; primaries were relatively unimportant, and voter caucuses were almost unheard of. Adlai Stevenson in 1952 and Hubert Humphrey in 1968 won the Democratic presidential nominations without even entering a primary. Harry Truman once described primaries as "eyewash."[25] After 1972, the vast majority of delegates were selected in primaries and caucuses. In 1992, forty states and territories held primaries, and twenty held caucuses (some places had primaries and caucuses).

Only about half as many people vote in primaries as in general elections. If these primary voters have more extreme political views than rank-and-file party followers, then they might support presidential delegates who also have extreme views. However, little evidence suggests that such is the case. Studies comparing the ideological orientations of primary voters with those of rank-and-file party voters show few strong differences.[26]

When it comes to presidential primaries, a good fight draws a crowd. For example, in 12 of the first 18 Republican presidential primaries in 2000, voter turnout hit record highs as Governor George W. Bush battled state by state to stay ahead of Senator John McCain. But the "crowd" represented only 13.6 percent of the voting-age population, up 4.3 percent from the 1996 turnout, and the highest since Senator Barry Goldwater's campaign for the nomination divided Republicans in 1964.[27] In the states that voted after Bush had the nomination all but won, turnout was considerably lower. Likewise, the contest between Vice President Al Gore and Senator Bill Bradley resulted in the second-lowest Democratic presidential primary turnout since 1960.

Primaries differ from caucuses. A **caucus** is a meeting of party followers, often lasting for hours and held in the dead of winter in a schoolhouse sometimes miles from home, in which party delegates are picked. Only the most dedicated partisans attend. For the Democrats, these have been liberals; for the Republicans, conservatives. In 1988, the most liberal Democratic candidate, Jesse Jackson, got more delegates in the Alaska, Delaware, Michigan, and Vermont caucuses than Michael Dukakis, the eventual nominee. Republican evangelist Pat Robertson did not win any primary, but he won the caucuses in Alaska, Hawaii, and Washington. Barack Obama gained momentum in his presidential campaign with his upset victory in the 2008 Iowa caucuses; Hillary Rodham Clinton had been expected to secure the Democratic nomination early in the campaign, but after she narrowly came in third in Iowa, the race for the nomination became hotly competitive and was not resolved definitively until she conceded to Obama in June.

WHO ARE THE NEW DELEGATES?

However delegates are chosen, they are a different breed today than they once were. Whether picked by caucuses or primaries, and whatever their sex and race, a far larger proportion of convention delegates, both Republican and Democratic, are issue-oriented activists—people with an "amateur" or "purist" view of politics. Far fewer delegates are in it for the money (there is no longer much patronage to pass around) or to help their own reelection prospects. For example, in 1980 only 14 percent of the Democratic senators and 15 percent of the Democratic members of the House were delegates to the national convention. In 1956, by contrast, 90 percent of the senators and 33 percent of the representatives were delegates.[28] Party activists, especially those who work without pay and who are in politics out of an interest in issues, are not likely to resemble the average citizen for whom politics is merely an object of observation, discussion, and occasional voting.

The changing incentives for participation in party work, in addition to the effects of the primary system, have contributed to the development of a national presidential nominating system different from that which once existed. The advantage of the new system is that it increases the opportunity for those with strong policy preferences to play a role in the party and thus reduces the chance that they will bolt the party and form a factional minor party. The disadvantage of the system is that it increases the chances that one or both parties may nominate presidential candidates who are not appealing to the average voter or even to a party's rank and file.

RESEARCH FRONTIERS

Will a New Political Party Develop in the United States?

Since the Founding era, there have been five lasting shifts in the popular coalition supporting one or both major parties. The third of these so-called realigning periods occurred in 1850s when the Whig party collapsed.

In the 1830s, the Whigs were born in opposition to President Andrew Jackson and the day's Democratic party. Two Whigs (William Henry Harrison and Zachary Taylor) won the presidency. Lincoln himself had been a Whig leader in Illinois. But in 1852, many Whigs like Lincoln who opposed the expansion of slavery defected to the new Republican party.

In 2009, Republican Party leaders were publicly debating whether "the party of Lincoln" might go the way of the Whigs. In 2006, Republicans had lost control of the U.S. House of Representatives. In 2008, they had lost the White House. But the debates about the Republican Party's condition were also fueled by fresh survey evidence indicating a deep and wide decline in post-2001 Republican affiliation among American voters:

- Between 2001 and 2009, only frequent churchgoers maintained their level of support for the GOP, with conservative voters and senior citizens dropping off only slightly, and with long-anemic levels of support among African Americans unchanged.
- Among every other demographic group in every region of the country (men, women, old, young, rich, middle class, poor, married, unmarried, college graduates, and others), affiliation with the Republican Party fell significantly.
- Whereas in 2001 partisan self-identification was split between the two parties, by mid-2009 the electorate was running 53 percent Democratic versus 39 percent Republican.

The 2010 congressional midterm elections, however, demonstrated the resilience of the Republican Party, as it won a landslide victory in and regained control of the U.S. House of Representatives, and also picked up seats in the U.S. Senate. Whether the election results should be interpreted as a rejection of the Democratic Party's agenda, strong support for the Republican Party platform, or voter frustration with the incumbent party in a time of economic crisis remains to be seen.

Still, the Republican Party's concerns in 2009 appear to have been premature, as it is highly unlikely that the Republicans will follow their Whig forbearers into political party oblivion, at least not anytime soon. First, Republicans remain relatively strong in parts of the country that are experiencing robust population growth. Second, over the next several election cycles, Republicans are likely to recruit and run more candidates who appeal to broad popular coalitions. Third, in the past, realignments have occurred only when a new issue of utmost importance to the voters (like slavery in the 1850s) has cut across existing party divisions.

- Do you think that there is any such issue on the political horizon today?
- Regardless, what is the relative strength of two parties where you reside?
- If you were a political consultant with no partisan loyalties toward either party, what would you advise the Republican Party's leaders to do in order to continue their electoral success in 2012, and what would you advise the Democratic Party's leaders to do to regain their popularity?

Sources: Gallup Organization, "GOP Losses Span Nearly All Demographic Groups," May 2009, reporting data from January–April 2009 nationwide telephone interviews with 7,139 adults aged 18 and older; James L. Sundquist, *Dynamics of the Party System*, 2nd ed. (Brookings Institution Press, 1983); William Nisbet Chambers et al., eds., *The American Party Systems: Stages of Political Development*, 2nd ed. (Oxford University Press, 1975); Jeffrey M. Stonecash, "The 2010 Elections: Party Pursuits, Voter Perceptions, and the Chancy Game of Politics," *The Forum* 8, no. 4 (2010), art. 11.

In sum, presidential nominating conventions are now heavily influenced by ideologically motivated activists. Democratic conventions have heavy representation from organized feminists, unionized schoolteachers, and abortion rights activists; Republican conventions have large numbers of antiabortion activists and Christian conservatives, and small numbers of government libertarians. As a result, the presidential nominating system is now fundamentally different from what it was as late as the mid-1960s.

WHAT WOULD YOU DO?

MEMORANDUM

To: *Elizabeth Ramos, campaign manager*

From: *Isaac Marx, political consultant*

Subject: *Independent voters in the upcoming presidential election*

As you prepare for the upcoming presidential campaign, you need to consider how your candidate can build support among the growing number of independent voters. To do so, she must establish a centrist party platform that will appeal to voters beyond the party faithful.

Arguments for:

1. Independent and third-party voters can garner votes for president or tip an election result. In 1992, Ross Perot won nearly a fifth of the votes. In 2000, Green party candidate Ralph Nader got only 3 percent, but that included 100,000 votes in Florida where Republican Bush was credited with only 600 votes more than Democrat Gore.
2. Third-party voters can make a mark on American politics. Third parties have advocated policies later championed by the two main parties: abolishing slavery (Free-Soil party), women's right to vote (Woman's party), direct election of U.S. senators (Progressive party), and many others. The candidate can break out of the field of contenders by advocating far-reaching policy change that will appeal to independent voters.
3. In a tight presidential race, independent voters will be decisive.

Arguments against:

1. Independent and third-party voters do not direct the national agenda. It is virtually impossible for their candidates to win, thanks to the winner-take-all system of elections. Since the 1850s, more than a hundred third parties have come and gone. Better to be attentive to concerns within the major party than to be distracted by issues that are not central to victory.
2. The two major parties have a long history of taking issues that are important to independent voters and making them more palatable to the larger electorate, which is more effective than appealing directly to independent voters. In the 1930s, for example, the Democrats plucked Social Security from the Socialist party's far-reaching plan. In the 1980s, the Republicans' position on taxes only faintly echoed the Libertarian party's.
3. In a close election, building support among likely and predictable voters is a more effective strategy than reaching out to possible but unpredictable voters.

News »

Who Will Independent Voters Support in the Presidential Race?

A recent public opinion poll finds that independent voters are noncommital about which candidate they will support in the upcoming presidential race. A majority say issues, such as reducing the national debt, are more important than party labels. They have concerns about candidates who offer a stark choice between tax increases or spending cuts, saying a more moderate policy agenda is needed.

Your decision:

Create a centrist platform ________ Keep the platform focused on core party issues ________

Parties versus Voters

Since 1968, the Democratic party has had no trouble winning congressional elections but great difficulty winning presidential contests. Except for 1994–2006, the Democrats have controlled both houses of Congress; except for 1976, 1992, 1996, and 2008, they have lost every presidential election. The Republican Party has had the opposite problem: though it won five out of seven presidential elections between 1968 and 1992, it did not control Congress for the 40 years preceding its big win in 1994.

There are many reasons for this odd state of affairs, most of which will be discussed later. But one requires attention here. The difficulty the Democrats have had in competing for the presidency is in part because their candidates for the presidency have had, on certain issues—chiefly social and taxation issues—views very different from those of the average voter. That disparity to a large degree mirrors (and may be caused by) the gulf that separates the opinions of delegates to Democratic nominating conventions from the opinions of most citizens.

The Republicans have not been immune to this problem. In 1964, they nominated Barry Goldwater, whose beliefs placed him well to the right of most voters. Not surprisingly, he lost. And the delegates to recent Republican conventions have held opinions on some matters that continue to be very different from most people's. Still, the problem has been somewhat more acute for the Democrats.

The problem is illustrated in Table 9.3. A lot of information is shown there; to understand it, study the table step by step. First, look at the middle column, which summarizes the views of voters in 2008. (Because there are about the same number of Democratic and Republican voters, the opinion of the average voter is about halfway between those of the followers of the two parties.) Now look at the columns on the far left and the far right. These show the views of delegates to the 2008 Democratic and Republican conventions. On almost every issue, the delegates are in sharp disagreement. There were hardly any conservatives at the Democratic convention or liberals at the Republican convention. On each and every issue, the delegates were at opposite ends of the spectrum.

Still, either party can win if its delegates nominate a candidate whose views put him or her closer to the average citizen than to the average delegate or if the campaign is fought out over issues on which the delegates and the voters agree. For example, if the election turned on what to do about an economic recession, the delegates, the voters, and the candidate would probably all agree: do whatever is necessary to end the recession. Exactly that happened in 1992, and the Democrats won.

Of course, even without a scandal, recession, or some other unifying issue, the need to win an election will lead all candidates to move toward the middle of the road. That is where the votes are. But this creates a dilemma for a candidate of either party. The stance one takes to win support from party activists in the caucuses and primaries often will be quite different from the stance one should take to win votes from the general public. In the next chapter, we will look more closely at how politicians try to cope with that dilemma.

Table 9.3 Political Opinions of Delegates and Voters, 2008

	Democratic Delegates	Voters	Republican Delegates
Who They Are			
Male	50%	46%	68%
Female	50	54	32
African American	23	12	2
Hispanic	11	8	5
Income over $75,000	70	31	66
Union member	24	9	5
What They Think			
Government should do more to solve national problems.	83	43	3
America should have stayed out of Iraq.	95	59	13
Abortion should be generally available.	70	33	9
Religion is extremely important in daily life.	23	28	37
Gun laws should be more restrictive.	62	52	8
There should be no legal recognition of a gay couple's relationship.	5	39	46

Source: 2008 CBS/*New York Times* polls.

LEARNING OBJECTIVES

WHAT YOU NEED TO KNOW

☑ What is a political party, and why were the Framers of the Constitution concerned about their influence?

A political party is an organization that works to elect candidates to public office and identifies candidates by a clear name or label. The Framers of the Constitution viewed political parties as "factions" that would promote the interests of a few over the public good. By the early 19th century, though, public parties were viewed as an inevitable feature of democratic politics.

☑ Why does the United States have a two-party system?

The United States has a two-party political system because of two structural features in American politics: single-member districts and winner-take-all elections. Both features encourage the existence of two major parties, as smaller parties face great difficulty in winning elective office.

☑ What are the prospects for a viable third party in the United States?

A third political party in the United States may build popular support and influence the two major parties, perhaps even ultimately replacing one of them, but the structural features of the American political system make establishment of a third party in electoral politics highly unlikely.

RECONSIDERING WHO GOVERNS?

1. How has America's two-party system changed, and how does it differ from the party systems of other representative democracies?

American parties during the 19th century and the first half of the 20th century were strong organizations that picked their candidates for office. Parties in European democracies still do that, but America has changed. Now, candidates usually are picked by direct primary elections, as the American voters' loyalty to parties has weakened.

2. How much do parties affect how Americans vote?

Registered Democrats are more likely to vote for Democratic candidates, and registered Republicans are more likely to vote for Republican candidates, but more voters now register as independents, the proportion of people identifying with one or the other party has declined, and split-ticket voting has been common in the American electorate. The declining attachment of voters to parties and their weaknesses as organizations have led many candidates for president and other offices to run more as individuals than as party members.

RECONSIDERING TO WHAT ENDS?

1. Did the Founding Fathers think political parties were a good idea?

No. For example, George Washington denounced parties as "factions." But as soon as it was time to select his replacement, the republic's first leaders realized they had to organize their followers to win the election, and parties were born. It was not, however, until well into the 19th century that the idea of a permanent two-party system was considered legitimate by virtually all of the country's political leaders.

2. How, if at all, should America's two-party system be reformed?

Any answer should depend, at least in part, on how one evaluates the many reforms already made. For instance, some argue that the parties should become more open to popular influences. To a large extent, however, that has already happened. Whereas once presidential candidates were selected by party leaders, today they are selected by primaries. Others maintain that there is little real difference between the two parties. That opinion, however, is at variance with the wide differences on many important issues one finds in party platforms, as well as with the fact that delegates to the Republican and Democratic national conventions differ widely on the issues. Still others contend that the plurality system in which the winner is the candidate with the most votes, even if he or she does not receive a majority, is unfair to minor or third-party candidates. Perhaps, but Bill Clinton was twice (1992 and 1996) a popular plurality president. Besides, America has had little experience with other voting or party systems, and democracies that have proportional voting or multiparty systems have other shortcomings (such as unduly empowering small parties with extreme views).

QUESTIONS TO CONSIDER

1. **How does the two-party system create constraints and opportunities in American politics?**
2. **Which major political party is most likely to face a realignment in the coming years, and why?**
3. **Which variables are most important in understanding the success or failure of minor parties?**
4. **How many voters in the United States identify as Independent rather than Democrat or Republican?**
5. **Which smaller parties in the United States have national support, and from which of the major parties are they drawing voters?**
6. **How do the political parties appeal to existing members while reaching out to new voters in their platforms and information?**

TO LEARN MORE

Democratic National Committee: **www.democrats.org**

Republican National Committee: **www.rnc.org**

Green party: **www.greens.org**

Libertarian party: **www.lp.org**

Reform party: **www.reformparty.org**

Aldrich, John H. *Why Parties?: The Origin and Transformation of Political Parties in America* (Chicago: University of Chicago Press, 1995). Explains why we have parties.

Goldwin, Robert A., ed. *Political Parties in the Eighties.* Washington, D.C.: American Enterprise Institute, 1980. Essays evaluating parties and efforts at reform.

Key, V. O., Jr. *Southern Politics.* New York: Knopf, 1949. A classic account of the one-party South.

Mayhew, David R. *Placing Parties in American Politics.* Princeton, N.J.: Princeton University Press, 1986. A state-by-state description of state party organizations.

Nader, Ralph. *Crashing the Party: Taking on the Corporate Government in an Age of Surrender.* New York: St. Martin's Press, 2002. An impassioned attack on the two-party system by a well-known activist who ran for president as a minor-party candidate in 2000 and 2004.

Polsby, Nelson W. *Consequences of Party Reform.* New York: Oxford University Press, 1983. Fine analysis of how changed party rules have affected the parties and the government.

Ranney, Austin. *Curing the Mischiefs of Faction: Party Reform in America.* Berkeley: University of California Press, 1975. History and analysis of party "reforms," with special attention to the 1972 changes in the Democratic Party rules.

Riordan, William L. *Plunkitt of Tammany Hall.* New York: Knopf, 1948. (First published in 1905.) Insightful account of how an old-style party boss operated.

Schattschneider, E. E. *Party Government.* New York: Holt, Rinehart and Winston, 1942. An argument for a more disciplined and centralized two-party system.

Shafer, Byron E. *Quiet Revolution: The Struggle for the Democratic Party and the Shaping of Post-Reform Politics.* New York: Russell Sage Foundation, 1983. Detailed, insightful history of how the Democratic Party came to be reformed.

Sundquist, James L. *Dynamics of the Party System*, Rev. ed. Washington, D.C.: Brookings Institution, 1983. History of the party system, emphasizing the impact of issues on voting.

Wilson, James Q. *The Amateur Democrat.* Chicago: University of Chicago Press, 1962. Analysis of the issue-oriented political clubs that rose in the 1950s and 1960s.

10 Elections and Campaigns

LEARNING OBJECTIVES

WHAT YOU NEED TO KNOW

- ☑ What is the difference between a primary election and a general election?
- ☑ Does the federal government provide funding for political campaigns?
- ☑ How do voters typically decide on a candidate?

WHO GOVERNS?

1. How do American elections determine the kind of people who govern us?
2. What matters most in deciding who wins presidential and congressional elections?

TO WHAT ENDS?

1. Do elections make a real difference in what laws get passed?

National elections in the United States in the 21st century would be virtually unrecognizable to politicians in the early republic. As we saw in Chapter 9, political parties once determined, or powerfully influenced, who got nominated. In the 19th century, the members of Congress from a given caucus would meet to pick their presidential candidate. After the caucuses were replaced by the national nominating conventions, the real power was wielded by local party leaders, who came together (sometimes in the legendary "smoke-filled rooms") to choose the candidate, whom the rest of the delegates would then endorse. Congressional candidates were also often hand-picked by local party bosses. Most people voted a straight party ticket. This system endured until well into the 20th century.

THEN In 1968, Vice President Hubert Humphrey won the Democratic presidential nomination without competing in a single state primary. His party's bosses pretty much delivered the nomination to him. He competed in a three-way race for president without having to raise nearly as much money as candidates routinely do today. (He lost in a close race to Republican Richard M. Nixon.)

In 1988, Vice President George H. W. Bush won the Republican presidential nomination. He had to win primaries and raise tens of millions of dollars. His party's leaders played a big role in his campaign, but so did consultants, pollsters, and others with no traditional ties to the party organization. (He won in a landslide over Democrat Michael Dukakis.) Still, even his 1988 campaign would not be close to presidential politics in 2008.

NOW The 2008 presidential sweepstakes started in 2006. By early 2007, more than a dozen candidates had come forward, and at least one had declared and then dropped out. For the first time in four-score years, neither a sitting president nor a sitting vice president was in the race. With hundreds of days left to go before election day in November 2008, several frontrunners were each on their way to raising around $100 million. While the 2012 presidential race would not have the same early start, since no incumbent was running for reelection and only one party would hold nominating contests, the cost of participating in those contests would almost certainly match or exceed the 2008 figure.

Many things have changed, but the key changes are related to one another: parties are less important; media (or "media buys") are more important; polling is ubiquitous; and money—or the nonstop fundraising that keeps it coming—matters more than ever.

Campaigns Today

With the parties' ability to control nominations weakened, candidates are now pretty much on their own. Most, however, do not go it alone. Rather, they hire people to perform several separate but related campaign tasks:[1]

- *Media consultants* who create advertisements and buy airtime from stations and networks.
- *Direct-mail firms* that design and produce mailings to promote the candidate or solicit money.
- *Polling firms* to survey voters on their attitudes toward issues and candidates and to run focus groups.
- *Political technology firms* to supply services such as Web site design, online advertising, online fundraising, and voter-targeting.

To pay for all this help, today's candidates must raise and spend enormous sums of money. As Table 10.1 shows, in the 2010 midterm elections, all candidates for national office raised and spent more than $1.8 billion: more than $1 billion in House races, and about $765 million `in Senate races. These campaign finance sums are unprecedented.

In the 2004 elections, all candidates for national office raised and spent "only" about $1.85 billion; the leap to more than $3.7 billion in the 2010 congressional

Table 10.1 The 2010 Midterm Elections: Money Raised and Spent

	Total Raised	Total Spent
House Candidates	$ 1,102,340,257	$ 1,094,911,271
Senate Candidates	$ 766,716,134	$ 764,967,246
Total, All Candidates	$ 1,869,056,391	$ 1,859,878,517

Source: Federal Election Commission, 2010 House and Senate Campaign Finance Summary.

Table 10.2 Presidential Fundraising and Expenditures, 1976–2008

			Percent change from previous election	
Year	$ Raised	$ Spent	Raised	Spent
1976	$171 million	$70 million	–%	–%
1980	$162 million	$92 million	–5.2	+31.4
1984	$202 million	$104 million	+24.6	+13.0
1988	$324 million	$211 million	+60.3	+102.6
1992	$331 million	$192 million	-00.9	–9.00
1996	$426 million	$240 million	+28.7	+25.0
2000	$529 million	$343 million	+24.1	+42.9
2004	$881 million	$718 million	+66.6	+109
2008	$1.81 billion	$1.76 billion	+105	+145
1976–2008 Increase	+$1.63 billion	+$1.69 billion	+853	+2,314
Inflation-Adjusted	+$436 million	+$452 million	+255	+645

Source: Adapted from Federal Election Commission summary reports, January 2009 and May 2009. Dollar figures rounded. Inflation adjustment keyed to consumer price index 1976–2008, 3.74 (i.e., assumes that what cost $1.00 in 1976 cost $3.74 in 2008).

elections more than doubled that amount, and the 2010 figure does not even include costs for a presidential election. Presidential campaign fundraising and expenditures more than doubled between 2004 and 2008; presidential campaign spending in 2008 (about $1.81 billion) rivaled total 2004 House, Senate, and presidential campaign spending (about $1.85 billion). As Table 10.2 shows, even adjusted for inflation, the amounts of money raised and spent by presidential candidates have exploded since 1976.

Today's presidential candidates spend more on media consultants, television and radio ads, and diverse other forms of "media messages" than on any other category of campaign expenses. For example, 2008 presidential candidates spent about $569 million on media, representing about 31 percent of all their campaign expenditures (see Figure 10.1).

With so much money spent by candidates for media outlets and media consultants, you might think there is clear and convincing evidence that media exposure makes a critical difference in who wins elections, or that some types of televised appeals work better than others, or both.

Figure 10.1

2008 Presidential Campaigns' Spending on Media

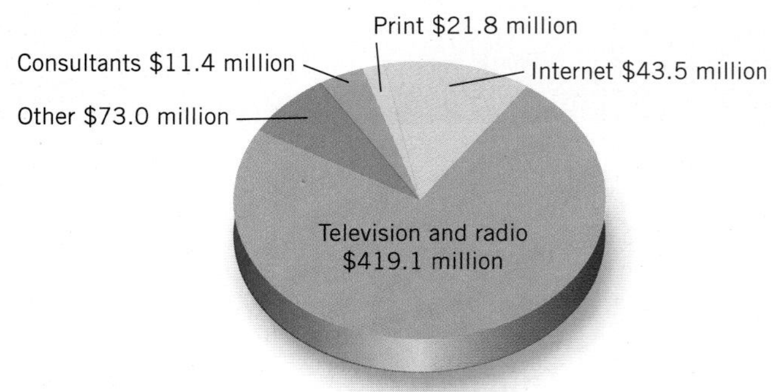

Total: $568.8 million

Source: Federal Election Commission summary reports, May 2009. Figures rounded.

But you would be wrong. About the only safe generalization one can presently make on the subject is not that "media buys" matter, but how common it is for today's candidates to purchase political ads embodying emotional appeals.

A comprehensive 2006 study carefully analyzed thousands of political ads broadcast from 1999 through 2004.[2] A plurality, it found, were purposely designed (everything from the images used to the music playing in the background) to appeal mainly to voters' fears (impending war, losing a job, and so on). A smaller but significant fraction was more focused on stirring positive emotions (patriotism and community pride). You might suppose that candidates favor ads that appeal to such emotions because they are particularly effective in reaching voters who know little and care less about politics.

Once again, you would be wrong. The political ads, televised and other, that appealed to emotion (fear or enthusiasm, mainly) wielded the greatest influence over voters with the greatest interest in politics and the most information about government.[3] Still, experts do not know how or whether televised political ads influence election outcomes.

BETTER OR WORSE?

There is less mystery in political polling than in trying to determine how campaign ads affect election results. Today, even many candidates running in relatively low-budget local races do extensive pre- and post-election voter polling, and often use the results to shape television ads, other campaign communications, positions on the issues, and even what words candidates repeat (or eschew) and how they dress when in public.

It is, however, still only in the national political big leagues that many candidates do extensive polling designed not merely to test voters' existing attitudes, but also to discover how to change them. And it is still only in presidential races and especially well-funded contests for Congress (mostly for the Senate) that sophisticated surveys, much like those traditionally done by big corporations to identify markets where their goods or services are especially likely to sell, are used to mobilize voters.

In the elections of 2004, 2006, and again in 2008, these survey techniques "micro-targeted" people by using data about their consumer and recreational habits (small car or SUV, drink high-cost coffees or cheap brews, like watching professional sports or loathe it, and more). In 2008, micro-targeting software, databases, and techniques became highly refined and were used intensively by both the Obama and the McCain presidential campaigns.[4]

Of course, it is one thing to know where "your voters" are, but quite another thing to reach them through door-to-door drives like the ones that once were the political parties' chief stock-in-trade. In 2008, both parties' national leaders stressed building or expanding grassroots get-out-the-vote organizations not dissimilar from those that, precinct by precinct, once dominated election days in most American cities. Such "high-tech canvassing," if it continues, may yet re-create something somewhat like the party organizations of old.

Patrick Caddell pioneered present-day political polling techniques when he served as Jimmy Carter's consultant in the mid-1970s. By the time Ronald Reagan followed Carter as president in 1980, pollsters like Caddell were the new political bosses, at least in presidential campaigns. As veteran political reporter Joe Klein has reflected, when they "endorsed" a candidate, "fund-raising, media buzz, and support from the party's special interests suddenly became easier."[5]

In 2006, republican presidential hopeful Senator John McCain hired into his campaign political consultants who had previously worked against him and developed harshly negative ads that he had in years past objected to as dishonest (and worse). But nobody who knows how the game is played today was really surprised. Today, candidates in both parties, whether ideologically liberal, conservative, or in between, routinely practice what the political professionals preach and purchase what they produce.

This is the main reason for the unceasing spiral in campaign spending, and hence for the fact that "campaigning" has become largely synonymous with "fundraising." Candidates for major offices have two top needs: money for television ads, followed by time for fundraising to generate the cash needed to pay for the ads.[6] Once elected, the permanent fundraising campaign continues for House members, and almost as much for senators and even for the president (who, especially when popular, also makes many trips to raise money for his party's candidates).

The American Association for Political Consultants (AAPC) is a trade association. In 1980, it had about 50 members. By 1990, it had around 700 members. Today, it has more than 1,100 members representing a campaign industry with more than 2,500 firms.[7] The industry's expansion coincided with decreased political participation, and—the only development that can definitely be laid at its door—a dramatic rise in negative, slick, and super-costly political ads. If that leads you to wonder whether, all told, campaigns were better for democracy when party bosses in smoke-filled rooms were more common than political consultants in high-tech firms, you are not alone.

HERE AND ABROAD

Even the best American political consultants probably would have trouble exporting their wares. A campaign plan that will work here would be useless in almost any other democratic nation; one that would work abroad would be useless here.

Unlike in many other democratic nations, in America, elections have not one but two crucial phases—getting nominated and getting elected. Getting nominated means getting your name on the ballot. In the great majority of states, winning your party's nomination for either the presidency or Congress requires an *individual* effort—*you* decide to run, *you* raise money, *you* and your friends collect signatures to get your name on the ballot, and *you* appeal to voters in primary elections on the basis of your personality and your definition of the issues. In most European nations, winning your party's nomination for parliament involves an *organizational* decision—*the party* looks you over, *the party* decides whether to allow you to run, and *the party* puts your name on its list of candidates.

American political parties do play a role in determining the outcome of the final election, but even that role involves parties more as labels in the voters' minds than as organizations that get out the vote. By contrast, many other democratic nations conduct campaigns almost entirely as a contest between parties as organizations. In Israel and the Netherlands, the names of the candidates for the legislature do not even appear on the ballot; only the party names are listed there. And even where candidate names are listed, as in Great Britain, the voters tend to vote "Conservative" or "Labour" more than they vote for Smith or Jones. European nations (except France) do not have a directly elected president; instead, the head of the government—the prime minister—is selected by the party that has won the most seats in parliament.

incumbent The person already holding an elective office.

g36/g36/ZUMA Press/Newscom

Senator Lisa Murkowski of Alaska held onto her seat in 2010 despite losing the Republican primary—she successfully ran in the general election as a write-in candidate, the first person to do this in any state since 1954.

Presidential versus Congressional Campaigns

Presidential and congressional races differ in important ways. The most obvious, of course, is size: more voters participate in the former than the latter contests, and so presidential candidates must work harder and spend more. But there are some less obvious differences that are equally important.

First, presidential races are more competitive than those for the House of Representatives. In the 39 elections from 1932 to 2008 the Republicans won control of the House only eight times (20 percent of the time); in the 20 presidential elections during the same period the Republicans won the White House on nine occasions (45 percent of the time). In the typical presidential race, the winner gets less than 55 percent of the two-party vote; in the typical House race, the **incumbent** wins with over 60 percent of the vote.

Second, a much smaller proportion of people vote in congressional races during off years (that is, when there is no presidential contest) than vote for president. This lower turnout (around 36 percent of the voting-age population) means that candidates in congressional races must be appealing to the more motivated and partisan voter.

Third, members of Congress can do things for their constituents that a president cannot. They take credit—sometimes deserved, sometimes not—for every grant, contract, bridge, canal, and highway that the federal government provides the district or state. They send letters (at the government's expense) to large factions of their constituents and visit their districts every weekend. Presidents get little credit for district improvements and must rely on the mass media to communicate with voters.

Fourth, a candidate for Congress can deny that he or she is responsible for "the mess in Washington," even when the candidate is an incumbent. Incumbents tend to run as individuals, even to the point of denouncing the very Congress of which they are a part. An incumbent president cannot get away with this; rightly or wrongly, he often is held responsible for whatever has gone wrong, not only in the government but in the nation as a whole.

These last three factors—low voter turnout, services to constituents, and the ability to duck responsibility—probably help explain why so high a percentage of congressional incumbents get reelected. But they do not enjoy a completely free ride. Members of Congress who belong to the same party as the president often feel voters' anger about national affairs, particularly economic conditions. When the economy turns sour and a Republican is in the White House, Republican congressional candidates lose votes; if a Democrat is in the White House, Democratic congressional candidates lose votes.

coattails The alleged tendency of candidates to win more votes in an election because of the presence at the top of the ticket of a better-known candidate, such as the president.

At one time the **coattails** of a popular presidential candidate could help congressional candidates in his or her own party. But there has been a sharp decline in the value of presidential coattails; indeed, some scholars doubt they still exist.

The net effect of all these factors is that, to a substantial degree, congressional elections have become independent of presidential ones. Though economic factors may still link the fate of a president and some members of his or her party, by and large the incumbent members of Congress enjoy enough of a cushion to protect them against whatever political storms engulf an unpopular president. This fact further reduces the meaning of party—members of Congress can get reelected even though their party's "leader" in the White House has lost popular support, and nonincumbent candidates for Congress may lose despite the fact that a very popular president from their party is in the White House.

RUNNING FOR PRESIDENT

The first task facing anyone who wishes to be president is to get "mentioned" as someone who is of "presidential caliber." No one is quite sure why some people are mentioned and others are not. Journalist David Broder once suggested that somewhere there is "The Great Mentioner" who announces from time to time who is of presidential caliber (and only The Great Mentioner knows how big that caliber is).

But if The Great Mentioner turns out to be as unreal as the Easter Bunny, you have to figure out for yourself how to get mentioned. One way is to let it be known to reporters, "off the record," that you are thinking about running for president. Another is to travel around the country making speeches (Ronald Reagan, while working for General Electric, made a dozen or more speeches *a day* to audiences all over the country). Another way is to already have a famous name (John Glenn, the former astronaut, was in the public eye long before he declared for the presidency in 1984). Another way to get mentioned is to be identified with a major piece of legislation. Former Senator Bill Bradley of New Jersey was known as an architect of the Tax Reform Act of 1986; Representative Richard Gephardt of Missouri was known as an author of a bill designed to reduce foreign imports. Still another way is to be the governor of a big state. Former New York governors, such as Mario Cuomo, often are viewed as presidential prospects, partly because New York City is the headquarters of the television and publishing industries.

Once you are mentioned, it is wise to set aside a lot of time to run, especially if you are only "mentioned" as opposed to being really well known. Ronald Reagan devoted the better part of six years to running; Walter Mondale spent four years campaigning; Howard Baker resigned from the Senate in 1984 to prepare to run in 1988 (he finally dropped out of the race). However, many post-1988 candidates—senators Bob Dole, John Kerry, John McCain, and Barack Obama; governors Michael Dukakis, Bill Clinton, and George W. Bush; vice presidents George Bush and Al Gore; and House members Ron Paul and Dennis Kucinich—made the run while holding elective office.

Though presidential candidates come from various backgrounds, in general the voters tend to prefer those with experience as governors or military leaders rather than those who come immediately from Congress. Some candidates, such as John F. Kennedy, have been elected president directly after being a senator, but most are either war heroes (Dwight Eisenhower), former governors (George W. Bush, Bill Clinton, Ronald Reagan, Jimmy Carter, and Franklin D. Roosevelt), or former members of Congress who have already had experience as vice

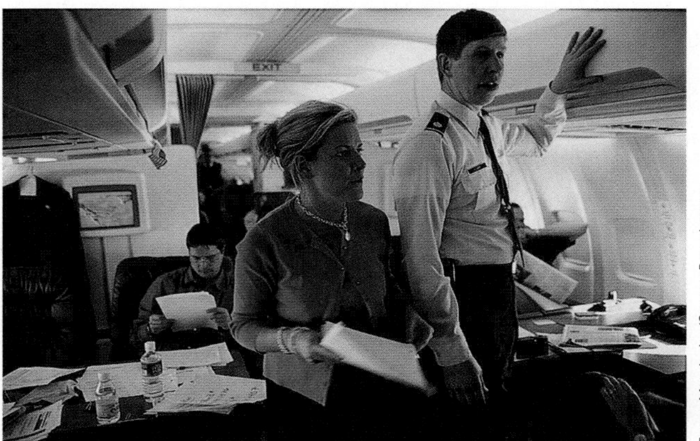

Tomas Muscionico/Contact Press Images

Political campaigns are hard work, even when you get to fly on the vice president's airplane.

presidents (Gerald Ford, Richard Nixon, Lyndon Johnson, and Harry Truman).

Money

One reason why running takes so much time is that it takes so long to raise the necessary money and build up an organization of personal followers. As we shall see later in this chapter, federal law restricts the amount that any single individual can give a candidate to $2,000 in each election. (A **political action committee,** or **PAC,** which is a committee set up by and representing a corporation, labor union, or other special-interest group, can give up to $5,000.) Moreover, to be eligible for federal matching grants to pay for your primary campaign, you must first raise at least $5,000, in individual contributions of $250 or less, in each of 20 states.

political action committee (PAC) A committee set up by a corporation, labor union, or interest group that raises and spends campaign money from voluntary donations.

Organization

Raising and accounting for money to campaign requires a staff of fundraisers, lawyers, and accountants. You also need a press secretary, a travel scheduler, an advertising specialist, a direct-mail company, and a pollster, all of whom must be paid, plus a large number of volunteers in at least those states that hold early primary elections or party caucuses. These volunteers will brief you on the facts of each state, try to line up endorsements from local politicians and celebrities, and put together a group of people who will knock on doors, make telephone calls, organize receptions and meetings, and try to keep you from mispronouncing the name of the town in which you are speaking. Finally, you have to assemble advisers on the issues. These advisers will write "position papers" for you on all sorts of things you are supposed to know about (but probably don't). Because a campaign usually is waged around a few broad themes, these position papers rarely get used or even read. The papers exist so you can show important interest groups that you have taken "sound" positions, so you can be prepared to answer tough questions, and so journalists can look up your views on matters that may become topical.

Strategy and Themes

Every candidate picks a strategy for the campaign. In choosing one, much depends on whether you are the incumbent. Incumbents must defend their records, like it or not. (An incumbent ran for president in 1964, 1972, 1976, 1980, 1984, 1992, 1996, and 2004.) The challenger attacks the incumbent. When there is no incumbent (as in 1960, 1968, 1988, 2000, and 2008), both candidates can announce their own programs; however, the candidate from the party that holds the White House must take, whether or not the candidate thinks he deserves it, some of the blame for whatever has gone wrong in the preceding four years. Within these limits, a strategy consists of the answers to questions about tone, theme, timing, and targets:

- What *tone* should the campaign have? Should it be a positive (build-me-up) or negative (attack-the-opponent) campaign? In 1988, George H. W. Bush began with a negative campaign; Michael Dukakis followed suit.
- What *theme* can I develop? A theme is a simple, appealing idea that can be repeated over and over again. For Jimmy Carter in 1976, it was "trust"; for Ronald Reagan in 1980, it was "competence" and in 1984, it was "it's morning again in America"; for Bush in 1988, it was "stay the course"; for Clinton in 1992, it was "we need to change"; for George W. Bush in 2000, it was "compassionate

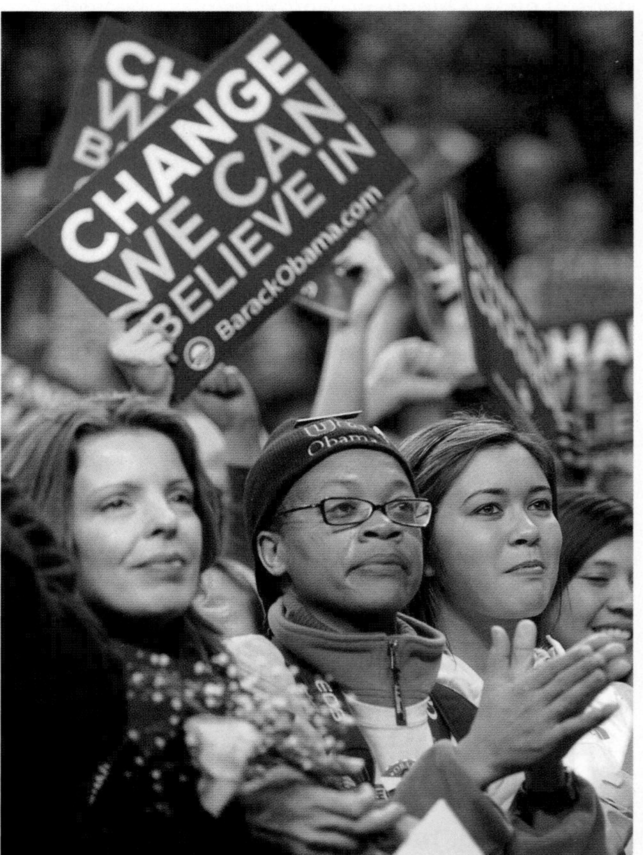

Stephen Brashear/Getty Images

Barack Obama campaigned on the slogan "Change We Can Believe In."

conservatism"; for Barack Obama in 2008, it was "yes we can" and "change you can believe in."

- What should be the *timing* of the campaign? If you are relatively unknown, you will have to put everything into the early primaries and caucuses, try to emerge a frontrunner, and then hope for the best. If you are already the frontrunner, you may either go for broke early (and try to drive out all your opponents) or hold back some reserves for a long fight.
- Whom should you *target?* Only a small percentage of voters change their vote from one election to the next. Who is likely to change this time—unemployed steelworkers? Unhappy farmers? People upset by inflation?

GETTING ELECTED TO CONGRESS

A president cannot serve more than two terms, so at least once every eight years you have a chance of running against a nonincumbent; members of Congress can serve for an unlimited number of terms, and so chances are you will run against an incumbent. If you decide to run for the House, the odds are very much against you. Since 1962, over 90 percent of the House incumbents who sought reelection won it.

But the incredible incumbency advantage enjoyed by modern-day House members is hardly the whole story of getting elected to Congress. Who serves in Congress, and what interests are represented there, is affected by how its members are elected. Each state is entitled to two senators who serve six-year terms and at least one representative who serves a two-year term. How many more representatives a state has depends on its population; what local groups these representatives speak for depends in part on how the district lines are drawn.

The Constitution says very little about how representatives will be selected except to require that they be inhabitants of the states from which they are chosen. It says nothing about districts and originally left it up to the states to decide who would be eligible to vote for representatives. The size of the first House was set by the Constitution at 65 members, and the apportionment of the seats among the states was spelled out in Article I, section 2. From that point on, it has been up to Congress to decide how many representatives each state would have (provided that each had at least one).

Initially, some states did not create congressional districts; all their representatives were elected at large. In other states, representatives were elected from multimember as well as single-member districts. In time, all states with more than one representative elected each from a single-member district. How those district boundaries were drawn, however, could profoundly affect the outcomes of elections. There were two problems. One was **malapportionment,** which results from having districts of very unequal size. If one district is twice as populous as another, twice as many votes are needed in the larger district to elect a representative. Thus, a citizen's vote in the smaller district is worth twice as much as a vote in the larger.

malapportionment Drawing the boundaries of legislative districts so that they are unequal in population.

gerrymandering Drawing the boundaries of legislative districts in bizarre or unusual shapes to favor one party.

The other problem was **gerrymandering,** which means drawing a district boundary in some bizarre or unusual shape to make it easy for the candidate of one party to win election in that district. In a state entitled to 10 representatives, where half the voters are Democrats and half are Republicans, district lines could be drawn so that eight districts would have a slight majority of citizens from one party and two districts would have lopsided majorities from the other. Thus, it can be made easy for one party to win eight of the 10 seats.

Malapportionment and gerrymandering have been conspicuous features of American congressional politics. In 1962, for example, one district in Texas had nearly a million residents, while another had less than a quarter million. In California, Democrats in control of the state legislature drew district lines in the early 1960s so that two pockets of Republican strength in Los Angeles separated by many miles were connected by a thin strip of coastline. In this way, most Republican voters were thrown into one district, while Democratic voters were spread more evenly over several.

Hence, there are four problems to solve in deciding who gets represented in the House:

1. Establishing the total size of the House
2. Allocating seats in the House among the states
3. Determining the size of congressional districts within states
4. Determining the shape of those districts

By and large, Congress has decided the first two questions, and the states have decided the last two—but under some rather strict Supreme Court rules.

In 1911, Congress decided the House had become large enough and voted to fix its size at 435 members. There it has remained ever since (except for a brief period when it had 437 members owing to the admission of Alaska and Hawaii to the Union in 1959). Once the size was decided, it was necessary to find a formula for performing the painful task of apportioning seats among the states as they gained and lost population. The Constitution requires such reapportionment every 10 years. A more or less automatic method was selected in 1929 based on a complex statistical system that has withstood decades of political and scientific testing. Since 1990, under this system 18 states have lost representation in the House and 11 have gained it. Florida and California posted the biggest gains, while New York and Pennsylvania suffered the largest losses (see Table 10.3).

The states did little about malapportionment and gerrymandering until ordered to do so by the Supreme Court. In 1964, the Court ruled that the Constitution requires districts be drawn so that, as nearly as possible, one person's vote would be worth as much as another's.[8] The Court rule, "one person, one vote," seems clear but in fact leaves a host of questions unanswered. How much deviation from equal size is allowable? Should other factors be considered besides population? (For example, a state legislature might want to draw district lines to make it easier for African Americans, Italian Americans, farmers, or some other group with a distinct interest to elect a representative; the requirement of exactly equal districts might make this impossible.) And the gerrymandering problem remains: districts of the same size can be drawn to favor one party or another. The courts have struggled to find answers to these questions, but they remain far from settled.

sophomore surge An increase in the votes congressional candidates usually get when they first run for reelection.

Winning the Primary

However the district lines are drawn, getting elected to Congress first requires getting one's name on the ballot. At one time, the political parties nominated candidates and even printed ballots with the party slates listed on them. All the voter had to do was take the ballot of the preferred party and put it in the ballot box. Today, with rare exceptions, a candidate wins a party's nomination by gathering enough voter signatures to get on the ballot in a primary election, the outcome of which often is beyond the ability of political parties to influence. Candidates tend to form organizations of personal followings and win "their party's" nomination simply by getting more primary votes than the next candidate. It is quite unusual for an incumbent to lose a primary: from 1990 through 2008, only about 10 percent of incumbent senators and 5 percent of incumbent representatives seeking reelection failed to win renomination in primaries. These statistics suggest how little opportunity parties have to control or punish their congressional members.

Most newly elected members become strong in their districts very quickly; this is called the **sophomore surge.** It is the difference between the votes candidates get the first time they are elected (and thus

Table 10.3 Changes in State Representation in the House of Representatives

	Number of Seats			
States	**After 1990 Census**	**After 2000 Census**	**After 2010 Census**	**Change**
Gained/Maintained Seats				
Arizona	6	8	9	+3
California	52	53	53	+1
Florida	23	25	27	+4
Georgia	11	13	14	+3
North Carolina	12	13	13	+1
Texas	30	32	36	+6
Lost Seats				
Illinois	20	19	18	−2
Michigan	16	15	14	−2
New York	31	29	27	−4
Ohio	19	18	16	−3
Pennsylvania	21	19	18	−3

Source: U.S. Bureau of the Census.

become freshman members) and the votes they get when they run for reelection (in hopes of becoming sophomore members). Before the 1960s, House candidates did not do much better the second time they ran. Beginning then, however, the sophomore surge kicked in, so that today freshman candidates running for reelection will get 8 to 10 percent more votes than when they were first elected. Senate candidates also benefit now from a sophomore surge, though to a lesser degree.

The reason for this surge is that members of Congress have figured out how to use their offices to run *personal* rather than party campaigns. They make use of free ("franked") mail, frequent trips home, radio and television broadcasts, and the distribution of services to their districts to develop among their constituents a good opinion of themselves, not their party. They also cater to their constituents' distrust of the federal government by promising to "clean things up" if reelected. They run *for* Congress by running *against* it.[9]

To the extent that they succeed, they enjoy great freedom in voting on particular issues and have less need to explain away votes that their constituents might not like. If, however, any single-issue groups are actively working in their districts for or against abortion, gun control, nuclear energy, or tax cuts, muting the candidates' voting record may not be possible.

Staying in Office

The way people get elected to Congress has two important effects. First, it produces legislators closely tied to local concerns (their districts, their states), and second, it ensures that party leaders will have relatively weak influence over them (because those leaders cannot determine who gets nominated for office).

The local orientation of legislators has some important effects on how policy is made. For example:

- Every member of Congress organizes his or her office to do as much as possible for people back home.
- If your representative serves on the House Transportation and Infrastructure Committee, your state has a much better chance of getting a new bridge or canal than if you do not have a representative on this committee.[10]
- If your representative serves on the House Appropriations Committee, your district is more likely to get approval for a federal grant to improve your water and sewage-treatment programs than if your representative does not serve on that committee.[11]

Former House Speaker Thomas P. "Tip" O'Neill had this in mind when he said, "All politics is local." Some people think this localism is wrong; in their view members of Congress should do what is best for "the nation as a whole." This argument is about the role of legislators: are they supposed to be *delegates* who do what their district wants or *trustees* who use their best judgment on issues without regard to the preferences of their district?

Naturally, most members are some combination of delegate and trustee, with the exact mix depending on the nature of the issue. But some, as we shall see, definitely lean one way or the other. All members want to be reelected, but "delegates" tend to value this over every other consideration and so seek out committee assignments and projects that will produce benefits for their districts. On the other hand, "trustees" will seek out committee assignments that give them a chance to address large questions, such as foreign affairs, that may have no implications at all for their districts.

Primary versus General Campaigns

When you run for federal office, you must run in two elections, not just one. The first consists of primary elections designed to choose each party's nominee, and the second is the general election that picks the winner who will hold office. If you are running for president, some states, such as Iowa, hold caucuses instead of primary elections. A caucus is a meeting of people, often in an auditorium or church basement, where they vote on who they would like for their party's nominee.

Each election or caucus attracts a different mix of voters. What may help you win a primary or a caucus may be very different from what will help you win the general election. To win a primary or a caucus, you must mobilize political activists who will give money, do volunteer work, and attend local caucuses. As we saw in Chapters 7 and 8, activists are more ideologically stringent than the voters at large. To motivate these activists, you must be more liberal (if you are a Democrat) in your tone and theme than rank-and-file Democrats, or more conservative (if you are a Republican) than rank-and-file Republicans.

Consider the caucuses held in Iowa in the winter preceding a presidential election year. This is the first real test of the candidates vying for the nomination. Anyone who does poorly here is at a disadvantage, in terms of media attention and

clothespin vote
The vote cast by a person who does not like either candidate and so votes for the less objectionable of the two, putting a clothespin over his or her nose to keep out the unpleasant stench.

position issue
An issue about which the public is divided and rival candidates or political parties adopt different policy positions.

contributor interest, for the rest of the campaign. The several thousand Iowans who participate in their parties' caucuses are not representative of the followers of their party in the state, much less nationally. In 1988, Senator Robert Dole came in first and evangelist Pat Robertson came in second in the Iowa Republican caucus, with Vice President George Bush finishing third. As it turned out, there was little support for Dole or Robertson in the rest of the country.

Democrats who participate in the Iowa caucus tend to be more liberal than Democrats generally. Moreover, the way the caucuses are run is a far cry from how most elections are held. To vote in the Republican caucus, you need not prove you are a Republican or even a voter. The Democratic caucus is not an election at all; instead, a person supporting a certain candidate stands in one corner of the room with people who also support that candidate, while those supporting other candidates stand in other corners with other groups. There is a lot of calling back and forth, intended to persuade people to leave one group and join another. No group with fewer than 15 percent of the people in attendance gets to choose any delegates, so people in these small groups then go to other, larger ones. It is a cross between musical chairs and fraternity pledge week.

Suppose you are a Democrat running for president and you do well in the Iowa caucus. Suppose you go on to win your party's nomination. Now you have to go back to Iowa to campaign for votes in the general election. Between 1940 and 2008, Iowa has voted Republican in every presidential election but seven (1948, 1964, 1988, 1992, 1996, 2000, and 2008). Your Republican opponent is not going to let you forget all of the liberal slogans you uttered nine months before. The Republican candidate faces the mirror image of this problem—sounding very conservative to get support from Republican activists in states such as Massachusetts and New York and then having to defend those speeches when running against his or her Democratic opponent in those states.

The problem is not limited to Iowa but exists in every state where activists are more ideologically polarized than the average voter. To get activist support for the nomination, candidates move to the ideological extremes; to win the general election, they try to move back to the ideological center. The typical voter looks at the results and often decides that neither candidate appeals to him or her very much, and so casts a "**clothespin vote.**"

Early in the 2004 presidential caucuses and primaries, John Kerry claimed he was an opponent of the American invasion of Iraq in order to defeat Howard Dean, the Vermont governor who seemed to be capturing the antiwar vote among Democrats. But after he won his party's nomination, Kerry backed away from an antiwar stance in order to be more attractive to centrist voters. He had learned a lesson that George McGovern did not understand in 1972. McGovern maintained his liberal views on the war in Vietnam, decriminalizing marijuana, and providing amnesty for draft dodgers.[12] His opponent, Richard Nixon, defeated him easily by taking more centrist positions.

One last thing: if you decide to run for president as a Democrat, do not trust too much in the early polls indicating the frontrunner for the nomination. Edmund Muskie (1972), George Wallace (1976), Ted Kennedy (1980), Gary Hart (1988), Mario Cuomo (1992), and Joseph Lieberman (2004) were all early frontrunners among Democrats, but none got the party's nomination. Only frontrunners Walter Mondale (1984) and Al Gore (2000) prevailed (though neither went on to win the office). By contrast, since 1972, every early Republican frontrunner except one has won the nomination. In 2007, the Republican frontrunner was former New York City Mayor Rudolph Guiliani, and the Democratic frontrunner was then New York State Senator Hillary Rodham Clinton. By early 2008, Guiliani faded, and Arizona Senator John McCain went on to win the Republican nomination. McCain lost the general election to Illinois Senator Barack Obama following Obama's protracted nomination battle with Clinton.

TWO KINDS OF CAMPAIGN ISSUES

In election campaigns, there are two different kinds of issues.[13] A **position issue** is one in which the rival candidates have opposing views on a question that also divides the voters. For example, in the 2008 election, John McCain wanted to let people put some of their Social Security money into private savings accounts; Barack Obama opposed this.

Since 1860, many of the great party realignments have been based on differing position issues. After the Civil War, the question was whether African Americans should be slaves or free. In the 1890s, it

How Things Work

Qualifications for Entering Congress and Privileges of Serving in Congress

Representative

- Must be 25 years of age (when seated, not when elected)
- Must have been a citizen of the United States for seven years
- Must be an inhabitant of the state from which elected (*Note:* Custom, but *not* the Constitution, requires that a representative live in the district that he or she represents.)

Senator

- Must be 30 years of age (when seated, not when elected)
- Must have been a citizen of the United States for nine years
- Must be an inhabitant of the state from which elected

Judging Qualifications

Each house is the judge of the "elections, returns, and qualifications" of its members. Thus, Congress alone can decide disputed congressional elections. On occasion, it has excluded a person from taking a seat on the grounds that the election was improper. Either house can punish a member—by reprimand, for example—or, by a two-thirds vote, expel a member.

Privileges

Members of Congress have certain privileges, the most important of which, conferred by the Constitution, is that "for any speech or debate in either house they shall not be questioned in any other place." This doctrine of "privileged speech" has been interpreted by the Supreme Court to mean that members of Congress cannot be sued or prosecuted for anything that they say or write in connection with their legislative duties.

When Senator Mike Gravel read the Pentagon Papers—some then-secret government documents about the Vietnam War—into the *Congressional Record* in defiance of a court order restraining their publication, the Court held that this was "privileged speech" and beyond challenge (*Gravel v. United States*, 408 U.S. 606, 1972). But when Senator William Proxmire issued a press release critical of a scientist doing research on monkeys, the Court decided the scientist could sue him for libel because a press release was not part of the legislative process (*Hutchinson v. Proxmire*, 443 U.S. 111, 1979).

valence issue An issue about which the public is united and rival candidates or political parties adopt similar positions in hopes that each will be thought to best represent those widely shared beliefs.

was whether tariffs should be high or low and whether the dollar should be made cheaper. In the 1960s, it was whether broad new civil rights legislation was needed.

But sometimes voters are not divided on important issues. Instead, the question is whether a candidate fully supports the public's view on a matter about which nearly everyone agrees. These are called **valence issues.** For example, everybody wants a strong economy and low crime rates, and so no candidate favors high unemployment or more crime. What voters look for on valence issues is which candidate seems most closely linked to a universally shared view.

Valence issues are quite common. In 1968, Richard Nixon seemed more supportive of anticrime measures than his rival; in 1976, Jimmy Carter seemed more likely to favor honesty in government than his opponent; in 1984, Ronald Reagan seemed more closely identified with a strong economy than his opponent; in 1988, George H. W. Bush seemed more closely linked to patriotism than his opponent. Notice that we have said "seemed." This is how voters perceived the winners; it does not mean the opponents favored crime, corruption, unemployment, or anti-Americanism.

In 1992, Bill Clinton was beset with charges that he was guilty of dodging the draft, marital infidelity, and smoking pot. But his strategists decided to focus the campaign on the valence issue of the economy, and they went about rescuing Clinton from the other criticisms. One observer later reported, "Retooling the image of a couple who had already been in the public eye for five battering months required a campaign of behavior modification and media manipulation so elaborate that its outline ran to 14 single-spaced pages."[14] Bill and Hillary Clinton made joint appearances on television during which they demonstrated their affection for each other. The plan even called for staging an event where Bill Clinton and his daughter would surprise Hillary Clinton on Mother's Day.[15]

The 2008 campaign relied on both valence issues (Obama and McCain supported "reforming" the health care system to make it more "affordable," while differing on many details related to government-paid health insurance) and position issues (McCain supported tax cuts while Obama favored increasing taxes for people earning over $200,000 a year).

Campaigns usually combine both position and valence questions, but the latter have increased in importance in recent years. This has happened in part because presidential campaigns are now conducted largely on television, where it is important to project popular symbols and manipulate widely admired images. Candidates try to show they are likable, and they rely on televised portraits of their similarity to ordinary people.

general election An election held to choose which candidate will hold office.

primary election An election held to choose candidates for office.

closed primary A primary election in which voting is limited to already registered party members.

open primary A primary election in which voters may choose in which party to vote as they enter the polling place.

TELEVISION, DEBATES, AND DIRECT MAIL

Once campaigns mostly involved parades, big rallies, "whistle-stop" train tours, and shaking hands outside factory gates and near shopping centers. These types of activities still occur, but increasingly presidential and senatorial candidates (and those House candidates with television stations in their districts) use broadcasting to reach potential voters.

Television can be used in two ways—by running paid advertisements and by getting on the nightly news broadcasts. Short television ads are called *spots,* and a campaign activity that appears on a news broadcast is called a *visual.* Much has been written about the preparation of spots, usually under titles such as "the selling of the president" or "packaging the candidate" (and mostly by advertising executives, who are not especially known for underestimating their own influence). No doubt spots can have an important effect in some cases. A little-known candidate can increase his or her visibility by frequent use of spots (this is what Jimmy Carter did in the 1976 presidential primaries).

The effect of television advertising on general elections is probably a good deal less than its effect on primaries; indeed, as we shall see in Chapter 12, most scientific studies of television's influence on voting decisions have shown that either it has no effect or the effect is subtle and hard to detect. Nor is it surprising that this should be the case. In a general election, especially one for a high-visibility office (such as president or governor), the average voter has many sources of information—his or her own party or ideological preference, various kinds of advertising, the opinions of friends and family, and newspaper and magazine stories. Furthermore, both sides will use TV spots; if well done, they are likely to cancel each other out. In short, it is not yet clear that a gullible public is being sold a bill of goods by slick Madison Avenue advertisers, whether the goods are automobiles or politicians.

Visuals are a vital part of any major campaign effort because, unlike spots, they cost the campaign little and, as "news," they may have greater credibility with the viewer. A visual is a brief, filmed episode showing the candidate doing something that a reporter thinks is newsworthy. Simply making a speech, unless the speech contains important new facts or charges, often is thought by TV editors to be uninteresting: television viewers are not attracted by pictures of "talking heads," and in the highly competitive world of TV, audience reactions are all-important determinants of what gets on the air. Knowing this, campaign managers will strive to have their candidates do something visually interesting every day, no later than 3:00 P.M. (if the visual is to be on the 6:00 P.M. news)—talk to elderly folks in a nursing home, shake hands with people waiting in an unemployment line, or sniff the waters of a polluted lake. Obviously, all these efforts are for naught if a TV camera crew is not around; great pains therefore are taken to schedule these visuals at times and in places that make it easy for photographers to be present.

Ironically, visuals—and television newscasts generally—may give the viewer less information than commercial spots. This, of course, is the exact opposite of what many people believe. It is commonplace to deplore political advertising, especially the short spot, on the grounds that it is either devoid

How Things Work

Kinds of Elections

There are two kinds of elections in the United States: general and primary. A **general election** is used to fill an elective office. A **primary election** is used to select a party's candidates for an elective office, though in fact those who vote in a primary election may not consider themselves party members. Some primaries are closed. In a **closed primary,** you must declare in advance (sometimes several weeks in advance) that you are a registered member of the political party in whose primary you wish to vote. About 40 states have closed primaries.

Other primaries are open. In an **open primary,** you can decide when you enter the voting booth which party's primary you wish to participate in. You are given every party's ballot; you may vote on one. Idaho, Michigan, Minnesota, Montana, North Dakota, Utah, Vermont, and Wisconsin have open primaries. A variant on the open primary is the **blanket** (or "free love") **primary**—in the voting booth, you mark a ballot that lists the candidates of all the parties, and thus you can help select the Democratic candidate for one office and the Republican candidate for another. Alaska and Washington have blanket primaries.

The differences among these kinds of primaries should not be exaggerated, for even the closed primary does not create any great barrier for a voter who wishes to vote in the Democratic primary in one election and the Republican in another. Some states also have a **runoff primary:** if no candidate gets a majority of the votes, there is a runoff between the two with the most votes. Runoff primaries are common in the South.

A special kind of primary, a presidential primary, is used to pick delegates to the presidential nominating conventions of the major parties. Presidential primaries come in a bewildering variety. A simplified list looks like this:

- **Delegate selection only** Only the names of prospective delegates to the convention appear on the ballot. They may or may not indicate their presidential preferences.
- **Delegate selection with advisory presidential preference** Voters pick delegates and indicate their preferences among presidential candidates. The delegates are not legally bound to observe these preferences.
- **Binding presidential preference** Voters indicate their preferred presidential candidates. Delegates must observe these preferences, at least for a certain number of convention ballots. The delegates may be chosen in the primary or by a party convention.

In 1981, the Supreme Court ruled that political parties, not state legislatures, have the right to decide how delegates to national conventions are selected. Thus, Wisconsin could not retain an open primary if the national Democratic Party objected (*Democratic Party v. La Follette,* 101 S. Ct. 1010, 1981). Now the parties can insist that only voters who declare themselves Democrats or Republicans can vote in presidential primaries. The Supreme Court's ruling may have relatively little practical effect, however, since the "declaration" might occur only an hour or a day before the election.

of information or manipulative, and to praise television news programs, especially longer debates and interviews, because they are informative and balanced. In fact, the best research we have so far suggests that the reverse is true: news programs covering elections tend to convey very little information (they often show scenes of crowds cheering or candidates shouting slogans) and make little or no impression on viewers, if indeed they are watched at all. Paid commercials, on the other hand, especially the shorter spots, often contain a good deal of information that is seen, remembered, and evaluated by a public quite capable of distinguishing between fact and humbug.[16]

A special kind of television campaigning is the campaign debate. Incumbents or well-known candidates have little incentive to debate their opponents; by so doing, they only give more publicity to lesser-known rivals. Despite the general rule among politicians never to help an opponent, Vice President Nixon debated the less-well-known John Kennedy in 1960, and President Gerald Ford debated

blanket primary A primary election in which each voter may vote for candidates from both parties.

runoff primary A second primary election held when no candidate wins a majority of the votes in the first primary.

the less-well-known Jimmy Carter in 1976. Nixon and Ford lost. Lyndon Johnson would not debate Barry Goldwater in 1964, nor would Nixon debate Humphrey in 1968 or McGovern in 1972. Johnson and Nixon won. Carter debated the equally well-known Reagan in 1980 (but refused to join in a three-way debate with Reagan and John Anderson). Carter lost.

It is hard to know what effect TV debates have on election outcomes, but poll data suggest that in 1980 voters who watched the debates were reassured by Reagan's performance; after the second debate with Carter, he took a lead in the polls that he never relinquished.[17] In 1984, most people thought that Mondale did better than Reagan in the first debate, but there is little evidence that the debate affected the outcome of the election. In 1992 and 1996, Clinton was probably the better debater, but he most likely would have won even if he had stumbled. In 2008, Barack Obama and John McCain held three televised debates. Opinions differ as to who did better, but there is little evidence that these encounters affected the election results.

Though TV visuals and debates are free, they are also risky. The risk is the slip of the tongue. You may have spent 30 years of your life in unblemished public service, you may have thought through your position on the issues with great care, you may have rehearsed your speeches until your dog starts to howl,

In the 1888 presidential campaign, supporters of Benjamin Harrison rolled a huge ball covered with campaign slogans across the country. The gimmick, first used in 1840, gave rise to the phrase "keep the ball rolling."

Library of Congress

but just make one verbal blunder and suddenly the whole campaign focuses on your misstep. In 1976, President Ford erroneously implied that Poland was not part of the Soviet bloc. For days, the press dwelt on this slip. His opponent, Jimmy Carter, admitted in a *Playboy* interview that he sometimes had lust in his heart. It is hard to imagine anyone who has not, but apparently presidents are supposed to be above that sort of thing. In 1980, Ronald Reagan said trees cause pollution—oops, here we go again.

Because of the fear of a slip, because the voters do not want to hear long speeches about complex issues, and because general-election campaigns are fights to attract the centrist voter, the candidates will rely on a stock speech that sets out the campaign theme as well as on their ability to string together several proven applause-getting lines. For reporters covering the candidate every day, it can be a mind-numbing experience. Nelson Rockefeller spoke so often of the "brotherhood of man and the fatherhood of God" that the reporters started referring to it as his BOMFOG speech. Occasionally this pattern is interrupted by a "major" address—that is, a carefully composed talk on some critical issue, usually delivered before a live audience and designed to provide issue-related stories for the reporters to write.

If you dislike campaign oratory, put yourself in the candidate's shoes for a moment. Every word you say will be scrutinized, especially for slips of the tongue. Interest group leaders and party activists will react sharply to any phrase that departs from their preferred policies. Your opponent stands ready to pounce on any error of fact or judgment. You must give countless speeches every day. The rational reaction to this state of affairs is to avoid controversy, stick to prepared texts and tested phrases, and shun anything that sounds original (and hence untested). You therefore wind up trying to sell yourself as much as or more than your ideas. Voters may *say* they admire a blunt, outspoken person, but in a tough political campaign they would probably find such bluntness a little unnerving.

Television is the most visible example of modern technology's effect on campaigns. Since 1960, presidential elections have been contested largely through television. Without television, the campaign waged in 1992 by independent candidate Ross Perot might not have happened at all. Perot launched his candidacy with successive appearances on Cable News Network's call-in program "Larry King Live," and he bought several half-hour chunks of television time to air his views on the federal budget deficit. In early October, before the first of three televised debates featuring Perot, Republican incumbent

George H. W. Bush, and Democratic challenger Bill Clinton, most national polls showed Perot with only 10 percent of the vote. But after the debates, Perot's support in the polls doubled, and he ended up with about 19 percent of the votes cast on election day.

In 1996, the big television networks agreed to make some free television time available to the major presidential candidates. The Federal Communications Commission approved the plan to limit the free TV to "major" candidates, thus denying it to minor third-party nominees.

Less visible than television but perhaps just as important is the Internet. The computer makes possible sophisticated direct-mail campaigning, and this in turn makes it possible for a candidate to address specific appeals to particular voters easily and rapidly solicit campaign contributions. In the 2004 presidential campaign, Vermont Governor Howard Dean, at first largely unknown, raised a huge amount of money from Internet appeals in which he emphasized his opposition to our war in Iraq. Other candidates will no doubt do the same. However, the Internet lends itself to ideological appeals that motivate small contributions, and not every candidate will want to make such arguments.

Whereas television is heard by everybody—and thus leads the candidate using it to speak in generalities to avoid offending anyone—direct mail is aimed at particular groups (college students, Native Americans, bankers, autoworkers) to whom specific views can be expressed with much less risk of offending someone. So important are the lists of names of potential contributors to whom a computer may send appeals that a prized resource of any candidate, guarded as if it were a military secret, is "The List." Novices in politics must slowly develop their own lists or beg sympathetic incumbents for a peek at theirs.

AP Images

Alaska Governor Sarah Palin debates Senator Joe Biden during the 2008 campaign.

The chief consequence of the new style of campaigning is not, as some think, that it is more manipulative than old-style campaigning (picnics with free beer and $5 bills handed to voters can be just as manipulative as TV ads); rather, it is that running campaigns has become divorced from the process of governing. Previously, the party leaders who ran the campaigns would take part in the government once it was elected, and since they were *party* leaders, they had to worry about getting their candidate *re*elected. Modern political consultants take no responsibility for governing, and by the time the next election rolls around, they may be working for someone else.

Money

As we outlined earlier in this chapter, all these consultants, TV ads, and computerized mailings cost money—lots of it. A powerful California politician once observed that "money is the mother's milk of politics," and many people think that our democracy is drowning in it. In Chapter 11, we will consider what, if anything, interest groups get for the money they give to politicians; in Chapter 12, we shall summarize what we know about the effects of television advertising on elections. Here let us try to answer four questions: Where does campaign money come from? What rules govern how it is raised and spent? What has been the effect of campaign finance reform? What does campaign spending buy?

THE SOURCES OF CAMPAIGN MONEY

Presidential candidates get part of their money from private donors and part from the federal government; congressional candidates get all of their money from private sources. In the presidential primaries, candidates raise money from private citizens and interest groups. The federal government will provide matching funds, dollar for dollar, for all monies raised from individual donors who contribute no more than $250. (To prove they are serious candidates, they must first raise $5,000 in each of 20 states from such small contributors.) The government also gives a lump-sum grant to each political party to help pay the costs of its nominating convention. In the general election, the government pays all the costs (up to a legal limit) of major-party candidates and part of the costs of minor-party candidates (those winning between 5 and 25 percent of the vote).

© Bettmann/CORBIS

Candidates first made phonographic recordings of their speeches in 1908. Warren G. Harding is shown here recording a speech during the 1920 campaign.

Paul Schutzer/Time Life Pictures/Getty Images

John F. Kennedy and Richard Nixon debate during the 1960 presidential campaign.

Congressional candidates get no government funds; all their money must come out of their own pockets or be raised from individuals, interest groups (PACs), or the political parties. Contrary to what many people think, most of that money comes from—and has always come from—individual donors. Because the rules sharply limit how much any individual can give, these donors tend not to be fat cats but people of modest means who contribute $100 or $200 per person.

CAMPAIGN FINANCE RULES

During the 1972 presidential election, men hired by President Nixon's campaign staff broke into the headquarters of the Democratic National Committee in the Watergate office building. They were caught by an alert security guard. The subsequent investigation disclosed that the Nixon people had engaged in dubious or illegal money-raising schemes, including taking large sums from wealthy contributors in exchange for appointing them to ambassadorships. Many individuals and corporations were indicted for making illegal donations (since 1925, it had been against the law for corporations or labor unions to contribute money to candidates, but the law had been unenforceable). Some of the accused had given money to Democratic candidates as well as to Nixon.

When the break-in was discovered, the Watergate scandal unfolded. It had two political results: President Nixon was forced to resign, and a new campaign finance law was passed.

Under the new law, individuals could not contribute more than $1,000 to a candidate during any single election. Corporations and labor unions had for many decades been prohibited from spending money on campaigns, but the new law created a substitute: political action committees. A PAC must have at least 50 members (all of whom enroll voluntarily), give to at least five federal candidates, and must not give more than $5,000 to any candidate in any election or more than $15,000 per year to any political party. In addition, the law made federal tax money available to help pay for presidential primary campaigns and for paying all of the campaign costs of a major-party candidate and a fraction of the costs of a minor-party candidate in a presidential general election.

The new law helped increase the amount of money spent on elections and, in time, changed the way money was spent. There are now more than 4,000 PACs (see Figure 10.2). In each election since 2002, PACs have given over $250 million to congressional candidates. But PACs are not a dominant influence on candidates because they give rather little (often no more than $500). A small contribution is enough to ensure that a phone call to a member of Congress from a PAC sponsor will be returned but not enough, in most cases, to guarantee that the member will act as the PAC wishes.

Moreover, most money for congressional candidates still comes from individuals. But since the limit until 2002 was $1,000 per election (a limit set in the early 1970s), candidates had to devise clever ways of reaching a lot of individuals to raise the amount of money they needed. This usually meant direct-mail and telephone solicitations. If you are bothered by constant appeals for campaign funds, remember—that's what the law requires.

How Things Work

Major Federal Campaign Finance Rules

General

- All federal election contributions and expenditures are reported to a Federal Election Commission.
- All contributions over $100 must be disclosed, with name, address, and occupation of contributor.
- No *cash* contributions over $100 or foreign contributions.
- No ceiling on how much candidates may spend out of their own money (unless they accept federal funding for a presidential race).

Individual Contributions

- An individual may not give more than $2,000 to any candidate in any election.
- An individual may not make federal political gifts exceeding $95,000 every two years, of which only $37,500 may go to candidates.

Political Action Committees (PACs)

- Each corporation, union, or association may establish one.
- A PAC must register six months in advance, have at least 50 contributors, and give to at least five candidates.
- PAC contributions may not exceed $5,000 per candidate per election or $15,000 to a national political party.

Ban on Soft Money

- No corporation or union may give money from its own treasury to any national political party.

Independent Expenditures

- Corporations, unions, and associations may use their own money to fund "electioneering communications." PACs may fund electioneering communications up to their expenditure limits.

Presidential Primaries

- Federal matching funds can be given to match individual contributions of $250 or less.
- To be eligible, a candidate must raise $5,000 in each of 20 states in contributions of $250 or less.

Presidential Election

- The federal government will pay all campaign costs (up to a legal limit) of major-party candidates and part of the costs of minor-party candidates (those winning between 5 and 25 percent of the vote).

Figure 10.2

Growth of PACs 1979–2010

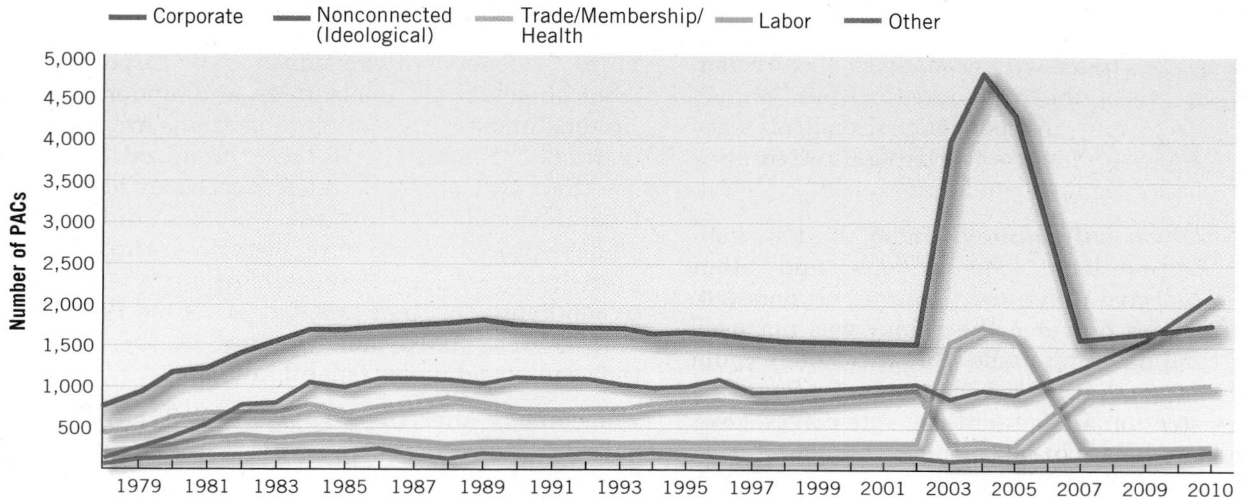

Source: Federal Election Commission.

By contrast, when George McGovern ran against Richard Nixon in 1972, he was chiefly supported by the large contributions of one wealthy donor, and when Eugene McCarthy ran against Lyndon Johnson in 1968, he benefited from a few big donations and did not have to rely on massive fundraising appeals.

A candidate gets federal money to match, dollar for dollar, what he or she has raised in contributions of $250 or less. But a presidential candidate can decide to forgo federal primary funding and raise his or her own money. In 2000, George W. Bush relied entirely on his own fundraising, while his chief rival, John McCain, used federal matching funds. In 2004, Bush, Kerry, and Dean all declined federal matching funds in the primary elections. In 2008, John McCain declined public financing for the primaries but accepted it for the general election; Barack Obama relied entirely on his own fundraising for both the primaries and the general election.

If you are a minor-party candidate, you can get some support from the federal government provided you have won at least 5 percent of the vote in the last election. In 2000, both Pat Buchanan (Reform party) and Ralph Nader (Green party) got partial support from Washington because their parties had won more than 5 percent of the vote in 1996. But no minor party won more than 5 percent in either 2004 or 2008, so none received partial support.

independent expenditures Spending by political action committees, corporations, or labor unions to help a party or candidate but done independently of them.

soft money Funds obtained by political parties that are spent on party activities, such as get-out-the-vote drives, but not on behalf of a specific candidate.

The 1973 campaign finance law produced two problems. The first was **independent expenditures.** A PAC, a corporation, or a labor union could spend whatever it wanted supporting or opposing a candidate, so long as this spending was "independent," that is, not coordinated with or made at the direction of the candidate's wishes. Simply put, independent expenditures are ordinary advertising directed at or against candidates.

The second was **soft money.** Under the law, individuals, corporations, labor unions, and other groups could give unlimited amounts of money to political parties provided the money was not used to back candidates by name. But the money could be used in ways that helped candidates by financing voter registration and get-out-the-vote drives. Over half a billion dollars in soft money was spent during each of the last three presidential campaigns (2000, 2004, 2008).

A SECOND CAMPAIGN FINANCE LAW

Reform is a tricky word. We like to think it means fixing something gone wrong. But some reforms can make matters worse. For example, the campaign finance reforms enacted in the early 1970s helped matters in some ways by ensuring that all campaign contributors would be identified by name. But they made things worse in other ways by, for example, requiring candidates to raise small sums from many donors. This made it harder for challengers to run (incumbents are much better known and raise more money) and easier for wealthy candidates to run because, under the law as interpreted by the Supreme Court, candidates can spend as much of their own money as they want.

After the 2000 campaign, a strong movement developed in Congress to reform the reforms of the 1970s. The result was the Bipartisan Campaign Finance Reform Act of 2002, which passed easily in the House and Senate and was signed by President Bush. After the 1970s laws were passed, the Supreme Court, in *Buckley v. Valeo* (424 U.S. 1, 1976), upheld federal limits on campaign contributions even as it ruled that spending money to influence elections is a form of constitutionally protected free speech (hence candidates were free to give unlimited amounts of money to their own campaigns). That precedent had pretty much held, but the new law made three important changes.

First, it banned "soft money" contributions to national political parties from corporations and unions. After the federal elections in 2002, no national party or party committee can accept soft money. Any money the national parties get must come from "hard money"—that is, individual donations or PAC contributions as limited by federal law.

Second, the limit on individual contributions was raised from $1,000 per candidate per election to $2,000.

Third, "independent expenditures" by corporations, labor unions, trade associations, and (under certain circumstances) nonprofit organizations are sharply restricted. Now none of these organizations can use their own money to refer to a clearly identified federal candidate in any advertisement during the 60 days preceding a general election or the 30 days preceding a primary contest. (PACs can still refer to candidates in their ads, but of course PACs are restricted to "hard money"—that is, the amount they can spend under federal law.)

Immediately after the law was signed, critics filed suit in federal court claiming it was unconstitutional. The suit brought together a number of organizations that rarely work together, such as the American

The 2010 Elections

Just four years after they regained control of Congress, Democrats faced devastating results in the 2010 midterm elections. They lost more than 60 seats and majority control in the House, and they narrowly kept control of the Senate (though they already had lost their filibuster-proof majority after a special race in January 2010). What happened?

Although President Barack Obama was not running for election in 2010, many viewed the congressional election results as a referendum on his first two years in office. Exit polls showed that voters were concerned about what the White House and Congress were doing—Obama's popularity had dropped below 50 percent before the elections, and Congress's approval ratings were just half of that. Despite Obama's success in enacting his top policy priority, health care reform, less than 20 percent of voters viewed health care as the country's top priority, while more than 60 percent said the economy was the most important issue. Nearly 90 percent said they were concerned about the direction of the economy in the coming year.

Additionally, the youth voters who turned out in high numbers for Obama in 2008 did not return to the polls as strongly in 2010. Only about one-tenth of voters were in the 18–29 age group, while more than two-thirds of voters were 44 and older. So-called "swing" voters—those who will shift party loyalties and thus can be decisive in an election—including women, independents, and suburban voters, largely voted for Republican candidates. Voters were roughly divided over whether the next generation would fare better than its predecessors.

The Tea Party movement, which gained traction in 2009 by opposing the White House's stimulus package and calling for major reductions in government spending, also played a role in the 2010 elections. About 4 in 10 voters expressed support for the movement, with the overwhelming majority of those voters in the Republican Party. Candidates with Tea Party support won key Senate races in Wisconsin and Kentucky, as well as the gubernatorial race in South Carolina. But Tea Party candidates also suffered major losses in states where they had prevailed in Republican primaries and subsequently gained significant national attention, including Delaware and Nevada.

After the 2010 elections, Obama famously admitted in a press conference that his party had suffered a "shellacking," and he promised to pursue bipartisanship more vigorously in the rest of his term. But as the president prepared to run for reelection, he faced the challenge of working with the opposition party while campaigning to keep his most faithful supporters and draw in independents who had turned away from the Democrats in 2010. The delicate balance of campaigning and governing would be critical in 2012, with the president's name on the ballot.

Sources: National Public Radio, "2010 Exit Polls: What Happened Election Night"; CNN exit polls; Clint Hendler, "Six Nuggets from the 2010 Exit Polls: Who Voted for Whom, and What Did They Think?," *Columbia Journalism Review*, November 3, 2010; ABC News, "Which Tea Party Candidates Won?"; PBS NewsHour, "Obama on Midterm Shellacking: 'It Feels Bad,'" November 3, 2010.

Civil Liberties Union and the National Right to Life Committee. The suit claimed that the ban on independent spending that "refers to" clearly identified candidates 60 days before an election is unconstitutional because it is an abridgement of the right of free speech. Under the law, an organization need not even endorse or oppose a candidate; it is enough that it mention a politician. This means that 60 days before an election, an organization cannot say it "supports (or opposes) a bill proposed by Congresswoman Pelosi."

Newspapers, magazines, and radio and television stations are not affected by the law, so they can say whatever they want for or against a candidate. One way of evaluating the law is to observe that it shifts influence away from businesses and unions and toward the media.

In *McConnell v. Federal Election Commission* (2002), the Supreme Court decided to uphold almost all of the law. As we saw in Chapter 5, it rejected the argument of those who claimed that speech requires money and decided it was no violation of the free speech provisions of the First Amendment to eliminate the ability of corporations and labor unions (and the organizations that use their money) to even *mention* a candidate for federal office for 60 days before the national election. In 2007, however, the Court

Table 10.4 2010 Congressional Exit Poll Results

	Voted for Democrat (D)	Voted for Republican (R)
SEX		
Male 48% of Respondents	44%	56%
Female 52% of Respondents	49	51
RACE AND ETHNICITY		
White 72% of Respondents	40	60
Black 12% of Respondents	85	15
Hispanic/Latino 8% of Respondents	54	46
Asian 3% of Respondents	50	50
Other 5% of Respondents	50	50
AGE		
18–29 17% of Respondents	54	46
30–44 29% of Respondents	46	54
45–64 39% of Respondents	46	54
65+ 15% of Respondents	42	58
EDUCATION		
No high school diploma 22% of Respondents	48	52
High school graduate 20% of Respondents	46	54
Some college/assoc. degree 21% of Respondents	45	55
College graduate 21% of Respondents	46	54
Postgraduate study 16% of Respondents	48	52
RELIGION		
Protestant/Other Christian 35% of Respondents	45	55
Catholic 12% of Respondents	49	51
Jewish 11% of Respondents	46	54
Something Else 29% of Respondents	47	53
None 13% of Respondents	49	51
APPROVE/DISAPPROVE OF HOW OBAMA IS DOING HIS JOB		
Approve 42% of Respondents	73%	27%
Disapprove 53% of Respondents	26%	74%
APPROVE/DISAPPROVE OF HOW CONGRESS IS DOING ITS JOB		
Approve 54% of Respondents	46%	54%
Disapprove 41% of Respondents	45%	55%
FEELING ABOUT TEA PARTY MOVEMENT		
Support 41% of Respondents	11%	86%
Neutral 24% of Respondents	47%	50%
Oppose 30% of Respondents	86%	12%
WHICH OF FOUR ISSUES IS THE MOST IMPORTANT FACING THE COUNTRY		
The War in Afghanistan 7% of Respondents	58%	40%
Health Care 18% of Respondents	51%	47%
The Economy 63% of Respondents	43%	54%
Illegal Immigration 8% of Respondents	26%	68%

Source: ABC News/Politics 2010 National Exit Poll, November 2, 2010, reporting data on more than 17,000 respondents.

backed away from this view. An ad by a right-to-life group urged people to write to Senator Russell Feingold to convince him to vote for certain judicial nominees, but it did not tell people how to vote. The Court decided this was "issue advocacy" protected by the First Amendment and so could not be banned by the McCain-Feingold law. Three years later, the Court narrowly decided, in a 5-4 decision, to overturn the ban on corporate and union funding of campaign ads.

If the past is any guide, neither recent changes nor the existing legal maze will do much to keep individuals, PACs, party leaders, and others from funding the candidates they favor. Nor should we be surprised if groups continue to steer contributions much as one might expect.

For instance, PACs dedicated to a party, a policy position, or a cause (for example, pro-choice PACs that favor Democrats and pro-life PACs that favor Republicans) generally do not change how they give to candidates depending on who is in power. By contrast, trade and corporate PAC money tends to follow power: after the Democrats regained the House in 2006, scores of trade and corporate PACs started giving Democrats far more money and Republicans far less. The Wine and Spirits Wholesalers PAC gave 23 percent of its money to Democrats in 2005 and 65 percent of its money to Democrats in 2007; the Home Depot Inc. PAC gave 13 percent of its money to Democrats in 2005 and 46 percent of its money to Democrats in 2007—and so it went for numerous other trade or corporate PACs (see Table 10.5 for a list of the top 20 PAC contributors in 2009–2010). With the Republican Party winning control of the House in 2010, shifts in PAC spending will happen again.

NEW SOURCES OF MONEY

If money is, indeed, the mother's milk of politics, efforts to make the money go away are not likely to work. The Bipartisan Campaign Reform Act, once enforced, immediately stimulated people to find other ways to spend political money.

527 organizations Organizations under section 527 of the Internal Revenue Code that raise and spend money to advance political causes.

The most common were **527 organizations.** These groups, named after a provision of the

Table 10.5 Top 20 PAC Contributors to Candidates, 2009–10

PAC Name	Total Amount	Democratic	Republican
National Assn of Realtors	$3,791,296	55%	44%
Honeywell International	$3,654,700	54	45
National Beer Wholesalers Assn	$3,300,000	53	47
AT&T Inc.	$3,262,375	45	55
Intl Brotherhood of Electrical Workers	$2,993,373	98	2
American Bankers Assn	$2,880,154	32	68
American Assn for Justice	$2,820,500	97	3
Operating Engineers Union	$2,799,220	88	11
National Auto Dealers Assn	$2,483,400	44	55
International Assn of Fire Fighters	$2,372,500	82	18
Credit Union National Assn	$2,367,846	57	43
American Federation of Teachers	$2,361,250	99	0
Teamsters Union	$2,330,900	97	2
American Fedn of St/Cty/Mun Employees	$2,314,000	99	0
Carpenters & Joiners Union	$2,275,375	88	12
Laborers Union	$2,220,500	96	4
Boeing Co	$2,215,000	53	47
National Education Assn	$2,169,800	95	4
American Crystal Sugar	$2,147,500	68	32
National Assn of Home Builders	$2,131,000	37%	63%

Source: Center for Responsive Politics, based on FEC data.

Internal Revenue Code, are designed to permit the kind of soft money expenditures once made by political parties. In 2004, the Democrats created the Media Fund, America Coming Together, America Votes, and many other groups. George Soros, the wealthy businessman, gave more than $23 million to organizations pledged to defeat George Bush. The Republicans responded by creating Progress for America, The Leadership Forum, America for Job Security, and other groups. Under the law, as it is now interpreted, 527 organizations can spend their money on politics so long as they do not coordinate with a candidate or lobby directly for that person. In 2004, 527 organizations raised and spent over one-third of a billion dollars. So far, the lesson seems to be this: campaign finance laws are not likely to take money out of politics.

MONEY AND WINNING

In the general election for president, money does not make much difference, because both major-party candidates have the same amount, contributed by the federal government. During peacetime, presidential elections usually are decided by three things: political party affiliation, the state of the economy, and the character of the candidates.

For all the talk about voting for "the person, not the party," history teaches that at least 80 percent of the presidential vote will go to the candidates of the two main parties. This means that a presidential election will normally be decided by the 20 percent of voters who cannot be counted on to vote either Democratic or Republican.

In good economic times, the party holding the White House normally does well; in poor times, it does badly. This is sometimes called the "pocketbook vote." But it is not clear whose pocketbook determines how a person will vote. Many who are doing well financially will vote against the party in power if the country as a whole is not doing well. A person doing well may have friends or family members who are doing poorly. Or the well-off voter may think that if the country is doing poorly, he or she will soon feel the pinch by losing a job or losing customers.

Voters also care about character, and so some money from presidential campaign coffers goes to fund "character ads." *Character* here means several things: Is the candidate honest and reliable? Does the candidate think as the voter thinks about social issues such as crime, abortion, and school prayer? Does the candidate act presidential? Acting presidential seems to mean being an effective speaker, displaying dignity and compassion, sounding like someone who can take charge and get things done, and coming across consistently as a reasonable, likable person. Rash, disagreeable extremists need not apply.

Landmark Cases

Financing Elections

- ***Buckley v. Valeo* (1976):** Held that a law limiting contributions to political campaigns was constitutional but that one restricting a candidate's expenditures of his or her own money was not.
- ***McConnell v. Federal Election Commission* (2002):** Upheld 2002 Bipartisan Campaign Reform Act (popularly known as "McCain-Feingold" law) prohibiting corporations and labor unions from running ads that mention candidates and their positions for 60 days before a federal general election.
- ***Federal Election Commission v. Wisconsin Right to Life, Inc.* (2007):** Held that issue ads may not be prohibited before a primary or general election.
- ***Citizens United v. Federal Election Commission* (2010):** Overturned part of 2002 law that had prohibited corporate and union funding of campaign ads.

Since both major candidates usually get the same amount of federal money for the general election campaign, money does not make much of a difference in determining the winner. Other factors that also do not make a difference include the following:

- *Vice-presidential nominee:* There has rarely been an election in which his or her identity has made a difference.
- *Political reporting:* It may make a difference in some elections, but not in presidential ones.
- *Religion:* Being a Catholic was once a barrier, but since John F. Kennedy was elected president in 1960, this is no longer true. Still, no president or vice president to date has had a non-Christian religious affiliation (though some have had no religious affiliation at all).
- *Abortion:* This probably affects who gets a party's nomination, but in the general election ardent supporters and ardent opponents are about evenly balanced.

In congressional races, however, in general it seems that money does make a decisive difference. Scholars are not entirely agreed on the facts, but strong evidence suggests that how much the challenger spends is most important, because the challenger usually must become known to the public. Buying name recognition is expensive. Gary Jacobson has shown that, other things being equal, in every congressional election from 1972 to the mid-1980s, challengers who spent more money did better than those who spent less.[18] Jacobson also suggested that how much the incumbents spent was not very important, presumably because they already had all the name recognition they needed (as well as the other benefits of holding office, such as free mail and travel). Other scholars, applying different statistical methods to the same facts, have come to different conclusions. It now seems that, other things being equal, high-spending incumbents do better than low-spending ones.[19] "Million-dollar challengers" are becoming more common in House races, but it remains to be seen if that will continue, and if so, whether it narrows the gap with incumbents.

Incumbents find it easier to raise money than challengers; incumbents provide services to their districts that challengers cannot; incumbents regularly send free ("franked") mail to their constituents, while challengers must pay for their mailings; incumbents can get free publicity by sponsoring legislation or conducting an investigation. Thus, it is hardly surprising that incumbents who run for reelection win in the overwhelming majority of races.

How We Compare

Public Funding for National Political Campaigns

In the United States, national political campaigns are funded primarily through private donations by individuals, political parties, and interest groups. Only presidential campaigns are eligible to receive public funding, and even there, candidates may decide not to accept the funds so they are not restricted by a federal cap on spending. Despite efforts to regulate campaign contributions since the 1970s, American democracy has a longstanding tradition of applying the First Amendment protection of free speech to campaign spending, a position recently endorsed by the Supreme Court. Other advanced industrialized democracies take a different view.

Many democracies around the world rely much more heavily on public funding for elections than the United States, and have stricter regulations on campaign contributions and expenditures. Australia, Germany, France, and Israel all provide public funds for political campaigns, typically granting funds to parties that received a certain percentage of votes in the previous election. France and the United Kingdom ban paid political ads, and both countries as well as Israel provide free broadcasting time for candidates. All three countries also impose limits on campaign spending.

How do campaign finance rules affect elections? In many ways, campaigns in the United States run much longer than in other democracies—the countries listed above typically hold national elections in about six weeks, whereas the 2008 presidential race in the United States began two years earlier. This is because public funding typically strengthens political parties, whose leaders decide which candidates they will support. Unlimited campaign contributions may permit relatively unknown candidates to prevail in party nominating contests without initial support from the top leadership. But winning requires time and money in the United States, and the financial costs increase in every election cycle. Is money a form of free speech? Democracies disagree.

Sources: Law Library of Congress, "Campaign Finance: Comparative Summary;" Brennan Center for Justice, "Breaking Free with Fair Elections: A New Declaration of Independence," March 2007; Debate between Bradley Smith and Thomas E. Mann, "Campaign Finance Reloaded," *Los Angeles Times*, July 2007.

What Decides the Election?

To the voter, it all seems quite simple—he or she votes for "the best person" or maybe "the least-bad person." To scholars, it is all a bit mysterious. How do voters decide who the best person is? What does "best" mean, anyway?

PARTY

One answer to these questions is party identification. People may say they are voting for the "best person," but for many people the best person is always a Democrat or a Republican. Moreover, we have seen in Chapter 7 that many people know rather little about the details of political issues. They may not even know what position their favored candidate has taken on issues the voters care about. Given these facts, many scholars have argued that party identification is the principal determinant of how people vote.[20]

If it were only a matter of party identification, though, the Democrats would always win the presidency, since usually more people identify with the Democratic than the Republican party. But we know that the Democrats lost seven of the 11 presidential elections between 1968 and 2008. There are three reasons for this.

First, those people who consider themselves Democrats were less firmly wedded to their party than Republicans. Table 10.6 shows how people identifying themselves as Democrats, Republicans, or independents voted in presidential elections from 1960 to 2008. In every election except 1992, at least 80 percent of Republican voters supported the Republican candidate in each election. By contrast, there have been more defections among Democratic

Table 10.6 Percentage of Popular Vote by Groups in Presidential Elections, 1960–2008

		National	Republicans	Democrats	Independents
1960	Kennedy	50%	5%	84%	43%
	Nixon	50	95	16	57
1964	Johnson	61	20	87	56
	Goldwater	39	80	13	44
1968	Humphrey	43	9	74	31
	Nixon	43	86	12	44
	Wallace	14	5	14	25
1972	McGovern	38	5	67	31
	Nixon	62	95	33	69
1976	Carter	51	11	80	48
	Ford	49	89	20	52
1980[a]	Carter	41	11	66	30
	Reagan	51	84	26	54
	Anderson	7	4	6	12
1984	Mondale	41	7	73	35
	Reagan	59	92	26	63
1988	Dukakis	46	8	82	43
	Bush	54	91	17	55
1992	Clinton	43	10	77	38
	Bush	38	73	10	32
	Perot	19	17	13	30
1996	Clinton	49	13	84	43
	Dole	41	80	10	35
	Perot	8	6	5	17
2000	Gore	49	8	86	45
	Bush	48	91	11	47
2004	Kerry	49	6	89	49
	Bush	51	93	11	48
2008	Obama	52	9	89	52
	McCain	46	89	10	44

[a]The figures for 1980, 1984, 1988, and 1996 fail to add up to 100 percent because of missing data.

voters—in 1972, a third of Democrats supported Nixon, and in 1984, 26 percent supported Reagan.

The second reason, also clear from Table 10.6, is that the Republicans did much better than the Democrats among the self-described "independent" voters. In the dozen presidential elections since 1960, the Democratic candidate won a large share of the independent vote five times (1964, 1992, 1996, 2004, and 2008) while the Republican candidate won it seven times (1968, 1972, 1976, 1980, 1984, 1988, and 2000).

Finally, a higher percentage of Republicans than Democrats vote in elections. In every presidential contest in the past 34 years, those describing themselves as "strongly Republican" have been more likely to vote than those describing themselves as "strongly Democratic."

ISSUES, ESPECIALLY THE ECONOMY

Even though voters may not know a lot about the issues, that does not mean issues play no role in elections or that voters respond irrationally to them. For example, V. O. Key, Jr., looked at those voters who switched from one party to another between elections and found that most of them switched in a direction consistent with their own interests. As Key put it, the voters are not fools.[21]

Moreover, voters may know a lot more than we suppose about issues that really matter to them. They may have hazy, even erroneous, views about monetary policy, business regulation, and the trade deficit, but they likely have a very good idea about whether unemployment is up or down, prices at the supermarket are stable or rising, or crime is a problem in their neighborhoods. And on some issues—such as abortion, school prayer, and race relations—they likely have some strong principles they want to see politicians obey.

Contrary to what we learn in our civics classes, representative government does not require voters to be well informed on the issues. If it were our duty as citizens to have accurate facts and sensible ideas about how best to negotiate with foreign adversaries, stabilize the value of the dollar, revitalize failing industries, and keep farmers prosperous, we might as well forget about citizenship and head for the beach. It would be a full-time job, and then some, to be a citizen. Politics would take on far more importance in our lives than most of us would want, given our need to earn a living and our belief in the virtues of limited government.

To see why our system can function without well-informed citizens, we must understand the differences between two ways in which issues can affect elections.

Prospective Voting

Prospective means "forward-looking"—we vote prospectively when we examine the views the rival candidates have on the issues of the day and then cast our ballots for the person we think has the best ideas for handling these matters. **Prospective voting** requires a lot of information about issues and candidates. Some of us vote prospectively. Those who do tend to be political junkies. They are either willing to spend a lot of time learning about issues or are so concerned about some big issue (abortion, school busing, nuclear energy) that all they care about is how a candidate stands on that question.

Prospective voting is more common among people who are political activists, have a political ideology that governs their voting decision, or are involved in interest groups with a big stake in the election. They are a minority of all voters, but (as we saw in Chapters 7 and 8) they are more influential than their numbers would suggest. Some prospective voters (by no means all) are organized into single-issue groups, to be discussed in the next section.

Retrospective Voting

Retrospective means "backward-looking"—**retrospective voting** involves looking at how things have gone in the recent past and then voting for the party that controls the White House if we like what has happened and voting against that party if we do not like what has happened. Retrospective voting does not require us to have a lot of information—all we need to know is whether things have, in our view, gotten better or worse.

prospective voting Voting for a candidate because you favor his or her ideas for handling issues.

retrospective voting Voting for a candidate because you like his or her past actions in office.

Elections are decided by retrospective voters.[22] In 1980, they decided to vote against Jimmy Carter because inflation was rampant, interest rates were high, and we seemed to be getting the worst of things overseas. The evidence suggests rather clearly that they did not vote *for* Ronald Reagan; they voted for *an alternative to* Jimmy Carter. (Some people did vote for Reagan and his philosophy; they were voting prospectively, but they were in the minority.) In 1984, people voted for Ronald Reagan because unemployment, inflation, and interest rates were down and because we no longer seemed to be getting pushed around overseas. In 1980, retrospective voters wanted change; in 1984, they wanted continuity. In 1988, there was no incumbent running, but George H. W. Bush portrayed himself as the candidate who would continue the policies that had led to prosperity and depicted Michael Dukakis as a "closet liberal" who would change those policies. In 1992, the economy had once again turned sour, and so voters turned away from Bush and toward his rivals, Bill Clinton and Ross Perot.

Though most incumbent members of Congress get reelected, those who lose do so, it appears, largely because they are the victims of retrospective voting. After Reagan was first elected, the economy went into a recession in 1981–1982. As a result, Republican members of Congress were penalized by the voters, and Democratic challengers were helped. But it is not just the economy that can hurt congressional candidates. In most midterm elections, the party holding the White House has lost seats in Congress. Just why this should be is not entirely clear, but it probably has something to do with the tendency of some voters to change their opinions of the presidential party once that party has had a chance to govern—which is to say, a chance to make some mistakes, disappoint some supporters, and irritate some interests.

Some scholars believe that retrospective voting is based largely on economic conditions. Figure 10.3 certainly provides support for this view. Each dot represents a presidential election (16 of them, from 1948 to 2008). The horizontal axis is the percentage increase or decrease in per capita disposable income (adjusted for inflation) during the election year. The vertical axis is the percentage of the two-party vote won by the party already occupying the White House. You can see that, as per capita income goes up (as you move to the right on the horizontal axis), the incumbent political party tends to win a bigger share of the vote.

Figure 10.3
The Economy and Vote for President 1948–2008

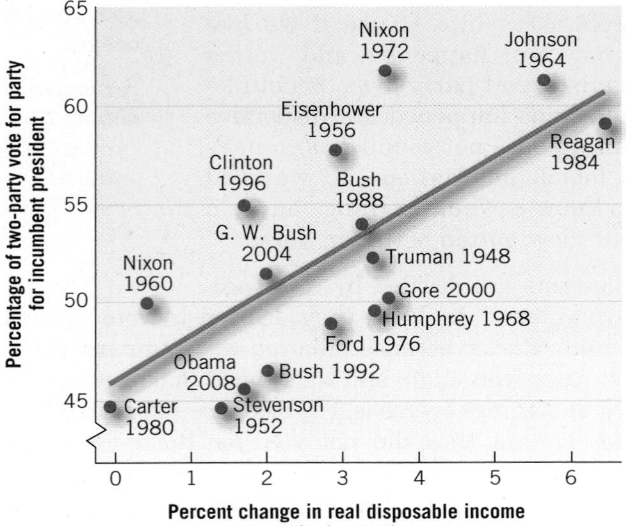

Notes: (1) Each dot represents a presidential election, showing the popular vote received by the incumbent president's party. (2) 1992 data do not include votes for independent candidate H. Ross Perot. (3) 2004 value on RDI is projection from data available in December 2004.

Source: From *American Public Opinion*, 5th ed., by Robert S. Erikson and Kent L. Tedin. Copyright © 1995 by Addison-Wesley Educational Publishers, Inc. Reprinted by permission of Pearson Education, Inc. 2008 update from Bureau of Economic Analysis, U.S. Department of Commerce.

Other scholars feel that matters are more complicated than this. As a result, a small industry has grown up consisting of people who use different techniques to forecast the outcome of elections. If you know how the president stands in the opinion polls several months before the election and how well the economy is performing, you can make a pretty good guess as to who is going to win the presidency. For congressional races, predicting the result is a lot tougher because so many local factors affect these contests. Election forecasting remains an inexact science. As one study of the performance of presidential election forecasting models concluded: "Models may be no improvement over pundits."[23]

THE CAMPAIGN

If party loyalty and national economic conditions play so large a role in elections, is the campaign just sound and fury, signifying nothing?

No. Campaigns can make a difference in three ways. First, they reawaken the partisan loyalties of voters. Right after a party's nominating convention selects a presidential candidate, that person's standing with voters of both parties goes way up in the polls. The reason is that the just-nominated candidate has received a lot of media attention during the summer months, when not much else is happening. When the campaign gets under way, however, both candidates get publicity, and voters return to their normal Democratic or Republican affiliations.

Second, campaigns give voters a chance to watch how the candidates handle pressure, and they give candidates a chance to apply that pressure. The two rivals, after promising to conduct a campaign "on the issues" without mudslinging, immediately start searching each other's personal histories and records to find acts, statements, or congressional votes that can be shown in the worst possible light in newspaper or television ads. Many voters don't like these "negative ads"—but they work. Careful statistical studies based on actual campaigns (as opposed to voter surveys or laboratory-like focus group studies) suggest that negative ads work by stimulating voter turnout.[24] As a result, every politician constantly

AP Images

Union members were once heavily Democratic, but since Ronald Reagan began winning white union votes in 1980, these votes have been up for grabs.

worries about how an opponent might portray his or her record, a fact that helps explain why so many politicians never do or say anything that cannot be explained in a 30-second television spot.

Third, campaigns allow voters an opportunity to judge the character and core values of the candidates. Most voters don't study in detail a candidate's positions on issues; even if they had the time, they know you can't predict how politicians will behave just from knowing what a campaign manager has written in a position paper. The voters want some guidance as to how a candidate will behave once elected. They get that guidance by listening not to the details of what a candidate says but to the themes and tone of those statements. Is the candidate tough on crime and drugs? Are his or her statements about the environment sincere or perfunctory? Does the candidate favor having a strong military? Does the candidate care more about not raising taxes or more about helping the homeless?

The desire of voters to discern character, combined with the mechanics of modern campaigning—short radio and television ads and computer-targeted direct mail—lend themselves to an emphasis on themes at the expense of details. This tendency is reinforced by the expectations of ideological party activists and single-issue groups.

Thematic campaigning, negative ads, and the demands of single-issue groups are not new; they are as old as the republic. In the 19th century, the theme was slavery and the single-issue groups were abolitionists and their opponents; their negative ads make the ones we have today sound like Sunday school sermons. At the turn of the century, the themes were temperance and the vote for women; both issues led to no-holds-barred, rough-and-tumble campaigning. In the 1970s and 1980s, new themes were advanced by fundamentalist Christians and by pro- and antiabortion groups.

What has changed is not the tone of campaigning but the advent of primary elections. Once, political parties picked candidates out of a desire to win elections. Today, activists and single-issue groups influence the selection of candidates, sometimes out of a belief that it is better to lose with the "right" candidate than to win with the wrong one. In a five-candidate primary, a minority of the voters can pick the winner. Single-issue groups can make a big difference under these conditions, even though they may not have much influence in the general election.

FINDING A WINNING COALITION

Putting together a winning electoral coalition means holding on to your base among committed partisans and attracting the swing voters who cast their ballots in response to issues (retrospectively or prospectively) and personalities.

There are two ways to examine the nature of the parties' voting coalitions. One is to ask what percentage of various identifiable groups in the population

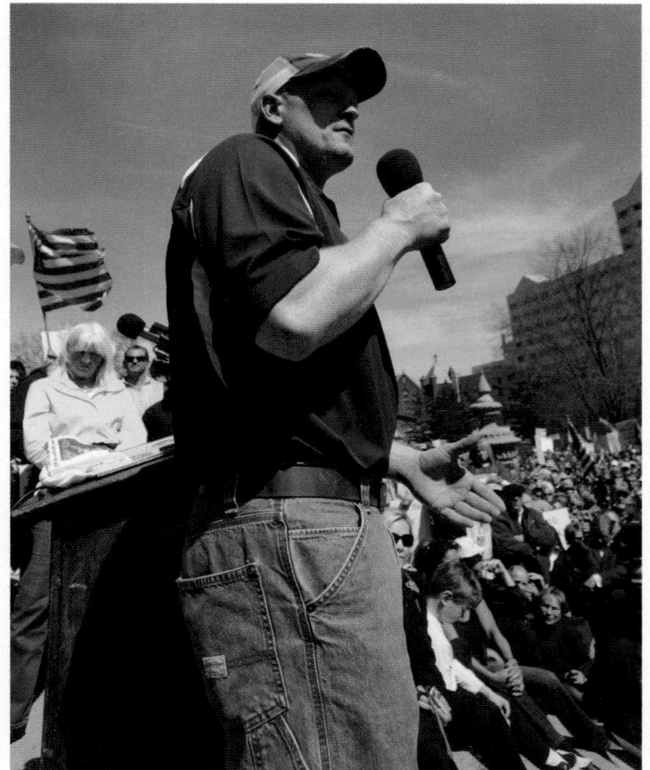
AP Images

At a public meeting, Samuel Joseph Wurzelbacher challenged Barack Obama on his tax plan and quickly became known as "Joe the Plumber."

supported the Democratic or Republican candidate for president. The other is to ask what proportion of a party's total vote came from each of these groups. The answer to the first question tells us how *loyal* African Americans, farmers, union members, and others are to the Democratic or Republican party or candidate; the answer to the second question tells us how *important* each group is to a candidate or party.

For the Democratic coalition, African Americans are the most loyal voters. In every election but one since 1952, two-thirds or more of all African Americans voted Democratic; since 1964, four-fifths have gone Democratic. Usually, Jewish voters are almost as solidly Democratic. Most Hispanics have been Democrats, though the label "Hispanic" conceals differences among Cuban Americans (who often vote Republican) and Mexican Americans and Puerto Ricans (who are strongly Democratic). The turnout among most Hispanic groups has been quite low (many are not yet citizens), so their political power is not equivalent to their numbers.

The Democrats have lost their once strong hold on Catholics, southerners, and union members. In 1960, Catholics supported John F. Kennedy (a Democrat and fellow Catholic), but they also voted for Eisenhower, Nixon, and Reagan—all Republicans. Union members deserted the Democrats in 1968 and 1972, came back in 1980 and 1988, and divided about evenly between the two parties in 1952, 1956, and 1980. White southerners have voted Republican in national elections but Democratic in many local ones (see Table 10.7).

Table 10.7 Who Likes the Democrats?

	1968[a]	1972	1976	1980[c]	1984	1988	1992[d]	1996	2000	2004	2008
Percentage of various groups saying they voted for the Democratic presidential candidate, 1964–2008											
Sex											
Men	41%	37%	53%	37%	37%	41%	41%	43%	42%	45%	49%
Women	45	38	48	45	42	49	46	54	54	52	56
Race											
White	38	32	46	36	34	40	39	43	42	42	43
Nonwhite	85	87	85	82	90	86	82	84	90	89	95
Education											
College	37	37	42	35	40	43	44	47	45	47	50
Graduate school	52	49	58	43	49	56	55	52	52	55	58
Age											
Under 30	47	48	53	43	41	47	44	53	48	54	66
50 and over	41	36	52	41[e]	39	49	50	48[g]	48	49	48
Religion											
Protestant	35	30	46	NA	NA	33[f]	33	36	42	41	45
Catholic	59	48	57	40	44	47	44	53	50	48	54
Jewish[b]	85	66	68	45	66	64	78	78	79	76	78
Southerners	31	29	54	47	36	41	42	46	NA	41	45

[a] 1968 election had three major candidates (Humphrey, Nixon, and Wallace).

[b] Jewish vote estimated from various sources; since the number of Jewish persons interviewed often is less than 100, the error in this figure, as well as that for nonwhites, may be large.

[c] 1980 election had three major candidates (Carter, Reagan, and Anderson).

[d] 1992 election had three major candidates (Clinton, Bush, and Perot).

[e] For 1980–1992, refers to age 60 and over.

[f] For 1988, white Protestants only.

[g] For 1996, refers to age 45 and over.

Sources: For 1964–1976: Gallup poll data, as tabulated in Jeane J. Kirkpatrick, "Changing Patterns of Electoral Competition," in *The New American Political System*, ed. Anthony King (Washington, D.C.: American Enterprise Institute, 1978), 254–256. For 1980–1992: Data from *New York Times*/CBS News exit polls. For 1996: *Congressional Quarterly Weekly Report*, 1997, p. 188. For 2000: Exit polls supplied by ABC News. For 2004 and 2008: CNN exit polls.

The Republican party often is described as the party of business and professional people. The loyalty of these groups to Republicans is strong: only in 1964 did they desert the Republican candidate to support Lyndon Johnson. Farmers usually have been Republican, but they are a volatile group, highly sensitive to the level of farm prices—and thus quick to change parties. In sum, the loyalty of most identifiable groups of voters to either party is not overwhelming. Only African Americans, businesspeople, and Jews usually give two-thirds or more of their votes to one party or the other; other groups display tendencies, but none that cannot be overcome.

The contribution that each of these groups makes to the party coalitions is a different matter. Though African Americans are overwhelmingly and persistently Democratic, they make up so small a portion of the total electorate that they have never accounted for more than a quarter of the total Democratic vote. The groups that make up the largest part of the Democratic vote—Catholics, union members, southerners—are also the least dependable parts of that coalition.[25]

When representatives of various segments of society make demands on party leaders and presidential

RESEARCH FRONTIERS

Candidate Positions Drive Voter Choices

When asked why they voted for one candidate over another, most people will say they chose the best person for the job. But how do voters decide who the "best person" is?

In a 2008 article, political scientists Michael Tomz and Robert P. Van Houweling address this question with surveys and other data regarding candidate positions and voter choice. Their focus is mainly on health care policy, but their research spans dozens of studies of how voters make decisions and tests three leading theories—proximity, discounting, and direction:

Proximity: Voters believe candidates will deliver on campaign pledges and prefer candidates whose positions on the issues are closest to their own.

Discounting: Doubting candidates will deliver on campaign pledges, voters discount pledges and prefer candidates who—whatever their positions—voters think might get something good done in government.

Direction: Voters see issues as essentially two-sided; prefer candidates who take their side or "direction"; and, given a choice between two candidates who are both on their side, will prefer the candidate whose position is most intense.

As Tomz and Van Houweling emphasize, each theory yields a different prediction about the relationship between candidate positioning and voter choice. For example, if a voter has a position on an issue (abortion, for example), but does not feel strongly about it (say the voter is moderately pro-choice), proximity theory predicts that the voter will choose the candidate closest to his or her position even if that candidate is on the opposite side (say a candidate who is moderately pro-life). Direction theory predicts that the voter will instead choose the competing candidate who advocates his or her side of the issue most intensely (say, a candidate who is very strongly pro-choice).

And the winner is?

Proximity: Tomz and Van Houweling find proximity voting about twice as common as discounting and four times as common as direction voting. Thus, a voter who favors a 5 percent increase in government spending on health care will most likely prefer a candidate who advocates much the same position.

- **Does that finding surprise you, and just how inclined are you to behave like a proximity voter?**
- **Do you strongly prefer candidates whose positions on the issues are closest to your own? Or might you vote for a candidate who—though he or she espouses positions at odds with your own—seems more likely than an opponent whose positions more nearly mirror your own to "get things done" in government?**
- **Do you think candidates who advocate extreme positions are more likely to stay committed if elected than candidates who advocate more moderate positions on the same issues?**
- **In sum, what most influences your way of deciding who is the "best person" for the job?**

Source: Michael Tomz and Robert P. Van Houweling, "Candidate Positioning and Voter Choice," *American Political Science Review* 102 (August 2008): 303–318.

candidates, they usually stress their numbers or their loyalty, but rarely both. African American leaders, for example, sometimes describe the black vote as of decisive importance to Democrats and thus deserving of special consideration from a Democratic president. But African Americans are so loyal that a Democratic candidate can almost take their votes for granted, and in any event they are not as numerous as other groups. Union leaders emphasize how many union voters there are, but a president will know that union leaders cannot "deliver" the union vote and that this vote may go to the president's opponent, whatever the leaders say. For any presidential candidate, a winning coalition must be put together anew for each election. Only a few voters can be taken for granted or written off as a lost cause.

The Effects of Elections on Policy

To the candidates, and perhaps to the voters, the only interesting outcome of an election is who won. To a political scientist, the interesting outcomes are the broad trends in winning and losing and what they imply about the attitudes of voters, the operation of the electoral system, the fate of political parties, and the direction of public policy.

Figure 10.4 shows the trend in the popular vote for president since before the Civil War. From 1876 to 1896, the Democrats and Republicans were hotly competitive. The Republicans won three times, the Democrats twice in close contests. Beginning in 1896, the Republicans became the dominant party, and except for 1912 and 1916, when Woodrow Wilson, a Democrat, was able to win owing to a split in the Republican party, the Republicans carried every presidential election until 1932. Then Franklin Roosevelt put together what has since become known as the "New Deal coalition," and the Democrats became the dominant party. They won every election until 1952, when Eisenhower, a Republican and a popular military hero, was elected for the first of his two terms. In the presidential elections since 1952, power has switched hands between the parties frequently.

Still, cynics complain that elections are meaningless: no matter who wins, crooks, incompetents, or self-serving politicians still hold office. The more charitable argue that elected officials usually are decent enough, but that public policy remains more or less the same no matter which official or party is in office.

There is no brief and simple response to this latter view. Much depends on which office or policy you examine. One reason it is so hard to generalize about the policy effects of elections is that the

Figure 10.4
Partisan Division of the Presidential Vote in the Nation, 1856–2008

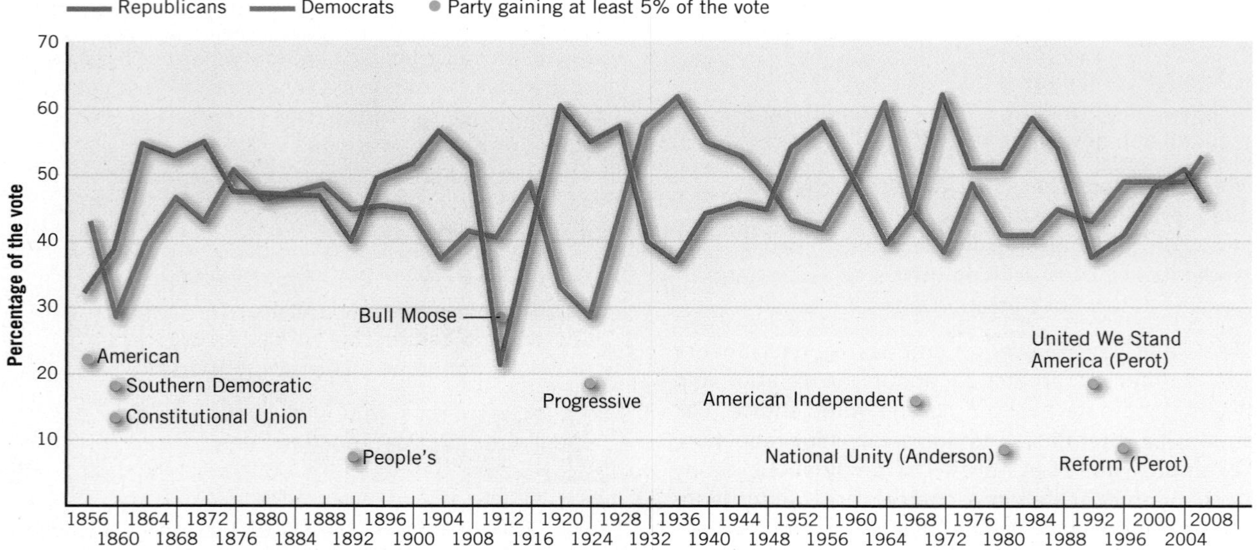

Sources: Information for 1856–1988, updated from Historical Data Archive, Inter-University Consortium for Political Research, as reported in William H. Flanigan and Nancy H. Zingale, *Political Behavior of the American Electorate*, 3rd ed., 32. For 1992: *World Almanac and Book of Facts 1994*, 73.

WHAT WOULD YOU DO?

MEMORANDUM

To: *Arjun Bruno, National party chairperson*

From: *Arlene Marcus, State party chairperson*

Subject: *Supporting a national primary*

In the past few election cycles, our state's role in the party nomination for president virtually has disappeared with a May primary date. Several states have leapfrogged ahead of us, and party leaders have indicated that they do not want any more states to move up their primary date. The national party needs to find a way to ensure that all states, large and small, have a real voice in nominating a presidential candidate.

News »

Would a National Primary Date Give All States an Equal Voice?

With the increasing cost and length of presidential nominating contests, several political strategists favor creating a single national primary date. But party leaders are divided over the consequences for candidates and voters.

Arguments for:

1. A single national primary permits equal participation by all states and presents a fair compromise with the increased number of delegates that larger states send to the national conventions, much like the compromises during the original constitutional debates.
2. The nominating process needs to be less costly, particularly when presidential candidates realistically need to raise $100 million a year before the general election to be competitive for the nomination. Holding all primaries and caucuses on a single day will reduce overall election expenses significantly.
3. If the American electorate knows presidential nominations will be decided by each party on one day, then they will be more likely to vote, a significant factor for elections in which, historically, fewer than 20 percent of eligible voters typically participate.

Arguments against:

1. Each state decides in conjunction with the national party when its primary or caucus will take place, and the federal system of government designed by the Framers did not guarantee that all states would be treated equally at all times.
2. A national primary would favor candidates with high name recognition and funding to further that recognition and would severely disadvantage lesser-known candidates within the party.
3. Even though the general election takes place on one day, voter turnout in the United States still is lower than in other advanced industrialized democracies, which suggests that other factors influence who participates.

Your decision:

Support national primary ____________________

Oppose national primary ____________________

offices to be filled by the voters are so numerous and the ability of the political parties to unite these officeholders behind a common policy is so weak that any policy proposal must run a gauntlet of potential opponents. Though we have but two major parties, and though only one party can win the presidency, each party is a weak coalition of diverse elements that reflect the many divisions in public opinion. The proponents of a new law must put together a majority coalition almost from scratch, and a winning coalition on one issue tends to be somewhat different—quite often dramatically different—from a winning coalition on another issue.

In a parliamentary system with strong parties, such as that in Great Britain, an election often can have a major effect on public policy. When the Labour party won office in 1945, it put several major industries under public ownership and launched a comprehensive set of social services, including a nationalized health care plan. Its ambitious and controversial campaign platform was converted, almost item by item, into law. When the Conservative party returned to power in 1951, it accepted some of these changes but rejected others (for example, it denationalized the steel industry).

American elections, unless accompanied by a national crisis such as a war or a depression, rarely produce changes of the magnitude of those that occurred in Britain in 1945. The constitutional system within which our elections take place was designed to moderate the pace of change—to make it neither easy nor impossible to adopt radical proposals. But the fact that the system is intended to moderate the rate of change does not mean it will always work that way.

The election of 1860 brought to national power a party committed to opposing the extension of slavery and southern secession; it took a bloody war to vindicate that policy. The election of 1896 led to the dominance of a party committed to high tariffs, a strong currency, urban growth, and business prosperity—a commitment that was not significantly altered until 1932. The election of that year led to the New Deal, which produced the greatest single enlargement of federal authority since 1860. The election of 1964 gave the Democrats such a large majority in Congress (as well as control of the presidency) that there began to issue forth an extraordinary number of new policies of sweeping significance—Medicare and Medicaid, federal aid to education and to local law enforcement, two dozen environmental and consumer protection laws, the Voting Rights Act of 1965, a revision of the immigration laws, and a new cabinet-level Department of Housing and Urban Development.

The election of 1980 brought into office an administration determined to reverse the direction of policy over the preceding half century. Reagan's administration succeeded in obtaining large tax cuts, significant reductions in spending (or in the rate of increase of spending) on some domestic programs, and changes in the policies of some regulatory agencies. The election of 1982, in which the Democrats made gains in the House of Representatives, stiffened congressional resistance to further spending cuts and stimulated renewed interest in tax increases as a way of reducing the deficit. Following the election of 1984, a major tax reform plan was passed. After the 1996 election, Clinton and Republican congressional leaders agreed on a plan to balance the budget.

In view of all these developments, it is hard to argue that the pace of change in our government is always slow or that elections never make a difference. Studies by scholars confirm that elections often are significant, despite the difficulty of getting laws passed. One analysis of about 1,400 promises made between 1944 and 1964 in the platforms of the two major parties revealed that 72 percent were put into effect.[26]

Another study examined the party platforms of the Democrats and Republicans from 1844 to 1968 and all the laws passed by Congress between 1789 and 1968. By a complex statistical method, the author of the study was able to show that during certain periods the differences between the platforms of the two parties were especially large (1856, 1880, 1896, 1932) and that there was at about the same time a high rate of change in the kinds of laws being passed.[27] This study supports the general impression conveyed by history that elections often can be central to important policy changes.

Why then do we so often think elections make little difference? It is because public opinion and the political parties enter a phase of consolidation and continuity between periods of rapid change. During this phase, the changes are digested, and party leaders adjust to the new popular consensus, which may (or may not) evolve around the merits of these changes. During the 1870s and 1880s, Democratic politicians had to come to terms with the failure of the southern secessionist movement and the abolition of slavery; during the 1900s, the Democrats had to adjust again, this time to the fact that national economic policy was going to support industrialization and urbanization, not farming; during the 1940s and 1950s, the Republicans had to learn to accept the popularity of the New Deal.

Elections in ordinary times are not "critical"—they do not produce any major party realignment, they are not fought out over a dominant issue, and they provide the winners with no clear mandate. In most cases, an election is little more than a retrospective judgment on the record of the incumbent president and the existing congressional majority. If times are good, incumbents win easily; if times are bad, incumbents may lose—even though their opponents may have no clear plans for change. But even a "normal" election can produce dramatic results if the winner is a person such as Ronald Reagan, who helped give his party a distinctive political philosophy, or Barack Obama, the nation's first African American president.

LEARNING OBJECTIVES

WHAT YOU NEED TO KNOW

☑ What is the difference between a primary election and a general election?

A primary election selects a political party's nominee for office, while a general election determines who will hold that office.

☑ Does the federal government provide funding for political campaigns?

The federal government does not fund congressional elections, but it does provide public funding for presidential candidates (and their party conventions), though candidates may choose not to accept public funds and raise unlimited funding on their own, as happened in 2008.

☑ How do voters typically decide on a candidate?

Voters typically evaluate an incumbent's performance and vote for reelection if they are pleased; if not, then they cast a vote against the incumbent, but that may not necessarily mean they endorse the opponent's platform. Evaluating an incumbent's term is retrospective voting, while trying to determine how a candidate will act in office is prospective voting.

RECONSIDERING WHO GOVERNS?

1. How do American elections determine the kind of people who govern us?

American democracy rewards candidates who have personal appeal rather than party endorsements. Politics here produces individualists who usually have a strong ideological orientation toward liberal or conservative causes, but only a weak sense of loyalty to the political parties who endorse those ideologies.

2. What matters most in deciding who wins presidential and congressional elections?

The party identification of the voters matters the most. Only 10 to 20 percent of the voters are available to have their votes changed. For them, the state of the economy, and in wartime the success or failures we have while fighting abroad, make the most difference. Closely allied with those issues, at least for presidential candidates, is the voters' assessment of their character.

RECONSIDERING TO WHAT ENDS?

1. Do elections make a real difference in what laws get passed?

Yes. During campaigns parties may try to sound alike, in order to attract centrist voters, but when in office they differ greatly in the policies they put into law.

QUESTIONS TO CONSIDER

1. **How do presidential nominating contests test candidates?**
2. **Should American elections be restricted in length and cost? Why or why not?**
3. **How do fixed terms of office for Congress and the presidency affect opportunities for policymaking?**
4. **Who spent the most money in the last House and Senate elections?**
5. **How many incumbents won reelection in Congress, and when did challengers prevail?**
6. **How do presidential candidates balance negative and positive campaigning, and which commercials are most effective?**

TO LEARN MORE

Federal Election Commission: **www.fec.gov**

Project Vote Smart: **www.vote-smart.org**

Election history: **clerkweb.house.gov**

Electoral college: **www.fec.gov/pages/ecmenu2**

Campaign finance: **www.opensecrets.org**

Bader, Ted. *Campaigning for Hearts and Minds: How Emotional Appeals in Political Ads Work.* Chicago: University of Chicago Press, 2006. Masterful analysis of how ads move voters and influence people who are most well-informed about politics.

Black, Earl, and Merle Black. *Divided America: The Ferocious Power Struggle in American Politics.* New York: Simon and Schuster, 2007. Detailed account of how evenly balanced the two parties are in all parts of the country.

Burnham, Walter Dean. *Critical Elections and the Mainsprings of American Politics.* New York: Norton, 1970. An argument about the decline in voting participation and the significance of the realigning election of 1896.

Klein, Joe. *Politics Lost? How American Democracy Was Trivialized by People Who Think You're Stupid.* New York: Doubleday, 2006. A veteran political reporter claims that political consultants are to blame for negative political developments.

Sundquist, James L. *Dynamics of the Party System: Alignment and Realignment of Political Parties in the United States,* Rev. ed. Washington, D.C.: Brookings Institution, 1983. Historical analysis of realigning elections from 1860 to the nonrealignment of 1980.

11 Interest Groups

LEARNING OBJECTIVES

WHAT YOU NEED TO KNOW

- ☑ What are interest groups and how did they arise in America?
- ☑ What are the different kinds of interest groups and which types have been proliferating of late?
- ☑ How do interest groups attempt to influence public policy, and how does government regulate interest group activities?

WHO GOVERNS?

1. Do interest groups dominate government, and is any particular lobby politically unbeatable?
2. Why do people join interest groups?

TO WHAT ENDS?

1. Is the proliferation of political action committees (PACs) and other groups good or bad for America's representative democracy?
2. Should interest groups' political activities be restricted by law?

You probably do not think of yourself or of people you know as belonging to an "interest group." But are you or friends of yours part of an effort to improve the environment? Does your father build houses? Does your mother teach school or go to PTA meetings? Is your sister a lawyer? If the answer to any of these questions is yes, then you and your friends may help support the Sierra Club or the Audubon Society, your father probably belongs to a labor union, your mother to the American Federation of Teachers, and your sister to the American Bar Association. In short, if you examine your own activities and affiliations and those of at least some people you know well, chances are that you or they belong to one or more interest groups.

An **interest group** is an organization of people sharing a common interest or goal that seeks to influence public policy. The size and diversity of our country, the decentralizing effects of our Constitution, the vast number of nonprofit organizations, and the weakness of our political parties make it certain that interest groups will be an important way for people to have their voices heard. But while interest groups are as old as the republic itself, the number of interest groups has grown rapidly since 1960, and the number of interest groups that have lobbyists working full-time in Washington has reached new highs in just the last decade.

THEN During the 1770s, many groups arose to agitate for American independence; during the 1830s and 1840s, the number of religious associations increased sharply, and the antislavery movement

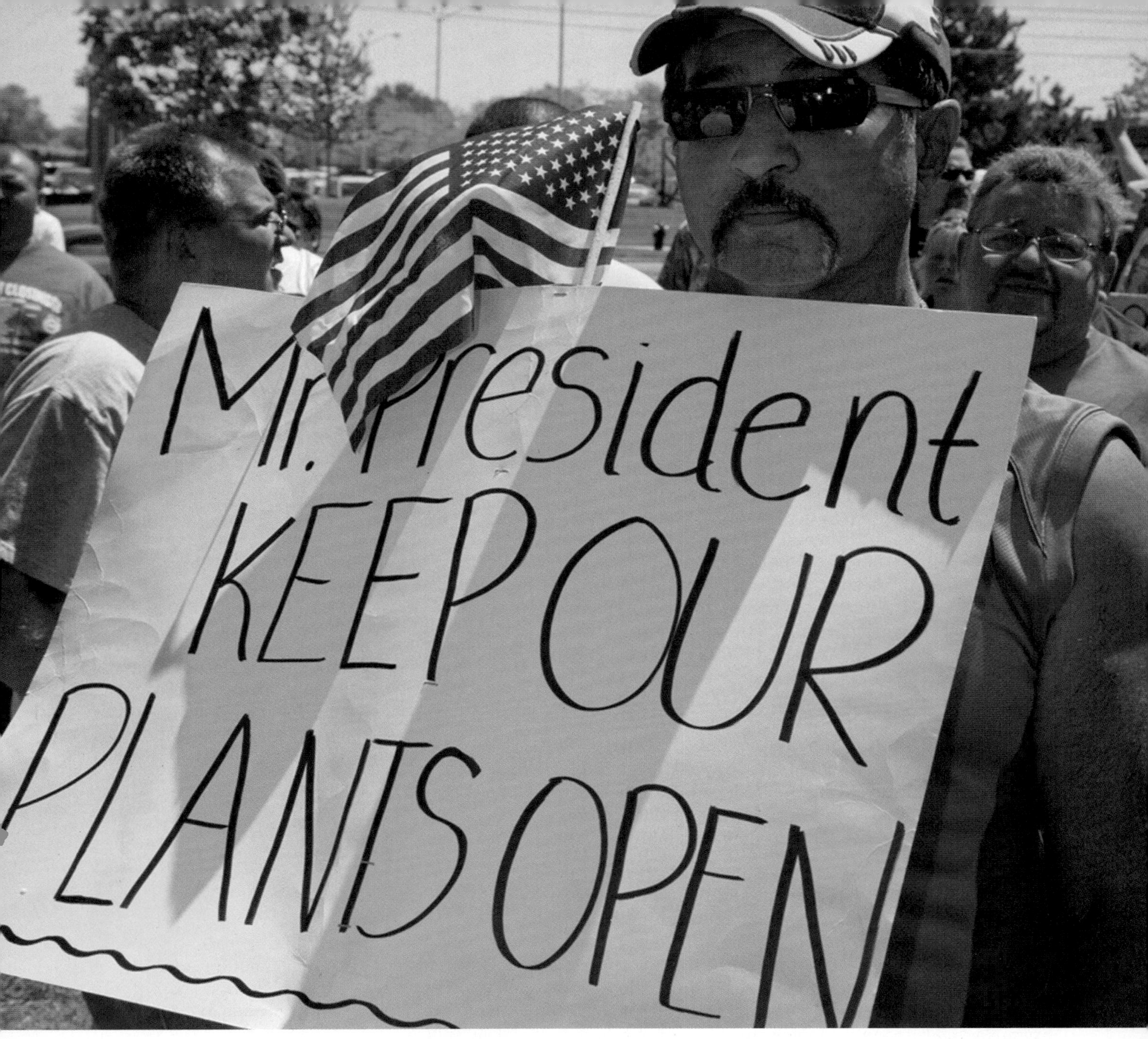

began. In the 1860s, trade unions based on crafts emerged in significant numbers, farmers formed the Grange, and various fraternal organizations were born. In the 1880s and 1890s, business associations proliferated.

The great era of organization building, however, was in the first two decades of the 20th century. Within this 20-year period, many of the best-known and largest associations with an interest in national politics were formed: the Chamber of Commerce, the National Association of Manufacturers, the American Medical Association, the National Association for the Advancement of Colored People (NAACP), the Urban League, the American Farm Bureau Federation, the Farmers' Union, the National Catholic Welfare Conference, the American Jewish Committee, and the Anti-Defamation League.

NOW The wave of interest group formation that occurred in the 1960s led to the emergence of environmental, consumer, and political reform organizations such as those sponsored by consumer activist Ralph Nader. In 1973, a new federal campaign finance law made it legal

interest group An organization of people sharing a common interest or goal that seeks to influence public policy.

political action committee (PAC) A committee set up by a corporation, labor union, or interest group that raises and spends campaign money from voluntary donations.

lobbyist A person who tries to influence legislation on behalf of an interest group.

for interest groups to create political action committees. A **political action committee (PAC)** is an organization created by a business firm, labor union, trade association, or ideological group that recruits members from whom it obtains campaign contributions. By the mid-1990s, there were about six times as many PACs (more than 4,000) as there had been in the mid-1970s, about a quarter of them ideological in character.

The growth in ideological groups has been equaled and, of late, exceeded only by the growth in business groups. For instance, between 1981 and 2005, the number of full-time and part-time **lobbyists**—persons who try to influence legislation on behalf of an interest group—in Washington representing just the S&P 500 corporations increased from 1,475 to 2,765.[1] Today about 14,000 lobbyists for business, union, and other groups are listed in the (over 2,000-page) *Washington Directory*, up from about 7,000 lobbyists (and 531 pages) three decades ago. Adjusted for inflation, the roughly $3.5 billion spent on lobbying in 2009 was nearly seven times the amount spent on lobbying a quarter-century earlier.[2]

Why are associations in general and political interest groups in particular created more rapidly in some periods than in others? After all, there have always been farmers in this country, but there were no national farm organizations until the latter part of the 19th century. Blacks were victimized by various white-supremacy policies from the end of the Civil War on, but the NAACP did not emerge until 1910. Men and women worked in factories for decades before industrial unions were formed. Every political era featured activists who believed strongly in liberal or conservative ideology, but only in recent decades have ideological groups become so pervasive. Organized business interests have battled organized labor interests over public policy for more than a hundred years, but only in recent decades has the big business lobbying presence in Washington expanded so dramatically both in absolute terms and relative to big labor.

Four factors have helped shape how and when given interest groups arose in America. We now turn to a consideration of them.

How We Compare

Interest Groups in America, Great Britain, and Germany

Suppose we were a small country that had no state governments and operated under a parliamentary system that made the prime minister the only important official. Suppose further that strong parties dominated how policies were made and that our tax laws made it hard to support nonprofit organizations. If these things were true, then interest groups would be much less important. Most of the political decisions would be made by the ruling party. If you wanted to affect how those decisions were made, you would have to be a leader of that party or part of one or two very powerful interest groups.

But in America these things are not true. This country has a great variety of ethnic groups, scores of religious organizations, and a Constitution that requires power to be shared by three branches of government and that ensures independent authority for 50 state governments. In our diverse nation, political authority is so decentralized that it invites the creation of interest groups that try to affect some part of every decision. And the Constitution makes it clear that lobbyists are protected: they are exercising freedom of speech and petitioning the government for a redress of grievances, just as the First Amendment guarantees them the right to do.

Compare the United States with Great Britain. Both nations are democratic, but in Great Britain only a few big interest groups exist; here, there are thousands. In Britain, only one lobbying organization represents farmers; here, there are at least three.

Or compare the United States and Germany. Both countries are democratic, but German environmentalists formed an influential political party (the Green Party), which by 2005 had won more than 50 seats in the national legislature. In this country, the Green Party has won no seats in Congress; most environmentalists have instead worked through a score of interest groups.

The Birth of Interest Groups

At least four factors help explain the rise of interest groups. The first consists of broad economic developments that create new interests and redefine old ones. Farmers had little reason to become organized for political activity so long as most of them consumed what they produced. The importance of regular political activity became evident only after most farmers began to produce cash crops for sale in markets that were unstable or affected by forces (the weather, the railroads, foreign competition) that farmers could not control. Similarly, for many decades most workers were craftspeople working alone or in small groups. Such unions as existed were little more than craft guilds interested in protecting members' jobs and in training apprentices. The reason for large, mass-membership unions did not exist until there arose mass-production industry operated by large corporations.

Second, government policy itself helps to create interest groups. Wars create veterans, who in turn demand pensions and other benefits. The first large veterans' organization, the Grand Army of the Republic, was made up of Union veterans of the Civil War. By the 1920s, these men were receiving about a quarter of a billion dollars a year from the government, and naturally they created organizations to watch over the distribution of this money. The federal government encouraged the formation of the American Farm Bureau Federation (AFBF) by paying for county agents who would serve the needs of farmers under the supervision of local farm organizations; these county bureaus eventually came together as the AFBF. The Chamber of Commerce was launched at a conference attended by President William Howard Taft. Professional societies, such as those made up of lawyers and doctors, became important in part because state governments gave to such groups the authority to decide who was qualified to become a lawyer or a doctor.

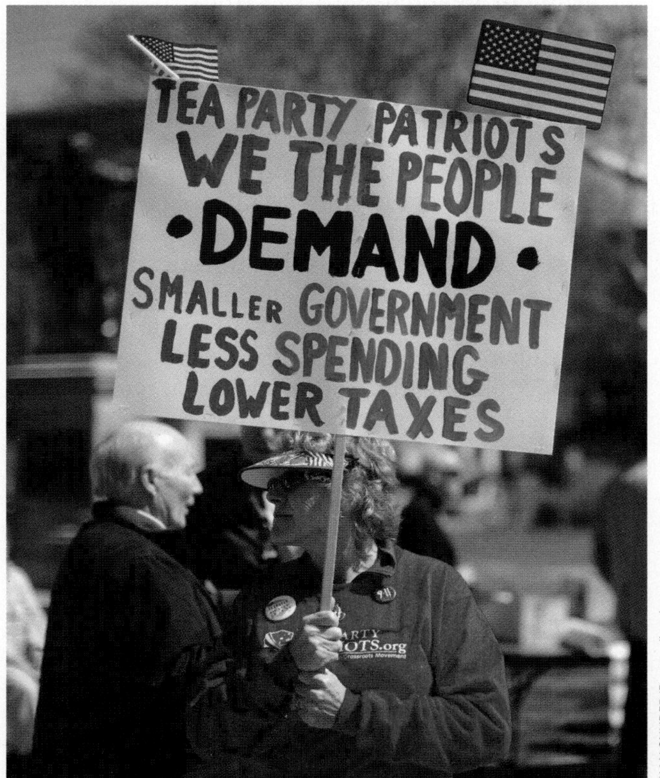

BRIAN SNYDER/Reuters/Landov

A woman holds a Tea Party sign at a rally in Concord, New Hampshire.

Workers had a difficult time organizing as long as the government, by the use of injunctions enforced by the police and the army, prevented strikes. Unions, especially those in mass-production industries, began to flourish after Congress passed laws in the 1930s that prohibited the use of injunctions in private labor disputes, that required employers to bargain with unions, and that allowed a union representing a majority of the workers in a plant to require all workers to join it.[3]

Third, political organizations do not emerge automatically, even when government policy permits them and social circumstances seem to require them. Somebody must exercise leadership, often at substantial personal cost. These organizational entrepreneurs are found in greater numbers at certain times than at others. Often they are young, caught up in a social movement, drawn to the need for change, and inspired by some political or religious doctrine.

Antislavery organizations were created in the 1830s and 1840s by enthusiastic young people influenced by a religious revival sweeping the country. The period from 1890 to 1920, when so many national organizations were created, was a time when the college-educated middle class was growing rapidly. (The number of men and women who received college degrees each year tripled between 1890 and 1920.)[4] During this era, natural science and fundamentalist Christianity were locked in a bitter contest, with the Gospels and Darwinism offering competing ideas about personal salvation and social progress. The 1960s, when many new organizations were born, was a decade in which young people were powerfully influenced by the civil rights and antiwar movements and when college enrollments more than doubled.

Finally, the more government does, the more interest groups will arise or expand and try to influence public policy. Most Washington offices representing corporations, labor unions, and trade and professional associations were established before 1960—in some cases many decades before—because it was during the 1930s or even earlier that the government began making policies important to business and labor. The great majority of "public-interest" lobbies (those concerned with the environment or consumer protection), social welfare associations, and organizations concerned with civil rights, the elderly, and the handicapped established offices in Washington after major new federal laws in these respective areas were enacted.

The most recent and dramatic example is what happened in the post-9/11 years after the USA Patriot Act was enacted in 2001 and the Department of Homeland Security (DHS) was created in 2002. By 2010, with billions of dollars a year in federal funding for the purpose flowing, more than 500 new private companies specializing in work related to security and counterterrorism had come into being, and most of another 1,400 or so private companies that existed and did related work prior to 2001 had expanded.[5] New lobbies quickly formed to represent those firms and keep their homeland security grants and contracts coming; for example, the "full body scanner" lobby represents firms that sell body-scanning equipment used in airports to a DHS subunit, the Transportation Security Administration (TSA).[6] Moreover, many local governments, from big cities to small towns, have hired lobbyists to work on getting or sustaining their fair share of federal homeland security money.

Kinds of Organizations

When we think of an organization, we usually think of something like the Boy Scouts or the League of Women Voters—a group consisting of individual members. In Washington, however, many organizations do not have individual members at all but are offices—corporations, law firms, public relations firms, or "letterhead" organizations that get most of their money from other organizations or from the government—out of which a staff operates. It is important to understand the differences between the two kinds of interest groups—institutional and membership interests.[7]

INSTITUTIONAL INTERESTS

Institutional interests are individuals or organizations representing other organizations. For example, long before the government bailed it out in 2008, General Motors had representatives in Washington, and it is now not uncommon for even mid-sized corporations to have one or more full-time representatives plus part-time lawyers or public relations consultants working for them in Washington. Another kind of institutional interest is the trade or governmental association, such as the National Independent Retail Jewelers and the National Association of Counties.

Individuals or organizations that represent other organizations tend to be interested in bread-and-butter issues of vital concern to their clients. Some of the people who specialize in this work can earn very large fees. Top public relations experts and Washington lawyers can charge $500 an hour or more for their time. Since they earn a lot, they are expected to deliver a lot.

Just what they are expected to deliver, however, varies with the diversity of the groups making up the organization. The American Cotton Manufacturers Institute represents southern textile mills. Those mills are few enough in number and similar enough in outlook to allow the institute to carry out clear policies squarely based on the business interests of its clients. For example, the institute works hard to get the federal government to adopt laws and rules that will keep foreign-made textiles from competing too easily with American-made goods. Sometimes the institute is successful, sometimes not, but it is never hard to explain what it is doing.

By contrast, the U.S. Chamber of Commerce represents thousands of different businesses in hundreds of different communities. The Chamber has led all interest groups in annual lobbying expenditures. All told, from 1998 to 2010, it spent nearly $750 million on lobbying (see Figure 11.1), a figure much larger than what was spent by any other organization over the same period, including corporate giants like Exxon Mobil and membership giants like AARP.

Landmark Cases

Lobbying Congress

- ***United States v. Harriss* (1954):** The Constitution protects the lobbying of Congress, but the government may require information from groups that try to influence legislation.

Figure 11.1
What the Top Lobby Spent, 1998–2010

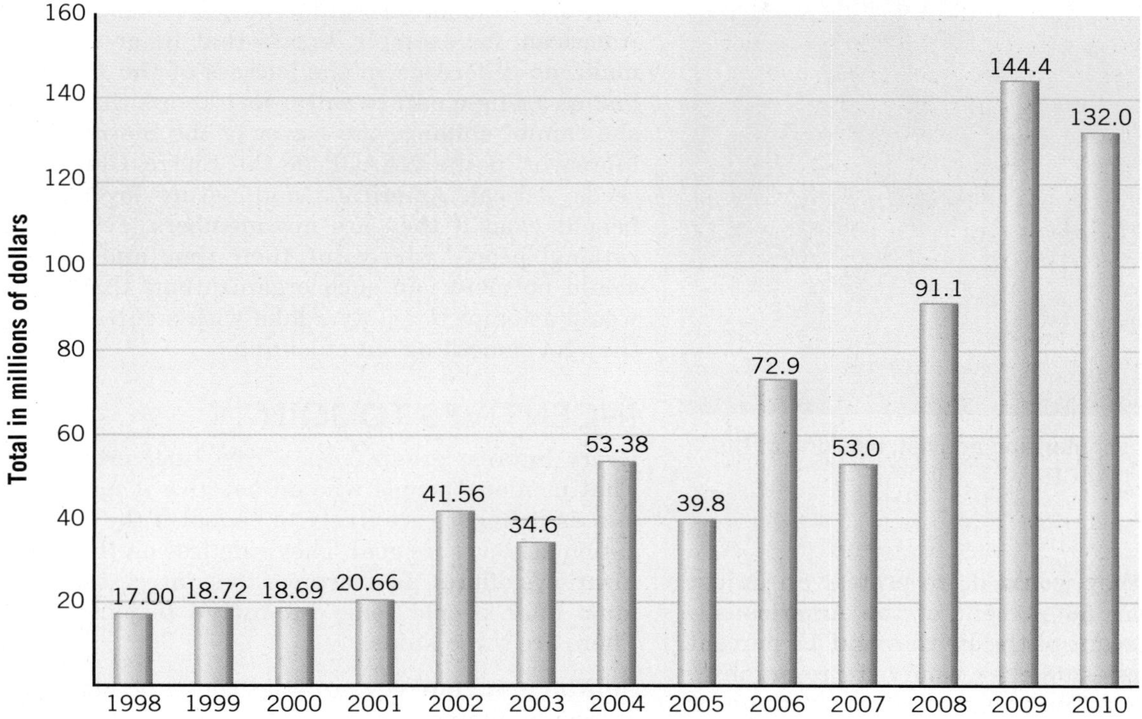

Source: Center for Public Integrity, Georgetown University, Washington, D.C., 2011.

Indeed, in 2010 alone, the Chamber spent $132 million on lobbying, a sum nearly equal to the combined spending on lobbying by the next four largest spenders (PG&E Corporation, General Electric, FedEx Corporation, and the American Medical Association, respectively). Its membership is so large and diverse that the Chamber in Washington can speak out clearly and forcefully on only those relatively few matters in which all, or most, businesses take the same position. Since all businesses would like lower taxes, the Chamber favors that. On the other hand, since some businesses (those that import goods) want lower tariffs and other businesses (those that face competition from imported goods) want higher tariffs, the Chamber says little or nothing about tariffs.

Institutional interests do not just represent business firms; they also represent governments, foundations, and universities. For example, the American Council on Education speaks for most institutions of higher education, the American Public Transit Association represents local mass-transit systems, and the National Association of Counties argues on behalf of county governments.

MEMBERSHIP INTERESTS

It often is said that Americans are a nation of joiners, and so we take for granted the many organizations around us supported by the activities and contributions of individual citizens. But we should not take this multiplicity of organizations for granted; in fact, their existence is something of a puzzle.

Americans join only certain kinds of organizations more frequently than citizens of other democratic countries. We are no more likely than the British, for example, to join social, business, professional, veterans', or charitable organizations, and we are *less* likely to join labor unions. Our reputation as a nation of joiners arises chiefly out of our unusually high tendency to join religious and civic or political associations.

This proclivity of Americans to get together with other citizens to engage in civic or political action reflects, apparently, a greater sense of political efficacy and a stronger sense of civic duty than that found in some nations. In a classic study, Gabriel Almond and Sidney Verba asked citizens of five

C M Battey/Hulton Archive/Getty Images

W.E.B. Du Bois, scholar and activist, was one of the founders of the NAACP.

nations what they would do to protest an unjust local regulation; 56 percent of the Americans—but only 34 percent of the British and 13 percent of the Germans—said they would try to organize their neighbors to write letters, sign petitions, or otherwise act in concert.[8] Americans are also more likely than Europeans to think organized activity is an effective way to influence the national government, remote as that institution may seem. And even scholars who emphasize how this willingness to form civic or political groups seems to have declined in recent decades still generally agree that, compared to most other democratic peoples, Americans of every socioeconomic status and demographic description are joiners.[9]

incentive Something of value one cannot get without joining an organization.

solidary incentives The social rewards (sense of pleasure, status, or companionship) that lead people to join political organizations.

material incentives Money or things valued in monetary terms.

But explaining the American willingness to join politically active groups by saying that Americans feel a "sense of political efficacy" is not much of an explanation; we might as well say people vote because they think their vote makes a difference. One vote clearly makes no difference at all in almost any election; similarly, one member, more or less, in the Sierra Club, the National Rifle Association, or the NAACP clearly will make no difference in the success of those organizations. And most people who are sympathetic to the aims of a mass-membership interest group do not join it. The NAACP, for example, enrolls as members only a tiny fraction of all African Americans. This is not because people are selfish or apathetic but because they are rational and numerous. A single African American, for example, knows that he or she can make no difference in the success of the NAACP, just as a single nature enthusiast knows that he or she cannot enhance the power of the Sierra Club. Moreover, if the NAACP or the Sierra Club succeeds, African Americans and nature lovers will benefit even if they are not members. Therefore, rational people who value their time and money would no more join such organizations than they would attempt to empty a lake with a cup—unless they got something out of joining.

INCENTIVES TO JOIN

Every interest group faces a free rider problem.[10] That is, many people who do not give it money or join as members are likely to benefit if the organization achieves its goal. They ride free on the organization's efforts. To overcome this, interest groups must offer people some **incentive** to join them. There are three kinds.

Solidary incentives are the sense of pleasure, status, or companionship that arises out of meeting together in small groups. Such rewards are extremely important, but because they tend to be available only from face-to-face contact, national interest groups offering them often have to organize themselves as coalitions of small local units. For example, the League of Women Voters, the Parent Teacher Association (PTA), the NAACP, the Rotary Club, and the American Legion all consist of small local chapters that support a national staff. It is the task of the local chapters to lure members and obtain funds from them; the state or national staff can then pursue political objectives by using these funds.

Forming organizations made up of small local chapters is probably easier in the United States than in Europe because of the great importance of local government in our federal system. There is plenty for a PTA, an NAACP, or a League of Women Voters to do in its own community, and so its members can be kept busy with local affairs while the national staff pursues larger goals.

A second kind of incentive consists of **material incentives**—that is, money, or things and services readily valued in monetary terms. Farm organizations have recruited many members by offering a wide range of services. The Illinois Farm Bureau, for example, offers to its members—and *only* to its

Bill Clark/CQ-Roll Call Group/Roll Call/Getty Images

The Service Employees International Union, a large and growing force, listens to Andy Stern, its president until 2010.

members—a chance to buy farm supplies at discount prices, market their products through cooperatives, and purchase low-cost insurance. These material incentives help explain why the Illinois Farm Bureau has been able to enroll nearly every farmer in the state as well as many nonfarmers who also value these rewards.

Similarly, the American Association of Retired Persons (AARP) has recruited tens of millions of members by supplying them with everything from low-cost life insurance and mail-order discount drugs to tax advice and group travel plans. Almost half of the nation's population aged 50 and older—one out of every four registered voters—belongs to the AARP. With an annual operating budget of about $800 million and a yearly cash flow of several billion dollars, the AARP seeks to influence public policy in many areas, from health and housing to taxes and transportation. To gain additional benefits for members, interest groups like the AARP also seek to influence how public laws are administered and who gets government grants.

purposive incentive A benefit that comes from serving a cause or principle.

ideological interest groups Political organizations that attract members by appealing to their political convictions or principles.

The third—and most difficult—kind of incentive is the *purpose* of the organization. Many associations rely chiefly on this **purposive incentive**—the appeal of their stated goals—to recruit members. If the attainment of those goals will also benefit people who do not join, individuals who do join will have to be those who feel passionately about the goal, who have a strong sense of duty (or who cannot say no to a friend who asks them to join), or for whom the cost of joining is so small that they are indifferent to joining or not. Organizations that attract members by appealing to their interest in a coherent set of (usually) controversial principles are sometimes called **ideological interest groups**.

Public-Interest Law Firms

A special kind of public-interest lobby is an organization that advances its cause by bringing lawsuits to challenge existing practices or proposed regulations. A public-interest law firm will act in one of two ways: First, it will find someone who has been harmed by some public or private policy and bring suit on his or her behalf. Second, it will file a brief with a court supporting somebody else's lawsuit (this is called an amicus curiae brief; it is explained in Chapter 16).

Here are some examples of liberal and conservative public-interest law firms:

Liberal

American Civil Liberties Union

Asian American Legal Defense Fund

Lawyers' Committee for Civil Rights

Mexican American Legal Defense Fund

NAACP Legal Defense and Education Fund

Natural Resources Defense Council

Women's Legal Defense Fund

Conservative

Atlantic Legal Foundation

The Center for Individual Rights

Criminal Justice Legal Foundation

Landmark Legal Foundation

Mountain States Legal Foundation

Pacific Legal Foundation

Washington Legal Foundation

public-interest lobby A political organization whose goals will principally benefit nonmembers.

When the purpose of the organization, if attained, will principally benefit nonmembers, it is customary to call the group a **public-interest lobby**. (Whether the public at large will really benefit, of course, is a matter of opinion, but at least the group members think they are working selflessly for the common good.)

Though some public-interest lobbies may pursue relatively noncontroversial goals (for example, persuading people to vote or raising money to house orphans), the most visible of these organizations are highly controversial. It is precisely the controversy that attracts the members, or at least those members who support one side of the issue. Many of these groups can be described as markedly liberal or decidedly conservative in outlook.

Perhaps the best known of the liberal public-interest groups are those founded by or associated with Ralph Nader. Nader became a popular figure in the mid-1960s after General Motors made a clumsy attempt to investigate and discredit his background at a time when he was testifying in favor of an auto-safety bill. Nader won a large out-of-court settlement against General Motors, his books began to earn royalties, and he was able to command substantial lecture fees. Most of this money was turned over to various organizations he created that dealt with matters of interest to consumers. In addition, he founded a group called Public Citizen that raised money by direct-mail solicitation from thousands of small contributors and sought foundation grants. Finally, he helped create Public Interest Research Groups (PIRGs) in a number of states, supported by donations from college students (voluntary at some colleges, a compulsory assessment levied on all students at others) and concerned with organizing student activists to work on local projects.

Conservatives, though slow to get started, also have adopted the public-interest organizational strategy. As with such associations run by liberals, they are of two kinds: those that engage in research and lobbying and those that bring lawsuits designed to advance their cause. The boxes on this page and page 277 list some examples of public-interest organizations that support liberal or conservative causes.

Membership organizations that rely on purposive incentives, especially appeals to deeply controversial purposes, tend to be shaped by the mood of the times. When an issue is hot—in the media or with the public—such organizations can grow rapidly. When the spotlight fades, the organization may lose

Think Tanks in Washington

Think tanks are public-interest organizations that do research on policy questions and disseminate their findings in books, articles, conferences, op-ed essays for newspapers, and (occasionally) testimony before Congress. Some are nonpartisan and ideologically more or less neutral, but others—and many of the most important ones—are aligned with liberal or conservative causes. Here are some examples of each:

Liberal	*Conservative*
Center on Budget and Policy Priorities	American Enterprise Institute
Center for Defense Information	Cato Institute
Children's Defense Fund	Center for Strategic and International Studies
Economic Policy Institute	Competitive Enterprise Institute
Institute for Policy Studies	Ethics and Public Policy Center
Joint Center for Political and Economic Studies	Free Congress Foundation
Progressive Policy Institute	Heritage Foundation

Note that the labels "liberal" and "conservative," while generally accurate, conceal important differences among the think tanks in each list.

support. Thus, such organizations have a powerful motive to stay in the public eye. To remain visible, public-interest lobbies devote a lot of attention to generating publicity by developing good contacts with the media and issuing dramatic press releases about crises and scandals.

Because of their need to take advantage of a crisis atmosphere, public-interest lobbies often do best when the government is in the hands of an administration that is *hostile,* not sympathetic, to their views. Environmentalist organizations could mobilize more resources when James Watt, an opponent of much of the environmental movement, was secretary of the interior than they could when Cecil D. Andrus, his pro-environment predecessor, was in office. By the same token, many conservative interest groups were able to raise more money with the liberal Jimmy Carter or Bill Clinton in the White House than with the conservative Ronald Reagan or George W. Bush there.

RESEARCH FRONTIERS

No Lobby Can't Be Beat

Nobody doubts that interest groups have proliferated, but is any one lobby so powerful as to dominate policymaking on certain issues? Three interest groups strike many observers as uniquely powerful:

- *NRA:* The National Rifle Association lobbies for promoting gun ownership as a civil liberty protected by the Second Amendment to the Constitution; it opposes most gun-control legislation. It has about four million members and takes in over $200 million a year.
- *AIPAC:* The American Israel Public Affairs Committee lobbies for U.S. foreign aid and diplomatic policies favorable to Israel. It has about 100,000 members. Together with other pro-Israel groups, it steers millions of dollars in campaign contributions to candidates it favors.
- *AARP:* The AARP lobbies for policies that provide financial benefits and services to people over age 50. The 40-million-member AARP is widely considered to be the dominant lobby on issues relating to such mammoth federal programs as Social Security and Medicare.

The NRA has won legislative battles for "shall-carry" laws, giving people the right to bear concealed weapons; the AIPAC boasts national leaders in both parties who support spending billions of dollars a year in U.S. financial and military aid to Israel; and the AARP has driven successive health care policy debates, like one in 2003 that resulted in increased federal subsidies for prescription drugs.

But recent and often highly critical writings on each lobby by political scientists and others remind us that no one group controls policymaking on any big issue:

- The NRA's legislative battles over "shall-carry" laws were protracted in many states. In 2004 it successfully stymied the renewal of the 1994 federal ban on various assault weapons, but it had lost its fight against that ban a decade earlier.
- The AIPAC has made U.S. support for Israel a bipartisan norm, but it has hardly always had its aid proposals adopted; and it has been subjected to espionage allegations and criticized by diverse past and present top U.S. government officials.
- The AARP has loomed large in debates over Social Security and Medicare, but it has often been more successful at blocking proposals that it opposes than in getting proposals that it favors into law; and it has faced congressional investigations.

Do a little research of your own on these three important, but not all-powerful or never-defeated, lobbies.

- What, if any, influence do each of these three lobbies wield in your state?
- What would you say are the main sources of each lobby's significant but not solitary influence over federal policy?

Sources: Richard Feldman, *Ricochet: Confessions of a Gun Lobbyist* (Wiley, 2007); John J. Mearsheimer and Stephen M. Walt, *The Israel Lobby and U.S. Foreign Policy* (Farrar, Straus, and Giroux, 2008); and Dale Van Natta, *Trust Betrayed: Inside the AARP* (Regnery, 1998), and "This Isn't the Old AARP," *Los Angeles Times*, November 24, 2003.

THE INFLUENCE OF THE STAFF

We often make the mistake of assuming that what an interest group does politically is simply to exert influence on behalf of its members. That is indeed the case when all the members have a clear and similar stake in an issue. But many issues affect different members differently. In fact, if the members joined to obtain solidary or material benefits, they may not care at all about many of the issues with which the organization gets involved. In such cases, what the interest group does may reflect more what the staff wants than what the members believe.

For example, a survey of the white members of a large labor union showed that one-third of them believed the desegregation of schools, housing, and job opportunities had gone too fast; only one-fifth thought it had gone too slowly. But among the staff members of the union, *none* thought desegregation had gone too fast, and over two-thirds thought it had gone too slowly.[11] As a result, the union staff aggressively lobbied Congress for the passage of tougher civil rights laws, even though most of the union's members did not feel they were needed. The members stayed in the union for reasons unrelated to civil rights, giving the staff the freedom to pursue its own goals.

Interest Groups and Social Movements

Because it is difficult to attract people with purposive incentives, interest groups employing them tend to arise out of social movements. A **social movement** is a widely shared demand for change in some aspect of the social or political order. The civil rights movement of the 1960s was such an event, as was the environmentalist movement of the 1970s.

social movement A widely shared demand for change in some aspect of the social or political order.

A social movement need not have liberal goals. In the 19th century, for example, there were various nativist movements that sought to reduce immigration to this country or to keep Catholics or Masons out of public office. Broad-based religious revivals are social movements. In recent years, the conservative Tea Party movement, which has taken hold around issues like restraining government growth, has played a role in both local and national elections.[12]

No one is quite certain why social movements arise. At one moment, people are largely indifferent to some issue; at another moment, many of these same people care passionately about religion, civil rights, immigration, or conservation. A social movement may be triggered by a scandal (an oil spill on the Santa Barbara beaches helped launch the environmental movement), the dramatic and widely publicized activities of a few leaders (lunch counter sit-ins helped stimulate the civil rights movement), or the coming of age of a new generation that takes up a cause advocated by eloquent writers, teachers, or evangelists.

Whatever its origin, the effect of a social movement is to increase the value some people attach to purposive incentives. As a consequence, new interest groups are formed that rely on these incentives.

THE ENVIRONMENTAL MOVEMENT

The environmental movement provides a good example of how a social movement gives rise to interest groups formed from reliance on purposive incentives. In the 1890s, as a result of the emergence of conservation as a major issue, the Sierra Club was organized. In the 1930s, conservation once again became popular, and the Wilderness Society and the National Wildlife Federation took form. In the 1960s and 1970s, environmental issues again came to the fore, and we saw the emergence of the Environmental Defense Fund and Environmental Action.

The smallest of these organizations (Environmental Action and the Environmental Defense Fund) tend to have the most liberal members. This often is the case with organizations that arise from social movements. A movement will spawn many organizations. The most passionately aroused people will be the fewest in number, and they will gravitate toward the organizations that take the most extreme positions; as a result, these organizations are small but vociferous. The more numerous and less passionate people will gravitate toward more moderate, less vociferous organizations, which will tend to be larger.

As happens over the years to most politically successful movements, the environmental movement has become more fragmented than it was in the 1970s. Different leading voices and organizations within it have begun to advocate somewhat different policy approaches to achieving the same basic (in this case, environmental protection and sustainability) goals.[13]

THE FEMINIST MOVEMENT

There have been several feminist social movements in this country's history—in the 1830s, in the 1890s, in the 1920s, and in the 1960s. Each period brought about new organizations, some of which have endured to the present. For example, the League of Women Voters was founded in 1920 to educate and organize women for the purpose of using effectively their newly won right to vote.

Though a strong sense of purpose may lead to the creation of organizations, each will strive to find some incentive that will sustain it over the long haul. These permanent incentives will affect how the organization participates in politics.

At least three kinds of feminist organizations exist. First, there are those that rely chiefly on solidary incentives, enroll middle-class women with relatively high levels of schooling, and tend to support those causes that command the widest support among women generally. The League of Women Voters and the Federation of Business and Professional Women are examples. Both supported the campaign to ratify the Equal Rights Amendment (ERA), but as Jane Mansbridge has observed in her history of the ERA, they were uneasy with the kind of intense, partisan fighting displayed by some other women's organizations and with the tendency of more militant groups to link the ERA to other issues, such as abortion. The reason for their uneasiness is clear: to the extent they relied on solidary incentives, they had a stake in avoiding issues and tactics that would divide their membership or reduce the extent to which membership provided camaraderie and professional contacts.[14]

Second, there are women's organizations that attract members with purposive incentives. The National Organization for Women (NOW) and the National Abortion Rights Action League (NARAL) are two of the largest such groups, though there are many smaller ones. Because they rely on purposes, these organizations must take strong positions, tackle divisive issues, and employ militant tactics. Anything less would turn off the committed feminists who make up the rank and file and contribute the funds. But because these groups take controversial stands, they are constantly embroiled in internal quarrels between those who think they have gone too far and those who think they have not gone far enough, between women who want NOW or NARAL to join with lesbian and socialist organizations and those who want them to steer clear. Moreover, as Jane Mansbridge showed, purposive organizations often cannot make their decisions stick on the local level (local chapters will do pretty much as they please).[15]

Larry Downing/Reuters

The Million Moms March in 2004 demanded a federal ban on assault weapons.

The third kind of women's organization is the caucus that takes on specific issues that have some material benefit to women. The Women's Equity Action League (WEAL) is one such group. Rather than relying on membership dues for financial support, it obtains grants from foundations and government agencies. Freed of the necessity of satisfying a large rank-and-file membership, WEAL has concentrated its efforts on bringing lawsuits aimed at enforcing or enlarging the legal rights of women in higher education and other institutions. In electoral politics, the National Women's Political Caucus (officially nonpartisan, but generally liberal and Democratic) and the National Federation of Republican Women (openly supportive of the Republican Party) work to get more women active in politics and more women elected or appointed to office.

The feminist movement has, of course, spawned an antifeminist movement, and thus feminist organizations have their antifeminist counterparts. The campaign by NOW for the ERA was attacked by a women's group called STOP ERA; the pro-choice position of NARAL has been challenged by the various organizations associated with the right-to-life movement. These opposition groups have their own tactical problems, which arise in large part from their reliance on different kinds of incentives. In the chapter on civil rights, we shall see how the conflict between these opposing groups shaped the debate over the ERA.

THE UNION MOVEMENT

When social movements run out of steam, they leave behind organizations that continue the fight. But with the movement dead or dormant, the organizations often must struggle to stay alive. This has happened to labor unions.

The major union movement in this country occurred in the 1930s when the Great Depression, popular support, and a sympathetic administration in Washington led to a rapid growth in union membership. In 1945, union membership peaked; at that time, nearly 36 percent of all nonfarm workers were union members.

Since then, union membership has fallen more or less steadily. Today, only about 12 percent of all workers are covered by unions. Between 1983 and 2010, the number of union members fell by about 3 million. This decline was caused by several factors. There has been a shift in the nation's economic life away from industrial production (where unions have traditionally been concentrated) and toward service delivery (where unions have usually been weak). But accompanying this decline, and perhaps contributing to it, has been a decline in popular approval of unions. Approval has moved down side by side with a decline in membership and declines in union victories in elections held to see whether workers in a plant want to join a union. The social movement that supported unionism has faded.

But unions will persist because most can rely on incentives other than purposive ones to keep them going. In many states, they can require workers to join unions if they wish to keep their jobs; in other places, workers believe they get sufficient benefits from the union to make even voluntary membership worthwhile. And in a few industries, such as teaching and government, there has been a growth in membership as some white-collar workers have turned to unions to advance their interests.

Unions composed of government workers are becoming the most important part of the union movement. Indeed, according to the U.S. Bureau of Labor Statistics, in 2010, 7.6 million public-sector employees belonged to a union, compared with 7.1 million union workers in the private sector; and the union membership rate for public-sector workers (36.2 percent) was more than five times that for private-sector workers (6.9 percent). In 2011, Wisconsin and several other states considered legislation that would restrict or eliminate certain bargaining rights and benefits enjoyed by public-employee unions including those representing public-school teachers.

Still, public-sector unions, led by groups like the American Federation of State County and Municipal Employees (AFSCME) and the American Federation of Teachers (AFT), remain robust, relatively well funded, and significant sources of campaign contributions. The Federal Elections Commission (FEC) reported that, in 2009, AFSCME's PAC contributed over $1.2 million to candidates while AFT's PAC contributed over $800,000 to candidates, making them the ninth and twenty-sixth entries, respectively, on the FEC's list of the top fifty PAC contributors for that year.

Unions can more or less reliably raise at least a portion of the funds they need by charging their members dues, but many interest groups struggle with raising money; some cannot easily predict what their budget will be from one quarter to the next. This is especially true for membership organizations that rely on appeals to purpose—to accomplishing stated goals. As a result, the Washington office of a public-interest lobbying group is likely to be small, stark, and crowded, whereas that of an institutional lobby, such as the AFL-CIO or the American Council on Education, will be rather lavish.

To make ends meet and maintain such influence as they each may have, diverse interest groups attempt to fund themselves through some combination of private foundation grants, government grants, direct-mail solicitation, and online appeals and donations (some tied in to the group leaders' blogs or social media sites). After the 2007 recession began, each of those funding sources became more precarious, but at least through mid-2011 fundraising challenges had not led to any easily observable changes in the landscape of America's organized interest groups.

UPPER-CLASS BIAS?

Observers often believe that interest groups active in Washington reflect an upper-class bias. There are two reasons for this belief: first, well-off people are more likely than poor people to join and be active in interest groups; and second, interest groups representing business and the professions are much more numerous and better financed than organizations representing minorities, consumers, or the disadvantaged.

Many scholars have shown that people with higher incomes, those whose schooling went through college or beyond, and those in professional or technical jobs are much more likely to belong to a voluntary association than people with the opposite characteristics. Just as we would expect, higher-income people can afford more organizational memberships than lower-income ones; people in business and the professions find it easier to attend meetings (they have more control over their own work schedules) and more necessary to do so than people in blue-collar jobs; and people with college degrees often have a wider range of interests than those without.

One study found that between 1981 and 2006, the ratio of business lobbyists to union plus public-interest lobbyists prone to oppose business interests rose from about 12 to 1 to nearly 16 to 1.[16] Some now argue that the nation's 2007–2010 economic crises were due in part to the disproportionate political influence wielded during the preceding decade by rich Wall Street executives and related business interests. There is some truth to this view. In 1999, corporate lawyers and lobbyists won a long legislative battle to repeal the Banking Act of 1933, better known as the Glass-Steagall Act, which strictly separated investment from commercial banking and imposed many other restrictions on financial companies. The repeal permitted the home mortgage business to change in ways that made it easier to lend money to poor credit risks, and it gave birth to new financial products and services that were weakly regulated by government and incomprehensible to most consumers.

But note that the 1933 law, albeit with certain changes made in subsequent decades, remained on the books for more than 60 years before it was repealed. And, strongly opposed though it was by myriad powerful business interests, today the Wall Street Reform and Consumer Protection Act of 2010 is law. Better known as Dodd-Frank, this law did not restore the Glass-Steagall act's strict separation between depository banking and financial trading, but it did tighten regulations on virtually all financial companies and broaden consumer protections for all, including first-time mortgage-seekers and small investors.

As this example suggests, even if it is true that financial moguls, big business executives, and the economically well off typically have more (and more high-priced) lobbyists looking out for their interests than other citizens do, the question of an upper-class bias is by no means entirely settled.

In the first place, lobbyists are only certain *inputs* into the political system; what matters are the *outputs*—that is, who wins and who loses on particular issues. For instance, even if scores and scores of groups inside the Washington beltway are pushing to protect the oil industry and those who benefit financially from it the most, this is important only if the oil industry in fact gets protected. Sometimes it does; sometimes it does not. At one time, when oil prices were low, oil companies were able to get Congress to pass a law that sharply restricted the importation of foreign oil. A few years later, after oil prices had risen and people were worried about energy issues, these restrictions were ended.

In the second place, business-oriented interest groups often are divided among themselves. Take one kind of business: farming. Once, farm organizations seemed so powerful in Washington that scholars spoke of an irresistible "farm bloc" in Congress that could get its way on almost anything. Today, dozens of agricultural organizations operate in the capital, with some (such as the Farm Bureau) attempting to speak for all farmers and others (such as the Tobacco

JP Laffront/Sygma/Corbis

Farmers once had great influence in Congress and could get their way with a few telephone calls. Today, they often must use mass-protest methods.

Institute and Mid-America Dairymen) representing particular commodities and regions.

Whenever American politics is described as having an upper-class bias, it is important to ask exactly what this bias is. Most of the major conflicts in American politics—over foreign policy, economic affairs, environmental protection, and equal rights for women—are conflicts *within* the upper class; that is, they are conflicts among politically active elites. As we saw in Chapter 7, profound cleavages of opinion exist among these elites. Interest group activity reflects these cleavages.

It would be a mistake to ignore the overrepresentation of business in Washington. A student of politics should always take differences in the availability of political resources as an important clue to possible differences in the outcomes of political conflicts. Nonetheless, the differences are only clues, not conclusions.

The Activities of Interest Groups

Size and wealth are no longer entirely accurate measures of an interest group's influence—if indeed they ever were. Depending on the issue, the key to political influence may be the ability to generate a dramatic newspaper headline, mobilize a big letter-writing campaign, stage a protest demonstration, file a suit in federal court to block (or compel) some government action, or quietly supply information to key legislators. All of these things require organization, but only some of them require big or expensive organizations.

INFORMATION

Of all these tactics, the single most important one—in the eyes of virtually every lobbyist and every academic student of lobbying—is supplying credible information. The reason why information is so valuable is that, to busy legislators and bureaucrats, information is in short supply. Legislators in particular must take positions on a staggering number of issues about which they cannot possibly become experts.

Nobody needs a lobbyist to access publicly available information via the Internet, but politicians often covet information that is highly detailed, specific, up-to-date, and not publicly available in any easy-to-find form. This kind of information ordinarily will be gathered only by a group that has a strong interest in some issue. Lobbyists, for the most part, are not flamboyant, party-giving arm-twisters; they are specialists who gather information (favorable to their clients, naturally) and present it in as organized, persuasive, and factual a manner as possible. All lobbyists no doubt exaggerate, but few can afford to misrepresent the facts or mislead a legislator, and for a very simple reason: almost every lobbyist must develop and maintain the confidence of a legislator over the long term, with an eye on tomorrow's issues as well as today's.

Misrepresentation or bad advice can embarrass a legislator who accepts it or repel one who detects it, leading to distrust of the lobbyist. Maintaining contacts and channels of communication is vital; to that end, maintaining trust is essential.

The value of the information provided by a lobbyist often is greatest when the issue is fairly narrow, involving only a few interest groups or a complex economic or technical problem. The value of information, and thus the power of the lobbyist, is likely to be least when the issue is one of broad and highly visible national policy.

political cue A signal telling a legislator what values are at stake in a vote, and how that issue fits into his or her own political views on party agenda.

ratings Assessments of a representative's voting record on issues important to an interest group.

Sometimes the nature of an issue or the governmental process by which an issue is resolved gives a great advantage to the suppliers of certain information and imposes a great burden on would-be suppliers of contrary information. This is an example of "client politics." For example, the Civil Aeronautics Board (CAB) once set airline fares and decided what airlines would fly to what cities. Historically, the only organizations with any incentive to appear before the CAB and supply the necessary information were, naturally, the airlines. Until the CAB began to deregulate civil aviation, CAB decisions often tended to favor the established airlines.

Public officials not only want technical information, but they also want political cues. A **political cue** is a signal telling the official what values are at stake in an issue—who is for, who against a proposal—and how that issue fits into his or her own set of political beliefs. Some legislators feel comfortable when they are on the liberal side of an issue, and others feel comfortable when they are on the conservative side, especially when they are not familiar with the details of the issue. A liberal legislator will look to see whether the AFL-CIO, the NAACP, the Americans for Democratic Action, the Farmers' Union, and various consumer organizations favor a proposal; if so, that is often all he or she has to know. If these liberal groups are split, then the legislator will worry about the matter and try to look into it more closely. Similarly, a conservative legislator will feel comfortable taking a stand on an issue if the Chamber of Commerce, the National Rifle Association, the American Medical Association, various business associations, and Americans for Constitutional Action are in agreement about it; he or she will feel less comfortable if such conservative groups are divided. As a result of this process, lobbyists often work together in informal coalitions based on general political ideology.

One important way in which these cues are made known is by **ratings** that interest groups make of legislators. These are regularly compiled by the AFL-CIO (on who is pro-labor), by the Americans for Democratic Action (on who is liberal), by the Americans for Constitutional Action (on who is conservative), by the Consumer Federation of America (on who is pro-consumer), and by the League of Conservation Voters (on who is pro-environment). These ratings are designed to generate public support for (or opposition to) various legislators. They can be helpful sources of information, but they are sometimes biased by the arbitrary determination of what constitutes a liberal, pro-consumer, or conservative vote.

Both political information and political cues now arrive in the offices of politicians at a faster rate than ever before, thanks to fax machines and the Internet. Many interest groups and political activists have banks of computer-operated fax machines that can get a short, snappy document into the hands of every legislator within minutes. William Kristol, a Republican activist, used this technique to good effect in 1993 when he bombarded Republican members of Congress with arguments concerning why they should oppose President Clinton's health care plan. Many believe he played a major role in the defeat of that plan.

EARMARKS

Information can be linked to influence. Lobbyists not only tell members of Congress facts, but they also learn from these members what Washington is doing and then look for ways to sell that information to their clients. What often results is an **earmark**, that is, a provision in a law that provides a direct benefit to a client without the benefit having been reviewed on the merits by all of Congress.

earmark A provision in a law that provides a direct benefit to a client without the benefit having been reviewed on the merits by all of Congress.

Earmarks have always existed, but they became much more common in the 1970s and later. There are two reasons for this. First, the federal government was doing much more and thus affecting more parts of the society. Second, lobbying organizations figured out they could sell to their clients information about how to convert some bit of federal activity to their benefit.

One recent study showed how a new kind of lobbying firm was born. Cassidy and Associates prospered by helping clients get earmarks. The firm charged a flat fee ($10,000 or more per month) and devoted its energy to studying congressional laws in order to find opportunities for its clients.[17]

Its first big client was a university that wanted federal money to pay for a nutrition center it hoped to build. The Cassidy firm discovered that Congress had authorized a "national" nutrition center and then set about persuading key congressional leaders that such a center should be located at the university that was paying Cassidy a fee. Soon many more universities pushed for earmarks for their pet ideas (a foreign-service school, defense software institutes, and computer centers). Not long after that, business firms joined the hunt.

In 2008, the Office of Management and Budget estimated that more than 11,000 earmarks had been approved by Congress at a cost of more than $16 billion. Soon a movement started among some legislators to stop earmarks. But they have faced a problem. Many members of Congress think earmarks are good: why should only the president or congressional committees decide on what things Congress should spend its money? Why not let individual legislators do good things for their constituents? One way to attempt to balance these competing views is to try to tell the difference between a good and a bad earmark. Is a university nutrition center a good thing but a study on wood utilization a bad one? Is a computer center desirable but a bridge to a (largely) uninhabited island in Alaska undesirable? There is no easy way to make these judgments, and so earmarks continue to thrive in Washington. Interest groups suggest ways legislators can help people who vote for them.

PUBLIC SUPPORT: THE RISE OF THE NEW POLITICS

Once upon a time, when the government was small, Congress was less individualistic, and television was nonexistent, lobbyists mainly used an *insider strategy:* they worked closely with a few key members of Congress, meeting them privately to exchange information and (sometimes) favors. Matters of mutual interest could be discussed at a leisurely pace, over dinner or while playing golf. Public opinion was important on some highly visible issues, but there were not many of these.

Following an insider strategy is still valuable, but increasingly interest groups have turned to an *outsider strategy.* The newly individualistic nature of Congress has made this tactic useful, and modern technology has made it possible. Radio, fax machines, and the Internet can now get news out almost immediately. Satellite television can be used to link interested citizens in various locations across the country. Toll-free phone numbers can be publicized, enabling voters to call the offices of their members of Congress without charge. Public opinion polls can be done by telephone, virtually overnight, to measure (and help generate) support for or opposition to proposed legislation. Mail can be directed by computers to people already known to have an interest in a particular matter.

This kind of *grassroots lobbying* is central to the outsider strategy. It is designed to generate public pressure directly on government officials. The "public" that exerts this pressure is not every voter or even most voters; it is that part of the public (sometimes called an *issue public*) directly affected by or deeply concerned with a government policy. What modern technology has made possible is the overnight mobilization of specific-issue publics.

Not every issue lends itself to an outsider strategy: it is hard to get many people excited about, for example, complex tax legislation affecting only a few firms. But as the government does more and more, and its policies affect more and more people, many more will join in grassroots lobbying efforts over matters such as abortion, Medicare, Social Security, environmental protection, and affirmative action.

Undoubtedly, the new politics creates new conflicts. Since conflict is the essence of politics, it may seem strange that politicians dislike controversy. But they do, and for perfectly human reasons: no one enjoys dealing with people who are upset or who find one's viewpoint objectionable or unworthy. Consequently, most legislators tend to hear what they want to hear and deal with interest groups that agree with them. Two senators from the same state may choose to listen to very different constituencies in that state and to take very different policy positions. Neither senator may feel "pressured" or "lobbied," because each has heard mostly from groups or persons who share his or her views. (Politicians define "pressure" as arguments and inducements supplied by somebody with whom they disagree.)

Members of interest groups also tend to work primarily with legislators with whom they agree; lobbyists do not like to argue with people who are suspicious of them or who are unlikely to change their minds no matter what is said. For the lobbyist, the key target is the undecided or wavering legislator or bureaucrat. Sometimes lobbyists make a major effort to persuade an undecided legislator that public opinion is strongly inclined in one direction. A lobbyist will do this by commissioning public opinion polls, stimulating local citizens to write letters or send telegrams, arranging for constituents to pay personal visits to the legislator, or getting newspapers to run editorials supporting the lobbyist's position.

Though most lobbying organizations cultivate the goodwill of government officials, there are important exceptions. Some groups, especially those that use an ideological appeal to attract supporters or that depend for their maintenance and influence on media publicity, will deliberately attack actual or potential allies in government in order to embarrass them.

Of late, interest groups have placed great emphasis on developing grassroots support. Sometimes it is impossible to develop such support, as when a complicated tax regulation of interest to only a few firms is changed. But sometimes a proposed bill touches a public nerve such that even businesses can help generate an outpouring of mail: a few decades ago, when the Food and Drug Administration announced it was going to ban saccharin on the grounds that it caused cancer in laboratory animals, the Calorie Control Council (closely tied to the Coca-Cola Company, a big user of saccharin in soft drinks such as Tab) ran newspaper ads denouncing the policy. The public, worried about losing access to an artificial sweetener important to dieters, responded with an avalanche of mail to Congress, which promptly passed a law reversing the ban.

MONEY AND PACS

Contrary to popular suspicions, money is probably one of the less effective ways by which interest groups advance their causes. That was not always the case. Only a few decades ago, powerful interests used their bulging wallets to buy influence in Congress. The passage of the Campaign Finance Reform Law of 1973 changed that. The law had two effects. First, it sharply restricted the amount any interest could give to a candidate for federal office (see Chapter 10). Second, it made it legal for organizations to create political action committees (PACs) that could make political contributions.

Once PACs became legal, they grew rapidly in numbers. Today there are more than 4,500 PACs. Over the last few years, so-called Leadership PACs and Super PACs have proliferated and received media attention. The former type of PAC is headed by a member of Congress who raises money for other candidates, while the latter type of PAC is an "independent expenditure-only committee" that is not allowed to coordinate with candidates or political party leaders. Among the best-known Leadership PACs is the one formed by former House Speaker Nancy Pelosi to help fund Democratic candidates (Team Majority). Among the best-known Super PACs is the one launched by former White House aide to President George W. Bush, Karl Rove, to assist Republican candidates (American Crossroads). The Leadership PACs are a type of so-called Non-Connected PACs that do not act on behalf of a particular corporation, labor union, or trade association, but are instead commonly organized around ideological views, particular issues, or leading political personalities. Still, the vast majority of PACs, including most of the fifty largest PAC contributors, are traditional so-called Connected PACs set up by and connected to business corporations, labor unions, or other interest groups that raise and spend campaign money from voluntary donations. The top ten PAC contributors alone combine to give millions of dollars a year to candidates of their choice (see Table 11.1). But there are strict limits on how much a member can contribute and how much the PAC can give to candidates and parties. How they work is shown in Table 11.2.

Table 11.1 Ten Largest PAC Contributors, 2009

PAC Affiliation	Amount
Engineers Political Education Committee	$1,924,500
International Brotherhood of Electrical Workers	$1,726,800
AT&T	$1,666,025
Honeywell International	$1,577,900
National Beer Wholesalers Association	$1,496,500
American Association for Justice	$1,428,500
American Bankers Association	$1,287,000
National Community Pharmacists Association	$1,279,750
American Federation of State County & Municipal Employees	$1,258,000
Boeing Company	$1,141,000

Source: Federal Election Committee, "Top 50 PACs by Contributions to Candidates and Other Committeees, January 1, 2009–December 31, 2009," 2010.

Table 11.2 Political Action Committees (PACs)

Can be formed by:
• Business firms
• Labor unions
• Trade associations
• Ideological organizations
Must have at least 50 individual members
• Each member can give up to $5,000 per election
• The sponsoring firm, union, association, or ideological group cannot contribute money
Each PAC may contribute:
• $5,000 to any federal candidate in any election (must give to at least five candidates)
• $15,000 to any national political party
• $5,000 to any state or local party
Where the money goes:
• Business PACs give slightly more to Republicans than to Democrats
• Labor unions give more than 90 percent to Democrats
• Ideological PACs give to Democrats and Republicans in about equal amounts

Some people worry that the existence of all this political money has resulted in our having, as the late Senator Edward Kennedy put it, "the finest Congress that money can buy." More likely, the increase in the number of PACs has had just the opposite effect. The reason is simple: with PACs so numerous and so easy to form, it is now probable that money will be available on every side of almost every conceivable issue. As a result, members of Congress can take money and still decide for themselves how to vote. As we shall see, there is not much scholarly evidence that money buys votes in Congress.

Indeed, some members of Congress tell PACs what to do rather than take orders from them. Members will frequently inform PACs that they "expect" money from them; grumbling PAC officials feel they have no choice but to contribute for fear of alienating the members. Moreover, some members have created their *own* PACs—organizations set up to raise money from individual donors that is then given to favored political allies in and out of Congress or used to advance the members' own political ambitions. When Charles Rangel, congressman from New York, was hoping to be elected whip of the Democratic Party in the House, he set

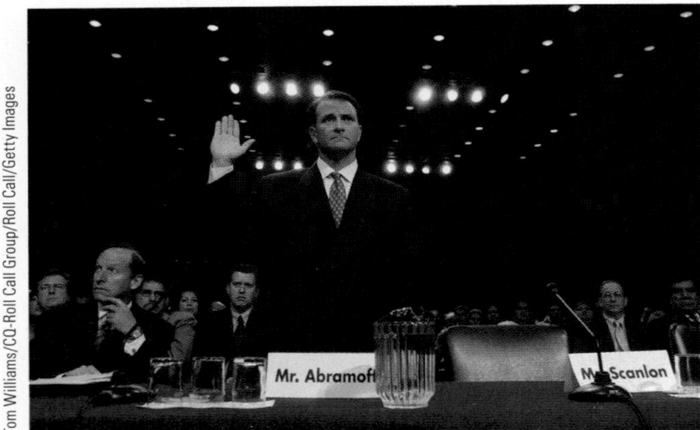

Tom Williams/CQ-Roll Call Group/Roll Call/Getty Images

Jack Abramoff, convicted of corruption in handling lobbying claims by certain Indian tribes, is sworn in before a congressional committee investigating this.

up a PAC that made campaign contributions to fellow representatives in hopes that they might vote for him as whip. There are many other examples from both sides of the aisle. An ironic consequence of this is that a conservative Republican may give money to a PAC set up by a moderate Democrat, who then gives the money to a liberal Democrat (or vice versa), with the result that the original donor winds up having his or her money go to somebody that he or she profoundly dislikes.

Almost any kind of organization—corporation, labor union, trade association, public-interest lobby, citizens group—can form a PAC. Over half of all PACs are sponsored by corporations or trade associations, about 6 percent by labor unions, and the rest by various groups, including independent and ideological ones. The rise of ideological PACs has been the most remarkable development in interest group activity in recent years. At various points over the last several decades, they have increased in number at a faster rate than business or labor PACs, and in several elections they raised more money than either business or labor.

In the 2007–2008 election cycle, PACs gave more than $380 million to candidates running for the House and Senate. Of the 10 PACs that gave the most money to candidates in the 2008 election, most were labor unions, business organizations, and groups that represented doctors, lawyers, realtors, and government employees. Incumbents received more PAC money than challengers. Labor PACs gave almost exclusively to Democrats. Business PACs favored Republicans.

Both parties have become dependent on PAC money. Still, the popular image of rich PACs stuffing huge sums into political campaigns and thereby buying the attention and possibly the favors of the grateful candidates is a bit overdrawn. For one thing, the typical PAC contribution is rather small. The average PAC donation to a House candidate is only a few hundred dollars. Most PACs spread small sums of money over many candidates, and despite their great growth in numbers and expenditures, PACs still provide only about one-third of all the money spent by candidates for the House ($123 million of $361 million in 2010).

Moreover, scholars have yet to find systematic evidence that PAC contributions generally affect how members of Congress vote. On most issues, how legislators vote can be explained primarily by their general ideological outlooks and the characteristics of their constituents; how much PAC money they have received turns out to be a small factor. On the other hand, when an issue arises in which most of their constituents have no interest and ideology provides little guidance, there is a slight statistical correlation between PAC contributions and votes. But even here the correlation may be misleading. The same groups that give money also wage intensive lobbying campaigns, flooding representatives with information, press releases, and letters from interested constituents.

In 2010, in *Citizens United v. Federal Election Commission*, the U.S. Supreme Court struck down as unconstitutional provisions of a 2002 federal campaign finance law that prohibited independent expenditures by business corporations, nonprofit organizations, and unions to fund "electioneering communications" within 30 days of a primary election or 60 days of a general election. This decision was the seedbed for the aforementioned Super PACs, but it is too soon to know whether, as many observers seem to fear, the decision will increase still further the amount of money that interests groups of all sorts are spending to influence lawmakers. But even if that fear is realized, it is not entirely certain that increased expenditures will result in increased influence over how lawmakers vote.

Of course, it is possible that money affects legislative behavior in ways that will never appear in studies of roll-call votes in Congress. Members of Congress may be more willing to set aside time in their busy schedules for a group that has given money than for a group that has not. In that case, what the money has bought is access: it has helped open the door. Or contributions might influence how legislators behave on the committees on which they serve, subtly shaping the way in which they respond to arguments and the facts on which they rely. No one knows, because the research has not been done.

In any event, if interest group money makes a difference at all, it probably makes it on certain kinds of issues more than others. In the chapter on policy-making, we define the kind of issues—we call them "client politics"—on which a given interest group is likely to be especially influential, whether by means of arguments, money, or both. After reading that chapter and considering the examples given there, it will be easier to put the present discussion of PAC money into context.

THE "REVOLVING DOOR"

Every year, hundreds of people leave important jobs in the federal government to take more lucrative positions in private industry. Some go to work as lobbyists, others as consultants to business, still others as key executives in corporations, foundations, and universities. Many people worry that this "revolving door" may give private interests a way of improperly influencing government decisions. If a federal official uses his or her government position to do something for a corporation in exchange for a cushy job after leaving government, or if a person who has left government uses his or her personal contacts in Washington to get favors for private parties, then the public interest may suffer.

From time to time, certain incidents stir these fears. For instance, as *The Washington Post* reported, following the attempted bombing of a U.S. airliner on Christmas day 2009, Michael Chertoff, the former secretary of the Department of Homeland Security (DHS), "gave dozens of media interviews touting the need for the federal government to buy more full body-scanners for airports"; but in that media blitz Chertoff did not always make clear what his security consulting firm, the Chertoff Group, had disclosed in a statement issued before he made the media rounds, namely, that the former DHS chief represented a client that manufactured the machines and sold them to a DHS subunit, the Transportation Safety Administration.[18]

Over the years, more than a few scandals have taken place concerning corrupt dealings between federal department officials and industry executives. Many have involved contractors or their

How Things Work

Conflict of Interest

In 1978, a new federal law, the Ethics in Government Act, codified and broadened the rules governing possible conflicts of interest among senior members of the executive branch. The key provisions were as follows.

The president, vice president, and top-ranking (GS-16 and above) executive branch employees must each year file a public financial disclosure report that lists:

- The source and amount of all earned income as well as income from stocks, bonds, and property; the worth of any investments or large debts; and the source of a spouse's income, if any
- Any position held in business, labor, or certain non-profit organizations

Employment after government service is restricted. Former executive branch employees may *not:*

- Represent anyone before their former agencies in connection with any matter that the former employees had been involved in before leaving the government
- Appear before an agency, for two years after leaving government service, on matters that came within the former employees' official sphere of responsibility, even if they were not personally involved in the matter
- Represent anyone on any matter before their former agencies, for one year after leaving them, even if the former employees had no connection with the matter while in the government

In addition, another law prohibits bribery. It is illegal to ask for, solicit, or receive anything of value in return for being influenced in the performance of one's duties.

Finally, an executive order forbids outside employment. An official may not hold a job or take a fee, even for lecturing or writing, if such employment or income might create a conflict of interest or an apparent conflict of interest.

Sources: National Journal (November 19, 1977): 1796–1803; *Congressional Quarterly Weekly Report* (October 28, 1978): 3121–3127.

consultants bribing procurement officials. Far more common, however, have been major breakdowns in the procurement process itself. For example, in 2006, the Department of Homeland Security revealed the results from an internal audit.[19] In the previous year, the department had spent $17.5 billion on contracts for airport security, radiation-monitor detectors, and other goods and services. But records for nearly three dozen contracts were completely missing, and records for many other contracts lacked evidence that the department had followed federal rules in negotiating best prices. (The internal audit itself was performed by private consultants, presumably in compliance with all relevant rules.)

Agencies differ in their vulnerability to outside influences. If the Food and Drug Administration is not vigilant, people in that agency who help decide whether a new drug should be placed on the market may have their judgment affected somewhat by the possibility that, if they approve the drug, the pharmaceutical company that makes it will later offer them a lucrative position. On the other hand, lawyers in the Federal Trade Commission who prosecute businesses that violate the antitrust laws may decide that their chances for getting a good job with a private law firm later on will increase if they are particularly vigorous and effective prosecutors. The firm, after all, wants to hire competent people, and winning a case is a good test of competence.[20]

CIVIL DISOBEDIENCE

Public displays and disruptive tactics—protest marches, sit-ins, picketing, and violence—have always been a part of American politics. Indeed, they were among the favorite tactics of the American colonists seeking independence in 1776.

Both ends of the political spectrum have used display, disruption, and violence. On the left feminists, antislavery agitators, coal miners, autoworkers, welfare mothers, African Americans, antinuclear power groups, public housing tenants, the American Indian Movement, the Students for a Democratic Society, and the Weather Underground have created "trouble" ranging from peaceful sit-ins at segregated lunch counters to bombings and shootings. On the right, the Ku Klux Klan has used terror, intimidation, and murder; parents opposed to forced busing of schoolchildren have demonstrated; business firms have used strong-arm squads against workers; right-to-life groups have blockaded abortion clinics; and an endless array of "anti-" groups (anti-Catholics, anti-Masons, anti-Jews, anti-immigrants, antisaloons, antiblacks, antiprotesters, and probably even anti-antis) have taken their disruptive turns on stage. These various activities are not morally the same—a sit-in demonstration is quite different from a lynching—but politically they constitute a similar problem for a government official.

An explanation of why and under what circumstances disruption occurs is beyond the scope of this book. To understand interest group politics, however, it is important to remember that making trouble has, since the 1960s, become a quite conventional political resource and is no longer simply the last resort of extremist groups. Making trouble is now an accepted political tactic of ordinary middle-class citizens as well as the disadvantaged or disreputable.

There is of course a long history of the use of disruptive methods by "proper" people. For example, in a movement that began in England at the turn of the 20th century and then spread to America, feminists would chain themselves to lampposts or engage in what we now call "sit-ins" as part of a campaign to win the vote for women. The object then was much the same as the object of similar tactics today: to disrupt the working of some institution so that it is forced to negotiate with you, or, failing that, to enlist the sympathies of third parties (the media, other interest groups) who will come to your aid and press your target to negotiate with you, or, failing that, to goad the police into making attacks and arrests so that martyrs are created.

The civil rights and antiwar movements of the 1960s gave experience in these methods to thousands of young people and persuaded others of the effectiveness of such methods under certain conditions. Though these movements have abated or

Fred Prouser/Reuters/Landov

Lawsuits, such as this one against Proposition 8 which banned same-sex marriage in California, are often more effective than protest demonstrations in changing policies.

disappeared, their veterans and emulators have put such tactics to new uses—trying to block the construction of a nuclear power plant, for example, or occupying the office of a cabinet secretary to obtain concessions for a particular group.

Government officials dread this kind of trouble. They usually find themselves in a no-win situation. If they ignore the disruption, they are accused of being "insensitive," "unresponsive," or "arrogant." If they give in to the demonstrators, they encourage more demonstrations by proving that this is a useful tactic. If they call the police, they run the risk of violence and injuries, followed not only by bad publicity but also by lawsuits.

Regulating Interest Groups

Interest group activity is a form of political speech protected by the First Amendment to the Constitution: it cannot lawfully be abolished or even much curtailed. In 1946, Congress passed the Federal Regulation of Lobbying Act, which requires groups and individuals seeking to influence legislation to register with the secretary of the Senate and the clerk of the House and to file quarterly financial reports. The Supreme Court upheld the law but restricted its application to lobbying efforts involving direct contacts with members of Congress.[21] More general "grassroots" interest group activity may not be restricted by the government. The 1946 law had little practical effect. Not all lobbyists took the trouble to register, and there was no guarantee that the financial statements were accurate. There was no staff in charge of enforcing the law.

After years of growing popular dissatisfaction with Congress, prompted in large measure by the (exaggerated) view that legislators were the pawns of powerful special interests, Congress in late 1995 unanimously passed a bill that tightened up the registration and disclosure requirements. Signed by the president, the law restated the obligation of lobbyists to register with the House and Senate, but it broadened the definition of a lobbyist to include the following:

- People who spend at least 20 percent of their time lobbying
- People who are paid at least $5,000 in any six-month period to lobby
- Corporations and other groups that spend more than $20,000 in any six-month period on their own lobbying staffs

The law covered people and groups who lobbied the executive branch and congressional staffers as well as elected members of Congress, and it included law firms that represent clients before the government. Twice a year, all registered lobbyists were required to report the following:

- The names of their clients
- Their income and expenditures
- The issues on which they worked

The registration and reporting requirements did not, however, extend to so-called grassroots organizations—that is, campaigns (sometimes led by volunteers, sometimes by hired professionals) to mobilize citizens to write or call the government about some issue. Nor was any new enforcement organization created, although congressional officials could refer violations to the Justice Department for investigation. Fines for breaking the law could amount to $50,000. In addition, the law barred tax-exempt, nonprofit advocacy groups that lobby from getting federal grants.

Just as the Republicans moved expeditiously to pass new regulations on interest groups and lobbying when they regained majorities in Congress in the November 1994 elections, the Democrats' first order of business after retaking Congress in the November 2006 elections was to adopt sweeping reforms. Beginning March 1, 2007, many new regulations took effect, including the following:

- No gifts of any value from registered lobbyists or firms that employ lobbyists
- No reimbursement for travel costs from registered lobbyists or firms that employ lobbyists
- No reimbursement for travel costs, no matter the source, if the trip is in any part organized or requested by a registered lobbyist or firm that employs lobbyists

Strictly speaking, these and related new rules mean that a House member cannot go on a "fact-finding" trip to a local site or a foreign country and have anyone associated with lobbying arrange to pay for it. Even people who are not themselves registered lobbyists, but who work for a lobbying firm, are not permitted to take members of Congress to lunch or give them any other "thing of value," no matter how small.

But if past experience is any guide, "strictly speaking" is not how the rules will be followed or enforced. For instance, buried in the fine print of the new rules are provisions that permit members of Congress to accept reimbursement for travel from lobbyists if

WHAT WOULD YOU DO?

MEMORANDUM

To: *Kathleen Moore, Senate majority leader*

From: *Christopher Franklin, chief of staff*

Subject: *Full federal financing of presidential campaigns*

Every presidential election since 1976 has been financed in part by federal funds. Now presidential candidates say they will forego public funding for the general election, given the vastly greater resources available through private fundraising. Congress needs to decide whether elections are a public investment or a political free market for citizens and candidates.

Arguments for:

1. Legal precedents are promising. Federal matching funds already go to presidential primary candidates who have raised at least $5,000, in contributions of $250 or less, in each of twenty states. For the general election, each major party nominee already is eligible for federal funding if he or she agrees to spend no more than that amount.
2. The funding required would be small. Allocating $1 billion out of the public treasury for a presidential election every four years is hardly a fiscal drain on a nearly $2 trillion annual budget.
3. The effects would be pervasive. Candidates and party leaders would stop covertly courting big donors with phone calls, lunches, and personal visits, and would focus instead on the needs of average citizens.

Arguments against:

1. Constitutional precedent for requiring political candidates to accept public funds is weak. In *Buckley v. Valeo* (1976), the Supreme Court upheld limits on campaign contributions for candidates who accept public money, but it also defined spending money for political purposes as expression protected by the First Amendment, thereby giving individuals the right to raise and spend as much of their own money as they choose, if they forego federal funds.
2. Campaign spending would soon spiral once again. The federal government may not restrict spending by individuals or organizations working independently from the political parties, and federal funds would merely supplement, not supplant, private fundraising.
3. Less than 10 percent of taxpayers currently supports public financing through voluntary federal income tax checkoffs, and voters likely would view bankrolling elections as serving politicians, not the people.

News »

Bipartisan Group in Senate Proposes Full Public Financing of Presidential Campaigns

With the upcoming presidential election expected to cost more than $1 billion, a bipartisan group of senators has proposed that Congress control those expenses by fully funding and setting an upper limit on financing for presidential campaigns. Presidential contenders so far have refrained from taking a position on the legislation.

Your decision:

Support legislation ____________ Oppose legislation ____________ the travel is for "one-day trips," so long as the lobbyists themselves do not initiate the trip, make the reservations, or pick up incidental expenses unrelated to the visit. Moreover, these rules have not yet been adopted in precisely the same form by the Senate; and neither chamber has yet clarified language or closed loopholes related to lobbying registration and reporting.

Do not suppose, however, that such remaining gaps in lobbying laws render the system wide open to abuses or evasions. For one thing, loopholes and all, the lobbying laws are now tighter than ever. For another, as we intimated earlier in this chapter, the most significant legal constraints on interest groups come not from the current federal lobbying law (though that may change) but from the tax code and the campaign finance laws. A nonprofit organization—which includes not only charitable groups but also almost all voluntary associations that have an interest in politics—need not pay income taxes, and financial contributions to it can be deducted on the donor's income tax return, provided that the organization does not devote a "substantial part" of its activities to "attempting to influence legislation."[22] Many tax-exempt organizations do take public positions on political questions and testify before congressional committees. If the organization does any serious lobbying, however, it will lose its tax-exempt status (and thus find it harder to solicit donations and more expensive to operate). Exactly this happened to the Sierra Club in 1968 when the Internal Revenue Service revoked its tax-exempt status because of its extensive lobbying activities. Some voluntary associations try to deal with this problem by setting up separate organizations to collect tax-exempt money—for example, the NAACP, which lobbies, must pay taxes, but the NAACP Legal Defense and Education Fund, which does not lobby, is tax-exempt.

Finally, the campaign finance laws, described in detail in Chapter 10, limit to $5,000 the amount any political action committee can spend on a given candidate in a given election. These laws have sharply curtailed the extent to which any *single* group can give money, though they have increased the *total* amount that different groups are providing.

Beyond making bribery or other manifestly corrupt forms of behavior illegal and restricting the sums that campaign contributors can donate, there is probably no system for controlling interest groups that would both make a useful difference and leave important constitutional and political rights unimpaired. Ultimately, the only remedy for imbalances or inadequacies in interest group representation is to devise and sustain a political system that gives all affected parties a reasonable chance to be heard on matters of public policy. That, of course, is exactly what the Founders thought they were doing. Whether they succeeded or not is a question to which we shall return at the end of this book.

LEARNING OBJECTIVES

WHAT YOU NEED TO KNOW

☑ What are interest groups and how did they arise in America?

An interest group is an organization of people sharing a common interest or goal that seeks to influence public policy. Interest groups were present from the first days of the republic, but they proliferated thereafter in several different periods. The latest period of interest group expansion began in the 1960s and has accelerated over the last decade.

☑ What are the different kinds of interest groups and which types have been proliferating of late?

There are two kinds of interest groups: institutional and membership. Institutional groups represent other organizations (like lobbying firms that represent corporations or trade groups in Washington), while membership groups represent their own members and their members' policy preferences and beliefs (like the National Association for the Advancement of Colored People, an historic civil rights membership organization). Membership groups organized around ideological beliefs and institutional groups representing corporate interests have proliferated in recent decades. Over just the last decade, there has been an especially large increase in the number of lobbyists representing business interests in Washington.

☑ How do interest groups attempt to influence public policy, and how does government regulate interest group activities?

Among other things, interest groups use specialized information, political cues, ratings of legislators, and earmarks to sway politicians and influence policy. Government influences interest groups as much as interest groups influence government: detailed rules and regulations now govern most aspects of what lobbyists do.

RECONSIDERING WHO GOVERNS?

1. Do interest groups dominate government, and is any particular lobby politically unbeatable?

The answers are "not really" and "no," respectively. There are so many governmental institutions in which power may be exercised that no single group can dominate most public policy decisions. What the government does is often the outcome of a complex pattern of political haggling, innumerable compromises, and shifting alliances among and between different groups and their leaders. Even supposedly all-powerful lobbies (like the National Rifle Association [NRA] on gun control, or the American Association of Retired Persons [AARP] on senior citizens' health care benefits) sometimes find themselves on the losing side of legislative decisions and court opinions.

2. Why do people join interest groups?

Pretty much for the same basic reasons that people join any organization. There are three kinds of incentives: solidary, material, and purposive. Organizations, including interest groups, can attract members through one, two, or all three incentives. Some interest groups rely mainly on one incentive. For example, ideological political action committees (PACs) rely largely on purposive incentives, attracting members by appealing to their beliefs in a coherent set of principles or their passions on a particular set of issues. Even these groups, however, normally provide their members with certain tangible, members-only benefits (for example, magazines or special discounts on various products). Organizations that principally benefit nonmembers are sometimes called public-interest lobbies.

RECONSIDERING TO WHAT ENDS?

1. Is the proliferation of political action committees (PACs) and other groups good or bad for America's representative democracy?

What would James Madison say? Go back to the Appendix and Federalist No. 10. Madison recognized that freedom begat factions, but he hoped that the government proposed under the Constitution would succeed in "regulating these various and interfering interests" in ways that secured the "public good." The mere proliferation of interest groups in our time does not justify a negative answer to that question. Rather, one would also have to believe the political process is dominated by groups that seek to serve their members with little or no regard for the well-being and rights of other citizens. To some pro-choice voters, certain pro-life groups may appear as factions, and to some pro-life citizens, certain pro-choice groups may appear as factions. Both these and other ideological groups have proliferated in recent decades. Whether this is good or bad for American's representative democracy is a question on which reasonable minds can and do differ. But this much is clear: in contemporary American politics, one citizen's special-interest group often is another citizen's public-interest lobby.

2. Should interest groups' political activities be restricted by law?

In fact, interest groups' activities are restricted by literally scores of laws that are already on the books. For example, Washington lobbyists must register with the House or Senate. All registered lobbyists must publicly divulge their client list and expenditures. There are legal limits on PAC contributions. Every new wave of campaign finance laws (see Chapter 10) has resulted in more rules regulating interest groups. The Internal Revenue Service (IRS) has tightly restricted political activity by religious groups, private schools, and other organizations as a condition for their exemption from federal income tax. The courts have consistently upheld such restrictions and ruled that they do not, under most circumstances, violate freedom of speech or other constitutional protections. On the other hand, the courts have effectively afforded even tax-exempt groups ways of legally, but indirectly, engaging in political activity. Finally, states and cities have their own laws regulating interest groups, and some places are more restrictive than others.

QUESTIONS TO CONSIDER

1. **What general criteria (that is, principles that transcend your own personal policy preferences) would you suggest using in order to distinguish between a "special-interest group" and a "public-interest lobby" in any given area of public policy (abortion, environmental protection, gun control, health care, others)?**
2. **Should former high-ranking government officials be subject to lifetime bans on paid employment that involves them in representing or lobbying for any organizations with even the slightest connections to their old public service positions, or are there other and better ways to deal with the "revolving door"?**
3. **How much money was received by candidates for the House and Senate from your state in the last national election, how much of it came from PACs, and which PACs were the largest contributors?**
4. **What, if any, membership organizations are headquartered in your state or city, how do these groups present themselves on their respective Web sites, and how are they funded?**
5. **What were the main issues that divided the majority and the minority in *Citizens United v. Federal Election Commission* (2010), does the ruling apply only to businesses or to all "corporations" including incorporated labor unions, and do you suppose that the decision will significantly increase campaign-related or other political spending by interest groups in the future?**

TO LEARN MORE

Conservative interest groups

American Conservative Union: **www.conservative.org**

Christian Coalition: **www.cc.org**

Liberal interest groups

American Civil Liberties Union: **www.aclu.org**

Americans for Democratic Action: **www.adaction.org**

Environmental groups

Environmental Defense: **www.environmentaldefense.org**

National Resources Defense Council: **www.nrdc.org**

Civil rights groups

NAACP: **www.naacp.org**

Center for Equal Opportunity: **www.ceousa.org**

Feminist group

National Organization for Women: **www.now.org**

Bauer, Raymond A., Ithiel de Sola Pool, and Lewis A. Dexter. *American Business and Public Policy.* New York: Atherton, 1963. A classic study of how business groups tried to shape foreign-trade legislation, set in a broad analysis of pressure groups and Congress.

Cigler, Allan J., and Burdett A. Loomis, eds. *Interest Group Politics,* 7th ed. Washington, D.C.: Congressional Quarterly Press, 2007. Essays on several interest groups active in Washington.

Lowi, Theodore J. *The End of Liberalism.* New York: Norton, 1969. A critique of the role of interest groups in American government.

Mansbridge, Jane J. *Why We Lost the ERA.* Chicago: University of Chicago Press, 1986. Insightful analysis of the relationship between organizational incentives and tactics in the ERA campaign.

Olson, Mancur. *The Logic of Collective Action.* Cambridge: Harvard University Press, 1965. An economic analysis of interest groups, especially the "free-rider" problem.

Sabato, Larry. *PAC Power.* New York: Norton, 1985. A full discussion of the nature and activities of political action committees.

Schlozman, Kay Lehman, and John T. Tierney. *Organized Interests and American Democracy.* New York: Harper and Row, 1985. Comprehensive treatise on interest groups based on original research.

Truman, David B. *The Governmental Process,* 2d ed. New York: Knopf, 1971. First published in 1951, this was the classic analysis—and defense—of interest group pluralism.

Wilson, James Q. *Political Organizations,* Rev. ed. Princeton, N.J.: Princeton University Press, 1995. A theory of interest groups emphasizing the incentives they use to attract members.

12 The Media

LEARNING OBJECTIVES

WHAT YOU NEED TO KNOW

☑ What role do the media play in American politics?

☑ Why are there so few restrictions on media coverage of politics and politicians in the United States?

☑ How has technology changed interactions between public officials and the media?

WHO GOVERNS?

1. How much power do the media have?
2. Can we trust the media to be fair?

TO WHAT ENDS?

1. What public policies will the media support?

Suppose you want to influence how other people think about health, politics, sports, or celebrities. What would you do? At one time, you might write a book or publish an essay in a newspaper or magazine. But unless you were very lucky, the book or article would only reach a few people. Today, you will have a much bigger impact if you can get on television or invent a controversial Web log (or blog). Vastly more people watch *American Idol* than read newspaper editorials; many more get opinions from blogs—such as the Daily Kos on the left or Power Line on the right—than read essays in magazines.

Television and the Internet are key parts of the New Media; newspapers and magazines are part of the Old Media. And when it comes to politics, the New Media are getting stronger and the Old Media weaker.

THEN In 1972–1974, the Nixon administration's efforts to cover up the burglary of Democratic National Committee headquarters at the Watergate hotel in Washington, D.C., were revealed through a series of articles published in *the Washington Post*, which gained national fame for its riveting news coverage by journalists Bob Woodward and Carl Bernstein.[1] In the summer of 1987, Congress held live, televised hearings about the Iran-Contra scandal, which viewers watched at home as well as in stores and other public venues that broadcast the hearings on their televisions.[2]

NOW In 2004, "60 Minutes," a CBS television news program, ran a story claiming that President Bush had performed poorly during his time in the Air National Guard. Within a few hours, bloggers produced evidence that the documents underlying this charge were forgeries, something CBS later conceded was true. Not long afterward, the producer and newscaster responsible for the charges left CBS. In 2008, then-presidential candidate Barack Obama stated at a private fundraiser that voters in economic distress "cling to guns or religion," and a freelance writer for *The Huffington Post* who attended the event decided to publish Obama's remarks, creating an uproar in his campaign.[3] In 2011, reports that the United States had captured and killed Osama bin Laden first appeared on the online site Twitter.

In 2011, more than 40 percent of Americans said they received most national and international news through the Internet. While two-thirds of Americans

said television remained their main news source, that number had dropped from almost three-quarters of Americans citing television as their primary source for news in 2008. The Internet is particularly important for young people: In 2010, for the first time, more people under 30 identified the Internet over television as their main news source.[4]

But not all of the users are convinced that the Internet is entirely trustworthy. One-third think it lets the loudest and most extreme voices prevail and feel that it is full of misinformation. And though newspapers are rapidly losing their audience, they remain vitally important: much of what is on the Internet comes from newspaper reporters, and politicians devote at least as much time to getting good newspaper coverage as they devote to expanding their Internet coverage.

The Media and Politics

The Internet is an important new way for politics to be carried on, but it is only the latest episode in the love-hate relationship between politicians and the nations' changing ways of communicating with one another. From the beginning of the Republic, public officials have tried to get the media on their side while knowing that, since the media love controversy, they are as likely to attack as to praise. The Internet may strike some politicians as the solution to this problem: they think that if they put their own Web pages out there, they can reach the voters directly. They can, but so can rival politicians with their own Web pages and with their allies attacking their competitors.

All of this takes place in a country so committed to a free press that there is little the government can do to control the process. As we shall see, there have been efforts to control radio and television as a result of the government's right to license broadcasters, but most of these attempts have evaporated.

Even strongly democratic nations restrict the press more than the United States. For example, the laws governing libel are much stricter in Great Britain than in the United States. As a result, it is easier in Great Britain for politicians to sue newspapers for publishing articles that defame or ridicule them. In this country, the libel laws make it almost impossible to prevent press criticisms of public figures. Moreover, England has an Official Secrets Act that can be used to punish any past or present public officials who leak information to the press.[5] In this country, leaking information occurs all the time, and our Freedom of Information Act makes it relatively easy for the press to extract documents from the government.

European governments can be much tougher on what people say than the American one. In 2006, an Austrian court sentenced a man to three years in prison for having denied that the Nazi death camp at Auschwitz killed its inmates. A French court convicted a distinguished American historian for telling a French newspaper that the slaughter of Armenians may not have been the result of planned effort. An Italian journalist stood trial for having written things "offensive to Islam." In this country, such statements would be protected by the Constitution even if, as with the man who denied the existence of the Holocaust, they were profoundly wrong.[6]

America has a long tradition of privately owned media. By contrast, private ownership of television has come only recently to France. And the Internet is not owned by anybody: here and in many nations, people can say or read whatever they want on their computers. Newspapers in this country require no government permission to operate, but radio and television stations need licenses granted by the Federal Communications Commission (FCC). These licenses must be renewed periodically. On occasion, the White House has made efforts to use license renewals as a way of influencing station owners who were out of political favor, but of late the level of FCC control over what is broadcast has lessened.

There are two potential limits to the freedom of privately owned newspapers and broadcast stations. First, they must make a profit. Some critics believe the need for profit will lead media outlets to distort the news in order to satisfy advertisers or to build an audience. Though there is some truth to this argument, it is too simple. Every media outlet must satisfy a variety of people—advertisers, subscribers, listeners, reporters, and editors—and balancing those demands is complicated and will be done differently by different owners.

The second problem is media bias. If most of the reporters and editors have similar views about politics and if they act on those views, then the media will give us only one side of many stories. Later in this chapter, we shall take a close look at this possibility.

Journalism in American Political History

Important changes in the nature of American politics have gone hand in hand with major changes in the organization and technology of the press. It is the nature of politics, essentially a form of communication, to respond to changes in how communications are carried on. This can be seen by considering five important periods in journalistic history.

THE PARTY PRESS

In the early years of the Republic, politicians of various factions and parties created, sponsored, and controlled newspapers to further their interests. This was possible because circulation was of necessity small (newspapers could not easily be distributed to large audiences, owing to poor transportation) and newspapers were expensive (the type was set by hand and the presses printed copies slowly). Furthermore, there were few large advertisers to pay the bills. These newspapers circulated chiefly among the political and commercial elites who could afford the high subscription prices. Even with high prices, the newspapers often required subsidies that frequently came from the government or a political party.

During the Washington administration, the Federalists, led by Alexander Hamilton, created the *Gazette of the United States*. The Republicans, led by Thomas Jefferson, retaliated by creating the *National Gazette* and made its editor, Philip Freneau, "clerk for foreign languages" in the State Department at $250 a year to help support him. After Jefferson became president, he induced another publisher, Samuel Harrison Smith, to start the *National Intelligencer*, subsidizing him by giving him a contract to print government documents. Andrew Jackson, when he became president, aided in the creation of the *Washington Globe*. By some estimates, there were more than 50 journalists on the government payroll during this era. Naturally, these newspapers were relentlessly partisan in their views. Citizens could choose among different party papers, but only rarely could they find a paper that presented both sides of an issue.

THE POPULAR PRESS

Changes in society and technology made possible the rise of a self-supporting, mass-readership daily

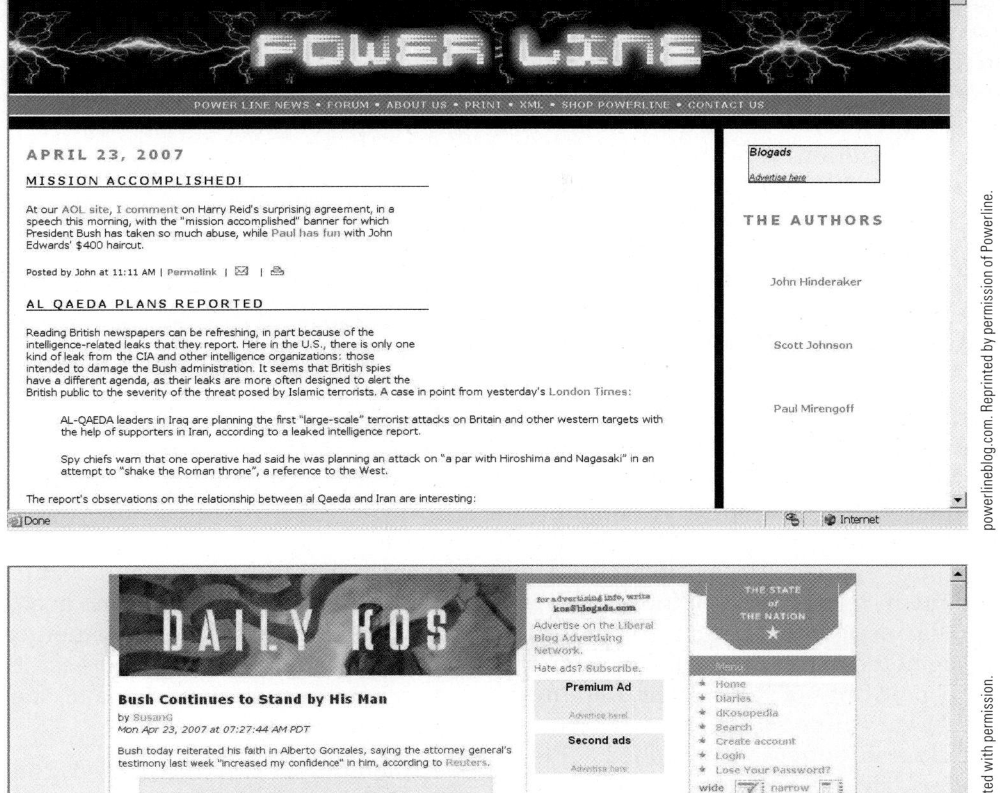

Blogs, both conservative and liberal, have become an important form of political advertising.

newspaper. The development of the high-speed rotary press enabled publishers to print thousands of copies of a newspaper cheaply and quickly. The invention of the telegraph in the 1840s meant that news from Washington could be flashed almost immediately to New York, Boston, Philadelphia, and Charleston, thus providing local papers with access to information that once only the Washington papers enjoyed. The creation in 1848 of the Associated Press allowed telegraphic dissemination of information to newspaper editors on a systematic basis. Since the AP provided stories that had to be brief and that went to newspapers of every political hue, it could not afford to be partisan or biased; to attract as many subscribers as possible, it had to present the facts objectively.

Meanwhile, the nation was becoming more urbanized, with large numbers of people brought together in densely settled areas. These people could support a daily newspaper by paying only a penny per copy and by patronizing merchants who advertised in its pages. Newspapers no longer needed political patronage to prosper, and soon such subsidies began to dry up. In 1860, the Government Printing Office was established, thereby putting an end to most of the printing contracts that Washington newspapers had once enjoyed.

The mass-readership newspaper was scarcely nonpartisan, but the partisanship it displayed arose from the convictions of its publishers and editors rather than from the influence of its party sponsors. And these convictions blended political beliefs with economic interest. The way to attract a large readership was with sensationalism: violence, romance, and patriotism, coupled with exposés of government, politics, business, and society. As practiced by Joseph Pulitzer and William Randolph Hearst, founders of large newspaper empires, this editorial policy had great appeal for the average citizen and especially for the immigrants flooding into the large cities.

Strong-willed publishers could often become powerful political forces. Hearst used his papers to agitate for war with Spain when the Cubans rebelled against Spanish rule. Conservative Republican political leaders were opposed to the war, but a steady diet of newspaper stories about real and imagined Spanish brutalities whipped up public opinion in favor of intervention. At one point, Hearst sent the noted artist Frederic Remington to Cuba to supply paintings of the conflict. Remington cabled back: "Everything is quiet.... There will be no war." Hearst supposedly replied: "Please remain. You furnish the pictures and I'll furnish the war."[7] When the battleship USS *Maine* blew up in Havana harbor, President William McKinley felt helpless to resist popular pressure, and war was declared in 1898.

For all their excesses, the mass-readership newspapers began to create a common national culture, to establish the feasibility of a press free of government control or subsidy, and to demonstrate how exciting (and profitable) could be the criticism of public policy and the revelation of public scandal.

MAGAZINES OF OPINION

The growing middle class often was repelled by what it called "yellow journalism" and was developing around the turn of the century a taste for political reform and a belief in the doctrines of the progressive movement. To satisfy this market, a variety of national magazines appeared that—unlike those devoted to manners and literature—discussed issues of public policy. Among the first of these were the *Nation,* the *Atlantic Monthly,* and *Harper's,* founded in the 1850s and 1860s; later came the more broadly based mass-circulation magazines such as *McClure's, Scribner's,* and *Cosmopolitan.* They provided the means for developing a national constituency for certain issues such as regulating business (or in the language of the times, "trustbusting"), purifying municipal politics, and reforming the civil service system. Lincoln Steffens and other so-called muckrakers were frequent contributors to the magazines, setting a pattern for what we now call "investigative reporting."

The national magazines of opinion provided an opportunity for individual writers to gain a nationwide following. The popular press, though initially under the heavy influence of founder-publishers, made the names of certain reporters and columnists household words. In time, the great circulation wars between the big-city daily newspapers started to wane, as the more successful papers bought up or otherwise eliminated their competition. This reduced the need for the more extreme forms of sensationalism, a change reinforced by the growing sophistication and education of America's readers. And the founding publishers gradually were replaced by less flamboyant managers. All of these changes—in circulation needs, audience interests, managerial style, the emergence of nationally known writers—helped increase the power of editors and reporters and make them a force to be reckoned with.

Although politics dominated the pages of most national magazines in the late 19th century, today national magazines that focus mainly on politics and government affairs account for only a small and declining portion of the national magazine market. Among all magazines in circulation today, only a fraction focus on politics—the majority of today's magazines focus on popular entertainment and leisure activities.

ELECTRONIC JOURNALISM

Radio came on the national scene in the 1920s, television in the late 1940s. They represented a major change in the way news was gathered and disseminated, though few politicians at first understood the importance of this change. A broadcast permits public officials to speak directly to audiences without their remarks being filtered through editors and reporters. This was obviously an advantage to politicians, provided they were skilled enough to use it: they could in theory reach the voters directly on a national scale without the services of political parties, interest groups, or friendly editors.

But there was an offsetting disadvantage—people could easily ignore a speech broadcast on a radio or television station, either by not listening at all or by tuning to a different station. By contrast,

Bettman/Corbis

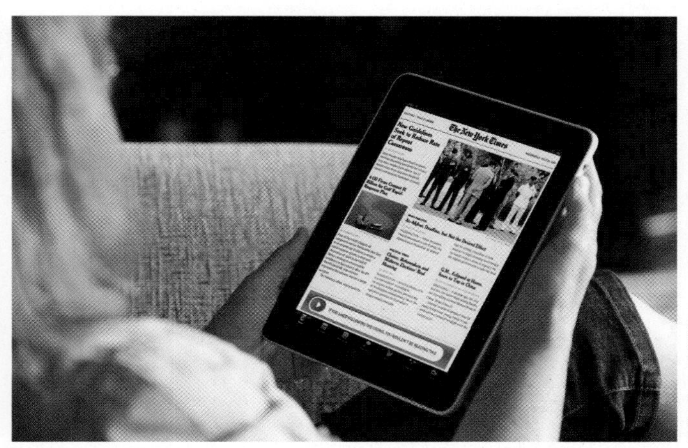
© Pixellover RM 3/Alamy

News used to come by radio, but today many people read newspapers on iPads and other electronic devices.

the views of at least some public figures would receive prominent and often unavoidable display in newspapers, and in a growing number of cities there was only one daily paper. Moreover, space in a newspaper is cheap compared to time on a television broadcast.

Adding one more story, or one more name to an existing story, costs the newspaper little. By contrast, less news can be carried on radio or television, and each news segment must be quite brief to avoid boring the audience. As a result, the number of political personalities that can be covered by radio and television news is much smaller than is the case with newspapers, and the cost (to the station) of making a news item or broadcast longer often is prohibitively large.

Thus, to obtain the advantages of electronic media coverage, public officials must do something sufficiently bold or colorful to gain free access to radio and television news—or they must find the money to purchase radio and television time. The president of the United States, of course, is routinely covered by radio and television and can ordinarily get free time to speak to the nation on matters of importance. All other officials must struggle for access to the electronic media by making controversial statements, acquiring a national reputation, or purchasing expensive time.

The rise of the talk show as a political forum has increased politicians' access to the electronic media, as has the televised "town meeting." But such developments need to be understood as part of a larger story.

Until the 1990s, the "big three" television networks (ABC, CBS, and NBC) together claimed 80 percent or more of all viewers. Their evening newscasts dominated electronic media coverage of politics and government affairs. When it came to presidential campaigns, for example, the three networks were the only television games in town—they reported on the primaries, broadcast the party conventions, and covered the general election campaigns, including any presidential debates. But over the last few decades, the networks' evening newscasts have changed in ways that have made it harder for candidates to use them to get their messages across. For instance, the average **sound bite**—a video clip of a presidential contender speaking—dropped from about 42 seconds in 1968 to 7.3 seconds in 2000.[8] Furthermore, as Figure 12.1 shows, the audience for the evening news has been in decline since the 1980s.

sound bite A radio or video clip of someone speaking.

Today, politicians have sources other than the network news for sustained and personalized television exposure. Cable television, early-morning news and entertainment programs, and prime-time "newsmagazine" shows have greatly increased and diversified politicians' access to the electronic media.

Naturally, many politicians favor the call-in format, town-meeting setups, lengthy human interest interviews, and casual appearances on entertainment shows to televised confrontations on policy issues with seasoned network journalists who push, probe, and criticize. And naturally, they favor being a part of visually interesting programs rather than traditional "talking heads" news shows. But what is

Figure 12.1
Evening News Audience Continues a 30-Year Decline

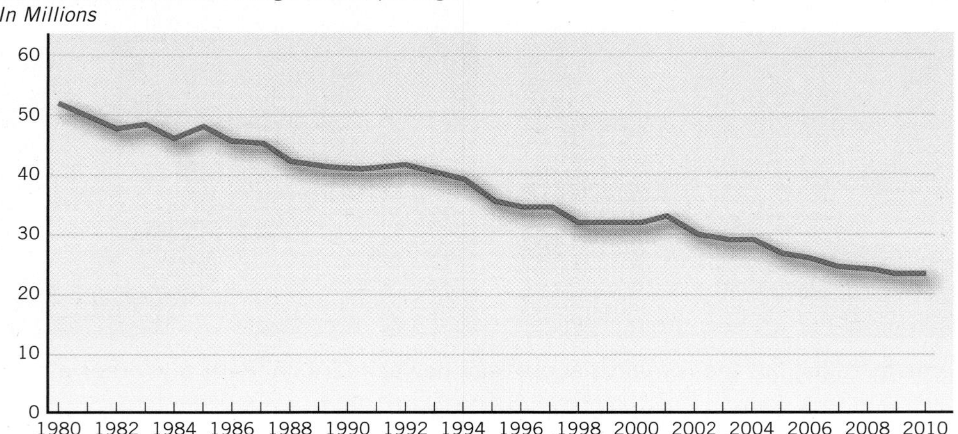

Source: Nielsen Media Research, used under license. Pew Research Center's Project for Excellence in Journalism, 2011 State of the News Media.

preferable to candidates is not necessarily helpful to the selection process that voters must go through in choosing a candidate.

One thing is clear: most politicians crave the media spotlight, both on the campaign trail and in office. The efforts made by political candidates to get "visuals"—filmed stories—on television continue after they are elected. Since the president is always news, a politician wishing to make news is well advised to attack the president.

THE INTERNET

More than half of all Americans used the Internet to get political news about the 2010 midterm elections.[9] The political news found there ranges from summaries of stories from newspapers and magazines to political rumors and hot gossip. Many **blogs** exist on which viewers can scan political ideas posted there; many blogs specialize in offering liberal, conservative, or libertarian perspectives. The Internet is the ultimate free market in political news: no one can ban, control, or regulate it, and no one can keep facts, opinions, or nonsense off of it.

blog A series, or log, of discussion items on a page of the World Wide Web.

The Internet is beginning to play a big role in politics. When Howard Dean ran for the Democratic presidential nomination in 2004, he raised most of his money from Internet appeals. When John Kerry, who won the nomination, was campaigning, the Internet and the blogs on it were a major source of discussion of the criticisms made of him by former Vietnam War veterans. Now every candidate for important offices has a Web site.

The rise of the Internet has completed a remarkable transformation in American journalism. In the days of the party press, only a few people read newspapers. When mass-circulation newspapers arose, mass politics also arose. When magazines of opinion developed, interest groups also developed. When radio and television became dominant, politicians could build their own bridges to voters without party or interest group influence. And now, with the Internet, voters and political activists can talk to each other. This is true in many dictatorships. When popular revolutions broke out against the autocratic leaders of Egypt and Libya, the activists used the Internet and Twitter to inform their colleagues. It is becoming much harder for a powerful leader to control what other people can learn.

Most users think the Internet is a wonderful device, but some worry that using e-mail, YouTube, Facebook, text messaging, blogs, and Twitter to communicate will isolate people from one another and make public opinion more extreme. There have been several studies of this possibility, but they have not produced a clear answer. A Stanford study argued that the Internet isolates people from ordinary human contact and makes them become anonymous. A study at Carnegie Mellon University came to much the same conclusion. By contrast, a study done at UCLA found that Internet users are more likely to consult newspapers and magazines and that they spend just as much time on the telephone as people not on the Internet. And a Pew survey suggested that e-mail makes people feel more, not less, connected to others.[10]

But one thing is clear: the Internet has profoundly affected politics by making it easier to (1) raise money in small donations, (2) organize people to attend meetings, (3) take instant (though probably unreliable) opinion polls, (4) disseminate instant criticism of your opponent, (5) mobilize local followers, and (6) target campaigners with the names of people they should contact.

The Structure of the Media

The relationship between journalism and politics is a two-way street: though politicians take advantage as best they can of the communications media available to them, these media in turn attempt to use politics and politicians as a way of both entertaining and informing their audiences. The mass media, whatever their disclaimers, are not simply a mirror held up to reality or a messenger that carries the news. There is inevitably a process of selection, of editing, and of emphasis, and this process reflects, to some degree, the way in which the media are organized, the kinds of audiences they seek to serve, and the preferences and opinions of the members of the media.

DEGREE OF COMPETITION

There has been a large decline in the number of daily newspapers that serve large communities. There were competing papers in 60 percent of American cities in 1900 but in only 4 percent in 1972. Several large cities—Boston, Chicago, Detroit, Los Angeles, New York, Philadelphia, and Washington, D.C.—have more than one paper, but in some of these the same business owns both papers. And newspaper circulation has fallen in recent years, with more and more people getting their news from radio and television. Young people especially have turned away from political news. In the 1940s and 1950s, age did not make much difference; people under the age of 30 read about the same amount of news as people over the age of 50. But by the 1970s, that had changed dramatically; from then until now, young people read less political news than older people. In Figure 12.2, we can see that today only half as many people between the ages of 18 and 34 read newspapers as was true in 1970.

Figure 12.2

Percentage of Newspaper Readers Ages 18–34

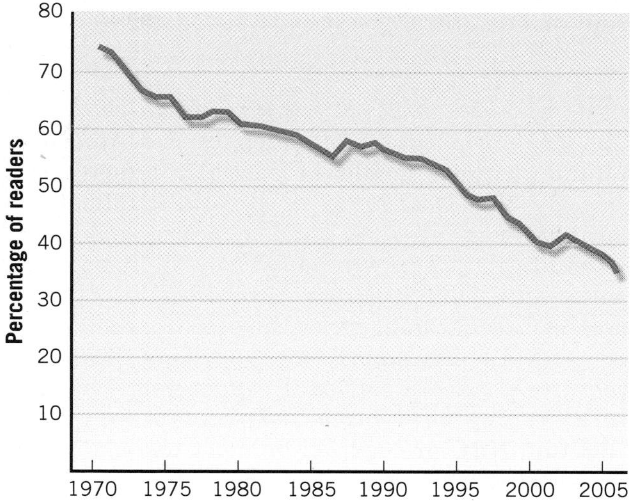

Note: 18–34 readership represents the average of 18–24 readership and 25–34 readership. 2006 data is through September

Source: *The Wall Street Journal* (February 15, 2007). The Wall Street Journal by News Corporation. Copyright 2007 Reproduced with permission of DOW JONES & COMPANY, INC. in the format Textbook and Other book via Copyright Clearance Center.

To a degree that would astonish most foreigners, the American press—radio, television, and newspapers—is made up of locally owned and managed enterprises. In Britain, France, Germany, Japan, Sweden, and elsewhere, the media are owned and operated with a national audience in mind. The *Times* of London may be published in that city, but it is read throughout Great Britain, as are the *Guardian,* the *Daily Telegraph,* and the *Daily Mirror.* Radio and television broadcasts are centrally planned and nationally aired.

The American newspaper, however, is primarily oriented to its local market and local audience, and there is typically more local than national news in it. Radio and television stations accept network programming, but the early- and late-evening news programs provide a heavy diet of local political, social, and sports news. Government regulations developed by the Federal Communications Commission (FCC) are in part responsible for this. Until the mid-1990s, no one could own and operate more than one newspaper, one AM radio station, one FM radio station, or one television station in a given market. The networks still today may not compel a local affiliate to accept any particular broadcast. (In fact, almost all network news programs are carried by the affiliates.) The result has been the development of a decentralized broadcast industry.

THE NATIONAL MEDIA

The local orientation of much of the American communications media is partially offset, however, by the emergence of certain publications and broadcast services that constitute a kind of national press. The wire services—the Associated Press and United Press International—supply most of the national news that local papers publish. Certain newsmagazines, such as *Time* and *Newsweek*, have a national readership. The network evening news broadcasts produced by ABC, CBS, and NBC are carried by most television stations with a network affiliation. Both CNN (Cable News Network) and Fox News broadcast news around the clock and have large audiences, as does MSNBC. Though most newspapers have only local audiences, several have acquired national influence. The *New York Times* and the *Wall Street Journal* are printed in several locations and can be delivered to many homes early in the morning. *USA Today* was created as a national newspaper and is distributed everywhere, aimed especially at people who travel a lot.

These newspapers have national standing for several reasons. First, they distribute a lot of copies: more than 1 million each day for the *Times* and the *Journal,* and more than 2 million a day for *USA Today.* Second, these papers, as well as the *Washington Post,* are carefully followed by political elites. Unlike most people, the elites even read the editorials. By contrast, local newspapers and radio stations may be invisible to Washington politicians. Third, radio and television stations often decide what to broadcast by looking at the front pages of the *Times* and the *Post.* The front page of the *Times* is a model for each network's evening news broadcast.[11] Finally, the editors and reporters for the national press tend to be better educated and more generously paid than their counterparts in local outlets. And as we shall see, the writers for the national press tend to have distinctly liberal political views. Above all they seek—and frequently obtain—the opportunity to write stories that are not accounts of a particular news event but "background," investigative, or interpretive stories about issues and policies.

The national press plays the role of gatekeeper, scorekeeper, and watchdog for the federal government.

Gatekeeper

As gatekeeper, the national media can influence what subjects become national political issues and for how long. Automobile safety, water pollution, and the quality of prescription drugs were not major political issues before the national press began giving substantial attention to these matters and thus helped place them on the political agenda. When crime rates rose in the early 1960s, the subject was given little political attention in Washington, in part because the media did not cover it extensively. Media attention to crime increased in the late 1960s and early 1970s, slackened in the late 1970s, and rose again in the 1980s and early 1990s. Throughout most of these years, crime went up. In short, *reality* did not change during this time; only the focus of media and political attention shifted. Elite opinion about the war in Vietnam also changed significantly as the attitude toward the war expressed by the national media changed.

Scorekeeper

As scorekeepers, the national media keep track of and help make political reputations, note who is "mentioned" as a presidential candidate, and help decide who is winning and losing in Washington politics. When Jimmy Carter, a virtually unknown former governor of Georgia, was planning his campaign to get the Democratic nomination for president, he understood clearly the importance of being "mentioned." So successful was he in cultivating members of the national press that, before the first primary election was held, he was the subject of more stories in the *New York Times,* the *Washington Post,* and the *Columbus Dispatch* than any other potential Democratic presiden-tial candidate.

The scorekeeper role of the media often leads the press to cover presidential elections as if they were horse races rather than choices among policies. Consider the enormous attention the media give to the Iowa caucus and the New Hampshire primary election, despite the fact that these states produce only a tiny fraction of the delegates to either party's nominating convention and that neither state is representative of the nation as a whole. The results of the Iowa caucus, the first in the nation, are given great importance by the press. Consequently, the coverage received by a candidate who does well in Iowa constitutes a tremendous amount of free publicity that can help him or her in the New Hampshire primary election. Doing well in that primary results in even more media attention, thus boosting the candidate for the next primaries, and so on.

Watchdog

Once the scorekeepers decide you are the person to watch, they adopt their watchdog role. When Gary Hart was the front-runner for the 1988 Democratic presidential nomination, the press played its watchdog role right from the start. When rumors circulated that he was unfaithful to his wife, the *Miami Herald* staked out his apartment in Washington, D.C., and discovered he had spent several evening hours there with an attractive young woman, Donna Rice. Soon other stories appeared about his having taken Rice on a boat trip to Bimini. Not long thereafter, Hart dropped out of the presidential race, accusing the press of unfair treatment.

This close scrutiny is natural. The media have an instinctive—and profitable—desire to investigate personalities and expose scandals. To some degree, all reporters probably share the belief that the role of the press is to "comfort the afflicted and afflict the comfortable." They tend to be tolerant of underdogs, tough on front-runners. Though some reporters develop close relations with powerful personages, many—especially younger ones—find the discovery of wrongdoing both more absorbing and more lucrative. Bob Woodward and Carl Bernstein, who wrote most of the Watergate stories for the *Washington Post,* simultaneously performed an important public service, received the accolades of their colleagues, and earned a lot of money.

Newspapers and television stations play these three roles in somewhat different ways. A newspaper can cover more stories in greater depth than a TV station and faces less competition from other papers than TV stations face from other broadcasters. A TV station faces brutal competition, must select its programs in part for their visual impact, and must keep its stories short and punchy. As a result, newspaper reporters have more freedom to develop their own stories, but they earn less money than television news broadcasters. The latter have little freedom (the fear of losing their audience is keen), but they can make a lot of money (if they are attractive personalities who photograph well).

Rules Governing the Media

Ironically, the least competitive media outlets—the big-city newspapers—are almost entirely free from government regulation, while the most competitive ones—radio and television stations—must have a government license to operate and must adhere to a variety of government regulations.

Newspapers and magazines need no license to publish, their freedom to publish may not be restrained in advance, and they are liable for punishment for what they do publish only under certain highly restricted circumstances. The First Amendment has been interpreted as meaning that no government, federal or state, can place "prior restraints" (that is, censorship) on the press except under very narrowly defined circumstances.[12] When the federal government sought to prevent the *New York Times* from publishing the Pentagon Papers, a set of secret government documents stolen by an antiwar activist, the Court held that the paper was free to publish them.[13]

Once something is published, a newspaper or magazine may be sued or prosecuted if the material is libelous or obscene or if it incites someone to commit an illegal act. But these usually are not very serious restrictions, because the courts have defined *libelous, obscene,* and *incitement* so narrowly as to make it more difficult here than in any other nation to find the press guilty of such conduct. For example, for a paper to be found guilty of libeling a public official or other prominent person, the person must not only show that what was printed was wrong and damaging but must also show, with "clear and convincing evidence," that it was printed maliciously—that is, with "reckless disregard" for its truth or falsity.[14] When in 1984 Israeli General Ariel Sharon sued *Time* magazine for libel, the jury decided the story *Time* printed was false and defamatory but that *Time* had not published it as the result of malice, and so Sharon did not collect any damages.

There are also laws intended to protect the privacy of citizens, but they do not really inhibit newspapers. In general, your name and picture can be printed without your consent if they are part of a news story of some conceivable public interest. And if a paper attacks you in print, the paper has no legal obligation to give you space for a reply.[15]

It is illegal to use printed words to advocate the violent overthrow of the government if by your advocacy you incite others to action, but this rule has only rarely been applied to newspapers.[16]

CONFIDENTIALITY OF SOURCES

Reporters believe they should have the right to keep confidential the sources of their stories. Some states agree and have passed laws to that effect. Most states and the federal government do not agree, so the courts must decide in each case whether the need of a journalist to protect confidential sources does or does not outweigh the interest of the government in gathering evidence in a criminal investigation. In general, the Supreme Court has upheld the right of the government to compel reporters to divulge information as part of a properly conducted criminal investigation, if it bears on the commission of a crime.[17]

This conflict arises not only between reporters and law enforcement agencies but also between reporters and persons accused of committing a crime. Myron Farber, a reporter for the *New York Times,* wrote a series of stories that led to the indictment and trial of a physician on charges he had murdered five patients. The judge ordered Farber to show him his notes to determine whether they should be given to the defense lawyers. Farber refused, arguing that revealing his notes would infringe upon the confidentiality he had promised to his sources. Farber was sent to jail for contempt of court. On appeal, the New Jersey Supreme Court and the U.S. Supreme Court decided against Farber, holding that the accused person's right to a fair trial includes the right to compel the production of evidence, even from reporters.

In 2005, two reporters were sentenced to jail when they refused to give prosecutors information about who in the Bush administration had told them that a woman was in fact a CIA officer. A federal court decided they were not entitled to any protection for their sources in a criminal trial. The *New York Times* reporter, Judith Miller, spent 85 days in jail; she was released after a government official authorized her to talk about their conversation. There is no federal shield law that will protect journalists, though such laws exist in 34 states.

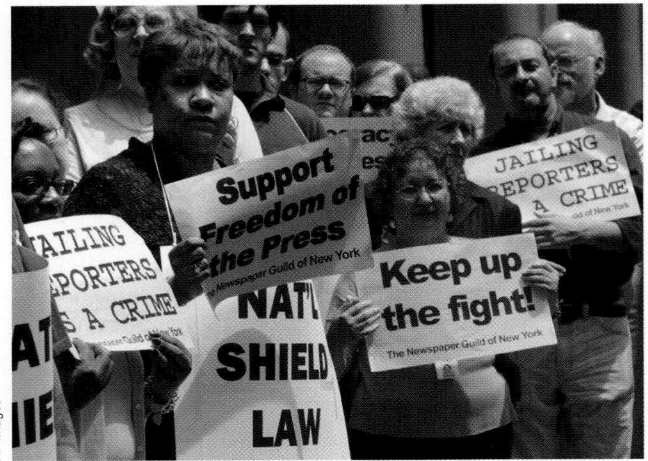

AP Images

Activists urge Congress to pass a law shielding reporters from being required to testify about their sources.

In another case, the Supreme Court upheld the right of the police to search newspaper offices, so long as they have a warrant. But Congress then passed a law forbidding such searches (except in special cases), requiring instead that the police subpoena the desired documents.[18]

REGULATING BROADCASTING

Although newspapers and magazines by and large are not regulated, broadcasting is regulated by the government. No one may operate a radio or television station without a license from the Federal Communications Commission, renewable every seven years for radio and every five for television stations. An application for renewal is rarely refused, but until recently the FCC required the broadcaster to submit detailed information about its programming and how it planned to serve "community needs" in order to get a renewal. Based on this information or on the complaints of some group, the FCC could use its powers of renewal to influence what the station put on the air. For example, it could induce stations to reduce the amount of violence shown, increase the proportion of "public service" programs on the air, or alter the way it portrayed various ethnic groups.

Of late a movement has arisen to deregulate broadcasting, on the grounds that so many stations are now on the air that competition should be allowed to determine how each station defines and serves community needs. In this view, citizens can choose what they want to hear or see without the government's shaping the content of each station's programming. For example, since the early 1980s, a station can simply submit a postcard requesting that its license be renewed, a request automatically granted unless some group formally opposes the renewal. In that case, the FCC holds a hearing. As a result, some of the old rules—for instance, that each hour on TV could contain only 16 minutes of commercials—are no longer rigidly enforced.

Radio broadcasting has been deregulated the most. Before 1992, one company could own one AM and one FM station in each market. In 1992, this number was doubled. And in 1996, the Telecommunications Act allowed one company to own as many as eight stations in large markets (five in smaller ones) and as many as it wished nationally. This trend has had two results. First, a few large companies now own most of the big-market radio stations. Second,

Landmark Cases

The Rights of the Media

- ***Near v. Minnesota* (1931):** Freedom of the press applies to state governments, so that they cannot impose prior restraint on newspapers.
- ***New York Times v. Sullivan* (1964):** Public officials may not win a libel suit unless they can prove that the statement was made knowing it to be false or with reckless disregard of its truth.
- ***Miami Herald v. Tornillo* (1974):** A newspaper cannot be required to give someone a right to reply to one of its stories.

the looser editorial restrictions that accompanied deregulation mean that a greater variety of opinions and shows can be found on radio. There are many more radio talk shows than would have been heard when content was more tightly controlled.

Deregulation has also lessened the extent to which the federal government shapes the content of broadcasting. At one time, for example, a "fairness doctrine" required broadcasters that air one side of a story to give time to opposing points of view. But there are now so many radio and television stations that the FCC relies on competition to manage differences of opinion. The abandonment of the fairness doctrine permitted the rise of controversial talk radio shows. If the doctrine had stayed in place, there would be no Rush Limbaugh or Al Franken. The FCC decided that competition among news outlets protected people by giving them many different sources of news.

equal time rule An FCC rule that if a broadcaster sells time to one candidate, it must sell equal time to other candidates.

There still exists an **equal time rule** that obliges stations that sell advertising time to one political candidate to sell equal time to that person's opponents. When candidates wish to campaign on radio or television, the equal time rule applies.

CAMPAIGNING

During campaigns, a broadcaster must provide equal access to candidates for office and charge them rates no higher than the cheapest rate applicable to commercial advertisers for comparable time. At one time, this rule meant that a station or network could not broadcast a debate between the Democratic and Republican candidates for an office without inviting all other candidates as well—Libertarian, Prohibitionist, or whatever. Thus, a presidential debate in 1980 could be limited to the major candidates, Reagan and Carter (or Reagan and Anderson), only by having the League of Women Voters sponsor it and then allowing radio and TV to cover it as a "news event." Now stations and networks can themselves sponsor debates limited to major candidates.

Though laws guarantee that candidates can buy time at favorable rates on television, not all candidates take advantage of this. The reason is that television is not always an efficient way to reach voters. A television message is literally "broad cast"—spread out to a mass audience without regard to the boundaries of the district in which a candidate is running. Presidential candidates, of course, always use television because their constituency is the whole nation. Candidates for senator or representative, however, may or may not use television, depending on whether the boundaries of their state or district conform well to the boundaries of a television market.

A *market* is an area easily reached by a television signal; there are about 200 such markets in the country. If you are a member of Congress from South Bend, Indiana, you come from a television market based there. You can buy ads on the TV stations in South Bend at a reasonable fee. But if you are a member of Congress from northern New Jersey, the only television stations are in nearby New York City. In that market, the costs of a TV ad are very high because they reach a lot of people, most of whom are not in your district and so cannot vote for you. Buying a TV ad is a waste of money. As a result, a much higher percentage of Senate than House candidates use television ads.

One aspect of campaigning that worries scholars is the media's reliance on **horse-race journalism**, that is, covering a campaign based on guesses about who is ahead rather than on candidates' positions on the issues. For example, in 2008 the journalists talked about how Barack Obama would win the New Hampshire primary because that is what the polls and political insiders told them. But then Hillary Clinton won. Nowhere in the press coverage was any attention given to the

horse-race journalism News coverage that focuses on who is ahead rather than on the issues.

positions Clinton and Obama had on the issues. The public says they want more such coverage, though one suspects that they actually like horse-race journalism.

Are the National Media Biased?

Everyone believes the media have a profound effect, for better or for worse, on politics. Many think the political opinions of writers and editors influence that effect. To decide whether these statements are true, we must answer three questions:

1. Do members of the media have a distinctive political attitude?
2. Does that attitude affect what they write or say?
3. Does what they write or say affect what citizens believe?

The answers to these questions, to be discussed below, are yes, yes, and probably.

A LIBERAL MAJORITY

Many studies, dating back to the early 1980s, have concluded that members of the national press are more liberal than the average citizen.[19] In 1992, 91 percent of the media members interviewed said they had voted for the Democratic candidate for president. By contrast, only 43 percent of the public voted that way.[20]

Not only are the media more liberal, they also tend to be secular. About 70 percent say they never or only a few times a year attend a religious service. And in recent years, the surveys suggest they have become more liberal. For example, between 1980 and 1995, the proportion of media members who believe the government should guarantee jobs to people rose, and the proportion who think government should reduce the regulation of business fell. A 2004 study found that a majority of journalists identified themselves as liberal.[21]

The public certainly believes that members of the media are liberals. A Gallup Poll done in 2003 found that 45 percent of Americans believe the media are "too liberal" (15 percent thought they were "too conservative"). In another study, even Democrats agreed with this view. A survey taken just a few weeks before the 2008 presidential election found that more than two-thirds of voters believed that the media favored Barack Obama over John McCain.[22]

Conservative media outlets have become more visible in recent years. Radio talk shows, such as those hosted by Rush Limbaugh and Sean Hannity, are conservative, as is some of the TV reporting broadcast on Fox News, such as on the *O'Reilly Factor*. Limbaugh and Hannity have large audiences, and Fox News has grown in popularity.

Senator Barack Obama campaigning for president in Los Angeles.

One-fifth of all Americans listen to radio talk shows every day and another tenth listen several times a week. A puzzling fact is that talk radio, which has grown rapidly in importance, is predominately conservative. Almost half of the 28 largest talk shows have been hosted by outspoken conservatives.

None of this dominance is the result of radio station owners plotting to put conservatives on the air. Media owners are interested in ratings—that is, in measures of how big their audiences are. Liberal talk-show hosts have had big corporate sponsors that dropped away when the shows did not get good ratings. If Fidel Castro got high ratings by playing the harmonica, Castro would be on the air.

William G. Mayer, a political scientist, has speculated as to why conservative talk shows are so common. First, there are more self-described conservatives than liberals in this country. Second, conservative listeners do not think their views are reflected in what big-city newspapers, the major television networks, and the leading newsmagazines display. Liberals, by contrast, think their views are encouraged by newspapers and television stations. Third, much of the liberal audience is broken up into distinctive racial and ethnic groups that have their own radio outlets. Many Hispanics listen to stations that broadcast in Spanish; many African Americans prefer stations that have black hosts and focus on black community issues.[23]

NEUTRAL AND OBJECTIVE?

In the United States, the journalistic philosophy in many media documents is that the press, when it reports the news (though not in editorial pages), should be neutral and objective. That view, of course, does not cover radio talk shows, but it is supposed to cover newspapers. A different view can be found in France or Great Britain where newspapers often clearly identify with one party or another.

But it is hard to measure whether the American commitment to objectivity is actually achieved. One would have to take into account not only how much space a politician or policy receives, but also the tone in which it is handled and the adjectives used to describe people who are part of those stories.

routine stories Media stories about events regularly covered by reporters.

New stories differ significantly in the opportunity for bias. **Routine stories** cover major political events that will be covered by many reporters and that involve relatively simple matters. For example: the president takes a trip, Congress passes a major bill, or the Supreme Court issues a ruling. **Feature stories** cover events that, though public, a reporter has to seek out because they are not routinely covered by the press. The reporter has to find the story and persuade an editor to publish it. For example: an interest group works hard to get a bill passed, a government agency adopts a new ruling, or a member of Congress conducts an unusual investigation. **Insider stories** cover things that are often secret. Investigative reporters are often credited with uncovering these stories, though it is often the case that some government insider has leaked the story to the press. Which leak a reporter picks up on may be influenced by the reporter's view of what is important, that is, by what is important to the reporter.

feature stories Media stories about events that, though public, are not regularly covered by reporters.

insider stories Media stories about events that are not usually made public.

Routine stories often are covered in much the same way by reporters. The space given to the story and the headline attached to it may reflect the political views of the editor, but the story itself often is written about the same way by every reporter. Feature and insider stories, by contrast, may more easily reflect the political views of reporters and editors. On these stories, journalists have to make choices.

Early in American history, newspapers had virtually no routine stories; almost everything they printed was an expression of opinion. By the 20th century, with the advent of telephone and telegraph lines that made it easy for news organizations such as the Associated Press to send the same story to almost every newspaper, routine stories became commonplace. But with the advent of radio and television and the rise of around-the-clock news broadcasting, feature and insider stories became much more important to newspapers. If people got their routine news from radio and television, newspapers had to sell something different; feature and insider stories were different.

A conservative newspaper might print feature or insider stories about crime, drug abuse, or welfare cheats, while a liberal newspaper might run ones on feminism, the environment, or civil rights. There are, however, very few conservative newspapers with a national audience.

A key question is whether there are facts to back up these generalizations. There are no definitive answers; here we can take a look at a few of the better studies.

How to Read a Newspaper

Newspapers don't simply report the news; they report somebody's idea of what is news, written in language intended to persuade as well as inform. To read a newspaper intelligently, look for three things: what is covered, who are the sources, and how language is used.

Coverage

Every newspaper will cover a big story, such as a flood, fire, or presidential trip, but newspapers can pick and choose among lesser stories. One paper will select stories about the environment, business fraud, and civil rights; another will prefer stories about crime, drug dealers, and "welfare cheats." What do these choices tell you about the beliefs of the editors and reporters working for these two papers? What do these people want you to believe are the important issues?

Sources

For some stories, the source is obvious: "The Supreme Court decided ...," "Congress voted ...," or "The president said...." For others, the source is not so obvious. There are two kinds of sources you should beware of. The first is an anonymous source. When you read phrases such as "a high official said today ..." or "White House sources revealed that ...," always ask yourself this question: Why does the source want me to know this? The answer usually will be this: because if I believe what he or she said, it will advance his or her interests. This can happen in one of three ways. First, the source may support a policy or appointment and want to test public reaction to it. This is called floating a **trial balloon**. Second, the source may oppose a policy or appointment and hope that by leaking word of it, the idea will be killed. Third, the source may want to take credit for something good that happened or shift blame onto somebody else for something bad that happened. When you read a story based on anonymous sources, ask yourself these questions: Judging from the tone of the story, is this leak designed to support or kill an idea? Is it designed to take credit or shift blame? In whose interest is it to accomplish these things? By asking these questions, you often can make a pretty good guess as to the identity of the anonymous source.

Some stories depend on the reader's believing a key fact, previously unknown. For example: "The world's climate is getting hotter because of manmade pollution," "drug abuse is soaring," "the death penalty will prevent murder," "husbands are more likely to beat up on their wives on Super Bowl Sunday." Each of these "facts" is wrong, grossly exaggerated, or stated with excessive confidence. But each comes from an advocate organization that wants you to believe it, because if you do, you will take that organization's solution more seriously. Be skeptical of key facts if they come from an advocacy source. Don't be misled by the tendency of many advocacy organizations to take neutral or scholarly names like "Center for the Public Interest" or "Institute for Policy Research." Some of these really are neutral or scholarly, but many aren't.

Language

Everybody uses words to persuade without actually making a clear argument. This is called using **loaded language**. For example: if you like a politician, call him "Senator Smith"; if you don't like him, refer to him as "right-wing (or left-wing) senators such as Smith." If you like an idea proposed by a professor, call her "respected"; if you don't like the idea, call her "controversial." If you favor abortion, call somebody who agrees with you "pro-choice" ("choice" is valued by most people); if you oppose abortion, call those who agree with you "pro-life" ("life," like "choice," is a good thing). Recognizing loaded language in a newspaper article can give you important clues to the writer's own point of view.

One study looked at 12 years' worth of political stories published in the *New York Times* and the *Washington Post*. It asked how these papers described the 10 most liberal and the 10 most conservative senators. The authors found that conservative senators were about three times more likely to be called conservative than liberal senators were to be called liberal.[24] The difference in the use of adjectives may influence how readers feel about the story. Politically independent readers might (no one knows) take more seriously the views of senators who are given no ideological labels than they will of those to whom such labels have been attached.

There have been efforts to see how newspapers and magazines cover specific issues. When *Time* and *Newsweek* ran stories about nuclear power, scholars found they tended to avoid quoting scientists and engineers working in this field because these specialists were in favor of nuclear power at a time when the magazines were opposed to it.[25]

Another study looked at how the top 10 newspapers and the Associated Press cover economic news when there is either a Democratic or Republican president in office. The news was based on government reports about sales, unemployment, and economic growth over a 13-year period. The authors decided whether a newspaper's headline covering that news (on the day it was released) was either positive, negative, or neutral. In general, these headlines gave a more positive spin when there was a Democrat in the White House and a more negative one when there was a Republican there.[26]

Newspapers are privately owned, so perhaps some of their bias comes from decisions made by the publishers. When scholars looked at 400 daily newspapers, they found that the "ideology of the owners doesn't correlate in any significant way with the political slant of their newspapers' coverage." Instead, a newspaper's bias tends to reflect the political views of its readers. If the same person owns several newspapers, each paper's style is tailored to its own market more than to the owner's beliefs.[27]

But perhaps the easiest evidence to understand comes from reporters themselves. The *New York Times* has a "public editor," that is, a person charged with receiving complaints from the public. When asked, "Is the *New York Times* a liberal newspaper?" he answered, in print, very simply: "Of course it is."

Public distrust of the media has grown. As shown in Figure 12.3, the proportion of people saying that news stories are often inaccurate has grown significantly since 1985.

Figure 12.3

Public Perception of Accuracy in the Media

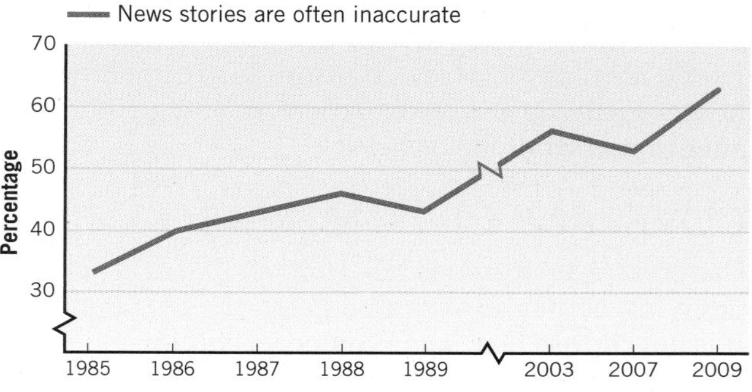

Source: Pew Research Center for the People & the Press, "Press Accuracy Rating Hits Two-Decade Low: Public Evaluations of the News Media: 1985–2009," September 2009.

MEDIA'S INFLUENCE

Some people will be influenced by what they read or hear, but others will not be. There is a well-known psychological process called **selective attention.** It means that people remember or believe only what they want to. If they see or hear statements inconsistent with their existing beliefs, they will tune out these messages.[28]

trial balloon Information leaked to the media to test public reaction to a possible policy.

loaded language Words that imply a value judgment, used to persuade a reader without having made a serious argument.

selective attention Paying attention only to those news stories with which one already agrees.

But after the 1964 presidential election, one study suggested that in the northern part of the United States a newspaper endorsement favoring Democratic candidate Lyndon Johnson added about five percentage points to the vote he received.[29]

Another study examined the vote in more than 60 contests for the U.S. Senate held over a five-year period. Newspaper stories about the rival candidates were scored as positive, negative, or neutral. Voters' feelings about the candidates were learned from public opinion polls. Obviously, many things other than newspaper stories will affect how voters feel, and so the authors of this study tried to control for these factors. They held constant the seniority of incumbent candidates, the level of political experience of challengers, the amount of campaign spending, how close each race was, and the political ideology and party identification of voters. After doing all of this, they discovered two things. First, newspapers that endorsed incumbents on their editorial pages gave more positive news coverage to them than newspapers that did not endorse them. Second, the voters had more positive feelings about endorsed incumbents than they did about nonendorsed ones. In short, editorial views affect news coverage, and news coverage affects public attitudes.[30]

A fascinating natural experiment occurred when Fox News, a network that generally favors Republicans, went on the air at different times in different cities. When two scholars compared the effects on voting patterns in cities where Fox News was on the air with similar cities in which it was not, they found that there was a 3 to 8 percent increase in the vote for Republican candidates and about a half a percent increase in the Republican vote for president in the Fox towns.[31] Another study even manufactured an experiment: the authors gave, at no charge, the *Washington Post* (a liberal newspaper) or the

Washington Times (a conservative newspaper) to people who subscribed to neither in a northern Virginia county. In the next election, those people receiving the *Post* were more likely to vote for the Democratic candidate for governor.[32]

What the press covers affects the policy issues that people think are important. Experiments conducted in New Haven, Connecticut, and a study done in North Carolina show that what citizens believe about some policy questions reflects what newspapers and television stations say about them.[33]

But there are limits to media influence. If people are unemployed, the victims of crime, or worried about high gasoline prices, they do not have to be told these things by the media.[34] But most people have no personal knowledge of highway fatalities, the condition of the environment, or American foreign policy in Europe. On these matters, the media are likely to have much more influence.

The best evidence of how important the media are comes from the behavior of people trying to get elected. In 1950, Estes Kefauver was a little-known senator from Tennessee. Then he chaired a Senate committee investigating organized crime. When these dramatic hearings were televised, Kefauver became a household name. In 1952, he ran for the Democratic nomination for president and won a lot of primary votes before losing to Adlai Stevenson.

From that time on, developing a strong media presence became a top priority for political candidates. Sometimes it backfires. In 2004, Howard Dean, then a candidate for the Democratic presidential nomination, saw his campaign start to sputter after television carried a speech he gave to his supporters that seemed to end in a kind of anguished scream. And every White House staffer spends a lot of time worrying about how to get the press, especially television, to cover the president. Studies show that television commentary about presidents affects their popularity.[35] President Lyndon Johnson reportedly concluded that the war he was supporting in Vietnam was a hopeless cause after Walter Cronkite, then the star of the popular CBS News program, turned against the war.

Government and the News

Every government agency, every public official, spends a great deal of time trying to shape public opinion. From time to time, somebody publishes an exposé of the efforts of the Pentagon, the White House, or some bureau to "sell" itself to the people, but in a government of separated powers, weak parties, and a decentralized legislature, any government agency that fails to cultivate public opinion will sooner or later find itself weak, without allies, and in trouble.

PROMINENCE OF THE PRESIDENT

Theodore Roosevelt was the first president to raise the systematic cultivation of the press to an art form. From the day he took office, he made it clear that he would give inside stories to friendly reporters and withhold them from hostile ones. He made sure that scarcely a day passed without his doing something newsworthy. In 1902, he built the West Wing of the White House and included in it, for the first time, a special room for reporters near his office, and he invited the press to become fascinated by the antics of his children. In return, the reporters adored him. Teddy's nephew Franklin Roosevelt institutionalized this system by making his press secretary (a job created by Herbert Hoover) a major instrument for cultivating and managing, as well as informing, the press.

Today, the press secretary heads a large staff that meets with reporters, briefs the president on questions he is likely to be asked, attempts to control the flow of news from cabinet departments to the press, and arranges briefings for out-of-town editors (to bypass what many presidents think are the biases of the White House press corps).

All this effort is directed primarily at the White House press corps, a group of men and women who have a lounge in the White House where they wait for a story to break, attend the daily press briefing, or take advantage of a "photo op"—an opportunity to photograph the president with some newsworthy person.

No other nation in the world has brought the press into such close physical proximity to the head of its government. The result is that the actions of our government are personalized to a degree not found in most other democracies. Whether the president rides a horse, comes down with a cold, greets a Boy Scout, or takes a trip, the press is there. The prime minister of Great Britain does not share his home with the press or expect to have his every sneeze recorded for posterity.

COVERAGE OF CONGRESS

Congress has watched all this with irritation and envy. It resents the attention given the president, but it is not certain how it can compete. The 435 members of the House are so numerous and play such specialized roles that they do not get much individualized press attention. In the past, the House was quite restrictive about television or radio coverage of its

The Maxims of Media Relations

The importance of the national media to politicians has given rise to some shared understandings among officeholders about how one deals with the media. Some of these are caught in the following maxims:

- All secrets become public knowledge. The more important the secret, the sooner it becomes known.
- All stories written about me are inaccurate; all stories written about you are entirely accurate.
- The rosier the news, the higher ranking the official who announces it.
- Always release bad news on Saturday night. Fewer people notice it.
- Never argue with a person who buys ink by the barrel.

proceedings. Until 1978, it prohibited television cameras on the floor except on purely ceremonial occasions (such as the annual State of the Union message delivered by the president). From 1952 to 1970, the House would not even allow electronic coverage of its committee hearings (except for a few occasions during those periods when the Republicans were in the majority). Significant live coverage of committee hearings began in 1974 when the House Judiciary Committee was discussing the possible impeachment of President Nixon. Since 1979, cable TV (C-SPAN) has provided gavel-to-gavel coverage of speeches on the House floor.

The Senate has used television much more fully, heightening the already substantial advantage that senators have over representatives in getting the public eye. Although radio and television coverage of the Senate floor was not allowed until 1978 (when the debates on the Panama Canal treaties were broadcast live), Senate committee hearings have frequently been televised for either news films or live broadcasts ever since Estes Kefauver demonstrated the power of this medium in 1950. Since 1986, the Senate has allowed live C-SPAN coverage of its sessions.

Senatorial use of televised committee hearings has helped turn the Senate into the incubator for presidential candidates. At least in most states, if you are a governor, you are located far from network television news cameras; the best you can hope for is that some disaster—a flood or a blizzard—will bring the cameras to you and focus them on your leadership. But senators all work in Washington, a city filled with cameras. No disaster is necessary to get on the air; only an investigation, a scandal, a major political conflict, or an articulate and telegenic personality is needed.

How We Compare

Freedom of the Press

The Anti-Federalists insisted on adding a Bill of Rights to the Constitution because they feared government intrusion into citizens' lives. Their first concern, as reflected in the First Amendment, was to protect speech and expression, which includes freedom of the press. Although the protection is not absolute—the Supreme Court has ruled that there are times when that freedom may be restricted by the government for national security, for example—the burden of proof is on the government to demonstrate when imposing a restriction is constitutionally necessary.

Not all advanced industrialized democracies provide such broad protection for the media. In the United Kingdom, for example, libel laws are stricter than in the United States, which is why celebrities and business sometimes seek restitution in the former over the latter. Some European democracies have prohibitions on hate speech, which the United States does not (though the United States does impose restrictions on other types of speech that can appear in media outlets, such as obscenity or threats of violence). According to a recent report by Freedom House, an organization that tracks various measurements of freedom cross-nationally, access to free and independent media has declined worldwide to its lowest level in more than ten years. Of 196 countries and territories for which Freedom House evaluated media coverage, 68 were rated Free, 65 were rated Partly Free, and 63 were rated Not Free.

(continued)

How We Compare (*continued*)

Countries at Top of Global Press Freedom Rankings, Freedom House, 2011

1. Finland
2. Norway
3. Sweden
4. Belgium
5. Iceland
6. Luxembourg

(The United States ranks 17.)

Countries at Bottom of Global Press Freedom Rankings, Freedom House, 2011

1. Burma
2. Eritrea
3. Libya
4. Uzbekistan
5. Turkmenistan
6. North Korea

Sources: Robert Barr, Associated Press, "U.K. Government Prepares to Offer Changes to Libel Law," *Deseret News*, March 15, 2011; Freedom House, "Freedom of the Press 2011: A Global Survey of Media Independence."

WHY DO WE HAVE SO MANY NEWS LEAKS?

American government is the leakiest in the world. The bureaucracy, members of Congress, and the White House staff regularly leak stories favorable to their interests. Of late, the leaks have become geysers, gushing forth torrents of insider stories. Many people in and out of government find it depressing that our government seems unable to keep anything secret for long. Others think the public has a right to know even more and that there are still too many secrets.

However you view leaks, you should understand why we have so many. The answer is found in the Constitution. Because we have separate institutions that must share power, each branch of government competes with the others to get power. One way to compete is to try to use the press to advance your pet projects and to make the other side look bad. There are far fewer leaks in other democratic nations in part because power is centralized in the hands of a prime minister, who does not need to leak in order to get the upper hand over the legislature, and because the legislature has too little information to be a good source of leaks. In addition, we have no Official Secrets Act of the kind that exists in England; except for a few matters, it is not against the law for the press to receive and print government secrets.

Even if the press and the politicians loved each other, the competition between the various branches of government would guarantee plenty of news leaks. But since the Vietnam War, the Watergate scandal, and the Iran-Contra affair, the press and the politicians have come to distrust one another. As a result, journalists today are far less willing to accept at face value the statements of elected officials and are far more likely to try to find somebody who will leak "the real story." We have come, in short, to have an **adversarial press**—that is, one that (at least at the national level) is suspicious of officialdom and eager to break an embarrassing story that will win for its author honor, prestige, and (in some cases) a lot of money.

adversarial press The tendency of the national media to be suspicious of officials and eager to reveal unflattering stories about them.

This cynicism and distrust of government and elected officials have led to an era of attack journalism—seizing upon any bit of information or rumor that might call into question the qualifications or character of a public official. Media coverage of gaffes—misspoken words, misstated ideas, clumsy moves—has become a staple of political journalism. At one time, such "events" as President Ford slipping down some stairs, Governor Dukakis dropping the ball while playing catch with a Boston Red Sox player, or Vice President Quayle misspelling the word *potato* would have been ignored, but now they are hot news items. Attacking public figures has become a professional norm, where once it was a professional taboo.

Brown Brothers

When President Theodore Roosevelt cultivated the media, reporters usually were unknown and poorly paid.

During the 1992 election, most of the national press clearly supported Bill Clinton. The love affair between Clinton and reporters lasted for several months after his inauguration. But when stories began to appear about Whitewater (an Arkansas real estate deal in which the Clintons were once involved), Clinton's alleged sexual escapades, and Hillary Rodham Clinton's profits in commodities trading, the press went into a feeding frenzy. The Clintons learned the hard way the truth of an old adage: if you want a friend in Washington, buy a dog.

Many people do not like this type of journalism, and the media's rising cynicism about the government is mirrored by the public's increasing cynicism about the media. In a national survey of registered voters conducted shortly before the 2000 presidential election, 89 percent of respondents agreed that the media's "political views influence coverage" often (57 percent) or sometimes (32 percent); 47 percent believed that "most journalists" were "pulling for" Gore to win; and 23 percent believed that most journalists were partial to Bush.[36] Most Americans really dislike biased journalism (or journalism they perceive as biased): 53 percent say they would require a license to practice journalism, and 70 percent favor court-imposed fines for inaccurate or biased reporting.[37]

Given their experiences with Watergate and Irangate, given the highly competitive nature of national newsgathering, and given their political ideology (which tends to put them to the left of the administration in power), American editors and reporters, at least at the national level, are likely to have an adversarial relationship with government for a long time to come. Given our constitutional system, there will always be plenty of people in government eager to help them with leaks hostile to one faction or another.

SENSATIONALISM IN THE MEDIA

Back in the 1930s, newspaper reporters knew President Franklin Roosevelt had a romantic affair with a woman other than his wife. They did not report it. In the early 1960s, many reporters knew President John Kennedy had many sexual affairs outside his marriage. They did not report this. In 1964, the director of the Federal Bureau of Investigation played for reporters secret tape recordings of the Reverend Martin Luther King, Jr., having sex with women other than his wife. They did not report it.

By the 1980s, sex and politics were extensively covered. When presidential candidate Gary Hart was caught in adultery and when President Bill Clinton was accused of adultery by Gennifer Flowers, of asking for sexual favors by Paula Jones, and of having sex with Monica Lewinsky in the Oval Office, these were headline news stories.

What had changed? Not politics: all of the people whom the press protected or reported on were Democrats. The big change was in the economics of journalism and the ideas of reporters. Until the 1970s, Americans gathered their political news from one of three networks—ABC, CBS, or NBC. For a long time, these networks had only one half-hour news show a day. Today, however, viewers have the same three networks plus three cable news networks, two sports networks, 10 weekly news-magazine shows, countless radio talk shows, and the Internet. Many of the cable networks, such as CNN, carry news 24 hours a day. The result of this intense competition is that each radio or television network has a small share of the audience. Today, less than half the public watches the evening network news shows. Dozens of news programs are trying to reach a shrinking audience, with the result that the audience share of each program is small. To attract any audience at all, each program has a big incentive to rely on sensational news stories—sex, violence, and intrigue. Reinforcing this desire to go with sensationalism is the fact that covering such stories is cheaper than investigating foreign policy or analyzing the tax code. During its first month, the Lewinsky story consumed more than one-third of the on-air time of the news networks—more than the U.S. showdown with Iran, the Winter Olympics, the pope's visit to Cuba, and the El Niño weather pattern combined.

Since the days of Vietnam and Watergate, journalists have become adversaries of the government. They instinctively distrust people in government. But to that attitude change can be added an economic one: in their desperate effort to reclaim market share, journalists are much more likely to rely on unnamed sources than once was the case. When the *Washington Post* broke the Watergate story in the 1970s, it required the reporters to have at least two sources for their stories. Now many reporters break stories that have only one unnamed source, and often not a source at all but a rumor posted on the Internet.

Before the terrorist attack on the United States on September 11, 2001, the big stories were the sexual conduct of President Clinton and the connection between California representative Gary Condit and a missing young woman. After September 11, the press focused on a more important matter—defeating terrorism at home and abroad. By early 2002, surveys indicated that the number of people who said they followed national news closely had increased slightly from 48 percent to 53 percent, and the number who said the media usually get the facts straight rose from 35 percent to 46 percent (the best public grade for accuracy in a decade). But within a year after the terrorist attack, public confidence in the media had collapsed, with more people than before saying the press was often inaccurate.[38] The television networks did not seem to gain any viewers back as a result of the crisis: fully 53 percent cited cable as their primary source for news on terrorism, versus 18 percent for local television and 17 percent for national networks.[39]

GOVERNMENT CONSTRAINTS ON JOURNALISTS

An important factor works against the influence of ideology and antiofficial attitudes on reporters—the need every reporter has for access to key officials. A reporter is only as good as his or her sources, and it is difficult to cultivate good sources if you regularly antagonize them. Thus, Washington reporters must constantly strike a balance between expressing their own views (and risk losing a valuable source) and keeping a source (and risk becoming its mouthpiece).

The great increase in the number of congressional staff members has made striking this balance easier than it once was. Since it is almost impossible to keep anything secret from Congress, the existence of 15,000 to 20,000 congressional staffers means there is a potential source for every conceivable issue and cause. Congress has become a gold mine for reporters. If a story annoys one congressional source, another source can easily be found.

The government is not without means to fight back. The number of press officers on the payroll of the

© Bettman/CORBIS

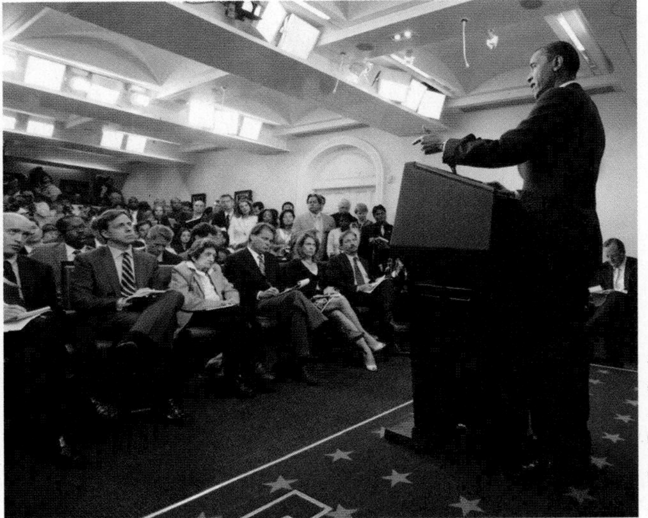

Jason Reed/Reuters/Landov

In 1993, White House press conferences were informal affairs, as when reporters gathered around Franklin Roosevelt's desk in the Oval Office. Today, they are huge gatherings held in a special conference room, as shown on the right.

White House, Congress, and the executive agencies has grown sharply in recent decades. Obviously, these people have a stake in putting out news stories that reflect favorably on their elected superiors. They can try to do this with press releases, but adversarial journalists are suspicious of "canned news" (although they use it nonetheless). Or the press officers can try to win journalistic friends by offering leaks and supplying background stories to favored reporters.

There are four ways in which reporters and public officials, or their press officers, can communicate:

- On the record: The reporter can quote the official by name.
- Off the record: What the official says cannot be used.
- On **background:** What the official says can be used but may not be attributed to him or her by name. Reporters often call such an anonymous source "a high-ranking official" or "a knowledgeable member of Congress."
- On deep background: What the official says can be used but not attributed to anybody, even an anonymous source.

background
A public official's statement to a reporter given on condition that the official not be named.

To get around the national press, public officials and their press officers can try to reach the local media directly by giving interviews or appearing on radio talk shows. The local media are a bit less likely than the national media to have an adversarial attitude toward the national government, and one can select talk-show hosts on the basis of their known ideology.

The ultimate weapon in the government's effort to shape the press to its liking is the president's rewarding of reporters and editors who treat him well and his punishing of those who treat him badly. President Kennedy regularly called in offending reporters for brutal tongue-lashings and favored friendly reporters with tips and inside stories. Johnson did the same, with special attention to television reporters. Nixon made the mistake of attacking the press publicly, thereby allowing it to defend itself with appeals to the First Amendment. (Kennedy's and Johnson's manipulative skills were used privately.) Probably every president tries to use the press with whatever means are at his disposal, but in the long run it is the press, not the president, who wins. Johnson decided not to run again in 1968 in part because of press hostility to him; Nixon was exposed by the press; Carter and Bush came to be disliked by national reporters. The press and the president need but do not trust one another; it is inevitably a stormy relationship.

RESEARCH FRONTIERS

Are "Tweeting" Politicians and "Digital Democracy" to Be Desired?

At 12:01 P.M. Tuesday, January 20, 2009, just one minute after the constitutional transfer of power from George W. Bush to Barack Obama, the White House Web site posted a message from President Obama's director of new media, announcing a White House blog. The public can follow the Obama administration's activities through Facebook, Twitter, YouTube, and numerous other online Web sites. Obama is the first president to use e-mail—his two predecessors did not do so while in office (Bush wrote to close friends shortly before his inauguration explaining that he would no longer use e-mail as president because messages would be considered part of the public record)—and he continues to have his BlackBerry for personal use, despite initial concerns about security.

The new media bring many opportunities for public officials to disseminate information and build political support. But they can result in political disasters as well. Two members of the U.S. House of Representatives in the 112th Congress were publicly humiliated when news reports revealed that they had sent inappropriate pictures of themselves to people online. The permanent public record that electronic technology creates

(continued)

allows repeated viewings of images, one-time mistakes, and patterns of conduct that become impossible to erase because they are distributed so quickly and so widely.

Given the growing popularity of tweeting and related high-technology communications, as well as the complications that can arise from these new technologies, you might suppose that researchers have identified their effect on campaigns, elections, and policymaking You might, but you would be wrong. Believe it or not, as late as the early 1980s, many reputable scholars still actually argued that television's influence on politics was minimal or ambiguous. It wasn't that they claimed that most voters did not watch television or were totally unaffected by what they watched. Rather, the claim was essentially that, all things considered, most citizens' opinions, partisan attachments, and voting behavior was pretty much what it would have been had they not been "exposed" to television or been regular consumers of televised political news reports or the like.

Today, nobody doubts that television, other electronic communications, and the Internet in all its manifestations matter to campaign politics, legislative agenda-setting, and more. In the 2008 presidential election, for example, the Obama campaign's savvy use of electronic media was instrumental in building the candidate's name recognition and drawing in young voters.

Still, the nature, scope, and direction of these "media effects," and how they vary under different conditions, are points on which the experts don't all agree. Many unresolved research questions divide scholars who study the media and politics. For example, some argue that the Internet revolution has improved political coverage, while others argue that the Internet (and instant communications more generally) has created a shallow "digital democracy."

How do the new media present opportunities and challenges for American democracy? We can't say definitively until we amass more evidence to identify long-term patterns of causes and effects for public officials as well as the general public.

Sources: Jennings Bryant and Susan Thompson, *Fundamentals of Media Effects* (New York: McGraw Hill, 2008); Megan Boler, ed., *Digital Media and Democracy: Tactics in Hard Times* (Cambridge, Mass.: MIT University Press, 2008); Diane J. Heith, "The Virtual Primary Campaign: Connecting with Constituents in a Multimedia Age," in *From Votes to Victory: Winning and Governing the White House in the Twenty-First Century*, ed. Meena Bose (College Station, Tex.: Texas A&M University Press, 2011); Richard L. Berke, "The Last (E-mail) Goodbye, from 'gwb' to His 42 Buddies," *New York Times*, March 17, 2001; "Suzanne Choney, "President Obama Gets to Keep His BlackBerry," msnbc.com, January 22, 2009.

WHAT WOULD YOU DO?

MEMORANDUM

To: *Matthew Wilson, senator*

From: *Margaret Drinker, legislative assistant*

Subject: *Protecting journalists*

The Supreme Court has held that forcing a reporter to testify does not violate the First Amendment to the Constitution. But Congress could pass a law, similar to that in many states, banning such testimony if it reveals a confidential source.

Arguments for:

1. Thirty-four states now have shield laws similar to the one proposed by Congress.
2. Effective journalism requires protecting sources from being identified; without protection, a lot of important stories would not be written.
3. The government should be able to collect sufficient information to prosecute cases without relying on journalists to do this work for them.

Arguments against:

1. Every person accused in a criminal trial has a right to know all of the evidence against him or her and to confront witnesses. A shield law would deprive people of this right.
2. A shield law would allow any government official to leak secret information with no fear of being detected.
3. The Supreme Court already has imposed a high barrier to forcing reporters to reveal confidential information, but that barrier should not be absolute, as situations can and do arise where a reporter is the only person who has the information necessary to investigate alleged criminal activity that threatens national security.

News »

Should a Shield Law Be Passed to Protect Journalists?

Efforts by the White House to find out who is the "high-ranking official" cited in recent news stories about possible ethics violations by some Cabinet secretaries have renewed calls by media groups for a "shield law" for journalists. Congress may hold hearings later this week.

Your decision:

Support bill ____________________ Oppose bill ____________________

LEARNING OBJECTIVES

WHAT YOU NEED TO KNOW

☑ What role do the media play in American politics?

The media serve three major roles in American politics: gatekeeper, scorekeeper, and watchdog. They identify priorities for policymaking, keep track of which candidates are doing well and which are doing poorly in political campaigns, and oversee the workings of government to ensure that public officials are meeting their responsibilities.

☑ Why are there so few restrictions on media coverage of politics and politicians in the United States?

The First Amendment to the Constitution explicitly guarantees that Congress may not pass a law abridging freedom of speech or of the press. While this protection is not absolute—journalists may be required by courts, for example, to divulge information about confidential sources in the interest of national security—the burden of proof is on the government to explain why violating this constitutional guarantee is necessary. Government officials have fewer protections from media coverage of their actions than private citizens because of their public responsibilities.

☑ How has technology changed interactions between public officials and the media?

Changes in technology, particularly the advent of the World Wide Web, have fundamentally changed how politicians and the media interact. Elected officials now can reach constituents directly via e-mail, Web sites, instant messages, and so forth, whereas previously they were primarily dependent on the media for conveying their messages. Electronic media, in turn, are able to cover elected officials 24 hours a day, further narrowing the zone of privacy that politicians may realistically expect.

RECONSIDERING WHO GOVERNS?

1. How much power do the media have?

A lot, but it is limited by selective attention and personal knowledge. Selective attention means that people tend to believe only those arguments consistent with their own beliefs. Personal knowledge means people know a lot based on their own experiences regardless of what the press says. Politicians in and out of office spend a great deal of time cultivating the media, but in many campaigns it is clear that the press is more likely to favor some people over others.

2. Can we trust the media to be fair?

The public does not believe we can trust the press, and that hostility has increased in recent years. Members of the national media are disproportionately liberal and secular, and there is evidence that these liberal views affect what they say or write. The extent of that political influence will differ, however, depending on whether a story is a routine feature or an insider account.

RECONSIDERING TO WHAT ENDS?

1. What public policies will the media support?

The media will lead the public to think about issues remote from their personal experiences, such as foreign policy. But the press can take up or drop issues, not because the issue has changed, but because the issue has become, to journalists, stale. Crime and drug abuse may be big topics some years and minor ones in other years. Liberal newspapers, such as the *New York Times,* will be much more interested in gay rights, gun control, and the environment than will conservative newspapers or even the general public.

QUESTIONS TO CONSIDER

1. **In an era of 24/7 news and a blurry division, at best, between public and private life, what qualifies as a "news" media outlet, and why?**
2. **Is the decline in news readership in the United States, as well as the decline in overseas news bureaus for U.S. media, a source of concern? Why or why not?**
3. **Would the United States benefit from a national public news service, as other industrialized democracies have? Why or why not?**
4. **How often do the White House and members of Congress update their Web sites, and with what types of information?**
5. **How do media outlets differ in their coverage of major political events, and what may help to explain those differences?**
6. **How do the media in other countries cover American politics?**

TO LEARN MORE

To search many newspapers: **www.ipl.org**

To get analyses of the press

Nonpartisan view: **www.cmpa.org**

Liberal view: **www.fair.org**

Conservative view: **www.mrc.org**

Public opinion about the press

Pew Research Center: **people-press.org**

National media:

New York Times: **www.nytimes.com**

Wall Street Journal: **www. wsj.com**

Washington Post: **www.washingtonpost.com**

Crouse, Timothy. *The Boys on the Bus.* New York: Random House, 1973. A lively, irreverent account by a participant of how reporters cover a presidential campaign.

Epstein, Edward J. *Between Fact and Fiction: The Problem of Journalism.* New York: Random House, 1975. Essays by a perceptive student of the press on media coverage of Watergate, the Pentagon Papers, the deaths of Black Panthers, and other major stories.

___. *News from Nowhere.* New York: Random House, 1973. Analysis of how television network news programs are produced and shaped.

Garment, Suzanne. *Scandal.* New York: Random House, 1991. A careful look at the role of the media (and others) in fostering the "culture of mistrust."

Graber, Doris A. *Mass Media and American Politics,* 8th ed. Washington, D.C.: Congressional Quarterly Press, 2009. A good summary of what we know about the press and politics.

Groseclose, Tim. *Left Turn: How Liberal Media Bias Distorts the American Mind.* New York: St. Martin's Press, 2011. Excellent study, written for the general reader, of new findings about media bias.

Iyengar, Shanto, and Donald R. Kinder. *News That Matters.* Chicago: University of Chicago Press, 1987. The report of experiments testing the effect of television news on public perceptions of politics.

Lichter, S. Robert, Stanley Rothman, and Linda S. Lichter. *The Media Elite.* Bethesda, Md.: Adler and Adler, 1986. A study of the political beliefs of "elite" journalists and how those beliefs influence what we read and hear.

McGowan, William. *Coloring the News.* San Francisco: Encounter Books, 2001. An argument about the harmful effects of affirmative action and "identity politics" on news coverage.

Stroud, Natalie Jomini. *Niche News: The Politics of News Choice.* New York: Oxford University Press, 2011. Extensive empirical analysis of how political partisanship shapes the news sources that people use.

Part 3

Institutions of Government

13 **Congress** 326

14 **The Presidency** 364

15 **The Bureaucracy** 408

16 **The Judiciary** 438

But the great security against a gradual concentration of the several powers in the same department consists in giving to those who administer each department the necessary constitutional means and personal motives to resist encroachments of the others.

**** Federalist No. 51***

13 Congress

LEARNING OBJECTIVES

WHAT YOU NEED TO KNOW

- ☑ In what respects is Congress "the first branch" of American national government?
- ☑ Why do most Americans and many experts now view Congress as "the broken branch"?
- ☑ What are the main differences between a congress and a parliament?
- ☑ How has the legislative productivity of the U.S. Congress varied over time?
- ☑ Are the American people as deeply divided in partisan and ideological terms as their representatives in Congress now appear to be?

WHO GOVERNS?

1. How closely do members of Congress mirror the American people in terms of gender, race, and other demographic characteristics?
2. Does Congress normally do what most citizens want it to do?

TO WHAT ENDS?

1. Should Congress run under strong leadership?
2. Should Congress act more quickly?

If you are like most Americans, you trust the Supreme Court, respect the presidency (whether or not you like the president), and dislike Congress (even if you like your own representative and senators). Congress is the most unpopular branch of government. But it is also the most important one. You cannot understand the national government without first understanding Congress. Glance at the Constitution and you will see why Congress is so important: the first four and a half pages are about Congress, while the presidency gets only a page and a half and the Supreme Court about three-quarters of one page.

To the Framers of the Constitution, the bicameral (two-chamber) Congress was "the first branch." They expected Congress to wield most of the national government's powers, including its most important ones like the "power of the purse" (encompassing taxation and spending decisions) and the ultimate authority to declare war. They understood Congress as essential to sustaining federalism (guaranteeing two senators to each state without regard to state population) and maintaining the separation of powers (ensuring that no lawmaker would be allowed to serve in either of the other two branches while in Congress). They also viewed Congress as the linchpin of the system of checks and balances, constitutionally empowered as it was both to override presidential vetoes and to determine the structure and the appellate jurisdiction of the federal judiciary, including the one Supreme Court.

Most contemporary Americans and many experts, however, think of Congress not as the first branch but as "the broken branch," unable to address the nation's

most pressing domestic, economic, and international problems in an effective way; unduly responsive to powerful organized special interests; awash in nonstop campaign fundraising and other activities that many believe border on political corruption; and unlikely to fix itself through real reforms.[1]

Consistent with this broken branch view, in recent decades, public approval of Congress has rarely ranged much above a third. In the 2000s, ratings in the 20s or 30s were the norm. In recent years, several ratings in the teens have been recorded. In July 2008, the Gallup Organization, which has tracked public approval of Congress for decades, recorded an all-time low of 14 percent public approval. In March 2010, public approval of Congress stood at 16 percent. In November 2010, Republicans regained control of the House after four years of Democratic control; and in March 2011, public approval of Congress was at 18 percent.

Many academic analysts and veteran Washington journalists echo the popular discontent with Congress as the broken branch, but the experts focus more on two things, the first a paradox and the second a puzzle. The paradox is that most Americans consistently disapprove of Congress yet routinely reelect their own members to serve in it. In political scientist Richard F. Fenno's famous phrase, if "Congress is the broken branch then how come we love our congressmen so much more than our Congress?"[2] Despite public approval ratings that almost never reach as high as half, since 1980 over 90 percent of all congressional incumbents who have sought reelection have won it, most by comfortable margins. Even in elections in

How Things Work

The Powers of Congress

The powers of Congress are found in Article I, section 8, of the Constitution.

- To lay and collect taxes, duties, imposts, and excises
- To borrow money
- To regulate commerce with foreign nations and among the states
- To establish rules for naturalization (that is, becoming a citizen) and bankruptcy
- To coin money, set its value, and punish counterfeiting
- To fix the standard of weights and measures
- To establish a post office and post roads
- To issue patents and copyrights to inventors and authors
- To create courts inferior to (below) the Supreme Court
- To define and punish piracies, felonies on the high seas, and crimes against the law of nations
- To declare war
- To raise and support an army and navy and make rules for their governance
- To provide for a militia (reserving to the states the right to appoint militia officers and to train the militia under congressional rules)
- To exercise exclusive legislative powers over the seat of government (the District of Columbia) and other places purchased to be federal facilities (forts, arsenals, dockyards, and "other needful buildings")
- To "make all laws which shall be necessary and proper for carrying into execution the fore-going powers, and all other powers vested by this Constitution in the government of the United States." (*Note*: This "necessary and proper," or "elastic," clause has been generously interpreted by the Supreme Court, as explained in Chapter 16.)

party polarization A vote in which a majority of Democratic legislators oppose a majority of Republican legislators.

which "anti-incumbent" public sentiment seems rife and voters effect a change in party control of one or both chambers of Congress, incumbents prevail and dominate the institution. For example, in the 2010 midterm elections, Democrats suffered historic losses in the House, but most Democratic and Republican incumbents alike who sought reelection won it. In the 112th Congress that began in 2011, 80 percent of House members, and 70 percent of Senators, were incumbents. Even though they have been fussing over it for several decades now, political scientists are still not sure how to answer Fenno's question and resolve the paradox.

The puzzle is why the post-1970 Congress has become ever more polarized by partisanship and divided by ideology, and whether this development reflects ever-widening political cleavages among average Americans or instead constitutes a disconnect between the people and their representatives on Capitol Hill.

THEN During 1890–1910, about two-thirds of all votes in Congress evoked a party split, and in several sessions more than half the roll calls found about 90 percent of each party's members opposing the other party.[3] But, during the 1970s, such **partisan polarization** in Congress was very much the exception to the rule. Well into the 1960s, Congress commonly passed major legislation on most issues on a bipartisan basis, and there were liberal members and conservative members in leadership positions in both parties and in both chambers. Such liberal and conservative voting blocs as existed typically crossed party lines, like the mid-20th-century conservative bloc featuring Republicans and southern Democrats. Leaders in Congress in each party were usually veteran politicians interested mainly in winning elections, dispensing patronage, obtaining tangible benefits for their own districts or states and constituents, and keeping institutional power and perks. Even members with substantial seniority did not get the most coveted committee chairmanships unless they were disposed to practice legislative politics as the art of the possible and the art of the deal. This meant forging interparty coalitions and approaching interbranch (legislative-executive) relations in ways calculated to result ultimately in bipartisan bargains and compromises, and doing so even on controversial issues and even when congressional leaders and the president were not all in the same party.

NOW When the 91st Congress ended in 1970, the more liberal half of the House had 29 Republicans and the more conservative half of the House had 59 Democrats.[4] By the time the 105th Congress ended in 1998, the more liberal half of the House had only ten Republicans while the more conservative half of the House had zero Democrats.[5] (Zero!) In the 2000s, liberal Republicans and conservative Democrats became virtually extinct in both the House and the Senate. For example, in 2010, the major health care reform bill (the Patient Protection and Affordable Care Act) proposed by Democrats passed in the House without a single Republican member of the House voting for it. In 2011, the far-reaching Fiscal Year 2012 budget plan (cutting trillions of dollars in spending over the next decade) drafted by Republicans passed in the House without a single Democratic member of the House voting for it. The 112th Congress began in January 2011, and during its first quarter-year a post-1945 record high of about 80 percent of all roll-call votes in the House pitted a majority of Democrats against a majority of Republicans.[6]

As we discuss in more detail later in this chapter, some scholars insist that the "disappearing center" in Congress reflects partisan and ideological divisions among average Americans,[7] while other scholars seem equally sure that we are instead witnessing a "disconnect" between a still nonideological and politically centrist mass public and its representatives on Capitol Hill.[8] Whichever side is more right, three things remain clear.

First, Congress has never perfectly embodied the Founders' fondest hopes for the first branch, not when the First Congress met in 1789–1791 (and wrangled endlessly over the Bill of Rights); not during the decades before, during, and just after the Civil War; not during the late nineteenth century through 1970; and certainly not since. James Madison envisioned members of Congress as "proper guardians of the public weal," public-spirited representatives of the people who would govern by intelligently mediating and dispassionately resolving conflicts among and between the large republic's diverse and competing financial, religious, and other interests.[9] Representatives or senators who might instead fan partisan passions, stir civic discord while refusing all compromises, or otherwise fuel rather than frustrate "factions" that trample citizens' rights or toy with the public's true needs, were disparaged by Madison as selfish, unenlightened, or "theoretic politicians" (what today we might call "extremists," "hyper-partisans," or "ideologues").[10] At least if judged by the Founders' highest aspirations for the first branch and its members, Congress has always been something of a broken branch.

Second, Congress is now home to ideologically distinct political parties that seem more unified than ever with respect to how their respective members vote, but the body still does not come close to matching the near-total party unity that has been typical in the national legislatures of Great Britain and other parliamentary democracies.

Third, Madison and the other Framers expressly rejected a parliamentary system like Great Britain's in favor of a system featuring both a separation of powers and checks and balances. They understood the fundamental differences between a "congress" and a "parliament," and so must every present-day student who hopes to really understand the U.S. Congress.

Congress versus Parliament

The United States (along with many Latin American nations) has a congress; Great Britain (along with most Western European nations) has a parliament. A hint as to the difference between the two kinds of legislatures can be found in the original meanings of the words. *Congress* derives from a Latin term that means "a coming together," a meeting, as of representatives from various places. *Parliament* comes from a French word, *parler,* that means "to talk."

There is of course plenty of talking—some critics say there is nothing *but* talking—in the U.S. Congress, and certainly members of a parliament represent to a degree their local districts. But the differences implied by the names of the lawmaking groups are real ones, with profound significance for how laws are made and how the government is run. These differences affect two important aspects of lawmaking bodies: how one becomes a member and what one does as a member.

Ordinarily, a person becomes a member of a parliament (such as the British House of Commons) by persuading a political party to put his or her name on the ballot. Though usually a local party committee selects a person to be its candidate, that committee often takes suggestions from national party headquarters. The local group selects as its candidate someone willing to support the national party program and leadership. In the election, voters in the district choose not between two or three personalities running for office, but between two or three national parties.

By contrast, a person becomes a candidate for representative or senator in the U.S. Congress by running in a primary election. Except in a very few places, political parties exercise little control over the choice of who is nominated to run for congressional office. (This is the case even though the person who wins the primary will describe himself or herself in the general election as a Democrat or a Republican.) Voters select candidates in the primaries because of their personalities, positions on issues, or overall reputation. Even in the general election, where the party label affects who votes for whom, many citizens vote "for the man" (or for the woman), not for the party.

As a result of these different systems, a parliament tends to be made up of people loyal to the national party leadership who meet to debate and vote on party issues. A congress, on the other hand, tends to be made up of people who think of themselves as independent representatives of their districts or states and who, while willing to support their party on many matters, expect to vote as their (or their constituents') beliefs and interests require.

Once they are in the legislature, members of a parliament discover they can make only one important decision—whether or not to support the government. The government in a parliamentary system such as Britain's consists of a prime minister and various cabinet officers selected from the party that has the most seats in parliament. As long as the members of that party vote together, that government will remain in power (until the next election). Should members of a party in power in parliament decide to vote against their leaders, the leaders lose office, and a new government must be formed. With so much at stake, the leaders of a party in parliament have a powerful incentive to keep their followers in line. They insist that all members of the party vote together on almost all issues. If someone refuses, the penalty is often drastic: the party does not renominate the offending member in the next election.

Members of the U.S. Congress do not select the head of the executive branch of government—that is done by the voters when they choose a president. Far from making members of Congress less powerful, this makes them more powerful. Representatives and senators can vote on proposed laws without worrying that their votes will cause the government to collapse and without fearing that a failure to support their party will lead to their removal from the ballot in the next election. Congress has independent powers, defined by the Constitution, that it can exercise without regard to presidential preferences. Political parties do not control nominations for office, and thus they cannot discipline members of Congress who fail to support the party leadership. Because Congress is constitutionally independent of the president, and because its members are not tightly disciplined by a party leadership, individual members of Congress are free to express their views

In January 2011, Democratic Speaker Nancy Pelosi turned over her gavel to Republican John Boehner who became speaker after the large Republican victory in the 2010 election.

Three powerful Speakers of the House: Thomas B. Reed (1889–1891, 1895–1899) (left), Joseph G. Cannon (1903–1911) (center), and Sam Rayburn (1941–1947, 1949–1953, 1955–1961) (right). Reed put an end to a filibuster in the House by refusing to allow dilatory motions and by counting as "present"—for purposes of a quorum—members in the House even though they were not voting. Cannon further enlarged the Speaker's power by refusing to recognize members who wished to speak without Cannon's approval and by increasing the power of the Rules Committee, over which he presided. Cannon was stripped of much of his power in 1910. Rayburn's influence rested more on his ability to persuade than on his formal powers.

and vote as they wish. They are also free to become involved in the most minute details of lawmaking, budget making, and supervision of the administration of laws. They do this through an elaborate set of committees and subcommittees.

A real parliament, such as that in Britain, is an assembly of party representatives who choose a government and discuss major national issues. The principal daily work of a parliament is debate. A congress, such as that in the United States, is a meeting place of the representatives of local constituencies—districts and states. Members of the U.S. Congress can initiate, modify, approve, or reject laws, and they share with the president supervision of the administrative agencies of the government. The principal work of a congress is representation and action, most of which takes place in committees.

What this means in practical terms to the typical legislator is easy to see. Since members of the British House of Commons have little independent power, they get rather little in return. They are poorly paid, may have no offices of their own and virtually no staff, are allowed only small sums to buy stationery, and can make a few free local telephone calls. Each is given a desk, a filing cabinet, and a telephone, but not always in the same place.

By contrast, a member of the U.S. House of Representatives, even a junior one, has power and is rewarded accordingly. For example, in 2011, each member earned a substantial base salary ($174,000) plus generous health care and retirement benefits, and was entitled to a large office (or "clerk-hire") allowance, to pay for about two dozen staffers. (Each chamber's majority and minority leaders earned $193,400 a year, and the Speaker of the House earned $223,400.) Each member also received individual allowances for travel, computer services, and the like. In addition, each member could mail newsletters and certain other documents to constituents for free using the "franking privilege." Senators, and representatives with seniority, received even larger benefits. Each senator is entitled to a generous office budget and legislative assistance allowance and is free to hire as many staff members as he or she wishes with the money. These examples are not given to suggest that members of Congress are overrewarded, but only that their importance as individuals in our political system can be inferred from the resources they command.

Because the United States has a congress made up of people chosen to represent their states and districts, rather than a parliament made up to represent competing political parties, no one should be surprised to learn that members of the U.S. Congress are more concerned with their own constituencies and careers than with the interests of any organized party or program of action. And since Congress does not choose the president, members of Congress know that worrying about the voters they represent is much more important than worrying about whether the president succeeds with his programs. These two factors taken together mean that Congress tends to be a decentralized institution, with each member more interested in his or her own views and those of his or her voters than with the programs proposed by the president.

Indeed, Congress was designed by the Founders in ways that almost inevitably make it unpopular with voters. Americans want government to take action, follow a clear course of action, and respond to strong leaders. Americans dislike political arguments, the activities of special-interest groups, and the endless pulling and hauling that often precede any congressional decision. But the people who feel this way are deeply divided about what government should do: Be liberal? Be conservative? Spend money? Cut taxes? Support abortions? Stop abortions? Since they are divided, and since members of Congress must worry about how voters feel, it is inevitable that on controversial issues Congress will engage in endless arguments, worry about what interest groups (who represent different groups of voters) think, and work out compromise decisions. When it does those things, however, many people feel let down and say they have a low opinion of Congress.

Of course, a member of Congress might explain all these constitutional facts to the people, but not many members are eager to tell their voters that they do not really understand how Congress was created and organized. Instead they run for reelection by promising voters they will go back to Washington and "clean up that mess."

The Evolution of Congress

The Framers chose to place legislative powers in the hands of a congress rather than a parliament for philosophical and practical reasons. They did not want to have all powers concentrated in a single governmental institution, even one that was popularly elected, because they feared such a concentration could lead to rule by an oppressive or impassioned majority. At the same time, they knew the states were jealous of their independence and would never consent to a national constitution if it did not protect their interests and strike a reasonable balance between large and small states. Hence, they created a **bicameral** (two-chamber) **legislature**—with a House of Representatives, elected directly by the people, and a Senate, consisting of two members from each state, chosen by the legislatures of each state. Though "all legislative powers" were vested in Congress, those powers would be shared with the president (who could veto acts of Congress), limited to powers explicitly conferred on the federal government, and, as it turned out, subject to the power of the Supreme Court to declare acts of Congress unconstitutional.

bicameral legislature A lawmaking body made up of two chambers or parts.

For decades, critics of Congress complained that the body cannot plan or act quickly. They are right, but two competing values are at stake: centralization versus decentralization. If Congress acted quickly and decisively as a body, then there would have to be strong central leadership, restrictions on debate, few opportunities for stalling tactics, and minimal committee interference. If, on the other hand, the interests of individual members—and the constituencies they represent—were protected or enhanced, then there would have to be weak leadership, rules allowing for delay and discussion, and many opportunities for committee activity.

Though there have been periods of strong central leadership in Congress, the general trend, especially since the mid-20th century, has been toward decentralizing decision making and enhancing the power of the individual member at the expense of the congressional leadership. This decentralization may not have been inevitable. Most American states have constitutional systems quite similar to the federal one, yet in many state legislatures, such as those in New York, Massachusetts, and Indiana, the leadership is quite powerful. In part, the position of these strong state legislative leaders may be the result of the greater strength of political parties in some states than in the nation as a whole. In large measure, however, it is a consequence of permitting state legislative leaders to decide who shall chair what committee and who shall receive what favors.

The House of Representatives, though always powerful, often has changed the way in which it is organized and led. In some periods, it has given its leader, the Speaker, a lot of power; in other periods, it has given much of that power to the chairs of the House committees; and in still other periods, it has allowed individual members to acquire great influence. To simplify a complicated story, the box starting on page 333 outlines six different periods in the history of the House.

The House faces fundamental problems: it wants to be big (it has 435 members) and powerful, and its members want to be powerful as individuals and as a group. But being big makes it hard for the House to be powerful unless some small group is given

House History: Six Phases

Phase One: The Powerful House

During the first three administrations—of George Washington, John Adams, and Thomas Jefferson—leadership in Congress often was supplied by the president or his cabinet officers. Rather quickly, however, Congress began to assert its independence. The House of Representatives was the preeminent institution, overshadowing the Senate.

Library of Congress/LC-DIG-ppmsca-09398

One of the most powerful Speakers of the House, Henry Clay, is shown here addressing the U.S. Senate around 1850.

Phase Two: The Divided House

In the late 1820s, the preeminence of the House began to wane. Andrew Jackson asserted the power of the presidency by vetoing legislation he did not like. The party unity necessary for a Speaker, or any leader, to control the House was shattered by the issue of slavery. Of course, representatives from the South did not attend during the Civil War, and their seats remained vacant for several years after it ended. A group called the Radical Republicans, led by men such as Thaddeus Stevens of Pennsylvania, produced strong majorities for measures aimed at punishing the defeated South. But as time passed, the hot passions the war had generated began to cool, and it became clear that the leadership of the House remained weak.

Phase Three: The Speaker Rules

Toward the end of the 19th century, the Speaker of the House gained power. When Thomas B. Reed of Maine became Speaker in 1889, he obtained by vote of the Republican majority more authority than any of his predecessors, including the right to select the chairs and members of all committees. He chaired the Rules Committee and decided what business would come up for a vote, any limitations on debate, and who would be allowed to speak and who would not. In 1903, Joseph G. Cannon of Illinois became Speaker. He tried to maintain Reed's tradition, but he had many enemies within his Republican ranks.

Phase Four: The House Revolts

In 1910–1911, the House revolted against "Czar" Cannon, voting to strip the Speaker of his right to appoint committee chairs and to remove him from the Rules Committee. The powers lost by the Speaker flowed to the party caucus, the Rules Committee, and the chairs of the standing committees. It was not, however, until the 1960s and 1970s that House members struck out against all forms of leadership.

(continued)

(continued)

Phase Five: The Members Rule

Newly elected Democrats could not get the House to vote on a meaningful civil rights bill until 1964 because powerful committee chairs, most of them from the South, kept such legislation bottled up. In response, Democrats changed their rules so that chairpersons lost much of their authority. Beginning in the 1970s, committee chairs would no longer be selected simply on the basis of seniority: they had to be elected by the members of the majority party. Chairpersons could no longer refuse to call committee meetings, and most meetings had to be public. Committees without subcommittees had to create them and allow their members to choose subcommittee chairs. Individual members' staffs were greatly enlarged, and half of all majority-party members were chairs of at least one committee or subcommittee.

Phase Six: The Leadership Returns

Since every member had power, it was harder for the House to get anything done. By slow steps, culminating in some sweeping changes made in 1995, there were efforts to restore some of the power the Speaker had once had. The number of committees and subcommittees was reduced. Republican Speaker Newt Gingrich dominated the choice of committee chairs, often passing over more senior members for more agreeable junior ones. But Gingrich's demise was as quick as his rise. His decision not to pass some appropriations bills forced many government offices to close for a short period, he had to pay a fine for using tax-exempt funds for political purposes, and then the Republicans lost a number of seats in the 1998 election. Gingrich resigned as Speaker and as a member of the House and was replaced by a more moderate Speaker, Republican Dennis Hastert of Illinois, with a penchant for accommodating his colleagues. When the 110th Congress began in 2007, Democrat Nancy Pelosi of California held the Speaker's gavel. Pelosi was the sixtieth Speaker in House history but the first woman to lead the House. She presided over many battles with the House's GOP leaders, but her most memorable role as Speaker occurred in 2010 when she struck assorted (and some critics claimed sordid) deals with members of her own party to garner their votes for the president's sweeping health care overhaul plan. Following heavy Democratic losses in the 2010 midterm elections, in January 2011 Pelosi was succeeded as Speaker by Republican John Boehner of Ohio. Even some liberal Democratic members of his state's congressional delegation (for example, Ohio Representative Dennis Kucinich) characterized Boehner as a committed but pragmatic conservative and professional legislator, but opinions differed widely over how (and how well) he would lead the 112th Congress.

the authority to run it. If a group runs the place, however, the individual members lack much power. Individuals can gain power, but only at the price of making the House harder to run and thus reducing its collective power in government. There is no lasting solution to these dilemmas, and so the House will always be undergoing changes.

The Senate does not face any of these problems. It is small enough (100 members) that it can be run without giving much authority to any small group of leaders. In addition, it has escaped some of the problems the House once faced. During the period leading up to the Civil War, it was carefully balanced so that the number of senators from slave-owning states exactly equaled the number from free states. Hence, fights over slavery rarely arose in the Senate.

From the first, the Senate was small enough that no time limits had to be placed on how long a senator could speak. This meant there never was anything like a Rules Committee that controlled the amount of debate.

Finally, senators were not elected by the voters until the 20th century. Prior to that, they were picked instead by state legislatures. Thus senators often were the leaders of local party organizations, with an interest in funneling jobs back to their states.

The big changes in the Senate came not from any fight about how to run it (nobody ever really ran it), but from a dispute over how its members should be chosen. For more than a century after the Founding, members of the Senate were chosen by state legislatures. Though often these legislatures picked popular local figures to be senators, just as often there was intense political maneuvering among the leaders of various factions, each struggling to win (and sometimes buy) the votes necessary to become senator. By the end of the 19th century, the Senate was known as the Millionaires' Club because of the number of wealthy party leaders

New York Public Library

A cartoon from *Puck* in 1890 expressed popular resentment over the "Millionaires Club," as the Senate had become known.

and businessmen in it. There arose a demand for the direct, popular election of senators.

Naturally the Senate resisted, and without its approval the necessary constitutional amendment could not pass Congress. When some states threatened to demand a new constitutional convention, the Senate feared that such a convention would change more than just the way in which senators were chosen. A protracted struggle ensued, during which many state legislatures devised ways to ensure that the senators they picked would already have won a popular election. The Senate finally agreed to a constitutional amendment that required the popular election of its members, and in 1913 the Seventeenth Amendment was approved by the necessary three-fourths of the states. Ironically, given the intensity of the struggle over this question, no great change in the composition of the Senate resulted; most of those members who had first been chosen by state legislatures managed to win reelection by popular vote.

filibuster An attempt to defeat a bill in the Senate by talking indefinitely, thus preventing the Senate from taking action on the bill.

The other major issue in the development of the Senate was the filibuster. A **filibuster** is a prolonged speech, or series of speeches, made to delay action in a legislative assembly. It had become a common—and unpopular—feature of Senate life by the end of the 19th century. It was used by liberals and conservatives alike and for lofty as well as self-serving purposes. The first serious effort to restrict the filibuster came in 1917, after an important foreign policy measure submitted by President Wilson had been talked to death by, as Wilson put it, "eleven willful men." Rule 22 was adopted by a Senate fearful of tying a president's hands during a wartime crisis. The rule provided that debate could be cut off if two-thirds of the senators present and voting agreed to a "cloture" motion (it has since been revised to allow 60 senators to cut off debate). Two years later, it was first invoked successfully when the Senate voted cloture to end, after 55 days, the debate over the Treaty of Versailles. Despite the existence of Rule 22, the tradition of unlimited debate remains strong in the Senate.

Who Is in Congress?

With power so decentralized in Congress, the kind of person elected to it is especially important. Since each member exercises some influence, the beliefs and interests of each individual affect policy. Viewed simplistically, most members of Congress seem the same: the typical representative or senator is a middle-aged white Protestant male lawyer. If all such persons usually thought and voted alike, that would be an interesting fact, but they do not, and so it is necessary to explore the great diversity of views among seemingly similar people.

GENDER AND RACE

Congress has gradually become less male and less white. Between 1950 and 2011, the number of women in the House increased from nine to 75 and the number of African Americans from two to 42. There are also 30 Latino members.

Until recently, the Senate changed much more slowly (see Table 13.1). Before the 1992 election, there were no African Americans and only two women in the Senate. But in 1992, four more women, including one black woman, Carol Mosely Braun of Illinois, were elected. Two more were elected in 1994, when a Native American, Ben Nighthorse Campbell of Colorado, also became a senator. Today there are 17 women in the Senate.

The relatively small number of African Americans and Latinos in the House understates their influence, at least when the Democrats are in the majority. In 1994, four House committees were chaired by blacks and three by Latinos. In the same year, however, no woman chaired a committee. The reason for

Table 13.1 Blacks, Hispanics, and Women in Congress, 1971–2011

Congress	Senate Blacks	Senate Hispanics	Senate Women	House Blacks	House Hispanics	House Women
112th (2011–2012)	0	2	17	42	30	75
111th	1	3	17	42	25	77
110th	1	3	16	38	23	74
109th	1	0	14	37	23	59
108th	0	0	13	39	23	62
107th	0	0	13	36	19	59
106th	0	0	9	39	19	58
105th	1	1	9	37	18	51
104th	1	0	8	38	18	48
103rd	1	0	6	38	17	47
102nd	0	0	2	26	10	29
101st	0	0	2	24	11	25
100th	0	0	2	23	11	23
99th	0	0	2	20	11	22
98th	0	0	2	21	10	22
97th	0	0	2	17	6	19
96th	0	0	1	16	6	16
95th	1	0	2	16	5	18
94th	1	1	0	15	5	19
93rd	1	1	0	15	5	14
92nd (1971–1972)	1	1	2	12	5	13

Source: *Congressional Quarterly*, various years.

this difference in power is that the former tend to come from districts in which incumbents have normally won reelection by comfortable margins and thus have more seniority than the latter. When the Democrats retook control of Congress in 2007, African Americans and Latinos became chairpersons of several important committees.

ROD LAMKEY JR./The Washington Times/Landov

Rep. Paul Ryan (R-WI) in 2011 became the new chair of the House Budget Committee where he oversaw the preparation of a response to Pres. Obama's budget plan.

Similarly, the first woman to become Speaker (Nancy Pelosi in 2007) was a Democrat, and the post-1970 increase of women in Congress has been led by Democrats: in 2011, 12 of the 17 women in the Senate, and 51 of the 75 women in the House, were Democrats. Among the notable women in the 112th Congress was Gabrielle Dee "Gabby" Giffords, a 41-year-old Democrat of Arizona elected to her third House term in 2010, and only the third woman from Arizona to serve in Congress. Representative Giffords served on the House Armed Services Committee and was a member of the "Blue Dog" Caucus of moderately conservative House Democrats. In January 2011, she was shot in the head by a would-be assassin but made such remarkable and rapid progress toward recovery that in spring 2011 she was able to attend the scheduled but aborted launch of a NASA shuttle co-commanded by her husband.

Middle-aged white males with law degrees are still the norm in Congress, but as Table 13.2 shows,

Rep. Gabrielle Giffords (D-AZ) recovering from being shot in the head by a homicidal maniac.

Table 13.2 Who's in Congress, 1991–1992 Versus 2011–2012

	102nd Congress (1991–1992)	112th Congress (2011–2012)
Average Age		
House	53	57
Senate	57	62
Occupation		
Law	244	200
Business	189	209
Military		
Had served	277	118
Incumbency		
In first term	44	103

Source: Adapted from chart based on Congressional Research Service and Military Officers Association data in John Harwood, "For New Congress, Data Shows Why Polarization Abounds," *New York Times*, March 6, 2011.

compared to the makeup of the 102nd Congress that began in 1991, the 112th Congress that began in 2011 had not only more women, blacks, and Latinos, but also fewer lawyers, fewer persons who had served in the armed forces, more businesspeople, more people over the age of 55, and more members (about 1 in 5 overall) serving their first term.

INCUMBENCY

The recent spike in first-termers in Congress is interesting, but the most important change that has occurred in the composition of Congress has been so gradual that most people have not noticed it. In the 19th century, a large fraction—often a majority—of congressmen served only one term. In 1869, for example, more than half the members of the House were serving their first term in Congress. Being a congressman in those days was not regarded as a career. This was in part because the federal government was not very important (most of the interesting political decisions were made by the states); in part because travel to Washington, D.C. was difficult and the city was not a pleasant place in which to live; and in part because being a congressman did not pay well. Furthermore, many congressional districts were highly competitive, with the two political parties fairly evenly balanced in each.

By the 1950s, however, serving in Congress had become a career. Between 1863 and 1969, the proportion of first-termers in the House fell from 58 percent to 8 percent.[11] As the public took note of this shift, people began to complain about "professional politicians" being "out of touch with the people." A movement to impose term limits was started. In 1995, the House approved a constitutional amendment to do just that, but it died in the Senate. Then the Supreme Court struck down an effort by a state to impose term limits on its own members of Congress.

As it turned out, natural political forces were already doing what the term limits amendment was supposed to do. The 1992 and 1994 elections brought scores of new members to the House, with the result that by 1995 the proportion of members who were serving their first or second terms had risen sharply. Three things were responsible for this change. First, when congressional district lines were redrawn after the 1990 census, a lot of incumbents found themselves running in new districts they couldn't carry. Second, voter disgust at a variety of Washington political scandals made them receptive to appeals from candidates who could describe themselves as "outsiders." And third, the Republican victory in 1994—made possible in part by the conversion of the South from a Democratic bastion to a Republican stronghold—brought a lot of new faces to the Capitol. In the 2006 midterm elections, the Democrats regained control of the House from Republicans; they retained it in 2008, but then lost it again in the 2010 midterm elections.

marginal districts Political districts in which candidates elected to the House of Representatives win in close elections, typically by less than 55 percent of the vote.

safe districts Districts in which incumbents win by margins of 55 percent or more.

As in 1994, in 2006 and in 2010 there was an influx of freshmen members.

But these periodic power-shifts accompanied by the arrival of scores of new faces in Congress should not obscure an important fact that was documented decades ago by political scientists[12] and is still true today: even in elections that result in the out party regaining power, most incumbent House members who seek reelection not only win but win big in their districts. And while Senators have been somewhat less secure than House members, most Senate incumbents who have sought reelection have won it by a comfortable margin.

Figure 13.1 shows the 1964–2010 reelection rates for incumbent House and Senate members who sought reelection. Over that span of two dozen elections, the average reelection rate for House incumbents was 93 percent and the average reelection rate for Senate incumbents was 82 percent. For the 15 elections from 1980 through 2010, the House and Senate incumbent reelection averages are 94 percent and 87 percent, respectively. In the 2010 midterm election, despite polls showing mass disaffection with Congress and a strongly "anti-incumbent" mood, 87 percent of House incumbents who sought reelection won it (53 House incumbents who sought reelection lost), and 84 percent of Senate incumbents who sought reelection won it (4 Senate incumbents who sought reelection lost, two in primary elections and two in the general election).

House incumbents who seek reelection normally beat their opponents by 10 points or more. Political scientists call districts that have close elections (when the winner gets less than 55 percent of the vote) **marginal districts** and districts where incumbents win by wide margins (55 percent or more) **safe districts.** Even by a more exacting standard—winning with 60 percent or more of the vote—in all but one of the 24 elections from 1964 to 2010 (the election of 1994), between 60 and 80 percent of House incumbents who were reelected won with 60 percent or more of the vote.[13] By contrast, over the same period, well under half of all Senate incumbents who won reelection did so by such a wide margin. In 1998 and again in 2008, about two-thirds of Senate incumbents won with 60 percent or more of the vote, but "safe states" remain far less common than safe districts.

Why congressional seats have become less marginal—that is, safer—is a matter on which scholars do not agree. Some feel it is the result of television and other media. But challengers can go on television, too, so why should this benefit incumbents? Another possibility is that voters are becoming less and less likely to automatically support whatever candidate wins the nomination of their own party. They are more likely, in short, to vote for the person rather than the party. And they are more likely to have heard of a person who is an incumbent: incumbents can deluge the voter

Figure 13.1

Reelection Rates for House and Senate Incumbents, 1964–2010

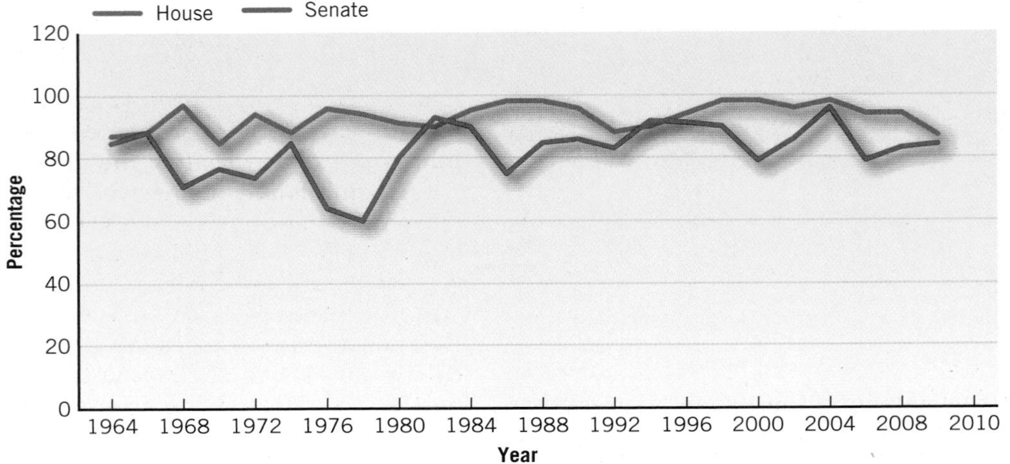

Sources: For 1964–2008 data, The Center for Responsive Politics; 2010 data compiled by author.

with free mailings, they can travel frequently (and at public expense) to meet constituents, and they can get their names in the headlines by sponsoring bills or conducting investigations. Simply having a familiar name is important in getting elected, and incumbents find it easier than challengers to make their names known.

Finally, some scholars argue that incumbents can use their power to get programs passed or funds spent to benefit their districts—and thereby to benefit themselves.[14] They can help keep an army base open, support the building of a new highway (or block the building of an unpopular one), take credit for federal grants to local schools and hospitals, make certain a particular industry or labor union is protected by tariffs against foreign competition, and so on.

Probably all of these factors make some difference. Whatever the explanation, the tendency of voters to return incumbents to office means that in ordinary times no one should expect any dramatic changes in the composition of Congress. Even when elections effect a change in party control in one or both chambers, even when new leaders are in charge and new members abound, many old hands will still be on hand in Congress.

PARTY

Forty Congresses convened between 1933 and 2011 (a new Congress convenes every two years). The Democrats controlled both houses in 27 of these Congresses and at least one house in 30 of them. Scholars differ in their explanations of why the Democrats have so often had the upper hand in Congress. Most of the research on the subject has focused on the reasons for Democratic control of the House.

In every election from 1968 to 1992, the percentage of the popular vote for Republican candidates to the House was higher than the percentage of House seats that actually went to Republicans. For example, in 1976 the Republicans won 42.1 percent of the vote but received only 32.9 percent of the seats. Some argued that this gap between votes and seats occurred because Democratic-controlled state legislatures redrew congressional district maps in ways that make it hard for Republicans to win House seats. Some striking anecdotal evidence supports this conclusion. For example, following the 1990 census, the Democratic-controlled Texas legislature crafted a new congressional district map clearly designed to benefit Democrats. In 1992, Republicans won 48 percent of the House vote in Texas but received only 30 percent of the seats. But after Republicans won control of more state legislatures, matters began to change. In Texas, a new districting plan was adopted that ensured more House seats would be won by Republicans. And when a court, rather than the Democratic legislature, redrew California's district lines, both parties won the same proportion of seats as their share of the popular vote.[15] In 2006, things had evened out nationally: both parties won about the same share of House seats as their percentage of the vote.

Partisan tinkering with district maps and other structural features of House elections is not a sufficient explanation of why Democrats dominated the House in the four decades prior to 1994. As one study concluded, "Virtually all the political science evidence to date indicates that the electoral system has little or no partisan bias, and that the net gains nationally from redistricting for one party over another are very small."[16] To control the redistricting process, one party must control both houses of the legislature, the governor's office, and, where necessary, the state courts. These conditions simply do not exist in most states.

For these and related reasons, the gains made by Republicans in the 2010 elections are unlikely to be expanded to any significant degree in the decade ahead purely by virtue of the redistricting required by the results of the 2010 Census. That is true even for Texas, which will gain more new House seats than any other state (four), but where Democrats already hold only nine of the state's 32 House seats.[17]

Congressional incumbents have come to enjoy certain built-in electoral advantages over challengers. Democrats were in the majority as the advantages of incumbency grew, but Republicans enjoyed the same or greater advantages from 1994 to 2006. Studies suggest the incumbency advantage was worth about two percentage points prior to the 1960s but has grown to six to eight points today.

It is important to remember that from time to time major electoral convulsions do alter the membership of Congress. For example, in the election of 1938 the Democrats lost 70 seats in the House; in 1942, they lost 50; in 1950, they lost 29; and, in 1966, they lost 48. Despite these big losses, the Democrats retained a majority in the House in each of these years. Not so, however, in 1994, when the Democrats lost 52 House seats (the largest loss by either party since the Republicans had lost 75 seats in 1948), and Republicans gained majorities in both the House and the Senate. And not so in 2010, when Republicans gained more than 60 House seats and narrowly failed to take the Senate as well.

Just as it is not easy to explain why Democrats dominated Congress for half a century, so it is not easy to explain why that domination ended when and as it did in 1994, or why Democrats regained control in 2006 only to lose it again just four years later. Several reasons, however, stand out.

By the 1990s, certain advantages of incumbency had turned into disadvantages: voters increasingly came to dislike "professional politicians," whom they held responsible for "the mess in Washington." Just what "the mess" was varied according to which voter you asked, but it included chronic budget deficits, the congressional habit of exempting itself from laws that affected everybody else, constant bickering between Congress and the White House, and various congressional scandals. During the 1980s, about 40 members of Congress were charged with misconduct ranging from having sex with minors to accepting illegal gifts. When it was disclosed that the House had its own bank that would cash checks even for members who (temporarily) had no funds in their accounts, public indignation exploded, even though almost no taxpayer money was lost. Public respect for Congress, as measured by the polls, plummeted. The Democrats had the misfortune of being the majority party in Congress when all of this happened. The anti-incumbent mood, coupled with the effects of redistricting after the 1990 census and the shift of the South to the Republican Party, brought the Republicans into power in the House and Senate in the 1994 elections.

By 2006, however, with an unpopular Republican president in the White House and most voters blaming congressional leaders for moving the country in the "wrong direction," Democrats regained control of both chambers. And, in 2010, with a Democrat in the White House and three years into a deep economic recession that had more people than ever feeling that the country was heading in the "wrong direction," Republicans reclaimed the House, nearly retook the Senate, and also made historic gains in races for governorships and state legislatures.

In the past, the Democratic party was more deeply divided than the Republicans because of the presence in Congress of conservative Democrats from the South. These southern Democrats often would vote with the Republicans in the House or Senate, thereby forming what came to be called the **conservative coalition.** During the 1960s and 1970s, that coalition came together in about one-fifth of all roll-call votes. When it did, it usually won, defeating northern Democrats. But since the 1980s, and especially since the watershed election of 1994, the conservative coalition has become much less important. The reason is simple: many southern Democrats in Congress have been replaced by southern Republicans, and the southern Democrats who remain (many of them African Americans) are as liberal as northern Democrats. The effect of this change is to make Congress, and especially the House, more ideologically partisan—Democrats are liberals, Republicans are conservatives—and this in turn helps explain why there is more party unity in voting—no matter which party is in charge.

conservative coalition An alliance between Republican and conservative Democrats.

Representation and Polarization

In a decentralized, individualistic institution such as Congress, it is not obvious how its members will behave. They could be devoted to doing whatever their constituents want or, since most voters are not aware of what their representatives do, act in accordance with their own beliefs, the demands of pressure groups, or the expectations of congressional leaders. You may think it would be easy to figure out whether members are devoted to their constituents by analyzing how they vote, but that is not quite right. Members can influence legislation in many ways other than by voting: they can conduct hearings, help mark up bills in committee meetings, and offer amendments to the bills proposed by others. A member's final vote on a bill may conceal as much as it reveals: some members may vote for a bill that contains many things they dislike because it also contains a few things they value.

There are at least three theories about how members of Congress behave: representational, organizational, and attitudinal. The *representational* explanation is based on the reasonable assumption that members want to get reelected, and therefore they vote to please their constituents. The *organizational* explanation is based on the equally reasonable assumption that since most constituents do not know how their legislator has voted, it is not essential to please them. But it is important to please fellow members of Congress, whose goodwill is valuable in getting things done and in acquiring status and power in Congress. The *attitudinal* explanation is based on the assumption that there are so many conflicting pressures on members of Congress that they cancel one another out, leaving them virtually free to vote on the basis of their own beliefs. Political scientists have studied, tested, and argued about these (and other) explanations for decades, and nothing like a consensus has emerged. Some facts have been established, however, in regard to these three views.

REPRESENTATIONAL VIEW

The representational view has some merit under certain circumstances—namely, when constituents have a clear view on some issue and a legislator's vote on that issue is likely to attract their attention. Such is often the case for civil rights laws: representatives with significant numbers of black voters in their districts are not likely to oppose civil rights bills; representatives with few African Americans in their districts are comparatively free to oppose such bills. Until the late 1960s, many southern representatives were able to oppose civil rights measures because the African Americans in their districts were prevented from voting. On the other hand, many representatives without black constituents have supported civil rights bills, partly out of personal belief and partly perhaps because certain white groups in their districts—organized liberals, for example—have insisted on such support.

From time to time, an issue arouses deep passions among the voters, and legislators cannot escape the need either to vote as their constituents want, whatever their personal views, or to anguish at length about which side of a divided constituency to support. Gun control has been one such question and the use of federal money to pay for abortions has been another. Some fortunate members of Congress get unambiguous cues from their constituents on these matters, and no hard decision is necessary. Others get conflicting views, and they know that whichever way they vote, it may cost them dearly in the next election.

Keith Ellison (D-Minn.), the first Muslim elected to Congress.

Occasionally, members of Congress in this fix will try to be out of town when the matter comes up for a vote.

You might think that members of Congress who won a close race in the last election—who come from a "marginal" district—would be especially eager to vote the way their constituents want. Research so far has shown that is not generally the case. There seem to be about as many independent-minded members of Congress from marginal as from safe districts. Perhaps it is because opinion is so divided in a marginal seat that one cannot please everybody; as a result, the representative votes on other grounds.

In general, the problem with the representational explanation is that public opinion is not strong and clear on most measures on which Congress must vote. Many representatives and senators face constituencies that are divided on key issues. Some constituents go to special pains to make their views known (these interest groups were discussed in Chapter 11). But as we indicated, the power of interest groups to affect congressional votes depends, among other things, on whether a legislator sees them as united and powerful or as disorganized and marginal.

This does not mean that constituents rarely have a direct influence on voting. The influence they have probably comes from the fact that legislators risk defeat should they steadfastly vote in ways that can be held against them by a rival in the next election. Though most congressional votes are not known to most citizens, blunders (real or alleged) quickly become known when an electoral opponent exploits them.

Still, any member of Congress can choose the positions he or she takes on most roll-call votes (and on all voice or standing votes, where names are not recorded). And even a series of recorded votes against constituency opinion need not be fatal: a member of Congress can win votes in other ways—for example, by doing services for constituents or by appealing to the party loyalty of the voters.

ORGANIZATIONAL VIEW

When voting on matters where constituency interests or opinions are not vitally at stake, members of Congress respond primarily to cues provided by their colleagues. This is the organizational explanation of their votes. The principal cue is party; as already noted, what party a member of Congress belongs to explains more about his or her voting record than any other single factor. Additional organizational cues come from the opinions of colleagues with whom the member of Congress feels a close ideological affinity: for liberals in the House, it is the Democratic Study Group; for conservatives, it often has been the Republican Study Committee or the Wednesday Club. But party and other organizations do not have clear positions on all matters. For the scores of votes that do not involve the "big questions," a representative or senator is especially likely to be influenced by the members of his or her party on the sponsoring committee.

It is easy to understand why. Suppose you are a Democratic representative from Michigan who is summoned to the floor of the House to vote on a bill to authorize a new weapons system. You haven't the faintest idea what issues might be at stake. There is no obvious liberal or conservative position on this matter. How do you vote? Simple. You take your cue from several Democrats on the House Armed Services Committee that handled the bill. Some are liberal; others are conservative. If both liberals and conservatives support the bill, you vote for it unhesitatingly. If they disagree, you vote with whichever Democrat is generally closest to your own political ideology. If the matter is one that affects your state, you can take your cue from members of your state's delegation to Congress.

ATTITUDINAL VIEW

There is evidence that the ideology of a member of Congress affects how he or she votes. This should not be entirely surprising. As we saw in Chapter 7, political elites generally think more ideologically than the public. But, as we suggested at the start of this chapter, Congress has become an increasingly ideological organization, that is, its members are more sharply divided by political ideology than they once were. Today, all of Congress's most liberal members are Democrats, and all of its most conservative ones are Republicans.

Why attitudes have hardened along ideological and partisan lines in Congress is a topic of much scholarly debate. The representational view would suggest that members are simply behaving the way their constituents wish them to behave. The organizational view would suggest that members are responding to cues from their colleagues and party leaders. Of course, the representational and organizational influences on members' attitudes could be mutually reinforcing, and one important recent study explains the "disappearing center" in Congress based on certain evidence suggesting that they are.[18]

According to this theory, growing ideological and partisan splits among voters themselves have resulted in ever more partisan polarization among congressional leaders and senior members from safe districts where the only serious threats to an incumbent's reelection prospects are primary election challenges from the right (if a Republican) or the left (if a Democrat).[19] Only about 20 percent of Americans who harbor moderate views and favor bipartisanship are politically attentive, while the rest are largely "disengaged moderates."[20] By contrast, a majority of the growing number of citizens who identify themselves as "strongly liberal" or "strongly conservative" are engaged in obtaining political news (often from sources like talk radio or preferred Internet blogs that mainly serve to reinforce their preexisting views), debating controversial issues, and influencing others (either in person or via the Internet and other means of communication) to think, join groups, *and* vote as they do.[21]

Most scholars agree that in recent decades, the parties in Congress have "sorted" themselves ever more clearly on ideological hot-button issues like abortion, and increasingly favored candidates and leaders, including relative political novices, with ideologically consistent profiles.[22] But many dispute the notion that the American electorate on the whole has become so highly partisan and ideological. Studies like the one summarized above claiming that it has, say their critics, generally rely too much on voters' ideological self-identifications and focus too narrowly on only the most ideologically loaded issues.[23] Measured across dozens of domestic, economic, and other issues, the policy differences and ideological distances between registered Republicans and registered Democrats have increased only a bit since the mid-1980s; and, depending on how the survey questions are worded, there is substantial overlap among voters even on a topic like abortion.[24] In short, this theory holds that we are witnessing, not a "disappearing center," but rather a breakdown of representation in American politics, an attitudinal "disconnect" between average voters and national lawmakers that has made the post-1970 Congress far less representative of the American people than the pre-1970 Congress was.[25]

By the same token, how much congresspersons' attitudes are influenced by committee chairpersons and other party leaders is also a matter of some scholarly dispute. The most sophisticated studies to date indicate that, while these organizational influences matter, individual members' ideological views probably matter more. "Members of Congress," one study concluded, "come to Washington with a staked-out position on the (liberal-conservative) continuum, and then, largely 'die with their ideological boots on.' "[26] Everything from which "ideological boots" a given member chooses to wear in the first place to how he or she votes on a particular issue "may result as much from external pressures of campaign donors and primary voters as from the internal pressures of the congressional party."[27]

The Organization of Congress: Parties and Interests

Congress is not a single organization; it is a vast and complex collection of organizations by which the business of Congress is carried on and through which members of Congress form alliances. Unlike the British Parliament, in which the political parties are the only important kind of organization, parties are only one of many important units in Congress. In fact, other organizations have grown in number as party influence has declined.

PARTY ORGANIZATIONS

The Democrats and Republicans in the House and the Senate are organized by party leaders, who in turn are elected by the full party membership within the House and Senate.

THE SENATE

The majority party chooses one of its members—usually the person with the greatest seniority—to be president pro tempore of the Senate. This is usually an honorific position, required by the Constitution so that the Senate will have a presiding officer when the vice president of the United States (according to the Constitution, the president of the Senate) is absent. In fact, both the president pro tem and the vice president usually assign the tedious chore of presiding to a junior senator.

majority leader The legislative leader elected by party members holding the majority of seats in the House or the Senate.

minority leader The legislative leader elected by party members holding a minority of seats in the House or the Senate.

The real leadership is in the hands of the majority and minority leaders. The principal task of the **majority leader** is to schedule the business of the Senate, usually in consultation with the **minority leader.** A majority leader who has a strong personality and is skilled at political bargaining (such as Lyndon Johnson, the Democrats' leader in the 1950s) may also acquire much influence over the substance of Senate business.

A **whip**, chosen by each party, helps party leaders stay informed about what the party members are thinking, rounds up members when important votes are taken, and attempts to keep a nose count of how voting on a controversial issue is likely to go. Several senators assist each party whip.

whip A senator or representative who helps the party leader stay informed about what party members are thinking.

Each party also chooses a Policy Committee composed of a dozen or so senators who help the party leader schedule Senate business, choosing what bills will be given major attention and in what order.

For individual senators, however, the key party organization is the group that assigns senators to the Senate's standing committees: for the Democrats, a 22-member Steering Committee; for the Republicans, an 18-member Committee on Committees. For newly elected senators, their political careers, opportunities for favorable publicity, and chances for helping their states and constituents depend in great part on the committees to which they are assigned.

Achieving ideological and regional balance is a crucial—and delicate—aspect of selecting party leaders, making up important committees, and assigning freshmen senators to committees. Liberals and conservatives in each party fight over the choice of majority and minority leaders.

THE HOUSE OF REPRESENTATIVES

The party structure is essentially the same in the House as in the Senate, though the titles of various posts are different. But leadership carries more power in the House than in the Senate because of the House rules. Being so large (435 members), the House must restrict debate and schedule its business with great care; thus leaders who manage scheduling and determine how the rules shall be applied usually have substantial influence.

The **Speaker**, who presides over the House, is the most important person in that body and is elected by whichever party has a majority. Unlike the president pro tem of the Senate, this position is anything but honorific, for the Speaker is also the principal leader of the majority party. Though Speakers as presiders are expected to be fair, Speakers as party leaders are expected to use their powers to help pass legislation favored by their party.

Speaker The presiding officer of the House of Representatives and the leader of his party in the House.

How Things Work

Key Facts About Congress

Qualifications

Representative

- Must be 25 years of age (when seated, not when elected).
- Must have been a citizen of the United States for seven years.
- Must be an inhabitant of the state from which elected. (*Note:* Custom, but *not* the Constitution, requires that a representative live in the district he or she represents.)

Senator

- Must be 30 years of age (when seated, not when elected).
- Must have been a citizen of the United States for nine years.
- Must be an inhabitant of the state from which elected.

Judging Qualifications

Each house is the judge of the "elections, returns, and qualifications" of its members. Thus, Congress alone decides disputed congressional elections. On occasion it has excluded a person from taking a seat on the grounds that the election was improper.

Privileges

Members of Congress have certain privileges, the most important of which, conferred by the Constitution, is that "for any speech or debate in either house they shall not be questioned in any other place." This doctrine of "privileged speech" has been interpreted by the Supreme Court to mean that members of Congress cannot be sued or prosecuted for anything they say or write in connection with their legislative duties.

When Senator Mike Gravel read the Pentagon Papers—some then-secret government documents about the Vietnam War—into the *Congressional Record* in defiance of a court order restraining their publication, the Court held this was "privileged speech" and beyond challenge (*Gravel* v. *United States,* 408 U.S. 606, 1972). But when Senator William Proxmire issued a press release critical of a scientist doing research on monkeys, the Court decided the scientist could sue him for libel because a press release was not part of the legislative process (*Hutchinson* v. *Proxmire,* 443 U.S. 111, 1979).

The Size of Congress

Congress decides the size of the House of Representatives. The House began with 65 members in 1790 and has had 435 members since 1912. Each state must have at least one representative. Regardless of its population, each state has two senators. Equal suffrage for states in the Senate is enshrined in Article I of the Constitution, the only provision that cannot be amended (see Article V).

In helping his or her party, the Speaker has some important formal powers. He or she decides who shall be recognized to speak on the floor of the House, rules whether a motion is relevant and germane to the business at hand, and decides (subject to certain rules) the committees to which new bills shall be assigned. He or she influences what bills are brought up for a vote and appoints the members of special and select committees. Since 1975, the Speaker has been able to select the majority-party members of the Rules Committee, which plays an important role in the consideration of bills.

The Speaker also has some informal powers. He or she controls some patronage jobs in the Capitol building and the assignment of extra office space. Though now far less powerful than some of his or her predecessors, the Speaker is still an important person to have on one's side.

In the House, as in the Senate, the majority party elects a floor leader, called the majority leader. The other party chooses the minority leader. Traditionally, the majority leader becomes Speaker when the person in that position dies or retires—provided, of course, that his or her party is still in the majority. Each party also has a whip, with several assistant whips in charge of rounding up votes. For the Democrats, committee assignments are made and the scheduling of legislation is discussed in a Steering and Policy Committee chaired by the Speaker. The Republicans have divided responsibility for committee assignments and policy discussion between two committees. Each party also has a congressional campaign committee to provide funds and other assistance to party members running for election or reelection to the House.

PARTY VOTING

The effect of this elaborate party machinery can be crudely measured by the extent to which party members vote together in the House and the Senate. A **party vote** can be defined in various ways; naturally, the more stringent the definition, the less party voting we will observe.

Figure 13.2 shows two measures of party voting in the House of Representatives during the last century. By the strictest measure, a party vote occurs when 90 percent or more of the Democrats vote together against 90 percent or more of the Republicans. A looser measure counts as a party vote one in which at least 50 percent of the Democrats vote together against 50 percent of the Republicans. By the 90 percent measure, the extent of party voting is low and has declined since the turn of the century. By the 50 percent measure, it is as high today as it was in 1920 and has risen sharply since 1970.

Given that political parties as organizations do not tightly control a legislator's ability to

party vote There are two measures of such voting. By the stricter measure, a party vote occurs when 90 percent or more of the Democrats in either house of Congress vote together against 90 percent or more of the Republicans. A looser measure counts as a party vote any case where at least 50 percent of the Democrats vote together against at least 50 percent of the Republicans.

Figure 13.2

Party Votes in the House, 1877–2010

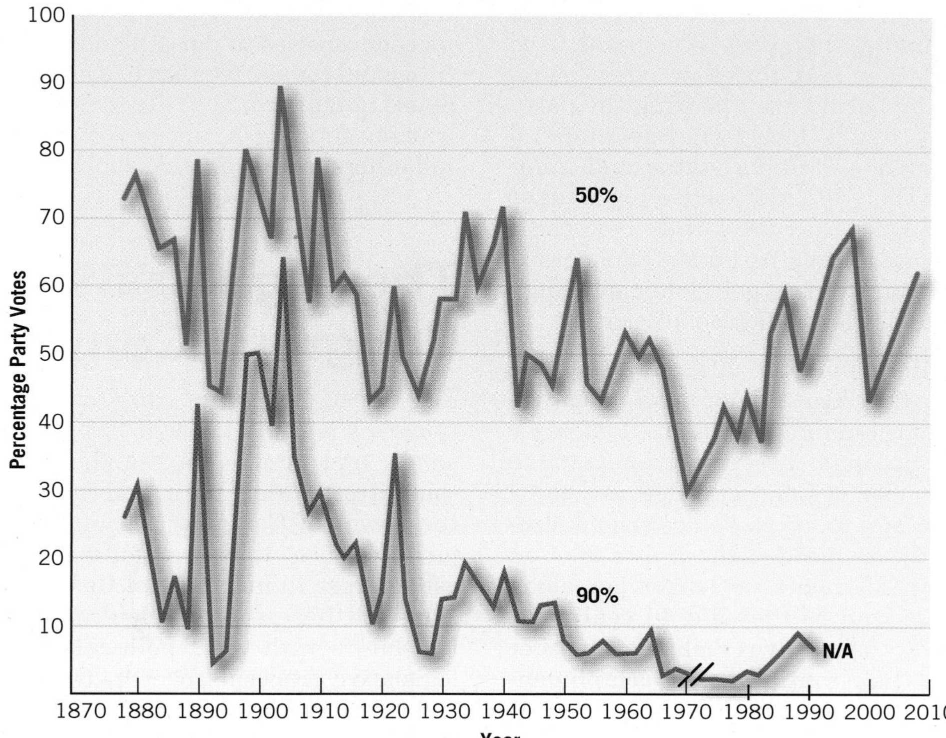

Note: A party vote occurs when the specified percentage (or more) of one party votes against the specified percentage (or more) of the other party.

Sources: Updated through 2008 by Zach Courser; NES data as reported in *2001–2002;* Harold W. Stanley and Richard G. Niemi, *Vital Statistics on American Politics* (CQ Press, 2001), 211. Reprinted by permission of Congressional Quarterly, Inc.

caucus An association of congressional members created to advance a political ideology or a regional, ethnic, or economic interest.

get elected, what is surprising is not that strict party votes are relatively rare, but that they occur at all. There are several reasons that congressional members of one party sometimes do vote together against a majority of the other party. First, members of Congress do not randomly decide to be Democrats or Republicans; at least for most members, these choices reflect some broad policy agreements. By tabulating the ratings that several interest groups give members of Congress for voting on important issues, it is possible to rank each member of Congress from most to least liberal in three policy areas: economic affairs, social questions, and foreign and military affairs. Democrats in the House and Senate are much more liberal than Republicans, and this has been true for many years. The ideological differences between the parties are so pronounced that even the average southern Democrat in the House is more liberal than the average northern Republican.

In addition to their personal views, members of Congress have other reasons for supporting their party's position at least some of the time. On many matters that come up for vote, members of Congress often have little information and no opinions. It is only natural that they look to fellow party members for advice. Furthermore, supporting the party position can work to the long-term advantage of a member interested in gaining status and influence in Congress. Though party leaders are weaker today than in the past, they are hardly powerless. Sam Rayburn reputedly told freshman members of Congress that "if you want to get along, go along." That is less true today, but still good advice.

In short, party *does* make a difference—not as much as it did 90 years ago and not nearly as much as it does in a parliamentary system—but party affiliation is still the single most important thing to know about a member of Congress. Because party affiliation in the House today embodies strong ideological preferences, the mood of the House is often testy and strident. Members no longer get along with each other as well as they did 40 years ago. Many liberals and conservatives dislike each other intensely, despite their routine use of complimentary phrases.

Although political parties may be less powerful in Congress than once was the case, ideology is more influential. In the last several Congresses, the 20 most liberal representatives were all Democrats and the 20 most conservative were all Republicans.

CAUCUSES

Congressional caucuses are a growing rival to the parties as a source of policy leadership. A **caucus** is an association of members of Congress created to advocate a political ideology or to advance a regional, ethnic, or economic interest. In 1959, only four such caucuses existed; by the early 1980s, there were more than 70. The more important among them have included the Democratic Study Group (uniting more than 200 liberal Democrats, though their names are not publicized to avoid embarrassing them with constituents), the Coalition (more popularly known as the Blue Dog Democrats), a group of moderate-to-conservative Democrats, and the Tuesday Lunch Bunch. Other caucuses include the delegations from certain large states who meet on matters of common interest, as well as the countless groups dedicated to racial, ethnic, regional, and policy interests. The Congressional Black Caucus in the House is one of the best known of these and is probably typical of many in its operations. It meets regularly and employs a staff. As with most other caucuses, some members are very active, others only marginally so. On some issues it simply registers an opinion; on others it attempts to negotiate with leaders of other blocs so that votes can be traded in a mutually advantageous way. It keeps its members informed and on occasion presses to put a member on a regular congressional committee that has no blacks. In 1995, the House Republican majority decided to eliminate government funding of caucuses, forcing some to shrivel and others to seek outside support.

The Organization of Congress: Committees

The most important organizational feature of Congress is the set of legislative committees of the House and Senate. In the chairmanship of these committees, and their subcommittees, most of the power of Congress is found. The number and jurisdiction of these committees are of the greatest interest to members of Congress because decisions on these subjects determine what groups of legislators with what political views will pass on legislative proposals, oversee the workings of agencies in the executive branch, and conduct investigations. A typical Congress has, in each house, about two dozen committees and well over one hundred subcommittees.

Periodically, efforts have been made to cut the number of committees to give each a broader jurisdiction and to reduce conflict between committees over a single bill. But as the number of committees declined, the number of subcommittees rose, leaving matters much as they had been.

There are three kinds of committees: **standing committees** (more or less permanent bodies with specific legislative responsibilities), **select committees** (groups appointed for a limited purpose, which do not introduce legislation and which exist for only a few years), and **joint committees** (on which both representatives and senators serve). An especially important kind of joint committee is the **conference committee**, made up of representatives and senators appointed to resolve differences in the Senate and House versions of a bill before final passage. Though members of the majority party could in theory occupy all the seats on all the committees, in practice they take the majority of the seats, name the chairperson, and allow the minority party to have the remainder of the seats. The number of seats varies from about six to more than fifty.

Usually the ratio of Democrats to Republicans on a committee roughly corresponds to their ratio in the House or Senate. Standing committees are more important because, with a few exceptions, they are the only committees that can propose legislation by reporting a bill out to the full House or Senate. Each member of the House usually serves on two standing committees (but members of the Appropriations, Rules, or Ways and Means committees are limited to one committee). Each senator may serve on two major committees and one minor committee (see the boxes on this page and page 349), but this rule is not strictly enforced.

In the past, when party leaders were stronger, committee chairs were picked on the basis of loyalty to the leader. When this leadership weakened, seniority on the committee came to govern the selection of chairpersons. Of late, however, seniority has been under attack. In 1971,

standing committees Permanently established legislative committees that consider and are responsible for legislation within a certain subject area.

select committees Congressional committees appointed for a limited time and purpose.

joint committees Committees on which both senators and representatives serve.

conference committees Joint committees appointed to resolve differences in the Senate and House versions of the same bill.

How Things Work

Standing Committees of the Senate

Major Committees

*No senator is supposed to serve on more than two.**

Agriculture, Nutrition, and Forestry

Appropriations

Armed Services

Banking, Housing, and Urban Affairs

Budget Commerce, Science, and Transportation Energy and Natural Resources

Environment and Public Works

Finance

Foreign Relations

Health, Education, Labor, and Pensions

Homeland Security and Governmental Affairs

Judiciary

Minor Committees

No senator is supposed to serve on more than one.

Rules and Administration

Small Business and Entrepreneurship

Veterans' Affairs

Select Committees

Aging

Ethics

Indian Affairs

Intelligence

*Despite the rules, some senators serve on more than two major committees.

House Democrats decided in their caucus to elect committee chairs by secret ballot; four years later, they used that procedure to remove three committee chairs who held their positions by seniority. Between 1971 and 1992, the Democrats replaced a total of seven senior Democrats with more junior ones as committee chairs. When Republicans took control of the House in 1995, Speaker Newt Gingrich ignored seniority in selecting several committee chairs, picking instead members who he felt would do a better job. In this and other ways, Gingrich enhanced the Speaker's power to a degree not seen since 1910.

Throughout most of the 20th century, committee chairs dominated the work of Congress. In the early 1970s, their power came under attack, mostly from liberal Democrats upset at the opposition by conservative southern Democratic chairs to civil rights legislation. The liberals succeeded in getting the House to adopt rules that weakened the chairs and empowered individual members. Among the changes were these:

- Committee chairs must be elected by the majority party, voting by secret ballot.
- The ability of committee chairs to block legislation by refusing to refer it to a subcommittee for a hearing is banned.
- All committees and subcommittees must hold public meetings unless the committee has voted to close them.
- Subcommittee chairs must be elected by committee members.
- Subcommittee chairs can hire their own staffs, independent of the committee chair.

The effect of these and other changes was to give individual members more power and committee chairs less. When the Republicans took control of the House in 1995, they made more changes, including the following:

- They reduced the number of committees and subcommittees.
- They authorized committee chairs to hire subcommittee staffs.
- They imposed term limits on committee and subcommittee chairs of three consecutive terms (or six years) and on the Speaker of four consecutive terms (or eight years).
- They prohibited chairs from casting an absent committee member's vote by proxy.

The House Republican rules gave back some power to chairpersons (for example, by letting them pick all staff members) but further reduced it in other ways (for example, by imposing term limits and banning proxy voting). The commitment to public meetings remained.

In the Senate there have been fewer changes, in part because individual members of the Senate have always had more power than their counterparts in the House. There were, however, three important changes made by the Republicans in 1995:

- A six-year term limit was set on all committee chairs (but not on the term of majority leader).
- Committee members were required to select their chairs by secret ballot
- Beginning in 1997, the chairs of Senate committees were limited to one six-year term.

Despite these new rules, the committees remain the place where the real work of Congress is done. These committees tend to attract different kinds of members. Some, such as the committees that draft tax legislation (the Senate Finance Committee and the House Ways and Means Committee) or that oversee foreign affairs (the Senate and House Foreign Relations Committees), have been attractive to members who want to shape public policy, become expert on important issues, and have influence with their colleagues. Others, such as the House and Senate committees dealing with public lands, small business, and veterans' affairs, are attractive to members who want to serve particular constituency groups.[28]

The Organization of Congress: Staffs and Specialized Offices

In 1900, representatives had no personal staff, and senators averaged fewer than one staff member each. By 1979, the average representative had 16 assistants and the average senator had 36. Since then the numbers have remained about the same. To the more than 10,000 people on the personal staffs of members of Congress must be added another 3,000 who work for congressional committees and yet another 3,000 employed by various congressional research agencies. Congress has produced the most rapidly growing bureaucracy in Washington: The personal staffs of legislators have increased more than fivefold since 1947.[29] Though many staffers perform routine chores, many others help draft legislation, handle constituents, and otherwise shape policy and politics.

How Things Work

Standing Committees of the House

Exclusive Committees

Member may not serve on any other committee, except Budget.

Appropriations

Rules

Ways and Means

Major Committees

Member may serve on only one major committee.

Agriculture

Armed Services

Education and Labor

Energy and Commerce

Financial Services

Foreign Affairs

Homeland Security

Judiciary

Transportation and Infrastructure

Nonmajor Committees

Member may serve on one major and one nonmajor or two nonmajor committees.

Budget

House Administration

Natural Resources

Oversight and Government Reform

Science and Technology

Small Business

Standards of Official Conduct

Veterans' Affairs

Select Committees

Energy Independence and Global Warming

Intelligence

Note: In 1995, the House Republican majority abolished three committees—District of Columbia, Post Office and Civil Service, and Merchant Marine and Fisheries—and gave their duties to other standing committees.

AP Photo/Haraz N. Ghanbari

Rep. Steve Scalise, R-La., holds a photo of an oil-covered pelican as he questions BP CEO Tony Hayward on Capitol Hill in Washington, June 17, 2010, during the House Oversight and Investigations subcommittee hearing on the role of BP in the Deepwater Horizon explosion and oil spill.

TASKS OF STAFF MEMBERS

A major function of a legislator's staff is to help constituents solve problems and thereby help that member of Congress get reelected. Indeed, over the last two decades, a growing portion of congressional staffs have worked in the local (district or state) offices of the legislator rather than in Washington. Almost all members of Congress have at least one such home office, and most have two or more. Some scholars believe that this growth in constituency-serving staff helps explain why it is so difficult to defeat an incumbent.[30]

The legislative function of congressional staff members is also important. With each senator serving on an average of more than two committees and seven subcommittees, it is virtually impossible for members of Congress to become familiar with the details of all the proposals that come before them or to write all the bills that they feel ought to be introduced.[31] The role of staff members has expanded in proportion to the tremendous growth in Congress's workload.

The orientation of committee staff members differs. Some think of themselves as—and to a substantial degree they are—politically neutral professionals whose job it is to assist members of a committee, whether Democrats or Republicans, in holding hearings or revising bills. Others see themselves as partisan advocates, interested in promoting Democratic or Republican causes, depending on who hired them.

Those who work for individual members of Congress, as opposed to committees, see themselves entirely as advocates for their bosses. They often assume an entrepreneurial function, taking the initiative in finding and selling a policy to their boss—a representative or senator—who can take credit for it. Lobbyists and reporters understand this completely and therefore spend a lot of time cultivating congressional staffers.

The increased reliance on staff has changed Congress, mainly because the staff has altered the environment within which Congress does its work. In addition to their role as entrepreneurs promoting new policies, staffers act as negotiators: Members of Congress today are more likely to deal with one another through staff intermediaries than through personal contact. Congress has thereby become less collegial, more individualistic, and less of a deliberative body.[32]

STAFF AGENCIES

In addition to increasing the number of staff members, Congress also has created a set of staff agencies that work for Congress as a whole. These have come into being in large part to give Congress specialized knowledge equivalent to what the president has by virtue of his or her position as chief of the executive branch. One of these, the *Congressional Research Service (CRS),* is part of the Library of Congress and employs almost 900 people; it is politically neutral, responding to requests by members of Congress for information and giving both sides of arguments. The *General Accountability Office (GAO),* once merely an auditing agency, now has about 5,000 employees and investigates policies and makes recommendations on almost every aspect of government; its head, though appointed by the president for a 15-year term, is very much the servant of Congress rather than the president. The *Congressional Budget Office (CBO),* created in 1974, advises Congress on the likely impact of different spending programs and attempts to estimate future economic trends.

simple resolution An expression of opinion either in the House or Senate to settle procedural matters in either body.

concurrent resolution An expression of opinion without the force of law that requires the approval of both the House and the Senate, but not the president.

How a Bill Becomes Law

Some bills zip through Congress; others make their way painfully and slowly, sometimes emerging in a form very different from their original one. Congress is like a crowd, moving either sluggishly or, when excited, with great speed. While reading the following account of how a bill becomes law (see Figure 13.3), keep in mind that the complexity of congressional procedures ordinarily gives powerful advantages to the opponents of any new policy. There are many points at which action can be blocked. This does not mean that nothing gets done, but that to get something done, a member of Congress must *either* slowly and painstakingly assemble a majority coalition or take advantage of enthusiasm for some new cause that sweeps away the normal obstacles to change.

INTRODUCING A BILL

Any member of Congress may introduce a bill—in the House by handing it to a clerk or dropping it in a box; in the Senate by being recognized by the presiding officer and announcing the bill's introduction. Bills are then numbered and printed. If a bill is not passed within one session of Congress, it is dead and must be reintroduced during the next Congress.

We often hear that legislation is initiated by the president and enacted by Congress. The reality is more complicated. Congress often initiates legislation (for example, most consumer and environmental laws passed since 1966 originated in Congress), and even laws formally proposed by the president have often been incubated in Congress. Even when he is the principal author of a bill, a president usually submits it (if he is prudent) only after careful consultation with key congressional leaders. In any case, he cannot himself introduce legislation; he must get a member of Congress to do it for him.

In addition to bills, Congress can also pass resolutions. Either house can use **simple resolutions** for such matters as establishing operating rules. **Concurrent resolutions** settle housekeeping and

Figure 13.3
How a Bill Becomes Law

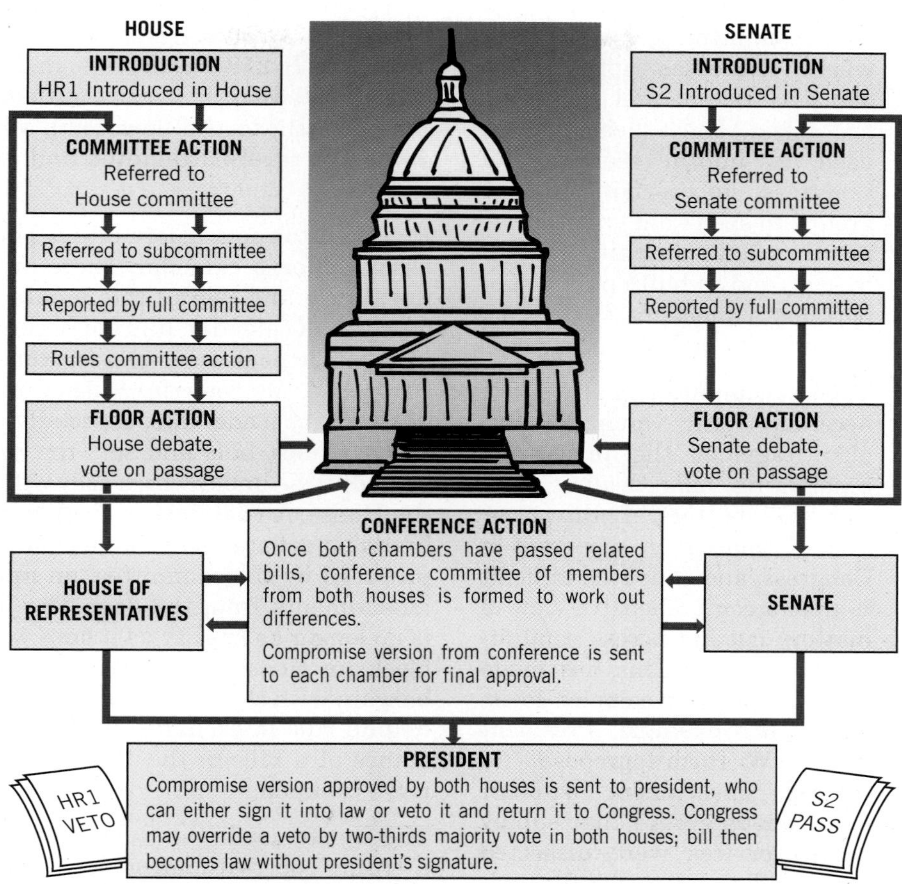

joint resolution A formal expression of congressional opinion that must be approved by both houses of Congress and by the president; constitutional amendments need not be signed by the president.

procedural matters that affect both houses. Simple and concurrent resolutions are not signed by the president and do not have the force of law. A **joint resolution** requires approval by both houses and a presidential signature; it is essentially the same as a law. A joint resolution is also used to propose a constitutional amendment, in which case it must be approved by a two-thirds vote in each house, but does not require the signature of the president.

STUDY BY COMMITTEES

A bill is referred to a committee for consideration by either the Speaker of the House or the Senate's presiding officer. If a chairperson or committee is known to be hostile to a bill, assignment can be a crucial matter. Rules govern which committee will get which bill, but sometimes a choice is possible. In the House, the Speaker's right to make such a choice (subject to appeal to the full House) is an important source of his or her power.

The Constitution requires that "all bills for raising revenue shall originate in the House of Representatives." The Senate can and does amend such bills, but only after the House has acted first. Bills that are not for raising revenue—that is, that do not alter tax laws—can originate in either chamber. In practice, the House also originates *appropriations bills* (bills that direct the spending of money). Because of the House's special position on revenue legislation, the committee that handles tax bills—the Ways and Means Committee—is particularly powerful.

Most bills die in committee. They are often introduced only to get publicity for various members of Congress or to enable them to say to a constituent or pressure group that they "did something" on some matter. Bills of general interest—many of them

discharge petition A device by which any member of the House, after a committee has had the bill for 30 days, may petition to have it brought to the floor.

restrictive rule An order from the House Rules Committee that permits certain kinds of amendments but not others to be made into a bill on the floor.

closed rule An order from the House Rules Committee that sets a time limit on debate; forbids a bill from being amended on the floor.

open rule An order from the House Rules Committee that permits a bill to be amended on the floor.

quorum The minimum number of members who must be present for business to be conducted in Congress.

drafted in the executive branch though introduced by members of Congress—are assigned to a subcommittee for a hearing where witnesses appear, evidence is taken, and questions are asked. These hearings are used to inform members of Congress, to permit interest groups to speak out (whether or not they have anything helpful to say), and to build public support for a measure favored by the majority on the committee.

Though committee hearings are necessary and valuable, they also fragment the process of considering bills dealing with complex matters. Both power and information are dispersed in Congress, and thus it is difficult to take a comprehensive view of matters cutting across committee boundaries. This has made it harder to pass complex legislation. For example, President George W. Bush's proposals to expand government support for religious groups that supply social services were dissected into small sections for the consideration of the various committees that had jurisdiction; after three years, no laws emerged. But strong White House leadership and supportive public opinion can push through controversial measures without great delay, as in the cases of Bush's tax cuts in 2001 and homeland security plans in 2002.

After the hearings, the committee or subcommittee makes revisions and additions (sometimes extensive) to the bill, but these changes do not become part of the bill unless they are approved by the entire house. If a majority of the committee votes to report a bill favorably to the House or Senate, it goes forward, accompanied by an explanation of why the committee favors it and why it wishes to see its amendments, if any, added; committee members who oppose the bill may include their dissenting opinions.

If the committee does not report the bill out to the house favorably, that ordinarily kills it, though there are complex procedures whereby the full House can get a bill that is stalled in committee out and onto the floor. The process involves getting a majority of all House members to sign a **discharge petition.** If 218 members sign, then the petition can be voted on; if it passes, then the stalled bill goes directly to the floor for a vote. These procedures are rarely attempted and even more rarely succeed.

For a bill to come before either house, it must first be placed on a calendar. There are five of these in the House and two in the Senate. Though the bill goes onto a calendar, it is not necessarily considered in chronological order or even considered at all. In the House, the powerful Rules Committee—an arm of the party leadership, especially of the Speaker—reviews most bills and sets the *rule*— that is, the procedures—under which they will be considered by the House. A **restrictive** or **closed rule** sets strict limits on debate and confines amendments to those proposed by the committee; an **open rule** permits amendments from the floor. The Rules Committee is no longer as mighty as it once was, but it can still block any House consideration of a measure and can bargain with the legislative committee by offering a helpful rule in exchange for alterations in the substance of a bill. In the 1980s, closed rules became more common.

The House needs the Rules Committee to serve as a traffic cop; without some limitations on debate and amendment, nothing would ever get done. The House can bypass the Rules Committee in a number of ways, but it rarely does so unless the committee departs too far from the sentiments of the House.

No such barriers to floor consideration exist in the Senate, where bills may be considered in any order at any time whenever a majority of the Senate chooses. In practice, bills are scheduled by the majority leader in consultation with the minority leader.

FLOOR DEBATE

Once on the floor, the bills are debated. In the House all revenue and most other bills are discussed by the *Committee of the Whole*—that is, whoever happens to be on the floor at the time, so long as at least 100 members are present. The Committee of the Whole can debate, amend, and generally decide the final shape of a bill but technically cannot pass it—that must be done by the House itself, for which the **quorum** is half the membership (218 representatives). The sponsoring committee

How Things Work

House and Senate Differences: A Summary

House	Senate
435 members serving two-year terms	100 members serving six-year terms
House members have only one major committee assignment, and thus tend to be policy specialists	Senators have two or more major committee assignments, and thus tend to be policy generalists
Speaker referral of bills to committee is hard to challenge	Referral decisions easy to challenge
Committees almost always consider legislation first	Committee consideration easily bypassed
Scheduling and rules controlled by majority party	Scheduling and rules generally agreed to by majority and minority leaders
Rules Committee powerful; controls time of debate, admissibility of amendments	Rules Committee weak; few limits on debate or amendments
Debate usually limited to one hour	Unlimited debate unless shortened by unanimous consent or by invoking cloture
Nongermane amendments may not be introduced from floor	Nongermane amendments may be introduced

riders Amendments on matters unrelated to a bill that are added to an important bill so that they will "ride" to passage through the Congress. When a bill has many riders, it is called a Christmas-tree bill.

cloture rule A rule used by the Senate to end or limit debate.

double tracking A procedure to keep the Senate going during a filibuster in which the disputed bill is shelved temporarily so that the Senate can get on with other business.

guides the discussion, and normally its version of the bill is the version that the full House passes.

Procedures are a good deal more casual in the Senate. Measures that have already passed the House can be placed on the Senate calendar without a committee hearing. There is no Committee of the Whole and no rule (as in the House) limiting debate, so that filibusters (lengthy speeches given to prevent votes from being taken) and irrelevant amendments, called **riders,** are possible. Filibusters can be broken if three-fifths of all senators agree to a **cloture resolution.** This is a difficult and rarely used procedure. (Both conservatives and liberals have found the filibuster useful, and therefore its abolition is unlikely.)

The sharp increase in Senate filibusters has been made easier by a new process called **double tracking.** When a senator filibusters against a bill, it is temporarily put aside so the Senate can move on to other business. Because of double tracking, senators no longer have to speak around the clock to block a bill. Once they talk long enough, the bill is shelved. So common has this become that, for all practical purposes, any controversial bill can pass the Senate only if it gets enough votes (60) to end a filibuster.

The Senate has made an effort to end filibusters aimed at blocking the nomination of federal judges. In 2005, seven Democrats and seven Republicans agreed not to filibuster a nomination except in "exceptional circumstances." A few nominees whose appointment had been blocked managed to get confirmed by this arrangement. Whether it holds for the future depends on how senators define "exceptional circumstances."

One rule was once common to both houses: Courtesy, often of the most exquisite nature, was required. Members always referred to each other as "distinguished" even if they were mortal political enemies. Personal or ad hominem criticism was frowned upon, but of late it has become more

voice vote A congressional voting procedure in which members shout "yea" in approval or "nay" in disapproval, permitting members to vote quickly or anonymously on bills.

division vote A congressional voting procedure in which members stand and are counted.

roll-call vote A congressional voting procedure that consists of members answering "yea" or "nay" to their names.

teller vote A congressional voting procedure in which members pass between two tellers, the "yeas" first and the "nays" second.

common. In recent years, members of Congress—especially of the House—have become more personal in their criticisms of one another, and human relationships have deteriorated.

METHODS OF VOTING

There are several methods of voting in Congress, which can be applied to amendments to a bill as well as to the question of final passage. Some observers of Congress make the mistake of deciding who was for and who against a bill by the final vote. This can be misleading. Often, a member of Congress will vote for final passage of a bill after having supported amendments that, if they had passed, would have made the bill totally different. To keep track of someone's voting record, therefore, it is often more important to know how that person voted on key amendments than how he or she voted on the bill itself.

Finding that out is not always easy, though it has become simpler in recent years. The House has three procedures for voting. A **voice vote** consists of the members shouting "aye" or "no"; a **division** (or standing) **vote** involves the members standing and being counted. In neither case are the names recorded of who voted which way. This is done only with a **roll-call vote.** Since 1973, an electronic voting system has been in use that greatly speeds up roll-call votes, and the number of recorded votes has thus increased sharply. To ensure a roll-call vote, one-fifth of house members present must request it. Voting in the Senate is simpler: It votes by voice or by roll call; there are no **teller votes** or electronic counters.

If a bill passes the House and Senate in different forms, the differences must be reconciled if the bill is to become law. If they are minor, the last house to act may simply refer the bill back to the other house, which then accepts the alterations. Major differences must be ironed out in a conference committee, though only a minority of bills requires a conference. Each house must vote to form such a committee. The members are picked by the chairs of the standing committees that have been handling the legislation; the minority as well as the majority party is represented. No decision can be made unless approved by a majority of *each* delegation. Bargaining is long and hard; in the past it was also

Photo courtesy of the Office of the Clerk of the House

The electronic voting system in the House of Representatives displays each member's name on the wall of the chamber. By inserting a plastic card in a box fastened to the chairs, a member can vote "Yea," "Nay," or "Present," and the result is shown opposite his or her name.

secret, but some sessions are now public. Often—as with Carter's energy bill—the legislation is substantially rewritten in conference. Theoretically nothing already agreed to by both the House and Senate is to be changed, but in the inevitable give-and-take, even those matters already approved may be modified.

Conference reports on spending bills usually split the difference between the House and Senate versions. Overall, the Senate tends to do slightly better than the House.[33] But whoever wins, conferees report their agreement back to their respective houses, which usually consider the report immediately. The report can be accepted or rejected; it cannot be amended. In the great majority of cases, it is accepted—the alternative is to have no bill at all, at least for that Congress.

veto Literally, "I forbid": It refers to the power of a president to disapprove a bill; it may be overridden by a two-thirds vote of each house of Congress.

The bill, now in final form, goes to the president for signature or **veto**. A vetoed bill returns to the house of origin, where an effort can be made to override the veto. Two-thirds of those present (provided there is a quorum) must vote, by roll call, to override. If both houses override, the bill becomes law without the president's approval.

LEGISLATIVE PRODUCTIVITY

In recent years, political scientists have studied how productive Congress has been and whether the post-9/11 Congress has performed especially well or especially poorly. The first issue concerns how best to measure the body's major and minor "legislative productivity." It is clear that Congress passed and funded an enormous number of bills in response to the Great Depression in the 1930s and in the mid-1960s, mainly in conjunction with that era's "war on poverty." And most scholars agree that in recent decades the body's legislative output has often slowed or declined.[34]

The second issue is how best to evaluate changes in the legislation Congress produces from one time period to the next. For instance, some scholars argue that the relatively low levels of legislative output of the late 1990s, together with decreases in the body's oversight hearings and related activities, betokened an institutional decline of Congress; others, however, reject the view that Congress, by passing fewer laws and holding fewer hearings, had thereby become a "broken branch."[35]

divided government One party controls the White House and another party controls one or both houses of Congress.

How We Compare

Number of Legislators

Writing in *Federalist* paper No. 55, James Madison insists that in any legislative body the number of legislators "ought at most to be kept within a certain limit, in order to avoid the confusion and intemperance of a multitude."

America has heeded Madison's advice. With 435 members of the House and 100 members of the Senate, the Congress has a total of 535 members representing more than 300 million citizens, or roughly one national legislator for every 561,000 citizens.

In most democracies, the ratio of national legislators to citizens is far higher than it is in the United States. For example, with a population of just over 60 million, the British Parliament's two houses total more than 1,300 members, or roughly one national legislator for every 46,000 citizens; and, with a population of about 10 million, Sweden's legislature has nearly 350 members, or roughly one national legislator for every 28,600 citizens.

At the same time, however, America has more numerous and more powerful subnational legislators (more than 7,300 in all) than most other nations do, including, in Madison's home state of Virginia, 140 state lawmakers representing about 8 million citizens, or roughly one state lawmaker for every 57,000 citizens.

Also, the U.S. Constitution would permit the U.S. House to expand enough to approximate the representation ratios of nations like Britain and Sweden and states like Virginia: Article 1, section 2 states that "the Number of Representatives shall not exceed one for every thirty Thousand."

Thus, given 300 million citizens, the Constitution would allow there to be as many as 10,000 members of the U.S. House (300 million divided by 30,000). But the mere thought heralds Madison's warning, harkening back to ancient Greece's large legislatures, that even if "every Athenian citizen had been a Socrates, every Athenian assembly would have been a mob."

The third issue is whether **divided government** (one party in control of the presidency and the other in charge of one or both chambers of Congress) decreases legislative productivity. Although there are

unified government The same party controls the White House and both houses of Congress.

earmarks "Hidden" congressional provisions that direct the federal government to fund specific projects or that exempt specific persons or groups from paying specific federal taxes or fees.

pork-barrel legislation Legislation that gives tangible benefits to constituents in several districts or states in the hope of winning their votes in return.

franking privilege The ability of members to mail letters to their constituents free of charge by substituting their facsimile signature for postage.

some exceptions, most studies of the subject suggest that divided party government only reduces the passage of the most far-reaching and costly legislation.[36] As we shall discuss in Chapter 14, divided party government does not lead inevitably to "policy gridlock" any more than having **unified government** (a single party in power in the White House and in both chambers of Congress) makes enacting ever more sweeping laws easy or inevitable.

The fourth issue involves so-called **earmarks**—congressional provisions that direct the federal government to fund specific projects or exempt specific persons or groups from needing to pay specific federal taxes or fees. Earmarks have tripled since 1994; in 2006 alone, nearly 13,000 earmarks cost about $64 billion.[37] Earmarks are legally binding, but few appear in a bill's text; rather, most are "hidden" in conference reports not subject to amendment.

This form of "legislative productivity" is criticized by most scholars and, in principle at least, by most citizens. Earmarks figured in the scandals surrounding lobbyist Jack Abramoff and the convicted Congressman Randy "Duke" Cunningham; Barack Obama and John McCain argued against earmarks during the 2008 presidential campaign. Still, earmarks, in one form or another, have proliferated because individuals and institutions—including not just businesses but also private universities, hospitals, and other nonprofit organizations—persist in demanding them from constituency-oriented members of Congress.

The fifth issue is how the post-9/11 Congress has legislated on matters directly relevant to homeland security, especially its own. The Framers crafted Congress as an institution that favors deliberation over dispatch; to act boldly only when backed by a persistent popular majority, or a broad consensus among its leaders, or both; and to be slow to change its time-honored procedures and structures.

But intelligence officials believe that a fourth plane involved in the 9/11 terrorist attacks was headed for the Capitol. In its June 2003 report, the bipartisan Continuity of Government Commission concluded that "the greatest hole in our constitutional system is the possibility of a terrorist attack that would kill or injure many members of Congress."[38]

This "hole" is relatively small with respect to the Senate. The Seventeenth Amendment allows the emergency replacement of senators by the governors of their states provided the state legislature allows it; otherwise, the governors must call for new elections. But the problem is greater for the House, where vacancies can only be filled by special elections, a process that can take many months.

Congress has enacted some, but by no means all, of the 9/11 Commission's recommendations.[39] But, as of 2011, a decade after the 9/11 attacks on the United States, it had failed to enact comprehensive legislation or proposals for constitutional amendments to ensure that "the first branch" can continue to function should a terrorist attack kill or incapacitate many or most of its members.

REFORMING CONGRESS

While most citizens are only vaguely familiar with the rules and procedures under which Congress operates, they do care whether Congress as an institution serves the public interest and fulfills its mission as a democratic body. Over the last several decades, many proposals have been made to reform and improve Congress—term limitations, new ethics and campaign finance laws, and organizational changes intended to reduce the power and perks of members while making it easier for Congress to pass needed legislation in a timely fashion. Some of these proposals—for example, campaign finance reforms (see Chapter 10)—have recently become law.

Many would-be reformers share the view that Congress is overstaffed and self-indulgent. It is, they complain, quick to impose new laws on states, cities, businesses, and average citizens but slow to apply those same laws to itself and its members. It is quick to pass **pork-barrel legislation**—bills that give tangible benefits (highways, dams, post offices) to constituents in the hope of winning their votes in return—but slow to tackle complex and controversial questions of national policy. The reformers' image of Congress is unflattering, but is it wholly unwarranted?

No perk is more treasured by members of Congress than the frank. Members of Congress are allowed by law to send material through the mail free of charge by substituting their facsimile signature (*frank*) for postage. But rather than using this **franking privilege** to keep their constituents informed about the government, most members use franked newsletters and questionnaires as campaign literature. That is why use of the frank soars in the months before an election. Thus, the frank amounts to a taxpayer subsidy of members' campaigns, a perk that bolsters the electoral fortunes of incumbents. Some reformers do not believe it is possible to fence in congressional use of the frank for public education or other legitimate purposes, and so they propose abolishing it outright. Other reformers argue that the frank can be fenced in by prohibiting mailings just before primaries and general elections.

For years, Congress routinely exempted itself from many of the laws it passed. In defense of this practice, members said that if members of Congress were subject to, for example, the minimum wage laws, the executive branch, charged with enforcing these laws, would acquire excessive power over Congress. This would violate the separation of powers. But as public criticism of Congress grew and confidence in government declined, more and more people demanded that Congress subject itself to the laws that applied to everybody else. In 1995, the 104th Congress did this by passing a bill that obliges Congress to obey 11 important laws governing things such as civil rights, occupational safety, fair labor standards, and family leave.

The bipartisan Congressional Accountability Act of 1995 had to solve a key problem: under the constitutional doctrine of separated powers, it would have been unwise and perhaps unconstitutional for the executive branch to enforce congressional compliance with executive-branch regulations. So Congress created the independent Office of Compliance and an employee grievance procedure to deal with implementation. Now Congress, too, must obey laws such as the Civil Rights Act, the Equal Pay Act, the Age Discrimination Act, and the Family and Medical Care Leave Act.

As already mentioned, bills containing money for local dams, bridges, roads, and monuments are referred to disparagingly as pork-barrel legislation. Reformers complain that when members act to "bring home the bacon," Congress misallocates tax dollars by supporting projects with trivial social benefits in order to bolster their reelection prospects.

No one can doubt the value of trimming unnecessary spending, but pork is not necessarily the villain it is made out to be. For example, the main cause of the budget deficit was the increase in spending on entitlement programs (like health care and interest on the national debt) without a corresponding increase in taxes. Spending on pork is a small fraction of total annual federal spending (about 2.5 percent, on average, from 1993 to 2005).[40] But many categories of pork spending have increased in the last 10 or 15 years. Of course, one person's

How Things Work

Rules on Congressional Ethics

Senate

Gifts: No gifts (in money, meals, or things) totaling $100 or more from anyone except a spouse or personal friend.

Lobbyists may not pay for gifts, official travel, legal defense funds, or charitable contributions to groups controlled by senators.

Fees: No fees for lectures or writing ("honoraria"), except that fees of up to $2,000 may go to a senator-designated charity.

Outside earned income may not exceed 15 percent of a senator's salary.

Ex-senators may not try to influence members of Congress for one year after leaving the Senate.

Mass mailings: No senator may receive more than $50,000 from the Senate to send out a mailing to constituents.

House

Gifts: No gifts (in money, meals, or things) totaling $100 or more from anyone except a spouse or personal friend.

Lobbyists may not offer gifts or pay for travel, even if a lobbyist is a spouse or personal friend.

Travel: House members may travel at the expense of others if travel is for officially connected meetings.

Fees: No honoraria for House members.

Ex-House members may not lobby Congress for one year after leaving office.

How Things Work

How Congress Raises Its Pay

For more than 200 years, Congress has tried to find a politically painless way to raise its own pay. It has managed to vote itself a pay increase 23 times in those two centuries, but usually at the price of a hostile public reaction. Twice during the 19th century, a pay raise led to a massacre of incumbents in the next election.

Knowing this, Congress has invented various ways to get a raise without actually appearing to vote for it. These have included the following:

- Voting for a tax deduction for expenses incurred as a result of living in Washington
- Creating a citizens' commission that could recommend a pay increase that would take effect automatically, provided Congress did not vote against it
- Linking increases in pay to decreases in honoraria (that is, speaking fees)

In 1989, a commission recommended a congressional pay raise of over 50 percent (from $89,500 to $135,000) and a ban on honoraria. The House planned to let it take effect automatically. But the public wouldn't have it, demanding that Congress vote on the raise—and vote it down. It did.

Embarrassed by its maneuvering, Congress retreated. At the end of 1989, it voted itself (as well as most top executive and judicial branch members) a small pay increase (7.9 percent for representatives, 9.9 percent for senators) that also provided for automatic cost-of-living adjustments (up to 5 percent a year) in the future. But the automatic adjustments in congressional pay have been rejected every year in recorded roll-call votes. Apparently nobody in Congress wants to be accused of "getting rich" at the taxpayers' expense.

pork is another person's necessity. No doubt some congressional districts get an unnecessary bridge or highway, but others get bridges and highways that are long overdue. The notion that every bridge or road a member of Congress gets for his or her district is wasteful pork is tantamount to saying that no member attaches any importance to merit.

Even if all pork were bad, it would still be necessary. Congress is an independent branch of government, and each member is, by constitutional design, the advocate of his or her district or state. No member's vote can be won by coercion, and few can be had by mere appeals to party loyalty or presidential needs. Pork is a way of obtaining consent. The only alternative is bribery, but bribery, besides being wrong, would benefit only the member, whereas pork usually benefits voters in the member's district. If you want to eliminate pork, you must eliminate Congress, by converting it into a parliament under the control of a powerful party leader or prime minister. In a tightly controlled parliament, no votes need be bought; they can be commanded. But members of such a parliament can do little to help their constituents cope with government or to defend them against bureaucratic abuses, nor can they investigate the conduct of the executive branch. The price of a citizen-oriented Congress is a pork-oriented Congress.

WHAT WOULD YOU DO?

MEMORANDUM

To: *Representative Peter Skerry*

From: *Martha Bayles, legislative aide*

Subject: *The size of the House of Representatives*

The House can decide how big it wishes to be. When it was created, there was one representative for every 30,000 people. Now there is one for every 600,000. In most other democracies, each member of parliament represents far fewer than 600,000 people. Doubling the size of the House may be a way of avoiding term limits.

News »

Should We Have a Bigger Congress?

A powerful citizens' organization has demanded that the House of Representatives be made larger so that voters can feel closer to their members. Each representative now speaks for about 600,000 people—far too many, the group argues, to make it possible for all points of view to be heard.

Arguments for:

1. Doubling the size of the House would reduce the huge demand for constituent services each member now faces.
2. A bigger House would represent more shades of opinion more fairly.
3. Each member could raise less campaign money because his or her campaign would be smaller.

Arguments against:

1. A bigger House would be twice as hard to manage, and it would take even longer to pass legislation.
2. Campaigns in districts of 300,000 people would cost as much as ones in districts with 600,000 people.
3. Interest groups do a better job of representing public opinion than would a House with more members.

Your decision:

Increase size of House: ____________________

Do not increase size of House: ____________________

LEARNING OBJECTIVES

WHAT YOU NEED TO KNOW

☑ In what respects is Congress "the first branch" of American national government?

Congress is one of three co-equal branches, but it is "the first branch" by virtue of the especially extensive and important powers bestowed on it by Article I of the Constitution, and with respect to the Framers' belief that Congress was pivotal to making federalism, the separation of powers, and checks and balances work.

☑ Why do most Americans and many experts now view Congress as "the broken branch"?

Most Americans and many experts express disapproval of Congress and believe that it is ineffective at solving important problems, beholden to contributors and special interests, and unable to reform itself. Yet upward of 90 percent of the "broken branch's" incumbents who seek reelection win it, usually by wide margins. And the experts offer conflicting views regarding why Congress remains "broken" and how, if at all, it can be fixed.

☑ What are the main differences between a congress and a parliament?

A congress differs from a parliament in two basic ways: how one becomes a member and what one does as a member. To run for a seat in a parliament like Great Britain's, you first need a political party to put your name on a ballot, but to become a candidate for representative or senator in Congress, you first need to enter a primary election (political parties exercise relatively little control over who runs). In a parliament, the head of the executive branch (the prime minister) is selected by the majority party from among its members, and once in office a member of parliament has only one important decision to make—whether or not to support the government. By contrast, the voters, not the congress, pick the president, and once elected a member of congress has powers that he or she can exercise without regard to presidential preferences.

☑ How has the legislative productivity of the U.S. Congress varied over time?

In some periods, like the 1930s (the New Deal) and the 1960s (the Great Society), Congress has produced lots of major legislation. In other periods, however, its legislative output has been less robust. But scholars disagree about what explains these changes and also over how to measure "legislative productivity" in the first place.

☑ Are the American people as deeply divided in partisan and ideological terms as their representatives in Congress now appear to be?

Nobody disputes that Congress in recent decades has become more polarized in partisan and ideological terms, but some leading scholars argue that the trend reflects the growing political polarization in the American electorate, while others argue instead that voters remain far less polarized than those elected political elites who now represent them.

RECONSIDERING WHO GOVERNS?

1. How closely do members of Congress mirror the American people in terms of gender, race, and other demographic characteristics?

Demographically, not at all closely: most Americans, unlike most members of Congress, are not middle-aged white males with law degrees or past political careers. Some groups (for example, women, African Americans, and Latinos) are much less prevalent in Congress than they are in the nation as a whole, while other groups (for example, Catholics) constitute about the same fraction of Congress as they do of the American people. Ideologically, Republican members of Congress are more conservative than average Americans, and Democratic members of Congress are more liberal than average Americans.

2. Does Congress normally do what most citizens want it to do?

On most issues most of the time, Congress is in step with the public. But on some issues, most representatives' opinions generally are out of sync with mass public preferences. For example, most Americans have long favored protectionist trade policies, but most members of Congress have consistently voted for free-trade policies. Likewise, most citizens are less solicitous of laws that reinforce civil liberties than the Congress has traditionally been. This, however, is much as the Framers of the Constitution had hoped and expected. They believed that representatives should refine, not reflect, public wishes, and mediate, not mirror, public views.

RECONSIDERING TO WHAT ENDS?

1. Should Congress run under strong leadership?

Congress has tried it both ways. Sometimes the House has had a strong Speaker, sometimes a weak one; sometimes committee chairs were selected by seniority, sometimes by the Speaker, and sometimes by party vote. If we want a Congress that can act quickly and decisively as a body, then we should desire strong leadership, place restrictions on debate, provide few opportunities for stalling tactics, and brook only minimal committee interference. But if we want a Congress in which the interests of individual members and the people they represent are routinely protected or enhanced, then we must reject strong leadership, proliferate rules allowing for delay and discussion, and permit many opportunities for committee activity. Unfortunately, the public often wants both systems to operate, the first for some issues and the second for others.

2. Should Congress act more quickly?

The Framers of the Constitution knew that Congress would normally proceed slowly and err in favor of deliberative, not decisive, action. Congress was intended to check and balance strong leaders in the executive branch, not automatically cede its authority to them, not even during a war or other national crisis. Today, the increased ideological and partisan polarization among members has arguably made Congress even less capable than it traditionally has been of planning ahead or swiftly adopting coherent changes in national policies. There is, however, only conflicting evidence concerning whether so-called policy gridlock has become more common than in decades past. Since the September 11, 2001, terrorist attacks on the United States, Congress has passed a host of new laws intended to enhance America's homeland security. Still, Congress took its time with several major proposals to reorganize the government around homeland security priorities. Some cite this as but the latest, and potentially the gravest, example of what's wrong with Congress. But others cite it as a salutary reminder that a Congress that could move swiftly to enact wise homeland security or other policies could also move swiftly to adopt unwise ones.

QUESTIONS TO CONSIDER

1. **What's your take on why most Americans seem to like their own congresspersons far more than they like the Congress?**
2. **If you could change only one thing about how Congress works, what would that be?**
3. **Do you think parliamentary democracy could have worked well in America much as it apparently has in Great Britain and other nations, and why—or why not?**
4. **What is the partisan breakdown of your own state's congressional delegation (how many Democrats and Republicans), and how long has each member been in office?**
5. **How do various public policy advocacy and other groups rate the House member and senators who represent you?**
6. **How was your state affected by the 1990, 2000, and 2010 census counts (lost House seats, gained House seats, or stayed the same)?**

TO LEARN MORE

House of Representatives: **www.house.gov**

Senate: **www.senate.gov**

Library of Congress: **www.loc.gov**

For news about Congress

Roll Call magazine: **www.rollcall.com**

C-SPAN: **www.c-span.org**

Abramowitz, Alan I. *The Disappearing Center: Engaged Citizens, Polarization, and American Democracy*. New Haven and London: Yale University Press, 2010. Claims that polarization in Congress reflects how politically attentive and active voters are polarized, while less informed but more moderate voters are disengaged.

Arnold, R. Douglas. *The Logic of Congressional Action*. New Haven and London: Yale University Press, 1990. Masterful analysis of how Congress sometimes passes bills that serve the general public, not just special interests.

Black, Amy E. *From Inspiration to Legislation: How an Idea Becomes a Bill*. Upper Saddle River, N.J.: Pearson, 2007. An insider's account of the creation of the Safe Haven Act of 2001.

Fenno, Richard F., Jr. *Congressmen in Committees*. Boston: Little, Brown, 1973. Classic study of the styles of 12 standing committees.

Fiorina, Morris P. *Disconnect: The Breakdown of Representation in American Politics*. Oklahoma: University of Oklahoma Press, 2009. Offers evidence suggesting that the increasingly ideological and partisan Congress represents the still-centrist and moderate American people far less well than it did in the past.

Fiorina, Morris P. *Congress: Keystone of the Washington Establishment,* 2nd ed. New Haven, Conn.: Yale University Press, 1989. Argues that congressional behavior is aimed at guaranteeing the members' chances for reelection.

Jacobson, Gary. *The Politics of Congressional Elections,* 6th ed. New York: Longman, 2004. Authoritative study of how members of Congress are elected.

Maass, Arthur. *Congress and the Common Good*. New York: Basic Books, 1983. Insightful account of congressional operations, especially those involving legislative-executive relations. Disputes Fiorina's argument that reelection needs explain congressional behavior.

Mann, Thomas E., and Norman J. Ornstein, *Broken Branch: How Congress Is Failing America and How to Get It Back on Track*, 2nd ed. New York: Oxford University Press, 2008. Critically compares the post-1994 Congress to its predecessors and suggests several major reforms.

Poole, Keith T., and Howard Rosenthal. *Congress: A Political-Economic History of Roll Call Voting*. New York: Oxford University Press, 1997. Sophisticated study of why members of Congress vote as they do and how relatively stable congressional voting patterns have been throughout American history.

Sundquist, James L. *The Decline and Resurgence of Congress*. Washington, D.C.: Brookings Institution, 1981. A history of the fall and, after 1973, the rise of congressional power vis-à-vis the president.

14 The Presidency

LEARNING OBJECTIVES

WHAT YOU NEED TO KNOW

- ☑ How do presidents differ from prime ministers?
- ☑ How have the constitutional and political powers of the presidency evolved from the founding of the United States to the present?
- ☑ How do presidents make policy?

WHO GOVERNS?

1. Did the Founders expect the presidency to be the most important political institution?
2. How important is the president's character in determining how he governs?

TO WHAT ENDS?

1. Should we abolish the electoral college?
2. Is it harder to govern when the presidency and the Congress are controlled by different political parties?

THEN When the Framers wrote the Constitution in the summer of 1787, they did not have a ready consensus on how to select the chief executive or define the powers of the office. James Wilson of Pennsylvania wanted the president to be elected by the people, Roger Sherman of Connecticut wanted him elected by Congress. Wilson's view got almost no support because the size of the United States (in 1787 it was as large as England, Ireland, France, Germany, and Italy combined) made it unlikely that anybody save George Washington could obtain a popular majority. Sherman's view got a lot of support, but many delegates worried that the president would become nothing more than a tool of Congress. Ultimately, a small subset of the group, the Committee on Postponed Matters, came up with the idea of creating an electoral college to choose the president. The Framers approved the plan, but they expected that most elections would ultimately be decided by the House of Representatives, as they thought candidates would have difficulty winning a majority in the electoral college.

NOW More than two hundred years later, the electoral college endures, and the House has not chosen a president since 1824. The stability of this institution is surprising, given that the Framers settled on it as a last-minute compromise, and yet it is the only part of the presidential campaign process that the Framers would recognize in the 21st century. The lengthy road to the nomination, extensive fundraising required (in the 2008 presidential race, competitive candidates had raised more than $100 million before the first primary or caucus), and 24-hour media coverage are all standard features of modern presidential selection, and the weighty demands of winning the White House affect how the victorious candidate governs as president. As you read this chapter, think about which features of the American presidency make sense today and which might merit change, keeping in mind that the Framers were not necessarily wedded to all aspects of the institution they created, nor could they have anticipated how technology and other factors would change it.

Professor Jones speaks to his political science class:

The president of the United States occupies one of the most powerful offices in the world. Presidents Kennedy and Johnson sent American troops to Vietnam, President Bush sent them to Saudi Arabia, and President Clinton sent them to Kosovo, all without war being declared by Congress. In fact, Clinton ordered our air force to bomb parts of the old Yugoslavia despite the fact that the House of Representatives had rejected a resolution that would have authorized the bombing. President Nixon imposed wage and price controls on the country. Between them, Presidents Carter and Reagan selected most of the federal judges now on the bench; thus the political philosophies of these two men were stamped on the courts. President George W. Bush created military tribunals to try captured terrorists and persuaded Congress to toughen antiterrorist laws. President Barack Obama, within just months of taking office, got Congress to go along with his plans for giving the executive branch new and sweeping powers to regulate financial markets. No wonder people talk about our having an "imperial presidency."

A few doors down the hall, Professor Smith speaks to her class:

The president, compared to the prime ministers of other democratic nations, is one of the weakest chief executives anywhere. President Carter signed an arms-limitation treaty with the Soviets, but the Senate wouldn't ratify it. President Reagan was not allowed even to test antisatellite weapons, and in 1986 Congress rejected his budget before the ink was dry. President Clinton's health care plan was ignored, and the House voted to impeach him. The federal courts struck down several parts of President Bush's antiterrorist policies. Even with his party in control of both houses of Congress, President Obama's first budget proposals were nixed on Capitol Hill, and his first health care reform plans were quickly recast by congressional committee chairpersons. Regularly, subordinates who are supposed to be loyal to the president leak his views to the press and undercut his programs before Congress. No wonder people call the U.S. president a "pitiful, helpless giant."

Can Professors Jones and Smith be talking about the same office? Who is right? In fact, they are both right. The American presidency is a unique office, with elements of great strength and profound weakness built into it by its constitutional origins.

Presidents and Prime Ministers

The popularly elected president is an American invention. Of the roughly five dozen countries in which there is some degree of party competition and thus, presumably, some measure of free choice for the voters, only 16 have a directly elected president, and 13 of these are nations of North and South America. The democratic alternative is for the chief executive to be a prime minister, chosen by and responsible to the parliament. This system prevails in most Western European countries as well as in Israel and Japan. There is no nation with a purely presidential political system in Europe; France combines a directly elected president with a prime minister and parliament.[1]

In a parliamentary system, the prime minister is the chief executive. The prime minister is chosen not by the voters but by the legislature, and he or she in turn selects the other ministers from the members of parliament. If the parliament has only two major parties, the ministers usually will be chosen from the majority party; if there are many parties (as in Israel), several parties may participate in a coalition cabinet. The prime minister remains in power as long as his or her party has a majority of the seats in the legislature or as long as the coalition he or she has assembled holds together. The voters choose who is to be a member of parliament—usually by voting for one or another party—but cannot choose who is to be the chief executive officer. Whether a nation has a presidential or a parliamentary system makes a big difference in the identity and powers of the chief executive.

PRESIDENTS ARE OFTEN OUTSIDERS

People become president by winning elections, and sometimes winning is easier if you can show the voters that you are not part of "the mess in Washington." Prime ministers are selected from among people already in parliament, and so they are always insiders.

Jimmy Carter, Ronald Reagan, Bill Clinton, and George W. Bush did not hold national office before becoming president. Franklin Roosevelt had been assistant secretary of the navy, but his real political experience was as governor of New York. Dwight Eisenhower was a general, not a politician. John F. Kennedy, Lyndon Johnson, and Richard Nixon had been in Congress, but only Nixon had had top-level experience in the executive branch (he had been vice president). George H. W. Bush had had a great deal of executive experience in Washington—as vice president, director of the CIA, and representative to China, whereas Bill Clinton and George W. Bush both served as governors. Barack Obama is the third president to be elected directly from the U.S. Senate to the White House—the other two were Warren G. Harding and John F. Kennedy.

Thirty-one different people were elected president between 1828 and 2000. Of these, the great majority were governors, military leaders, or vice presidents; only 13 percent were legislators just before becoming president.

Bettman/Corbis

The first cabinet: left to right, Secretary of War Henry Knox, Secretary of State Thomas Jefferson, Attorney General Edmund Randolph, Secretary of the Treasury Alexander Hamilton, and President George Washington.

PRESIDENTS CHOOSE CABINET MEMBERS FROM OUTSIDE CONGRESS

Under the Constitution, no sitting member of Congress can hold office in the executive branch. The persons chosen by a prime minister to be in the cabinet are almost always members of parliament.

Of the 15 heads of cabinet-level departments in the first George W. Bush administration, only four had been members of Congress. The rest, as is customary with most presidents, were close personal friends or campaign aides, representatives of important constituencies (for example, farmers, blacks, or women), experts on various policy issues, or some combination of all three. The prime minister of Great Britain, by contrast, picks all of his or her cabinet ministers from among members of Parliament. This is one way by which the prime minister exercises control over the legislature. If you were an ambitious member of Parliament, eager to become prime minister yourself someday, and if you knew that your main chance of realizing that ambition was to be appointed to a series of ever-more-important cabinet posts, then you would not likely antagonize the person doing the appointing.

PRESIDENTS HAVE NO GUARANTEED MAJORITY IN THE LEGISLATURE

A prime minister's party (or coalition) always has a majority in parliament; if it did not, somebody else would be prime minister. A president's party often does not have a congressional majority; instead, Congress often is controlled by the opposite party, creating a divided government. Divided government means that cooperation between the two branches, hard to achieve under the best of circumstances, is often further reduced by partisan bickering. Even when one party controls both the White House and Congress, the two branches often work at cross-purposes. The U.S. Constitution created a system of separate branches sharing powers. The authors of the document expected there would be conflict between the branches, and they have not been disappointed.

When Kennedy was president, his party, the Democrats, held a big majority in the House and the Senate. Yet Kennedy was frustrated by his inability to get Congress to approve proposals to enlarge civil rights, supply federal aid for school construction, create a Department of Urban Affairs and Housing, or establish a program of subsidized medical care for the elderly. During his last year in office, Congress passed only about one-fourth of his proposals. Carter did not fare much better; even though the Democrats controlled Congress, many of his most important proposals were defeated or greatly modified. Only Franklin Roosevelt (1933–1945) and Lyndon Johnson (1963–1969) had even brief success in leading Congress, and for Roosevelt most of that success was confined to his first term or to wartime.

PRESIDENTS AND PRIME MINISTERS AT WAR

These differences in political position are illustrated by how George W. Bush and Tony Blair managed the war in Iraq.

- Once Bush decided to fight, he had to cajole Congress, even though it was controlled by his own party, to support him. Once Blair decided to fight, there could not be any meaningful political resistance in Parliament.
- When public opinion turned against Bush, he continued the fight because he could not be removed from office. When public opinion turned against Blair, he announced he would resign from office and turn over the job of prime minister to another person in his party.

Divided Government

In the 58 years between 1952 and 2010, there were 29 congressional elections and 14 presidential elections. Nineteen of the 29 produced **divided government**—a government in which one party controls the White House and a different party controls one or both houses of Congress. When Barack Obama became president in 2009, it was only the fourth time since 1969 that the same party controlled the White House and Congress, creating a **unified government.** Eight years earlier, the inauguration of President George W. Bush marked the first time since 1953 that the Republicans were fully in charge of both branches of government (they controlled the White House and the Senate from 1981 to 1987). But not long after the Senate convened, one Republican, James Jeffords of Vermont, announced that he was an independent and voted

divided government One party controls the White House and another party controls one or both houses of Congress.

unified government The same party controls the White House and both houses of Congress.

gridlock The inability of the government to act because rival parties control different parts of the government.

with the Democrats. Divided government returned until an additional Republican was elected to the Senate in 2002. But the Democrats retook control in 2007 and increased their majorities in both chambers two years later, even gaining the 60 votes necessary to halt filibusters in the Senate following a contested Minnesota race that ended with Democrat Al Franken being declared the winner and seated. They lost their filibuster-proof majority in 2010, when Republican Scott Brown won a surprise victory to fill the seat of recently deceased Senator Ted Kennedy of Massachusetts. And President Obama faced partially divided government when the 111th Congress convened in January 2011, with a Republican-led House and a narrowly Democratic Senate.

Americans say they don't like divided government. They, or at least the pundits who claim to speak for them, think divided government produces partisan bickering, political paralysis, and policy gridlock. During the 1990 battle between President Bush and a Democratic Congress, one magazine compared it to a movie featuring the Keystone Kops, characters from the silent movies who wildly chased each other around while accomplishing nothing.[2] In the 1992 campaign, Bush, Clinton, and Ross Perot bemoaned the "stalemate" that had developed in Washington. When Clinton was sworn in as president, many commentators spoke approvingly of the "end of gridlock."

There are two things wrong with these complaints. First, it is not clear that divided government produces a gridlock that is any worse than that which exists with unified government. Second, it is not clear that, even if **gridlock** does exist, it is always, or even usually, a bad thing for the country.

DOES GRIDLOCK MATTER?

Despite the well-publicized stories about presidential budget proposals being ignored by Congress (Democrats used to describe Reagan's and Bush's budgets as being "dead on arrival"), it is not easy to tell whether divided governments produce fewer or worse policies than unified ones. The scholars who have looked closely at the matter have, in general, concluded that divided governments do about as well as unified ones in passing important laws, conducting important investigations, and ratifying significant treaties.[3] Political scientist David Mayhew studied 267 important laws that were enacted between 1946 and 1990. These laws were as likely to be passed when different parties controlled the White House and Congress as when the same party controlled both branches.[4] For example, divided governments produced the 1948 Marshall Plan to rebuild war-torn Europe and the

Divided Government at Work: Six Examples

President George W. Bush and the Democratic-controlled Congress expanded federal laws that fund health care for low-income and elderly citizens.

President Bill Clinton and the Republican-controlled Congress overhauled the nation's welfare system and balanced the federal budget.

President George H. W. Bush and the Democratic-controlled Congress enacted historic legislation to aid disabled persons.

President Ronald Reagan and the Democratic-controlled Congress reformed the federal tax system.

President Richard Nixon and the Democratic-controlled Congress created many new federal environmental policies and programs.

President Dwight D. Eisenhower and the Democratic-controlled Congress established the interstate highway system.

Source: Eisenhower to Clinton examples adapted from Associated Press, "Major Laws Passed in Divided Government," November 9, 2006.

1986 Tax Reform Act. The box on page 368 lists six examples of divided government in action.

Why do divided governments produce about as much important legislation as unified ones? The main reason is that "unified government" is something of a myth. Just because the Republicans control both the presidency and Congress does not mean that the Republican president and the Republican senators and representatives will see things the same way. For one thing, Republicans are themselves divided between conservatives (mainly from the South) and liberals (mainly from the Northeast and Midwest). They disagree about policy almost as much as Republicans and Democrats disagree. For another thing, the Constitution ensures that the president and Congress will be rivals for power and thus rivals in policymaking. That's what the separation of powers and checks and balances are all about.

As a result, periods of unified government often turn out not to be so unified. Democratic president Lyndon Johnson could not get many Democratic members of Congress to support his war policy in Vietnam. Democratic president Jimmy Carter could not get the Democratic-controlled Senate to ratify his strategic arms-limitation treaty. Democratic president Bill Clinton could not get the Democratic Congress to go along with his policy on gays in the military or his health proposals; and when the heavily revised Clinton budget did pass in 1993, it was by just one vote.

The only time there really is a unified government is when not just the same party but the same *ideological wing* of that party is in effective control of both branches of government. This was true in 1933 when Franklin Roosevelt was president and change-oriented Democrats controlled Congress, and it was true again in 1965 when Lyndon Johnson and liberal Democrats dominated Congress. Both were periods when many major policy initiatives became law: Social Security, business regulations, Medicare, and civil rights legislation. But these periods of ideologically unified government are very rare.

IS POLICY GRIDLOCK BAD?

An American president has less ability to decide what laws get passed than does a British prime minister. If you think the job of a president is to "lead the country," that weakness will worry you. The only cure for that weakness is either to change the Constitution so that our government resembles the parliamentary system in effect in Great Britain, or always to vote into office members of Congress who not only are of the same party as the president but also agree with him on policy issues.

We suspect that even Americans who hate gridlock and want more leadership aren't ready to make sweeping constitutional changes or to stop voting for presidents and members of Congress from different parties. This unwillingness suggests they like the idea of somebody being able to block a policy he or she doesn't like. Since all of us don't like something, we all have an interest in some degree of gridlock.

And we seem to protect that interest. In a typical presidential election, about one-fourth of all voters will vote for one party's candidate for president and the other party's candidate for Congress. As a result, about one-fourth of all congressional districts will be represented in the House by a person who does not belong to the party of the president who carried that district. Some scholars believe that voters split tickets deliberately in order to create divided government and thus magnify the effects of the checks and balances built into our system, but the evidence supporting this belief is not conclusive.

Gridlock, to the extent that it exists, is a necessary consequence of a system of representative democracy. Such a system causes delays, intensifies deliberations, forces compromises, and requires the creation of broad-based coalitions to support most new policies. This system is the opposite of direct democracy. If you believe in direct democracy, you believe that what the people want on some issue should become law with as little fuss and bother as possible. Political gridlocks are like traffic gridlocks—people get overheated, things boil over, nothing moves, and nobody wins except journalists who write about the mess and lobbyists who charge big fees to steer their clients around the tie-up. In a direct democracy, the president would be a traffic cop with broad powers to decide in what direction the traffic should move and to make sure that it moves that way.

But if unified governments are not really unified—if in fact they are split by ideological differences within each party and by the institutional rivalries between the president and Congress—then this change is less important than it may seem. What *is* important is the relative power of the president and Congress. That has changed greatly.

HOW WE COMPARE

Presidential Systems

Most modern democracies feature one of three systems:

- Parliamentary systems (like the United Kingdom) in which prime ministers are selected by a legislative majority and can be removed by a legislative majority at virtually any time;
- Presidential systems (like the United States) in which the president and the legislators are separately elected and serve fixed terms, with the president subject to removal by the legislature only under extreme circumstances (for example, in the United States, impeachment by the House and removal from office by the Senate); or
- Semi-presidential systems (like France) in which there is a prime minister selected and subject to removal by a parliamentary majority, as well as a president who is separately elected.

Using a multidimensional definition of "democratic," in 1950, about 60 percent of democratic nations had parliamentary systems, 30 percent had semi-presidential systems, and 10 percent had presidential systems. Today, however, about two-thirds of all democratic nations have either semi-presidential (about 36 percent) or presidential (about 30 percent) systems.

Are elected officials and party leaders in presidential systems like that in the United States more or less likely to deliver on campaign promises than are their counterparts in the other two systems? The most in-depth studies to date say "less likely": The rate at which a party in power pursues the policies it offered to voters in its platform is generally lower in presidential systems; and the incidence of "policy-switching" (pursuing policies directly contrary to those promised during the campaign) is more than four times as common in presidential systems as it is in parliamentary systems, with semi-presidential systems being in the middle.

Source: David Samuels and Matthew Shugart, *Presidents, Parties, and Prime Ministers: How the Separation of Powers Affects Party Organization and Behavior* (Cambridge University Press, 2010); "Presidents, Prime Ministers, and Mandate Representation: A Global Test," paper prepared for presentation at the 2006 Annual Meeting of the American Political Science Association, Philadelphia, Pennsylvania.

The Powers of the President

Though the president, unlike a prime minister, cannot command an automatic majority in the legislature, he does have some formidable, albeit vaguely defined, powers. These are mostly set forth in Article II of the Constitution and are of two sorts: those he can exercise in his own right without formal legislative approval, and those that require the consent of the Senate or of Congress as a whole.

POWERS OF THE PRESIDENT ALONE

- Serve as commander in chief of the armed forces
- Commission officers of the armed forces
- Grant reprieves and pardons for federal offenses (except impeachment)
- Convene Congress in special sessions
- Receive ambassadors

Mark Wilson/Getty Images News/Getty Images

A military officer carrying "the football"—the briefcase containing the secret codes the president can use to launch a nuclear attack.

- Take care that the laws be faithfully executed
- Wield the "executive power"
- Appoint officials to lesser offices

POWERS THE PRESIDENT SHARES WITH THE SENATE

- Make treaties
- Appoint ambassadors, judges, and high officials

POWERS THE PRESIDENT SHARES WITH CONGRESS AS A WHOLE

- Approve legislation

Taken alone and interpreted narrowly, this list of powers is not very impressive. Obviously, the president's authority as commander in chief is important, but literally construed, most of the other constitutional grants seem to provide for little more than a president who is chief clerk of the country. A hundred years after the Founding, that is about how matters appeared to even the most astute observers. In 1884, Woodrow Wilson wrote a book about American politics titled *Congressional Government,* in which he described the business of the president as "usually not much above routine," mostly "*mere* administration." The president might as well be an officer of the civil service. To succeed, he need only obey Congress and stay alive.[5]

But even as Wilson wrote, he was overlooking some examples of enormously powerful presidents, such as Lincoln, and was not sufficiently attentive to the potential for presidential power to be found in the more ambiguous clauses of the Constitution as well as in the political realities of American life. The president's authority as commander in chief has grown—especially, but not only, in wartime—to encompass not simply the direction of the military forces, but also the management of the economy and the direction of foreign affairs as well. A quietly dramatic reminder of the awesome implications of the president's military powers occurs at the precise instant that a new president assumes office. A military officer carrying a locked briefcase moves from the side of the outgoing president to the side of the new one. In the briefcase are the secret codes and orders that permit the president to authorize the launching of American nuclear weapons.

The president's duty to "take care that the laws be faithfully executed" has become one of the most elastic phrases in the Constitution. By interpreting this broadly, Grover Cleveland was able to use federal troops to break a labor strike in the 1890s, and Dwight Eisenhower was able to send troops to help integrate a public school in Little Rock, Arkansas, in 1957.

The greatest source of presidential power, however, is not found in the Constitution at all but in politics and public opinion. Increasingly since the 1930s, Congress has passed laws that confer on the executive branch broad grants of authority to achieve some general goals, leaving it up to the president

How Things Work

The President: Qualifications and Benefits

Qualifications

- A natural-born citizen (can be born abroad of parents who are American citizens)
- 35 years of age
- A resident of the United States for at least 14 years (but not necessarily the 14 years just preceding the election)

Benefits

- A nice house
- A salary of $400,000 per year (taxable)
- An expense account of $50,000 per year (tax-free)
- Travel expenses of $100,000 per year (tax-free)
- A pension, on retirement, equal to the pay of a cabinet member (taxable)
- Staff support and Secret Service protection for 10 years on leaving the presidency
- A White House staff of 400 to 500
- A place in the country—Camp David
- A personal airplane—Air Force One
- A fine chef

and his deputies to define the regulations and programs that will actually be put into effect. In Chapter 15, we shall see how this delegation of legislative power to the president has contributed to the growth of the bureaucracy. Moreover, the American people—always in times of crisis, but increasingly as an everyday matter—look to the president for leadership and hold him responsible for a large and growing portion of our national affairs. The public thinks, wrongly, that the presidency is the "first branch" of government.

The Evolution of the Presidency

Ironically, given the preeminence of the presidency in American politics today, few issues inspired as much debate or concern among the Framers in 1787 as the problem of defining the chief executive. The delegates feared anarchy and monarchy in about equal measure. When the Constitutional Convention met, the existing state constitutions gave most, if not all, power to the legislatures. In eight states, the governor actually was chosen by the legislature, and in ten states, the governor could not serve more than one year. Only in New York, Massachusetts, and Connecticut did governors have much power or serve for any length of time.

Some of the Framers proposed a plural national executive (that is, several people would each hold the executive power in different areas, or they would exercise the power as a committee). Others wanted the executive power checked, as it was in Massachusetts, by a council that would have to approve many of the chief executive's actions. Alexander Hamilton strongly urged the exact opposite: in a five-hour speech, he called for something very much like an elective monarchy, patterned in some respects after the British kind. No one paid much attention to this plan or even, at first, to the more modest (and ultimately successful) suggestion of James Wilson for a single, elected president.

In time, those who won out believed that the governing of a large nation, especially one threatened by foreign enemies, required a single president with significant powers. Their cause was aided, no doubt, by the fact that everybody assumed George Washington would be the first president, and confidence in him—and in his sense of self-restraint—was widely shared. Even so, several delegates feared the presidency would become, in the words of Edmund Randolph of Virginia, "the foetus of monarchy."

CONCERNS OF THE FOUNDERS

The delegates in Philadelphia, and later the critics of the new Constitution during the debate over its ratification, worried about aspects of the presidency that were quite different from those that concern us today. In 1787–1789, some Americans suspected that the president, by being able to command the state militia, would use the militia to overpower state governments. Others were worried that if the president were allowed to share treaty-making power with the Senate, he would be "directed by minions and favorites" and become a "tool of the Senate."

But the most frequent concern was over the possibility of presidential reelection: Americans in the late 18th century were sufficiently suspicious of human nature and sufficiently experienced in the arts of mischievous government to believe that a president, once elected, would arrange to stay in office in perpetuity by resorting to bribery, intrigue, and force. This might happen, for example, every time the presidential election was thrown into the House of Representatives because no candidate had received a majority of the votes in the electoral college, a situation that most people expected to happen frequently.

In retrospect, these concerns seem misplaced, even foolish. The power over the militia has had little significance; the election has gone to the House only twice (1800 and 1824); and though the Senate dominated the presidency off and on during the second half of the 19th century, it has not done so recently. The real sources of the expansion of presidential power—the president's role in foreign affairs, his ability to shape public opinion, his position as head of the executive branch, and his claims to have certain "inherent" powers by virtue of his office—were hardly predictable in 1787. And not surprisingly. There was nowhere in the world at that time, nor had there been at any time in history, an example of an American-style presidency. It was a unique and unprecedented institution, and the Framers and their critics can easily be forgiven for not predicting accurately how it would evolve. At a more general level, however, they understood the issue quite clearly. Gouverneur Morris of Pennsylvania put the problem of the presidency this way: "Make him too weak: the Legislature will usurp his powers. Make him too strong: he will usurp on the Legislature."

The Framers knew very well that the relations between the president and Congress and the manner in which the president is elected were of profound importance, and they debated both at great length. The first plan was for Congress to elect the president—in short, for the system to be quasi-parliamentary. But if that were done, some delegates pointed out, Congress could dominate an honest or lazy president, while a corrupt or scheming president might dominate Congress.

After much discussion, it was decided that the president should be chosen directly by voters. But by which voters? The emerging nation was large and diverse. It seemed unlikely that every citizen would be familiar enough with the candidates to cast an informed vote for a president directly. Worse, a direct popular election would give inordinate weight to the large, populous states, and no plan with that outcome had any chance of adoption by the smaller states.

THE ELECTORAL COLLEGE

Thus the **electoral college** was invented, whereby each of the states would select electors in whatever manner it wished. The electors would then meet in each state capital and vote for president and vice president. Many Framers expected that this procedure would lead to each state's electors' voting for a favorite son, and thus no candidate would win a majority of the popular vote. In this event, it was decided, the House of Representatives should make the choice, with each state delegation casting one vote.

The plan seemed to meet every test: large states would have their say, but small states would be protected by having a minimum of three electoral votes no matter how tiny their population. The small states together could wield considerable influence in the House, where, it was widely expected, most presidential elections would ultimately be decided. Of course, it did not work out quite this way: the Framers did not foresee the role that political parties would play in producing nationwide support for a slate of national candidates.

Once the manner of electing the president was settled, the question of his powers was much easier to decide. After all, if you believe the procedures are fair and balanced, then you are more confident in assigning larger powers to the president within this system. Accordingly, the right to make treaties and the right to appoint lesser officials, originally reserved for the Senate, were given to the president "with the advice and consent of the Senate."

THE PRESIDENT'S TERM OF OFFICE

Another issue was put to rest soon thereafter. George Washington, the unanimous choice of the electoral college to be the first president, firmly limited himself to two terms in office (1789–1797), and no president until Franklin D. Roosevelt (1933–1945) dared to run for more (though Ulysses S. Grant tried). In 1951, the Twenty-second Amendment to the Constitution was ratified, formally limiting all subsequent presidents to two terms. The remaining issues concerning the nature of the presidency, and especially the relations between the president and Congress, have been the subject of continuing dispute. The pattern of relationships that we see today is the result of an evolutionary process that has extended over more than two centuries. The first problem was to establish the legitimacy of the presidency itself: that is, to ensure, if possible, public acceptance of the office, its incumbent, and its powers and to establish an orderly transfer of power from one incumbent to the next.

electoral college The people chosen to cast each state's votes in a presidential election. Each state can cast one electoral vote for each senator and representative it has. The District of Columbia has three electoral votes, even though it cannot elect a representative or senator.

Today, we take this for granted. When George W. Bush was inaugurated in January 2001 as our 43rd president, Bill Clinton, the 42nd, quietly left the White House. In the world today, such an uneventful succession is unusual. In many nations, a new chief executive comes to power with the aid of military force or as a result of political intrigue; his predecessor often leaves office disgraced, exiled, or dead. At the time the Constitution was written, the Founders could only hope that an orderly transfer of power from one president to the next would occur. France had just undergone a bloody revolution; England in the not-too-distant past had beheaded a king; and in Poland the ruler was elected by a process so manifestly corrupt and so open to intrigue that Thomas Jefferson, in what may be the first example of ethnic humor in American politics, was led to refer to the proposed American presidency as a "bad edition of a Polish king."

Yet by the time Abraham Lincoln found himself at the helm of a nation plunged into a bitter, bloody civil war, 15 presidents had been elected, served their time, and left office without a hint of force being used to facilitate the process and with the people accepting the process—if not admiring all the presidents. This orderly transfer of authority occurred despite passionate opposition and deeply divisive elections (such as that which brought Jefferson to power). And it did not happen by accident.

THE FIRST PRESIDENTS

Those who first served as president were among the most prominent men in the new nation, all active either in the movement for independence or in the Founding or in both. Of the first five presidents,

Library of Congress

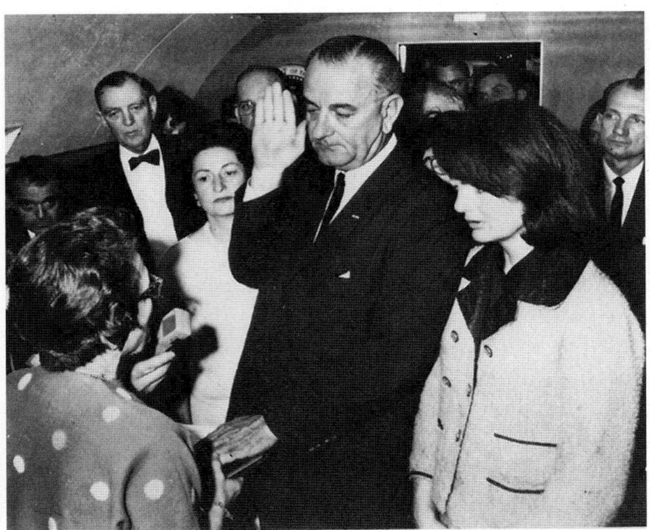

AP Photo/White House, Cecil Stoughton

America witnessed peaceful transfers of power not only between leaders of different parties (such as Woodrow Wilson and William Howard Taft in 1913), but also after a popular leader was assassinated (Lyndon Johnson is sworn in after John F. Kennedy's death).

four (all but John Adams) served two full terms. Washington and Monroe were not even opposed. The first administration had at the highest levels the leading spokesmen for all of the major viewpoints: Alexander Hamilton was Washington's secretary of the treasury (and was sympathetic to the urban commercial interests), and Thomas Jefferson was secretary of state (and more inclined toward rural, small-town, and farming views). Washington spoke out strongly against political parties, and though parties soon emerged, there was a stigma attached to them: many people believed that it was wrong to take advantage of divisions in the country, to organize deliberately to acquire political office, or to make legislation depend upon party advantage. As it turned out, this hostility to party (or "faction," as it was more commonly called) was unrealistic: parties are as natural to democracy as churches are to religion.

Establishing the legitimacy of the presidency in the early years was made easier by the fact that the national government had relatively little to do. It had, of course, to establish a sound currency and to settle the debt accrued during the Revolutionary War. The Treasury Department inevitably became the principal federal office, especially under the strong leadership of Hamilton. Relations with England and France were important—and difficult—but otherwise government took little time and few resources.

In appointing people to federal office, a general rule of "fitness" emerged: those appointed should have some standing in their communities and be well thought of by their neighbors. Appointments based on partisanship soon arose, but community stature could not be neglected. The presidency was kept modest. Washington clearly had not sought the office and did not relish the exercise of its then modest powers. He traveled widely so that as many people as possible could see their new president. His efforts to establish a semi-regal court etiquette were quickly rebuffed; the presidency was to be kept simple. Congress decided that not until after a president was dead might his likeness appear on a coin or on currency; no president until Eisenhower was given a pension on his retirement.

The president's relations with Congress were correct but not close. Washington appeared before the Senate to ask its advice on a proposed treaty with some Indian tribes. He got none and instead was politely told that the Senate would like to consider the matter in private. He declared that he would be "damned if he ever went there again," and he never did. Thus ended the responsibility of the Senate to "advise" the president. Vetoes were sometimes cast by the president, but sparingly, and only when the president believed the law was not simply unwise but unconstitutional. Washington cast only two vetoes; Jefferson and Adams cast none.

THE JACKSONIANS

At a time roughly corresponding to the presidency of Andrew Jackson (1829–1837), broad changes began to occur in American politics. These changes, together with the personality of Jackson himself, altered the relations between the president and

The Granger Collection

President Andrew Jackson thought of himself as the "Tribune of the People," and he symbolized this by throwing a White House party that anyone could attend. Hundreds of people showed up and ate or carried away most of a 1,400-pound block of cheese.

Congress and the nature of presidential leadership. As so often happens, few people at the time Jackson took office had much sense of what his presidency would be like. Though he had been a member of the House of Representatives and of the Senate, he was elected as a military hero—and an apparently doddering one at that. Sixty-one years old and seemingly frail, he nonetheless used the powers of his office as no one before him had.

Jackson vetoed 12 acts of Congress, more than all his predecessors combined and more than any subsequent president until Andrew Johnson 30 years later. His vetoes were not simply on constitutional grounds but on policy ones: as the only official elected by the entire voting citizenry, he saw himself as the "Tribune of the People." None of his vetoes were overridden. He did not initiate many new policies, but he struck out against the ones he did not like. He did so at a time when the size of the electorate was increasing rapidly, and new states, especially in the West, had entered the Union. (There were then 24 states in the Union, nearly twice the original number.)

Jackson demonstrated what could be done by a popular president. He did not shrink from conflict with Congress, and the tension between the two branches of government that was intended by the Framers became intensified by the personalities of those in government: Jackson in the White House, and Henry Clay, Daniel Webster, and John Calhoun in Congress. These powerful figures walked the political stage at a time when bitter sectional conflicts—over slavery and commercial policies—were beginning to split the country. Jackson, though he was opposed to a large and powerful federal government and wished to return somehow to the agrarian simplicities of Jefferson's time, was nonetheless a believer in a strong and independent presidency. This view, though obscured by nearly a century of subsequent congressional dominance of national politics, was ultimately to triumph—for better or for worse.

THE REEMERGENCE OF CONGRESS

With the end of Jackson's second term, Congress quickly reestablished its power, and except for the wartime presidency of Lincoln and brief flashes of presidential power under James Polk (1845–1849) and Grover Cleveland (1885–1889, 1893–1897), the presidency for a hundred years was the subordinate branch of the national government. Of the eight presidents who succeeded Jackson, two (William H. Harrison and Zachary Taylor) died in office, and none of the others served more than one term. Schoolchildren, trying to memorize the list of American presidents, always stumble in this era of the "no-name" presidents. This is hardly a coincidence: Congress was the leading institution, struggling, unsuccessfully, with slavery and sectionalism.

It was also an intensely partisan era, a legacy of Jackson that lasted well into the 20th century. Public opinion was closely divided. In nine of the 17 presidential elections between the end of Jackson's term in 1837 and Theodore Roosevelt's election in 1904, the winning candidate received less than half the popular vote. Only two candidates (Lincoln in 1864 and Ulysses S. Grant in 1872) received more than 55 percent of the popular vote.

During this long period of congressional—and usually senatorial—dominance of national government, only Lincoln broke new ground for presidential power. Lincoln's expansive use of that power, like Jackson's, was totally unexpected. He was first elected in 1860 as a minority president, receiving less than 40 percent of the popular vote in a field of four candidates. Though a member of the new Republican party, he had been a member of the Whig party, a group that had stood for limiting presidential power. He had opposed America's entry into the Mexican War and had been critical of Jackson's use of executive authority. But as president during the Civil War, he made unprecedented use of the vague powers in Article II of the Constitution, especially those that he felt were "implied" or "inherent" in the phrase "take care that the laws be faithfully executed" and in the express authorization for him to act as commander in chief. Lincoln raised an army, spent money, blockaded southern ports, temporarily suspended the writ of habeas corpus, and

How Things Work

The Electoral College

Until November 2000, it was almost impossible to get a student interested in the electoral college. But in the 2000 presidential election, Florida's electoral vote hung in the balance for weeks, with Bush finally winning it and (though he had fewer popular votes than Al Gore) the presidency.

Here are the essential facts: each state gets electoral votes equal to the number of its senators and representatives (the District of Columbia also gets 3, even though it has no representatives in Congress). There are 538 electoral votes. To win, a candidate must receive at least half, or 270.

In all but two states, the candidate who wins the most popular votes wins all of the state's electoral votes. Maine and Nebraska have a different system. They allow electoral votes to be split by awarding some votes on the basis of a candidate's statewide total and some on the basis of how the candidate did in each congressional district.

Electoral Votes per State

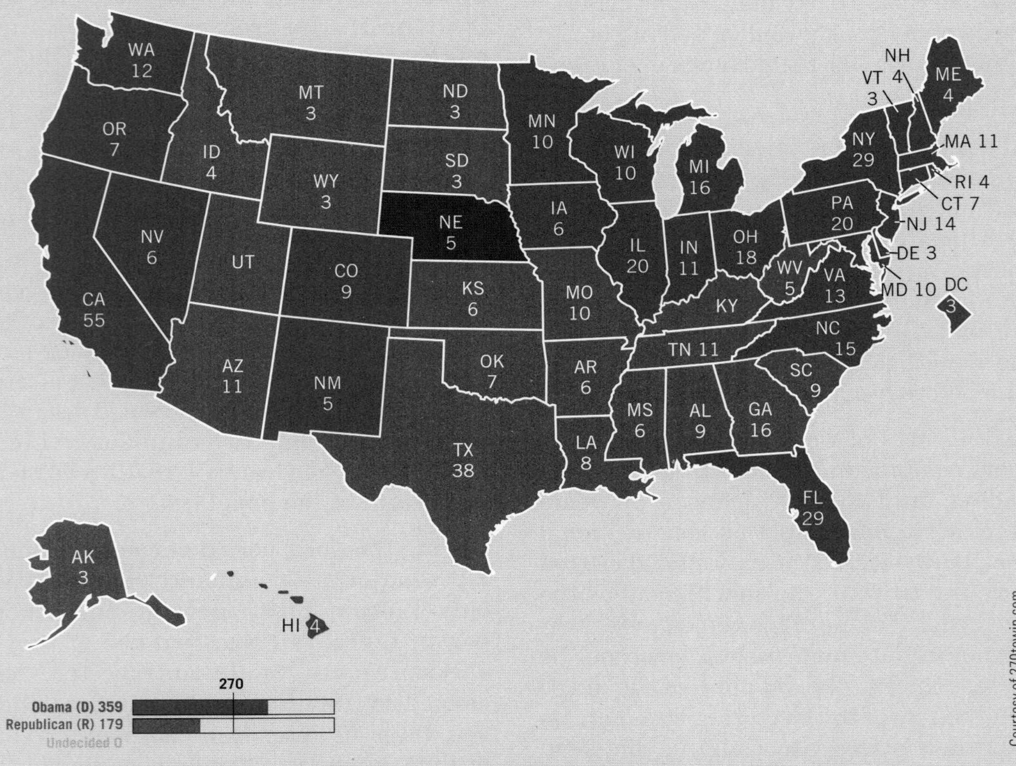

The distribution of electoral college votes per state is for the 2012 presidential election, based on the 2010 Census. The colors indicate which states voted Democratic and Republican (or both, in one case) in 2008, but the distribution of electoral college votes per state was different in 2008. In 2008, Obama won 365 electoral college votes, but the same states in 2012 would bring 359 electoral votes, as the bar graph shows (which is still well above the 270-vote minimum required to win in the electoral college).

issued the Emancipation Proclamation to free the slaves—all without prior congressional approval. He justified this, as most Americans probably would have, by the emergency conditions created by civil war. In this he acted little differently from Thomas Jefferson, who while president waged undeclared war against various North African pirates.

After Lincoln, Congress reasserted its power and became, during Reconstruction and for many decades thereafter, the principal federal institution. But it had become abundantly clear that a national emergency could equip the president with great powers and that a popular and strong-willed president could expand his powers even without an emergency.

The winning slates of electors assemble in their state capitals about six weeks after the election to cast their ballots. Ordinarily this is a pure formality. Occasionally, however, an elector will vote for a presidential candidate other than the one who carried the state. Such "faithless electors" have appeared in several elections since 1796. The state electoral ballots are opened and counted before a joint session of Congress during the first week of January. The candidate with a majority is declared elected.

If no candidate wins a majority, the House of Representatives chooses the president from among the three leading candidates, with each state casting one vote. By House rules, each state's vote is allotted to the candidate preferred by a majority of the state's House delegation. If there is a tie within a delegation, that state's vote is not counted.

The House has had to decide two presidential contests. In 1800, Thomas Jefferson and Aaron Burr tied in the electoral college because of a defect in the language of the Constitution—each state cast two electoral votes, without indicating which was for president and which for vice president. (Burr was supposed to be vice president, and after much maneuvering he was.) This problem was corrected by the Twelfth Amendment, ratified in 1804. The only House decision under the modern system was in 1824, when it chose John Quincy Adams over Andrew Jackson and William H. Crawford, even though Jackson had more electoral votes (and probably more popular votes) than his rivals.

Today the winner-takes-all system in effect in 48 states makes it possible for a candidate to win at least 270 electoral votes without winning a majority of the popular votes. This happened in 2000, 1888, and 1876, and almost happened in 1960 and 1884. Today a candidate who carries the 10 largest states wins 256 electoral votes, only 14 short of a presidential victory.

This means that the candidates have a strong incentive to campaign hard in big states they have a chance of winning. In 2000, Gore worked hard in California, New York, and Pennsylvania but pretty much ignored Texas, where Bush was a shoo-in. Bush campaigned hard in Florida, Illinois, and Ohio, but not so much in New York, where Gore was an easy winner.

But the electoral college can also help small states. South Dakota, for example, has 3 electoral votes (about 0.5 percent of the total), even though it casts only about 0.3 percent of the popular vote. South Dakota and other small states are thus overrepresented in the electoral college.

Most Americans would like to abolish the electoral college. But doing away with it entirely would have some unforeseen effects. If we relied just on the popular vote, there might have to be a runoff election among the two leading candidates if neither got a majority because third-party candidates won a lot of votes. This would encourage the formation of third parties (we might have a Jesse Jackson party, a Pat Buchanan party, a Pat Robertson party, and a Ralph Nader party). Each third party would then be in a position to negotiate with one of the two major parties between the first election and the runoff about favors it wanted in return for its support. American presidential politics might come to look like the multiparty systems in France and Italy.

There are other changes that could be made. One is for each state to allocate its electoral votes proportional to the popular vote the candidates receive in that state. Voters in Colorado acted on that measure in November 2004, but that proposal failed. If every state did that, several past elections would have been decided in the House of Representatives because no candidate got a majority of the popular vote.

And the electoral college serves a larger purpose: it makes candidates worry about carrying states as well as popular votes, and so heightens the influence of states in national politics.

Except for the administrations of Theodore Roosevelt (1901–1909) and Woodrow Wilson (1913–1921), the president was, until the New Deal, at best a negative force—a source of opposition to Congress, not a source of initiative and leadership for it. Grover Cleveland was a strong personality, but for all his efforts he was able to do little more than veto bills that he did not like. He cast 414 vetoes—more than any other president until Franklin Roosevelt. A frequent target of his vetoes were bills to confer special pensions on Civil War veterans.

Today we are accustomed to thinking that the president formulates a legislative program to which

Congress then responds, but until the 1930s the opposite was more the case. Congress ignored the initiatives of such presidents as Grover Cleveland, Rutherford Hayes, Chester Arthur, and Calvin Coolidge. Woodrow Wilson in 1913 was the first president since John Adams to deliver personally the State of the Union address, and he was one of the first to develop and argue for a presidential legislative program.

Our popular conception of the president as the central figure of national government, devising a legislative program and commanding a large staff of advisers, is very much a product of the modern era and of the enlarged role of government. In the past, the presidency became powerful only during a national crisis (the Civil War, World War I) or because of an extraordinary personality (Andrew Jackson, Theodore Roosevelt, Woodrow Wilson). Since the 1930s, however, the presidency has been powerful no matter who occupied the office and whether or not there was a crisis. Because government now plays such an active role in our national life, the president is the natural focus of attention and the titular head of a huge federal administrative system (whether he is the real boss is another matter).

But the popular conception of the president as the central figure of national government belies the realities of present-day legislative-executive relations. During national policymaking from the Eisenhower years through the Reagan administration, Congress, not the president, often took the lead in setting the legislative agenda.[6] For example, the 1990 Clean Air Act, like the 1970 Clean Air Act before it, was born and bred mainly by congressional, not presidential, action. Indeed, administration officials played almost no role in the legislative process that culminated in these laws.[7] When President Bush signed the 1990 Clean Air Act or President Clinton signed the 1996 Welfare Reform Act, each took credit for it, but in fact both bills were designed by members of Congress, not by the president.[8] Likewise, although presidents dominated budget policymaking from the 1920s into the early 1970s, they no longer do. Instead, the "imperatives of the budgetary process have pushed congressional leaders to center stage."[9] Thus, as often as not, Congress proposes, the president disposes, and legislative-executive relations involve hard bargaining and struggle between these two branches of government.

The Power to Persuade

The sketchy constitutional powers given the president, combined with the lack of an assured legislative majority, mean that he must rely heavily on persuasion if he is to accomplish much. Here, the Constitution gives him some advantages: he and the vice president are the only officials elected by the whole nation, and he is the ceremonial head of state as well as the chief executive of the government. The president can use his national constituency and ceremonial duties to enlarge his power, but he must do so quickly: the second half of his first term in office will be devoted to running for reelection, especially if he faces opposition for his own party's nomination (as was the case with Carter and Ford).

THE THREE AUDIENCES

The president's persuasive powers are aimed at three audiences. The first, and often the most important, is his Washington, D.C., audience of fellow politicians and leaders. As Richard Neustadt points out in his book *Presidential Power*, a president's reputation among his Washington colleagues is of great importance in affecting how much deference his views receive and thus how much power he can wield.[10] If a president is thought to be "smart," "sure of himself," "cool," "on top of things," or "shrewd," and thus "effective," he *will* be effective. Franklin Roosevelt had that reputation, and so did Lyndon Johnson, at least for his first few years in office. Truman, Ford, and Carter often did not have that reputation, and they lost ground accordingly. Power, like beauty, exists largely in the eye of the beholder.

A second audience is composed of party activists and officeholders outside Washington—the partisan grassroots. These persons want the president to exemplify their principles, trumpet their slogans, appeal to their fears and hopes, and help them get reelected. Since, as we explained in Chapter 9, partisan activists increasingly have an ideological orientation toward national politics, these people will expect "their" president to make fire-and-brimstone speeches that confirm in them a shared sense of purpose and, incidentally, help them raise money from contributors to state and local campaigns.

The third audience is "the public." But of course that audience is really many publics, each with a different view or set of interests. A president on the campaign trail speaks boldly of what he will accomplish; a president in office speaks quietly of the problems that must be overcome. Citizens often are irritated at the apparent tendency of officeholders, including the president, to sound mealy-mouthed and equivocal. But it is easy to criticize the cooking when you haven't been the cook. A president learns quickly that every utterance will be scrutinized closely by the media and by organized groups here and abroad, and errors of fact, judgment, timing, or even inflection will be immediately and forcefully pointed out. Given the risks of saying too much, it is a wonder that presidents say anything at all.

Presidents have made fewer and fewer impromptu remarks in the years since Franklin Roosevelt held office and have instead relied more and more on prepared speeches from which political errors can be removed in advance. Hoover and Roosevelt held six or seven press conferences each month, but every president from Nixon through Clinton has held barely one a month. Instead, modern presidents make formal speeches. A president's use of these speeches often is called the **bully pulpit,** a phrase that means taking advantage of the prestige and visibility of the presidency to try to guide or mobilize the American people.

bully pulpit The president's use of his prestige and visibility to guide or enthuse the American public.

RESEARCH FRONTIERS

Do a President's Communication Skills Matter?

Barack Obama garnered national attention in 2004 for his eloquent keynote address at the Democratic National Convention about "the audacity of hope" (a phrase that he later used as a book title). Four years later, his speeches propelled his successful candidacy for the White House. Obama's rhetorical skills were important for his presidential campaign, but for governing, how much does a president's ability to communicate matter?

The Framers of the Constitution probably would have said, "not much." After all, they wanted to keep some distance between the president and the public, as their creation of an electoral college to select the president indicates (see box on p. 376). The Constitution states that the president "shall from time to time give to the Congress Information of the State of the Union," but it does not require a presidential speech; indeed, presidents from Thomas Jefferson through William Howard Taft sent their state of the union messages in writing to Congress.

Presidential public communication has become more important since the early 20th century. Woodrow Wilson resumed the custom started by the first two presidents of delivering state of the union messages in person to Congress. Presidential scholar Richard E. Neustadt wrote in 1960 of the need for presidents to appeal to multiple constituencies, and he emphasized the importance of "public prestige," for which a president must be "effective as a teacher to the public."[1]

Political scientists and communication scholars have identified the use of public rhetoric as a political strategy by presidents in modern American politics. Samuel Kernell shows how modern presidents routinely employ a practice of "going public" to build popular support for their policies, and Jeffrey K. Tulis examines the development of the "rhetorical presidency," in which presidents use public speeches to exercise popular leadership. Mary E. Stuckey finds that advances in media technology shape what presidents say and how they do so, while Karlyn Kohrs Campbell and Kathleen Hall Jamieson evaluate how presidents use rhetorical opportunities to exercise political influence with the other institutions of government.

Despite all of the time and energy that presidents invest in their public communications, however, their efforts may not yield the results they seek. Based on extensive analysis of public opinion polls, George C. Edwards III argues that presidential speeches serve to bolster existing public views rather than to change them—the "bully pulpit," he says, falls "on deaf ears." Jeffrey E. Cohen examines media coverage of the presidency and finds that presidents can influence segments of the public through local news coverage, but that national strategies of "going public" are less successful.

Will presidents continue to devote significant resources to their public communications? Absolutely. Will doing so help them to achieve their political and policy goals? Probably not very much. The Framers appear to be correct, albeit for different reasons—they did not think presidents should "go public," and while presidents do so routinely today, they typically don't get a lot for their efforts.

[1]Richard E. Neustadt, *Presidential Power and the Modern Presidents: The Politics of Leadership from Roosevelt to Reagan* (New York: The Free Press, 1990), 84.

Sources: Richard E. Neustadt, *Presidential Power and the Modern Presidents: The Politics of Leadership from Roosevelt to Reagan* (New York: The Free Press, 1990); Samuel Kernell, *Going Public: New Strategies of Presidential Leadership,* 4th ed. (Washington, D.C.: CQ Press, 2007); Jeffrey K. Tulis, *The Rhetorical Presidency* (Princeton, N.J.: Princeton University Press, 1987); Mary E. Stuckey, *The President as Interpreter-in-Chief* (Chatham, N.J.: Chatham House Publishers, 1991); Karlyn Kohrs Campbell and Kathleen Hall Jamieson, *Presidents Creating the Presidency: Deeds Done in Words* (Chicago: University of Chicago Press, 2008); George C. Edwards III, *On Deaf Ears: The Limits of the Bully Pulpit* (New Haven, Ct.: Yale University Press, 2003); Jeffrey E. Cohen, *Going Local: Presidential Leadership in the Post-Broadcast Age* (New York: Cambridge University Press, 2010).

POPULARITY AND INFLUENCE

The object of all this talk is to convert personal popularity into congressional support for the president's legislative programs (and improved chances for reelection). It is not obvious, of course, why Congress should care about a president's popularity. After all, as we saw in Chapter 13, most members of Congress are secure in their seats, and few need fear any "party bosses" who might deny them renomination. Moreover, the president cannot ordinarily provide credible electoral rewards or penalties to members of Congress. By working for their defeat in the 1938 congressional election, President Roosevelt attempted to "purge" members of Congress who opposed his program, but he failed. Nor does presidential support help a particular member of Congress: most representatives win reelection anyway, and the few who are in trouble are rarely saved by presidential intervention. When President Reagan campaigned hard for Republican senatorial candidates in 1986, he, too, failed to have much impact.

For a while, scholars thought congressional candidates might benefit from the president's coattails: they might ride into office on the strength of the popularity of a president of their own party. It is true, as can be seen from Table 14.1, that a winning president will often find that his party's strength in Congress increases.

But there are good reasons to doubt whether the pattern observed in Table 14.1 is the result of presidential coattails. For one thing, there are some exceptions.

Table 14.1 Partisan Gains or Losses in Congress in Presidential Election Years

			Gains or Losses of President's Party In:	
Year	President	Party	House	Senate
1932	Roosevelt	Dem.	+90	+9
1936	Roosevelt	Dem.	+12	+7
1940	Roosevelt	Dem.	+7	-3
1944	Roosevelt	Dem.	+24	-2
1948	Truman	Dem.	+75	+9
1952	Eisenhower	Rep.	+22	+1
1956	Eisenhower	Rep.	-3	-1
1960	Kennedy	Dem.	-20	+1
1964	Johnson	Dem.	+37	+1
1968	Nixon	Rep.	+5	+7
1972	Nixon	Rep.	+12	-2
1976	Carter	Dem.	+1	+1
1980	Reagan	Rep.	+33	+12
1984	Reagan	Rep.	+16	-2
1988	Bush	Rep.	-3	-1
1992	Clinton	Dem.	-9	+1
1996	Clinton	Dem.	+9	-2
2000	Bush	Rep.	-3	-4
2004	Bush	Rep.	+4	+4
2008	Obama	Dem.	+21	+9

Sources: Updated from Congressional Quarterly, *Guide to U.S. Elections*, 928; and *Congress and the Nation*, vol. 4 (1973–1976), 28.

Figure 14.1
Presidential Popularity

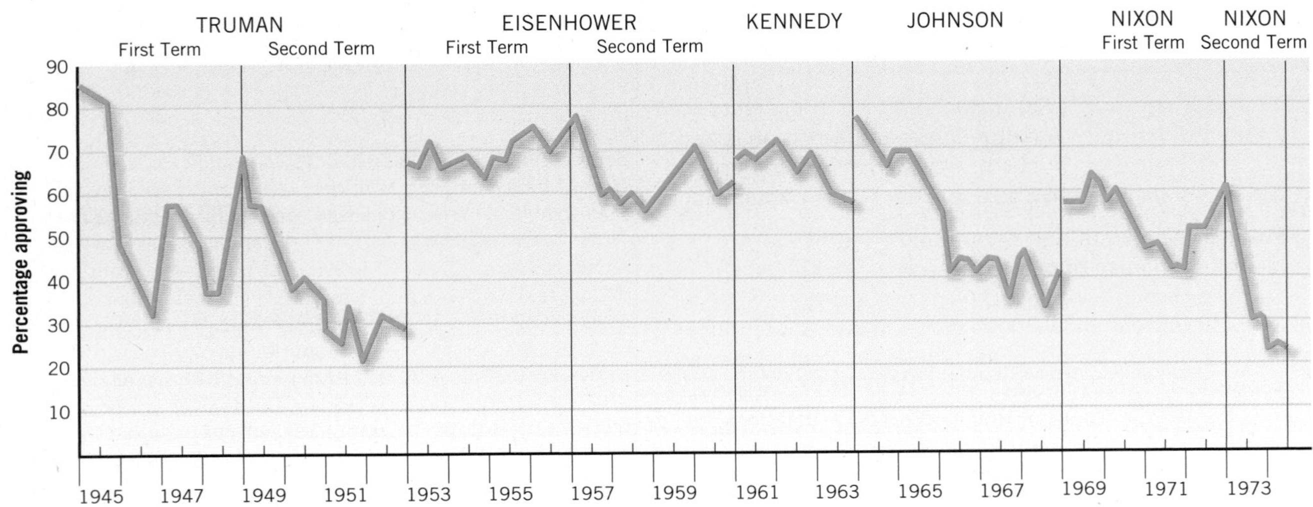

Eisenhower won 57.4 percent of the vote in 1956, but the Republicans lost seats in the House and Senate. Kennedy won in 1960, but the Democrats lost seats in the House and gained but one in the Senate. When Nixon was reelected in 1972 with one of the largest majorities in history, the Republicans lost seats in the Senate.

Careful studies of voter attitudes and of how presidential and congressional candidates fare in the same districts suggest that, whatever may once have been the influence of coattails, their effect has declined in recent years and is quite small today. The weakening of party loyalty and of party organizations, combined with the enhanced ability of members of Congress to build secure relations with their constituents, has tended to insulate congressional elections from presidential ones. When voters choose as members of Congress people of the same party as an incoming president, they probably do so out of desire for a general change and as an adverse judgment about the outgoing party's performance as a whole, not because they want to supply the new president with members of Congress favorable to him.[11] The big increase in Republican senators and representatives that accompanied the election of Ronald Reagan in 1980 was probably as much a result of the unpopularity of the outgoing president and the circumstances of various local races as it was of Reagan's coattails.

Nonetheless, a president's personal popularity may have a significant effect on how much of his program Congress passes, even if it does not affect the reelection chances of those members of Congress. Though they do not fear a president who threatens to campaign against them (or cherish one who promises to support them), members of Congress do have a sense that it is risky to oppose too adamantly the policies of a popular president. Politicians share a sense of a common fate: they tend to rise or fall together. Statistically, a president's popularity, as measured by the Gallup poll (see Figure 14.1), is associated with the proportion of his legislative proposals approved by Congress (see Figure 14.2). Other things equal, the more popular the president, the higher the proportion of his bills Congress will pass.

But use these figures with caution. How successful a president is with Congress depends not just on the numbers reported here, but on a lot of other factors as well. First, he can be "successful" on a big bill or on a trivial one. If he is successful on a lot of small matters and never on a big one, the measure of presidential victories does not tell us much. Second, a president can keep his victory score high by not taking a position on any controversial measure. (President Carter made his views known on only 22 percent of the House votes, while President Eisenhower made his views known on 56 percent of those votes.) Third, a president can appear successful if a few bills he likes are passed, but most of his legislative program is bottled up in Congress and never comes to a vote. Given these problems, "presidential victories" are hard to measure accurately.

A fourth general caution: presidential popularity is hard to predict and can be greatly influenced by factors over which nobody, including the president, has much control. For example, when he took

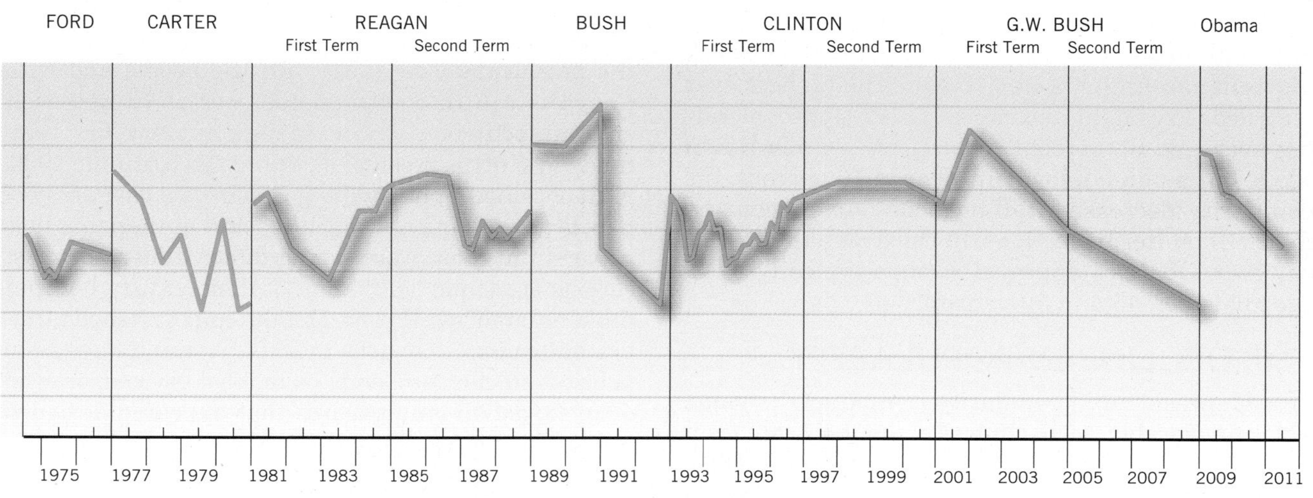

Note: Popularity was measured by asking every few months, "Do you approve of the way __________ is handling his job as president?"

Source: Thomas E. Cronin, The State of the Presidency (Boston: Little, Brown, 1975), 110–111. Updated with Gallup poll data, 1976–2004. Reprinted by permission of the Gallup Poll News Service.

Figure 14.2
Presidential Victories on Votes in Congress, 1953–2010

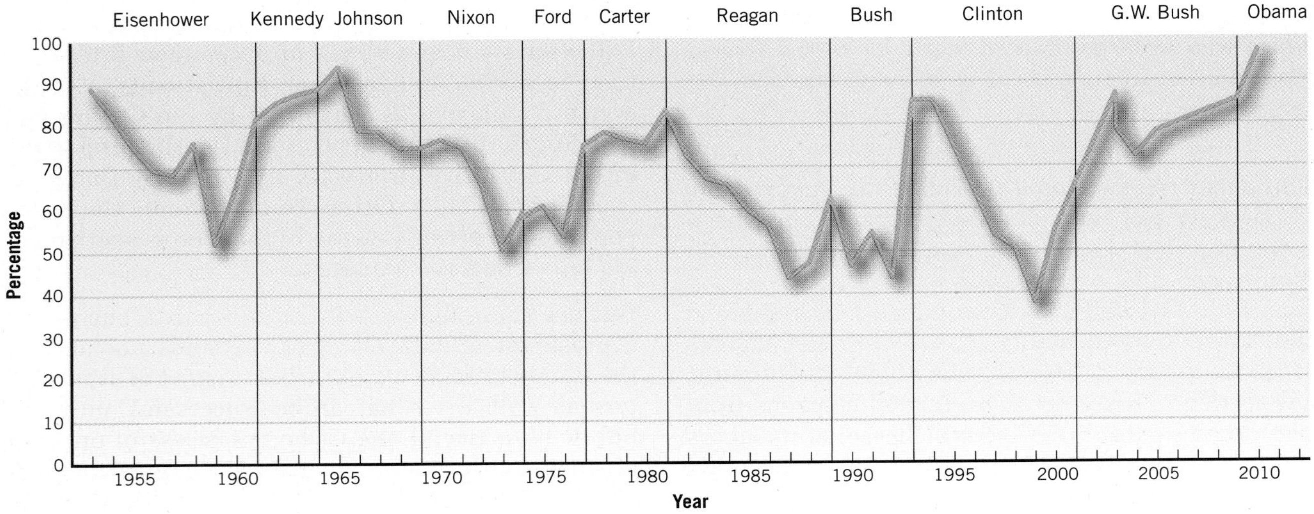

Note: Percentages indicate number of congressional votes supporting the president divided by the total number of votes on which the president has taken a position.

Source: *Congressional Quarterly Weekly Report*, various years. Data for 2010 from Schatz, Joseph J., "2010 Vote Studies: Presidential Support," *CQ Weekly* (January 3, 2011): 18–24.

office in 2001, President George W. Bush's approval rating was 57 percent, nearly identical to what President Bill Clinton received in his initial rating (58 percent) in 1993. But Bush also had the highest initial *dis*approval rating (25 percent) of any president since polling began. This was undoubtedly partly due to his becoming president on the heels of the Florida vote-count controversy (see Chapter 10). Bush's approval ratings through his first six months were fairly typical for post-1960 presidents. But from the terrorist attack on the United States on September 11, 2001 through mid-2002, his approval ratings never dipped below 70 percent, and the approval ratings he received shortly after the attack (hovering around 90 percent) were the highest ever recorded. President Barack Obama's approval rating averaged 63 percent in his first six months in office, but as unemployment neared 10 percent, his popularity decreased, falling below 45 percent by the 2010 midterm elections. In the first half of 2011, however, Obama's approval ratings typically averaged between 45 and 50 percent.

THE DECLINE IN POPULARITY

Though presidential popularity is an asset, its value tends inexorably to decline. As can be seen from Figure 14.1, every president except Eisenhower, Reagan, and Clinton lost popular support between his inauguration and the time that he left office, except when his reelection gave him a brief burst of renewed popularity. Truman was hurt by improprieties among his subordinates and by the protracted Korean War; Johnson was crippled by the increasing unpopularity of the Vietnam War; Nixon was severely damaged by the Watergate scandal; Ford was hurt by having pardoned Nixon for his part in Watergate; Carter was weakened by continuing inflation, staff irregularities, and the Iranian kidnapping of American hostages; George H. W. Bush was harmed by an economic recession. George W. Bush suffered from public criticism of the war in Iraq.

Because a president's popularity tends to be highest right after an election, political commentators like to speak of a "honeymoon," during which, presumably, the president's love affair with the people and with Congress can be consummated. Certainly, Roosevelt enjoyed such a honeymoon. In the legendary "first hundred days" of his presidency, from March to June 1933, FDR obtained from a willing Congress a vast array of new laws creating new agencies and authorizing new powers. But those were extraordinary times: the most serious economic depression of that century had put millions out of work, closed banks, impoverished farmers, and ruined the stock market. It would have been political suicide for Congress to have blocked, or even delayed, action on measures that appeared designed to help the nation out of the crisis.

Other presidents, serving in more normal times, have not enjoyed such a honeymoon. Truman had little success with what he proposed; Eisenhower proposed little. Kennedy, Nixon, Ford, and Carter had some victories in their first year in office, but nothing that could be called a honeymoon. Only Lyndon Johnson enjoyed a highly productive relationship with Congress; until the Vietnam War sapped his strength, he rarely lost. Reagan began his administration with important victories in his effort to cut expenditures and taxes, but in his second year in office he ran into trouble.

The decay in the reputation of the president and his party in midterm is evident in Table 14.2. Since 1934, in every off-year election but two, the president's party has lost seats in one or both houses of Congress. In 1998, the Democrats won five seats in the House and lost none in the Senate; in 2002, the Republicans gained eight House seats and two in the Senate. The ability of the president to persuade is important but limited. However, he also has a powerful bargaining chip to play: the ability to say no.

Table 14.2 Partisan Gains or Losses in Congress in Off-Year Elections

			Gains or Losses of President's Party in:	
Year	**President**	**Party**	**House**	**Senate**
1934	Roosevelt	Dem.	+9	+9
1938	Roosevelt	Dem.	−70	−7
1942	Roosevelt	Dem.	−50	−8
1946	Truman	Dem.	−54	−11
1950	Truman	Dem.	−29	−5
1954	Eisenhower	Rep.	−18	−1
1958	Eisenhower	Rep.	−47	−13
1962	Kennedy	Dem.	−5	+2
1966	Johnson	Dem.	−48	−4
1970	Nixon	Rep.	−12	+1
1974	Ford	Rep.	−48	−5
1978	Carter	Dem.	−12	−3
1982	Reagan	Rep.	−26	0
1986	Reagan	Rep.	−5	−8
1990	Bush	Rep.	−9	−1
1994	Clinton	Dem.	−52	−9
1998	Clinton	Dem.	+5	0
2002	G. W. Bush	Rep.	+8	+2
2006	G. W. Bush	Rep.	−30	−6
2010	Obama	Dem.	−64	−6

Sources: Norman J. Ornstein, Thomas E. Mann, and Michael J. Malbin, *Vital Statistics on Congress, 2001–2002* (Washington, D.C.: Congressional Quarterly Press, 2001), 207; Web sites of U.S. House of Representatives and U.S. Senate. Note: See the Web links on the front inside cover to visit the House and Senate Web sites.

The Power to Say No

The Constitution gives the president the power to veto legislation. In addition, most presidents have asserted the right of "executive privilege," or the right to withhold information that Congress may want to obtain from the president or his subordinates, and some presidents have tried to impound funds appropriated by Congress. These efforts by the president to say no are not only a way of blocking action but also a way of forcing Congress to bargain with him over the substance of policies.

VETO

If a president disapproves of a bill passed by both houses of Congress, he may veto it in one of two ways. One is by a **veto message.** This is a statement that the president sends to Congress accompanying the bill, within 10 days (not counting Sundays) after the bill has been passed. In it he sets forth his reasons for not signing the bill. The other is the **pocket veto.** If the president does not sign the bill within 10 days *and* Congress has adjourned within that time, then the bill will not become law. Obviously, a pocket veto can be used only during a certain time of the year—just before Congress adjourns at the end of its second session. At times, however, presidents have pocket-vetoed a bill just before Congress recessed for a summer vacation or to permit its members to campaign during an off-year election. In 1972, Senator Edward M. Kennedy of Massachusetts protested that this was unconstitutional, since a recess is not the same thing as an adjournment. In a case brought to federal court, Kennedy was upheld, and it is now understood that the pocket veto can be used only just before the life of a given Congress expires.

veto message A message from the president to Congress stating that he will not sign a bill it has passed. Must be produced within 10 days of the bill's passage.

pocket veto A bill fails to become law because the president did not sign it within 10 days before Congress adjourns.

A bill not signed or vetoed within 10 days while Congress is still in session becomes law automatically, without the president's approval. A bill returned to Congress with a veto message can be passed over the president's objections if at least two-thirds of each house votes to override the veto. A bill that has received a pocket veto cannot be brought back to life by Congress (since Congress has adjourned), nor does such a bill carry over to the next session of Congress. If Congress wants to press the matter, it will have to start all over again by passing the bill anew in its next session, and then hope the president will sign it or, if he does not, that they can override his veto.

line-item veto An executive's ability to block a particular provision in a bill passed by the legislature.

The president must either accept or reject the entire bill. Presidents do not have the power, possessed by most governors, to exercise a **line-item veto,** with which the chief executive can approve some provisions of a bill and disapprove others. Congress could take advantage of this by putting items the president did not like into a bill he otherwise favored, forcing him to approve those provisions along with the rest of the bill or reject the whole thing. In 1996, Congress passed a bill, which the president signed into law, that gives the president the power of "enhanced rescission." This means the president could cancel parts of a spending bill passed by Congress without vetoing the entire bill. The president had five days after signing a bill to send a message to Congress rescinding some parts of what he had signed. These rescissions would take effect unless Congress, by a two-thirds vote, overturned them. Congress could choose which parts of the president's cancellations it wanted to overturn. But the Supreme Court has decided that this law is unconstitutional. The Constitution gives the president no such power to carve up a bill: he must either sign the whole bill, veto the whole bill, or allow it to become law without his signature.[12]

Nevertheless, the veto power is a substantial one, because Congress rarely has the votes to override it. From George Washington to Bill Clinton, more than 2,500 presidential vetoes were cast; about 4 percent were overridden (see Table 14.3). Cleveland, Franklin Roosevelt, Truman, and Eisenhower made the most extensive use of vetoes, accounting for 65 percent of all vetoes ever cast. George W. Bush did not veto a single bill in his first term, though he issued 12 vetoes in his second term, of which four were overridden. In his first two years in office, Barack Obama vetoed just two bills. Often the vetoed legislation is revised by Congress and passed in a form suitable to the president. There is no tally of how often this happens, but it is frequent enough so that both branches of government recognize that the veto, or even the threat of it, is part of an elaborate process of political negotiation in which the president has substantial powers.

Table 14.3 Presidential Vetoes, 1789–2010

	Regular Vetoes	Pocket Vetoes	Total Vetoes	Vetoes Overridden
Washington	2	—	2	—
Madison	5	2	7	—
Monroe	1	—	1	—
Jackson	5	7	12	—
Tyler	6	3	9	1
Polk	2	1	3	—
Pierce	9	—	9	5
Buchanan	4	3	7	—
Lincoln	2	4	6	—
A. Johnson	21	8	29	15
Grant	45	49	94	4
Hayes	12	1	13	1
Arthur	4	8	12	1
Cleveland	304	109	413	2
Harrison	19	25	44	1
Cleveland	43	127	170	5
McKinley	6	36	42	—
T. Roosevelt	42	40	82	1
Taft	30	9	39	1
Wilson	33	11	44	6
Harding	5	1	6	—
Coolidge	20	30	50	4
Hoover	21	16	37	3
F. Roosevelt	372	263	635	9
Truman	180	70	250	12
Eisenhower	73	108	181	2
Kennedy	12	9	21	—
L. Johnson	16	14	30	—
Nixon	26	17	43	7
Ford	48	18	66	12
Carter	13	18	31	2
Reagan	39	39	78	9
Bush	29	15	44	1
Clinton	36	1	37	2
G. W. Bush	12	0	12	4
Obama	0	2	2	0

Sources: Norman J. Ornstein, Thomas E. Mann, and Michael J. Malbin, *Vital Statistics on Congress, 2002–2003* (Washington, D.C.: Congressional Quarterly Press, 2003), 207; The American Presidency Project of the University of California at Santa Barbara.

EXECUTIVE PRIVILEGE

The Constitution says nothing about whether the president is obliged to divulge private communications between himself and his principal advisers, but presidents have acted as if they do have that privilege of confidentiality. The presidential claim is based on two grounds. First, the doctrine of the separation of powers means that one branch of government does not have the right to inquire into the internal workings of another branch headed by constitutionally named officers. Second, the principles of statecraft and of prudent administration require that the president have the right to obtain confidential and candid advice from subordinates; such advice could not be obtained if it would quickly be exposed to public scrutiny.

For almost 200 years, there was no serious challenge to the claim of presidential confidentiality. The Supreme Court did not require the disclosure of confidential communications to or from the president.[13] Congress was never happy with this claim but until 1973 did not seriously dispute it. Indeed, in 1962, a Senate committee explicitly accepted a claim by President Kennedy that his secretary of defense, Robert S. McNamara, was not obliged to divulge the identity of Defense Department officials who had censored certain speeches by generals and admirals.

In 1974, the Supreme Court for the first time met the issue directly. A federal special prosecutor sought tape recordings of White House conversations between President Nixon and his advisers as part of his investigation of the Watergate scandal. In the case of *United States v. Nixon,* the Supreme Court, by a vote of eight to zero, held that while there may be a sound basis for the claim of executive privilege, especially where sensitive military or diplomatic matters are involved, there is no "absolute unqualified Presidential privilege of immunity from judicial process under all circumstances."[14] To admit otherwise would be to block the constitutionally defined function of the federal courts to decide criminal cases.

Thus, Nixon was ordered to hand over the disputed tapes and papers to a federal judge so that the judge could decide which were relevant to the case at hand and allow those to be introduced into evidence. In the future, another president may well persuade the Court that a different set of records or papers is so sensitive as to require protection, especially if there is no allegation of criminal misconduct requiring the production of evidence in court. As a practical matter, it seems likely that presidential advisers will be able, except in unusual cases such as Watergate, to continue to give private advice to the president.

In 1997 and 1998, President Clinton was sued while in office by a private person, Paula Jones, who claimed he had solicited sex from her in ways that hurt her reputation. In defending himself against that and other matters, his lawyers attempted to claim executive privilege for Secret Service officers and government-paid lawyers who worked with him, but federal courts held that not only could a president be sued, but these other officials could not claim executive privilege.[15] One unhappy consequence of this episode is that the courts have greatly weakened the number of officials with whom the president can speak in confidence. It is not easy to run an organization when the courts can later compel your associates to testify about everything you said.

IMPOUNDMENT OF FUNDS

From time to time, presidents have refused to spend money appropriated by Congress. Truman did not spend all that Congress wanted spent on the armed forces, and Johnson did not spend all that Congress made available for highway construction. Kennedy refused to spend money appropriated for new weapons systems that he did not like. Indeed, the precedent for impounding funds goes back at least to the administration of Thomas Jefferson.

But what has precedent is not thereby constitutional. The Constitution is silent on whether the president *must* spend the money that Congress appropriates; all it says is that the president cannot spend money that Congress has *not* appropriated. The major test of presidential power in this respect occurred during the Nixon administration. Nixon wished to reduce federal spending. He proposed in 1972 that Congress give him the power to reduce federal spending so that it would not exceed $250 billion for the coming year. Congress, under Democratic control, refused. Nixon responded by pocket-vetoing 12 spending bills and then impounding funds appropriated under other laws that he had not vetoed.

Landmark Cases

Powers of the President

- **United States v. Nixon (1974):** Though the president is entitled to receive confidential advice, he can be required to reveal material related to a criminal prosecution.
- **Nixon v. Fitzgerald (1982):** The president may not be sued while in office.
- **Clinton v. Jones (1997):** The president may be sued for actions taken before he became president.

Congress in turn responded by passing the Budget Reform Act of 1974, which, among other things, requires the president to spend all appropriated funds unless he first tells Congress what funds he wishes not to spend and Congress, within 45 days, agrees to delete the items. If he wishes simply to delay spending the money, he need only inform Congress, but Congress then can refuse the delay by passing a resolution requiring the immediate release of the money. Federal courts have upheld the rule that the president must spend, without delay for policy reasons, money that Congress has appropriated.

SIGNING STATEMENTS

Since at least the presidency of James Monroe, the White House has issued statements at the time the president signs a bill that has been passed by Congress. These statements have had several purposes: to express presidential attitudes about the law, to tell the executive branch how to implement it, or to declare that the president thinks some part of the law is unconstitutional. President Andrew Jackson, for example, issued a statement in 1830 saying that a law designed to build a road from Chicago to Detroit should not cross the Michigan boundary (and so not get to Chicago). Congress complained, but Jackson's view prevailed and the road did not get to Chicago.

In the 20th century, these statements became common. President Reagan issued 71, President George H. W. Bush signed 141, and President Clinton inked 105. By the late 1980s, they were published in legal documents as part of the legislative history of a bill.[16] During his two terms, President George W. Bush signed more than 150, and in so doing, he challenged more than 1,200 sections of legislation, about double the number challenged by all of his predecessors. Between his inauguration and early 2011, President Obama (who campaigned against the use of signing statements) signed 14.[17]

Naturally, members of Congress are upset by this practice. To them, a **signing statement** often blocks the enforcement of a law Congress has passed and so it is equivalent to an unconstitutional line-item veto. But presidential advisers have defended these documents, arguing (as did an assistant attorney general in the Clinton administration) that they not only clarify how the law should be implemented but also allow the president to declare what part of the law is in his view unconstitutional and thus ought not to be enforced at all.[18]

signing statement A presidential document that reveals what the president thinks of a new law and how it ought to be enforced.

While the Supreme Court has allowed signing statements to clarify the unclear legislative intent of a law, it has never given a clear verdict about the constitutional significance of such documents.[19] By 2007, the Democratic Congress was considering a challenge to the practice, and President Barack Obama issued a memo less than three months after taking office stating that he would use signing statements only to protest unconstitutional provisions on legislation, not for policy disagreements. But even with unified government, President Obama issued a few signing statements during his first year in office, and members of Congress criticized him for doing so. The struggle over signing statements is another illustration of what one scholar has called the "invitation to struggle" that the Constitution has created between the president and Congress.[20]

Presidential Character

Although all presidents share certain constitutional and political powers, every president brings to the White House a distinctive personality; the way the White House is organized and run will reflect that personality. Moreover, the public will judge the president not only in terms of what he accomplishes, but also in terms of its perception of his character. Thus, personality plays a more important role in explaining the presidency than it does in explaining Congress.

Dwight Eisenhower brought an orderly, military style to the White House. He was accustomed to delegating authority and to having careful and complete staff work done for him by trained specialists. Though critics often accused him of having a bumbling, incoherent manner of speaking, in fact much of that was a public disguise—a strategy for avoiding being pinned down in public on matters where he wished to retain freedom of action. His private papers reveal a very different Eisenhower—sharp, precise, deliberate.

John Kennedy brought a very different style to the presidency. He projected the image of a bold, articulate, and amusing leader who liked to surround himself with talented amateurs. Instead of clear, hierarchical lines of authority, there was a pattern of personal rule and an atmosphere of improvisation. Kennedy did not hesitate to call very junior subordinates directly and tell them what to do, bypassing the chain of command.

Lyndon Johnson was a master legislative strategist who had risen to be majority leader of the Senate on the strength of his ability to persuade other politicians in face-to-face encounters. He was a consummate deal maker who, having been in Washington for 30 years before becoming president, knew everybody and everything. As a result he tried to make every decision himself. But the style that served him well in political negotiations did not serve him well in speaking to the country at large, especially when trying to retain public support for the war in Vietnam.

Richard Nixon was a highly intelligent man with a deep knowledge of and interest in foreign policy, coupled with a deep suspicion of the media, his political rivals, and the federal bureaucracy. In contrast to Johnson, he disliked personal confrontations and tended to shield himself behind an elaborate staff system. Distrustful of the cabinet agencies, he tried first to centralize power in the White House and then to put into key cabinet posts former White House aides loyal to him. Like Johnson, his personality made it difficult for him to mobilize popular support. Eventually, he was forced to resign under the threat of impeachment arising out of his role in the Watergate scandal.

Gerald Ford, before being appointed vice president, had spent his political life in Congress and was at home with the give-and-take, discussion-oriented procedures of that body. He was also a genial man who liked talking to people. Thus, he preferred the circular to the pyramid system of White House organization. But this meant that many decisions were made in a disorganized fashion in which key people—and sometimes key problems—were not taken into account.

Jimmy Carter was an outsider to Washington and boasted of it. A former Georgia governor, he was determined not to be "captured" by Washington insiders. He also was a voracious reader with a wide range of interests and an appetite for detail. These dispositions led him to try to do many things and to do them personally. Like Ford, he began with a circular structure; unlike Ford, he based his decisions on reading countless memos and asking detailed questions. His advisers finally decided that he was trying to do too much in too great detail, and toward the end of his term he shifted to a pyramid structure.

Ronald Reagan was also an outsider, a former governor of California. But unlike Carter, he wanted to set the broad directions of his administration and leave the details to others. He gave wide latitude to subordinates and to cabinet officers, within the framework of an emphasis on lower taxes, less domestic spending, a military buildup, and a tough line with the Soviet Union. He was a superb leader of public opinion, earning the nickname "The Great Communicator."

George H. W. Bush lacked Reagan's speaking skills and was much more of a hands-on manager. Drawing on his extensive experience in the federal government (he had been vice president, director of the CIA, ambassador to the United Nations, representative to China, and a member of the House), Bush made decisions on the basis of personal contacts with key foreign leaders and Washington officials.

Bill Clinton, like Carter, paid a lot of attention to public policy and preferred informal, ad hoc arrangements for running his office. Unlike Carter, he was an effective speaker who could make almost any idea sound plausible. He was elected as a centrist Democrat but immediately pursued liberal policies such as comprehensive health insurance. When those failed and the Republicans won control of Congress in 1994, Clinton became a centrist again. His sexual affairs became the object of major investigations, and he was impeached by the House but acquitted by the Senate.

George W. Bush, the 43rd president, entered office as an outsider from Texas, but he was an outsider with a difference: his father had served as the 41st president of the United States, his late paternal grandfather had served as a U.S. senator from Connecticut, and he won the presidency only after the U.S. Supreme Court halted a recount of ballots in Florida, where his brother was governor. During the campaign, he focused almost entirely on domestic issues, especially cutting taxes and reforming education. A deeply religious man, he talked openly about how he had stopped excessive drinking only after he had found God. He ran as a "compassionate conservative" concerned about America's needy children and families. Bush, who had earned an advanced degree in business administration from Harvard, ran a very tight White House ship, insisting that meetings run on time and that press contacts be strictly controlled. He turned back public doubts about his intellect through self-deprecating humor. Following the terrorist attack on America on September 11, 2001, his agenda shifted almost entirely to foreign and military affairs, the war on terror, and the issue of homeland security.

Barack Obama succeeded Bush in 2009. He was the first African American to win a major party's presidential nomination and only the third person elected to the presidency while a sitting U.S. Senator. After Harvard, he taught constitutional law part-time at the University of Chicago. After entering politics and winning an Illinois State

Senate seat, he was elected to the U.S. Senate in 2004. His electrifying speech at the 2004 Democratic National Convention catapulted him to national attention. He criticized Democratic presidential candidates who had supported military action against Iraq, and he campaigned in 2008 as the candidate of change and hope ("Yes we can!" was his most popular mantra). He came to office in January 2009 amid a global economic crisis that included devastating losses in America's real-estate sector and financial markets. In his first two years in office, he passed the largest budget in U.S. history and enacted legislation for comprehensive health insurance.

The Office of the President

It was not until 1857 that the president was allowed to have a private secretary paid for with public funds, and it was not until after the assassination of President McKinley in 1901 that the president was given a Secret Service bodyguard. The president was not able to submit a single presidential budget until after 1921, when the Budget and Accounting Act was passed and the Bureau of the Budget (now called the Office of Management and Budget) was created. Grover Cleveland personally answered the White House telephone, and Abraham Lincoln often answered his own mail.

pyramid structure A president's subordinates report to him through a clear chain of command headed by a chief of staff.

circular structure Several of the president's assistants report directly to him.

ad hoc structure Several subordinates, cabinet officers, and committees report directly to the president on different matters.

Today, of course, the president has hundreds of people assisting him, and the trappings of power—helicopters, guards, limousines—are plainly visible. The White House staff has grown enormously. (Just how big the staff is, no one knows. Presidents like to pretend that the White House is not the large bureaucracy that it in fact has become.) Add to this the opportunities for presidential appointments to the cabinet, the courts, and various agencies, and the resources at the disposal of the president would appear to be awesome. That conclusion is partly true and partly false, or at least misleading, and for a simple reason. If the president was once helpless for lack of assistance, he now confronts an army of assistants so large that it constitutes a bureaucracy he has difficulty controlling.

The ability of a presidential assistant to affect the president is governed by the rule of propinquity: in general, power is wielded by people in the room when a decision is made. Presidential appointments can thus be classified in terms of their proximity, physical and political, to the president. There are three degrees of propinquity: the White House Office, the Executive Office, and the cabinet.

THE WHITE HOUSE OFFICE

The president's closest assistants have offices in the White House, usually in the West Wing of that building. Their titles often do not reveal the functions that they actually perform: "counsel," "counselor," "assistant to the president," "special assistant," "special consultant," and so forth. The actual titles vary from one administration to another, but in general the men and women who hold them oversee the political and policy interests of the president. As part of the president's personal staff, these aides do not have to be confirmed by the Senate; the president can hire and fire them at will. In 2001, the Bush White House had 400 staff members and a budget of $35.4 million.

There are essentially three ways in which a president can organize his personal staff—through the "pyramid," "circular," and "ad hoc" methods. In a **pyramid structure,** used by Eisenhower, Nixon, Reagan, Bush, and (after a while) Clinton, most assistants report through a hierarchy to a chief of staff, who then deals directly with the president. In a **circular structure,** used by Carter, cabinet secretaries and assistants report directly to the president. In an **ad hoc structure,** used for a while by President Clinton, task forces, committees, and informal groups of friends and advisers deal directly with the president. For example, the Clinton administration's health care policy planning was spearheaded not by Health and Human Services secretary Donna E. Shalala, but by First Lady Hillary Rodham Clinton and a White House adviser, Ira Magaziner. Likewise, its initiative to reform the federal bureaucracy (the National Performance Review) was led not by Office of Management and Budget director Leon E. Panetta, but by an adviser to Vice President Gore, Elaine Kamarck.[21]

It is common for presidents to mix methods. For example, Franklin Roosevelt alternated between the circular and ad hoc methods in the conduct of his domestic policy and sometimes employed a pyramid structure when dealing with foreign affairs and military policy.

Taken individually, each method of organization has advantages and disadvantages. A pyramid structure provides for an orderly flow of information and decisions, but does so at the risk of isolating or misinforming the president. The circular method has the virtue of giving the president a great deal of information, but at the price of confusion and conflict among cabinet secretaries and assistants. An ad hoc structure allows great flexibility, minimizes bureaucratic inertia, and generates ideas and information from disparate channels, but it risks cutting the president off from the government officials who are ultimately responsible for translating presidential decisions into policy proposals and administrative action.

All presidents claim they are open to many sources of advice, and some presidents try to guarantee that openness by using the circular method of staff organization. President Carter liked to describe his office as a wheel with himself as the hub and his several assistants as spokes. But most presidents discover, as did Carter, that the difficulty of managing the large White House bureaucracy and of conserving their own limited supply of time and energy makes it necessary for them to rely heavily on one or two key subordinates. Carter, in July 1979, dramatically altered the White House staff organization by elevating Hamilton Jordan to the post of chief of staff, with the job of coordinating the work of the other staff assistants.

At first, President Reagan adopted a compromise between the circle and the pyramid, putting the White House under the direction of three key aides. At the beginning of his second term in 1985, however, the president shifted to a pyramid, placing all his assistants under a single chief of staff. Clinton began with an ad hoc system and then changed to one more like a pyramid. Each assistant has, of course, others working for him or her, sometimes a large number. There are, at a slightly lower level of status, "special assistants to the president" for various purposes. (Being "special" means, paradoxically, being less important.)

Typically, senior White House staff members are drawn from the ranks of the president's campaign staff—longtime associates in whom he has

How Things Work

The Myth and Reality of the White House Office

The Myth

The White House Office was created in the 1930s following recommendations made by the President's Commission on Administrative Management. The principles underlying those recommendations have been endorsed by almost every presidential chief of staff since then. The key ones are:

1. *Small is beautiful.* The presidential staff should be small. At first, there were only six assistants.
2. *A passion for anonymity.* The president's personal assistants should stay out of the limelight.
3. *Honest brokers.* The presidential staff should not make decisions for the president; it should only coordinate the flow of information to the president.

The Reality

Increasingly, the operations of the White House Office seem to reflect almost the exact opposite of these principles.

1. *Big is better.* The White House staff has grown enormously in size. Hundreds now work there.
2. *Get out front.* Key White House staffers have become household words—Henry Kissinger (under Nixon and Ford), H. R. Haldeman (under Nixon), Hamilton Jordan (under Carter), Howard Baker (under Reagan), George Stephanopoulos (under Clinton), and Karl Rove (under G. W. Bush).
3. *Be in charge.* Cabinet officers regularly complain that White House staffers are shutting them out and making all the important decisions. Congressional investigations have revealed the power of such White House aides as Haldeman, John Poindexter, and Lieutenant Colonel Oliver North.

Why the Gap Between Myth and Reality?

The answer is—the people and the government. The people expect much more from presidents today; no president can afford to say, "We're too busy here to worry about that." The government is much more complex, and so leadership requires more resources. Even conservatives such as Ronald Reagan have been activist presidents.

Source: Adapted from Samuel Kernell and Samuel L. Popkin, eds., *Chief of Staff* (Berkeley: University of California Press, 1986), 193–232.

confidence. A few members, however, will be experts brought in after the campaign: such was the case, for example, with Henry Kissinger, a former Harvard professor who became President Nixon's assistant for national security affairs. The offices these men and women occupy often are small and crowded (Kissinger's was not much bigger than the one he had while a professor at Harvard), but their occupants willingly put up with any discomfort in exchange for the privilege (and the power) of being *in* the White House. The arrangement of offices—their size, and especially their proximity to the president's Oval Office—is a good measure of the relative influence of the people in them.

To an outsider, the amount of jockeying among the top staff for access to the president may seem comical or even perverse. The staff attaches enormous significance to whose office is closest to the president's, who can see him on a daily as opposed to a weekly basis, who can get an appointment with the president and who cannot, and who has a right to see documents and memoranda just before they go to the Oval Office. To be sure, there is ample grist here for Washington political novels. But there is also something important at stake: it is not simply a question of power plays and ego trips. Who can see the president and who sees and "signs off" on memoranda going to the president affect in important ways who influences policy and thus whose goals and beliefs become embedded in policy.

For example, if a memo from a secretary of the treasury who believes in free trade can go directly to the president, the president may be more likely to support free trade (low tariffs). On the other hand, if that memo must be routed through the office of the assistant to the president for political affairs, who is worried about the adverse effects of foreign competition on jobs in the American steel industry because the votes of steelworkers are important to the president's reelection campaign, then the president may be led to support higher tariffs.

THE EXECUTIVE OFFICE OF THE PRESIDENT

Agencies in the Executive Office report directly to the president and perform staff services for him but are not located in the White House itself. Their members may or may not enjoy intimate contact with him; some agencies are rather large bureaucracies. The top positions in these organizations are filled by presidential appointment, but unlike the White House staff positions, these appointments must be confirmed by the Senate.

cabinet The heads of the 15 executive branch departments of the federal government.

The principal agencies in the Executive Office are:

- Office of Management and Budget (OMB)
- Director of National Intelligence (DNI)
- Council of Economic Advisers (CEA)
- Office of Personnel Management (OPM)
- Office of the U.S. Trade Representative

Of all the agencies in the Executive Office of the President, perhaps the most important in terms of the president's need for assistance in administering the federal government is the Office of Management and Budget. First called the Bureau of the Budget when it was created in 1921, it became OMB in 1970 to reflect its broader responsibilities. Today it does considerably more than assemble and analyze the figures that go each year into the national budget the president submits to Congress. It also studies the organization and operations of the executive branch, devises plans for reorganizing various departments and agencies, develops ways of getting better information about government programs, and reviews proposals that cabinet departments want included in the president's legislative program.

The OMB has a staff of more than 500 people, almost all career civil servants, many of high professional skill and substantial experience. Traditionally, OMB has been a nonpartisan agency—experts serving all presidents, without regard to party or ideology. Starting with the Reagan administration, however, OMB has played a major role in advocating policies rather than merely analyzing them. David Stockman, President Reagan's OMB director, was the primary architect of the 1981 and 1985 budget cuts proposed by the president and enacted by Congress. Stockman's proposals often were adopted over the objections of the affected department heads. In 2001, President George W. Bush's OMB director, Mitch Daniels, also participated fully in West Wing political strategy sessions; he later was elected governor of Indiana. In 2009, President Obama appointed Peter Orzag, a former think-tank and university researcher who had served as an economic adviser to President Clinton and as a budget analyst in Congress, to head OMB. Whether Orzag's appointment presaged a return to OMB's earlier tradition as a mostly nonpartisan body remains to be seen.

THE CABINET

The **cabinet** is a product of tradition and hope. At one time, the heads of the federal departments met regularly with the president to discuss matters, and some people, especially those critical of strong presidents, would like to see this kind of collegial decision making reestablished. But in fact this role of the cabinet is largely a fiction. Indeed, the Constitution does not even mention the cabinet (though the Twenty-fifth Amendment implicitly defines it as consisting of "the principal offices of the executive departments"). When Washington tried to get his cabinet members to work together, its two strongest members—Alexander Hamilton and Thomas Jefferson—spent most of their time feuding. The cabinet, as a presidential committee, did not work any better for John Adams or Abraham Lincoln, for Franklin Roosevelt or John Kennedy. Dwight Eisenhower is almost the only modern president who came close to making the cabinet a truly deliberative body: he gave it a large staff, held regular meetings, and listened to opinions expressed there. But even under Eisenhower, the cabinet did not have much influence over presidential decisions, nor did it help him gain more power over the government.

By custom, cabinet officers are the heads of the 15 major executive departments. These departments, together with the dates of their creation and the approximate number of their employees, are given in Table 14.4. The order of their creation is unimportant except in terms of protocol: where one sits at cabinet meetings is determined by the age of the department that one heads. Thus, the secretary of state sits next to the president on one side and the secretary of the treasury next to him on the other. Down at the foot of the table are the heads of the newer departments.

The president appoints or directly controls vastly more members of his cabinet departments than does the British prime minister. The reason is simple: the president must struggle with Congress for control of these agencies, while the prime minister has no rival branch of government that seeks this power. Presidents get more appointments than prime ministers to make up for what the separation of powers denies them.

This abundance of political appointments, however, does not give the president ample power over the departments. The secretary of Health and Human Services (HHS) reports to the president and has a few hundred political appointees to assist him or her in responding to the president's wishes. But the secretary of HHS heads an agency with more than 60,000 employees, 11 operating divisions, hundreds of grant-making programs, and a budget of more than $460 billion. Likewise, the secretary of Housing and Urban Development (HUD) spends most of his or her time on departmental business and vastly less on talking to the president. It is hardly surprising that the secretary is largely a representative of HUD to the president than his representative to HUD. And no one should be surprised that the secretary of HUD rarely finds much to talk about with the secretary of defense at cabinet meetings.

Table 14.4 The Cabinet Departments

Department	Created	Approximate Employment (2009)
State	1789	36,762
Treasury	1789	110,686
Defense[a]	1947	714,483
Justice	1789	111,214
Interior	1849	71,536
Agriculture[b]	1889	97,803
Commerce	1913	74,305
Labor	1913	16,316
Health and Human Services[c]	1953	65,389
Housing and Urban Development	1965	9,636
Transportation	1966	56,310
Energy	1977	15,613
Education	1979	4,097
Veterans Affairs	1989	289,335
Homeland Security	2002	177,428

[a]Formerly the War Department, created in 1789. Figures are for civilians only.

[b]Agriculture Department created in 1862; made part of cabinet in 1889.

[c]Originally Health, Education and Welfare; reorganized in 1979.

Source: *Statistical Abstract of the United States, 2011,* table 497.

Having the power to make these appointments does give the president one great advantage: he has a lot of opportunities to reward friends and political supporters. In the Education Department, for example, President Clinton found jobs for onetime mayors, senators, state legislators, and campaign aides.

INDEPENDENT AGENCIES, COMMISSIONS, AND JUDGESHIPS

The president also appoints people to four dozen or so agencies and commissions that are not considered part of the cabinet and that by law often have a quasi-independent status. The difference between an "executive" and an "independent" agency is not precise. In general, it means the heads of executive agencies serve at the pleasure of the president and can be removed at his discretion. On the other hand, the heads of many independent agencies serve for fixed terms of office and can be removed only "for cause" (see box on page 393).

The president can also appoint federal judges, subject to the consent of the Senate. Judges serve for life unless they are removed by impeachment and conviction. The reason for the special barriers to the removal of judges is that they represent an independent branch of government as defined by the Constitution, and limits on presidential removal powers are necessary to preserve that independence.

One new feature of appointing top government officials is the increasing use of "acting" appointments. An acting appointee holds office until the Senate acts on his or her nomination. In 1998, acting officials held one-fifth of all of the Clinton administration's cabinet-level (or subcabinet-level)* jobs. Some were in office for many months. Many senators feel that this violates their right to consent to appointments and in particular violates the Vacancies Act passed in 1868. That law limits acting appointees to 120 days in office. If the Senate takes no action during those 120 days, the acting official may stay in office until he or she, or someone else, is confirmed for the post. Administration officials defend the practice as necessary given the slow pace of confirmations; senators attack it as an opportunity for a president to fill up his administration with unconfirmed officials.

Who Gets Appointed

As we have seen, a president can make a lot of appointments, but he rarely knows more than a few of the people whom he does appoint.

Unlike cabinet members in a parliamentary system, the president's cabinet officers and their principal deputies usually have not served with the chief executive in the legislature. Instead they come from private business, universities, think tanks, foundations, law firms, labor unions, and the ranks of former and present members of Congress as well as past state and local government officials. A president is fortunate if most cabinet members turn out to agree with him on major policy questions. President Reagan made a special effort to ensure that his cabinet members were ideologically in tune with him, but even so Secretary of State Alexander Haig soon got into a series of quarrels with senior members of the White House staff and had to resign.

The men and women appointed to the cabinet and to the subcabinet usually will have had some prior federal experience. One study of more than a thousand such appointments made by five presidents (Franklin Roosevelt through Lyndon Johnson) found that about 85 percent of the cabinet, subcabinet, and independent-agency appointees had some prior federal experience. In fact, most were in government service (at the federal, state, or local levels) just before they received their cabinet or subcabinet appointment.[22] Clearly, the executive branch is not, in general, run by novices.

Many of these appointees are what Richard Neustadt has called "in-and-outers": people who alternate between jobs in the federal government and ones in the private sector, especially in law firms and in universities. Donald Rumsfeld, before becoming secretary of defense to President George W. Bush, had been secretary of defense and chief of staff under President Ford and before that a member of Congress. Between his Ford and Bush services, he was an executive in a large pharmaceutical company. This pattern is quite different from that of parliamentary systems, where all the cabinet officers come from the legislature and typically are full-time career politicians.

At one time, the cabinet had in it many people with strong political followings of their own—former senators and governors and powerful local party leaders. Under Franklin Roosevelt, Truman, and Kennedy, the postmaster general was the president's campaign manager. George Washington, Abraham Lincoln, and other presidents had to contend with cabinet members who were powerful figures in their own right: Alexander Hamilton and Thomas Jefferson worked with Washington; Simon Cameron (a Pennsylvania political boss) and Salmon P. Chase (formerly governor of Ohio) worked for—and against—Lincoln. Before 1824, the post of secretary of state was regarded as a stepping stone to the presidency; and after that at least 10 persons ran for president who had been either secretary of state or ambassador to a foreign country.[23]

Of late, however, a tendency has developed for presidents to place in their cabinets people known for their expertise or administrative experience rather than for their political following. This is in part because political parties are now so weak that party leaders can no longer demand a place in the cabinet and in part because presidents want (or think they want) "experts." A remarkable illustration of this is the number of people with Ph.Ds who have entered

* *Subcabinet* refers to undersecretary, deputy secretary, and assistant secretaries in each cabinet department.

the cabinet. President Nixon, who supposedly did not like Harvard professors, appointed two—Henry Kissinger and Daniel Patrick Moynihan—to important posts; Gerald Ford added a third, John Dunlop.

A president's desire to appoint experts who do not have independent political power is modified—but not supplanted—by his need to recognize various politically important groups, regions, and organizations. Since Robert Weaver became the first African American to serve in the cabinet (as secretary of HUD under President Johnson), it is clear that it would be quite costly for a president *not* to have one or more blacks in his cabinet. The secretary of labor must be acceptable to the AFL-CIO, the secretary of agriculture to at least some organized farmers. Each of the last three presidents (Bill Clinton, George W. Bush, and Barack Obama) appointed several women and minorities to his cabinet.

Because political considerations must be taken into account in making cabinet and agency appointments and because any head of a large organization will tend to adopt the perspective of that organization, there is an inevitable tension—even a rivalry—between the White House staff and the department heads. Staff members see themselves as extensions of the president's personality and policies; department heads see themselves as repositories of expert knowledge (often knowledge of why something will not work as the president hopes). White House staffers, many of them young men and women in their 20s or early 30s with little executive experience, will call department heads, often persons in their 50s with substantial executive experience, and tell them "the president wants" this or that or "the president asked me to tell you" one thing or another. Department heads try to conceal their irritation and then maneuver for some delay so they can develop their own counterproposals. On the other hand, when department heads call a White House staff person and ask to see the president, unless they are one of the privileged few in whom the president has special confidence, they often are told that "the president can't be bothered with that" or "the president doesn't have time to see you."

How Things Work

Federal Agencies

The following agencies are classified by whether the president has unlimited or limited right of removal.

"Executive" Agencies

Head can be removed at any time.

- Action
- Arms Control and Disarmament Agency
- Commission on Civil Rights
- Energy Research and Development Agency
- Environmental Protection Agency
- Federal Mediation and Conciliation Service
- General Services Administration
- National Aeronautics and Space Administration
- Postal Service
- Small Business Administration
- All cabinet departments
- Executive Office of the President

"Independent" or "Quasi-Independent" Agencies

Members serve for a fixed term.

- Federal Reserve Board (14 years)
- Consumer Product Safety Commission (6 years)
- Equal Employment Opportunity Commission (5 years)
- Federal Communications Commission (7 years)
- Federal Deposit Insurance Corporation (6 years)
- Federal Energy Regulatory Commission (5 years)
- Federal Maritime Commission (5 years)
- Federal Trade Commission (7 years)
- National Labor Relations Board (5 years)
- National Science Foundation (6 years)
- Securities and Exchange Commission (5 years)
- Tennessee Valley Authority (9 years)

Bettman/CORBIS

Bob Daemmrich/PhotoEdit

Secretary of Labor Frances Perkins (left), appointed by President Franklin Roosevelt, was the first woman cabinet member. When Condoleezza Rice was selected by President George W. Bush to be National Security Advisor, she became the first woman to hold that position (and later the first African American woman to be Secretary of State).

The President's Program

Imagine you have just spent three or four years running for president, during which time you have given essentially the same speech over and over again. You have had no time to study the issues in any depth. To reach a large television audience, you have couched your ideas largely in rather simple—if not simple-minded—slogans. Your principal advisers are political aides, not legislative specialists.

You win. You are inaugurated. Now you must *be* a president instead of just talking about it. You must fill hundreds of appointive posts, but you know personally only a handful of the candidates. You must deliver a State of the Union message to Congress only two or three weeks after you are sworn in. It is quite possible you have never read, much less written, such a message before. You must submit a new budget; the old one is hundreds of pages long, much of it comprehensible only to experts. Foreign governments, as well as the stock market, hang on your every word, interpreting many of your remarks in ways that totally surprise you. What will you do?

The Constitution is not much help. It directs you to report on the state of the union and to recommend "such measures" as you shall judge "necessary and expedient." Beyond that, you are charged to "take care that the laws be faithfully executed."

At one time, of course, the demands placed on a newly elected president were not very great, because the president was not expected to do very much. The president, on assuming office, might speak of the tariff, or relations with England, or the value of veterans' pensions, or the need for civil service reform, but he was not expected to have something to say (and offer) to everybody. Today he is.

PUTTING TOGETHER A PROGRAM

To develop policies on short notice, a president will draw on several sources, each with particular strengths and weaknesses:

- **Interest groups**

Strength: Will have specific plans and ideas.
Weakness: Will have narrow view of the public interest.

- **Aides and campaign advisers**

Strength: Will test new ideas for their political soundness.
Weakness: Will not have many ideas to test; inexperienced in government.

- **Federal bureaus and agencies**

Strength: Will know what is feasible in terms of governmental realities.
Weakness: Will propose plans that promote own agencies and will not have good information on whether plans will work.

- **Outside, academic, and other specialists and experts**

Strength: Will have many general ideas and criticisms of existing programs.
Weakness: Will not know the details of policy or have good judgment as to what is feasible.

There are essentially two ways for a president to develop a program. One, exemplified by Presidents Carter and Clinton, is to have a policy on almost everything. To do this, they worked endless hours and studied countless documents, trying to learn something about and then state their positions on, a large number of issues. The other method, illustrated by President Reagan, is to concentrate on three or four major initiatives or themes and leave everything else to subordinates.

But even when a president has a governing philosophy, as did Reagan, he cannot risk plunging ahead on his own. He must judge public and congressional reaction to this program before he commits himself fully to it. Therefore, he often will allow parts of his program to be "leaked" to the press, or "floated" as a trial balloon. Reagan's commitment to a 30 percent tax cut and larger military expenditures was so well known that it required no leaking, but he did have to float his ideas on Social Security and certain budget cuts to test popular reaction. His opponents in the bureaucracy did exactly the same thing, hoping for the opposite effect. They leaked controversial parts of the program in an effort to discredit the whole policy. This process of testing the winds by a president and his critics helps explain why so many news stories coming from Washington mention no person by name but only an anonymous "highly placed source."

In addition to the risks of adverse reaction, the president faces three other constraints on his ability to plan a program. One is the sheer limit of his time and attention span. Every president works harder than he has ever worked before. A 90-hour week is typical. Even so, he has great difficulty keeping up with all the things he is supposed to know and make decisions about. For example, Congress during an average year passes between 400 and 600 bills, each of which the president must sign, veto, or allow to take effect without his signature. Scores of people wish to see him. Hundreds of phone calls must be made to members of Congress and others in order to ask for help, to smooth ruffled feathers, or to get information. He must receive all newly appointed ambassadors and visiting heads of state and in addition have his picture taken with countless people, from a Nobel Prize winner to a child whose likeness will appear on the Easter Seal.

The second constraint is the unexpected crisis. Franklin Roosevelt obviously had to respond to a depression and to the mounting risks of world war. But most presidents get their crises when they least expect them. Consider these crises:

Kennedy

- Failure of Bay of Pigs invasion of Cuba
- Soviets put missiles in Cuba
- China invades India
- Federal troops sent to the South to protect blacks

Johnson

- Vietnam War
- Black riots in major cities
- War between India and Pakistan
- Civil war in Dominican Republic
- Arab-Israeli war
- Civil rights workers murdered in South

Nixon

- Watergate scandal
- Arab-Israeli war
- Value of dollar falls in foreign trade
- Arabs raise the price of oil

Carter

- OMB director Bert Lance accused of improprieties
- Lengthy coal strike
- Seizure of American hostages in Iran
- Soviet invasion of Afghanistan

Reagan

- Poland suppresses Solidarity movement
- U.S. troops sent to Lebanon
- U.S. hostages held in Lebanon
- Civil war in Nicaragua
- Iran-Contra crisis

George H.W. Bush

- Soviet Union dissolves
- Iraq invades Kuwait

Clinton

- Civil war continues in Bosnia and other parts of the former Yugoslavia

- Investigation of possible wrongdoing of President and Mrs. Clinton in Whitewater real estate development
- Clinton impeached

George W. Bush

- Terrorist attacks on World Trade Center and Pentagon kill close to 3,000 people
- U.S.-led wars against terrorists in Afghanistan and Iraq

Obama

- Economic crisis affecting financial markets, industry, and employment

The third constraint is that the federal government and most federal programs, as well as the federal budget, can only be changed marginally, except in special circumstances. The vast bulk of federal expenditures are beyond control in any given year: the money must be spent whether the president likes it or not. Many federal programs have such strong congressional or public support that they must be left intact or modified only slightly. And this means that most federal employees can count on being secure in their jobs, whatever a president's views on reducing the bureaucracy.

The result of these constraints is that the president, at least in ordinary times, has to be selective about what he wants. He can be thought of as having a stock of influence and prestige the way that he might have a supply of money. If he wants to get the most "return" on his resources, he must "invest" that influence and prestige carefully in enterprises that promise substantial gains—in public benefits and political support—at reasonable costs. Each president tends to speak in terms of changing everything at once, calling his approach a "New Deal," a "New Frontier," a "Great Society," or the "New Federalism." But beneath the rhetoric, he must identify a few specific proposals on which he wishes to bet his resources, mindful of the need to leave a substantial stock of resources in reserve to handle the inevitable crises and emergencies. In recent decades, events have required every president to devote much of his time and resources to two key issues: the state of the economy and foreign affairs. What he manages to do beyond this will depend on his personal views and his sense of what the nation, as well as his reelection, requires.

And it will depend on one other thing: opinion polls. The last president who never used polls was Herbert Hoover. Franklin Roosevelt began making heavy use of them, and every president since has relied on them. Bill Clinton had voters polled about almost everything—where he should go on vacation (the West) and how to deal with Bosnia (no ground troops).

A group of Civilian Conservation Corps workers hired by the government during the Great Depression.

Once, when polls did not exist, politicians often believed they should do what they thought the public interest required. Now that polls are commonplace, some politicians act on the basis of what their constituents want. Scholars call the first view the trustee approach: do what the public good requires, even if the voters are skeptical. The second view is the delegate model: do what your constituents want you to do.

But there is another way of looking at polls. They may be a device not for picking a policy, but for deciding what language to use in explaining that policy. Choose a policy that helps you get reelected or that satisfies an interest group, but then explain it with poll-tested words. President Clinton wanted to keep affirmative action (described in the chapter titled "Civil Rights"), but knew that most voters disliked it. So he used a poll-tested phrase—"mend it but don't end it"—and then did nothing to mend it.

Finally, a president's program can be radically altered by a dramatic event or prolonged crisis. George W. Bush ran as a candidate interested in domestic issues and with little background in foreign affairs, but the terrorist attack of September 11, 2001, on the World Trade Center and the Pentagon dramatically changed his presidency into one preoccupied with foreign and military policy. Barack Obama campaigned against the war in Iraq but spent the first months of his presidency focused mainly on the country's sagging economy.

ATTEMPTS TO REORGANIZE

One item on the presidential agenda has been the same for almost every president since Herbert Hoover: reorganizing the executive branch of government. In the wake of the terrorist attack on the United States on September 11, 2001, the president, by executive order, created a new White House Office of Homeland Security, headed by his friend and former Pennsylvania governor, Tom Ridge. In the months that followed, it became clear to all, including the president, that he had given Ridge an impossible job. For one thing, despite its obvious importance, Ridge's office, like most units with the Executive Office of the President, had only a dozen or so full-time staff, little budgetary authority, and virtually no ability to make and enforce decisions regarding how cabinet agencies operated. Nobody could meaningfully coordinate the literally dozens of administrative units that the administration's new homeland security blueprint required Ridge's office to somehow manage.

To address this problem, President Bush called for a reorganization that would create the third-largest cabinet department encompassing 22 federal agencies, nearly 180,000 employees, and an annual budget of close to $40 billion. Among the federal agencies placed under the new Department of Homeland Security are the Coast Guard, the Customs Service, the Federal Emergency Management Agency, and the Immigration and Naturalization Service. A law authorizing the new Department of Homeland Security was enacted in November 2002, but it will take years and much effort for the new agency to become fully operational.

Important as it is, the ongoing attempt to reorganize the federal government around homeland security goals is neither the first, nor even the largest, reorganization effort made by a sitting president. With few exceptions, every president since 1928 has tried to change the structure of the staff, departments, and agencies that are theoretically subordinate to him. Every president has been appalled by the number of agencies that report to him and by the apparently helter-skelter manner in which they have grown up. But this is only one—and often not the most important—reason for wanting to reorganize. If a president wants to get something done, put new people in charge of a program, or recapture political support for a policy, it often is easier to do so by creating a new agency or reorganizing an old one than by abolishing a program, firing a subordinate, or passing a new law. Reorganization serves many objectives and thus is a recurring theme.

Legally, the president can reorganize his personal White House staff anytime he wishes. To reorganize in any important way the larger Executive Office of the President or any of the executive departments or agencies, however, Congress must first be consulted. For more than 40 years, this consultation usually took the form of submitting to Congress a reorganization plan that would take effect provided that neither the House nor the Senate passed, within 60 days, a concurrent resolution disapproving the plan (such a resolution was called a **legislative veto**). This procedure, first authorized by the Reorganization Act of 1939, could be used to change, but not create or abolish, an executive agency. In 1981, authority under that act expired, and Congress did not renew it. Two years later, the Supreme Court declared all legislative vetoes unconstitutional (see Chapter 15), and so today any presidential reorganization plan would have to take the form of a regular law, passed by Congress and signed by the president.

legislative veto The authority of Congress to block a presidential action after it has taken place. The Supreme Court has held that Congress does not have this power.

What has been said so far may well give the reader the impression that the president is virtually helpless. That is not the case. The *actual* power of the president can only be measured in terms of what he can accomplish. What this chapter has described so far is the office as the president finds it—the burdens, restraints, demands, complexities, and resources that he encounters on entering the Oval Office for the first time. Every president since Truman has commented feelingly on how limited the powers of the president seem from the inside compared to what they appear to be from the outside. Franklin Roosevelt compared his struggles with the bureaucracy to punching a feather bed; Truman wrote that the power of the president was chiefly the power to persuade people to do what they ought to do anyway. After in office a year or so, Kennedy spoke to interviewers about how much more complex the world appeared than he had first supposed. Johnson and Nixon were broken by the office and the events that happened there.

Yet Franklin Roosevelt helped create the modern presidency, with its vast organizational reach, and directed a massive war effort. Truman ordered two atomic bombs dropped on Japanese cities. Eisenhower sent American troops to Lebanon; Kennedy supported an effort to invade Cuba. Johnson sent troops to the Dominican Republic and to Vietnam; Nixon ordered an invasion of Cambodia;

Reagan launched an invasion of Grenada and sponsored an antigovernment insurgent group in Nicaragua; Bush invaded Panama and sent troops to the Persian Gulf to fight Iraq; Clinton sent troops to Haiti and Bosnia; George W. Bush ordered U.S. military operations in Afghanistan and Iraq; Barack Obama approved air strikes in Libya. Obviously Europeans, Russians, Vietnamese, Panamanians, Iraqis, and others do not think the American president is "helpless."

Presidential Transition

No president but Franklin Roosevelt has ever served more than two terms, and since the ratification of the Twenty-second Amendment in 1951, no president will ever again have the chance. But more than tradition or the Constitution escorts presidents from office. Only about one-third of the presidents since George Washington have been elected to a second term. Of the 27 not reelected, four died in office during their first term. But the remainder either did not seek or (more usually) could not obtain reelection.

Of the eight presidents who died in office, four were assassinated: Lincoln, Garfield, McKinley, and Kennedy. At least six other presidents were the objects of unsuccessful assassination attempts: Jackson, Theodore Roosevelt, Franklin Roosevelt, Truman, Ford, and Reagan. (There may have been attempts on other presidents that never came to public notice; the attempts mentioned here involved public efforts to fire weapons at presidents.)

Michael Evans/The White House

President Reagan, moments before he was shot on March 30, 1981, by a would-be assassin. The Twenty-fifth Amendment solves the problem of presidential disability by providing for an orderly transfer of power to the vice president.

The presidents who served two or more terms fall into certain periods, such as the Founding (Washington, Jefferson, Madison, Monroe) or wartime (Lincoln, Wilson, Roosevelt), or they happened to be in office during especially tranquil times (Monroe, McKinley, Eisenhower, Clinton), or some combination of the above. When the country was deeply divided, as during the years just before the Civil War and during the period of Reconstruction after it, it was the rare president who was reelected.

THE VICE PRESIDENT

Eight times a vice president has become president because of the death of his predecessor. It first happened to John Tyler, who became president in 1841 when William Henry Harrison died peacefully after only one month in office. The question for Tyler and for the country was substantial: was Tyler simply to be the acting president and a kind of caretaker until a new president was elected, or was he to be *president* in every sense of the word? Despite criticism and despite what might have been the contrary intention of the Framers of the Constitution, Tyler decided on the latter course and was confirmed in that opinion by a decision of Congress. Ever since, the vice president has automatically become president, in title and in powers, when the occupant of the White House has died or resigned.

But if vice presidents frequently acquire office because of death, they rarely acquire it by election. Since the earliest period of the Founding, when John Adams and Thomas Jefferson were each elected president after having first served as vice president under their predecessors, there have only been three occasions when a vice president was later able to win the presidency without his president's having died in office. One was in 1836, when Martin Van Buren was elected president after having served as Andrew Jackson's vice president; the second was in 1968, when Richard Nixon became president after having served as Dwight Eisenhower's vice president eight years earlier; the third was in 1988, when George Bush succeeded Ronald Reagan. Many vice presidents who entered the Oval Office because their predecessors died were subsequently elected to terms in their own right—Theodore Roosevelt, Calvin Coolidge, Harry Truman, and Lyndon Johnson. But no one who wishes to become president should assume that to become vice president first is the best way to get there.

The vice-presidency is just what so many vice presidents have complained about its being: a rather empty job. John Adams described it as "the most insignificant office that ever the invention of man contrived or his imagination conceived," and most of his successors would have agreed. Thomas Jefferson, almost alone, had a good word to say for it: "The second office of the government is honorable and easy, the first is but a splendid misery."[24] Daniel Webster rejected a vice-presidential nomination in 1848 with the phrase, "I do not choose to be buried until I am really dead."[25] (Had he taken the job, he would have become president after Zachary Taylor died in office, thereby achieving a remarkable secular resurrection.) For all the good and bad jokes about the vice-presidency, however, candidates still struggle mightily for it. John Nance Garner gave up the speakership of the House to become Franklin Roosevelt's vice president (a job he valued as "not worth a pitcher of warm spit"*), and Lyndon Johnson gave up the majority leadership of the Senate to become Kennedy's. Truman, Nixon, Humphrey, Mondale, and Gore all left reasonably secure Senate seats for the vice-presidency.

The only official task of the vice president is to preside over the Senate and to vote in case of a tie. Even this is scarcely time-consuming, as the Senate chooses from among its members a president pro tempore, as required by the Constitution, who (along with others) presides in the absence of the vice president. The vice president's leadership powers in the Senate are weak, especially when the vice president is of a different party from the majority of the senators. But on occasion the vice president can become very important. Right after the terrorists attacked the United States in 2001, President Bush was in his airplane while his advisers worried that he might be attacked next. Vice President Cheney was quickly hidden away in a secret, secure location so he could run the government if anything happened to President Bush. And for many months thereafter, Cheney stayed in this location in case he suddenly became president. But absent a crisis, the vice president is, at best, only an adviser to the president.

PROBLEMS OF SUCCESSION

If the president should die in office, the right of the vice president to assume that office has been clear since the time of John Tyler. But two questions remain: What if the president falls seriously ill, but does not die? And if the vice president steps up, who then becomes the new vice president?

The first problem has arisen on a number of occasions. After President James A. Garfield was shot in 1881, he lingered through the summer before he died. President Woodrow Wilson collapsed from a stroke and was a virtual recluse for seven months in 1919 and an invalid for the rest of his term. Eisenhower had three serious illnesses while in office; Reagan was shot during his first term and hospitalized during his second.

The second problem has arisen on eight occasions when the vice president became president owing to the death of the incumbent. In these cases, no elected person was available to succeed the new president, should he die in office. For many decades, the problem was handled by law. The Succession Act of 1886, for example, designated the secretary of state as next in line for the presidency should the vice president die, followed by the other cabinet officers in order of seniority. But this meant that a vice president who became president could pick his own successor by choosing his own secretary of state. In 1947, the law was changed to make the Speaker of the House and then the president pro tempore of the Senate next in line for the presidency. But that created still other problems: a Speaker or a president pro tempore is likely to be chosen because of seniority, not executive skill, and in any event might well be of the party opposite to that occupying the White House.

Both problems were addressed in 1967 by the Twenty-fifth Amendment to the Constitution. It deals with the disability problem by allowing the vice president to serve as "acting president" whenever the president declares he is unable to discharge the powers and duties of his office or whenever the vice president and a majority of the cabinet declare that the president is incapacitated. If the president disagrees with the opinion of his vice president and a majority of the cabinet, then Congress decides the issue. A two-thirds majority is necessary to confirm that the president is unable to serve.

The amendment deals with the succession problem by requiring a vice president who assumes the presidency (after a vacancy is created by death or resignation) to nominate a new vice president. This person takes office if the nomination is confirmed by a majority vote of both houses of Congress. When there is no vice president, then the 1947 law governs: next in line are the Speaker, the Senate president, and the 15 cabinet officers, beginning with the secretary of state.

* The word he actually used was a good deal stronger than *spit,* but historians are decorous.

The disability problem has not arisen since the adoption of the amendment, but the succession problem has. In 1973, Vice President Spiro Agnew resigned, having pleaded no contest to criminal charges. President Nixon nominated Gerald Ford as vice president, and after extensive hearings he was confirmed by both houses of Congress and sworn in. Then on August 9, 1974, Nixon resigned the presidency—the first man to do so—and Ford became president. He nominated as his vice president Nelson Rockefeller, who was confirmed by both houses of Congress—again, after extensive hearings—and was sworn in on December 19, 1974. For the first time in history, the nation had as its two principal executive officers men who had not been elected to either the presidency or the vice-presidency. It is a measure of the legitimacy of the Constitution that this arrangement caused no crisis in public opinion.

IMPEACHMENT

There is one other way—besides death, disability, or resignation—by which a president can leave office before his term expires, and that is by impeachment. Not only the president and vice president, but also all "civil officers of the United States" can be removed by being impeached and convicted. As a practical matter civil officers—cabinet secretaries, bureau chiefs, and the like—are not subject to impeachment, because the president can remove them at any time and usually will if their behavior makes them a serious political liability. Federal judges, who serve during "good behavior"† and who are constitutionally independent of the president and Congress, have been the most frequent objects of impeachment.

An **impeachment** is like an indictment in a criminal trial: a set of charges against somebody, voted by (in this case) the House of Representatives. To be removed from office, the impeached officer must be convicted by a two-thirds vote of the Senate, which sits as a court, is presided over by the Chief Justice, hears the evidence, and makes its decision under whatever rules it wishes to adopt. Sixteen persons have been impeached by the House, and seven have been convicted by the Senate. The last conviction was in 1989, when two federal judges were removed from office.

impeachment Charges against a president approved by a majority of the House of Representatives.

† "Good behavior" means a judge can stay in office until he retires or dies, unless he or she is impeached and convicted.

Only two presidents have ever been impeached—Andrew Johnson in 1868 and Bill Clinton in 1998. Richard Nixon would surely have been impeached in 1974, had he not resigned after the House Judiciary Committee voted to recommend impeachment.

The Senate did not convict either Johnson or Clinton by the necessary two-thirds vote. The case against Johnson was entirely political—Radical Republicans, who wished to punish the South after the Civil War, were angry at Johnson, a southerner, who had a soft policy toward the South. The argument against him was flimsy.

The case against Clinton was more serious. The House Judiciary Committee, relying on the report of independent counsel Kenneth Starr, charged Clinton with perjury (lying under oath about his sexual affair with Monica Lewinsky), obstruction of justice (trying to block the Starr investigation), and abuse of power (making false written statements to the Judiciary Committee). The vote to impeach was passed by the House along party lines. The Senate vote fell far short of the two-thirds required for conviction.

Why did Clinton survive? There were many factors. The public disliked his private behavior, but did not think it amounted to an impeachable offense. (In fact, right after Lewinsky revealed her sexual affair with him, his standing in opinion polls went up.) The economy was strong, and the nation was at peace. Clinton was a centrist Democrat who did not offend most voters.

The one casualty of the entire episode was the death of the law creating the office of the Independent Counsel. Passed in 1978 by a Congress that was upset by the Watergate crisis, the law directed the attorney general to ask a three-judge panel to appoint an independent counsel whenever a high official is charged with serious misconduct. (In 1993, when the 1978 law expired, President Clinton asked that it be passed again. It was.) Eighteen people were investigated by various independent counsels from 1978 to 1999. In about half the cases, no charges were brought to court.

For a long time, Republicans disliked the law because the counsels were investigating them. After Clinton came to office, the counsels started investigating him and his associates, and so the Democrats began to oppose it. In 1999, when the law expired, it was not renewed.

A problem remains, however. How will any high official, including the president, be investigated when the attorney general, who does most investigations, is part of the president's team? One answer is to let Congress do it, but Congress may be controlled by the president's party. No one has yet solved this puzzle.

Some Founders may have thought that impeachment would be used frequently against presidents, but as a practical matter it is so complex and serious an undertaking that we can probably expect it to be reserved in the future only for the gravest forms of presidential misconduct. No one quite knows what a high crime or misdemeanor is, but most scholars agree that the charge must involve something illegal or unconstitutional, not just unpopular. Unless a president or vice president is first impeached and convicted, many experts believe he is not liable to prosecution as would be an ordinary citizen. (No one is certain, because the question has never arisen.) President Ford's pardon of Richard Nixon meant that he could not be prosecuted under federal law for things he may have done while in office.

Students may find the occasions of misconduct or disability remote and the details of succession or impeachment tedious. But the problem is not remote—succession has occurred nine times and disability at least twice—and what may appear tedious goes, in fact, to the heart of the presidency. The first and fundamental problem is to make the office legitimate. That was the great task George Washington set himself, and that was the substantial accomplishment of his successors. Despite bitter and sometimes violent partisan and sectional strife, beginning almost immediately after Washington stepped down, presidential succession has always occurred peacefully, without a military coup or a political plot. For centuries, in the bygone times of kings as well as in the present times of dictators and juntas, peaceful succession has been a rare event among the nations of the world. Many of the critics of the Constitution believed in 1787 that peaceful succession would not happen in the United States either: somehow the president would connive to hold office for life or to handpick his successor. Their predictions were wrong, though their fears are understandable.

How Powerful Is the President?

Just as members of Congress bemoan their loss of power, so presidents bemoan theirs. Can both be right?

In fact, they can. If Congress is less able to control events than it once was, it does not mean that the president is thereby more able to exercise control. The federal government *as a whole* has become more constrained, so it is less able to act decisively. The chief source of this constraint is the greater complexity of the issues with which Washington must deal.

It was one thing to pass the Social Security Act in 1935; it is quite another thing to keep the Social Security system adequately funded. It was one thing for the nation to defend itself when attacked in 1941; it is quite another to maintain a constant military preparedness while simultaneously exploring possibilities for arms control. It was not hard to give pensions to veterans; it seems almost impossible today to find the cure for drug abuse or juvenile crime.

In the face of modern problems, all branches of government, including the presidency, seem both big and ineffectual. Add to this the much closer and more critical scrutiny of the media and the proliferation of interest groups, and it is small wonder that both presidents and members of Congress feel that they have lost power.

Presidents have come to acquire certain rules of thumb for dealing with their political problems. Among them are these:

- *Move it or lose it.* A president who wants to get something done should do it early in his term, before his political influence erodes.
- *Avoid details.* President Carter's lieutenants regret having tried to do too much. Better to have three or four top priorities and forget the rest.
- *Cabinets don't get much accomplished; people do.* Find capable White House subordinates and give them well-defined responsibility; then watch them closely.[26]

WHAT WOULD YOU DO?

MEMORANDUM

To: *White House Chief of Staff Ann Martin*

From: *Office of Legislative Affairs Director Sean Rivera*

Subject: *Passing budget bills under divided government*

With the opposition party in control of Congress, media pundits and other commentators are calling for the president to accept the other party's agenda for the next round of budget bills.

Arguments for:

1. With a reelection battle around the corner, the president cannot afford to get caught up in a budget battle with Congress.
2. The president's ability to gain public support for his agenda is limited, and even increased public support will not improve leverage with Congress.
3. The president should defer to Congress as the primary representative of the people in American politics.

Arguments against:

1. American politics is guided too often by campaigns, and the president will build support for reelection by acting presidential—that is, by setting the agenda for the budget and not backing down.
2. The president can build public support through speeches and other forms of communication, and this support can be used as political capital to negotiate with Congress.
3. The president is the only nationally elected official in American politics (other than the vice president), and therefore is responsible for identifying and promoting public priorities, even if this means legislative battles with Congress.

News »

Will the White House and Congress Agree on a Budget?

In the latest budget battle between the White House and Congress, the pressure on the president to accept a compromise with his political opponents is great, given the looming threat of not only a government shutdown, but also a debt default by the United States for the first time in the history of the American republic.

Your decision:

Favor plan ____________ Oppose ban ____________

LEARNING OBJECTIVES

WHAT YOU NEED TO KNOW

☑ **How do presidents differ from prime ministers?**

Unlike prime ministers, American presidents are elected independently of Congress, which gives them both more independence in governing and more challenges in building political coalitions.

☑ **How have the constitutional and political powers of the presidency evolved from the founding of the United States to the present?**

Presidential power has grown significantly from its constitutional origins. Since the 1930s, the president has become the central figure in American politics, even though the president's ability to achieve political success remains highly dependent on other individuals and institutions.

☑ **How do presidents make policy?**

To make policy, a president must work closely with Congress and the federal bureaucracy, while being attentive to public and political party expectations, as well as media scrutiny.

RECONSIDERING WHO GOVERNS?

1. Did the Founders expect the presidency to be the most important political institution?

Most did not. They worried about whether the presidency would be too strong or too weak, but designed a Constitution hoping that Congress would be the most important institution. And it was, with a few exceptions, until the 20th century. Today, the strength of the presidency depends chiefly on two things: the importance of military and foreign affairs and the president's personal popularity.

2. How important is the president's character in determining how he governs?

Very important. Presidents with great personal skills, such as Franklin Roosevelt, Dwight Eisenhower, Ronald Reagan, and Bill Clinton can influence public opinion and that in turn influences Congress. But character is not the whole story. Having a majority of fellow believers in Congress, though rare, is important (as it was for Roosevelt and Lyndon Johnson), and so are unexpected events, such as wars and other crises.

RECONSIDERING TO WHAT ENDS?

1. Should we abolish the electoral college?

There are big risks in doing that. If no president were to win a majority of the popular vote (which happens quite often), there would either have to be a runoff election or the House would make the final decision. Without an electoral college, small parties would play a bigger role and the United States could politically come to look like France or Italy. And without the college, a presidential campaign might be waged in just a few big states with the candidates ignoring most places.

2. Is it harder to govern when the presidency and Congress are controlled by different political parties?

Not really. Both the Democratic and Republican parties have legislators who often vote with their party rivals. Unless the president has a big ideological majority in Congress, something that does not happen too often, he can easily lose legislative struggles. Gridlock does not in fact prevent major new pieces of legislation from being passed.

QUESTIONS TO CONSIDER

1. **How are presidents more and less powerful than prime ministers?**
2. **How has the balance of power between the presidency and Congress changed over time?**
3. **In the modern era, how does the president influence policymaking?**
4. **Is constitutional reform of the presidency needed? What changes, if any, are most important in the 21st century?**
5. **Who works in the White House?**
6. **How closely do the president and Congress share policy priorities?**
7. **How often does the president communicate with the public?**
8. **How do the legacies of modern presidents compare with those of their predecessors?**

TO LEARN MORE

Official White House blog:
www.whitehouse.gov
Studies of presidents:
Miller Center of Public Affairs, University of Virginia:
www.millercenter.virginia.edu/academic/americanpresident
The American Presidency Project, University of California at Santa Barbara:
www.presidency.ucsb.edu/

GENERAL

Cohen, Jeffrey E. *Going Local: Presidential Leadership in the Post-Broadcast Age*. New York: Cambridge University Press, 2010. Examines how party polarization and an increasingly decentralized media have led presidents to target their public communications to local audiences over the national arena.

Corwin, Edward S. *The President: Office and Powers,* 5th ed. New York: New York University Press, 1985. Historical, constitutional, and legal development of the office.

Greenstein, Fred I. *The Presidential Difference: Leadership Style from FDR to Barack Obama,* 3rd ed. Princeton, N.J.: Princeton University Press, 2009. Explores how, independent of other influences, modern presidents' respective leadership styles account for consequential changes in domestic and foreign policy decisions.

Kernell, Samuel. *Going Public: New Strategies of Presidential Leadership,* 4th ed. New Haven, Conn.: Yale University Press, 2007. Examines how modern presidents develop policies with an eye fixed on how best to communicate with multiple public audiences.

Neustadt, Richard E. *Presidential Power and the Modern Presidents: The Politics of Leadership from Roosevelt to Reagan*. New York: The Free Press, 1990 (original edition published in 1960). How presidents try to acquire and hold political power in the competitive world of official Washington, by a man who was both a scholar and an insider.

Peterson, Mark A. *Legislating Together: The White House and Congress from Eisenhower to Reagan*. Cambridge: Harvard University Press, 1990. Challenges the conventional view that "the president proposes, Congress disposes." Contains many excellent examples of bargaining and cooperation between Congress and the executive branch.

Polsby, Nelson W., and Aaron Wildavsky. *Presidential Elections,* 10th ed. New York: Chatham House, 2000. Excellent analysis of how campaigns and the electoral college shape the presidency.

Tulis, Jeffrey K. *The Rhetorical Presidency.* Princeton, N.J.: Princeton University Press, 1987. Fascinating study of how once-powerful constitutional customs that proscribed presidents rallying the public for political support on a routine basis changed in the early 20th century.

ON FRANKLIN D. ROOSEVELT

Leuchtenberg, William E. *Franklin D. Roosevelt and the New Deal, 1932–1940*. New York: Harper & Row, 1963.

Maney, Richard J. *The Roosevelt Presence.* New York: Twayne, 1992.

ON HARRY S. TRUMAN

Hamby, A. L. *Beyond the New Deal: Harry S. Truman and American Liberalism*. New York: Columbia University Press, 1973.

McCullough, David. *Truman*. New York: Simon and Schuster, 1984.

ON DWIGHT D. EISENHOWER

Ambrose, Stephen E. *Eisenhower.* New York: Simon and Schuster, 1984.

Greenstein, Fred I. *The Hidden-Hand Presidency: Eisenhower as Leader*. New York: Basic Books, 1982.

ON JOHN F. KENNEDY

Paper, Lewis J. *The Promise and the Performance: The Leadership of John F. Kennedy*. New York: Crown, 1975.

Parmet, Herbert C. *Jack*. New York: Dial Press, 1980.

ON LYNDON B. JOHNSON

Caro, Robert A. *The Years of Lyndon Johnson.* 3 vols. New York: Alfred Knopf, 1982–2002.

Dallek, Robert. *Lone Star Rising and Flawed Giant*. New York: Oxford University Press, 1991 and 1996.

Kearns, Doris. *Lyndon Johnson and the American Dream*. New York: Harper and Row, 1976.

ON RICHARD M. NIXON

Ambrose, Stephen E. *Nixon.* 3 vols. New York: Simon and Schuster, 1987, 1989, 1991.

ON JIMMY CARTER

Bourne, Peter G. *Jimmy Carter.* New York: Scribner, 1997.

ON RONALD REAGAN

Cannon, Lou. *President Reagan.* New York: Simon and Schuster, 1991.

ON GEORGE H. W. BUSH

Parmet, Herbert C. *George Bush.* New York: Scribner, 1997.

ON BILL CLINTON

Klein, Joe. *The Natural: The Misunderstood Presidency of Bill Clinton.* New York: Doubleday, 2002.

ON GEORGE W. BUSH

Draper, Robert. *Dead Certain: The Presidency of George W. Bush.* New York; Free Press, 2007.

Jacobson, Gary C. *A Divider, Not A Uniter: George W. Bush and the American People.* 2d ed. (New York: Longman, 2010).

Pfiffner, James P. *Power Play: The Bush Presidency and the Constitution.* Washington, D.C.: Brookings Institution Press, 2008.

ON BARACK OBAMA

Remnick, David. *The Bridge: The Life and Rise of Barack Obama.* New York: Knopf, 2010.

Renshon, Stanley A. *Barack Obama and the Politics of Redemption.* New York: Routledge, 2011.

15 The Bureaucracy

LEARNING OBJECTIVES

WHAT YOU NEED TO KNOW

- ☑ What is "bureaucracy" and in what ways is the American bureaucracy distinctive?
- ☑ What is "discretionary authority" and why do some bureaucrats have lots of it?
- ☑ How does Congress exert control over the bureaucracy?

WHO GOVERNS?

1. What happened to make the bureaucracy a "fourth branch" of American national government?
2. What are the actual size and scope of the federal bureaucracy?

TO WHAT ENDS?

1. What should be done to improve bureaucratic performance?
2. Is "red tape" all bad?

There is probably not a man or woman in the United States who has not, at some time or other, complained about "the bureaucracy." Your letter was slow in getting to Aunt Minnie? The Internal Revenue Service took months to send you your tax refund? The Defense Department paid $400 for a hammer? The Occupational Safety and Health Administration told you that you installed the wrong kind of portable toilet for your farm workers? The "bureaucracy" is to blame.

bureaucracy A large, complex organization composed of appointed officials.

For most people and politicians, *bureaucracy* is a pejorative word implying waste, confusion, red tape, and rigidity. But for scholars—and for bureaucrats themselves—*bureaucracy* is a word with a neutral, technical meaning. A **bureaucracy** is a large, complex organization composed of appointed officials. By *complex*, we mean that authority is divided among several managers; no one person is able to make all the decisions. A large corporation is a bureaucracy; so also are a big university and a government agency. With its sizable staff, even Congress has become, to some degree, a bureaucracy.

What is it about complex organizations in general, and government agencies in particular, that leads so many people to complain about them? In part, the answer is to be found in their very size and complexity. But in large measure the answer is to be found in the political context within which such agencies must operate. If we examine that context carefully, we will discover that many of the problems that we blame on "the bureaucracy" are in fact the result of what Congress, the courts, and the president do. And, if we dig just a bit deeper, we will also discover that behind just about every government bureaucracy is some set of new or old public demands. Consider, for example, Washington bureaucracies' roles with respect to keeping us safe from street criminals, cleaning up toxic waste sites, and making sure that poor children have nutritional school lunches.

THEN The U.S. Department of Justice (USDOJ—this is bureaucracy, so enjoy all the alphabet soup) was established in 1789, but until a series of federal "crime bills" was enacted beginning in the 1960s, it had only an incidental role in crime control. For the most part, it neither funded nor worked at all closely with state and

local criminal justice agencies. A USDOJ subunit, the Federal Bureau of Prisons (FBOP), was a tiny agency that held fewer inmates than many small state prison systems did.

NOW With public support for successive federal "wars on crime" and "wars on drugs," the USDOJ and other federal agencies now spend billions of dollars each year to fund federal, state, and local agencies engaged in combating street crime, and the FBOP now runs one of the largest prison systems in the world.

THEN Before the Environmental Protection Agency (EPA) was launched in 1970, the federal government's environmental protection activities were virtually nonexistent.

NOW The media stories and public outcries that accompanied the discovery of lethal toxic waste sites in and around New York's Love Canal area led in 1978 to the creation of the so-called Superfund program. To administer Superfund, in 1980, the EPA expanded, and there has been an expansion in federal environmental protection efforts, and in federally directed state and local efforts as well, in most years ever since.

THEN The first federal law providing for subsidized school lunches was passed in 1946, but it was not until the 1960s that Washington began expanding its programs in this area to include ever greater numbers of children eligible for both free (or reduced price) breakfasts and lunches.

NOW It was only in 2010 that the U.S. Department of Agriculture (USDA)—created in 1862, made into a cabinet department in 1889, and long concerned mainly with the nation's farms and agri-businesses—was mandated by law to work with local school districts and other organizations so as to make nutritional meals (breakfasts, lunches, and snacks) available to low-income children year-round, including in the summer months when school is out.

Whatever else it may be, bureaucracy is an outgrowth of representative democracy: if people demanded that government do less or do nothing, in due course public laws would change and the agencies that exist to translate those laws into administrative action would dissolve. But that has rarely happened. Instead, six of the federal government's 15 cabinet agencies, including (next to the U.S. Department of Defense) its two largest and newest (the U.S. Department of Veterans Affairs, created in 1989, and the U.S. Department of Homeland Security, created in 2002), were created after 1964.

Distinctiveness of the American Bureaucracy

As you might expect, much the same can be said for the growth of bureaucracy in other democratic nations. Indeed, bureaucratic government has become an obvious feature of all modern societies, democratic and nondemocratic alike.

In the United States, however, three aspects of our constitutional system and political traditions give to the bureaucracy a distinctive character. First, political authority over the bureaucracy is not in one set of hands but is shared among several institutions. In a parliamentary regime, such as in Great Britain, the appointed officials of the national government work for the cabinet ministers, who are in turn dominated by the prime minister. In theory, and to a considerable extent in practice, British bureaucrats report to and take orders from the ministers in charge of their departments, do not deal directly with Parliament, and rarely give interviews to the press. In the United States, the Constitution permits both the president and Congress to exercise authority over the bureaucracy. Every senior appointed official has at least two masters: one in the executive branch and the other in the legislative. Often there are many more than two: Congress, after all, is not a single organization but a collection of committees, subcommittees, and individuals. This divided authority encourages bureaucrats to play one branch of government against the other and to make heavy use of the media.

Second, most of the agencies of the federal government share their functions with related agencies in state and local government. Though some federal agencies deal directly with American citizens—the Internal Revenue Service collects taxes from them, the Federal Bureau of Investigation looks into crimes for them, the Postal Service delivers mail to them—many agencies work with other organizations at other levels of government. For example, the Department of Education gives money to local school systems; the Health Care Financing Administration in the Department of Health and Human Services reimburses states for money spent on health care for the poor; the Department of Housing and Urban Development gives grants to cities for community development; and the Employment and Training Administration in the Department of Labor supplies funds to local governments so that they can run job-training programs. In France, by contrast, government programs dealing with education, health, housing, and employment are centrally run, with little or no control exercised by local governments.

Third, the institutions and traditions of American life have contributed to the growth of what some writers have described as an "adversary culture," in which the definition and expansion of personal rights, and the defense of rights and claims through lawsuits as well as political action, are given central importance. A government agency in this country operates under closer public scrutiny and with a greater prospect of court challenges to its authority than in almost any other nation. Virtually every important decision of the Occupational Safety and Health Administration or of the Environmental Protection Agency is likely to be challenged in the courts or attacked by an affected party; in Sweden the decisions of similar agencies go largely uncontested.

The scope as well as the style of bureaucratic government differs. In most Western European nations, the government owns and operates large parts of the economy: the French government operates the railroads and owns companies that make automobiles and cigarettes, and the Italian government owns many similar enterprises and also the nation's oil refineries. In just about every large nation except the United States, the telephone system is owned by the government. Publicly operated enterprises account for about 12 percent of all employment in France but less than 3 percent in the United States.[1] The U.S. government regulates privately owned enterprises to a degree not found in many other countries, however. Why we should have preferred regulation to ownership as the proper government role is an interesting question to which we shall return.

Proxy Government

government by proxy Washington pays state and local governments and private groups to staff and administer federal programs.

Much of our federal bureaucracy operates on the principle of **government by proxy.**[2] In every representative government, the voters elect legislators who make the laws, but in this country the bureaucrats often pay other people to do the work. These "other people" include state and local governments, business firms, and nonprofit organizations.

Among the programs run this way are Social Security, Medicare, much environmental protection, and the collection of income taxes by withholding money from your paycheck. Even many military duties are contracted out.[3] In the first Gulf War in 1991, American soldiers outnumbered private contractors in the region by 60 to one. But by 2006, there were nearly as many private workers as soldiers in Iraq. One company was paid $7.2 billion to get food and supplies to our troops there.[4]

When Hurricanes Katrina and Rita hit our Gulf Coast, the nation's response was managed by a small and weak group, the Federal Emergency Management Agency (FEMA). When the levees broke, it had only 2,600 employees; most of the help it was to provide came through "partners," such as state and local agencies, and some of these were not very competent.

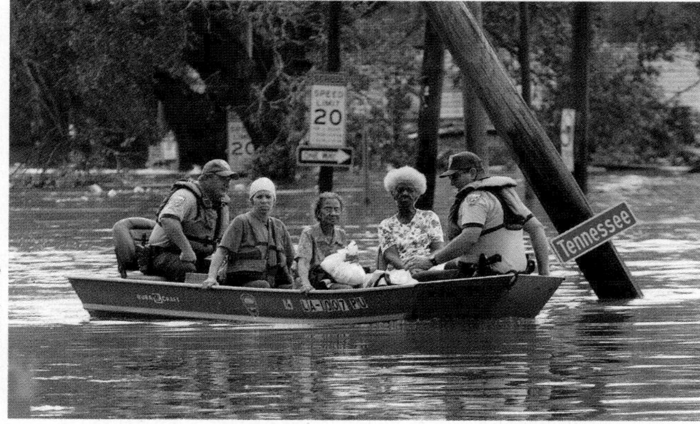

Mario Tama/Getty Images

People taken by boat away from their New Orleans homes that were struck by Hurricane Katrina in 2008.

Critics of our government-by-proxy system argue that it does not keep track of how the money we send to public and private agencies is used. Congress, of course, could change matters around, but it has an interest in setting policies and defining goals, not in managing the bureaucracy or levying taxes. Moreover, the president and Congress like to keep the size of the federal bureaucracy small by giving jobs to people not on the federal payroll.[5]

Defenders of government by proxy claim that the system produces more flexibility, takes advantage of private and nonprofit skills, and defends the principle of federalism embodied in our Constitution. The defenders make fair points, but the system does produce certain everyday oddities like the fact that many average citizens receive costly federal government services over long periods of time without ever directly interacting with civil servants. In 2008, Donald F. Kettl, a University of Maryland political scientist, dubbed this the "Mildred Paradox": in her last several years of life, his aged and ill mother-in-law, Mildred, applied successfully for multiple federal health insurance programs and received several years' worth of different types of expensive institutional care and top-quality medical treatment—all at government expense—but without ever actually encountering a single government worker.[6]

Or look a bit closer at what we noted above regarding the U.S. Department of Agriculture (USDA). As a result of a new federal law (the Healthy, Hunger-Free Kids Act of 2010), the USDA is now required to expand and improve its "food security" programs by, among other measures, seeing to it that all eligible low-income children have daily access to free meals (breakfast or lunch plus a snack) during the summer months when school is out. The new law, however, does not even begin to specify just how the USDA and its scores and scores of state and local government proxy agencies (not to mention their tens of thousands of administrative partners) are to accomplish that objective. Among big cities, Philadelphia has had the largest USDA-funded summer food program in the country (almost 4 million meals served each summer through more than 1,000 local "sites" including churches, recreation centers, and private homes on streets closed off for the purpose by local police). But the city's summer participation rate among eligible children has still been only about 50 percent.

The Growth of the Bureaucracy

The Constitution made scarcely any provision for an administrative system other than to allow the president to appoint, with the advice and consent of the Senate, "ambassadors, other public ministers and consuls, judges of the Supreme Court, and all other officers of the United States whose appointments are not herein otherwise provided for, and which shall be established by law."[7] Departments and bureaus were not mentioned.

In the first Congress, in 1789, James Madison introduced a bill to create a Department of State to assist the new secretary of state, Thomas Jefferson, in carrying out his duties. People appointed to this department were to be nominated by the president and approved by the Senate, but they were "to be removable by the president" alone. These six words, which would confer the right to fire government officials, occasioned six days of debate in the House. At stake was the locus of power over what was to become the bureaucracy. Madison's opponents argued that the Senate should consent to the removal of officials as well as their appointment. Madison responded that, without the unfettered right of removal, the president would not be able to control his subordinates, and without this control he would not be able to discharge his constitutional obligation to "take care that the laws be faithfully executed."[8] Madison won, 29 votes to 22. When the issue went to the Senate, another debate resulted in a tie vote, broken in favor of the president by Vice President John Adams. The Department of State, and all cabinet departments subsequently created, would be run by people removable only by the president.

That decision did not resolve the question of who would really control the bureaucracy, however. Congress retained the right to appropriate money, to investigate the administration, and to shape the laws that would be executed by that administration—more than ample power to challenge any president who claimed to have sole authority over his subordinates. And many members of Congress expected the cabinet departments, even though headed by people removable by the president, to report to Congress.

The government in Washington was at first minuscule. The State Department started with only nine employees; the War Department did not have 80 civilian employees until 1801. Only the Treasury Department, concerned with collecting taxes and finding ways to pay the public debt, had much power, and only the Post Office Department provided any significant service.

THE APPOINTMENT OF OFFICIALS

Small as the bureaucracy was, people struggled, often bitterly, over who would be appointed to it. From George Washington's day to modern times, presidents have found appointment to be one of their most important and difficult tasks. The officials they select affect how the laws are interpreted (thus the political ideology of the job holders is important), what tone the administration will display (thus personal character is important), how effectively the public business is discharged (thus competence is important), and how strong the political party or faction in power will be (thus party affiliation is important). Presidents trying to balance the competing needs of ideology, character, fitness, and partisanship have rarely pleased most people. As John Adams remarked, every appointment creates one ingrate and 10 enemies.

Because Congress, during most of the 19th and 20th centuries, was the dominant branch of government, congressional preferences often controlled the appointment of officials. And since Congress was, in turn, a collection of people who represented local interests, appointments were made with an eye to rewarding the local supporters of members of Congress or building up local party organizations. These appointments made on the basis of political considerations—patronage—were later to become a major issue. They galvanized various reform efforts that sought to purify politics and to raise the level of competence of the public service. Many of the abuses the reformers complained about were real enough, but patronage served some useful purposes as well. It gave the president a way to ensure that his subordinates were reasonably supportive of his policies; it provided a reward the president could use to induce recalcitrant members of Congress to vote for his programs; and it enabled party organizations to be built up to perform the necessary functions of nominating candidates and getting out the vote.

Though at first there were not many jobs to fight over, by the middle of the 19th century, there were a lot. From 1816 to 1861, the number of federal employees increased eightfold. This expansion was not, however, the result of the government's taking on new functions but simply a result of the increased demands on its traditional functions. The Post Office alone accounted for 86 percent of this growth.[9]

The Civil War was a great watershed in bureaucratic development. Fighting the war led, naturally, to hiring many new officials and creating many new offices. Just as important, the Civil War revealed the administrative weakness of the federal government and led to demands by the civil service reform movement for an improvement in the quality and organization of federal employees. And finally, the war was followed by a period of rapid industrialization and the emergence of a national economy. The effects of these developments could no longer be managed by state governments acting alone. With the creation of a nationwide network of railroads, commerce among the states became increasingly important. The constitutional powers of the federal government to regulate interstate commerce, long dormant for want of much commerce to regulate, now became an important source of controversy.

A SERVICE ROLE

From 1861 to 1901, new agencies were created, many to deal with particular sectors of society and the economy. More than 200,000 new federal employees were added, with only about half of this increase in the Post Office. The rapidly growing Pension Office began paying benefits to Civil War veterans; the Department of Agriculture was created in 1862 to help farmers; the Department of Labor was founded in 1882 to serve workers; and the Department of Commerce was organized in 1903 to assist businesspeople. Many more specialized agencies, such as the National Bureau of Standards, also came into being.

These agencies had one thing in common: their role was primarily to serve, not to regulate. Most did research, gathered statistics, dispensed federal lands, or passed out benefits. Not until the Interstate Commerce Commission (ICC) was created in 1887 did the federal government begin to regulate the economy (other than by managing the currency) in any large way. Even the ICC had, at first, relatively few powers.

There were several reasons why federal officials primarily performed a service role. The values that had shaped the Constitution were still strong: these included a belief in limited government, the importance of states' rights, and the fear of concentrated discretionary power. The proper role of government in the economy was to promote, not to regulate, and a commitment to **laissez-faire**—a freely competitive economy—was strongly held. But just as important, the Constitution said nothing about giving any regulatory powers to bureaucrats. It gave to *Congress* the power to regulate commerce among the states. Now obviously Congress could not make the necessary day-to-day decisions to regulate, for example, the rates that interstate railroads charged to farmers and other shippers. Some agency or commission composed of appointed officials and experts would have to be created to do that. For a long time, however, the prevailing interpretation of the Constitution was that no such agency could exercise such regulatory powers unless Congress first set down clear standards that would govern the agency's decisions. As late as 1935, the Supreme Court held that a regulatory agency could not make rules on its own; it could only apply the standards enacted by Congress.[10] The Court's view was that the legislature may not delegate its powers to the president or to an administrative agency.[11]

laissez-faire An economic theory that government should not regulate or interfere with commerce.

These restrictions on what administrators could do were set aside in wartime. During World War I, for example, President Woodrow Wilson was authorized by Congress to fix prices, operate the railroads, manage the communications system, and even control the distribution of food.[12] This kind of extraordinary grant of power usually ended with the war.

Some changes in the bureaucracy did not end with the war. During the Civil War, World War I, World War II, the Korean War, and the war in Vietnam, the number of civilian (as well as military) employees of the government rose sharply. These increases were not simply in the number of civilians needed to help serve the war effort; many of the additional people were hired by agencies, such as the Treasury Department, not obviously connected with the war. Furthermore, the number of federal officials did not return to prewar levels after each war. Though there was some reduction, each war left the number of federal employees larger than before.[13]

It is not hard to understand how this happens. During wartime, almost every government agency argues that its activities have *some* relation to the war effort, and few legislators want to be caught voting against something that may help that effort. Hence in 1944, the Reindeer Service in Alaska, an agency of the Interior Department, asked for more employees because reindeer are "a valued asset in military planning."

A CHANGE IN ROLE

Today's bureaucracy is largely a product of two events: the depression of the 1930s (and the concomitant New Deal program of President Roosevelt) and World War II. Though many agencies have been added since then, the basic features of the bureaucracy were set mainly as a result of changes in public attitudes and in constitutional interpretation that occurred during these periods. The government was now expected to play an active role in dealing with economic and social problems. In the late 1930s, the Supreme Court reversed its earlier decisions (see Chapter 16) on the question of delegating legislative powers to administrative agencies and upheld laws by which Congress merely instructs agencies to make decisions that serve "the public interest" in some area.[14] As a result, it was possible for President Nixon to set up in 1971 a system of price and wage controls based on a statute that simply authorized the president "to issue such orders and regulations as he may deem appropriate to stabilize prices, rents, wages, and salaries."[15] The Cost of Living Council and other agencies that Nixon established to carry out this order were run by appointed officials who had the legal authority to make sweeping decisions based on general statutory language.

World War II was the first occasion during which the government made heavy use of federal income taxes—on individuals and corporations—to finance its activities. Between 1940 and 1945, total federal tax collections increased from about $5 billion to nearly $44 billion. The end of the war brought no substantial tax reduction: the country believed that a high level of military preparedness continued to be necessary and that various social programs begun before the war should enjoy the heavy funding made possible by wartime taxes. Tax receipts continued, by and large, to grow. Before 1913, when the Sixteenth Amendment to the Constitution was passed, the federal government could not collect income taxes at all (it financed itself largely from customs duties and excise taxes). From 1913 to 1940, income taxes were small (in 1940, the average American paid only $7 in federal income taxes). World War II created the first great financial boom for the government, permitting the sustained expansion of a wide variety of programs and thus entrenching a large number of administrators in Washington.[16]

Although it is still too soon to tell, a third event—the September 11, 2001, terrorist attacks on the United States—could affect bureaucracy as profoundly as the depression of the 1930s and World War II. A law creating a massive new cabinet agency, the Department of Homeland Security (DHS), was passed in late 2002. Within two years of its creation, the DHS had consolidated under its authority 22 smaller federal agencies with nearly 180,000 federal employees (third behind Defense and Veterans Affairs) and over $40 billion in budgets (fourth behind Defense, Health and Human Services, and Education). In addition, dozens of intergovernmental grant-making programs came under the authority of the DHS. In late 2004, Congress passed another law that promised, over time, to centralize under a single director of national intelligence the work of the more than 70 federal agencies authorized to spend money on counterterrorist activities. But even after related reforms in 2006, dozens of different agencies were still authorized to spend money on counterterrorism activities; and in 2008, the General Accountability Office (GAO) once again ranked the DHS, which by then employed more than 155,000 employees, among those agencies with especially serious management problems.[17]

The Federal Bureaucracy Today

No president wants to admit that he has increased the size of the bureaucracy. He can avoid saying this by pointing out that the number of civilians working for the federal government, excluding postal workers, has not increased significantly in recent years and is about the same today (2 million persons) as it was in 1960, and less than it was during World War II. This explanation is true but misleading, for it neglects the roughly 13 million people who work *indirectly* for Washington as employees of private firms and state or local agencies that are largely, if not entirely, supported by federal funds. There are nearly three persons earning their living indirectly from the federal government for every one earning it directly. While federal employment has remained quite stable, employment among federal contractors and consultants and in state and local governments has mushroomed. Indeed, most federal bureaucrats, like most other people who work for the federal government, live outside Washington, D.C.

As Table 15.1 shows, from 1990 to 2007, nearly every federal executive department reduced its workforce. The U.S. Department of State grew by over a third, but that represented fewer than 10,000 new staff. The single major exception was the U.S. Department of Justice (DOJ). This exception is explained almost entirely by the growth in just one DOJ unit—and one of the few federal agencies anywhere in the bureaucracy that was slow to join the trend toward what we described earlier in this chapter as government by proxy—the Federal Bureau of Prisons (BOP). The BOP administers more than 100 facilities, from maximum-security prisons to community corrections centers, all across the country. Between 1990 and 2009, its staff grew by 90 percent, or about 17,000 new employees; but the prisoner populations these federal workers supervised grew by 355 percent, or nearly 150,000.

Table 15.1 Federal Civilian Employment, 1990–2007

	1990	2007	Percent Change
All executive departments (in millions)	2.065	1.696	−17.8%
(In thousands)			
State	25.2	34.6	+37.3
Treasury	158.6	111.5	−29.6
Defense	1,034	673.7	−34.8
Justice	83.9	106.9	+27.4
Interior	77.6	70.2	−9.5
Agriculture	122.5	99.6	−18.6
Commerce	69.9	40.1	−42.6
Labor	17.7	15.8	−10.7
Health and Human Services	123.9	61.2	−50.6
Housing and Urban Development	13.5	9.7	−28.1
Transportation	67.3	53.5	−20.5
Energy	17.7	14.6	−17.5
Education	4.70	4.1	−12.7
Veterans Affairs	248.1	245.5	−1
Homeland Security	N/A	155.3	N/A

Source: *Statistical Abstract of the United States 2009*, Table 481.

Federal Bureau of Prisons	1990	2009	Percent Change
Staff	19.0	36.2	+90.5%
Inmates	58.0	206.1	+355

Sources: Federal Bureau of Prisons Weekly Population Report and Quick Facts, available at http://www.bop.gov/locations/weekly_report.jsp; and http://www.bop.gov/news/quick.jsp#5.

The power of the federal bureaucracy cannot be measured by the number of employees, however. A bureaucracy of 5 million persons would have little power if each employee did nothing but type letters or file documents, whereas a bureaucracy of only 100 persons would have awesome power if each member were able to make arbitrary life-and-death decisions affecting the rest of us. The power of the bureaucracy depends on the extent to which appointed officials have **discretionary authority**—that is, the ability to choose courses of action and to make policies not spelled out in advance by laws. As Figure 15.1 shows, the volume of regulations issued has risen much faster than the rate of government spending (relative to gross domestic product) and the number of federal employees who write the regulations and spend the money (federal employees who, as we have explained, often work mainly through state and local government employees and other administrative proxies).

discretionary authority The extent to which appointed bureaucrats can choose courses of action and make policies not spelled out in advance by laws.

By this test, the power of the federal bureaucracy has grown enormously. Congress has delegated substantial authority to administrative agencies in three areas: (1) paying subsidies to particular groups and organizations in society (farmers, veterans, scientists, schools, universities, hospitals); (2) transferring money from the federal government to state and local governments (the grant-in-aid programs described in Chapter 3); and (3) devising and enforcing regulations for various sectors of society and the economy. Some of these administrative functions, such as grants-in-aid to states, are closely monitored by Congress; others, such as the regulatory programs, usually operate with a greater degree of independence. These delegations of power, especially in the areas of paying subsidies and regulating

Figure 15.1

The Growth of the Federal Government in Money, People, and Rules, 1940–2010

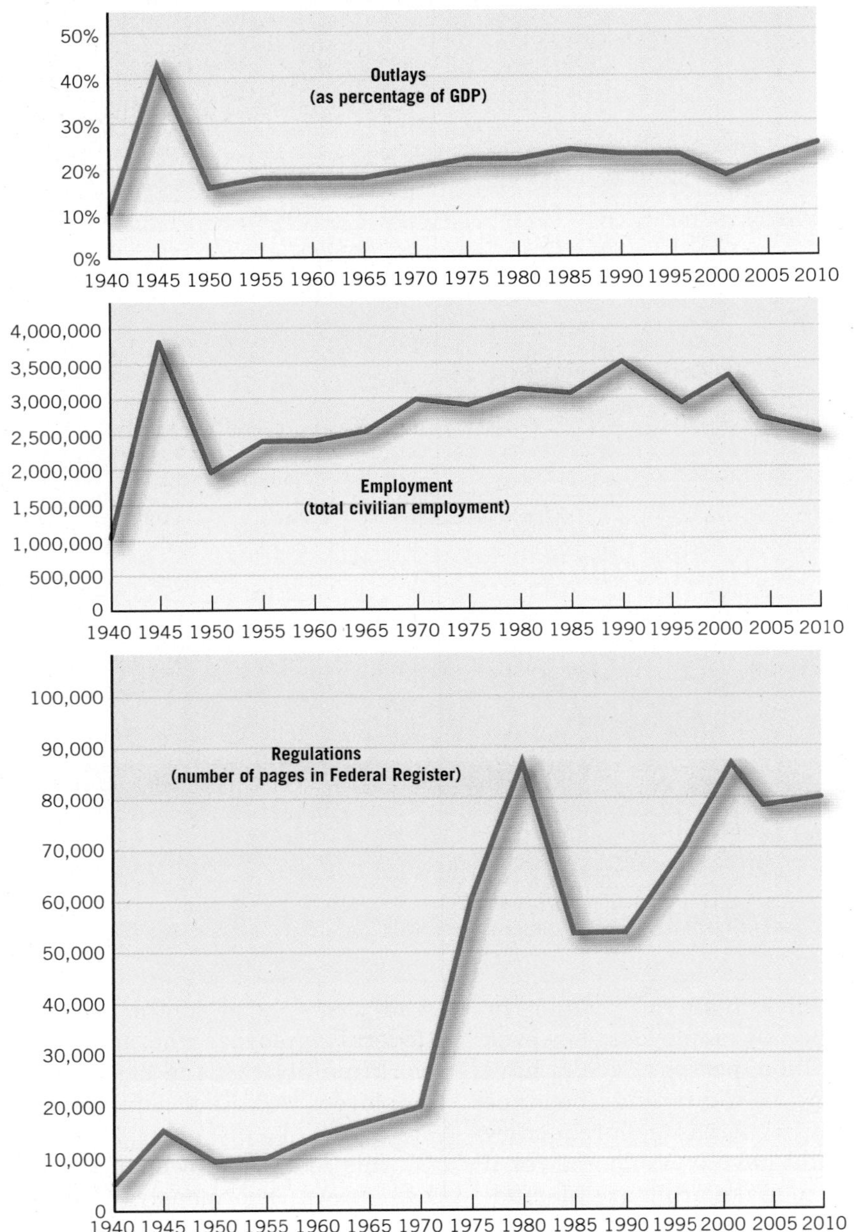

Source: Outlays: *Statistical Abstract of the United States, 2004–2005,* Table 461, and *Historical Statistics of the United States*, Series F-32 and Y-340. Civilian employment and pages in the *Federal Register*: Harold W. Stanley and Richard G. Niemi, *Vital Statistics on American Politics* (Washington, D.C.: Congressional Quarterly Press, 2010), 255.

the economy, did not become commonplace until the 1930s, and then only after the Supreme Court decided that such delegations were constitutional. Today, by contrast, appointed officials can decide, within rather broad limits, who shall own a television station, what safety features automobiles shall have, what kinds of scientific research shall be specially encouraged, what drugs shall appear on the market, which dissident groups shall be investigated, what fumes an industrial smokestack may emit, which corporate mergers shall be allowed, what use shall be made of national forests, and what prices crop and dairy farmers shall receive for their products.

If appointed officials have this kind of power, then how they use it is of paramount importance in understanding modern government. There are, broadly, four factors that may explain the behavior of these officials:

1. The manner in which they are recruited and rewarded
2. Their personal attributes, such as their socioeconomic backgrounds and their political attitudes
3. The nature of their jobs
4. The constraints that outside forces—political superiors, legislators, interest groups, journalists—impose on their agencies

RECRUITMENT AND RETENTION

The federal civil service system was designed to recruit qualified people on the basis of merit, not political patronage, and to retain and promote employees on the basis of performance, not political favoritism. Many appointed federal officials belong to the **competitive service.** This means they are appointed only after they have passed a written examination administered by the Office of Personnel Management (OPM) or met certain selection criteria (such as training, educational attainments, or prior experience) devised by the hiring agency and approved by the OPM. Where competition for a job exists and candidates can be ranked by their scores or records, the agency must usually appoint one of the three top-ranking candidates.

competitive service The government offices to which people are appointed on the basis of merit, as ascertained by a written exam or by applying certain selection criteria.

In recent years, the competitive service system has become decentralized, so that each agency now hires its own people without an OPM referral, and examinations have become less common. In 1952, more than 86 percent of all federal employees were civil servants hired by the competitive service; by 1996, that figure had fallen to less than 54 percent. This decentralization and the greater use of ways other than exams to hire employees were caused by three things. First, the old OPM system was cumbersome and often not relevant to the complex needs of departments. Second, these agencies had a need for more professionally trained employees—lawyers, biologists, engineers, and computer specialists—who could not be ranked on the basis of some standard exam. And third, civil rights groups pressed Washington to make the racial composition of the federal bureaucracy look more like the racial composition of the nation.

Moreover, the kinds of workers being recruited into the federal civil service have changed. For example, blue-collar employment has fallen while the federal government's white-collar workforce has become more diverse occupationally. As one expert on civil service reform has noted, the "need to recruit and retain physicists, biologists, oceanographers, nurses, statisticians, botanists, and epidemiologists, as well as large numbers of engineers, lawyers, and accountants, now preoccupies federal personnel managers."[18]

Employees hired outside the competitive service are part of the excepted service. They now make up almost half of all workers. Though not hired by the OPM, they still are typically hired in a nonpartisan fashion. Some are hired by agencies—such as the CIA, the FBI, and the Postal Service—that have their own selection procedures.

About 3 percent of the excepted employees are appointed on grounds other than or in addition to merit. These legal exceptions exist to permit the president to select, for policymaking and politically sensitive posts, people who are in agreement with his policy views. Such appointments are generally of three kinds:

1. Presidential appointments authorized by statute (cabinet and subcabinet officers, judges, U.S. marshals and U.S. attorneys, ambassadors, and members of various boards and commissions).
2. "Schedule C" appointments to jobs described as having a "confidential or policy-determining character" below the level of cabinet or subcabinet posts (including executive assistants, special aides, and confidential secretaries).
3. Noncareer executive assignments (NEAs) given to high-ranking members of the regular competitive civil service or to persons brought into the civil service at these high levels. These people are deeply involved in the advocacy of presidential programs or participate in policymaking.

These three groups of excepted appointments constitute the patronage available to a president and his

HO/AFP/Getty Images/Newscom

Fire erupting from the offshore oil rig operated by BP in the Gulf of Mexico near American land.

administration. When President Kennedy took office in 1961, he had 451 political jobs to fill. When President Barack Obama took office in 2009, he had more than four times that number, including nearly four times the number of top cabinet posts. Scholars disagree over whether this proliferation of political appointees has improved or worsened Washington's performance, but one thing is clear: widespread presidential patronage is hardly unprecedented. In the 19th century, practically every federal job was a patronage job. For example, when Grover Cleveland, a Democrat, became president in 1885, he replaced some 40,000 Republican postal employees with Democrats.

Ironically, two years earlier, in 1883, the passage of the Pendleton Act had begun a slow but steady transfer of federal jobs from the patronage to the merit system. It may seem strange that a political party in power (the Republicans) would be willing to relinquish its patronage in favor of a merit-based appointment system. Two factors made it possible for the Republicans to pass the Pendleton Act: (1) public outrage over the abuses of the spoils system, highlighted by the assassination of President James Garfield by a man always described in the history books as a "disappointed office seeker" (*lunatic* would be a more accurate term); and (2) the fear that if the Democrats came to power on a wave of anti-spoils sentiment, existing Republican officeholders would be fired. (The Democrats won anyway.)

The merit system spread to encompass most of the federal bureaucracy, generally with presidential support. Though presidents may have liked in theory the idea of hiring and firing subordinates at will, most felt that the demands for patronage were impossible either to satisfy or to ignore. Furthermore, by increasing the coverage of the merit system a president could "blanket in" patronage appointees already holding office, thus making it difficult or impossible for the next administration to fire them.

THE BUDDY SYSTEM

The actual recruitment of civil servants, especially in middle and upper-level jobs, is somewhat more complicated, and slightly more political, than the laws and rules might suggest. Though many people enter the federal bureaucracy by learning of a job, filling out an application, perhaps taking a test, and being hired, many also enter on a "name-request" basis. A **name-request job** is one that is filled by a person whom an agency has already identified. In this respect, the federal government is not so different from private business. A person learns of a job from somebody who already has one, or the head of a bureau decides in advance whom he or she wishes to hire. The agency must still send a form describing the job to the OPM, but it also names the person whom the agency wants to appoint. Sometimes the job is even described in such a way that the person named is the only one who can qualify for it. Occasionally, this tailor-made, name-request job is offered to a person at the insistence of a member of Congress who wants a political supporter taken care of; more often it is made available because the bureaucracy itself knows whom it wishes to hire and wants to circumvent an elaborate search. This is the "buddy system."

name-request job A job filled by a person whom an agency has already identified.

The buddy system does not necessarily produce poor employees. Indeed, it is frequently a way of hiring people known to the agency as capable of handling the position. It also opens up the possibility of hiring people whose policy views are congenial to those already in office. Such networking is based on shared policy views, not (as once was the case) on narrow partisan affiliations. For example, bureaucrats in consumer protection agencies recruit new staff from private groups with an interest in consumer protection, such as the various organizations associated with Ralph Nader, or from academics who have a pro-consumer inclination.

There has always been an informal "old boys' network" among those who move in and out of high-level government posts; with the increasing appointment of women to these jobs, there has begun to emerge an old girls' network as well.[19] In a later section, we will consider whether, or in what ways, these recruitment patterns make a difference.

FIRING A BUREAUCRAT

The great majority of bureaucrats who are part of the civil service and who do not hold presidential appointments have jobs that are, for all practical purposes, beyond reach. An executive must go through elaborate steps to fire, demote, or suspend a civil servant. Realistically, this means no one is fired or demoted unless his or her superior is prepared to invest a great deal of time and effort in the attempt. In 1987, about 2,600 employees who had completed their probationary period were fired for misconduct or poor performance. That is about one-tenth of 1 percent of all federal employees. It is hard to believe that a large private company would fire only one-tenth of 1 percent of its workers in a given year. It's also impossible to believe that, as is often the case in Washington, it would take a year to fire anyone. To cope with this problem, federal executives have devised a number of stratagems for bypassing or forcing out civil servants

How Things Work

Firing a Bureaucrat

To fire or demote a member of the competitive civil service, these procedures must be followed:

1. The employee must be given written notice at least 30 days in advance that he or she is to be fired or demoted for incompetence or misconduct.
2. The written notice must contain a statement of reasons, including specific examples of unacceptable performance.
3. The employee has the right to an attorney and to reply, orally or in writing, to the charges.
4. The employee has the right to appeal any adverse action to the Merit Systems Protection Board (MSPB), a three-person, bipartisan body appointed by the president with the consent of the Senate.
5. The MSPB must grant the employee a hearing, at which the employee has the right to have an attorney present.
6. The employee has the right to appeal the MSPB decision to a U.S. court of appeals, which can hold new hearings.

with whom they cannot work—denying them promotions, transferring them to undesirable locations, or assigning them to meaningless work.

With the passage of the Civil Service Reform Act of 1978, Congress recognized that many high-level positions in the civil service have important policy-making responsibilities and that the president and his cabinet officers ought to have more flexibility in recruiting, assigning, and paying such people. Accordingly, the act created the Senior Executive Service (SES), about 8,000 top federal managers who can (in theory) be hired, fired, and transferred more easily than ordinary civil servants. Moreover, the act stipulated that members of the SES would be eligible for substantial cash bonuses if they performed their duties well. (To protect the rights of SES members, anyone who is removed from the SES is guaranteed a job elsewhere in the government.)

Things did not work out quite as the sponsors of the SES had hoped. Though most eligible civil servants joined it, there was only a modest increase in the proportion of higher-ranking positions in agencies that were filled by transfer from another agency; the cash bonuses did not prove to be an important incentive (perhaps because the base salaries of top bureaucrats did not keep up with inflation); and hardly any member of the SES was actually fired. Two years after the SES was created, less than one-half of 1 percent of its members had received an unsatisfactory rating, and none had been fired. Nor does the SES give the president a large opportunity to make political appointments: only 10 percent of the SES can be selected from outside the existing civil service. And no SES member can be transferred involuntarily.

THE AGENCY'S POINT OF VIEW

When one realizes that most agencies are staffed by people recruited by those agencies, sometimes on a name-request basis, and virtually immune from dismissal, it becomes clear that the recruitment and retention policies of the civil service work to ensure that most bureaucrats will have an "agency" point of view. Even with the encouragement for transfers created by the SES, most government agencies are dominated by people who have not served in any other agency and who have been in government service most of their lives. This fact has some advantages: it means that most top-tier bureaucrats are experts in the procedures and policies of their agencies and that there will be a substantial degree of continuity in agency behavior no matter which political party happens to be in power.

But the agency point of view has its costs as well. A political executive entering an agency with responsibility for shaping its direction will discover that he or she must carefully win the support of career subordinates. A subordinate has an infinite capacity for discreet sabotage and can make life miserable for a political superior by delaying action, withholding information, following the rule book with literal exactness, or making an "end run" around a superior to mobilize members of Congress sympathetic to the bureaucrat's point of view. For instance, when one political executive wanted to downgrade a bureau in his department, he found, naturally, that the bureau chief was opposed. The bureau chief spoke to some friendly lobbyists and a key member of Congress. When the political executive asked the congressman whether he had any problem with the contemplated reorganization, the congressman replied, "No, you have the problem, because if you touch that bureau, I'll cut your job out of the budget."[20]

PERSONAL ATTRIBUTES

A second factor that might shape the way bureaucrats use their power is their personal attributes. These include their social class, education, and personal political beliefs. The federal civil service as a whole looks very much like a cross section of American society in the education, sex, race, and social origins of its members (see Figure 15.2). But as with many other employers, African Americans and other minorities are most likely heavily represented in the lowest grade levels and tend to be underrepresented at the executive level. At the higher-ranking levels, where the most power is found—say, in the supergrade ranks of GS 16 through GS 18—the typical civil servant is a middle-aged white male with a college degree whose father was somewhat more advantaged than the average citizen. In the great majority of cases, this individual is in fact very different from the typical American in both background and personal beliefs.

Because political appointees and career bureaucrats are unrepresentative of the average American, and because of their supposed occupational self-interest, some critics have speculated that the people holding these jobs think about politics and government in ways very different from the public at large. Some surveys do find that career bureaucrats are more likely than other people to hold liberal views, to trust government, and to vote for Democrats.[21]

It is important, however, not to overgeneralize from such differences. For example, whereas Clinton appointees (virtually all of them strong Democrats) were more liberal than average citizens, Reagan appointees (virtually all of them loyal Republicans) were undoubtedly more conservative than average citizens. Likewise, career civil servants are more pro-government than the public at large, but on most specific policy questions, federal bureaucrats do not have extreme positions. Still, those employed in "activist" agencies such as the Federal Trade Commission, Environmental Protection Agency, and Food and Drug Administration tend to have more liberal views than those who work for the more "traditional" agencies such as the departments of Agriculture, Commerce, and the Treasury. Even when the bureaucrats come from roughly the same social backgrounds, their policy views seem to reflect the type of government work that they

Figure 15.2
Characteristics of Federal Civilian Employees, 1960 and 2005

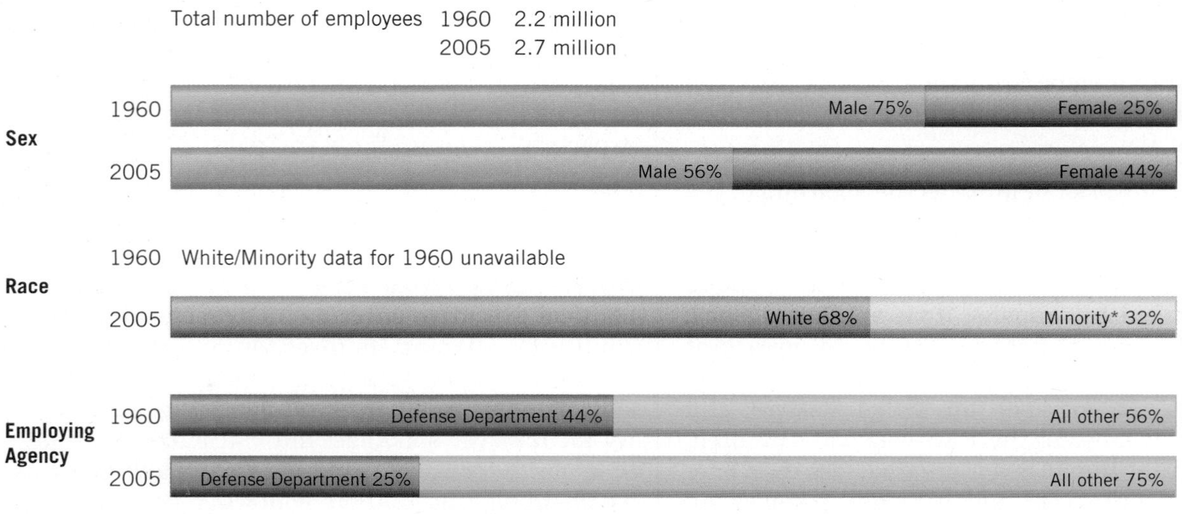

*Blacks, Native Americans, Hispanics, Asians, and Pacific Islanders

Sources: *Statistical Abstract of the United States, 1961,* 392–394; *Statistical Abstract of the United States, 2009,* Table 482.

Peter Steiner/Alamy

An Amtrak train speeding along its tracks. Amtrak service costs the federal government much more than the train earns in fares.

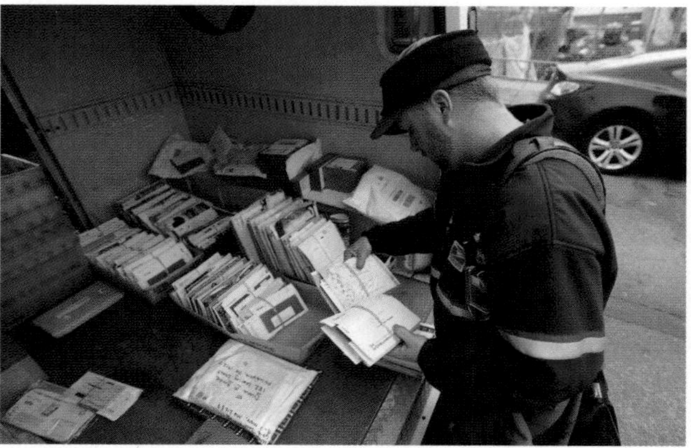

AP Images

A letter carrier picks up mail; his employer, the U.S. Postal Service, is running a huge deficit.

do. For example, studies dating back decades have found that Democrats and people with liberal views tend to be overrepresented in social service agencies, whereas Republicans and people with conservative views tend to be overrepresented in defense agencies.[22] But it is not clear whether such differences in attitudes are produced by the jobs that people hold or whether certain jobs attract people with certain beliefs. Probably both forces are at work.

DO BUREAUCRATS SABOTAGE THEIR POLITICAL BOSSES?

Because it is so hard to fire career bureaucrats, it is often said that these people will sabotage any actions by their political superiors with which they disagree. And since civil servants tend to have liberal views, it has been conservative presidents and cabinet secretaries who have usually expressed this worry.

There is no doubt that some bureaucrats will drag their heels if they don't like their bosses, and a few will block actions they oppose. However, most bureaucrats try to carry out the policies of their superiors even when they personally disagree with them. When David Stockman was director of the OMB, he set out to make sharp cuts in government spending programs in accordance with the wishes of his boss, President Reagan. He later published a book complaining about all the people in the White House and Congress who worked against him.[23] But nowhere in the book is there any major criticism of the civil servants at the OMB. It appears that whatever these people thought about Stockman and Reagan, they loyally tried to carry out Stockman's policies.

Bureaucrats tend to be loyal to political superiors who deal with them cooperatively and constructively. An agency head who tries to ignore or discredit them can be in for a tough time, however. The powers of obstruction available to aggrieved bureaucrats are formidable. Such people can leak embarrassing stories to Congress or to the media, help interest groups mobilize against the agency head, and discover a thousand procedural reasons why a new course of action won't work.

The exercise of some of those bureaucratic powers is protected by the Whistle Blower Protection Act. Passed in 1989, the law created the Office of Special Counsel, charged with investigating complaints from bureaucrats that they were punished after reporting to Congress about waste, fraud, or abuse in their agencies.

It may seem odd that bureaucrats, who have great job security, would not always act in accordance with their personal beliefs instead of in accordance with the wishes of their bosses. Bureaucratic sabotage, in this view, ought to be very common. But bureaucratic cooperation with superiors is not odd, once you take into account the nature of a bureaucrat's job.

If you are a voter at the polls, your beliefs will clearly affect how you vote (see Chapter 7). But if you are the second baseman for the Boston Red Sox, your political beliefs, social background, and education will have nothing to do with how you field ground balls. Sociologists like to call the different things that people do in their lives "roles" and to distinguish between roles that are loosely structured (such as the role of voter) and those that are highly structured (such as that of second baseman). Personal attitudes greatly affect loosely structured roles and only slightly affect highly structured ones. Applied to the federal bureaucracy, this suggests that civil servants performing tasks that are routinized (such as filling out forms), tasks that are closely defined by laws and rules (such as issuing welfare checks), or tasks that are closely monitored by others (supervisors, special-interest groups, the media) will probably perform them in ways that can only partially be explained, if at all, by their personal attitudes. Civil servants performing complex, loosely defined tasks that are not closely monitored may carry out their work in ways powerfully influenced by their attitudes.

Among the loosely defined tasks are those performed by professionals, and so the values of these people may influence how they behave. An increasing number of lawyers, economists, engineers, and physicians are hired to work in federal agencies. These men and women have received extensive training that produces not only a set of skills, but also a set of attitudes as to what is important and valuable. For example, the Federal Trade Commission (FTC), charged with preventing unfair methods of competition among businesses, employs two kinds of professionals—lawyers, organized into a Bureau of Competition, and economists, organized into a Bureau of Economics. Lawyers are trained to draw up briefs and argue cases in court and are taught the legal standards by which they will know whether they have a chance of winning a case or not. Economists are trained to analyze how a competitive economy works and what costs consumers must bear if the goods and services are produced by a monopoly (one firm controlling the market) or an oligopoly (a small number of firms dominating the market).

Because of their training and attitudes, lawyers in the FTC prefer to bring cases against a business firm that has done something clearly illegal, such as attending secret meetings with competitors to rig the prices that will be charged to a purchaser. These cases appeal to lawyers because there is usually a victim (the purchaser or a rival company) who complains to the government, the illegal behavior can be proved in a court of law, and the case can be completed rather quickly.

Economists, on the other hand, are trained to measure the value of a case not by how quickly it can be proved in court, but by whether the illegal practice imposes large or small costs on the consumer. FTC economists often dislike the cases that appeal to lawyers. The economists feel that the amount of money that such cases save the consumer is often small and that the cases are a distraction from the major issues—such as whether IBM unfairly dominates the computer business or whether General Motors is too large to be efficient. Lawyers, in turn, are leery of big cases, because the facts are hard to prove and they may take forever to decide (one blockbuster case can drag through the courts for 10 years). In many federal agencies divergent professional values such as these help explain how power is used.

CULTURE AND CAREERS

Unlike the lawyers and economists working in the FTC, the government bureaucrats in a typical agency don't have a lot of freedom to choose a course of action. Their jobs are spelled out not only by the laws, rules, and routines of their agency, but also by the informal understandings among fellow employees as to how they are supposed to act. These understandings are the *culture* of the agency.[24]

If you belong to the air force, you can do a lot of things, but only one thing really counts: flying airplanes, especially advanced jet fighters and bombers. The culture of the air force is a pilots' culture. If you belong to the navy, you have more choices: fly jet aircraft or operate nuclear submarines. Both jobs provide status and a chance for promotion to the highest ranks. By contrast, sailing minesweepers or transport ships (or worse, having a desk job and not sailing anything at all) is not a very rewarding job. The culture of the CIA emphasizes working overseas as a clandestine agent; staying in Washington as a report writer is not as good for your career. The culture of the State Department rewards skill in political negotiations; being an expert on international economics or embassy security is much less rewarding.

You can usually tell what kind of culture an agency has by asking an employee, "If you want to get ahead here, what sort of jobs should you take?" The jobs that are career enhancing are part of the culture; the jobs that are not career enhancing (NCE in bureaucratic lingo) are not part of it.

Being part of a strong culture is good—up to a point. It motivates employees to work hard in order to win the respect of their coworkers as well as the approval of their bosses. But a strong culture also makes it hard to change an agency. FBI agents for many years resisted getting involved in civil rights or organized crime cases, and diplomats in the State Department didn't pay much attention to embassy security. These important jobs were not a career-enhancing part of the culture.

CONSTRAINTS

The biggest difference between a government agency and a private organization is the vastly greater number of constraints on the agency.

The "Rules" of Politics

"Laws" of Bureaucratic Procedure

Acheson's Rule A memorandum is written not to inform the reader but to protect the writer.

Boren's Laws

When in doubt, mumble.

When in trouble, delegate.

When in charge, ponder.

Chapman's Rules of Committees

Never arrive on time, or you will be stamped a beginner.

Don't say anything until the meeting is half over; this stamps you as being wise.

Be as vague as possible; this prevents irritating others.

When in doubt, suggest that a subcommittee be appointed.

Meskimen's Law There's never time to do it right but always time to do it over.

Murphy's Law If anything can go wrong, it will.

O'Toole's Corollary to Murphy's Law Murphy was an optimist.

Parkinson's First Law Work expands to fill the time available for its completion.

Parkinson's Second Law Expenditure rises to meet income.

Peter Principle In every hierarchy, each employee tends to rise to his level of incompetence; thus, every post tends to be filled by an incompetent employee.

Robertson's Rule The more directives you issue to solve a problem, the worse it gets.

Smith's Principle Never do anything for the first time.

Unlike a business firm, the typical government bureau cannot hire, fire, build, or sell without going through procedures set down in laws. How much money it pays its members is determined by statute, not by the market. Not only the goals of an agency but often its exact procedures are spelled out by Congress.

At one time, the Soil Conservation Service was required by law to employ at least 14,177 full-time workers. The State Department has been forbidden by law from opening a diplomatic post in Antigua or Barbuda but forbidden from closing a post anywhere else. The Agency for International Development (which administers our foreign-aid program) has been given by Congress 33 objectives and 75 priorities and must send to Congress 288 reports each year. When it buys military supplies, the Defense Department must give a "fair proportion" of its contracts to small businesses, especially those operated by "socially and economically disadvantaged individuals," and must buy from American firms even if, in some cases, buying abroad would be cheaper.

Some of the more general constraints include the following:

- Administrative Procedure Act (1946). Before adopting a new rule or policy, an agency must give notice, solicit comments, and (often) hold hearings.
- Freedom of Information Act (1966). Citizens have the right to inspect all government records except those containing military, intelligence, or trade secrets or revealing private personnel actions.
- National Environmental Policy Act (1969). Before undertaking any major action affecting the environment, an agency must issue an environmental impact statement.
- Privacy Act (1974). Government files about individuals, such as Social Security and tax records, must be kept confidential.
- Open Meeting Law (1976). Every part of every agency meeting must be open to the public unless certain matters (for example, military or trade secrets) are being discussed.

One of the biggest constraints on bureaucratic action is that Congress rarely gives any job to a single agency. Stopping drug trafficking is the task of the Customs Service, the FBI, the Drug Enforcement Administration, the Border Patrol, and the Defense Department (among others). Disposing of the assets of failed savings-and-loan associations is the job of the Resolution Funding Corporation, Resolution Trust Corporation, Federal Housing Finance Board, Office of Thrift Supervision in the Treasury Department, Federal Deposit Insurance Corporation, Federal Reserve Board, and Justice Department (among others).

The effects of these constraints on agency behavior are not surprising.

- The government will often act slowly. (The more constraints that must be satisfied, the longer it will take to get anything done.)
- The government will sometimes act inconsistently. (What is done to meet one constraint—for example, freedom of information—may endanger another constraint—for example, privacy.)
- It will be easier to block action than to take action. (The constraints ensure that lots of voices will be heard; the more voices heard, the more they may cancel each other out.)
- Lower-ranking employees will be reluctant to make decisions on their own. (Having many constraints means having many ways to get into trouble; to avoid trouble, let your boss make the decision.)
- Citizens will complain of red tape. (The more constraints to serve, the more forms to fill out.)

AP Images

The F-35 Joint Strike Fighter made by Lockheed Martin for the American military and some of its allies.

These constraints do not mean government bureaucracy is powerless, only that, however great its power, it tends to be clumsy. That clumsiness arises not from the fact that the people who work for agencies are dull or incompetent, but from the complicated political environment in which that work must be done.

The moral of the story: the next time you get mad at a bureaucrat, ask yourself, Why would a rational, intelligent person behave that way? Chances are you will discover there are good reasons for that action. You would probably behave the same way if you were working for the same organization.

Why So Many Constraints?

Government agencies behave as they do in large part because of the many different goals they must pursue and the complex rules they must follow. Where does all this red tape come from?

From us. From us, the people.

Every goal, every constraint, every bit of red tape, was put in place by Congress, the courts, the White House, or the agency itself responding to the demands of some influential faction. Civil rights groups want every agency to hire and buy from women and minorities. Environmental groups want every agency to file environmental impact statements. Industries being regulated want every new agency policy to be formulated only after a lengthy public hearing with lots of lawyers present. Labor unions also want those hearings so that they can argue against industry lawyers. Everybody who sells something to the government wants a "fair chance" to make the sale, and so everybody insists that government contracts be awarded only after complex procedures are followed. A lot of people don't trust the government, and so they insist that everything it does be done in the sunshine—no secrets, no closed meetings, no hidden files.

If we wanted agencies to pursue their main goal with more vigor and less encumbering red tape, we would have to ask Congress, the courts, or the White House to repeal some of these constraints. In other words, we would have to be willing to give up something we want in order to get something else we want even more. But politics does not encourage people to make these trade-offs; instead it encourages us to expect to get everything—efficiency, fairness, help for minorities—all at once.

AGENCY ALLIES

Despite these constraints, government bureaucracies are not powerless. In fact, some of them actively seek certain constraints. They do so because it is a way of cementing a useful relationship with a congressional committee or an interest group.

iron triangle
A close relationship between an agency, a congressional committee, and an interest group.

At one time scholars described the relationship between an agency, a committee, and an interest group as an **iron triangle.** For example, the Department of Veterans Affairs, the House and Senate committees on veterans' affairs, and veterans' organizations (such as the American Legion) would form a tight, mutually advantageous alliance. The department would do what the committees wanted and in return get political support and budget appropriations; the committee members would do what the veterans' groups wanted and in return get votes and campaign contributions. Iron triangles are examples of what are called *client politics*.

Many agencies still have important allies in Congress and the private sector, especially those bureaus that serve the needs of specific sectors of the economy or regions of the country. The Department of Agriculture works closely with farm organizations, the Department of the Interior with groups interested in obtaining low-cost irrigation or grazing rights, and the Department of Housing and Urban Development with mayors and real-estate developers.

Sometimes these allies are so strong that they can defeat a popular president. For years, President Reagan tried to abolish the Small Business Administration (SBA), arguing that its program of loans to small firms was wasteful and ridden with favoritism. But Congress, reacting to pressures from small-business groups, rallied to the SBA's defense. As a result, Reagan had to oversee an agency that he didn't want.

But iron triangles are much less common today than once was the case. Politics of late has become far more complicated. For one thing, the number and variety of interest groups have increased so much in recent years that scarcely any agency is not subject to pressures from several competing interests instead of only from one powerful interest. For another, the growth of subcommittees in Congress has meant most agencies are subject to control by many different legislative groups, often with very different concerns. Finally, the courts have made it much easier for all kinds of individuals and interests to intervene in agency affairs.

As a result, nowadays government agencies face a bewildering variety of competing groups and legislative subcommittees that constitute not a loyal group of allies, but a fiercely contentious collection of critics. The Environmental Protection Agency is caught between the demands of environmentalists and those of industry organizations, the Occupational Safety and Health Administration between the pressures of labor and those of business, and the Federal Communications Commission between the desires of broadcasters and those of cable television companies. Even the Department of Agriculture faces not a unified group of farmers, but many different farmers split into rival groups, depending on the crops they raise, the regions in which they live, and the attitudes they have toward the relative merits of farm subsidies or free markets.

Political scientist Hugh Heclo has described the typical government agency today as being embedded not in an iron triangle, but in an **issue network.**[25] These issue networks consist of people in Washington-based interest groups, on congressional staffs, in universities and think tanks, and in the mass media, who regularly debate government policy on a certain subject—say, health care or auto safety. The networks are contentious, split along political, ideological, and economic lines. When a president takes office, he often recruits key agency officials from those members of the issue network who are most sympathetic to his views.

issue network
A network of people in Washington, D.C.–based interest groups, on congressional staffs, in universities and think tanks, and in the mass media, who regularly discuss and advocate public policies.

When Jimmy Carter, a Democrat, became president, he appointed to key posts in consumer agencies people who were from that part of the consumer issue network associated with Ralph Nader. Ronald Reagan, a conservative Republican, filled these same jobs with people who were from that part of the issue network holding free-market or antiregulation views. When George Bush the elder, a more centrist Republican, took office, he filled these posts with more centrist members of the issue network. Bill Clinton brought back the consumer activists. George W. Bush reversed Clinton, and Barack Obama reversed Bush.

Congressional Oversight

The main reason why some interest groups are important to agencies is that they are important to Congress. Not every interest group in the country has substantial access to Congress, but those that do and that are taken seriously by the relevant committees or subcommittees must also be taken seriously by the agency. Furthermore, even apart from interest groups, members of Congress have constitutional powers over agencies and policy interests in how agencies function.

Congressional supervision of the bureaucracy takes several forms. First, no agency may exist (except for a few presidential offices and commissions) without congressional approval. Congress influences—and sometimes determines precisely—agency behavior by the statutes it enacts.

authorization legislation Legislative permission to begin or continue a government program or agency.

appropriation A legislative grant of money to finance a government program or agency.

trust funds Funds for government programs collected and spent outside the regular government budget.

Second, no money may be spent unless it has first been authorized by Congress. **Authorization legislation** originates in a legislative committee (such as Agriculture, Education and Labor, or Public Works) and states the maximum amount of money that an agency may spend on a given program. This authorization may be permanent, it may be for a fixed number of years, or it may be annual (that is, it must be renewed each year, or the program or agency goes out of business).

Third, even funds that have been authorized by Congress cannot be spent unless (in most cases) they are also appropriated. Appropriations usually are made annually, and they originate not with the legislative committees but with the House Appropriations Committee and its various (and influential) subcommittees. An **appropriation** (money formally set aside for a specific use) may be, and often is, for less than the amount authorized. The Appropriations Committee's action thus tends to have a budget-cutting effect. There are some funds that can be spent without an appropriation, but in virtually every part of the bureaucracy, each agency is keenly sensitive to congressional concerns at the time that the annual appropriations process is going on.

But is fidelity to the constitutional principle of separation of powers (see Chapter 2) called into question when Congress engages in oversight of agencies that are in the executive branch? Members of Congress themselves once debated that issue, but the aforementioned Administrative Procedure Act of 1946 and a dozen subsequent laws that built on it (the latest being the Data Quality Act of 2000, and all upheld when challenged in the courts) are predicated on the idea that agencies are "adjuncts for legislative functions. . . . Congress lacks the capacity to legislate on all matters it touches and perforce must delegate a great deal of legislative authority to the agencies."[26]

This idea was challenged during the George W. Bush presidency by administration officials and others who, especially but not exclusively with respect to military, national, and homeland security issues, argued that agencies were bound to act in accordance with the president's directives whenever they conflicted with directives from Congress. While Bush's executive-centered approach sparked many controversies, most scholars seem to think that it effected no major or lasting changes, and some suggest that it stirred Congress to pursue even more comprehensive (and aggressive) oversight policies and practices.[27]

THE APPROPRIATIONS COMMITTEE AND LEGISLATIVE COMMITTEES

The fact that an agency budget must be both authorized and appropriated means that each agency serves not one congressional master but several, and that these masters may be in conflict. The real power over an agency's budget is exercised by the Appropriations Committee; the legislative committees are especially important when a substantive law is first passed or an agency is first created, or when an agency is subject to annual authorization.

In the past, the power of the Appropriations Committee was rarely challenged: from 1947 through 1962, fully 90 percent of the House Appropriations Committee's recommendations on expenditures were approved by the full House without change.[28] Furthermore, the Appropriations Committee tends to recommend less money than an agency requests (though some specially favored agencies, such as the FBI, the Soil Conservation Service, and the Forest Service, have tended to get almost everything that they have asked for). Finally, the process of "marking up" (revising, amending, and approving) an agency's budget request gives to the Appropriations Committee, or one of its subcommittees, substantial influence over the policies that the agency follows.

Of late, the appropriations committees have lost some of their great power over government agencies. This has happened in three ways:

First, Congress has created trust funds to pay for the benefits many people receive. The Social Security trust fund is the largest of these. In 2008, it took in $695 billion in Social Security taxes and paid out $516 billion in old-age benefits. There are several other trust funds as well. **Trust funds** operate outside the regular government budget, and the appropriations committees have no control over these expenditures. They are automatic.

Second, Congress has changed the authorization of many programs from permanent or multiyear to annual authorizations. This means that every year the legislative committees, as part of the reauthorization process, get to set limits on what these agencies can spend. This limits the ability of the appropriations committees to determine the spending limits. Before 1959, most authorizations were permanent or multiyear. Now a long list of agencies must be reauthorized every year—the State Department, NASA, military procurement programs of the Defense Department, the Justice Department, the Energy Department, and parts or all of many other agencies.

Third, the existence of huge budget deficits during the 1980s and in the 2000s has meant that much of Congress's time has been taken up with trying (usually not very successfully) to keep spending down. As a result, there has rarely been much time to discuss the merits of various programs or how much ought to be spent on them; instead, attention has been focused on meeting a target spending limit. In 1981, the budget resolution passed by Congress mandated cuts in several programs before the appropriations committees had even completed their work.[29]

In addition to the power of the purse, there are informal ways by which Congress can control the bureaucracy. An individual member of Congress can call an agency head on behalf of a constituent. Most such calls merely seek information, but some result in, or attempt to obtain, special privileges for particular people. Congressional committees may also obtain the right to pass on certain agency decisions. This is called **committee clearance,** and though it usually is not legally binding on the agency, few agency heads will ignore the expressed wish of a committee chair that he or she be consulted before certain actions (such as transferring funds) are taken.

committee clearance
The ability of a congressional committee to review and approve certain agency decisions in advance and without passing a law.

legislative veto
The authority of Congress to block a presidential action after it has taken place. The Supreme Court has held that Congress does not have this power.

THE LEGISLATIVE VETO

For many decades, Congress made frequent use of the legislative veto to control bureaucratic or presidential actions. A **legislative veto** is a requirement that an executive decision must lie before Congress for a specified period (usually 30 or 90 days) before it takes effect. Congress could then veto the decision if a resolution of disapproval was passed by either house (a "one-house veto") or both houses (a "two-house veto"). Unlike laws, such resolutions were not signed by the president. Between 1932 and 1980, about 200 laws were passed providing for a legislative veto, many of them involving presidential proposals to sell arms abroad.

But in June 1983, the Supreme Court declared the legislative veto to be unconstitutional. In the *Chadha* case, the Court held that the Constitution clearly requires in Article I that "every order, resolution, or vote to which the concurrence of the Senate and House of Representatives may be necessary" (with certain minor exceptions) "shall be presented to the President of the United States," who must either approve it or return it with his veto attached. In short, Congress cannot take any action that has the force of law unless the president concurs in that action.[30] At a stroke of the pen parts of 200 laws suddenly became invalid.

At least that happened in theory. In fact, since the *Chadha* decision, Congress has passed a number of laws that contain legislative vetoes, despite the Supreme Court's having ruled against them! (Someone will have to go to court to test the constitutionality of these new provisions.)

Opponents of the legislative veto hope future Congresses will have to pass laws that state much more clearly than before what an agency may or may not do. But it is just as likely that Congress will continue to pass laws stated in general terms and require that agencies implementing those laws report their plans to Congress, so that it will have a chance to enact and send to the president a regular bill disapproving the proposed action. Or Congress may rely on informal (but scarcely weak) means of persuasion, including threats to reduce the appropriations of an agency that does not abide by congressional preferences.

CONGRESSIONAL INVESTIGATIONS

Perhaps the most visible and dramatic form of congressional supervision of an agency is the investigation. Since 1792, when Congress investigated an army defeat by a Native American tribe, congressional investigations of the bureaucracy have been a regular feature—sometimes constructive, sometimes destructive—of legislative-executive relations. The investigative power is not mentioned in the Constitution, but has been inferred from the power to legislate. The Supreme Court has consistently upheld this interpretation, though it has also said that such investigations should not be solely for the purpose of exposing the purely personal affairs of private individuals and must not operate to deprive citizens of their basic rights.[31] Congress may compel a person to attend an investigation by issuing a subpoena; anyone who ignores the subpoena may be punished for contempt. Congress can vote to send the person to jail or can refer the matter to a court for further action. As explained in Chapter 14, the president and his principal subordinates have refused to answer certain congressional inquiries on grounds of "executive privilege."

Although many areas of congressional oversight—budgetary review, personnel controls, investigations—are designed to control the exercise of bureaucratic discretion, other areas are intended to ensure the freedom of certain agencies from effective control, especially by the president. In dozens of cases, Congress has authorized department heads and bureau chiefs to operate independent of presidential preferences. Congress has resisted, for example, presidential efforts to ensure that policies to regulate pollution do not impose excessive costs on the economy, and interest groups have brought suit to prevent presidential coordination of various regulatory agencies. If the bureaucracy sometimes works at cross-purposes, it usually is because Congress—or competing committees in Congress—wants it that way.

Bureaucratic "Pathologies"

Everyone complains about bureaucracy in general (though rarely about bureaucratic agencies that everyone believes are desirable). This chapter should persuade you that it is difficult to say anything about bureaucracy "in general"; there are too many different kinds of agencies, kinds of bureaucrats, and kinds of programs to label the entire enterprise with some single adjective. Nevertheless, many people who recognize the enormous variety among government agencies still believe they all have some general features in common and suffer from certain shared problems or pathologies.

This is true enough, but the reasons for it—and the solutions, if any—are often not understood. There are five major (or at least frequently mentioned) problems with bureaucracies: red tape, conflict, duplication, imperialism, and waste. **Red tape** refers to the complex rules and procedures that must be followed to get something done.

red tape Complex bureaucratic rules and procedures that must be followed to get something done.

Conflict exists because some agencies seem to be working at cross-purposes with other agencies. (For example, the Agricultural Research Service tells farmers how to grow crops more efficiently, while the Agricultural Stabilization and Conservation Service pays farmers to grow fewer crops or to produce less.) *Duplication* (usually called "wasteful duplication") occurs when two government agencies seem to be doing the same thing, as when the Customs Service and the Drug Enforcement Administration both attempt to intercept illegal drugs being smuggled into the country. *Imperialism* refers to the tendency of agencies to grow without regard to the benefits that their programs confer or the costs that they entail. *Waste* means spending more than is necessary to buy some product or service.

These problems all exist, but they do not necessarily exist because bureaucrats are incompetent or power-hungry. Most exist because of the very nature of government itself. Take red tape: partly we encounter cumbersome rules and procedures because any large organization, governmental or not, must have some way of ensuring that one part of the organization does not operate out of step with another. Business corporations have red tape also; it is to a certain extent a consequence of bigness. But a great amount of governmental red tape is also the result of the need to satisfy legal and political requirements. Government agencies must hire on the basis of "merit," must observe strict accounting rules, must supply Congress with detailed information on their programs, and must allow for citizen access in countless ways. Meeting each need requires rules; enforcing the rules requires forms.

Or take conflict and duplication: they do not occur because bureaucrats enjoy conflict or duplication. (Quite the contrary!) They exist because Congress,

David McNew/Getty Images

At the world's busiest border crossing, cars line up to enter the United States in Tijuana, Mexico.

in setting up agencies and programs, often wants to achieve a number of different, partially inconsistent goals or finds that it cannot decide which goal it values the most. Congress has 535 members and little strong leadership; it should not be surprising that 535 people will want different things and will sometimes succeed in getting them.

Imperialism results in large measure from government agencies' seeking goals so vague and so difficult to measure that it is hard to tell when they have been attained. When Congress is unclear as to exactly what an agency is supposed to do, the agency will often convert that legislative vagueness into bureaucratic imperialism by taking the largest possible view of its powers. It may do this on its own; more often it does so because interest groups and judges rush in to fill the vacuum left by Congress. As we saw in Chapter 3, the 1973 Rehabilitation Act was passed with a provision barring discrimination against people with disabilities in any program receiving federal aid. Under pressure from people with disabilities, that lofty but vague goal was converted by the Department of Transportation into a requirement that virtually every big-city bus have a device installed to lift people in wheelchairs onboard.

Waste is probably the biggest criticism that people have of the bureaucracy. Everybody has heard stories of the Pentagon's paying $91 for screws that cost 3 cents in the hardware store. President Reagan's "Private Sector Survey on Cost Control," generally known as the Grace Commission (after its chairman, J. Peter Grace), publicized these and other tales in a 1984 report. No doubt there is waste in government. After all, unlike a business firm worried about maximizing profits, in a government agency there are only weak incentives to keep costs down. If a business employee cuts costs, he or she often receives a bonus or raise, and the firm gets to add the savings to its profits. If a government official cuts costs, he or she receives no reward, and the agency cannot keep the savings—they go back to the Treasury.

But many of the horror stories are either exaggerations or unusual occurrences.[32] Most of the screws, hammers, and light bulbs purchased by the government are obtained at low cost by means of competitive bidding among several suppliers. When the government does pay outlandish amounts, the reason typically is that it is purchasing a new or one-of-a-kind item not available at your neighborhood hardware store—for example, a new bomber or missile.

Even when the government is not overcharged, it still may spend more money than a private firm in buying what it needs. The reason is red tape—the rules and procedures designed to ensure that when the government buys something, it will do so in a way that serves the interests of many groups. For example, it often must buy from American rather than foreign suppliers, even if the latter charge a lower price; it must make use of contractors that employ minorities; it must hire only union laborers and pay them the "prevailing" (that is, the highest) wage; it must allow public inspection of its records; it frequently is required to choose contractors favored by influential members of Congress; and so on. Private firms do not have to comply with all these rules and thus can buy for less.

From this discussion, it should be easy to see why these five basic bureaucratic problems are so hard to correct. To end conflicts and duplication, Congress would have to make some policy choices and set some clear priorities, but with all the competing demands that it faces, Congress finds it difficult to do that. You make more friends by helping people than by hurting them, and so Congress is more inclined to add new programs than to cut old ones, whether or not the new programs are in conflict with existing ones. To check imperialism, some way would have to be found to measure the benefits of government, but that is often impossible; government exists in part to achieve precisely those goals—such as national defense—that are least measurable. Furthermore, what might be done to remedy some problems would make other problems worse: if you simplify rules and procedures to cut red tape, you are also likely to reduce the coordination among agencies and thus to increase the extent to which there is duplication or conflict. If you want to reduce waste, you will have to have more rules and inspectors—in short, more red tape. The problem of bureaucracy is inseparable from the problem of government generally.

Just as people are likely to say they dislike Congress but like their own member of Congress, they are inclined to express hostility toward "the bureaucracy" but goodwill for that part of the bureaucracy with which they have dealt personally. While most Americans have unfavorable impressions of government agencies and officials in general, they have quite favorable impressions about government agencies and officials with whom they have had direct contact or about which they claim to know something specific.

For example, Table 15.2 shows that wide majorities have very or somewhat favorable impressions of diverse federal government agencies. Surveys dating back decades suggest that, despite persistent public complaints about "the bureaucracy," most

Table 15.2 How the Public Views Particular Federal Agencies

Percent reporting a "favorable or unfavorable impression"*

AGENCY	% FAVORABLE Very/Somewhat/Total	% UNFAVORABLE Very/Somewhat/Total	Favorable Minus Unfavorable
Postal Service	58/31/89	5/5/10	+79
FBI	31/46/77	10/7/17	+60
Defense Department	31/34/65	15/2/17	+48
Social Security Admin.	24/40/64	19/13/32	+32
EPA	23/40/63	15/15/31	+32
CIA	22/36/58	16/14/30	+28
Homeland Security	24/36/60	17/17/34	+26
Transportation Safety	15/41/56	16/9/25	+26
Education Department	22/37/59	19/19/38	+21
IRS	14/42/56	21/18/39	+17
FEMA	16/33/49	24/26/50	−1

*Other response categories were "never heard of" and "can't rate," and only the newest agency, the Transportation Safety Administration, drew significant numbers in each category (9 percent for each).

Source: Adapted from results of a nationally representative Associated Press/IPSOS Public Agenda poll conducted December 17–19, 2007.

Americans have judged, and continue to judge, each federal agency to be fair and useful.[33] Even the tax-collecting IRS has more public fans than foes, as did the new Transportation Safety Administration (TSA) whose workers people routinely encounter at airport security checkpoints.

Politically Speaking

Red Tape

As early as the seventh century, legal and government documents in England were bound together with a tape of pinkish-red color. In the 1850s, historian Thomas Carlyle described a British politician as "little other than a red tape Talking Machine," and later the American writer Washington Irving said of an American figure that "his brain was little better than red tape and parchment."

Since then *red tape* has come to mean "bureaucratic delay or confusion," especially that accompanied by unnecessary paperwork.

Source: From *Safire's Political Dictionary* by William Safire. Copyright © 1968, 1972, 1978 by William Safire. Reprinted by permission of Random House, Inc. and the author.

This finding helps explain why government agencies are rarely reduced in size or budget: whatever the popular feelings about the bureaucracy, any given agency tends to have many friends. Even the much-criticized FEMA, viewed unfavorably by half the public, was able to fend off budget cuts in the several years following its failed response to Hurricane Katrina.

Reforming the Bureaucracy

The history of American bureaucracy has been punctuated with countless efforts to make it work better and cost less. There were 11 major attempts in the 20th century alone. The latest was the National Performance Review (NPR)—popularly called the plan to "reinvent government"—led by Vice President Al Gore.

The NPR differed from many of the preceding reform efforts in one important way. Most of the earlier ones suggested ways of increasing central (that is, presidential) control of government agencies: the Brownlow Commission (1936–1937) recommended giving the president more assistants, the First Hoover Commission (1947–1949) suggested ways of improving top-level management, and the Ash Council (1969–1971) called for consolidating existing agencies into a few big "super departments."

HOW WE COMPARE

Outsourcing Government

In the United States, government by proxy is the norm. Bureaucrats in Washington pay state and local governments and private groups to staff and administer most federal programs.

For instance, Medicaid, the main federal health program for low-income citizens, is administered mainly by state agencies. The federal government has co-funded nonprofit groups to lead recovery efforts in the hurricane-ravaged Gulf Coast. At points during the second Gulf War, there were nearly as many for-profit workers as U.S. soldiers in Iraq.

The Canadian and Indian central governments each administer many policies via provincial or territorial governments; and every European government uses private contractors for at least some functions.

But most other democracies restrict and regulate outsourcing more than the United States does; for example, German law directs that all persons involved in administering national policies must be directly supervised by a government official.

And no other nation follows the American practice whereby government bureaucracies give tax-exempt organizations, including local faith-based groups, grants to administer myriad health and human services programs.

Many experts argue that outsourcing and proxy government have gone too far in this country; but none is sure whether or how it can be reined in, and most admit that public administration in other democracies is also far from perfect.

Sources: Donald F. Kettl, *The Next Government of the United States: Why Our Institutions Fail Us and How to Fix Them* (New York: W. W. Norton, 2008); Paul R. Verkuil, *Outsourcing Sovereignty: Why Privatization of Government Functions Threatens Democracy and What We Can Do About It* (Cambridge: Cambridge University Press, 2007); John J. DiIulio, Jr., "Government by Proxy: A Faithful Overview," *Harvard Law Review*, March 2003, pp. 1271–1284.

The intent was to make it easier for the president and his cabinet secretaries to run the bureaucracy. The key ideas were efficiency, accountability, and consistent policies.

The NPR, by contrast, emphasized customer satisfaction (the "customers" in this case being the citizens who come into contact with federal agencies). To the authors of the NPR report, the main problem with the bureaucracy was that it had become too centralized, too rule-bound, too little concerned with making programs work, and too much concerned with avoiding scandal. The NPR report contained many horror stories about useless red tape, excessive regulations, and cumbersome procurement systems that make it next to impossible for agencies to do what they were created to do. (For example, before it could buy an ashtray, the General Services Administration issued a nine-page document that described an ashtray and specified how many pieces it must break into, should it be hit with a hammer.)[34]

To solve these problems, the NPR called for less centralized management and more employee initiative, fewer detailed rules and more emphasis on customer satisfaction. It sought to create a new kind of organizational culture in government agencies, one more like that found in the more innovative, quality-conscious American corporations. The NPR was reinforced legislatively by the Government Performance and Results Act (GPRA) of 1993, which required agencies "to set goals, measure performance, and report on the results."

President George W. Bush built on the Clinton-Gore NPR efforts and the GPRA using the Performance Assessment Rating Tool (PART). The main goal of the PART was to link management reform to the budget process. During the 2008 presidential campaign, Barack Obama harkened back to the Clinton-Gore NPR but also pledged to keep but improve Bush's PART. By 2011, however, administrative reform was not widely mentioned among Obama's main priorities or accomplishments in office.

Reforming the bureaucracy is easier said than done. Most of the rules and red tape that make it hard for agency heads to do a good job are the result either of the struggle between the White House and Congress for control over the agencies or of the agencies' desire to avoid irritating influential voters. Silly as the rules for ashtrays may sound, they were written so that the government could say it had an "objective" standard for buying ashtrays. If it simply went out and bought ashtrays at a department store the way ordinary people do, it would risk being accused by the Acme Ashtray Company of buying trays from its competitor, the A-1 Ashtray Company, because of political favoritism.

The rivalry between the president and Congress for control of the bureaucracy makes bureaucrats nervous about irritating either branch, and so they issue

David McNew/Getty Images

Mayor Villaraigosa goes through a full-body scanner at Los Angeles International Airport.

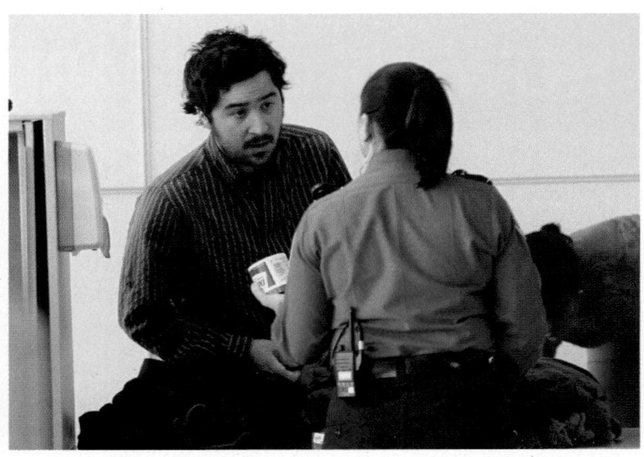

REUTERS/Mike Segar

An airline passenger is questioned by Transportation Security Administration inspector at Newark airport.

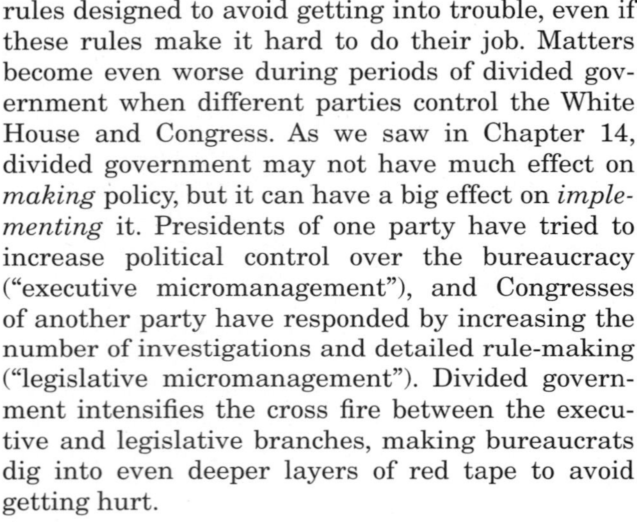

rules designed to avoid getting into trouble, even if these rules make it hard to do their job. Matters become even worse during periods of divided government when different parties control the White House and Congress. As we saw in Chapter 14, divided government may not have much effect on *making* policy, but it can have a big effect on *implementing* it. Presidents of one party have tried to increase political control over the bureaucracy ("executive micromanagement"), and Congresses of another party have responded by increasing the number of investigations and detailed rule-making ("legislative micromanagement"). Divided government intensifies the cross fire between the executive and legislative branches, making bureaucrats dig into even deeper layers of red tape to avoid getting hurt.

This does not mean that reform is impossible, only that it is very difficult. For example, despite a lack of clear-cut successes in other areas, the NPR's procurement reforms stuck: government agencies can now buy things costing as much as $100,000 without following any complex regulations. Still, the main effect of the NPR, the GPRA, and the PART was to get federal agencies collecting far more information than in the past concerning what they do without, however, using the information to improve the way they do it.[35]

It might be easier to make desirable changes if the bureaucracy were accountable to only one master—say, the president—instead of to several. But that situation, which exists in many parliamentary democracies, creates its own problems. When the bureaucracy has but one master, it often ends up having none: it becomes so powerful that it controls the prime minister and no longer listens to citizen complaints. A weak, divided bureaucracy, such as exists in the United States, may strike us as inefficient, but that very inefficiency may help protect our liberties.

WHAT WOULD YOU DO?

MEMORANDUM

To: *Dr. Robert Smith, president of Cybersystems Engineering*

From: *James Logan, secretary of defense*

Subject: *Becoming an assistant secretary of defense*

As both secretary and a dear old college buddy of yours, I write again to express my hope that you will accept the president's call to service. We all desperately want you aboard. Yes, conflict-of-interest laws will require you to sell your stock in your present company and drop out of its generous pension plan. No, the government won't even pay moving costs. And once you leave office, you will be barred for life from lobbying the executive branch on matters in which you were directly involved while in office, and you will be barred for two years from lobbying on matters that were under your general official authority. Your other concerns have teeth, too, but let me help you weigh your options.

News »

New Administration Struggling to Fill Top Posts—Cabinet Secretaries Say "The President Needs Help!"

Four months into the new administration, hundreds of assistant secretary and deputy assistant secretary positions remain unfilled. In 1960 the total number of presidential political appointees was just 450. Today the total is closer to 3,000 but sheer growth is not the whole story. Rather, say experts on federal bureaucracy, plum public service posts go unfilled because the jobs have become so unrewarding, even punishing.

Arguments for:

1. I hate to preach, but it is one's duty to serve one's country when called. Your sacrifice would honor your family and benefit your fellow Americans for years to come.
2. As an accomplished professional and the head of a company that has done business with the government, you could help the president succeed in reforming the department so that it works better and costs less.
3. Despite the restrictions, you could resume your career once your public service was complete.

Arguments against:

1. Since you will have to be confirmed by the Senate, your life will be put under a microscope, and everything (even some of our old college mischief together) will be fair game for congressional staffers and reporters.
2. You will face hundreds of rules telling you what you can't do and scores of congresspersons telling you what you should do. Old friends will get mad at you for not doing them favors. The president will demand loyalty. The press will pounce on your every mistake, real or imagined.
3. Given the federal limits on whom in the government you can deal with after you leave office, your job at Cybersystems may well suffer.

Your decision:

Accept position ________________ Reject position ________________

LEARNING OBJECTIVES

WHAT YOU NEED TO KNOW

☑ What is "bureaucracy" and in what ways is the American bureaucracy distinctive?

A bureaucracy is a large, complex organization composed of appointed officials. American bureaucracy is distinctive in three ways: political authority over the bureaucracy is shared by several institutions; most national government agencies share their functions with state and local government agencies; and government agencies are closely scrutinized and frequently challenged by both individuals and nongovernmental groups.

☑ What is "discretionary authority" and why do some bureaucrats have lots of it?

Discretionary authority refers to the extent to which appointed bureaucrats can choose courses of action and make policies not spelled out in advance by laws. It is impossible for Congress to specify every last detail regarding how a law it passes is to be implemented. Many laws are administered by persons with special information and expertise, and many private citizens administer public laws by working as government contractors or grantees.

☑ How does Congress exert control over the bureaucracy?

Congress exerts control over the bureaucracy in many different ways. It decides whether an agency may exist and how much money an agency spends. It can hold oversight hearings and launch investigations into just about any aspect of agency decision making or operations it chooses. And it traditionally has enjoyed wide latitude from the president in exercising its oversight functions.

RECONSIDERING WHO GOVERNS?

1. What happened to make the bureaucracy a "fourth branch" of American national government?

The Constitution made no provision for an administrative system other than to allow the president to appoint, with the advice and consent of the Senate, ambassadors, Supreme Court judges, and "all other officers . . . which shall be provided by law."

By the early 20th century, however, Washington's role in making, administering, and funding public policies had already grown far beyond what the Framers had contemplated. Two world wars, the New Deal, and the Great Society each left the government with expanded powers and requiring new batteries of administrative agencies to exercise them. Today, the federal bureaucracy is as vast as most people's expectations about Washington's responsibility for every public concern one can name. It is the appointed officials—the bureaucrats—not the elected officials or policymakers, who command the troops, deliver the mail, audit the tax returns, run the federal prisons, decide who qualifies for public assistance, and do countless other tasks. Unavoidably, many bureaucrats exercise discretion in deciding what public laws and regulations mean and how to apply them. Still, the president, cabinet secretaries, and thousands of political appointees are ultimately their bosses. Congress and the courts have ample, if imperfect, means of checking and balancing even the biggest bureaucracy, old or new.

2. What are the actual size and scope of the federal bureaucracy?

A few million civil servants work directly for the federal government, but more than five times as many people work indirectly for Washington as employees of business firms or of nonprofit organizations that receive federal grants or contracts, or as state and local government employees working under federal mandates. For example, the U.S. Department of Health and Human Services (HHS) has about 60,000 employees, runs more than 300 different programs, and makes more than 60,000 grants a year. But millions more people work indirectly for the HHS—as state and local government employees whose entire jobs involve the administration of one or more HHS programs (for example, Medicaid), and as people who work for community-serving nonprofit organizations that receive HHS grants to administer social services.

RECONSIDERING TO WHAT ENDS?

1. What should be done to improve bureaucratic performance?

There have been numerous efforts to make the bureaucracy work better and cost less, including 11 presidential or other major commissions in the 20th century. Among the latest was the National Performance Review (NPR), popularly called the plan to "reinvent government." Vice President Gore led the NPR during the two terms of the Clinton administration. The NPR was predicated on the view that bureaucracy had become too centralized, too rule-bound, too little concerned with program results, and too much concerned with avoiding scandal. In the end, the NPR produced certain money-saving changes in the federal procurement process (how government purchases goods and services from private contractors), and it also streamlined parts of the federal personnel process (how Washington hires career employees). Most experts, however, gave the NPR mixed grades. The Bush Administration abolished the NPR but began the Performance Assessment Rating Tool (PART). Most experts judged the PART to be only mildly successful.

2. Is "red tape" all bad?

No, not all. Red tape refers to the complex rules and procedures that must be follo
to get something done. All large organizations, including business firms, have som
red tape. Some red tape in government agencies is silly and wasteful (or worse), b
try imagining government without any red tape at all. Imagine no rules about hir
on the basis of merit, no strict financial accounting procedures, and no regulations
concerning citizen access to information or public record keeping. As the Yale polit
scientist Herbert Kaufman once quipped, one citizen's "red tape" often is another's
"treasured procedural safeguard."

QUESTIONS TO CONSIDER

1. **Even though reforming the bureaucracy is difficult, in what respects do you think federal government agencies are most badly in need of reform?**
2. **Why do you suppose it is that the news media tend to focus on how laws get administered only when something goes oddly or horribly wrong, or when the agencies obviously fail to get the job done (as most agencies failed in responding to Hurricane Katrina)? (And don't be bashful in saying so if you think the answer is quite simply "bureaucracy is boring.")**
3. **According to opinion polls, what federal agencies are most popular and least popular with the general public today?**
4. **Does your school receive any federal funding, grants, or contracts, and, if so, via what federal agencies?**
5. **Which agencies in your state or city are proxy administrators for federal crime, environmental protection, or food security and nutrition policies or programs?**

TO LEARN MORE

For addresses and reports of various cabinet departments:

Web addresses: **www.whitehouse.gov**

Documents and bulletin boards: **www.fedworld.gov**

National Performance Review: **www.npr.gov**

A few specific Web sites of federal agencies:

Department of Defense: **www.defenselink.mil**

Department of Education: **www.ed.gov**

Department of Health and Human Services: **www.dhhs.gov**

Department of State: **www.state.gov**

Federal Bureau of Investigation: **www.fbi.gov**

Department of Labor: **www.dol.gov**

Burke, John P. *Bureaucratic Responsibility*. Baltimore: Johns Hopkins University Press, 1986. Examines the problem of individual responsibility—for example, when to be a whistle blower—in government agencies.

Downs, Anthony. *Inside Bureaucracy*. Boston: Little, Brown, 1967. An economist's explanation of why bureaucrats and bureaus behave as they do.

Durant, Robert F., ed. *The Oxford Handbook of American Bureaucracy*. New York: Oxford University Press, 2010. Thirty-three largely up-to-date academic essays covering just about every facet of the subject.

Halperin, Morton H. *Bureaucratic Politics and Foreign Policy*. Washington, D.C.: Brookings Institution, 1974. Insightful account of the strategies by which diplomatic and military bureaucracies defend their interests.

Heclo, Hugh. *A Government of Strangers*. Washington, D.C.: Brookings Institution, 1977. Analyzes how political appointees attempt to gain control of the Washington bureaucracy and how bureaucrats resist those efforts.

Kettl, Donald F. *Government by Proxy*. Washington, D.C.: Congressional Quarterly Press, 1988. An account of how the federal government pays others to staff and run its programs.

Kettl, Donald F. *The Next Government of the United States: Why Our Institutions Fail Us and How to Fix Them*. New York: W. W. Norton, 2008. A masterful study of how proxy government functions and often fails today, and what might be done to remedy its worst failures.

Moore, Mark H. *Creating Public Value: Strategic Management in Government*. Cambridge: Harvard University Press, 1995. A thoughtful account of how wise bureaucrats can make government work better.

Parkinson, C. Northcote. *Parkinson's Law*. Boston: Houghton Mifflin, 1957. Half-serious, half-joking explanation of why government agencies tend to grow.

Wilson, James Q. *Bureaucracy: What Government Agencies Do and Why They Do It*. New York: Basic Books, 1989. A comprehensive review of what we know about bureaucratic behavior in the United States.

16 The Judiciary

LEARNING OBJECTIVES

WHAT DO YOU NEED TO KNOW?

- ☑ Where in the Constitution does it say that the Supreme Court has the power of judicial review?
- ☑ What is meant by an "Article III" federal judge?
- ☑ Does England have a Supreme Court?
- ☑ What is the difference between original and appellate jurisdiction?

WHO GOVERNS?

1. Why should federal judges serve for life?

TO WHAT ENDS?

1. Why should federal courts be able to declare laws unconstitutional?
2. Should federal judges only interpret existing laws or should they be able to create new laws?

THEN When the states were debating the ratification of the Constitution, Alexander Hamilton wrote in *Federalist* paper No. 78 that the new system of federal courts would be "the least dangerous" branch of government because, unlike the president, it would not command the sword and, unlike Congress, it would not control the purse strings. The courts, he argued, could take "no active resolution whatever." Nowhere in the Constitution was the Supreme Court given the right to declare laws of Congress or decisions of the president to be unconstitutional, though Hamilton argued that such a power was necessary. That document was our fundamental law and expressed the will of the people, and so it ought to be preferred to a law passed by Congress if there were an "irreconcilable variance between the two."

NOW Within a few years after the Constitution was ratified, the Supreme Court took Hamilton's position by asserting that the Court could decide if a law was unconstitutional. A dozen years later, the same Court said that Congress could not only pass laws on the basis of powers explicitly given it by the Constitution, but also do things that were "necessary and proper" in order to implement those powers. By the middle of the 19th century, the Supreme Court had begun to declare many federal and scores of state laws to be unconstitutional.

As a result of its newfound powers, justices began serving on the Supreme Court for much longer periods. The 11 justices nominated by President George Washington served, on average, seven years, while the five nominated 40 years later by President Andrew Jackson served on average 20 years. The Court had become not the least dangerous branch, but a powerful one.

In time, the identity of these justices became an important political issue. Until recently, most justices were confirmed by the Senate, and from 1947 to 1985, almost

all persons nominated to be a federal appeals court judge were approved. But of late, these nominations have had a less certain reception in the Senate. When President Ronald Reagan nominated Antonin Scalia, he was confirmed by the Senate in 1986 by a vote of 98–0. But one year later, when President Reagan nominated Robert Bork, he was rejected by the Senate. Four years after that, Clarence Thomas barely survived a confirmation vote, and in 2005, Samuel Alito won a narrow confirmation victory. By 2000, the percentage of appeals court judges confirmed by the Senate had fallen to 40 percent (see Figure 16.3 on page 449).

Why the change? One reason is partisanship. A Senate under Democratic control is suspicious of the nominees chosen by a Republican president. In recent years, Stephen Breyer, Ruth Bader Ginsburg, Anthony Kennedy, and David Souter were easily confirmed. One reason for this difference may have been that Bork, Thomas, and Alito were regarded as conservatives, whereas Breyer, Ginsburg, and Souter were regarded as liberals (or, in the case of Souter, as having unknown views). For Supreme Court nominees, the Senate tends to be tougher on conservatives than on liberals. But for the federal courts of appeal, the Senate is tough on the left as well as the right. As you can see in Figure 16.3 (page 449), there has been a sharp drop since the early 1980s in the speed at which appeals court candidates are confirmed no matter which party controls the Senate.

But an equally important and closely related reason is that the federal judiciary has played an increasingly important role in making public policy. It, and not Congress, decided that abortions should be legal, settled the closely contested 2000 presidential election, and allowed private homes to be seized in order to build a residential hotel and other private structures aimed at affluent clientele. In these and many other cases, the federal courts have become major political actors; as a result, Congress has become concerned about who will be federal judges. As you will see on page 449, by the 1980s, the senatorial habit of confirming every nominee to federal appeals courts had collapsed. As federal judges make more policy decisions, however, the Senate pays more close attention to who they are.

They do this because tradition allows senators from the home state of an appeals court nominee to file a private objection—what is called registering a negative "blue slip" complaint. If filed by a Judiciary Committee member, this will prevent a hearing on the nominee from being held. Sometimes these blue slips indicate that a senator doesn't like the nominee's political views, but other times it can mean that the senator is blocking a judicial appointment as a way of inducing the president to do something he wants on a totally unrelated matter.

judicial review The power of courts to declare laws unconstitutional.

judicial restraint approach The view that judges should decide cases strictly on the basis of the language of the laws and the Constitution.

activist approach The view that judges should discern the general principles underlying laws or the Constitution and apply them to modern circumstances.

Judicial Review

One aspect of the power of the federal courts is **judicial review**—the right of the federal courts to declare laws of Congress and acts of the executive branch void and unenforceable if they are judged to be in conflict with the Constitution. Since 1789, the Supreme Court has declared more than 160 federal laws to be unconstitutional. In Britain, by contrast, Parliament is supreme, and no court may strike down a law that it passes. As the second earl of Pembroke supposedly said, "A parliament can do anything but make a man a woman and a woman a man." All that prevents Parliament from acting contrary to the (unwritten) constitution of Britain are the consciences of its members and the opinions of the citizens.

About 60 nations do have something resembling judicial review, but in only a few cases does this power mean much in practice. Where it means something—in Australia, Canada, Germany, India, and some other nations—one finds a stable, federal system of government with a strong tradition of an independent judiciary.[1] Some other nations—France, for example—have special councils, rather than courts, that can under certain circumstances decide that a law is not authorized by the constitution.

Judicial review is the federal courts' chief weapon in the system of checks and balances on which the American government is based. Today, few people would deny to the courts the right to decide that a legislative or executive act is unconstitutional, though once that right was controversial. What remains controversial is the method by which such review is conducted.

There are two competing views, each ardently pressed during the fight to confirm Clarence Thomas. The first holds that judges should only judge—that is, they should confine themselves to applying those rules stated in or clearly implied by the language of the Constitution. This often is called the **judicial restraint approach.** The other argues that judges should discover the general principles underlying the Constitution and its often vague language, amplify those principles on the basis of some moral or economic philosophy, and apply them to cases. This is sometimes called the **activist approach.**

Note that the difference between activist and strict-constructionist judges is not necessarily the same as the difference between liberals and conservatives. Judges can be political liberals and still believe they are bound by the language of the Constitution. A liberal justice, Hugo Black, once voted to uphold a state law banning birth control because nothing in the Constitution prohibited such a law. Or judges can be conservative and still think they have a duty to use their best judgment in deciding what is good public policy. Rufus Peckham, one such conservative, voted to overturn a state law setting maximum hours of work because he believed the Fourteenth Amendment guaranteed something called "freedom of contract," even though those words are not in the amendment. Seventy years ago, judicial activists tended to be conservatives and strict-constructionist judges tended to be liberals; today the opposite usually is the case.

Table 16.1 Chief Justices of the United States

Chief Justice	Appointed by	Years of Service
John Jay	Washington	1789–1795
Oliver Ellsworth	Washington	1796–1800
John Marshall	Adams	1801–1835
Roger B. Taney	Jackson	1836–1864
Salmon P. Chase	Lincoln	1864–1873
Morrison R. Waite	Grant	1874–1888
Melville W. Fuller	Cleveland	1888–1910
Edward D. White	Taft	1910–1921
William Howard Taft	Harding	1921–1930
Charles Evans Hughes	Hoover	1930–1941
Harlan Fiske Stone	F. Roosevelt	1941–1946
Fred M. Vinson	Truman	1946–1953
Earl Warren	Eisenhower	1953–1969
Warren E. Burger	Nixon	1969–1986
William H. Rehnquist	Reagan	1986–2005
John G. Roberts, Jr.	Bush	2005–present

Note: Omitted is John Rutledge, who served for only a few months in 1795 and who was not confirmed by the Senate.

The Development of the Federal Courts

Most of the Founders probably expected the Supreme Court to have the power of judicial review (though they did not say that in so many words in the Constitution), but they did not expect federal courts to play so large a role in making public policy. The traditional view of civil courts was that they judged disputes between people who had direct dealings with each other—they had entered into a contract, for example, or one had dropped a load of bricks on the other's toe—and decided which of the two parties was right. The court then supplied relief to the wronged party, usually by requiring the other person to pay him or her money ("damages").

This traditional understanding was based on the belief that judges would find and apply existing law. The purpose of a court case was not to learn what the judge believes but what the law requires. The later rise of judicial activism occurred when judges questioned this traditional view and argued instead that judges do not merely find the law, they make the law.

The view that judges interpret the law and do not make policy made it easy for the Founders to justify the power of judicial review and led them to predict that the courts would play a relatively neutral, even passive, role in public affairs. Alexander Hamilton, writing in *Federalist* No. 78, described the judiciary as the branch "least dangerous" to political rights. The president is commander in chief and thus holds the "sword of the community"; Congress appropriates money and thus "commands the purse" as well as decides what laws shall govern. But the judiciary "has no influence over either the sword or the purse" and "can take no active resolution whatever." It has "neither force nor will but merely judgment," and thus is "beyond comparison the weakest of the three departments of power." As a result, "liberty can have nothing to fear from the judiciary alone." Hamilton went on to state clearly that the Constitution intended to give to the courts the right to decide whether a law is contrary to the Constitution. But this authority, he explained, was designed not to enlarge the power of the courts but to confine that of the legislature.

Obviously, things have changed since Hamilton's time. The evolution of the federal courts, especially the Supreme Court, toward the present level of activism and influence has been shaped by the political, economic, and ideological forces of three historical eras. From 1787 to 1865, nation building, the legitimacy of the federal government, and slavery were the great issues; from 1865 to 1937, the great issue was the relationship between the government and the economy; from 1938 to the present, the major issues confronting the Court have involved personal liberty and social equality and the potential conflict between the two. In the first period, the Court asserted the supremacy of the federal government; in the second, it placed important restrictions on the powers of that government; and in the third, it enlarged the scope of personal freedom and narrowed that of economic freedom.

NATIONAL SUPREMACY AND SLAVERY

"From 1789 until the Civil War, the dominant interest of the Supreme Court was in that greatest of all the questions left unresolved by the Founders—the nation-state relationship."[2] The answer the Court gave, under the leadership of Chief Justice John Marshall, was that national law was in all instances the dominant law, with state law having to give way, and that the Supreme Court had the power to decide what the Constitution meant. In two cases of enormous importance—*Marbury v. Madison* in 1803 and *McCulloch v. Maryland* in 1819—the Court, in decisions written by Marshall, held that the Supreme Court could declare an act of Congress unconstitutional; that the power granted by the Constitution to the federal government flows from the people and thus should be generously construed (and thus any federal laws that are "necessary and proper" to the attainment of constitutional ends are permissible); and that federal law is supreme over state law, even to the point that a state may not tax an enterprise (such as a bank) created by the federal government.[3]

The supremacy of the federal government was reaffirmed by other decisions as well. In 1816, the Supreme Court rejected the claim of the Virginia courts that the Supreme Court could not review the decisions of state courts. The Virginia courts were ready to acknowledge the supremacy of the U.S. Constitution but believed they had as much right as the U.S. Supreme Court to decide what the Constitution meant. The Supreme Court felt otherwise, and in this case and another like it, the Court asserted its own broad powers to review any state court decision if that decision seemed to violate federal law or the federal Constitution.[4]

The power of the federal government to regulate commerce among the states was also established. When New York gave to Robert Fulton, the inventor of the steamboat, the monopoly right to operate his steamboats on the rivers of that state, the Marshall Court overturned the license because the rivers connected New York and New Jersey and thus trade on those rivers would involve *inter*state commerce, and federal law in that area was supreme. Since there was a conflicting federal law on the books, the state law was void.[5]

All of this may sound rather obvious to us today, when the supremacy of the federal government is largely unquestioned. In the early 19th century, however, these were almost revolutionary decisions. The Jeffersonian Republicans were in power and had become increasingly devoted to states' rights; they were aghast at the Marshall decisions. President Andrew Jackson attacked the Court bitterly for defending the right of the federal government to create a national bank and for siding with the Cherokee Indians in a dispute with Georgia. In speaking of the latter case, Jackson is supposed to have remarked, "John Marshall has made his decision; now let him enforce it!"[6]

Though Marshall seemed to have secured the supremacy of the federal government over the state governments, another even more divisive issue had arisen; that, of course, was slavery. Roger B. Taney succeeded Marshall as chief justice in 1836. He was deliberately chosen by President Jackson because he was an advocate of states' rights, and he began to chip away at federal supremacy, upholding state claims that Marshall would have set aside. But the decision for which he is famous—or infamous—came in 1857 when, in the *Dred Scott* case, he wrote perhaps the most disastrous judicial opinion ever issued. A slave, Dred Scott, had been taken by his owner to a territory (near what is now St. Paul, Minnesota) where slavery was illegal under federal law. Scott claimed that since he had resided in a free territory, he was now a free man. Taney held that Negroes were not citizens of the United States and could not become so, and that the federal law—the Missouri Compromise—prohibiting slavery in northern territories was unconstitutional.[7] The public outcry against this view was enormous, and the Court and Taney were discredited in the North, at least. The Civil War was ultimately fought over what the Court mistakenly had assumed was a purely legal question.

GOVERNMENT AND THE ECONOMY

The supremacy of the federal government may have been established by John Marshall and the Civil War, but the scope of the powers of that government or even of the state governments was still to be defined. During the period from the end of the Civil War to the early years of the New Deal, the dominant issue the Supreme Court faced was deciding when the economy would be regulated by the states and when by the nation.

The Court revealed a strong though not inflexible attachment to private property. In fact, that attachment had always been there: the Founders thought political and property rights were inextricably linked, and Marshall certainly supported the sanctity of contracts. But now, with the muting of the federal supremacy issue and the rise of a national economy with important unanticipated effects, the property question became the dominant one. In general, the Court developed the view that the Fourteenth Amendment, adopted in 1868 primarily to protect African American claims to citizenship from hostile state action, also protected private property and the corporation from unreasonable state action. The crucial phrase was this: no state shall "deprive any person of life, liberty, or property, without due process of law." Once it became clear that a "person" could be a firm or a corporation as well as an individual, business and industry began to flood the courts with cases challenging various government regulations.

The Court quickly found itself in a thicket: it began ruling on the constitutionality of virtually every effort by any government to regulate any aspect of business or labor, and its workload rose sharply. Judicial activism was born in the 1880s and 1890s

Marbury v. Madison

The story of *Marbury v. Madison* is often told, but it deserves another telling because it illustrates so many features of the role of the Supreme Court—how apparently small cases can have large results, how the power of the Court depends not simply on its constitutional authority but also on its acting in ways that avoid a clear confrontation with other branches of government, and how the climate of opinion affects how the Court goes about its task.

When President John Adams lost his bid for reelection to Thomas Jefferson in 1800, he—and all members of his party, the Federalists—feared that Jefferson and the Republicans would weaken the federal government and turn its powers to what the Federalists believed were wrong ends (states' rights, an alliance with the French, hostility to business). Feverishly, as his hours in office came to an end, Adams worked to pack the judiciary with 59 loyal Federalists by giving them so-called midnight appointments before Jefferson took office.

John Marshall, as Adams's secretary of state, had the task of certifying and delivering these new judicial commissions. In the press of business, he delivered all but 17; these he left on his desk for the incoming secretary of state, James Madison, to send out. Jefferson and Madison, however, were furious at Adams's behavior and refused to deliver the 17. William Marbury and three other Federalists who had been promised these commissions hired a lawyer and brought suit against Madison to force him to produce the documents. The suit requested the Supreme Court to issue a writ of mandamus (from the Latin, "we command") ordering Madison to do his duty. The right to issue such writs had been given to the Court by the Judiciary Act of 1789.

Marshall, the man who had failed to deliver the commissions to Marbury and his friends in the first place, had become the chief justice and was now in a position to decide the case. These days a justice who had been involved in an issue before it came to the Court would probably disqualify himself or herself, but Marshall had no intention of letting others decide this question. He faced, however, not simply a partisan dispute over jobs but what was nearly a constitutional crisis. If he ordered the commission delivered, Madison might still refuse, and the Court had no way—if Madison was determined to resist—to compel him. The Court had no police force, whereas Madison had the support of the president of the United States. And if the order were given, whether or not Madison complied, the Jeffersonian Republicans in Congress would probably try to impeach Marshall. On the other hand, if Marshall allowed Madison to do as he wished, the power of the Supreme Court would be seriously reduced.

Marshall's solution was ingenious. Speaking for a unanimous Court, he announced that Madison was wrong to withhold the commissions, that courts could issue writs to compel public officials to do their prescribed duty—*but* that the Supreme Court had no power to issue such writs in this case because the law (the Judiciary Act of 1789) giving it that power was unconstitutional. The law said the Supreme Court could issue such writs as part of its "original jurisdiction"—that is, persons seeking such writs could go *directly* to the Supreme Court with their request (rather than go first to a lower federal court and then, if dissatisfied, appeal to the Supreme Court). Article III of the Constitution, Marshall pointed out, spelled out precisely the Supreme Court's original jurisdiction; it did not mention issuing writs of this sort and plainly indicated that on all matters not mentioned in the Constitution, the Court would have only appellate jurisdiction. Congress may not change what the Constitution says; hence, the part of the Judiciary Act attempting to do this was null and void.

The result was that a showdown with the Jeffersonians was avoided—Madison was not ordered to deliver the commissions—but the power of the Supreme Court was unmistakably clarified and enlarged. As Marshall wrote, "It is emphatically the province and duty of the judicial department to say what the law is." Furthermore, "a law repugnant to the Constitution is void."

as the Court set itself up as the arbiter of what kind of regulation was permissible. In the first 75 years of this country's history, only two federal laws were held to be unconstitutional; in the next 75 years, 71 were.[8] Of the roughly 1,300 state laws held to be in conflict with the federal Constitution since 1789, about 1,200 were overturned after 1870. In one decade alone—the 1880s—five federal and 48 state laws were declared unconstitutional.

Many of these decisions provided clear evidence of the Court's desire to protect private property: it upheld the use of injunctions to prevent labor strikes,[9] struck down the federal income tax,[10] sharply limited the reach of the antitrust law,[11] restricted the powers of the Interstate Commerce Commission to set railroad rates,[12] prohibited the federal government from eliminating child labor,[13] and prevented the states from setting maximum hours of work.[14] In 184 cases between 1899 and 1937, the Supreme Court struck down state laws for violating the Fourteenth Amendment, usually by economic regulation.[15]

But the Court also rendered decisions that authorized various kinds of regulation. It allowed states to regulate businesses "affected with a public interest,"[16] changed its mind about the Interstate Commerce Commission and allowed it to regulate railroad rates,[17] upheld rules requiring railroads to improve their safety,[18] approved state antiliquor laws,[19] approved state mine safety laws,[20] supported state workers' compensation laws,[21] allowed states to regulate fire-insurance rates,[22] and in time upheld a number of state laws regulating wages and hours. Indeed, between 1887 and 1910, in 558 cases involving the Fourteenth Amendment, the Supreme Court upheld state regulations over 80 percent of the time.[23]

To characterize the Court as pro-business or antiregulation is both simplistic and inexact. More accurate, perhaps, is to characterize it as supportive of the rights of private property but unsure how to draw the lines that distinguish "reasonable" from "unreasonable" regulation. Nothing in the Constitution clearly differentiates reasonable from unreasonable regulation, and the Court has been able to invent no consistent principle of its own to make this determination. For example, what kinds of businesses are "affected with a public interest"? Grain elevators and railroads are, but are bakeries? Sugar refiners? Saloons? And how much of commerce is "interstate"—anything that moves? Or only something that actually crosses a state line? The Court found itself trying to make detailed judgments that it was not always competent to make and to invent legal rules where no clear legal rules were possible.

In one area, however, the Supreme Court's judgments were clear: the Fourteenth and Fifteenth Amendments were construed so narrowly as to give African Americans only the most limited benefits of their provisions. In a long series of decisions, the Court upheld segregation in schools and on railroad cars and permitted blacks to be excluded from voting in many states.

GOVERNMENT AND POLITICAL LIBERTY

After 1936, the Supreme Court stopped imposing any serious restrictions on state or federal power to regulate the economy, leaving such matters in the hands of the legislatures. From 1937 to 1974, the Supreme Court did not overturn a single federal law designed to regulate business but did overturn 36 congressional enactments that violated personal political liberties. It voided as unconstitutional laws that restricted freedom of speech,[24] denied passports to communists,[25] permitted the government to revoke a person's citizenship,[26] withheld a person's mail,[27] or restricted the availability of government benefits.[28]

This new direction began when one justice changed his mind, and it continued as the composition of the Court changed. At the outset of the New Deal, the Court was by a narrow margin dominated by justices who opposed the welfare state and federal regulation based on broad grants of discretionary authority to administrative agencies. President Franklin Roosevelt, who was determined to get just such legislation implemented, found himself powerless to alter the composition of the Court during his first term (1933–1937): because no justice died or retired, he had no vacancies to fill. After his overwhelming reelection in 1936, he moved to remedy this problem by "packing" the Court.

Roosevelt proposed a bill that would have allowed him to appoint one new justice for each one over the age of 70 who refused to retire, up to a total membership of 15. Since there were six men in this category then on the Supreme Court, he would have been

Landmark Cases

Power of the Supreme Court

- ***Marbury v. Madison* (1803):** Upheld judicial review of congressional acts.
- ***Martin v. Hunter's Lessee* (1816):** The Supreme Court can review the decisions of the highest state courts if they involve a federal law or the federal Constitution.
- ***McCulloch v. Maryland* (1819):** Said that creating a federal bank, though not mentioned in the Constitution, was a "necessary and proper" exercise of the government's right to borrow money.
- ***Ex parte McCardle* (1869):** Allowed Congress to change the appellate jurisdiction of the Supreme Court.

Figure 16.1

Economics and Civil Liberties Laws Overturned by the U.S. Supreme Court, by Decade, 1900–2006

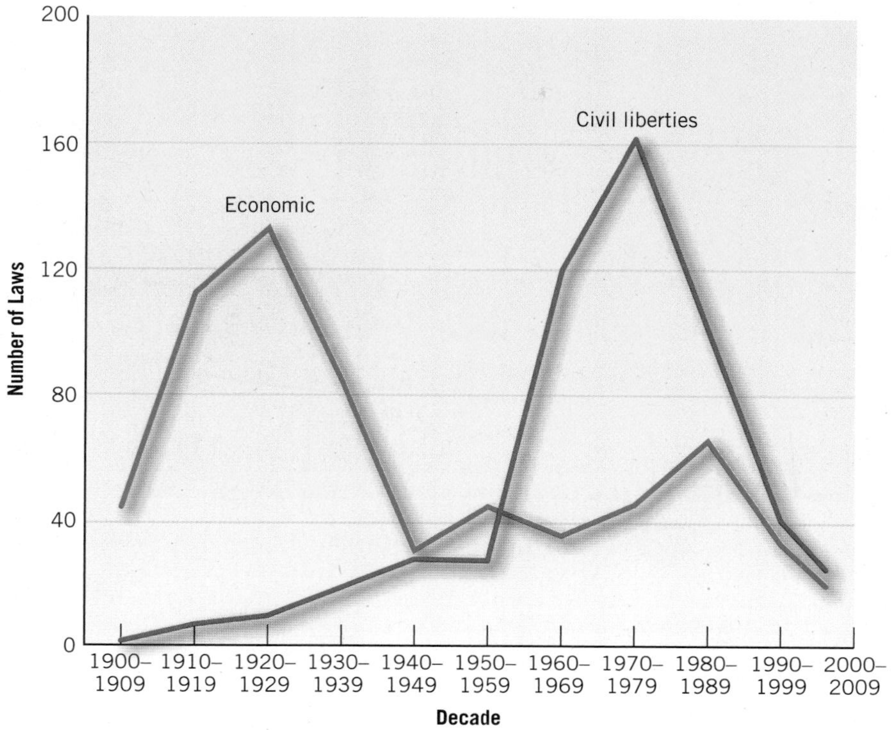

Note: Civil liberties category does not include laws supportive of civil liberties. Laws include federal, state, and local.

Source: Harold W. Stanley and Richard G. Niemi, Vital Statistics on American Politics, 2007–2008, 5th ed., p. 302 (Washington, D. C.: CQ Press, 2008).

able to appoint six new justices, enough to ensure a comfortable majority supportive of his economic policies. A bitter controversy ensued, but before the bill could be voted on, the Supreme Court, perhaps reacting to Roosevelt's big win in the 1936 election, changed its mind. Whereas it had been striking down several New Deal measures by votes of 5 to 4, now it started approving them by the same vote. One justice, Owen Roberts, had switched his position. This was called the "switch in time that saved nine," but in fact Roberts had changed his mind *before* the FDR plan was announced.

The "Court-packing" bill was not passed, but it was no longer necessary. Justice Roberts had yielded before public opinion in a way that Chief Justice Taney a century earlier had not, thus forestalling an assault on the Court by the other branches of government. Shortly thereafter, several justices stepped down, and Roosevelt was able to make his own appointments (he filled seven seats during his four terms in office). From then on, the Court turned its attention to new issues—political liberties and, in time, civil rights.

With the arrival in office of Chief Justice Earl Warren in 1953, the Court began its most active period yet. Activism now arose to redefine the relationship of citizens to the government and especially to protect the rights and liberties of citizens from governmental trespass. Although the Court has always seen itself as protecting citizens from arbitrary government, before 1937 that protection was of a sort that conservatives preferred; after 1937, it was of a kind that liberals preferred.

THE REVIVAL OF STATE SOVEREIGNTY

For many decades, the Supreme Court allowed Congress to pass almost any law authorized by the Constitution, no matter how it affected the states.

Map 16.1

U.S. District and Appellate Courts

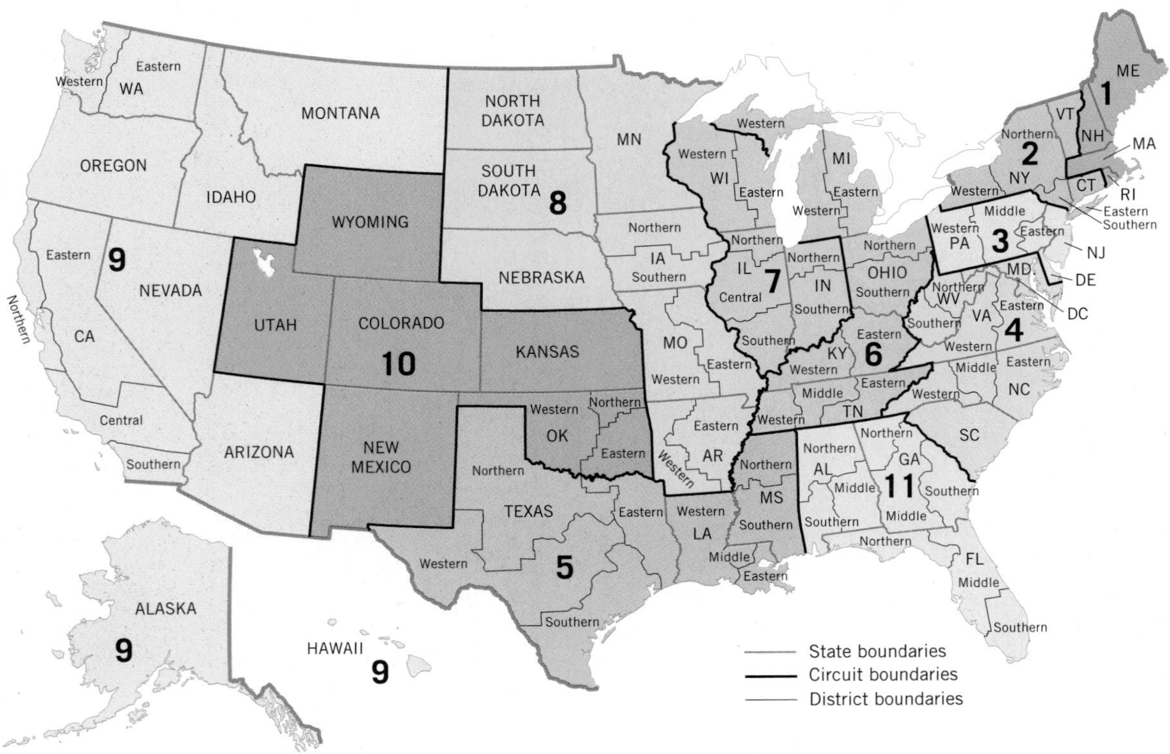

Note: Washington, D.C., is in a separate court. Puerto Rico is in the first circuit; the Virgin Islands are in the third; Guam and the Northern Mariana Islands are in the ninth. The Court of Appeals for the Federal Circuit, located in Washington, D.C., is a Title 3 court that hears appeals regarding patents, trademarks, international trade, government contracts, and from civil servants who claim they were unjustly discharged.

Source: Administrative Office of the United States Courts (January 1983).

As we saw in Chapter 3, the Court had long held that Congress could regulate almost any activity if it affected interstate commerce, and in the Court's opinion virtually every activity did affect it. The states were left with few rights to challenge federal power. But since around 1992, the Court has backed away from this view. By narrow majorities, it has begun to restore the view that states have the right to resist some forms of federal action.

When Congress passed a bill that forbade anyone from carrying a gun near a school, the Court held that carrying guns did not affect interstate commerce, and so the law was invalid.[29] One year later, it struck down a law that allowed Indian tribes to sue the states in federal courts, arguing that Congress lacks the power to ignore the "sovereign immunity" of states—that is, the right, protected by the Eleventh Amendment, not to be sued in federal court. (It has since upheld that view in two more cases.) And the next year, it held that the Brady gun control law could not be used to require local law enforcement officers to do background checks on people trying to buy weapons.[30] These cases are all hints that there are some real limits to the supremacy of the federal government created by the existence and powers of the several states.

After the enactment of President Obama's health care plan, several states argued that its requirement that everyone purchase health insurance was unconstitutional. Some district courts agreed with the claims and others disagreed. The issue is whether Congress's authority to levy taxes or to regulate interstate commerce gives it the right to require citizens to purchase a product. The Supreme Court will ultimately decide this issue.

The Structure of the Federal Courts

The only federal court the Constitution requires is the Supreme Court, as specified in Article III. All other federal courts and their jurisdictions are creations of Congress. Nor does the Constitution indicate how many justices shall be on the Supreme Court (there

constitutional court A federal court authorized by Article III of the Constitution that keeps judges in office during good behavior and prevents their salaries from being reduced. They are the Supreme Court (created by the Constitution) and appellate and district courts created by Congress.

district court The lowest federal courts; federal trials can be held only here.

courts of appeals Federal courts that hear appeals from district courts; no trials.

legislative courts Courts created by Congress for specialized purposes whose judges do not enjoy the protections of Article III of the Constitution.

were originally six, now there are nine) or what its appellate jurisdiction shall be.

Congress has created two kinds of lower federal courts to handle cases that need not be decided by the Supreme Court: constitutional and legislative courts. A **constitutional court** is one exercising the judicial powers found in Article III of the Constitution, and therefore its judges are given constitutional protection: they may not be fired (they serve during "good behavior"), nor may their salaries be reduced while they are in office. The most important of the constitutional courts are the **district courts** (a total of 94, with at least one in each state, the District of Columbia, and the commonwealth of Puerto Rico) and the **courts of appeals** (one in each of 11 regions, plus one in the District of Columbia and one federal circuit). There are also various specialized constitutional courts, such as the Court of International Trade.

A **legislative court** is one set up by Congress for some specialized purpose and staffed with people who have fixed terms of office and can be removed or have their salaries reduced. Legislative courts include the Court of Military Appeals and the territorial courts.

SELECTING JUDGES

Party background makes a difference in how judges behave. An analysis has been done of more than 80 studies of the link between party and either liberalism or conservatism among state and federal judges in cases involving civil liberties, criminal justice, and economic regulation. It shows that judges who are Democrats are more likely to make liberal decisions and Republican judges are more likely to make conservative ones.* The party effect is not small.[31]

Topham/The Image Works

Louis Brandeis, creator of the "Brandeis Brief" that developed court cases based on economic and social more than legal arguments, became the first Jewish Supreme Court justice. He served in the Court from 1916 until 1939.

We should not be surprised by this, since we have already seen that among political elites (and judges are certainly elites), party identification influences personal ideology.

But ideology does not entirely determine behavior. So many other things shape court decisions—the facts of the case, prior rulings by other courts, the arguments presented by lawyers—that there is no reliable way of predicting how judges will behave in all matters. Presidents sometimes make the mistake of thinking they know how their appointees will behave, only to be surprised by the facts. Theodore Roosevelt appointed Oliver Wendell Holmes to the Supreme Court, only to remark later, after Holmes had voted in a way that Roosevelt did not like, that "I could carve out of a banana a judge with more backbone than that!" Holmes, who had plenty of backbone, said he did not "give a damn" what Roosevelt thought. Richard Nixon, an ardent foe of court-ordered school busing, appointed Warren Burger chief justice. Burger promptly sat down and wrote the opinion upholding busing. Another Nixon appointee, Harry Blackmun, wrote the opinion declaring the right to an abortion to be constitutionally protected.

*A "liberal" decision is one that favors a civil right, a criminal defendant or an economic regulation; a "conservative" one opposes the right or the regulation or supports the criminal prosecutor.

Federal judges tend to be white, male, and Protestant, and increasingly have been judges on some other court. There has been a decline in the proportion of Supreme Court justices who come directly from private law practice; almost all have been promoted from a lower-ranking judgeship. For example, of the nine justices chosen by President Franklin D. Roosevelt, only two had been judges, while of the 10 nominated by presidents Ronald Reagan, George H. W. Bush, Bill Clinton, and George W. Bush, nine had been judges. Sex, race, and ethnicity also have become important factors in selecting judges, as is evident in Figure 16.2. No one is quite certain what these changes mean.

SENATORIAL COURTESY

In theory, the president nominates a "qualified" person to be a judge, and the Senate approves or rejects the nomination based on those "qualifications." In fact, the tradition of *senatorial courtesy* gives heavy weight to the preferences of the senators from the state where a federal district judge is to serve. Ordinarily, the Senate will not confirm a district court judge if the senior senator from the state where the district is located objects (if he is of the president's party). The senator can exercise this veto power by means of the "blue slip"—a blue piece of paper on which the senator is asked to record his or her views on the nominee. A negative opinion, or even failure to return the blue slip, usually kills the nomination. This means that as a practical matter the president nominates only persons recommended to him by that key senator. Someone once suggested that, at least with respect to district judges, the Constitution has been turned on its head. To reflect reality, he said, Article II, section 2, ought to read: "The senators shall nominate, and by and with the consent of the President, shall appoint" federal judges.

THE "LITMUS TEST"

Of late, presidents have tried to exercise more influence on the selection of federal district and appellate court judges by getting the Justice Department to find candidates that not only are supported by their party's senators, but also reflect the political and judicial philosophy of the president. Presidents Carter and Clinton sought out liberal, activist judges; President Reagan sought out conservative, strict-constructionist ones. The party membership of federal judges makes a difference in how they vote.[32]

Because different courts of appeals have different combinations of judges, some will be more liberal than others. For example, there are more liberal judges in the court of appeals for the ninth circuit (which includes most of the far western states) and more conservative ones in the fifth circuit (Texas, Louisiana, and Mississippi). The ninth circuit takes liberal positions, the fifth more conservative ones. Since the Supreme Court does not have time to settle every disagreement among appeals courts, different interpretations of the law may exist in different circuits. In the fifth, for instance, it was for a while unconstitutional for state universities to have affirmative action programs, but in the ninth circuit that was permitted.

Figure 16.2

Female and Minority Judicial Appointments, 1963–2004

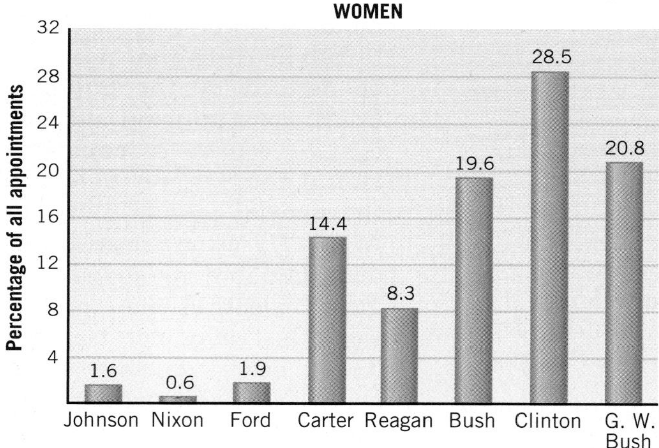

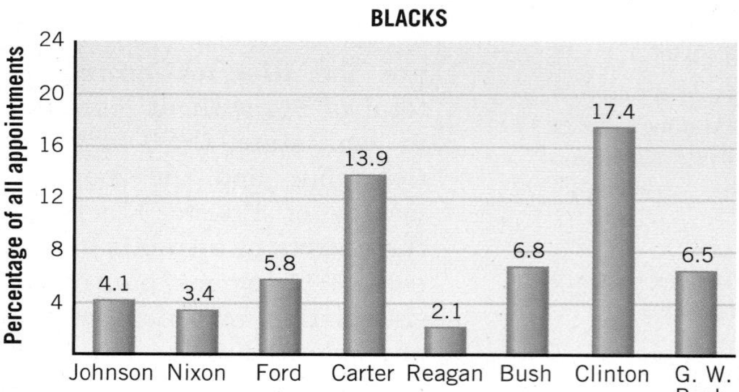

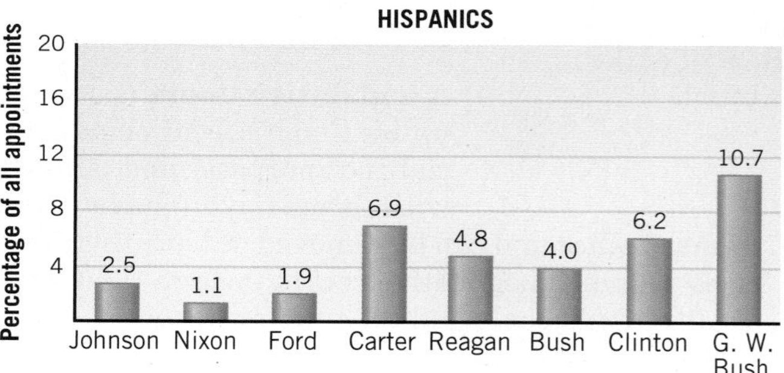

Source: Updated from Harold W. Stanley and Richard G. Niemi, *Vital Statistics on American Politics, 2005–2006* (Washington, D.C.: Congressional Quarterly, 2006), Table 7.5.

litmus test An examination of the political ideology of a nominated judge.

These differences make some people worry about the use of a political **litmus test**—a test of ideological purity—in selecting judges. When conservatives are out of power, they complain about how liberal presidents use such a test; when liberals are out power, they complain about how conservative presidents use it. Many people would like to see judges picked on the basis of professional qualifications, without reference to ideology, but the courts are now so deeply involved in political issues that it is hard to imagine what an ideologically neutral set of professional qualifications might be.

The litmus test has grown in importance. There has been a sharp drop in the percentage of nominees to federal appeals courts who are confirmed (see Figure 16.3). From 1945 until 1970, almost every nominee was confirmed, but by 1995 only about half got through the Senate and by 2000 it was less than 40 percent. (Nominees to the federal district court are, obviously, much less controversial because the president rarely nominates someone who is not supported by the state's senators.)

A judicial nominee's view on abortion is the chief motive for using the litmus test. Since it is easy to mount a filibuster and it takes 60 votes to end one, the nominee usually must be assured of 60 Senate votes to be confirmed. In theory, the Senate could adopt a rule preventing filibusters of nominations—but it never has. In 2005, a group of 14 senators, half from each party, agreed they would vote to block a filibuster on court nominees unless there were "extraordinary circumstances." This group—called the Gang of Fourteen—made it possible for several nominees (including Samuel Alito) to be confirmed even though they had fewer than 60 votes (but still, of course, more than 50).

The litmus test issue is of greatest importance in selecting Supreme Court justices. Here, there is no tradition of senatorial courtesy. The president takes a keen personal interest in the choices and, of late, has sought to find nominees who share his philosophy. In the Reagan administration, there were bruising fights in the Senate over the nomination of William Rehnquist to be chief justice (he won) and Robert Bork to be an associate justice (he lost), with liberals pitted against conservatives. When President George H. W. Bush nominated David Souter, there were lengthy hearings as liberal senators tried to pin down Souter's views on issues such as abortion. Souter refused to discuss matters on which he might later have to judge, however. Clarence Thomas, another Bush nominee, also tried to avoid the litmus test by saying he had not formed an opinion on prominent abortion cases. In his case, however, the litmus test issue was overshadowed by sensational allegations from a former employee, Anita Hill, that Thomas had sexually harassed her.

Figure 16.3

Confirmation Rates for Nominees to the U.S. Court of Appeals (1947–2005)

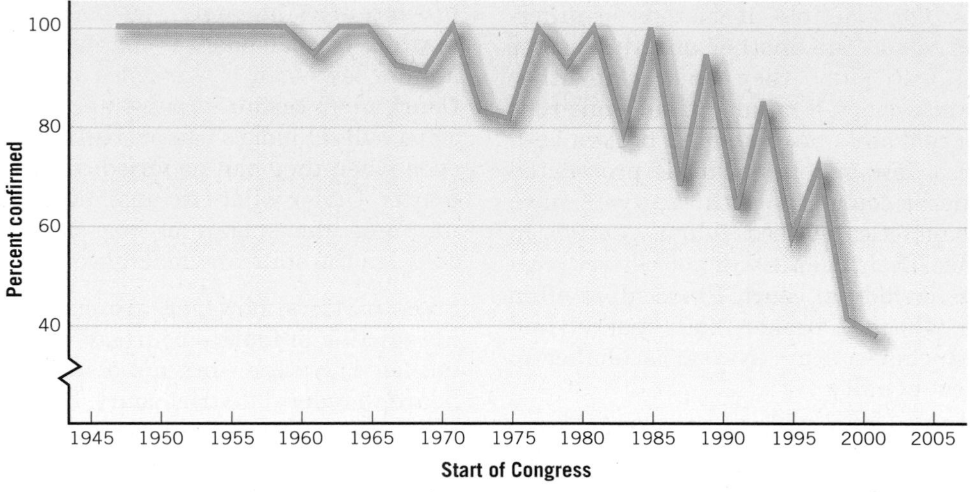

Source: Sarah A. Binder, "The Consequences of Polarization: Congress and the Courts," in David Brady and Pietro Nivola, eds., *Red and Blue Nation?* (Vol. 2) *Consequences and Correction of America's Polarized Politics* (figure 3.3, p. 116). Brookings Institution Press. Reprinted by permission of the author.

Of the 160 Supreme Court nominees presented to it, 36 failed to be confirmed by the Senate. The reasons for rejecting a Supreme Court nominee are complex—each senator may have a different reason—but have involved such matters as the nominee's alleged hostility to civil rights, questionable personal financial dealings, a poor record as a lower-court judge, and Senate opposition to the nominee's political or legal philosophy. Nominations of district court judges are rarely defeated, because typically no nomination is made unless the key senators approve in advance.

KAREN BLEIER/AFP/Getty Images

Sonia Sotomayor answers questions before the Senate committee considering her nomination to be a Supreme Court justice.

The Jurisdiction of the Federal Courts

We have a dual court system—one state, one federal—and this complicates enormously the task of describing what kinds of cases federal courts may hear and how cases beginning in the state courts may end up before the Supreme Court. The Constitution lists the kinds of cases over which federal courts have jurisdiction (in Article III and the Eleventh Amendment); by implication, all other matters are left to state courts. Federal courts (see Figure 16.4) can hear all cases "arising under the Constitution, the laws of the United States, and treaties" (these are **federal-question cases**), and cases involving citizens of different states (called **diversity cases**).

federal-question cases Cases concerning the Constitution, federal laws, or treaties.

diversity cases Cases involving citizens of different states who can bring suit in federal courts.

Some kinds of cases can be heard in either federal or state courts. For example, if citizens of different states wish to sue one another and the matter involves more than $75,000, they can do so in either a federal or a state court. Similarly, if someone robs a federally insured bank, he or she has broken both state and federal law and thus can be prosecuted in state or federal courts, or both. Lawyers have become quite sophisticated in deciding whether, in a given civil case, their clients will get better treatment in a state or federal court. Prosecutors often send a person who has broken both federal and state law to whichever court system is likelier to give the toughest penalty.

Sometimes defendants may be tried in both state and federal courts for the same offense. In 1992, four Los Angeles police officers accused of beating Rodney King were tried in a California state court and acquitted of assault charges. They were then prosecuted in federal court for violating King's civil rights. This time, two of the four were convicted. Under the dual sovereignty doctrine, state and federal authorities can prosecute the same person for the same conduct. The Supreme Court has upheld this doctrine on two grounds: first, each level of government has the right to enact laws serving its own purposes.[33] As a result, federal civil rights charges could have been brought against the officers even if they had already been convicted of assault in state court (though as a practical matter this would have been unlikely). Second, neither level of government wants the other to be able to block prosecution of an accused person who has the sympathy of the authorities at one level. For example, when certain southern state courts were in sympathy with whites who had lynched blacks, the absence of the dual sovereignty doctrine would have meant that a trumped-up acquittal in state court would have barred federal prosecution.

Furthermore, a matter that is exclusively within the province of a state court—for example, a criminal case in which the defendant is charged with violating only a state law—can be appealed to the U.S. Supreme Court under certain circumstances (described below). Thus federal judges can overturn state court rulings even when they had no jurisdiction over the original matter. Under what circumstances this should occur has been the subject of long-standing controversy between the state and federal courts.

Some matters, however, are exclusively under the jurisdiction of federal courts. When a federal criminal law is broken—but not a state one—the case is heard in federal district court. If you wish to appeal the decision of a federal regulatory agency, such as the Federal Communications Commission, you can do so only before a federal court of appeals. And if you wish to declare bankruptcy, you do so in federal court. If there is a controversy between two state

Figure 16.4
The Jurisdiction of the Federal Courts

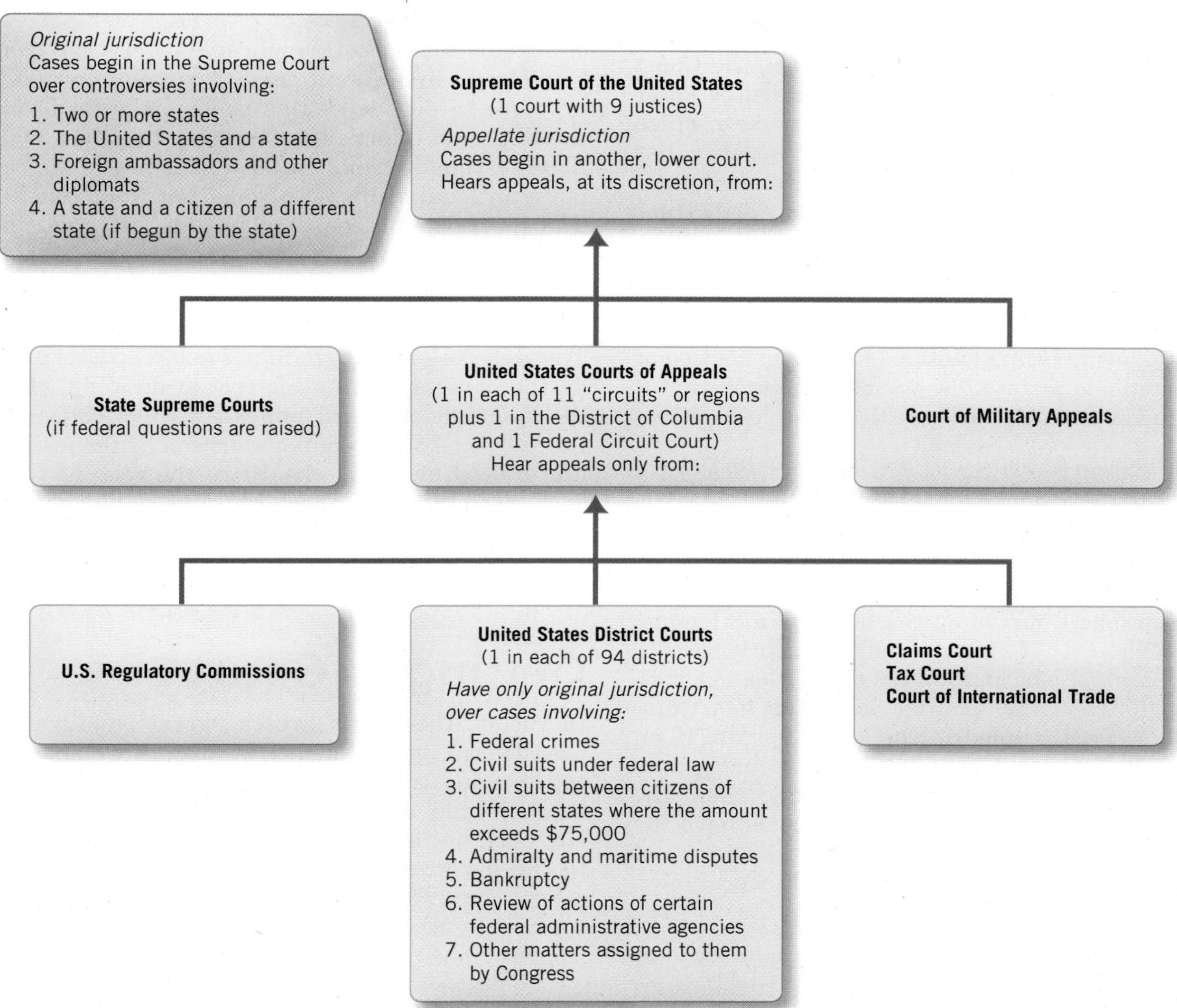

governments—say, California and Arizona sue each other over which state is to use how much water from the Colorado River—the case can be heard only by the Supreme Court.

Original jurisdiction
Cases begin in the Supreme Court over controversies involving:
1. Two or more states
2. The United States and a state
3. Foreign ambassadors and other diplomats
4. A state and a citizen of a different state (if begun by the state)
Supreme Court of the United States
(1 court with 9 justices)
Appellate jurisdiction
Cases begin in another, lower court.
Hears appeals, at its discretion, from:
State Supreme Courts
(if federal questions are raised)
United States Courts of Appeals
(1 in each of 11 "circuits" or regions plus 1 in the District of Columbia and 1 Federal Circuit Court)
Hear appeals only from:
Court of Military Appeals
U.S. Regulatory Commissions
United States District Courts
(1 in each of 94 districts)
Have only original jurisdiction, over cases involving:
1. Federal crimes
2. Civil suits under federal law
3. Civil suits between citizens of different states where the amount exceeds $75,000
4. Admiralty and maritime disputes
5. Bankruptcy
6. Review of actions of certain federal administrative agencies
7. Other matters assigned to them by Congress
Claims Court
Tax Court
Court of International Trade

The vast majority of all cases heard by federal courts begin in the district courts. The volume of business there is huge. In 2009, the 667 district court judges received 276,397 cases (more than 400 per judge). Most of the cases heard in federal courts involve rather straightforward applications of law; few lead to the making of new public policy. Cases that do affect how the law or the Constitution is interpreted can begin with seemingly minor events. For example, a major broadening of the Bill of Rights—requiring for the first time that all accused persons in *state* as well as federal criminal trials be supplied with a lawyer, free if necessary—began when impoverished Clarence Earl Gideon, imprisoned in Florida, wrote an appeal in pencil on prison stationery and sent it to the Supreme Court.[34]

The Supreme Court does not have to hear any appeal it does not want to hear. At one time, it was required to listen to certain appeals, but Congress has changed the law so that now the Court can pick the cases it wants to consider. It does this by issuing a **writ of certiorari.** *Certiorari* is a Latin word meaning, roughly, "made more certain"; lawyers and judges have abbreviated it

writ of certiorari An order by a higher court directing a lower court to send up a case for review.

to *cert*. It works this way: the Court considers all the petitions it receives to review lower-court decisions. If four justices agree to hear a case, cert is issued and the case is scheduled for a hearing.

In deciding whether to grant certiorari, the Court tries to reserve its time for cases decided by lower federal courts or by the highest state courts in which a significant federal or constitutional question has been raised. For example, the Court often will grant certiorari when one or both of the following is true:

- Two or more federal circuit courts of appeals have decided the same issue in different ways.
- The highest court in a state has held a federal or state law to be in violation of the Constitution or has upheld a state law against the claim that it is in violation of the Constitution.

In a typical year, the Court may consider more than 7,000 petitions asking it to review decisions of lower or state courts. It rarely accepts more than about 100 of them for full review.

In exercising its discretion in granting certiorari, the Supreme Court is on the horns of a dilemma. If it grants it frequently, it will be inundated with cases. As it is, the Court's workload has quintupled in the last 50 years. If, on the other hand, the Court grants certiorari only rarely, then the federal courts of appeals have the last word on the interpretation of the Constitution and federal laws, and since there are 12 of these, staffed by about 167 judges, they may well be in disagreement. In fact this has already happened: because the Supreme Court reviews only about 1 or 2 percent of appeals court cases, applicable federal law may be different in different parts of the country.[35] One proposal to deal with this dilemma is to devote the Supreme Court's time entirely to major questions of constitutional interpretation and to create a national court of appeals that would ensure that the 12 circuit courts of appeals are producing uniform decisions.[36]

in forma pauperis A method whereby a poor person can have his or her case heard in federal court without charge.

Flip Schulke

Clarence Earl Gideon studied law books while in prison so that he could write an appeal to the Supreme Court. His handwritten appeal asked that his conviction be set aside because he had not been provided with an attorney. His appeal was granted.

Because the Supreme Court has a heavy workload, the influence wielded by law clerks has grown. These clerks—recent graduates of law schools hired by the justices—play a big role in deciding which cases should be heard under a writ of certiorari. Indeed, some of the opinions written by the justices are drafted by the clerks. Since the reasons for a decision may be as important as the decision itself, and since these reasons are sometimes created by the clerks, the power of the clerks can be significant.

Getting to Court

In theory, the courts are the great equalizer in the federal government. To use the courts to settle a question, or even to alter fundamentally the accepted interpretation of the Constitution, one need not be elected to any office, have access to the mass media, be a member of an interest group, or be otherwise powerful or rich. Once the contending parties are before the courts, they are legally equal.

It is too easy to believe this theory uncritically or to dismiss it cynically. In fact, it is hard to get before the Supreme Court: it rejects over 96 percent of the applications for certiorari that it receives. And the costs involved in getting to the Court can be high. To apply for certiorari costs only $300 (plus 40 copies of the petition), but if certiorari is granted and the case is heard, the costs—for lawyers and for copies of the lower-court records in the case—can be very high. And by then one has already paid for the cost of the first hearing in the district court and probably one appeal to the circuit court of appeals. Furthermore, the time it takes to settle a matter in federal court can be quite long.

But there are ways to make these costs lower. If you are indigent—without funds—you can file and be heard as a pauper for nothing; about half the petitions arriving before the Supreme Court are **in forma pauperis** (such as the one from

Gideon, described earlier). If your case began as a criminal trial in the district courts and you are poor, the government will supply you with a lawyer at no charge. If the matter is not a criminal case and you cannot afford to hire a lawyer, interest groups representing a wide spectrum of opinion sometimes are willing to take up the cause if the issue in the case seems sufficiently important. The American Civil Liberties Union (ACLU), a liberal group, represents some people who believe their freedom of speech has been abridged or their constitutional rights in criminal proceedings have been violated. The Center for Individual Rights, a conservative group, represents some people who feel that they have been victimized by racial quotas.

But interest groups do much more than just help people pay their bills. Many of the most important cases decided by the Court got there because an interest group organized the case, found the plaintiffs, chose the legal strategy, and mobilized legal allies. The NAACP has brought many key civil rights cases on behalf of individuals. Although in the past most such cases were brought by liberal interest groups, of late conservative interest groups have entered the courtroom on behalf of individuals. One helped sue CBS for televising a program that allegedly libeled General William Westmoreland, once the American commander in Vietnam. (Westmoreland lost the case.) And many important issues are raised by attorneys representing state and local governments. Several price-fixing cases have been won by state attorneys general on behalf of consumers in their states.

FEE SHIFTING

Unlike what happens in most of Europe, each party to a lawsuit in this country must pay its own way. (In England, by contrast, if you sue someone and lose, you pay the winner's costs as well as your own.) But various laws have made it easier to get someone else to pay. **Fee shifting** enables the **plaintiff** (the party that initiates the suit) to collect its costs from the defendant if the defendant loses, at least in certain kinds of cases. For example, if a corporation is found to have violated the antitrust laws, it must pay the legal fees of the winner. If an environmentalist group sues the Environmental Protection Agency, it can get the EPA to pay the group's legal costs. Even more important to individuals, Section 1983 of Chapter 42 of the *United States Code* allows a citizen to sue a state or local government official—say, a police officer or a school superintendent—who has deprived the citizen of some constitutional right or withheld some benefit to which the citizen is entitled. If the citizen wins, he or she can collect money damages and lawyers' fees from the government. Citizens, more aware of their legal rights, have become more litigious, and a flood of such "Section 1983" suits has burdened the courts. The Supreme Court has restricted fee shifting to cases authorized by statute,[37] but it is clear that the drift of policy has made it cheaper to go to court—at least for some cases.

> ***fee shifting*** A rule that allows a plaintiff to recover costs from the defendant if the plaintiff wins.
>
> ***plaintiff*** The party that initiates a lawsuit.

STANDING

There is, in addition, a nonfinancial restriction on getting into federal court. To sue, one must have **standing,** a legal concept that refers to who is entitled to bring a case. It is especially important in determining who can challenge the laws or actions of the government itself. A complex and changing set of rules governs standings; some of the more important ones are these:

> ***standing*** A legal rule stating who is authorized to start a lawsuit.

- There must be an actual controversy between real adversaries. (You cannot bring a "friendly" suit against someone, hoping to lose in order to prove your friend right. You cannot ask a federal court for an opinion on a hypothetical or imaginary case or ask it to render an advisory opinion.)
- You must show that you have been harmed by the law or practice about which you are complaining. (It is not enough to dislike what the government or a corporation or a labor union does; you must show that you were actually harmed by that action.)
- Merely being a taxpayer does not ordinarily entitle you to challenge the constitutionality of a federal governmental action. (You may not want your tax money to be spent in certain ways, but your remedy is to vote against the politicians doing the spending; the federal courts will generally require that you show some other personal harm before you can sue.)

Congress and the courts have recently made it easier to acquire standing. It has always been the rule that a citizen could ask the courts to order federal officials to carry out some act that they were under a legal obligation to perform or to refrain from some action that was contrary to law. A citizen can also sue a government official personally to collect damages if the official acted contrary to law. For example, it was for long the case that if an FBI agent broke into your office without a search warrant, you could sue the agent and, if you won, collect money. However, you cannot sue the government itself without its consent. This is the doctrine of **sovereign immunity.** For instance, if the army accidentally kills your cow while testing a new cannon, you cannot sue the government to recover the cost of the cow unless the government agrees to be sued. (Since testing cannons is legal, you cannot sue the army officer who fired the cannon.) By statute, Congress has given its consent for the government to be sued in many cases involving a dispute over a contract or damage done as a result of negligence (for example, the dead cow). Over the years, these statutes have made it easier to take the government into court as a defendant.

sovereign immunity The rule that a citizen cannot sue the government without the government's consent.

Even some of the oldest rules defining standing have been liberalized. The rule that merely being a taxpayer does not entitle you to challenge in court a government decision has been relaxed where the citizen claims that a right guaranteed under the First Amendment is being violated. The Supreme Court allowed a taxpayer to challenge a federal law that would have given financial aid to parochial (or church-related) schools on the grounds that this aid violated the constitutional requirement of separation between church and state. On the other hand, another taxpayer suit to force the CIA to make public its budget failed because the Court decided that the taxpayer did not have standing in matters of this sort.[38]

CLASS-ACTION SUITS

Under certain circumstances, a citizen can benefit directly from a court decision, even though the citizen himself or herself has not gone into court. This can happen by means of a **class-action suit:** a case brought into court by a person on behalf not only of himself or herself, but of all other persons in similar circumstances. Among the most famous of these was the 1954 case in which the Supreme Court found that Linda Brown, a black girl attending the fifth grade in the Topeka, Kansas, public schools, was denied the equal protection of the laws (guaranteed under the Fourteenth Amendment) because the schools in Topeka were segregated. The Court did not limit its decision to Linda Brown's right to attend an unsegregated school but extended it—as Brown's lawyers from the NAACP had asked—to cover all "others similarly situated."[39] It was not easy to design a court order that would eliminate segregation in the schools, but the principle was clearly established in this class action.

class-action suit A case brought by someone to help both himself or herself and all others who are similarly situated.

Since the *Brown* case, many other groups have been quick to take advantage of the opportunity created by class-action suits. By this means, the courts could be used to give relief not simply to a particular person but to all those represented in the suit. A landmark class-action case challenged the malapportionment of state legislative districts (see Chapter 13).[40] There are thousands of class-action suits in the federal courts involving civil rights, the rights of prisoners, antitrust suits against corporations, and other matters. These suits became more common partly because people were beginning to have new concerns that were not being met by Congress and partly because some class-action suits became quite profitable. The NAACP got no money from Linda Brown or from the Topeka Board of Education in compensation for its long and expensive labors, but beginning in the 1960s court rules were changed to make it financially attractive for lawyers to bring certain kinds of class-action suits.

Suppose, for example, that you think your telephone company overcharged you by $75. You could try to hire a lawyer to get a refund, but not many lawyers would take the case, because there would be no money in it. Even if you were to win, the lawyer would stand to earn no more than perhaps one-third of the settlement, or $25. Now suppose you bring a class action against the company on behalf of everybody who was overcharged. Millions of dollars might be at stake; lawyers would line up eagerly to take the case, because their share of the settlement, if they won, would be huge. The opportunity to win profitable class-action suits, combined with the possibility of having the loser pay the attorneys' fees, led to a proliferation of such cases.

In response to the increase in its workload, the Supreme Court decided in 1974 to tighten drastically the rules governing these suits. It held that it would no longer hear (except in certain cases defined by Congress, such as civil rights matters) class-action suits seeking monetary damages unless each and every ascertainable member of the class was individually notified of the case. To do this often is prohibitively expensive (imagine trying to find and send a letter to every customer that may have been overcharged by the telephone company!), and so the

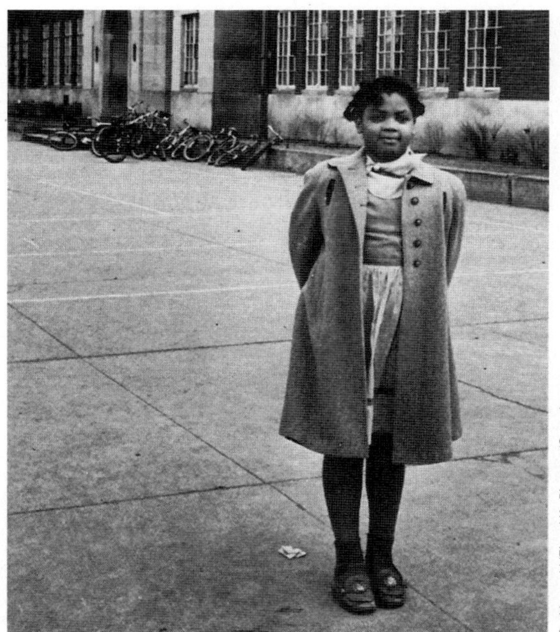

Carl Iwasaki/Time Life Pictures/Getty Images

Linda Brown was refused admission to a white elementary school in Topeka, Kansas. On her behalf, the NAACP brought a class-action suit that resulted in the 1954 landmark Supreme Court decision *Brown v. Board of Education.*

number of such cases declined and the number of lawyers seeking them out dropped.[41]

But it remains easy to bring a class-action suit in most state courts. State Farm automobile insurance company was told by a state judge in a small Illinois town that it must pay over $1 billion in damages on behalf of a "national" class, even though no one in this class had been notified. Big class-action suits powerfully affect how courts make public policy. Such suits have forced into bankruptcy companies making asbestos and silicone breast implants and have threatened to put out of business tobacco companies and gun manufacturers. (Ironically, in some of these cases, such as the one involving breast implants, there was no scientific evidence showing that the product was harmful.) Some class-action suits, such as the one ending school segregation, are good, but others are frivolous efforts to get companies to pay large fees to the lawyers who file the suits.

In sum, getting into court depends on having standing and having resources. The rules governing standing are complex and changing, but generally they have been broadened to make it easier to enter the federal courts, especially for the purpose of challenging the actions of the government. Obtaining the resources is not easy but has become easier because laws in some cases now provide for fee shifting, private interest groups are willing to finance cases, and it is sometimes possible to bring a class-action suit that lawyers find lucrative.

The Supreme Court in Action

If your case should find its way to the Supreme Court—and of course the odds are that it will not—you will be able to participate in one of the more impressive, sometimes dramatic ceremonies of American public life. The Court is in session in its white marble building for 36 weeks out of each year, from early October until the end of June. The nine justices read briefs in their individual offices, hear oral arguments in the stately courtroom, and discuss their decisions with one another in a conference room where no outsider is ever allowed.

Table 16.2 Supreme Court Justices in Order of Seniority, 2011

Name (Birth Date)	Home State	Prior Experience	Appointed by (Year)
John G. Roberts, Jr., Chief Justice (1955)	Maryland	Federal judge	G. W. Bush (2005)
Antonin Scalia (1936)	Virginia	Federal judge	Reagan (1986)
Anthony Kennedy (1936)	California	Federal judge	Reagan (1988)
Clarence Thomas (1948)	Georgia	Federal judge	G. H. W. Bush (1991)
Ruth Bader Ginsburg (1933)	New York	Federal judge	Clinton (1993)
Stephen Breyer (1938)	Massachusetts	Federal judge	Clinton (1994)
Samuel Alito (1950)	New Jersey	Federal judge	G. W. Bush (2006)
Sonia Sotomayor (1954)	New York	Federal judge	Obama (2009)
Elena Kagan (1960)	New York	Law school dean	Obama (2010)

brief A written statement by an attorney that summarizes a case and the laws and rulings that support it.

Most cases, as we have seen, come to the Court on a writ of certiorari. The lawyers for each side may then submit their briefs. A **brief** is a document that sets forth the facts of the case, summarizes the lower-court decision, gives the arguments for the side represented by the lawyer who wrote the brief, and discusses the other cases that the Court has decided bear on the issue. Then the lawyers are allowed to present their oral arguments in open court. They usually summarize their briefs or emphasize particular points in them, and they are strictly limited in time—usually to no more than a half hour. (The lawyer speaks from a lectern that has two lights on it. When the white light goes on, the attorney has five minutes remaining; when the red flashes, he or she must stop—instantly.) The oral arguments give the justices a chance to question the lawyers, sometimes searchingly.

Since the federal government is a party—as either plaintiff or defendant—to about half the cases that the Supreme Court hears, the government's top trial lawyer, the solicitor general of the United States, appears frequently before the Court. The solicitor general is the third-ranking officer of the Department of Justice, right after the attorney general and deputy attorney general. The solicitor general decides what cases the government will appeal from lower courts and personally approves every case the government presents to the Supreme Court. In recent years, the solicitor general often has been selected from the ranks of distinguished law school professors.

amicus curiae A brief submitted by a "friend of the court."

per curiam opinion A brief, unsigned court opinion.

opinion of the Court A signed opinion of a majority of the Supreme Court.

concurring opinion A signed opinion in which one or more members agree with the majority view but for different reasons.

dissenting opinion A signed opinion in which one or more justices disagree with the majority view.

In addition to the arguments made by lawyers for the two sides in a case, written briefs and even oral arguments may also be offered by "a friend of the court," or **amicus curiae.** An amicus brief is from an interested party not directly involved in the suit. For example, when Allan Bakke complained that he had been the victim of "reverse discrimination" when he was denied admission to a University of California medical school, 58 amicus briefs were filed supporting or opposing his position. Before such briefs can be filed, both parties must agree or the Court must grant permission. Though these briefs sometimes offer new arguments, they are really a kind of polite lobbying of the Court that declare which interest groups are on which side. The ACLU, the NAACP, the AFL-CIO, and the U.S. government itself have been among the leading sources of such briefs.

These briefs are not the only source of influence on the justices' views. Legal periodicals such as the *Harvard Law Review* and the *Yale Law Journal* are frequently consulted, and citations to them often appear in the Court's decisions. Thus the outside world of lawyers and law professors can help shape, or at least supply arguments for, the conclusions of the justices.

The justices retire every Friday to their conference room, where in complete secrecy they debate the cases they have heard. The chief justice speaks first, followed by the other justices in order of seniority. After the arguments they vote, traditionally in reverse order of seniority: the newest justice votes first, the chief justice last. By this process an able chief justice can exercise considerable influence—in guiding or limiting debate, in setting forth the issues, and in handling sometimes temperamental personalities. In deciding a case, a majority of the justices must be in agreement: if there is a tie, the lower-court decision is left standing. (There can be a tie among nine justices if one is ill or disqualifies himself or herself because of prior involvement in the case.)

Though the vote is what counts, by tradition the Court usually issues a written opinion explaining its decision. Sometimes the opinion is brief and unsigned (called a **per curiam opinion**); sometimes it is quite long and signed by the justices agreeing with it. If the chief justice is in the majority, he will either write the opinion or assign the task to a justice who agrees with him. If he is in the minority, the senior justice on the winning side will decide who writes the Court's opinion. There are three kinds of opinions—an **opinion of the Court** (reflecting the majority's view), a **concurring opinion** (an opinion by one or more justices who agree with the majority's conclusion but for different reasons that they wish to express), and a **dissenting opinion** (the opinion of the justices on the losing side). Each justice has three or four law clerks to help him or her review the many petitions the Court receives, study cases, and write opinions.

Many Supreme Court decisions, perhaps two-fifths of them, are decided unanimously. In these cases, the law is clear and no difficult questions of interpretation exist. But for the remaining ones, there appear to be two main blocs and one swing vote on today's Court:

- A conservative bloc of Samuel Alito, John Roberts, Antonin Scalia, and Clarence Thomas
- A liberal bloc of Stephen Breyer, Ruth Bader Ginsburg, Elena Kagan, and Sonia Sotomayor.
- A swing vote of Anthony Kennedy. He often votes with the conservatives on criminal law but on some other cases (abortion, gay rights, and foreign combatants detained at Guantanamo Bay) votes with the liberals.

The Power of the Federal Courts

The great majority of the cases heard in the federal courts have little or nothing to do with changes in public policy: people accused of bank robbery are tried, disputes over contracts are settled, personal-injury cases are heard, and the patent law is applied. In most instances, the courts are simply applying a relatively settled body of law to a specific controversy.

THE POWER TO MAKE POLICY

The courts make policy whenever they reinterpret the law or the Constitution in significant ways, extend the reach of existing laws to cover matters not previously thought to be covered by them, or design remedies for problems that involve the judges' acting in administrative or legislative ways. By any of these tests the courts have become exceptionally powerful.

One measure of that power is the fact that more than 160 federal laws have been declared unconstitutional. And as we shall see, on matters where Congress feels strongly, it can often get its way by passing slightly revised versions of a voided law.

Another measure, and perhaps a more revealing one, is the frequency with which the Supreme Court changes its mind. An informal rule of judicial decision making has been **stare decisis,** meaning "let the decision stand." It is the principle of precedent: a court case today should be settled in accordance with prior decisions on similar cases. (What constitutes a similar case is not always clear; lawyers are especially gifted at finding ways of showing that two cases are different in some relevant way.) There are two reasons why precedent is important. The practical reason should be obvious: if the meaning of the law continually changes, if the decisions of judges become wholly unpredictable, then human affairs affected by those laws and decisions become chaotic. A contract signed today might be invalid tomorrow. The other reason is at least as important: if the principle of equal justice means anything, it means that similar cases should be decided in a similar manner. On the other hand,

stare decisis "Let the decision stand," or allowing prior rulings to control the current case.

TIM SLOAN/AFP/Getty Images

The U.S. Supreme Court Justices in 2010. Front row: Justices Clarence Thomas and Antonin Scalia, Chief Justice John Roberts, Justices Anthony Kennedy and Ruth Bader Ginsburg; second row: Sonia Sotomayor, Stephen Breyer, Samuel Alito, and Elena Kagan.

times change, and the Court can make mistakes. As Justice Felix Frankfurter once said, "Wisdom too often never comes, and so one ought not to reject it merely because it comes late."[42]

However compelling the arguments for flexibility, the pace of change can become dizzying. By one count, the Court has overruled its own previous decisions in more than 260 cases since 1810.[43] In fact, it may have done it more often, because sometimes the Court does not say that it is abandoning a precedent, claiming instead that it is merely distinguishing the present case from a previous one.

A third measure of judicial power is the degree to which courts are willing to handle matters once left to the legislature. For example, the Court refused for a long time to hear a case about the size of congressional districts, no matter how unequal their populations.[44] The determination of congressional district boundaries was regarded as a **political question**—that is, as a matter that the Constitution left entirely to another branch of government (in this case, Congress) to decide for itself. Then in 1962, the Court decided that it was competent after all to handle this matter, and the notion of a "political question" became a much less important (but by no means absent) barrier to judicial power.[45]

political question An issue the Supreme Court will allow the executive and legislative branches decide.

remedy A judicial order enforcing a right or redressing a wrong.

By all odds the most powerful indicator of judicial power can be found in the kinds of remedies that the courts will impose. A **remedy** is a judicial order setting forth what must be done to correct a situation that a judge believes to be wrong. In ordinary cases, such as when one person sues another, the remedy is straightforward: the loser must pay the winner for some injury that he or she has caused, the loser must agree to abide by the terms of a contract he or she has broken, or the loser must promise not to do some unpleasant thing (such as dumping garbage on a neighbor's lawn).

Today, however, judges design remedies that go far beyond what is required to do justice to the individual parties who actually appear in court. The remedies now imposed often apply to large groups and affect the circumstances under which thousands or even millions of people work, study, or live. For example, when a federal district judge in Alabama heard a case brought by a prison inmate in that state, he issued an order not simply to improve the lot of that prisoner but to revamp the administration of the entire prison system. The result was an improvement in the living conditions of many prisoners, at a cost to the state of an estimated $40 million a year. Similarly, a person who feels entitled to welfare payments that have been denied him or her may sue in court to get the money, and the court order will in all likelihood affect all welfare recipients. In one case certain court orders made an additional 100,000 people eligible for welfare.[46]

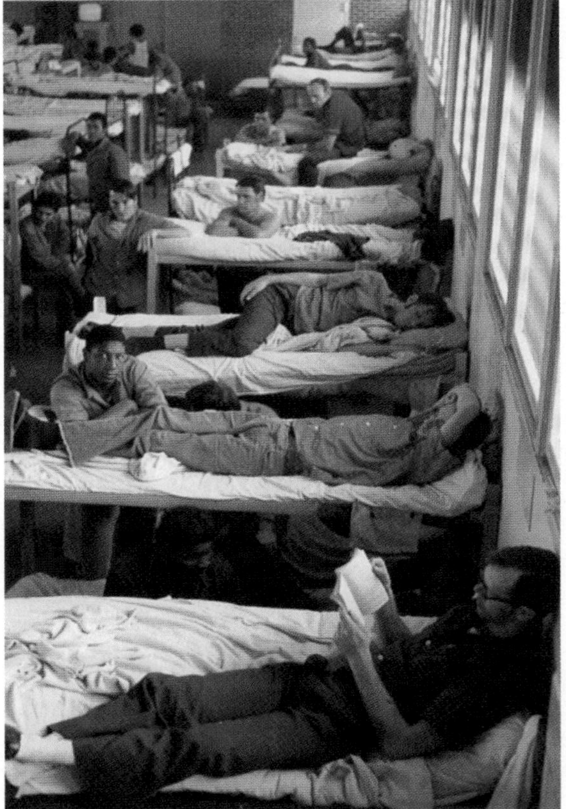
Alex Webb/Magnum Photos

The activism of federal courts is exemplified by the sweeping orders they have issued to correct such problems as overcrowded prisons.

The basis for sweeping court orders can sometimes be found in the Constitution; the Alabama prison decision, for example, was based on the judge's interpretation of the Eighth Amendment, which prohibits "cruel and unusual punishments."[47] Others are based on court interpretations of federal laws. The Civil Rights Act of 1964 forbids discrimination on grounds of "race, color, or national origin" in any program receiving federal financial assistance. The Supreme Court interpreted that as meaning the San Francisco school system was obliged to teach English to Chinese students unable to speak it.[48] Since a Supreme Court decision is the law of the land, the impact of that ruling was not limited to San Francisco. Local courts and legislatures elsewhere decided that that decision meant that classes must be taught in Spanish for Hispanic children. What Congress meant by the Civil Rights Act is not clear; it may or may not have believed that teaching Hispanic children in English rather than Spanish was a form of discrimination. What is important is that it was the Court, not Congress, that decided what Congress meant.

VIEWS OF JUDICIAL ACTIVISM

Judicial activism has, of course, been controversial. Those who support it argue that the federal courts must correct injustices when the other branches of the federal government, or the states, refuse to do so. The courts are the institution of last resort for those without the votes or the influence to obtain new laws, and especially for the poor and powerless. After all, Congress and the state legislatures tolerated segregated public schools for decades. If the Supreme Court had not declared segregation unconstitutional in 1954, it might still be law today.

Those who criticize judicial activism rejoin that judges usually have no special expertise in matters of school administration, prison management, environmental protection, and so on; they are lawyers, expert in defining rights and duties but not in designing and managing complex institutions. Furthermore, however desirable court-declared rights and principles may be, implementing those principles means balancing the conflicting needs of various interest groups, raising and spending tax monies, and assessing the costs and benefits of complicated alternatives. Finally, federal judges are not elected; they are appointed and are thus immune to popular control. As a result, if they depart from their traditional role of making careful and cautious interpretations of what a law or the Constitution means and instead begin formulating wholly new policies, they become unelected legislators.

Some people think we have activist courts because we have so many lawyers. The more we take matters to courts for resolution, the more likely it is that the courts will become powerful. It is true that we have more lawyers in proportion to our population than most other nations. There is one lawyer for every 325 Americans, but only one for every 970 Britons, every 1,220 Germans, and every 8,333 Japanese.[49] But that may well be a symptom, not a cause, of court activity. As we suggested in Chapter 4, we have an adversary culture based on an emphasis on individual rights and an implicit antagonism between the people and the government. Generally speaking, lawyers do not create cases; contending interests do, thereby generating a demand for lawyers.[50] Furthermore, we had more lawyers in relation to our population in 1900 than in 1970, yet the courts at the turn of the 20th century were far less active in public affairs. In fact, in 1932 there were more court cases per 100,000 people than there were in 1972.

A more plausible reason for activist courts has been the developments discussed earlier in this chapter that have made it easier for people to get standing in the courts, to pay for the costs of litigation, and to bring class-action suits. The courts and Congress have gone a long way toward allowing private citizens to become "private attorneys general." Making it easier to get into court increases the number of cases being heard. For example, in 1961, civil rights cases, prisoners' rights cases, and cases under the Social Security laws were relatively uncommon in federal court. Between 1961 and 1990, the increase in the number of such matters was phenomenal: civil rights cases rose more than sixtyfold and prisoners' petitions more than fortyfold. Such matters are the fastest-growing portion of the courts' civil workload.

LEGISLATION AND THE COURTS

An increase in cases will not by itself lead to sweeping remedies. For that to occur, the law must be sufficiently vague to permit judges wide latitude in interpreting it, and the judges must want to exercise that opportunity fully. The Constitution is filled with words of seemingly ambiguous meaning—"due process of law," the "equal protection of the laws," the "privileges or immunities of citizens." Such phrases may have been clear to the Framers, but to the Supreme Court they have become equivocal or elastic. How the Court has chosen to interpret such phrases has changed greatly over the last two centuries in ways that can be explained in part by the personal political beliefs of the justices.

Increasingly, Congress has passed laws that also contain vague language, thereby adding immeasurably to the courts' opportunities for designing remedies. Various civil rights acts outlaw discrimination but do not say how one is to know whether discrimination has occurred or what should be done to correct it if it does occur. That is left to the courts and the bureaucracy. Various regulatory laws empower administrative agencies to do what the "public interest" requires but say little about how the public interest is to be defined. Laws intended to alleviate poverty or rebuild neighborhoods speak of "citizen participation" or "maximum feasible participation" but do not explain who the citizens are that should participate, or how much power they should have.

In addition to laws that require interpretation, other laws induce litigation. Almost every agency that regulates business will make decisions that cause the agency to be challenged in court—by business firms if the regulations go too far, by consumer or labor organizations if they do not go far enough.

One study showed that the federal courts of appeals heard more than 3,000 cases in which they had to review the decision of a regulatory agency. In two-thirds of them, the agency's position was supported; in the other third, the agency was overruled.[51] Perhaps one-fifth of these cases arose out of agencies or programs that did not even exist in 1960. The federal government today is much more likely to be on the defensive in court than it was 20 or 30 years ago.

Finally, the attitudes of the judges powerfully affect what they will do, especially when the law gives them wide latitude. Their decisions and opinions have been extensively analyzed—well enough, at least, to know that different judges often decide the same case in different ways. Conservative southern federal judges in the 1950s, for example, often resisted plans to desegregate public schools, while judges with a different background authorized bold plans.[52] Some of the greatest disparities in judicial behavior can be found in the area of sentencing criminals.[53]

Checks on Judicial Power

No institution of government, including the courts, operates without restraint. The fact that judges are not elected does not make them immune to public opinion or to the views of the other branches of government. How important these restraints are varies from case to case, but in the broad course of history they have been significant.

One restraint exists because of the very nature of courts. A judge has no police force or army; decisions that he or she makes can sometimes be resisted or ignored, *if* the person or organization resisting is not highly visible and is willing to run the risk of being caught and charged with contempt of court. For example, long after the Supreme Court's controversial decisions that praying and Bible reading could not take place in public schools,[54] schools all over the country were still allowing prayers and Bible reading.[55] Years after the Court declared segregated schools to be unconstitutional, scores of school systems remained segregated. On the other hand, when a failure to comply is easily detected and punished, the courts' power is usually unchallenged. When the Supreme Court declared the income tax to be unconstitutional in 1895, income tax collections promptly ceased. When the Court in 1952 declared illegal President Truman's effort to seize the steel mills in order to stop a strike, the management of the mills was immediately returned to their owners.

CONGRESS AND THE COURTS

Congress has a number of ways of checking the judiciary. It can gradually alter the composition of the judiciary by the kinds of appointments the Senate is willing to confirm, or it can impeach judges it does not like. Fifteen federal judges have been the object of impeachment proceedings in our history, and nine others have resigned when such proceedings seemed likely. Of the 15 who were impeached, seven were acquitted, four were convicted, and one resigned.

How We Compare

Judicial Review in Canada and Europe

Courts outside the United States can declare laws to be unconstitutional, but most can do so in ways that are very different from that in the United States.

Canada: The highest court can declare a law unconstitutional, but not if the legislature has passed it with a special provision that says the law will survive judicial scrutiny notwithstanding the country's Charter of Rights. Such laws must be renewed every five years.

Europe: The European Court of Human Rights in Strasbourg can decide human rights cases that begin in any of the nations that make up the European Community.

France: Its Constitutional Council can declare a law unconstitutional, but only if asked to do so by government officials and only before (not after) the law goes into effect.

Germany: The Federal Constitutional Court can declare in an advisory opinion, before a case has emerged, that a law is unconstitutional, and it can judge the constitutionality of laws when asked to do so by a lower court (which itself cannot rule a law unconstitutional). The Federal Constitutional Court may hold an administrative or judicial action to be unjustified when a citizen, having exhausted all other remedies, files a petition.

The most recent convictions were those of Alcee Hastings of Florida and Walter Nixon of Mississippi, both in 1989.[56] In practice, however, confirmation and impeachment proceedings do not make much of an impact on the federal courts because simple policy disagreements are not generally regarded as adequate grounds for voting against a judicial nominee or for starting an impeachment effort.

Congress can alter the number of judges, though, and by increasing the number sharply, it can give a president a chance to appoint judges to his liking. As described above, a "Court-packing" plan was proposed (unsuccessfully) by Franklin Roosevelt in 1937 specifically to change the political persuasion of the Supreme Court. In 1978, Congress passed a bill creating 152 new federal district and appellate judges to help ease the workload of the federal judiciary. This bill gave President Carter a chance to appoint over 40 percent of the federal bench. In 1984, an additional 84 judgeships were created; by 1988, President Reagan had appointed about half of all federal judges. In 1990, an additional 72 judges were authorized. During and after the Civil War, Congress may have been trying to influence Supreme Court decisions when it changed the size of the Court three times in six years (raising it from nine to 10 in 1863, lowering it again from 10 to seven in 1866, and raising it again from seven to nine in 1869).

Congress and the states can also undo a Supreme Court decision interpreting the Constitution by amending that document. This happens, but rarely: the Eleventh Amendment was ratified to prevent a citizen from suing a state in federal court; the Thirteenth, Fourteenth, and Fifteenth were ratified to undo the *Dred Scott* decision regarding slavery; the Sixteenth was added to make it constitutional for Congress to pass an income tax; and the Twenty-sixth was added to give the vote to 18-year-olds in state elections.

On more than 30 occasions, Congress has merely repassed a law that the Court has declared unconstitutional. In one case, a bill to aid farmers, voided in 1936, was accepted by the Court in slightly revised form three years later.[57] (In the meantime, of course, the Court had changed its collective mind about the New Deal.)

One of the most powerful potential sources of control over the federal courts, however, is the authority of Congress, given by the Constitution, to decide what the entire jurisdiction of the lower courts and the appellate jurisdiction of the Supreme Court shall be. In theory, Congress could prevent matters on which it did not want federal courts to act from ever coming before the courts. This happened in 1868. A Mississippi newspaper editor named McCardle was jailed by federal military authorities who occupied the defeated South. McCardle asked the federal district court for a writ of habeas corpus to get him out of custody; when the district court rejected his plea, he appealed to the Supreme Court. Congress at that time was fearful that the Court might find the laws on which its Reconstruction policy was based (and under which McCardle was in jail) unconstitutional. To prevent that from happening, it passed a bill withdrawing from the Supreme Court appellate jurisdiction in cases of this sort. The Court conceded that Congress could do this and thus dismissed the case because it no longer had jurisdiction.[58]

Congress has threatened to withdraw jurisdiction on other occasions, and the mere existence of the threat may have influenced the nature of Court decisions. In the 1950s, for example, congressional opinion was hostile to Court decisions in the field of civil liberties and civil rights, and legislation was proposed that would have curtailed the Court's jurisdiction in these areas. It did not pass, but the Court may have allowed the threat to temper its decisions.[59] On the other hand, as congressional resistance to the Roosevelt Court-packing plan shows, the Supreme Court enjoys a good deal of prestige in the nation, even among people who disagree with some of its decisions, and so passing laws that would frontally attack it would not be easy except perhaps in times of national crisis.

Furthermore, laws narrowing jurisdiction or restricting the kinds of remedies that a court can impose often are blunt instruments that might not achieve the purposes of their proponents. Suppose that you, as a member of Congress, would like to prevent the federal courts from ordering schoolchildren to be bused for the purpose of achieving racial balance in the schools. If you denied the Supreme Court appellate jurisdiction in this matter, you would leave the lower federal courts and all state courts free to do as they wished, and many of them would go on ordering busing. If you wanted to attack that problem, you could propose a law that would deny to all federal courts the right to order busing as a remedy for racial imbalance. But the courts would still be free to order busing (and of course a lot of busing goes on even without court orders), provided that they did not say that it was for the purpose of achieving racial balance. (It could be for the purpose of "facilitating desegregation" or making possible "redistricting.") Naturally you could always make it illegal for children to enter a school bus for any reason, but then many children would not be able to get to school at all. Finally, the Supreme Court might well decide that if busing were essential to achieve a constitutional right, then any congressional law prohibiting such busing would itself be unconstitutional. Trying to think through how *that* dilemma would be resolved is like trying to visualize two kangaroos simultaneously jumping into each other's pouches.

PUBLIC OPINION AND THE COURTS

Though they are not elected, judges read the same newspapers as members of Congress, and thus they, too, are aware of public opinion, especially elite opinion. Though it may be going too far to say the Supreme Court follows the election returns, it is nonetheless true that the Court is sensitive to certain bodies of opinion, especially of those elites—liberal or conservative—to which its members happen to be attuned. The justices will keep in mind historical cases in which their predecessors, by blatantly disregarding public opinion, very nearly destroyed the legitimacy of the Court itself. This was the case with the *Dred Scott* decision, which infuriated the North and was widely disobeyed. No such crisis exists today, but it is altogether possible that changing political moods affect the kinds of remedies that judges will think appropriate.

Opinion not only restrains the courts; it may also energize them. The most activist periods in Supreme Court history have coincided with times when the political system was undergoing profound and lasting changes. The assertion by the Supreme Court, under John Marshall's leadership, of the principles of national supremacy and judicial review occurred at the time when the Jeffersonian Republicans were coming to power and their opponents, the Federalists, were collapsing as an organized party. The pro-slavery decisions of the Taney Court came when the nation was so divided along sectional and ideological lines as to make almost any Court decision on this matter unpopular. Supreme Court review of economic regulation in the 1890s and 1900s came at a time when the political parties were realigning and the Republicans were acquiring dominance that would last for several decades. The Court decisions of the 1930s corresponded to another period of partisan realignment. (The meaning of a realigning election was discussed in Chapter 10.)

Pollsters have been measuring how much confidence the public has in the Supreme Court. The results are shown in Figure 16.5. The percentage of people saying that they had a "great deal of confidence" in the Court rose sharply from 1971 to 1974, fell again until 1976, seesawed up and down until 1989, took a sharp dip and then recovered from 1989 to 1991, and again seesawed before rising in 1996. These movements seem to reflect the public's reaction not only to what the Court does but also to what the government as a whole is doing. The upturn in the early 1970s was probably caused by the Watergate scandal, an episode that simultaneously discredited the presidency and boosted

Figure 16.5
Patterns of Public Confidence in the Court, 1974–2006

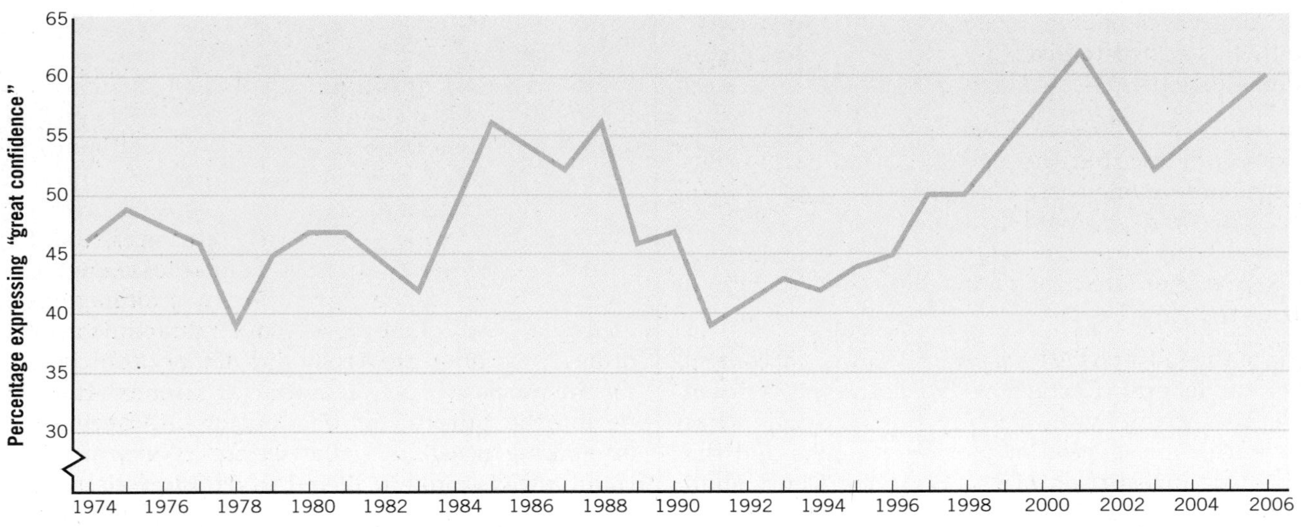

Source: The Gallup Poll.

the stock of those institutions (such as the courts) that seemed to be checking the abuses of the White House. The gradual upturn in the 1980s may have reflected a general restoration of public confidence in government during that decade.[60]

Though popular support for the Supreme Court often declines, these drops have so far not resulted in any legal checks placed on it. In the 1970s and 1980s, several bills were introduced in Congress that would have restricted the jurisdiction of federal courts over busing for purposes of racial integration or altered the Supreme Court's decisions regarding school prayer and abortion. None passed.

The changes that have occurred in the Court have been caused by changes in its personnel. Presidents Nixon and Reagan attempted to produce a less activist Court by appointing justices who were more inclined to be strict constructionists and conservatives. To some extent, they succeeded: Justices Kennedy, O'Connor, Rehnquist, and Scalia were certainly less inclined than Justice Thurgood Marshall to find new rights in the Constitution or to overturn the decisions of state legislatures. But as of yet, there has been no wholesale retreat from the positions staked out by the Warren Court. As noted above, a Nixon appointee, Justice Blackmun, wrote the decision making antiabortion laws unconstitutional; and another Nixon appointee, Chief Justice Burger, wrote the opinion upholding court-ordered school busing to achieve racial integration. A Reagan appointee, Justice O'Connor, voted to uphold a right to an abortion. The Supreme Court has become somewhat less willing to impose restraints on police practices, and it has not blocked the use of the death penalty. But in general, the major features of Court activism and liberalism during the Warren years—school integration, sharper limits on police practice, greater freedom of expression—have remained intact.

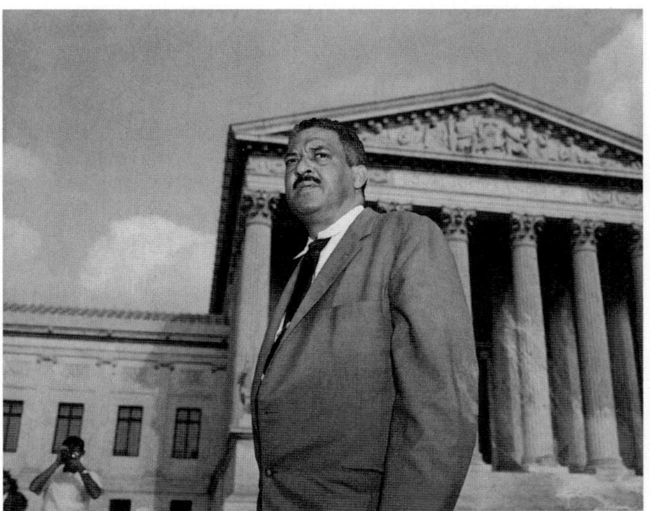

Thurgood Marshall became the first black Supreme Court justice. As chief counsel for the NAACP, Marshall argued the 1954 *Brown v. Board of Education* case in front of the Supreme Court. He was appointed to the Court in 1967 and served until 1991.

The reasons for the growth in court activism are clear. One is the sheer growth in the size and scope of the government as a whole. The courts have come to play a larger role in our lives because Congress, the bureaucracy, and the president have come to play larger ones. In 1890, hardly anybody would have thought of asking Congress—much less the courts—to make rules governing the participation of women in college sports or the district boundaries of state legislatures. Today such rules are commonplace, and the courts are inevitably drawn into interpreting them. And when the Court decided how the vote in Florida would be counted during the 2000 presidential election, it created an opportunity in the future for scores of new lawsuits challenging election results.

The other reason for increased activism is the acceptance by a large number of judges, conservative as well as liberal, of the activist view of the function of the courts. If courts once existed solely to "settle disputes," today they also exist in the eyes of their members to "solve problems."

Though the Supreme Court is the pinnacle of the federal judiciary, most decisions, including many important ones, are made by the several courts of appeals and the 94 district courts. The Supreme Court can control its own workload by deciding when to grant certiorari. It has become easier for citizens and groups to gain access to the federal courts (through class-action suits, by amicus curiae briefs, by laws that require government agencies to pay legal fees, and because of the activities of private groups such as the NAACP and the ACLU).

At the same time, the courts have widened the reach of their decisions by issuing orders that cover whole classes of citizens or affect the management of major public and private institutions. However, the courts can overstep the bounds of their authority and bring upon themselves a counterattack from both the public and Congress. Congress has the right to control much of the courts' jurisdiction, but it rarely does so. As a result, the ability of judges to make law is only infrequently challenged directly.

WHAT WOULD YOU DO?

MEMORANDUM

To: *Senator Ann Gilbert*

From: *Amy Wilson, legislative assistant*

Re: *Federal law legalizing assisted suicide*

The Supreme Court has held that the attorney general cannot use his authority over federally controlled drugs to block the implementation of the Oregon "Death with Dignity" law. Now some of your colleagues want to enact a federal equivalent of that law that would allow physicians to prescribe deadly drugs to patients who request them.

News »

Legalizing Assisted Suicide

Congress is discussing a federal law that would allow physicians to administer drugs that will lead to the death of patients who request them. Oregon already has a "Death with Dignity" statute.

Arguments for:

1. The law respects the people's right to choose the time and place of their own death.
2. It is already permissible to post "Do Not Resuscitate" orders on the charts of terminally ill patients.
3. Physicians can be held to high standards in implementing the law.

Arguments against:

1. The law will corrupt the role of doctors, as many think has happened in Holland, where a similar law has led some physicians to kill patients prematurely or without justification.
2. Such a law will lead some physicians to neglect or ignore the desires of the patient.
3. This law will undermine the more important goal of helping patients overcome pain and depression.

Your decision:

Support the law ________________ Oppose the law ________________

LEARNING OBJECTIVES

WHAT YOU NEED TO KNOW

☑ **Where in the Constitution does it say that the Supreme Court has the power of judicial review?**

Nowhere in the Constitution does it say that the Supreme Court has the power of judicial review. The Constitution is silent on this matter, but the Court has asserted, and almost every scholar has agreed, that our system of separated powers means that the Court must be able to defend the Constitution. Otherwise, Congress and the President would be free to ignore it.

☑ **What is an "Article III" federal judge?**

An "Article III" federal judge is a federal judge who benefits from Article III of the Constitution, which guarantees judges that they can serve during good behavior. The Supreme Court, courts of appeal, and all district courts are all Title 3 courts. Congress has also established "legislative" courts whose members serve for fixed terms. Examples are the Tax Court and the Court of Appeals for the Armed Forces.

☑ **Does England have a supreme court?**

England does not have a supreme court. In most parliamentary governments, such as England's, the parliament is supreme and cannot be challenged. But most European nations, including England, are part of the European Union that has created the rough equivalent of a supreme court.

☑ **What is the difference between original and appellate jurisdiction?**

Original jurisdiction refers to a trial held before a court; appellate jurisdiction refers to an appeal a court hears from a trial in another court. Even the Supreme Court has original jurisdiction. For example, it will hear a trial involving ambassadors or a controversy between two or more states.

RECONSIDERING WHO GOVERNS?

1. Why should federal judges serve for life?

Strictly speaking, they serve during "good behavior," but that means they would have to be impeached and convicted in order to be removed. The reason for this protection is clear: the judiciary cannot be independent of the other two branches of government if judges could be easily removed by the president or Congress, and this independence ensures that they are a separate branch of government.

RECONSIDERING TO WHAT ENDS?

1. Why should federal courts be able to declare laws unconstitutional?

Though the Constitution does not explicitly give them that power, they have acquired it on the reasonable assumption that the Constitution would become meaningless if the president and Congress could ignore its provisions. The Constitution, after all, states that it shall be the "supreme law of the land."

2. Should federal judges only interpret existing laws or should they be able to create new laws?

The federal courts rarely think their decisions create entirely new laws, but in fact their interpretations sometimes come close to just that. One reason is that many provisions of the Constitution are vague. What does the Constitution mean by "respecting an establishment of religion," the "equal protection of the law," or a "cruel and unusual punishment"? The courts must give concrete meaning to these phrases. But another reason is the personal ideology of judges. Some think a free press is more important than laws governing campaign finance, while others think a free press must give way to such laws. Some believe the courts ought to use federal law to strike down discrimination, but others think affirmative action programs must be put in place.

QUESTIONS TO CONSIDER

1. **Imagine yourself to be an attorney with a case that is similar to one recently decided by the Supreme Court. How could you use the various opinions written by the justices to guide your case?**
2. **Should the process of appointing Federal judges be political? What are the advantages and disadvantages to the politics of judicial confirmation?**
3. **Do you think judges should exercise restraint or be activists? Explain in detail why you prefer one over the other and give examples of cases to justify your answer.**
4. **Should there be greater limits on judicial review? Explain why or why not.**

TO LEARN MORE

Federal Judicial Center: **www.fjc.gov**
Federal courts: **www.uscourts.gov**
Supreme Court decisions: **www.law.cornell.edu**
Finding laws and reports: **www.findlaw.com**

Abraham, Henry J. *The Judicial Process,* 7th ed. New York: Oxford University Press, 1998. An excellent, comprehensive survey of how the federal courts are organized and function.

Abraham, Henry J., and Barbara A. Perry. *Freedom and the Court,* 8th ed. Lawrence, Kan.: University of Kansas Press, 2003. Careful summary of civil liberties and civil rights cases.

Cardozo, Benjamin N. *The Nature of the Judicial Process*. New Haven, Conn.: Yale University Press, 1921. Important statement of how judges make decisions, by a former Supreme Court justice.

Ely, John Hart. *Democracy and Distrust*. Cambridge: Harvard University Press, 1980. Effort to create a theory of judicial review that is neither strict-constructionist nor activist.

Greenburg, Jan Crawford. *Supreme Conflict*. New York: Penguin, 2007. A fascinating journalistic account of how the Supreme Court operates.

Hall, Kermit L., and James W. Ely, Jr., eds. *The Oxford Guide to the United States Supreme Court Decisions*, 2nd ed. New York: Oxford University Press, 2009. Summarizes the 440 most important decisions of the Supreme Court and includes a comprehensive bibliography of books about the Court.

Lasser, William. *The Limits of Judicial Power*. Chapel Hill: University of North Carolina Press, 1988. Shows how the Court through history has withstood the political storms created by its more controversial decisions.

McCloskey, Robert G. *The American Supreme Court,* 4th ed. Edited by Sanford Levinson. Chicago: University of Chicago Press, 2005. Superb brief history of the Supreme Court, updated by one of McCloskey's former students who now teaches law at the University of Texas.

Rabkin, Jeremy. *Judicial Compulsions*. New York: Basic Books, 1989. Explains (and argues against) the extensive Court intervention in the work of administrative agencies.

Wolfe, Christopher. *The Rise of Modern Judicial Review*. New York: Basic Books, 1986. An excellent history of judicial review from 1787 to the present.

Part 4

The Politics of Public Policy

17 The Policymaking Process 470

18 Economic Policy 492

19 Social Welfare 514

20 Foreign and Military Policy 534

21 Environmental Policy 564

In the extended republic of the United States, and among the great variety of interests, parties, and sects, which it embraces, a coalition of a majority of the whole society could seldom take place on any other principles than those of justice and the general good.

**** Federalist No. 51***

17 The Policymaking Process

LEARNING OBJECTIVES

WHAT YOU NEED TO KNOW

- ☑ What is a political agenda?
- ☑ What is meant by logrolling?
- ☑ What is a policy entrepreneur?

WHO GOVERNS?

1. Does some political elite dominate American politics?
2. Do powerful interest groups decide what policies our government should adopt?

TO WHAT ENDS?

1. Why are Social Security payments popular but welfare payments to unwed mothers unpopular?
2. Why were government regulations on certain industries repealed over the objection of those industries?

If all you wanted to know about American politics is how our leaders are chosen and the ways in which they operate, you could close this book now. But if you are interested in how our public policies get made, you should keep reading because not all policies are made the same way.

Of course, some people claim that big business, or top bureaucrats, or powerful interest groups decide everything. But the Marxist, the Weberian, and the pluralist views are only partially correct.

THEN Certain oil companies were once able to persuade the government to restrict sharply the amount of foreign oil imported into the United States, to give them preferential tax treatment, and to permit them to drill for new oil just about anywhere they liked. Automobile manufacturers once faced virtually no federal controls on the products they manufactured.

NOW Today, the restrictions on foreign oil imports have ended, the tax breaks the oil companies enjoy have been reduced considerably (though they still exist), and the freedom of oil companies to drill in certain places, particularly offshore locations, has been restricted. Auto companies are heavily regulated regarding the safety of the vehicles they make, and two of them (GM and Chrysler) have been partially owned by the federal government.

Business regulation is now a complicated story. In the past, some corporations have been regulated in ways that increased their profitability (the airlines), reduced it (the railroads), or had no appreciable effect one way or the other (electric utilities). These outcomes of government action or inaction are not easily explained. To understand why they happen, we need some theory of policymaking. This chapter will provide one; subsequent chapters will apply it.

Setting the Agenda

The most important decision that affects policymaking is also the least noticed one: deciding what to make policy *about,* or in the language of political science, deciding what belongs on the **political agenda.** We take for granted that politics is about certain familiar issues such as taxes, energy, welfare, and civil rights. We forget that there is nothing inevitable about having these issues—rather than some other ones—on the nation's agenda. At one time, it was unconstitutional for the federal government to levy income taxes; energy was a nonissue because everybody (or at least everybody who could chop down trees for a fireplace) had enough; welfare was something for cities and towns to handle; and civil rights were supposed to be a matter of private choice rather than government action. Until the 1930s, the national political agenda was quite short, and even in the 1950s many people would have been astonished or upset to be told that the federal government was supposed to worry about the environment, consumerism, or civil rights.

"He who decides what politics is about runs the country."[1] This is a statement of profound significance, though it exaggerates the extent to which somebody—some person—actually "decides" what politics is all about. The statement correctly suggests that, at any given time, certain shared beliefs determine what is legitimate (proper, right) for the government to do. This legitimacy is affected by several forces:

- Shared political values—for example, if many people believe that poverty is the result of individual failure rather than social forces, then there is no reason for a government program to combat poverty.

political agenda Issues that people believe require governmental action.

- The weight of custom and tradition—people will usually accept what the government has customarily done, even if they are leery of what it proposes to do.
- The impact of events—wars, depressions, and the like—alter our sense of the proper role of government.
- Changes in the way political elites think and talk about politics.

THE LEGITIMATE SCOPE OF GOVERNMENT ACTION

Because many people believe that whatever the government now does it ought to continue doing, and because changes in attitudes and the impact of events tend to increase the number of things that government does, the scope of legitimate government action is always getting larger. As a result, the scope of what is illegitimate for the government to do steadily gets smaller. This means that today we hear far fewer debates about the legitimacy of a proposed government policy than we heard in the 1920s or the 1930s. The existence of "big government" is sustained by these expanded beliefs about legitimacy and is not the consequence of some sinister power grab by politicians or bureaucrats. When President Gerald Ford, a Republican, ran for election in 1976, a favorite slogan of his was that a government big enough to give you everything you want is also big enough to take away everything you have. No doubt he thought he was criticizing liberal Democrats. But it was his immediate predecessor, President Nixon, also a Republican, who had imposed peacetime wage and price controls and proposed a guaranteed annual income for every family, working or not working. It was another Republican president, Dwight Eisenhower, who had sent federal troops to Little Rock, Arkansas, to enforce a school-desegregation order. And it was yet another Republican president, Ronald Reagan, who was in office when federal payments to farmers grew to be six times larger than they had been in the 1970s. For better or worse, the expansion of government has been the result, fundamentally, of a nonpartisan process.

Popular views on the legitimate scope of government action, and thus on the kinds of issues that ought to be on the political agenda, are changed by the impact of events. During wartime or after a terrorist attack on this country, the people expect the government to do whatever is necessary to win, whether or not such actions are clearly authorized by the Constitution. (As we saw in Chapter 15, the federal bureaucracy enjoys its most rapid growth in wartime.) A depression, such as the ones that began in 1929 and 2008, also leads people to expect the government to do something. As we shall see in Chapter 19, public opinion favored federal action to deal with the problems of the unemployed, the elderly, and the poor well in advance of the actual decisions of the government to take action. A coal mine disaster leads to an enlarged role for the government in promoting mine safety. A series of airplane hijackings leads to a change in public opinion so great that what once would have been unthinkable—requiring all passengers at airports to be searched before boarding their flights—becomes routine.

But sometimes the government enlarges its agenda of policy issues, often dramatically, without any crisis or widespread public demand. This may happen even at a time when the conditions at which a policy is directed are improving. There was no public demand for government action to make automobiles safer before 1966, when a law was passed imposing safety standards on cars. Though the number of auto fatalities (per 100 million miles driven) had gone up slightly just before the law was passed, the long-term trend in highway deaths had been more or less steadily downward. The Occupational Safety and Health Act was passed in 1970 at a time when the number of industrial deaths (per 100,000 workers) had been steadily dropping for almost 20 years.[2] Programs to combat urban poverty and unemployment were adopted in the mid-1960s at a time when the number of persons, black as well as white, living below the poverty line was declining and when the adult unemployment rate—for blacks as well as whites—was lower than it had been at any time in the preceding 10 years.[3] Affirmative action programs were introduced to increase the flow of minorities into jobs and colleges at a time when minorities were already making rapid progress.

It is not easy to explain why the government adds new issues to its agenda and adopts new programs when there is little public demand and when, in fact, there has been an improvement in the conditions to which the policies are addressed. In general, the explanation may be found in the behavior of groups, the workings of institutions, the opinions of political elites, and the action of state governments.

GROUPS

Many policies are the result of small groups of people enlarging the scope of government by their demands. Sometimes these are organized interests (for example, corporations or unions); sometimes they are intense but unorganized groups (urban minorities). The organized groups often work quietly, behind the scenes; the intense, unorganized ones may take their causes to the streets.

Organized labor favored a tough federal safety law governing factories and other workplaces not because it was unaware that factory conditions had been improving but because the standards by which union leaders and members judged working conditions had risen even faster. As people became better off, conditions that once were thought normal suddenly became intolerable. When Alexis de Tocqueville sought to explain the French Revolution, he observed that citizens are most restless and easily aroused not when they are living in abject poverty or under grinding repression but when they have started to become better off.[4] Social scientists sometimes refer to this as a sense of "relative deprivation."

On occasion, a group expresses in violent ways its dissatisfaction with what it judges to be intolerable conditions. The black riots in American cities during the mid-1960s had a variety of causes, and people participated out of a variety of motives. For many, rioting was a way of expressing pent-up anger at what they regarded as an unresponsive and unfair society. This sense of relative deprivation—of being worse off than one thinks one *ought* to be—helps explain why so large a proportion of the rioters were not uneducated, unemployed recent migrants to the city, but rather young men and women born in the North, educated in its schools, and employed in its factories.[5] Life under these conditions turned out to be not what they had come to expect or what they were prepared to tolerate.

The new demands of such groups need not result in an enlarged political agenda, and they do not when society and its governing institutions are confident of the rightness of the existing state of affairs. Unions could have been voted down on the occupational safety bill; rioting blacks could have been jailed and ignored. At one time, exactly this would have happened. But society itself had changed: many people who were not workers sympathized with the plight of the injured worker and distrusted the good intentions of business in this matter. Many whites felt that a constructive as well as a punitive response to the urban riots was required and thus urged the formation of commissions to study—and the passage of laws to deal with—the problems of inner-city life. Such changes in the values and beliefs of people generally—or at least of people in key government positions—are an essential part of any explanation of why policies not demanded by public opinion nonetheless become part of the political agenda.

INSTITUTIONS

Among the institutions whose influence on agenda-setting has become especially important are the courts, the bureaucracy, and the Senate.

The courts can make decisions that force the hand of the other branches of government. When in 1954 the Supreme Court ordered schools desegregated, Congress and the White House could no longer ignore the issue. Local resistance to implementing the order led President Eisenhower to send troops to Little Rock, Arkansas, despite his dislike for using force against local governments. When the Supreme Court ruled in 1973 that the states could not ban abortions during the first trimester of pregnancy, abortion suddenly became a national political issue. Right-to-life activists campaigned to reverse the Court decision or, failing that, to prevent federal funds from being used to pay for abortions. Pro-choice activists fought to prevent the Court from changing its mind and to get federal funding for abortions. In these and many other cases, the courts act like trip wires: when activated, they set off a chain reaction of events that alters the political agenda and creates a new constellation of political forces.

Indeed, they are more than trip wires. As the government agenda has expanded, the courts have become the favorite method for doing things for which there is no popular majority. There may be no electoral support for allowing abortion on demand, eliminating school prayer, creating affirmative action, ordering school busing, or attacking tobacco companies, but in the courts elections do not matter. The courts are the preferred vehicles for the advocates of unpopular causes.

The bureaucracy has acquired a new significance in American politics not simply because of its size or power but also because it is now a source of political innovation. At one time, the federal government *reacted* to events in society and to demands from segments of society; ordinarily it did not itself propose changes and new ideas. Today, the bureaucracy is so large and includes within it so great a variety of experts and advocates, that it has become a *source* of policy proposals as well as an implementer of those that become law. Daniel Patrick Moynihan called this the "professionalization of reform," by which he meant, in part, that the government bureaucracy had begun to think up problems for government to solve rather than simply to respond to the problems identified by others.[6] In the 1930s, many of the key elements of the New Deal—Social Security, unemployment compensation, public housing, old-age benefits—were ideas devised by nongovernment experts and intellectuals here and abroad and then, as the crisis of the depression deepened, taken up by the federal government. In the 1960s, by contrast, most of the measures that became known as part of Lyndon Johnson's "Great Society"—federal aid to education, manpower development and training, Medicare and Medicaid, the "War on Poverty," the "safe-streets" act providing federal aid to local law enforcement agencies—were developed, designed, and advocated by government officials, bureaucrats, and their political allies.

Chief among these political allies are U.S. senators and their staffs. Once the Senate was best described as a club that moved slowly, debated endlessly, and resisted, under the leadership of conservative southern Democrats, the plans of liberal presidents. With the collapse of the one-party South and the increase in the number of liberal activist senators, the Senate became in the 1960s an incubator for developing new policies and building national constituencies.[7] As the Senate became more conservative in the 1980s, it retained the initiative, but now on behalf of reversing some of the changes wrought earlier. The Senate has thus become one of the sources of political change rather than, as the Founders intended, a balance wheel designed to moderate change.[8]

MEDIA

The national press can either help place new matters on the agenda or publicize those matters placed there by others. There was a close correlation between the political attention given in the Senate to proposals for new safety standards for industry, coal mines, and automobiles and the amount of space devoted to these questions in the pages of the *New York Times*. Newspaper interest in the matter, low before the issue was placed on the agenda, peaked at about the time the bill was passed.[9] It is hard, of course, to decide which is cause and which effect. The press may have stimulated congressional interest in the matter or merely reported on what Congress had already decided to pursue. Nonetheless, the press must choose which of thousands of proposals it will cover. The beliefs of editors and reporters led it to select the safety issue. In later chapters, we shall discuss the kinds of issues for which the national press is important.

In short, the political agenda can change because of changes in popular attitudes, elite interest, critical events, or government actions. An overly simple but essentially correct generalization might be this: popular attitudes usually change slowly, often in response to critical events; elite attitudes and government actions are more volatile and interdependent and thus change more quickly, often in response to each other.

ACTION BY THE STATES

National policy is increasingly being made by the actions of state governments. You may wonder how. After all, a state can only pass laws that affect its own people. Of course, the national government

JASON REED/Reuters/Landov

Comedians Jon Stewart (right) and Stephen Colbert (left) sing during the "Rally to Restore Sanity and/or Fear" on the Washington Mall, October 30, 2010.

Spencer Grant/PhotoEdit

Computers are lined up on the desks of members of the California state legislature.

may later adopt ideas pioneered in the states, as it did when Congress passed a "Do Not Call" law to reduce how many phone calls you will get from salespeople while you are trying to eat dinner. The states had taken the lead in this.

But there is another way in which state governments can make national policy directly without Congress ever voting on the matter. The attorneys general of states may sue a business firm and settle the suit with an agreement that binds the industry throughout the country. The effect of one suit was to raise prices for consumers and create a new set of regulations. This is what happened in 1998 with the tobacco agreement negotiated between cigarette companies and some state attorneys general. The companies agreed to raise their prices, pay more than $240 billion to state governments (to use as they wished) and several billion dollars to private lawyers, and to agree to a massive regulatory program. A decade later, the federal government passed laws that reinforced the states' regulations, culminating in the Family Smoking Prevention Tobacco Control Act of 2009.

Making a Decision

Once an issue is on the political agenda, its nature affects the kind of politicking that ensues. Some issues provoke intense interest group conflict; others allow one group to prevail almost unchallenged. Some issues involve ideological appeals to broad national constituencies; others involve quiet bargaining in congressional offices. We all know that private groups try to influence government policies; we often forget that the nature of the issues with which government is dealing influences the kinds of groups that become politically active.

One way to understand how an issue affects the distribution of political power among groups and institutions is to examine what appear to be the costs and benefits of the proposed policy. The **cost** is any burden, monetary or nonmonetary, that some people must bear, or think they must bear, if the policy is adopted. The costs of a government spending program are the taxes it entails; the cost of a foreign policy initiative may be the increased chance of having the nation drawn into war. The **benefit** is any satisfaction, monetary or nonmonetary, that people believe they will enjoy if the policy is adopted. The benefits of a government spending program are the payments, subsidies, or contracts received by some people; the benefits of a foreign policy initiative may include the enhanced security of the nation, the protection of a valued ally, or the vindication of some important principle such as human rights.

cost A burden that people believe they must bear if a policy is enacted.

benefit A satisfaction that people believe they will enjoy if a policy is adopted.

Two aspects of these costs and benefits should be borne in mind. First, it is the *perception* of costs and benefits that affects politics. People may think the cost of an auto emissions control system is paid by the manufacturer, when it is actually passed on to the consumer in the form of higher prices and reduced performance. Political conflict over pollution control will take one form when people think that Ford and GM pay the costs and another form when they think that the consumers pay.

Second, people take into account not only who benefits but also whether it is *legitimate* for that group to benefit. When programs providing financial assistance to women with dependent children were first developed in the early part of the 20th century, they were relatively noncontroversial because people saw the money as going to widows and orphans who deserved such aid. Later on, giving aid to mothers with dependent children became controversial because some people now perceived the recipients not as deserving widows but as sexually loose women who had never married. Whatever the truth of the matter, the program had lost some of its legitimacy because the beneficiaries were no longer seen as "deserving." By the same token, groups once thought undeserving, such as men out of work, were later thought to be entitled to aid, and thus the unemployment compensation program acquired a legitimacy that it once lacked.

Politics is in large measure a process of raising and settling disputes over who *will* benefit or pay for a program and who *ought* to benefit or pay. Since beliefs about the results of a program and the rightness of those results are matters of opinion, it is evident that ideas are at least as important as interests in shaping politics. In recent years, ideas have become especially important with the rise of issues whose consequences are largely intangible, such as abortion, school prayer, and racial integration.

Though perceptions about costs and benefits change, most people most of the time prefer government programs that provide substantial benefits to them at low cost. This rather obvious fact can have important implications for how politics is carried out. In a political system based on some measure of popular rule, public officials have a strong incentive to offer programs that confer—or appear to confer—benefits on people with costs either small in amount, remote in time, or borne by "somebody else." Policies that seem to impose high, immediate costs in return for small or remote benefits will be avoided, enacted with a minimum of publicity, or proposed only in response to a real or apparent crisis.

Ordinarily, no president would propose a policy that would immediately raise the cost of fuel, even if he were convinced that future supplies of oil and gasoline were likely to be exhausted unless higher prices reduced current consumption. But when a crisis occurs, such as the Arab oil cartel's price increases beginning in 1973, it becomes possible for the president to offer such proposals—as did Nixon, Ford, and Carter in varying ways. Even then, however, people are reluctant to bear increased costs, and thus many are led to dispute the president's claim that an emergency actually exists.

These entirely human responses to the perceived costs and benefits of proposed policies can be organized into a simple theory of politics.[10] It is based on the observation that the costs and benefits of a policy may be *widely distributed* (spread over many, most, or even all citizens) or *narrowly concentrated* (limited to a relatively small number of citizens or to some identifiable, organized group). For instance, a widely distributed cost would include an income tax, a Social Security tax, or a high rate of crime; a widely distributed benefit might include retirement benefits for all citizens, clean air, national security, or low crime rates. Examples of narrowly concentrated costs include the expenditures by a factory to reduce its pollution, government regulations imposed on doctors and hospitals participating in the Medicare program, or restrictions on freedom of speech imposed on a dissident political group. Examples of narrowly concentrated benefits include subsidies to farmers or merchant ship companies, the enlarged freedom to speak and protest afforded a dissident group, or protection against competition given to an industry because of favorable government regulation.

majoritarian politics A policy in which almost everybody benefits and almost everybody pays.

The perceived distribution of costs and benefits shapes the *kinds of political coalitions that will form*—but it will not necessarily determine *who wins*. A given popular majority, interest group, client, or entrepreneur may win or lose depending on its influence and the temper of the times.

In the remainder of this chapter, we shall describe the politics of four kinds of policies and then illustrate each kind with examples drawn from government efforts to regulate business.

Majoritarian Politics: Distributed Benefits, Distributed Costs

Some policies promise benefits to large numbers of people at a cost that large numbers of people will have to bear (see Figure 17.1). For example, almost everybody will sooner or later receive Social Security benefits, and almost everybody who works has to pay Social Security taxes. Similarly, defending the nation against military attack benefits everyone, and every taxpayer contributes to its cost. If government-sponsored research to find cures for cancer and heart disease is successful, a large proportion of the citizenry will benefit from a program that all taxpayers have been obliged to support.

Such **majoritarian politics** are usually not dominated by pulling and hauling among rival interest groups; instead they involve making appeals to large blocs of voters and their representatives in hopes of finding a majority. The reason why interest groups are not so important in majoritarian politics is that, as we saw in Chapter 11, citizens rarely will have much incentive to join an interest group if the policy that such a group supports will benefit everybody, whether or not they are members of the group. This is the "free-rider" problem. Why join the Committee to Increase (or Decrease) the Defense Budget when what you personally contribute to that committee makes little difference in the outcome and when you will enjoy the benefits of more (or less) national defense even if you have stayed on the sidelines?

Figure 17.1
A Way of Classifying and Explaining the Politics of Different Policy Issues

		PERCEIVED COSTS	
		Distributed	Concentrated
PERCEIVED BENEFITS	Distributed	**Majoritarian Politics**	**Entrepreneurial Politics**
	Concentrated	**Client Politics**	**Interest Group Politics**

Majoritarian politics may be controversial, but the controversy is usually over matters of cost or ideology, not between rival interest groups. For example, there was intense controversy over the health care plan that President Obama signed into law, but it did not involve many interest groups; it was a majoritarian issue where people disagreed about whether it would help or hurt the public. The military budget went up during the early 1980s, down in the late 1980s, up after 2001, and down again after 2010. These changes reflected different views on how much we need to spend on our miliary operations abroad.

Interest Group Politics: Concentrated Benefits, Concentrated Costs

In **interest group politics,** a proposed policy will confer benefits on some relatively small, identifiable group and impose costs on another small, equally identifiable group. For example, when Congress passed a bill requiring companies to give 60 days' notice of a plant closing or a large-scale layoff, labor unions (whose members would benefit) backed the bill, and many business firms (which would pay the costs) opposed it.

interest group politics A policy in which one small group benefits and another small group pays.

Issues of this kind tend to be fought out by organized interest groups. Each side will be so powerfully affected by the outcome that it has a strong incentive to mobilize: union members who worry about layoffs will have a personal stake in favoring the notice bill; business leaders who fear government control of investment decisions will have an economic stake in opposing it.

Interest group politics often produces decisions about which the public is uninformed. The bitter debates between television broadcasters and cable companies over who may send what kind of signals to which homes hardly draw any public

Topham/The Image Works

During the Great Depression, depositors besiege a bank hoping to get their savings out.

notice—until after a law is passed and people can see their cable charges. Similarly, the long struggle to give banks the right to sell insurance involved not the public, but banks and insurance companies. In time, the public will discover whether they like the results.

Though many issues of this type involve monetary costs and benefits, they can also involve intangible considerations. If the American Nazi party wants to march through a predominantly Jewish neighborhood carrying flags with swastikas on them, the community may organize itself to resist out of revulsion against the disgraceful treatment of Jews by Nazi Germany. Each side may hire lawyers to debate the issue before the city council and in the courts.

Client Politics: Concentrated Benefits, Distributed Costs

With **client politics** some identifiable, often small group will benefit, but everybody—or at least a large part of society—will pay the costs. Because the benefits are concentrated, the group to receive those benefits has an incentive to organize and work to get them. But because the costs are widely distributed, affecting many people only slightly, those who pay the costs may be either unaware of any costs or indifferent to them, because per capita they are so small.

client politics A policy in which one small group benefits and almost everybody pays.

pork-barrel legislation Legislation that gives tangible benefits to constituents in several districts or states in the hope of winning their votes in return.

logrolling A legislator supports a proposal favored by another in return for support of his or hers.

This situation gives rise to client politics (sometimes called clientele politics); the beneficiary of the policy is the "client" of the government. For example, many farmers benefit substantially from agricultural price supports, but the far more numerous food consumers have no idea what these price supports cost them in taxes and higher food prices. In the same way, airlines for a long time benefited from the higher prices they were able to charge on certain routes as a result of government regulations that restricted competition over prices. But the average passenger was either unaware that his or her costs were higher or did not think the higher prices were worth making a fuss about.

Not all clients are economic interests. Localities can also benefit as clients when, for example, a city or county obtains a new dam, a better harbor, or an improved irrigation system. Some of these projects may be worthwhile, others may not; by custom, however, they are referred to as *pork-barrel projects.* Usually several pieces of "pork" are put into one barrel—that is, several projects are approved in a single piece of **pork-barrel legislation,** such as the "rivers and harbors" bill that Congress passes almost every year. Trading votes in this way attracts the support of members of Congress from each affected area; with enough projects a majority coalition is formed. This process is called **logrolling.**

Not every group that wants something from government at little cost to the average citizen will get it. Welfare recipients cost the typical taxpayer a small amount each year, yet there was great resistance to increasing these benefits. The homeless have not organized themselves to get benefits; indeed, most do not even vote. Yet benefits are being provided (albeit in modest amounts so far). These examples illustrate the importance of popular views concerning the legitimacy of client claims as a factor in determining the success of client demands. As we shall see in Chapter 19, welfare recipients have never enjoyed much legitimacy in the public's eye, and so programs to increase their benefits have been hard to sell to Congress. The plight of the homeless, on the other hand, has aroused a good deal of sympathy and has produced bipartisan agreement on a bill providing emergency aid. Moreover, that agreement seems to have persisted.

By the same token, groups can lose legitimacy that they once had. People who grow tobacco once were supported simply because they were farmers, and were thus seen as both "deserving" and politically important. But when people began worrying about

Paul S. Howell/Liaison/Getty Images

A Superfund site in Houston, Texas, where bacteria were used to clean up harmful industrial waste.

the health risks associated with using tobacco, farmers who produce tobacco lost some legitimacy compared to those who produce corn or cotton. As a result, it became harder to get votes for maintaining tobacco price supports and easier to slap higher taxes on cigarettes.

Entrepreneurial Politics: Distributed Benefits, Concentrated Costs

In **entrepreneurial politics,** society as a whole or some large part of it benefits from a policy that imposes substantial costs on some small, identifiable segment of society. The antipollution and safety requirements for automobiles were proposed as ways of improving the health and well-being of all people at the expense (at least initially) of automobile manufacturers. Similarly, Congress enacted the Brady bill, which requires a background check on gun buyers before they can purchase a firearm.

No policies exist unchallenged; for example, the entrepreneurial politics that got the Brady bill enacted failed to keep certain of its key provisions from being eliminated a decade later. Still, it is remarkable that policies of this sort are ever adopted, and in fact many are not. After all, the American political system creates many opportunities for checking and blocking the actions of others. The Founders deliberately arranged things so that it would be difficult to pass a new law; a determined minority therefore has an excellent chance of blocking a new policy. And any organized group that fears the loss of some privilege or the imposition of some burden will become a very determined minority indeed. The opponent has every incentive to work hard; the large group of prospective beneficiaries may be unconvinced of the benefit or regard it as too small to be worth fighting for.

entrepreneurial politics A policy in which almost everybody benefits and a small group pays the cost.

policy entrepreneurs Activists in or out of government who pull together a political majority on behalf of unorganized interests.

Nonetheless, policies with distributed benefits and concentrated costs are in fact adopted, and in recent decades they have been adopted with increasing frequency. A key element in the adoption of such policies has been the work of people who act on behalf of the unorganized or indifferent majority. Such people, called **policy entrepreneurs,** are those both in and out of government who find ways of pulling together a legislative majority on behalf of interests that are not well represented in the government. These policy entrepreneurs may or may not represent the interests and wishes of the public at large, but they do have the ability to dramatize an issue in a convincing manner. Ralph Nader is perhaps the best-known example of a policy entrepreneur, or as he might describe himself, a "consumer advocate." But there are other examples from both ends of the political spectrum, conservative as well as liberal.

Entrepreneurial politics can occur without the leadership of a policy entrepreneur if voters or legislators in large numbers suddenly become disgruntled by the high cost of some benefit that a group is receiving (or become convinced of the urgent need for a new policy to impose such costs). For example, voters may not care about government programs that benefit the oil industry when gasoline costs only one dollar a gallon, but they might care very much when the price rises to three dollars a gallon, even if the government benefits had nothing to do with the price increase. By the same token, legislators may not worry much about the effects of smog in the air until a lot of people develop burning eyes and runny noses during an especially severe smog attack.

Likewise, most legislators did not worry very much about toxic or hazardous wastes until 1977, when the Love Canal dump site near Buffalo, New York, spilled some of its toxic waste into the backyards of an adjacent residential neighborhood and people were forced to leave their homes. Five years later, anyone who had forgotten about Love Canal was reminded of it when the town of Times Beach, Missouri, had to be permanently evacuated because it had become contaminated with the chemical dioxin. Only then did it become widely known that there were more than 30,000 toxic waste sites nationwide that posed public safety risks. Although researchers have yet to find any conclusive evidence of health damage at either site, the Superfund program was born in 1980 of the political pressure that developed in the wake of these and other highly publicized tales of toxic waste dangers. Superfund was intended to force industries to clean up their own toxic waste sites. It also authorized the Environmental Protection Agency (EPA) to act speedily, with or without cooperation from industries, in identifying and cleaning up any sites that posed a large or imminent danger.

Superfund has suffered a number of political and administrative problems, and only a few of the 1,300 sites initially targeted by the EPA had been cleaned up a dozen years after the program went into effect.[11] However, Superfund is a good illustration of entrepreneurial politics in action. Special taxes on once largely unregulated oil and chemical companies have funded the program. Previously, these companies enjoyed special tax privileges as beneficiaries of client politics; today they face special tax burdens as the targets of entrepreneurial politics.

For many reasons—including the enlarged political role of the media, the decentralization of Congress, and a change in the attitudes of many citizens—entrepreneurial politics has become more common and policy entrepreneurs more visible in recent decades.

The Case of Business Regulation

Efforts by government to regulate business not only illustrate these four kinds of policymaking processes, but also shed light on an issue that many people think is central to the study of politics—namely, the relationship between wealth and power.

To some observers, the very existence of large corporations is a threat to popular rule. Economic power will dominate political power, they believe, for one or more of three reasons: first, because wealth can be used to buy influence; second, because politicians and business leaders have similar class backgrounds and thus similar beliefs about public policy; and third, because elected officials must defer to the preferences of business so as to induce corporations to keep the economy healthy and growing. Karl Marx, of course, proposed the most sweeping version of the view that economics controls politics; for him the state in a capitalist society was nothing more than the executive committee of the propertied classes.[12] But there are other non-Marxist or neo-Marxist versions of the same concern.[13]

To other observers, politics, far from being subordinate to economic power, is a threat to the very existence of a market economy and the values—economic growth, private property, personal freedom—that they believe such an economy protects. In this view, politicians will find it in their interest, in their struggle for votes, to take the side of the nonbusiness majority against that of the business minority. The heads of large corporations, few in number but great in wealth, fear that they will be portrayed as a sinister elite on whom politicians can blame war, inflation, unemployment, and pollution. Defenders of business worry that corporations will be taxed excessively to pay for social programs that in turn will produce more votes for politicians. Just as bad, in this view, is the tendency of universities (on which corporations must rely for technical experts) to inculcate antibusiness values in their students.[14]

The theory of the policymaking process presented earlier in this chapter should suggest that neither of these two extreme views of business-government relations is entirely correct. These relations depend on many things, including the *kind* of policy proposed. Instead of clenching our fists and shouting pro-business or antibusiness slogans at each other, we should be able, after applying this theory to the available facts, to make more careful and exact statements of the following sort: "If certain conditions exist, then business-government relations will take certain forms."

MAJORITARIAN POLITICS

Not all efforts to regulate business pit one group against another. From time to time, laws are passed that reflect the views of a majority of voters that is neither imposing its will on a hostile business community nor acceding to the desires of a privileged industry.

Much of the antitrust legislation passed in this country, including the Sherman Act (1890) and parts of the Federal Trade Commission Act (1914) and the Clayton Act (1914), has been the result of majoritarian politics. Toward the end of the 19th century, a broadly based criticism arose of business monopolies (then called trusts) and, to a lesser extent, of large corporations, whether or not they monopolized trade. The Grange, an organization of farmers, was especially outspoken in its criticism, and popular opinion generally—insofar as we can know it in an era without pollsters—seems to have been indignant about trusts and in favor of "trust-busting." Newspaper editorials and magazine articles frequently dwelt on the problem.[15]

But though antitrust feeling was strong, it was also relatively unfocused: no single industry was the special target of this criticism (the oil industry, and especially the Standard Oil Company, came as close as any), and no specific regulation was proposed. In fact, there was no general agreement about how to define the problem: for some it was monopoly; for others sheer bigness; and for still others the legal basis of the modern corporation. The bill proposed by Senator John Sherman did not clarify matters much: while it made it a crime to "restrain" or "monopolize" trade, it did not define these terms, nor did it create any new regulatory agency charged with enforcing the law.[16]

No doubt some large corporations worried about what all this would mean for them, but few felt sufficiently threatened to try very hard to defeat the bill. It passed the Senate by a voice vote and the House by a vote of 242 to 0.

Laws are not self-executing, and vague laws are especially likely to lie dormant unless political leaders work hard at bringing them to life. For the first decade or so after 1890, only one or two antitrust cases a year were filed in the courts. In 1904, President Theodore Roosevelt persuaded Congress to provide enough money to hire five full-time lawyers, and soon the number of prosecutions increased to about seven a year. Then in 1938, President Franklin Roosevelt appointed as head of the Antitrust Division of the Justice Department a vigorous lawyer named Thurman Arnold, who began bringing an average of 50 cases a year.[17] Today, more than 400 lawyers in the division sift through complaints alleging monopolistic or other unfair business practices. Though controversy exists over the kinds of cases that should be brought, there is no serious effort among either politicians or business leaders to abandon the commitment to a firm antitrust policy, the strongest such policy found in any industrial nation.

The antitrust laws were strengthened in 1914 by bills that created the Federal Trade Commission and made (via the Clayton Act) certain specific practices, such as price discrimination, illegal. As with the earlier Sherman Act, the advocates of these measures had a variety of motives. Some proponents favored these laws because they would presumably help consumers (by preventing unfair business practices); other proponents supported them because they might help business (by protecting firms against certain tactics that competitors might employ).

President Woodrow Wilson endorsed both of these bills and helped create a broad coalition on behalf of the legislation; the Federal Trade Commission Act and the Clayton Act passed Congress by lopsided majorities.[18]

As with the Sherman Act, there has been continual controversy about how these laws should be administered. But this controversy, like the debate over the initial passage of the laws, has not been dominated by interest groups.[19] The reason for the relative absence of interest group activity is that these laws do not divide society into permanent and identifiable blocs of proponents and opponents. Any given business firm can be either helped or hurt by the enforcement of the antitrust laws. One year, the XYZ Widget Company may be sued by the government to prevent it from unfairly advertising its widgets, and the next year the same XYZ Company may ask the government to prosecute its competitor for trying to drive XYZ out of business by selling widgets at prices below cost.

The amount of money the federal government devotes to antitrust enforcement and the direction those enforcement efforts take are determined more by the political ideology and personal convictions of the administration in power than by interest group pressures. For example, the Reagan administration decided the benefits of trying to break up IBM were not worth the costs, and thus it ended its antitrust prosecution of the giant computer firm. At the same time, however, it decided it was desirable to break up American Telephone and Telegraph (AT&T), making the local phone companies independent of AT&T and forcing AT&T to compete with other long-distance service providers. In the 1990s, the Clinton administration brought an antitrust suit against computer software giant Microsoft.

Between 2001 and 2008, the Bush administration, through a high-level White House task group led by Vice President Dick Cheney, reversed many Clinton-era policies and reinstated Reagan-era ones. Then, in 2009, with the country beset by a major economic crisis, the Obama administration proposed overhauling antitrust policies yet again, folding its plan into a proposal that would centralize all

The Grange sought to warn famers of the dangers of a railroad monopoly.

The Granger Collection, New York

relevant financial regulatory powers in just a few federal agencies. And Christine Varney, a strong antitrust enforcement advocate, was appointed to head the new administration's antitrust investigations within the U.S. Department of Justice.

In sum, as with most majoritarian policies, antitrust regulation tends to reflect broad philosophies of governance more than interest group activity.

INTEREST GROUP POLITICS

Organized interest groups are very powerful, however, when the regulatory policies confer benefits on a particular group and costs on another, equally distinct group.

In 1935, labor unions sought government protection for their right to organize, to bargain collectively with industry, and to compel workers in unionized industries to join the unions. Business firms opposed these plans. The struggle was fought out in Congress, where the unions won. The Wagner Act, passed that year, created the National Labor Relations Board (NLRB) to regulate the conduct of union organizing drives and to hear complaints of unfair labor practices brought by workers against management.

But the struggle was far from over. In 1947, management sought to reverse some of the gains won by unions by pressing for a law (the Taft-Hartley Act) that would make illegal certain union practices (such as the closed shop and secondary boycotts) and would authorize the president to obtain a court order blocking for up to eighty days any strike that imperiled the "national health or safety." Business won.

Business and labor fought round three in 1959 over a bill (the Landrum-Griffin Act) intended to prevent corruption in unions, to change the way in which organizing drives were carried out, and to prohibit certain kinds of strikes and picketing. Business won.

In each of these cases, the struggle was highly publicized. The winners and losers were determined by the partisan composition of Congress (Republicans and southern Democrats tended to support business, northern Democrats to support labor) and by the existence of economic conditions (a depression in 1935, revelations of labor racketeering in 1959) that affected public opinion on the issue.

But the interest group struggle did not end with the passage of the laws; it continued throughout their administration. The National Labor Relations Board, composed of five members appointed by the president, had to adjudicate countless disputes between labor and management over the interpretation of these laws. The losing party often appealed the NLRB decision to the courts, where the issue was fought out again. Moreover, each president has sought to tilt the NLRB in one direction or another by means of whom he appoints to it. Democratic presidents favor labor and thus tend to appoint pro-union board members; Republican presidents favor business and thus tend to appoint pro-management members. Since NLRB members serve five-year terms, a new president cannot immediately appoint all of the board's members; thus there is often a split on the board between two factions.

But one vote can make a difference. When President Obama appointed a Democrat to the NLRB, it acquired a Democratic majority. The Board then issued an order that would prevent Boeing from building its 787 aircraft in South Carolina, a state with a "right to work" law that prevents workers from being required to join a union. The issue was, of course, appealed; by mid-2011, we did not know whether the ruling would be enforced.

A similar pattern of interest group influence is revealed by the history of the Occupational Safety and Health Act, passed in 1970. Labor unions wanted a strict bill with tough standards set by a single administrator; business organizations wanted a more flexible bill with standards set by a commission that would include some business representatives. After a long struggle labor won, and the Occupational Safety and Health Administration (OSHA), headed by a single administrator, was set up inside the Department of Labor.

As with the NLRB, conflict did not end with the passage of the law, and OSHA decisions were frequently appealed to the courts. The politics swirling about OSHA were all the more contentious because of the vast mandate of the agency: it is supposed to determine the safe limits for worker exposure to hundreds of chemicals and to inspect tens of thousands of workplaces to see whether they should be cited for violating any standards. During the Carter administration, an appointed OSHA administrator was sympathetic to the labor view and thus set many standards and issued many citations; during the Reagan administration, the selected administrator was admired by business because he set fewer standards and issued fewer citations.

CLIENT POLITICS

Many people suppose that when government sets out to regulate business, the firms that are supposed to be regulated will in fact "capture" the agency that is supposed to do the regulating. But as we have already seen, certain kinds of policies—those that give rise to majoritarian and interest group politics—do not usually lead to capture, because the agency either faces no well-organized, enduring opponent (as with majoritarian politics) or is caught in a crossfire of competing forces (as with interest group politics).

But when a policy confers a benefit on one group at the expense of many other people, client politics arises, and so agency "capture" is likely. More precisely, nothing needs to be captured at all, since the agency will have been created from the outset to serve the interests of the favored group. We sometimes think regulations are always resisted. But a regulation need not be a burden; it can be a great benefit.

How this works can be seen close to home. State and city laws regulate the practice of law and medicine as well as a host of other occupations—barbers, beauticians, plumbers, dry cleaners, taxi drivers, and undertakers. These regulations are sometimes designed and always defended as ways of preventing fraud, malpractice, and safety hazards. But they also have the effect of restricting entry into the regulated occupation, thereby enabling its members to charge higher prices than they otherwise might.[20] Ordinarily, citizens do not object to this, in part because they believe, rightly or wrongly, that the regulations in fact protect them, and in part because the higher prices are spread over so many customers as to be unnoticed.

Much the same thing can be found at the national level. In the early 1930s, the American dairy industry was suffering from rapidly declining prices for milk. As the farmers' incomes fell, many could no longer pay their bills and were forced out of business. Congress responded with the Agricultural Adjustment Act, which authorized an agency of the Department of Agriculture to regulate the milk industry. This agency, the Dairy Division of the Agricultural Marketing Service, would issue "market orders" that had the effect of preventing price competition among dairy farmers and thus kept the price of milk up. If this guaranteed minimum price leads to the production of more milk than people want to drink, then another part of the Agriculture Department—the Commodity Credit Corporation—stands ready to buy up the surplus with tax dollars.[21]

Consumers wind up paying more for milk than they otherwise would, but they have no way of knowing the difference between the regulated and unregulated price of milk (economists estimate that it amounts to between five and 21 cents per gallon).[22] Consumers have little incentive to organize politically to do much about it. The total cost, however, can be very high; in 2006 it was over $4 billion. Although consumers are not helped by high prices, not every dairy farmer is helped either. More milk is produced than people will buy, and so many dairy farmers have gone out of business.

A similar system works with sugar. Sugar produced abroad, in countries such as Brazil and the Philippines, costs much less than sugar produced here, in states such as Louisiana. To keep the incomes of U.S. sugar producers high, Congress decided to restrict the importation of cheap foreign sugar by imposing quotas. This costs the consumer money—maybe as much as $3 billion a year—but the extra cost per pound of sugar is not noticeable.[23]

From time to time, various officials attempt to change the regulations that benefit a client group. But they must confront some sobering political facts. Dairy farmers are found scattered through scores of congressional districts; sugar beet growers are concentrated in southern states important in any presidential election. Efforts have been made in Congress to cut milk subsidies and sugar quotas, but with only limited success.

In 1996, Congress passed and President Clinton signed a bill that began, at least for wheat and corn crops, to phase out the practice of paying farmers the difference between what they can sell their crops for and what the government thinks the crops ought to be worth. It replaced these crop subsidies with direct cash payments to farmers that they can use for anything, including not farming.

But the 1996 plan to lure farmers into a free-market economy did not last. Between 1996 and 2001, the subsidies they got increased rather than decreased. In 2002, President Bush signed a new farm bill that did away with the 1996 law and authorized paying farmers $171 billion in new subsidies by 2012. Though defended as a way of protecting "the little

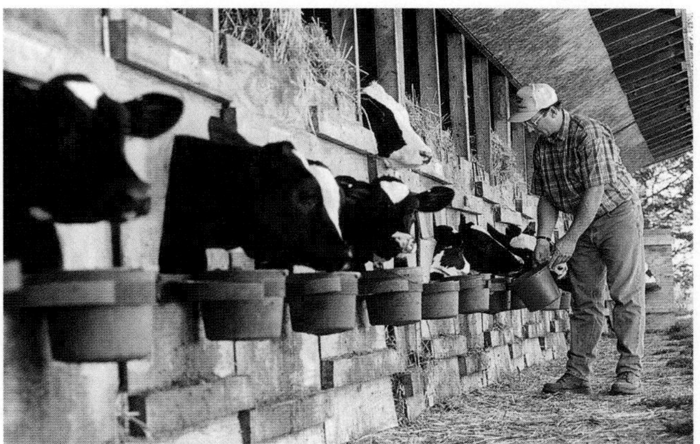

Bob Mahoney/The Image Works

Dairy farmers get government subsidies for their milk production.

farmer," most of the money will go to big farmers who produce wheat, corn, rice, cotton, and soybeans (but not to those who produce cattle, hogs, poultry, fruits, or vegetables).

Farm subsidies are justified by the fact that the prices farmers earn swing wildly, but subsidies don't go to people who make computer chips or raise cattle even though they also experience big swings in the prices they can charge. The existence of farm subsidies is the result of history (a legacy of the time, during the Great Depression, when the government wanted to help nearly one-fourth of all employed Americans who then worked on farms) and politics (farmers are key and changeable voters in many important states).

Client politics has become harder to practice in this country unless a group is widely thought to be a "deserving" client. Dairy farmers, sugar producers, and tobacco growers struggle (sometimes successfully, sometimes unsuccessfully) to keep their benefits, but the struggle relies on "insider politics"—that is, on dealing with key Washington decision makers and not on building widespread public support. By contrast, when a devastating flood, tornado, earthquake, or hurricane strikes a community, the victims are thought to be eminently deserving of help. After all, people say, it was not their fault that their homes were destroyed. (In some cases, it was because they built homes in areas they knew were at high risk for hurricanes or floods.) They receive client benefits.

Although client politics for "special interests" seems to be on the decline, that is true mostly for programs that actually send certain groups money. Pietro Nivola reminds us of a different form of client politics: using regulations instead of cash to help groups. For example, regulations encourage the use of ethanol (a kind of alcohol made from corn) in gasoline, which benefits corn farmers and ethanol manufacturers. Clients that might not be thought legitimate increasingly get their way by means of regulations rather than subsidies.[24]

But regulation that starts out by trying to serve a client can end up hurting it. Radio broadcasters supported the creation of the Federal Communications Commission (FCC), which would, broadcasters and telephone companies thought, bring order and stability to their industries. It did. But then it started doing a bit more than the industries had hoped for. It began reviewing efforts by companies to merge. When one telephone company tried to merge with another, the FCC said it would have to review the consolidation even though the law did not give it the power to do so. After long (and secret) negotiations, it extracted concessions from the companies as a condition of their merger. Because there was no law requiring such concessions, the firms accepted them "voluntarily." But if they had not agreed, they would have been in deep trouble with the FCC in the future.

Regulatory agencies created to help clients can become burdens to those clients when the laws the agencies enforce are sufficiently vague so as to provide freedom of action for the people who run them. For a long time, most of these laws were hopelessly vague. The FCC, for example, was told to award licenses as "the public interest, convenience, and necessity" required. In time, such language can give an agency wide, undefined powers.

ENTREPRENEURIAL POLITICS

During the 1960s and 1970s some two dozen consumer and environmental protection laws were passed, including laws that regulated the automobile industry, oil companies, toy manufacturers, poultry producers, the chemical industry, and pharmaceutical companies.*

When measures such as these become law, it is often because a policy entrepreneur has dramatized an issue, galvanized public opinion, and mobilized congressional support. Sometimes that entrepreneur is in the government (a senator or an outspoken bureaucrat); sometimes that entrepreneur is a private person (the best known, of course, is Ralph Nader). The motives of such entrepreneurs can be either self-serving or public-spirited; the policies they embrace may be either good or bad. (Just because someone succeeds in regulating business does not mean that the public will necessarily benefit; by the same token, just because business claims that a new regulation will be excessively costly does not mean that business will in fact have to pay those costs.)

An early example of a policy entrepreneur inside the government was Dr. Harvey Wiley, a chemist in the Department of Agriculture, who actively campaigned for what was to become the Pure Food and Drug Act of 1906. Later, Senator Estes Kefauver held hearings that built support for the 1962 drug laws (and incidentally for his presidential bid), and Senator Edmund Muskie called

*The Motor Vehicle Air Pollution Control Act of 1965, the National Traffic and Motor Vehicle Safety Act of 1966, the Clean Air Act of 1970, the Water Quality Improvement Act of 1970, the Children's Protection and Toy Safety Act of 1969, the Wholesome Poultry Act of 1968, the Toxic Substances Control Act of 1976, and the 1962 amendments to the Pure Food and Drug Act.

attention to the need for air and water pollution control legislation (and incidentally to his own 1972 presidential aspirations).

When a policy entrepreneur is outside the government, he or she will need a sympathetic ear within it. Occasionally, the policy needs of the entrepreneur and the political needs of an elected official coincide. When Ralph Nader was walking the corridors of the Capitol looking for someone interested in auto safety, he found Senators Abraham Ribicoff and Warren Magnuson, who themselves were looking for an issue with which they could be identified.

The task of the policy entrepreneur is made easier when a crisis or scandal focuses public attention on a problem. Upton Sinclair's book *The Jungle*[25] dramatized the frightful conditions in meat-packing plants at the turn of the century and helped pave the way for the Meat Inspection Act of 1906. The stock market collapse of 1929 helped develop support for the Securities and Exchange Act. When some people who had taken a patent medicine (elixir of sulfanilamide) died as a result, the passage of the 1938 drug laws became easier. Oil spilled on the beaches of Santa Barbara, California, drew attention to problems addressed by the Water Quality Improvement Act of 1970.

The dramatic event need not be an actual crisis; in some cases, a political scandal will do. Highway fatalities were not a matter of great concern to most citizens when Congress began considering the auto safety act in 1965–1966, but support for the bill grew when it was revealed that General Motors had hired a private detective who made a clumsy effort to collect (or manufacture) gossip harmful to Ralph Nader, whose book *Unsafe at Any Speed* had criticized the safety of certain GM cars.

In some cases, no dramatic event at all is required for entrepreneurial politics to succeed. Most of the air and water pollution control bills were passed despite the absence of any environmental catastrophe.[26] Support for such measures was developed by holding carefully planned committee hearings that were closely followed by the media. For example, by drawing attention to the profits of the pharmaceutical companies, Senator Kefauver was able to convince many people that these firms were insensitive to public needs. By drawing on information made available to him by environmentalists, Senator Muskie was able to capitalize on and help further a growing perception in the country during the early 1970s that nature was in danger.

Because political resistance must be overcome without the aid of a powerful economic interest group, policy entrepreneurs seeking to regulate an industry often adopt a moralistic tone, with their opponents portrayed as devils, their allies viewed with suspicion, and compromises fiercely resisted. When Senator Muskie was drafting an air pollution bill, Ralph Nader issued a highly publicized report *attacking* Muskie, his nominal ally, for not being tough enough. This strategy forced Muskie—who wanted acclaim, not criticism, for his efforts—to revise the bill so that it imposed even more stringent standards.[27] Other allies of Nader, such as Dr. William Haddon, Jr., and Joan Claybrook, got the same treatment when they later became administrators of the National Highway Traffic Safety Administration. They came under attack not only from the auto industry for designing rules that the companies thought were too strict, but also from Nader, for devising rules that he thought were not strict enough.

Once a policy entrepreneur manages to defeat an industry that is resisting regulation, he or she creates—at least for a while—a strong impetus for additional legislation of the same kind. A successful innovator produces imitators, in politics as in rock music. After the auto safety law was passed in 1966, it became easier to pass a coal mine safety bill in 1969 and an occupational safety and health bill in 1970.

The great risk faced by policy entrepreneurs is not that their hard-won legislative victories will later be reversed but that the agency created to do the regulating will be captured by the industry it is supposed to regulate. The Food and Drug Administration (FDA), which regulates the pharmaceutical industry, has fallen victim during much of its history to precisely this kind of capture. Once the enthusiasm

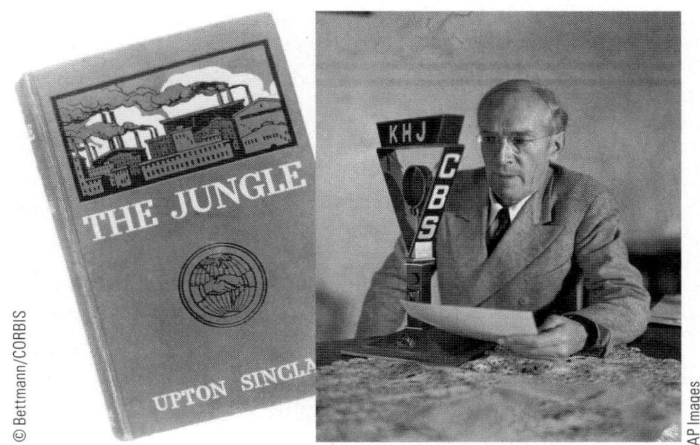

Entrepreneurial politics: Upton Sinclair's book *The Jungle*, published in 1906, shocked readers with its description of conditions in the meat-packing industry and helped bring about passage of the Meat Inspection Act of 1906.

of its founders had waned and public attention had turned elsewhere, the FDA seemed to develop a cozy and rather uncritical attitude toward the drug companies. (In 1958, the head of the FDA received an award from the Pharmaceutical Manufacturers' Association.)[28] In the mid-1960s, under the spur of renewed congressional and White House attention, the agency was revitalized. During the Reagan administration, environmentalists worried that the leadership of the Environmental Protection Agency had been turned over to persons who were unduly sympathetic to polluters.

There are at least five reasons, however, why the newer consumer and environmental protection agencies may not be as vulnerable to capture as some critics contend. First, these agencies often enforce laws that impose specific standards in accordance with strict timetables, and so they have relatively little discretion. (The Environmental Protection Agency, for example, is required by law to reduce certain pollutants by a fixed percentage within a stated number of years.) Second, the newer agencies, unlike the FDA, usually regulate many different industries and so do not confront a single, unified opponent. The Occupational Safety and Health Administration, for example, deals with virtually every industry. Third, the very existence of these agencies has helped strengthen the hand of the "public-interest" lobbies that initially demanded their creation. Fourth, these lobbies can now call upon many sympathetic allies in the media who will attack agencies thought to have a pro-business bias.

Finally, as explained in Chapter 16, it has become easier for groups to use the federal courts to put pressure on the regulatory agencies. These groups do not have to be large or broadly representative of the public; all they need are the services of one or two able lawyers. If the Environmental Protection Agency (EPA) issues a rule disliked by a chemical company, the company will promptly sue the EPA; if it issues a ruling that pleases the company, the Environmental Defense Fund will sue.

Perceptions, Beliefs, Interests, and Values

The politics of business regulation provides a good illustration of the theory of policymaking offered in this book, but the reader should not be misled by a discussion of costs and benefits into thinking that all or even most of politics is about getting or losing money or that it is an easy matter to classify the costs and benefits of a policy and thus put it into the correct pigeonhole.

For one thing, what constitutes a cost or a benefit is a matter of opinion, and opinions change. We have already said it is the *perception* of costs and benefits that affects politics. If people think that laws requiring factories to install devices to remove from their smokestacks chemicals that contribute to acid rain can be implemented in ways that make the companies but not the consumers pay the bills, they will favor such measures, and the affected industries will oppose them. But if people believe that the cost of preventing acid rain will be borne by them—in the form of fewer jobs or higher prices—then these citizens may be less enthusiastic about such measures.

Some people favor having the government regulate the price of natural gas, and others oppose it. One reason for the conflict, obviously, is that people who use natural gas in their homes want to buy it cheaply, whereas people who work in the natural gas industry want gas prices to go up so they can earn more. Interests are clearly in conflict.

Yet some users may oppose regulating the price of gas because they believe that keeping the price of gas artificially low now will discourage exploration for new gas fields, thereby creating shortages—and much higher prices—in the future. Thus, *beliefs* are also in conflict; in this case, some users believe that it is more important to take the long view and worry about gas shortages 10 years from now, while others believe that what counts is how much you have to pay for natural gas today.

A political conflict is in large measure a struggle to make one definition of the costs and benefits of a proposal prevail over others; that is, it is a struggle to alter perceptions and beliefs. Material interests do play a part in all this: the more you stand to gain or lose in hard cash from a proposal, the harder it will be for someone else to change your mind about your position. But many, perhaps most, government proposals will not have an immediate, unambiguous impact on your pocketbook, and so your perceptions and beliefs about what will happen in the future become the prize for which political activists compete.

In that competition, certain arguments enjoy a natural advantage over others. One might be called the *here-and-now* argument. What happens now or in the near future is more important to most people than what happens in the distant future. (Economists refer to this as the human tendency to "discount the future.") Thus, most users of natural gas probably care more about present prices than future shortages, and so many will tend to favor price regulation today.

Another political tactic that enjoys a natural advantage might be called the *cost* argument. People seem to react more sharply to what they will lose if a policy is adopted than to what they may gain. Thus, there usually will be strong opposition to putting a tax on imported oil, even if the benefit gained will be to reduce our dependence on foreign oil.

Politicians know the value of the here-and-now and the cost arguments and so try to present their proposals in ways that take advantage of these sentiments. Regulations aimed at new drugs, for example, will emphasize the harm that will be prevented now from keeping dangerous drugs off the market, not the harm that may come later if lifesaving drugs with some dangerous side effects are kept off the market. Plans to solve the problems of our Social Security system stress keeping intact the benefits now received by people already retired, postponing into the future the tax increases necessary to pay for these benefits.

Policies are affected not only by our perceptions and beliefs about where our interests lie but also by our *values*—that is, by our conceptions of what is good for the country or for our community. Many whites, for example, want to see opportunities increased for minorities, not because such opportunities will make whites better off but because they think it is the right thing to do. Many citizens worry about political conditions in the Middle East, not because they fear having to fight a war there or because they work for a company that does business there but because they wish a better life for people who live in that region and want them to be free of terrorists and dictatorships. Some citizens oppose restrictions on the sale of obscene magazines and others favor those restrictions; neither group stands to benefit—those who oppose censorship usually don't plan to read the publications, and those who favor it would not thereby have their own lives improved—yet both groups often advocate their opposing views with great passion.

All this may seem obvious, but the reader should recall how often he or she assumes that people are only "looking out for themselves" and so politics is only about "who gets what." We all have a tendency to be a bit cynical about government—that is, to impute self-seeking motives to whoever is involved. Since there is plenty of self-interest in politics, this assumption is often a pretty good one. But following it blindly can lead us to ignore those cases in which ideas—beliefs, perceptions, and values—are the decisive forces in political conflict.

DEREGULATION

In the 1980s, several industries were deregulated over the objections of those industries. Airline fares were once set by the Civil Aeronautics Board. The airlines liked it that way—it kept competition down and prices up. But today airline fares are set by the market, with the result that in some (but not all) areas fares are lower than they once were. Not only did most airlines fight tooth and nail to prevent this deregulation from occurring, but some couldn't adjust to the new era of competition and, like Eastern Airlines, went bankrupt.

Long-distance telephone services were once provided on a monopoly basis by AT&T; its prices were set by the Federal Communications Commission. Today there are several long-distance telephone systems—MCI, Sprint, AT&T—and prices are heavily influenced by competition. AT&T was not eager to have this happen, but it couldn't prevent it.

Once, the number of trucking companies and the prices they charged were set by the Interstate Commerce Commission (ICC). The trucking companies and the Teamsters Union favored this pattern of regulation—as with the airlines, the system kept competition down and prices up. But then Congress changed the law, and in January 1996 the ICC was abolished.

People who think politics is simply the result of deals struck between certain favored industries and friendly or "captured" agencies would have a hard time explaining this period of deregulation. Client politics—the cozy relationship (or "iron triangle") between a private client, a government agency, and a supportive Congress—was ended. How did it happen?

Martha Derthick and Paul Quirk, two political scientists, answered the question in their book *The Politics of Deregulation.*[29] The key to that answer is the power of ideas. Academic economists were in agreement that regulating prices in industries that were competitive, or could easily be made so, was a bad idea; the regulations hurt consumers by keeping prices artificially high. But academic ideas by themselves are powerless. In the three cases described above, key political leaders—Presidents Carter, Ford, and Reagan, and Senators Edward Kennedy and Howard Cannon—accepted and acted on these ideas, albeit for very different reasons. The regulatory commissions—the Civil Aeronautics Board (CAB), the Federal Communications Commission (FCC), the ICC—were led by people who wanted to deregulate. In one case, the breakup of AT&T, a federal judge made many of the key decisions. The public did not support deregulation, but it was concerned about inflation, and deregulation could be defended as a way of bringing prices down. Finally, the industries that fought to save their client relationships with government—the airlines, the trucking companies, the phone company—were not wildly popular businesses; once they were subjected to political criticism, they found that they had relatively few allies.

Since the mid-1970s, every president has put in place machinery to bring government regulation of industry under more central review. President Ford in 1974 ordered all regulatory agencies to assess the inflationary impact of their decisions. President Carter in 1978 directed each agency to consider alternative ways of achieving the goals of regulation. President Reagan in 1981 created the Task Force on Regulatory Relief and instructed those agencies under his control not to issue a regulation if, in the judgment of the Office of Management and Budget, its potential benefits to society did not outweigh its costs.[30] President Bush the elder essentially continued the Reagan system.

process regulation Rules governing commercial activities designed to improve consumer, worker, or environmental conditions. Also called social regulation.

Deregulation is opposed, of course, by groups that benefit from regulation. But it is controversial in at least two other ways. First, some members of the public do not like the results, especially if the world becomes more complicated as a result of relying on the market. Many people liked CAB control of the airlines, for example, because the higher prices kept the number of air travelers down, and so airports were less congested. Second, some people who favor deregulating *prices* oppose deregulating *processes.* **Process regulation** (sometimes called social regulation) includes rules aimed at improving consumer or worker safety and reducing environmental damage. There are good and bad ways of achieving these goals, and much of the dispute about regulation concerns the question of means, not ends. The intensity of that dispute shows how important perceptions and beliefs are even when economic interests are at stake.

It is too soon to know, but we might be entering into a new period in which "deregulation," whether of financial markets, consumer products, telecommunications, or other domains, is treated by many politicians in both parties as a dirty word.

For instance, among the many reasons widely believed to be behind the financial meltdown that many observers date to September 2008 is how the Securities and Exchange Commission (SEC) and other financial regulatory bodies exempted brokerage firms from old regulations that limited the amount of debt they could take on, and thereby freed them to make unconventional and, as it turned out, unsafe and unstable investments (such as so-called mortgage-backed securities and credit derivatives).

Similarly, in 2008 and 2009, opinion polls suggested that most average Americans did not believe that the Food and Drug Administration (FDA) does enough to regulate the safety of drugs; meanwhile, the Consumer Product Safety Commission (CPSC) was challenged regarding public scares about lead paint in imported toys, and the Federal Communications Commission (FCC) was widely criticized regarding rising cell phone, cable television, and Internet service bills.

Whether what critics call the "drive to deregulate" actually has weakened these or other agencies or otherwise produced perverse and unintended consequences that obviate the benefits of deregulation is less important politically than what most people and their elected representatives believe to be true.

THE LIMITS OF IDEAS

Ideas can be powerful, but there are limits to their power. There are many forms of client politics that persist—some because people agree that the client deserves to benefit, others because the conditions do not exist for mounting an effective challenge to the client.

Dairy, sugar, and other agricultural price supports are paid for by taxpayers. Regulations that increased above market levels the prices charged by airlines and trucking companies were successfully challenged; regulations that increased above market levels the prices charged by oceangoing freighters were not. The wages paid to airline pilots and truck drivers are no longer protected by federal rules; the wages paid to merchant seamen and construction workers employed on federal projects still are.

It is not entirely clear why it is easier to challenge client politics in some industries and occupations than in others. We can say, however, why it generally is harder to maintain client politics free of challenge today than once was the case.

WHAT WOULD YOU DO?

MEMORANDUM

To: *J. Peter, assistant to the president*

From: *Daniel Gilbert, special assistant to the president*

Subject: *Department of Energy nuclear waste plan*

The president must decide whether to sign the bill allowing the department to establish a safe repository for the nation's nuclear waste beneath mountains in Nevada. The waste is produced mainly by 131 commercial nuclear reactors and by national defense weapons programs. It is presently stored at 126 sites in more than three dozen states.

News »

Congress Approves Plan to Store Nuclear Waste in Nevada

Yesterday the U.S. Congress approved a bill allowing the U.S. Department of Energy to proceed with a plan to site 70,000 tons of highly radioactive nuclear waste in Nevada. Under the plan, beginning in 2010, irradiated fuel from nuclear reactors would be shipped to Nevada from cities all over the country.

Arguments for:

1. For more than 50 years, radioactive waste that remains deadly to humans for 10,000 years has been accumulating in cities and towns throughout the country.
2. According to many experts, encasing the waste in well-engineered tunnels beneath mountains in remote locations is both safer and more cost-effective than such alternatives as storing it in ocean tunnels or propelling it into space.
3. The bill achieved a bipartisan majority. Polls find that most people know little about the problem but believe that something should be done to increase safety.

Arguments against:

1. The department admits that transporting nuclear waste to the Nevada site through dozens of states on trucks, trains, and barges would take decades and pose safety risks.
2. Some experts argue that constructing a 100-mile network of tunnels that safely stores nuclear waste in disposal canisters for 10,000 years will prove technologically difficult and financially burdensome.
3. The plan is strongly opposed by many elected officials in Nevada and surrounding states, and a coalition of environmental groups is threatening to challenge it in court.

Your decision:

Advise president to sign ____________________

Advise president not to sign ____________________

LEARNING OBJECTIVES

WHAT YOU NEED TO KNOW

☑ What is a political agenda?

A political agenda is a general agreement about what issues the federal government should act on. That agenda has expanded enormously in the last half century.

☑ What is meant by logrolling?

Logrolling, a word drawn from the old practice of two loggers standing on a log and rolling it in the water, means two legislators supporting each other's proposals.

☑ What is a policy entrepreneur?

A policy entrepreneur is an activist who pulls together a political majority on behalf of unorganized interests.

RECONSIDERING WHO GOVERNS?

1. Does some political elite dominate American politics?

People active in politics are an elite in the sense that they play a larger role than most citizens. But there are so many American elections and so many places where political action can be blocked that no single elite can dominate. Business corporations, for example, are an important interest group, but they only dominate client politics, and even then their influences can be overcome by entrepreneurial politics.

2. Do powerful interest groups decide what policies our government should adopt?

Over the last half century, there has been a sharp increase in the number and variety of interest groups so that in interest group politics there are always rival organizations competing for influence. In client politics, one interest group can dominate decision making, but client politics is becoming rarer as new interest groups emerge.

RECONSIDERING TO WHAT ENDS?

1. Why are Social Security payments popular but welfare payments to unwed mothers unpopular?

For two reasons: First, people who get retirement benefits have paid money into the program, while those who get welfare benefits have not. Second, many people think elderly people who have retired are legitimate recipients of payments but that unwed mothers are not.

were government regulations on certain industries repealed over the objection of e industries?

re were several reasons, but the most important were new ideas. When enough ical leaders became convinced that government-regulated airfares, bank interest s, and trucking charges made people pay more money than would fares, rates, and ges set by the market, government regulation was abandoned.

QUESTIONS TO CONSIDER

1. **Study an issue that affects your state and see if you can determine whether the debate over it was chiefly influenced by majoritarian, client, interest group, or entrepreneurial politics. Don't be surprised if some issues involve more than one kind of policy debate.**

TO LEARN MORE

Nonpartisan reviews of public policy issues

www.policy.com

www.publicagenda.org

For partisan discussion of issues, use the World Wide Web addresses of the Washington, D.C., think tanks listed in Chapter 11.

Derthick, Martha. *Up in Smoke.* Washington, D.C.: Congressional Quarterly Press, 2002. Fascinating account of how lawyers and tobacco companies created a private regulation of smoking.

Derthick, Martha, and Paul J. Quirk. *The Politics of Deregulation.* Washington, D.C.: Brookings Institution, 1985. A brilliant analysis of how three industries—airlines, trucking, and telecommunications—were deregulated, often in the teeth of industry opposition.

Kingdon, John W. *Agendas, Alternatives, and Public Policies.* Boston: Little, Brown, 1984. An insightful account of how issues, especially those involving health and transportation, get on (or drop off) the federal agenda.

Lowi, Theodore J. "American Business, Public Policy, Case Studies, and Political Theory." *World Politics* 16 (July 1964). A theory of policymaking somewhat different from that offered in this book.

Nadel, Mark V. *The Politics of Consumer Protection,* 2d ed. Indianapolis: Bobbs-Merrill, 1975. An analysis of the sources and uses of political influence in consumer legislation.

Polsby, Nelson W. *Political Innovation in America.* New Haven, Conn.: Yale University Press, 1984. Explains how eight policy innovations were adopted by the federal government.

Wilson, James Q., ed. *The Politics of Regulation.* New York: Basic Books, 1980. Analyzes regulatory politics in nine agencies and provides a more detailed statement of the theory presented in this text.

18 Economic Policy

LEARNING OBJECTIVES

WHAT YOU NEED TO KNOW

- ☑ How do you define deficit, national debt, and gross domestic product?
- ☑ What makes the politics of taxing and spending so difficult?
- ☑ On which programs does the federal government spend most of its money?

WHO GOVERNS?

1. Who in the federal government can make our economy strong?
2. How do you end a recession?

TO WHAT ENDS?

1. Why does the federal government ever have a budget deficit?
2. Who was responsible for the 2007–2009 recession?

Like most Americans, you probably think about the way the government spends its money the same way you think about how you ought to spend yours. If you spend more than you earn, you will have to borrow money and pay it back to the bank. If you want to buy a car or a house, you will have to get a loan and make monthly payments on it. It you run up so many charges on your credit card that it is maxed out, you won't be able to charge anything more on it. If you keep spending more than you earn, you will have to declare bankruptcy. Surely, the government ought to work the same way: spend no more than it earns and pay back its loans.

But it doesn't. With just a few exceptions, the government has spent more money than it takes in every year since at least 1960. The amount it spends in excess of what it takes in each year is called the **deficit** (see Figure 18.1). It is financed by selling government bonds, issued by the Treasury Department, to Americans and foreigners. The total amount of all deficits is the **national debt.** In 2011, the national debt rose to over $14 trillion, and it was widely projected to reach $20 trillion by 2015.

For the last four decades, the government in Washington got away with routine deficit spending and nonstop increases in the national debt. But over the last several years, for both economic and political reasons, this has begun to change rather dramatically.

THEN Deficits that result in debt are important economically only insofar as the government cannot make the payments on its bonds in a currency that people regard as stable and valuable. Happily, almost everybody around the world has regarded the American dollar as stable and valuable. As a result, people have lined up to buy U.S. Treasury bonds whenever they are sold. But to keep our currency stable, people must believe that the dollar will always be valuable and that the government is not borrowing more than it can pay back. Prior to 1980, annual deficit spending was relatively minor and large deficits occurred only during wartime. Washington began its deficit spending and debt accumulation spree in the mid-1970s, interrupted only by several years during the 1990s when the government ran surpluses. Despite the huge deficits and mounting debt, most people, including most major domestic and foreign investors and experts on public finances, nonetheless considered America to be a good credit risk. In particular, concerns about "too much debt" were often dismissed as unduly alarmist, and presidents

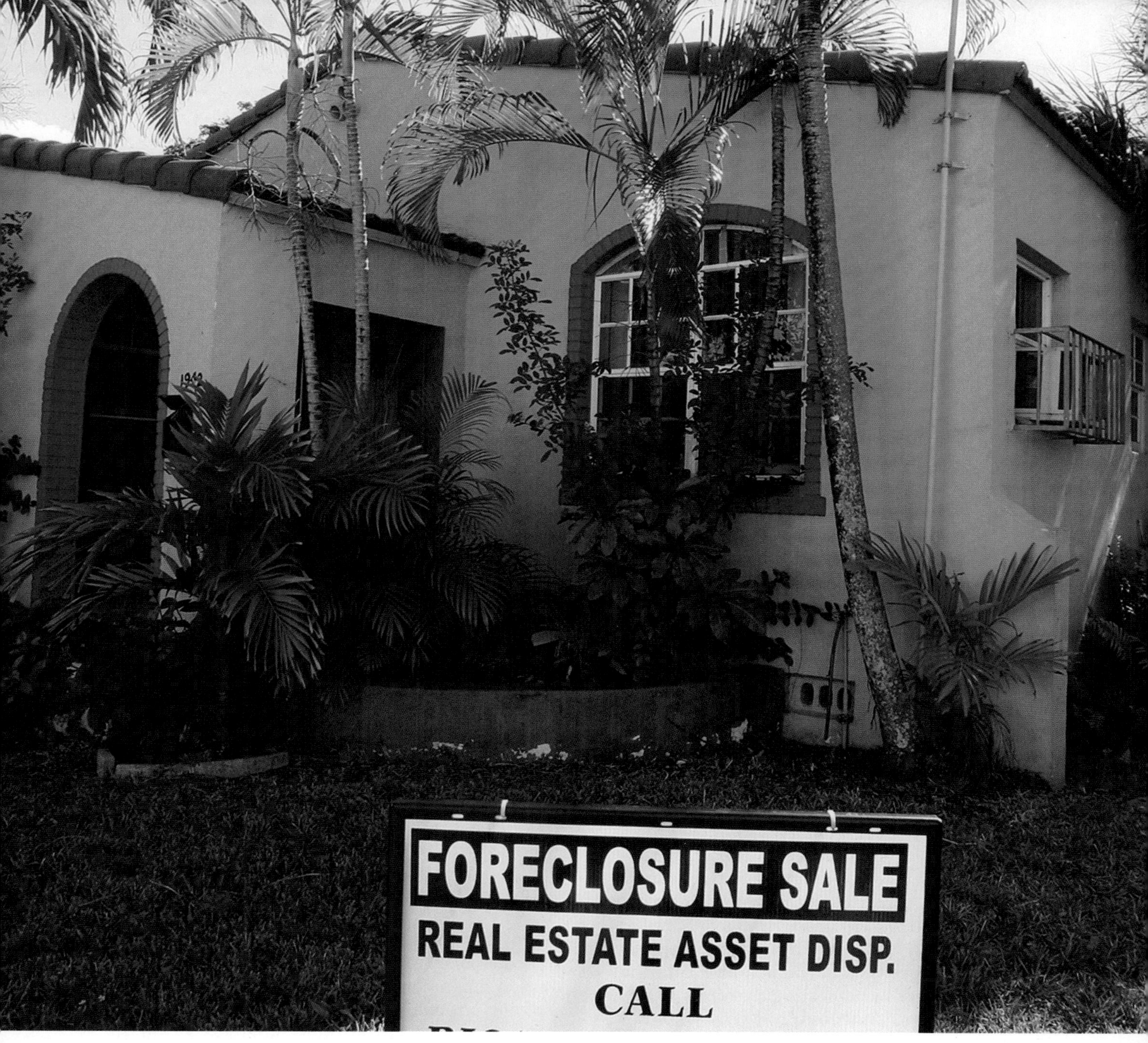

and congressional leaders in both parties quietly and consistently increased the national debt ceiling so that Washington could keep right on spending and borrowing.

NOW In April 2011, Standard & Poor's, a credit ratings agency that has been grading U.S. Treasury bonds since the 1930s, issued a first-ever warning about America's national debt, downgrading it from "stable" to "negative," and forecasting a one-third chance that the country would lose its "triple-A" credit rating before 2014. It did not take that long. In August 2011, Standard & Poor's itself downgraded the United States to "double-A" status. The annual federal deficit topped a trillion dollars for the first time in 2009, and in 2010 another trillion-dollar deficit was recorded. In December 2010, members of a bipartisan presidential commission, the National Commission on Fiscal Responsibility and Reform, proclaimed that dire, long-term economic consequences would follow unless Washington acted at once to rein in deficit spending and slow debt accumulation. For example, the total value of all the goods and services the nation produces each year is called **gross domestic product,** or GDP. The Commission warned that the national debt would soon exceed the nation's annual GDP, and that annual interest payments on the national debt could rise to almost 4 percent of GDP (from about 1.2 percent of GDP in 2009) over the next decade. In 2011, several competing deficit and debt reduction plans were circulated by members of Congress and by the White House, but bitterly partisan and ideological politics greeted each plan, and a heated public debate

Figure 18.1
Federal Budget Deficit (or Surplus), FY 1960–2012 in Billions of Constant FY 2005 Dollars (President's Proposals)

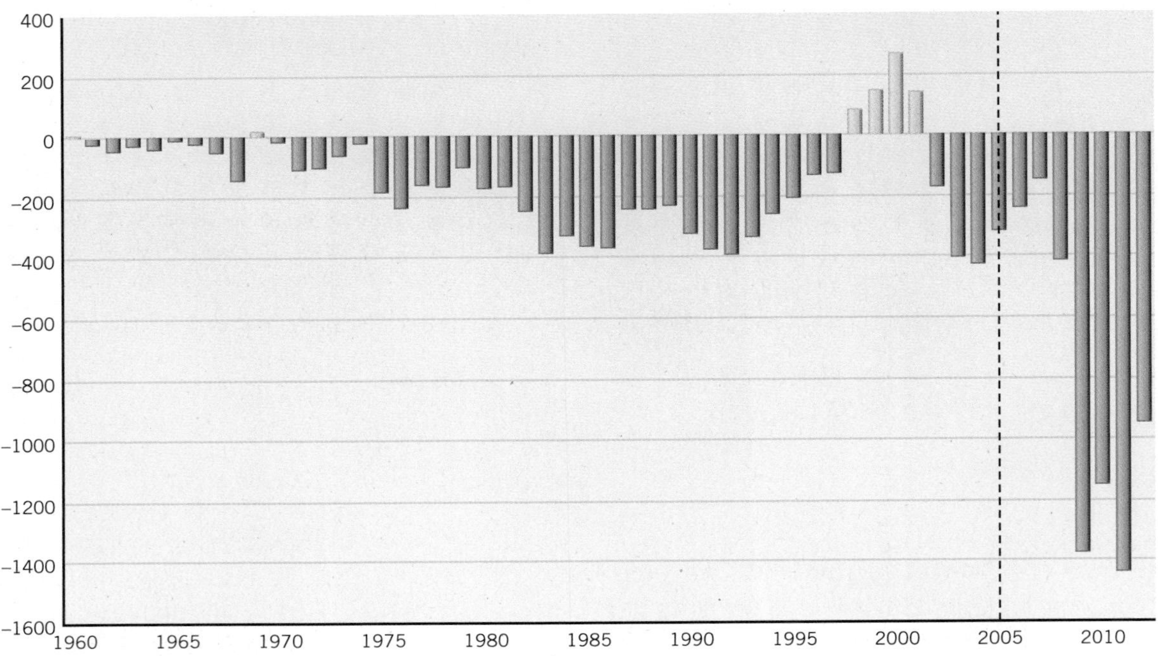

Source: Adapted from Office of Management and Budget (OMB), Historical Tables, February 1, 2010, Table 1.3.

ensued regarding the once-routine business of raising the national debt ceiling. In accordance with key provisions of the final bipartisan deal that raised the debt ceiling, in August 2011, a dozen members of Congress (half from the House and half from the Senate, half Democrats and half Republicans) were appointed to a "super committee" and charged with identifying $1.5 trillion in additional debt reduction; if they failed to agree, or if Congress rejected their plan, then across-the-board spending cuts (half in defense and half in domestic programs) were to be "triggered."

deficit The result of when the government in one year spends more money than it takes in from taxes.

national debt The total deficit from the first presidency down to the present.

gross domestic product The total of all goods and services produced in the economy during a given year.

Today's debates about deficit spending and debt accumulation are so rancorous in part because they have taken shape in the midst of a weak economy. A serious recession occurs when businesses fail, unemployment rises, and economic growth stops. This happened, starting in 2007 and continuing through 2010 and (depending on which economists one believes) perhaps beyond. The debates are also made more intense by the fiscal challenges that policymakers see just over the horizon. One such challenge is that our population is getting older. This creates huge new demands for Social Security retirement benefits and medical payments under Medicare and the part of Medicaid that covers long-term care (see Chapter 19). When a recession and an older population occur together, our national debt and interest payments to support it will shoot up.

But the core reason why ongoing debates over economic policy are so divisive is that people disagree, often fundamentally, not so much over the sheer size of our national debt but over what we buy with all this borrowed money. Most families borrow to buy long-lasting items, like a home, a new car, or a college education. We don't really know what the federal debt is used for. It would be nice if we knew that we borrowed only to pay for long-lasting things that enhance security and economic growth, such as schools, aircraft carriers, and basic health care research. But our government borrows whenever it needs the money without much regard for what it gets.

It should not be surprising that politicians typically avoid seriously debating, let alone making, hard choices on economic policy. Since they know the public is opposed to the government going into debt, politicians will also oppose the debt, but they offer two opposed ways to combat it. One, advanced mainly by conservatives, is by cutting spending; the other, offered mainly by liberals, is raising taxes. But since the people do not want less spending on programs they favor and certainly don't want higher taxes, these contradictory political strategies are hard to reconcile, maybe now more than ever. National polls in 2010 and 2011 found most Americans thinking that big government and big business work together against them, doubting that cuts to huge and hugely popular programs like Medicare were really necessary to rein in deficits and debt, and believing that eliminating government "waste, fraud, and abuse" could pretty nearly set things right. Thus, any truly far-reaching fiscal reforms will require politicians in both parties to win back public trust while telling the people what few care to hear.

The Politics of Economic Prosperity

In more normal economic times, however, economic policy is not nearly so hard for politicians to fashion without fighting big legislative battles or risking public ire. The health of the American economy creates majoritarian politics. Hardly anyone wants inflation or unemployment; everyone wants rapid increases in income and wealth. But this fact is a bit puzzling. You might think that people would care about their own jobs and worry only about avoiding their own unemployment. If that were the case, they would vote for politicians who promised to award contracts to firms that would hire them or who would create programs that would benefit them, regardless of how well other people were getting along. In fact, though, people see connections between their own well-being and that of the nation, and they tend to hold politicians responsible for the state of the country.

Everybody knows that just before an election politicians worry about the *pocketbook issue.* We have seen in Chapter 10 that economic conditions are strongly associated with how much success the incumbent party has in holding on to the White House and to the seats held by the White House's party in Congress. But whose pocketbook are voters worried about?

In part, of course, it is their own. We know that low-income people are more likely to worry about unemployment and to vote Democratic, and higher-income people are more likely to worry about inflation and to vote Republican.[1] We also know that people who tell pollsters that their families' finances have gotten worse are more likely than other people to vote against the incumbent president.[2] In 1980, about two-thirds of those who said they had become worse off economically voted for Ronald Reagan, the challenger, while over half of those who felt they had become better off voted for Jimmy Carter, the incumbent.[3] In 1992, people who felt economically pinched were more likely to vote for Clinton than for Bush. Clinton campaign aides often reminded each other, "It's the economy, stupid!"

But people do not simply vote their own pocketbooks. In any recession, the vast majority of people still have jobs; nevertheless, these people say unemployment is the nation's biggest problem, and many of them vote accordingly—against the incumbent during whose watch unemployment went up.[4] Why should employed people worry about other people's unemployment?

By the same token, younger voters—whose incomes tend to go up each year—often worry less about inflation than retired people living on fixed incomes, the purchasing power of which goes down with inflation.[5] In presidential elections, those who think national economic trends are bad are much more likely to vote against the incumbent, *even when* their own personal finances have not worsened.[6]

In technical language, voting behavior and economic conditions are strongly correlated at the national level but not at the individual level, and this is true both in the United States and in Europe.[7] Such voters are behaving in an "other-regarding" or "sociotropic" way. In ordinary language, voters seem to respond more to the condition of the national economy than to their own personal finances.

It is not hard to understand why this might be true. Part of the explanation is that people understand what government can and cannot be held accountable for. If you lose your job at the aircraft plant because the government has not renewed the plant's contract, you will be more likely to hold the government responsible than if you lose your job because you were always showing up drunk or because the plant moved out of town.

And part of the explanation is that people see general economic conditions as having indirect effects on them even when they are still doing pretty well. They may not be unemployed, but they may have friends who are, and they may worry that if unemployment grows worse, they will be the next to lose their jobs.

WHAT POLITICIANS TRY TO DO

Elected officials, who have to run for reelection every few years, are strongly tempted to take a short-run view of the economy and to adopt those policies that will best satisfy the self-regarding voter. They would dearly love to produce low unemployment rates and rising family incomes just before an election. Some scholars think that they do just this.

Since the 19th century, the government has used money to affect elections. At first this mostly took the form of patronage passed out to the party faithful and money benefits given to important blocs of voters. The massive system of Civil War pensions for Union army veterans was run in a way that did no harm to the political fortunes of the Republican party. After the Social Security system was established, Congress voted to increase the benefits in virtually every year in which there was an election (see Chapter 19).

But it is by no means clear that the federal government can or will do whatever is necessary to reduce unemployment, cut inflation, lower interest rates, and increase incomes just to win an election. For one thing, the government does not know how to produce all of these desirable outcomes. Moreover, doing one of these things often may be possible only at the cost of not doing another. For example, reducing inflation can, in many cases, require the government to raise interest rates, and this in turn can slow down the economy by making it harder to sell houses, automobiles, and other things purchased with borrowed money.

If it were easy to stimulate the economy just before an election, practically every president would serve two full terms. But because of the uncertainties and complexities of the economy, presidents can lose elections over economic issues they do not manage to the satisfaction of voters. Ford lost in 1976, Carter in 1980, and George H. W. Bush in 1992. In all cases, economic conditions played a major role.

All this means that politicians must make choices about economic policy, choices affected by uncertainty and ignorance. Those choices are shaped significantly by the ideological differences between the two political parties over what ought to be the principal goal of economic policy. Democrats and Republicans alike would prefer to have low unemployment and no inflation, but if they must choose (and choose they must), then the Democrats mainly attempt to reduce unemployment and the Republicans chiefly attempt to reduce inflation.[8]

This tendency mirrors to some degree what Democratic and Republican voters want their parties to do. Polls regularly show that those who think of themselves as Democrats are much more worried about unemployment than those who think of themselves as Republicans.[9] (There is not as much of a difference between Democratic and Republican voters in worrying about inflation.) Because of these beliefs, voters concerned about unemployment not only are more likely to vote against the incumbent but also are more likely to vote Democratic.

The Politics of Taxing and Spending

People want prosperity, but they also want no tax increases, no government deficit, and continued (or higher) government spending on the things they like, such as education, medical care, the environment, and retirement benefits. Politicians confront two inconsistent kinds of majoritarian politics: everybody wants general prosperity, and large majorities want more government spending on popular

© Harrison Mcclary/Reuters/Corbis

Thousands of Tea Party members gather in Nashville, Tennessee, in early 2009. The movement was named in part after the Boston Tea Party that in 1773 stimulated American resistance to the British. Others have said that "tea" stands for "taxed enough already."

programs. But the more the government spends on popular programs, the more money it requires, and the more it takes in, the less that is left over for private investment that produces prosperity.

Most voters would like to have all three things—lower taxes, less debt, and new programs. But the difficulty with this is that the policies endorsed are inconsistent with one another. We cannot have lower taxes, no debt, and higher spending on politically popular programs such as health care, education, the environment, and retirement benefits. If we have more spending, we have to pay for it, either with higher taxes or with more borrowing.

What Caused the Recession?

It was a perfect storm. The Federal Reserve Bank made borrowed money cheap by lowering interest rates (see page 502). Firms invented new ways of selling mortgages to investors. The government made it easy for poor people to get mortgages. They were called "subprime" because they went to people with low credit ratings who put up a small (if any) deposit. Investment firms invented new ways of selling mortgages. Cheap money combined with a big market for mortgages produced a housing boom and made it easy to get loans.

In 1999, the Banking Act of 1933, better known as the Glass-Steagall Act, was repealed. That law had separated investment from commercial banking and imposed many other restrictions on financial companies. In the 2000s, investment banks packaged good and subprime mortgages together and sold them as "mortgage-backed securities." The theory was that since each of these securities was backed by so many mortgages, a few could fail without hurting the value of the stock. Credit agencies were optimistic and said these were good deals. Many new financial products and services followed, several of them largely unregulated by the government or so complicated as to be beyond the intelligent grasp of average consumers.

For a while, it was a great success. More people bought homes, the price of these homes shot up, and people and firms used borrowed money to buy whatever they wanted. The unemployment rate was low. Everybody was happy.

But these changes led people and businesses to borrow more money than they could afford to pay back. The problem began with banks. Under federal rules, banks must have at least $1 of their own capital for every $12 dollars of deposits they accept. This makes it easier to fund mortgages. But there is a risk: if a lot of people who have mortgages stop making payments, then the bank may go out of business. Suppose a bank has $10 million in capital and issues mortgages worth $100 million. Suppose further that these mortgages decline in value by $10 million. The bank's capital ($10 million) is wiped out. Worried depositors will start withdrawing their money, and worried investors will sell their stock in the bank. The bank will fail.

The recession began when some people could no longer make their mortgage payments. Private and public regulatory agencies told the people who owned these mortgages that they had to write down their value. Suddenly, banks and investment companies with valueless mortgages began to fail. The firms that had insured these loans could not afford to pay for them. The market for credit froze. Many firms started firing people and others went out of business. The recession was underway.

Some people think all of this simply showed a weakness in America's private economy. They are wrong. Government was a big part of the problem. The two biggest purchasers of bank mortgages were the Federal National Mortgage Association (known as Fannie Mae) and the Federal Home Loan Mortgage Corporation (known as Freddie Mac). By 2007, they owned $5 *trillion* worth of mortgages.

These firms were created and sponsored by the federal government, but they were owned by private investors. Despite being privately owned, many people believed the federal government would stand behind Fannie Mae and Freddie Mac. One reason for this belief was that Washington politicians told the two firms how to behave. In particular, they told them to issue "subprime" mortgages. The goal was to extend home ownership to poor people. The problem is that poor people often cannot afford a mortgage.

When some people stopped paying for their mortgages, the federal government took over Fannie Mae and Freddie Mac because they were bankrupt. Private investment houses were also in trouble; a few went out of business or were sold to other firms.

(continued)

(continued)

The credit squeeze was on. Banks were reluctant to lend money and people were worried about borrowing it. Without credit, contractors stopped building homes and auto dealers stopped selling cars. As firms lost business, they began laying off workers. The unemployment rate went up. The value of homes sharply declined. The stock market collapsed. The recession was in full swing.

As the recession lingered and public outcries against government-funded corporate "bailouts" mounted, the U.S. Securities and Exchange Commission filed charges including some against a big investment bank that had allegedly manipulated subprime mortgage borrowers and markets while indemnifying itself from any losses and even posting big profits. In 2010, Congress enacted the Wall Street Reform and Consumer Protection Act, reinstituting some of the financial regulations that had been repealed in 1999. In 2010, economists debated whether the nation's economy was in recovery; and in 2011 they debated whether the country was heading into another deep recession.

People who want new programs have to either cut existing programs, let the government go deeper in debt, or raise taxes. But how do you raise taxes without alienating voters? The answer is that you raise taxes on *other people.*

The "other people" are always a minority of the voters. For example, if you want to put more money into medical research (something that everybody likes), you raise taxes on cigarettes (only a minority smoke them). If you want to pay for new education programs or bigger environmental programs, you raise taxes on affluent voters. In this way, you can find a majority of voters who will support—or at least not oppose very strongly—tax increases on a small group of voters—cigarette smokers or high-income people.

monetarism The belief that inflation occurs when too much money is chasing too few goods.

Legislators who like high rates say that "people who can afford it should pay a lot." Legislators who want low rates say that their opponents are trying to "soak the rich" by denying tax cuts to the people who now pay the biggest share of taxes.

Economic Theories and Political Needs

There are four main theories about how to improve the economy. When presidents select economic advisers, they often choose people who identify with one of these theories. In general, conservative economists tend to support monetarism and supply-side economics, while liberal economists are more likely to embrace Keynesianism and planning. Here, we give a highly simplified account of them and what each implies about ending a recession.

MONETARISM

A monetarist, such as the late economist Milton Friedman, believes that inflation occurs when too much money chases too few goods. The federal government has the power to create money (in ways to be described on page 502); according to monetarists, inflation occurs when it prints too much money. When inflation becomes rampant and government tries to do something, it often cuts back sharply on the amount of money in circulation. Then a recession will occur, with slowed economic growth and an increase in unemployment. Since the government does not understand that economic problems result from its own start-and-stop habit of issuing new money, it will try to cure some of these problems with policies that make matters worse—such as having an unbalanced budget or creating new welfare programs. **Monetarism** suggests that the proper thing for government to do is to have a steady, predictable increase in the money supply at a rate about equal to the growth in the economy's productivity. When the economy goes into a recession, however, many monetarists think the Federal Reserve Bank ("the Fed") should cut interest rates to make it easier for people and businesses to borrow money. That is what the Fed did during 2008.

KEYNESIANISM

John Maynard Keynes, an English economist who died in 1946, believed that the market will not automatically operate at a full-employment, low-inflation level. Its health depends on what fraction of people's incomes they save or spend. If they save too much, there will be too little demand, production will decline, and unemployment will rise. If they spend too much, demand will rise too fast, prices will go up, and shortages will develop. According to **Keynesianism,** the key is to create the right level of demand. This is the task of government. When demand is too little, the government should pump more money into the economy (by spending more than it takes in in taxes and by creating public-works programs). When demand is too great, the government should take money out of the economy (by increasing taxes or cutting federal expenditures). There is no need for the government's budget to be balanced on a year-to-year basis; what counts is the performance of the economy.

Keynesianism
The belief the government must manage the economy by spending more money when in a recession and cutting spending when there is inflation.

PLANNING

Some economists have too little faith in the workings of the free market to be pure Keynesians, much less monetarists. They believe the government should plan, in varying ways, some part of the country's economic activity. One form of **economic planning** is price and wage controls, as advocated by John Kenneth Galbraith and others. In this view, big corporations can raise prices because the forces of competition are too weak to restrain them, and labor unions can force up wages because management finds it easy to pass the increases along to consumers in the form of higher prices. Thus, during inflationary times, the government should regulate the maximum prices that can be charged and wages that can be paid, at least in the larger industries.

economic planning
The belief that government plans, such as wage and price controls or the direction of investment, can improve the economy.

Washington Tries to Stimulate the Economy

First Stimulus Bill (February 2008)

- $125 billion paid to people in checks of $600 each

Troubled Asset Relief Program (October 2008)

- $700 billion invested
- Buy shares in troubled banks and insurance companies
- Make loans to Chrysler and General Motors
- Make payments to troubled mortgage owners

American Recovery and Reinvestment Act (February 2009)

- $787 billion (over 11 years)
- Tax cuts and benefit checks for people earning less than $75,000 (total = $237 billion)
- Tax cuts for some businesses (total = $51 billion)
- Paying for unemployment benefits, health insurance, food stamps, etc. (total = $322 billion)
- Grants to states for Medicaid, highways, school construction, etc. (total = $155 billion)
- Money to repair or manage federal facilities (total = $57 billion).

Federal Reserve Board

- Federal Reserve spending $1.8 trillion (The Fed can create money by writing a check).
- Fed will help banks borrow money at low rates, purchase some corporate debt, and help bail out some investment houses and insurance companies (AIG).

Public-Private Investment Program (March 23, 2009)

- A program to help banks and others get rid of bad loans
- An auction will be held in which investors can buy up bad loans at low prices, with the federal government paying for much of the cost.

Source: Updated from "Sorting Out the Bailouts," *Congressional Quarterly Weekly* (February 23, 2009).

Planning has never been popular in America, but when the TARP program began investing in banks, some people began to suggest that perhaps the government should own the banks. That way, they said, the government might get back some of the money it had spent on them. The government was already the largest single stockholder in Bank of America and Citigroup (though in each case it owned less than half the stocks).

SUPPLY-SIDE TAX CUTS

Exactly the opposite remedy for declining American productivity is suggested by people who call themselves supply-siders. The view of economists such as Arthur Laffer and Paul Craig Roberts is that the market, far from having failed, has not been given an adequate chance. According to **supply-side theory,** what is needed is not more planning but less government interference. In particular, sharply cutting taxes will increase people's incentive to work, save, and invest. Greater investments will then lead to more jobs, and if the earnings from these investments and jobs are taxed less, it will lessen the tendency of many individuals to shelter their earnings from the tax collector by taking advantage of various tax loopholes or cheating on their income tax returns. The greater productivity of the economy will produce more tax revenue for the government. Even though tax *rates* will be lower, the total national income to which these rates are applied will be higher.

supply-side theory The belief that lower taxes and fewer regulations will stimulate the economy.

DID THE FEDERAL GOVERNMENT END THE RECESSION?

The box on page 499 summarizes the complicated efforts the federal government made to end the recession that began in 2007. If you take a course in economics, you may be able to learn what effect these efforts have had. But here you can learn about the *politics* of these attempts.

Proponents (in Congress, almost entirely the Democrats) of the second stimulus law enacted in early 2009 believed that several things had to be done:

- Give money to people so they could spend more.
- Spend more money on state, local, and federal projects to create jobs.
- Borrow the money to pay for these programs.

Landmark Cases

Federal Laws About Commerce

- ***Lochner v. New York* (1905):** Struck down as unconstitutional a New York law limiting the number of hours that may be worked by bakers.
- ***Muller v. Oregon* (1980):** Upheld as constitutional an Oregon law limiting the number of hours worked by women; in effect, it overruled the *Lochner* decision.
- ***West Coast Hotel Co. v. Parrish* (1937):** Upheld as constitutional a Washington State minimum wage law for women.
- ***Youngstown Sheet & Tube Co. v. Sawyer* (1952):** The president does not have the authority to seize private steel mills even in wartime.

Critics of the second stimulus plan (in Congress, almost every Republican) believed this approach was wrong because:

- Spending more money on government projects would not help because much of it would not produce benefits for several years.
- Borrowing a lot of money would vastly increase the federal debt.
- More could be accomplished by sharply cutting tax rates on people and businesses so that they would spend and invest more.

The Machinery of Economic Policymaking

Predicting what will happen to the economy is very hard. Few economists, for example, foresaw the recession that began in 2007. But even if the president knew exactly the right thing to do, he would still have to find some way of doing it. In our government, that is no easy task. The machinery for making decisions about economic matters is complex and not under the president's full control. Within the executive branch, three people other than the president are of special importance.

Karen Vismara/Black Star

Milton Friedman

© Bettmann/CORBIS

John Maynard Keynes

© Bettmann/CORBIS

John Kenneth Galbraith

Walter Bennett/Time Life Pictures/Getty Images

Arthur B. Laffer

Sometimes called the troika,* these are the chairman of the Council of Economic Advisers (CEA), the director of the Office of Management and Budget (OMB), and the secretary of the treasury.

The CEA, composed of three professional economists plus a small staff, has existed since 1946. In theory, it is an impartial group of experts responsible for forecasting economic trends, analyzing economic issues, and helping prepare the economic report that the president submits to Congress each year. Though quite professional in tone, the CEA is not exactly impartial in practice, since each president picks members sympathetic to his point of view. Kennedy picked Keynesians; Reagan picked supply-siders and monetarists. But whatever its philosophical tilt, the CEA is seen by other executive agencies as the advocate of the opinion of professional economists, who despite their differences generally tend to favor reliance on the market.

The OMB originally was the Bureau of the Budget, which was created in 1921 and made part of the executive office of the president in 1939; in 1970, it was renamed the Office of Management and Budget. Its chief function is to prepare estimates of the amount that will be spent by federal agencies, to negotiate with other departments over the size of their budgets, and to make certain (insofar as it can) that the legislative proposals of these other departments are in accord with the president's program. Of late it has acquired something of a split personality; it is in part an expert, nonpartisan agency that analyzes spending and budget patterns and in part an activist, partisan organization that tries to get the president's wishes carried out by the bureaucracy.

*From the Russian word for a carriage pulled by three horses.

The secretary of the treasury often is close to or drawn from the world of business and finance and is expected to argue the point of view of the financial community. (Since its members do not always agree, this is not always easy.) The secretary provides estimates of the revenue that the government can expect from existing taxes and what will be the result of changing tax laws. He or she represents the United States in its dealings with the top bankers and finance ministers of other nations.

A good deal of pulling and hauling takes place among members of the troika, but if that were the extent of the problem, presidential leadership would be fairly easy. The problem is far more complex. One study found 132 separate government bureaus engaged in formulating economic policy. They regulate business, make loans, and supply subsidies. For example, as foreign trade becomes increasingly important to this country, the secretary of state (among many others) acquires an interest in economic policy. One-third of corporate profits come from overseas investments, and one-fourth of farm output is sold abroad.

THE FED

Among the most important of these other agencies is the board of governors of the Federal Reserve System (the "Fed"). Its seven members are appointed by the president, with the consent of the Senate, for 14-year, nonrenewable terms and may not be removed except for cause. (No member has been removed since it was created in 1913.) The chairperson serves for four years. In theory, and to some degree in practice, the Fed is independent of both the president and Congress. Its most important function is to regulate, insofar as it can, the supply of money (both in circulation and in bank deposits) and the price of money (in the form of

monetary policy Managing the economy by altering the supply of money and interest rates.

interest rates). The Fed sets **monetary policy,** that is, the effort to shape the economy by controlling the amount of money and bank deposits and the interest rates charged for money. The box on this page shows how the Fed does this. In 2001, it lowered interest rates 11 times in order to help reduce the recession. From 2004 to 2007, it raised these rates 17 times in order to prevent inflation.

Just how independent the Fed is can be a matter of dispute. During the 1980 election, Fed policies helped keep interest rates at a high level, a circumstance that did not benefit President Carter's reelection bid. On the other hand, whenever a president is determined to change monetary policy, he usually can do so. For example, the term of Fed chairman Arthur F. Burns, appointed by President Nixon, came up for renewal in 1978. President Carter, seeking to influence Burns's decisions, held out the prospect of reappointing him chairman. When Burns balked, he was passed over, and G. William Miller was appointed in his stead. Presidents Truman, Johnson, and Nixon were all able to obtain changes in monetary policy. When Alan Greenspan, a conservative, became Fed chairman in 1987 under President Reagan, he was so successful in curbing inflation that he was reappointed by President Clinton, a Democrat.

CONGRESS

The most important part of the economic policy-making machinery, of course, is Congress. It must approve all taxes and almost all expenditures; there can be no wage or price controls without its consent;

How Things Work

The Federal Reserve Board

The Tools by Which the Fed Implements Its Monetary Policy

1. **Buying and selling federal government securities** (bonds, Treasury notes, and other pieces of paper that constitute government IOUs). When the Fed buys securities, it in effect puts more money into circulation and takes securities out of circulation. With more money around, interest rates tend to drop, and more money is borrowed and spent. When the Fed sells government securities, it in effect takes money out of circulation, causing interest rates to rise and making borrowing more difficult.
2. **Regulating the amount of money that a member bank must keep in hand as reserves** to back up the customer deposits it is holding. A bank lends out most of the money deposited with it. If the Fed says that it must keep in reserve a larger fraction of its deposits, then the amount that it can lend drops, loans become harder to obtain, and interest rates rise.
3. **Changing the interest charged banks** that want to borrow money from the Federal Reserve System. Banks borrow from the Fed to cover short-term needs. The interest that the Fed charges for this is called the *discount* rate. The Fed can raise or lower that rate; this will have an effect, though usually rather small, on how much money the banks will lend.

Federal Reserve Board (7 members)

- Determines how many government securities will be bought or sold by regional and member banks.
- Determines interest rates to be charged by regional banks and amount of money member banks must keep in reserve in regional banks.

Regional Federal Reserve Banks (12)

- Buy and sell government securities.
- Loan money to member banks.
- Keep percentage of holdings for member banks.

Member Banks (6,000)

- Buy and sell government securities.
- May borrow money from regional banks.
- Must keep percentage of holdings in regional banks.
- Interest rates paid to regional banks determine interest rates charged for business and personal loans and influence all bank interest rates.

and it has the ability to alter the policy of the nominally independent Federal Reserve Board by threatening to pass laws that would reduce its powers. And Congress itself is fragmented, with great influence wielded by the members of key committees, especially the House and Senate Budget Committees, the House and Senate Appropriations Committees, the House Ways and Means Committee, and the Senate Finance Committee. The decisions Congress makes about how high taxes should be and how much money the government should spend create the nation's **fiscal policy.**

fiscal policy Managing the economy by the use of tax and spending laws.

In sum, no matter what economic theory the president may have, if he is to put that theory into effect he needs the assistance of many agencies within the executive branch, such independent agencies as the Federal Reserve Board, and the various committees of Congress. Though members of the executive and legislative branches are united by their common desire to get reelected (and thus have a common interest in producing sound economic growth), each part of this system may also be influenced by different economic theories and will be motivated by the claims of interest groups.

The effect of these interest group claims is clearly shown in the debate over trade restriction. Usually the economic health of the nation affects everyone in pretty much the same way—we are all hurt by inflation or helped by stable prices; the incomes of all of us tend to grow (or remain stagnant) together. In these circumstances, the politics of economic health is majoritarian.

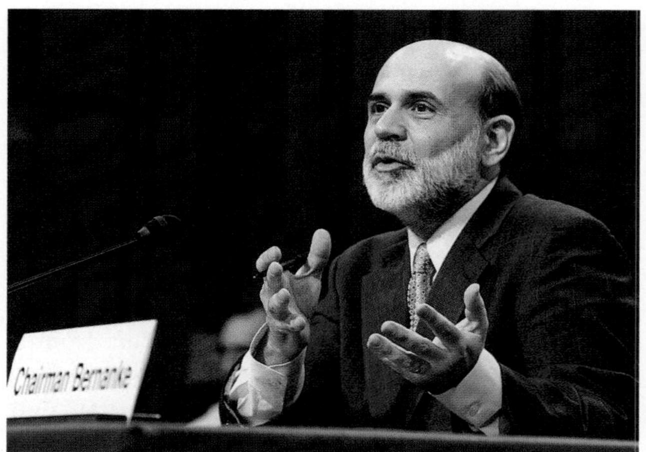

Mark Wilson/Getty Images

Ben Bernanke, chairman of the Federal Reserve, speaks to a congressional committee.

Suppose, however, that most of us are doing pretty well but that the people in a few industries or occupations are suffering. That is sometimes the result of foreign competition. In many countries, labor costs are much lower than in the United States. That means these countries can ship to American buyers goods—such as shoes, textiles, and beef—that sell at much lower prices than American producers can afford to charge. By contrast, if the price of a product is based chiefly on having advanced technology rather than low labor costs, American manufacturers can beat almost any foreign competitor.

When Congress passes laws governing foreign trade, it is responding to interest group politics. Industries that find it easy to sell American products abroad want free trade—that is, they want no taxes or restrictions on international exchanges. Industries that find it hard to compete with foreign imports oppose free trade—that is, they want tariffs and other limitations on imports.

When the North American Free Trade Agreement (NAFTA) was passed by Congress in 1993, the free traders won, and tariffs on our commerce with Canada and Mexico were largely abolished. But when the government later suggested creating free trade with all of Latin America, the critics of free trade opposed the idea, and it died. This is a good example of how people who bear the costs of a policy are often much more effective in influencing the votes on it than are those who stand to benefit from it.

Not only has the United States not extended the NAFTA idea to other countries, but it has done things that reward certain economic interest groups. Even though Republicans tend to support free trade, President George W. Bush imposed sharp increases in the taxes that must be paid on imported steel. The reason is not hard to find. Steel is produced in certain states, such as Ohio and Pennsylvania, that the president wanted to carry in 2004.

GLOBALIZATION

Trying to block free trade is a part of the opposition of some people to **globalization,** the growing integration of the economies and societies of the world. You can experience globalization easily: if your computer develops a problem and you call technical support, you are likely to speak with a technician based in India.

globalization The growing integration of the economies and societies of the world.

Supporters of globalization argue that it has increased the income, literacy, and standard of living of people in almost every country involved in the worldwide process of economic growth. These supporters favor free trade because it makes products cheaper. Opponents of globalization make several different and not always consistent arguments. Some (such as labor union leaders) argue that free trade undercuts the wages of American workers as less expensive foreign workers make things that are sold here. Others argue that globalization is driven by selfish corporate interests that exploit people in poor countries when they work for American firms. Still others feel that globalization means imposing one culture on everyone in ways that hurt local cultures.

budget A document that states tax collections, spending levels, and the allocation of spending among purposes.

fiscal year For the federal government, October 1 through the following September 30.

Spending Money

If only the economic health of the nation mattered, then majoritarian politics would dominate, and the president and Congress would both work to improve economic conditions. Although they still might work at cross-purposes because they held to different economic theories, the goal would be the same.

But the government must also respond to the demands of voters and interest groups. While these demands are no less legitimate than the voters' general interest in economic health, they produce not majoritarian but client and interest group politics.

The sources of this conflict can be seen in public opinion polls. Voters consistently say they want a balanced budget and lower government spending. They believe the government spends too much and that if it wanted to, it could cut spending. When the government runs a deficit, the reason in the voters' eyes is that it is spending too much, not that it is taxing too little. But these same polls show that the voters believe the government should spend more on education, homelessness, child care, and crime control.

The voters are not irrational, thinking they can have more spending and less spending simultaneously. Nor are they selfish or hypocritical, wanting less spending overall but more for programs that benefit them. They are simply expressing a variety of concerns. They want a limited government with no deficit; they also want good schools, cleaner air, better health care, and less crime. They believe a frugal government could deliver what they want by cutting out waste.

What this means for the government is easy to imagine. Politicians have an incentive to make two kinds of appeals: The first is, "Vote for me and I will keep government spending down and cut the deficit." The second is, "Vote for me and I will make certain that your favorite program gets more money." Some people will vote for the candidate because of the first appeal; some will vote for him or her because of the second. But acting on these two appeals is clearly going to lead to inconsistent policies. These inconsistencies become evident in the budget.

The Budget

A **budget** is a document that announces how much the government will collect in taxes and spend in revenues and how those expenditures will be allocated among various programs. (Each budget covers a **fiscal year,** which runs from October 1 of one year through September 30 of the next. A fiscal year is named after the year in which it *ends:* thus, "fiscal 2012" or "FY 2012" means the year ending on September 30, 2012.

In theory, the federal budget should be based on *first* deciding how much money the government is going to spend and *then* allocating that money among different programs and agencies. That is the way a household makes up its budget: "We have this much in the paycheck, and so we will spend X dollars on rent, Y dollars on food, and Z dollars on clothing, and what's left over on entertainment. If the amount of the paycheck goes down, we will cut something out—probably entertainment."

In fact, the federal budget is a list of everything the government is going to spend money on, with only slight regard (sometimes no regard at all) for how much money is available to be spent. Instead of being a way of *allocating* money to be spent on various purposes, it is a way of *adding up* what is being spent.

Indeed, there was no federal budget at all before 1921, and there was no unified presidential budget until the 1930s. Even after the president began submitting a single budget, the committees of Congress acted on it separately, adding to or subtracting from the amounts he proposed. (Usually they followed his lead, but they were certainly free to depart from it as they wished.) If one committee wanted to spend more on housing, no effort was made to take that amount away from the committee that was spending money on health (in fact, there was no machinery for making such an effort).

budget resolution A congressional decision that states the maximum amount of money the government should spend.

The Congressional Budget Act of 1974 changed this somewhat. Now after the president submits his budget in February, two budget committees—one in the House, one in the Senate—study his overall package and obtain an analysis of it from the Congressional Budget Office (CBO). Each committee then submits to its house a **budget resolution** that proposes a total budget ceiling and a ceiling for each of several spending areas (such as health or defense). Each May, Congress is supposed to adopt, with some modifications, these budget resolutions, intending them to be targets to guide the work of each legislative committee as it decides what should be spent in its area. During the summer Congress then takes up the specific appropriations bills, informing its members as it goes along whether or not the spending proposed in these bills conforms to the May budget resolution. The object, obviously, is to impose some discipline on the various committees. After each committee approves its appropriations bill and Congress passes it, it goes to the president for his signature.

These appropriations bills, however, can rarely make big changes in government spending. About two-thirds of what the government spends is mandatory—that is, the money goes to people who are entitled to it. **Entitlements** include Social Security and Medicare payments, veterans' benefits, food stamps, and money the government owes investors who have bought Treasury bonds (that is, the interest on the national debt). In theory, the government could change these entitlements by, for example, cutting Social Security payments, but that would be a political disaster. In reality, the government can change only about one-third of federal spending in any year.

entitlements A claim for government funds that cannot be changed without violating the rights of the claimant.

There is a big loophole in the current budget process: nothing in the process requires Congress to tighten the government's financial belt. It can pass a budget resolution authorizing spending that is more or less than what the president has proposed. Nonetheless, the process has made a difference. Congress is now conscious of how its spending decisions match up with estimates of tax revenues.

When President Reagan took office, he and his allies in Congress took advantage of the Congressional Budget Act to start the controversial process of cutting federal spending. The House and Senate budget committees, with the president's support, used the first budget resolution in May 1981 not simply to set a budget ceiling that, as in the past, looked pretty much like the previous year's budget but to direct each committee of Congress to make *cuts*—sometimes deep cuts—in the programs for which it was responsible. These cuts were to be made in the authorization legislation (see Chapter 15) as well as in the appropriations.

The object was to get members of Congress to vote for a total package of cuts before they could vote on any particular cut. Republican control of the Senate and an alliance between Republicans and conservative southern Democrats in the House allowed this strategy to succeed. The first budget resolution ordered Senate and House committees to reduce federal spending during fiscal 1982 by about $36 billion—less than the president had first asked, but a large sum nonetheless. Then the individual committees set to work trying to find ways of making these cuts.

Note how the *procedures* used by Congress can affect the *policies* adopted by Congress. If the Reagan plan had been submitted in the old piecemeal way, it is unlikely that cuts of this size would have occurred in so short a time, or at all. The reason is not that Congress would have wanted to ignore the president but that, then as now, Congress reflects public opinion on economic policy. As stated at the beginning of the chapter, the public wants less total federal spending but more money spent on specific federal programs. Thus, if you allow the public or Congress to vote first on specific programs, spending is bound to rise. But if you require Congress to vote first on a budget ceiling, then (unless it changes its mind as it goes along) total spending will go down, and tough choices will have to be made about the component parts of the budget. That, at least, is the theory. It worked once, in 1981, but it did not work very well thereafter.

Reducing Spending

Because the 1974 Congressional Budget Act did not automatically lead to spending cuts, people concerned about the growing federal deficit decided to find ways to put a cap on spending. The first such cap was the Balanced Budget Act of 1985, called the Gramm-Rudman Act after two of its sponsors, Senators Phil Gramm (R-Tex.) and Warren Rudman (R-N.H.). The law required that each year from 1986

Figure 18.2

Federal Revenues in 2010

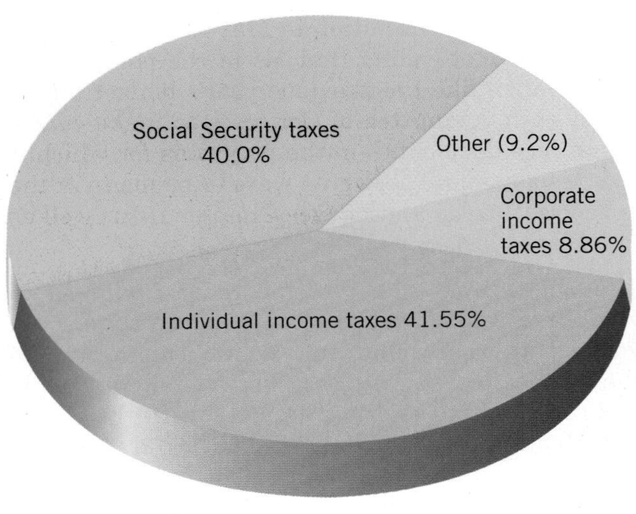

Federal Outlays in 2010

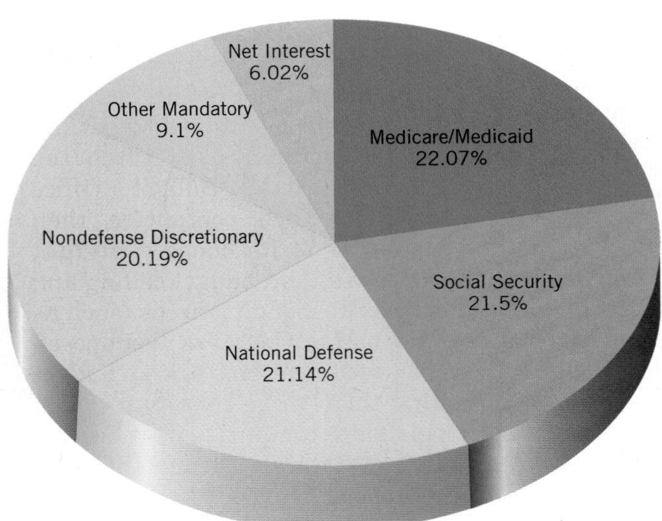

Source: Office of Management and Budget (OMB), Receipts and Outlays, Tables 2.1, 8.5, and 8.7, *OMB Review*, 2010.

sequester Automatic spending cuts.

to 1991 the budget would automatically be cut until the federal deficit had disappeared. What made the cuts automatic, its authors hoped, was a provision in the bill, called a **sequester,** that required across-the-board percentage cuts in all federal programs (except for entitlements) if the president and Congress failed to agree on a total spending level that met the law's targets.

But nobody much liked the idea, and the plan failed. By various devices that people began to call "smoke and mirrors," Congress and the president found ways to get new spending that was higher than the targeted amounts. By 1990, it was evident that a new strategy was needed if the government was going to help eliminate the deficit.

discretionary spending Spending that is not required to pay for contracts, interest on the national debt, or entitlement programs such as Social Security.

That strategy had two parts. First, Congress voted for a tax increase. Second, it passed the Budget Enforcement Act of 1990 that set limits on **discretionary spending.** This phrase refers to those government expenditures that are not required by existing contracts, payments on the national debt, or entitlement programs such as Social Security. As Figure 18.2 indicates, today only about a fifth of the budget involves discretionary spending, but back when the 1990 act was debated, the fraction was closer to a third. According to the 1990 act, if Congress were to spend more on a discretionary program, it would have to cut spending on another discretionary program or raise taxes. The law expired in 2001. As Figure 18.3 makes clear, something has to be done to manage huge future increases in spending on Social Security and Medicare.

Levying Taxes

Tax policy reflects a mixture of majoritarian politics ("What is a 'fair' tax law?") and client politics ("How much is in it for me?"). In the United States, a fair tax law generally has been viewed as one that keeps the overall tax burden rather low, requires everyone to pay something, and requires the better-off to pay at

Figure 18.3

Social Security and Medicare Cost as a Percentage of GDP

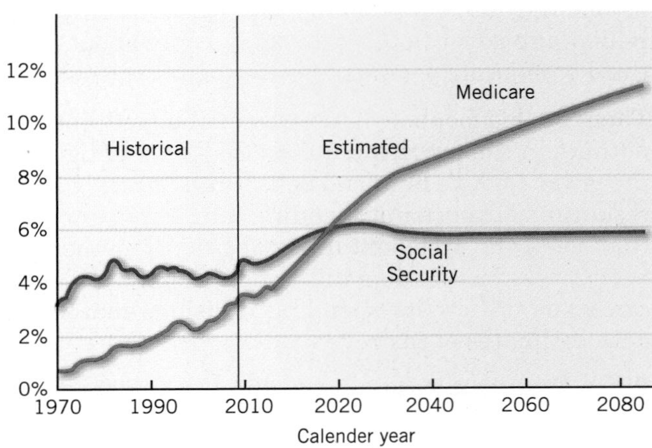

Source: *Trustees' Report*, 2009.

a higher rate than the less-well-off. The law, in short, was viewed as good if it imposed modest burdens, prevented cheating, and was mildly progressive.

Americans have had their first goal satisfied. The tax burden in the United States is lower than it is in most other democratic nations (see "How We Compare" on this page). There is some evidence that they have also had their second goal met—there is reason to believe that Americans evade their income taxes less than do citizens of, say, France or Italy. (That is one reason why many nations rely more on sales taxes than we do—they are harder to evade.) And federal income taxes here are progressive: according to the Congressional Budget Office data for 2007, the 40 percent of Americans who earn the least money pay no individual income taxes, while the 10 percent who earn the most money pay over 72 percent of all individual income taxes.

Keeping the burden low and the cheating at a minimum are examples of majoritarian politics: most people benefit, most people pay. The loopholes, however, are another matter—all manner of special interests can get some special benefit from the tax law that the rest of us must pay for but, given the complexity of the law, rarely notice. Loopholes are client politics par excellence.

Because of that, hardly any scholars believed tax reform (dramatically reducing the loopholes) was politically possible. Every interest that benefited from a loophole—and these included not just corporations but universities, museums, states, cities, and investors—would lobby vigorously to protect it.

Nevertheless, in 1986 a sweeping tax reform act was passed. Many of the most cherished loopholes were closed or reduced. What happened? It is as if scientists who had proved that a bumblebee could not fly got stung by a flying bumblebee.

How We Compare

Tax Burdens in Democratic Nations

Measured by taxes as a percentage of income of a family with two children, America as of 2008 had one of the lightest such tax burdens anywhere in the democratic world.

Denmark	28.8%
Turkey	25.7%
Greece	25.4%
Netherlands	22.6%
Finland	22.6%
Norway	21.8%
Germany	20.8%
Belgium	20.2%
UK	18.5%
Sweden	17.9%
Poland	17.8%
France	17.1%
Italy	15.1%
Japan	13.8%
Spain	12.0%
Canada	8.8%
Australia	8.6%
Switzerland	8.1%
U.S.	5.2%

Source: Organization for Economic Cooperation and Development (OECD), Comparative Table 1361, 2010.

THE RISE OF THE INCOME TAX

To understand what happened in 1986, one must first understand the political history of taxation in the United States. Until almost the end of the 19th century, there was no federal income tax (except for a brief period during the Civil War). The money the government needed came mostly from tariffs (that is, taxes on goods imported into this country). And when Congress did enact a peacetime income tax, the Supreme Court in 1895 struck it down as unconstitutional.[10] To change this, Congress proposed, and in 1913 the states ratified, the Sixteenth Amendment, which authorized such a tax.

For the next 40 years or so, tax rates tended to go up during wartime and down during peacetime (see Figure 18.4). The rates were progressive—that is, the wealthiest individuals paid at a higher rate than the less affluent. For example, during World War II incomes in the highest bracket were taxed at a rate of 94 percent. (The key tax rate is called by economists the "marginal rate." This is the percentage of the last dollar you earn that must be paid out in taxes.)

An income tax offers the opportunity for majoritarian politics to become class politics. The majority of the citizenry earn average incomes and control most of the votes. In theory there is nothing to prevent the

Figure 18.4
Federal Taxes on Income, Top Percentage Rates, 1913–2010

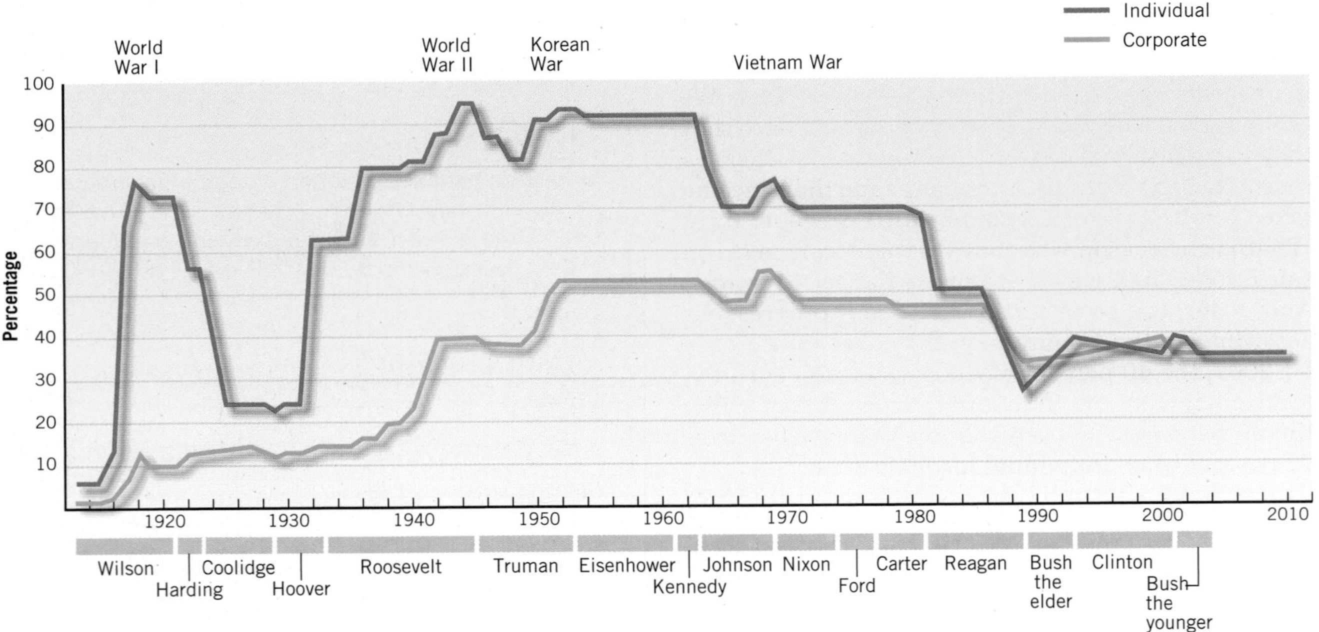

Source: Updated from *Congressional Quarterly Weekly Report* (various years).

mass of people from voting for legislators who will tax only the rich, who, as a minority, will always be outvoted. During the early decades of the 20th century, that is exactly what the rich feared would happen. Since the highest marginal tax rate was 94 percent, you might think that is in fact what did happen.

You would be wrong. Offsetting the high rates were the deductions, exemptions, and exclusions by which people could shelter some of their income from taxation. These loopholes were available for everyone, but they particularly helped the well-off. In effect, a political compromise was reached during the first half of the 20th century. The terms were these: the well-off, generally represented by the Republican party, would drop their bitter opposition to high marginal rates provided that the less-well-off, generally represented by the Democratic party, would support a large number of loopholes. The Democrats (or more accurately, the liberals) were willing to accept this compromise because they feared that if they insisted on high rates with no loopholes, the economy would suffer as people and businesses lost their incentive to save and invest.

For at least 30 years after the adoption of the income tax in 1913, only a small number of high-income people paid any significant amount in federal income taxes. The average citizen paid very little in such taxes until World War II. After the war, taxes did not fall to their prewar levels.

Most people did not complain too much, because they, too, benefited greatly from the loopholes. They could deduct from their taxable income the interest they paid on their home mortgages, the state and local taxes they paid, much of what they paid in medical insurance premiums, and the interest they paid on consumer loans (such as those used to buy automobiles). On the eve of the Tax Reform Act of 1986, an opinion poll showed that more people favored small cuts in tax rates coupled with many large deductions than favored big cuts in tax rates coupled with fewer and smaller deductions.[11]

Interest groups organized around each loophole. Home builders organized to support the mortgage-interest deduction; universities supported the charitable-contribution deduction; insurance companies supported the deduction for medical insurance premiums; and automakers supported the deduction for interest on consumer loans.

In addition to these well-known loopholes, there were countless others, not so well known and involving much less money, that were defended and enlarged through the efforts of other interest groups: for instance, oil companies supported the deduction for drilling costs, heavy industry supported the investment tax credit, and real estate developers supported special tax write-offs for apartment and office buildings.

WHAT WOULD YOU DO?

MEMORANDUM

To: *Elizabeth Gilbert, chairperson, Council of Economics*

From: *Edward Larson, White House speechwriter*

Subject: *Flat tax proposal*

The President would like your advice on whether to endorse a flat tax. His likely opponent is pushing this issue.

Arguments for:

1. A flat tax is fair because it treats all income groups the same. We could leave the lowest income group with no taxes.
2. With a flat tax, we could eliminate almost all deductions and loopholes from the tax code.
3. Countries with a flat tax, such as Lithuania, have achieved great economic prosperity.

Arguments against:

1. A flat tax is unfair because it treats all income groups the same. The rich should be taxed more heavily.
2. Many tax deductions, such as the one for home mortgages, are desirable.
3. We could eliminate undesirable tax loopholes without creating a flat tax.

News »

Should We Have a Flat Tax?

White House candidate David Wilson declared yesterday that he would seek a fundamental overhaul of the nation's tax system by creating a single rate for all taxpayers. The President is expected to respond to this in his State of the Union address.

Your decision:

Support ____________ Oppose ____________

Until 1986, the typical tax fight was less about rates than about deductions. Rates were important, but not as important as tax loopholes. "Loophole politics" was client politics. When client groups pressed for benefits, they could take advantage of the decentralized structure of Congress to find well-placed advocates who could advance these interests through low-visibility bargaining. In effect, these groups were getting a subsidy from the federal government equal to the amount of the tax break. However, the tax break was even better than a subsidy, because it did not have to be voted on every year as part of an appropriations bill: once part of the tax code, it lasted for a long time, and given the length and complexity of that code, scarcely anyone would notice it was there.

Many of these loopholes could be justified by arguments about economic growth. Low tax rates on a certain kind of investment encouraged more investment of that kind. Deductions for mortgage interest and property taxes encouraged people to own their own homes and boosted the construction industry.

Then the Tax Reform Act of 1986 turned the decades-old compromise on its head: instead of high rates with big deductions, we got low rates with much smaller deductions. The big gainers were individuals; the big losers were businesses.

But soon the old system began to reassert itself. Not long after the 1986 bill became law, tax rates started to go up again, this time with far fewer of the deductions that had once made it easy for affluent citizens to keep their rates low. In 1990, President Bush, after having campaigned on the slogan "Read my lips, no new taxes," signed a tax increase. The top rate was 31 percent. In 1993 President Clinton proposed another tax increase, one that would raise the top rate to over 39 percent (it had been 28 percent in 1986) and make most Social Security benefits taxable for upper-income retirees. His bill narrowly passed by a vote of 218 to 216 in the House, a vote of 51 to 50 in the Senate, with Vice President Al Gore casting the deciding vote. Not a single Republican voted for it. It was the first time since 1945 that the majority party in Congress had passed a major bill without one vote from the minority party.

When President George W. Bush got his tax cut plan through Congress in 2002, many Democrats as well as most Republicans voted for it. The next issue was clear: should the tax cuts, now expiring at the end of 2010, be made permanent? The issue deeply divided the parties in Congress. But, in December 2010, President Barack Obama signed into law a compromise bill featuring a two-year extension of the Bush tax cuts (favored by most Republicans) as well as additional money for unemployment insurance (favored by most Democrats).

LEARNING OBJECTIVES

WHAT YOU NEED TO KNOW

☑ **How do you define deficit, national debt, and gross domestic product?**

The deficit is what results when the government in one year spends more money than it takes in from taxes. The national debt is the total deficit from the first presidency down to the present. The gross domestic product, or GDP, is the total of all goods and services produced in the economy during a given year. In recent years, deficits and the national debt, both in absolute terms and relative to GDP, have reached record highs.

☑ **What makes the politics of taxing and spending so difficult?**

The politics of taxing and spending are so difficult mainly because most people don't like being taxed but do value government-funded programs that benefit themselves, their families and communities, and other citizens more generally. Most voters want lower taxes, less debt, and new programs, but if we have more spending, we have to pay for it, either with higher taxes or with more borrowing (and hence more, not less, debt). The recession that began in 2007 has lingered. Both deficits and the national debt hit new highs in 2008 and 2009. In 2011, for the first time, America's top credit rating was called into serious question. Thus, it has become harder and harder for politicians to avoid debating and making hard economic policy choices.

☑ **On which programs does the federal government spend most of its money?**

The federal government now spends about a fifth of its money on each of four things: Social Security, health care (Medicare and Medicaid), national defense, and nondefense programs. It spends the remaining fifth on other things including interest on the national debt.

RECONSIDERING WHO GOVERNS?

1. Who in the federal government can make our economy strong?

Nobody. The president, the Congress, the Federal Reserve Board, and countless small agencies play a role. And opinions as to what is the correct course of action (cut or increase taxes, decrease or increase regulations, spend more or less money) are deeply divided. The party that controls the White House usually must take the blame if the economy is in bad shape, but it is limited in what it can do to make it better.

2. How do you end a recession?

Who knows? The government has pumped billions of dollars into the economy with only slight effects. Somehow banks must become willing to make loans, borrowers must be willing to repay loans, and big investment firms (including government-sponsored ones) must stop buying up dubious mortgages.

RECONSIDERING TO WHAT ENDS?

1. Why does the federal government ever have a budget deficit?

It is not because politicians like deficits; it is because events may cause them while leaders disagree over how to fix them. Since the 1930s we have had deficits whenever the economy went into a depression or we had to take part in a war. In fact, a lot of things the government buys, such as new buildings and military supplies, ought to be considered as investments to be paid for over time, just as when private citizens buy cars and houses. And when the deficit goes up, some politicians will want to cut it by raising taxes while others will prefer cutting spending.

2. Who was responsible for the 2007–2009 recession?

Everybody. Borrowers, banks, credit rating agencies, investment firms, and two big government-sponsored enterprises, Fannie Mae and Freddie Mac.

QUESTIONS TO CONSIDER

1. **If you were an economic policymaker, what would you do to reduce deficits, and how might your approach please some voters at the expense of displeasing others?**
2. **How aware do you think most people your age are of either the economic problems facing the nation, or the government's problems with deficits and debt, or both?**
3. **Do you think that the top federal individual tax rates are too high or too low, and what's the highest tax rate that you think anyone, regardless of income, should be required to pay?**
4. **What is the latest figure for the national debt, and how does it compare to the latest estimate of gross domestic product (GDP)?**
5. **The federal government has run deficits for decades, but few states have done the same, in part because many state constitutions have provisions forbidding deficit spending: does yours?**
6. **The fiscal health of the federal government aside, since 2007 many state and local governments have also faced hard times: what is the latest financial word on your state government or local government?**

TO LEARN MORE

Internal Revenue Service: **www.irs.gov**
Tax Foundation: **www.taxfoundation.org**

Birnbaum, Jeffrey H., and Alan S. Murray. *Showdown at Gucci Gulch*. New York: Random House, 1987. Lively journalistic account of the passage of the Tax Reform Act of 1986.

Kiewiet, D. Roderick. *Macroeconomics and Micropolitics*. Chicago: University of Chicago Press, 1983. Argues that citizens vote on the basis of their estimate of national economic conditions as well as their own financial circumstances.

Morgenson, Gretchen, and Joshua Rosner. *Reckless Endangerment: How Outside Ambition, Greed, and Corruption Led to Economic Armageddon*. New York: Times Books/Henry Holt, 2011. The subtitle says it all.

Samuelson, Robert J. *The Good Life and Its Discontents*. New York: Times Books/Random House, 1995. A readable, intelligent account of American economic life since the Second World War.

Schick, Allen. *The Federal Budget*. Washington, D.C.: Brookings Institution, 2000. Excellent overview of how Washington allocates money.

Sorkin, Andrew Ross. *Too Big to Fail: The Inside Story of How Wall Street and Washington Fought to Save the Financial System—and Themselves*. New York: Viking, 2009. The captivating tale of how certain top Washington officials and Wall Street leaders reacted to the near-collapse of the financial system.

Stein, Herbert, and Murray Foss. *The New Illustrated Guide to the American Economy*, 3rd ed. Washington, D.C.: American Entervprise Institute, 1999. A vivid collection of graphs, all clearly explained, that describes the American economy and government spending from the 1950s through the 1990s.

19 Social Welfare

LEARNING OBJECTIVES

WHAT YOU NEED TO KNOW

- ☑ What are the federal government's largest social welfare programs?
- ☑ How have the politics of given social welfare programs changed in recent years?
- ☑ Is there a political consensus about how to address the solvency challenges facing major social welfare programs?

WHO GOVERNS?

1. How, if at all, have Americans' views of government's responsibility to help the "deserving poor" changed over time?
2. Why are some government social welfare programs politically protected while others are politically imperiled?

TO WHAT ENDS?

1. What does the Constitution mean by "promote the general Welfare"?
2. Should religious groups be eligible to administer some federal welfare programs?

Among the reasons given in the Preamble to the United States Constitution for establishing the national government is a desire to "promote the general Welfare." Article I, Section 8 of the Constitution states the power of Congress to "provide for the . . . general Welfare."

From the first, however, the Constitution's defenders disagreed about what the phrase was supposed to mean. Some, like James Madison, argued that it was meant to restrict Congress to taxing and spending only for things that the Constitution specifically empowered Congress to do (like regulating interstate commerce or maintaining the military). Others, like Alexander Hamilton, argued for a broader meaning that would allow Congress to tax and spend for things that it was not specifically empowered by the Constitution to do, but which might reasonably be expected to meet national needs and benefit some or all citizens.

In the 1930s, asserting a constitutional authority to advance the "general welfare," Congress enacted a host of new national policies and programs in response to the economic hardships wrought by the Great Depression. The biggest was the Social Security Act of 1935. Among other provisions, the law created a national system of old-age pensions and, to pay for it, imposed an income tax on workers that was deducted from their wages and paid by their employers. In 1937, in the case of *Helvering v. Davis*, the U.S. Supreme Court upheld the constitutionality of that provision, ruling that Congress has broad discretion to tax and spend "in aid of the 'general welfare,'" including policies and programs designed to ease the "plight of men and women" who lose their jobs and provide for others who are either temporarily or permanently "needy and dependent." Nobody, however, foresaw just how far Congress would go in exercising that power, or where doing so would lead.

THEN Before the 1960s, neither most Washington lawmakers nor most citizens believed that the federal government should ensure that all retirees, whatever their work history, have enough money to live on; that all veterans of foreign wars have grants for college and subsidized medical care for life; that all poor children are guaranteed free or reduced price meals in schools

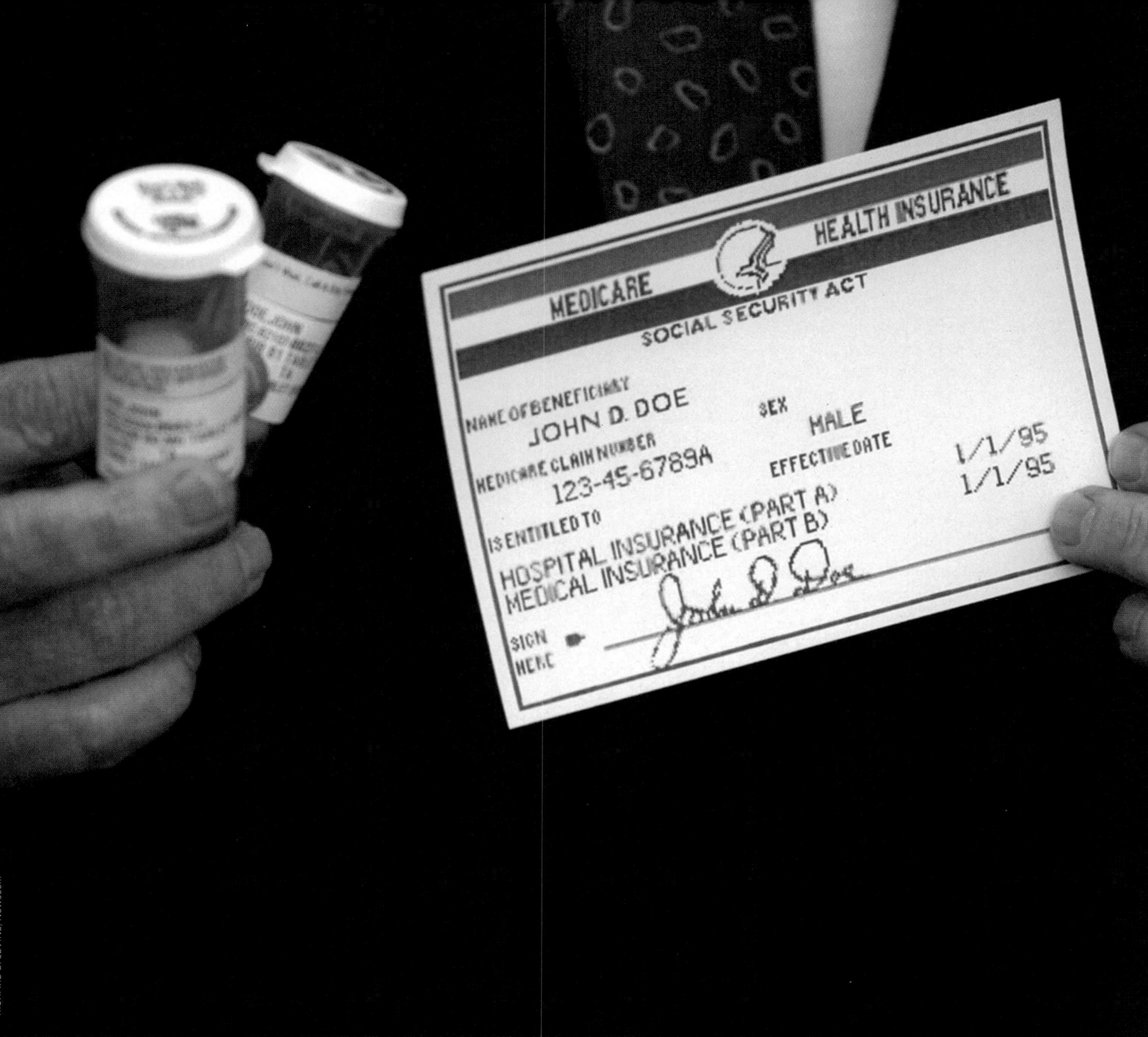

and during summers; that all physically, mentally, or developmentally disabled people, like all people with life-threatening medical maladies, are insured for hospital stays and treatment including long-term nursing care; that all low-wage workers receive tax credits that effectively boost their wages; that all citizens who may need it have access to affordable housing; that all low-income children are able to attend preschools; that all special needs children receive special education; and that all full-time workers who lose their jobs receive unemployment benefits and (in many cases) job training. If they existed at all, national laws touching on these social welfare matters were few and thin, and federal departments, bureaus, or programs to fund or administer such social welfare benefits were virtually nonexistent.

NOW Washington sets, funds, and implements policies on all these social welfare matters and others besides. By 2010, three giant programs—the aforementioned Social Security (established in 1935) plus Medicare and Medicaid (each established in 1965)—together accounted for over 40 percent of the federal budget (double what was spent on national defense). They were flanked by scores of smaller federal social welfare programs, most of them either established or expanded since 1965. The U.S. Department of Health and Human Services and the U.S. Department of Veterans Affairs are two of the main bureaucracies responsible for federal social welfare policies and programs, but benefits also emanate from several other federal departments. For instance, the U.S. Department of Justice has supported myriad programs for "at-risk youth" including

Landmark Cases

Federal Laws About "General Welfare"

- ***United States v. Butler* (1936):** Found particular federal regulations on agricultural production to be unconstitutional, but proclaimed that Congress has wide power to tax and spend for whatever it deems to be for the "general welfare."
- ***Helvering v. Davis* (1937):** Upheld key provisions of the Social Security Act of 1935, and declared that Congress has broad discretion to tax and spend "in aid of the 'general welfare.'"
- ***South Dakota v. Dole* (1987):** Ruled that Washington could condition the receipt of federal highway funds on a state's compliance with a 21-year-old drinking age, and declared that Congress's power to define the "general welfare" and to spend in pursuit of it is virtually unlimited.

ones that provide mentors to the children of prisoners and "second chance" job training to young adult ex-prisoners.

Still, even now, Americans and their leaders are far from agreeing on all federal social welfare polices and programs, and even farther from any consensus concerning what, if any, new such policies or programs are both feasible and desirable. Indeed, one of the most heated political controversies of recent years surrounded the passage of the latest major federal health care law, the Patient Protection and Affordable Care Act of 2010, dubbed by certain of its critics "Obamacare" (see box on page 517).

majoritarian politics A policy in which almost everybody benefits and almost everybody pays.

client politics A policy in which one small group benefits and almost everybody pays.

Two Kinds of Social Welfare Programs

Both the policy process by which social welfare programs are adopted, altered, or expanded and the administrative means by which they are put into action vary, but there are two kinds of social welfare programs.

To illustrate, many groups of senior citizens take day trips from Philadelphia to Atlantic City, New Jersey, where they stroll or gamble. On the bus ride, they are usually relaxed and talkative, but this wasn't the case in 2005. Then they had their noses buried in a booklet sent to them by the federal government. Entitled *Medicare & You,* it explained that if they were old enough to be on Medicare, then starting in January 2006, Uncle Sam would help them pay for their prescription drugs. The new program had a lot of complicated choices, but seniors were helped by a massive government-sponsored public relations program that explained everything to them. By 2009, most eligible senior citizens had signed up, and even with robust enrollments, the program actually was costing taxpayers a little less than the government had projected it would cost—a rarity, since most social welfare programs end up costing far more than was originally predicted.

Another welfare program is for certain poor people who get help to buy food by acquiring Food Stamps. Mary Summers, an expert on this program at the University of Pennsylvania, discovered that even bright college students with easy access to computer-based information systems required nearly four hours to figure out who could apply. She described it as "an administrative maze." Unlike with the Medicare prescription drug benefit, however, there has never been a massive public relations campaign to explain how to sign up for the Food Stamp program.

The key difference in this regard involves *who* benefits. Two kinds of social welfare programs exist in this country: those that benefit most or all of the people and those that help only a small number of them. In the first category are Social Security and Medicare, programs that provide retirement benefits or medical assistance to almost every citizen who has reached a certain age. In the second are programs such as Medicaid and Food Stamps that offer help only to people with low incomes.

Legally, the difference between the two kinds of programs is that the first have no *means test* (they are available to everyone without regard to income) while the second are *means tested* (you must fall below a certain income level to enjoy them). Politically, the programs differ in how they get money from the government. The first kind of welfare program represents **majoritarian politics:** nearly everyone benefits, nearly everyone pays. The second kind represents **client politics:** a (relatively) few number of people benefit, but almost everyone pays. The biggest problem facing majoritarian welfare programs

The Changing Politics of Health Care

When Medicare was enacted in 1965, Democrats in the House and Senate voted for it by a wide margin, but roughly half of the Republicans in each chamber also supported it. But the 2010 health care bill was passed without any Republican support. The Medicare bill went to President Johnson with broad bipartisan backing, but the 2010 health care bill went to President Obama with narrow partisan backing. Using the model of the policy process explained in Chapter 17, here is a summary of how the costs and benefits of the Obama plan affected the political coalitions that formed around health care.

Majoritarian Politics: The bill was opposed by a majority of Americans for a variety of reasons. Many thought it too expensive ($940 billion over 10 years) or worried about the government regulations the law contained.

Client Politics: Drug manufacturers looked forward to having many new customers as more people owned health insurance. To get this benefit, the pharmaceutical companies agreed to pay up to $85 billion in higher taxes. Many hospitals thought they would be helped by having more patients who could pay their bills with health insurance.

Interest Group Politics: Labor unions wanted health care coverage, but business firms were upset by the higher taxes and fees they would have to pay. Poorer people liked it, but those earning $200,000 a year or more would see their taxes escalate. Elderly people on Medicare and many doctors worried that the new law promised to cut payments to physicians, but the American Medical Association and the AARP (the largest organization representing senior citizens) endorsed the law.

Policy Entrepreneurs: In early 2010, the winners were President Obama and the Democratic leaders in the House who got a bill passed over popular and interest group opposition. In the latter half of 2010, however, the winners were the Republicans who opposed "Obamacare" and used the issue on the way to sweeping GOP victories in the November 2010 elections.

When the 112th Congress began in 2011, Republicans in the House made good on a pledge to vote for the outright repeal of the new law (the symbolic bill died in the Senate), and several state attorneys general challenged the law's constitutionality in the federal courts (focusing mainly on the provision mandating that individuals purchase health insurance).

The Medicare law and the new health care law mobilized very different coalitions because, between 1965 and 2010, Congress became a far more polarized institution (see Chapter 13). Most major pieces of social legislation in the past reflect majoritarian politics, but the health care bill was based on a combination of client, interest group, and entrepreneurial politics.

is their cost: who will pay, and how much will they pay? The biggest problem facing client-oriented programs is their legitimacy: who should benefit, and how should they be served?

This political difference between these programs has a huge impact on how the government acts in regard to them. Social Security and Medicare are sacrosanct. The thought of making any changes that might lower the benefits these programs pay is so politically risky that most politicians never even discuss them. When programs such as these run into trouble because of rising expenses (Medicare is in deep trouble today, and Social Security will be in deep trouble in a few decades), politicians scramble to look for ways of maintaining benefits while hiding the rising costs or postponing dealing with them. As we shall see later in this chapter, there has been a sharp growth in the proportion of people who are retired and are thus entitled to Social Security and Medicare. To keep benefits flowing to these individuals, people who are not retired will have to pay more and more in taxes. No politician wants to raise taxes or cut benefits, so they adopt a variety of halfhearted measures (like slowly increasing the age at which people can get these benefits) designed to postpone the tough decisions until they are out of office.

Client-based welfare programs—those that are means tested—are a very different matter. Like many other client-based programs, their political appeal changes as popular opinion about them changes. Take the old Aid to Families with Dependent Children (AFDC) program. When it was started in 1935, people thought of it as a way of helping poor women whose husbands had been killed in war or had died in mining accidents. The goal was to help these women support their children, who had been made fatherless by death or disaster. Most people thought of these women as the innocent victims of a tragedy. No one thought that they would take AFDC for very long. It was a program to help smooth things over for them until they could remarry.

About 30 years later, however, the public's opinion of AFDC had begun to change. People started to think AFDC was paying money to women who had never married and had no intention of marrying. The government, according to this view, was subsidizing single-parent families, encouraging out-of-wedlock births, and creating social dependency. Moreover, some people thought that African Americans were taking undue advantage of the program. (In fact, when this opinion emerged, African Americans were still a minority among AFDC recipients.) From the mid-1960s, through the mid-1990s, these views became stronger. AFDC had lost the legitimacy it needed, as a client program, to survive politically.

Whenever a client program loses political legitimacy, the program is in trouble. Client politics depends on the beneficiaries' being thought of as legitimate. Almost any means-tested program risks losing its political legitimacy because some people will always wonder whether the program itself causes people to avoid working in order to claim the benefits. Some people think that about Food Stamps, the program that gives low-income people free stamps that they can exchange for food. There have been a few publicized cases of people using food stamps to buy luxury items. But no powerful opposition to the program has developed, because in general the only thing the beneficiaries have in common is that they have low incomes. Many Americans can imagine becoming poor, and so they probably are willing to allow such a program to operate as part of a government-supplied safety net that might, someday, help them.

But AFDC was a different matter. Having to accept AFDC was not something the typical taxpayer thought would ever happen to him or her. Moreover, the beneficiaries weren't just poor; some of them did things—such as having babies without getting married—that most Americans thought were simply wrong. The legitimacy of AFDC was thus in jeopardy, because it either made possible or actually encouraged behavior that most Americans found improper. As a result, something happened to AFDC that almost never happens to decades-old government programs: it was abolished.

In this chapter, we provide examples of both majoritarian and client welfare programs and describe how they have been reformed over the years. There are far too many social welfare programs to describe them all here; rather the main purpose of this chapter is to explain the key features of the two main kinds of programs.

Social Welfare in the United States

Before analyzing how these programs came into being, it is first necessary to understand that social welfare policy in the United States is shaped by four factors that make it different from what exists in many other nations. First, Americans generally have taken a more restrictive view of who is entitled to government assistance. Second, America has been slower than other countries to embrace the welfare state. Third, we have insisted that the states (and to a degree private enterprise) play a large role in running welfare programs. Fourth, nongovernmental organizations play a large role in welfare.

The first distinctive feature of the American welfare state involves who benefits. To Americans, who benefits has been a question of who *deserves* to benefit. We usually have insisted that public support be given only to those who cannot help themselves. But what does it mean to say that a person cannot help himself or herself? Surely a disabled, blind, elderly woman deserted by her family cannot do much to help herself, but would she still be deserving of public aid were she merely disabled? Or merely elderly? And to what extent should we require that her family support her? As we shall see, American welfare policy since the 1930s has been fundamentally shaped by a slow but steady change in how we have separated the "deserving" from the "undeserving" poor.

That we have always thought this way may make us forget there are other ways of thinking about welfare. The major alternative view is to ask not who deserves help but what each person's "fair share" of the national income is. Seen this way, the role of government is to take money from those who have a lot and give it to those who have only a little, until each person has, if not the same amount, then at least a fair share. But defining a "fair share" is even more difficult than defining the "deserving poor." Moreover, Americans have generally felt that giving money to people who are already working, or who could work if they chose to, is unfair. In some nations—Sweden is an example—government policy is aimed at redistributing income from better-off to not-so-well-off persons, without regard to who "deserves" the money.

Thus Americans base welfare policy on the concept of "help for the deserving poor" rather than

The attorneys general of several states have filed suit challenging the constitutionality of President Obama's health care law. Here supporters of the law denounce the Washington state attorney general for joining the suit.

"redistribution to produce fair shares."[1] They have done so, one suspects, because they believe citizens should be encouraged to be self-reliant, people who work hard will get what they deserve, and giving money to people who could help themselves will produce a class of "welfare chiselers." If Americans believed success at work was a matter of luck rather than effort or was dictated by forces over which they had no control, they might support a different concept of welfare.

Moreover, we have always been a bit uneasy about giving money to people. Though we recognize that many people through no fault of their own cannot buy groceries and thus need funds, we would prefer that, to the extent possible, people who deserve help be given *services* (education, training, medical care) rather than money. Throughout much of our history, our welfare policies have reflected a general philosophical disposition in favor of providing services to deserving persons.

The second striking fact about American welfare policy is how late in our history it arrived (at least at the national level) compared to other nations. By 1935, when Congress passed the Social Security Act, at least 22 European nations already had similar programs, as did Australia and Japan.[2] Germany was the first to create a nationwide social security program when it developed sickness and maternity insurance in 1883. Six years later, it added old-age insurance and in 1927 unemployment insurance.

England offers perhaps the clearest contrast with the United States. In 1908, a national system of old-age pensions was set up, followed three years later by a plan for nationwide health and unemployment insurance.[3] England had a parliamentary regime in which a political party with liberal sentiments and a large majority had come to power. With authority concentrated in the hands of the prime minister and his cabinet, there was virtually no obstacle to instituting measures, such as welfare programs, that commended themselves to party leaders on grounds of either principle or party advantage. Furthermore, the British Labour party was then beginning to emerge. Though the party was still small (it had only 30 seats in Parliament in 1908), its leaders included people who had been influential in formulating welfare programs that the leaders of the dominant Liberal party backed. And once these programs were approved, they were in almost all cases nationally run: there were no state governments to which authority had to be delegated or whose different experiences had to be accommodated.

Moreover, the British in 1908 were beginning to think in terms of social classes, to accept the notion

charitable choice Name given to four federal laws passed in the late 1990s specifying the conditions under which nonprofit religious organizations could compete to administer certain social service delivery and welfare programs.

of an activist government, and to make welfare the central political issue. Americans at that time also had an activist leader, Theodore Roosevelt; there was a progressive movement; and labor was well along in its organizing drives. But the issues were defined differently in the United States. Progressives, or at least most of them, emphasized the reform of the political process—by eliminating corruption, by weakening the parties, and by improving the civil service—and attacked bigness by breaking up industrial trusts. Though some progressives favored the creation of a welfare state, they were a distinct minority. They had few allies in organized labor (which was skeptical of public welfare programs) and could not overcome the general distrust of big government and the strong preference for leaving matters of welfare in state hands. In sum, what ordinary politics brought to England in 1908–1911, only the crisis politics of 1935 would bring to the United States. But once started, the programs grew. By 1983, almost one-third of all Americans received benefits from one or more social welfare programs, and today some estimates put the fraction closer to one-half.

The third factor involves the degree to which federalism has shaped national welfare policy. Since the Constitution was silent on whether Congress had the power to spend money on welfare and since powers not delegated to Congress were reserved to the states, it was not until the constitutional reinterpretation of the 1930s (see Chapter 16) that it became clear that the federal government could do anything in the area of social policy. At the same time, federalism meant that any state so inclined could experiment with welfare programs. Between 1923 and 1933, thirty states enacted some form of an old-age pension. By 1935 all but two states had adopted a "mother's pension"—a program whereby a widow with children was given financial assistance, provided that she was a "fit mother" who ran a "suitable home." The poor were given small doles by local governments, helped by private charities, or placed in almshouses. Only one state, Wisconsin, had an unemployment insurance program.

Politically the state programs had a double-edged effect: they provided opponents of a federal welfare system with an argument (the states were already providing welfare assistance), but they also supplied a lobby for federal financial assistance (state authorities would campaign for national legislation to help them out). Some were later to say that the states were the laboratories for experimentation in welfare policy. When the federal government entered the field in 1935, it did so in part by spending money through the states, thereby encouraging the formation in the states of a strong welfare bureaucracy whose later claims would be difficult to ignore.

A fourth distinctive feature of welfare policy in the United States is that much of it is administered via grants and contracts to nongovernmental institutions, both for-profit firms and nonprofit organizations. For example, many large national nonprofit organizations, such as Big Brothers Big Sisters of America, Youth Build, Jewish Federation, and Catholic Charities, have received large federal grants and long participated in the administration of federal social programs. The 1996 law that abolished the Aid to Families with Dependent Children program contained a provision directing that religious nonprofit organizations, including small community-based groups, be permitted to compete for government grants with which to administer federal welfare-to-work and related policies. The latter provision, known as **charitable choice,** enjoyed bipartisan support. The provision prohibited religious organizations from using any public funds for proselytizing, religious instruction, or worship services, but also prohibited the government from requiring them to remove religious art or iconography from buildings where social service delivery programs funded in whole or in party by Washington might be administered.

In 2001, President George W. Bush's call to expand the role of religious organizations in administering federal social programs led to a political firestorm.[4] Some religious conservatives demanded that the Bush administration act to permit faith-based organizations to proselytize with public funds and also allow them to hire only coreligionists if they wished. But some civil libertarians sought to reduce or eliminate most existing public-private partnerships involving religious organizations.

Between 2002 and 2003, HHS and HUD grants to faith-based groups increased 41 percent and 16 percent, respectively, and five federal agencies awarded $1.17 billion to such organizations.[5] Today, faith-based organizations figure ever more prominently in the administration of welfare-to-work programs in many big cities, from about 14 percent of all such programs in Los Angeles to about 41 percent in Philadelphia.[6] Fewer than one in 10 of these urban faith-based organizations give preferences to coreligionists in hiring, and virtually all accept beneficiaries without regard to religion.[7] This approach

Major Social Welfare Programs

Insurance, or "Contributory," Programs

Old Age, Survivors, and Disability Insurance (OASDI) Monthly payments to retired or disabled people and to surviving members of their families. This program, popularly called Social Security, is paid for by a payroll tax on employers and employees. *No means test.*

Medicare Federal government pays for part of the cost of medical care for retired or disabled people covered by Social Security. Paid for by payroll taxes on employees and employers. *No means test.*

Assistance, or "Noncontributory," Programs

Unemployment Insurance (UI) Weekly payments to workers who have been laid off and cannot find work. Benefits and requirements determined by states. Paid for by taxes on employers. *No means test.*

Temporary Assistance for Needy Families (TANF) Payments to needy families with children. Replaced the old AFDC program. Partially paid for by block grants from the federal government to the states. *Means test.*

Supplemental Security Income (SSI) Cash payments to aged, blind, or disabled people whose income is below a certain amount. Paid for from general federal revenues. *Means test.*

Food Stamps (now part of the **Supplemental Nutrition Assistance Program, SNAP**) Vouchers, given to people whose income is below a certain level, that can be used to buy food at grocery stores. Paid for out of general federal revenues. *Means test.*

Medicaid Pays medical expenses of persons receiving TANF or SSI payments. *Means test.*

Earned Income Tax Credit Pays cash or tax credit to poor working families. *Means test.*

reflects mass opinion on the subject: three-quarters want government to help fund community-serving, faith-based organizations and deem them to be "more caring and compassionate" than professional providers of the same services; but the same three-fourths majority opposes government support for faith-based programs that require beneficiaries to "take part in religious practices" or "only hire people of the same faith."[8]

MAJORITARIAN WELFARE PROGRAMS: SOCIAL SECURITY AND MEDICARE

At the time the Great Depression began in 1929, the job of providing relief (food, money, medicine, and other services) to needy people fell almost entirely to state and local governments or to private charities, and even these sources were primarily concerned with widows, orphans, and the elderly.[9] Hardly any state had a systematic program for supporting the unemployed, though many states provided some kind of help if it was clear that the person was out of work through no fault of his or her own. When the economy suddenly ground to a near standstill and the unemployment rate rose to include one-fourth of the workforce, private charities and city relief programs nearly went bankrupt.

Earned Income Tax Credit (EITC) A provision of a 1975 law that entitles working families with children to receive money from the government if their total income is below a certain level. The program was expanded in the early 1990s.

The election of 1932 produced an overwhelming congressional majority for the Democrats and placed Franklin D. Roosevelt in the White House. Almost immediately, a number of emergency measures were adopted to cope with the depression by supplying federal cash to bail out state and local relief agencies and by creating public works jobs under federal auspices. These measures were recognized as temporary expedients, however, and were unsatisfactory to those who believed the federal government had a permanent and major responsibility for welfare. Roosevelt created the Cabinet Committee on Economic Security to consider long-term policies. The committee drew heavily on the experience of European nations and on the ideas of various American scholars and social workers, but it understood that it would have to

Topham/The Image Works

In 1932, unemployed workers line up at a soup kitchen during the Great Depression.

© Bettmann/CORBIS

In 1934, Huey Long, the popular governor of Louisiana, claimed that Roosevelt was not doing enough to help the common man. But before he could become a serious threat to Roosevelt in the 1936 election, Long was assassinated in 1935.

adapt these proposals to the realities of American politics. Chief among these was the widespread belief that any direct federal welfare program might be unconstitutional. The Constitution nowhere explicitly gave to Congress the authority to set up an unemployment compensation or old-age retirement program. And even if a welfare program were constitutional, many believed, it would be wrong because it violated the individualistic creed that people should help themselves unless they were physically unable to do so.

insurance program A self-financing government program based on contributions that provide benefits to unemployed or retired persons.

assistance program A government program financed by general income taxes that provides benefits to poor citizens without requiring contribution from them.

means test An income qualification program that determines whether one is eligible for benefits under government programs reserved for lower-income groups.

But failure by the Roosevelt administration to produce a comprehensive social security program, his supporters felt, might make the president vulnerable in the 1936 election to the leaders of various radical social movements. Huey Long of Louisiana was proposing a "Share Our Wealth" plan; Upton Sinclair was running for governor of California on a platform calling for programs to "End Poverty in California"; and Dr. Francis E. Townsend was leading an organization of hundreds of thousands of elderly people on whose behalf he demanded government pensions of $200 a month.

The plan that emerged from the cabinet committee was carefully designed to meet popular demands within the framework of constitutional understandings. It called for two kinds of programs: (1) an **insurance program** for the unemployed and elderly, to which workers would contribute and from which they would benefit when they became unemployed or retired; and (2) an **assistance program** for the blind, dependent children, and the aged. (Giving assistance as well as providing "insurance" for the aged was necessary because for the first few years the insurance program would not pay out any benefits.) The federal government would use its power to tax to provide the funds, but all of the programs (except for old-age insurance) would be administered by the states. Everybody, rich or poor, would be eligible for the insurance programs. Only the poor, as defined by a **means test** (a measure to determine that incomes are below a certain level), would be eligible for the assistance programs. Though bitterly opposed by some, the resulting Social Security Act passed swiftly and virtually unchanged through Congress. It was introduced in January 1935 and signed by President Roosevelt in August of that year.

The idea of having the government pay the medical and hospital bills of the elderly and the poor had been discussed in Washington since the drafting of the Social Security Act. President Roosevelt and his Committee on Economic Security sensed that medical care would be very controversial, and so health programs were left out of the 1935 bill in order not to jeopardize its chances of passage.[10]

The proponents of the idea did not abandon it, however. Working mostly within the executive branch, they continued to press, sometimes publicly, sometimes behind the scenes, for a national health care plan. Democratic presidents, including Truman, Kennedy, and Johnson, favored it; Republican president Eisenhower opposed it; Congress was deeply divided on it. The American Medical Association attacked it as "socialized medicine." For 30 years, key policy entrepreneurs, such as Wilbur Cohen, worked to find a formula that would produce a congressional majority.

The first and highest hurdle to overcome, however, was not Congress as a whole but the House Ways and Means Committee, especially its powerful chairman from 1958 to 1975, Wilbur Mills of Arkansas. A majority of the committee members opposed a national health care program. Some members believed it wrong in principle; others feared that adding a costly health component to the Social Security system would jeopardize the financial solvency and administrative integrity of one of the most popular government programs. By the early 1960s, a majority of the House favored a health care plan, but without the approval of Ways and Means it would never reach the floor.

The 1964 elections changed all that. The Johnson landslide produced such large Democratic majorities in Congress that the composition of the committees changed. In particular, the membership of the Ways and Means Committee was altered. Whereas before it had three Democrats for every two Republicans, after 1964 it had two Democrats for every one Republican. The House leadership saw to it that the new Democrats on the committee were strongly committed to a health care program. Suddenly the committee had a majority favorable to such a plan, and Mills, realizing that a bill would pass and wanting to help shape its form, changed his position and became a supporter of what was to become Medicare.

The policy entrepreneurs in and out of the government who drafted the Medicare plan attempted to anticipate the major objections to it. First, the bill would apply only to the aged—those eligible for Social Security retirement benefits. This would reassure legislators worried about the cost of providing tax-supported health care for everybody. Second, the plan would cover only hospital expenses, not doctors' bills. Since doctors were not to be paid by the government, they would not be regulated by it; thus, presumably, the opposition of the American Medical Association would be blunted.

Unexpectedly, however, the Ways and Means Committee broadened the coverage of the plan beyond what the administration had thought was politically feasible. It added sections providing medical assistance, called Medicaid, for the poor (defined as those already getting public assistance payments) and payment of doctors' bills for the aged (a new part of Medicare). The new, much-enlarged bill passed both houses of Congress with ease. The key votes pitted a majority of the Democrats against a majority of the Republicans.

Johnson's Great Society programs and "war on poverty" went far beyond Roosevelt's New Deal programs. But neither the chief political architects of Social Security in 1935 nor the main political movers behind Medicare and Medicaid in 1965 ever envisioned scores of millions of Americans receiving food, money, medicine, and other benefits through programs funded largely by the federal government.

Lyndon Baines Johnson Library/MCT/Newscom

President Lyndon Johnson signs the Medicare Act in 1965.

Chip Somodevilla/Getty Images

President Barack Obama signs the Affordable Health Care for America Act in 2010.

And no one contemplated that middle-class and even upper-income citizens would one day become as likely to receive federally financed health care as the poorest of the poor.

But that day has long since arrived. In 2010, about 60 million Americans received Medicaid benefits, 54 million Americans received Social Security benefits, and 52 million Americans (45 million senior citizens and 7 million younger adults with permanent disabilities) received Medicare benefits.

The two largest federal social welfare programs, Social Security and Medicare, are bound for big increases in beneficiaries over the next several decades as the primary beneficiary population each program serves, persons age 65 and older, grows and grows. For example, between 2010 and 2030, the number of Medicare beneficiaries is expected to rise by about 50 percent to 78 million.

When Medicare was enacted in 1965, the government said that by 1990 it would cost $12 billion a year. When 1990 rolled around, Medicare actually cost $110 billion. Today, it costs more than $500 billion a year. As the population gets older and new (and expensive) life-prolonging technologies are developed, the cost of the program will rise even faster. Post-1970 growth in government health care spending has been higher in the United States than in many other countries (see Table 19.1), a fact for which Medicare's growth is largely responsible.

Medicare allows people to visit the doctor or go to the hospital whenever they feel they need to (see

Table 19.1 Post-1970 Government Health Care Spending in Ten Countries

Country	Average Annual Real Per-Capita Increase (%)
Australia	4.1
Austria	4.0
Canada	3.1
Germany	3.6
Japan	4.9
Norway	5.3
Spain	5.1
Sweden	2.6
United Kingdom	3.7
United States	5.1
Average	4.1

Source: Laurence Kotlilkoff and Christian Hagist, National Bureau of Economic Research, Working paper no. 11833, 2005, reporting OECD data and rounded averages for the period 1970–2002, as cited in National Center for Policy Analysis, *Health Care Spending Trends*, 2004, table 1.

How Things Work

Medicare ABCDs

Medicare is a federal health insurance program that covers most senior citizens 65 or older, some younger people with disabilities, and people with end-stage renal disease. Today, it covers about 52 million elderly and disabled persons.

Part A: Hospital Insurance

It covers inpatient care in hospitals, and also helps cover skilled nursing facility care, hospice care, and home health care. Some people pay a monthly premium; others do not.

Part B: Medical Insurance

It covers doctors' services, hospital outpatient care, and some preventive services. The standard monthly premium in 2009 was $96.40. It gets deducted automatically from your Social Security check.

Part C: Medicare Advantage Plus

Basically, it sets the terms under which companies that contract with the Medicare program must provide benefits.

Part D: Prescription Drug Coverage

Participation is voluntary, and the monthly premium depends on how much coverage you have.

the box on page 524). The doctor or hospital is paid a fee for each visit. This creates three problems: (1) a lot of people use medical services when they don't really need them; (2) some doctors and hospitals overcharge the government for their services; and (3) doctors and hospitals are paid on the basis of a government-approved payment plan that can change whenever the government wants to save money.

Social Security, which provides the majority of income for about half of Americans over age 65, has a $2.6 trillion trust fund (essentially Treasury bonds), but far more is needed to cover the program's long-term projected expenses. The key problem for Social Security is that, as the population ages, soon there will not be enough people paying Social Security taxes to provide benefits for every retired person. By 2020, there will be fewer than two workers for every retiree, and the payroll taxes on these workers would have to more than double to pay that retiree's bills. In 2011, the trustees of each program issued reports: Medicare was forecast to become almost totally insolvent by 2017, and Social Security was predicted to be at least 25 percent short of what would be needed to cover all benefits by 2037.

That is, of course, unless things change. One change is contained in President Obama's plan: it creates a government commission that would cut Medicare payments starting in 2014. The public is not likely to want this, but there is only shallow public support for changing Medicare and Social Security in ways that reduce or slow benefits or increase taxes (see Table 19.2). In 2011, a Medicare reform plan proposed by Representative Paul Ryan, Republican of Wisconsin, would have transformed the program into a voucher-like system. Under his plan, federal

AP Images

When members of Congress went home in August 2009, they encountered a long line of voters angry over the health care debate.

How We Compare

Social Security

Most European democracies began social security systems earlier than the United States did. Even for its time, the U.S. Social Security program that began in 1935 was a relatively modest insurance-based retirement program.

Today, more than seven decades later, the U.S. Social Security program has grown dramatically and covers more than "old age, disability, and survivors." Still, European nations not only started sooner but have developed far more comprehensive—and expensive—social security systems than America has yet known.

In many European countries, social security programs extend well beyond retirement benefits or pensions to funding for work-related injuries, sickness, maternity leaves, and more; the retirement age for eligibility is lower than it is in the United States; and the benefits are, on average, greater.

For example, while the average American has received maybe half of his or her working-life income in benefits, a typical French or German worker has retired several years earlier and received as much as 70 percent of his or her working-life income in benefits. Social security benefits here are earnings-related, but many European nations (Ireland, Switzerland, and the United Kingdom, to name just three) provide a flat-rate pension independent of earnings.

Nothing is free: Europeans have paid two to three times as much as Americans in program-related taxes. And, unlike some European and other nations, the United States has avoided " dual Social Security taxation" via bilateral agreements and policies that do not require either foreign workers in America or Americans who work abroad to pay social security to both countries.

Sources: U.S. Social Security Administration, Social Security Programs Throughout the World, September 2008, and "U.S. International Social Security Agreements," 2009, accessed May 27, 2010, at www.ssa.gov/international/agreements_overview.html.

Table 19.2 Public Opinion on Changing Medicare and Social Security, 2011

Support (%)	
SOCIAL SECURITY	
Major Reduction in Benefits	8
Minor Reduction in Benefits	27
Raise Retirement Age from 67 to 68	42
Increase Program Tax Rates	35
Increase Benefits at a Slower Rate	45
MEDICARE	
Major Reduction in Benefits	8
Minor Reduction in Benefits	35
Raise Eligibility Age from 67 to 70	32
Increase Program Tax Rates	49
Replace program with a voucher system	35

Source: Adapted from ABC News/Washington Post Poll, March 10–13, 2011; Kaiser Family Foundation/Harvard School of Public Health Poll, January 4–14, 2011; and School of Public Policy, University of Maryland and Center on Policy Attitudes, "How Americans Would Deal with the Budget Deficit," February 3, 2011, p. 49.

money would go to Medicare recipients who would then use it to buy private health insurance. Total Medicare costs, beyond what the insurance covered, would be capped at $6,000 a person (which would grow every year at the same rate as the growth in GDP plus one percent); poor people who could not pay the cap would receive a subsidy from the government. As of mid-2011 congressional Democrats had not submitted a rival plan.

CLIENT WELFARE PROGRAMS: AID TO FAMILIES WITH DEPENDENT CHILDREN

One part of the Social Security Act of 1935 created what came to be called Aid to Families with Dependent Children (AFDC). It was scarcely noticed at the time. The federal government, in response to the depression, promised to provide aid to states that were, in many cases, already running programs to help poor children who lacked a father.

Because AFDC involved giving federal aid to existing state programs, it allowed the states to define what constituted "need," to set benefit levels, and to administer the program. Washington did set (and, over the years, continued to increase) a number of rules governing how the program would work, however. Washington told the states how to calculate applicants' incomes and required the states to give Medicaid to AFDC recipients. The states had to establish mandatory job-training programs for many AFDC recipients and to provide child-care programs for working AFDC parents. Washington also required that women on AFDC identify their children's fathers. In addition to the growing list of requirements, Washington created new programs for which AFDC recipients were eligible, such as Food Stamps, the Earned Income Tax Credit (EITC—a cash grant to poor parents who were working), free school meals, various forms of housing assistance, and certain other benefits. But while all this was happening, public opinion moved against the AFDC program.

The combination of souring public opinion, increasing federal regulations, and a growing roster of benefits produced a program that irritated almost everyone. The states disliked having to conform to a growing list of federal regulations. The public disliked the program because it was viewed as weakening the family by encouraging out-of-wedlock births (since AFDC recipients received additional benefits for each new child). The public worried that AFDC recipients were working covertly on the side; the data proved that this was true of at least half of them in several large cities. AFDC recipients saw the actual (inflation-adjusted) value of their AFDC checks was going down. Critics countered that if you added together all the benefits they were receiving (Food Stamps, Medicaid, housing assistance, and so on), benefit levels were actually going up. Politicians complained that healthy parents were living off AFDC instead of working. The AFDC law was revised many times, but never in a way that satisfied all, or even most, of its critics. Though AFDC recipients were only a small fraction of all Americans, they had become a large political problem.

MILLER EMILY/SIPA/Newscom

An Electronic Benefits Transfer card is like a debit card that allows a person to use food stamps and spend TANF money.

What made matters worse was that the composition of the people in the program had changed. In 1970, about half of the mothers on AFDC were there because their husbands had died or divorced them; only a quarter had never been married. By 1994, the situation had changed dramatically: only about a quarter of AFDC mothers were widowed or divorced, and over half had never been married at all. And though most women on AFDC for the first time got off it after just a few years, almost two-thirds of the women on AFDC at any given moment had been on it for eight years or more.

These facts, combined with the increased proportion of out-of-wedlock births in the country as a whole, made it virtually impossible to sustain political support for what had begun as a noncontroversial client program. In 1996 the program was abolished. It was replaced by a block grant program, Temporary Assistance for Needy Families (TANF), that set strict federal requirements about work and limited how long families can receive federally funded benefits. Under TANF, by 2006, welfare caseloads nationally had declined by 62 percent.

Majoritarian versus Client Politics

The programs just described illustrate two patterns of policymaking. The old-age pensions created by the Social Security Act of 1935 and the health care benefits created by the Medicare Act of 1965 are examples of *majoritarian politics*: almost everybody benefits, and almost everybody pays. The TANF program is an example of *client politics*: a relatively few people benefit, but everybody pays.

MAJORITARIAN POLITICS

When both the benefits and the costs of a proposed program are widely distributed, the proposal will be adopted if the beneficiaries believe their benefits will exceed their costs *and* if political elites believe it is legitimate for the federal government to adopt the program.

Initially, the benefits people received from the retirement program greatly exceeded its costs to them. Older people were able to get an old-age pension or health care even though they had paid in taxes only a small fraction of what these benefits cost. Social Security and Medicare seemed initially like the nearest thing to a free lunch.

The big debate in 1935 and 1965 was not over whether the people wanted these programs—the polls showed that they did—but over whether it was legitimate for the federal government to provide them.[11] In 1935, conservatives argued that as desirable as Social Security might be, nothing in the Constitution authorized the federal government to spend money for this purpose; welfare, they said, was a policy area reserved to the states. Liberals rejoined that the federal government had an obligation to help people avoid poverty in their old age. Besides, they said, as an "insurance" program, retirement benefits were not really a federal expenditure at all: Washington was merely collecting payments and holding them in a trust fund until the people who paid them were ready to retire. In the midst of the Great Depression and at a time when liberals had large majorities in Congress, it was an easy argument to make, and so the Social Security bill readily crossed over the legitimacy barrier.

In 1965, the same issues were raised. Conservatives argued that medical care was a private, not a governmental, matter and that any federal involvement would subject doctors and hospitals to endless red tape and harm the quality of the doctor-patient relationship. Liberals rejoined that the elderly had health needs they could not meet without help and that only the federal government had the resources to provide that assistance. Because the 1964 elections, when Lyndon Johnson defeated Barry Goldwater, had swept into the House and Senate large majorities of liberal Democrats, there was no chance that a conservative coalition of Republicans and southern Democrats could defeat Medicare, and so it passed.

The votes in Congress on Social Security and Medicare followed party lines. Since the Democratic opponents of these bills typically were conservative southerners, the vote followed ideological lines even more closely.

CLIENT POLITICS

When the benefits of a proposal are to go to a relatively small group but the public at large pays, we have client politics. Proposals to benefit clients will pass if the cost to the public at large is not perceived to be great *and* if the client receiving the benefit is thought to be "deserving."

As noted previously, when AFDC was first enacted, it was relatively noncontroversial. Originally, it seemed intended to help deserving people. In 1935, the typical welfare mother was perceived to be a woman living in a small town, whose husband had been killed in a mining accident. Who could object to giving some modest help to a person who was the victim of circumstances?

Who Governs? To What Ends?

Reforming Majoritarian Education Programs

America is home to about 50 million public-school children. Most citizens, even the elderly and young adults with no children in public schools, tend to think of public education in majoritarian terms: everyone benefits, everyone pays.

Until recently, Democrats pretty much owned this majoritarian issue. With the exception of some Democratic mayors, most Democratic leaders have opposed plans to give parents school vouchers (public monies that can be used to pay for private or religious school tuitions). Meanwhile, most Republican leaders have favored vouchers. In 2000, voucher referenda were defeated soundly in California and Michigan.

Three days after taking office in January 2001, Republican president George W. Bush proposed an education reform plan that he then described as "the cornerstone of my administration." It contained voucher language and related provisions that would have effected sweeping changes in the Elementary and Secondary Education Act (ESEA). But just a few months into negotiations on the bill with Senate Democrats, virtually every aspect of the original Bush plan that could not be credibly couched in majoritarian terms, reconciled with existing ESEA programs, or otherwise justified as "recruiting high-quality teachers," "promoting informed parental choice," or "improving the academic achievement of the disadvantaged" was abandoned.

On January 8, 2002, Congress easily passed the No Child Left Behind Act of 2001. The president's major ally in getting the 670-page education reform plan into law was Democratic senator Ted Kennedy of Massachusetts. Democrats applauded the act mainly for increasing federal education funding under the ESEA by 49 percent over 2000 levels, to more than $22 billion a year. Republicans, led by House conservatives, complained about the increased ESEA spending and lamented that the new law did nothing to advance the cause of school vouchers.

On February 17, 2009, President Barack Obama signed the American Recovery and Reinvestment Act. It had something in it for just about everyone: about $5 billion for early learning programs like Head Start, $30 billion for college loans and other support for higher education, and federal grants totaling nearly $50 billion for elementary and secondary schools, among other provisions.

In the several years after Bush's No Child Left Behind bill became law, Republicans pulled even with Democrats on public trust with respect to education policy; but just a few months after the Obama administration's majoritarian push for education reform, by mid-2009, Democrats had regained a big edge on the issue.

service strategy A policy providing poor people with education and job training to help lift them out of poverty.

income strategy A policy giving poor people money to help lift them out of poverty.

Right or wrong, American values on this subject changed. Today, most Americans believe that able-bodied people on welfare should be made to work for their benefits. The work-based welfare provisions of TANF plainly reflect this belief. In 2002, during the largely consensual congressional debate over reauthorizing TANF, even many who had opposed these strategies in 1996 (when TANF replaced AFDC) now supported them. There remains, however, some popular sentiment for giving welfare recipients job training or even creating government jobs for them. This **service strategy** (providing training and education) is strongly preferred to an **income strategy** (giving people money)—unless, of course, the income can be called "insurance."[12]

Indeed, some critics of welfare, such as Charles Murray, have argued that AFDC actually increased the number of people living in poverty. Murray claimed that high welfare benefits made it more attractive for some people to go on welfare than to look for a job and more attractive for some women to have babies than to get married. This kept them

WHAT WOULD YOU DO?

MEMORANDUM

To: *Ursula Marx, Senate Committee chair*

From: *Cindy Fried, senior staff member*

Subject: *Universal health care legislation*

You and the committee have two fairly distinct sets of options on this universal health care package.

Arguments for:

1. With more than 47 million Americans, or one in seven, lacking health care coverage, the government needs to enact far-reaching reform to ensure that everyone receives quality medical care.
2. The soaring cost of health care (which is expected to reach approximately one-fifth of the federal budget in the next decade) can be contained only by a public system that has the power to set prices and control costs.
3. Universal health care is a logical expansion of the Medicare and Medicaid programs created in 1965; nearly half a century later, health care should be a fundamental right guaranteed for everyone who lives in the United States.

Arguments against:

1. Though many people lack health insurance, most of them get health care in hospital emergency rooms and from doctors who donate their services.
2. Medical services in the United States are the best in the world, and government controls on costs will serve only to reduce the quality of care available.
3. In an era of budget deficits and trillions of dollars in national debt, the United States cannot afford to expand social welfare programs.

News »

Universal Health Care Gets Strong Backing in Senate

A bill sponsoring universal health care in the United States is likely to be reviewed by the full Senate next week. After vigorous hearings over coverage and costs, the chair of the Senate Committee on Health, Education, Labor, and Pensions said the committee would approve the bill. But it faces an uphill battle in the main chamber, as 42 senators say they will not support such drastic reform. Public opinion is divided, with a recent poll showing that Americans want everyone to have basic health care, but they do not want a new "health" tax to fund the program.

Your decision:

Support ____________________ Oppose ____________________

poor. Other scholars have criticized Murray's thesis. They have argued that there is no direct evidence that welfare encourages family breakup and have suggested that the rise in the number of illegitimate children occurred during a period (the 1970s) when welfare benefits, in real (that is, inflation-adjusted) dollars, were going down.[13]

In short, the clients of these programs never acquired in the public's mind the legitimacy necessary for their programs to prosper. As a result, whereas for 40 years it was thought to be good politics to increase old-age benefits, it increasingly became considered bad politics to do anything but attack, investigate, and curtail "welfare" programs.

Still, as we stressed in Chapter 17, the politics of policy issues can be affected by changes in people's perceptions concerning who bears the burdens and who receives the benefits. Thus, under TANF, after 1996, able-bodied adults had a harder time getting welfare benefits, but welfare-related child-care spending in most states rose significantly. The average AFDC (and later TANF) benefit amount, adjusted for inflation, has fallen since 1980. In addition, many poor parents who are eligible for an EITC grant are unaware of the program and so do not receive benefits.

In November 2009, a much-publicized report by the U.S. Department of Agriculture indicated that the number of "highly food insecure" (bureaucratic jargon for "hungry") children in America had risen from under a half a million in 2006 to over 1 million. The economic recession and unemployment surge that began in 2007 was largely responsible for a steep and steady increase in Food Stamp beneficiaries, from about 27 million that year to 44 million in 2011. And, as the economy worsened, the number of TANF beneficiaries rose a bit to about 4.5 million in 2010, though it was still way down from the pre-reform 1996 "welfare caseload" of 12.3 million.

The politics of the policy process is always hard to predict, but in the years just ahead, needy children, youth, and families might well prove more politically popular, and be more widely perceived as "deserving" government aid, than baby-boomer retirees.

LEARNING OBJECTIVES

WHAT YOU NEED TO KNOW

☑ What are the federal government's largest social welfare programs?

The federal government's largest social welfare programs are Social Security, Medicare, and Medicaid. Together, these three programs now account for over 40 percent of the federal budget. All three are still growing.

☑ How have the politics of given social welfare programs changed in recent years?

The politics of certain social welfare programs have become more polarized in recent years. One example is the politics of Medicare in 1965 versus the politics of the Patient Protection and Affordable Care Act in 2010. In terms of the model discussed in Chapter 17, majoritarian politics has become somewhat less the norm where major social welfare policies and programs are concerned.

☑ Is there a political consensus about how to address the solvency challenges facing major social welfare programs?

Barring changes, Medicare is likely to become insolvent around 2017, and by 2037 Social Security will be unable to cover all its obligations. In both cases, however, a majority opposes changes that would reduce or slow benefits or increase taxes. Many members of Congress have proposed plans, but as of mid-2011, none had any real chance of attracting bipartisan support and being enacted into law.

RECONSIDERING WHO GOVERNS?

1. How, if at all, have Americans' views of government's responsibility to help the "deserving poor" changed over time?

American welfare policy since the 1930s has undergone a slow but steady change in how it has separated the "deserving" from the "undeserving" poor. In essence, today we separate them less and are more willing to have people rely solely on the government for help. For example, even before the New Deal, most Americans would surely have counted a poor, disabled, blind, elderly woman deserted by her family as deserving of public aid. Today, however, a majority of citizens would also favor giving her aid even if she were only disabled, without regard to her income or family situation. Likewise, whereas once most Americans were inclined to provide public aid only if the beneficiary's family helped too, today most citizens do not believe in strictly conditioning public aid on family support.

2. Why are some government social welfare programs politically protected while others are politically imperiled?

Majoritarian programs (nearly everyone benefits, nearly everyone pays) like Social Security and Medicare are politically sacrosanct. Client-based programs (a relatively few number of people benefit, but almost everyone pays) like the now-defunct Aid to Families with Dependent Children (AFDC) are politically shaky. Debates about the former normally concern only how to keep the benefits flowing; debates about the latter often concern whether to keep the program ongoing. But certain client-based programs are less politically vulnerable than others—it all depends on who the clients are, or are widely perceived to be. Medicaid was protected largely because its clients included middle-class retirees who received nursing home benefits and medically needy low-income children. AFDC was targeted because its clients were perceived by many to include able-bodied adults who chose to receive public aid rather than go to work.

RECONSIDERING TO WHAT ENDS?

1. What does the Constitution mean by "promote the general Welfare"?

The phrase "promote the general Welfare" appears in the Constitution's Preamble, and Article I, Section 8 of the Constitution references "the general Welfare" again in relation to the powers of Congress. We know that the Framers of the Constitution disagreed about what the phrase was supposed to mean, but this much is certain: to none of them did it mean that government has a duty to provide cash assistance or other benefits to citizens in economic need, or that the president or Congress has to manage the economy. Regardless, since the 1930s Congress has repeatedly asserted, and the federal courts have rather consistently upheld, a constitutional power to tax and spend in accordance with antipoverty, economic recovery, and other national policy goals deemed by Congress to be in "the general welfare."

2. Should religious groups be eligible to administer some federal welfare programs?

Under four charitable choice laws, the federal government may not discriminate against community-serving faith-based organizations in the grant-making process, but these organizations are strictly prohibited from using any public funds to proselytize, provide religious instruction, or perform worship services; may not hire only coreligionists; and must serve all eligible persons without regard to religion. The courts have consistently upheld their legality and constitutionality.

QUESTIONS TO CONSIDER

1. **If it were left to you to decide how to solve the fiscal problems facing Social Security and Medicare, what mix of benefits cuts or tax increases might you propose, and how would you justify those particular changes?**
2. **If some or all federal social welfare programs did not exist, do you suppose that citizens now dependent on those programs would find alternate reliable sources of food, money, medicine, or other services?**

3. To ponder the previous question in a more personal way: do you know anyone your age (yourself included!) who plans to save money in order to help support their parents in retirement or to help pay for their parents' prescription drugs should they ever be needed?

4. How much, if at all, has the number of people receiving food stamps in your state increased over the last several years? (Hint: The U.S. Department of Agriculture tracks "food security" in America.)

5. Medicaid is a federal-state program that benefits the poor as well as elderly middle-class individuals who have spent down their savings and need long-term nursing care: how many Medicaid beneficiaries are elderly, how many are children, and how much does the program spend on each group? (Hint: The U.S. Department of Health and Human Services tracks Medicaid expenditures and compiles related data.)

6. Many citizens who have been eligible to participate in the federal earned income tax credit (EITC) program have failed to participate: what can you discover about participation rates for EITC and other federal social welfare programs?

TO LEARN MORE

Social welfare programs

Medicare: **www.medicare.gov**

Social Security: **www.ssa.gov**

TANF: **www.acf.dhhs.gov/programs/ofa/**

Views on Social Security reform

www.socialsecurityreform.org

www.socialsecurity.org

www.socsec.org

Derthick, Martha. *Policymaking for Social Security*. Washington, D.C.: Brookings Institution, 1979. A detailed analysis of how the Social Security program grew.

Eberstadt, Nicholas. *The Poverty of "The Poverty Rate": Measure and Mismeasure of Want in Modern America*. Washington, D.C.: American Enterprise Institute, 2008. A searching analysis of the official poverty rate as a measure of social welfare in America.

Heclo, Hugh. *Modern Social Politics in Britain and Sweden*. New Haven, Conn.: Yale University Press, 1974. Comparative analysis of how social welfare programs came to Britain and Sweden.

Monsma, Stephen V. *Putting Faith in Partnerships: Welfare-to-Work in Four Cities*. Ann Arbor: University of Michigan Press, 2004. Careful study of the six different types of organizations that administer welfare-to-work programs in big cities today.

Moynihan, Daniel Patrick. *Family and Nation*. New York: Harcourt Brace Jovanovich, 1986. Argument for the importance of federal policy to aid families.

Murray, Charles. *Losing Ground: American Social Policy, 1950–1980*. New York: Basic Books, 1984. An argument that federal spending on the poor actually increased poverty during the 1960s and 1970s.

Wilson, William J. *The Truly Disadvantaged*. Chicago: University of Chicago Press, 1987. Disputes Murray's explanation, arguing instead that ghetto poverty has been the result of the movement of jobs out of cities.

20 Foreign and Military Policy

LEARNING OBJECTIVES

WHAT YOU NEED TO KNOW

- ☑ Define isolationism, containment, and appeasement.
- ☑ What is meant by "rally round the flag"?
- ☑ Explain how a bipolar and a unipolar world differ.

WHO GOVERNS?

1. Is American foreign policy set by public wishes or elite views?
2. If only Congress can declare war, why has the president become so powerful in military affairs?

TO WHAT ENDS?

1. Why do we go to war against some dictatorships and not others?
2. Should our foreign policy be based on American interests or some conception of human rights?

Every American knows we struggle against terrorists—that is, against private groups that attack unarmed civilians. But this is not a recent development.

THEN Between 1801 and 1805 President Thomas Jefferson sent our navy to fight the Barbary Pirates who operated out of various North African countries against merchant shipping in the Mediterranean. They were sponsored by the Ottoman Empire, a Muslim organization based in Turkey. In the 19th century, American warships did battle with pirates in the Caribbean and along our Atlantic coast. Some terrorists operated inside the country. John Brown fought against slavery by raiding the supplies of the American military at Harper's Ferry. One might sympathize with his antislavery views, but he and his followers killed innocent civilians. He was caught and hanged.

After the Civil War the Ku Klux Klan (KKK) was formed to block the emancipation of blacks by lynching them and shooting into their homes as well those of sympathetic whites. The first KKK, created in the 19th century, was replaced by a second one created in the 20th; each of them enrolled several million members and continued the policy of harassment and murder. Although a KKK still exists, it only has a few thousand members and rarely commits an illegal act. To defeat the Klan, in 1871 Congress passed the "Klan Act" that gave the president the power to suspend the writ of habeas corpus in any state where ordinary law enforcement procedures were unavailable and afforded people the right to sue officials who violated their rights.

In the 1960s and 1970s, the Weather Underground, a radical leftist organization, bombed police stations, the Pentagon, and a townhouse; threw Molotov cocktails through a judge's window; and robbed a Brink's armored car. Though several of its leaders have abandoned radical action and taken respectable jobs, they denounce conservatives in and out of government in the strongest language.

NOW The 9/11 attacks by hijacked aircraft against the World Trade Center and the Pentagon ushered in a new phase and represented a much more deadly form of terrorism than what we have encountered in the past. The evidence suggests that this attack, as well as the bombing of two American embassies and the suicide attack on the USS *Cole,* were carried out by al Qaeda, a radical Islamic group founded by Osama bin Laden

and his colleagues. ("Al Qaeda" means "the base.") But these attacks were different from that on Pearl Harbor: the latter attack had, so to speak, a return address—we knew who did it and where they lived. But 9/11 had no return address: it was a terrorist attack waged by small groups that could be located anywhere.

In response, the United States launched an attack on Afghanistan where the ruling party, the Taliban, had supported and helped train al Qaeda, and passed the Patriot Act that improved cooperation among intelligence and law enforcement agencies. The federal government amended the Foreign Intelligence Surveillance Act (FISA) that makes it possible for us to eavesdrop on communications that cross our national borders. In 2011, Osama bin Laden, the founder of al Qaeda, was found in Pakistan and killed by American special forces operatives.

Such choices must be made in a democracy, and some observers think democratic politics makes managing foreign and military policy harder. Tocqueville said the conduct of foreign affairs requires precisely those qualities most lacking in a democratic nation: "A democracy can only with great difficulty regulate the details of an important undertaking, persevere in a fixed design, and work out its execution in spite of serious obstacles. It cannot combine its measures with secrecy or await their consequences with patience."[1] In plain language, a democracy is forced to play foreign policy poker with its cards turned up. As a result, aggressors from Hitler to Saddam Hussein can bluff or misjudge us.

But other writers disagree with Tocqueville. To them, the strength of democracy is that, though it rarely if ever wages an unjustified war on another country, its

© PPImages / Demotix/Demotix/Corbis

In May 2011 Osama bin Laden was killed by U.S. special forces in the house behind this wall, located in Abbottabad, Pakistan.

people, when mobilized by the president, will support our overseas engagements even when many deaths occur.[2]

Kinds of Foreign Policy

The majoritarian component of foreign policy includes those decisions (and nondecisions) perceived to confer widely distributed benefits and impose widely distributed costs. The decision to go to war is an obvious example of this. So, too, are the establishment of military alliances with Western Europe, the negotiation of a nuclear test ban treaty or a strategic arms limitation agreement, the response to the placement of Soviet offensive missiles in Cuba, and the opening up of diplomatic relations with the People's Republic of China. These may be good or bad policies, but the benefits and costs accrue to the nation generally.

Some argue that the costs of many of these policies are in fact highly concentrated—for example, soldiers bear the burden of a military operation—but that turns out, on closer inspection, not to shape the positions that people take on issues of war and peace. Though soldiers and their immediate families may feel the costs of a war to an especially high degree, public opinion surveys taken during the Vietnam War showed that having a family member in the armed forces did not significantly affect how people evaluated the war.[3] There is a sense that, during wartime, we are all in this together.

Foreign policy decisions may also reflect interest group politics. Tariff decisions confer benefits on certain business firms and labor unions and impose costs on other firms and unions. If the price of Japanese steel imported into this country is increased by tariffs, quotas, or other devices, this helps the American steel industry and the United Steel Workers of America. On the other hand, it hurts those firms (and associated unions) that had been purchasing the once-cheap Japanese steel.

Examples of client politics also occur in foreign affairs. Washington often provides aid to American corporations doing business abroad because the aid helps those firms directly without imposing any apparent costs on an equally distinct group in society. Americans support Israel partly because Jewish organizations back her and partly because they admire that embattled democracy. Arab Americans have begun to organize and to press on the government concerns that are very different from the pro-Israel arguments.

Who has power in foreign policy depends very much on what kind of foreign policy we have in mind. Where it is of a majoritarian nature, the president is clearly the dominant figure, and much, if not everything, depends on his beliefs and skills and on those of his chief advisers. Public opinion will ordinarily support this presidential leadership, but it will not guide it. Woe to the president who by his actions forfeits that trust.

When interest group or client politics is involved, Congress plays a much larger role. Although Congress has a subsidiary role in the conduct of foreign diplomacy, the decision to send troops overseas, or the direction of intelligence operations, it has a large one in decisions involving foreign economic aid, the structure of the tariff system, the shipment of weapons to foreign allies, the creation of new weapons systems, and the support of Israel.

And Congress is the central political arena on those occasions when entrepreneurial politics shapes

Fars/Abaca/Newscom

A nuclear reactor in southern Iran. America suspects that Iran will build nuclear weapons somewhere in that country.

foreign policy. If a multinational corporation is caught in a scandal, congressional investigations shake the usual indifference of politicians to the foreign conduct of such corporations. If presidential policies abroad lead to reversals, as when in 1986 presidential aides sought to trade arms for U.S. hostages in Iran and then use some profits from the arms sales to support the anti-Marxist contras fighting in Nicaragua, Congress becomes the forum for investigations and criticism. At such moments Congress often seeks to expand its power over foreign affairs.

In this chapter, we will be chiefly concerned with foreign policy insofar as it displays the characteristics of majoritarian politics. Limiting the discussion in this way permits us to focus on the grand issues of foreign affairs—war, peace, and global diplomacy. It allows us to see how choices are made in a situation in which public majorities support but do not direct policy, in which opinion tends to react to events, and in which interest groups are relatively unimportant.

The Constitutional and Legal Context

The Constitution defines the authority of the president and of Congress in foreign affairs in a way that, as Edward Corwin put it, is an "invitation to struggle."[4] The president is commander in chief of the armed forces, but Congress must authorize and appropriate money for those forces. The president appoints ambassadors, but they must be confirmed by the Senate. The president may negotiate treaties, but the Senate must ratify these by a two-thirds vote. Only Congress may regulate commerce with other nations and "declare" war. (In an early draft of the Constitution, the Framers gave Congress the power to "make" war but changed this to "declare" so that the president, acting without Congress, could take military measures to repel a sudden attack.) Because power over foreign affairs is shared by the president and Congress, conflict between them is to be expected.

Yet almost every American thinks instinctively that the president is in charge of foreign affairs, and what popular opinion supposes, the historical record confirms. Presidents have asserted the right to send troops abroad on their own authority in more than 125 instances. Only six of the 13 major wars that this country has fought have followed a formal declaration of war by Congress.[5] The State Department, the Central Intelligence Agency, and the National Security Agency are almost entirely "presidential" agencies, with only modest congressional control. The Defense Department, though keenly sensitive to congressional views on weapons procurement and the location of military bases, is very much under the control of the president on matters of military strategy. While the Senate has since 1789 ratified well over 1,000 treaties signed by the president, the president during this period also has signed around 7,000 executive agreements with other countries that did not require Senate ratification and yet have the force of law.[6]

PRESIDENTIAL BOX SCORE

When the president seeks congressional approval for foreign policy matters, he tends to win more often than when he asks for support on domestic matters. One student of the presidency, Aaron Wildavsky, concluded that the American political system has "two presidencies"—one in domestic affairs that is relatively weak and closely checked, and another in foreign affairs that is quite powerful.[7] As we shall see, this view considerably overstates presidential power in certain areas.

When it comes to international diplomacy and the use of American troops, the president is indeed strong, much stronger than the Framers may have intended and certainly stronger than many members of Congress would prefer. Examples abound:

- 1861: Abraham Lincoln blockaded southern ports and declared martial law.
- 1940: Franklin D. Roosevelt sent 50 destroyers to England to be used against Germany, with which we were then technically at peace.
- 1950: Harry Truman sent American troops into South Korea to help repulse a North Korean attack on that country.
- 1960s: John F. Kennedy and Lyndon Johnson sent American forces into South Vietnam without a declaration of war.
- 1983: Ronald Reagan sent troops to overthrow a pro-Castro regime in Grenada.
- 1989: George H. W. Bush ordered the U.S. invasion of Panama to depose dictator Manuel Noriega.
- 1990: Bush ordered troops to Saudi Arabia in response to Iraq's invasion of Kuwait.
- 1999: Bill Clinton ordered the military to attack, with bombs and cruise missiles, Serbian forces that were trying to control Kosovo.
- 2001: George W. Bush sent U.S. troops to liberate Afghanistan from the Taliban, a regime supportive of Osama bin Laden, the architect of the September 11 terrorist attacks.

- 2003: Bush, with some allies, invaded Iraq.
- 2010: President Obama had to decide how to react to popular revolts in Egypt, Libya, Syria, and Tunisia (the "Arab Spring").

However, by the standards of other nations, even other democratic ones, the ability of an American president to act decisively often appears rather modest. England was dismayed at the inability of Woodrow Wilson in 1914–1915 and Franklin Roosevelt in 1939–1940 to enter into an alliance when England was engaged in a major war with Germany. Wilson was unable to bring this country into the League of Nations. Gerald Ford could not intervene covertly in Angola in support of an anti-Marxist faction. Ronald Reagan was heavily criticized in Congress for sending 55 military advisers to El Salvador and a few hundred Marines to Lebanon. After George H. W. Bush sent U.S. troops to the Persian Gulf in 1990, he began a long debate with Congress over whether he would need a formal declaration of war before the troops were sent into combat. George W. Bush's decision to invade Iraq in 2003 became bitterly controversial in the 2004, 2006, and 2008 elections.

Furthermore, a treaty signed by the president is little more than his promise to try to get the Senate to go along. He can sign executive agreements without Senate consent, but most of these are authorized in advance by Congress.[8]

By contrast, the leaders of other democratic nations (to say nothing of totalitarian ones) often are able to act with much greater freedom. While Reagan was arguing with Congress over whether we should assign any military advisers to El Salvador, the president of France, François Mitterrand, ordered 2,500 combat troops to Chad with scarcely a ripple of opposition. A predecessor of Mitterrand, Charles de Gaulle, brought France into the European Common Market over the explicit opposition of the French Assembly and granted independence to Algeria, then a French colony, without seriously consulting the Assembly.[9] The British prime minister brought his country into the Common Market despite popular opposition and can declare war without the consent of Parliament.[10]

Shifting Patterns of Leadership in Foreign Policy

Depending on the personalities, skills, and interests of those involved, leadership in making American foreign policy may be found centered in the White House (the president and his national security adviser) or in the State Department (the secretary of state).

Periods of White House Dominance

President	*Secretary of State*
Franklin D. Roosevelt	Cordell Hull (1933–1944)
John F. Kennedy (and National Security Adviser McGeorge Bundy)	Dean Rusk (1961–1969)
Richard M. Nixon (and National Security Adviser Henry A. Kissinger)	William P. Rogers (1969–1973)

Periods of Leadership by the Secretary of State

Secretary of State	*President*
George C. Marshall (1947–1949) and Dean Acheson (1949–1953)	Harry S. Truman
John Foster Dulles (1953–1959)	Dwight D. Eisenhower
Henry A. Kissinger (1973–1977)	Gerald R. Ford
Warren Christopher (1993–1996)	Bill Clinton

Periods of Tension between the White House and Secretary of State

President	*Secretary of State*
Jimmy Carter	Cyrus Vance (1977–1980)
Ronald Reagan	George Shultz (1982–1989)

EVALUATING THE POWER OF THE PRESIDENT

Whether one thinks the president is too strong or too weak in foreign affairs depends not only on whether one holds a domestic or international point of view but also on whether one agrees or disagrees with his policies. Historian Arthur M. Schlesinger, Jr., thought that President Kennedy exercised commendable presidential vigor when he made a unilateral decision to impose a naval blockade on Cuba to induce the Soviets to remove missiles installed there. However, he viewed President Nixon's decision to extend U.S. military action in Vietnam into neighboring Cambodia as a deplorable example of the "imperial presidency."[11] To be sure, there were important differences between these two actions, but that is precisely the point: a president strong enough to do something that one thinks proper is also strong enough to do something that one finds wrong.

The Supreme Court has fairly consistently supported the view that the federal government has powers in the conduct of foreign and military policy beyond those specifically mentioned in the Constitution. The leading decision, rendered in 1936, holds that the right to carry out foreign policy is an inherent attribute of any sovereign nation:

> *The power to declare and wage war, to conclude peace, to make treaties, to maintain diplomatic relations with other sovereignties, if they had never been mentioned in the Constitution, would have vested in the Federal Government as necessary concomitants of nationality.*[12]

The individual states have few rights in foreign affairs.

© Bettmann/CORBIS

In 1962 President Kennedy forced the Soviet Union to withdraw the missiles it had placed in Cuba after their presence was revealed by aerial photograph.

Moreover, the Supreme Court has been reluctant to intervene in disputes over the conduct of foreign affairs. When various members of Congress brought suit challenging the right of President Nixon to enlarge the war in Vietnam without congressional approval, the court of appeals handled the issue, as one scholar was later to describe it, with all the care of porcupines making love. The Court said it was a matter for the president and Congress to decide and that if Congress was unwilling to cut off the money to pay for the war, it should not expect the courts to do the job for it.[13]

The Supreme Court upheld the extraordinary measures taken by President Lincoln during the Civil War and refused to interfere with the conduct of the Vietnam War by Presidents Johnson and Nixon.[14] After Iran seized American hostages in 1979, President Carter froze Iranian assets in this country. To win the hostages' freedom the president later agreed to return some of these assets and to nullify claims on them by American companies. The Court upheld the nullification because it was necessary for the resolution of a foreign policy dispute.[15]

How great the deference to presidential power may be is vividly illustrated by the actions of President Franklin Roosevelt in ordering the army to move more than 100,000 Japanese Americans—the great majority of them born in this country and citizens of the United States—from their homes on the West Coast to inland "relocation centers" for the duration of World War II. Though this action was a wholesale violation of the constitutional rights of U.S. citizens and was unprecedented in American history, the Supreme Court decided that with the West Coast vulnerable to attack by Japan, the president was within his rights to declare that people of Japanese ancestry might pose a threat to internal security; thus the relocation order was upheld.[16] (No Japanese American was ever found guilty of espionage or sabotage.) One of the few cases in which the Court denied the president broad wartime powers occurred in 1952, when by a 5-to-4 vote it reversed President Truman's seizure of the steel mills—a move that he had made in order to avert a strike that, in his view, would have imperiled the war effort in Korea.[17]

CHECKS ON PRESIDENTIAL POWER

If there is a check on the powers of the federal government or the president in foreign affairs, it is chiefly political rather than constitutional. The most important check is Congress's control of the purse strings. In addition, Congress has imposed three important kinds of restrictions on the president's freedom of action, all since Vietnam:

LIMITATIONS ON THE PRESIDENT'S ABILITY TO GIVE MILITARY OR ECONOMIC AID TO OTHER COUNTRIES

For example, between 1974 and 1978 the president could not sell arms to Turkey because of a dispute between Turkey and Greece over control of the island of Cyprus. The pressure on Congress from groups supporting Greece was much stronger than that from groups supporting Turkey. In 1976, Congress prevented President Ford from giving aid to the pro-Western faction in the Angolan civil war. Until the method was declared unconstitutional, Congress for many years could use a legislative veto, a resolution disapproving of an executive decision (see Chapter 15), to block the sale by the president of arms worth more than $25 million to another country.

THE WAR POWERS ACT

Passed in 1973 over a presidential veto, this law placed the following restrictions on the president's ability to use military force:

- He must report in writing to Congress within 48 hours after he introduces U.S. troops into areas where hostilities have occurred or are imminent.
- Within 60 days after troops are sent into hostile situations, Congress must, by declaration of war or other specific statutory authorization, provide for the continuation of hostile action by U.S. troops.
- If Congress fails to provide such authorization, the president must withdraw the troops (unless Congress has been prevented from meeting as a result of an armed attack).
- If Congress passes a concurrent resolution (which the president may not veto) directing the removal of U.S. troops, the president must comply.

Until recently the War Powers Act has had very little influence on American military actions. Since its passage every president—Ford, Carter, Reagan, Bush the elder, Clinton, Bush the younger, and Obama—has sent American forces abroad without any explicit congressional authorization. (Bush the elder asked for that support when he attacked Iraq and, by a narrow margin, received it.) No president has acknowledged that the War Powers Act is constitutional. In its 1983 decision in the *Chadha* case, the Supreme Court struck down the legislative veto, which means that this section of the act is already in constitutional trouble.[18]

National Archives

Following the attack on Pearl Harbor, in 1942 President Roosevelt ordered that all Japanese Americans living on the West Coast be interned in prison camps.

Even if the act is constitutional, politically it is all but impossible to use. Few members of Congress would challenge a president who carried out a successful military operation (for example, those in Grenada, Panama, and Afghanistan). More might challenge the president if, after a while, the military action were in trouble, but the easiest way to do that would be to cut off funding for the operation. But even during the Vietnam War, a conflict that preceded the War Powers Act, Congress, though it contained many critics of U.S. policy, never stopped military appropriations.

In 2011, however, after this country, working with the North Atlantic Treaty Organization (NATO), used military resources in support of rebels attacking the despotic regime of Muammar Gaddafi in Libya, Republicans in Congress (who in the past had shown little interest in the War Powers Act) attacked President Obama over his failure to comply with it.

INTELLIGENCE OVERSIGHT

Owing to the low political stock of President Nixon during the Watergate scandal and the revelations of illegal operations by the Central Intelligence Agency (CIA) within the United States, Congress required that the CIA notify appropriate congressional committees about any proposed covert action (between 1974 and 1980 it had to notify *eight* different committees). Today it must keep two groups, the House and the Senate Intelligence Committees, "fully and currently informed" of all intelligence activities, including covert actions. The committees do not have the authority to disapprove such actions.

However, from time to time Congress will pass a bill blocking particular covert actions. This happened when the Boland Amendment (named after its sponsor, Representative Edward Boland) was passed on several occasions between 1982 and 1985. Each version of the amendment prevented, for specifically stated periods, intelligence agencies from supplying military aid to the Nicaraguan contras.

The 9/11 surprise terrorist attacks left everyone wondering why our intelligence agencies had not foreseen them. After the attacks, there was an investigation to find out why the CIA had not warned the country of this risk. In an effort to improve matters,

Rivalry Versus Cooperation: The President and the Senate

Because the Senate must ratify treaties and consent to the appointment of ambassadors and other high foreign policy officials, it has the opportunity to play a large role in the conduct of foreign affairs. The key figure in the Senate is usually the chairman of the Senate Foreign Relations Committee.

Depending on personalities and circumstances, the president and the chairman have sometimes been able to work together closely but at other times have been bitter, outspoken rivals. In general, cooperation occurs when there is a widely shared foreign policy worldview; rivalry erupts when worldviews diverge.

Periods of Shared Worldviews and Political Cooperation

President	*Chairman of Foreign Relations Committee*
Franklin D. Roosevelt	Tom Connally (1941–1947, 1949–1953)
Harry S. Truman	Arthur H. Vandenberg (1947–1949)

Periods of Competing Worldviews and Political Rivalry

President	*Chairman of Foreign Relations Committee*
Woodrow Wilson	Henry Cabot Lodge (1919–1924)
Lyndon B. Johnson	J. William Fulbright (1959–1975)
Richard M. Nixon	J. William Fulbright (1959–1975)
Bill Clinton	Jesse Helms (1995–1999)

Congress passed and President Bush signed a law creating the Office of the Director of National Intelligence (DNI). It was designed to coordinate the work of the CIA, the FBI, the Defense Intelligence Agency (DIA), and the intelligence units of several other government agencies. The DNI replaced the director of the CIA as the president's chief adviser. It is too early to tell how much real coordination will occur; the DNI's office is another large bureaucracy placed on top of other big ones.

The Machinery of Foreign Policy

From the time that Thomas Jefferson took the job in Washington's first administration until well into the 20th century, foreign policy was often made and almost always carried out by the secretary of state. No more. When America became a major world power during and after World War II, our commitments overseas expanded dramatically. With that expansion two things happened. First, the president began to put foreign policy at the top of his agenda and to play a larger role in directing it. Second, that policy was shaped by the scores of agencies (some brand-new) that had acquired overseas activities.

Today Washington, D.C., has not one State Department but many. The Defense Department has military bases and military advisers abroad. The Central Intelligence Agency has intelligence officers abroad, most of them assigned to "stations" that are part of the American embassy but not under the full control of the American ambassador there. The Departments of Agriculture, Commerce, and Labor have missions abroad. The Federal Bureau of Investigation and the Drug Enforcement Administration have agents abroad. The Agency for International Development has offices to dispense foreign aid in host countries. The U.S. Information Agency runs libraries, radio stations, and educational programs abroad.

Every new secretary of state bravely announces he or she is going to "coordinate" and "direct" this enormous foreign policy establishment. He or she never does. The reason is partly that the job is too big for any one person and partly that most of these agencies owe no political or bureaucratic loyalty to the secretary of state. If anyone is to coordinate them, it will have to be the president. But the president cannot keep track of what all these organizations are doing in the more than 190 nations and 50 international organizations where we have representatives, or in the more than 800 international conferences that we attend each year.

So he has hired a staff to do the coordinating for him. That staff is part of the National Security Council (NSC), a committee created by statute and chaired by the president, whose members include by law the vice president and the secretaries of state and defense, by custom the director of national intelligence (DNI), the chairman of the Joint Chiefs of Staff, and often the attorney general. Depending on the president, the NSC can be an important body in which to hammer out foreign policy. Attached to it is a staff headed by the national security adviser. That staff, which usually numbers a few dozen men and women, can be (again, depending on the president) an enormously powerful instrument for formulating and directing foreign policy.

Presidents Truman and Eisenhower made only limited use of the NSC staff, but beginning with President Kennedy it has grown greatly in influence. Its head, the national security adviser, has come to rival the secretary of state for foreign policy leadership, especially when the adviser is a powerful personality such as Henry Kissinger. President Reagan attempted to downgrade the importance of the national security adviser, but ironically it was one of his relatively low-visibility appointees, Admiral John Poindexter, and his subordinate, Lieutenant Colonel Oliver North, who precipitated the worst crisis of the Reagan presidency when, allegedly without informing the president, they tried to use cash realized from the secret sale of arms to Iran to finance guerrillas fighting against the Marxist government of Nicaragua. The sale and the diversion became known, North was fired, a congressional investigation ensued, criminal charges were filed against Poindexter and North, and the president's political position was weakened. But even in ordinary times the NSC staff has been the rival of the secretary of state, except during that period in the Ford administration when Henry Kissinger held *both* jobs.

The way in which the machinery of foreign policymaking operates has two major consequences for the substance of that policy. First, as former secretary of state George Shultz asserted, "It's never over." Foreign policy issues are endlessly agitated, rarely settled. The reason is that the rivalries *within* the executive branch intensify the rivalries *between* that branch and Congress. In ways already described, Congress has steadily increased its influence over the conduct of foreign policy. Anybody in the executive branch who loses out in a struggle over foreign policy can take his or her case (usually by means of a well-timed leak) to a sympathetic member of Congress, who then can make a speech, hold a hearing, or introduce a bill.

Second, the interests of the various organizations making up the foreign policy establishment profoundly affect the positions that they take. Because the State Department has a stake in diplomacy, it tends to resist bold or controversial new policies that might upset established relationships with other countries. Part of the CIA has a stake in gathering and analyzing information; that part tends to be skeptical of the claims of other agencies that their overseas operations are succeeding. Another part of the CIA conducts covert operations abroad; it tends to resent or ignore the skepticism of the intelligence analysts. The air force flies airplanes and so tends to be optimistic about what can be accomplished through the use of air power in particular and military power in general; the army, on the other hand, which must fight in the trenches, is often dubious about the prospects for military success. During the American war in Iraq, the conflict between the CIA and the Defense Department was great, with each side leaking information to the press.

Landmark Cases

Foreign Affairs

- ***Curtiss-Wright Export Corp. v. United States* (1936):** American foreign policy is vested entirely in the federal government where the president has plenary power.
- ***Korematsu v. United States* (1944):** Sending Japanese Americans to relocation centers during World War II was based on an acceptable military justification.
- ***Youngstown Sheet & Tube Co. v. Sawyer* (1952):** The president may not seize factories during wartime without explicit congressional authority even when they are threatened by a strike.
- ***Hamdi v. Rumsfeld* (2004):** An American citizen in jail because he allegedly joined the Taliban extremist group should have access to a "neutral decision maker."
- ***Rasul v. Bush* (2004):** Foreign nationals held at Guantanamo Bay because they are believed to be terrorists have a right to bring their cases before an American court.

Americans often worry that their government is keeping secrets from them. In fact, there are no secrets in Washington—at least not for long.

Foreign Policy and Public Opinion

These organizational conflicts shape the details of foreign policy, but its broad outlines are shaped by public and elite opinion.

World War II was the great watershed event in American foreign policy. Before that time, a clear majority of the American public opposed active involvement in world affairs. The public saw the costs of such involvement as being substantially in excess of the benefits, and only determined, skillful leaders were able, as was President Roosevelt during 1939–1940, to affect in even a limited fashion the diplomatic and military struggles then convulsing Europe and Asia.

In 1937, 94 percent of the American public preferred the policy of doing "everything possible to keep out of foreign wars" to the policy of doing "everything possible to prevent war, even if it means threatening to fight countries that fight wars." In 1939, after World War II had begun in Europe but before Pearl Harbor was attacked, only 13 percent of Americans polled thought that we should enter the war against Germany. Just a month before Pearl Harbor, only 19 percent felt that the United States should take steps, at the risk of war, to prevent Japan from becoming too powerful.[19] Congress reflected the noninterventionist mood of the country: in the summer of 1941, with war breaking out almost everywhere, the proposal to continue the draft passed the House of Representatives by only one vote.

The Japanese attack on Pearl Harbor on December 7 changed all that. Not only was the American war effort supported almost unanimously, not only did Congress approve the declaration of war with only one dissenting vote, but World War II—unlike World War I—produced popular support for an active assumption of international responsibilities that continued after the war had ended.[20] Whereas after World War I a majority opposed U.S. entry into the League of Nations, after World War II a clear majority favored our entry into the United Nations.[21]

This willingness to see the United States remain a world force persisted. Even during the Vietnam War the number of people thinking that we should "keep independent" in world affairs as opposed to "working closely with other nations" rose from 10 percent in 1963 to only 22 percent in 1969.[22] In 1967, after more than two years of war in Vietnam, 44 percent of Americans believed that this country had an obligation to "defend other Vietnams if they are threatened by communism."[23]

Before 9/11, hardly any American thought we should fight a war in Afghanistan, but after that attack we fought exactly that war in order to get rid of the Taliban regime. The Taliban, a group of radical young Muslims, had taken control of that country and allowed Osama bin Laden, the head of al Qaeda, to use the nation as a place to train and direct terrorists. Though al Qaeda designed and carried out the 9/11 attacks on America, it is not a single organization located in one place and thus easily defeated. It is instead a network of terrorist cells found all over the world that is allied with other terrorist groups.

But the support for an internationalist American foreign policy was, and is, highly general and heavily dependent on the phrasing of poll questions, the opinions expressed by popular leaders, and the impact of world events. Public opinion, while more internationalist than once was the case, is both mushy and volatile. Just prior to President Nixon's decision to send troops into Cambodia, only 7 percent of the people said they supported such a move. After the troops were sent and Nixon made a speech explaining his move, 50 percent of the public said they supported it.[24] Similarly, only 49 percent of the people favored halting the American bombing of North Vietnam before President Johnson ordered such a halt in 1968; afterward 60 percent of the people said they supported such a policy.[25]

BACKING THE PRESIDENT

Much of this volatility in specific opinions (as opposed to general mood) reflects the already-mentioned deference to the "commander in chief" and a desire to support the United States when it confronts other nations. Table 20.1 shows the proportion of people who said that they approved of the way the president was doing his job before and after various major foreign policy events. Almost every foreign crisis increased the level of public approval of the president, often dramatically. The most vivid illustration of this was the Bay of Pigs fiasco: an American-supported, American-directed invasion of Cuba by anti-Castro Cuban émigrés was driven back into the sea. President Kennedy accepted responsibility for the aborted project. His popularity *rose.* (Comparable data for domestic crises tend to show no similar effect.)

This tendency to "rally round the flag" operates for some but not all foreign military crises.[26] The rally not only helped Kennedy after the Bay of Pigs, but it also helped Ronald Reagan when he invaded Grenada and George Bush the elder when he sent troops to fight Iraq. But it did not help Bill Clinton when he sent forces to Bosnia or launched bombing attacks on

Table 20.1 Popular Reactions to Foreign Policy Crises

Percentage of public saying that they approve of the way the president is handling his job

Foreign Policy Crisis		Before	After
1960	American U-2 spy plane shot down over Soviet Union	62%	68%
1961	Abortive landing at Bay of Pigs in Cuba	73	83
1962	Cuban missile crisis	61	74
1975	President Ford sends forces to rescue the American ship	40	51
1979	American embassy in Teheran seized by Iranians	32	61
1980	Failure of military effort to rescue hostages in Iran	39	43
1983	U.S. invasion of Grenada	43	53
1989	U.S. invasion of Panama	71	80
1990	U.S. troops to Persian Gulf	60	75
1995	U.S. troops to Bosnia	59	54
1999	U.S. troops to Kosovo	55	51
2001	U.S. combat in Afghanistan	51	86
2003	U.S. invasion of Iraq	58	71
2011	U.S. kills Osama bin Laden	46	52

Source: Updated from Theodore J. Lowi, *The End of Liberalism* (New York: Norton, 1969), 184. Poll data are from Gallup poll. Time lapse between "before" and "after" samplings of opinion was in no case more than one month.

Iraq. If there is an attack on America, the president will do very well. Just before September 11, 2001, George Bush's favorability rating was 51 percent; just after the attack, it was 86 percent.

Sometimes people argue that whatever support a president gets during a military crisis will disappear once dead soldiers in body bags begin returning home. There are two things wrong with this statement. First, dead soldiers do not come home in body bags; they come home in coffins. Second, a close study of how casualty rates affect public opinion showed that although deaths tend to reduce how "favorable" people are toward a war, what they then support is not withdrawal but an *escalation* in the fighting so as to defeat the enemy more quickly. This was true during Korea, Vietnam, and the Persian Gulf War.[27]

In sum, people tend to be leery of overseas military expeditions by the United States—until they start. Then they support them and want to win, even if it means more intense fighting. When Americans began to dislike our involvement in Korea and Vietnam,[28] they did not conclude that we should pull out; they concluded instead that we should do whatever was necessary to win. The invasion of Iraq did not raise large questions for Americans until terrorist attacks on the American military continued after the Iraqi army had been defeated.

Despite the tendency for most Americans to rally round the flag, there has been for many decades some public opposition to almost any war in which the United States participates. About one-fifth of Americans opposed our invading Iraq, about the same level of opposition to our wars in Korea and Vietnam. Opposition has generally been highest among Democrats, African Americans, and people with a postgraduate degree.[29]

MASS VERSUS ELITE OPINION

The public is poorly informed about foreign affairs. It probably has only a vague idea where Kosovo is, how far it is from Baghdad to Kuwait, or why the Palestinians and the Jews disagree about the future of Israel. But that is to be expected. Foreign affairs are, well, foreign. They do not have much to do with the daily lives of American citizens, except during wartime. But the public, since World War II, has consistently felt that the United States should play an important international role.[30] And if our troops go abroad, it is a foolish politician who will try to talk the public out of supporting them.

Political elites, however, have a different perspective. They are better informed about foreign policy issues, but their opinions are more likely to change rapidly. Initially, college-educated people gave *more* support to the war in Vietnam than those without college training; by the end of the war, however, that support had decreased dramatically. Whereas the average citizen was upset when the United States seemed to be on the *defensive* in Vietnam, college-educated voters tended to be more upset when the United States was on the *offensive*.[31]

Though the average citizen did not want our military in Vietnam in the first place, he or she felt that we should support our troops once they were there. The average person also was deeply opposed to the antiwar protests taking place on college campuses. When the Chicago police roughed up antiwar demonstrators at the 1968 Democratic convention, public sentiment was overwhelmingly on the side of the police.[32] Contrary to myths much accepted at the time, younger people were *not* more opposed to the war than older ones. There was no "generation gap."

By contrast, college-educated citizens, thinking at first that troops should be involved, soon changed their minds, decided that the war was wrong, and grew increasingly upset when the United States seemed to be enlarging the war (by invading Cambodia, for example). College students protested against the war largely on moral grounds, and their protests received more support from college-educated adults than from other citizens.

Elite opinion changes more rapidly than public opinion. During the Vietnam War, upper-middle-class people who regularly read several magazines and newspapers underwent a dramatic change in opinion between 1964 (when they supported the war) and 1968 (when they opposed it). But the views of blue-collar workers scarcely changed at all.[33]

The cleavage between mass and elite opinion is even wider if you restrict the definition of *elite* to only those involved in making foreign policy rather than including all college-educated people. In Table 20.2, we see the differences in foreign policy views of a cross section of American citizens and a group of 450 leaders active in government, academia, the mass media, and various organizations concerned with foreign affairs.[34]

In general the leaders have a more liberal and internationalist outlook than the public: they are more likely to favor giving economic aid to other countries and defending our allies. The public, on the other hand, wants the United States to be less active overseas and worries about protecting the jobs of American workers. Accordingly, it wants the United States to protect American jobs from foreign competition and give less economic aid to other nations.

Table 20.2 How the Public and the Elite See Foreign Policy 2004

	Percentage Agreeing	
	Public	Leaders
Combating international terrorism should be very important	71	84
Protect jobs of American workers	78	41
Reduce illegal immigration	59	21
Support U.S. troops in Afghanistan	60	92
Use U.S. troops to defend South Korea if attacked by North	43	82
Take Israel's side in conflicts with Palestinians	17	15
Expand economic aid to other countries	8	61

Source: *Global Views 2004* (Chicago: Chicago Council on Foreign Relations, 2004).

Cleavages Among Foreign Policy Elites

As we have seen, public opinion on foreign policy is permissive and a bit mushy: it supports presidential action without giving it much direction. Elite opinion therefore acquires extraordinary importance. Of course events and world realities are also important, but since events have no meaning except as they are perceived and interpreted by people who must react to them, the attitudes and beliefs of those people in and out of government who are actively involved in shaping foreign policy often assume decisive importance.

Contrary to the views of people who think that some shadowy, conspiratorial group of insiders runs our foreign policy, the foreign policy elite in this country is deeply divided. That elite consists not only of those people with administrative positions in the foreign policy field—the senior officials of the State Department and the staff of the National Security Council—but also the members and staffs of the key congressional committees concerned with foreign affairs (chiefly the Senate Foreign Relations Committee and the House International Relations Committee) and various private organizations that help shape elite opinion, such as the members of the Council on Foreign Relations and the editors of two important publications, *Foreign Affairs* and *Foreign Policy.* To these must be added influential columnists and editorial writers whose work appears regularly in the national press. One could extend the list by adding ever-wider circles of people with some influence (lobbyists, professors, leaders of veterans' organizations); this would complicate without changing the central point: elite beliefs are probably more important in explaining foreign policy than in accounting for decisions in other policy areas.

worldviews A comprehensive opinion of how the United States should respond to world problems.

HOW A WORLDVIEW SHAPES FOREIGN POLICY

These beliefs can be described in simplified terms as **worldviews** (or, as some social scientists put it, as paradigms)—more or less comprehensive mental pictures of the critical problems facing the United States in the world and of the appropriate and inappropriate ways of responding to these problems. The clearest, most concise, and perhaps most influential statement of one worldview that held sway for many years was in an article published in 1947 in *Foreign Affairs,* titled "The Sources of Soviet Conduct."[35] Written by a "Mr. X" (later revealed to be George F. Kennan, director of the Policy Planning Staff of the State Department and thereafter ambassador to Moscow), the article argued that the Russians were pursuing a policy of expansion that could only be met by the United States' applying "unalterable counterforce at every point where they show signs of encroaching upon the interests of a peaceful and stable world." This he called the strategy of "containment," and it became the governing principle of American foreign policy for at least two decades.

There were critics of the containment policy at the time—Walter Lippmann, in his book *The Cold War,* argued against it in 1947[36]—but the criticisms were less influential than the doctrine. A dominant worldview is important precisely because it prevails over alternative views. One reason why it prevails is that it is broadly consistent with the public's mood. In 1947, when Kennan wrote, popular attitudes toward the Soviet Union, favorable during World War II when Russia and America were allies, had turned quite hostile. In 1946, less than one-fourth of the American people believed Russia could be trusted to cooperate with this country,[37] and by 1948 over three-fourths were convinced the Soviet Union was trying not simply to defend itself but to become the dominant world power.[38]

Such a worldview was also influential because it was consistent with events at the time: Russia had occupied most of the previously independent countries of Eastern Europe and was turning them into puppet regimes. When governments independent of both the United States and the Soviet Union attempted to rule in Hungary and Czechoslovakia, they were overthrown by Soviet-backed coups. A worldview also becomes dominant when it is consistent with the prior experiences of the people holding it.

FOUR WORLDVIEWS

Every generation of political leaders comes to power with a foreign policy worldview shaped, in large measure, by the real or apparent mistakes of the previous generation.[39] This pattern can be traced back, some have argued, to the very beginnings of the nation. Frank L. Klingberg traces the alteration since 1776 between two national "moods" that favored first "extroversion" (or an active, internationalist policy) and then "introversion" (a less active, even isolationist posture).[40]

isolationism The opinion that the United States should withdraw from world affairs.

containment The belief that the United States should resist the expansion of aggressive nations, especially the former Soviet Union.

Since the 1920s, American elite opinion has moved through four dominant worldviews: isolationism, containment (or antiappeasement), disengagement, and human rights. **Isolationism** was the view adopted as a result of our unhappy experience in World War I. Our efforts to help European allies had turned sour: thousands of American troops had been killed in a war that had seemed to accomplish little and certainly had not made the world, in Woodrow Wilson's words, "safe for democracy." As a result, in the 1920s and 1930s elite opinion (and popular opinion) opposed getting involved in European wars.

The **containment** (or antiappeasement) paradigm was the result of World War II. Pearl Harbor was the death knell for isolationism. Senator Arthur H. Vandenberg of Michigan, a staunch isolationist before the attack, became an ardent internationalist not only during but after the war. He later wrote of the Japanese attack on Pearl Harbor on December 7, 1941, "that day ended isolationism for any realist."[41] At a conference in Munich, efforts of British and French leaders to satisfy Hitler's territorial demands in Europe had led not to "peace in our time," as Prime Minister Neville Chamberlain of Britain had claimed, but to ever-greater territorial demands and ultimately to world war. This crisis brought to power men determined not to repeat their predecessors' mistakes: "Munich" became a synonym for weakness, and leaders such as Winston Churchill made antiappeasement the basis of their postwar policy of resisting Soviet expansionism. Churchill summed up the worldview that he had acquired from the Munich era in a famous speech delivered in 1946 in Fulton, Missouri, in which he coined the term *iron curtain* to describe Soviet policy in Eastern Europe.

The events leading up to World War II were the formative experiences of those leaders who came to power in the 1940s, 1950s, and 1960s. What they took to be the lessons of Pearl Harbor and Munich were applied repeatedly—in building a network of defensive alliances in Europe and Asia during the late 1940s and 1950s, in operating an airlift to aid West Berlin when road access to it was cut off by the Russians, in coming to the aid of South Korea, and finally in intervening in Vietnam. Most of these applications of the containment worldview were successful in the sense that they did not harm American interests, they proved welcome to allies, or they prevented a military conquest.

A meeting that named an era: In Munich in 1938, British prime minister Neville Chamberlain attempted to appease the territorial ambitions of Hitler. Chamberlain's failure brought World War II closer.

disengagement The belief that the United States was harmed by its war in Vietnam and so should avoid supposedly similar events.

human rights The view that we should try to improve the lives of people in other countries.

The **disengagement** (or "Vietnam") view resulted from the experience of the younger foreign policy elite that came to power in the 1970s. Unlike previous applications of the antiappeasement view, our entry into Vietnam had led to a military defeat and a domestic political disaster. There were three ways of interpreting that crisis: (1) we applied the correct worldview in the right place but did not try hard enough; (2) we had the correct worldview but tried to apply it in the wrong place under the wrong circumstances; (3) the worldview itself was wrong. By and large, the critics of our Vietnam policy tended toward the third conclusion, and thus when they supplanted in office the architects of our Vietnam policy, they inclined toward a worldview based on the slogan "no more Vietnams." Critics of this view called it the "new isolationism," arguing that it would encourage Soviet expansion.

The language of Vietnam colored many discussions of foreign policy. Almost every military initiative since then has been debated in terms of whether it would lead us into "another Vietnam": sending the Marines to Lebanon, invading Grenada, dispatching military advisers to El Salvador, supporting the contras in Nicaragua, helping South American countries fight drug producers, and sending troops to invade Iraq.

How elites thought about Vietnam affected their foreign policy views for many years. If they thought the war was "immoral," they were reluctant to see American military involvement elsewhere. These elites played a large role in the Carter administration but were replaced by rival elites—those more inclined to a containment view—during the Reagan presidency.[42] When George H. W. Bush sought to expel Iraqi troops from Kuwait, the congressional debate pitted those committed to containment against those who believed in disengagement. The Senate vote on Bush's request for permission to use troops was narrowly carried by containment advocates.

When Clinton became president in 1992, he brought to office a lack of interest in foreign policy coupled with advisers who were drawn from the ranks of those who believed in disengagement. His strongest congressional supporters were those who had argued against the Gulf War. But then a remarkable change occurred. When Slobodan Milosevic, the Serbian leader, sent troops into neighboring Kosovo to suppress the ethnic Albanians living there, the strongest voices for American military intervention came from those who once advocated disengagement. During the Gulf War 47 Senate Democrats voted to oppose U.S. participation. A few years later, 42 Senate Democrats voted to support our role in Kosovo.

U.S. Navy

The battleship USS *West Virginia* burns after being hit by Japanese warplanes at Pearl Harbor on December 7, 1941.

What had happened? The change was inspired by the view that helping the Albanians was required by the doctrine of **human rights.** Liberal supporters of U.S. air attacks on Serbian forces believed that we were helping Albanians escape mass killing. By contrast, many conservative members of Congress who had followed a containment policy in the Gulf War now felt that disengagement ought to be followed in Kosovo. Of course, politics also mattered. Clinton was a Democratic president; Bush had been a Republican one.

But politics was not the whole story. American liberal elites had persuaded themselves that the attack in Kosovo resembled the genocide—that is, the mass murder of people because of their race or ethnicity—that the Jews had suffered in Nazi Germany. They held that we must "never again" permit a whole people to be killed.

There are some problems with this view. Hardly any human rights advocates had called for U.S. intervention in Rwanda, China, or Iraq—all countries that massacred millions of their own citizens.

In addition, the historical record suggests that the Serbs and the Albanians have been killing each other for centuries. Now that the Serbian army has withdrawn from Kosovo, Serbian civilians who stayed behind are being killed by the Albanians whom they once killed. The response that some human rights advocates would give to these criticisms is that America owes a special obligation to Europe and that even if Albanians kill Serbs, a Western military presence there will at least prevent organized military killing.

In the aftermath of 9/11, a new issue has arisen that may divide foreign policy elites in the future. Should the United States "go it alone" against its enemies abroad, or do so only on the basis of a broad coalition of supporting nations? President Bush the elder assembled just such a coalition to force Iraq out of Kuwait, but President Bush the younger acted without UN support in invading Afghanistan and later Iraq, though he received crucial support from Great Britain, Australia, and Poland.

POLITICAL POLARIZATION

For as long as we have records, public opinion has been slow to favor our military actions overseas in the abstract but quick to support them once they occur. However, that pattern ended with our invasion of Iraq in 2003. Public opinion became deeply divided about that war, with most Democrats strongly opposing it and most Republicans favoring it.

That was not how things worked out during our wars in Korea and Vietnam. The war in Korea produced angry divisions in Congress, especially after General Douglas MacArthur, the allied commander in Korea, was fired in 1951 for having disobeyed the president. He received a hero's welcome when he returned to this country and gave an emotional speech to a joint session of Congress. Many Republicans demanded that President Truman be impeached. Despite this public support for MacArthur and these angry congressional words, the country was not split along partisan lines. Slightly more Republicans than Democrats said the war was a mistake (roughly half of each party), but the differences between these voters was not great.

The war in Vietnam split American political elites even more deeply. Journalists and members of Congress took sharply opposing sides, and some Americans traveled to North Vietnam to express their support for the Communist cause. When the North Vietnamese launched a major offensive to destroy American and South Vietnamese troops during the Tet holidays in 1968, it failed, but the American press reported it as a Communist victory, and demands to bring our troops home were heard during the presidential campaign that year. But public opinion did not divide along party lines; in 1968, Democratic and Republican voters had just about the same views (a little over half thought the war was a mistake, about a third thought it wasn't).

polarization A deep and wide conflict over some government policy.

Our invasion of Iraq was a different story. From the very first, Democratic voters strongly opposed it and Republican ones favored it. By 2006, 76 percent of Democrats said we should have stayed out of Iraq, while 71 percent of Republicans said that the invasion was the right thing to do.[43]

American public opinion has become more polarized by our foreign policy. **Polarization** means a deep and wide conflict, usually along party lines, over some government policy. It has replaced the bipartisan foreign policy of the Second World War and the modest differences in public opinion during Korea and Vietnam.[44]

It is clear from Table 20.3 that what political party we belong is strongly linked to our views on foreign policy. The public is deeply divided about these matters, and so, we think, will be the people for whom they vote.

Table 20.3 Party Affiliation and Foreign Policy

Issue	Democrats	Republicans
Reducing illegal immigration is very important	47%	74%
Globalization very good for our economy	58	34
Government should do more about climate change	62	27
Very important to strengthen United Nations	50	24
U.S. troops should aid Israel if it is attacked	40	60
I favor torture to get information from terrorists	29	53
Expand offshore drilling for oil	45	77

Source: Chicago Council on Global Affairs, "Constrained Internationalism" (Chicago, 2010).

The Use of Military Force

Foreign policy takes many forms—discussions are held, treaties are signed, organizations are joined—but in many cases it depends on the ability to use military force. Troops, ships, and aircraft are not the only ways of influencing other countries; international trade and foreign aid are also useful. But in modern times, as in the past, the nations of the world know the difference between a "great power" (that is, a heavily armed one) and a weak nation.

With the collapse of the Soviet Union and the end of the cold war, one might think that military power has become less important. But in fact it remains as important as ever. Since the Soviet Union was dissolved and the Berlin Wall came down in 1989, the United States has used military force to attack Iraq, maintain order in Bosnia, defend Kosovo, and go to war in Afghanistan. Various rogue nations, such as Iran and North Korea, have acquired or are about to acquire long-range rockets and weapons of mass destruction (that is, nuclear, chemical, and biological arms). Many nations that feel threatened by their neighbors, such as China, India, Pakistan, and Israel, have nuclear bombs. And Russia still has many of the nuclear weapons that the old Soviet Union built. It would be foolish to assume that the end of the cold war means the end of war.

There are two views about the role of the military in American life. One is majoritarian: the military exists to defend the country or to help other nations defend themselves. When troops are used, almost all Americans benefit and almost all pay the bill. (Some Americans, such as those who lose a loved one in war, pay much more than the rest of us.) The president is the commander in chief, and Congress plays a largely supportive role.

Although the other view does not deny that the armed forces are useful, it focuses on the extent to which the military is a large and powerful client.

U.S. Military Intervention in the Middle East

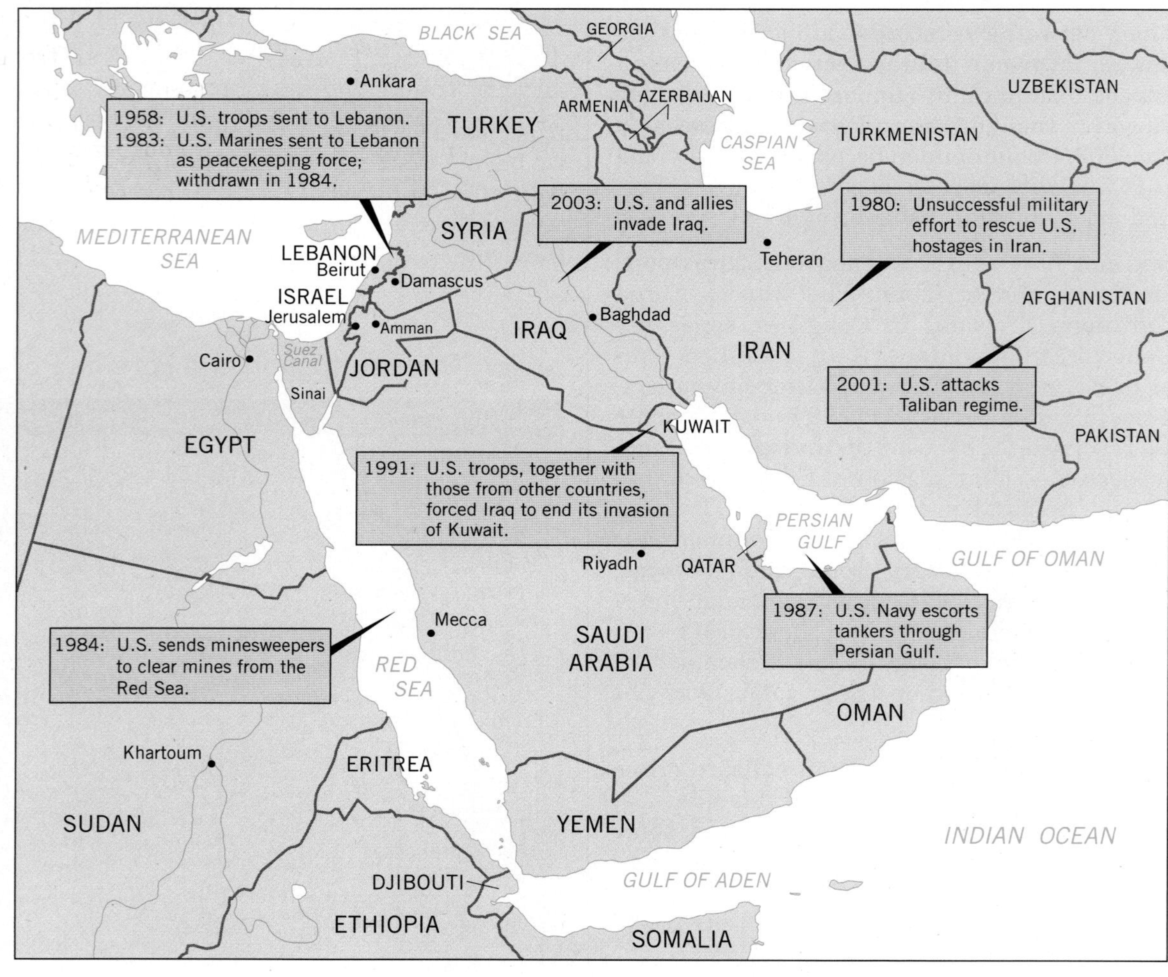

military-industrial complex An alleged alliance between military leaders and corporate leaders.

The real beneficiaries of military spending are the generals and admirals, as well as the big corporations and members of Congress whose districts get fat defense contracts. Everyone pays, but these clients get most of the benefits. What we spend on defense is shaped by the **military-industrial complex,** a supposedly unified bloc of Defense Department leaders and military manufacturers.

WAR IN IRAQ

After the Iraqi army under Saddam Hussein had invaded neighboring Kuwait in 1990, the United Nations passed a resolution demanding that Iraq withdraw and authorizing force to expel it. In January 1991 the United States led a coalition of forces from several nations that attacked Iraq; within 100 days, the Iraqi army had retreated from Kuwait and fled home. The U.S.-led military ended its attack, allowing Saddam to remain in power in Baghdad, the Iraqi capital.

After the war, a no-fly zone was established under which Iraqi flights in certain areas were prohibited. This ban was enforced for twelve years by U.S., British, and French planes that shot down Iraqi aircraft violating the rule.

Throughout this time, United Nations (UN) inspectors were sent to Iraq to look for weapons of mass destruction (WMDs): chemical, biological, and nuclear materials that could be used to attack others. There was no doubt such weapons existed, as Saddam had dropped chemical weapons on people living in his own country. The UN inspectors found evidence of such a program, but in 1997 Saddam expelled them from his country, only to allow them to return a few years later. Saddam's misleading statements led American and British leaders to conclude that his regime was a threat to peace.

Unable to convince the United Nations to support a war, America, Great Britain, and other countries decided to act alone. On March 30, 2003, they invaded Iraq in a campaign called Operation Iraqi Freedom; within about six weeks, the Iraqi army was defeated and the American-led coalition occupied all of the country. After the war, a large group of inspectors toured Iraq looking for WMDs, but they found virtually none. Later a bipartisan commission concluded that Saddam had apparently cancelled his WMD program, but had told hardly any of his own military leaders about this.[45]

The newly freed Iraqi people voted first for an interim parliament, then for a new constitution, and finally for a regular government. But this process was offset by the terrorist activities of various insurgents, first aimed at American troops and later at Iraqi civilians, killing several tens of thousands of them. The situation in Iraq became a major American political issue, contributing to the loss of the Republican congressional majority in the 2006 elections.

As we shall see (page 561), a new military strategy began in 2007 that improved conditions in Iraq.

Politically Speaking

Third World

Originally a French term (*tiers monde*) referring to nations neutral in the cold war between the United Nations and the Soviet Union, the *Third World* now means almost any underdeveloped nation in Africa, Asia, Latin America, or the Middle East.

When the oil-producing nations, such as Saudi Arabia, became wealthy after having succeeded in raising oil prices in the early 1970s, some observers began to use a new phrase, the *Fourth World*, to refer to underdeveloped nations that had no oil reserves and thus had to pay heavily for imported oil.

And some nations, such as Taiwan and the Republic of Korea, once thought to be part of the Third World because they were underdeveloped have made such startling economic progress that they are now referred to as the "newly industrialized nations" (NINs).

Source: Adapted from ***Safire's Political Dictionary*** by William Safire.

The Defense Budget

To sort out these competing claims, one has to understand how America raises and spends its defense dollars. There are two important things to know: how much money we spend and how it is divided up. The first reflects majoritarian politics, the second, interest group bargaining.

TOTAL SPENDING

Throughout most of our history the United States has not maintained large military forces during peacetime. For instance, the percentage of the gross national product (GNP) spent on defense in 1935, on the eve of World War II, was about the same as it was in 1870, when we were on the eve of nothing in particular. We armed when a war broke out, then we disarmed when the war ended.

But all of that changed after World War II, when defense spending declined sharply but did not return to its prewar levels. And in 1950, our defense expenditures soared again. In that year, we rearmed to fight a war in Korea, but when it was over, we did not completely disarm. The reason was our containment policy toward the Soviet Union. For about 40 years—from the outbreak of the Korean War in 1950 to the collapse of the Soviet Union in 1991—American military spending was driven by our desire to contain the Soviet Union and its allies. The Soviet Union had brought under its control most of Eastern Europe; would it also invade Western Europe? Russia had always wanted access to the oil and warm-water ports of the Middle East; would the Soviets someday invade or subvert Iran or Turkey? The Soviet Union was willing to help North Korea invade South Korea and North Vietnam to invade South Vietnam; would it next use an ally to threaten the United States? Soviet leaders supported "wars of national liberation" in Africa and Latin America; would they succeed in turning more and more nations against the United States?

To meet these threats, the United States built up a military system designed to repel a Soviet invasion of Western Europe and at the same time help allies resist smaller-scale invasions or domestic uprisings. Figure 20.1 depicts the dramatic increase in military spending in 1950. It also shows that even after we decided to have a large military force, there were many ups and downs in the actual level of spending. After the Korean War was over, we spent less; when

U.S. Military Intervention in Central America and the Caribbean Since 1950

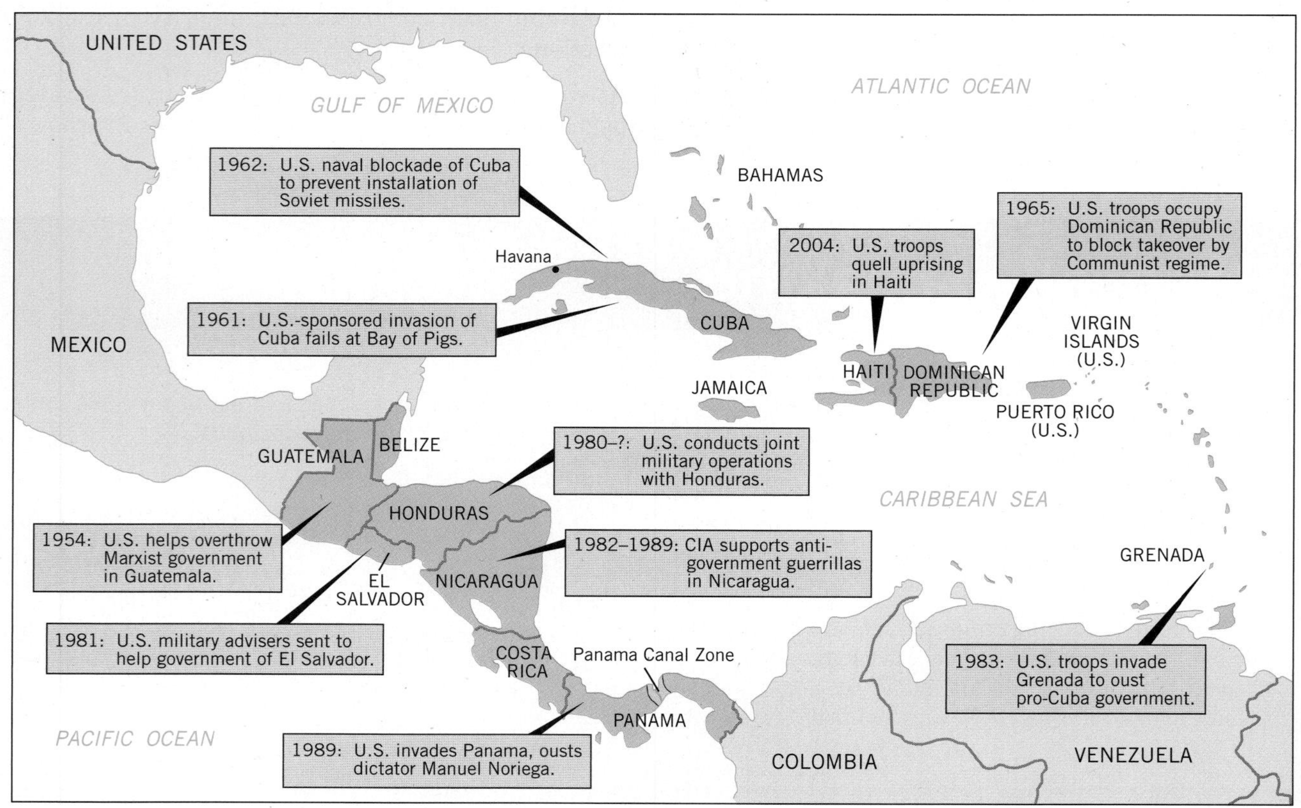

Figure 20.1
Trends in Military Spending (outlays in constant dollars)

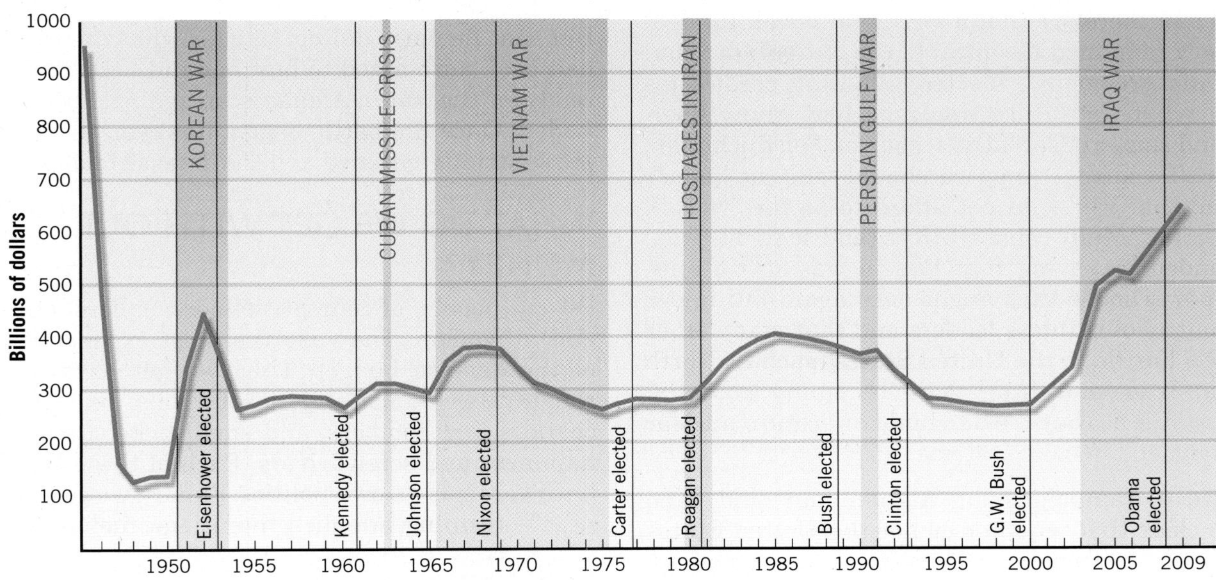

Source: Office of the Under Secretary of Defense (Comptroller), "National Defense Budget Estimates for FY 2007."

we became involved in Vietnam, we spent more; when the Soviet Union invaded Afghanistan and we invaded Iraq, we spent more again. These changes in spending tended to reflect changes in public opinion about the defense budget.

As Figure 20.2 shows, a majority of Americans have said that our defense program is either "about right" or "not strong enough," but other studies show that popular support for spending more money on defense changes from year to year.

After the collapse of the Soviet Union, there has been a debate about defense strategy. Liberals demanded sharp cuts in defense spending, weapons procurement, and military personnel, arguing that with the Soviet threat ended, it was time to collect our "peace dividend" and divert funds from the

Figure 20.2
Most Americans Think National Defense Is Either "About Right" or "Not Strong Enough"

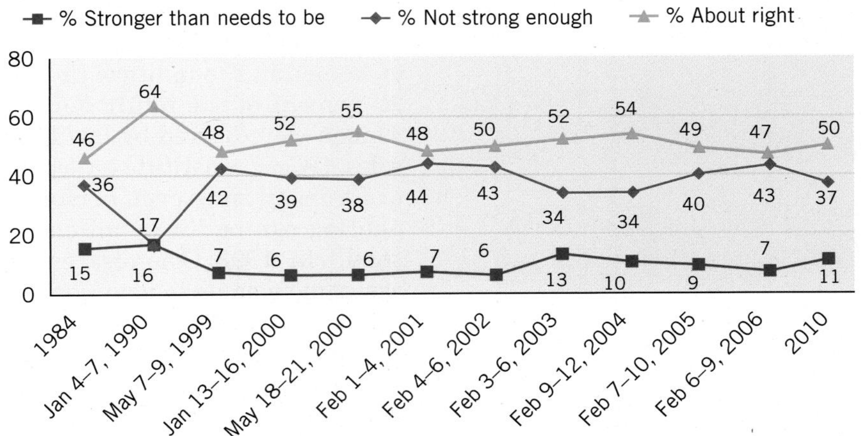

Source: Gallup Poll.

military to domestic social programs. Conservatives agreed that some military cuts were in order, but they argued that the world was still a dangerous place and therefore that a strong (and well-funded) military remained essential to the nation's defense. This disagreement reflected different predictions about what the future would be like. Many liberals (and some conservatives, such as Pat Buchanan, who believed that America should "stay at home") argued that we could not afford to be the "world's policeman." Many conservatives (and some liberals) responded by saying that Russia was still a military powerhouse that might once again fall under the control of ruthless leaders and that many other nations hostile to the United States (such as North Korea, Iran, and Iraq) were becoming potential adversaries as they tried to build or acquire nuclear weapons and missile systems.

American campaigns in Afghanistan and Iraq made clear that whether or not the United States was the "world's police officer," there was no escaping its need to use military force. They also made clear that the United States had reduced its armed forces so sharply since Desert Storm (there were half a million fewer people in the military in 1996 than in 1991) that it was hard-pressed to carry out any sustained military campaign (see Table 20.4).

Table 20.4 U.S. Military Forces Before and After the Breakup of the Soviet Union

Service	Before 1991	End FY 1998
Army		
Active divisions	18	10
National Guard divisions	10	8
Navy		
Aircraft carriers	15	11
Training carriers	1	2
Ships	546	346
Air Force		
Active fighter wings	24	13
Reserve fighter wings	12	7
Marine Corps		
Active divisions	3	3
Reserve divisions	1	1
Strategic Nuclear Forces		
Ballistic missile submarines	31	18
Strategic bombers	324	182
ICBMs	1,000	550

Source: *Statistical Abstract of the United States, 1998,* 363.

When the national budget deficit was eliminated in 1999, both President Clinton and the Republican Congress called for more military spending.

But that increase did not pay for what the military had been authorized to buy, and did little to get us ready for the war in Afghanistan against Osama bin Laden. Once the battle began, however, the federal purse strings loosened and the defense budget grew.

WHAT DO WE GET WITH OUR MONEY?

We get people, of course—soldiers, sailors, airmen, and airwomen. They are the most expensive part of the defense budget. Then we get hardware of roughly two kinds—big-ticket items, like aircraft carriers and bombers, and small-ticket items, like hammers and screwdrivers. Each of these kinds of hardware has its own politics. Finally, we get "readiness"—training, supplies, munitions, fuel, and food.

PERSONNEL

Efforts to develop our military forces before World War II reflected the considerable American discomfort with a strong central government. The United States did not institute a peacetime draft until 1940, when the rest of the world was already at war, and the draft was renewed the following year (only a few months before Pearl Harbor) by only a one-vote margin in the House. Until 1973, the United States relied on the draft to obtain military personnel. Then, at the end of the Vietnam War, it replaced the draft with the all-volunteer force (AVF). After getting off to a rocky start, the AVF began to improve thanks to increases in military pay and rising civilian unemployment. Abolishing the draft had been politically popular: nobody likes being drafted, and even in congressional districts that otherwise are staunch supporters of a strong defense, the voters tell their representatives that they do not want to return to the draft.

There has been a steady increase in the percentage of women in the military (in 2005, they constituted 20 percent of the total). For a long time, however, women were barred by law from serving in combat roles. (What constitutes a "combat role" is a bit difficult to say, since even personnel far from the main fighting can be hit by an enemy bomb or artillery shell.) In 1993 Congress ended the legal ban on assigning women to navy combat ships and air force fighter jets, and soon women were serving on three aircraft carriers. Congress must still be consulted in advance if women are to serve in ground combat forces (such as in front-line infantry or tank units).

The presence of homosexuals in the military has proved much harder to resolve. Until 1993, it was the long-standing policy of the U.S. armed forces to bar homosexuals from entering the military and to discharge them if they were discovered serving. Gay and lesbian rights organizations had long protested this exclusion. In 1993, a gay soldier won a lawsuit against the army for having discharged him; he settled for back pay and retirement benefits in exchange for a promise not to reenlist. In 1993, a judge ordered the navy to reinstate a discharged sailor who had revealed on national television that he was a homosexual. In response to the growing controversy, presidential candidate Bill Clinton promised to lift the official ban on gays and lesbians serving in the military if he were elected to office.

Once in office, he discovered that it was not that easy. Many members of the armed forces believed that knowingly serving alongside and living in close quarters with gays and lesbians would create unnecessary tension and harm military morale and troop solidarity. The Joint Chiefs of Staff opposed lifting the ban, and several key members of Congress said they would try to pass a law reaffirming it. President Clinton was forced to settle for a compromise: "don't ask, don't tell." Under this policy, persons entering or serving in the military will not be asked to reveal their sexual orientation and will be allowed to serve, provided they do not engage in homosexual conduct. If a person says he or she is a homosexual, it will not be automatic grounds for discharge, but it may be grounds for launching an investigation to see whether rules against homosexual conduct have been violated.

Vandenberg Air Force Base

The United States has tried to decide whether to build interceptors like this one to shoot down incoming missiles from enemies.

In 1994, the new Pentagon rules designed to implement "don't ask, don't tell" went into effect. In 2010 a law passed to ban the policy, and in 2011 it ended after the secretary of defense and the chairman of the Joint Chiefs said that this would not harm military readiness.

BIG-TICKET ITEMS

Whenever the Pentagon buys a new submarine, airplane, or missile, we hear about **cost overruns.** In the 1950s, actual costs were three times greater than estimated costs; by the 1960s, things were only slightly better—actual costs were twice estimated costs.

cost overruns When the money actually paid to military suppliers exceeds the estimated costs.

gold plating The tendency of Pentagon officials to ask weapons contractors to meet excessively high requirements.

There are five main reasons for these overruns. First, it is hard to know in advance what something that has never existed before will cost once you build it. People who have remodeled their homes know this all too well. So do government officials who build new subways or congressional office buildings. It is no different with a B-2 bomber.

Second, people who want to persuade Congress to appropriate money for a new airplane or submarine have an incentive to underestimate the cost. To get the weapon approved, its sponsors tell Congress how little it will cost; once the weapon is under construction, the sponsors go back to Congress for additional money to cover "unexpected" cost increases.

Third, the Pentagon officials who decide what kind of new aircraft they want are drawn from the ranks of those who will fly it. These officers naturally want the best airplane (or ship or tank) that money can buy. As air force general Carl "Tooey" Spaatz once put it, "A second-best aircraft is like a second-best poker hand. No damn good."[46] But what exactly is the "best" airplane? Is it the fastest one? Or the most maneuverable one? Or the most reliable one? Or the one with the longest range? Pentagon officials have a tendency to answer, "All of the above." Of course, trying to produce all of the above is incredibly expensive (and sometimes impossible). But asking for the expensive (or the impossible) is understandable, given that the air force officers who buy it will also fly it. This tendency to ask for everything at once is called **gold plating.**

Fourth, many new weapons are purchased from a single contractor. This is called sole-sourcing. A contractor is hired to design, develop, and build an airplane. As a result there is no competition, and so the manufacturer has no strong incentive to control costs. And if the sole manufacturer gets into financial trouble, the government, seeking to avoid a shutdown of all production, has an incentive to bail the company out.

Fifth, when Congress wants to cut the military budget, it often does so not by canceling a new weapons system but by stretching out the number of years during which it is purchased. Say that Congress wants to buy one hundred F-22s, twenty-five a year for four years. To give the appearance of cutting the budget, it will decide to buy only fifteen the first year and take five years to buy the rest. Or it will authorize the construction of twenty now and then ask again next year for the authority to build more. But start-and-stop production decisions and stretching out production over more years drives up the cost of building each unit. If Toyota built cars this way, it would go broke.

There are ways to cope with four of these five problems. You cannot do much about the first, ignorance, but you can do something about low estimates, gold plating, sole-sourcing, and stretch-outs. If the Pentagon would give realistic cost estimates initially (perhaps verified by another agency); if it would ask for weapons that meet a few critical performance requirements instead of every requirement that can be thought of; if two or more manufacturers were to compete in designing, developing, and manufacturing new weapons; and if Congress were to stop trying to "cut" the budget using the smoke-and-mirrors technique of stretch-outs, then we would hear a lot less about cost overruns.

Scott Olson/Getty Images News

Women Marine recruits go through close combat training.

© Paul Chinn/San Francisco Chronicle/Corbis

Retired Navy commander Zoe Dunning (2nd from left) and her friends celebrate the end of "Don't Ask, Don't Tell" in San Francisco.

Some of these things are being done. There is more competition and less sole-sourcing in weapons procurement today than once was the case. But the political incentives to avoid other changes are very powerful. Pentagon officers will always want "the best." They will always have an incentive to understate costs. Congress will always be tempted to use stretch-outs as a way of avoiding hard budget choices.

READINESS

Presumably, we have a peacetime military so that we will be ready for wartime. Presumably, therefore, the peacetime forces will devote a lot of their time and money to improving their readiness.

Not necessarily. The politics of defense spending is such that readiness often is given a very low priority. Here is why.

Client politics influences the decision. In 1990, Congress was willing to cut almost anything, provided it wasn't built or stationed in some member's district. That doesn't leave much. Plans to stop producing F-14 fighters for the navy were opposed by members from Long Island, where the Grumman manufacturing plant was located. Plans to kill the Osprey aircraft for the Marines were opposed by members from the places where it was to be built. Plans to close bases were opposed by every member with a base in his or her district.

That leaves training and readiness. These things, essential to military effectiveness, have no constituencies and hence few congressional defenders. When forced to choose, the services themselves often prefer to allocate scarce dollars to developing and buying new weapons than to spending for readiness. Moreover, the savings from buying less fuel or having fewer exercises shows up right away, while the savings from canceling an aircraft carrier may not show up for years. Not surprisingly, training and readiness are usually what get the ax.

BASES

At one time, the opening and closing of military bases was pure client politics, which meant that a lot of bases were opened and hardly any were closed. Almost every member of Congress fought to get a base in his or her district, and *every* member fought to keep an existing base open. Even the biggest congressional critics of the U.S. military, people who would vote to take a gun out of a soldier's hand, would fight hard to keep bases in their districts open and operating.

In 1988, Congress finally concluded that no base would ever be closed unless the system for making decisions was changed. It created a Commission on Base Realignment and Closure (BRAC), consisting of private citizens (originally 12, later 8) who would consider recommendations from the secretary of defense. By law Congress would have to vote within 45 days for or against the commission's list as a whole, without having a chance to amend it. Since 1988, there have been five BRAC reports. Congress approved each one, resulting in the closing of more than 350 bases.

Congress, it appears, has finally figured out how to make some decisions that most members know are right but that each member individually finds it politically necessary to oppose.

The Structure of Defense Decision Making

The formal structure within which decisions about national defense are made was in large part created after World War II, but it reflects concerns that go back at least to the time of the Founding. Chief among these is the persistent desire by citizens to ensure civilian control over the military.

The National Security Act of 1947 and its subsequent amendments created the Department of Defense. It is headed by the secretary of defense, under whom serve the secretaries of the army, the air force, and the navy as well as the Joint Chiefs of Staff. The secretary of defense, who must be a civilian (though one former general, George C. Marshall, was allowed by Congress to be the secretary), exercises, on behalf of the president, command authority over the defense establishment. The secretary of the army, the secretary of the navy,* and the secretary of the air force also are civilians and are subordinate to the secretary of defense. Unlike him, they do not attend cabinet meetings or sit on the National Security Council. In essence, they manage the "housekeeping" functions of the various armed services, under the general direction of the secretary of defense and his deputy and assistant secretaries of defense.

The four armed services are separate entities; by law, they cannot be merged or commanded by a single military officer, and each has the right to communicate directly with Congress. There are two reasons for having separate uniformed services functioning within a single department: the fear of many citizens that a unified military force might become too powerful politically, and the desire of each service to preserve its traditional independence and autonomy. The result, of course, is a good deal of interservice rivalry and bickering, but this is precisely what Congress intended when it created the Department of Defense. Rivalry and bickering, it was felt, would ensure that Congress would receive the maximum amount of information about military affairs and would enjoy the largest opportunity to affect military decisions.

Since the end of World War II, Congress has aimed both to retain a significant measure of control over the military's decision making and to ensure the adequacy of the nation's defenses. Congress does not want a single military command headed by an all-powerful general or admiral, but neither does it want the services to be so autonomous or their heads so equal that coordination and efficiency suffer. In 1986, Congress passed and the president signed a defense reorganization plan known as the Goldwater-Nichols Act, which increased the power of the officers who coordinate the activities of the different services. The 1947 structure was left in place, but with revised procedures.

JOINT CHIEFS OF STAFF

The Joint Chiefs of Staff (JCS) is a committee consisting of the uniformed heads of each of the military services (the army, navy, air force, and Marine Corps), plus a chairman and a (nonvoting) vice chairman, also military officers, who are appointed by the president and confirmed by the Senate. The JCS does not have command authority over troops, but it plays a key role in national defense planning. Since 1986, the chairman of the joint chiefs has been designated the president's principal military adviser, in an effort to give him more influence over the JCS.

Assisting the JCS is the Joint Staff, consisting of several hundred officers from each of the four services. The staff draws up plans for various military contingencies. Before 1986, each staff member was

*The secretary of the navy manages two services, the navy and the Marine Corps.

loyal to the service whose uniform he or she wore. As a result, the staff was often "joint" in name only, since few members were willing to take a position opposed by their service for fear of being passed over for promotion. The 1986 law changed this in two ways: first, it gave the chairman of the JCS control over the Joint Staff; now it works for the chairman, not for the JCS as a group. Second, it required the secretary of defense to establish guidelines to ensure that officers assigned to the Joint Staff (or to other interservice bodies) are promoted at the same rate as officers whose careers are spent entirely with their own services.

THE SERVICES

bipolar world A political landscape with two superpowers.

unipolar world A political landscape with one superpower.

Each military service is headed by a civilian secretary—one for the army, the navy (including the Marine Corps), and the air force—plus a senior military officer: the chief of staff of the army, the chief of naval operations, the commandant of the Marine Corps, and the chief of staff of the air force. The civilian secretaries are in charge of purchasing, auditing, congressional relations, and public affairs. The military chiefs oversee the discipline and training of their uniformed forces and in addition represent their services on the Joint Chiefs of Staff.

THE CHAIN OF COMMAND

Under the Constitution the president is the commander in chief of the armed forces. The chain of command runs from him to the secretary of defense (also a civilian), and from him to the various unified and specified commands. These orders may be transmitted through the Joint Chiefs of Staff or its chairman, but by law the chairman of the JCS does not have command authority over the combat forces. Civilians are in charge at the top to protect against excessive concentration of power.

No one yet knows how well the 1986 changes will work, though many analysts viewed the quick victory in the 1991 Persian Gulf War as evidence of its success. Critics of the Pentagon have been urging changes along these lines at least since 1947. But others say that unless the armed services are actually merged, interservice rivalry will continue. Still others argue that even the coordination achieved by the 1986 act is excessive. The country, in their view, is better served by having wholly autonomous services. What is striking is that so many members of Congress who once would have insisted on the anticoordination view voted for the 1986 law, thereby indicating a greater willingness to permit some degree of central military leadership.

The New Problem of Terrorism

Since 9/11, both our foreign policy and our military policy have had to focus on terrorism and what to do with nations we have conquered that harbored terrorists. When the cold war was on, this was easy. For a half century, each president, operating through the National Security Council, made it clear that our chief goal was to prevent the Soviet Union from overrunning Western Europe, bombing the United States, or invading other nations.

But the Soviet Union has disappeared and no other nation has acquired the power to take its place. During the cold war, we lived in a **bipolar world** made up of two superpowers. Now we live in a **unipolar world** made up of the United States as the only superpower. But our superpower status, though it means no other country can challenge us militarily, still leaves us vulnerable here and abroad to terrorist attacks, as 9/11 amply confirms.

To respond, President George W. Bush in September 2002 issued a document that emphasized a new view of our policies. Instead of waiting to be attacked, the president said that America "will act against such emerging threats before they are fully formed" because we "cannot defend America and our friends by hoping for the best." We will identify and destroy a terrorist threat "before it reaches our borders" and "we will not hesitate to act alone."[47] In the case of Iraq, this meant a commitment to "regime change"; that is, getting rid of a hostile government, even if the United Nations did not support us.

This has been called a doctrine of preemption; that is, of attacking a determined enemy before it can launch an attack against us or an ally. In fact, it is not really new. President Bill Clinton launched cruise missile strikes against training camps that followers of Osama bin Laden were using in the aftermath of their bombing of American embassies in Kenya and Tanzania in 1998. President Bush elevated the policy of preemption into a clearly stated national doctrine.

Supporters of this view hailed it as a positive step to defeat terrorists abroad before they could attack us at home. Critics attacked the argument as justifying

WHAT WOULD YOU DO?

MEMORANDUM

To: *The president*

From: *National security adviser*

Subject: *Hostages*

The six Americans held hostage in the Middle East are beginning their second year of captivity. One, a CIA officer, is undergoing torture. It has been the policy of this administration not to negotiate with terrorists. Criticism of this refusal is being heard from hostage families and their sympathizers. The terrorist groups are demanding that we end our support of Israel. A government in the region has secretly indicated that, in exchange for military supplies, it may be able to help win the release of "some" hostages.

News »

American Hostages Begin Second Year of Captivity

Families Urge President to Negotiate Freedom

The families of the six American hostages held captive in the Middle East today criticized the president for failing to win their release.

Your options:

1. Maintain the "no-negotiations" policy but use quiet diplomacy with friendly nations in the region to see whether they can intercede with the terrorist groups on behalf of the hostages.

   Advantages: (a) Our "no-negotiations" policy remains credible, and this will deter other terrorist groups from thinking that they can win concessions by capturing Americans. (b) This policy is consistent with our insistence that U.S. allies not negotiate with terrorists.

   Disadvantages: (a) There is no evidence that our traditional policy will get the hostages released. (b) Public sympathy for the hostages may increase, and this will lead to more criticism of this administration for failing to free captive Americans.

2. Secretly exchange arms for the release of Americans.

   Advantages: (a) Some or all hostages may be released. (b) We may earn the goodwill of more moderate elements in the area and thereby increase our influence there.

   Disadvantages: (a) We may deliver arms and no hostages will be released. (b) If secret arms deliveries become public, we will be heavily criticized for abandoning our "no-negotiations" policy.

3. Use military units to find and free the hostages.

   Advantage: The hostages may be freed without our having to make any concessions.

   Disadvantages: (a) The military is not optimistic that it can find and free the hostages, who are being kept in hidden, scattered sites. (b) The hostages may be killed during the rescue effort.

Your decision:

Option 1 ________ Option 2 ________ Option 3 ________

The Paradoxes of Fighting Insurgents

The U.S. Army Field Manual lists some paradoxes of fighting terrorists and insurgents. It is the manual used by Petraeus in Iraq.

Sometimes, the more you protect your force, the less secure you are.

You may be safe staying barricaded in compounds, but you lose contact with the people.

Some of the best weapons for fighting insurgents do not shoot.

Diplomacy, communications, and economic development can be more effective than guns.

Many important decisions are not made by generals.

Teaching lower-ranking personnel how to think and adapt is more important than teaching them what to think.

Sometimes the more force is used, the less effective it is.

Using too much force can hurt civilians and generate sympathy for insurgents.

preemptive and possibly unjust wars and abandoning the United Nations. This debate has divided Congress in a way that puts an end to the old adage that partisanship ends at the water's edge.

Since the end of the cold war, we have not had a common enemy that, in the opinion of critics of our overseas efforts, should justify a nonpartisan view. Most liberal Democrats opposed both our effort to get Iraq out of Kuwait in 1991 and our invasion of Iraq in 2003; most Republicans supported both efforts.[48] But when President Clinton launched attacks on hostile forces in Kosovo, he was supported by many liberal Democrats and opposed by many conservative Republicans.[49] Party differences and political ideology now make a big difference in foreign policy.

Sometimes we have sought and obtained United Nations support, as we did when going to war in Korea (1950) and in launching our effort to force Iraqi troops out of Kuwait (1991). We did not seek it in fighting against North Vietnam (in the 1960s), in occupying Haiti (1994), or in going to the assistance of friendly forces in Bosnia (1994) or Kosovo (1999). When we invaded Iraq in 2003, we asked for but did not get UN support; we went anyway, aided by allies, such as Britain and Australia, that joined with us.

After we conquered Afghanistan and Iraq, we faced the problem of rebuilding these nations. The United States has had a lot of experience, some good and some bad, with this problem. We helped put Germany and Japan back on their feet after World War II. From 1992 to 1994, we tried to bring peace among warring factions to Somalia. From 1994 to 1996, we worked to install a democratically elected president and rebuild the local police force in the Caribbean country Haiti. Starting in 1995, we worked with European allies to restore order to Bosnia and Kosovo, located in what used to be Yugoslavia. In 2001, we began helping Afghans create a new government and economy, and in 2003 we started doing the same thing in Iraq.

We succeeded in Germany and Japan, failed in Somalia and Haiti, and made progress in Bosnia and Kosovo.[50]

IRAQ AND AFGHANISTAN

After easily defeating the Iraqi army in 2003, we tried to bring stability and democracy to the country in mistaken ways. We abolished the Iraqi army (and so had no native defense force), relied on too few American troops (and so could not pacify the country), and kept these troops when they were not fighting in American compounds (thus leaving Iraqi civilians unprotected). Iran funneled arms and terrorists into the country to help attack American soldiers. Public opinion in this country, though deeply divided along party lines, became hostile to our efforts there.

To deal with this problem, President Bush (over the objections of many subordinates) announced a new strategy. We would send another 30,000 troops to Iraq (the "surge") and instruct these troops to work in Iraqi neighborhoods and build alliances with local groups. He assigned General David Petraeus to be our military leader.

The surge worked. Deaths of American forces and Iraqi civilians fell dramatically, an elected Iraqi government began to function effectively, and new Iraqi elections in 2009 were held peacefully. The American government negotiated an agreement with Iraqi leaders that called for withdrawing most American troops from the country by 2011. Because of this progress and because our economy went into a recession, American public opinion began to lose interest in Iraq.

Afghanistan is a more difficult problem. Unlike Iraq, it has never been a unified nation and lacks a large middle class or many populous cities. We easily defeated the Taliban regime and managed to put in office a moderate leader. Troops from other nations arrived to help out. But creating an effective central government in a country that has rarely had one and ending terrorist attacks has proved to be a difficult assignment. During the 2008 presidential campaign, Barack Obama promised to send more forces to that country, and beginning in 2009 he did so. By the middle of the year we had 60,000 troops there, but they were not enough. In 2009 the general leading our forces there asked President Obama for another 40,000 troops; the president sent 30,000.

LEARNING OBJECTIVES

WHAT YOU NEED TO KNOW

☑ Define isolationism, containment, and appeasement.

Isolationism means focusing on America and staying out of world affairs; containment means resisting the expansion of hostile foreign powers; appeasement means yielding to hostile foreign powers in order to induce them to stay their hands.

☑ What is meant by "rally round the flag"?

"Rally round the flag" means the tendency of the American public to support the president when he takes bold action. The increased support usually does not last for very long.

☑ Explain how a bipolar and a unipolar world differ.

A bipolar world exists when two powerful nations confront one another, as did the United States and the Soviet Union between 1945 and the 1980s; unipolar means a world with only one superpower, such as the United States since the collapse of the USSR.

RECONSIDERING WHO GOVERNS

1. Is American foreign policy set by public wishes or elite views?

Elite views matter greatly because most Americans pay little attention to foreign affairs most of the time. And on many key issues, the public disagrees with the elite. But when the president sends troops overseas to fight, the public will rally around him.

2. If only Congress can declare war, why has the president become so powerful in military affairs?

The Constitution makes him the commander in chief of the military, and the Supreme Court has made it clear that he has great powers on foreign affairs. The president often has sent troops to fight without a declaration of war, but Congress has invariably supported him. Technically, he should get Congress's approval under the War Powers Act, but if Americans are already fighting it would be very hard for Congress to say no.

RECONSIDERING TO WHAT ENDS?

1. Why do we go to war against some dictatorships and not others?

Some threaten our interests directly and some do not. And even when they do not threaten us, as in Bosnia, Haiti, Kosovo, and Somalia, we may intervene to protect citizens from brutality. Or we may not, as in Rwanda. Everything depends on how the government assesses each situation.

2. Should our foreign policy be based on American interests or some conception of human rights?

Sometimes this is not a problem because in a few cases a threat to our interests and a violation of human rights coincide. But at other times, they do not. This is a continuing issue that divides American foreign policy elites. In Congress, liberal members supported and conservative ones opposed our intervention in Bosnia and Kosovo even though neither country threatened us; in Iraq, conservative ones supported and many liberal ones opposed our intervention.

QUESTIONS TO CONSIDER

1. **Explain what leads political parties in Congress to support or oppose the War Powers Act.**
2. **We now have an all-volunteer military force. What arguments could be made for and against reinstating the draft?**

TO LEARN MORE

U.S. Army: **www.army.mil**

U.S. Air Force: **www.af.mil**

U.S. Navy: **www.navy.mil**

Central Intelligence Agency: **www.odci.gov**

Department of State: **www.state.gov**

Allison, Graham T. *Essence of Decision: Explaining the Cuban Missile Crisis.* Boston: Little, Brown, 1971. Shows how the decision made by a president during a major crisis was shaped by bureaucratic and organizational factors.

Barnett, Thomas P. M. *The Pentagon's New Map: War and Peace in the Twenty-First Century.* New York: Berkley Books, 2004. Discusses what America's foreign and military policy should be in the global war against terror.

Commission on the Intelligence Capabilities of the United States Regarding Weapons of Mass Destruction. *Report to the President of the United States.* Washington, D.C.: Government Printing Office, 2005. Thorough examination by a bipartisan group of why American intelligence agencies did not understand Iraq's WMD efforts.

Kissinger, Henry. *White House Years.* Boston: Little, Brown, 1979. A brilliant insider's account of the politics and tactics of "high diplomacy" during the Nixon administration.

Mead, Walter Russell. *Special Providence.* New York: Knopf, 2001. Argues that American foreign policy, though often criticized, has been remarkably successful.

Mueller, John E. *War, Presidents, and Public Opinion.* New York: Wiley, 1973. Best summary of the relationship between presidential foreign policy decisions and public opinion.

21 Environmental Policy

LEARNING OBJECTIVES

WHAT YOU NEED TO KNOW

- ☑ Who makes environmental policy?
- ☑ Why are environmental policies designed and enforced differently in the United States than in other industrialized nations?
- ☑ How important are environmental issues in American politics in the 21st century?

WHO GOVERNS?

1. Why have environmental issues become so important in American politics and policymaking?
2. Does the public get the environmental laws it wants?

TO WHAT ENDS?

1. If we wish to have cleaner air and water, how far should we go in making them cleaner when the cost of each additional gain goes up?
2. What is the best way for the government to achieve an environmental goal: by issuing orders or offering incentives?

Environmental policies in the United States gained widespread public attention in the 1960s, when reports of water and air pollution, pesticide use, and other threats to natural resources prompted the passage of legislation to control such activity. The Environmental Protection Agency was created in 1970 to set standards for environmental safety, track violations, and enforce compliance.[1] Since then, the field has expanded to encompass concerns about broader national and international environmental threats, such as the continuing debate about whether global warming is a danger that must be addressed.[2] But public interest and attention can be unpredictable, and can shift when other concerns, such as economic prosperity, become pressing. Consider the following:

THEN In the 2008 presidential race, environmental politics was a major concern for the electorate, particularly young voters. A CBS News/MTV poll in the spring of 2008 found that 18 percent of voters aged 18–29 viewed environmental problems as the biggest challenge in the coming years, exceeded only by the economy, which was ranked first by 34 percent of voters in that age group. (Education came in third with 13 percent of voters, and war and terrorism ranked fourth with 11 percent of voters.)[3] Both presidential candidates discussed the need to protect the environment for future generations: Barack Obama declared that the country faced a "defining moment in our history: Our nation is at war. The planet is in peril," while John McCain called for the need to "restore the health of our planet."[4]

NOW Since the 2008 presidential race, environmental issues have not been central to the American political agenda. Even after the disastrous oil spill in the Gulf of Mexico in 2010, neither the White House nor Congress pressed forward with a long-term plan for U.S. energy independence. The public is not aggressively advocating environmental policies either: One recent survey found that two-thirds of Americans view the

development of clean-energy sources as a high national priority, but another survey showed that voters aged 18–34—the age group that had historic voter turnout in 2008—were divided about the importance of global warming.[5] In the spring of 2011, President Obama met with a group of young leaders at the White House who were in Washington, D.C., for the third youth summit on clean energy and climate reform, but how this youth mobilization will influence policymaking remains to be seen.[6]

Why is environmental policy so controversial and complicated? There are four reasons. First, every governmental policy, including one established to protect the environment, creates both winners and losers. The losers are the people who must pay the costs without getting enough of the benefits. Sometimes those losers are influential interest groups. But sometimes the losers are average citizens. They may love the environment, but not enough to change the way they live in order to enhance it. For example, automobile exhausts are a major cause of smog, but not many people like the idea of being told to leave their cars at home and take the bus to work.

Second, many environmental issues are enmeshed in scientific uncertainty: the experts either do not know or they disagree about what is happening and how to change it. For example, many scientists worry that society is burning so much fuel (thus producing a lot of carbon dioxide) and cutting down so many trees (thus reducing the plants available to convert carbon dioxide back into oxygen) that the earth will soon become a greenhouse: the excess carbon dioxide in the earth's atmosphere will prevent heat from escaping, and so the earth will get warmer with disastrous effects for humanity. But there are some scientists who say human activity is not a major cause of global warming; instead, they argue, it is the result of natural changes in the earth's temperature.[7]

Third, much environmental policy takes the form of entrepreneurial politics—mobilizing decision makers with strong, often emotional appeals in order to overcome the political advantages of the client groups that oppose a change. To make these appeals, people who want change must stir up controversy and find villains. Many times this produces desirable changes. But it can also lead to distorted priorities. For example, making dramatic and politically powerful arguments about a pesticide that causes a minute increase in the risk of cancer may achieve results because the "villain" will be a single company or a small group of them that manufactures the pesticide. But dramatizing the problems from runoff of polluted water from farms and city streets into our rivers and oceans is more difficult because the source of trouble may include individuals, groups, and businesses.

Finally, environmental politics profoundly affect how the federal government deals with states and with other nations. The states have passed more than three dozen laws to lower the emission of various greenhouse gases and have influenced how Washington handles cleaning up toxic waste sites.[8] During the Clinton administration, the government participated in drafting the 1997 Kyoto Protocol that called for a 5 percent reduction worldwide in greenhouse gases, but aware that the Senate was strongly opposed to this treaty, President Clinton never pushed for its ratification. Senators had noted that the treaty would allow several countries, such as China and India, to keep generating greenhouse gases but would require that the United States cut energy use by 25 percent by 2012.[9] The George W. Bush administration scrapped the treaty.

It would take a book almost as long as this one to describe all the environmental laws and regulations now in effect in this country and to discuss the endless controversies over how those rules should be changed or expanded. Since 1963, more than three dozen major federal environmental laws have been enacted. This is not a book about environmental policy; instead, we focus here on the politics that create the policy.

In this chapter, we explain how environmental policy is made. Controversies over controlling pollution from stationary sources, such as factories and power plants, take the form of *entrepreneurial politics*—many people hope to benefit from rules that impose costs on a few firms. Policies intended to reduce air pollution caused by automobiles involve *majoritarian politics*—many people hope to benefit, but many people (anyone who owns a car) will have to pay the cost. The fight over acid rain has largely been a case of *interest group politics*—regions hurt by acid rain (mainly in the Northeast) argue with regions that produce a lot of acid rain (mainly in the Midwest) about who should pay. Finally, there are examples of *client politics* at work—for example, when farmers manage to minimize federal controls over the use of pesticides. Most people are unaware of what food contains what pesticide or which, if any, are harmful; farmers are keenly aware of the economic benefits of pesticides and are well organized to defend them.

Entrepreneurial Politics: Global Warming

When an offshore well spewed thousands of gallons of oil onto the beaches of Santa Barbara, California, at the very time (January 1969) when protest politics was in the air, it became difficult or impossible for the government or business firms to resist the demand that threats to our natural surroundings be curtailed. The emerging environmental movement created an occasion—Earth Day, first celebrated on April 22, 1970—to celebrate its beginning.

The movement was hugely successful. In 1970, President Nixon created the Environmental Protection Agency (EPA) and Congress toughened the existing Clean Air Act and passed the Water Quality Improvement Act. Two years later, it passed laws designed to clean up the water; three years later, it adopted the Endangered Species Act. New laws were passed right into the 1990s. Existing environmental organizations grew in size, and new ones were formed. Public opinion rallied around environmental issues. One was global warming.

The phrase *global warming* means that gases, such as carbon dioxide, produced by people when they burn fossil fuels—wood, oil, or coal—get trapped in the atmosphere and cause the earth's temperature to rise. When the temperature goes up, bad things may follow—floods on coastal areas as the polar ice caps melt, wilder weather as more storms are created, and the spread of tropical diseases to North America.

Robert Nickelsberg/Getty Images

The fight over climate change pits people who use coal with those who oppose burning it.

Scott Olson/Getty Images News/Getty Images

A rider drives the new Chevrolet Volt that, like the Toyota Prius, combines electric and gasoline power. The Volt costs over $42,000, but there is a government subsidy that goes to purchasers.

WHAT WOULD YOU DO?

MEMORANDUM

To: *Senator Diane Gray*

From: *Keith Mays, legislative assistant*

Subject: *Incentives for buying hybrid vehicles*

Until recently, you could get a tax credit if you bought a hybrid car. Now that the credit has expired, Congress needs to decide if it will continue supporting the hybrid car market to promote clean energy.

News »

Subsidizing Hybrid Cars

Congress is going to consider a plan to give government tax breaks to people who buy hybrid vehicles.

Arguments for:

1. We need to reduce gasoline consumption and our dependence on foreign oil.
2. Hybrid cars consume much less gasoline.
3. A tax break to buyers of hybrid vehicles that rely on both electric and gasoline engines will provide a stable market that will encourage sales.

Arguments against:

1. We can more easily cut fuel consumption by raising taxes on gasoline.
2. Many hybrids get worse gas mileage than several conventional cars.
3. The past tax breaks were essentially a support for domestic car builders who were being beaten in the market by Japanese producers.

Your decision:

Support ________________ Oppose ________________

But our natural concern for global warming must address three difficult questions. First we need to know by how much greenhouse gases cause the earth's temperature to rise. Various scientific groups, such as a panel from the National Science Foundation (NSF), and certain government organizations, such the Intergovernmental Panel on Climate Change (IPCC), have argued that it is "very likely" that greenhouse gases produced by humans have made and will continue to make the earth warmer.

But other organizations, such as the Nongovernmental International Panel on Climate Change (NIPCC), have produced reports arguing that greenhouse gases have not caused the earth to warm. The NIPCC argues that the IPCC neglects the effect the sun and other natural forces have had in making the earth warmer and ignores periods in the past when, long before greenhouse gases had been produced, people were managing farms in Greenland.

Second, if human activity has caused global warming, what would it cost in lost productivity and income to reduce greenhouse gases? Since America acting alone cannot eliminate greenhouse gases, we have to figure out how to get other countries, especially rapidly growing ones such as China and India, to absorb their share of the cost.

Third, how large would be the gains to humankind, and when would they occur? On the one hand, a warmer globe will cause sea levels to rise, threatening coastal communities; on the other hand, greater warmth will make it easier and cheaper to grow crops and avoid high heating bills.[10]

As with most kinds of entrepreneurial politics, global warming has resulted in a conflict among elites who often base their arguments on ideology as much as on facts. Environmental activists raise

"Yeah, yeah, maybe it's cyclical but I don't feel any better."

Major Environmental Laws

Smog Clean Air Act (passed in 1970; amended in 1977 and 1990)

- **Stationary sources:** EPA sets national air quality standards; states must develop plans to attain them. If the state plan is inadequate, EPA sets a federal plan. Local sources that emit more than a certain amount of pollutants must install pollution control equipment.
- **Gasoline-powered vehicles:** Between 1970 and 1990, pollution from cars was cut by between 60 and 80 percent. Between 1991 and 1998 there was another 30 percent reduction. All states must have an auto pollution inspection system.
- **Cities:** Classifies cities in terms of how severe their smog problem is and sets deadlines for meeting federal standards.

Water Clean Water Acts of various years state that there is to be no discharge of wastewater into lakes and streams without a federal permit; to get a permit, cities and factories must meet federal discharge standards.

Toxic wastes EPA is to clean up abandoned dump sites with money raised by a tax on the chemical and petroleum industries and from general revenues. (Many thousands of such sites exist.)

Environmental impact statements Since 1969, any federal agency planning a project that would significantly affect the human environment must prepare in advance an environmental impact statement (EIS).

Acid rain The Clean Air Act of 1990 requires a reduction of 10 million tons of sulfur dioxide (mostly from electric-generating plants that burn coal) by 1995. The biggest sources must acquire government allowances (which can be traded among firms) setting emission limits.

money with scary statements about the harm global warming will cause; conservatives raise money with scary statements about the economic pain an American cut in greenhouse gases will cause.[11]

Another environmental example of entrepreneurial politics is the Endangered Species Act (ESA). Passed in 1973, it forbids buying or selling a bird, fish, animal, or plant the government regards as "endangered"—that is, likely to become extinct unless it receives special protection—or engaging in any economic activity (such as building a dam or running a farm) that would harm an endangered species. Currently there are more than 600 species on the protected list; about half are plants. The regulations forbid not only killing a protected species but also adversely affecting its habitat.

The ESA is run by the Fish and Wildlife Service and the National Oceanic and Atmospheric Administration. They can add species to the endangered or threatened list or in response to a private petition. Trafficking in an endangered species can lead to criminal penalties; fines may be imposed for managing private land in ways that might harm a species. Several species (such as bald eagles, grizzly bears, gray wolves, and sea otters) have increased in number since being listed and a few (such as bald eagles and gray wolves) have been taken off the list.

Firms and government agencies that wish to build a dam, bridge, factory, or farm in an area where an endangered species lives must comply with federal regulations. The complaints of such clients about these regulations are outweighed by the public support for the law. Sometimes the law preserves a creature, such as the bald eagle, that almost everyone admires; sometimes it protects a creature, such as the snail darter, that no one has ever heard of.

Majoritarian Politics: Pollution from Automobiles

The Clean Air Act of 1970 imposed tough restrictions on the amount of pollutants that could come out of automobile tailpipes. Indeed, most of the debate over that bill centered on this issue.

Initially, the auto emissions control rules followed the pattern of entrepreneurial politics: an aroused public with media support demanded that automobile companies be required to make their cars less polluting. It seemed to be "the public" against "the interests," and the public won: by 1975, new cars would have to produce 90 percent less of two pollutants (hydrocarbons and carbon monoxide), and by 1976 achieve a 90 percent reduction in another (nitrous oxides). This was a tall order. There was no time to redesign automobile engines or to find an alternative to the internal combustion engine; it would be necessary to install devices (called catalytic converters) on exhaust pipes that would transform pollutants into harmless gases.

But a little-noticed provision in the 1970 law soon shoved the battle over automobile pollution into the arena of majoritarian politics. That provision required states to develop land-use and transportation rules to help attain air quality standards. What that meant in practice was that in any area where smog was still a problem, even after emission controls had been placed on new cars, there would have to be rules restricting the public's use of cars. There was no way for cities such as Denver, Los Angeles, and New York to get rid of smog just by requiring people to buy less-polluting cars—the increase in the number of cars or in the number of miles driven in those places outweighed the gain from making the average car less polluting. That meant the government would have to impose such unpopular measures as bans on downtown parking, mandatory use of buses and carpools, and even gasoline rationing. But efforts to do this failed. Popular opposition to such rules was too great, and the few such rules put into place didn't work. Congress reacted by postponing the deadlines by which air quality standards in cities would have to be met; the EPA reacted by abandoning any serious effort to tell people when and where they could drive.[12]

Even the effort to clean up the exhausts of new cars ran into opposition. Some people didn't like the higher cost of cars with catalytic converters; others didn't like the loss in horsepower these converters caused (many people disconnected them). The United Auto Workers union began to worry that antismog rules would hurt the U.S. auto industry and cost them their jobs. Congress took note of these complaints and decided that despite a lot of effort, new cars could not meet the 90 percent emission reduction standard by 1975–1976, and so in 1977 it amended the Clean Air Act to extend these deadlines by up to six years.

The Clean Air Act, when revised again in 1990, set new, tougher auto emission control standards—but it pushed back the deadline for compliance. It reiterated the need for getting rid of smog in the smoggiest cities and proposed a number of ways to do it—but it set the deadline for compliance in the worst area (Los Angeles) at 20 years in the future.

Most clean-air laws passed since 1990 have targeted particular industries. For example, in 2004 the Bush administration approved a new measure to dramatically reduce emissions from heavy-use diesel engines used in construction, agricultural, and other industrial machinery. The public will support such tough environmental laws when somebody else pays or when the costs are hidden (as in the price of a car); it will not give as much support when it believes it is paying, especially when the payment takes the form of changing how and when it uses the family car. Here are more examples of each kind of majoritarian politics.

Landmark Cases

Government and the Environment

- ***Union Electric Co. v. Environmental Protection Agency* (1976):** EPA rules must be observed without regard to their cost or technological feasibility.
- ***Chevron v. National Resources Defense Council* (1984):** States should comply with EPA decisions, even if not explicitly authorized by statute, provided they are reasonable efforts to attain the goal of the law.
- ***Whitman v. American Trucking Associations* (2001):** Allows Congress to delegate broad authority to regulatory agencies.
- ***Massachusetts v. Environmental Protection Agency* (2007):** The EPA must hear a petition asking it to regulate greenhouse gases.

MAJORITARIAN POLITICS WHEN PEOPLE BELIEVE THE COSTS ARE LOW

The National Environmental Policy Act (NEPA), passed in 1969, contained a provision requiring that an **environmental impact statement** (EIS) be written before any federal agency undertakes an activity that will "significantly" affect the quality of the human environment. (Similar laws have been passed in many states, affecting not only what government does but also what private developers do.) Because it required only a "statement" rather than some specific action and because it was a pro-environment law, NEPA passed by overwhelming majorities.

As it turned out, the EIS provision was hardly innocuous. Opponents of virtually any government-sponsored project have used the EIS as a way of blocking, changing, or delaying the project. Hundreds of lawsuits have been filed to challenge this or that provision of an EIS or to claim that a project was not supported by a satisfactory EIS. In this way, environmental activists have challenged the Alaska pipeline, a Florida canal, and several nuclear power plants, as well as countless dams, bridges, highways, and office buildings. Usually the agency's plan is upheld, but this does not mean the EIS is unimportant: the EIS induces the agency to think through what it is doing, and it gives critics a chance to examine, and often to negotiate, the content of those plans.

environmental impact statement A report required by federal law that assesses the possible effect of a project on the environment if the project is subsidized in whole or part by federal funds.

Despite the grumbling of many people adversely affected by fights over an EIS (someone once complained that Moses would never have been able to part the Red Sea if he had had to file an EIS first), popular support for it remains strong because the public at large does not believe it is paying a high price and does believe it is gaining a significant benefit.

MAJORITARIAN POLITICS WHEN PEOPLE BELIEVE THE COSTS ARE HIGH

From time to time, someone proposes that gasoline taxes be raised sharply. Such taxes would discourage driving, and this not only would conserve fuel but also would reduce smog. Almost everyone would pay, but almost everyone would benefit. However, it is only with great difficulty that the public can be persuaded to support such taxes. The reason is that the people pay the tax first, and the benefit, if any, comes later, and may be a general, rather than individual, result. Unlike Social Security, where the taxes we pay now support cash benefits we get later, gasoline taxes support noncash benefits (cleaner air, less congestion) that many people doubt will ever appear or, if they do, may not be meaningful to them.[13]

When gasoline taxes have been raised, it has usually been because the politicians did not push the tax hike as an environmental measure. Instead, they promised that in return for paying higher taxes the public would receive some concrete benefits—more highways, more buses, or a reduction in the federal deficit (as happened with the gas tax hike of 1990 and again in 1993).

Since it cannot easily cut gasoline use by raising taxes, the government has turned to other approaches. One is to provide tax breaks and other incentives to companies that seek to develop alternative energy sources. Another is to offer incentives to car manufacturers to build vehicles that consume less fuel by relying in whole or in part on electricity.

Interest Group Politics: Acid Rain

Sometimes the rain, snow, or dust particles that fall onto the land are acidic. This is called *acid rain*. One source of that acid precipitation is burning fuel, such as certain types of coal, that contains a lot of sulfur. Some of the sulfur (along with nitrogen) will turn into sulfuric (or nitric) acid as it comes to earth. Steel mills and electric power plants that burn high-sulfur coal are concentrated in the Midwest and Great Lakes regions of the United States. The prevailing winds tend to carry those sulfurous fumes eastward, where some fall to the ground.

That much seems certain. Everything else has been surrounded by controversy. Many lakes and rivers in the eastern United States and in Canada have become more acidic, and some forests in these areas have died back. Some part of this is the result of acid rain from industrial smokestacks, but some part of it is also the result of naturally occurring acids in the soils and rainfall. How much of the acidification is man-made and how much is a result of the actions of Mother Nature is unclear. Some lakes are not affected by acid rain; some are. Why some are affected more than others is unclear. The long-term effects of higher acid levels in lakes and forests are also unclear.

These scientific uncertainties are important because they have provided some support for each side in a fierce interest group battle. Residents of Canada and New England have complained bitterly of the loss of forests and the acidification of lakes, blaming it on midwestern smokestacks. Midwestern businesses, labor unions, and politicians have denied that their smokestacks are the major cause of the problem (if, indeed, there is a problem) and have argued that, even if they are the cause, they shouldn't have to pay the cost of cleaning up the problem.

An attempt to deal with the issue in 1977 reflected the kind of bizarre compromises that sometimes result when politically opposed forces have to be reconciled. There were essentially two alternatives. One was to require power plants to burn low-sulfur coal. This would undoubtedly cut back on sulfur emissions, but it would cost money, because low-sulfur coal is mined mostly in the West, hundreds of miles away from the midwestern coal-burning industries. The other way would be to require power plants to install scrubbers—complicated and very expensive devices that would take sulfurous fumes out of the gas before it came out of the smokestack. In addition to their cost, the trouble with scrubbers was that they didn't always work and that they generated a lot of unpleasant sludge that would have to be hauled away and buried somewhere. Their great advantage, however, was that they would allow midwestern utilities to continue their practice of using cheap, high-sulfur coal.

Congress voted for the scrubbers for all new coal-burning plants, even if they burned low-sulfur coal. In the opinion of most economists, this was the wrong decision,[14] but it had four great political advantages. First, the jobs of miners in high-sulfur coal mines would be protected. They had powerful allies in Congress. Second, environmentalists liked scrubbers, which they seemed to regard as a definitive, technological "solution" to the problem, an approach far preferable to relying on incentives to induce power plants to buy low-sulfur coal. Third, scrubber manufacturers liked the idea, for obvious reasons. Finally, some eastern governors liked scrubbers because if all new plants had to have them, it would be more costly, and thus less likely, for existing factories in their states to close down and move into the West.

The 1977 law in effect required scrubbers on all new coal-burning plants—even ones located right next to mines where they could get low-sulfur coal. As two scholars later described the law, it seemed to produce "clean coal and dirty air."[15]

The 1977 bill did not solve much. Many of the scrubbers, as predicted, didn't work very well. And there remained the question of what to do about existing power plants and factories.

When a solution was finally agreed upon, it was a compromise. President Bush the elder proposed a two-step regulation. In the first phase, 111 power plants would be required to reduce their emission of sulfur by a fixed amount. They could decide for themselves how to do it: buy low-sulfur coal, install scrubbers, or use some other technology. This would be done by 1995. In the second phase, with a deadline in the year 2000, there would be sharper emission reductions for many more plants, and this

Figure 21.1
Which Should Take Precedence: Environmental Protection or Economic Growth? 1984–2011

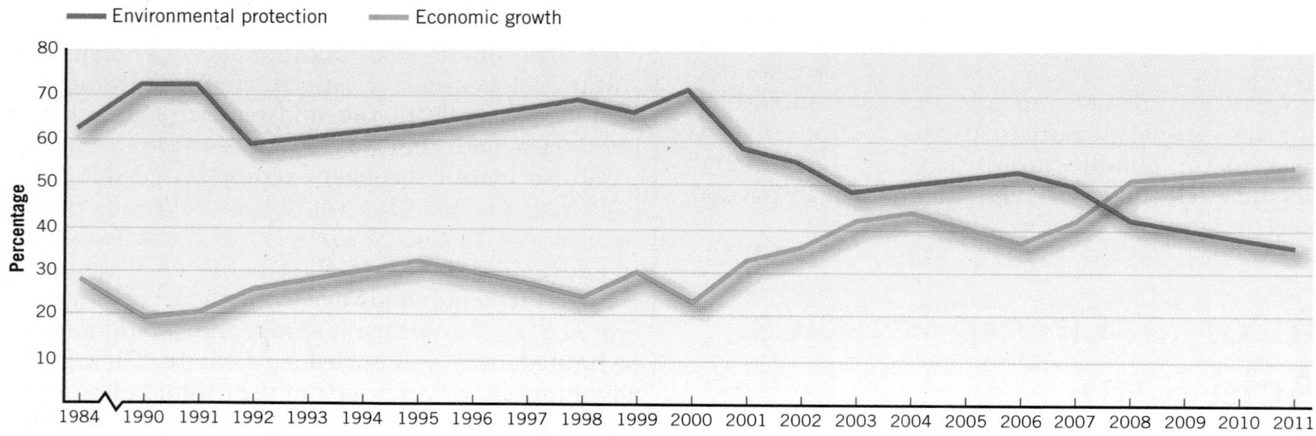

Source: Gallup Poll and Roper Center.

would probably require the use of scrubbers. To create some flexibility in how much each utility must cut its emissions, a system of sulfur dioxide allowances that could be bought and sold was established. This compromise became part of the Clean Air Act of 1990. By 2005, interest groups, advocates, and experts on all sides of the issue were once again poised to battle each other.

Interest group politics permeates many aspects of environmental policymaking. When cities or states consider land-use controls and zoning ordinances, they are weighing the competing demands of established residents (who often want as little new growth in their communities as possible) against demands of developers who want to build additional housing.

The heady victories of the early 1970s are hard to duplicate today because groups that were once unorganized are now well organized. For example, there is now a large and growing industry that makes products designed to improve the environment. As we saw in the acid rain controversy, industry can play an important role in supporting laws that favor their machines, whether or not they are the best solution to the problem. Industry is far better organized today than in 1970 to use its employees and political allies to defend its interests. Similarly, public-interest groups, such as the Environmental Defense Fund, that did not exist in 1965 now compete with other environmental groups for money and publicity. Labor unions, such as the United Auto Workers, that once fought for tough air pollution laws now are worried about whether some of these laws may cost them their jobs.

When the public is asked which should be more important, economic growth or environmental protection, their answers change. In the 1980s and 1990s, they overwhelmingly preferred environmental protection, but by the mid-2000s, a preference for economic growth had risen (see Figure 21.1). However, overall, citizens are environmentalists first.

Client Politics: Agricultural Pesticides

Some client groups have so far escaped this momentum. One such group is organized farmers, who have more or less successfully resisted efforts to restrict, sharply, the use of pesticides or to control the runoff of pesticides from farmlands.

For a while, it seemed as though farmers would also fall before the assaults of policy entrepreneurs. When Rachel Carson published *Silent Spring* in 1962, she set off a public outcry about the harm to wildlife caused by the indiscriminate use of DDT, a common pesticide. In 1972, the EPA banned the use of DDT.

That same year, Congress directed the EPA to evaluate the safety of all pesticides on the market; unsafe ones were to be removed. However, that is easier said than done. One reason is that there are more than 50,000 pesticides now in use, with 5,000 new ones introduced every year.[16] Testing all of these chemicals is a huge, vastly expensive, and very time-consuming job, especially since any health effects on people may not be observed for several years.[17] Another reason is that pesticides have many beneficial uses; therefore, someone has to balance the gains and the risks of using a given

© William Campbell/Corbis

Environmentalists have used the protection of endangered species, such as the spotted owl, as a way of reducing timber harvests.

pesticide and compare the relative gains and risks of two similar pesticides.

But even if the science were easy, the politics would not be. American farmers are the most productive in the world, and most of them believe they cannot achieve that output (and thus their present incomes) without using pesticides. These farmers are well organized to express their interests and well represented in Congress (especially on the House and Senate Agricultural Committees). Complicating matters is the fact that the subsidies the taxpayers give to farmers often encourage them to produce more food than they can sell and thus to use more pesticides than they really need. Though many of these chemicals do not remain in the crops harvested, large amounts sink into the soil, contaminating water supplies. But these problems are largely invisible to the public and are much harder to dramatize than, say, the discovery of a toxic waste dump like that at Love Canal, New York.

Though attacked by environmental organizations, farm groups have been generally successful at practicing client politics. The EPA's budget for reviewing pesticides has been kept small.[18] Very few pesticides have been taken off the market, and those that have been removed have tended to be ones that, because they were involved in some incident receiving heavy media coverage (such as the effect of DDT on birds), easily fell prey to entrepreneurial politics.

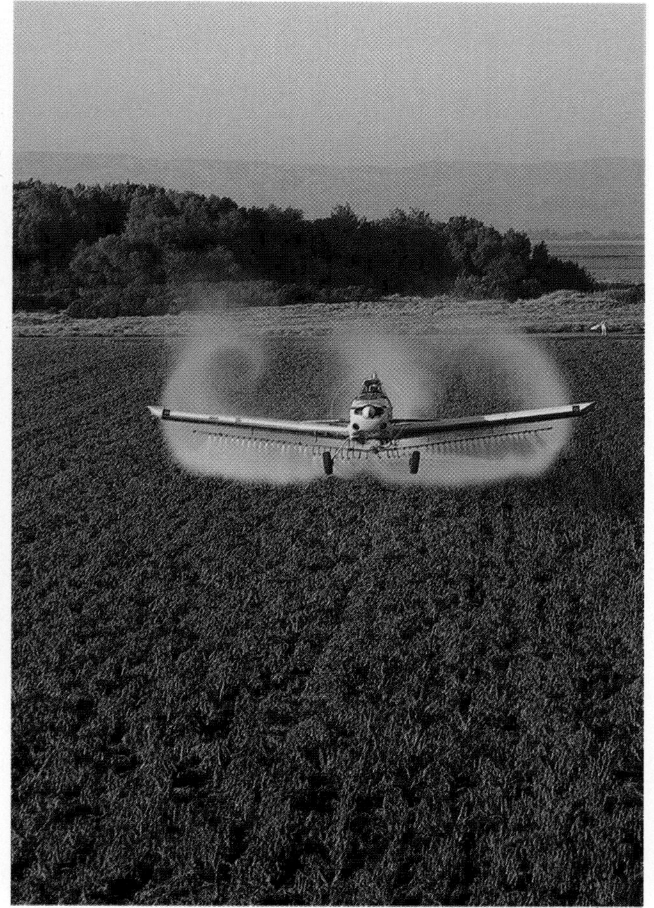

Jack Clark/The Image Works

Pesticides help grow better crops, but some worry they may harm the environment.

One of the reasons client politics has been able to protect the use of pesticides despite a political atmosphere that heavily favors environmental safety is that in fact pesticides have trivial effects on long-term human health problems, such as cancer. The most scholarly studies of the tendency of pesticides to cause cancer suggest that they are "unimportant" because "there is no convincing evidence" that they produce cancer.[19]

A similar kind of client politics exists in the timber industry. Wood product companies and loggers want access to forests under the control of the U.S. Forest Service. Though only 13 percent of all cut timber comes from these forests and two-thirds of the U.S. forest system is already off-limits to logging, environmentalists want further restrictions, especially to prevent clear-cutting (cutting down all the trees in a given area) and to prevent harvesting trees from the old-growth forests of

How We Compare

Environmental Policy

First, environmental policymaking in the United States is much more adversarial than it is in most European nations. In this country, there have been bitter and lasting conflicts over the contents of the Clean Air Act. Minimum auto emissions standards are uniform across the nation, regardless of local conditions (states can set higher standards if they wish). Many rules for improving air and water quality have strict deadlines and require expensive technology. Hundreds of inspectors enforce these rules, and hundreds of lawyers bring countless lawsuits to support or challenge this enforcement. Government and business leaders have frequently denounced each other for being unreasonable or insensitive. So antagonistic are the interests involved in environmental policy that it took 13 years, from 1977 to 1990, to agree on a congressional revision of the Clean Air Act.

In England, by contrast, rules designed to reduce air pollution were written by government and business leaders acting cooperatively. The rules are neither rigid nor nationally uniform; they are flexible and allow plenty of exceptions to deal with local variations in business needs. Compliance with the rules depends mostly on voluntary action, not formal enforcement. Lawsuits are rare. You might think all this sweetness and light were the result of having meaningless rules, but not so. As David Vogel has shown, the improvement in air and water quality in England has been at least as great as, if not greater than, that in the United States.[20]

Second, environmental policy here, as in so many other policy areas, depends heavily on the states. Though there are uniform national air quality standards, how those standards are achieved is left to the states (subject to certain federal controls). Though sewage treatment plants are in large measure paid for by Washington, they are designed, built, and operated by state and local governments.

Though the federal government decrees that radioactive waste must be properly disposed of somewhere, the states have a big voice in where that is. Federalism reinforces adversarial politics: one of the reasons environmental issues are so contentious in this country is that cities and states fight over what standards should apply where.

Third, the separation of powers guarantees that almost anybody who wants to wield influence over environmental policy will have an opportunity to do so. In England and in most European nations, the centralized, parliamentary form of government means that the opponents of a policy have less leverage. Here, environmental pressures are brought by interest groups; in Europe, where such groups have less influence, environmentalists form political parties, such as the Green party, so as to be represented in the legislature.

Oregon and Washington. But Congress has generally supported the timber industry, ordering the Forest Service to sell harvesting rights at below-market prices, in effect subsidizing the industry. Some activists hope to convert this client politics into entrepreneurial politics by demanding that clear-cutting in certain forests be stopped in order to protect endangered species, such as the spotted owl.

The Environmental Uncertainties

Making environmental policy strikes many people as easy—identify a problem, raise a fuss, defeat "the interests," and enjoy the benefits. In fact it is much harder than that to have a sane environmental policy.

First, what is the problem? Nobody likes smog, and human waste or oil slicks floating off our beaches are obviously bad. But many other problems are much less clear-cut. Science doesn't know how bad the greenhouse effect is. Pesticides that cause cancer in animals when given in megadoses may or may not cause cancer in people when absorbed in nominal amounts.

Second, if there is a problem, what goals do we want to achieve? We want reasonably clean air and water, of course, but how clean is reasonably clean? Since the cost of removing from the air the last 10 percent of some pollutants often is greater than the cost of removing the first 90 percent, how clean is clean enough? If making air and water cleaner is costly in terms of jobs, energy, and economic growth, how big a price are we willing to pay?

Third, how do we want to achieve our goals? Issuing rules and enforcing them in court often seem the easiest things to do, but they are not always the wisest.

command-and-control strategy A strategy to improve air and water quality, involving the setting of detailed pollution standards and rules.

That **command-and-control strategy** assumes that the rule makers and rule enforcers know how to achieve the greatest environmental gain at the least cost. In fact, no one knows how to do that, because local circumstances, technological problems, and economic costs are so complex. Under what circumstances can we use incentives and market prices to get people voluntarily to clean up their act by using their own imagination?

All of these uncertainties have become part of the endless political controversies surrounding the administration of the Environmental Protection Agency. Here are some specific examples.

WHAT IS THE PROBLEM?

The EPA was given the responsibility to administer certain laws governing air, water, and pesticides (among others). But it is rarely left alone to define these problems; any new environmental scandal leads to popular and congressional demands that it drop everything and solve that crisis. When toxic chemicals were found at Love Canal and Virginia Beach, these dramatic discoveries put other, less dramatic, but often more important problems on the back burner.

Who Governs? To What Ends?

Superfund: Cleaning Up Toxic Wastes

During the 1970s, hazardous waste sites were discovered all across America. Dangerous chemicals, many used decades before anybody worried about the environment and in some cases involving substances no one knew to be toxic, were found in the soil and near drinking water. These new investigations understandably alarmed many people. They and their legislators wanted this junk cleaned up.

What could be simpler? Find the dangerous stuff and take it out. In 1980, President Carter signed the Comprehensive Environmental Response, Compensation, and Liability Act (CERCLA), commonly known as Superfund. The law did two things: First, it taxed chemical and petroleum industries and put the proceeds, along with general tax revenues, into a trust fund to pay for cleaning up abandoned hazardous waste sites. Second, the law gave the government the power to sue any person or company (if they could be found) that had dumped the waste. In 1986, the law was strengthened when President Reagan signed a bill that gave the Environmental Protection Agency (EPA) more power and increased the size of Superfund to $8.5 billion.

But a decade later, the results were mixed. Superfund and related laws were associated with steep reductions in levels of toxic chemical releases (few new hazardous waste sites were created), but only 14 of 1,200 known hazardous waste sites had been cleaned up. By 2005, there were still more than 2,000 waste sites that had not been treated. What had gone wrong?

First, finding and suing the responsible parties was very difficult. These "potentially responsible parties" included present and past owners of a site, their insurance companies, and any firm that deposited waste long before a law had been passed saying it was illegal. Some companies had dumped the junk knowingly, others by accident; still others had long since gone out of business or were bankrupt. Finding them and getting them to pay were slow and difficult processes. As a result a lot of the Superfund money went to hire lawyers, not waste removers.

Second, it is complicated and time-consuming to clean up a site. Some sites had become big industrial plants or suburban housing developments. The EPA never had a staff equal to these high demands. There was a rapid turnover in EPA Superfund managers.

Third, as the environmental lobby got stronger, it put more and more pressure on the EPA to expand the list of hazardous sites and raise the standard for what constituted a cleaned-up site. No one seemed to be interested in developing a clear list of top-priority sites; instead, the whole list just got longer.

Nobody wants to live on a toxic waste site. But how do you clean it up? Just by hiring more lawyers to sue more people? The Superfund problem highlights the difficulty of designing an effective strategy and a good administrative system for doing what almost everyone wants done.

WHAT ARE THE COSTS AND BENEFITS?

Everyone wants a healthy environment, but people do not distinguish accurately between realistic and unrealistic threats or between reasonable and unreasonable costs. The biggest scare is cancer, even though every form of cancer has been steadily declining for many years (except lung cancer, which is caused primarily by smoking, not environmental hazards). People fear the unknown—many are afraid of flying, for example, even though flying is vastly safer than driving. People fear strange threats, such as toxic chemicals, even though they may never hurt anyone. People applaud dramatic governmental steps without asking whether they actually help anyone. For example, the government has mandated that all asbestos must be removed from public school buildings. Though intense exposure to asbestos can cause health problems, removing all the asbestos from old school buildings helps almost no one and may hurt the asbestos removers. The problem for government officials is to keep policies aimed at real risks—they do exist—and not to be diverted by popular concerns over unreal ones. In a free society, that is not easy.

WHAT ARE OUR GOALS?

When the EPA was told by Congress to eliminate *all* pollutants entering our waterways by 1985, to cut auto emissions by 90 percent within five years, and to eliminate smog in *all* cities, Congress should have known that these goals were utterly unrealistic. When the EPA realized it could not achieve these goals, it was forced to ask for extensions in deadlines and for revisions in laws. This gave it the appearance of knuckling under to industry pressure.[21]

HOW DO WE ACHIEVE OUR GOALS?

Initially, the EPA was zealous about using a command-and-control strategy to improve air and water quality. For example, to reduce water pollution discharged from factories, the EPA issued rules broken down into 642 industry subcategories, and even then there was a lot of local variation that it could not take into account. When the cost of doing this sort of thing got out of control, the EPA during the Carter administration began to devise incentives to replace some rules. These included offsets, bubbles, and banks:

- **Offsets.** If a company wants to open a new plant in an area with polluted air, it can do so if the pollution it generates is offset by a reduction in pollution from another source in that area. To achieve that reduction, the new company may buy an existing company and close it down.
- **Bubble standard.** A bubble is the total amount of air pollution that can come from a given factory. A company is free to decide which specific sources within that factory must be reduced in order to meet the bubble standard.
- **Pollution allowances (or banks).** If a company reduces its polluting emissions by more than the law requires, it can either use this excess to cover a future plant expansion or sell it to another company as an offset.

Once, only affected businesses complained about the high cost, slow progress, and legal complexity of environmental regulations. Increasingly, however, pro-environment interest groups and the government itself have become aware of the difficulties that arise when the government relies on a command-and-control strategy that is indifferent to costs and excessively reliant on lawsuits.

CAP AND TRADE

To deal with global warming, the House of Representatives in mid-2009 passed a bill that would set maximum emissions of carbon dioxide for most large firms. The emissions allowed imposed by these caps would decline as the years passed. If a firm produced less than the maximum emissions, it could sell part of its permit to another firm. The theory was that firms would take the least costly way to meet the standards: either lowering their emissions or, if that was too expensive, buying an additional permit from another firm. This strategy was used in the 1990s to reduce the emission of sulphur dioxide that people believed caused acid rain. This plan was similar to the cap-and-trade requirements imposed by the Kyoto Treaty of 1997, but the Senate had never ratified that bill in part because China, India, and other growing economies were not bound by it.

Some liberal critics of the 2009 bill argued that it allowed firms to pay money in order to pollute and was not an efficient method to reduce pollution. Many of them argued that it should be replaced by a tax on carbon. Some conservative critics said it would only work if the permits were auctioned off (instead, the plan allowed the government to give most away), that it required an unrealistically large decrease in carbon dioxide (85 percent by 2050), and that the decreased emissions would impose taxes on Americans and slow economic growth.

Despite the efforts of a small bipartisan group of senators, the bill did not come to a vote in their chamber. The White House was focused on passing health care reform, and the president's advisers were divided over how much the president should engage in the legislative negotiations about the environmental bill. Then the Senate majority leader, Democrat Harry Reid of Nevada, declared that immigration reform needed to pass before environmental reform, in an effort to win support from immigration activists in his home state, where he faced a tough (though ultimately successful) reelection campaign. Finally, the disastrous oil spill in the Gulf of Mexico doomed any prospects of passing legislation that had promised (with White House support) an expansion of offshore oil drilling in return for capping carbon emissions.[22]

After his failure to make headway on one of his signature campaign issues, Obama, like his recent predecessors, has pursued environmental reforms through regulation instead of legislation. For example, the EPA has imposed stricter guidelines for coal mines to receive permits in compliance with the Clean Water Act. And the U.S. Fish and Wildlife Service was debating in 2011 whether a small desert lizard belonged on its endangered species list, which would mean prohibiting oil and gas production in the areas where the lizard resides. Interest group politics typically dominate regulatory efforts, while large-scale reform more often requires majoritarian support, which is more difficult for the administration to build in a time of economic turmoil.

The Results

Though Americans think their environment has gotten worse, in fact many aspects of it have gotten better since 1970. There is now much less carbon monoxide, sulfur dioxide, and lead in the atmosphere than once was the case. It is less clear whether there have been equally noticeable improvements in water quality, in large part because much of the gunk that flows into our rivers, lakes, and oceans does not come from some fixed source (such as a sewer) that can be easily isolated; a lot comes from runoff from the ground as a result of rain washing pollutants off urban streets and farmlands and into the water.

Hazardous waste is found at thousands of known locations (and perhaps hundreds more unknown ones). The cleanup job is so great that it will be years before much progress can be shown. Getting big reductions in dangerous pesticides requires first reaching agreement on what is a dangerous pesticide and then finding a way of minimizing the harm to agriculture that would be caused by the reduction.

LEARNING OBJECTIVES

WHAT YOU NEED TO KNOW

☑ Who makes environmental policy?

As with other policy areas, several people and groups shape environmental policy in the United States, including elected and appointed officials, interest groups, and the general public. Depending on the specific issue, one person or group may dominate the discussion.

☑ Why are environmental policies designed and enforced differently in the United States than in other industrialized nations?

The adversarial nature of American politics as well as the system of federalism complicate policymaking in the United States, as illustrated by efforts to pass and enforce legislation on automobile emissions, clean air and water, safe disposal of radioactive waste, and other environmental issues.

☑ How important are environmental issues in American politics in the 21st century?

While economic issues typically matter most to voters, environmental politics have become increasingly visible in the United States in the 21st century, even if the public does not have a clear consensus on such controversies as the sources and consequences of climate change.

RECONSIDERING WHO GOVERNS?

1. Why have environmental issues become so important in American politics and policymaking?

Today, almost everybody loves the environment and thinks government has a duty to protect and improve it. Despite post-1970 improvements in many environmental conditions, most people think the environment is getting worse, not better, and worry about acute environmental threats to public health and safety. Nevertheless, environmental issues have attracted the interest and energy of talented policy entrepreneurs. These issues figure prominently not only in Washington politics, but also at the state and local levels as well as in international relations.

2. Does the public get the environmental laws it wants?

Yes and no. Most people say they want the government to do whatever it takes to protect and improve the environment, and most support laws and regulations that force particular industries to reduce pollution or take other pro-environment actions at their own expense. Many such laws and regulations have been enacted and enforced since the early 1970s. But most people waver when it comes to laws and regulations that would impose substantial financial costs on them (substantially higher gasoline taxes, for example) or force them to change how they live (prohibiting them from driving their cars to work, for instance). Typically, politicians echo the public's pro-environment sentiments without, however, enacting policies or enforcing regulations that impose large and visible costs on most people.

RECONSIDERING TO WHAT ENDS?

1. If we wish to have cleaner air and water, how far should we go in making them cleaner when the cost of each additional gain goes up?

We have cut the pollutants coming out of cars dramatically, but it will cost a lot to cut them to zero. The key question is whether spending scarce dollars that way makes more sense than spending the same amount of money on something else, like preventing diseases or funding schools. Choosing between spending money on clean air, less disease, and better schools may strike some readers as wrongheaded; shouldn't we have all of these? But governing means using limited resources to deal with many different desires. It is almost impossible to have air that is entirely clean (natural fires and dust storms will make it dirty), and even reducing auto pollutants to zero will have to await the invention of engines powered by things like fuel cells that have as a waste product only water. If we spend huge sums on making air or water entirely pure, we will inevitably be spending less on something else that we also want. Americans love the environment, but even for things we love we have to worry about costs.

2. What is the best way for the government to achieve an environmental goal: by issuing orders or offering incentives?

For a lot of people, issuing orders makes sense. That way we tell people what they have to do and can punish them if they don't do it. But for most economists and policy analysts, incentives make more sense because they give people the opportunity to choose the most efficient way to help the environment. For example, we can tell utilities not to let any sulphur dioxide out of their smokestacks, but that may impose huge costs on utilities that already produce very little sulphur dioxide or even drive them out of business. If instead we tell utilities they will get rewards for reducing pollutants, those that can do so easily will make big changes and, if they reduce them by more than a specified amount, will be allowed to sell the extra gains to another company to help it meet its goals. Still, when the gains are huge and the costs minimal, issuing orders makes sense.

QUESTIONS TO CONSIDER

1. **How important have environmental politics been in recent presidential and congressional elections?**
2. **Do environmental policies need to be developed locally, nationally, or internationally? What are the consequences, pro and con, of each approach?**
3. **How have American public attitudes on the importance of environmental politics shifted, if at all, in the 21st century, and why?**

TO LEARN MORE

Environmental Protection Agency: **www.epa.gov**

Environmental activists

Environmental Defense Fund: **www.edf.org**

National Resources Defense Council: **www.nrdc.org**

Sierra Club: **www.sierraclub.org**

Environmental skeptics

American Enterprise Institute: **www.aei.org**

Competitive Enterprise Institute: **www.cei.org**

Easterbrook, Gregg. *A Moment on Earth.* New York: Viking, 1995. A comprehensive account of what we have accomplished and what remains to be done regarding the environment, written by a hard-headed environmentalist.

Gore, Al. *Earth in the Balance.* Boston: Houghton Mifflin, 2000. Revised edition of a pro-environment argument first written when Gore was a senator.

Hayward, Steven F. *Index of Leading Environmental Indicators.* Washington, D.C.: American Enterprise Institute, 2005. Annual review of various measures of environmental change.

Intergovernmental Panel on Climate Change. *Fourth Assessment Report,* 2007. Latest study by the IPCC, created by two United Nations organizations.

Lomborg, Bjorn. *Cool It: The Skeptical Environmentalist's Guide to Global Warming.* New York: Knopf, 2007. A liberal agrees that global warming is occurring but urges more moderate steps to deal with it.

Nongovernmental International Panel on Climate Change. *Climate Change Reconsidered.* Chicago, Ill.: Heartland Institute, 2009. A lengthy argument by scientists who disagree with the IPCC report.

Rosenbaum, Walter A. *Environmental Politics and Policy,* 8th ed. Washington, D.C.: Congressional Quarterly Press, 2010. Analysis of the politics of environmental issues, including air and water pollution, the use of chemicals, nuclear power, and preserving outer space.

Vogel, David. *National Style of Regulation: Environmental Policy in Great Britain and the United States.* Ithaca, N.Y.: Cornell University Press, 1986. An explanation of why environmental politics in the United States is so adversarial.

Part 5

The Nature of American Democracy

22 Who Governs? To What Ends? 582

Justice is the end of government. It is the end of civil society. It ever has been and ever will be pursued until it be obtained, or until liberty be lost in the pursuit.

*** Federalist No. 51**

22 Who Governs? To What Ends?

LEARNING OBJECTIVES

WHAT YOU NEED TO KNOW

- ☑ Name two things that for many years kept the agenda of the federal government short.
- ☑ Name two things that have expanded the agenda of the federal government.

Like most Americans, you probably worry about some social problems. These might include abortion, crime, drug abuse, civil rights, gun control, homelessness, or school quality. Maybe you have argued about these matters with your friends, discussing what Washington should do about these things. While you argue, remember this: until about a half-century ago, when our parents were alive, all of this talk would have been nonsense. None of these things were matters that people believed the federal government could or should do anything about.

Restraints on the Growth of Government

When Dwight Eisenhower was president, none of these issues except civil rights was even thought to be a matter for federal policy, and on civil rights Congress didn't do very much. Our national political agenda was very short. During the Eisenhower administration, we decided to build an interstate highway system, admit Alaska and Hawaii into the union, and fight over the power of labor unions. For *eight years,* these were about the only major domestic political issues. The rest of the time, Washington worried about foreign affairs.

This was about what the Founders had expected, though many of them would have objected to some things that were done in the Eisenhower administration. Some would have thought Washington shouldn't build any highways because the Constitution did not authorize Congress to make laws about such matters. The federal government, in their view, should limit itself to war, peace, interstate commerce, establishing a national currency, and delivering the mail. And for a long time, the prevailing interpretation of the Constitution sharply limited what policies the federal government could adopt. The Supreme Court restricted the authority of the government to regulate business and prevented it from levying an income tax. Most important, the Supreme Court refused, with some exceptions, to allow the delegation of broad discretionary power to administrative agencies.

The Supreme Court could not have maintained this position for as long as it did if it had acted in the teeth of popular opposition. But popular opinion was also against the growth of government. It was not thought legitimate for the federal government to intervene deeply in the economy (even the American Federation of Labor, led by Samuel Gompers, resisted federal involvement in labor-management issues). It was certainly not thought proper for Washington to upset racial segregation as it was practiced in both the North and the South. It took constitutional amendments to persuade Congress that it had the authority to levy an income tax or to prohibit the sale of alcoholic beverages. Even in the 1930s, public opinion polls showed that as many as half the voters were skeptical of a federal unemployment compensation program.

That was the Old System. Today, under the New System, federal politics is not about some small list of problems thought to be truly national; it is about practically everything. It is almost impossible to think of a problem about which Washington has no policy at all or around which it does not carry on intense debates. Listen to radio talk shows, and you will hear discussions about why Washington has a good or bad policy on almost any issue you can imagine.

What is puzzling about this change from the Old System to the New System is that the Constitution is filled with arrangements designed to make it hard, not easy, for the federal government to act. The separation of powers

John Moore/Staff/Getty Images

permits the president, Congress, and the courts to check one another; federalism guarantees that states will have an important role to play; and the division of legislative authority between the House and the Senate ensures that each body will be inclined to block the other. To get a new law passed, you have to please a large number of political actors; to get a new one blocked, you only have to convince one congressional committee.

That system made the national government relatively unimportant for many decades. Until well into the 20th century, governors and mayors were more important than the president. Most members of Congress did not serve more than one or two terms in Washington; there didn't seem to be much point in becoming a career legislator because Congress didn't do much, didn't pay much, and wasn't in session for very long.

Relaxing the Restraints

As we have said, the constraints on federal action have now weakened or disappeared altogether. First, the courts have altered their interpretation of the Constitution in ways that have not only permitted but sometimes even required government action. The Bill of Rights has been extended so that almost all its important provisions are now regarded as applying to the states (by having been incorporated into the due process clause of the Fourteenth Amendment). This means that a citizen can use the federal courts to alter state policy to a greater degree than ever before. (Overturning state laws that ban abortions or require racially separate schools are two important examples of this change.) The special protection the courts once granted property rights has been substantially reduced so that business can be regulated to a greater degree than previously. The Court has permitted Congress to give broad discretionary powers to administrative agencies, allowing bureaucrats to make decisions that once only Congress could make.

Second, public opinion has changed in ways that support an expanded role for the federal government. The public demanded action to deal with the Great Depression (the programs that resulted, such as Social Security, survived in part because the Supreme Court changed its mind about the permissible scope of federal action). Political elites changed their minds faster than the average citizen. Well-educated, politically active people began demanding federal policies regarding civil rights, public welfare, environmental protection, consumer safety, and foreign aid well before the average citizen became concerned with such things.

Once in place, most of these programs proved popular, so their continuance was supported by mass as well as elite opinion. The cumulative effect of this process was to blur, if not erase altogether, the line that once defined what the government had the authority to do. At one time, a new proposal was debated in terms of whether it was *legitimate* for the federal government to do it all. Federal aid to education, for example, usually was opposed because many people feared it would lead to federal control of local schools. But after so many programs (including federal aid to education) had been passed, people stopped arguing about whether a certain policy was legitimate and argued instead about whether it was *effective.*

Third, political resources have become more widely distributed. The number and variety of interest groups have increased enormously. The funds available from foundations for organizations pursuing specific causes have grown. It is now easier to get access to the federal courts than formerly was the case, and once in the courts the plaintiffs are more likely to encounter judges who believe that the law and the Constitution should be interpreted broadly to permit particular goals (for example, prison reform) to be attained by legal rather than legislative means. Hundreds of magazines, newsletters, and World Wide Web pages have arisen to provide policy information to specialized segments of opinion. The techniques of mass protest, linked to the desire of television to show visually interesting accounts of social conflict, have been perfected in ways that convey the beliefs of a few into the living rooms of millions.

Campaign finance laws and court rulings have given legal status and constitutional protection to thousands of political action committees (PACs) that raise and spend tens of millions of dollars from millions of small contributors. College education, once the privilege of a tiny minority, has become the common experience of millions of people, so that the effects of college—in encouraging political participation and in shaping political beliefs (usually in a liberal direction)—are now widely shared. The ability of candidates to win nomination for office no longer depends on their ability to curry favor with a few powerful bosses; it now reflects their skill at raising money, mobilizing friends and activists, cultivating a media image, and winning a primary election.

So great have been the changes in the politics of policymaking in this country starting in the 1930s that we can refer, with only slight exaggeration, to one policymaking system having been replaced by another (see box on page 586).

The Old System

The Old System had a small agenda. Though people voted at a high rate and often took part in torchlight parades and other mass political events, political leadership was professionalized in the sense that the leadership circle was small, access to it was difficult, and the activists in social movements generally were kept out. Only a few major issues were under discussion at any time. A member of Congress had a small staff (if any at all), dealt with his or her colleagues on a personal basis, deferred to the prestige of House and Senate leaders, and tended to become part of some stable coalition (the farm bloc, the labor bloc, the southern bloc) that persisted across many issues.

When someone proposed adding a new issue to the public agenda, a major debate often arose over whether it was legitimate for the federal government to take action at all on the matter. A dominant theme in this debate was the importance of "states' rights." Except in wartime, or during a very brief period when the nation expressed interest in acquiring colonies, the focus of policy debate was on domestic affairs. Members of Congress saw these domestic issues largely in terms of their effect on local constituencies. The presidency was small and somewhat personal; there was only a rudimentary

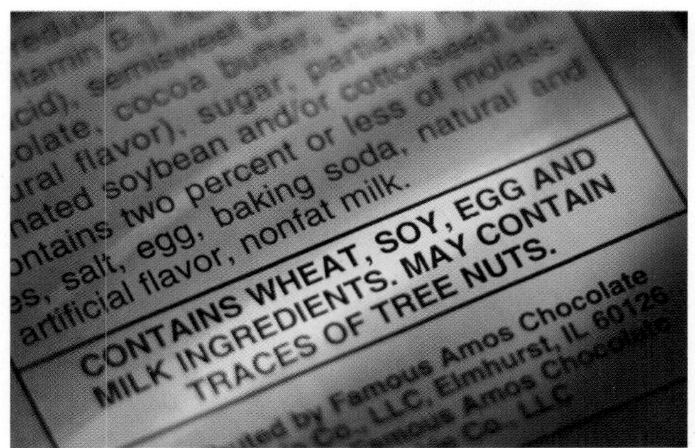

© Envision/Corbis

Food products now contain health warnings, such as nuts in this package of cookies.

White House staff. The president would cultivate the press, but there was a clear understanding that what he said in a press conference was never to be quoted directly.

For the government to take bold action under this system, the nation usually had to be facing a crisis. War presented such crisis, and so the federal government during the Civil War and World Wars I and II acquired extraordinary powers to conscript soldiers, control industrial production, regulate the flow of information to citizens, and restrict the scope of personal liberty. Each succeeding crisis left the government bureaucracy somewhat larger than it had been before, but when the crisis ended, the exercise of extraordinary powers ended. Once again, the agenda of political issues became small, and legislators argued about whether it was legitimate for the government to enter some new policy area, such as civil rights or industrial regulation.

The New System

The New System began in the 1930s but did not take its present form until the 1970s. It is characterized by a large policy agenda, the end of the debate over the legitimacy of government action (except in the area of First Amendment freedoms), the diffusion and decentralization of power in Congress, and the multiplication of interest groups. The government has grown so large that it has a policy on almost every conceivable subject, and so the debate in Washington is less often about whether it is right and prudent to take some bold new step and more often about how the government can best cope with the strains and problems that arise from implementing existing policies. As someone once said, the federal government is now more concerned with managing than with ruling.

For example, in 1935 Congress debated whether the nation should have a Social Security system at all; in the 1980s, it debated whether the system could best be kept solvent by raising taxes or by cutting benefits; in 2004 and 2005, it debated whether some part of each person's Social Security payments could be invested in the stock market. In the 1960s, Congress argued over whether there should be any federal civil rights laws at all; by the 1980s and 1990s, it was arguing over whether those laws should be administered in a way that simply eliminated legal barriers to equal opportunity for racial minorities or in a way (by affirmative action) that made up for the disadvantages that burdened such minorities in the past. As late as the 1950s, the president and Congress argued over whether it was right to adopt a new program if it meant the government had to borrow money to pay for it. As late as the 1960s, many members of Congress believed the federal government had no business paying for the health care of its citizens; today hardly anyone argues against having Medicare but many worry about how best to control its rising cost.

The differences between the Old and New Systems should not be exaggerated. The Constitution still makes it easier for Congress to block the proposals of the president, or for some committee of Congress to defeat the preferences of the majority of Congress, than in almost any other democratic government. The system of checks and balances operates as before. The essential differences between the Old and the New Systems are these:

1. Under the Old System, the checks and balances made it difficult for the federal government to *start* a new program, and so the government remained relatively small. Under the New System, these checks and balances have made it hard to *change* what the government is already doing, and so the government has remained large.
2. Under the Old System, power was *somewhat centralized* in the hands of party and congressional leaders. There was still plenty of conflict, but the number of people who had to agree before something could be done was not large. Under the New System, power is much more *decentralized,* and so it is harder to resolve conflict because so many more people—party activists, interest group leaders, individual members of Congress, heads of government agencies—must agree.

The transition from the Old to the New System occurred chiefly during two periods in American politics. The first was in the early 1930s when a catastrophic depression led the government to explore new ways of helping the needy, regulating business, and preventing a recurrence of the disaster.

How American Politics Has Changed

Old System		New System
	Congress	
Chairs relatively strong		Chairs relatively weak
Small staffs		Large staffs
Few subcommittees		Many subcommittees
	Interest Groups	
A few large blocs (farmers, business, labor)		Many diverse interests that form ad hoc coalitions
Rely on "insider" lobbying		Mobilize grassroots
	Presidency	
Small staff		Large staff
Reaches public via press conferences		Reaches public via radio and television
	Courts	
Allow government to exercise few economic powers		Allow government to exercise broad economic power
Take narrow view of individual freedoms		Take broad view of individual freedoms
	Political Parties	
Dominated by state and local party leaders meeting in conventions		Dominated by activists chosen in primaries and caucuses
	Policy Agenda	
Brief		Long
	Key Question	
Should the federal government enter a new policy area?		How can we fix and pay for an existing policy?
	Key Issue	
Would a new federal program abridge states' rights?		Would a new federal program prove popular?

Franklin Roosevelt's New Deal was the result. The huge majorities enjoyed by the Democrats in Congress, coupled with popular demands to solve the problem, led to a vast outpouring of new legislation and the creation of dozens of new government agencies. Though initially the Supreme Court struck down some of these measures as unconstitutional, a key member of the Court changed his mind and others retired from the bench; by the late 1930s, the Court had virtually ceased opposing any economic legislation.

The second period was in the mid-1960s, a time of prosperity. There was no crisis akin to the Great Depression or World War II, but two events helped change the face of American politics. One was an intellectual and popular ferment that we now refer to as the spirit of "the sixties"—a militant civil rights movement, student activism on college campuses aimed at resisting the Vietnam War, growing concern about threats to the environment, the popular appeal of Ralph Nader and his consumer protection movement, and an optimism among many political and

AP Images/Charlie Riedel

The Ford Motor company did not accept federal support during the recent recession and has begun to show a profit.

Jim West/Alamy

A Chevrolet Volt being assembled in Detroit. Federal subsidies go to people who buy one.

intellectual leaders that the government could solve whatever problems it was willing to address. The other was the 1964 election that returned Lyndon Johnson to the presidency with a larger share of the popular vote than any other president in modern times. Johnson swept into office and with him, liberal Democratic majorities in both the House and Senate.

The combination of organized demands for new policies, elite optimism about the likely success of those policies, and extraordinary majorities in Congress meant that President Johnson was able, for a few years, to get almost any program he wanted enacted into law. So large were his majorities in Congress that the conservative coalition of Republicans and southern Democrats was no longer large enough to block action; northern Democratic liberals were sufficiently numerous in the House and Senate to take control of both bodies. And so, much of Johnson's "Great Society" legislation became law. This included the passage of Medicare (to help pay the medical bills of retired people) and Medicaid (to help pay the medical bills of people on welfare), greatly expanded federal aid to the states (to assist them in fighting crime, rebuilding slums, and running transit systems), the enactment of major civil rights laws and of a program to provide federal aid to local schools, the creation of a "War on Poverty" that included various job-training and community-action agencies, and the enactment of a variety of laws regulating business for the purpose of reducing auto fatalities, improving the safety and health of industrial workers, cutting back on pollutants entering the atmosphere, and safeguarding consumers from harmful products.

These two periods—the early 1930s and the mid-1960s—changed the political landscape in America. Of the two, the latter was perhaps the more important, for not only did it witness the passage of so much unprecedented legislation, but also it saw major changes in the pattern of political leadership. It was during this time that the great majority of the members of the House of Representatives came to enjoy relatively secure seats, the primary elections came to supplant party conventions as the decisive means of selecting presidential candidates, interest groups increased greatly in number, and television began to play an important role in shaping the political agenda and perhaps influencing the kinds of candidates nominated.

Consequences of Activist Government

One way of describing the New System is to call it an "activist" government. It is tempting to make a sweeping judgment about such a government, either praising it because it serves a variety of popular needs or condemning it because it is a bureaucratic affliction. Such generalizations are not entirely empty, but neither are they very helpful. The worth of any given program, or of any collection of programs, can be assessed only by a careful consideration of its costs and benefits, of its effects and side effects. But we may discover some general political consequences of the enlarged scope of government activity.

First, as the government gets bigger, its members must spend more time managing the consequences—intended and unintended—of existing programs and less time debating at length new ideas. As a result, all parts of the government, not just the executive agencies, become more bureaucratized. The White House Office and the Office of Management and Budget (OMB) grow in size and influence, as do the staffs of Congress. At the same time, private organizations (corporations, unions, universities) that deal with the government must also become more bureaucratic. The government hires more people when it is running 80 programs concerned with employment than when it is running two. By the same token, a private employer will hire (and give power to) more people when it is complying with 80 sets of regulations than when it is complying with two.

Second, the more government does, the more it will appear to be acting in inconsistent, uncoordinated, and cumbersome ways. When people complain of red tape, bureaucracy, stalemates, and confusion, they often assume these irritants are caused by incompetent or self-seeking public officials. There is incompetence and self-interest in government just as in every other part of society, but these character traits are not the chief cause of the problem. As citizens, we want many different and often conflicting things. The result is the rise of competing policies, the division of labor among separate administrative agencies, the diffusion of accountability and control, and the multiplication of paperwork. And because Americans are especially energetic about asserting their rights, we must add to the above list of problems the regular use of the courts to challenge policies that we do not like.

Third, an activist government is less susceptible to control by electoral activity than a passive one. When the people in Washington did little, elections made a larger difference in policy than when they began to do a lot. We have pointed out in this book the extent to which both political parties and voter turnout have declined. There are many reasons for this, but an important one often is forgotten. If elections make less of a difference—because the few people for whom one votes can do little to alter the ongoing programs of government—then it may make sense for people to spend less time on party or electoral activities and more on interest group activities aimed at specific agencies and programs.

The rapid increase in the number and variety of interest groups and their enlarged role in government are not pathological. They are a rational response to the fact that elected officials can tend to only a few things, and therefore we must direct our energies at the appointed officials (and judges) who tend to all other government matters. Every president tries to accomplish more, usually by trying to reorganize the executive branch. But no president and no reorganization plan can affect more than a tiny fraction of the millions of federal employees and thousands of government programs. "Coordination" from the top can at best occur selectively, for a few issues of exceptional importance.

Ronald Reagan learned this when he took office in 1981 after promising to reduce the size of government. He did persuade Congress to cut taxes, but his plans to cut domestic spending resulted in only small declines in some programs and actual increases in many others. Though some programs, such as public housing, were hard hit, most were not, and agricultural subsidies increased dramatically.

When George W. Bush became president in 2001, his philosophy was summarized by the phrase "compassionate conservatism," words that implied that, though he was a conservative, he was not much interested in simply cutting the size of the federal government. And while in office, he proposed policies that would increase spending on many programs. His actions suggest a fact: cutting down on what Washington does is virtually impossible because the people want so much of what it does.

Finally, the more government tries to do, the more things it will be held responsible for and the greater the risk of failure. From time to time in the 19th century, the business cycle made many people unhappy with the federal government—recall the rise of various protest parties—though then the government did very little. If federal officials were lucky, popular support would rise as soon as economic conditions improved. If they were unlucky and a depression lasted into the election campaign, they would be thrown out of office. Today, however, the government—and the president in particular—is held responsible for crime, drug abuse, abortion, civil rights, the environment, the elderly, the status of women, the decay of central cities, the price of gasoline, and international tensions in half a dozen places on the globe.

No government and no president can do well on all or even most of these matters most of the time. Indeed, most of these problems, such as crime, may be totally beyond the reach of the federal government, no matter what its policy. It should not be surprising, therefore, that opinion surveys taken since the early 1960s have shown a steep decline in public confidence in government. There is no reason to believe that this represents a loss of faith in our form of government or even in the design of its institutions, but it clearly reflects a disappointment in, and even cynicism about, the performance of government.

It is too soon to know how, if at all, public sentiments about the performance of government will change as Washington (in response to the 2008–2009 economic crisis) has expanded government activity faster than it has grown in any periods since the late 1930s and the mid-1960s. President Barack Obama proposed a budget for Fiscal Year 2012 that contemplated a

What Would You Do?

MEMORANDUM

To: *President Daniel Gilbert*

From: *Fowler Brown, legislative liaison*

Subject: *Replacing Social Security*

You face a difficult decision. Despite past reforms, the program can no longer be funded without large tax increases. Here are the arguments for and against allowing workers to invest their taxes in private mutual funds.

Arguments for:

1. Workers pay 15 percent of their salary to Social Security, with no guarantee that they will get their money back when they retire.
2. There are only two workers for every retired person (in the 1930s, there were 16 for every retiree). People must be encouraged to invest in their own retirement.
3. The federal government spends a quarter of its budget on Social Security, far more than it devotes to national defense.

News »

Policies for the Future

The President will make a major announcement about Social Security in his 2021 State of the Union message next week. The program, while popular, is running out of money.

Arguments against:

1. Workers will have no guarantee that the mutual funds in which they put their tax money will earn them enough.
2. We should raise taxes on all high-income workers to save Social Security.
3. Social Security is more important than national defense.

Your decision:

Approve ______________ Oppose ______________

deficit of $1.645 trillion. Congressional Republicans, who won control of the House in 2010, objected. After long negotiations with the White House, the two sides agreed on a compromise that made some cuts in spending, thereby avoiding a shutdown of the federal government until November 2011. The large spending increases, however, are only half the story. The other half concerns the federal government taking on new responsibilities and challenges: It has become the majority stockholder in what was once the world's largest automotive company, General Motors; it has more closely controlled dozens of other companies and diverse financial markets; and it has enacted a large, new government-regulated health care system.

The 2009 stimulus bill allowed people to get money if they traded in an old car that burned a lot of gas.

University of Maryland political scientist Donald F. Kettl has argued that the "financial meltdown accelerated our expectations that government will keep us safe. . . . We've gone from debates over privatizing the public sector to big steps toward governmentalizing the private sector."[1] The far-reaching changes include "more public money in the private economy, more rules to shape how the private sector behaves, and more citizen expectations that government will manage the risks we face."[2]

We cannot yet say whether multi-trillion-dollar budget deficits and policies that betoken government-guaranteed corporate capitalism will persist for years to come. But it seems a fair bet that the New System is entering a new era which, not unlike the expansion that began in the late 1930s, has been fueled by economic problems that have afflicted or threatened most Americans.

It also seems likely that, if anything, public disenchantment with government performance will continue to grow along with government's role in people's lives. Such disenchantment is hardly unique to the United States; it appears to be a feature of almost every democratic political system. The disenchantment is in fact probably greater elsewhere. Americans who complain of high taxes might feel somewhat differently if they lived in Sweden, where taxes are nearly twice as high as here. Those who grouse about bureaucrats in this country probably have never dealt with the massive, centralized bureaucracies of Italy or France. People who are annoyed by congestion, pollution, and inflation ought to arrange a trip to Beijing, Mexico City, or Tokyo. However frustrating private life and public affairs may be in this country, every year thousands living in other nations become immigrants to this country. Few Americans choose to emigrate to other places.

The enormous expansion of the scope and goals of the federal government has not been random or unguided. The government has tended to enlarge its powers more in some directions than in others; certain kinds of goals have been served more frequently than others. Though many factors shape this process of selection, two are of special importance. One is our constitutional structure, and the other our political culture.

The Influence of Structure

To see the influence of structure, it is necessary to perform a mental experiment. Suppose the Founders had adopted a centralized, parliamentary regime instead of a decentralized, congressional one. They had the British model right before their eyes. Every other European democracy adopted it. What difference would it have made had we followed the British example?

No one can be certain, of course, because the United States and Great Britain differ in many ways, and not just in their political forms. At best, our mental experiment will be an educated guess. But the following possibilities seem plausible.

A parliamentary regime of the British sort centralizes power in the hands of an elected prime minister with a disciplined partisan majority in the legislature and frees him or her from most of the constraints created by independent congressional committees or independent, activist courts. Had the Framers adopted a parliamentary system, we might see these features in the political life of the United States today:

- *Quicker adoption of majoritarian policies, such as those in the area of social welfare.* Broad popular desires would be translated sooner into national policy when they are highly salient and conform to the views of party leaders.
- *More centralization of bureaucratic authority—more national planning, and less local autonomy.* More decisions would be made bureaucratically, both because bureaucracies would be proportionately larger and because they would have wider discretionary authority delegated to them. (If the prime minister heads *both* the executive branch and the legislature, he or she sees no reason why decisions cannot be made as easily in one place as the other.) Local authorities would not have been able to prevent groups of citizens (such as African Americans) from voting or otherwise participating in public life by maintaining segregated facilities at the local level.
- *Fewer opportunities for citizens to challenge or block government policies of which they disapprove.* Without independent and activist courts, without local centers (state and city) of autonomous power, U.S. citizens would have less of a chance to organize to stop a highway or an urban-renewal project, for example, and hence fewer citizen organizations with these and similar purposes would exist.
- *Greater executive control of government.* If a situation like Watergate occurred, we would never know about it. No legislative investigating committees would be sufficiently independent of executive control to be able to investigate claims of executive wrongdoing.

- *Similar foreign policy.* We probably would have fought in about the same number of wars and under pretty much the same circumstances.
- *Higher and more centralized taxation.* Taxes would be higher, and a larger share of our tax money would be collected at the national level. Thus we would find it harder to wage a "tax revolt" (since it is easier to block local spending decisions than national ones).

If this list of guesses is even approximately correct, it means that you would get more of some things that you want and less of others. In general, it would be easier for temporary majorities to govern and harder for individuals and groups to protect their interests.

The Founders would probably not be surprised at this list of differences. Though they could not have foreseen all the events and issues that would have led to these outcomes, they would have understood them, because they thought they were creating a system designed to keep central power weak and to enhance local and citizen power. They would have been amazed, of course, at the extent to which central power has been enhanced and local power weakened in the United States, but if they visited Europe, they would learn that by comparison American politics remains far more sensitive to local concerns than does politics abroad.

The Influence of Ideas

The broadly shared political culture of Americans has also influenced the policies adopted by the U.S. government. Paramount among these attitudes is the preoccupation with rights. More than the citizens of perhaps any other nation, Americans define their relations with one another and with political authority in terms of rights. The civil liberties protected by the Bill of Rights have been assiduously defended and their interpretation significantly broadened even while the power of government has been growing.

For example, we expect that the groups affected by any government program will have a right to play a role in shaping and administering that program. In consequence, interest groups have proliferated. We think citizens should have the right to select the nominees of political parties as well as to choose between the parties; hence primary elections have largely replaced party conventions in selecting candidates. Individual members of Congress assert their rights, and thus the power of congressional leaders and committee chairs has steadily diminished. We probably use the courts more frequently than the citizens of any other nation to make or change public policy; in doing so, we are asserting one set of rights against a competing set. The procedural rules that set forth how government is to act—the Freedom of Information Act, the Privacy Act, the Administrative Procedure Act—are more complex and demanding than the rules under which any other democratic government must operate. Each rule exists because it embodies what somebody has claimed to be a right: the right to know information, to maintain one's privacy, to participate in making decisions, and to bring suit against rival parties.

The more vigorously we assert our rights, the harder it is to make government decisions or to manage large institutions. We recognize this when we grumble about red tape and bureaucratic confusion, but we rarely give much support to proposals to centralize authority or simplify decision making. We seem to accept whatever it costs in efficiency or effectiveness in order to maintain the capacity for asserting our rights.

We do not always agree on which rights are most important, however. In addition to the influence of the widely shared commitment to rights generally, government is also shaped by the views that certain political elites have about which rights ought to be given the highest priority. Elite opinion tends to favor freedom of expression over freedom to manage or dispose of property. Mass opinion, though it has changed a good deal in the last few decades, is less committed to the preferred position of freedom of expression. Rank-and-file citizens often complain that what the elite calls essential liberty should instead be regarded as excessive permissiveness. People who own or manage property often lament the extent to which the rights governing its use have declined.

The changes in the relative security of personal and property freedom are linked to a fundamental and enduring tension in American thought. Tocqueville said it best: Americans, he wrote, "are far more ardently and tenaciously attached to equality than to freedom." Though democratic communities have a "natural taste for freedom," that freedom is hard to preserve, because its excesses are immediate and obvious and its advantages are remote and uncertain. The advantages of equality, on the other hand, are readily apparent, and its costs are obscure and deferred.[3] For example, Americans believe in free speech, but most of us rarely take advantage of that right and notice the problem only when somebody says something we don't like. We have to remind ourselves that freedom has to be protected even when

Some "Rules" of Politics

Here are some generalizations about American politics, distilled from what has been said in this book, and offered in nervous awareness that our political system has a way of proving everybody wrong. (Before the 1960s, it was a "rule" of politics that no Catholic could be elected president. John F. Kennedy took care of that.)

- Policies, once adopted, tend to persist whatever their value. (It is easier to start new programs than to end old ones.)
- Almost all electoral politics is local politics. (Members of Congress who forget "home base" tend not to remain in Congress for long.)
- Whatever the size of their staff and budget, Congress and the White House will always be overworked. (More resources produce more work, which requires more resources.)
- Each branch of government tends to emulate the others. (Congress will become more bureaucratized to cope with an executive branch that becomes more bureaucratized; judges will become more activist as Congress becomes more activist.)
- Proposals that seem to confer widespread and immediate benefits will be enacted whatever their long-term costs.
- Proposals that seem to confer delayed benefits will be enacted only if their costs are unknown, concealed, or deferred.
- Nobody—businesspeople, bureaucrats, members of Congress, judges, professors—likes competition, and everybody will do whatever he or she can to reduce or eliminate it.
- "Planning" in government takes place after a crisis takes place.
- The mass media never cover a story about things that are going well. Thus the number of "problems" in society is a function of the number of reporters.
- If you want something, you are claiming a right; if your opponent wants something, he or she is protecting a vested interest.

it does not help us directly. By contrast, we notice equality immediately, as when everybody of a certain age gets Social Security even when they are already rich. Equality makes us feel comfortable even if a few people don't need the benefits they are getting.

Tocqueville, however, may have underestimated the extent to which political liberties would endure, because he did not foresee the determination of the courts to resist, in the long run if not the short, the passions of temporary majorities seeking to curtail such liberties. But he did not underestimate the extent to which in the economic and social realms Americans would decide that improving the conditions of life would justify restrictions on the right to dispose of property and to manage private institutions. At first, the conflict was between liberty and equality of opportunity; more recently it has become a conflict—among political elites if not within the citizenry itself—between equality of opportunity and equality of results.

The fact that decisions can be influenced by opinions about rights indicates that decisions can be influenced by opinions generally. As the political system has become more fragmented and more individualized as a result of our collective assertion of rights, it has come more under the sway of ideas. When political parties were strong and congressional leadership was centralized (as in the latter part of the 19th and the early part of the 20th centuries), gaining access to the decision-making process in Washington was difficult, and the number of new ideas that stood a chance of adoption was small. However, those proposals that could command leadership support were more easily adopted: though there were powerful organizations that could say no, those same organizations could also say yes.

Today, these and other institutions are fragmented and in disarray. Individual members of Congress are far more important than congressional leaders. Political parties no longer control nominations for office. The media have given candidates direct access to the voters; campaign finance laws have restricted, but not eliminated, the influence that interest groups can wield by spending money. Forming new, issue-oriented lobbying groups is much easier today than formerly, thanks to the capability of computers and direct-mail advertising.

These idea-based changes in institutions affect how policy is made. When there is widespread enthusiasm for an idea—especially among political elites but also in the public at large—new programs can be formulated and adopted with great speed. This happened when Lyndon Johnson's Great Society legislation was proposed, when the environmental and consumer protection laws first arrived on the public agenda, and when campaign finance reform was proposed in the wake of Watergate. So long as such symbols have a powerful appeal, so long as a consensus persists, change is possible. But when these ideas lose their appeal—or are challenged by new ideas—the competing pressures make change extremely difficult. Environmentalism today is challenged by concerns about creating jobs and economic growth; social legislation is challenged by skepticism about its effectiveness and concern over its cost; campaign finance reforms are, to some critics, merely devices for protecting incumbents.

This may all seem obvious to a reader raised in the world of contemporary politics. But it is different in degree if not in kind from the way in which politics was once carried out. In the 1920s, the 1930s, the 1940s, and even the 1950s, people described politics as a process of bargaining among organized interests, or "blocs," representing business, farming, labor, ethnic, and professional groups. With the expansion of the scope of government policy, there are no longer a few major blocs that sit astride the policy process. Instead, thousands of highly specialized interests and constituencies seek above all to protect whatever benefits, intangible as well as tangible, they get from government.

We have a large government—and large expectations about what it can achieve. But the government finds it increasingly difficult to satisfy those expectations. The public's acceptance of an activist role for government has been accompanied by a decline in public confidence in those who manage that government. We expect more and more from government but are less and less certain that we will get it, or get it in a form and at a cost that we find acceptable. This perhaps constitutes the greatest challenge to statesmanship in the years ahead: to find a way to serve the true interests of the people while restoring and retaining their confidence in the legitimacy of government itself.

LEARNING OBJECTIVES

WHAT YOU NEED TO KNOW

☑ **Name two things that for many years kept the agenda of the federal government short.**

(a) The Supreme Court restricted the ability of Congress to delegate broad discretionary powers to administrative agencies.

(b) Public opinion supported the idea of a limited federal government.

(c) Washington could not levy an income tax.

☑ **Name two things that have expanded the agenda of the federal government.**

(a) The Supreme has allowed the delegation of broad discretionary powers to top administrative agencies.

(b) Public opinion has supported a more activist government.

(c) The Constitution has been amended to allow for an income tax.

The Declaration of Independence

In Congress, July 4, 1776

The Unanimous Declaration of the Thirteen United States of America

When, in the course of human events, it becomes necessary for one people to dissolve the political bands which have connected them with another, and to assume, among the powers of the earth, the separate and equal station to which the laws of nature and of nature's God entitle them, a decent respect to the opinions of mankind requires that they should declare the causes which impel them to the separation.

We hold these truths to be self-evident: That all men are created equal; that they are endowed by their Creator with certain unalienable rights; that among these are life, liberty, and the pursuit of happiness; that, to secure these rights, governments are instituted among men, deriving their just powers from the consent of the governed; that whenever any form of government becomes destructive of these ends, it is the right of the people to alter or to abolish it, and to institute new government, laying its foundation on such principles, and organizing its power in such form, as to them shall seem most likely to effect their safety and happiness. Prudence, indeed, will dictate that governments long established should not be changed for light and transient causes; and accordingly all experience hath shown that mankind are more disposed to suffer, while evils are sufferable, than to right themselves by abolishing the forms to which they are accustomed. But when a long train of abuses and usurpations, pursuing invariably the same object, evinces a design to reduce them under absolute despotism, it is their right, it is their duty, to throw off such government, and to provide new guards for their future security. Such has been the patient sufferance of these colonies; and such is now the necessity which constrains them to alter their former systems of government. The history of the present King of Great Britain is a history of repeated injuries and usurpations, all having in direct object the establishment of an absolute tyranny over these states. To prove this, let facts be submitted to a candid world.

He has refused to assent to laws, the most wholesome and necessary for the public good.

He has forbidden his governors to pass laws of immediate and pressing importance, unless suspended in their operation till his assent should be obtained; and, when so suspended, he has utterly neglected to attend to them.

He has refused to pass other laws for the accommodation of large districts of people, unless those people would relinquish the right of representation in the legislature, a right inestimable to them, and formidable to tyrants only.

He has called together legislative bodies at places unusual, uncomfortable, and distant from the depository of their public records, for the sole purpose of fatiguing them into compliance with his measures.

He has dissolved representative houses repeatedly, for opposing, with manly firmness, his invasions on the rights of the people.

He has refused for a long time, after such dissolutions, to cause others to be elected; whereby the legislative powers, incapable of annihilation, have returned to the people at large for their exercise; the state remaining, in the mean time, exposed to all dangers of invasions from without and convulsions within.

He has endeavored to prevent the population of these states; for that purpose obstructing the laws for naturalization of foreigners; refusing to pass others to encourage their migration hither, and raising the conditions of new appropriations of lands.

He has obstructed the administration of justice, by refusing his assent to laws for establishing judiciary powers.

He has made judges dependent on his will alone, for the tenure of their offices, and the amount and payment of their salaries.

He has erected a multitude of new offices, and sent hither swarms of officers to harass our people, and eat out their substance.

He has kept among us, in times of peace, standing armies, without the consent of our legislatures.

He has affected to render the military independent of, and superior to, the civil power.

He has combined with others to subject us to a jurisdiction foreign to our constitution, and unacknowledged by our laws, giving his assent to their acts of pretended legislation:

For quartering large bodies of armed troops among us:

For protecting them, by a mock trial, from punishment for any murders which they should commit on the inhabitants of these states;

For cutting off our trade with all parts of the world;

For imposing taxes on us without our consent;

For depriving us, in many cases, of the benefits of trial by jury;

For transporting us beyond seas, to be tried for pretended offenses;

For abolishing the free system of English laws in a neighboring province, establishing therein an arbitrary government, and enlarging its boundaries, so as to render it at once an example and fit instrument for introducing the same absolute rule into these colonies;

For taking away our charters, abolishing our most valuable laws, and altering fundamentally the forms of our governments;

For suspending our own legislatures, and declaring themselves invested with power to legislate for us in all cases whatsoever.

He has abdicated government here, by declaring us out of his protection and waging war against us.

He has plundered our seas, ravaged our coasts, burned our towns, and destroyed the lives of our people.

He is at this time transporting large armies of foreign mercenaries to complete the works of death, desolation, and tyranny already begun with circumstances of cruelty and perfidy scarcely paralleled in the most barbarous ages, and totally unworthy the head of a civilized nation.

He has constrained our fellow-citizens, taken captive on the high seas, to bear arms against their country, to become the executioners of their friends and brethren, or to fall themselves by their hands.

He has excited domestic insurrection among us, and has endeavored to bring on the inhabitants of our frontiers the merciless Indian savages, whose known rule of warfare is an undistinguished destruction of all ages, sexes, and conditions.

In every stage of these oppressions we have petitioned for redress in the most humble terms; our repeated petitions have been answered only by repeated injury. A prince, whose character is thus marked by every act which may define a tyrant, is unfit to be the ruler of a free people.

Nor have we been wanting in our attentions to our British brethren. We have warned them, from time to time, of attempts by their Legislature to extend an unwarrantable jurisdiction over us. We have reminded them of the circumstances of our emigration and settlement here. We have appealed to their native justice and magnanimity; and we have conjured them, by the ties of our common kindred, to disavow these usurpations, which would inevitably interrupt our connections and correspondence. They, too, have been deaf to the voice of justice and of consanguinity. We must, therefore, acquiesce in the necessity which denounces our separation, and hold them, as we hold the rest of mankind, enemies in war, in peace friends.

We, therefore, the representatives of the United States of America, in General Congress assembled, appealing to the Supreme Judge of the world for the rectitude of our intentions, do, in the name and by the authority of the good people of these colonies, solemnly publish and declare, that these United Colonies are, and of right ought to be, FREE AND INDEPENDENT STATES; that they are absolved from all allegiance to the British crown, and that all political connection between them and the state of Great Britain is, and ought to be, totally dissolved; and that, as free and independent states, they have full power to levy war, conclude peace, contract alliances, establish commerce, and do all other acts and things which independent states may of right do. And for the support of this declaration, with a firm reliance on the protection of Divine Providence, we mutually pledge to each other our lives, our fortunes, and our sacred honor.

JOHN HANCOCK [*President*]
[*and fifty-five others*]

The Constitution of the United States

Preamble

We the People of the United States, in Order to form a more perfect Union, establish Justice, insure domestic Tranquility, provide for the common defence, promote the general Welfare, and secure the Blessings of Liberty to ourselves and our Posterity, do ordain and establish this Constitution for the United States of America.

Article I.

Bicameral Congress

Section 1. All legislative Powers herein granted shall be vested in a Congress of the United States, which shall consist of a Senate and House of Representatives.

Membership of the House

Section 2. The House of Representatives shall be composed of Members chosen every second Year by the People of the several States, and the Electors in each State shall have the Qualifications requisite for Electors of the most numerous Branch of the State Legislature.

No person shall be a Representative who shall not have attained to the age of twenty five Years, and been seven Years a Citizen of the United States, and who shall not, when elected, be an Inhabitant of that State in which he shall be chosen.

Representatives and direct Taxes shall be apportioned among the several States which may be included within this Union, according to their respective Numbers, which shall be determined by adding to the whole Number of free Persons, including those bound to Service for a Term of Years, and excluding Indians not taxed, three fifths of all other Persons.[1] The actual Enumeration shall be made within three Years after the first Meeting of the Congress of the United States, and within every subsequent Term of ten Years, in such Manner as they shall by Law direct. The Number of Representatives shall not exceed one for every thirty Thousand, but each State shall have at Least one Representative; and until such enumeration shall be made, the State of New Hampshire shall be entitled to chuse three, Massachusetts eight, Rhode-Island and Providence Plantations one, Connecticut five, New-York six, New Jersey four, Pennsylvania eight, Delaware one, Maryland six, Virginia ten, North Carolina five, South Carolina five, and Georgia three.

When vacancies happen in the Representation from any State, the Executive Authority thereof shall issue Writs of Election to fill such Vacancies.

Power to impeach

The House of Representatives shall chuse their Speaker and other Officers; and shall have the sole Power of Impeachment.

Membership of the Senate

Section 3. The Senate of the United States shall be composed of two Senators from each State, *chosen by the Legislature thereof*,[2] for six Years; and each Senator shall have one Vote.

Immediately after they shall be assembled in Consequence of the first Election, they shall be divided as equally as may be into three Classes. The Seats of the Senators of the first class shall be vacated at

---

NOTE: The topical headings are not part of the original Constitution. Excluding the Preamble and Closing, those portions set in italic type have been superseded or changed by later amendments.

1. Changed by the Fourteenth Amendment, section 2.

2. Changed by the Seventeenth Amendment.

the Expiration of the second Year, of the second Class at the Expiration of the fourth Year, and of the third Class at the Expiration of the sixth Year, so that one third may be chosen every second Year; *and if Vacancies happen by Resignation, or otherwise, during the Recess of the Legislature of any State, the Executive thereof may make temporary Appointments until the next Meeting of the Legislature, which shall then fill such Vacancies*.[3]

No Person shall be a Senator who shall not have attained to the Age of thirty Years, and been nine Years a Citizen of the United States, and who shall not, when elected, be an Inhabitant of that State for which he shall be chosen.

The Vice President of the United States shall be President of the Senate, but shall have no Vote, unless they be equally divided.

Power to try impeachments

The Senate shall chuse their other Officers, and also a President pro tempore, in the Absence of the Vice President, or when he shall exercise the Office of President of the United States.

The Senate shall have the sole Power to try all Impeachments. When sitting for that Purpose, they shall be on Oath or Affirmation. When the President of the United States is tried the Chief Justice shall preside: And no Person shall be convicted without the Concurrence of two thirds of the Members present.

Judgment in Cases of Impeachment shall not extend further than to removal from Office, and disqualification to hold and enjoy any Office of honor, Trust or Profit under the United States: but the Party convicted shall nevertheless be liable and subject to Indictment, Trial, Judgment and Punishment, according to Law.

Laws governing elections

Section 4. The Times, Places and Manner of holding Elections for Senators and Representatives, shall be prescribed in each State by the Legislature thereof; but the Congress may at any time by Law make or alter such Regulations, except as to the Places of chusing Senators.

The Congress shall assemble at least once in every Year, and such Meeting shall be on the *first Monday in December, unless they shall by Law appoint a different Day*.[4]

Rules of Congress

Section 5. Each House shall be the Judge of the Elections, Returns and Qualifications of its own Members, and a Majority of each shall constitute a Quorum to do Business; but a smaller number may adjourn from day to day, and may be authorized to compel the Attendance of absent Members, in such Manner, and under such Penalties as each House may provide.

Each House may determine the Rules of its Proceedings, punish its Members for disorderly Behaviour, and, with the Concurrence of two thirds, expel a Member.

Each House shall keep a Journal of its Proceedings, and from time to time publish the same, excepting such Parts as may in their Judgment require Secrecy; and the Yeas and Nays of the Members of either House on any question shall, at the Desire of one fifth of those Present, be entered on the Journal.

Neither House, during the Session of Congress, shall, without the Consent of the other, adjourn for more than three days, nor to any other Place than that in which the two Houses shall be sitting.

---

3. Changed by the Seventeenth Amendment.
4. Changed by the Twentieth Amendment, section 2.

Salaries and immunities of members

Section 6. The Senators and Representatives shall receive a Compensation for their Services, to be ascertained by Law, and paid out of the Treasury of the United States. They shall in all Cases, except Treason, Felony and Breach of the Peace, be privileged from Arrest during their Attendance at the Session of their respective Houses, and in going to and returning from the same; and for any Speech or Debate in either House, they shall not be questioned in any other Place.

Bar on members of Congress holding federal appointive office

No Senator or Representative shall, during the Time for which he was elected, be appointed to any civil Office under the Authority of the United States, which shall have been created, or the Emoluments whereof shall have been encreased during such time; and no Person holding any Office under the United States, shall be a Member of either House during his Continuance in Office.

Money bills originate in House

Section 7. All Bills for raising Revenue shall originate in the House of Representatives; but the Senate may propose or concur with Amendments as on other Bills.

Procedure for enacting laws; veto power

Every Bill which shall have passed the House of Representatives and the Senate, shall, before it become a Law, be presented to the President of the United States; If he approve he shall sign it, but if not he shall return it, with Objections to that House in which it shall have originated, who shall enter the Objections at large on their Journal, and proceed to reconsider it. If after such Reconsideration two thirds of that House shall agree to pass the Bill, it shall be sent, together with the Objections, to the other House, by which it shall likewise be reconsidered, and if approved by two thirds of that House, it shall become a Law. But in all such Cases the Votes of both Houses shall be determined by yeas and Nays, and the Names of the Persons voting for and against the Bill shall be entered on the Journal of each House respectively. If any Bill shall not be returned by the President within ten Days (Sundays excepted) after it shall have been presented to him, the Same shall be a Law, in like Manner, as if he had signed it, unless the Congress by their Adjournment prevent its Return, in which Case it shall not be a Law.

Every Order, Resolution, or Vote to which the Concurrence of the Senate and House of Representatives may be necessary (except on a question of Adjournment) shall be presented to the President of the United States; and before the Same shall take Effect, shall be approved by him, or being disapproved by him, shall be repassed by two thirds of the Senate and House of Representatives, according to the Rules and Limitations prescribed in the Case of a Bill.

Powers of Congress *—taxes*

Section 8. The Congress shall have Power To lay and Collect Taxes, Duties, Imposts and Excises, to pay the Debts and provide for the common Defence and general Welfare of the United States; but all Duties, Imposts and Excises shall be uniform throughout the United States.

—borrowing

To borrow Money on the credit of the United States;

—regulation of commerce

To regulate Commerce with foreign Nations, and among the several States, and with the Indian Tribes;

—naturalization and bankruptcy

To establish an uniform Rule of Naturalization, and uniform Laws on the subject of Bankruptcies throughout the United States;

—money

To coin Money, regulate the Value thereof, and of foreign Coin, and fix the Standard of Weights and Measures;

—counterfeiting

To provide for the Punishment of counterfeiting the Securities and current Coin of the United States;

—post office

To establish Post Offices and post Roads;

—patents and copyrights

To promote the Progress of Science and useful Arts, by securing for limited Times to Authors and Inventors the exclusive Right to their respective Writings and Discoveries;

—create courts

To constitute Tribunals inferior to the Supreme Court;

—punish piracies

To define and punish Piracies and Felonies committed on the high Seas, and Offences against the Law of Nations;

—declare war

To declare War, grant Letters of Marque and Reprisal, and make Rules concerning Captures on Land and Water;

—create army and navy

To raise and support Armies, but no Appropriation of Money to that Use shall be for a longer Term than two Years;

To provide and maintain a Navy;

To make Rules for the Government and Regulation of the land and naval Forces;

—call the militia

To provide for calling forth the Militia to execute the Laws of the Union, suppress Insurrections and repel Invasions;

To provide for organizing, arming, and disciplining, the Militia, and for governing such Part of them as may be employed in the Service of the United States, reserving to the States respectively, the Appointment of the Officers, and the Authority of training the Militia according to the discipline prescribed by Congress;

—govern District of Columbia

To exercise exclusive Legislation in all Cases whatsoever, over such District (not exceeding ten Miles square) as may, by Cession of Particular States, and the Acceptance of Congress, become the Seat of the Government of the United States, and to exercise like Authority over all Places purchased by the Consent of the Legislature of the State in which the Same shall be, for the Erection of Forts, Magazines, Arsenals, dock-Yards and other needful Buildings;—And

—"necessary-and-proper" clause

To make all Laws which shall be necessary and proper for carrying into Execution the foregoing Powers, and all other Powers vested by this Constitution in the Government of the United States, or in any Department or Officer thereof.

Restrictions on powers of Congress
—slave trade

Section 9. The Migration or Importation of such Persons as any of the States now existing shall think proper to admit, shall not be prohibited by the Congress prior to the Year one thousand eight hundred and eight, but a Tax or duty may be imposed on such Importation, not exceeding ten dollars for each Person.

—habeas corpus

The Privilege of the Writ of Habeas Corpus shall not be suspended, unless when in Cases of Rebellion or Invasion the public Safety may require it.

—no bill of attainder or ex post facto law

No bill of Attainder or ex post facto Law shall be passed.

No Capitation, or other direct, Tax shall be laid, *unless in Proportion to the Census or Enumeration herein before directed to be taken.*[5]

—no interstate tariffs

No Tax or Duty shall be laid on Articles exported from any State.

—no preferential treatment for some states

No Preference shall be given by any Regulation of Commerce or Revenue to the Ports of one State over those of another; nor shall Vessels bound to, or from, one State, be obliged to enter, clear or pay Duties in another.

—appropriations

No Money shall be drawn from the Treasury, but in Consequence of Appropriations made by Law; and a regular Statement and Account of the Receipts and Expenditures of all public Money shall be published from time to time.

---

5. Changed by the Sixteenth Amendment.

—no titles of nobility

No Title of Nobility shall be granted by the United States: And no Person holding any Office of Profit or Trust under them, shall, without the Consent of the Congress, accept of any present, Emolument, Office, or Title, of any kind whatever, from any King, Prince, or foreign State.

Restrictions on powers of states

Section 10. No State shall enter into any Treaty, Alliance, or Confederation; grant Letters of Marque and Reprisal; coin Money; emit Bills of Credit; make any Thing but gold and silver Coin a Tender in Payment of Debts; pass any Bill of Attainder, ex post facto Law, or Law impairing the Obligation of Contracts, or grant any Title of Nobility.

No State shall, without the Consent of Congress, lay any Imposts or Duties on Imports or Exports, except what may be absolutely necessary for executing its inspection Laws; and the net Produce of all Duties and Imposts, laid by any State on Imports or Exports, shall be for the Use of the Treasury of the United States; and all such Laws shall be subject to the Revision and Controul of the Congress.

No State shall, without the Consent of Congress, lay any Duty of Tonnage, keep Troops, or Ships of War in time of Peace, enter into any Agreement or Compact with another State, or with a foreign Power, or engage in War, unless actually invaded, or in such imminent Danger as will not admit of delay.

Article II.

Office of president

Section 1. The executive Power shall be vested in a President of the United States of America. He shall hold his Office during the Term of four Years, and, together with the Vice President, chosen for the same Term, be elected, as follows:

Election of president

Each State shall appoint, in such Manner as the Legislature thereof may direct, a Number of Electors, equal to the whole Number of Senators and Representatives to which the State may be entitled in the Congress: but no Senator or Representative, or Person holding an Office of Trust or Profit under the United States, shall be appointed an Elector.

The Electors shall meet in their respective States, and vote by Ballot for two Persons, of whom one at least shall not be an Inhabitant of the same State with themselves. And they shall make a List of all the Persons voted for, and of the Number of Votes for each; which List they shall sign and certify, and transmit sealed to the Seat of the Government of the United States, directed to the President of the Senate. The President of the Senate shall, in the Presence of the Senate and House of Representatives, open all the Certificates, and the Votes shall then be counted. The Person having the greatest Number of Votes shall be the President, if such Number be a Majority of the whole Number of Electors appointed; and if there be more than one who have such Majority, and have an equal Number of Votes, then the House of Representatives shall immediately chuse by Ballot one of them for President; and if no Person have a Majority, then from the five highest on the List said House shall in like Manner chuse the President. But in chusing the President, the Votes shall be taken by States, the Representation from each State having one Vote; a quorum for this Purpose shall consist of a Member or Members from two thirds of the States, and a Majority of all the States shall be necessary to a Choice. In every Case, after the Choice of the President, the Person having the greatest Number of Votes of the Electors shall be the Vice President. But if there should remain two or more who have equal Votes, the Senate shall chuse from them by Ballot the Vice President.[6]

The Congress may determine the Time of chusing the Electors, and the Day on which they shall give their Votes, which Day shall be the same throughout the United States.

Requirements to be president

No Person except a natural born Citizen, or a Citizen of the United States, at the time of the Adoption of this Constitution, shall be eligible to the Office of President; neither shall any person be eligible to that Office who shall not have attained to the Age of thirty five Years, and been fourteen Years a Resident within the United States.

In Case of the Removal of the President from Office, or of his Death, Resignation, or Inability to discharge the Powers and Duties of the said Office, the Same shall devolve on the Vice President, and the Congress may by Law provide for the Case of Removal, Death, Resignation or Inability, both of the President and Vice President, declaring what Officer shall then act as President, and such Officer shall act accordingly, until the Disability be removed, or a President shall be elected.[7]

Pay of president

The President shall, at stated Times, receive for his Services, a Compensation, which shall neither be increased nor diminished during the Period for which he shall have been elected, and he shall not receive within that Period any other Emolument from the United States, or any of them.

Before he enter on the Execution of his Office, he shall take the following Oath or Affirmation:—"I do solemnly swear (or affirm) that I will faithfully execute the Office of President of the United States, and will to the best of my Ability preserve, protect and defend the Constitution of the United States."

Powers of president
—commander in chief

Section 2. The President shall be Commander in Chief of the Army and Navy of the United States, and of the Militia of the several States, when called into the actual Service of the United States; he may require the Opinion, in writing, of the principal Officer in each of the executive Departments, upon any Subject relating to the Duties of their respective Offices, and he shall have Power to grant Reprieves and Pardons for Offences against the United States, except in Cases of Impeachment.

—pardons

— treaties and appointments

He shall have Power, by and with the Advice and Consent of the Senate, to make Treaties, provided two thirds of the Senators present concur; and he shall nominate, and by and with the Advice and Consent of the Senate, shall appoint Ambassadors, other public Ministers and Consuls, Judges of the supreme Court, and all other Officers of the United States, whose Appointments are not herein otherwise provided for, and which shall be established by Law: but the Congress may by Law vest the Appointment of such inferior Officers, as they think proper, in the President alone, in the Courts of Law, or in the Heads of Departments.

The President shall have Power to fill up all Vacancies that may happen during the Recess of the Senate, by granting Commissions which shall expire at the End of their next Session.

---

6. Superseded by the Twelfth Amendment.
7. Modified by the Twenty-fifth Amendment.

Relations of president with Congress

Section 3. He shall from time to time give to the Congress Information of the State of the Union, and recommend to their Consideration such Measures as he shall judge necessary and expedient; he may, on extraordinary Occasions, convene both Houses, or either of them, and in Case of Disagreement between them, with Respect to the Time of Adjournment, he may adjourn them to such Time as he shall think proper; he shall receive Ambassadors and other public Ministers; he shall take Care that the Laws be faithfully executed, and shall Commission all the Officers of the United States.

Impeachment

Section 4. The President, Vice President and all civil Officers of the United States, shall be removed from Office on Impeachment for, and Conviction of, Treason, Bribery, or other high Crimes and Misdemeanors.

Article III.

Federal courts

Section 1. The judicial Power of the United States, shall be vested in one supreme Court, and in such inferior Courts as the Congress may from time to time ordain and establish. The Judges, both of the supreme and inferior Courts, shall hold their Offices during good Behaviour, and shall, at stated Times, receive for their Services, a Compensation, which shall not be diminished during their Continuance in Office.

Jurisdiction of courts

Section 2. The judicial Power shall extend to all Cases, in Law and Equity, arising under this Constitution, the Laws of the United States, and Treaties made, or which shall be made, under their Authority;—to all Cases affecting Ambassadors, other public Ministers and Consuls;—to all Cases of admiralty and maritime Jurisdiction;—to Controversies to which the United States shall be a Party;—to Controversies between two or more States;—*between a State and Citizens of another State*;[8]—between Citizens of different States;—between Citizens of the same State claiming Lands under Grants of different States, and between a State, or the Citizens thereof, and foreign States, Citizens or Subjects.

—original

In all Cases affecting Ambassadors, other public Ministers and Consuls, and those in which a State shall be Party, the supreme Court shall have original Jurisdiction. In all the other Cases before mentioned, the supreme Court shall have appellate Jurisdiction, both as to Law and Fact, with such Exceptions, and under such Regulations as the Congress shall make.

—appellate

The Trial of all Crimes, except in Cases of Impeachment, shall be by Jury; and such Trial shall be held in the State where the said Crimes shall have been committed; but when not committed within any State, the Trial shall be at such Place or Places as the Congress may by Law have directed.

Treason

Section 3. Treason against the United States, shall consist only in levying War against them, or in adhering to their Enemies, giving them Aid and Comfort. No Person shall be convicted of Treason unless on the Testimony of two Witnesses to the same overt Act, or on Confession in open Court.

The Congress shall have Power to declare the Punishment of Treason, but no Attainder of Treason shall work Corruption of Blood, or Forfeiture except during the Life of the Person attainted.

8. Modified by the Eleventh Amendment.

Article IV.

Full faith and credit

Section 1. Full Faith and Credit shall be given in each State to the public Acts, Records, and judicial Proceedings of every other State. And the Congress may by general Laws prescribe the Manner in which such Acts, Records and Proceedings shall be proved, and the Effect thereof.

Privileges and immunities

Section 2. The Citizens of each State shall be entitled to all Privileges and Immunities of Citizens in the several States.

Extradition

A person charged in any State with Treason, Felony, or other Crime, who shall flee from Justice, and be found in another State, shall on Demand of the executive Authority of the State from which he fled, be delivered up, to be removed to the State having Jurisdiction of the Crime.

No Person held to Service or Labour in one State, under the Laws thereof, escaping into another, shall, in Consequence of any Law or Regulation therein, be discharged from such Service or Labour, but shall be delivered up on Claim of the Party to whom such Service or Labour may be due.[9]

Creation of new states

Section 3. New States may be admitted by the Congress into this Union; but no new State shall be formed or erected within the Jurisdiction of any other State; nor any State be formed by the Junction of two or more States, or Parts of States, without the Consent of the Legislatures of the States concerned as well as of the Congress.

Governing territories

The Congress shall have Power to dispose of and make all needful Rules and Regulations respecting the Territory or other Property belonging to the United States; and nothing in this Constitution shall be so construed as to Prejudice any Claims of the United States, or of any particular State.

Protection of states

Section 4. The United States shall guarantee to every State in this Union a Republican Form of Government, and shall protect each of them against Invasion; and on Application of the Legislature, or of the Executive (when the Legislature cannot be convened) against domestic Violence.

Article V.

Amending the Constitution

The Congress, whenever two thirds of both Houses shall deem it necessary, shall propose Amendments to this Constitution, or, on the Application of the Legislatures of two thirds of the several States, shall call a Convention for proposing Amendments, which, in either Case, shall be valid to all Intents and Purposes, as Part of this Constitution, when ratified by the Legislatures of three fourths of the several States, or by Conventions in three fourths thereof, as the one or the other Mode of Ratification may be proposed by the Congress; Provided that no Amendment which may be made prior to the Year One thousand eight hundred and eight shall in any Manner alter the first and fourth Clauses in the Ninth Section of the first Article; and that no State, without its Consent, shall be deprived of its equal Suffrage in the Senate.

Article VI.

Assumption of debts of Confederation

All Debts contracted and Engagements entered into, before the Adoption of this Constitution, shall be as valid against the United States under this Constitution, as under the Confederation.

---

9. Changed by the Thirteenth Amendment.

Supremacy of federal laws and treaties

This Constitution, and the Laws of the United States which shall be made in Pursuance thereof; and all Treaties made, or which shall be made, under the Authority of the United States, shall be the Supreme Law of the Land; and the Judges in every State shall be bound thereby, any Thing in the Constitution or Laws of any State to the Contrary notwithstanding.

No religious test

The Senators and Representatives before mentioned, and the Members of the several State Legislatures, and all executive and judicial Officers, both of the United States and of the several States, shall be bound by Oath or Affirmation, to support this Constitution; but no religious Test shall ever be required as a Qualification to any Office or public Trust under the United States.

Article VII.

Ratification procedure

The Ratification of the Conventions of nine States, shall be sufficient for the Establishment of this Constitution between the States so ratifying the Same.

Done in Convention by the Unanimous Consent of the States present the Seventeenth Day of September in the Year of our Lord one thousand seven hundred and Eighty seven and of the Independence of the United States of America the Twelfth In witness whereof We have hereunto subscribed our Names,

G°. WASHINGTON—*Presid*t.
and deputy from Virginia

New Hampshire: JOHN LANGDON, NICHOLAS GILMAN

Massachusetts: NATHANIEL GORHAM, RUFUS KING

New Jersey: WIL: LIVINGSTON, DAVID BREARLEY, WM: PATERSON, JONA: DAYTON

Pennsylvania: B FRANKLIN, THOMAS MIFFLIN, ROBT: MORRIS, GEO. CLYMER, THOS: FITZSIMONS, JARED INGERSOLL, JAMES WILSON, GOUV MORRIS

Connecticut: WM: SAML: JOHNSON, ROGER SHERMAN

New York: ALEXANDER HAMILTON

Maryland: JAMES MCHENRY, DAN OF ST THOS: JENIFER, DANL CARROLL

Virginia: JOHN BLAIR—, JAMES MADISON JR.

North Carolina: WM BLOUNT, RICHD: DOBBS SPAIGHT, HU WILLIAMSON

South Carolina: J. RUTLEDGE, CHARLES COTESWORTH PINCKNEY, CHARLES PINCKNEY, PIERCE BUTLER

Delaware: GEO: READ, GUNNING BEDFORD JUN, JOHN DICKINSON, RICHARD BASSETT, JACO: BROOM

Georgia: WILLIAM FEW, ABR BALDWIN

[The first ten amendments, known as the "Bill of Rights," were ratified in 1791.]

AMENDMENT I.

Freedom of religion, speech, press, assembly

Congress shall make no law respecting an establishment of religion, or prohibiting the free exercise thereof, or abridging the freedom of speech, or of the press; or the right of the people peaceably to assemble, and to petition the Government for a redress of grievances.

AMENDMENT II.

Right to bear arms

A well regulated Militia, being necessary to the security of a free State, the right of the people to keep and bear Arms, shall not be infringed.

AMENDMENT III.

Quartering troops in private homes

No Soldier shall, in time of peace be quartered in any house without the consent of the Owner, nor in time of war, but in a manner to be prescribed by law.

AMENDMENT IV.

Prohibition against unreasonable searches and seizures

The right of the people to be secure in their persons, houses, papers, and effects, against unreasonable searches and seizures, shall not be violated, and no Warrants shall issue, but upon probable cause, supported by Oath or affirmation, and particularly describing the place to be searched, and the persons or things to be seized.

AMENDMENT V.

Right when accused; "due-process" clause

No person shall be held to answer for a capital, or otherwise infamous crime, unless on a presentment or indictment of a Grand Jury, except in cases arising in the land or naval forces, or in the Militia, when in actual service in time of War or public danger; nor shall any person be subject for the same offence to be twice put in jeopardy of life or limb; nor shall be compelled in any criminal case to be a witness against himself, nor be deprived of life, liberty, or property, without due process of law, nor shall private property be taken for public use, without just compensation.

AMENDMENT VI.

Rights when on trial

In all criminal prosecutions, the accused shall enjoy the right to a speedy and public trial, by an impartial jury of the State and district wherein the crime shall have been committed, which district shall have been previously ascertained by law, and to be informed of the nature and cause of the accusation; to be confronted with the witnesses against him; to have compulsory process for obtaining witnesses in his favor, and to have the Assistance of Counsel for his defence.

AMENDMENT VII.

Common-law suits

In Suits at common law, where the value in controversy shall exceed twenty dollars, the right of trial by jury shall be preserved, and no fact tried by a jury, shall be otherwise reexamined in any Court of the United States, than according to the rules of the common law.

AMENDMENT VIII.

Bail; no "cruel and unusual" punishments

Excessive bail shall not be required, nor excessive fines imposed, nor cruel and unusual punishments inflicted.

AMENDMENT IX.

Unenumerated rights protected

The enumeration in the Constitution, of certain rights, shall not be construed to deny or disparage others retained by the people.

AMENDMENT X.

Powers reserved for states

The powers not delegated to the United States by the Constitution, nor prohibited by it to the States, are reserved to the States respectively, or to the people.

AMENDMENT XI.

[Ratified in 1795.]

Limits on suits against states

The Judicial power of the United States shall not be construed to extend to any suit in law or equity, commenced or prosecuted against one of the United States by Citizens of another state, or by Citizens or Subjects of any Foreign State.

AMENDMENT XII.

[Ratified in 1804.]

Revision of electoral-college procedure

The Electors shall meet in their respective states and vote by ballot for President and Vice President, one of whom, at least, shall not be an inhabitant of the same state with themselves; they shall name in their ballots the person voted for as President, and in distinct ballots the person voted for as Vice President, and they shall make distinct lists of all persons voted for as President, and of all persons voted for as Vice President, and of the number of votes for each, which lists they shall sign and certify, and transmit sealed to the seat of government of the United States, directed to the President of the Senate;—The President of the Senate shall, in the presence of the Senate and House of Representatives, open all the certificates and the votes shall then be counted;—The person having the greatest number of votes for President, shall be the President, if such number be a majority of the whole number of Electors appointed; and if no person have such majority, then from the persons having the highest numbers not exceeding three on the list of those voted for as President, the House of Representatives shall choose immediately, by ballot, the President. But in choosing the President, the votes shall be taken by states, the representation from each state having one vote; a quorum for this purpose shall consist of a member or members from two-thirds of the states, and a majority of all the states shall be necessary to a choice. *And if the House of Representatives shall not choose a President whenever the right of choice shall devolve upon them, before the fourth day of March next following, then the Vice President shall act as President, as in the case of the death or other constitutional disability of the President.*—[10] The person

10. Changed by the Twentieth Amendment, section 3.

having the greatest number of votes as Vice President, shall be the Vice President, if such number be a majority of the whole number of Electors appointed, and if no person have a majority, then from the two highest numbers on the list, the Senate shall choose the Vice President; a quorum for the purpose shall consist of two-thirds of the whole number of Senators, and a majority of the whole number shall be necessary to a choice. But no person constitutionally ineligible to the office of President shall be eligible to that of Vice President of the United States.

AMENDMENT XIII.

[Ratified in 1865.]

Slavery prohibited

Section 1. Neither slavery nor involuntary servitude, except as a punishment for crime whereof the party shall have been duly convicted, shall exist within the United States, or any place subject to their jurisdiction.

Section 2. Congress shall have power to enforce this article by appropriate legislation.

AMENDMENT XIV.

[Ratified in 1868.]

Ex-slaves made citizens

"Due-process" clause applied to states

"Equal-protection" clause

Section 1. All persons born or naturalized in the United States and subject to the jurisdiction thereof, are citizens of the United States and of the State wherein they reside. No State shall make or enforce any law which shall abridge the privileges or immunities of citizens of the United States; nor shall any State deprive any person of life, liberty, or property, without due process of law; nor deny to any person within its jurisdiction the equal protection of the laws.

Reduction in congressional representation for states denying adult males the right to vote

Section 2. Representatives shall be apportioned among the several States according to their respective numbers, counting the whole number of persons in each State, excluding Indians not taxed. But when the right to vote at any election for the choice of electors for President and Vice President of the United States, Representatives in Congress, the Executive and Judicial officers of a State, or the members of the Legislature thereof, is denied to any of the male inhabitants of such State, being *twenty-one*[11] years of age and citizens of the United States, or in any way abridged, except for participation in rebellion, or other crime, the basis of representation therein shall be reduced in the proportion which the number of such male citizens shall bear to the whole number of male citizens twenty-one years of age in such State.

Southern rebels denied federal office

Section 3. No person shall be a Senator or Representative in Congress, or elector of President and Vice President, or hold any office, civil or military, under the United States, or under any State, who, having previously taken an oath, as a member of Congress, or as an officer of the United States, or as a member of any State legislature, or as an executive or judicial officer of any State, to support the Constitution of the United States, shall have engaged in insurrection or rebellion against the same, or given aid or comfort to the enemies thereof. But Congress may by a vote of two-thirds of each House, remove such disability.

---

11. Changed by the Twenty-sixth Amendment.

Rebel debts repudiated

Section 4. The validity of the public debt of the United States, authorized by law, including debts incurred for payment of pensions and bounties for services in suppressing insurrection or rebellion, shall not be questioned. But neither the United States nor any State shall assume or pay any debt or obligation incurred in aid of insurrection or rebellion against the United States, or any claim for the loss or emancipation of any slave; but all such debts, obligations and claims shall be held illegal and void.

Section 5. The Congress shall have power to enforce, by appropriate legislation, the provisions of this article.

AMENDMENT XV.

[Ratified in 1870.]

Blacks given right to vote

Section 1. The right of citizens of the United States to vote shall not be denied or abridged by the United States or by any State on account of race, color, or previous condition of servitude.

Section 2. The Congress shall have power to enforce this article by appropriate legislation.

AMENDMENT XVI.

[Ratified in 1913.]

Authorizes federal income tax

The Congress shall have power to lay and collect taxes on incomes, from whatever source derived, without apportionment among the several States, and without regard to any census or enumeration.

AMENDMENT XVII.

[Ratified in 1913.]

Requires popular election of senators

The Senate of the United States shall be composed of two Senators from each State, elected by the people thereof, for six years; and each Senator shall have one vote. The electors in each State shall have the qualifications requisite for electors of the most numerous branch of the State legislatures.

When vacancies happen in the representation of any State in the Senate, the executive authority of such State shall issue writs of election to fill such vacancies: Provided, That the legislature of any State may empower the executive thereof to make temporary appointments until the people fill the vacancies by election as the legislature may direct.

This amendment shall not be so construed as to affect the election or term of any Senator chosen before it becomes valid as part of the Constitution.

AMENDMENT XVIII.

[Ratified in 1919.]

Prohibits manufacture and sale of liquor

Section 1. *After one year from the ratification of this article the manufacture, sale, or transportation of intoxicating liquors within, the importation thereof into, or the exportation thereof from the United States and all territory subject to the jurisdiction thereof for beverage purposes is hereby prohibited.*

Section 2. *The Congress and the several States shall have concurrent power to enforce this article by appropriate legislation.*

Section 3. *This article shall be inoperative unless it shall have been ratified as an amendment to the Constitution by the legislatures of the several States, as provided in the Constitution, within seven years from the date of the submission hereof to the States by the Congress.*[12]

AMENDMENT XIX.

[Ratified in 1920.]

Right to vote for women

The right of citizens of the United States to vote shall not be denied or abridged by the United States or by any State on account of sex.

Congress shall have power to enforce this article by appropriate legislation.

AMENDMENT XX.

[Ratified in 1933.]

Federal terms of office to begin in January

Section 1. The terms of the President and Vice President shall end at noon on the 20th day of January, and the terms of Senators and Representatives at noon on the 3d day of January, of the years in which such terms would have ended if this article had not been ratified; and the terms of their successors shall then begin.

Section 2. The Congress shall assemble at least once in every year, and such meeting shall begin at noon on the 3d day of January, unless they shall by law appoint a different day.

Emergency presidential succession

Section 3. If, at the time fixed for the beginning of the term of the President, the President elect shall have died, the Vice President elect shall become President. If a President shall not have been chosen before the time fixed for the beginning of his term, or if the President elect shall have failed to qualify, then the Vice President elect shall act as President until a President shall have qualified; and the Congress may by law provide for the case wherein neither a President elect nor a Vice President elect shall have qualified, declaring who shall then act as President, or the manner in which one who is to act shall be selected, and such person shall act accordingly until a President or Vice President shall have qualified.

Section 4. The Congress may by law provide for the case of the death of any of the persons from whom the House of Representatives may choose a President whenever the right of choice shall have devolved upon them, and for the case of the death of any of the persons from whom the Senate may choose a Vice President whenever the right of choice shall have devolved upon them.

Section 5. Sections 1 and 2 shall take effect on the 15th day of October following the ratification of this article.

---

12. Repealed by the Twenty-first Amendment.

Section 6. This article shall be inoperative unless it shall have been ratified as an amendment to the Constitution by the legislatures of three-fourths of the several States within seven years from the date of its submission.

AMENDMENT XXI.

[Ratified in 1933.]

Repeals Prohibition

Section 1. The eighteenth article of amendment to the Constitution of the United States is hereby repealed.

Section 2. The transportation or importation into any State, Territory, or possession of the United States for delivery or use therein of intoxicating liquors, in violation of the laws thereof, is hereby prohibited.

Section 3. This article shall be inoperative unless it shall have been ratified as an amendment to the Constitution by conventions in the several States, as provided in the Constitution, within seven years from the date of submission hereof to the States by the Congress.

AMENDMENT XXII.

[Ratified in 1951.]

Two-term limit for president

Section 1. No person shall be elected to the office of the President more than twice, and no person who has held the office of President, or acted as President, for more than two years of a term to which some other person was elected President shall be elected to the office of President more than once. But this Article shall not apply to any person holding the office of President when this Article was proposed by the Congress, and shall not prevent any person who may be holding the office of President, or acting as President, during the term within which this Article becomes operative from holding the office of President or acting as President during the remainder of such term.

Section 2. This Article shall be inoperative unless it shall have been ratified as an amendment to the Constitution by the legislatures of three-fourths of the several States within seven years from the date of its submission to the States by the Congress.

AMENDMENT XXIII.

[Ratified in 1961.]

Right to vote for president in District of Columbia

Section 1. The District constituting the seat of Government of the United States shall appoint in such manner as the Congress may direct:

A number of electors of President and Vice President equal to the whole number of Senators and Representatives in Congress to which the District would be entitled if it were a State, but in no event more than the least populous State; they shall be in addition to those appointed by the States, but they shall be considered, for the purposes of the election of President and Vice President, to be electors appointed by a State; and they shall meet in the District and perform such duties as provided by the twelfth article of amendment.

Section 2. The Congress shall have power to enforce this article by appropriate legislation.

AMENDMENT XXIV.

[Ratified in 1964.]

Prohibits poll taxes in federal elections

Section 1. The right of citizens of the United States to vote in any primary or other election for President or Vice President, for electors for President or Vice President, or for Senator or Representative in Congress, shall not be denied or abridged by the United States or any State by reason of failure to pay any poll tax or other tax.

Section 2. The Congress shall have the power to enforce this article by appropriate legislation.

AMENDMENT XXV.

[Ratified in 1967.]

Presidential disability and succession

Section 1. In case of the removal of the President from office or of his death or resignation, the Vice President shall become President.

Section 2. Whenever there is a vacancy in the office of the Vice President, the President shall nominate a Vice President who shall take office upon confirmation by a majority vote of both Houses of Congress.

Section 3. Whenever the President transmits to the President pro tempore of the Senate and the Speaker of the House of Representatives his written declaration that he is unable to discharge the powers and duties of his office, and until he transmits to them a written declaration to the contrary, such powers and duties shall be discharged by the Vice President as Acting President.

Section 4. Whenever the Vice President and a majority of either the principal officers of the executive departments or of such other body as Congress may by law provide, transmit to the President pro tempore of the Senate and the Speaker of the House of Representatives their written declaration that the President is unable to discharge the powers and duties of his office, the Vice President shall immediately assume the powers and duties of the office as Acting President.

Thereafter, when the President transmits to the President pro tempore of the Senate and the Speaker of the House of Representatives his written declaration that no inability exists, he shall resume the powers and duties of his office unless the Vice President and a majority of either the principal officers of the executive department[s] or of such other body as Congress may by law provide, transmit within four days to the President pro tempore of the Senate and the Speaker of the House of Representatives their written declaration that the President is unable to discharge the powers and duties of his office. Thereupon Congress shall decide the issue, assembling within forty-eight hours for that purpose if not in session. If the Congress, within twenty-one days after receipt of the latter written declaration, or, if Congress is not in session, within twenty-one days after Congress is required to assemble, determines by two-thirds vote of both Houses that the President is unable to discharge the powers and duties of his office, the Vice President shall continue to discharge the same as Acting President; otherwise, the President shall resume the powers and duties of his office.

AMENDMENT XXVI.

[Ratified in 1971.]

Voting age lowered to eighteen

Section 1. The right of citizens of the United States, who are eighteen years of age or older, to vote shall not be denied or abridged by the United States or by any State on account of age.

Section 2. The Congress shall have power to enforce this article by appropriate legislation.

AMENDMENT XXVII.

[Ratified in 1992.]

Congressional pay raises

No law varying the compensation for the services of the Senators and Representatives shall take effect, until an election of Representatives shall have intervened.

The Federalist No. 10

November 22, 1787

James Madison

TO THE PEOPLE OF THE STATE OF NEW YORK.

Among the numerous advantages promised by a well constructed Union, none deserves to be more accurately developed than its tendency to break and control the violence of faction. The friend of popular governments, never finds himself so much alarmed for their character and fate, as when he contemplates their propensity to this dangerous vice. He will not fail therefore to set a due value on any plan which, without violating the principles to which he is attached, provides a proper cure for it. The instability, injustice and confusion introduced into the public councils, have in truth been the mortal diseases under which popular governments have every where perished; as they continue to be the favorite and fruitful topics from which the adversaries to liberty derive their most specious declamations. The valuable improvements made by the American Constitutions on the popular models, both ancient and modern, cannot certainly be too much admired; but it would be an unwarrantable partiality, to contend that they have as effectually obviated the danger on this side as was wished and expected. Complaints are everywhere heard from our most considerate and virtuous citizens, equally the friends of public and private faith, and of public and personal liberty; that our governments are too unstable; that the public good is disregarded in the conflicts of rival parties; and that measures are too often decided, not according to the rules of justice, and the rights of the minor party; but by the superior force of an interested and over-bearing majority. However anxiously we may wish that these complaints had no foundation, the evidence of known facts will not permit us to deny that they are in some degree true. It will be found indeed, on a candid review of our situation, that some of the distresses under which we labor, have been erroneously charged on the operation of our governments; but it will be found, at the same time, that other causes will not alone account for many of our heaviest misfortunes; and particularly, for that prevailing and increasing distrust of public engagements, and alarm for private rights, which are echoed from one end of the continent to the other. These must be chiefly, if not wholly, effects of the unsteadiness and injustice, with which a factious spirit has tainted our public administrations.

By a faction I understand a number of citizens, whether amounting to a majority or minority of the whole, who are united and actuated by some common impulse of passion, or of interest, adverse to the rights of other citizens, or to the permanent and aggregate interests of the community.

There are two methods of curing the mischiefs of faction: the one, by removing its causes; the other, by controlling its effects.

There are again two methods of removing the causes of faction: the one by destroying the liberty which is essential to its existence; the other, by giving to every citizen the same opinions, the same passions, and the same interests.

It could never be more truly said than of the first remedy, that it is worse than the disease. Liberty is to faction, what air is to fire, an aliment without which it instantly expires. But it could not be a less folly to abolish liberty, which is essential to political life, because it nourishes faction, than it would be to wish the annihilation of air, which is essential to animal life, because it imparts to fire its destructive agency.

The second expedient is as impracticable, as the first would be unwise. As long as the reason of man continues fallible, and he is at liberty to exercise it, different opinions will be formed. As long as the connection subsists between his reason and his self-love, his opinions and his passions will have a reciprocal influence on each other; and the former will be objects to which the latter will attach themselves. The diversity in the faculties of men from which the rights of property originate, is not less an insuperable obstacle to a uniformity of interests. The protection of these faculties is the first object of Government. From the protection of different and unequal faculties of acquiring property, the possession of different degrees and kinds of property immediately results: and from the influence of these on the sentiments and views of the respective proprietors, ensues a division of the society into different interests and parties.

The latent causes of faction are thus sown in the nature of man; and we see them every where brought into different degrees of activity, according to the different circumstances of civil society. A zeal for different opinions concerning religion, concerning Government and many other points, as well of speculation as of practice; an attachment to different leaders ambitiously contending for pre-eminence and power; or to persons of other descriptions whose fortunes have been interesting to the human passions, have in turn divided mankind into parties, inflamed them with mutual animosity, and rendered them much more disposed to vex and oppress each other, than to cooperate for their common good. So strong is this propensity of mankind to fall into mutual animosities, that where no substantial occasion presents itself, the most frivolous and fanciful distinctions have been sufficient to kindle their unfriendly passions, and excite their most violent conflicts. But the most common and durable source of factions, has been the various and unequal distribution of property. Those who hold, and those who are without property, have ever formed distinct interests in society. Those who are creditors, and those who are debtors, fall under a like discrimination. A landed interest, a manufacturing interest, a mercantile interest, a monied interest, with many lesser interests, grow up of necessity in civilized nations, and divide them into different classes, actuated by different sentiments and views. The regulation of these various and interfering interests forms the principal task of modern Legislation, and involves the spirit of party and faction in the necessary and ordinary operations of Government.

No man is allowed to be judge in his own cause; because his interest would certainly bias his judgment, and, not improbably, corrupt his integrity. With equal, nay with greater reason, a body of men, are unfit to be judges and parties, at the same time; yet, what are many of the most important acts of legislation, but so many judicial determinations, not indeed concerning the rights of single persons, but concerning the rights of large bodies of citizens, and what are the different classes of legislators, but advocates and parties to the causes which they determine? Is a law proposed concerning private debts? It is a question to which the creditors are parties on one side, and the debtors on the other. Justice ought to hold the balance between them. Yet the parties are and must be themselves the judges; and the most numerous party, or, in other words, the most powerful faction must be expected to prevail. Shall domestic manufactures be encouraged, and in what degree, by restrictions on foreign manufactures? are questions which would be differently decided by the landed and the manufacturing classes; and probably by neither, with a sole regard to justice and the public good. The apportionment of taxes on the various descriptions of property, is an act which seems to require the most exact impartiality; yet, there is perhaps no legislative act in which greater opportunity and temptation are given to a predominant party, to trample on the rules of justice. Every shilling with which they over-burden the inferior number, is a shilling saved to their own pockets.

It is in vain to say, that enlightened statesmen will be able to adjust these clashing interests, and render them all subservient to the public good. Enlightened statesmen will not always be at the helm: Nor, in many cases, can such an adjustment be made at all, without taking into view indirect and remote considerations, which will rarely prevail over the immediate interest which one party may find in disregarding the rights of another, or the good of the whole.

The inference to which we are brought, is, that the *causes* of faction cannot be removed; and that relief is only to be sought in the means of controlling its *effects*.

If a faction consists of less than a majority, relief is supplied by the republican principle, which enables the majority to defeat its sinister views by regular vote: It may clog the administration, it may convulse the society; but it will be unable to execute and mask its violence under the forms of the Constitution. When a majority is included in a faction, the form of popular government on the other hand enables it to sacrifice to its ruling passion or interest, both the public good and the rights of other citizens. To secure the public good, and private rights, against the danger of such a faction, and at the same time to preserve the spirit and the form of popular government, is then the great object to which our inquiries are directed: Let me add that it is the great desideratum, by which alone this form of government can be rescued from the opprobrium under which it has so long labored, and be recommended to the esteem and adoption of mankind.

By what means is this object attainable? Evidently by one of two only. Either the existence of the same passion or interest in a majority at the same time, must be prevented; or the majority, having such co-existent passion or interest, must be rendered, by their number and local situation, unable to concert and carry into effect schemes of oppression. If the impulse and the opportunity be suffered to coincide, we well know that neither moral nor religious motives can be relied on as an adequate control. They are not found to be such on the injustice and violence of individuals, and lose their efficacy in proportion to the number combined together; that is, in proportion as their efficacy becomes needful.

From this view of the subject, it may be concluded, that a pure Democracy, by which I mean, a Society, consisting of a small number of citizens, who assemble and administer the Government in person, can admit of no cure for the mischiefs of faction. A common passion or interest will, in almost every case, be felt by a majority of the whole; a communication and concert results from the form of Government itself; and there is nothing to check the inducements to sacrifice the weaker party, or an obnoxious individual. Hence it is, that such Democracies have ever been spectacles of turbulence and contention; have ever been found incompatible with personal security, or the rights of property; and have in general been as short in their lives, as they have been violent in their deaths. Theoretic politicians, who have patronized this species of Government, have erroneously supposed, that by reducing mankind to a perfect equality in their political rights, they would, at the same time, be perfectly equalized and assimilated in their possessions, their opinions, and their passions.

A republic, by which I mean a government in which the scheme of representation takes place, opens a different prospect, and promises the cure for which we are seeking. Let us examine the points in which it varies from pure democracy, and we shall comprehend both the nature of the cure and the efficacy which it must derive from the union.

The two great points of difference, between a democracy and a republic, are, first, the delegation of the government, in the latter, to a small number of citizens, elected by the rest; secondly, the greater number of citizens, and greater sphere of country, over which the latter may be extended.

The effect of the first difference is, on the one hand, to refine and enlarge the public views, by passing them through the medium of a chosen body of citizens, whose wisdom may best discern the true interest of their country, and whose patriotism and love of justice, will be least likely to sacrifice it to temporary or partial considerations. Under such a regulation, it may well happen, that the public voice, pronounced by the representatives of the people, will be more consonant to the public good, than if pronounced by the people themselves, convened for the purpose. On the other hand the effect may be inverted. Men of factious tempers, of local prejudices, or of sinister designs, may by intrigue, by corruption, or by other means, first obtain the suffrages, and then betray the interest of the people. The question resulting is, whether small or extensive republics are most favorable to the election of proper guardians of the public weal, and it is clearly decided in favor of the latter by two obvious considerations.

In the first place, it is to be remarked that, however small the republic may be, the representatives must be raised to a certain number, in order to guard against the cabals of a few; and that however large it may be, they must be limited to a certain number, in order to guard against the confusion of a multitude. Hence, the number of representatives in the two cases not being in proportion to that of the constituents, and being proportionally greatest in the small republic, it follows, that if the proportion of fit characters be not less in the large than in the small republic, the former will present a greater option, and consequently a greater probability of a fit choice.

In the next place, as each Representative will be chosen by a greater number of citizens in the large than in the small Republic, it will be more difficult for unworthy candidates to practise with success the vicious arts, by which elections are too often carried; and the suffrages of the people being more free, will be more likely to center on men who possess the most attractive merit, and the most diffusive and established characters.

It must be confessed, that in this, as in most other cases, there is a mean, on both sides of which inconveniences will be found to lie. By enlarging too much the number of electors, you render the representatives too little acquainted with all their local circumstances and lesser interests; as by reducing it too much, you render him unduly attached to these, and too little fit to comprehend and pursue great and national objects. The Federal Constitution forms a happy combination in this respect; the great and aggregate interests being referred to the national, the local and particular, to the state legislatures.

The other point of difference is, the greater number of citizens and extent of territory which may be brought within the compass of Republican, than of Democratic Government; and it is this circumstance principally which renders factious combinations less to be dreaded in the former, than in the latter. The smaller the society, the fewer probably will be the distinct parties and interests composing it; the fewer the distinct parties and interests, the more frequently will a majority be found of the same party; and the smaller the number of individuals composing a majority, and the smaller the compass within which they are placed, the more easily they will concert and execute their plans of oppression. Extend the sphere, and you take in a greater variety of parties and interests; you make it less probable that a majority of the whole will have a common motive to invade the rights of other citizens; or if such a common motive exists, it will be more difficult for all who feel it to discover their own strength, and to act in unison with each other. Besides other impediments, it may be remarked, that where there is a consciousness of unjust or dishonorable purposes, communication is always checked by distrust, in proportion to the number whose concurrence is necessary.

Hence it clearly appears, that the same advantage, which a Republic has over a Democracy, in controlling the effects of factions, is enjoyed by a large over a small Republic—is enjoyed by the Union over the States composing it. Does this advantage consist in the substitution of Representatives, whose enlightened views and virtuous sentiments render them superior to local prejudices, and to schemes of injustice? It will not be denied, that the Representation of the Union will be most likely to possess these requisite endowments. Does it consist in the greater security afforded by a greater variety of parties, against the event of any one party being able to outnumber and oppress the rest? In an equal degree does the increase variety of parties, comprised within the Union, increase this security? Does it, in fine, consist in the greater obstacles opposed to the concert and accomplishment of the secret wishes of an unjust and interested majority? Here, again, the extent of the Union gives it the most palpable advantage.

The influence of factious leaders may kindle a flame within their particular States, but will be unable to spread a general conflagration through the other States: a religious sect, may degenerate into a political faction in a part of the Confederacy but the variety of sects dispersed over the entire face of it, must secure the national Councils against any danger from that source: a rage for paper money, for an abolition of debts, for an equal division of property, or for any other improper or wicked project, will be less apt to pervade the whole body of the Union, than a particular member of it; in the same proportion as such a malady is more likely to taint a particular county or district, than an entire State.

In the extent and proper structure of the Union, therefore, we behold a Republican remedy for the diseases most incident to Republican Government. And according to the degree of pleasure and pride, we feel in being Republicans, ought to be our zeal in cherishing the spirit, and supporting the character of Federalists.

PUBLIUS

The Federalist No. 51

February 6, 1788

James Madison

TO THE PEOPLE OF THE STATE OF NEW YORK.

To what expedient then shall we finally resort for maintaining in practice the necessary partition of power among the several departments, as laid down in the constitution? The only answer that can be given is, that as all these exterior provisions are found to be inadequate, the defect must be supplied, by so contriving the interior structure of the government, as that its several constituent parts may, by their mutual relations, be the means of keeping each other in their proper places. Without presuming to undertake a full development of this important idea, I will hazard a few general observations, which may perhaps place it in a clearer light, and enable us to form a more correct judgment of the principles and structure of the government planned by the convention.

In order to lay a due foundation for that separate and distinct exercise of the different powers of government, which to a certain extent, is admitted on all hands to be essential to the preservation of liberty, it is evident that each department should have a will of its own; and consequently should be so constituted, that the members of each should have as little agency as possible in the appointment of the members of the others. Were this principle rigorously adhered to, it would require that all the appointments for the supreme executive, legislative, and judiciary magistracies, should be drawn from the same fountain of authority, the people, through channels, having no communication whatever with one another. Perhaps such a plan of constructing the several departments would be less difficult in practice than in it may in contemplation appear. Some difficulties however, and some additional expense, would attend the execution of it. Some deviations therefore from the principle must be admitted. In the constitution of the judiciary department in particular, it might be inexpedient to insist rigorously on the principle; first, because peculiar qualifications being essential in the members, the primary consideration ought to be to select that mode of choice, which best secures these qualifications; secondly, because the permanent tenure by which the appointments are held in that department, must soon destroy all sense of dependence on the authority conferring them.

It is equally evident that the members of each department should be as little dependent as possible on those of the others, for the emoluments annexed to their offices. Were the executive magistrate, or the judges, not independent of the legislature in this particular, their independence in every other would be merely nominal.

But the great security against a gradual concentration of the several powers in the same department, consists in giving to those who administer each department, the necessary constitutional means, and personal motives, to resist encroachments of the others. The provision for defense must in this, as in all other cases, be made commensurate to the danger of attack. Ambition must be made to counteract ambition. The interest of the man must be connected with the constitutional right of the place. It may be a reflection on human nature, that such devices should be necessary to control the abuses of government. But what is government itself but the greatest of all reflections on human nature? If men were angels, no government would be necessary. If angels were to govern men, neither external nor internal controls on government would be necessary. In framing a government which is to be administered by men over men, the great difficulty lies in this: You must first enable the government to control the governed; and in the next place, oblige it to control itself. A dependence on the people is no doubt the primary control on the government; but experience has taught mankind the necessity of auxiliary precautions.

This policy of supplying by opposite and rival interests, the defect of better motives, might be traced through the whole system of human affairs, private as well as public. We see it particularly displayed in all the subordinate distributions of power; where the constant aim is to divide and arrange the several offices in such a manner as that each may be a check on the other; that the private interest of every individual, may be a sentinel over the public rights. These inventions of prudence cannot be less requisite in the distribution of the supreme powers of the state.

But it is not possible to give each department an equal power of self defense. In republican government the legislative authority, necessarily, predominates. The remedy for this inconvenience is, to divide the legislative into different branches; and to render them by different modes of election, and different principles of action, as little connected with each other, as the nature of their common functions, and their common dependence on the society, will admit. It may even be necessary to guard against dangerous encroachments by still further precautions. As the weight of the legislative authority requires that it should be thus divided, the weakness of the executive may require, on the other hand, that it should be fortified. An absolute negative, on the legislature, appears at first view to be the natural defense with which the executive magistrate should be armed. But perhaps it would be neither altogether safe, nor alone sufficient. On ordinary occasions, it might not be exerted with the requisite firmness, and on extraordinary occasions, it might be prefidiously abused. May not this defect of an absolute negative be supplied, by some qualified connection between this weaker department, and the weaker branch of the stronger department, by which the latter may be led to support the constitutional rights of the former, without being too much detached from the rights of its own department?

If the principles on which these observations are founded be just, as I persuade myself they are, and they be applied as a criterion, to the several state constitutions, and to the federal constitution, it will be found, that if the latter does not perfectly correspond with them, the former are infinitely less able to bear such a test.

There are moreover two considerations particularly applicable to the federal system of America, which place the system in a very interesting point of view.

First. In a single republic, all the power surrendered by the people, is submitted to the administration of a single government; and usurpations are guarded against by a division of the government into distinct and separate departments. In the compound republic of America, the power surrendered by the people, is first divided between two distinct governments, and then the portion allotted to each, subdivided among distinct and separate departments. Hence a double security arises to the rights of the people. The different governments will control each other; at the same time that each will be controlled by itself.

Second. It is of great importance in a republic, not only to guard the society against the oppression of its rulers; but to guard one part of the society against the injustice of the other part. Different interests necessarily exist in different classes of citizens. If a majority be united by a common interest, the rights of the minority will be insecure. There are but two methods of providing against this evil: The one by creating a will in the community independent of the majority, that is, of the society itself, the other by comprehending in the society so many separate descriptions of citizens, as will render an unjust combination of a majority of the whole, very improbable, if not impracticable. The first method prevails in all governments possessing an hereditary or self appointed authority. This at best is but a precarious security; because a power independent of the society may as well espouse the unjust views of the major, as the rightful interests, of the minor party, and may possibly be turned against both parties. The second method will be exemplified in the federal republic of the United States. While all authority in it will be derived from and dependent on the society, the society itself will be broken into so many parts, interests and classes of citizens, that the rights of individuals or of the minority, will be in little danger from interested combinations of the majority. In a free government, the security for civil rights must be the same as for religious rights. It consists in the one case in the multiplicity of interests, and in the other, in the multiplicity of sects. The degree of security in both cases will depend on the number of interests and sects; and this may be presumed to depend on the extent of country and number of people comprehended under the same government. This view of the subject must particularly recommend a proper federal system to all the sincere and considerate friends of republican government: Since it shows that in exact proportion as the territory of the union may be formed into more circumscribed confederacies or states, oppressive combinations of a majority will be facilitated, the best security under the republican form, for the rights of every class of citizens, will be diminished; and consequently, the stability and independence of some member of the government, the only other security, must be proportionally increased. Justice is the end of government. It is the end of civil society. It ever has been, and ever will be pursued, until it be obtained, or until liberty be lost in the pursuit. In a society under the forms of which the stronger faction can readily unite and oppress the weaker, anarchy may as truly be said to reign, as in a state of nature where the weaker individual is not secured against the violence of the stronger: And as in the latter state even the stronger individuals are prompted by the uncertainty of their condition, to submit to a government which may protect the weak as well as themselves: So in the former state, will the more powerful factions or parties be gradually induced by a like motive, to wish for a government which will protect all parties, the weaker as well as the more powerful. It can be little doubted, that if the state of Rhode Island was separated from the confederacy, and left to itself, the insecurity of rights under the popular form of government within such narrow limits, would be displayed by such reiterated oppressions of factious majorities, that some power altogether independent of the people would soon be called for by the voice of the very factions whose misrule had proved the necessity of it. In the extended republic of the United States, and among the great variety of interests, parties and sects which it embraces, a coalition of a majority of the whole society could seldom take place on any other principles than those of justice and the general good; and there being thus less danger to a minor from the will of the major party, there must be less pretext also, to provide for the security of the former, by introducing into the government a will not dependent on the latter; or in other words, a will independent of the society itself. It is no less certain than it is important, notwithstanding the contrary opinions which have been entertained, that the larger the society, provided it lie within a practicable sphere, the more duly capable it will be of self government. And happily for the *republican cause*, the practicable sphere may be carried to a very great extent, by a judicious modification and mixture of the *federal principle*.

PUBLIUS

Presidents and Congresses, 1789–2009

Year	President and Vice President	Party of President	Congress	House Majority Party	House Minority Party	Senate Majority Party	Senate Minority Party
1789–1797	**George Washington**	None	1st	38 Admin	26 Opp	17 Admin	9 Opp
	John Adams		2d	37 Fed	33 Dem-Rep	16 Fed	13 Dem-Rep
			3d	57 Dem-Rep	48 Fed	17 Fed	13 Dem-Rep
			4th	54 Fed	52 Dem-Rep	19 Fed	13 Dem-Rep
1797–1801	**John Adams**	Federalist	5th	58 Fed	48 Dem-Rep	20 Fed	12 Dem-Rep
	Thomas Jefferson		6th	64 Fed	42 Dem-Rep	19 Fed	13 Dem-Rep
1801–1809	**Thomas Jefferson**	Dem-Rep	7th	69 Dem-Rep	36 Fed	18 Dem-Rep	13 Fed
	Aaron Burr (to 1805)		8th	102 Dem-Rep	39 Fed	25 Dem-Rep	9 Fed
	George Clinton (to 1809)		9th	116 Dem-Rep	25 Fed	27 Dem-Rep	7 Fed
			10th	118 Dem-Rep	24 Fed	28 Dem-Rep	6 Fed
1809–1817	**James Madison**	Dem-Rep	11th	94 Dem-Rep	48 Fed	28 Dem-Rep	6 Fed
	George Clinton (to 1813)		12th	108 Dem-Rep	36 Fed	30 Dem-Rep	6 Fed
	Elbridge Gerry (to 1817)		13th	112 Dem-Rep	68 Fed	27 Dem-Rep	9 Fed
			14th	117 Dem-Rep	65 Fed	25 Dem-Rep	11 Fed
1817–1825	**James Monroe**	Dem-Rep	15th	141 Dem-Rep	42 Fed	34 Dem-Rep	10 Fed
	Daniel D. Tompkins		16th	156 Dem-Rep	27 Fed	35 Dem-Rep	7 Fed
			17th	158 Dem-Rep	25 Fed	44 Dem-Rep	4 Fed
			18th	187 Dem-Rep	26 Fed	44 Dem-Rep	4 Fed
1825–1829	**John Quincy Adams**	Nat-Rep	19th	105 Admin	97 Jack	26 Admin	20 Jack
	John C. Calhoun		20th	119 Jack	94 Admin	28 Jack	20 Admin
1829–1837	**Andrew Jackson**	Democrat	21st	139 Dem	74 Nat Rep	26 Dem	22 Nat Rep
	John C. Calhoun (to 1833)		22d	141 Dem	58 Nat Rep	25 Dem	21 Nat Rep
	Martin Van Buren (to 1837)		23d	147 Dem	53 AntiMas	20 Dem	20 Nat Rep
			24th	145 Dem	98 Whig	27 Dem	25 Whig
1837–1841	**Martin Van Buren**	Democrat	25th	108 Dem	107 Whig	30 Dem	18 Whig
	Richard M. Johnson		26th	124 Dem	118 Whig	28 Dem	22 Whig
1841	**William H. Harrison***	Whig					
	John Tyler						
1841–1845	**John Tyler**	Whig	27th	133 Whig	102 Dem	28 Whig	22 Dem
	(VP vacant)		28th	142 Dem	79 Whig	28 Whig	25 Dem
1845–1849	**James K. Polk**	Democrat	29th	143 Dem	77 Whig	31 Dem	25 Whig
	George M. Dallas		30th	115 Whig	108 Dem	36 Dem	21 Whig
1849–1850	**Zachary Taylor***	Whig	31st	112 Dem	109 Whig	35 Dem	25 Whig
	Millard Fillmore						
1850–1853	**Millard Fillmore**	Whig	32d	140 Dem	88 Whig	35 Dem	24 Whig
	(VP vacant)						
1853–1857	**Franklin Pierce**	Democrat	33d	159 Dem	71 Whig	38 Dem	22 Whig
	William R. King		34th	108 Rep	83 Dem	40 Dem	15 Rep
1857–1861	**James Buchanan**	Democrat	35th	118 Dem	92 Rep	36 Dem	20 Rep
	John C. Breckinridge		36th	114 Rep	92 Dem	36 Dem	26 Rep

NOTES: Only members of two major parties in Congress are shown; omitted are independents, members of minor parties, and vacancies. Party balance as of beginning of Congress.

Congresses in which one or both houses are controlled by party other than that of the president are shown in color.

During administration of George Washington and (in part) John Quincy Adams, Congress was not organized by formal parties; the split shown is between supporters and opponents of the administration.

ABBREVIATIONS: **Admin** = Administration supporters; **AntiMas** = Anti-Masonic; **Dem** = Democratic; **Dem-Rep** = Democratic-Republican; **Fed** = Federalist; **Jack** = Jacksonian Democrats; **Nat Rep** = National Republican; **Opp** = Opponents of administration; **Rep** = Republican; **Union** = Unionist; **Whig** = Whig.

*Died in office.

Year	President and Vice President	Party of President	Congress	House Majority Party	House Minority Party	Senate Majority Party	Senate Minority Party
1861–1865	**Abraham Lincoln***	Republican	37th	105 Rep	43 Dem	31 Rep	10 Dem
	Hannibal Hamlin (to 1865)		38th	102 Rep	75 Dem	36 Rep	9 Dem
	Andrew Johnson (1865)						
1865–1869	**Andrew Johnson**	Republican	39th	149 Union	42 Dem	42 Union	10 Dem
	(VP vacant)		40th	143 Rep	49 Dem	42 Rep	11 Dem
1869–1877	**Ulysses S. Grant**	Republican	41st	149 Rep	63 Dem	56 Rep	11 Dem
	Schuyler Colfax (to 1873)		42d	134 Rep	104 Dem	52 Rep	17 Dem
	Henry Wilson (to 1877)		43d	194 Rep	92 Dem	49 Rep	19 Dem
			44th	169 Dem	109 Rep	45 Rep	29 Dem
1877–1881	**Rutherford B. Hayes**	Republican	45th	153 Dem	140 Rep	39 Rep	36 Dem
	William A. Wheeler		46th	149 Dem	130 Rep	42 Dem	33 Rep
1881	**James A. Garfield***	Republican	47th	147 Rep	135 Dem	37 Rep	37 Dem
	Chester A. Arthur						
1881–1885	**Chester A. Arthur**	Republican	48th	197 Dem	118 Rep	38 Rep	36 Rep
	(VP vacant)						
1885–1889	**Grover Cleveland**	Democrat	49th	183 Dem	140 Rep	43 Rep	34 Dem
	Thomas A. Hendricks		50th	169 Dem	152 Rep	39 Rep	37 Dem
1889–1893	**Benjamin Harrison**	Republican	51st	166 Rep	159 Dem	39 Rep	37 Dem
	Levi P. Morton		52d	235 Dem	88 Rep	47 Rep	39 Dem
1893–1897	**Grover Cleveland**	Democrat	53d	218 Dem	127 Rep	44 Dem	38 Rep
	Adlai E. Stevenson		54th	244 Rep	105 Dem	43 Rep	39 Dem
1897–1901	**William McKinley***	Republican	55th	204 Rep	113 Rep	47 Rep	34 Dem
	Garret A. Hobart (to 1901)		56th	185 Rep	163 Rep	53 Rep	26 Dem
	Theodore Roosevelt (1901)						
1901–1909	**Theodore Roosevelt**	Republican	57th	197 Rep	151 Dem	55 Rep	31 Dem
	(VP vacant, 1901–1905)		58th	208 Rep	178 Dem	57 Rep	33 Dem
	Charles W. Fairbanks		59th	250 Rep	136 Dem	57 Rep	33 Dem
	(1905–1909)		60th	222 Rep	164 Dem	61 Rep	31 Dem
1909–1913	**William Howard Taft**	Republican	61st	219 Rep	172 Dem	61 Rep	32 Dem
	James S. Sherman		62d	228 Dem	161 Rep	51 Rep	41 Dem
1913–1921	**Woodrow Wilson**	Democrat	63d	291 Dem	127 Rep	51 Dem	44 Rep
	Thomas R. Marshall		64th	230 Dem	196 Rep	56 Dem	40 Rep
			65th	216 Dem	210 Rep	53 Dem	42 Rep
			66th	240 Rep	190 Dem	49 Rep	47 Dem
1921–1923	**Warren G. Harding***	Republican	67th	301 Rep	131 Dem	59 Rep	37 Dem
	Calvin Coolidge						
1923–1929	**Calvin Coolidge**	Republican	68th	225 Rep	205 Dem	51 Rep	43 Dem
	(VP vacant, 1923–1925)		69th	247 Rep	183 Dem	56 Rep	39 Dem
	Charles G. Dawes		70th	237 Rep	195 Dem	49 Rep	46 Dem
	(1925–1929)						
1929–1933	**Herbert Hoover**	Republican	71st	267 Rep	167 Dem	56 Rep	39 Dem
	Charles Curtis		72d	220 Dem	214 Rep	48 Rep	47 Dem
1933–1945	**Franklin D. Roosevelt***	Democrat	73d	310 Dem	117 Rep	60 Dem	35 Rep
	John N. Garner		74th	319 Dem	103 Rep	69 Dem	25 Rep
	(1933–1941)		75th	331 Dem	89 Rep	76 Dem	16 Rep
	Henry A. Wallace		76th	261 Dem	164 Rep	69 Dem	23 Rep
	(1941–1945)		77th	268 Dem	162 Rep	66 Dem	28 Rep
	Harry S. Truman (1945)		78th	218 Dem	208 Rep	58 Dem	37 Rep
1945–1953	**Harry S. Truman**	Democrat	79th	242 Dem	190 Rep	56 Dem	38 Rep
	VP vacant, 1945–1949		80th	245 Rep	188 Dem	51 Rep	45 Dem
	Alben W. Barkley		81st	263 Dem	171 Rep	54 Dem	42 Rep
	(1949–1953)		82d	234 Dem	199 Rep	49 Dem	47 Rep

*Died in office.

Year	President and Vice President	Party of President	Congress	House		Senate	
				Majority Party	Minority Party	Majority Party	Minority Party
1953–1961	**Dwight D. Eisenhower**	Republican	83d	221 Rep	211 Dem	48 Rep	47 Dem
	Richard M. Nixon		84th	232 Dem	203 Rep	48 Dem	47 Rep
			85th	233 Dem	200 Rep	49 Dem	47 Rep
			86th	283 Dem	153 Rep	64 Dem	34 Rep
1961–1963	**John F. Kennedy***	Democrat	87th	263 Dem	174 Rep	65 Dem	35 Rep
	Lyndon B. Johnson						
1963–1969	**Lyndon B. Johnson**	Democrat	88th	258 Dem	177 Rep	67 Dem	33 Rep
	(VP vacant, 1963–1965)		89th	295 Dem	140 Rep	68 Dem	32 Rep
	Hubert H. Humphrey (1965–1969)		90th	247 Dem	187 Rep	64 Dem	36 Rep
1969–1974	**Richard M. Nixon†**	Republican	91st	243 Dem	192 Rep	57 Dem	43 Rep
	Spiro T. Agnew††		92d	254 Dem	180 Rep	54 Dem	44 Rep
	Gerald R. Ford§						
1974–1977	**Gerald R. Ford**	Republican	93d	239 Dem	192 Rep	56 Dem	42 Rep
	Nelson A. Rockefeller§		94th	291 Dem	144 Rep	60 Dem	37 Rep
1977–1981	**Jimmy Carter**	Democrat	95th	292 Dem	143 Rep	61 Dem	38 Rep
	Walter Mondale		96th	276 Dem	157 Rep	58 Dem	41 Rep
1981–1989	**Ronald Reagan**	Republican	97th	243 Dem	192 Rep	53 Rep	46 Dem
	George Bush		98th	269 Dem	165 Rep	54 Rep	46 Dem
			99th	253 Dem	182 Rep	53 Rep	47 Dem
			100th	257 Dem	178 Rep	54 Dem	46 Rep
1989–1993	**George Bush**	Republican	101st	262 Dem	173 Rep	55 Dem	45 Rep
	Dan Quayle		102d	267 Dem	167 Rep	56 Dem	44 Rep
1993–2000	**Bill Clinton**	Democrat	103d	258 Dem	176 Rep	57 Dem	43 Rep
	Albert Gore, Jr.		104th	230 Rep	204 Dem	53 Rep	47 Dem
			105th	228 Rep	206 Dem	55 Rep	45 Dem
			106th	223 Rep	211 Dem	54 Rep	46 Dem
2000–2009	**George W. Bush**	Republican	107th	220 Rep	215 Dem	50 Rep	50 Dem
	Dick Cheney		108th	229 Rep	204 Dem	51 Rep	48 Dem
			109th	233 Rep	206 Dem	55 Rep	44 Dem
			110th	229 Dem	196 Rep	51 Dem	49 Rep
2009–2012	**Barack Obama**	Democrat	111th	256 Dem	179 Rep	60 Dem	40 Rep
	Joe Biden		112th	193 Dem	242 Rep	51 Dem	47 Rep

*Died in office. †Resigned from the presidency. ††Resigned from the vice presidency. §Appointed vice president.

CHAPTER 1

1. The text defines power as
   (A) the ability of one person to get another person to act in accordance with the first person's intentions.
   (B) the right to use one's authority.
   (C) legal or unofficial authority, capacity, or right to influence one's own outcome.
   (D) the ability to determine who gets what, when, and how.
   (E) the elected officials' ability to make policy.

2. The U.S. Constitution created a form of republican government called a representative democracy. Under this style of government,
   (A) ultimate power rests with elected officials.
   (B) popular sovereignty is in the hands of the ruling class.
   (C) the people hold the ultimate power over the government through the election process.
   (D) policy decisions will be made based on mutual agreement between the people and government officials.
   (E) impeachment of elected officials rests in the hands of the electorate.

3. The Framers of the Constitution were influenced by ________, who argued against powerful kings and in favor of popular consent.
   (A) Harold Lasswell
   (B) Karl Marx
   (C) Aristotle
   (D) Thomas Hobbes
   (E) John Locke

4. In the U.S., elected officials are the delegates of the people, acting as the people would act were the matter put to a popular vote. This is called
   (A) the power elite view.
   (B) bureaucratic policy.
   (C) legitimacy.
   (D) majoritarian politics.
   (E) political culture.

5. Which political view argues that political resources have become so widely distributed that no single entity can control them?
   (A) the class view
   (B) the power elite view
   (C) the bureaucratic view
   (D) the pluralist view
   (E) the federalism view

CHAPTER 2

1. The goal of the American Revolution was
   (A) liberty.
   (B) control.
   (C) power.
   (D) equality.
   (E) understanding.

2. The Articles of the Confederation
   (A) gave the federal government the power to levy taxes.
   (B) gave the federal government the power to regulate commerce.
   (C) retained state sovereignty and independence.
   (D) gave states the power to ratify treaties.
   (E) established a national judicial system.

3. The Great Compromise attempted to resolve the dispute between the Virginia Plan and the New Jersey Plan by recommending that
   (A) senators would be elected by the people.
   (B) states would have equal representation in the House of Representatives.
   (C) bills of revenue would originate in the Senate.
   (D) representation in the House of Representatives would be apportioned by population.
   (E) slaves would be counted in the total population of a state.

4. All of the following were proposed by the Antifederalists EXCEPT
   (A) creating a council to check the president's power.
   (B) narrowing the jurisdiction of the Supreme Court.
   (C) increasing the size of the House of Representatives to reflect more popular interests.
   (D) leaving military affairs in the hands of the state militias.
   (E) a stronger national government over state governments.

CHAPTER 3

1. _______ is a political system in which the national government shares power with state governments.
   (A) Federalism
   (B) Republicanism
   (C) Democracy
   (D) Antifederalism
   (E) Nationalism

2. What Supreme Court decision resulted in the *necessary and proper clause*, confirming the national government's right to charter a national bank?
   (A) *United States v. Morrison*
   (B) *United States v. Lopez*
   (C) *McCulloch v. Maryland*
   (D) *Printz v. United States*
   (E) *Gibbons v. Ogden*

3. The states play a key role in all of the following EXCEPT
   (A) social welfare.
   (B) law enforcement.
   (C) roads and highways.
   (D) managing water supplies.
   (E) interstate commerce.

4. By far, the largest grant-in-aid from the federal government to states is for
   (A) income security.
   (B) education and training.
   (C) Medicaid.
   (D) Medicare.
   (E) transportation.

5. In 1994, a renewed effort was led by Congress to cut total government spending, roll back federal regulations, and shift important functions back to the states. This demonstrates the process of
   (A) deregulation.
   (B) devolution.
   (C) revolution.
   (D) confederation.
   (E) republicanism.

CHAPTER 4

1. "A patterned and sustained way of thinking about how political and economic life ought to be carried out" is the definition of
   (A) public opinion.
   (B) political ideology.
   (C) political culture.
   (D) public policy.
   (E) policy agenda.

2. The text lists five important elements in the American view of the political system, including all of these EXCEPT
   (A) liberty.
   (B) civic duty.
   (C) individual responsibility.
   (D) education.
   (E) equality.

3. The constitutional prohibition of an official religion has resulted in an inevitable
   (A) religious diversity.
   (B) decline in membership in religious institutions.
   (C) increase in contentious religious differences.
   (D) decrease in the power of culture to shape the individual.
   (E) surge in new religious faiths.

4. Which statement about American's trust in the government is TRUE?
   (A) Recent polls show that three-quarters of Americans trust Washington most of the time or just about always.
   (B) Since the late 1950s, there has been a steady decline in the proportion of Americans who say they trust the government in Washington.
   (C) By and large, trust in government has been absent since about the mid-1990s.
   (D) Americans are less supportive of the country and its institutions than Europeans are of theirs.
   (E) Americans place more trust in big business than they do in Congress.

5. Only one institution has gained support in the past three decades in the U.S. Which one is it?
   (A) churches
   (B) public schools
   (C) big business
   (D) Congress
   (E) the military

CHAPTER 5

1. What law made it illegal to advocate the overthrow of the U.S. government by force or violence?
(A) the Internal Security Act in 1950
(B) the Smith Act in 1940
(C) the Communist Control Act in 1954
(D) the Sedition Act in 1798
(E) the Espionage Act in 1917

2. Originally, the liberties stated in the Bill of Rights applied only to the federal government. When did this change?
(A) after the Revolutionary War
(B) after the Civil War
(C) after WWI
(D) after the Civil Rights Movement in the 1960s
(E) during the 1990s

3. What is selective incorporation?
(A) a standard of equal treatment that must be observed by the government
(B) denies the government the right, without due process, to deprive people of life, liberty, and property
(C) the process whereby the Court has applied many parts of the Bill of Rights to the states
(D) censorship of a publication
(E) the law should not punish speech unless there is a clear and present danger of producing harmful actions

4. If the government tells a newspaper what it can or cannot print in advance of publication, it is
(A) prior restraint.
(B) a violation of the Second Amendment.
(C) a deprival of due process.
(D) selective incorporation.
(E) enforcing the clear and present danger test.

5. Burning the American flag has been determined to be an act of
(A) symbolic speech.
(B) treason.
(C) anti-Americanism.
(D) libel.
(E) slander.

6. Some feel that the Miranda protections are not a sufficient deterrent to police misconduct. However, the Court has refused to let Congress abolish Miranda because
(A) we have no better alternative.
(B) it is a constitutional rule.
(C) it has the support of law enforcement.
(D) it would cause a backlog of cases that would need to be reviewed on the basis of the change in the law.
(E) it believes Congress had political motives for wanting it abolished.

CHAPTER 6

1. The Supreme Court concluded that the Fourteenth Amendment "could not have been intended to abolish distinctions based upon color, or to enforce social . . . equality." This quote from the Supreme Court that established the principle of "separate but equal" came from the case of
(A) *Dred Scott v. Sanford.*
(B) *Brown v. Board of Education of Topeka.*
(C) *Sweat v. Painter.*
(D) *Plessy v. Ferguson.*
(E) *Smith v. Allwright.*

2. *De facto* segregation in the public schools was a result of
(A) laws that prohibited integration.
(B) whites living in their own part of town and the concept of attending schools closest to your home.
(C) state constitutions requiring it.
(D) decisions made by state courts.
(E) court-ordered busing to achieve absolute segregation.

3. Which of the Civil Rights Acts was the most far-reaching of all and dealt with voting, employment, schooling, and public accommodations?
(A) 1957
(B) 1960
(C) 1964
(D) 1965
(E) 1968

4. Which Amendment made it clear that no state may deny the right to vote on the basis of sex?
   (A) 12th
   (B) 14th
   (C) 16th
   (D) 19th
   (E) 21st

5. Using preferential hiring practices on the basis of sex or race is
   (A) illegal.
   (B) affirmative action.
   (C) discrimination.
   (D) prejudicial conduct.
   (E) inequality of results.

CHAPTER 7

1. Interviews with randomly selected voters conducted at polling places on election day are called
   (A) random samples.
   (B) election surveys.
   (C) focus groups.
   (D) exit polls.
   (E) sampling.

2. Citizens aged 18 to 29, compared to older Americans, have been more likely to favor all of the following EXCEPT
   (A) gay marriage.
   (B) women's rights.
   (C) giving parents tax money in the form of vouchers for private or religious schools.
   (D) letting people invest some of their Social Security contribution in the stock market.
   (E) the opinion that partisanship is important to the political process.

3. Which statement about racial difference in politics is TRUE?
   (A) Black Americans are overwhelmingly Republican.
   (B) Blacks are more likely than whites to support affirmative action.
   (C) Whites are more likely than blacks to oppose the use of military force.
   (D) Neither blacks nor whites believe our courts should be tougher in handling criminals.
   (E) Whites are more likely than blacks to think that believing in God is essential for a person to be moral.

4. Which of the following would NOT be considered a political elite?
   (A) George, who is running for office
   (B) Mary, who is the governor of her state
   (C) Fernando, who is working to get President Obama reelected
   (D) Nancy, who votes in every election
   (E) Diana, who speaks out against immigration policies

CHAPTER 8

1. Caro is 18 years old, and as such is _________; she is not a U.S. citizen so she is ________.
   (A) in the voting-age population; not eligible to vote
   (B) in the voting-eligible population; eligible to vote
   (C) in the voting-eligible population; not eligible to vote
   (D) in the voting-age population; eligible to vote
   (E) a registered voter; not eligible to vote

2. In most European nations, voter registration is done
   (A) in school.
   (B) at specialized facilities.
   (C) in banks and grocery stores.
   (D) at birth.
   (E) by the government.

3. Which method to keep blacks from voting involved whether or not a person's ancestors had voted before 1867?
   (A) the literacy test
   (B) the generation test
   (C) the poll tax
   (D) the grandfather clause
   (E) the historical voting test

4. Using Verba and Nie's six forms of participation in politics, which group comprises about 11% of the population, includes the highly educated with high incomes, tends to participate in all forms of politics and has the highest rate of voting participation?
   (A) voting specialists
   (B) activists
   (C) campaigners
   (D) communalists
   (E) parochial participants

5. Mr. Freeman doesn't vote and doesn't belong to any civic associations, but he often sends letters to his congressman about the empty houses on his street. According to Verba and Nie, Mr. Freeman is a
(A) campaigner.
(B) complainer.
(C) parochial participant.
(D) communalist.
(E) activist.

CHAPTER 9

1. The first organized political party in American history was
(A) Federalists.
(B) Republicans.
(C) Progressives.
(D) Madisonians.
(E) Jacksonians.

2. The modern Republican Party became a major party as a result of
(A) the Civil War.
(B) the defeat of Andrew Jackson.
(C) the advent of the party convention.
(D) the rise of the mugwumps.
(E) a press for civil service reform to eliminate patronage.

3. There are at least two kinds of realignments—one in which a major party is so badly defeated that it disappears and a new party emerges to take its place, and one in which
(A) a third party becomes so strong that there are three viable parties.
(B) the two existing parties continue, but voters shift their support from one to the other.
(C) the two parties become so similar that a third party is needed.
(D) both parties lose support and undergo a major revision of policy.
(E) neither existing party is sufficiently popular to gain enough votes and one party splits.

4. Which ballot lists all candidates of a given office under the name of that office?
(A) party-column
(B) split ticket
(C) office-bloc
(D) straight ticket
(E) straight office

5. A ________ is a party organization that recruits its members by the use of tangible incentives—money, political jobs, an opportunity to get favors from government— and is characterized by a high degree of leadership control over member activity.
(A) party platform
(B) party committee
(C) political faction
(D) party following
(E) political machine

6. A few minor parties have been able to carry states and win electoral votes. Which is NOT one of these?
(A) Republicans
(B) Populists
(C) States' Rights Democrats
(D) Green Party
(E) American Independent party

CHAPTER 10

1. ________ refers to the alleged tendency of candidates to win more votes in an election because of the presence at the top of the ticket of a better-known candidate, such as the president.
(A) Patronage
(B) Nepotism
(C) Coattails
(D) Caboose
(E) Favoritism

2. Drawing the boundaries of legislative districts in bizarre or unusual shapes to favor one party is
(A) gerrymandering.
(B) redlining.
(C) apportioning.
(D) rigging.
(E) jigsawing.

3. When a senatorial candidate runs a brief commercial during a television broadcast, it is known as a
(A) spot.
(B) sound bite.
(C) talking head.
(D) visual.
(E) photo op.

4. What event led to the passing of a new campaign finance law?
(A) the Bay of Pigs invasion
(B) Watergate
(C) the Iran-Contra affair
(D) the Florida election result in *Gore v. Bush*
(E) the impeachment of Clinton

5. One way of evaluating the ultimate effect of the Bipartisan Campaign Finance Reform Act of 2002 is to say that it
(A) bans all "hard money" contributions to national political parties.
(B) decreased the total amount of individual contributions to candidates.
(C) increased independent expenditures by corporations, labor unions and trade associations, in exchange for increased regulation.
(D) eliminates issue advocacy by anyone other than individuals.
(E) shifts influence away from businesses and unions and toward the media.

CHAPTER 11

1. Which of the following is the definition of an interest group?
(A) an organization of people sharing a common interest or goal that seeks to influence public policy
(B) a committee set up by a corporation, labor union, or interest group that raises and spends campaign money from voluntary donations
(C) a political organization whose goals will principally benefit nonmembers
(D) a group that shares a demand for change in some aspect of the social or political order
(E) a group that tells a legislator what values are at stake in a vote, and how that issue fits into his or her own political views or party agenda

2. The AARP provides health insurance, travel discounts, and other freebies to their members. These benefits are known as
(A) free riders.
(B) material incentives.
(C) solidary incentives.
(D) purposive incentives.
(E) latent interests.

3. Frederik is working on the Obama campaign because he believes in Obama's platform. Frederik's incentive for joining the campaign is
(A) material.
(B) solidary.
(C) purposive.
(D) coherent.
(E) public interest.

4. What organization was founded in 1920 to educate and organize women for the purpose of using effectively their newly won right to vote?
(A) the Women's Suffrage Organization
(B) the Federation of Business and Professional Women
(C) the Women's Equity Action League
(D) the National Women's Political Caucus
(E) the League of Women Voters

5. *Citizens United v. FEC* (2010) ruled that nonprofit organizations, labor unions and corporations
(A) were restricted in donating up to $10,000 to a candidate.
(B) could only endorse political parties and not individual candidates.
(C) could not create 527 organizations.
(D) were not allowed to spend money on any candidate.
(E) could fund "electioneering communications" within 30 days of a primary election or 60 days of a general election.

6. Campaign finance laws limit to________the amount any political action committee can spend on a given candidate in a given election.
(A) $2,000
(B) $5,000
(C) $12,000
(D) $15,000
(E) $50,000

CHAPTER 12

1. The creation in 1848 of the ________ allowed telegraphic dissemination of information to newspaper editors on a systematic basis.
(A) Associated Press
(B) high-speed rotary press
(C) teletype machine
(D) telegraph
(E) Government Printing Office

2. As a ________, the national media influence what subjects become national political issues and for how long.
   (A) scorekeeper
   (B) gatekeeper
   (C) watchdog
   (D) source
   (E) monitor

3. Which of these is an example of a conservative media outlet?
   (A) CNN
   (B) *The New York Times*
   (C) MSNBC
   (D) ABC
   (E) Fox News

4. Who was the first president to use the media to promote his agenda, sometimes on a daily basis?
   (A) Theodore Roosevelt
   (B) Woodrow Wilson
   (C) Franklin D. Roosevelt
   (D) John F. Kennedy
   (E) Bill Clinton

CHAPTER 13

1. *Congress* derives from a Latin term that means
   (A) to converse.
   (B) ruling body.
   (C) decision maker.
   (D) public forum.
   (E) a coming together.

2. The purpose of cloture is
   (A) to defeat legislation by using a procedural rule.
   (B) to bring an end to a filibuster in the Senate so the senators can vote on a bill.
   (C) to kill a bill in a standing committee.
   (D) to get a stalled bill out of committee.
   (E) to work out differences between the House and Senate versions of a bill.

3. The first woman to become Speaker of the House was
   (A) Gabrielle Gifford.
   (B) Hillary Clinton.
   (C) Jeannette Rankin.
   (D) Nancy Pelosi.
   (E) Olympia Snowe.

4. Most bills are sent to the committee that has jurisdiction on the subject of the bill. These committees are referred to as
   (A) joint committees.
   (B) standing committees.
   (C) conference committees.
   (D) select committees.
   (E) policy committees.

5. The policy that enables members of Congress to send material through the mail by substituting their facsimile signature for postage is known as
   (A) pork-barrel spending.
   (B) logrolling.
   (C) franking.
   (D) earmarking.
   (E) legislative oversight.

CHAPTER 14

1. Which of the following presidents did NOT hold national office before becoming president?
   (A) Franklin Roosevelt
   (B) Richard Nixon
   (C) George H.W. Bush
   (D) John F. Kennedy
   (E) Ronald Reagan

2. When the same party controls the White House and both houses of Congress, it is called
   (A) unified government.
   (B) divided government.
   (C) bicameral congress.
   (D) partisan government.
   (E) gridlock.

3. The Constitution requires that the president must be a natural-born citizen and at least
   (A) 40 years old.
   (B) 35 years old.
   (C) 30 years old.
   (D) 50 years old.
   (E) 25 years old.

4. When presidential candidates fail to receive the majority of the electoral college votes,
   (A) the top two candidates will face each other in a runoff election.
   (B) the Senate will choose from the top two candidates.
   (C) the electors will be released from their pledges to support a particular candidate and will continue voting until the candidate receives a majority of the electors.
   (D) the House of Representatives will choose from among the top three candidates.
   (E) the candidate with the greatest percentage of the popular vote will be declared the winner.

5. If the president does not sign the bill within 10 days *and* Congress has adjourned within that time, then the bill will not become law. This is called the
   (A) pocket veto.
   (B) line item veto.
   (C) message veto.
   (D) legislative veto.
   (E) end veto.

6. Which president was a highly intelligent man with a deep knowledge of and interest in foreign policy, coupled with a deep suspicion of the media, his political rivals, and the federal bureaucracy?
   (A) George H. W. Bush
   (B) Bill Clinton
   (C) Richard Nixon
   (D) Gerald Ford
   (E) Lyndon Johnson

CHAPTER 15

1. Publicly operated enterprises account for ________ of all employment in the United States.
   (A) almost 60%
   (B) about 35%
   (C) about 22%
   (D) about 15%
   (E) less than 3%

2. ________ was the first occasion during which the government made heavy use of federal income taxes—on individuals and corporations—to finance its activities.
   (A) The Civil War
   (B) The New Deal
   (C) World War II
   (D) World War I
   (E) The Vietnam War

3. When an agency submits the name of the person it wants to hire along with the form describing the job to the OPM, it is a form of the buddy system, called
   (A) a name-request job.
   (B) a partisan favor.
   (C) nepotism.
   (D) the merit system.
   (E) informal patronage.

4. When Congress sets aside money for a specific government program, such as disaster relief, that money is a(n)
   (A) budget.
   (B) appropriation.
   (C) grant.
   (D) funded program.
   (E) trust fund.

5. ________ refers to the tendency of agencies to grow without regard to the benefits that their programs confer or the costs that they entail.
   (A) Waste
   (B) Red tape
   (C) Conflict
   (D) Duplication
   (E) Imperialism

CHAPTER 16

1. This gave the courts the right to declare laws of Congress and acts of the executive branch void and unenforceable if they are judged to be in conflict with the Constitution.
   (A) judicial activism
   (B) judicial review
   (C) writs of mandamus
   (D) doctrine of political questions
   (E) original intent

2. What court(s) are required by the Constitution?
   (A) the Supreme Court
   (B) the Supreme Court and two federal courts: constitutional and legislative
   (C) the Supreme Court and courts of appeals
   (D) the Supreme Court, courts of appeals and district courts
   (E) the Supreme Court and legislative courts

3. In order to start a lawsuit, you must have ________, which means you are entitled to bring the case to court.
(A) a writ of certiorari
(B) a writ of habeas corpus
(C) a writ of mandamus
(D) standing
(E) immunity

CHAPTER 17

1. In ________ politics, a proposed policy will confer benefits on some relatively small, identifiable group and impose costs on another small, equally identifiable group.
(A) majoritarian
(B) entrepreneurial
(C) distributed
(D) interest group
(E) client

2. The ______ Act created the National Labor Relations Board (NLRB) to regulate the conduct of union organizing drives and to hear complaints of unfair labor practices brought by workers against management.
(A) Wagner
(B) Sherman
(C) Clayton
(D) Taft-Hartley
(E) Landrum-Griffin

3. The existence of farm subsidies is the result of
(A) price swings.
(B) normal economic downturns.
(C) history and politics.
(D) necessity in order to save small farms.
(E) entrepreneurial politics.

CHAPTER 18

1. What do monetarists believe the government should do when the economy goes into a recession?
(A) cut spending
(B) print more money
(C) increase taxes
(D) decrease taxes
(E) cut interest rates

2. What do Keynesians believe the government should do in a recession?
(A) cut spending
(B) spend more money
(C) increase taxes
(D) decrease taxes
(E) cut interest rates

3. The most important part of the economic policy-making machinery is
(A) Congress.
(B) the Fed.
(C) the OMB.
(D) the CEA.
(E) the executive branch.

CHAPTER 19

1. The biggest problem facing majoritarian welfare programs is
(A) their cost.
(B) their legitimacy.
(C) partisan politics.
(D) changing popular opinion.
(E) deciding who deserves the benefit.

2. Social Security and Medicare were initiated under the administration of
(A) Franklin D. Roosevelt.
(B) Woodrow Wilson.
(C) Herbert Hoover.
(D) Harry Truman.
(E) Dwight Eisenhower.

3. Which is an example of majoritarian politics?
(A) TANF
(B) ADFC
(C) Social Security
(D) food stamps
(E) Medicaid

4. A policy in which poor people are provided with education and job training to help get them out of poverty is called a(n) ________ strategy.
(A) income
(B) service
(C) welfare
(D) job
(E) antipoverty

CHAPTER 20

1. The majoritarian component of foreign policy-making includes decisions such as
   (A) the elimination of the military draft.
   (B) the establishment of military alliances.
   (C) the establishment of tariffs on a specific industry.
   (D) providing aid to American corporations doing business abroad.
   (E) Congressional investigations into scandals involving multinationals.

2. The power to regulate commerce with other nations lies with
   (A) the president.
   (B) the Supreme Court.
   (C) cabinet officials.
   (D) Congress.
   (E) the Secretary of State.

3. One of the few cases in which the Supreme Court denied the president broad wartime powers occurred
   (A) during the 1940s, when President Roosevelt ordered the relocation of more than 100,000 Japanese Americans.
   (B) during the 1950s, when President Truman seized the steel mills to avert a strike.
   (C) during the 1960s, when President Johnson escalated the war in Vietnam.
   (D) during the 1970s, when Iranian assets were frozen by President Carter during the hostage crisis.
   (E) during the 1860s, when President Lincoln took extraordinary measures to protect the union.

4. The advent of the containment paradigm in U.S. foreign policy was a direct result of
   (A) the War of 1812.
   (B) World War I.
   (C) World War II.
   (D) the Korean War.
   (E) the Cold War.

5. The disengagement view reflects the beliefs of younger foreign policymakers in response to
   (A) U.S. actions in Vietnam.
   (B) the Marshall Plan.
   (C) massive casualties during World War I.
   (D) ethnic cleansing in Kosovo.
   (E) the breakup of the Soviet Union.

6. The world of today can best be described as ______, with ______ as the reigning superpower(s).
   (A) multipolar; the United States, China and the European Union
   (B) unipolar; China
   (C) unipolar; the United States
   (D) bipolar; the United States and the European Union
   (E) bipolar; the United States and China

CHAPTER 21

1. Entrepreneurial politics, particularly as it involves the environment, is understood to mean
   (A) many people hope to benefit from rules that impose costs on just a few firms.
   (B) many people hope to benefit from regulation, and most will share the costs.
   (C) regions hurt by environmental concerns hope to force everyone to share their costs.
   (D) interest groups work to minimize the impact of environmental regulation on their industry.
   (E) the mobilizing of decision makers to establish exhaustive environmental regulations.

2. The Environmental Protection Agency was created by the administration of
   (A) John Kennedy.
   (B) Lyndon Johnson.
   (C) Richard Nixon.
   (D) Jimmy Carter.
   (E) Bill Clinton.

3. A provision of the National Environmental Policy Act requiring a(n) ______ has received popular support, and often works to block, change or delay government-sponsored projects.
   (A) global warming assessment
   (B) environmental impact statement
   (C) intergovernmental environment protection guarantee
   (D) uniform air quality standard
   (E) environmental damage assessment

4. In the United States, a major source of acid rain is
   (A) the New England nuclear power industry.
   (B) nitrogen-based fertilizers used in agriculture.
   (C) Western coal and natural gas mining operations.
   (D) Midwestern industries burning high-sulfur coal.
   (E) automotive emissions.

5. The international Kyoto Treaty of 1997 aimed at reducing greenhouse gases was not ratified by the Senate because
   (A) debate occurred during the time of President Clinton's impeachment trial.
   (B) China, India, and other growing economies were not bound by it.
   (C) a majority of senators did not believe in the concept of global warming.
   (D) the costs to major industries were considered to be too high.
   (E) it violated existing U.S. environmental policy.

CHAPTER 22

1. Under the Old System of government, the federal government was not required or expected to play a major role in
   (A) declaring and conducting war.
   (B) interstate commerce.
   (C) establishing a national currency.
   (D) regulating the economy.
   (E) delivering the mail.

2. In recent times, citizens have used the federal courts to alter state policy to a greater degree than ever before. An important example of this is
   (A) overturning state laws banning abortion.
   (B) restructuring campaign finance regulations.
   (C) the establishment of Social Security.
   (D) enforcing environmental regulatory policies.
   (E) welfare reform legislation.

3. The transition from the Old System to the New System of government took place during two periods in American politics:
   (A) the eras of Reconstruction and the Great Depression.
   (B) the eras of the Great War and the Cold War.
   (C) the eras of the New Deal and World War II.
   (D) the eras of the New Deal and the Great Society.
   (E) the eras of the Cold War and the New Frontier.

4. All of the following are consequences of modern enlarged government activity EXCEPT
   (A) more time managing existing programs, less time exploring new ideas.
   (B) decreasing the size and influence of interest groups.
   (C) appearing to act increasingly in inconsistent and uncoordinated ways.
   (D) being less susceptible to control by electoral activity.
   (E) increasing the programs/issues it is responsible for while increasing the risk of failure.

5. The Founders believed they were establishing a government system designed to
   (A) balance power equally between national and citizen interests.
   (B) keep local power weak and instill a strong central government.
   (C) keep central power weak and enhance local and citizen power.
   (D) enhance the role of special interests in formulating policy.
   (E) guarantee equal rights for every person living in the new republic.

AP* Practice Free-Response Questions

Essay 1: It is projected that in the 21st Century the demographics of the United States will make a radical shift. A mostly white baby boomer generation will enter their retirement years and the young generation will mostly belong to a number of racial and ethnic minority groups. Each will place demands on government for favorable policies for their groups. Discuss the policies that each group will demand from the government and the means of achieving those demands.

Essay 2: In *Federalist* 51 James Madison wrote the following: "In a republican government, the legislative authority necessarily predominates. The remedy for this inconveniency is to divide the legislature into different branches; and to render them by different modes of election, and different principles of action, as little connected with each other as the nature of their common functions and their common dependence on the society will admit. Discuss how the different modes of elections and different principles of action have created checks and balances in the Congress.

Essay 3: Since the Great Depression, the United States has moved from dual to cooperative federalism. However, the national government has been able to pursue its national objectives through the use of categorical and block grants. Additionally, the national government has attached strings to these grants and has issued federal mandates for the states to implement. Discuss how all of these have helped the national government to achieve its national goals.

Essay 4: The equal protection clause and the due process clause of the Fourteenth Amendment have been used by the Supreme Court to incorporate the Bill of Rights. Cite relevant Supreme Court cases that demonstrate how the Court has protected citizens from abusive state governments in the areas of the establishment clause and the rights of the accused.

Essay 5: Throughout American history, certain groups have faced discrimination including African Americans and women. Beginning in the mid-twentieth century, Congress and the courts have attempted to end discrimination of these groups. Discuss how Congress has changed past discrimination practices through the passage of the 1964 Civil Rights Act. Discuss the role of the Supreme Court by analyzing the impact of the decisions in *Brown v. Board of Education* and *Roe v. Wade*.

Essay 6: Voter participation is often linked to education, income, race and ethnicity, and age. Examine how each of these factors will influence who will vote.

Essay 7: Interest groups attempt to influence public policy at all levels of government. Their main strategies are lobbying, electioneering, and litigation in the courts. Discuss how interest groups achieve their policy objectives by using these three strategies. Cite examples of actual interest groups engaging in these strategies.

Essay 8: Dealignment, swing voters, and split-ticket voting have changed American politics since the 1960s. Define each of these terms and explain the impact that each has had on political parties and campaigns.

Essay 9: Third parties have made important contributions to the American political system, yet they have great difficulty winning elections. Explain important contributions third parties have made to the political system and how our traditional two-party system has deprived third parties from achieving electoral victory.

Essay 10: Since President Franklin D. Roosevelt, the way the media covers the presidents and how the presidents use the media, have evolved. Discuss the relationship between the media and the presidents and cite examples from two presidential administrations.

Essay 11: Most of the actual work in Congress is performed in committees and subcommittees. Explain the role of the Congressional committee system in both the legislative process and in their oversight functions.

Essay 12: The president and Congress are often in conflict on what foreign policy the United States should pursue. Discuss two formal powers and two informal powers that the president has in making foreign policy. Discuss two ways that Congress can use their formal powers to guide foreign policy.

Essay 13: Both the president and Congress have trouble controlling the bureaucracy. Explain why the president has a hard time bringing the bureaucracy under his control and what tools presidents have to accomplish this. How can Congress control the bureaucracy?

Essay 14: It has been argued that the Supreme Court should leave policymaking to the two elected branches. Yet, the courts have often engaged in making policy. Examine the role of the courts in making policy in the areas of civil rights and commerce.

Essay 15: Sometimes domestic policies seem to conflict. This is especially true with our energy and environmental policies. Discuss how Congress has tried to balance our appetite for oil with our desire for clean air and water.

Essay 16: The federal government has a number of tools to control the economy. Two of the tools are fiscal policy and monetary policy. Define each of these terms and explain how the government can use both to help the economy.

Essay 17: Since the end of World War II, American policy regarding the Soviet Union evolved from one of containment, to *détente*, to Reagan's military build up with his SDI proposals. Examine the presidencies of Truman, Nixon and Reagan regarding their approaches to the Cold War.

Essay 18: Both the national and state governments have a representative democracy. However, on the state level some citizens can experience direct democracy through their use of legislative initiatives and referendums. Define each term and explain how these two tools provide citizens with the ability to shape their state governments.

Essay 19: Describe the five policy making steps (agenda building, policy formulation, policy adoption, policy implementation, and policy evaluation) and discuss how this process reflects the will of the people.

Essay 20: The criticism of the original Constitution was that it seemed to focus on economic issues and not equality. Discuss how the Constitution has become more democratic and more egalitarian with the passage of the Bill of Rights and other amendments.

Glossary

527 organizations Organizations under section 527 of the Internal Revenue Code that raise and spend money to advance political causes. (10)

activist approach The view that judges should discern the general principles underlying laws or the Constitution and apply them to modern circumstances. (16)

activists People who tend to participate in all forms of politics. (8)

ad hoc structure Several subordinates, cabinet officers, and committees report directly to the president on different matters. (14)

adversarial press The tendency of the national media to be suspicious of officials and eager to reveal unflattering stories about them. (12)

affirmative action Programs designed to increase minority participation in some institution (businesses, schools, labor unions, or government agencies) by taking positive steps to appoint more minority-group members. (6)

amendment A new provision in the Constitution that has been ratified by the states. (2)

amicus curiae A brief submitted by a "friend of the court." (16)

Antifederalists Those who favor a weaker national government. (2)

appropriation A legislative grant of money to finance a government program or agency. (15)

Articles of Confederation A weak constitution that governed America during the Revolutionary War. (2)

assistance program A government program financed by general income taxes that provides benefits to poor citizens without requiring contribution from them. (19)

Australian ballot A government-printed ballot of uniform dimensions to be cast in secret that many states adopted around 1890 to reduce voting fraud associated with party printed ballots cast in public. (8)

authority The right to use power. (1)

authorization legislation Legislative permission to begin or continue a government program or agency. (15)

background A public official's statement to a reporter given on condition that the official not be named. (12)

benefit A satisfaction that people believe they will enjoy if a policy is adopted. (17)

bicameral legislature A lawmaking body made up of two chambers or parts. (13)

bill of attainder A law that declares a person, without a trial, guilty of a crime. (2)

Bill of Rights First ten amendments to the Constitution. (2)

bipolar world A political landscape with two superpowers. (20)

blanket primary A primary election in which each voter may vote for candidates from both parties. (10)

blog A series, or log, of discussion items on a page of the World Wide Web. (12)

brief A written statement by an attorney that summarizes a case and the laws and rulings that support it. (16)

budget A document that states tax collections, spending levels, and the allocation of spending among purposes. (18)

budget resolution A congressional decision that states the maximum amount of money the government should spend. (18)

bully pulpit The president's use of his prestige and visibility to guide or enthuse the American public. (14)

bureaucracy A large, complex organization composed of appointed officials. (15)

bureaucratic view View that the government is dominated by appointed officials. (1)

cabinet The heads of the 15 executive branch departments of the federal government. (14)

categorical grants Federal grants for specific purposes, such as building an airport. (3)

caucus A meeting of party members to select delegates backing one or another primary candidate. An association of congressional members created to advance a political ideology or a regional, ethnic, or economic interest. (9, 10, 13)

charitable choice Name given to four federal laws passed in the late 1990s specifying the conditions under which non-profit religious organizations could compete to administer certain social service delivery and welfare programs. (19)

checks and balances Authority shared by three branches of government. (2)

circular structure Several of the president's assistants report directly to him. (14)

civic competence A belief that one can affect government policies. (4)

civic duty A belief that one has an obligation to participate in civic and political affairs. (4)

civil disobedience Opposing a law considered unjust by peacefully disobeying it and accepting the resultant punishment. (6)

civil rights The rights of people to be treated without unreasonable or unconstitutional differences. (6)

civil society Voluntary action that makes cooperation easier. (4)

class-action suit A case brought by someone to help both himself or herself and all others who are similarly situated. (16)

class consciousness A belief that you are a member of an economic group whose interests are opposed to people in other such groups. (4)

class view View that the government is dominated by capitalists. (1)

clear-and-present-danger test Law should not punish speech unless there was a clear and present danger of producing harmful actions. (5)

client politics A policy in which one small group benefits and almost everybody pays. (17, 19)

closed primary A primary election in which voting is limited to already registered party members. (10)

closed rule An order from the House Rules Committee that sets a time limit on debate; forbids a bill from being amended on the floor. (13)

clothespin vote The vote cast by a person who does not like either candidate and so votes for the less objectionable of the two, putting a clothespin over his or her nose to keep out the unpleasant stench. (10)

cloture rule A rule used by the Senate to end or limit debate. (13)

coalition An alliance of factions. (2)
coattails The alleged tendency of candidates to win more votes in an election because of the presence at the top of the ticket of a better-known candidate, such as the president. (10)
command-and-control strategy A strategy to improve air and water quality, involving the setting of detailed pollution standards and rules. (21)
committee clearance The ability of a congressional committee to review and approve certain agency decisions in advance and without passing a law. (15)
competitive service The government offices to which people are appointed on the basis of merit, as ascertained by a written exam or by applying certain selection criteria. (15)
concurrent powers Powers shared by the national and state governments. (2)
concurrent resolution An expression of opinion without the force of law that requires the approval of both the House and the Senate, but not the president. (13)
concurring opinion A signed opinion in which one or more members agree with the majority view but for different reasons. (16)
conditions of aid Terms set by the national government that states must meet if they are to receive certain federal funds. (3)
conference committees Joint committees appointed to resolve differences in the Senate and House versions of the same bill. (13)
congressional campaign committee A party committee in Congress that provides funds to members and would-be members. (9)
conservative coalition An alliance between Republicans and conservative Democrats. (13)
Constitutional Convention A meeting in Philadelphia in 1787 that produced a new constitution. (2)
constitutional court A federal court authorized by Article III of the Constitution that keeps judges in office during good behavior and prevents their salaries from being reduced. They are the Supreme Court (created by the Constitution) and appellate and district courts created by Congress. (16)
containment The belief that the United States should resist the expansion of aggressive nations, especially the former Soviet Union. (20)
cost A burden that people believe they must bear if a policy is enacted. (17)
cost overruns When the money actually paid to military suppliers exceeds the estimated costs. (20)
courts of appeals Federal courts that hear appeals from district courts; no trials. (16)
critical or **realignment period** A period when a major, lasting shift occurs in the popular coalition supporting one or both parties. (9)
***de facto* segregation** Racial segregation that occurs in schools, not as a result of the law, but as a result of patterns of residential settlement. (6)
***de jure* segregation** Racial segregation that is required by law. (6)
deficit The result of when the government in one year spends more money than it takes in from taxes. (18)
democracy The rule of the many. (1)
direct or participatory democracy A government in which all or most citizens participate directly. (1)
discharge petition A device by which any member of the House, after a committee has had the bill for 30 days, may petition to have it brought to the floor. (13)
discretionary authority The extent to which appointed bureaucrats can choose courses of action and make policies not spelled out in advance by laws. (15)
discretionary spending Spending that is not required to pay for contracts, interest on the national debt, or entitlement programs such as Social Security. (18)
disengagement The belief that the United States was harmed by its war in Vietnam and so should avoid supposedly similar events. (20)
dissenting opinion A signed opinion in which one or more justices disagree with the majority view. (16)
district courts The lowest federal courts; federal trials can be held only here. (16)
diversity cases Cases involving citizens of different states who can bring suit in federal courts. (16)
divided government One party controls the White House and another party controls one or both houses of Congress. (13, 14)
division vote A congressional voting procedure in which members stand and are counted. (13)
double tracking A procedure to keep the Senate going during a filibuster in which the disputed bill is shelved temporarily so that the Senate can get on with other business. (13)
dual federalism Doctrine holding that the national government is supreme in its sphere, the states are supreme in theirs, and the two spheres should be kept separate. (3)
due process of law Denies the government the right, without due process, to deprive people of life, liberty, and property. (5)
earmarks "Hidden" congressional provisions that direct the federal government to fund specific projects or that exempt specific persons or groups from paying specific federal taxes or fees. A provision in a law that provides a direct benefit to a client without the benefit having been reviewed on the merits by all of Congress. (11, 13)
Earned Income Tax Credit (EITC) A provision of a 1975 law that entitles working families with children to receive money from the government if their total income is below a certain level. The program was expanded in the early 1990s. (19)
economic planning The belief that government plans, such as wage and price controls or the direction of investment, can improve the economy. (18)
electoral college The people chosen to cast each state's votes in a presidential election. Each state can cast one electoral vote for each senator and representative it has. The District of Columbia has three electoral votes, even though it cannot elect a representative or senator. (14)
elite People who have a disproportionate amount of some valued resource, like money or power. (1, 7)
entitlements A claim for government funds that cannot be changed without violating the rights of the claimant. (18)
entrepreneurial politics A policy in which almost everybody benefits and a small group pays the cost. (17)
enumerated powers Powers given to the national government alone. (2)
environmental impact statement A report required by federal law that assesses the possible effect of a project on the environment if the project is subsidized in whole or part by federal funds. (21)
equality of opportunity Giving people an equal chance to succeed. (6)
equality of results Making certain that people achieve the same result. (6)

equal protection of the law A standard of equal treatment that must be observed by the government. (5)
equal time rule An FCC rule that if a broadcaster sells time to one candidate, it must sell equal time to other candidates. (12)
establishment clause First Amendment ban on laws "respecting an establishment of religion." (5)
ex post facto law A law that makes an act criminal although the act was legal when it was committed. (2)
exclusionary rule Improperly gathered evidence may not be introduced in a criminal trial. (5)
exit polls Polls based on interviews conducted on election day with randomly selected voters. (7)
faction A group with a distinct political interest. (2)
feature stories Media stories about events that, though public, are not regularly covered by reporters. (12)
federalism Government authority shared by national and local governments. (2, 3)
Federalists Those who favor a stronger national government. (2)
federal-question cases Cases concerning the Constitution, federal laws, or treaties. (16)
fee shifting A rule that allows a plaintiff to recover costs from the defendant if the plaintiff wins. (16)
filibuster An attempt to defeat a bill in the Senate by talking indefinitely, thus preventing the Senate from taking action on the bill. (13)
fiscal policy Managing the economy by the use of tax and spending laws. (18)
fiscal year For the federal government, October 1 through the following September 30. (18)
franking privilege The ability of members to mail letters to their constituents free of charge by substituting their facsimile signature for postage. (13)
freedom of expression Right of people to speak, publish, and assemble. (5)
freedom of religion People shall be free to exercise their religion, and government may not establish a religion. (5)
free-exercise clause First Amendment requirement that law cannot prevent free exercise of religion. (5)
gender gap Difference in political views between men and women. (7)
general election An election held to choose which candidate will hold office. (10)
gerrymandering Drawing the boundaries of legislative districts in bizarre or unusual shapes to favor one party. (10)
globalization The growing integration of the economies and societies of the world. (18)
gold plating The tendency of Pentagon officials to ask weapons contractors to meet excessively high requirements. (20)
good-faith exception An error in gathering evidence sufficiently minor that it may be used in a trial. (5)
government by proxy Washington pays state and local governments and private groups to staff and administer federal programs. (15)
grandfather clause A clause in registration laws allowing people who do not meet registration requirements to vote if they or their ancestors had voted before 1867. (8)
grants-in-aid Money given by the national government to the states. (3)
Great Compromise Plan to have a popularly elected House based on state population and a state-selected Senate, with two members for each state. (2)
gridlock The inability of the government to act because rival parties control different parts of the government. (14)
gross domestic product The total of all goods and services produced in the economy during a given year. (18)
habeas corpus An order to produce an arrested person before a judge. (2)
horse-race journalism News coverage that focuses on who is ahead rather than on the issues. (12)
human rights The view that we should try to improve the lives of people in other countries. (20)
ideological interest groups Political organizations that attract members by appealing to their political convictions or principles. (11)
ideological party A party that values principled stands on issues above all else. (9)
impeachment Charges against a president approved by a majority of the House of Representatives. (14)
in forma pauperis A method whereby a poor person can have his or her case heard in federal court without charge. (16)
incentive Something of value one cannot get without joining an organization. (11)
income strategy A policy giving poor people money to help lift them out of poverty. (19)
incumbent The person already holding an elective office. (10)
independent expenditures Spending by political action committees, corporations, or labor unions to help a party or candidate but done independently of them. (10)
initiative Process that permits voters to put legislative measures directly on the ballot. (3)
insider stories Media stories about events that are not usually made public. (12)
insurance program A self-financing government program based on contributions that provide benefits to unemployed or retired persons. (19)
interest group An organization of people sharing a common interest or goal that seeks to influence public policy. (11)
interest group politics A policy in which one small group benefits and another small group pays. (17)
iron triangle A close relationship between an agency, a congressional committee, and an interest group. (15)
isolationism The opinion that the United States should withdraw from world affairs. (20)
issue network A network of people in Washington, D.C.– based interest groups, on congressional staffs, in universities and think tanks, and in the mass media who regularly discuss and advocate public policies. (15)
joint committees Committees on which both senators and representatives serve. (13)
joint resolution A formal expression of congressional opinion that must be approved by both houses of Congress and by the president; constitutional amendments need not be signed by the president. (13)
judicial restraint approach The view that judges should decide cases strictly on the basis of the language of the laws and the Constitution. (16)
judicial review The power of courts to declare laws unconstitutional. (2, 16)
Keynesianism The belief the government must manage the economy by spending more money when in a recession and cutting spending when there is inflation. (18)
laissez-faire An economic theory that government should not regulate or interfere with commerce. (15)
lame duck A person still in office after he or she has lost a bid for reelection. (14)

legislative courts Courts created by Congress for specialized purposes whose judges do not enjoy the protections of Article III of the Constitution. (16)
legislative veto The authority of Congress to block a presidential action after it has taken place. The Supreme Court has held that Congress does not have this power. (14, 15)
legitimacy Political authority conferred by law or by a state or national constitution. (1)
libel Writing that falsely injures another person. (5)
line-item veto An executive's ability to block a particular provision in a bill passed by the legislature. (2, 14)
literacy test A requirement that citizens show that they can read before registering to vote. (8)
litmus test An examination of the political ideology of a nominated judge. (16)
loaded language Words that imply a value judgment, used to persuade a reader without having made a serious argument. (12)
lobbyist A person who tries to influence legislation on behalf of an interest group. (11)
logrolling A legislator supports a proposal favored by another in return for support of his or hers. (17)
majoritarian politics A policy in which almost everybody benefits and almost everybody pays. (17, 19)
majority leader The legislative leader elected by party members holding the majority of seats in the House or the Senate. (13)
malapportionment Drawing the boundaries of legislative districts so they are unequal in population. (10)
mandates Terms set by the national government that states must meet whether or not they accept federal grants. (3)
marginal districts Political districts in which candidates elected to the House of Representatives win in close elections, typically by less than 55 percent of the vote. (13)
material incentives Money or things valued in monetary terms. (11)
means test An income qualification program that determines whether one is eligible for benefits under government programs reserved for lower-income groups. (19)
military-industrial complex An alleged alliance between military leaders and corporate leaders. (20)
minority leader The legislative leader elected by party members holding a minority of seats in the House or the Senate. (13)
monetarism The belief that inflation occurs when too much money is chasing too few goods. (18)
monetary policy Managing the economy by altering the supply of money and interest rates. (18)
mugwumps or **progressives** Republican party faction of the 1890s to the 1910s composed of reformers who opposed patronage. (9)
multiple referral A congressional process whereby a bill may be referred to several important committees. (13)
name-request job A job filled by a person whom an agency has already identified. (15)
national chair Day-to-day party manager elected by the national committee. (9)
national committee Delegates who run party affairs between national conventions. (9)
national convention A meeting of party delegates held every four years. (9)
national debt The total deficit from the first presidency down to the present. (18)
"necessary and proper" clause Section of the Constitution allowing Congress to pass all laws "necessary and proper" to its duties, and which has permitted Congress to exercise powers not specifically given to it (enumerated) by the Constitution. (3)
New Jersey Plan Proposal to create a weak national government. (2)
norm A standard of right or proper conduct. (7)
nullification The doctrine that a state can declare null and void a federal law that, in the state's opinion, violates the Constitution. (3)
office-bloc ballot A ballot listing all candidates of a given office under the name of that office; also called a *"Massachusetts" ballot.* (9)
open primary A primary election in which voters may choose in which party to vote as they enter the polling place. (10)
open rule An order from the House Rules Committee that permits a bill to be amended on the floor. (13)
opinion of the Court A signed opinion of a majority of the Supreme Court. (16)
orthodox A belief that morality and religion ought to be of decisive importance. (4)
party-column ballot A ballot listing all candidates of a given party together under the name of that party; also called an *"Indiana" ballot.* (9)
party polarization A vote in which a majority of Democratic legislators oppose a majority of Republican legislators. (13)
party vote There are two measures of such voting. By the stricter measure, a party vote occurs when 90 percent or more of the Democrats in either house of Congress vote together against 90 percent or more of the Republicans. A looser measure counts as a party vote any case where at least 50 percent of the Democrats vote together against at least 50 percent of the Republicans. (13)
per curiam opinion A brief, unsigned court opinion. (16)
personal following The political support provided to a candidate on the basis of personal popularity and networks. (9)
plaintiff The party that initiates a lawsuit. (16)
pluralist view The belief that competition among all affected interests shapes public policy. (1)
plurality system An electoral system in which the winner is the person who gets the most votes, even if he or she does not receive a majority; used in almost all American elections. (9)
pocket veto A bill fails to become law because the president did not sign it within 10 days before Congress adjourns. (14)
polarization A deep and wide conflict over some government policy. (20)
police power State power to enact laws promoting health, safety, and morals. (3, 6)
policy entrepreneurs Activists in or out of government who pull together a political majority on behalf of unorganized interests. (17)
political action committee (PAC) A committee set up by a corporation, labor union, or interest group that raises and spends campaign money from voluntary donations. (10, 11)
political agenda Issues that people believe require governmental action. (17)
political cue A signal telling a legislator what values are at stake in a vote, and how that issue fits into his or her own political views on party agenda. (11)

political culture A patterned and sustained way of thinking about how political and economic life ought to be carried out. (4)
political elites Persons with a disproportionate share of political power. (7)
political ideology A more or less consistent set of beliefs about what policies government ought to pursue. (7)
political machine A party organization that recruits members by dispensing patronage. (9)
political participation The many different ways that people take part in politics and government. (8)
political party A group that seeks to elect candidates to public office. (9)
political question An issue the Supreme Court will allow the executive and legislative branches to decide. (16)
political socialization Process by which background traits influence one's political views. (7)
poll A survey of public opinion. (7)
poll tax A requirement that citizens pay a tax in order to register to vote. (8)
pork-barrel legislation Legislation that gives tangible benefits to constituents in several districts or states in the hope of winning their votes in return. (13, 17)
position issue An issue about which the public is divided and rival candidates or political parties adopt different policy positions. (10)
power The ability of one person to get another person to act in accordance with the first person's intentions. (1)
power elite view View that the government is dominated by a few top leaders, most of whom are outside government. (1)
primary election An election held to choose candidates for office. (10)
prior restraint Censorship of a publication. (5)
private bill A legislative bill that deals only with specific, private, personal, or local matters. (13)
probable cause Reasonable cause for issuing a search warrant or making an arrest; more than mere suspicion. (5)
process regulation Rules governing commercial activities designed to improve consumer, worker, or environmental conditions; also called *social regulation*. (17)
progressive A belief that personal freedom and solving social problems are more important than religion. (4)
prospective voting Voting for a candidate because you favor his or her ideas for handling issues. (10)
public bill A legislative bill that deals with matters of general concern. (13)
public-interest lobby A political organization whose goals will principally benefit nonmembers. (11)
public opinion How people think or feel about particular things. (7)
purposive incentive A benefit that comes from serving a cause or principle. (11)
pyramid structure A president's subordinates report to him through a clear chain of command headed by a chief of staff. (14)
quorum The minimum number of members who must be present for business to be conducted in Congress. (13)
quorum call A roll call in either house of Congress to see whether the minimum number of representatives required to conduct business is present. (13)
random sample Method of selecting from a population in which each person has an equal probability of being selected. (7)
ratings Assessments of a representative's voting record on issues important to an interest group. (11)
Reaganomics The belief that a combination of monetarism, lower federal spending, and supply-side economics will stimulate the economy. (18)
recall Procedure whereby voters can remove an elected official from office. (3)
red tape Complex bureaucratic rules and procedures that must be followed to get something done. (15)
referendum Procedure enabling voters to reject a measure passed by the legislature. (3)
registered voters People registered to vote. (8)
remedy A judicial order enforcing a right or redressing a wrong. (16)
representative democracy A government in which leaders make decisions by winning a competitive struggle for the popular vote. (1)
republic A government in which elected representatives make the decisions. (2)
reserved powers Powers given to the state government alone. (2)
restrictive rule An order from the House Rules Committee that permits certain kinds of amendments but not others to be made into a bill on the floor. (13)
retrospective voting Voting for a candidate because you like his or her past actions in office. (10)
reverse discrimination Using race or sex to give preferential treatment to some people. (6)
riders Amendments on matters unrelated to a bill that are added to an important bill so that they will "ride" to passage through the Congress. When a bill has many riders, it is called a Christmas-tree bill. (13)
roll-call vote A congressional voting procedure that consists of members answering "yea" or "nay" to their names. (13)
routine stories Media stories about events regularly covered by reporters. (12)
runoff primary A second primary election held when no candidate wins a majority of the votes in the first primary. (10)
safe districts Districts in which incumbents win by margins of 55 percent or more. (13)
sampling error The difference between the results of random samples taken at the same time. (7)
search warrant A judge's order authorizing a search. (5)
select committees Congressional committees appointed for a limited time and purpose. (13)
selective attention Paying attention only to those news stories with which one already agrees. (12)
selective incorporation The process whereby the Court has applied many parts of the Bill of Rights to the states. (5)
separate-but-equal doctrine The doctrine established in *Plessy v. Ferguson* (1896) that African Americans could constitutionally be kept in separate but equal facilities. (6)
separation of powers Constitutional authority is shared by three different branches of government. (2)
sequential referral A congressional process by which a Speaker may send a bill to a second committee after the first is finished acting. (13)
sequester Automatic spending cuts. (18)
service strategy A policy providing poor people with education and job training to help lift them out of poverty. (19)
Shays's Rebellion A 1787 rebellion in which ex-Revolutionary War soldiers attempted to prevent foreclosures of farms as a result of high interest rates and taxes. (2)

signing statement A presidential document that reveals what the president thinks of a new law and how it ought to be enforced. (14)

simple resolution An expression of opinion either in the House or Senate to settle procedural matters in either body. (13)

social movement A widely shared demand for change in some aspect of the social or political order. (11)

soft money Funds obtained by political parties that are spent on party activities, such as get-out-the-vote drives, but not on behalf of a specific candidate. (10)

solidary incentives The social rewards (sense of pleasure, status, or companionship) that lead people to join political organizations. (9, 11)

sophomore surge An increase in the votes congressional candidates usually get when they first run for reelection. (10)

sound bite A radio or video clip of someone speaking. (12)

sovereign immunity The rule that a citizen cannot sue the government without the government's consent. (16)

Speaker The presiding officer of the House of Representatives and the leader of his party in the House. (13)

split ticket Voting for candidates of different parties for various offices in the same election. (9)

sponsored party A local or state political party largely supported by another organization in the community. (9)

standing A legal rule stating who is authorized to start a lawsuit. (16)

standing committees Permanently established legislative committees that consider and are responsible for legislation within a certain subject area. (13)

stare decisis "Let the decision stand," or allowing prior rulings to control the current case. (16)

straight ticket Voting for candidates of the same party. (9)

superdelegates Party leaders and elected officials who become delegates to the national convention without having to run in primaries or caucuses. (9)

supply-side theory The belief that lower taxes and fewer regulations will stimulate the economy. (18)

symbolic speech An act that conveys a political message. (5)

teller vote A congressional voting procedure in which members pass between two tellers, the "yeas" first and the "nays" second. (13)

trial balloon Information leaked to the media to test public reaction to a possible policy. (12)

trust funds Funds for government programs collected and spent outside the regular government budget. (15)

two-party system An electoral system with two dominant parties that compete in national elections. (9)

unalienable A human right based on nature or God. (2)

unified government The same party controls the White House and both houses of Congress. (13, 14)

unipolar world A political landscape with one superpower. (20)

valence issue An issue about which the public is united and rival candidates or political parties adopt similar positions in hopes that each will be thought to best represent those widely shared beliefs. (10)

veto Literally, "I forbid": It refers to the power of a president to disapprove a bill; it may be overridden by a two-thirds vote of each house of Congress. (13)

veto message A message from the president to Congress stating that he will not sign a bill it has passed. Must be produced within 10 days of the bill's passage. (14)

Virginia Plan Proposal to create a strong national government. (2)

voice vote A congressional voting procedure in which members shout "yea" in approval or "nay" in disapproval, permitting members to vote quickly or anonymously on bills. (13)

voting-age population (VAP) Citizens who are eligible to vote after reaching the minimum age requirement. (8)

voting-eligible population (VEP) Citizens who have reached the minimum age to be eligible to vote, excluding those who are not legally permitted to cast a ballot. (8)

waiver A decision by an administrative agency granting some other part permission to violate a law or rule that would otherwise apply to it. (3)

wall of separation Court ruling that government cannot be involved with religion. (5)

whip A senator or representative who helps the party leader stay informed about what party members are thinking. (13)

white primary The practice of keeping blacks from voting in the southern states' primaries through arbitrary use of registration requirements and intimidation. (8)

worldviews A comprehensive opinion of how the United States should respond to world problems. (20)

writ of certiorari An order by a higher court directing a lower court to send up a case for review. (16)

Chapter 1
The Study of American Government

1. *Federalist* No. 45.
2. Patrick Henry, Virginia Convention, June 12, 1788, in Bernard Bailyn, ed., *The Debate on the Constitution*, Part Two (New York: The Library of America, 1993), p. 683.
3. Rockefeller Institute of Government and Pew Center on the States, *States' Revenue Estimating: Cracks in the Crystal Ball*, March 2011.
4. John Michlethwait, "Taming Leviathan," *The Economist*, March 19, 2011, reporting data from the IMF and OECD, p. 4.
5. Ibid.
6. Government at a Glance 2011, OECD, Part III, Figure 4.2.
7. Aristotle, *Politics*, iv, 4, 1290b. More precisely, Aristotle's definition was this: *Democracy* is a "constitution in which the free-born and poor control the government—being at the same time a majority." He distinguished this from an oligarchy, "in which the rich and well-born control the government—being at the same time a minority." Aristotle listed several varieties of democracy, depending on whether, for example, there was a property qualification for citizenship.
8. Joseph A. Schumpeter, *Capitalism, Socialism, and Democracy*, 3d ed. (New York: Harper Torchbooks, 1950), 269. First published in 1942.
9. John Locke, *Second Treatise of Civil Government* (New York: Hafner Publishing Co., 1956). First published in 1690.
10. Thomas Hobbes, *Leviathan* (Oxford: Basil Blackwell, 1957). First published in 1651.
11. Karl Marx and Friedrich Engels, "The Manifesto of the Communist Party," in *The Marx-Engels Reader*, 2d ed., ed. Robert C. Tucker (New York: Norton, 1978), 469–500.
12. C. Wright Mills, *The Power Elite* (New York: Oxford University Press, 1956).
13. H. H. Gerth and C. Wright Mills, eds., *From Max Weber: Essays in Sociology* (London: Routledge and Kegan Paul, 1948), 232–235.
14. Among the authors whose interpretations of American politics are essentially pluralist is David B. Truman, *The Governmental Process*, 2d ed. (New York: Knopf, 1971).
15. Alexis de Tocqueville, *Democracy in America*, vol. 2, ed. Phillips Bradley (New York: Knopf, 1951), book 2, ch. 8, 122.

Chapter 2
The Constitution

1. Quoted in Bernard Bailyn, *The Ideological Origins of the American Revolution* (Cambridge: Harvard University Press, 1967), 61, n. 6.
2. Quoted in Bailyn, ibid., 135–137.
3. Quoted in Bailyn, ibid., 77.
4. Quoted in Bailyn, ibid., 160.
5. *Federalist* No. 37.
6. Gordon S. Wood, *The Creation of the American Republic* (Chapel Hill: University of North Carolina Press, 1969). See also *Federalist* No. 49.
7. Letter of George Washington to Henry Lee (October 31, 1787), in *Writings of George Washington*, vol. 29, ed. John C. Fitzpatrick (Washington, D.C.: Government Printing Office, 1939), 34.
8. Letters of Thomas Jefferson to James Madison (January 30, 1787) and to Colonel William S. Smith (November 13, 1787), in *Jefferson Himself*, ed. Bernard Mayo (Boston: Houghton Mifflin, 1942), 145.
9. *Federalist* No. 51.
10. *Federalist* No. 48.
11. *Federalist* No. 51.
12. Ibid.
13. Ibid.
14. "The Address and Reasons of Dissent of the Minority of the State of Pennsylvania to Their Constituents," in *The Anti-Federalist*, ed. Cecelia Kenyon (Indianapolis: Bobbs-Merrill, 1966), 39.
15. Max Farrand, *The Framing of the Constitution of the United States* (New Haven, Conn.: Yale University Press, 1913), 185.
16. See, for example, John Hope Franklin, *Racial Equality in America* (Chicago: University of Chicago Press, 1976), ch. 1, esp. 12–20.
17. Max Farrand, *The Records of the Federal Convention of 1787*, 4 vols. (New Haven, Conn.: Yale University Press), 1911–1937.
18. Theodore J. Lowi, *American Government: Incomplete Conquest* (Hinsdale, Ill.: Dryden Press, 1976), 97.
19. Article I, section 2, para. 3.
20. Gary Wills, *"Negro President": Jefferson and the Slave Power* (Boston: Houghton Mifflin, 2003).
21. Article I, section 9, para. 1.
22. Article IV, section 2, para. 3
23. Charles A. Beard, *An Economic Interpretation of the Constitution* (New York: Macmillan, 1913), esp. 26–51, 149–151, 324–325.
24. Forrest McDonald, *We the People* (Chicago: University of Chicago Press, 1958); Robert E. Brown, *Charles Beard and the Constitution* (Princeton: Princeton University Press, 1956).
25. Robert A. McGuire, "Constitution Making: A Rational Choice Model of the Federal Convention of 1787," *American Journal of Political Science* 32 (May 1988): 483–522. See also Forrest McDonald, *Novus Ordo Seclorum* (Lawrence: University of Kansas Press, 1985), 221.
26. McDonald, *Novus Ordo Seclorum*, 202–221.
27. Robert A. McGuire and Robert L. Ohsfeldt, "Economic Interests and the American Constitution: A Quantitative Rehabilitation of Charles A. Beard," *Journal of Economic History* 44 (June 1984): 509–519.
28. Lloyd N. Cutler, "To Form a Government," *Foreign Affairs* (Fall 1980): 126–143.

Chapter 3
Federalism

1. Woodrow Wilson, *Constitutional Government in the United States* (New York: Columbia University Press, 1961), 173. First published in 1908.
2. Martin Diamond, "The Federalists' View of Federalism," in *Essays in Federalism*, ed. George C. S. Benson (Claremont, Calif.: Institute for Studies in Federalism, 1961), 21–64; Samuel H. Beer, "Federalism, Nationalism, and Democracy in America," *American Political Science Review* 72 (March 1978): 9–21.
3. *United States v. Sprague*, 282 U.S. 716 (1931).

4. *Garcia v. San Antonio Metropolitan Transit Authority*, 105 S. Ct. 1005 (1985), overruling *National League of Cities v. Usery*, 426 U.S. 833 (1976).
5. *McCulloch v. Maryland*, 4 Wheat. 316 (1819).
6. *Pollock v. Farmers' Loan & Trust Co.*, 157 U.S. 429 (1895); *South Carolina v. Baker*, No. 94 (1988).
7. *Texas v. White*, 7 Wall. 700 (1869).
8. *Champion v. Ames*, 188 U.S. 321 (1903).
9. *Hoke v. United States*, 227 U.S. 308 (1913).
10. *Clark Distilling Co. v. W. Md. Ry.*, 242 U.S. 311 (1917).
11. *Hipolite Egg Co. v. United States*, 220 U.S. 45 (1911).
12. *United States v. E. C. Knight Co.*, 156 U.S. 1 (1895).
13. *Paul v. Virginia*, 8 Wall. 168 (1869).
14. *Veazie Bank v. Fenno*, 8 Wall. 533 (1869).
15. *Brown v. Maryland*, 12 Wheat. 419 (1827).
16. *Wickard v. Filburn*, 317 U.S. 111 (1942); *NLRB v. Jones & Laughlin Steel Corp.*, 301 U.S. 58 (1937).
17. *Kirschbaum Co. v. Walling*, 316 U.S. 517 (1942).
18. *Goldfarb v. Virginia State Bar*, 421 U.S. 773 (1975); *Flood v. Kuhn*, 407 U.S. 258 (1972); *Gonzales v. Raich*, No. 03-1454 (2005).
19. David B. Truman, "Federalism and the Party System," in *Federalism: Mature and Emergent*, ed. Arthur McMahon (Garden City, N.Y.: Doubleday, 1955), 123.
20. Harold J. Laski, "The Obsolescence of Federalism," *New Republic* (May 3, 1939): 367–369.
21. William H. Riker, *Federalism: Origin, Operation, Significance* (Boston: Little Brown, 1964), 154.
22. Daniel J. Elazar, *American Federalism: A View from the States* (New York: Crowell, 1966), 216.
23. Martha Derthick, *Keeping the Compound Republic: Essays on American Federalism* (Washington, D.C.: Brookings Institution, 2001), 140.
24. Donald F. Kettl, ed., *The Department of Homeland Security's First Year: A Report Card* (New York: Century Foundation Report, 2004), 18, 102.
25. Samuel H. Beer, "The Modernization of American Federalism," *Publius* 3 (Fall 1973): esp. 74–79; and Beer, "Federalism," 18–19.
26. Congressional Budget Office, *Federal Constraints on State and Local Government Actions* (Washington, D.C.: Government Printing Office, 1979).
27. William T. Gormley, Jr., "Money and Mandates: The Politics of Intergovernmental Conflict," *Publius: The Journal of Federalism* 36(4): 527.
28. Ibid., 535–537.
29. U.S. Advisory Commission on Intergovernmental Relations, *Federally Induced Costs Affecting State and Local Governments*, September 1994.
30. This is according to a study by a George Mason University researcher—see http://mercatus.org/publication/rapid-expansion-federal-spending-household.
31. Information taken from http://www.usgovernmentrevenue.com/downchart_gr.php?year=1900_2010&units=p&title=Revenue%20as%20percent%20of%20GDP.
32. Paul Teske, *Regulation in the States* (Washington, D.C.: Brookings Institution, 2004).
33. Stephen V. Monsma, *Putting Faith in Partnerships: Welfare-to-Work in Four Cities.* (Ann Arbor: University of Michigan Press, 2004).
34. Baylor University Institute for Studies of Religion, *Ohio Governor's Office of Faith-Based and Community Initiatives: A Case Study*, January 2007.
35. United States Governmental Accountability Office, "Opportunities to Reduce Potential Duplication in Government Programs, Save Tax Dollars, and Enhance Revenue," March 2011. Available at http://www.gao.gov/new.items/d11318sp.pdf.

Chapter 4

American Political Culture

1. Alexis de Tocqueville, *Democracy in America*, vol. 1, ed. Phillips Bradley (New York: Knopf, 1951), vol. 1, "Principal Causes Which Tend to Maintain the Democratic Republic in the United States" chapter. First published in 1835.
2. *The Public Perspective* (November/December 1991): 5, 7, reporting survey data from the Roper Center for Public Opinion Research.
3. Fred I. Greenstein, "The Benevolent Leader Revisited: Children's Images of Political Leaders in Three Democracies," *American Political Science Review* 69 (December 1975): 1387.
4. Alexis de Tocqueville, *Democracy in America*, vol. 1, 288.
5. Donald J. Devine, *The Political Culture of the United States* (Boston: Little, Brown, 1972), 185; Herbert McClosky and John *Zaller, The American Ethos: Public Attitudes Toward Capitalism and Democracy* (Cambridge: Harvard University Press, *1984), ch. 3, esp. 74–75.*
6. *McClosky and Zaller, The American Ethos*, 74–77.
7. Ibid., 66.
8. Gunnar Myrdal, *An American Dilemma: The Negro Problem in Modern Democracy* (New York: Harper, 1944), intro. and ch. 1.
9. Frank R. Westie, "The American Dilemma: An Empirical Test," *American Sociological Review* 30 (August 1965): 536–537.
10. Samuel P. Huntington, *American Politics* (Cambridge, Mass.: Harvard University Press, 1983), 202.
11. Eric L. McKitrick, "Party Politics and the Union and Confederate War Efforts," in *The American Party Systems*, 2d ed., ed. William Nisbet Chambers and Walter Dean Burnham (New York: Oxford University Press, 1975), 117–121.
12. Russell J. Dalton, *The Good Citizen* (Washington, D.C.: CQ Press, 2008), 38, 71, 168–171.
13. McClosky and Zaller, *The American Ethos*, 174.
14. Sidney Verba and Gary R. Orren, *Equality in America: The View from the Top* (Cambridge: Harvard University Press, 1985), 146–147.
15. McClosky and Zaller, *The American Ethos*, 82–84, 93, 95.
16. Verba and Orren, *Equality in America*, 72, 254.
17. Donald Kinder and David Sears, "Symbolic Racism Versus Racial Threats to the Good Life," *Journal of Personality and Social Psychology* 40 (1981): 414–431.
18. Paul M. Sniderman and Michael Gray Hagen, *Race and Inequality: A Study in American Values* (Chatham, N.J.: Chatham House, 1985), 111.
19. Ibid., 37–38.
20. Theodore Caplow and Howard M. Bahr, "Half a Century of Change in Adolescent Attitudes: A Replication of a Middletown Survey by the Lynds," *Public Opinion Quarterly* 43 (1979): 1–17, table 1.

21. Thomas J. Anton, "Policy-Making and Political Culture in Sweden," *Scandinavian Political Studies* 4 (1969): 88–100; M. Donald Hancock, *Sweden: The Politics of Post-Industrial Change* (Hinsdale, Ill.: Dryden Press, 1972); Sten Johansson, "Liberal-Democratic Theory and Political Processes," in *Readings in the Swedish Class Structure*, ed. Richard Scarse (New York: Pergamon Press, 1976); Steven J. Kelman, *Regulating America, Regulating Sweden: A Comparative Study of Occupational Safety and Health Policy* (Cambridge, Mass.: MIT Press, 1981), 118–123.
22. Lewis Austin, *Saints and Samurai: The Political Culture of American and Japanese Elites* (New Haven, Conn.: Yale University Press, 1975).
23. Gabriel Almond and Sidney Verba, *The Civic Culture* (Princeton, N.J.: Princeton University Press, 1963), 169, 185. See also Gabriel Almond and Sidney Verba, eds., *The Civic Culture Revisited* (Boston: Little, Brown, 1980).
24. Sidney Verba, et al., *Voice and Equality: Civic Voluntarism in American Politics* (Cambridge: Harvard University Press, 1995), 69, 70.
25. Kenneth Newton and Pipa Norris, "Confidence in Public Institutions: Faith, Culture or Performance?" Paper presented at the Annual Meeting of the American Political Science Association, Atlanta, Ga., September 1999, tables 8.1 and 8.3.
26. Paul M. Sniderman, *A Question of Loyalty* (Berkeley: University of California Press, 1981).
27. Verba and Orren, *Equality in America*, 255.
28. Pippa Norris and Ronald Ingelhart, *Sacred and Secular: Religion and Politics Worldwide* (Cambridge: Cambridge University Press, 2004); George Gallup, Jr., and Thomas Jones, *The Next American Spirituality* (Colorado Springs, Colo.: Cook, 2000).
29. Arthur C. Brooks, *Who Really Cares? America's Charity Divide* (New York: Basic Books, 2006), ch. 2; Ram A. Cnaan, *The Other Philadelphia Story: How Local Congregations Support Quality of Life in Urban America* (Philadelphia: University of Pennsylvania Press, 2006).
30. Max Weber, *The Protestant Ethic and the Spirit of Capitalism*, trans. Talcott Parsons (New York: Scribner's, 1930). First published in 1904.
31. Erik H. Erikson, *Childhood and Society* (New York: Norton, 1950), ch. 8.
32. James Davison Hunter, *Culture Wars: The Struggle to Define America* (New York: Basic Books, 1991), and Hunter, *Before the Shooting Begins* (New York: Macmillan, 1994).
33. Morris P. Fiorina, *Culture War? The Myth of a Polarized America*, rev. ed. (New York: Pearson Longman, 2006); and Fiorina and Matthew S. Levendusky, "Disconnected: The Political Class Versus the People," in Pietro S. Nivola and David W. Brady, eds., *Red and Blue Nation?* (Washington, D.C.: Brookings Institution, 2006), 49–71.
34. Alan I. Abramovitz, "Comment," in Nivola and Brady, op. cit., 72–85, 111–114; Gary C. Jacobson, "Comment," in Nivola and Brady, op. cit., 85–95.
35. Philip D. Zelikow and David C. King, eds., *Why People Don't Trust Government* (Cambridge, Mass.: Harvard University Press, 1997).
36. Marc J. Hetherington, *Why Trust Matters* (Princeton, N.J.: Princeton University Press, 2005).
37. Robert D. Putnam, *Bowling Alone: The Collapse and Revival of American Community* (New York: Simon & Schuster, 2000); and Putnam, et al., *Better Together: Report of the Saguaro Seminar* (Cambridge, Mass.: Kennedy School of Government, Harvard University), 2001.
38. James Q. Wilson, "Bowling with Others," *Commentary* (October 2007), 30–33.
39. James W. Prothro and Charles M. Grigg, "Fundamental Principles of Democracy: Bases of Agreement and Disagreement," *Journal of Politics* 22 (Spring 1960): 275–294.
40. General Social Survey of the National Opinion Research Center, University of Chicago.
41. Gallup Poll data compiled by Professor John Zaller, Department of Political Science, UCLA.
42. *The American Enterprise* (January/February 1999): 37, reporting data from various polls.
43. John L. Sullivan, James Piereson, and George F. Marcus, *Political Tolerance and American Democracy* (Chicago: University of Chicago Press, 1982), 194–202.

Chapter 5

Civil Liberties

1. P. Ford, ed., *Works of Thomas Jefferson*, 1905, vol. 9, p. 449.
2. *Zamora v. Pomeroy*, 639 F.2d 662 (1981); *Goss v. Lopez*, 419 U.S. 565 (1975); *Tinker v. Des Moines Community School District*, 393 U.S. 503 (1969); *Smith v. Goguen*, 415 U.S. 566 (1974); *New Jersey v. T.L.O.*, 469 U.S. 325 (1985); *Morse v. Frederick*, No. 06-278 (2007).
3. *Snyder v. Phelps*, 131 S. Ct. 1207 (2011); *New York Times Co. v. United States*, 403 U.S. 713 (1971); *Kunz v. New York*, 340 U.S. 290 (1951).
4. *Barron v. Baltimore*, 7 Pet. 243 (1833).
5. *Chicago, Burlington, and Quincy Railroad Co. v. Chicago*, 166 U.S. 226 (1987); *Gitlow v. New York*, 268 U.S. 652 (1925); *Palko v. Connecticut*, 302 U.S. 319 (1937).
6. *District of Columbia v. Heller*, 554 U.S. 570 (2008); McDonald v. Chicago, 130 S. Ct. 3020 (2010).
7. William Blackstone, *Commentaries*, vol. 4 (1765), 151–152.
8. Jefferson's remarks are from a letter to Abigail Adams (quoted in Walter Berns, *The First Amendment and the Future of American Democracy*, New York: Basic Books, 1976, 82), and from a letter to Thomas McKean, governor of Pennsylvania, February 19, 1803 (Paul L. Ford, ed., *The Writings of Thomas Jefferson: 1801–1806*, vol. 8, New York: Putnam, 1897, 218).
9. *Schenck v. United States*, 249 U.S. 47 (1919), 52.
10. *Gitlow v. New York*, 268 U.S. 652 (1925), 666.
11. *Fiske v. Kansas*, 274 U.S. 380 (1927); *Stromberg v. California*, 283 U.S. 359 (1931); *Near v. Minnesota*, 283 U.S. 697 (1931); *De Jonge v. Oregon*, 299 U.S. 353 (1937).
12. *Dennis v. United States*, 341 U.S. 494 (1951), 510ff. The test was first formulated by Judge Learned Hand of the court of appeals: see *Dennis v. United States*, 183 F.2d 201 (1950), 212.
13. *Yates v. United States*, 354 U.S. 298 (1957).
14. *Brandenburg v. Ohio*, 395 U.S. 444 (1969).

15. *Village of Skokie v. National Socialist Party*, 432 U.S. 43 (1977); 366 N.E.2d 349 (1977); and 373 N.E.2d 21 (1978).
16. *R.A.V. v. City of St. Paul*, 112 S. Ct. 2538 (1992).
17. *Wisconsin v. Mitchell*, No. 92–515 (1993).
18. C. Herman Pritchett, *Constitutional Civil Liberties* (Englewood Cliffs, N.J.: Prentice-Hall, 1984), 100.
19. *New York Times v. Sullivan*, 376 U.S. 254 (1964); but compare *Time, Inc. v. Firestone*, 424 U.S. 448 (1976).
20. Henry J. Abraham, *Freedom and the Court*, 4th ed. (New York: Oxford University Press, 1982), 193, fn 189.
21. Justice Stewart's famous remark was made in his concurring opinion in *Jacobellis v. Ohio*, 378 U.S. 184 (1964), 197.
22. *Miller v. California*, 413 U.S. 15 (1973).
23. *Jenkins v. Georgia*, 418 U.S. 153 (1974).
24. *Schad v. Borough of Mt. Ephraim*, 452 U.S. 61 (1981).
25. *Barnes v. Glen Theatre*, 111 S. Ct. 2456 (1991).
26. *American Booksellers Association v. Hudnut*, 771 F.2d 323 (1985), affirmed at 475 U.S. 1001 (1986).
27. *Renton v. Playtime Theatres*, 475 U.S. 41 (1986). See also *Young v. American Mini-Theatres, Inc.*, 427 U.S. 50 (1976).
28. *Reno v. American Civil Liberties Union*, 521 U.S. 844 (1997); *Ashcroft v. Free Speech Coalition*, 122 S. Ct. 1389 (2002).
29. *United States v. O'Brien*, 391 U.S. 367 (1968).
30. *Texas v. Johnson*, 109 S. Ct. 2533 (1989).
31. *United States v. Eichman*, 496 U.S. 310 (1990).
32. *First National Bank of Boston v. Bellotti*, 435 U.S. 765 (1978); *Federal Election Commission v. Massachusetts Citizens for Life, Inc.*, 479 U.S. 238 (1986).
33. *44 Liquormart v. Rhode Island*, 517 U.S. 484 (1996); *Greater New Orleans Broadcasting Association v. United States*, 527 U.S. 173 (1999).
34. *Pacific Gas and Electric Co. v. Public Utilities Commission*, 475 U.S. 1 (1986). Some limitations on corporate speech have been upheld, including a state law prohibiting a firm from spending money on candidates for elective office. *Austin v. Michigan Chamber of Commerce*, 100 S. Ct. 1391 (1990).
35. *Board of Trustees of the State University of New York v. Fox*, 492 U.S. 469 (1989).
36. *Bates v. State Bar of Arizona*, 433 U.S. 350 (1977); *Edenfield v. Bane*, 113 S. Ct. 1792 (1993).
37. *McConnell v. Federal Election Commission*, 124 S. Ct. 619 (2003); *Federal Election Commission v. Wisconsin Right to Life*, No. 06-969 (2007).
38. *Hazelwood School District v. Kuhlmeier et al.*, 484 U.S. 260 (1988).
39. *Murdock v. Pennsylvania*, 319 U.S. 105 (1943).
40. *Church of the Lukumi Babalu Aye v. City of Hialeah*, 508 U.S. 520 (1993).
41. *Reynolds v. United States*, 98 U.S. 145 (1878).
42. *Jacobson v. Massachusetts*, 197 U.S. 11 (1905).
43. *Employment Division, Department of Human Resources of Oregon v. Smith*, 110 S. Ct. 1595 (1990).
44. *Society for Krishna Consciousness v. Lee*, 112 S. Ct. 2701 (1992).
45. *Welsh v. United States*, 398 U.S. 333 (1970); Pritchett, *Constitutional Civil Liberties*, 140–141.
46. *Sherbert v. Verner*, 374 U.S. 398 (1963); *Wisconsin v. Yoder*, 406 U.S. 205 (1972); *Hobbie v. Unemployment Appeals Commission of Florida*, 480 U.S. 136 (1987); *Estate of Thornton v. Caldor, Inc.*, 472 U.S. 703 (1985).
47. Berns, *The First Amendment.*
48. Pritchett, *Constitutional Civil Liberties*, 145–147.
49. *Everson v. Board of Education*, 330 U.S. 1 (1947).
50. *Engel v. Vitale*, 370 U.S. 421 (1962).
51. *Lubbock Independent School District v. Lubbock Civil Liberties Union*, 669 F.2d 1038.
52. *School District of Abington Township v. Schempp*, 374 U.S. 203 (1963).
53. *Lee v. Weisman*, 112 S. Ct. 2649 (1992); *Santa Fe Independent School District v. Jane Doe*, 530 U.S. 290 (2000).
54. *Epperson v. Arkansas*, 393 U.S. 97 (1968); *McLean v. Arkansas Board of Education*, 529 F. Supp. 1255 (1982).
55. *McCollum v. Board of Education*, 333 U.S. 203 (1948); *Zorach v. Clauson*, 343 U.S. 306 (1952).
56. *Tilton v. Richardson*, 403 U.S. 672 (1971).
57. *Board of Education v. Allen*, 392 U.S. 236 (1968).
58. *Walz v. Tax Commission*, 397 U.S. 664 (1970).
59. *Mueller v. Allen*, 463 U.S. 388 (1983).
60. *Zobrest v. Catalina Foothills School District*, 509 U.S. 1 (1993); *Mitchell v. Helms*, 2000 Lexis 4485.
61. *Lemon v. Kurtzman*, 403 U.S. 602 (1971).
62. *Committee for Public Education v. Nyquist*, 413 U.S. 756 (1973).
63. *Meek v. Pittenger*, 421 U.S. 349 (1975); *Wolman v. Walter*, 433 U.S. 229 (1977).
64. *Edwards v. Aguillard*, 482 U.S. 578 (1987); *Board of Education of Kiryas Joel Village School v. Louis Grumet*, 114 S. Ct. 2481 (1994).
65. *Agostini v. Felton*, 521 U.S. 203 (1997), overruled *Aguilar v. Felton*, 473 U.S. 402 (1985).
66. *Zelman v. Simmons-Harris*, 536 U.S. 639 (2002).
67. *Lemon v. Kurtzman*, 403 U.S. 602 (1971).
68. *Lynch v. Donelly*, 465 U.S. 668 (1984); *Allegheny v. ACLU*, 109 S. Ct. 3086 (1989); *McCreary County, Kentucky, v. ACLU*, 125 S. Ct. 2722 (2005); *Van Orden v. Perry*, 125 S. Ct. 2854 (2005).
69. *Marsh v. Chambers*, 492 U.S. 573 (1983).
70. Yale Kamisar, "Does (Did) (Should) the Exclusionary Rule Rest on a 'Principled Basis' Rather Than an 'Empirical Proposition'?" *Creighton Law Review* 16 (1982–1983): 565–667.
71. *Wolf v. Colorado*, 338 U.S. 25 (1949).
72. *Mapp v. Ohio*, 367 U.S. 643 (1961).
73. *Chimel v. California*, 395 U.S. 752 (1969).
74. *Washington v. Chrisman*, 455 U.S. 1 (1982).
75. *Oliver v. United States*, 466 U.S. 170 (1984).
76. *Arkansas v. Sanders*, 442 U.S. 753 (1979); *Robbins v. California*, 453 U.S. 420 (1981).
77. *United States v. Ross*, 456 U.S. 798 (1982); *Maryland v. Dyson*, 199 S. Ct. 2013 (1999); *Wyoming v. Houghton*, 119 S. Ct. 1297 (1999); *Whren v. United States*, 517 U.S. 806 (1996).
78. *Winston v. Lee*, 470 U.S. 753 (1985).
79. *South Dakota v. Neville*, 459 U.S. 553 (1983); *Schmerber v. California*, 384 U.S. 757 (1966).
80. *United States v. Dunn*, 480 U.S. 294 (1987); *California v. Ciraolo*, 476 U.S. 207 (1986); *California v. Carney*, 471 U.S. 386 (1985).
81. *O'Connor v. Ortega*, 480 U.S. 709 (1987).
82. *Escobedo v. Illinois*, 378 U.S. 478 (1964); *Miranda v. Arizona*, 384 U.S. 436 (1966).

83. *Malloy v. Hogan*, 378 U.S. 1 (1964).
84. *Miranda v. Arizona*, 384 U.S. 436 (1966).
85. *Gilbert v. California*, 388 U.S. 263 (1967); *Kirby v. Illinois*, 406 U.S. 682 (1972).
86. *Estelle v. Smith*, 451 U.S. 454 (1981).
87. *Brewer v. Williams*, 430 U.S. 387 (1977).
88. *Illinois v. Perkins*, 496 U.S. 292 (1990).
89. *Missouri v. Seibert*, 542 U.S. 600 (2004).
90. *Dickerson v. United States*, 530 U.S. 428 (2000).
91. *Fare v. Michael C.*, 442 U.S. 707 (1979).
92. *United States v. Leon*, 468 U.S. 897 (1984); *Massachusetts v. Sheppard*, 468 U.S. 981 (1984); *Herring v. United States*, No. 07–513 (2008).
93. *New York v. Quarles*, 467 U.S. 649 (1984); *Arizona v. Fulminante*, 499 U.S. 279 (1991); Kentucky v. King, No. 09-1272 (2011).
94. *Nix v. Williams*, 467 U.S. 431 (1984).
95. *Ex parte Quirin*, 317 U.S. 1 (1942).
96. *Rasul v. Bush*, 542 U.S. 466 (2004).
97. *Hamdi v. Rumsfeld*, 542 U.S. 507 (2004).
98. Military Commissions Act, Public Law 109–366 (2006).
99. Public Law 109-13 (2005).
100. *In re Sealed Case*, Foreign Intelligence Review Court, No. 02-001 (2001).

Chapter 6

Civil Rights

1. *United States v. Carolene Products Co.*, 304 U.S. 144 (1938); *San Antonio Independent School District v. Rodriguez*, 411 U.S. 1 (1973).
2. Gunnar Myrdal, *An American Dilemma* (New York: Harper, 1944), ch. 27.
3. Richard Kluger, *Simple Justice* (New York: Random House/ Vintage Books, 1977), 89–90.
4. Paul B. Sheatsley, "White Attitudes Toward the Negro," in *The Negro American*, ed. Talcott Parsons and Kenneth B. Clark (Boston: Houghton Mifflin, 1966), 305, 308, 317.
5. *Strauder v. West Virginia*, 100 U.S. 303 (1880).
6. *Civil Rights Cases*, 109 U.S. 3 (1883).
7. *Plessy v. Ferguson*, 163 U.S. 537 (1896).
8. *Cumming v. Richmond County Board of Education*, 175 U.S. 528 (1899).
9. *Missouri ex rel. Gaines v. Canada*, 305 U.S. 337 (1938).
10. *Sipuel v. Board of Regents of the University of Oklahoma*, 332 U.S. 631 (1948).
11. *Sweatt v. Painter*, 339 U.S. 629 (1950); *McLaurin v. Oklahoma State Regents for Higher Education*, 339 U.S. 637 (1950).
12. *Brown v. Board of Education of Topeka*, 347 U.S. 483 (1954).
13. *Brown v. Board of Education of Topeka*, 349 U.S. 294 (1955). This case is often referred to as "Brown II."
14. Frederick S. Mosteller and Daniel P. Moynihan, eds., *On Equality of Educational Opportunity* (New York: Random House, 1972), 60–62.
15. *Brown v. Board of Education of Topeka*, 347 U.S. 483 (1954).
16. C. Herman Pritchett, *Constitutional Civil Liberties* (Englewood Cliffs, N.J.: Prentice-Hall, 1984), 250–251, 261.
17. *Green et al. v. County School Board of New Kent County*, 391 U.S. 430 (1968).
18. *Swann v. Charlotte-Mecklenburg Board of Education*, 402 U.S. 1 (1971).
19. Busing *within* the central city was upheld in *Armour v. Nix*, 446 U.S. 930 (1980); *Keyes v. School District No. 1*, Denver, 413 U.S. 189 (1973); *Milliken v. Bradley*, 418 U.S. 717 (1974); *Board of School Commissioners of Indianapolis v. Buckley*, 429 U.S. 1068 (1977); and *School Board of Richmond v. State Board of Education*, 412 U.S. 92 (1972). Busing *across* city lines was upheld in *Evans v. Buchanan*, 423 U.S. 963 (1975), and *Board of Education v. Newburg Area Council*, 421 U.S. 931 (1975).
20. *Pasadena City Board of Education v. Spangler*, 427 U.S. 424 (1976).
21. See, for example, Herbert McClosky and John Zaller, *The American Ethos* (Cambridge: Harvard University Press, 1984), 92, 100; and data reported in Chapter 5 of this text.
22. NES, *1952–1990 Cumulative Data File, 1992 NES Pre/Post Election Study* (1992).
23. *Freeman v. Pitts*, 112 S. Ct. 1430 (1992); *Parents v. Seattle School District*, No. 05-908 (2007).
24. Robert S. Erikson and Norman R. Luttbeg, *American Public Opinion* (New York: Wiley, 1973), 49; Hazel Erskine, "The Polls: Demonstrations and Race Riots," *Public Opinion Quarterly* 31 (Winter 1967–1968): 654–677.
25. Howard Schuman, Charlotte Steeh, and Lawrence Bobo, *Racial Attitudes in America* (Cambridge: Harvard University Press, 1985), 69, 78–79.
26. Ibid., 102, 110, 127–135.
27. *Grove City College v. Bell*, 465 U.S. 555 (1984).
28. *United States v. Armstrong*, 116 S. Ct. 1480 (1996).
29. *Promoting Cooperative Strategies to Reduce Racial Profiling: A Technical Guide*, ch. 9 (Santa Monica, Calif.: RAND, April 2004).
30. *Mueller v. Oregon*, 208 U.S. 412 (1908).
31. Equal Pay Act of 1963; Civil Rights Act of 1964, Title VII, and 1978 amendments thereto; Education Amendments of 1972, Title IX.
32. *Reed v. Reed*, 404 U.S. 71 (1971).
33. *Frontiero v. Richardson*, 411 U.S. 677 (1973).
34. *Stanton v. Stanton*, 421 U.S. 7 (1975).
35. *Craig v. Boren*, 429 U.S. 190 (1976).
36. *Dothard v. Rawlinson*, 433 U.S. 321 (1977).
37. *Cleveland Board of Education v. LaFleur*, 414 U.S. 632 (1974).
38. *Fortin v. Darlington Little League*, 514 F.2d 344 (1975).
39. *Roberts v. United States Jaycees*, 468 U.S. 609 (1984); *Board of Directors Rotary International v. Rotary Club of Duarte*, 481 U.S. 537 (1987).
40. *Arizona Governing Committee for Tax Deferred Annuity and Deferred Compensation Plans v. Norris*, 463 U.S. 1073 (1983).
41. *EEOC v. Madison Community Unit School District No. 12*, 818 F.2d 577 (1987).
42. *Michael M. v. Superior Court*, 450 U.S. 464 (1981).
43. *Vorchheimer v. School District of Philadelphia*, 430 U.S. 703 (1977).
44. *Kahn v. Shevin*, 416 U.S. 351 (1974).
45. *Schlesinger v. Ballard*, 419 U.S. 498 (1975).
46. *Bennett v. Dyer's Chop House*, 350 F. Supp. 153 (1972); *Morris v. Michigan State Board of Education*, 472 F.2d 1207 (1973); *Fitzgerald v. Porter Memorial Hospital*, 523 F.2d 716 (1975); *Kruzel v. Podell*, 226 N.W.2d 458 (1975).
47. *United States v. Virginia*, 116 S. Ct. 2264 (1996).
48. *Rostker v. Goldberg*, 453 U.S. 57 (1981).

49. *Gebser v. Lago Vista School District*, 118 S. Ct. 1989 (1998); *Faragher v. Boca Raton*, 118 S. Ct. 2275 (1998); *Burlington Industries v. Ellerth*, 118 S. Ct. 2257 (1998).
50. *Griswold v. Connecticut*, 381 U.S. 479 (1965).
51. *Roe v. Wade*, 410 U.S. 113 (1973).
52. Though the constitutionality of the Hyde Amendment was upheld in *Harris v. McRae*, 448 U.S. 297 (1980), other limitations on access to abortions were struck down in *Planned Parenthood Federation of Central Missouri v. Danforth*, 428 U.S. 52 (1976); *Akron v. Akron Center for Reproductive Health*, 462 U.S. 416 (1983); and *Thornburgh v. American College of Obstetricians and Gynecologists*, 476 U.S. 747 (1986).
53. *Planned Parenthood v. Casey*, 112 S. Ct. 2791 (1992).
54. *Gonzales v. Carhart*, No. 05-380 (2007).
55. For an argument in support of a color-blind Constitution, see Andrew Kull, *The Color-Blind Constitution* (Cambridge: Harvard University Press, 1992).
56. *Regents of the University of California v. Bakke*, 438 U.S. 265 (1978).
57. *Fullilove v. Klutznick*, 448 U.S. 448 (1980).
58. *City of Richmond v. J.A. Croson Co.*, 488 U.S. 469 (1989).
59. *Metro Broadcasting v. FCC*, 497 U.S. 547 (1990).
60. *Northeastern Florida Contractors v. Jacksonville*, 508 U.S. 656 (1993).
61. *Firefighters Local Union No. 1784 v. Stotts*, 467 U.S. 561 (1984); *Wygant v. Jackson Board of Education*, 476 U.S. 267 (1986); *City of Richmond v. J.A. Croson Co.*, 488 U.S. 469 (1989).
62. *Local No. 28 of the Sheet Metal Workers' International Association v. Equal Employment Opportunity Commission*, 478 U.S. 421 (1986); *Wards Cove Packing Co. v. Atonio*, 490 U.S. 642 (1989); *Price Waterhouse v. Hopkins*, 490 U.S. 228 (1989). (Note: *Wards Cove* and *Price* were both superseded in part by the Civil Rights Act of 1991.)
63. *Fullilove v. Klutznick*, 448 U.S. 448 (1980); *Metro Broadcasting v. FCC*, 497 U.S. 547 (1990).
64. *United Steelworkers of America v. Weber*, 443 U.S. 193 (1979); *Johnson v. Santa Clara County Transportation Agency*, 480 U.S. 616 (1987).
65. *Wygant v. Jackson Board of Education*, 476 U.S. 267 (1986); *United States v. Paradise*, 480 U.S. 149 (1987).
66. Seymour Martin Lipset and William Schneider, "An Emerging National Consensus," *The New Republic* (October 15, 1977): 8–9.
67. John R. Bunzel, "Affirmative Re-Actions," *Public Opinion* (February/March 1986): 45–49; *New York Times* (December 14, 1997).
68. *Adarand Constructors v. Pena*, 515 U.S. 200 (1995).
69. *Hopwood v. Texas*, 78 F.3d 932 (1996).
70. *Gratz v. Bollinger*, 539 U.S. 244 (2003).
71. *Grutter v. Bollinger*, 539 U.S. 306 (2003).
72. *Bowers v. Hardwick*, 478 U.S. 186 (1986).
73. *Romer v. Evans*, 517 U.S. 620 (1996).
74. *Lawrence v. Texas*, 539 U.S. 558 (2003).
75. *Goodridge v. Department of Public Health*, 440 Mass. 309 (2003) and 440 Mass. 1201 (2004).
76. *Boy Scouts of America v. Dale*, 530 U.S. 640 (2000).

Chapter 7

Public Opinion

1. *Federalist* No. 50.
2. *Federalist* No. 63.
3. George W. Bishop, Alfred J. Tuchfarber, and Robert W. Oldendick, "1984: How Much Can We Manipulate and Control People's Answers to Public Opinion Surveys?" Paper delivered at the 1984 annual meeting of the American Political Science Association; Howard Schuman and S. Presser, *Questions and Answers in Attitude Surveys* (New York: Academic Press, 1981), ch. 5.
4. For example, see Bernard Berelson, et al., *Voting: A Study of Opinion Formation in a Presidential Campaign* (Chicago: University of Chicago Press, 1954), and Phillip E. Converse, "The Nature of Belief Systems in Mass Publics," in *Ideology and Discontent*, ed. David E. Apter (New York: Free Press, 1964).
5. For example, see V. O. Key, *The Responsible Electorate* (Cambridge: Harvard University Press, 1966); Samuel Popkin, *The Reasoning Voter: Communication and Persuasion in Presidential Campaigns* (Chicago: University of Chicago Press, 1991); Benjamin I. Page and Robert Y. Shapiro, *The Rational Public: Fifty Years of Trends in Americans' Policy Preferences* (Chicago: University of Chicago Press, 1991).
6. Terry M. Moe, *Schools, Vouchers, and the American Public* (Washington, D.C.: Brookings Institution, 2001), 253.
7. James Q. Wilson, "The Press at War," *City Journal* (Autumn 2006): 54–63.
8. M. Kent Jennings and Richard G. Niemi, "The Transmission of Political Values from Parent to Child," *American Political Science Review* 62 (March 1968): 173; Robert D. Hess and Judith V. Tomey, *The Development of Political Attitudes in Children* (Chicago: Aldine, 1967), 90.
9. John R. Alford, Carolyn L. Funk, and John R. Hibbing, "Are Political Orientations Genetically Transmitted?" *American Political Science Review*, 99 (May 2005): 153–167; James Q. Wilson, "The DNA of Politics," *City Journal* (Winter 2009): 83–87; Thomas J. Bouchard, et al., "Evidence for the Construct Validity and Heritability of the Wilson-Patterson Conservatism Scale," *Personality and Individual Differences*, 24 (2003): 959–969.
10. Several studies of child-parent agreement on party preference are summarized in David O. Sears, "Political Behavior," in *The Handbook of Social Psychology*, 2d ed., ed. Gardner Lindzey and Elliot Aronson (Reading, Mass.: Addison-Wesley, 1969), vol. 5, 376.
11. Norman H. Nie, Sidney Verba, and John R. Petrocik, *The Changing American Voter* (Cambridge: Harvard University Press, 1976), ch. 4.
12. Richard Niemi and M. Kent Jennings, "Issues and Inheritance in the Formation of Party Identification," *American Journal of Political Science* (November 1991): 970–988.
13. Pew Forum on Religion and Public Life, "Support for Same-Sex Marriage Edges Upward," October 6, 2010.
14. Elizabeth Humel, et. al., "Younger Voters," *Public Perspective* (May/June 2003): 11.
15. Pew Forum on Religion and Public Life, *Survey: More Americans Question Religion's Role in Politics*, August 21, 2008.
16. Pew Forum on Religion and Public Life, *Survey: Religious Groups*

Agree—Fixing the Nation's Economy Is Job One, March 4, 2009.
17. V. O. Key, Jr., *Public Opinion and American Democracy* (New York: Knopf, 1961), 122–138.
18. Richard E. Dawson, *Public Opinion and Contemporary Disarray* (New York: Harper & Row, 1973), ch. 4.
19. David Bositis, *Public Opinion 1998: Political Attitudes* (Washington, D.C.: Joint Center for Political and Economic Studies, 1998), table 18A.
20. "The Black and White of Public Opinion," Pew Research Center for the People & the Press (October 31, 2005).
21. Ibid.
22. Lisa J. Montoya, et al., "Latina Politics: Gender, Participation, and Leadership," *PS: Political Science and Politics* 33 (September 2000): 557.
23. Bruce Cain and Roderick Kiewit, "California's Coming Minority Majority," *Public Opinion* (February/March 1986): 50–52.
24. Ibid.
25. Pew Hispanic Center, *Survey of Latino Attitudes on the War in Iraq,* Pew Research Center, February 7, 2005.
26. Richard Frey, et al., *Hispanics and the Social Security Debate,* Pew Research Center, March 16, 2005.
27. Ibid.
28. Nie, Verba, and Petrocik, *The Changing American Voter,* 247–250.
29. Lydia Saad, "Conservatives Maintain Edge as Top Ideological Group," Gallup Organization, October 26, 2009.
30. Adam J. Berinsky, *Silent Voices: Public Opinion and Political Participation in America* (Princeton, N.J.: Princeton University Press, 2004); Berinsky, "Two Faces of Public Opinion," *American Journal of Political Science* (October 1999): 1209–1230.
31. Ibid.
32. John Zaller, *The Nature and Origins of Mass Opinion* (Cambridge: Cambridge University Press, 1992).
33. Ibid.
34. Lawrence R. Jacobs and Robert Y. Shapiro, "Debunking the Myth of the Pandering Politician," *Public Perspective* (April/May 1997): 3–5.

Chapter 8
Political Participation

1. Michael McDonald and Samuel L. Popkin, "The Myth of the Vanishing Voter," *American Political Science Review* 95 (December 2001).
2. U.S. Bureau of the Census, *Current Population Survey,* "Reasons for Not Voting," June 2008, table 6.
3. John P. DiIulio, "The Liberalization of Absentee and Mail-In Voting, 1996–2008," unpublished paper, November 2008.
4. Raymond E. Wolfinger and Jonathan Hoffman, "Registering and Voting with Motor Voter," *PS: Political Science and Politics* 34 (March 2001): 90.
5. Donald P. Green and Alan S. Gerber, *Get Out the Vote: How to Increase Voter Turnout* (Washington, D.C.: The Brookings Institution Press, 2008).
6. Alan S. Gerber, et al., "Social Pressure and Voter Turnout: Evidence from a Large-Scale Field Experiment," *American Political Science Review* 102 (February 2008).
7. Morton Keller, *Affairs of State* (Cambridge, Mass.: Harvard University Press, 1977), 523.
8. *United States v. Reese,* 92 U.S. 214 (1876); *United States v. Cruikshank,* 92 U.S. 556 (1876); and *Ex Parte Yarbrough,* 110 U.S. 651 (1884).
9. *Guinn and Beall v. United States,* 238 U.S. 347 (1915).
10. *Smith v. Allright,* 321 U.S. 649 (1944).
11. *Schnell v. Davis,* 336 U.S. 993 (1949).
12. *Historical Statistics of the United States: Colonial Times to 1970,* part 2, 1071–1072.
13. Walter Dean Burnham, "The Changing Shape of the American Political Universe," *American Political Science Review* 59 (March 1965): 11; and William H. Flanigan and Nancy H. Zingale, *Political Behavior of the American Electorate,* 3d ed. (Boston, Mass.: Allyn and Bacon, 1975), 15.
14. Burnham, "The Changing Shape;" and E. E. Schattschneider, *The Semi-Sovereign People* (New York: Holt, Rinehart & Winston, 1960), chs. 5, 6.
15. Philip E. Converse, "Change in the American Electorate," in *The Human Meaning of Social Change,* ed. Angus Campbell and Philip E. Converse (New York: Russell Sage Foundation, 1972), 263–338.
16. Raymond Wolfinger and Benjamen Highton, "What If They Gave an Election and Everyone Came?," Public Affairs Report, University of California at Berkeley, June 1999, 11–13.
17. Sidney Verba and Norman H. Nie, *Participation in America* (New York: Harper and Row, 1972), 30.
18. Sidney Verba, et al., *Voice and Equality: Civic Voluntarism in American Politics* (Cambridge, Mass.: Harvard University Press, 1998), 79.
19. Ibid., 77.
20. Verba and Nie, *Participation in America,* ch. 6.
21. Catherine E. Wilson, *The Politics of Latino Faith: Religion, Identity and Urban Community* (New York: New York University Press, 2008).

Chapter 9
Political Parties

1. Leon D. Epstein, "Political Parties," in *Handbook of Political Science,* ed. Fred I. Greenstein and Nelson W. Polsby (Reading, Mass.: Addison-Wesley, 1975), vol. 4, 230.
2. Quoted in Henry Adams, *History of the United States of America During the Administrations of Jefferson and Madison,* ed. Ernest Samuels, abridged ed. (Chicago: University of Chicago Press, 1967), 147.
3. Walter Dean Burnham, *Critical Elections and the Mainsprings of American Politics* (New York: Norton, 1970), 10.
4. James L. Sundquist, *Dynamics of the Party System* (Washington, D.C.: Brookings Institution, 1973), ch. 7.
5. Edward G. Carmines and James A. Stimson, "Issue Evolution, Population Replacement, and Normal Partisan Change," *American Political Science Review* 75 (March 1981): 107–118; and Gregory Markus, "Political Attitudes in an Election Year," *American Political Science Review* 76 (September 1982): 538–560.
6. Ray Wolfinger and Michael G. Hagen, "Republican Prospects: Southern Comfort," *Public Opinion* (October/November 1985): 8–13. But compare Richard Scammon and James A. Barnes, "Republican Prospects: Southern Discomfort," *Public Opinion* (October/November 1985): 14–17.
7. Jerold G. Rusk, "The Effect of the Australian Ballot Reform on Split-Ticket Voting: 1876–1908," *American Political Science Review* 64 (December 1970): 1220–1238.
8. Morton Keller, *Affairs of State* (Cambridge: Harvard University Press, 1977), 239.
9. Quoted in Keller, ibid., 256.
10. Martin Shefter, "Parties, Bureaucracy, and Political Change in the United States," in *The*

Development of Political Parties, Sage Electoral Studies Yearbook, vol. 4, ed. Louis Maisel and Joseph Cooper (Beverly Hills, Calif.: Sage, 1978).

11. James Q. Wilson, *The Amateur Democrat: Club Politics in Three Cities* (Chicago: University of Chicago Press, 1962).
12. Samuel J. Eldersveld, *Political Parties: A Behavioral Analysis* (Chicago: Rand McNally, 1964), 278, 287.
13. Robert H. Salisbury, "The Urban Party Organization Member," *Public Opinion Quarterly* 29 (Winter 1965–1966): 550–564.
14. Ibid., 557, 559.
15. Eldersveld, *Political Parties;* and J. David Greenstone, *Labor in American Politics* (New York: Knopf, 1969), 187.
16. David R. Mayhew, *Placing Parties in American Politics* (Princeton, N.J.: Princeton University Press, 1986), chs. 2, 3.
17. *Boston Globe* (July 9, 1984): 1.
18. William Nisbet Chambers and Walter Dean Burnham, eds., *The American Party Systems: Stages of Political Development,* 2d ed. (New York: Oxford University Press, 1975), 6.
19. American National Election Studies, August 5, 2010, table 2B.4; reporting data for the period 1952–2008.
20. For example, see *The Public Perspective* (April/May 1998).
21. American National Election Survey, November 27, 2005, table 2B.3; reporting data for the period 1972–2000.
22. *Williams v. Rhodes*, 393 U.S. 23 (1968).
23. James Q. Wilson, *Political Organizations* (New York: Basic Books, 1973), ch. 12; and Samuel Stouffer, *Communism, Conformity, and Civil Liberties* (Garden City, N.Y.: Doubleday, 1955).
24. Updated from Jeane Kirkpatrick, *The New Presidential Elite* (New York: Russell Sage Foundation and Twentieth Century Fund, 1976), 297–315.
25. Nelson W. Polsby, *Consequences of Party Reform* (New York: Oxford University Press, 1983), 9–11, 64.
26. Ibid., 158. But compare John G. Geer, "Voting in Presidential Primaries," paper delivered to the 1984 annual meeting of the American Political Science Association.
27. Center for the Study of the American Electorate, April 2000.
28. Michael J. Malbin, "Democratic Party Rules Are Made to Be Broken," *National Journal* (August 23, 1980): 1388.

Chapter 10

Elections and Campaigns

1. The Center for Public Integrity, *Campaign Consultants,* Georgetown University, Washington, D.C., September 26, 2006, 1.
2. Ted Bader, *Campaigning for Hearts and Minds: How Emotional Appeals Work in Political Ads* (Chicago: University of Chicago Press, 2006).
3. Ibid., 140–143.
4. Steven Levy, "Every Voter a 'Microtarget,'" *Washington Post,* April 23, 2008, D1.
5. Joe Klein, *Politics Lost: How American Democracy Was Trivialized by People Who Think You're Stupid* (New York: Doubleday, 2006), 54.
6. Ibid., 14–16; and Bader, op. cit., 19–20.
7. Bader, op. cit., ch. 2, endnote 5, reporting data from AAPC, 220.
8. *Wesberry v. Sanders,* 376 U.S. 1 (1964).
9. Richard F. Fenno, Jr., "U.S. House Members and Their Constituencies: An Exploration," *American Political Science Review* 71 (September 1977): 883–917, esp. 914.
10. John A. Ferejohn, *Pork Barrel Politics* (Stanford, Calif.: Stanford University Press, 1974).
11. Douglas Arnold, *Congress and the Bureaucracy* (New Haven, Conn.: Yale University Press, 1979).
12. Arthur H. Miller, et al., "A Majority Party in Disarray: Policy Polarization in the 1972 Election," *American Political Science Review* 70 (1976): 757.
13. Donald E. Stokes and John J. DiIulio, Jr., "Valence Politics in Modern Elections," in *The 1992 Elections,* ed. Michael J. Nelson (Washington, D.C.: Congressional Quarterly Press, 1993), ch. 1.
14. Michael Kelley, "The Making of a First Family: A Blueprint," *New York Times* (November 14, 1992): 1, 9.
15. Ibid.
16. Thomas E. Patterson and Robert D. McClure, *The Unseeing Eye: The Myth of Television Power in National Politics* (New York: Putnam, 1976); and Xandra Kayden, *Campaign Organization* (Lexington, Mass.: D. C. Heath, 1978), ch. 6.
17. Gerald M. Pomper, et al., *The Election of 1980* (Chatham, N.J.: Chatham House, 1981), 75, 105–107.
18. Gary C. Jacobson, *The Politics of Congressional Elections,* 2d ed. (Boston: Little, Brown, 1987), 49.
19. Donald Philip Green and Jonathan S. Krasno, "Salvation for the Spendthrift Incumbent: Reestimating the Effects of Campaign Spending in House Elections," *American Journal of Political Science* 32 (1988): 884–960; Stephen Ansolabehre, "Winning Is Easy but It Sure Ain't Cheap," Working Paper 90–1, Center for American Politics and Public Policy, UCLA, 1990; Robert S. Erickson and Thomas R. Palfrey, "The Puzzle of Incumbent Spending in Congressional Elections," Social Science Working Paper 806, California Institute of Technology, August 1992.
20. Angus Campbell, Philip E. Converse, Warren E. Miller, and Donald E. Stokes, *The American Voter* (New York: Wiley, 1960), ch. 8.
21. V. O. Key, Jr., *The Responsible Electorate* (Cambridge: Harvard University Press, 1966).
22. Morris P. Fiorina, *Retrospective Voting in American National Elections* (New Haven, Conn.: Yale University Press, 1981).
23. Jay P. Greene, "Forewarned Before Forecast: Presidential Election Forecasting Models and the 1992 Election," *P.S.: Political Science and Politics* (March 1993): 20.
24. Paul Freedman and Ken Goldstein, "Measuring Media Exposure and the Effects of Negative Campaign Ads," *American Journal of Political Science* 43 (October 1999): 1189–1208.
25. Robert Axelrod, "Where the Votes Come From: An Analysis of Electoral Coalitions, 1952–1968," *American Political Science Review* 66 (1972): 11–20; and Axelrod, "Communication," *American Political Science Review* 68 (1974): 718–719.
26. Gerald M. Pomper, *Elections in America* (New York: Dodd, Mead, 1971), 178.

27. Benjamin Ginsberg, "Elections and Public Policy," *American Political Science Review* 70 (March 1976): 41–49.

Chapter 11

Interest Groups

1. Lee Jared Drutman, *The Business of America Is Lobbying: The Expansion of Corporate Activity and the Future of American Pluralism*, Ph.D. Dissertation, University of California, Berkeley, Fall 2010; Kay Lehrman Schlozman, et al., "Who Sings in the Heavenly Chorus? The Shape of Organized Interest Group Activity," paper presented at the annual meeting of the American Political Science Association, Boston, Mass., August 2008.
2. Ibid.
3. The use of injunctions in labor disputes was restricted by the Norris-LaGuardia Act of 1932; the rights to collective bargaining and to the union shop were guaranteed by the Wagner Act of 1935.
4. *Historical Abstract of the United States, Colonial Times to 1970*, vol. 1, 386.
5. Dana Priest and William M. Arkin, "A Hidden World, Growing Beyond Control" and "National Security Inc," *The Washington Post*, July 19–21, 2010.
6. Timothy P. Carney, "The TSA and the Full-Body Scanner Lobby," *The Washington Examiner*, December 29, 2009; Kimberly Kindy, "Ex-Homeland Security Chief Head Said to Abuse Public Trust by Touting Body Scanners," *The Washington Post*, January 1, 2010.
7. The distinction is drawn from Kay Lehman Schlozman and John T. Tierney, *Organized Interests and American Democracy* (New York: Harper and Row, 1985).
8. Gabriel A. Almond and Sidney Verba, *The Civic Culture* (Princeton, N.J.: Princeton University Press, 1963), 194.
9. Robert D. Putnam, *Bowling Alone: The Collapse and Revival of American Community* (New York: Simon and Shuster, 2001); and Robert D. Putnam and David Campbell, *American Grace: How Religion Unites and Divides Us* (New York: Simon and Shuster, 2010).
10. Mancur Olson, Jr., *The Logic of Collective Action* (Cambridge: Harvard University Press, 1965), 153–157.
11. Derek C. Bok and John T. Dunlop, *Labor and the American Community* (New York: Simon and Shuster, 1970), 134.
12. J. Scott Applewhite, "What Is the 'Tea Party' and How Is It Shaking Up American Politics?" *Christian Science Monitor*, September 15, 2010.
13. Walter A. Rosenbaum, *Environmental Politics and Policy*, 8th ed. (Washington, D.C.: Congressional Quarterly College Press, 2010).
14. Jane Mansbridge, *Why We Lost the ERA* (Chicago: University of Chicago Press, 1986), fj.
15. Ibid.
16. Drutman, *The Business of America*, 5.
17. Robert Kaiser, *So Damn Much Money* (New York: Knopf, 2009).
18. Kindy, "Ex-Homeland Security Chief."
19. Robert O'Harrow and Scott Higham, "Report Finds DHS Lax on Contracting Procedures," *The Washington Post*, November 22, 2006.
20. Susan Weaver, *Decision to Prosecute* (Cambridge, Mass.: MIT Press, 1977): 154–163.
21. *United States v. Harris*, 347 U.S. 612 (1954).
22. *United States Code*, Title 26, section 501(c)(3).

Chapter 12

The Media

1. See "The Watergate Story," *The Washington Post*, available at http://www.washingtonpost.com/wp-srv/politics/special/watergate/.
2. Coverage of the Iran-contra affair by selected news networks is available through the Vanderbilt University Television News Archive.
3. Mayhill Fowler, "Obama: No Surprise That Hard-Pressed Pennsylvanians Turn Bitter," *Huffington Post*, 11 April 2008.
4. Pew Research Center for the People & the Press, "Internet Gains on Television as Public's Main News Source," January 4, 2011.
5. David E. Butler, "Why America's Political Reporting Is Better than England's," *Harper's* (May 1963): 15–25.
6. Gerard Alexander, "Illiberal Europe," *Weekly Standard*, April 10, 2006.
7. Quoted in F. L. Mort, *American Journalism, 1690–1960*, 3rd ed. (New York: Macmillan, 1962), 529.
8. Center for Media and Public Affairs, "The Incredible Shrinking Sound Bite," press release, Washington, D.C., September 28, 2000.
9. Pew Internet & American Life Project, "The Internet and Campaign 2010," March 2011.
10. Updated from Times Mirror Center for the People and the Press, June 28, 1990.
11. Edward J. Epstein, *News from Nowhere: Television and the News* (New York: Random House, 1973), 37.
12. *Near v. Minnesota*, 283 U.S. 697 (1931).
13. *New York Times v. United States*, 403 U.S. 713 (1971).
14. *New York Times v. Sullivan*, 376 U.S. 254 (1964).
15. *Miami Herald Publishing Co. v. Tornillo*, 418 U.S. 241 (1974).
16. *Yates v. United States*, 354 U.S. 298 (1957).
17. *Branzburg v. Hayes*, 408 U.S. 665 (1972).
18. *Zurcher v. Stanford Daily*, 436 U.S. 547 (1978), overturned by the Privacy Protection Act of 1980 (P.L. 96–440).
19. S. Robert Lichter, Stanley Rothman, and Linda S. Lichter, *The Media Elite* (Bethesda, Md.: Adler and Adler, 1986); Stanley Rothman and Amy Black, "Elites Revisited: American Social and Political Leadership in the 1990s," *International Journal of Public Opinion Research* 11 (1999): 169–195; William Schneider and I. A. Lewis, "Views on the News," *Public Opinion* (August/September 1985): 7.
20. Rothman and Black, "Elites Revisited," 182.
21. Ibid., 177; Jeffrey A. Dvorkin, "Pew Study: Journalists and Liberal Bias," *National Public Radio*, June 2, 2004.
22. Gallup Poll, February 2003; Pew Research Center for the People and the Press poll, July 2003; Pew Research Center for the People & the Press, "Most Voters Say News Media Wants Obama to Win," October 22, 2008.
23. William G. Mayer, "Why Talk Radio Is Conservative," *The Public Interest* (Summer 2004): 86–103.
24. David W. Brady and Jonathan Ma, "Spot the Difference," *Wall Street Journal* (November 12, 2003).

25. Lichter, Rothman, and Lichter, *Media Elite.*
26. John R. Lott, Jr., and Kevin A. Hassett, "Is Newspaper Coverage of Economic Events Politically Biased?" unpublished paper, American Enterprise Institute (September 1, 2004). See also Tim Groseclose and Jeff Milyo, "A Measure of Media Bias," *Quarterly Journal of Economics*, 120 (November 2005): 1191–1237.
27. Matthew Gentzkow and Jesse M. Shapiro, "What Drives Media Slant?" NBER paper 1207 (Cambridge, Mass.: National Bureau of Economic Research, 2006).
28. David O. Sears and Richard E. Whitney, "Political Persuasion," in Pool, *Handbook of Communication*, 253–289.
29. Robert S. Erickson, "The Influence of Newspaper Endorsements in Presidential Elections: The Case of 1964," *American Journal of Political Science* 20 (May 1976): 207–233.
30. Kim Fridkin Kahn and Patrick J. Kenney, "The Slant of the News: How Editorial Endorsements Influence Campaign Coverage and Citizens' Views of Candidates," *American Political Science Review* 96 (2002): 381–394; James N. Druckman and Michael Parkin, "The Impact of Media Bias," *Journal of Politics 67* (2005): 1030–1049.
31. Stefano Della Vigna and Ethan Kaplan, "The Fox News Effect: Media Bias and Voting," Working paper 12160 (Cambridge, Mass.: National Bureau of Economic Research, 2006).
32. Alan Gerber, Dean Karlan, and Daniel Bergan, "Does the Media Matter? A Field Experiment," Unpub. paper, Department of Political Science, Yale University, January 2006. See also Gerber, et al., "How Large and How Long-lasting Are the Persuasive Effects of Televised Ads?" *American Political Science Review* 105 (2011): 135–150.
33. Maxwell E. McCombs and Donald R. Shaw, "The Agenda Setting Function of the Mass Media," *Public Opinion Quarterly* 36 (Summer 1972): 176–187; Shanto Iyengar and Donald R. Kinder, *News That Matters* (Chicago: University of Chicago Press, 1987).
34. G. Ray Funkhouser, "The Issues of the Sixties," *Public Opinion Quarterly* 37 (Spring 1973): 62–75.
35. Benjamin I. Page, Robert Y. Shapiro, and Glenn R. Dempsey, "What Moves Public Opinion?" *American Political Science Review* 81 (March 1987): 23–43; Benjamin I. Page, "The Media as Political Actors," *PS: Political Science and Politics* (March 1996): 21.
36. Pew Research Center for the People and the Press, "Media Seen as Fair, But Tilting to Gore," press release, Washington, D.C., October 15, 2000.
37. Center for Media and Public Affairs, "Public to Press: Keep in Touch!," press release, Washington, D.C., 1996.
38. Pew Center for the People and the Press, "Terror Coverage Boost News Media's Images," press release, November 28, 2001.
39. Will Lester, "Poll: Interest in News Stabilizes," *The Macon Telegraph* (June 9, 2002).

Chapter 13

Congress

1. Thomas E. Mann and Norman J. Ornstein, *The Broken Branch: How Congress Is Failing America and How to Get It Back on Track*, 2nd ed. (New York: Oxford University Press, 2008). Also see Richard F. Fenno, "If as Ralph Nader Says Congress Is the 'Broken Branch,' How Come We Love Our Congressmen So Much More than Our Congress?" in *Congress in Change: Evolution and Reform*, ed. Norman J. Ornstein (New York: Praeger Publishers, 1975).
2. Fenno, "If as Ralph Nader Says," 286.
3. Norman J. Ornstein and Thomas E. Mann, *Vital Statistics on Congress, 1995–1996* (Washington, D.C.: Congressional Quarterly Press, 1996), 199–200.
4. "A Polarized Congress," *National Journal* (January 21, 2006): 21, reporting data compiled by David Rhode and John Aldrich.
5. Ibid.
6. "Vicious or Virtuous? America's Political System May Have Become Too Polarized to Produce Compromise," *The Economist* (April 16, 2011): 38.
7. Alan I. Abramowitz, *The Disappearing Center: Engaged Citizens, Polarization, and American Democracy* (New Haven and London: Yale University Press, 2010).
8. Morris P. Fiorina, *Disconnect: The Breakdown of Representation in American Politics* (Oklahoma: Oklahoma University Press, 2009).
9. *Federalist* No. 10.
10. Ibid.
11. H. Douglas Price, "Careers and Committees in the American Congress," in *The History of Parliamentary Behavior*, ed. William O. Aydelotte (Princeton: Princeton University Press, 1977); John F. Bibby, et al., *Vital Statistics on Congress, 1980* (Washington, D.C.: American Enterprise Institute, 1980), 53–54.
12. David Mayhew, *Congress: The Electoral Connection* (New Haven: Yale University Press, 1974).
13. Harold W. Stanley and Richard G. Niemi, *Vital Statistics on American Politics, 1999–2000* (Washington, D.C.: Congressional Quarterly Press, 2000), table 1-18, and post-2000 data updated by Marc Siegel.
14. Mayhew, *Congress*; Morris P. Fiorina, *Congress: Keystone of the Washington Establishment* (New Haven: Yale University Press, 1977).
15. Rhodes Cook, "House Republicans Scored a Quiet Victory in '92," *Congressional Quarterly* (April 17, 1993): 966.
16. Bruce E. Cain and David Butler, "Redrawing District Lines: What's Going On and What's At Stake," *The American Enterprise* (July/August 1991): 37.
17. "Redistricting Rows: Not So Easy," *The Economist* (May 7, 2011): 27.
18. Abramowitz, *The Disappearing Center.*
19. Ibid.
20. Ibid.
21. Ibid.
22. Matthew Levendusky, *The Partisan Sort: How Liberals Became Democrats and Conservatives Became Republicans* (Chicago: University of Chicago Press, 2009); Fiorina, *Disconnect*; and Abramowitz, *The Disappearing Center.*
23. Fiorina, *Disconnect*; Morris P. Fiorina and Matthew Levendusky, "Disconnected: The Political Class and the People," in *Red and Blue Nation?* vol. I, eds. Pietro Nivola and David Brady (Washington, D.C., and Stanford: Brookings Institution and Hoover Institution, 2006).
24. Fiorina, *Disconnect,* ibid.
25. Ibid.
26. Keith T. Poole and Howard Rosenthal, *A Political Economic History of Roll Call Voting* (New York: Oxford University Press, 1997), 8.
27. Nolan McCarty, et al., "The Hunt for Party Discipline in Congress,"

American Political Science Review 95, no. 3 (September 2001): 66.

28. Richard F. Fenno, *Congressmen in Committees* (Boston: Little, Brown, 1973).
29. Bibby, et al., *Vital Statistics*, 65–74.
30. Fiorina, *Congress*.
31. Bibby, et al., *Vital Statistics*, 60.
32. Michael J. Malbin, "Delegation, Deliberation, and the New Role of Congressional Staff," in *The New Congress*, eds. Thomas E. Mann and Norman J. Ornstein (Washington, D.C.: American Enterprise Institute, 1981), 134–177, esp. 170–171.
33. Malcolm E. Jewell and Samuel C. Patterson, *The Legislative Process in the United States*, 3rd ed. (New York: Random House, 1977), 349.
34. Mann and Ornstein, *Broken Branch*; Joshua D. Clinton and John S. Lapinski, "Measuring Legislative Accomplishment," *American Journal of Political Science* 56 (2006): 232–249; J. Tobin Grant and Nathan J. Kelly, "Legislative Productivity of the U.S. Congress," *Political Analysis* 16 (2008): 303–323.
35. Mann and Ornstein, *Broken Branch*.
36. David Mayhew, *Divided We Govern: Party Control, Lawmaking, and Investigations* (New Haven: Yale University Press, 1991); Grant and Kelly, "Legislative Productivity."
37. Tom Coburn, "The Spending Process Is Broken," *Extensions: Journal of the Carl Albert Research and Studies Center* (Spring 2007): 16, reporting data from the Congressional Research Service and the Congressional Budget Office.
38. Continuity of Government Commission, *Preserving Our Institutions: The Continuity of Congress—First Report*, Washington, D.C. (June 3, 2003): 3, 4.
39. *The 9/11 Commission Report: Final Report of the National Commission on Terrorist Attacks Upon the United States* (New York and London: W.W. Norton & Company, 2004).
40. Diana Evans, "Appropriations in the Republican Era," *Extensions: Journal of the Carl Albert Congressional Research and Studies Center* (Spring 2007): 13.

Chapter 14
The Presidency

1. Jean Blondel, *An Introduction to Comparative Government* (New York: Praeger, 1969), as cited in Nelson W. Polsby, "Legislatures," in *Handbook of Political Science*, ed. Fred I. Greenstein and Nelson W. Polsby (Reading, Mass.: Addison-Wesley, 1975), vol. 5, 275.
2. Donald F. Kettl, *Deficit Politics: Public Budgeting in Its Institutional and Historical Context* (New York: Macmillan, 1992), 13.
3. Morris P. Fiorina, *Divided Government* (New York: Macmillan, 1992), 86–111.
4. David Mayhew, *Divided We Govern: Party Control, Lawmaking, and Investigations, 1946–1990* (New Haven, Conn.: Yale University Press, 1991), 76.
5. Woodrow Wilson, *Congressional Government* (New York: Meridian Books, 1956), 167–168, 170. First published in 1885.
6. Mark A. Peterson, *Legislating Together: The White House and Congress from Eisenhower to Reagan* (Cambridge: Harvard University Press, 1990).
7. Richard E. Cohen, *Washington at Work: Back Rooms and Clean Air* (New York: Macmillan, 1992), 154–155.
8. Ibid., 169.
9. Kettl, *Deficit Politics*, 138.
10. Richard E. Neustadt, *Presidential Power and the Modern Presidents: The Politics of Leadership from Roosevelt to Reagan* (New York: The Free Press, 1990), ch. 4.
11. Walter D. Burnham, "Insulation and Responsiveness in Congressional Elections," *Political Science Quarterly* 90 (Fall 1975): 412–413; George C. Edwards III, *Presidential Influence in Congress* (San Francisco: Freeman, 1980), 70–78; Warren E. Miller, "Presidential Coattails: A Study in Political Myth and Methodology," *Public Opinion Quarterly* 19 (Winter 1955–1956): 368; and Miller, "The Motivational Basis for Straight and Split Ticket Voting," *American Political Science Review* 51 (June 1957): 293–312.
12. *Clinton v. City of New York*, 118 S. Ct. 2091 (1998).
13. *Marbury v. Madison*, 1 Cranch 137 (1803).
14. *United States v. Nixon*, 418 U.S. 683 (1974).
15. *Clinton v. Jones*, 520 U.S. 681 (1997); *In re Grand Jury Subpoena Duces Tecum*, 112 F.3d 910 (1997); *In re Sealed Case*, 121 F.3d 729 (1997).
16. Christopher S. Kelley, "A Comparative Look at the Constitutional Signing Statement," paper presented at the Midwest Political Science Association meeting, April 2003; Kelley, "To Be (Unitarian) or Not to Be (Unitarian): Presidential Power in the George W. Bush Administration," *White House Studies* 10, no. 2 (2010): 115–129.
17. Charlie Savage, "Obama Looks to Limit Impact of Tactic Bush Used to Sidestep New Laws," *New York Times*, March 9, 2009.
18. Walter Dellinger, "Memorandum for Bernard N. Nussbaum, Counsel to the President," Office of Legal Counsel, U.S. Department of Justice, November 3, 1993.
19. *Chevron v. NRDC*, 467 U.S. 837 (1984).
20. Edwin S. Corwin, *The Presidency: Office and Powers* (New York: New York University Press, 1957), 171.
21. Stephen Hess, *Organizing the Presidency* (Washington, D.C.: Brookings Institution, 1976), 3; R. W. Apple, "Clinton's Refocusing," *New York Times*, May 6, 1993, A22; Michael K. Frisby, "Power Switch," *Wall Street Journal*, March 26, 1993, A1, A7.
22. David T. Stanley, et al., *Men Who Govern* (Washington, D.C.: Brookings Institution, 1967), 41–42, 50.
23. Daniel J. Elazar, "Which Road to the Presidency?" in *The Presidency*, ed. Aaron Wildavsky (Boston: Little, Brown, 1969), 340.
24. Marcus Cunliffe, *American Presidents and the Presidency* (New York: American Heritage Press/McGraw-Hill, 1972), 63, 65.
25. Ibid., 214.
26. Adapted from Paul C. Light, *The President's Agenda* (Baltimore, Md.: Johns Hopkins University Press, 1982), 217–225.

Chapter 15
The Bureaucracy

1. Charles E. Lindblom, *Politics and Markets* (New York: Basic Books, 1977), 114.
2. Donald F. Kettl, *Government by Proxy: (Mis?) Managing Federal Programs* (Washington, D.C.: Congressional Quarterly Press, 1988); John J. DiIulio, Jr., "Government by Proxy: A Faithful Overview," *Harvard Law Review* (March 2003): 1272–1284.
3. Mark Hemmingway, "Warriors for Hire," *Weekly Standard*, December 18, 2006, 25.
4. Ibid., 26.
5. Martha Derthick, *Keeping the Compound Republic: Essays on American Federalism* (Washington, D.C.: Brookings Institution, 2001), 63.

6. Donald F. Kettl, *The Next Government of the United States: Why Our Institutions Fail Us and How to Fix Them* (New York: W.W. Norton, 2008), 1–14.
7. Article II, section 2, para. 2.
8. Article II, section 3.
9. Calculated from data in *Historical Statistics of the United States: Colonial Times to 1970* (Washington, D.C.: Government Printing Office, 1975), vol. 2, 1102–1103.
10. *Panama Refining Co. v. Ryan*, 293 U.S. 388 (1935).
11. *Hampton Jr. & Co. v. United States*, 276 U.S. 394 (1928).
12. Edward S. Corwin, *The Constitution and What It Means Today*, 13th ed. (Princeton, N.J.: Princeton University Press, 1973), 151.
13. Bruce D. Porter, "Parkinson's Law Revisited: War and the Growth of American Government," *Public Interest* (Summer 1980): 50–68.
14. See the cases cited in Corwin, *The Constitution*, 8.
15. *U.S. Statutes*, vol. 84, sec. 799 (1970).
16. *Historical Statistics of the United States*, vol. 2, 1107.
17. Kettl, *The Next Government*, op. cit., 52.
18. Donald F. Kettl, et al., *Civil Service Reform: Building a Government That Works* (Washington, D.C.: Brookings Institution, 1996), 15.
19. Hugh Heclo, "Issue Networks and the Executive Establishment," in *The New American Political System*, ed. Anthony King (Washington, D.C.: American Enterprise Institute, 1978), 87–124.
20. Quoted in Hugh Heclo, *A Government of Strangers* (Washington, D.C.: Brookings Institution, 1977), 225.
21. Alexis Simendinger, "Of the People, for the People," *National Journal* (April 18, 1998): 852–855. Data from the Pew Charitable Trusts Research Center for the People and the Press.
22. Kenneth Meier and Lloyd Nigro, "Representative Bureaucracy and Policy References: A Study of the Attitudes of Federal Executives," *Public Administration Review* 36 (July/August 1976): 458–467; Bernard Mennis, *American Foreign Policy Officials* (Columbus: Ohio State University Press, 1971).
23. David Stockman, *The Triumph of Politics* (New York: Harper and Row, 1986).
24. James Q. Wilson, *Bureaucracy* (New York: Basic Books, 1989), ch. 6.
25. Heclo, "Issue Networks and the Executive Establishment," 87–124.
26. David H. Rosenbloom, "Reevaluating Executive-Centered Public Administrative Theory," in *The Oxford Handbook of American Bureaucracy*, ed. Robert F. Durant. Oxford University Press, 2010, p. 114.
27. Ibid., pp. 121–122.
28. Richard F. Fenno, Jr., *The Power of the Purse* (Boston: Little, Brown, 1966), 450, 597.
29. John E. Schwartz and L. Earl Shaw, *The United States Congress in Comparative Perspective* (Hinsdale, Ill.: Dryden Press, 1976), 262–263; *National Journal* (July 4, 1981): 1211–1214.
30. *Immigration and Naturalization Service v. Chadha*, 462 U.S. 919 (1983); *Maine v. Thiboutot*, 448 U.S. 1 (1980).
31. See cases cited in Corwin, *The Constitution*, 22.
32. Steven Kelman, "The Grace Commission: How Much Waste in Government?" *Public Interest* (Winter 1985): 62–87.
33. Daniel Katz, et al., *Bureaucratic Encounters* (Ann Arbor: Survey Research Center, University of Michigan, 1975), 63–69, 118–120, 184–188.
34. U.S. Government Accountability Office, *Government Performance Lessons Learned*, GAO Report, July 24, 2008, as cited in Kettl, *The Next Government*, op. cit., 173, 255.
35. Ibid.

Chapter 16

The Judiciary

1. Henry J. Abraham, *The Judicial Process*, 3d ed. (New York: Oxford University Press, 1975), 279–280.
2. Robert G. McCloskey, *The American Supreme Court* (Chicago: University of Chicago Press, 1960), 27.
3. *Marbury v. Madison*, 5 U.S. 137 (1803); and *McCulloch v. Maryland*, 17 U.S. 316 (1819).
4. *Martin v. Hunter's Lessee*, 14 U.S. 304 (1816); and *Cohens v. Virginia*, 19 U.S. (1821).
5. *Gibbons v. Ogden*, 22 U.S. (1824).
6. Quoted in Albert J. Beveridge, *The Life of John Marshall* (Boston: Houghton Mifflin, 1919), vol. 4, 551.
7. *Dred Scott v. Sandford*, 60 U.S. 393 (1857).
8. Abraham, *The Judicial Process*, 286.
9. *In re Debs*, 158 U.S. 564 (1895).
10. *Pollock v. Farmers' Loan & Trust Co.*, 157 U.S. 429 (1895).
11. *United States v. Knight*, 156 U.S. 1 (1895).
12. *Cincinnati, N.O. & T.P. Railway Co. v. Interstate Commerce Commission*, 162 U.S. 184 (1896).
13. *Hammer v. Dagenhart*, 247 U.S. 251 (1918).
14. *Lochner v. New York*, 198 U.S. 45 (1905).
15. McCloskey, *The American Supreme Court*, 151.
16. *Munn v. Illinois*, 94 U.S. 113 (1877).
17. *Dayton-Goose Creek Railway Co. v. United States*, 263 U.S. 456 (1924).
18. *Atchison, Topeka, and Santa Fe Railroad Co. v. Matthews*, 174 U.S. 96 (1899).
19. *Mugler v. Kansas*, 123 U.S. 623 (1887).
20. *St. Louis Consolidated Coal Co. v. Illinois*, 185 U.S. 203 (1902).
21. *New York Central Railroad Co. v. White*, 243 U.S. 188 (1917).
22. *German Alliance Insurance Co. v. Lewis*, 233 U.S. 389 (1914).
23. Morton Keller, *Affairs of State* (Cambridge: Harvard University Press, 1977), 369. See also Mary Cornelia Porter, "That Commerce Shall Be Free: A New Look at the Old Laissez-Faire Court," in *The Supreme Court Review*, ed. Philip B. Kurland (Chicago: University of Chicago Press, 1976), 135–159.
24. *Chief of Capitol Police v. Jeannette Rankin Brigade*, 409 U.S. 972 (1972).
25. *Aptheker v. Secretary of State*, 378 U.S. 500 (1964).
26. *Trop v. Dulles*, 356 U.S. 86 (1958); *Afroyim v. Rusk*, 387 U.S. 253 (1967); and *Schneider v. Rusk*, 377 U.S. 163 (1964).
27. *Lamont v. Postmaster General*, 381 U.S. 301 (1965); and *Blount v. Rizzi*, 400 U.S. 410 (1971).
28. *Richardson v. Davis*, 409 U.S. 1069 (1972); *U.S. Department of Agriculture v. Murry*, 413 U.S. 508 (1973); *Jimenez v. Weinberger*, 417 U.S. 628 (1974); and *Washington v. Legrant*, 394 U.S. 618 (1969).
29. *United States v. Lopez*, 514 U.S. 549 (1995).
30. *Seminole Tribe of Florida v. Florida*, 517 U.S. 44 (1996); *Alden v. Maine*, 527 U.S. 706 (1999); *Florida v. College Savings Bank*, 527 U.S. 627 (1999).

31. Daniel R. Pinello, "Linking Party to Judicial Ideology in American Courts: A Meta-Analysis," *Justice System Journal* 20 (1999): 219–254.
32. An opinion survey of federal judges shows how party affects ideology: see Althea K. Nagai, Stanley Rothman, and S. Robert Lichter, "The Verdict of Federal Judges," *Public Opinion* (November/December 1987): 52–56.
33. *United States v. Lanza*, 260 U.S. 377 (1922). Cf. *Abbate v. United States*, 359 U.S. 187 (1959), and *Bartkus v. Illinois*, 359 U.S. 121 (1989).
34. *Gideon v. Wainwright*, 372 U.S. 335 (1963). The story is told in Anthony Lewis, *Gideon's Trumpet* (New York: Random House, 1964).
35. Erwin Griswold, "Rationing Justice: The Supreme Court's Case Load and What the Court Does Not Do," *Cornell Law Review* 60 (1975): 335–354.
36. Joseph Weis, Jr., "Disconnecting the Overloaded Circuits—A Plan for a Unified Court of Appeals," *St. Louis University Law Journal* 39 (1995): 455.
37. *Alyeska Pipeline Service Co. v. Wilderness Society*, 421 U.S. 240 (1975).
38. *Flast v. Cohen*, 392 U.S. 83 (1968), which modified the earlier *Frothingham v. Mellon*, 262 U.S. 447 (1923); *United States v. Richardson*, 418 U.S. 166 (1947).
39. *Brown v. Board of Education of Topeka*, 347 U.S. 483 (1954).
40. *Baker v. Carr*, 369 U.S. 186 (1962).
41. See Louise Weinberg, "A New Judicial Federalism?" *Daedalus* (Winter 1978): 129–141.
42. Quoted in Abraham, *The Judicial Process*, 330.
43. Carolyn D. Richmond, "The Rehnquist Court: What Is in Store for Constitutional Precedent?" *New York Law Review* 39 (1994): 511.
44. *Colegrove v. Green*, 328 U.S. 549 (1946).
45. The Court abandoned the "political question" doctrine in *Baker v. Carr*, 369 U.S. 186 (1962), and began to change congressional-district apportionment in *Wesberry v. Sanders*, 376 U.S. 1 (1964).
46. Donald L. Horowitz, *The Courts and Social Policy* (Washington, D.C.: Brookings Institution, 1977), 6.
47. *Gates v. Collier*, 349 F. Supp. 881 (1972).
48. *Lau v. Nichols*, 414 U.S. 563 (1974).
49. Jane Burnbaum, "Guilty! Too Many Lawyers and Too Much Litigation," *Business Week* (April 13, 1992): 60–61.
50. Joel B. Grossman and Austin Sarat, "Litigation in the Federal Courts: A Comparative Perspective," *Law and Society Review* 9 (Winter 1975): 321–346.
51. Administrative Office of the U.S. Courts, *Annual Report, 1988*, 109.
52. Jack W. Peltason, *Fifty-Eight Lonely Men: Southern Federal Judges and School Desegregation* (New York: Harcourt Brace, 1961).
53. Anthony Partridge and William B. Eldridge, *The Second Circuit Sentencing Study* (Washington, D.C.: Federal Judicial Center, 1974).
54. *Abington School District v. Schempp*, 374 U.S. 203 (1963).
55. Robert H. Birkby, "The Supreme Court and the Bible Belt," *Midwest Journal of Political Science* 10 (1966): 3.
56. Cass R. Sunstein, "Impeaching the President," *University of Pennsylvania Law Review* 147 (1998): 279.
57. *United States v. Butler*, 297 U.S. 1 (1936).
58. *Ex parte McCardle*, 74 U.S. 506 (1869).
59. Walter F. Murphy, *Congress and the Court* (Chicago: University of Chicago Press, 1962); and C. Herman Pritchett, *Congress Versus the Supreme Court* (Minneapolis: University of Minnesota Press, 1961).
60. Gregory A. Caldeira, "Neither the Purse nor the Sword: Dynamics of Public Confidence in the U.S. Supreme Court," *American Political Science Review* 80 (1986): 1209–1226. See also Joseph T. Tannenhaus and Walter F. Murphy, "Patterns of Public Support for the Supreme Court: A Panel Study," *Journal of Politics* 43 (1981): 24–39.

Chapter 17

The Policymaking Process

1. E. E. Schattschneider, *The Semisovereign People* (New York: Holt, Rinehart and Winston, 1960), 68.
2. Jack L. Walker, "Setting the Agenda in the U.S. Senate: A Theory of Problem Selection," *British Journal of Political Science* 7 (1977): 343, 441.
3. *Statistical Abstract of the United States, 1975* (Washington, D.C.: Government Printing Office, 1975), 342–343, 349.
4. Alexis de Tocqueville, *The Old Regime and the French Revolution*, trans. Gilbert Stuart (Garden City, N.Y.: Doubleday Anchor Books, 1955), 176–177. First published in 1856.
5. David O. Sears and J. B. McConahay, *The Politics of Violence* (Boston: Houghton Mifflin, 1973). Compare Abraham H. Miller, et al., "The New Urban Blacks," *Ethnicity* 3 (1976): 338–367.
6. Daniel Patrick Moynihan, *Maximum Feasible Misunderstanding* (New York: Free Press, 1969), ch. 2.
7. Nelson W. Polsby, "Goodbye to the Senate's Inner Club," in *Congress in Change: Evolution and Reform*, ed. Norman J. Ornstein (New York: Praeger, 1975), 208–215.
8. *Federalist* No. 62.
9. Walker, "Setting the Agenda," 434, 439, 441.
10. This is a revised version of a theory originally presented in James Q. Wilson, *Political Organizations* (New York: Basic Books, 1973), ch. 16. There are other ways of classifying public policies, notably that of Theodore J. Lowi, "American Business, Public Policy, Case Studies, and Political Theory," *World Politics* 16 (July 1964).
11. Donald F. Kettl, *Sharing Power: Public Governance and Private Markets* (Washington, D.C.: Brookings Institution, 1993); Lawrence J. Hajna, "Superfund: Costly Program Under Fire," *Courier-Post* (February 13, 1994): 6A.
12. Edward S. Greenberg, *Serving the Few: Corporate Capitalism and the Bias of Government Policy* (New York: Wiley, 1974).
13. Charles E. Lindblom, *Politics and Markets* (New York: Basic Books, 1977).
14. Joseph Schumpeter, *Capitalism, Socialism, and Democracy* (New York: Harper and Row, 1950).
15. Louis Galambos, *The Public Image of Big Business in America, 1880–1940* (Baltimore: Johns Hopkins University Press, 1975).
16. Suzanne Weaver, *Decision to Prosecute: Organization and Public Policy in the Antitrust Division* (Cambridge, Mass.: MIT Press, 1977); Robert H. Bork, *The Antitrust Paradox* (New York: Basic Books, 1978).

17. Richard A. Posner, *Antitrust Law: An Economic Perspective* (Chicago: University of Chicago Press, 1976), 25.
18. Alan L. Seltzer, "Woodrow Wilson as 'Corporate-Liberal': Toward a Reconsideration of Left Revisionist Historiography," *Western Political Quarterly* 30 (June 1977): 183–212.
19. Weaver, *Decision to Prosecute*; and Robert A. Katzmann, *Regulatory Bureaucracy: The Federal Trade Commission and Antitrust Policy* (Cambridge, Mass.: MIT Press, 1980).
20. Charles R. Plott, "Occupational Self-Regulation: A Case Study of the Oklahoma Dry Cleaners," *Journal of Law and Economics* 8 (October 1965): 195–222.
21. Paul H. MacAvoy, ed., *Federal Milk Marketing Orders and Price Supports* (Washington, D.C.: American Enterprise Institute, 1977).
22. Ibid., 111.
23. *Congressional Quarterly Weekly Report* (April 21, 1990): 1184–1188.
24. Pietro Nivola, "The New Pork Barrel," *Brookings Review* (Winter 1998): 6–13.
25. Upton Sinclair, *The Jungle* (New York: Doubleday, Page and Co., 1906).
26. Mark V. Nadel, *The Politics of Consumer Protection* (Indianapolis, Ind.: Bobbs-Merrill, 1971), 143–144.
27. Alfred A. Marcus, *Promise and Performance: Choosing and Implementing an Environmental Policy* (Westport, Conn.: Greenwood Press, 1980).
28. Nadel, *Politics*, 66–80.
29. Martha Derthick and Paul J. Quirk, *The Politics of Deregulation* (Washington, D.C.: Brookings Institution, 1985).
30. Executive Orders 11821 (1974), 12044 (1978), and 12291 (1981).

Chapter 18
Economic Policy

1. Edward R. Tufte, *Political Control of the Economy* (Princeton, N.J.: Princeton University Press, 1978): 84; Douglas A. Hibbs, Jr., "The Mass Public and Macroeconomic Performance: The Dynamics of Public Opinion Toward Unemployment and Inflation," *American Journal of Political Science* 23 (1979): 705–731.
2. D. Roderick Kiewiet, *Macroeconomics and Micropolitics: The Electoral Effect of Economic Issues* (Chicago: University of Chicago Press, 1983); Morris P. Fiorina, "Economic Retrospective Voting in American National Elections: A Micro-Analysis," *American Journal of Political Science* 22 (1978): 426–443; Donald R. Kinder and D. Roderick Kiewiet, "Sociotropic Politics: The American Case," *British Journal of Political Science* 11 (1981): 129–161.
3. *New York Times*/CBS News poll cited in Douglas A. Hibbs, Jr., "President Reagan's Mandate from the 1980 Elections: A Shift to the Right?" *American Politics Quarterly* 10 (1982): 387–420.
4. Hibbs, "The Mass Public."
5. Ibid.
6. Kiewiet, *Macroeconomics and Micropolitics.*
7. Michael S. Lewis-Beck, "Comparative Economic Voting: Britain, France, Germany, Italy," *American Journal of Political Science* 30 (1986): 315–346.
8. Douglas A. Hibbs, Jr., "Political Parties and Macroeconomic Policy," *American Political Science Review* 71 (1977): 1467–1487.
9. Kiewiet, *Macroeconomics and Micropolitics*, 69.
10. *Pollock v. Farmers' Loan & Trust Co.*, 157 U.S. 429, affirmed at 158 U.S. 601 (1895).
11. NBC News/*Wall Street Journal* poll, as reported in *National Journal* (July 12, 1986): 1741.

Chapter 19
Social Welfare

1. For a general discussion see Charles E. Gilbert, "Welfare Policy," in *Handbook of Political Science*, ed. Fred I. Greenstein and Nelson W. Polsby (Reading, Mass.: Addison-Wesley, 1975), vol. 6, ch. 4.
2. *Congress and the Nation, 1945–1964* (Washington, D.C.: Congressional Quarterly Service, 1965), 1225.
3. Harold E. Raynes, *Social Security in Britain: A History* (London: Pitman, 1960), ch. 18. See also Hugh Heclo, *Modern Social Politics in Britain and Sweden* (New Haven, Conn.: Yale University Press, 1974).
4. Amy E. Black, Douglas Koopman, and David K. Ryder, *Of Little Faith: The Politics of George W. Bush's Faith-Based Initiatives* (Washington, D.C.: Georgetown University Press, 2004).
5. Anne Farris, Richard P. Nathan, and David Wright, *The Expanding Administrative Presidency: George W. Bush and the Faith-Based Initiative* (Albany, New York: Nelson A. Rockefeller Institute of Government, 2004), Executive Summary, 2.
6. Stephen V. Monsma, *Putting Faith in Partnerships: Welfare-to-Work in Four Cities* (Ann Arbor, Mich.: University of Michigan Press, 2004), ix, 70.
7. Ibid., x.
8. Surveys by Pew Forum on Religion and Public Life: *American Views on Religion, Politics, and Public Policy* (Washington, D.C.: Pew Forum, 2001); *Lift Every Voice: A Report on Religion in American Public Life* (Washington, D.C.: Pew Forum, 2002); *Americans Struggle with Religion's Role at Home and Abroad* (Washington, D.C.: Pew Forum, 2002).
9. Histories of the 1935 act include Edwin E. Witte, *The Development of the Social Security Act* (Madison: University of Wisconsin Press, 1962). A different view, offering a neo-Marxist interpretation of the act, can be found in Frances Fox Piven and Richard A. Cloward, *Regulating the Poor* (New York: Pantheon, 1971).
10. The development of Medicare is described in Theodore Marmor, "Doctors, Politics, and Health Insurance for the Aged: The Enactment of Medicare," in *Cases in Contemporary American Government*, ed. Allan Sindler (Boston: Little, Brown, 1969).
11. Michael E. Schiltz, *Public Attitudes Toward Social Security, 1935–1965*, Research Report No. 3, Social Security Administration, U.S. Department of Health, Education, and Welfare (Washington, D.C.: Government Printing Office, 1970), 36, 98, 128, 140.
12. Ibid., ch. 4, 154–165.
13. Charles Murray, *Losing Ground: American Social Policy, 1950–1980* (New York: Basic Books, 1984). A critique of Murray is William J. Wilson, *The Truly Disadvantaged* (Chicago: University of Chicago Press, 1987), esp. chs. 3 and 4.

Chapter 20
Foreign and Military Policy

1. Alexis de Tocqueville, *Democracy in America, vol. 1*, ed. Phillips Bradley (New York: Knopf, 1951), 235.
2. See Victor Davis Hanson, *Carnage and Culture* (New York: Anchor

Books, 2002); and Hanson, *The Soul of Battle* (New York: Free Press, 1999).

3. Richard Lau, Thad A. Brown, and David O. Sears, "Self-Interest and Civilians' Attitudes Toward the Vietnam War," *Public Opinion Quarterly* 42 (1978): 464–481.
4. Edward S. Corwin, *The President: Office and Powers* (New York: New York University Press, 1940), 200.
5. Louis W. Koenig, *The Chief Executive,* 3d ed. (New York: Harcourt Brace Jovanovich, 1975), 217.
6. Louis Fisher, *President and Congress* (New York: Free Press, 1972), 45; *United States v. Belmont,* 301 U.S. 324 (1937).
7. Aaron Wildavsky, "The Two Presidencies," in *The Presidency,* ed. Wildavsky (Boston: Little, Brown, 1969), 231.
8. Loch Johnson and James M. McCormick, "The Making of International Agreements: A Reappraisal of Congressional Involvement," *Journal of Politics,* 40 (1978): 468–478.
9. Bernard E. Brown, "The Decision to End the Algerian War," in *Cases in Comparative Politics,* ed. James B. Christoph (Boston: Little, Brown, 1965), 154–180; Roy C. Macridis, "De Gaulle and NATO," in *Modern European Governments,* ed. Macridis (Englewood Cliffs, N.J.: Prentice-Hall, 1968), 92–115; and John E. Schwartz and L. Earl Shaw, *The United States Congress in Comparative Perspective* (Hinsdale, Ill.: Dryden Press, 1976), 235–236.
10. Peter G. Richards, *Parliament and Foreign Affairs* (London: George Allen and Unwin, 1967), 37–38; Schwartz and Shaw, *The United States Congress in Comparative Perspective,* 235.
11. Arthur M. Schlesinger, Jr., *A Thousand Days: John F. Kennedy in the White House* (Boston: Houghton Mifflin, 1965), chs. 30, 31. Schlesinger, at p. 841, described Kennedy's actions as a "brilliantly controlled," "matchlessly calibrated" combination of "nerve and wisdom." His view of Nixon's actions was a good deal less charitable in *The Imperial Presidency* (Boston: Houghton Mifflin, 1974), ch. 7.
12. *United States v. Curtiss-Wright Export Co.,* 299 U.S. 304 (1936).
13. *Mitchell v. Laird,* 488 F.2d 611 (1973).
14. *Prize Cases,* 67 U.S. 635 (1863); *Mora v. McNamara,* 389 U.S. 934 (1964); *Massachusetts v. Laird,* 400 U.S. 886 (1970).
15. *Dames and Moore v. Regan,* 435 U.S. 654 (1981).
16. *Korematsu v. United States,* 323 U.S. 214 (1944).
17. *Youngstown Sheet & Tube Co. v. Sawyer,* 343 U.S. 579 (1952).
18. *Immigration and Naturalization Service v. Chadha,* 103 S. Ct. 2764 (1983).
19. Robert S. Erikson and Norman R. Luttbeg, *American Public Opinion* (New York: Wiley, 1973), 50–51.
20. William R. Caspary, "The 'Mood Theory': A Study of Public Opinion and Foreign Policy," *American Political Science Review* 64 (June 1970): 536–547.
21. Erikson and Luttbeg, *American Public Opinion,* 52.
22. John E. Mueller, *War, Presidents, and Public Opinion* (New York: Wiley, 1973), 110.
23. Ibid., 112.
24. Milton J. Rosenberg, Sidney Verba, and Philip E. Converse, *Vietnam and the Silent Majority* (New York: Harper and Row, 1970), 26–27.
25. Erikson and Luttbeg, *American Public Opinion,* 155.
26. John R. Oneal and Brad Lian, "Presidents, the Use of Military Force, and Public Opinion," Working Papers in International Security I–92–8, Hoover Institution, Stanford, Calif. (July 1992).
27. Benjamin C. Schwarz, *Casualities, Public Opinion, and U.S. Military Intervention* (Santa Monica, Calif.: RAND, 1994).
28. Mueller, *War, Presidents, and Public Opinion,* 45–47, 169.
29. James Q. Wilson and Karlyn Bowman, "Defining the Peace Party," *The Public Interest* (Fall 2003): 69–78.
30. Everett Carll Ladd, "Since World War II, Americans Have Persistently Looked Outward," *The Public Perspective* (August/September 1997): 5–34.
31. Howard Schuman, "Two Sources of Antiwar Sentiment in America," *American Journal of Sociology* 78 (1973): 513–536.
32. Philip E. Converse, Warren E. Miller, Jerrold G. Rusk, and Arthur C. Wolfe, "Continuity and Change in American Politics," *American Political Science Review* 63 (December 1969): 1083–1105; John P. Robinson, "Public Reaction to Political Protest: Chicago, 1968," *Public Opinion Quarterly* 34 (Spring 1970): 1–9.
33. James D. Wright, "Life, Time, and the Fortunes of War," *Transaction* 9 (January 1972).
34. John E. Rielly, *American Public Opinion and U.S. Foreign Policy, 1999* (Chicago: Chicago Council on Foreign Relations, 1999).
35. X, "The Sources of Soviet Conduct," *Foreign Affairs* 25 (July 1947): 566.
36. Walter Lippmann, *The Cold War* (New York: Harper Brothers, 1947).
37. Erikson and Luttbeg, *American Public Opinion,* 52.
38. Mueller, *War, Presidents, and Public Opinion,* 40.
39. Michael Roskin, "From Pearl Harbor to Vietnam: Shifting Generational Paradigms and Foreign Policy," *Political Science Quarterly* 89 (Fall 1974): 567.
40. Frank L. Klingberg, "The Historical Alternation of Moods in American Foreign Policy," *World Politics* 4 (1952): 239–273.
41. Roskin, "From Pearl Harbor," 567.
42. *American Public Opinion and U.S. Foreign Policy, 1987* (Chicago: Chicago Council on Foreign Relations, 1987), 33.
43. Carl M. Cannon, "Comment," in Pietro S. Nivola and David W. Brady, eds., *Red and Blue Nation?* (Washington, D.C.: Brookings Institution, 2006), 168; and Cannon, "Administration: A New Era of Partisan War," *National Journal,* March 18, 2006.
44. For a lively debate over the extent of political polarization, see Morris Fiorina and Matthew S. Levendusky, "Disconnected: The Political Class Versus the People"; Alan I. Abramowitz, "Comment"; and Gary C. Jacobson, "Comment,"—all in Nivola and Brady, op. cit.
45. Commission on the Intelligence Capabilities of the United States Regarding Weapons of Mass Destruction, *Report to the President* (Washington, D.C.: Government Printing Office, 2005), 43–249.
46. Quoted in Robert J. Art, *The TFX Decision* (Boston: Little, Brown, 1968), 126.
47. *The National Security Strategy of the United States of America,* September 2002, cover letter and p. 6.
48. The vote on the Persian Gulf War as reported in *Congress and the Nation,* vol. 8 (Washington, D.C.:

Congressional Quarterly Press, 1993), 310; the vote on the war in Iraq as reported in the *New York Times,* October 12, 2002, A11.

49. There were no congressional votes on our military efforts in Bosnia and Kosovo, but speeches supporting them were made by (among others) Democratic Senators Barbara Boxer, Carl Levin, and Paul Wellstone and Representative David Bonior; speeches opposing them were made by (among others) Republican Senators Don Nickles and John Warner and by Representatives Robert Barr and Dan Burton. In the vote on the invasion of Iraq, each group took the opposite position.
50. James Dobbins, et al., *America's Role in Nation Building* (Santa Monica, Calif.: RAND, 2003).

Chapter 21

Environmental Policy

1. Environmental Protection Agency Web site, www.epa.gov/aboutepa/history/index.html.
2. The debate over the existence, causes, and consequences of global warming is examined in detail in PBS Newshour's "The Global Warming Debate," at www.pbs.org/newshour/indepth_coverage/science/globalwarming/.
3. Gil Kaufman, "Young Voters Say Economy Is Most Important Factor in Choosing President, Not Race or Gender, CBS News/MTV Poll Finds," Mtv.com, April 21, 2008, available at www.mtv.com/news/articles/1585936/young-voters-economy-most-important-cbs-news-mtv-poll.jhtml.
4. Barack Obama, speech at Jefferson-Jackson dinner, Des Moines, Iowa, November 10, 2007, available at www.washingtonpost.com/wp-dyn/content/article/2008/12/17/AR2008121703661.html; John McCain, speech at Republican National Convention, Minneapolis, Minnesota, September 4, 2008, available at http://elections.nytimes.com/2008/president/conventions/videos/20080904_MCCAIN_SPEECH.html.
5. Yale Project on Climate Change Communication, "Public Support for Climate and Energy Policies in May 2011," June 13, 2011, available at http://environment.yale.edu/climate/; Yale Project on Climate Change Communication, "Youth Less Concerned About Global Warming Than Their Elders?" March 23, 2010, available at http://environment.yale.edu/climate/news/youth-less-concerned-about-global-warming-than-their-elders/.
6. Jeff Mann, "President Obama Meets with Power Shift Youth Clean Energy Leaders," April 15, 2011, available at www.wearepowershift.org/news/president-obama-meets-power-shift-youth-clean-energy-leaders.
7. Sallie Baliunas, "The Koyoto Protocol and Global Warming," *Imprimis* 31 (March 2002); National Research Council, *Climate Change: An Analysis of Some Key Questions* (Washington, D.C.: National Academy of Sciences, 2001); Bjørn Lomborg, *The Skeptical Environmentalist* (Cambridge: Cambridge University Press, 2001), ch. 24.
8. Barry G. Rabe, "Statehouse and Greenhouse: The States Are Taking the Lead on Climate Change," *Brookings Review* 20 (Spring 2002): 11–13.
9. Baliunas, "Koyoto Protocol," 2.
10. For arguments by activists, see Albert Gore, *Earth in the Balance* (Boston: Houghton Mifflin, 1992); and Stephen Schneider, *Global Warming* (San Francisco: Sierra Club Books, 1989). For arguments by skeptics, see Gregg Easterbrook, *A Moment on the Earth* (New York: Viking, 1995), ch. 17; Frederick Seitz, et al., "Environmental Effects of Increased Atmospheric Carbon Dioxide," on the World Wide Web at www.oism.org/project; and Patrick J. Michaels, "Global Deception," Policy Study 146, Center for the Study of American Business, Washington University (1998).
11. Easterbrook, *A Moment,* 309.
12. R. Shep Melnick, *Regulation and the Courts: The Case of the Clean Air Act* (Washington, D.C.: Brookings Institution, 1983), ch. 9.
13. Pietro S. Nivola, *The Politics of Energy Conservation* (Washington, D.C.: Brookings Institution, 1986), 11–12, 244–247.
14. Robert W. Crandall, "Pollution, Environmentalists, and the Coal Lobby," in *The Political Economy of Deregulation,* ed. Roger G. Noll and Bruce M. Own (Washington, D.C.: American Enterprise Institute, 1983), 84–96; Crandall, *Controlling Industrial Pollution* (Washington, D.C.: Brookings Institution, 1983).
15. Bruce A. Ackerman and William T. Hassler, *Clear Coal/Dirty Air* (New Haven, Conn.: Yale University Press, 1981).
16. Robert Dorfman, "Lessons of Pesticide Regulation," in *Reform of Environmental Regulation,* ed. Wesley A. Magat (Cambridge, Mass.: Ballinger, 1982), 13–30.
17. Easterbrook, *A Moment,* 386–395.
18. *Congressional Quarterly Weekly Report* (January 12, 1990): 166–170.
19. Richard Doll and Richard Peto, "The Causes of Cancer," *Journal of the National Cancer Institute* 66 (1981); World Cancer Research Fund, *Food, Nutrition, and the Prevention of Cancer* (Washington, D.C.: American Institute for Cancer Research, 1997).
20. David Vogel, *National Styles of Regulation* (Ithaca, N.Y.: Cornell University Press, 1986), 19–30.
21. R. Shep Melnick, "Deadlines, Cynicism, and Common Sense," *The Brookings Review* (Fall 1983): 21–24.
22. Ryan Lizza, "As the World Burns," *New Yorker,* October 22, 2010.

Chapter 22

Who Governs? To What Ends?

1. Donald F. Kettl, "Heading for Disaster, "*Government Executive,* February 1, 2009.
2. Ibid.
3. Alexis de Tocqueville, *Democracy in America,* vol. 2, ed. Phillips Bradley (New York: Knopf, 1951), book 2, ch. 1.

Index

Abramoff, Jack, 288, 356
Acheson's Rule, 412
Acid rain, 571–572
Activist approach, 440
Activist government, consequences of, 587–590
Activists, 192
Adams, John, 6
Ad hoc structure, 388
Administrative Procedure Act, 423
Adversarial press, 316
Affirmative action, 149–154
  defined, 149
  equality of results, 149
  landmark cases, 154
  opportunity, equality of, 149–154
Affordable Care Act ("Obamacare"), 52, 329, 516
African Americans
  affirmative action and, 149–150
  civil rights and, 131–133
  in Congress, 335–336
  as Democratic voters, 262–263
  interest groups and, 275–276
  political parties, 223–224
  political power and, 5
  political system and, 82
  racial profiling and, 144–145
  representational view of, 341
  separate-but-equal doctrine, 134
  social welfare and, 518
  voting and, 143, 188, 189
Agency allies, 425
Agricultural Adjustment Act, 483
Agricultural pesticides, 572–574
Aid to Families with Dependent Children (AFDC), 517–518, 526–527
Alger, Horatio, 89
Aliens
  defined, 151
  rights of, 151
Alito, Samuel, 457
Al Qaeda, defined, 535
Amending the Constitution, ways of, 43
Amendments, defined, 43
American Association for Political Consultants (AAPC), 237
American Association of Retired Persons (AARP), 277, 279
American bureaucracy, distinctiveness of, 410–411
American civic health index, 2009, 93
American Civil Liberties Union (ACLU), 102, 453
American Cotton Manufacturers Institute, 274
American electorate, rise of, 187–192
  state to Federal control, 187–190
  voter turnout, 190–192
American Farm Bureau Federation (AFBF), 271, 273
American Federation of State, County and Municipal Employees (AFSCME), 282
American Federation of Teachers (AFT), 282
American institutions, confidence in, 92
American Israel Public Affairs Committee (AIPAC), 279
American Jewish Committe, 271
American Medical Association, 271
American political history, journalism in, 300–305
  electronic journalism, 302–304
  Internet, 304–305
  magazines of opinion, 302
  party press, 300
  popular press, 300–302
American Recovery and Reinvestment Act, 499
American Revolution
  goal of, 20
  property rights and, 22–23
Americans with Disabilities Act (ADA), 152
Amicus curiae, 456
Anderson, John, two-party system and, 222
Anti-Defamation League, 271
Antifederalists
  defined, 32
  view of Constitution, 33–36
Anti-Masonic party, 207
Appropriations bills, 351
Appropriations Committee, 426–427
Aristotle, 7, 9, 10, 32
Arnold, Thurman, 481
Articles of Confederation
  defined, 24
  weaknesses of, 24–25
Assistance program, 522
Associated Press, 301, 306
Atlantic Monthly, 302
Attitudinal view, of Congress members, 342–343
Australian ballot, 191
Authority
  defined, 5
  formal, 5–6
Authorization legislation, 426

Background, communication method, 319
Balanced Budget Act, 1985, 505–506
Ballot initiatives, 9, 15
Bases, defense budget spending and, 556–557
Bayh, Birch, personal following and, 219
Beard, Charles, 39
Behavior theories of Congress members, 340–343
  attitudinal view, 342–343
  organizational view, 341–342
  representational view, 341
Benefit, defined, 475
Bernanke, Ben, 503
Bernstein, Carl, 307
Bicameral legislature, 332
Biden, Joe, 249
Big-ticket items, defense budget spending and, 555–556
Bill becoming law, procedure for, 350–358
  floor debate, 352–354
  introducing bill, 350–351
  legislative productivity and, 355–356
  reforming Congress and, 356–358
  study by committees, 351–352
  voting methods, 354–355
Bill of attainder, 36
Bill of Rights, 37
  applying to states, 105
  defined, 35
  need for, 36–37
Bin Laden, Osama, 534–535, 544, 554, 558
Bipartisan Campaign Finance Reform Act of 2002, 252–255
Bipolar world, 558
Black, Hugo, 440
Black elected officials, increase in, 143
Blackmun, Harry, 447
Black predicament, 132–133
Blackstone, William, 107
Blair, Tony, war in Iraq and, 367
Blanket primary, 247
Block grants, 66
Blogs
  defined, 304
  as political advertising form, 301
Boehner, John, 330
Boren's Laws, 423
Bork, Robert, 449
Boroughs, defined, 58
Bourgeoisie, 10
Boy Scouts of America v. Dale, 154
Bradley, Bill, 226, 239
Brandeis, Louis, 447
Brandenburg, Clarence, 108
Braun, Carol Mosely, 335
Breyer, Stephen, 457
Brief, defined, 456
Brown, John, 534

Brown, Linda, 134–135, 137, 454, 455
Brown, Pat, personal following and, 219
Brown, Ronald H., 216
Brown, Scott, 167, 368
Brown v. Board of Education, 135–139, 463
desegregation *vs.* integration, 137–139
implementation, 135–136
rationale, 136–137
Bryan, William Jennings, 210
Buckley v. Valeo, 252, 256
Buddy system, 418
Budget, defined, 504
Budget Enforcement Act, 1990, 506
Budget resolution, 505
Bully pulpit, 379
Bureaucracy, 408–432
agency allies, 425
agency point of view, 419–420
appointment of officials, 412–413
buddy system and, 418
change in role, 413–414
congressional oversight, 425–428
constraints of, 422–424
culture and careers, 422
defined, 408
distinctiveness of American, 410–411
federal, 414–424
federal civilian employees, 415, 420
firings in, 418–419
growth of, 412–414
growth of in money, people, and rules, 416
laws of procedure, 424
pathologies of, 428–430
personal attributes, 420–421
political boss sabotage in, 421–422
proxy government, 411
recruitment and retention, 417–418
reforming, 430–432
rules of politics in, 423
service role and, 413
then *vs.* now, 408–410
Bureaucratic view, 10
Burger, Warren, 138, 447, 463
Burns, Arthur F., 502
Bush, George H. W., 234, 548
character of, 387
negative campaign of, 240
as outsider, 366
personal following and, 219, 220
popularity decline of, 382
retrospective voting and, 259
Roe v. Wade and, 149
signing statements, 386
Souter nomination by, 449
unexpected crises of, 395
valence issues and, 245
Bush, George W., 558, 588
approval/disapproval ratings of, 382
character of, 387
grant-in-aid and, 64
Guantanamo prison inmates and, 124
line-item veto and, 45
No Child Left Behind, 222
as outsider, 366, 387
personal following and, 219, 220
popularity decline of, 382
presidential primaries and, 226
signing statements, 386
unexpected crises of, 396
unified government and, 367
war in Iraq and, 367
Bush, Jeb, personal following and, 219, 220
Business regulation, 480–486
client politics, 482–484
entrepreneurial politics, 484–486
interest group politics, 482
majoritarian politics, 480–482
Busing, mandatory, 138–139

Cabinet, 390–391
defined, 390
departments, 391
Caddell, Patrick, 237
Campaigners, 192
Campaign finance rules, 250–252
Campaigns
campaign issues in, 244–246
elections and, 234–266
money and, 249–257
presidential fundraising and expenditures, 1976–2008, 236
presidential *vs.* congressional, 238–243
primary *vs.* general, 243–249
tasks performed during, 235–238
today, 235–238
Campbell, Ben Nighthorse, 335
Cannon, Joseph G., 331
Carson, Rachel, 572
Carter, Jimmy
character of, 387
unexpected crises of, 395
unified government and, 369
Categorical grants, 66–67
defined, 66
Caucus, defined, 226, 346
Chain of command, armed forces, 558
Chamberlain, Neville, 547
Chamber of Commerce, 271, 273, 274–275
Chaplinksy v. New Hampshire, 113
Chapman's Rules of Committees, 423
Character ads, 256
Charitable choice, 520
Checks and balances, Constitution, U.S., 31
Chertoff, Michael, 289
Chevron v. National Resources Defense Council, 570
Chief Justices, 441
Chinese Revolution, goal of, 20
Christian Coalition, 88
Church and state, separation of, 113–117
America comparison to other nations, 115
wall of separation, 115
Churchill, Winston, 547
Circular structure, 388
Citizens United v. Federal Election Commission, 113, 256, 288
City, defined, 58
Civic competence, defined, 86
Civic duty
defined, 86
as element of political system, 81
Civil Aeronautics Board, 487, 488
Civil disobedience, 140
Civil liberties, 100–125
church and state, 113–117
commercial and youthful speech, 112–113
crime and due process, 117–125
culture and, 102–105
First Amendment interpretation and application, 106–109
overview, 101–102
speech, 109–112
terrorism and, 122–124
then *vs.* now, 100–101
Civil rights, 130–156
affirmative action, 149–154
black predicament, 132–133
court campaigns for, 133–139
defined, 132
gays and Constitution, 154–156
key provisions of, laws, 143
laws in Congress, 139–145
overview, 131–132
then and now, 130–131
women and equal rights, 145–149
Civil society, 92–93
American civic health index, 2009, 93
defined, 92
Civil War, 6
sectionalism and, 208
Clarity, restriction on expression and, 111
Class-action suit, 454–455
defined, 454
Class consciousness, 89
Class view, defined, 10
Clay, Henry, 333
Claybrook, Joan, 485
Clayton Act, 480, 481
Clean Air Act, 566, 569, 572
Clear-and-present-danger test, 107–108
Cleavages, of two-party system, 213
Cleveland, Grover, 375
Client politics, 425, 478–479, 516, 527–528
agricultural pesticides, 572–574
business regulation and, 482–484
defined, 478
health care and, 517

social welfare and, 527–530
welfare programs, 526–527
Clinton, Bill, 317, 558
approval rating of, 382
character of, 387
impeachment and, 400
unexpected crises of, 395–396
unified government and, 369
Clinton, Hillary Rodham, 226, 388
Clinton v. Jones, 385
Closed primary, 246, 247
Closed rule, 352
Clothespin vote, 244
Cloture resolution, 353
Coalition, defined, 34
Coattails, defined, 239
Colbert, Stephen, 474
Cold War, The (Lippmann), 546
Command-and-control strategy, 575
Commentaries (Blackstone), 107
Commission on Base Realignment and Closure (BRAC), 557
Committee clearance, 427
Committee of the Whole, 352
Communalists, 193
Communist Control Act, 103
Compensatory action, 153
Competing rights and duties, 102
Competitive service, 417
Concurrent powers, 31
Concurrent resolutions, 350–351
Concurring opinion, 456
Condit, Gary, 318
Conditions of aid, 69–70
defined, 68
Confederal system of government
defined, 59
lines of power in, 53
Confederation, 59
Conference committees, 347
Confessions, 121
Confirmation rates for court of appeals nominees, 449
Conflict
as bureaucracy problem, 428
persistence of, political culture and, 82–83
rights in, 102–104
Congress, 326–358
behavior theories of members, 340–343
bill to law procedure in, 350–358
caucuses, 346
checks and balances role of, 31
courts and, 460–462
economic policy making and, 502–503
ethics rules for, 357
evolution of, 332–335
federalism and, 71–72
key facts about, 344
member characteristics, 335–340
organization of, 343–350
overview of, 326–328
versus Parliament, 329–332
partisan gains or losses in, election year, 380
partisan gains or losses in, off-year election, 383
party voting and, 345–346
pay raises for, 358
powers of, 328
Presidential victories on votes in, 382
privileges of serving in, 245
qualifications for entering, 245
reemergence of, 375–378
then *vs.* now, 328–329
Congress, civil rights laws and, 139–145
changing congressional support for, 142
crime and, 143–144
early demonstrations, 139–140
Johnson, Lyndon B. election and, 141
Kennedy, John F. assassination and, 141
key provisions of, 143
public opinion change and, 140, 141
racial profiling, 144–145
violent reactions to demonstrators and, 140–141
Congress, organization of, 343–350
House of Representatives, 343–345
legislative committees, 346–348, 349
Senate, 343
staffs and specialized offices, 348–350
Congress, reforming, 356–358
Congressional Accountability Act, 357
Congressional Budget Act, 505
Congressional Budget Office (CBO), 350, 505
Congressional campaign committee, 213
Congressional election, cost of winnning, 2002–2010, 214
Congressional ethics, rules on, 357
Congressional Government (Wilson), 371
Congressional member characteristics, 335–340
gender and race, 335–337
incumbency, 337–339
party affiliation, 339–340
Congressional oversight, 425–428
Congressional Research Service (CRS), 350
Connor, Eugene "Bull," 140
Conservative coalition, 340
Constitution, U.S., 20–45
amending, 43
challenge of creating, 27–29
checks and balances, 31
Constitutional Convention and, 25–27
democracy and, 29–32
equality and, 40–41
Framers' motives for, 39–41
gays and, 154–156
liberties and, 21–25
liberty and, 32–39
reform views on, 41–45
slavery and, 37–39
sovereignty, federalism and, 59
states and, 56
Supreme Court as arbiter of, 55
then *vs.* now, 20
women and, 42
Constitutional Convention, 6, 14, 25–27
defined, 25
Framers, 26–27
Shays's Rebellion and, 26
state constitutions and, 25–26
Constitutional court, 447
Constitutional reform, views on, 41–45
making system less democratic, 44–45
separation of powers, reducing, 41–44
Consumer Product Safety Commission (CPSC), 488
Consumer Protection Act, 283
Containment, 547
Continuity, of two-party system, 213
Corwin, Edward, 537
Cosmopolitan, 302
Cost, defined, 475
Cost overruns, 555
Council of Economic Advisers (CEA), 390, 501
Counties, defined, 58
Counts, Dorothy, 135
Court campaigns, civil rights, 133–139
Brown v. Board of Education, 135–139
Cumming v. Richmond County Board of Education, 134
equal education cases, 134–135
Plessy v. Ferguson, 133–134
separate-but-equal doctrine, 134
Swann v. Charlotte-Mecklenburg Board of Education, 138
Courts, checks and balances role of, 31
Courts of appeals, 447
Craig v. Boren, 146
Crime, civil rights laws and, 143–144
Crime and due process, 117–125
confessions and self-incrimination, 121
exclusionary rule, 118
relaxing exclusionary rule, 121–122
search and seizure, 118–121
searches without warrants, 124–125
terrorism and civil liberties, 122–124
Crisis, The, magazine, 134
Critical periods, 210
Cronkite, Walter, 314
Cultural conflicts, 104–105
Culture, civil liberties and, 102–105
Bill of Rights, applying to states, 105
cultural conflicts, 104–105
rights in conflict, 102–104
Culture war, political, 89–91
Cumming v. Richmond County Board of Education, 134
Cunningham, Randy "Duke," 356
Curtiss-Wright Export Corp. v. United States, 543

Daniels, Mitch, 390
Dean, Howard, 314
  Internet appeals of, 304
Debs, Eugene, 222
Declaration of Independence, 21
  signing of, 22
De facto segregation, defined, 137
Defense budget, 552–557
  for bases, 556–557
  for big-ticket items, 555–556
  for personnel, 554–555
  public opinion concerning, 553
  for readiness, 556
  total spending, 552–554
Defense decision making, structure of, 557–558
Defense of Marriage Act, 155
Deficit, defined, 492, 494
De jure segregation, defined, 137
Democracy, 7–8
  defined, 7
  as element of political system, 81
  political change and, 12–13
  public opinion and, 163–164
  self-interest driving, 12
Democracy, Constitution and, 29–32
  checks and balances, 31
  government and human nature aspects of, 31–32
  key principles of, 30–31
  overview of, 29–30
Department of Agriculture, 483
Department of Homeland Security (DHS), 274, 414
Deregulation, 487–488
Derthick, Martha, 487
Devolution, 70–71
Dickerson v. United States, 124
Dillon's rule, 58
Direct democracy, 7–8
  defined, 7
Direct-mail firms, campaign tasks of, 235
Director of National Intelligence (DNI), 390
Disabled persons, rights of, 152
Discharge petition, 352
Discretionary authority, 415
Discretionary spending, 506
Discrimination, Supreme Court tests to determine, 146
Disengagement, 548
Dissenting opinion, 456
District courts, 447
Diversity cases, 450
Divided government, 367–369
  defined, 355, 367
  examples, 368
  gridlock and, 368–369
  policy gridlock of, 369
Division vote, 354
Double tracking, 353
Dual federalism doctrine, 56–57
  defined, 57
Du Bois, W.E.B., 276
Due process of law, 105
Dukakis, Michael, 226
Dunlop, John, 393
Duplication, as bureaucracy problem, 428

Earmark, defined, 285, 356
Earned Income Tax Credit (EITC), 521
Economic Interpretation of the Constitution, An (Beard), 39
Economic planning, 499–500
Economic policy, 492–510
  budget, 504–505
  levying taxes, 506–510
  machinery of policy making, 500–504
  politics of economic prosperity, 495–496
  reduced spending, 505–506
  spending money, 504
  taxing and spending politics, 496–498
  then *vs.* now, 492–495
  theories and political needs, 498–500
Economic policy making, machinery of, 500–504
  components of, 501
  Congress, 502–503
  Federal Reserve System (the "Fed"), 501–502
  globalization, 503–504
Economic prosperity, politics of, 495–496
Economic system
  America compared to other nations, 86–87
  Americans' view of, 83–85
  political culture and, 83–85
Economic theories, political needs and, 498–500
  economic planning, 499–500
  Keynesianism, 498–499
  monetarism, 498
  supply-side theory, 500
Economy, vote for president and, 1948–2008, 260
Economy stimulation attempts, 499
Eisenhower, Dwight, 582
  character of, 386
Election, determining factors, 257–264
  campaign as, 260–261
  issues as, 259–260
  party as, 257–259
  prospective voting and, 259
  retrospective voting and, 259–260
  winning coalition as, 261–264
Elections
  campaigns and, 234–266
  determining factors, 257–264
  midterm, 2010 money raised and spent, 236
  money and, 249–257
  policy effects of, 264–266
  presidential *vs.* congressional, 238–243
  primary *vs.* general, 243–249
  tasks performed, 235–238
  then *vs.* now, 234
  types of, 247
Electoral college, 373, 376–377
Electronic journalism, 302–304
Elite
  defined, 10, 167
  political, 10–11
Ellison, Keith, 341
Endangered Species Act, 566
Endangered Species Act (ESA), 569
Engel v. Vitale, 118
Enhanced rescission authority, 44
Entitlements, 505
Entrepreneurial politics, 479–480
  business regulation and, 484–486
  defined, 479
  Endangered Species Act, 569
  global warming, 566, 568–569
Enumerated powers, 31
Environmental Action, 280
Environmental Defense Fund, 280, 572
Environmental impact statement (EIS), 570
Environmental laws, 568
Environmental movement, 280
Environmental policy, 564–577
  acid rain, 571–572
  agricultural pesticides, 572–574
  American context of, 574
  automobile pollution, 569–571
  vs. economic growth, 572
  environmental uncertainties, 574–577
  global warming, 566, 568–569
  results of, 577
  then *vs.* now, 564–566
Environmental Protection Agency (EPA), 566, 575
  administration of, 575–577
  costs and benefits, 576
  goals of, 576
  toxic waste cleanup, 575
Equality
  Constitution and, 40–41
  as element of political system, 81
Equality of opportunity, 149–154
  defined, 150
  quota systems, 151–153
  reverse discrimination and, 149
Equality of results, 149
Equal protection of the laws, 105
Equal time rule, 309
Era of reform, 208–209
Espionage and Sedition Acts, 103
Establishment clause, 114–117
  defined, 114
Ethics in Government Act, 289
Ethnicity, public opinion and, 172–173
Everson v. Board of Education, 118
Exclusionary rule, 118
  relaxing, 121–122
Executive privilege, 384–385

Exit polls, 165
2010 Congressional results, 254
Ex parte McCardle, 444
Ex post facto law, 36

Faction, defined, 32
Factional parties, 222
Fairshare formulas, 65
Farber, Myron, 308
Farmers' Union, 271
Feature stories, 311
FEC v. Wisconsin Right to Life, 113
Federal aid, federal control and, 68–70
conditions of aid and, 69–70
mandates, 68–69
Federal civilian employees, 415
characteristics of, 420
Federal Communications Commission (FCC), 300, 305, 308, 484, 487, 488
Federal courts
development, 441–446
jurisdiction, 450–452
power, 457–460
structure, 446–450
Federal Election Commission v. Wisconsin Right to Life, Inc., 256
Federal Elections Commission (FEC), 282
Federal Emergency Management Agency (FEMA), 61, 411
Federal government, mistrust of, 91–93
Federal grants. *See* Grants-in-aid
Federalism, 50–72
American-style, *vs.* other nations, 60
Congress and, 71–72
defined, 30, 52
devolution and, 70–71
federal aid and control with, 68–70
federal-state relations and, 63–68
goal of, 52–54
government structure, 59–63
importance of, 51–52
meaning, debate of, 55–59
political activity, increased and, 62–63
sovereignty, and Constitution, 59
states' role in, 63
then *vs.* now, 50–51
Federalism, goal of, 52–54
language used and, 54
lines of power and, 53–54
Federalism, meaning of, 55–59
dual federalism doctrine and, 56–57
nullification and, 55–56
state sovereignty and, 57–59
Supreme Court, 55
Federalist
defined, 32
founding of, 206
Federalist papers, 25, 34–35
Federal-question cases, 450
Federal regime, defined, 59
Federal Regulation of Lobbying Act, 291
Federal Reserve Bank, 498
Federal Reserve Board, 499
Federal Reserve System (the "Fed")
economic policy making and, 501–502
monetary policy and, 502
Federal revenues/outlays 2010, 506
Federal spending, reducing, 505–506
Federal-state relations, 63–68
categorical grants, 66–67
grants-in-aid, 63–65
intergovernmental body, 66
landmark cases, 58
national needs, 65–66
rivalry among states, 67–68
Federal system of government
defined, 59
lines of power in, 53
Federal Trade Commission (FTC), 422, 481
Federal Trade Commission Act, 480
Federation of Business and Professional Women, 281
Fee shifting, 453
Feminine Mystique, The (Friedan), 145
Feminist movement, 280–281
Filibuster, 335
Fingerprinting, 6
Firing, bureaucrat, 418–419
First Amendment interpretation and application, 106–109
establishment clause, 114–117
free-exercise clause, 113–114
separation of church and state, 113–117
speech and national security, 107–109
First Great Awakening, 87
Fiscal policy, 503
Fiscal year, 504
Fish and Wildlife Service, 569
527 organizations, 255–256
Flowers, Gennifer, 317
Food and Drug Administration (FDA), 485–486, 488
Food Stamps, 521
Ford, Gerald, character of, 387
Foreign Affairs, 546
Foreign and military policy, 534–561
cleavages among elites, 546–549
constitutional and legal context, 537–542
defense budget, 552–557
defense decision-making structure, 557–558
kinds of, 536–537
machinery of, 542–543
party affiliation and, 549
presidency and, 537–538
public opinion and, 543–546
shifting patterns of leadership in, 538
terrorism, 558, 560–561
then *vs.* now, 534–536
use of military force, 550–551
Foreign Intelligence Surveillance Act (FISA), 535
Foreign policy, kinds of, 536–537
Foreign policy crises, reactions to, 544
Foreign policy elites, cleavages among, 546–549
polarization and, 549
worldviews and, 546–549
Formal authority, 5–6
Fourteenth Amendment, 133–139. *See also* Court campaigns, civil rights
Framers, Constitution, 9–10, 26–27
economic interests, 39
equality, 40–41
motives of, 39–41
Franken, Al, 368
Franking privilege, 356–357
Fraternal Order of the Police, 102
Freedom-of-choice plan, 137
Freedom of expression, 106, 107
restrictions on, constitutionally permissible, 111
Freedom of Information Act, 423
Freedom of religion, 106, 107
Free-exercise clause, 113–114
defined, 113
French Revolution, goal of, 20
Freneau, Philip, 300
Friedan, Betty, 145
Friedman, Milton, 498, 501
Frontrunners, nomination and, 244

Gaddafi, Muammar, 541
Gaines, Lloyd, 134
Galbraith, John Kenneth, 499, 501
Gang of Fourteen, 449
Garrity, W. Arthur, 138
Gatekeeper, national media as, 306
Gay rights
Constitution and, 154–156
landmark cases, 154
same-sex marriages and, 155
Gazette of the United States, 300
Gender, of Congressional members, 335–337
Gender gap
defined, 170
in partisan identification, 170
political socialization and, 170
General Accountability Office (GAO), 350, 414
General-act charter, 58
General election, defined, 246, 247
Gerrymandering, 241
Gibbons v. Ogden, 58
Gideon, Clarence Earl, 451, 452
Gideon v. Wainwright, 124
Giffords, Gabrielle Dee "Gabby," 336, 337
Gingrich, Newt, 348
Ginsburg, Ruth Bader, 457
Gitlow v. New York, 107
Globalization
defined, 503
economic policy making and, 503–504

Global warming, 566, 568–569
defined, 566
Gold plating, 555
Goldwater, Barry, 225, 226
Gonzales v. Carhart, 148
Good faith exception, defined, 122
Gore, Al, 226
Government
activist, consequences of, 587–590
economy and, 442–444
influence of, 4–5
influence of ideas, 591–593
influence of structure, 590–591
New System, 585–587
Old System, 584–585
political liberty and, 444–445
relaxing restraints on, 583–584
restraints on growth of, 582–583
Government, media and, 314–320
constraints on journalists, 318–319
coverage of Congress, 314–315
leaks in, 316–317
prominence of president, 314
sensationalism in, 317–318
Government action, scope of legitimate, 472
Government by proxy, 411
Government Printing Office, 301
Government structure, federalism and, 59–63
effects of, 62–63
overview, 59–62
public trust in, 61
states' roles in, 63
Gramm, Phil, 505
Gramm-Rudman Act, 505–506
Grandfather clause, 188
Grange, the, 480, 481
Grant, Ulysses S., term limits and, 373
Grants-in-aid
cash, 64
changing purpose of, 65
defined, 63
economic reasons for, 64
federal-state relations and, 63–65
land, 63–64
Grassroots lobbying, 285
Gratz v. Bollinger, 154
Great Compromise, 29
Greenspan, Alan, 502
Green v. County School Board of New Kent County, 139
Gridlock, defined, 368
Griswold v. Connecticut, 148
Gross domestic product (GDP), 493, 494
Social Security and Medicare cost percentages, 506
Groups, policymaking and, 472–473
Grutter v. Bollinger, 154

Habeas corpus, 36
Haddon, William, Jr., 485
Hagen, Michael Gray, 84
Haig, Alexander, 392
Hamdi v. Rumsfeld, 124, 543
Hamilton, Alexander, 6, 22, 26, 366
executive power and, 372
Gazette of the United States, 300
judicial review and, 441
party press of, 300
Hannity, Sean, 310
Harding, Warren G., 250
Harper's, 302
Harrison, Benjamin, 248
Harrison, William H., 375
Hart, Gary, 307, 317
Hatch Act, 217
Hayward, Tony, 349
Health care, politics of, 517
Hearst, William Randolph, 302
Helvering v. Davis, 514, 516
Hill, Anita, 449
Hispanics, in Congress, 335–336
Hobbes, Thomas, 9
Holmes, Oliver Wendell, 447
Home-rule charter, 58
Horse-race journalism, 309–310
House of Representatives, 343–345
state representation changes in, 242
Human rights, 548
Humphrey, Hubert, 222–223, 226
personal following and, 219
Hunt, James B., 215
Hunt Commission, 215
Hunter, James Davison, 90–91
Huntington, Samuel P., 82
Hussein, Saddam, 551
Hyde, Henry, 148

Ideas
influence of, 591–593
limits of, 488
Ideological interest groups, 277
Ideological party, 218
unified government and, 369
Ideological typology, 174, 175
Immigrants, U.S. citizenship and, 150
Imminent danger, restriction on expression and, 111
Impeachment, 400–401
defined, 400
Imperialism, as bureaucracy problem, 428, 429
Incentive, 276
Income strategy, 528
Income tax, rise of federal, 507–510
percentage rates,1913-2010, 508
Incumbency
Congress, 337–339
House and Senate, 338
Incumbent, 238
Independent expenditures, 252
Indiana ballot, 212
Individual responsibility, as element of political system, 81
Inevitable discovery, defined, 122
In forma pauperis, 452–453
Initiative, defined, 63, 209
Insider stories, 311
Insider strategy, explained, 285
Institutional interests, 274–275
Institutions, policymaking and, 473–474
Insurance program, 522
Interest group activities, 283–291
earmarks, 285
information, supplying credible, 284–285
political action committees, 286–289
public support, 285–286
Interest group politics, 477–478
acid rain, 571–572
business regulation and, 482
defined, 477
health care and, 517
Interest groups, 270–293
America *vs.* Great Britain and Germany, 272
birth of, 273–274
civil disobedience, 290–291
conflicts of interest, 289
defined, 270, 272
incentives to join, 276–279
institutional interests, 274–275
membership interests, 275–276
organization types, 274–280
regulating, 291–293
revolving door, 289–290
social movements and, 280–283
staff influence of, 280
then *vs.* now, 270–272
upper-class bias of, 282–283
Intergovernmental body, 66
Intergovernmental Panel on Climate Change (IPCC), 568
Intermediate scrutiny, sexual discrimination and, 145
Internal Security Act, 103
Internet, 304–305
Interstate commerce, 57
Interstate Commerce Commission (ICC), 413, 444, 487, 488
Intrastate commerce, 57
Investigative reporting, 302
Iraq war, 551
Iron triangle, 425
Isolationism, 547
Issue network, 425

Jackson, Andrew, 207, 300, 374–375
Jackson, Jesse, 226
Jacksonians, 207–208, 374–375
Jacobson, Gary, 257
Jefferson, Thomas, 6, 366
Barbary Pirates and, 534
Declaration of Independence and, 22–23
party press of, 300
slave trade clause, 37
Jeffords, James, 367
Johnson, Andrew, impeachment and, 400

Johnson, Lyndon B., 141, 314, 374, 587
character of, 386–387
congressional majority and, 367
Great Society legislation, 593
unexpected crises of, 395
unified government and, 369
Joint Chiefs of Staff (JCS), 557–558
Joint committees, 347
Joint resolutions, 351
Jones, Paula, 147, 317, 385
Jordan, Hamilton, 389
Judges, selecting, 447–448
Judicial restraint approach, 440
Judicial review, 440
in Canada and Europe, 460
defined, 30
Judiciary, 438–463
checks on power of, 460–463
federal courts development, 441–446
federal courts jurisdiction, 450–452
federal courts power, 457–460
federal courts structure, 446–450
female and minority appointments, 448
getting cases to court, 452–455
judicial review, 440
Supreme Court in action, 455–457
then *vs.* now, 438–440
Jungle, The (Sinclair), 485
Justices, by seniority, 455

Kagan, Elena, 457
Kamarck, Elaine, 388
Karzai, Hamid, 7
Katzenbach, Nicholas, 137
Kefauver, Estes, 314, 315, 484
Kelo v. City of New London, 51
Kennan, George F., 546
Kennedy, Anthony, 457
Kennedy, Edward M., personal following and, 219
Kennedy, John F., 141, 250, 374
character of, 386
personal following and, 219
unexpected crises of, 395
Kennedy, Joseph P., II, personal following and, 219
Kennedy, Robert, personal following and, 219
Kerry, John, Internet appeals of, 304
Kettl, Donald F., 411, 590
Keynes, John Maynard, 498, 501
Keynesianism, 498–499
Kinder, Donald, 84
King, Martin Luther, Jr., 131, 139, 141, 142, 317
Kissinger, Henry, 393, 542
Klein, Joe, 237
Klingberg, Frank L., 547
Knox, Henry, 366
Korematsu v. United States, 543
Ku Klux Klan (KKK), 534
Kyoto Protocol, 566, 576

Label, as political arena, 204
Laffer, Arthur, 500, 501
La Follette, Robert, personal following and, 220
Laissez-faire, 413
Land grants, 63–64
Laski, Harold, 61
Lawrence v. Texas, 154, 155
Leadership PAC, 286
League of Women Voters, 281
Least-restrictive means, restriction on expression and, 111
Lee v. Weisman, 118
Legal immigration, annual, 1850–2010, 104
Legislative committees, 346–348
America *vs.* other nations, 355
productivity of, 355–356
Legislative court, 447
Legislative veto, 397, 427
Legitimacy, defined, 6
Lemon v. Kurtzman, 118
Lewinsky, Monica, 317
Libel, defined, 109
Libel tourism, 109
Liberal majority, 310–311
Liberties, American colonists and, 21–25
Articles of Confederation and, 24–25
colonial mind and, 22–23
revolutionary ideas of, 23
Liberty, as element of political system, 81
Liberty, Constitution and, 32–39
Antifederalists' view of, 33–36
Bill of Rights and, 36–37
Federalist papers and, 34–35
overview of, 32–33
slavery and, 37–39
Limbaugh, Rush, 310
Lincoln, Abraham, 373
Line-item veto, 44, 384
Lines of power, 53–54
Lippmann, Walter, 546
Literacy test, 188
Litmus test, 448–450
defined, 449
importance of, 449
Liuzzo, Viola, 141
Loaded language, 312, 313
Lobbying expenditures, 275
Lobbyist, defined, 272. *See also* Interest groups
Local governance terms, 58
Lochner v. New York, 500
Locke, John, 9
Logrolling, 478
Long, Huey, 522
Lynchings, 132

MacArthur, Douglas, 549
Magazines, of opinion, 302
Magnuson, Warren, 485
Majoritarian politics, 10, 476–477, 516, 527
automobile pollution, 569–571
business regulation and, 480–482
defined, 476
education programs, 528
health care and, 517
high costs and, 570–571
low cost and, 570
social welfare and, 527–530
welfare programs, 521–526
Majority leader, 343
Malapportionment, 241
Mandates, 68–69
defined, 68
Mansbridge, Jane, 281
Mapp v. Ohio, 124
Marbury v. Madison, 441, 443, 444
March on Washington, 140–141
Marginal districts, 338
Market, defined, 309
Marshall, John, 55, 441–442, 462
Marshall, Thurgood, 463
Martin v. Hunter's Lessee, 444
Marx, Karl, 10
Mason, George, 6
Massachusetts ballot, 212
Massachusetts v. Environmental Protection Agency, 570
Material incentives, 276
Mayer, William G., 311
Mayhew, David, 220, 368
McCain, John, 226, 237
earmarks and, 356
environmental politics of, 564
McCarthy, Joseph, 83, 103
McClure's, 302
McConnell v. Federal Election Commission, 253, 255, 256
McCorvey, Norma, 149
McCulloch v. Maryland, 55, 441, 444
McDonald v. Chicago, 107
McGovern, George, 215
McKinley, William, 210
McLaurin, George, 134
McNamara, Robert S., 385
Means test, 516, 522
Meat Inspection Act, 485
Media, 298–320
bias of national, 310–314
campaigning and, 309–310
confidentiality of sources, 307–308
government and, 314–320
influence of, 313–314
journalism in American political history, 300–305
neutral or objective, 311–313
policymaking and, 474
politics and, 299–300
regulating broadcasting, 308–309
rules governing, 307–310
structure of, 305–307
then *vs.* now, 298–299

Media, government and, 314–320
    constraints on journalists, 318–319
    coverage of Congress, 314–315
    leaks in, 316–317
    prominence of president, 314
    sensationalism in, 317–318
Media consultants, campaign tasks of, 235
Media structure, 305–307
    competition and, 305–306
    national media, 306–307
Medicaid, 521, 587
Medicare, 515, 517, 521, 523–526, 587
Membership interest groups, 275–276
Meskimen's Law, 423
Miami Herald v. Tornillo, 309
Mikulski, Barbara, 215, 218
Military-industrial complex, 551
Military policy. *See* Foreign and military policy
Miller, G. William, 502
Miller, Judith, 308
Miller v. California, 113
Milosevic, Slobodan, 548
Minority leader, 343
Minor parties, 222–225
    factional parties, 222
    impact of, 224
    Socialist party, 222
    types of, 223
Miranda, Ernesto A., 121
Miranda v. Arizona, 124
Miranda warning, 121, 123
Moe, Terry M., 165
Monetarism, 498
Monetary policy, 502
Money, campaign, 240, 249–257
    Bipartisan Campaign Finance Reform Act of 2002, 252–255
    campaign finance rules, 250–252
    527 organizations, 255–256
    landmark cases, 256
    sources of, 249–250
    winning and, 256–257
Moral Majority, 88
Motor-voter law, 186
Moynihan, Daniel Patrick, 393, 473
Mugwumps, 208
Muller v. Oregon, 500
Municipal corporation, 58
Municipality, 58
Murkowski, Lisa, 238
Murphy's Law, 423
Muskie, Edmund, 484–485
Myrdal, Gunnar, 82

Nader, Ralph, 203, 278, 479, 485, 586–587
    third-party movement of, 225
Name-request job, 418
Narrowly concentrated costs and benefits, 476
Nation, 302
National Abortion Rights Action League (NARAL), 281
National Association for the Advancement of Colored People (NAACP), 134–135, 271, 276
National Association of Counties, 274
National Association of Manufacturers, 271
National Catholic Welfare Conference, 271
National chair, defined, 213
National committee, defined, 213
National conventions, 214–216
    apportioning delegates, 215
    commissions rules for, 215–216
    defined, 213
    time and place selection, 214
National debt, 492, 494
National Environmental Policy Act (NEPA), 423, 570
National Federation of Republican Women, 281
National Gazette, 300
National Highway Traffic Safety Administration, 485
National Independent Retail Jewelers, 274
National Intelligencer, 300
National Labor Relations Board (NLRB), 482
National media, 306–307
    bias of, 310–314
    as gatekeeper, 306
    as scorekeeper, 306
    as watchdog, 307
National Oceanic and Atmospheric Administration, 569
National Organization for Women (NOW), 281
National Performance Review (NPR), 430–432
National Rifle Association (NRA), 276, 279
National Science Foundation (NSF), 568
National supremacy and slavery, 441–442
National Wildlife Federation, 280
National Women's Political Caucus, 281
Near v. Minnesota, 111, 309
"Necessary and proper" clause, 55
Neustadt, Richard, 378, 392
Neutrality, restriction on expression and, 111
New Deal, 6, 586
New Jersey plan, 28–29
Newspaper, how to read, 312
New System, 585–587
    vs. Old System, 585–586
New York Times v. Sullivan, 113, 309
Nie, Norman, 192
Nivola, Pietro, 484
Nixon, Richard, 250
    character of, 387
    unexpected crises of, 395
Nixon v. Fitzgerald, 385
Nomenklatura, 175
Noncareer executive assignments (NEAs), 417
Nongovernmental International Panel on Climate Change (NIPCC), 568
Nonvoting, 184–187
    calculating voter turnout, 184–185
    voter registration/turnout by age, 185
Norm, defined, 176
North, Oliver, 542
North America, 1787 map of, 24
North American Free Trade Agreement (NAFTA), 503
North Atlantic Treaty Organization (NATO), 541
Nullification, 55–56
    defined, 56

Obama, Barack, 226, 310, 588–589
    approval ratings of, 382
    character of, 387–388
    earmarks and, 356
    environmental politics of, 564, 565
    unexpected crises of, 396
    unified government of, 367
Obscenity, 109–111
Occupational Safety and Health Act, 482
Occupational Safety and Health Administration (OSHA), 482
Office-bloc ballot, 212
Office of Management and Budget (OMB), 390, 501
Office of Personnel Management (OPM), 390, 417
Office of the Director of National Intelligence (DNI), 542
Office of the U.S. Trade Representative, 390
Old Age, Survivors, and Disability Insurance (OASDI), 521
Old System, 584–585
    vs. New System, 585–586
Open Meeting Law, 423
Open primary, defined, 246, 247
Open rule, 352
Opinion of the Court, 456
Opinion-policy congruence, 166
Opinion saliency, 166
Opinion stability, 166
Ordinances, defined, 58
O'Reilly Factor, 310
Organization, as political arena, 204
Organizational view, of Congress members, 341–342
Orren, Gary, 86–87
Orthodox, defined, 90
Orzag, Peter, 390
O'Toole's Corollary to Murphy's Law, 423
Outsider strategy, explained, 285

Palin, Sarah, 249
Palko v. Connecticut, 107
Palmer, A. Mitchell, 103

Panetta, Leon E., 388
Parents v. Seattle School District, 154
Parishes, defined, 58
Parkinson's First Law, 423
Parkinson's Second Law, 423
Parks, Rosa, 139
Parliament, *versus* Congress, 329–332
Parliamentary systems, 370
Parochial participants, 193
Participatory democracy, 7
Partisan polarization, defined, 328
Party-column ballot, 212
Party convention, founding of, 207–208
Party delegates, characteristics of, 216
Party press, 300
Party vote, 345
Patient Protection and Affordable Care Act, 2010, 516
Patriotism, by race and ethnicity, 83
Peckham, Rufus, 440
Pelosi, Nancy, 286, 330, 336
Pentagon terrorist attacks, 8
Per curiam opinion, 456
Perkins, Frances, 394
Perot, Ross
  third-party movement of, 225
  two-party system and, 222
Personal following, 219–220
  defined, 219
Personnel, defense budget spending and, 554–555
Peter Principle, 423
Petraeus, David, 561
Pierce v. Society of Sisters, 118
Plaintiff, 453
Planned Parenthood v. Casey, 148
Plessy, Adolph, 134
Plessy v. Ferguson, 133–134, 139
Plunkitt, George Washington, 217
Pluralist view, 11
Plurality system, 220
Pocket veto, 383
Poindexter, John, 542
Polarization, 549
Police powers, defined, 59, 148
Policy entrepreneurs, 479
  health care and, 517
Policymaking process, 470–488
  business regulation, 480–486
  client politics, 478–479
  decision making, 475–476
  entrepreneurial politics, 479–480
  groups and, 472–473
  institutions and, 473–474
  interest group politics, 477–478
  majoritarian politics, 476–477
  media and, 474
  perceptions, beliefs, interests, and values, 486–488
  setting agenda, 471–475
  state governments actions and, 474–475
  then *vs.* now, 470
Polis, 7
Political action committee (PAC), 240
  contributors, 287
  contributors to candidates, 2009–2010, 255
  defined, 272
  growth of, 1979–2010, 251
  money and, 286–289
Political agenda, 471, 472
Political cue, 284
Political culture, 78–85
  America comparison with other nations, 85–88
  civic role of religion, 87–88
  civil society, 92–93
  culture war, 89–91
  defined, 80
  economic system, 83–85
  Hispanics and American, 84
  mistrust of government, 91–93
  overview of, 79–81
  persistence of conflict, 82–83
  political system, 81–82
  political tolerance, 93–94
  sources of, 88–91
  then *vs.* now, 78–79
Political elites, 175–178
  Congress and, 176
  consistency in, 176
  defined, 175
  norms and, 176, 178
  public opinion and public policy, 176–178
Political ideology
  defined, 173
  liberal and conservative elites, 174–176
  public opinion and, 173–176
  typology of, 174
Political machine, 217–218
  defined, 217
Political opinion, of delegates and voters, 2008, 229
Political participation, 182–196
  American electorate, rise of, 187–192
  causes and meaning of, 193–196
  defined, 182, 184
  forms of, 192–193
  here and abroad, 194
  nonvoting, 184–187
  participants of, 192–196
  then and now, 182–184
Political parties, 202–229
  American and abroad, 204–206
  defined, 204
  identification, 1952–2008, 205
  minor parties, 222–225
  national party structure today, 212–216
  number of, in national legislatures, 206
  presidential nominations by, 225–226
  rise and decline of, 206–212
  state and local, 216–220
  then and now, 202–204
  two-party system, 220–222
  versus voters, 229
Political party, rise and decline of, 206–212
  Civil War and sectionalism, 208
  era of reform, 208–209
  founding, 206–207
  Jacksonians, 207–208
  party decline, 211–212
  party realignments, 209–211
Political party realignments, 209–211
Political party structure, national, 212–216
  national conventions, 214–216
  overview, 212–214
Political polarization, 549
Political power, 5–7
  distribution of, 10–11
Political question, 458
Political socialization, 166, 167–170
  gender gap and, 170
  genetic background and, 167–169
  religion and, 169
Political system
  America compared to other nations, 85–86
  elements of, 81
  political culture and, 81–82
Political technology firms, campaign tasks of, 235
Political tolerance, 93–94
Politics
  client, 478–479, 482–484
  entrepreneurial, 479–480, 484–486
  existence of, 4
  interest group, 477–478, 482
  majoritarian, 476–477, 480–482
  media and, 299–300
  nature of, 13–14
  rules of, 592
Politics of Deregulation, The (Derthick and Quirk), 487
Polk, James, 375
Poll, defined, 165
Polling, 165–166
Polling firms, campaign tasks of, 235
Poll tax, 188
Popular press, 300–302
Popular vote, percentage of by group in presidential elections, 1960–2008, 258–259
Pork-barrel legislation, 356, 478
Position issue, 244
Power, defined, 5
Power, of federal courts, 457–460
  legislation and, 459–460
  to make policy, 457–459
  views of judicial activism, 459
Power, political, 5–7
Power elite view
  defined, 10
  descriptions of, 10–11
Preferential treatment, 153

Preferred position, restriction on expression and, 111
Presidencial vetos, 384
Presidency
Cabinet of, 367, 390–391
checks on power of, 539–542
divided government, 367–369
electoral college, 373, 376–377
evolution of, 372–378
executive privilege of, 384–385
on foreign policy, 537–538
Founders' concerns, 372–373
founding presidents, 373–374
impeachment of, 400–401
impoundment of funds, 385–386
independent agencies, commissions, and judgeships, 391–392
Jacksonians, 374–375
persuasive power of, 378–383
popularity and influence of, 380–382
programs of, 394–398
reemergence of Congress and, 375–378
signing statements, 386
succession problems, 399–400
term of office, 373
then *vs.* now, 364
three audiences of, 378–379
transition of, 398–401
veto power of, 383–386
White House office, 388–390
Presidential appointments, 417
Presidential nominations, 225–226
primary voting and, 226
Presidential Power (Neustadt), 378
Presidential powers, 370–372
of President alone, 370–371
shared with Congress as whole, 371–372
shared with Senate, 371
Presidential prospects, 239
Presidential systems, 370
Presidential transition, 398–401
impeachment and, 400–401
succession problems, 399–400
vice president and, 398–399
Presidential *vs.* congressional campaigns, 238–243
Congress elections, 241–242
differences in, 238–239
money and, 240
organization, 240
remaining in office, 243
running for president, 239–240
strategy and themes, 240–241
winning primary, 242–243
President(s)
agency appointments of, 393
appointments made by, 392–393
character of, 386–388
checks and balances role of, 31
congressional majority and, 367
evaluating power of, 539
executive office of, 390
office of, 388–392
as outsiders, 366
popularity, 380, 381
popularity decline of, 382–383
powers of, 370–372, 401
Prime Ministers and, 366–367
public opinion supporting, 544–545
qualifications and benefits of, 371
victories on votes in Congress, 382
at war, 367
President's program, 394–398
assembling, 394–396
reorganizing attempts, 397–398
unexpected crises and, 395–396
Press freedom rankings, 315–316
Primary election, defined, 246, 247
Primary *vs.* general campaigns, 243–249
campaign issues, 244–246
debates, 247–248
direct-mail campaigning, 249
frontrunners in, 244
television, 246–249
Prime Ministers
cabinet members of, 367
majority in parliament and, 367
Presidents and, 366–367
at war, 367
Prior restraint, 107
Prior restraint, restriction on expression and, 111
Privacy, sex and, 148–149
Privacy Act, 423
Probable cause, defined, 119
Process regulation, 488
Progressive, defined, 90
Progressives, 208
Proletariat, 10
Prospective voting, 259
Public-interest law firms, 277
Public-interest lobby, 278
Public Interest Research Groups (PIRGs), 278
Public opinion, 162–178
cleavages in, 170–173
courts and, 462–463
defined, 162, 164–167
democracy and, 163–164
differences, 166–167
foreign policy and, 543–546
mass v. elite, 545–546
political elites, public policy and, 176–178
political ideology, 173–176
political socialization, 167–170
polling, 165–166
race and ethnicity, 172–173
region influencing, 173
social class and, 171–172
then *vs.* now, 162–163
Public policy, election effects on, 264–266
Public-Private Investment Program, 499
Public safety exception, defined, 122
Pulitzer, Joseph, 302
Pure Food and Drug Act, 484
Purposive incentive, 277
Putnam, Robert, 93
Pyramid structure, 388

Quirk, Paul, 487
Quorum, 352
Quota systems, 151–153

Race
of Congressional members, 335–337
public opinion and, 172–173
Racial profiling, 144–145
Randolph, Edmund, 366, 372
Random sample, 165
Rasul v. Bush, 124, 543
Ratification of Federal Constitution by state, map of, 33
Ratings, of legislators, 284
Rayburn, Sam, 331
Readiness, defense budget spending and, 556
Reagan, Ronald, 588
character of, 387
tax cuts of, 13
unexpected crises of, 395
Realignment periods, 210
Realignments, of political parties, 209–211
kinds of, 210
Reasonableness standard, sexual discrimination and, 145
Recall, defined, 63
Recession, causes of, 497–498
Red tape, 428, 430
Reed, Thomas B., 331
Reed v. Reed, 146
Referendum, defined, 63, 209
Reform era, 208–209
Regents of the University of California v. Bakke, 154
Region, public opinion influence by, 173
Registered voters, 184
Rehnquist, William, 449
Reid, Harry, 577
Religion
America compared to other nations, 87–88
political socialization and, 169
Remedy, 458
Reno v. ACLU, 113
Representational view, of Congress members, 341
Representative democracy, 8–10
defined, 7, 10
Republic, defined, 30
Republicans, founding of, 206
Research frontiers
candidate positions drive voter choices, 263
church and state debate, 40
guns as public nuisance, 144
Hispanics and American political culture, 84

"in your face" television and political tolerance, 106
new political party in United States, 224
political behavior, explaining, 11
powerful interest groups, 279
Presidential communication skills, 379
public trust in Federal government, 61
religion and voter participation, 195
2008 presidential primary polling, 166
White House blog and e-mail, 319–320
Reserved powers, 31
Restrictive rule, 352
Retrospective voting, 259–260
Reverse discrimination, defined, 149
Ribicoff, Abraham, 485
Rice, Condoleezza, 394
Rice, Donna, 307
Richmond v. Croson, 154
Riders, 353
Riker, William H., 61–62
Roberts, John, 457
Roberts, Owen, 445
Roberts, Paul Craig, 500
Robertson, Pat, 226
Robertson's Rule, 423
Roe v. Wade, 148–149
Roll-call vote, 354
Roosevelt, Franklin, 6, 314, 317, 481, 586
congressional majority and, 367
term limits and, 373
unified government and, 369
Roosevelt, Theodore, 314
welfare program and, 520
Rostker v. Goldberg, 146, 147
Routine stories, 311
Rove, Karl, 286
Rubio, Marco, 172
Rudman, Warren, 505
Rumsfeld, Donald, 392
Runoff primary, 247
Russian Revolution, goal of, 20
Ryan, Paul, 336

Safe districts, 338
Same-sex marriages, 155
Sampling error, 165
Santa Fe Independent School District v. Doe, 118
Scalia, Antonin, 457
Scalise, Steve, 349
Schedule C appointments, 417
Schenck v. United States, 113
Schlesinger, Arthur M., Jr., 539
Schumpeter, Joseph, 7–8
Scorekeeper, national media as, 306
Scott v. Sanford, 139
Scribner's, 302
Search and seizure, 118–121
Searches without warrants, 124–125
Search warrant, defined, 119
Sears, David, 84
Securities and Exchange Act, 485
Securities and Exchange Commission (SEC), 488
Sedition Act, 103, 107
Segregation, 137–138. *See also Brown v. Board of Education;* Court campaigns, civil rights
Select committees, 347
Selective attention, 313
Selective incorporation, 105
Self-incrimination, 121
Self-interest, democracy driven by, 12
Semi-presidential systems, 370
Senate, 343
Senatorial courtesy, 448
Seneca Falls Convention, 145
Separate-but-equal doctrine, 134
schools and, 134–135
Separation of powers, 32
reducing, 41–44
September 11 terrorist attacks, 8, 12, 64, 92, 122, 318, 362, 382, 387, 396, 397, 414
Sequester, defined, 506
Service Employees International Union, 277
Service strategy, 528
Set of leaders, as political arena, 204
Sexual discrimination examples, illegal, 146–147
Sexual distinctions, legal, 147–149
Sexual harassment, 147–148
Shalala, Donna E., 388
Sharon, Ariel, 307
Shays, Daniel, 26
Shays's Rebellion, 26
Sherman, John, 480
Sherman Act, 480
Shultz, George, 542
Sierra Club, 276, 280
Signing statement, 386
Silent Spring (Carson), 572
Simple resolutions, 350
Sinclair, Upton, 485
Sipuel, Ada Lois, 134
Slavery, 13
Constitution and, 37–39
national supremacy and, 441–442
Smith, Samuel Harrison, 300
Smith Act, 103
Smith's Principle, 423
Smith v. Allwright, 188
Sniderman, Paul M., 84
Social class, public opinion and, 171–172
Socialist party, 222
Social movements
defined, 280
environmental movement, 280
feminist movement, 280–281
interest groups and, 280–283
union movement, 281–282
Social Security, 515, 517, 523–526
Social welfare, 514–530
majoritarian *vs.* client politics, 527–530
programs of, 516–518
then *vs.* now, 514–516
in United States, 518–527
Soft money, 214, 252
Solidary incentives, 219, 276
Sophomore surge, 242–243
Sotomayor, Sonia, 450, 457
Sound bite, 303
Souter, David, 449
South Dakota v. Dole, 516
Sovereign immunity, 454
Sovereignty, defined, 59
Speaker, 343
Speakers of the House, 330–331
Special-act charter, 58
Speech
commercial and youthful, 112–113
libel, 109
national security and, 107–109
obscenity, 109–111
symbolic, 111–112
Speechwriters, power of, 5
Split ticket voting, 211–212
Sponsored party, 219
Spots, defined, 246
Standing, defined, 453
Standing committees, 347
of House, 349
of Senate, 347
Standing vote, 354
Stare decisis, 457
State and local political parties, 216–220
ideological party, 218
personal following, 219–220
political machine, 217–218
solidary groups, 218–219
sponsored parties, 219
State constitutions, 25–26
State governments, policymaking and, 474–475
State sovereignty, 57–59
revival of, 445–446
Steffens, Lincoln, 302
Stern, Andy, 277
Stevenson, Adlai, 226, 314
Stewart, Jon, 474
Stimulus Bill, 2008, 499
Straight ticket voting, 211
Strict scrutiny
affirmative action and, 153
sexual discrimination and, 145–146
Structure, influence of, 590–591
Succession, problems with, 399–400
Superdelegates, 215
Superfund program, 479–480, 575
Super PAC, 286
Supplemental Nutrition Assistance Program (SNAP), 521
Supplemental Security Income (SSI), 521
Supply-side theory, 500

Supreme Court, as Constitution arbiter, 55
Swann v. Charlotte-Mecklenburg Board of Education, 138, 139
Sweatt, Heman, 134
Symbolic speech, 111–112
  defined, 111

Taft, William Howard, 273, 374
Taney, Roger B., 442
Taxes, levying, 506–510
  America compared to other nations, 507
  politics of, 506–507
  rise of federal income tax, 507–510
Taxing and spending, politics of, 496–498
Taylor, Zachary, 375
Telecommunications Act, 308–309
Teller vote, 354
Temporary Assistance for Needy Families (TANF), 71, 521, 527, 528
Terrorism, 558, 560–561
  civil liberties and, 122–124
  democracy fighting against, 8
  paradoxes of fighting, 560
Texas v. Johnson, 113
Think tanks, as public-interest organizations, 278
Third parties, 222
Third World, explained, 551
Thomas, Clarence, 440, 457
Thurmond, J. Strom, 222
Time magazine, 307
Tinker v. Des Moines, 113
Tocqueville, Alexis de, 12, 80, 81, 473
Transportation Security Administration (TSA), 274
Trial balloon, 312, 313
Troubled Asset Relief Program, 499
Truman, David B., 60
Truman, Harry, 222, 226
Trumbull, John, 22
Trust funds, 426–427
Trusts, 480
Two-party system, 220–222
  cleavages and continuity of, 213
Tyler, John, 398

Unalienable, defined, 23
Unemployment Insurance (UI), 521
Unexpected crises of Presidents, 395–396
Unified government, 356, 367
Union Electric Co. v. Environmental Protection Agency, 570
Union movement, 281–282
Unipolar world, 558
Unitary system of government
  defined, 59
  lines of power in, 53
United Press International, 306
United States
  Constitution, 6
  foreigners entering, 6
  military forces before/after Soviet Union breakup, 554
  military intervention in Central America and Caribbean, 552
  military intervention in Middle East, 550
  political power in, 6
  September 11 and emotions of, 8
  social welfare in, 518–527
U.S. citizenship, obtaining, 150
U.S. Department of Agriculture (USDA), 411
U.S. Department of Health and Human Services, 515
U.S. Department of Veterans Affairs, 515
U.S. district and appellate courts, map, 446
United States v. Butler, 516
United States v. Harriss, 274
United States v. Leon, 124
United States v. Lopez, 58
United States v. Nixon, 385
United States v. Virginia, 146
United Steelworkers v. Weber, 154
Unsafe at Any Speed (Nader), 485
Urban League, 271
USS *West Virginia* (battleship), 548

Valance issue, 245–246
Van Buren, Martin, 207, 208
Vandenberg, Arthur H., 547
Varney, Christine, 482
Verba, Sidney, 86–87, 192
Veto, 355, 383–384
  defined, 383
Veto message, 383
Vice president, presidential transition and, 398–399
Virginia Plan, 28
Visual, defined, 246
Voice vote, 354
Voter registration methods, 187
Voter turnout, 190–192
  methods of calculating, 184–185
  presidential elections, 1860-2008, 190
Voting-age population (VAP), 184
Voting-eligible population (VEP), 184
Voting laws, 186
Voting rates by groups, 193
Voting specialists, 192

Wabash, St. Louis and Pacific Railroad v. Illinois, 58
Wagner Act, 482
Waiver, defined, 68
Wallace, George, 137
  personal following and, 220
  two-party system and, 222
Wallace, Henry, 222
Wall of separation, defined, 115
Wall Street Reform, 283
War in Iraq, 551
War on Poverty, 587
War Powers Act, 540–541
Warren, Earl, 445
Washington, George, 6, 366
  executive power and, 372
  term limits and, 373
Washington Globe, 300
Washington Post, 307
Waste, as bureaucracy problem, 428, 429
Watchdog, national media as, 307
Water Quality Improvement Act, 485, 566
Ways and Means Committee, 351, 523
Weather Underground, 534
Weaver, Robert, 393
Weber, Max, 10
Webster v. Reproductive Health Services, 148
Welfare. *See* Social welfare
West Coast Hotel Co. v. Parrish, 500
Whip, defined, 343
White flight, 138
White House office, 388–390
  myth and reality of, 389
White primary, 188, 189
Whitman v. American Trucking Associations, 570
Widely distributed costs and benefits, 476
Wildavsky, Aaron, 537
Wilderness Society, 280
Wiley, Harvey, 484
Wilson, James, executive power and, 372
Wilson, Woodrow, 371, 374, 481
Winograd, Morley, 215
Women
  Constitution, U.S. and, 42
  equal rights and, 145–149
  illegal discrimination against, 146–147
  landmark cases, rights, 146
  privacy and sex, 148–149
  sexual harassment and, 147–148
Women Hispanics, in Congress, 335–337
Women's Equity Action League (WEAL), 281
Woodward, Bob, 307
World Trade Center attacks, 8
Worldviews, 546
Writ of certiorari, 451–452
Wurzelbacher, Samuel Joseph, 261

Yellow journalism, 302
Youngstown Sheet & Tube Co. v. Sawyer, 500, 543

Zelman v. Simmons-Harris, 118
Zorauch v. Clauson, 118